The Jews of Czestochowa
(Częstochowa, Poland)

Translation of
"Tshenstokhover Yidn"

Edited by: Dr. Raphael Mahler

NY: United Czestochower Relief Committee and Ladies Auxiliary, 1947

Published by JewishGen

**An Affiliate of the Museum of Jewish Heritage—A Living Memorial to the Holocaust
New York**

The Jews of Czestochowa (Częstochowa, Poland)
Translation of "Tshenstokhover Yidn"

Project Coordinator and Translator: Gloria Berkenstat Freund
Layout: Donni Magid and Janice Sellers
Cover Design: Rachel Kolokoff Hopper

Published by JewishGen, Inc.
An Affiliate of the Museum of Jewish Heritage
A Living Memorial to the Holocaust
36 Battery Place, New York, NY 10280

JewishGen, Inc. is not responsible for inaccuracies or omissions in the original work and makes no representations regarding the accuracy of this translation. Digital images of the original book's contents can be seen online at the New York Public Library website.

The mission of the JewishGen organization is to produce a translation of the original work, and we cannot verify the accuracy of statements or alter facts cited.

Printed in the United States of America by Lightning Source, Inc.

Library of Congress Control Number (LCCN): 2019954867
ISBN: 978-1-939561-82-4 (hard cover: 824 pages, alk. paper)

Cover Designs: The front cover is composed of two images which are blended together. "The Old Synagogue", page 80, and "The map of the city with the ghettos and camps outlined", page 412.

The cover is composed of two images which are blended together. "The map of the large and small ghettos", page 283 and an untitled image from the original Yizkor book. The quote is from the forward from the original book: "The memory of Jewish Czenstochow was sanctified on a thousand layers by the martyred death of our brothers and sisters", page 1. All images are from the original book, "The Jews of Czestochowa."

JewishGen and the Yizkor Books in Print Project

This book has been published by the **Yizkor Books in Print Project**, as part of the **Yizkor Book Project** of JewishGen, Inc.

JewishGen, Inc. is a non-profit organization founded in 1987 as a resource for Jewish genealogy. Its website [www.jewishgen.org] serves as an international clearinghouse and resource center to assist individuals who are researching the history of their Jewish families and the places where they lived. JewishGen provides databases, facilitates discussion groups, and coordinates projects relating to Jewish genealogy and the history of the Jewish people. In 2003, JewishGen became an affiliate of the **Museum of Jewish Heritage—A Living Memorial to the Holocaust** in New York.

The **JewishGen Yizkor Book Project** was organized to make more widely known the existence of Yizkor (Memorial) Books written by survivors and former residents of various Jewish communities throughout the world. Later, volunteers connected to the different destroyed communities began cooperating to have these books translated from the original language—usually Hebrew or Yiddish—into English, thus enabling a wider audience to have access to the valuable information contained within them. As each chapter of these books was translated, it was posted on the JewishGen website and made available to the general public.

The **Yizkor Books in Print Project** began in 2011 as an initiative to print and publish Yizkor Books that had been fully translated, so that hard copies would be available for purchase by the descendants of these communities and also by scholars, universities, synagogues, libraries, and museums.

These Yizkor books have been produced almost entirely through the volunteer effort of researchers from around the world, assisted by donations from private individuals. The books are printed and sold at near cost, so as to make them as affordable as possible. Our goal is to make this important genre of Jewish literature and history available in English in book form, so that people can have the personal histories of their ancestral towns on their bookshelves for themselves and for their children and grandchildren.

A list of all published translated Yizkor Books in the project with prices and ordering information can be found at:
http://www.jewishgen.org/Yizkor/ybip.html

Binny Lewis, Yizkor Book Project Manager
Joel Alpert, Yizkor-Book-in-Print Project Coordinator

JewishGen
Yizkor Book Project

This book is presented by the
Yizkor Books in Print Project
Project Coordinator: Joel Alpert

Part of the
Yizkor Books Project of JewishGen, Inc.
Project Manager: Lance Ackerfeld

These books have been produced solely through volunteer effort
of individuals from around the world. The books are printed and
sold at near cost, so as to make them as affordable as possible.

Our goal is to make this history and important genre of Jewish
literature available in English in book form so that people can have
the near-personal histories of their ancestral towns on their bookshelves for themselves and for their children and grandchildren.

Any donations to the Yizkor Books Project are appreciated.

Please send donations to:
Yizkor Book Project
JewishGen
36 Battery Place
New York, NY 10280

JewishGen, Inc. is an affiliate of the
Museum of Jewish Heritage
A Living Memorial to the Holocaust

Notes to the Reader:

We apologize ahead of time for the poor quality of images in the book. Often these images had been scanned from the original Yizkor books which were of poor quality to begin with, being copies of old photographs. Each transfer results in loss of quality. We have done the best we could, given the original material and the resources and technology at hand. Even though images often appear of higher quality on computer screens that does not transfer to high quality images in print. A reader can view the original scans on the web sites listed below.

Toward the end of the book (starting on page 537), many pictures of people do not appear for two reasons: that they quality of the images are very poor and that this book is so long that by including these images would cause the book to have more pages than allowed by our printer. We apologize for these missing images and would refer the interested reader to view the pdf files of the original Yiddish book on the link below:
https://www.yiddishbookcenter.org/collections/yizkor-books/yzk-nybc313734/tshenstokhover-yidn

Or

To purchase a copy of the original
https://www.yiddishbookcenter.org/collections/digital-yiddish-library/buy-yiddish-book?spielberg_number=nybc313734&title=Ţshensţokhoyer%20Yidn&author=&url=https%3A//www.yiddishbookcenter.org/collections/yiddish-books/spb-nybc313734

Within the text the reader will note "{34}" standing ahead of a paragraph. This indicates that the material translated below was on page 34 of the original book. However, when a paragraph was split between two pages in the original book, the marker is placed in this book after the end of the paragraph for ease of reading.

Also please note that all references within the text of the book to page numbers, refer to the page numbers of the original Yizkor Book.

The original book can be seen online at the New York Public Library site:
http://yizkor.nypl.org/index.php?id=2099
or at the Yiddish Book Center web site:
https://www.yiddishbookcenter.org/collections/yizkor-books/yzk-nybc313734/tshenstokhover-yidn

In order to obtain a list of all Shoah victims from Czestochowa, the reader should access the Yad Vashem web site listed below; one can also search for specific family names using family name option. These lists are continually updated by Yad Vashem, so it is worthwhile to periodically search these lists.

There is much valuable information available on this web site, including the Pages of Testimony, etc.
http://yvng.yadvashem.org

A list of this book and all books available in the Yizkor-Book-In-Print Project along with prices is available at:
http://www.jewishgen.org/Yizkor/ybip.html

Acknowledgements and Dedication

I hope the translation of this Yizkor Book will serve as a memorial to this Polish city of approximately 30,000 Jewish men, women and children. Their lives were cut short and the vibrant spiritual, communal and cultural life they created throughout the generations were destroyed. We must never forget who they were, what they accomplished in their lives and the terrible sins committed against them by the Germans. I dedicate the translation of this book to the memory of my martyred cousins Moshe Berkenstat and his wife Rayzel Fajertag Berkenstat and all of the martyrs of Czenstochow.

Thank you to the JewishGen organization for making possible both the online publication and the publication of this hardcover edition of this translation.

The translation and production of this book would not have been possible without the help of the following very generous people:

Joyce Field, Emeritus Yizkor Book Project Manager, who gave me a copy of *Czenstochower Yidn* and encouraged me to translate it.

Pesakh Fiszman, of blessed memory, my incomparable Yiddish teacher, who taught me so well and encouraged me in my love of Yiddish and *Yiddishkeit*.

Larry Freund, my beloved husband, who read and reread each translated article and generously provided his editing skills.

Miriam Leberstein, who donated the translation of the chapter, "Remembering Those Who Left Us for Their Eternal Rest."

Joel Alpert, Yizkor-Books-in-Print Project Coordinator, who worked with a number of volunteers to publish this book.

Gloria Berkenstat Freund
Translator and Project Coordinator

Geopolitical Information

Częstochowa is located at 50°48' N, 19°07' E

Alternate names for the town are: Częstochowa [Pol], Chenstochov [Yid], Tschenstochau [Ger], Čenstochová [Cz], Chenstokhova [Rus], Chenstokhov, Chestokhova, Tshenstokhov

Period	Town	District	Province	Country
Before WWI (c. 1900):	Częstochowa	Częstochowa	Piotrków	Russian Empire
Between the wars (c. 1930):	Częstochowa	Częstochowa	Kielce	Poland
After WWII (c. 1950):	Częstochowa			Poland
Today (c. 2000):	Częstochowa			Poland

Nearby Jewish Communities:
Olsztyn 7 miles ESE
Mstów 8 miles ENE
Kamyk 9 miles NNW
Kłobuck 11 miles NW
Aurelów 13 miles NE
Truskolasy 13 miles WNW
Miedzno 14 miles NNW
Janów, (near Częstochowa) 15 miles ESE
Żarki 16 miles SE
Przyrów 17 miles E
Myszków 18 miles SE
Gidle 20 miles NE
Nowa Brzeźnica 20 miles N
Pławno 20 miles NE
Krzepice 20 miles NW

BALTIC SEA

LITHUANIA

Vilnius ●

RUSSIA

POLAND

BELARUS

GERMANY

● Poznan

Warsaw ●

● Lodz

● **Czestochowa**

● **Zabrze**

● Krakow

●**Jordanow**

● Prague

CZECH REPUBLIC

UKRAINE

SLOVAKIA

250 miles

0

0   250 Km   500 Km

POLAND - **Current Borders**

Map of Poland showing Czestochowa

Title Page of Original Yizkor Book

טשענסטאכאווער

יידן

אַרויסגעגעבן פֿון

יונײַטעד טשענסטאכאווער רעליף קאָמיטעט
און לײדיס אוקזילערי אין ניו־יאָרק

אונטער דער רעדאַקציע פֿון

ד״ר רפאל מאַהלער

מיטאַרבעטער פֿון דער רעדאַקציע־קאָלעגיע:

אלקנה כראָבאָלאָווסקי, רפאל פֿעדערמאַן, אבא קייממאַן
און װאָלף גליקסמאַן

קונסטלערישע רעפּראָדוקציעס

אַרטור שיק

גראַפֿישע אַרבעטן געצייכנט פֿון

נאַטע קאָזלאָווסקי

●

CZENSTOCHOVER YIDN

Copyright 1947 by

UNITED CZENSTOCHOVER RELIEF COMMITTEE

and LADIES AUXILIARY

●

Printed in U. S. A.

GRENICH PRINTING CORP.

151 West 25th Street

New York City 1, N. Y.

THE JEWS OF CZESTOCHOWA

Published by
United Czestochower Relief Committee
and the Ladies' Auxiliary of New York

Editor:
Dr. Raphael Mahler

Members of the Editorial Committee:
**Elkana Brovolovsky, Raphael Federman, Abba Koifman
and Wolf Gliksman**

Artistic Reproduction:
Arthur Shick

Graphic designs by
Note Kozlovsky

Table of Contents

[Page V]

Forward

While we were moving forward with the publication of this book, the Jews of Czenstochow were squirming under the bloody nails of the German villains. Now, as we give the book to the public, the disaster of the Czenstochower Jews is as deep as the ocean.

The *kehile* [organized Jewish community] of 30,000 Jewish souls in Czenstochow, with the exception of a small remnant, shared the fate of the 3,500,000 Polish Jews and of the six million Jewish victims of Nazism and Fascism in Europe. Yet our book, *Czenstochower Yidn*, was not conceived as a stone *matseyve* [headstone] at the cemetery of Jewish Czenstochow, but as a *Book of Life*. We held as a duty the writing of this *Book of Life* about all of the generations and layers of the Jewish population that struggled and created our home city. The memory of Jewish Czenstochow was sanctified on a thousand layers by the martyred death of our brothers and sisters.

Our *Book of Life, Czenstochower Yidn*, is also our *Book of Lineage*. The neighborhood of Czenstochow that Jews built and inhabited is now either utterly ruined or settled by non-Jews. A large number of institutions that were the pride of the Jewish *kehile* most likely will be taken over by strangers. All the Jewish streets, all of the Jewish houses, all Jewish institutions belong to us. We will always take pride in them and honor those who created them.

We are aware that this book in not in any way complete in every respect. Some of the communal movements and institutions in Czenstochow, as for example, the Zionist movement with its many branches and the religious institutions, were not handled with the necessary thoroughness. The abnormal conditions in which the preparations had to be made for this book, the destruction of the authoritative people who would have been able to give the necessary information, is the only reason for the blanks. Our sincere intention was to record the memories of all of the innovations of Jewish life and creativity in Czenstochow without distinction as to its direction.

[Page VI]

A consolation in our great misfortune is that large numbers of people from Jewish Czenstochow immigrated in time to America, to *Eretz-Yisroel*, and to other nations during the course of dozens of years. Everywhere they created their organizations, assisted in the development of Jewish life in the nations in which they now lived; they, who with generosity always supported their brothers in their old home, took upon themselves the great responsibility of publishing this book, *Czenstochower Yidn*, through the United Czenstochower Relief Committee. This book is also joined with the sacred work of fraternal aid. The income from this book will be used for the aid and building fund for the survivors of the Holocaust from our home city. Let us here express our great thanks and recognize our Czenstochower *landsleit* [people from the same city or town] in America, in *Eretz-Yisroel* and in all of the other countries who exerted themselves, sparing no effort or money, in order to see that this book saw the light. They all share a portion of this book and they deserve much pride and reward.

Let this book, *Czenstochower Yidn*, help still more to bind our *landsleit* all over the world as an integral conscious community among our severely tested people. Let this book be a reminder that the Czenstochower Jews will not give up the struggle for the survival and happiness of the Jewish people.

Editorial Board

Alkana Chrabalowski
Rafael Federman
Aba Koifman

Wolf Gliksman

Administrative Committee

Abraham Yakov Senzer
Josef Koifman
Yakov Ber Silver
Yanakl Kopinski (Kopin)

[Page VII]

Preface

The history of each large Jewish community in Poland reflects in miniature the most important aspects of the development of the great cultured and creative Jewish community that gave Polish Jewry its renown before the catastrophe. Our knowledge of the history of Polish Jewry – which formed the majority of East European Jewry – that comes from each new historical monograph about an important Jewish community in Poland is an achievement of very great significance, not only for Jewish historical knowledge, but, in general, also for the historical, national and cultural consciousness of the Jewish people all over the world.

However, a history of a Jewish *kehile* [organized Jewish community] in Poland is also more than an isolated fragment of the history of the settlements in the country. Each *kehile* was an important Jewish cultural center, not only with its wonderful traditions, but also because of its unique significance and its role in the life of the Jewish people. Each *kehile* possessed its own individuality that was a product of peculiar, specific development over the course of many generations.

The Czenstochower Jewish *kehile* shared the suffering and joy, the struggle for survival and the struggle for the cultural ascent of the entire courageous community in Poland. However, it possessed its own characteristic physiognomy, its peculiar charm and its proud consciousness about its own great achievements. Although much smaller than the Jewish *kehile* in Lodz, the second largest Jewish community in Poland, it displayed so many similar traits in its historical evolution and in its social-economic and cultural structure that it can rightly be labeled as "small Lodz." Lodz counted barely one Jewish *arendar* [tenant farmer] family at the end of the 18th century and in 1931 the *kehile* consisted of more than 200,000 Jewish souls. At the end of the era of old Poland, seven Jewish families were counted as inhabitants in Czenstochow and on the eve of the Second World War, a robust *kehile* of approximately 30,000 souls was there.

[Page VIII]

In Czenstochow, as in Lodz, the Jewish population grew with the rise of industry in the city and consisted in great proportion of factory workers. Both relatively young communities were not able to cite any lineage of old synagogues and houses of study, Torah geniuses and followers of the *misnagdim* [opponents of Hasidism] and Hasidim. Therefore, they were able to grow with the wonderful achievements of the Jewish entrepreneurial spirit, economic initiative and energy and with impressive accomplishments by Jewish workers and the common people in the areas of professional and political struggle, as well as in the area of modern Jewish cultural institutions. While Jewish Czenstochow was "small Lodz" and not large Lodz, it merged the attributes and virtues of being an industrial center with hominess and a warm, intimate atmosphere of a medium sized Jewish community. The geographical position near the German border also had an impact in that Czenstochower Jews, in general, were more enlightened than Jews in other medium sized communities in Poland. Czenstochow, as a Jewish community in an industrial city of middle size, was substantially unique in Polish Jewry.

The first hundred years of the history of the Jews in Czenstochow is one chain of persistent, courageous struggle against legal decrees for the right to live and reside in the city. In ancient Poland, the small Jewish community, a sub-district of the neighboring brave *kehile*, Janow

(Janowa), took the first stance against the feudal, clerical state and city administration that according to law did not permit Jews to settle in the city near the "Bright Mountain" [Translator's note: The hilltop monastery of Jasna Gora, where Czenstochow's famous "Black Madonna" is located]. Under the Prussian occupation, a ghetto for Jews in Czenstochow was legalized, although the poor Jews who did not pay taxes also had to use every means possible in order not to be thrown out of the city as a "useless element." In the half feudal Kingdom of Poland, the ghetto in Czenstochow was like those in a series of other Polish cities, officially recorded under the better sounding name, "Jewish District," and except for a few rich individuals, the Jewish population was squeezed into several narrow and dirty alleys.

With the reforms of Count Wielopolski in 1862, a new era began for the Jews in Czenstochow as well as in the rest of Poland. The struggle for the right to live in the city ended. However, the no less difficult struggle for economic existence, for a place in life, remained.

One is simply amazed when one reads the history of Jewish industry in Czenstochow. Without significant capital, without professional training, without any support from the Czarist and later Polish governments, Jews in the city built almost all intermediate-sized and small industries (the large factories belonged to foreigners, mainly Belgian and French firms). Young Jews, who received their entire education in houses of study and who would later, as "manufacturers," interrupt the work in the evening in order to go to the small synagogues for the *Minkhah-Maariv* [evening] prayers with their workers, built entire branches of new industries – toys and fancy goods, celluloid and paper, mirrors, paints and a series of others. The Jewish manufacturers who themselves had only once "smelled" a Leipziger cathedral, or a German factory*, had their production exported not only all over Russia, but even to the Balkans in competition with German manufacturers. Unlike Lodz, this industry not only had Jewish owners. Jewish workers from the back alleys of Szika Street and Jatka Street, Teper Street and Kasza Street contributed to the ascent with their toil and sweat and with their experience and proficiency were part of this impressive industrial rise, no less then the Jewish entrepreneurs with their initiative and agility. With heavy work, from dawn until late at night, through 12 and 14 hours a day, the Jewish workers – men, women and even children, who barely reached the work table, built up jobs for themselves and for the entire working class of the city. Many manufacturers who became wealthy through the work of Jews, later closed their factory gates to Jewish workers. That is how a condition came about that even in this significant industrial center, most Jewish labor was squeezed into the traditional Jewish trades of tailor, furrier, cap maker, shoemaker, butcher and baker.

*[Translator's note: in other words, the Jewish manufacturers may have visited larger cities but were provincial.]

[Page IX]

The old *shtetl* with its colorful, old fashioned appearance remained almost untouched under the layer of modern capitalist industry and wholesale trade. Haim Leib Szwarc's writings about the New Market in Czenstochow on the threshold of the 20th century describe the Jewish second hand goods dealers, fruit traders, herring and kasha [buckwheat groats] shops; with the stands of earthenware pots, bowls, baskets, chests, beds, closets, lime, string, *lokhshn-breter* [wooden boards for rolling out noodles] and graters on a Tuesday market day; with paint shops, cloth merchants and haberdasheries; Jews with small wagons and package carriers – the writings recall the fairs of Sholom Asch's *Shtetl*, in just the way his sellers of lemonade, skullcaps and the Kopls and the Shaya Stopes and Nakhum Yankls are blood brothers of Sholem Aleichem's *Motl Peyse der Khazan's* [*Motl Peyse the Son of the Cantor*]. A world of energy and a love of life bubbled among the petty bourgeois masses of shopkeepers, traders and craftsmen.

The awakener, the organizer and the leader of the Jewish masses, both economically and politically and in the cultural realm in Czenstochow, as in all of Poland, Lithuania and Ukraine, was the Jewish working class. Not forgetting that Jewish labor was splintered among small factories and workshops, and perhaps because of this abnormal condition and difficult national oppression, it showed a revolutionary spirit and energy for struggle like the neighboring established proletariat. The Czenstochower Jewish working class in the revolutionary years of 1905-6, organized by the stubborn, systematic work of enlightenment at illegal discussion meetings in the forest and at the cemetery, in the synagogue and in the "tea house," appeared as the recognized, leader of the Jewish masses in the city. The Jewish workers played a very important role in the struggle against czarism, not only with systematic political education, but also by organized struggle against the police (attempted bombings) and their underworld helpers.

A specific feature of the Jewish socialist movement in Czenstochow that lasted until the end of the First World War was the supremacy of the *S.S.* [Socialist Zionists] (Territorialists). A. Charabolowski notes in his section on the *S.S.* Party that the proportional strength of this party in Czenstochow was not only a result of chance, but because it possessed a series of leaders such as Dr. Ahron Singalowski and Dr. Josef Kruk. The geographical location of Czenstochow was important here. As a border city and an important point for passing emigrants, there were auspicious conditions for the growth of the worker's party that inevitably placed the regulation of emigration at the center of its program on the Jewish question.

[Page X]

After the failure of the 1905 revolution, the political and professional movement of the Jewish worker's unions (*Poalei-Zion* and the *Bund*) in Czenstochow dwindled, just as everywhere in Poland. Therefore, all legal possibilities were used for cultural work at that time. In 1911 the Jewish literary society joined with the *Lira* and carried on cultural work with the combined strength of worker activists and democratic Zionist intelligence, and it is worth recording as an example of the rise of secular Jewish culture in Poland. A dramatic section, choir and sports circle, public readings by prominent lecturers (Y.L. Peretz) and the first public Jewish library – this was the means by which modern Jewish culture was built in Poland after being under the yoke of Czarism. The local Yiddish press that began to publish before the First World War was also an important cultural achievement, as an organ of struggle against assimilation and to make the Jewish masses productive.

Thanks to the high state of enlightenment of the local community, Czenstochow was one of the rare Jewish communities that was not satisfied with its earlier productivity, although it was substantial in this field. The gardener school (farm) and the artisans' school that were founded on the threshold of the 20th century educated proficient agricultural workers, locksmiths, carpenters and wheelwrights. After the First World War, many of the graduates of both schools emigrated to *Eretz-Yisroel* and with their specialized abilities helped to build the Jewish nation.

Philanthropy was with reason a discredited institution in communal life. Yet, in the Czenstochwer *Dobroszinoczsz* (the Polish name for a charity), a positive example was achieved with Jewish communal self-help, initiative and energy. In addition to the organization of emergency help, of an old age home and orphan house, this society built a hospital in 1913 that was exemplary with its most modern accommodations and divisions for all fields of medicine.

This is how Jewish Czenstochow struggled, built and created under the yoke of Czarism until the First World War.

The First World War and the German occupation brought extraordinary desolation and need to the Jewish population in Czenstochow. Local Jewish labor again turned out to be the most agile and most responsible strength in Jewish communal life. Taking advantage of the new legal possibilities, professional unions were created in various industrial sectors. The worker unions also included, those who organized self-help institutions for the Jewish masses, such as a people's kitchen, a bakery, a children's home and who developed cultural work around a newly founded reading room.

The condition of the Jewish masses in aristocratic capitalistic Poland was determined by the changed political and economic conditions in the country. Legally, the Jews in Poland were citizens with equal rights. We also see in Czentochow how the changed legal conditions led to the development of a strong and widespread Jewish professional organization; the middle class organized itself in a respectable artisans club. A Jewish educational system was built with two children's home, two public schools, evening classes for workers and a Hebrew-Polish *gymnazie* [high school]. A large Jewish library grew and the Jewish sports movement spread.

[Page XI]

Although formal deprivations ended for Jews, the difficult economic conditions and, chiefly, the anti-Semitic reaction in the country also greatly oppressed the Jewish population, as in the time of Czarism. In Czarist times, particularly from the beginning of the 20ᵗʰ century, the fresh wind of the upcoming liberation was felt. In "independent" Poland, one watched with concern and anxiety how the [rightist] reaction grew increasingly strong from year to year. As a result, although Jewish communal and cultural life broadened and grew in size, the zest and the self confidence of the work before the First World War was missing. With the deepening of economic need and the sharpening of the political reaction, the level of Jewish cultural life also diminished. It is enough to remember that in the last years before the Second World War that in Czenstochow in the Jewish educational system in the Yiddish language, barely one children's home was supported with great self-sacrificing devotion.

The pogroms that the Czenstochower Jews lived through, the pogrom of 1919, a kind of omen for the brutal anti-Semitic course of the newly founded Polish government, and the second in 1937 that cast a dark shadow of the coming Hitler devastation, were a sorrowful symbol for the condition of the Jews in all of Poland in the era between the two world wars.

The brightest time in the history of the Jews in Czenstochow, as in the history of all of Poland, was during these 20 years with the extraordinary activity in the political realm. The Zionist movement spread widely and was strengthened with the growth of the national consciousness of Jewish citizens and, in particular, of the petty bourgeoisie. Class consciousness among great masses of Jewish labor found its expression in the growth of the movements of the proletarian parties.

The former *S.S.* reorganized as *Fareinikte* [United] and then as "inde-pendent socialists," lost even more of its former positions in 1938 when they were dissolved by the government powers. The strongest Jewish labor parties were the *Bund* and the communists. The left *Paolei-Zion*, the *heHalutz* movement [Zionist pioneer movement] and *Hatzeir Hashomer* [Youth Guard, a Socialist Zionist youth group], which dominated still wider circles of the Jewish young people, developed as a bridge between Zionism and Socialism. The Czenstochower young people entered a glorious page of the highest human idealism with their blood. Dozens of Jewish socialists and communists languished in Polish jails for years because of their struggle for the liberation of the Jewish and Polish people. Many Czenstochower young people gave their lives on the fields of Spain in the struggle against Franco's fascist Falanges. At the same time, dozens of Jewish young people from Czenstochow left for *Eretz-Yisroel* and, with their sweat and blood, dried up swamps, irrigated deserts and chiseled out new roads, in order to prepare the way for the old-new national home of the Jewish people. All of them, the *halutzim* [pioneers] and *shomrim* [volunteer patrols], right and left *Paolei-Zion*, *Bundists* and communists, later, in the dark hour of Hitlerist destruction raised their hands against the deadly enemy and they fell together in heroic struggle for the honor of the Jewish people.

[Page XII]

A book about Jewish Czenstochow would not be complete if it did not include an account of the activities of Czenstochower people throughout the entire world. The feelings of connection to the home city is particularly strong among Czenstochowers and wherever they emigrated, they organized themselves at first as a group with the purpose of coming to the aid of their brothers and sisters in Poland. In *Eretz-Yisroel* they majority of the approximately 2,000 Czenstochowers organized themselves into their own organization. In faraway Argentina a union of Czenstochower *landsleit* [people from the same town] has been active for approximately two dozen years. Here in South America the *landsleit* organization of Czenstochowers is so strongly united and so vigorously active that they can serve as an example for many other organizations of the same character.

* * *

The Czenstochower Jewish community suffered the horrible fate of all of Polish Jewry. There, where in the course of 200 years the Czenstochower Jewish community worked, struggled and created, there are ruins sown with ash and blackened, burned bricks. In the hellish ovens of Auschwitz and Treblinka, 50,000 Jews from Czenstochow and its surround-ing *shtetlekh* [towns] breathed out their last breath. The chapters about the frightening agony of death of the Jewish community of Czenstochow that are collected in this book are a very important contribution to the history of Jewish martyrdom under the Nazis: using the same vile system as in every large Jewish community in Eastern Europe, using the same devilish plan that the Germans carried out in Warsaw, in Lodz, in Bialystok and in Vilna, in Kovno and in Lemberg [Lvov or Lviv], they little by little exhausted the Jewish community in Czenstochow; first with hunger, torture and yellow patches; then the second stage – the imprisonment of all Jews from the city in a large ghetto jail; the liquidation of the ghetto and leaving a "small ghetto" in order to squeeze out the last working strength of the starving martyrs; the last act – the annihilation of the remnant in the ghetto.

However, the history of the Holocaust of the Czenstochower Jews is not only a *megilah* [scroll] of blood and tears, but an epic of Jewish heroism. Czenstochower Jews have shown that they are worthy brothers of the immortal Jewish heroes of the ghetto uprisings in Warsaw and Bialystok. The fighting courage of the sons and daughters of Jewish Czenstochow was erased.

If Jews in Czenstochow have recorded an important chapter in the history of Polish Jewry, they are immortalized in the history of the Jewish people, in general, by their heroic fight against the Nazis.

We all wish that the small number of Czenstochower Jewish survivors, who show so much energy and devotion to reconstructing their economic and cultural position, will withstand the storms of the fascist anti-Semitic wave that tried to drown the new Poland in Jewish blood. May they live to see happy times in Poland and not need to leave their home city, obliterating every trace of a Jewish community in Czenstochow. However, as the fate of a renewed Jewish community in Czenstochow is not inevitable, may the spirit of the 200 year Jewish history in the home city not go for naught for the Czenstochowers: the history of our own home city must be a source of inspiration, a reservoir of strength for the Czenstochowers across the world in the fight for a happy Jewish people in a liberated world.

[Page 3]

Development of the Community

Jews in Czenstochowa
Up to the First World War

by Dr. Yakov Szatzki

1. General History of the City

The city of Czenstochowa played an exceptional role in Polish history. There were times when this city was regarded as the most holy religious-national relic possessed by Congress Poland. In past times when Poland was independent, the name Czenstochowa was always revered, particularly in the moments of historical struggle for national existence. This was, for the most part, during wars, when foreign troops stormed the Fortress Czenstochowa, which was the gate that opened to Warsaw, the heart of Poland. However, when such wars would end with a victory for the Polish Army, this "miracle" would be inscribed to the "merit" of the holy "picture of Mary" that is found in the monastery of "*Jasna Gora*" or Klarenberg as it was called in all West European geographies or guidebooks.

However, in the "weeklies," when the storms of war subsided and the heroism and "merit" of intervention of "Godly" help was converted to legend that varied from the mediocre poets such as Kokhowski and Woronicz to such a genius as Adam Mickewicz, the city remained in the shadow of the nation. She was, however, the constant object of well-organized propaganda on the part of the Catholic Church. Czenstochowa did not occupy the kind of place in the history of Polish national thought as, for example, Krakow, Warsaw or even Lemberg [Lwow in Polish; now Lviv, Ukraine]. However, during the time of Russian rule, particularly in the second half of the 19th Century, when the Russification of the land clearly became the program's ultimate goal for the Czarist regime, Czenstochowa became for Russian-Poland that which Krakow was for the entire Polish people. In the larger debate that took place in Polish Socialist-Folkish circles in the 80's and 90's of the previous century [19th century], the city of Czenstochowa takes a central position, as a refuge for a reservoir of national resistance. In those interesting days, to this day's unsearching debate, it is a question of how can one propagandize socialism without debating the question of religion.

Jan Poplawski, the theoretician of Socialist Folkism, which was strongly influenced by the Russian "*narodnikes* [revolutionaries of the 1860's and 1870's]," developed a theory that only in Poland could a socialist not be indifferent to Catholicism; on the contrary, despite the fact that the official conduct of the Catholic Church strongly sinned in relation to Polish national aspirations, a Polish Socialist, he wrote, must first of all feel solidarity and unity with Catholicism, because in the political conditions in which the Polish people live at the present moment, Catholicism is literally a national faith. This faith helped conserve authentic national traditions and customs for the Polish people. Poland had many reasons to be indebted to the Catholic Church – Professor Poplawski wrote – not only language, but also patriotism.

As a "sacred place, Czenstochow" – Professor Poplawski wrote in his weekly *Glat* (Voice) (1890 and 1891) – "is not without reason a 'part' of the Catholic faith, the very heart of Polish national faith, which is the basis of the present faith."

[Page 4]

In a polemic with Aleksander Swietochowski, the leading spokesman of the Rationalistic School of Positivism, that contested clericalism, but not the religion, Popalowski enjoined the Polish intelligentsia to demonstrate its Polishness and make a pilgrimage together with the Polish peasants to Czenstochow. In such a procession, he wrote, is found the greatest Polishness that the political conditions permit to be revealed.

"Polish intellectual," Poplawski wrote, "put on a grey *sukmane* [long peasant coat] like the Mazowiecker peasant and walk with him to the holy relic of *Jasna Gora*. Sleep with him on the stones of the highways. Soak in the hard sweat of the peasant bodies, sing with them the old litany to the holy Mary of Czenstochow, in which is found the treasure of the old Polish language and deep Polish faith – and then you will feel that you live the only bit of Polish life for which history is still in envy of us and the external powers have not yet taken away."

The impression made by Poplawski's article was very great. In Congress Poland, penitent-radical types appeared who invited participation in processions by the Polish peasant masses to Czenstochow and even strove to organize such excursions by intellectuals and factory workers.

There was silence and no argument against this "Czenstochower political orientation," even in socialist circles in Poland that stood on Marxist terrain almost as if giving moral approval for this. In this regard, to present a little known fact, the famous Polish socialist writer, Stanislaw Brzozowski, published an article in which he professed his solidarity with the "Czenstochower political orientation."

It was written in the London *Przedswit* [*Dawn*], the theoretical organ of the Polish Socialist Party, that one cannot keep quiet and even more one cannot ignore the fact that the will of the Polish people can only be manifested legally in the procession to Czenstochow. This article was written by none other than the Jew, Feliks Perl.

In the well-known reportage of Wladyslaw Reymont about the religious procession to Czenstochow in which he took part with a group of prominent Polish writers and journalists – the role of Czenstochow at this national-religious moment was very clearly expressed.

The great events of 1859 – when there was success in obtaining permission to erect a monument for Father Kordecki, the heroic defender of the *Jasna Gora* against the Swedes (in 1655), thanks to the "liberal" course in Russia, – were the beginning of a revived national cult of Czenstochower "holiness." During the rebellion of 1853 pilgrimages were made there in order to ask for "help and protection for those who go to their death in her name." There are anthologies of poetry about Czenstochow. In 1859 Karl Kucz, then the editor of *Kurier Warszawski* [*Courier from Warsaw*] published an interesting reportage of his visit to Czenstochow. In 1860 a detailed travel guide, written by the well known Zalesice public worker, Josef Lompa, was published. In 1862, during the "moral revolution," a book was published in Warsaw entitled, *Czenstochow in Polish Poetry*, in which even two poems by Jewish writers are found, both students of the rabbinical school (Kon and Landau).

The sadly famous Macoch[1] murder trial (1910) that revealed the decadence of the "brothers" of *Jasna Gora* produced a terrible disappointment in Polish society. A "provocation" on the part of the Russian regime in order to "embarrass the holiest that Poland possessed" was even seen in this murder trial.

In this regard, the appeal by the Polish writers who wanted to disconnect this sad fact from life in the monastery and called for the "glorification of the holy that even the hand of a murderer cannot tarnish," signed by Sienkiewicz, Reymont and even Marya Konopnicka, is interesting.

After these general observations, let us focus on a short overview about the history of Czenstochow.

[Page 5]

The meaning of the name Czenstochowa produced so many fantasies and curious meanings that, in fact, the correct entomology of this word is not known to the present. In the 17th century one of the weavers of rhymes, who wrote an "epic" of 12 songs about the defense of *Jasna Gora*, interpreted the name by explaining, that "the holy mother" "often hides" the victims of calumny (*czensto* [often] *chowa* [hide]). This city arose from a village named Czenstochowka, in honor of a monastery that was erected nearby. It was probably begun in the 14th century on a hill that was given the name *Jasna Gora* (the bright mountain). This village gradually developed into a city. The history relates that in 1377 the Opoler Prince Wladyslaw conquered the Belzer castle. A picture of the "holy mother" that, according to tradition, was painted by the Apostle Luke, the "patron" of painters was found there in the Catholic Church. Prince Wladyslaw brought this picture with him and gave it to the wooden church that was found on *Jasna Gora*, near the village of Czenstochowka. This means that the church itself is a scepter [represents royal authority], and according to one historian of religious art in Poland, originates from the 12th century. The Prince brought the medal of the apostle Paul that was found in Hungary. He gave the Paulists two villages: Czenstochow and Kawadne. The income from these two villages was in time supposed to serve the purpose of building a brick church and monastery.

On 9 August 1382, the Polish king issued a privilege for a monastery. Thus this institution came about which, in time, gave rise to the growth and spread of this location's religious prestige not only in Poland, but in the entire Catholic world.

The Paulists proceeded to create a library and an archive. In spite of frequent wars and natural catastrophes, this library was barely hurt and possessed a large number of manuscripts, incunabulum [Translator's note: an incunabulum is a book, page or image printed in Europe prior to 1501], valuable objects and important documents. Among these rare books are many Hebrew religious books that were the object of a series of bibliographic investigations before the last war [World War II]. Unfortunately, however, it was not completed and as a matter of course, was never published (Balaban and Hirshberg).

The Czenstochower monastery in time became so famous all over Poland that people traveled there not only to pray, but also to loot. The gifts for the church grew and fantastic rumors spread about the golden treasures that were found there. In 1430 a gang of Polish nobles attacked the monastery, took some of the valuable items and even carried away the "holy picture."

The legend which is recorded in the unpublished chronicle of the monastery relates that when the robbers took the picture, "the picture began to cry." The robbers became frightened and in anger or awe began to cut the picture with a sword and escaped, leaving the cut picture not far from *Jasna Gora*. King Wladyslaw Jagiello asked that the picture be brought to Krakow. A "Brotherhood of Holy Lukasz," a group of monks solely engaged in painting "holy" pictures, was there. They repaired the picture and it was brought back to Czenstochow with a great ceremony. Incidentally, this procession of bare-footed pilgrims was the first large Catholic demonstration of a non-local character. Those who had dishonored the picture as well as robbing the treasures were caught and sentenced to death.

In the 16th century the monastery and its environs did not distinguish itself in any way. The "brotherly Paulines" sat *al hatoyre v'al hoavoyde*, that is, they studied theology and cultivated the villages that they received as a gift with the help of enslaved peasants. In comparison with other monasteries in Poland, such as Tyniec, for instance, *Jasna Gora* had no great scholarship in the field of Catholic theology and generated no publications. Aleksander Brikner, the great authority on religious literature in old Poland, maintains that the monastery in Czenstochow barely distinguished itself as an institute of learning, although the collections of old manuscripts and books always had a large cultural-historical value.

[Page 6]

Czenstochow first became known in the rest of Poland in the 17th century, although the fame of the city did not attain that of the French Lourdes. This was because while Lourdes became the center of Catholicism in Europe and its miracles of healing cripples was responsible for its prestige – Czenstochow became famous because of its strategic position which gave the state the idea to convert the city into a fortress. The fact itself that a holy picture was found in this city gave rise to this historic decision. Two possibilities were considered in this case. It was considered that such a fortress of the "holy mother" would strengthen the devotion of the military garrison that would feel that it protected both Poland along with the symbol and public image of the picture. On the other hand, the monastery itself would achieve grandeur because it was surrounded by a fortress with all kinds of garrisons of hired soldiers that would ascribe every victory not to their heroism, but to the influence of the "holy mother." Here, in this respect, not only were clear strategic themes realized; although from this standpoint there were many auspicious places for a fortress that would create a partnership between the supernatural protection and the physical resistance in Poland at that time. This was brought out very clearly by a series of travelers, in general, engineers who were invited from abroad by the Polish King, Zigmund III, and later his son, Wladyslaw IV. This happened in the ruthless time that Sienkiewicz described in his famous trilogy. Foreign armies entered Poland from all sides. A prologue came earlier: the revolt of the Cossacks and Chmelnicki's alliance against Poland. Later there was the war with Sweden. Czenstochow was then really transformed into a fortress which surrounded the monastery as a strong ring.

In 1655 the Swedish troops stood at the gates of the Czenstochow fortress. The fortress had to pass its first military test. The Swedish army consisted of 14,000 soldiers armed with 19 large cannons. The Czenstochower fortress counted in total 160 soldiers and 70 monks. At the head of these monks stood Augustyn Kordecki.

The siege of Czenstochow lasted from 18 November to 26 December 1655. The Swedes did not succeed in conquering the fortress and they had to retreat. This was immediately declared as a pure "miracle" and this helped to raise the prestige of Czenstochow both as a fortress and even more, as a "holy sanctuary."

Walenty Odimalski, in his long "epic" of several thousand lines, sang the praises of the "miracle-filled defense" and gave a sample of the kinds of works that in time grew in number to over 20.

The siege of 1655 and Kordecki's heroic accomplishment had made clear the function that this city had taken upon itself thanks to the fortress and the holy picture in the monastery. The fortress symbolized the physical resistance that could conquer a much greater enemy, because the "holy picture," the symbol of "moral power" protected the weak defenders.

In the 18th century, Czenstochow again became famous as a fortress that was the entrance to Warsaw, the capital city. This is how it was during the years 1702 and 1705 when the Swedes again attacked Poland.

During the Bar Confederation which fought to restrain the old privileges of the nobles and was the first anti-Russian movement in Poland, Czenstochow was in the hands of the followers of this movement starting in the year 1769.

The Russian army besieged the fortress for two weeks, which this time had to surrender. This was during the days of January 1 to January 15, 1771.

In 1793 the Prussians acquired Czenstochow. Although the *Jasna Gora* was well defended against the Prussians, the few Polish soldiers had to capitulate on 5 March, 1793. Prussia considered Czenstochow as a very important strategic point. The king wrote in a letter to the Prussian military commander, Melendorf, that both sides of the Warta River should be incorporated because this was a good protective flank for Silesia.

Dankelman, the Justice Minister, visited Klarenberg, that is *Jasna Gora*, on the same day as Czenstochow surrendered.

The birthday of the Prussian king was celebrated in Czenstochow on 25 September 1793 with more imposed pomp than for any celebration for a Polish king.

In the *Fosisher Zeitung* of 3 October 1793 there is a detailed report about this celebration that is worthwhile to provide in Yiddish.

"Last night, here in Czenstochow, the birthday of our gracious king was celebrated with great pageantry. The general field marshal, Excellency Lord Melendorf, the chief commandant of southern Prussia, brought good news. Poland would not obtain the holy picture of Mary that was found in the Klarenberg monastery. This calmed the mood of the local population and as a result the residents took part in the holiday, thanked and wished that the dear life of the father of our land would be maintained. The celebration of this happy and unforgettable day took place in this order:

[Page 7]

"There was a mass in the morning at the Paulists at which an orchestra played. There were three salvos from cannons in the walls of the fortress. At noon, General Lord Polic, the brigadier of the garrison that was located in the area, gave a celebratory banquet. Many individuals from the state were invited along with their wives. At lunch there were drinks to the health of the king and the royal court. Music was played and cannons were fired. At night there were fireworks. This celebratory day ended with a dance-ball that lasted until day break. Joy and delight reigned at the ball."

Presumably, the Prussians thought of the city of Czenstochow as the crown of their Prussian territorial conquests because, on his trip across this territory, the Prussian king stayed in Czenstochow for three days (28th-30th October 1793) and took great interest in the national-religious place occupied by this city in Polish history.

Czenstochow became part of southern Prussia and was chosen as the capital of an administrative region with 153 communities. Its first administrative head was a Germanized Pole, Mr. Futkamer.

On 18 November 1806, the Prussians returned the Czenstochower fortress to the Polish army of the Duchy of Warsaw. Three years later (1809) this fortress defended itself against the Austrians. In 1813 the Russians stormed Czenstochow. That year, the fortress was actually eliminated. It was shown, as a matter of course, that it was too old, without any military worth. However, the city of Czenstochow itself developed parallel to the growth of the importance of *Jasna Gora* and later, of the fortress that once surrounded it. Its importance came as a result of privileges that the Polish kings bestowed upon it. And as early as 1502 Czenstochow received from King Aleksander the rights of a city, the so-called Magdesliger [Magdeburg] right. The city was freed from the rights and jurisprudence of the nobles. King Stefan Batory certified the privileges of the citizens of Czenstochow at the Warsaw Seim because of the favorable geographic circumstances and the important political and diplomatic meetings taking place in Czenstochow. For example, the Polish King Zigmund III met Duke Karl of Breslau in Czenstochow in 1616 and negotiated for the intercession of military help for the Austrian Kaiser Fredinand II against the Czechs and the Hungarians.

In 1657, King Jan Kazimir called together a *senat* [Translator's note: at this time, the *senat* was a privy council and not the upper house of the Polish legislature] in Czenstochow that, at his request, decided on a general military mobilization of the nobles. This happened two years after the "miraculous" defense of the city against the Swedes. Thus, Czenstochow received the reputation as a center of political and, inevitably, military deeds. That Czenstochow played an important role in the political life of the state is shown by the fact that the same king again called together the *senat* there in 1661. This time there was a question of designating an heir to the throne while the king still lived, which was something new. The fact that the members of the *senat* consented to this, although it was entirely their responsibility to designate the place for such a convention, certifies that Czenstochow was thought of as an important political center. A royal wedding even took place in this city. This was in 1670. King Michael Wisniowiecki married the Austrian Duchess Leonora in the *Jasna Gora* monastery.

At that time, Czenstochow witnessed a convention of high state officials and nobles from Poland, Austria and other nations. This event was even worthy of being sung about in songs by every sort of court poet, who again placed the city in the center of political events in Europe.

It can be said that until the end of the 18ᵗʰ century Czenstochow had such a reputation that when someone had judged the city based on the number of writings, rhymes, liturgical poems, travel descriptions or newspaper articles about Czenstochow, one would have thought that this was a large city. Actually, Czenstochow was a small town. It was only at the start of the 19ᵗʰ century that the city had a population that was relatively large. In 1808 Czenstochow counted 3,349 souls. In 1826, new Czenstochow was united with old Czenstochow and one city was created. This almost doubled the number of residents. 6,168 souls were counted in the city in 1827, in 1859 – 8, 647, and a year later – 9,343. In 1826 the government of Congress Poland brought down artisans from Germany and encouraged foreign capitalists to settle in the city and to develop commerce and industry.

[Page 8]

Czenstochow played an important role during the uprising of 1831. As a result of the purchase of weapons for the Polish army in Bresla [possibly Breslau, now Wroclaw] and Konigsberg, the city became a transfer point. The fervent patriotic atmosphere of that generation of citizens of Czenstochow, the majority of German origin, best illustrates the rapid Polanization of the second and even the first generation of non-Poles.

The same was seen during the uprising of 1863. Many Polish uprising leaders came from Czenstochow. The role of Czenstochow in the national upsurge of Poland was made known in Polish patriotic poetry – in the hymns to the Czenstochower "mother" that the rebels sang.

After the uprising, when the positivist philosophy that was the credo of the young Polish capitalism held sway over literature and the press, Polish organized society in Czenstochow was governed by it. However, thanks to the direct influence of the church, the anti-positivistic forces were comparatively stronger in Czenstochow than in other Polish cities.

In 1847, the czarist regime built a Russian Orthodox church as a symbol of Russian rule. The anti-Russian activity at the solemn opening of the church was the first Polish demonstration in Czenstochow since 1863. Its consequences were: the first political trial in this city.

Meanwhile, Czenstochow grew and became greatly industrialized. In 1877 the city had many factories. Paper, wallpapers, soap, candles and candies were produced here. Later, whitewash and brick factories arrived. Czenstochow reached its greatest industrial success in the years 1880-1900. Then iron foundries, textiles and the steel industry arose. It should be understood that commerce developed around these industries. The export and import trade strongly increased thanks to the nearness of Prussia. Czenstochow began to play a heavy role in the economic life of the entire country as a transit point.

In 1897 Czenstochow numbered 43,863 souls. That is, approximately six times as many as 40 years earlier.

More rapid growth of the working class came with the development of Czenstochower industries. The first circle of Czenstochower socialists was founded by the followers of patriotic socialism. Later came the social-democrats, who did not have great influence in Czenstochow. A circle of socialist-revolutionaries was active there, thanks to those in the city's military garrison who were members of this party. This can be seen from the trial of a group of Russian soldiers in Czenstochow that took place in February 1906.

The Polish middleclass was far from having liberal or generally progressive ideas. The National Democratic Party had strong standing with the Polish bourgeoisie in Czenstochow. The Polish petit-bourgeoisie was very conservative, under the influence of Catholic clericalism, and was anti-Semitic as a matter of course. The individual progressive Poles felt very isolated and carried on a difficult struggle for cultural, humanistic activity in the city. This can be seen in a letters of the Czenstochower doctor, Wladyslaw Bieganski, who achieved a respected name beyond the borders of Poland with his medical and philosophical works.

The Polish Socialist Party was strong in Czenstochow. When the split between right and left *pepesovtses* [word derived from initials of *P.P.S.* – Polish Socialist Party] took place, the right, which took the name "revolutionary faction" of the P.P.S., won in Czenstochow. This was very clear at the famous trial of 82 members of this party that took place in January 1914. It is worth remembering that among the most active in this party who were on trial were Jews, such as Advocate Glikson, his daughter, the writer, Marya Glikson, Zaks and others.

At the First World War broke out, Czenstochow was occupied by the Germans on the third day. This was on 3 August 1914. On 8 August 1914, the Germans shot several residents of the city. People began to be dragged to work.

[Page 9]

Czenstochow found itself under German occupation. However, the *Jasna Gora* was under Austrian occupation. Austria, as a "Catholic monarchy," was better suited as a guard of the "holy picture" than Germany.

The population of the city grew greatly with the rise of independent Poland. The city became a part of the Kielce *wojewodztwo* [province or *guberniya*]. Czenstochow numbered 80,473 souls in 1921 and in 1939 – 130,000. Czenstochow had a progressive city managing committee that consisted of 42 councilmen, among them 12 to 14 Jews. In the years, 1917 – 1939, the general culture grew parallel with the economic growth of the city. The city library named for Dr. Wladyslaw Bieganski appeared in 1917. In 1938, this library had 60,000 books. Its foundation was Bieganski's private library. The school system also became more widespread. New *folks-shuls* [secular public schools] and a series of state and private *gymnazies* [high schools] sprang up. There were even plans to open an institution of higher learning.

Emblem of Czestochowa

The city had a series of arts organizations, sports clubs, communal unions and even publishing houses.

The professional intelligentsia was of a high caliber. The majority of the engineers studied abroad. The doctors had a good reputation in the profession. The Czenstochower division of the Medical Institute carried on independent scientific work. Although it held a respected place in the life of Poland, Czenstochow was the seventh largest city in Poland according to population. On the eve of the Second World War, Czenstochow had a major role in the economic activities of the nation. In1938, the city had 2,043 industrial certificates; of these 315 were for large factories, and 3,125 patents for commerce, of these 243 were for large firms.

The city had 6,100 buildings, 86 percent of them brick. Seventy-five percent of all houses had modern facilities, such as electricity, gas and plumbing.

Czenstochow was a modern city that went forward with sure steps until the bloody Second World War stopped its young, vehement march forward.

2. History of the Jews in Czenstochow

It is difficult to establish when Jews actually settled in Czenstochow. The first mention of Jewish matters concerning the city relates to the Frankist movement. When Jakob Frank (1726-1791) was convicted of blasphemy in a rabbinical court in 1760, he was sent to Czenstochow. He was imprisoned in the fortress there for 13 years until the Russian General Bibikow, who captured this fortress, freed him. These 13 years were a continuation of Frank's earlier adventurous life. He surrounded himself with a large retinue, pulled all of the strings, even brought his wife who died in Czenstochow. A number of his followers came here and settled in Czenstochow itself. However, in time this group dispersed. There is great doubt if even one Frankist family remained in Czenstochow.

It is possible that Jews lived in Czenstochow during the era of the last Polish King, Stanislaw August Poniatowski, who ruled in the years 1764-1794. There is information that this king permitted a Polish nobleman to settle seven Jewish families in his house. Such a privilege was entitled *juridike* [legal]. This information is a little suspect because, in general, a nobleman with a *juridike* did not need to ask for permission from the king because the *juridike* of the nobleman is "extraterritorial [exempt from the jurisdiction of local law]" on his small piece of land.

[Page 10]

It may well be that two facts were mixed together. Perhaps a nobleman had seven Jewish families in his house because such Jews paid as much as was wanted. In addition, the king probably permitted seven families to settle in Czenstochow. Who they were and where they lived – that we do not know.

One thing is certain. Jews lived in Czenstochow in the second half of the 18th century. There was already a *kehile* [organized Jewish community] in Janow at that time. The Jews from Czenstochow would be brought there for a Jewish burial. Czenstochow was thus a provincial *kahal*[community] of Janow. The Janower *kehile* carried on a long struggle for its hegemony and did not permit Czenstochow to become an independent *kehile*.

We also do not know the number of Jewish families in Czenstochow. It must not have been a small number because a Jewish *royfe* [old-time, untrained physician], one Reb Hersh, practiced there in the years 1787-1797.

The first concrete information about the Jews there comes from the time of the Prussian occupation when Czenstochow was absorbed into the new administrative portion of southern Prussia that was created after the second partition of Poland. In a report to the Prussian king that was sent by a special official whose task it was to describe the acquired provinces, it is said that "several Jewish peasants are found near Czenstochow." This is unquestionably an important and even peculiar fact. Since this is a statement of a Prussian official who traveled throughout the country and accurately recorded everything, there is no reason not to believe his report.

This is surely a very interesting fact – Jewish farmers at the cradle of the Jewish settlement in Czenstochow. From where were they attracted to Czenstochow? If they were already there, as the Prussian official describes, it means that they were there before the partitions of Poland. It could only mean that these are the seven Jewish families given the privilege by the last Polish king on the condition that they cultivate the earth. Since there were several similar cases of Jews at that time in various parts of Poland, it is plausible that these were the Jewish farmers. In addition, the fact that they were also a Jewish religious community in Czenstochow clinging to the dirty, wooden houses of a nobleman who had a *juridike* and drew a large income from the Jews for housing them is shown by the further fact:

According to a decree of the 17th April 1797, the Prussians permitted the Jews to move out of the dirty places in which they lived and to choose better residences for themselves. Unfortunately the Prussian official, who had been precise in giving the number of residents, Jewish and non-Jewish, in many cities and *shtetlekh*, was very stingy with the pertinent facts in relation to Czenstochow.

Consequently, the important fact about the number of Jews, who at that time were found in the ghetto in Czenstochow that was so dirty that the "good hearted" Prussian permitted them to move to a better ghetto, is not available to us.

We meet another type of Jew at that time around Czenstochow. The Prussian regime considered all Jews who could not show that they had a steady income as "beggar Jews" and drove them out of Prussia. Many of the "beggar Jews" began to wander through the forests and fields of the country in despair and hunger. They were organized into robber bands along with down graded Polish noblemen, burghers, peasants and even gypsies and were active throughout the country. It is said about one of these bands that had many Jews that it operated around Czenstochow.

Alas, there is no information about the internal life of Jews during the Prussian era. In 1806, the army of the Duchy of Warsaw, created by Napoleon on the ruins of the Prussian part of Poland, completed the Czenstochow fortress. The young state began to collect materials about the Jewish population in order to prepare the necessary projects of the planned reforms. We know from these reports that the city of Czenstochow numbered 3,349 souls, of them 496 Jews. This means that in 1808, the Jews made up 14.8 percent of the entire population. There were 6,963 souls in all of the cities and towns of Czenstochow *powiat* [county], of them 1,310 Jews. This means that more than a third of all Jews in the *powiat* lived in the city of Czenstochow. Thus the Jewish religious community in the city was the largest in the entire *powiat*. While Jews made up 18 percent of the city residents, their number in the villages was much smaller. On average they made up two percent of the village residents.

[Page 11]

It is unquestionable that some form of *kehile* organization existed in Czenstochow during the era of Prussian rule. Or else one cannot comprehend from where even the rudimentary form of a *kehile* managing committee originated that was found there in the era of the Duchy of Warsaw. The fiscal policies in relation to Jews under the Prussians dictated the necessity to create a *kehile* that would bear the responsibility for taxes that the Jews had to pay. In many cities, Warsaw included, the Prussians actually legalized the *kehile*. It was the same in Czenstochow. There must have been a *kehile* with leaders as there was everywhere. As there was no act from Prussian times about permitting Jews to have a *kehile* managing committee, it is clear that the conduct of the *kehile* that was active during the time of the Warsaw principality existed earlier under the Prussians.

The first activity of the Czenstochower *kehile* during the era of the Duchy of Warsaw was to open a permanent synagogue for praying. The second very important work was to choose a spiritual leader who would stand at the head of the *kehile*.

A session of the *kehile* took place in Czenstochow on 8 Av 5568 ([1 August] 1808). This surely was not the first session in the over two years that the city was under the new government. The character of this session attests that this was a routine continuation of a managing committee that had worked for a longer time on the part of the Jewish *kehile*. At that session, one Reb Yakov *ben* [son of] Eliezer Lewi was chosen as the head of the rabbinical court and also as chairman of the *kehile*. This Yakov *ben* Eliezer signed his name specifically as *Wierny Kahaku Czenstocowskiego* [Loyal Community of Czenstochow] (the name of the *kehile* in Czenstochow).

We know almost nothing about the origin of this first representative of the *kehile* in Czenstochow, whose name has reached us. We only know that he was a Jew, a scholar, a good organizer and probably also a wealthy man. This last can be deduced from the fact that he was the treasurer of the *kehile*, an office that as a rule was not entrusted to a poor man.

It was necessary to turn to him in all matters having to do with the *kehile*. It is very interesting that at this time Lewi signed a declaration of devotion and honesty in the carrying out of his functions, including the point that he, Lewi, "would work for the interests of the city, even if it brought harm to another *kehile*."

The "other *kehile*' was certainly Janow, which had frowned on Czenstochow's intentions of "emancipation" and tried with all of its strength to prevent Czenstochow from separating itself completely form Janow. The city itself had probably expected more benefits from an independent *kehile* than from being attached to Janow and therefore the Czenstochower city middle class supported the strivings for autonomy by the young Jewish community.

The *kehile* had three *parnosim* [elected heads of community, singular – *parnes*] who served according to a system of rotation, that is, alternating each month. Therefore, they were called *parnes-khodesh* [head for a month]. The treasurer was not permitted to pay out any monies without a note from a *parnes*.

The *parnes-khodesh* had the right to issue a note by himself, but not for more than six *gildn*.

A Regimental Flag from the Returning Remnant of the

Polish Army from Napoleon's 1813 Russian Campaign.

It was used as an ark curtain in the New Synagogue in Czenstochow.

[Page 12]

If it was a question of a larger amount, the signatures of all three *parnosim* was required.

The head of the rabbinical court was a paid office. Even when he himself did not want it to be. His wages were six *Reich's tolar* a month. His salary was 12 *Reich's tolar* a month during the months of Nisan and Tishrei. In addition, he received a free apartment. The head of the religious court also received three percent of the monies collected that came in from the surrounding settlements. At that session, it was also decided that as long as the city of Czenstochow did not have a rabbi, the head of the rabbinical court would also receive half of the rabbinical fees for certain functions.

The head of the rabbinical court was also permitted to go to the settlements around Czenstochow once a year and receive Chanukah money.

In addition to Reb Yakov Lewi, this document was signed by 40 more distinguished Czenstochower Jewish community leaders.

A Group of Children from Mrs. Wajzer's School

This is the oldest document saved in the records of the Czenstochower *kehile*. It can be seen from it that the salary for the head of the rabbinical court was not designed for Yakov Lewi, who in all probability did not need it, but as a principle for the future when another would take over this office. A second important fact is that around Czenstochow there were settlements that were bound administratively to the city. The best evidence is that funds would arrive from these communities and the head of the religious court had the right to receive three percent of this income. This can be deduced because the Czenstochower *kehile* was at that time already the head *kehile* in the district. This organization according to administrative counties or districts worked very actively during the era of the Duchy of Warsaw. Witnesses reported that in meetings of the *kehilus* of that time, a common effort was made to bring about the repeal of a series of severe fiscal edicts using their joint power.

The Janower *kehile* did not accept this effort by Czenstochow to become independent. It wanted to prevent it or else it would lose all of the surrounding small settlements, which very quickly came under the influence of the younger, more impetuous *kehile*.

The first dispute between Janow and Czenstochow was vividly displayed that year, that is, in 1808. Then Luszczewski, the Finance Minister of the marginal and smaller Duchy of Warsaw, imagined that a great deal of money could be extracted from the Jews through various precise taxes. He and the Education Minister Grabowski conducted a struggle against Jewish "fanaticism," whose main source was Jewish books.

The easiest thing would have been to confiscate Jewish books. However, such an edict would not have brought in any revenue. It was decided to tax the Jews who wanted to keep their Jewish books. This meant that everyone who had books had to permit them to be stamped and, it should be understood, there would be a payment for this. It is true that this did not exterminate "fanaticism," but the Jews who wished to remain "fanatics" were fiscally inconvenienced and had to pay for this "pleasure." The opinion was that many Jews would more quickly give up their books rather than pay the stamp tax. This would decrease the number of "fanatics." This was the calculation of the Education Minister, Stanislaw Grabowski.

When a circular arrived at the Czenstochower *kehile* that it should inform its Jews about the law for stamping books, they immediately sent a printed Yiddish proclamation from the rabbinical authority to all of the surrounding communities. These were Dzialoszyn, Krzepice, Amstow, Kejnckow [Cynkow], Kuznica, Klobuck, Lobodno, Mierzyce and others.

Until now this was the explicit territory of the Janower *kehile*. With the inclusion of these communities and the sending out of emissaries who stamped the books in the name of the Czenstochower *kehile*, gave receipts, provided exact accounts and so on, Janow lost its rights in relation to these communities and Czenstochow was established as the legal guardian of these communities.

[Page 13]

The decree is of such great cultural and historical value that we reprint it here. This decree is reprinted here without even the smallest changes so that the reader will have an idea of the language and orthography of that time.

[Translator's note: The reprint of the decree is not of the original, but a typeset version. The language and orthography are in the old Yiddish and Hebrew style and the text is a combination of Yiddish and Hebrew. The essence of the document is provided in the paragraphs below.]

From this important document we learn a great deal about the organization of the Jewish *kehile* in Czenstochow during the era of the Duchy of Warsaw. First of all, we see who the head of the *kehile* was at that time. He was named Berish Szapiro. Alas, we do not have any details about him. It can be seen from the text of the decree that the Jews had eight days to make a declaration about their books and have them stamped. Fines had to be paid in cases when the order was not carried out.

The *kehile* had special emissaries who would travel around and receive payment from the owners of the books. There were varying prices for the cities and for the villages. The residents of the villages paid a great deal less than the city property owners. The emissaries were probably collectors from the *kehile*. The head of the *kehile* used the opportunity of the emissaries being in the surrounding communities to stamp the books and he informed them that those who had not paid their yearly recruitment taxes must pay the same emissaries.

This tax was paid by Jews to free themselves from military service. In 1812, after long meetings and negotiations, the *kehilus* of the Duchy of Warsaw succeeded in freeing themselves of this tax for one large payment of 700,000 *gildn*.

At first, an emissary was nothing more than the presenter of an edict. In each *shtetl* or village, he would call all of the Jews and read aloud the proclamation of the rabbinical assembly. The representative of the communities in question would sign the proclamation stating that the Jews had heard it read or that he himself had read it. Each emissary was responsible for about 15 small adjacent towns. If they wanted to pay the book stamp tax or the recruitment taxes through him, it could be done. If not, the money had to be brought directly to the *kehile* in Czenstochow.

In the light of this document, it can be seen that the *kehile* in Czenstochow was a legal representative of the Jews not only from that city, but also from a series of surrounding *shtetlekh* and village settlements. True, it lacked many attributes of an independent *kehile*. For example, it did not yet have a rabbi and it also had no cemetery. This first came into being during the era of Congress Poland (1815-1830). However, its power was great enough, its population large enough so that it put many older and larger Jewish *kehilus* in the country in the shadows.

[Page 14]

First of all, the favorable geographical location of the city and the rapid industrialization of the entire surrounding area brought rapid growth of the Czenstochower *kehile*. The government encouraged foreign capitalists and fine craftsmen to enter the country and help in the development of industry and trade. In such a manner, many German capitalists and craftsmen came to Czenstochow from nearby Silesia. Among the first group were also Jews. It cannot be denied that among the older resident Jews who lived in Czenstochow, there were several who settled during the Prussian era. True, in the era of the Duchy of Warsaw, they were asked to leave the country. However, many remained, particularly in the smaller cities of the country. That there were at that time many among the Czenstochower Jews who had come from Germany can be seen by the fact that the well-to-do Jews employed teachers especially brought from abroad. This was not accomplished so easily because the local burghers fought each attempt to admit a "foreign" Jew and even the church was opposed to this. In 1818 it seems that there were two Jewish teachers in Czenstochow who gave lectures there. They were Leon Gotenberg of Glogau (Silesia) and Wilhelm Imier, who was brought from Praszka.

When they began to introduce "precincts" for the Jewish population, that is, actually ghettos, the Czenstochower city managing committee did not want to refuse this "privilege." Czenstochow then had a proportionally greater number of Europeanized Jews than, for example, Warsaw. In 1818, a group of Jews from the district turned to the regime with a proposal that they were prepared to dress in the European manner and to send their children to public schools. Therefore, they should be freed of the obligation to live in the Jewish precinct. It is not known how the city hall answered this. The fact that several of the rich Jews had houses outside the Jewish precinct gives witness that the "Europeanized" Jews actually lived in the Christian streets, just as in other Polish cities.

There is also the first information from that time about the role of the Jews in industry. In 1827 there were already descriptions of Jewish factories in the city that sold "Czenstochower products." We do not know the nature of these factories. Some Jews were involved with contraband. This can be seen from the frequent decrees about withdrawing from around Czenstochow. A large number of those involved with contraband later settled in Lodz.

The families that in time took a respected place in local Jewish communal life came from the first Czenstochower pioneers in industry and commerce. The head of the *kehile* in the 1830's was Herc Kon (1789-1862), the wealthy man and *maskhil* [follower of the Enlightenment]. He supported the efforts of the individual *maskhilim* [plural of *maskhil*] in spreading secular education among the local Jews and even opened a private school for Jewish children.

People began coming to Czenstochow from surrounding cities and *shtetlekh* searching for a livelihood. City hall was careful that "foreign" Jews not settle there, but it did not succeed. These illegal residents lived in constant fear of being ousted from the city. There was a time (around 1829) when the number of such families amounted to an entire 100, that is, almost half of the entire Jewish population. In 1827, the official number of Jews in Czenstochow was 1,141 souls and made up 18½ percent of the general city population.

The Jews without the right of residence probably had a livelihood in the city because they would spend a great deal of money for legal protection from the city administration. The city fathers and the police had an easy income from the systematic bribes paid by the illegal Jews.

A Jewish plutocracy [rule by the wealthy] began to evolve very early in Czenstochow, for whom the little respect that communal activity in the kehile life could give them in the narrow, enclosed residential area was no longer enough. It should not be forgotten that among the rich men in Czenstochow were many who received a general [i.e. secular] education in the nation's schools or abroad. Their frequent trips to Germany quickly "Europeanized" them and they wanted to carry out many of the reforms in Czenstochow that had been carried out in larger German communities.

Also among the Jewish artisan element were followers of modern Jewish life in the German style. In Czenstochow in 1841, there were 32 Jewish weavers with 160 weaving stools and 200 Jewish journeymen. The majority of their teachers were German master craftsmen. As a matter of course, they knew German and looked upon German culture as the last word in progress. Even the administration of the kehile in the years 1833-1862 was recorded in German, but printed with Yiddish letters.

It is no wonder that the individuals who already considered themselves progressive people looked for an entry into general communal life. This could be achieved either through an individual privilege or through conversion. The privilege was exemplified, first of all, by the right to live outside the Jewish ghetto. A higher form of the privilege was the right to own one's own estate.

[Page 15]

The history of Shimeon Landau-Gutenberg, the son of Wilhelm Landau, a German Jew who settled in Czenstochow during the time of the Duchy of Warsaw, is very interesting in this respect.

Shimeon Landau was a rich Czenstochower merchant and manufacturer. In a detailed petition, he turned to the regime in December 1833 with a request that the rights of a citizen be given to him. He wrote that he and his household read and write Polish and German. This – he asserted – could be easily established by the city management committee.

He further stated that his children attended the general [Polish secular] schools and he himself did not wear "the external signs that the Jews wear." Thus, he promised that no Jews would work in his businesses "who do not wear either Polish or German clothing nor speak one of these two languages well." Landau explains that since 1822 he has had a factory for calico and cotton production in the country.

The matter of giving him the rights of a citizen was drawn out for almost two years. The Warsaw regime answered (12 March 1835) that his service in relation to the country was not so remarkable that he was worthy to receive the rights of a citizen. Landau was able to live outside of the ghetto because he was rich, dressed as a "European" and sent his children to general schools.

However, his son had more luck. In 1863 he was permitted to buy an estate in Kielcer *gubernia* [province] and in that way the dream of the pioneer Jewish family in Czenstochow to become Polish lords and to have the privilege to enter the highest social group in the country came true.

It is worth remembering the other families that had the merit to receive the rights of a citizen – the banking family of Adam Bergman, Wilhelm Kon, the Walbergs and the Landowskis.

However, there were those who did not have any luck or enough capital in order to be able to present themselves and emerge from the Jewish community; they had to live in the crowded alleys of the Jewish precinct. They tried to better their circumstances through conversion. But they probably were ashamed of converting in Czenstochow itself. The Paulists of *Jasna Gora* even had a special fund to support converts, but these candidates for the Catholic Church actually traveled to Warsaw, in order to carry out the shameful act of betrayal far from their home and their relatives. The majority of those who converted in Czenstochow were not residents, but from the surrounding cities and *shtetlekh*.

In 1833 a Czenstochower, one Balzam, who immediately Polishized his name as Balzamowski, converted. In 1838 the local tailor, Borsztajn, left for Warsaw with his wife and converted there. In 1843, the local teacher, Gershom Wiszlicki, and his wife did it. One of the first capitalist entrepreneurs in the city, Jakov Jakubowicz, converted in 1848. The conversion in the house of Herc, the wealthy man and *parnes* [elected official] of the *kehile*, provoked great sorrow and tension. One of his sons converted in Warsaw in 1865.

The nickname, "Czenstochower *shmadnikes* [converts]" was not connected with the fact that there was a strongly felt affinity to the ideas of the Jewish Enlightenment in Czenstochow earlier than in other cities, but only with the actual conversions, which provoked great strain in the city.

The growth of the Jewish population in Czenstochow gave rise to the development of various charitable groups. Poverty remained in the community that had very quickly received a reputation as a rich *kehile*. However, with the arrival of the years 1847-1848, when the country lived through crisis and hunger took hold in many houses, the Czenstochower *kehile* had to organize immediate support for its poor. The effort to enable Jews to be employed in the nearby lime mines, even for temporary work, was rejected by the government.

The *kehile* was not prepared for such a charity effort. In general, they literally thought of the poor of their city as "strangers" who had come here in order to try their luck with the "residents." These "residents" prided themselves that they could show that their families had settled in Czenstochow at the time of the Duchy of Warsaw and, unavoidably they thought, before the "partition." Czenstochow was for many Jews from surrounding cities and *shtetlekh* a sort of transit point where one looked for a livelihood. If one had luck, he remained; if not, he left for Lodz, which at that time was tempting with the spell of pioneering enterprises that literally were surrounded by fantastically buzzing business adventures.

[Page 16]

The appeal by a pioneering Czenstochower *maskhil* [follower of the Enlightenment], Yitzhak Bursztyn or Bursztynski, the local correspondent of the *Algemeiner Zeitung Des Judentums* [*General Newspaper of Jewry*] that the well known Rabbi, Dr. Ludwig Filipson, had published in Magdeburg, stems from those years of crisis. Bursztynski appealed to the Czenstochower Jews to give charity systematically and not to throw donations at random when a poor person knocked at a Jewish door. He proposed that they should set a monthly payment over the course of six months for the victims of the crisis.

He wrote, "Where is fairness and justice that we would permit the needy of our religious community to die of hunger and die in the streets of our city before our eyes?"

He appealed to the Jews in the city to contribute to such a fund. The city had enough well-to-do proprietors and a contribution would hardly affect the wealthy person, but the poor might benefit greatly from a few pennies – he wrote in his half Hebrew and half German appeal.

This was the first and largest communal action on behalf of the local poor or impoverished Jews in the history of Czenstochow. The fact that this action was not organized by the *kehile* managing committee itself, but was an individual initiative by one person was a sign that although Czenstochow was a *kehile* with "progressive" leaders similar to Warsaw, in matters of *kehile* organization, it was still backward.

During the cholera epidemic of 1852 there was a more organized action. There were charity balls, money was collected and, in general, there was more interest in the victims of the epidemic. This was more a prophylactic charity that helped the rich element of the Jewish population protect itself from the plague.

Around that time the local Jewish population grew very quickly. In 1840, Jews made up about a third of the population. 5,004 Christians were then in Czenstochow, 2,999 Jews. However, the entire population of the city began to grow at a faster tempo and so did the Jewish population. This was because the city drew many new residents, particularly from the surrounding villages, who came to work in the factories in Czenstochow. For Jews, settling in the city was severely limited by the strict control of the Jewish precinct and the systematic regimentation of the Jewish residents. In 1857, the entire population of the city consisted of 8,637 souls, of them 2,976 Jews. This means 34.5 percent. In 1862, there were 3,360 Jews in Czenstochow (37.3 percent of the general population).

In 1862 Czenstochow met with a great misfortune. A terrible fire broke out on 4 November. The poor Jews suffered the most. This was at the time of "Polish-Jewish brotherhood." The joint action on behalf of the fire victims that was carried out by the Jews and the Poles actually was important in demonstrating the significance of "practical love." The priest and the rabbi joined the committee. Bernard Kon, an owner of the largest mill and a member of the city council, was the chairman. Many Christians gave money; 14,000 *zlotes* were collected.

This fire was used as a strong argument that the Jewish precinct must be abolished because the fire was a result of crowdedness and filth. In 1859 they began to urge that the Jewish precinct should be enlarged as far as "Panni Marja" Street, including the market. In 1862 the Czenstochower city council decided to entirely abolish the precinct. The city fathers were proud that their decision came earlier than the decree that in general abolished the ghettos in Congress Poland.

In general at that time, that is, in the years 1861-1863, a pro-Polish feeling held sway in Czenstochow that was expressed in identification with the Polish national idea. In addition to Bernard Kon, the property owners Bernard Mejzl, Yitzhak Ginsberg, Yitzhak Fajgenblat, and Jakov Zajdenman, were chosen for the city managing committee. These four Jews were representatives; Bernard Kon was the councilman.

The mood was so elevated that *Juczenka* [a weekly newspaper] published a letter from a Czenstochow Jew against Moshe Hess[2]. This Jew wrote that "*Eretz-Yisroel* is a dream" and that "our fatherland is Poland." The letter ostensibly was written to a Czenstochow Christian who wanted to know if Jews in the city felt themselves to be Poles.

[Page 17]

The fact itself that after Czenstochow, only Warsaw showed a great deal of activity that year in connection with the uprising of 1863 elicited an enthusiastic response in the Polish press.

In the years 1861-1863, Czenstochow had a significant group of young Jews who were already culturally Polish and were interested in Polish matters. The proximity of the Prussian border gave the young people easier access to political literature than the young people in Warsaw. It was easier to smuggle such literature simply because many people visited Breslau or Konigsberg more often from Czenstochow than from Warsaw. For example, therefore, a copy of *Rome and Jerusalem* by Moshe Hess fell into the hands of a member of the Enlightenment in Czenstochow much earlier than in Warsaw.

Therefore, Czenstochow also filled a significant role in the spread of forbidden works and in smuggling revolutionary literature and, later, in smuggling weapons during the uprising.

Those emigrating from Poland used Czenstochow as a more secure transit station as was done with the smuggling of literature. The local Jews, experienced in matters of contraband, distinguished themselves in this work. Among the young people were found many students from Warsaw schools in general and from the rabbinical schools, in particular.

They were very enthusiastic about the Polish patriotic movement before the uprising, brought news to the city, wrote in the Polish newspapers, sent correspondence to the weekly newspaper, *Juczenka,* later helped take care of the wounded insurgents and transferred them to Krakow. They were known in the revolutionary circles and, therefore, it is no wonder that in the secret instructions from the Polish revolutionary committee of 1863, the "connection to the

Poles of Moshe Rabbeinu's belief [a reference to the religion of Moses, i.e. Jews] in Czenstochow" are mentioned.

In 1862 a patriotic demonstration took place in Czenstochow, at which spoke Daniel Najfeld, about whom more will be written at length later. The Jewish students in the Czenstochow secular schools took part in this meeting. Also among those who took an active part in the uprising were several young Czenstochower Jews. Several Czenstochower Jews were arrested after the uprising of 1863, such as Shmuel Widowski, who was arrested and placed in the custody of the police for two years. One Josef Kon escaped abroad. When he returned, he was arrested and placed in the custody of the police, also for two years.

The most important one among the young Jewish patriots of the uprising was Shimeon Dankowicz, upon whose biography it is worthwhile to pause.

Dankowicz was born in Czenstochow in 1841. His mother was a midwife. He graduated from the secular elementary school and later was a student in the district school. He came to Warsaw in 1859 and entered the medical-surgical academy. Later, when this academy was closed, because a Polish university was opened (*Szkola Glowna*), Dankowicz transferred there and studied medicine. He was a member of the Warsaw youth circle that gave as its purpose the spreading of Polish assimilation among the young Jewish generation. In November 1860 Dankowicz gave a lecture to that circle about Jews that was bold and new. Dankowicz developed the idea that Jews did not cease to be a nation, although they had lost their land. No doubt this was the influence of Moshe Hess' *Rome and Jerusalem* that was published that year and provoked a mostly negative critique. In those sweet years of assimilation, publishing such a thesis in Warsaw required courage and independence of thought.

A passionate discussion developed around this report. The young Aleksander Krojzhar, who took an active part in this circle, described Dankowicz's report and the discussion in a letter to a friend.

Krojzhar wrote, "Voices were heard that there is no nation without a country, and only the land where they were born should be a fatherland for the Jews. This opinion found many supporters."

[Page 18]

The fact itself that Krojzhar wrote that many did not agree with Dankowicz, while one could have expected that everyone would not agree with him shows that not everyone then considered themselves Poles of Moshe Rabbeinu's belief. It is clear that Dankowicz also did not consider himself as such. He was the first nationally disposed Jew among the Jewish intelligencia in Poland at that time. Still clearer, this appears in connection with his article in the weekly newspaper, *Juczenka*, which was published in Warsaw in the years 1861-1863 under the editorship of Daniel Najfeld. This Najfeld met Dankowicz in Czenstochow. Najfeld invited him through the editor's mail box to send articles for his journal.

Dankowicz's article about "Proverbs and Fables in Rabbinic Literature" appeared in 1862, in *Juczenka* (number 12). Dankowicz wrote thusly in this article:

"Proverbs provide the philosophy of the people. Therefore, each nation (*narod* [nation in Polish]) collects these monuments of the past and carefully protects them, both those that are of a high cultural status and those that are of lower status."

Dankowicz expressed the desire "that our co-religionists should take up the collection of proverbs, reports and even characteristic expressions from Jewish *jargon*[3] from the mouths of the Jewish people."

This article evoked dissatisfaction in the radical-assimilated circles. However, Najfeld defended Dankowicz and agreed with him.

Dankowicz was one of the most dynamic personalities among the Jewish young people during the rebellion. He took an active part in a series of battles and was wounded. Thanks to the help of a group Poles, he was brought wounded to Krakow. He was healed there. He was a

Hebrew teacher at the beginning. In 1868 he was chosen as the preacher of the Krakow synagogue "of Jews, friends of progress." The intelligent sermon that he gave on 18 January 1868 was published by this synagogue.

Meanwhile Dankowicz received a doctorate from Krakow University and became a teacher of the Jewish religion in the district *gimnazie* [high school]. In the years 1868-1883 he held various positions as a rabbi and teacher of religion, all in smaller communities. He could not remain in Krakow because the Orthodox persecuted him. He left for Bulgaria and was the first chief rabbi of the young state. In 1893 he left there. What happened to him later and when he died is unknown.

This poor Czenstochower young man achieved a name as a Hebrew lexicographer. He published articles about Hebrew philology, about the influence of Hebrew on Slavic languages in the most significant periodicals of that time and intended to write a history of Jews in Poland.

A restless soul, Dankowicz could not find any permanent place for himself. His writings were lost; his name was forgotten. Many biographies indicate that he was was from Bohemia, because he was the rabbi there for a short time.

The Czenstochower son of a midwife was actually the first Jewish folklorist in Poland and the first herald of the Jewish national idea at a time when the idea of assimilation was entirely wrapped in the idea of "progress."

Translator's Footnotes

1. Damazy Macoch was a monk in Czenstochow's Pauline Convent. He killed his cousin and confessed to the murder, which took place after the monk, his cousin and his cousin's wife had committed a robbery at *Jasna Gora*, desecrating the robe and diamond encrusted crown of the "Black Madonna" and stealing and selling the jewels.

2. Moshe Hess was the author of *Rome and Jerusalem: The Last National Question,* in which he called for the creation of a Jewish socialist commonwealth in Palestine.

3. *Jargon* was originally a neutral term referring to a hybrid language; it became a derogatory term referring to Yiddish.

[Page 18]
3. Cultural History of Czenstochower Jews

It has already been mentioned that after Warsaw, Czenstochow was the city where the Enlightenment bloomed in Poland. As early as 1814, a private Jewish teacher from Germany was there, who taught the children of well-to-do proprietors. The best teachers from surrounding cities and *shtetlekh*, such as Dzialoszyn, Prazka, Wielun and others, would settle in Czenstochow. For example, one such person was Shlomoh Dovid Gutengot, a follower of the Enlightenment from Dzialoszyn, who would give private Hebrew lessons to the children who went to the public Czenstochower schools.

The wealthy young Jews would attend the government schools in Piotrkow, Kalisz and Warsaw. Young Jewish girls from Czenstochow were found in the schools of Breslau [Wroclaw], Konigsberg [Kaliningrad] and Berlin. There were private boarding schools there, "*für Izraelitshe Mädchen* [for Jewish girls]," where attention was given to the "daughters of Zion" and they guided them "to God and respectability."

It can be shown that the cultural language of the educated Jews in Czenstochow was German. The *Algemeine Zeitung des Judentums* [*General Newspaper of Jewry*] had 11 subscribers in Czenstochow and a special correspondent. Incidentally, even Warsaw did not always have this.

[Page 19]

When the rabbinical school was opened in Warsaw in 1826, many young men from Czenstochow attended this school. Bernard Cymerman, Moyrici Kon and Bernard Landau studied there in 1830. Cymerman was later a censor and even a teacher in the rabbinical school. Bernard Landau was a teacher. Moyrici Kon was a manufacturer and landowner.

After the rebellion of 1863 the number of Czenstochow young people in the rabbinical school rose and until the closing of the school (in 1863) amounted to a total of 12 [students].

During the years 1826-1840, the young Czenstochowers attended various learning institutions abroad. Several of them studied medicine and later practiced in their birthplace, such as Dr. Landowski, for example.

The *Algemeine Zeitung des Judentums* wrote in 1841 – "No *kehile* [organized Jewish community] in Poland has such a lively inclination for humanity as the local one [Czenstochow]. Almost every person, even those who wear Polish-Jewish clothing, develops a feeling for a better and more modern culture. Everyone rejoices because of the success the Enlightenment has had in Germany and other places. A considerable number of the local Jews read German and Polish books, mainly on themes of the Enlightenment, ethics and much beautiful literature. It can be said that religious fanaticism, superstition and nonsense have disappeared among the higher-class Jews over the past several years."

It was said in a second letter from Czenstochow published in the same German-Jewish weekly that the Enlightenment in general was stronger than Hasidism. There was a total of 25 Hasidic families out of 400 families in Czenstochow.

Czenstochow – it was said there – was the first of all of the organized communities in Poland to come into contact with education and culture thanks to its trade and contact with Silesia. This is partly a debt to the German language, to the European clothing and the feeling of cleanliness and order that the local Jews learned from the 'moral revolution' in Poland. That is, before the revolt of 1863, there was more educational activity in Polish than in German. In 1860 Czenstochower Jews could take pride in the hundreds of young Jews who studied in the general schools, *gymnazie* [secondary school] and in the Warsaw rabbinical school. In that year, nine Czenstochower Jews graduated from university.

This *kehile* began very early to lobby for its own elementary school for Jewish children.

This educational activity was connected to two names which had a place of honor in the history of the Czenstochow Enlightenment.

Bursztynski or Bursztyn was born in Zagorow (Konin *powiat* [county]) in 1790. He was a private Hebrew teacher and later an official translator of Yiddish and Hebrew with the Kalisz provincial government. He later settled in Praszka as a private teacher. When the Czenstochower city hall expelled two private Jewish teachers, Botenberg and Imler, because they did not have the right of residence, the local *kehile* invited Bursztynski as a *kehile* secretary. In addition, he was employed as a teacher and preacher in the city synagogue.

Thanks to the intervention of the head of the *kehile*, Herc Kon, Bursztynski had permission to live in Czenstochow for three years (1828-1831). However, he was not permitted to bring along his family.

Bursztynski knew Polish very well. This was a rarity among Jews at that time because, as was said, German was the cultural language of the educated Jews until about 1860. Therefore, it is no wonder that the Jewish population needed to have him. He wrote pleas in court, letters of commerce and was even chosen as a translator by the Czenstochower Friend's Court. His two sons were then in the Kalisz *gymnazie* [high school] and later studied medicine in Germany.

Thus, Bursztynski became a "private advocate" – that is, he wrote all kinds of pleas and letters. This situation did not please the local Polish advocates and they denounced him to the city regime. The city hall prohibited him from writing such letters. However, Bursztynski did not lose and in a memorandum to the city president showed that what he did was legal. Meanwhile the uprising of 1830-1831 silenced the controversy.

[Page 20]

At the end of 1831 they again began to persecute him. This time they relied on a legal basis. Since the three years that he was permitted to live in Czenstochow had passed, as a rule he had to leave the city. It was not itself important if his "private legal profession'" was legal or not. The city asked him to leave within five days. He himself felt that there was no legal basis for his remaining here because he was a "foreigner." Therefore, he had to carry on a fight alone and he carried it out. The *województwo* [administrative district] regime permitted him to remain in Czenstochow on the condition that he live in the Jewish precinct. Finally, after long official procedures he remained in the city where he died in 1852, falling victim to the cholera epidemic.

In the course of the years during which he lived in Czenstochow, Bursztynski did a great deal to spread worldly education among the Jews. It has already been mentioned that he was the Czenstochower correspondent of the *Algemeine Zeitung des Judentums*. His letters were an important source for the history of Jews in Czenstochow.

Bursztynski was convinced that the problem of education for the local Jews could not be solved with private teaching. He wrote that the majority of wealthy men have good teachers and *melamdim* for their children. They can pay as a matter of course and they choose and pay for the best pedagogues. On the contrary, the poor must approach the corner *melamdim*, send their children to the filthy, crowded religious elementary schools. Therefore, Bursztynski believed that a city such as Czenstochow needed to have a public elementary school for the lower economic strata. He submitted a detailed plan for this. The school was to have three classes with three teachers and, in addition, a manager. He himself volunteered to teach religion and ethics without pay. The school would be supported through tuition. In order to create communal prestige for the school, he proposed to organize a council of elders, at the head of which would stand the rabbi. He hoped to win over the pious circle with this. It should be understood that the orthodox fought Bursztynski's project. Therefore, his plan was supported by the followers of the Enlightenment headed by Herc Kon, the head of the *kehile*. It was proposed several times in the city synagogue and in the house of study. Signatures were collected from the prosperous merchants and a request was delivered to the regime. This was in 1840. The Polish city managing committee warmly received this proposal. Bursztynski himself wrote in a letter that the new City President, Pazerski, was favorably disposed toward the plan and recommended it to the higher state authorities. Bursztynski and his state supporters probably did not know that the Russian regime was against Polish schools for Jewish children. They waited until the general rules concerning elementary schools for Jews in Russia were completed. Paskewicz, the viceroy of Poland, blocked the permission granted for such schools.

Bursztynski was so sure of permission that he brought Daniel Najfeld, his student from Praszka, to Czenstochow who meanwhile was employed giving private lessons.

Bursztynski was also a writer. He knew German and Yiddish well, in addition to Polish and Hebrew. His Polish work written in 1820 remains in manuscript. This is a tractate against the blood libel.[4] This is the only work that has been preserved. Many other works of his have been lost. In those years, when there were no Jewish periodicals in Poland, not in Polish and not in Yiddish, it was difficult for a person such as Bursztynski to reach readers.

As someone who awoke people to education, as *kehile* secretary, private teacher, a lawyer with a small practice, organizer of charity in Czenstochow, Bursztynski earned the title as the first pioneer in the realm of Jewish instruction and education in Czenstochow.

The second educational worker in Czenstochow was the well known editor of the Polish-Yiddish periodical in Warsaw, *Jutrzenka* [*Morning Star*], which was published from 1861-1863. This was Daniel Josef Najfeld.

Najfeld was born in Praszka in 1814. In 1827 he became a student in the Wielun district school that was headed by priests. At that time there were very few Jewish students, particularly in the province, who attended a Polish school. He wanted to study medicine, but his family circumstances and the revolt of 1831 disturbed his plans. He settled in Dzialoszyn and became a private teacher. Later, he married in Praszka and from there he was brought to Czenstochow by Bursztynski. Meanwhile, Bursztynski worked at organizing a school and Najfeld was employed giving private Talmud lessons in Hebrew and Polish. Thanks to these lessons he became acquainted with the elite of the Jewish *kehile* and also with Polish society. He found great success in both circles. The Jews had great respect for him. Despite being a follower of the Enlightenment, he was a pious Jew and in addition a great scholar. The Polish also respected him because not only was he interested in Polish culture, but he also knew the Polish language and literature very well.

[Page 21]

Najfeld sent articles and reports from Czenstochow to the *Algemeiner Zeitung Des Judentums* [*General Newspaper of Jewry*]. This was his literary first fruit.

When Bursztynski's plan for a Jewish elementary school fell through, Najfeld decided to try out his own luck and seek permission to open a private school. In 1843, he turned from Czenstochow to educational trustee in Warsaw with a request for permission to open a private elementary school for Jewish children. However, he was refused. At that time several Czenstochower businessmen turned directly to Petersburg to Avarov, the education minister, asking that Najfeld be permitted to take up his teaching. After lengthy efforts, they succeeded in receiving permission for a school for Najfeld, but not in Czenstochow, but in Praszka. This was in 1847. This was interpreted legally that because Najfeld was not from Czenstochow, but from Praszka, he could participate in teaching in "his" city, but not in a "strange one."

However, Praszka was too small to support a Jewish private school. And Najfeld had already made a name in Czenstochow. He was very pleased with its followers of the Enlightenment. Therefore, he did not want to give up the hope that in the end, he would become a teacher and mentor of the Czenstochow Jews.

On 23 September 1850, Najfeld turned to the education trustee with a request that he be permitted to take an exam in order to receive a diploma as a teacher because the curriculum at the county school from which he had graduated was the equivalent of the curriculum of general instruction in the Rabbinical school: in such a manner, Najfeld, first of all, would be equally qualified as a teacher. Later, it would automatically be easier for him to receive permission for a school.

Two months later, he received a notice from the education trustee that he could not be permitted to take such an exam.

"The title of teacher" – the trustee clarified – "demands an exam after a full curriculum at a *gymnazie* [secondary school] or from a rabbinical school. The school from which Najfeld graduated, is the equivalent of a *powiat* [district or county] school and, therefore, I cannot agree that his request should be accommodated."

However, Najfeld did not give up. In April 1851 he wrote a detailed memorandum about his pedagogical activities in general and in particular, and based on his experiences, he asked to be permitted to open a private school in Czenstochow. This time Najfeld did not let the education trustee in Warsaw or the director of the provincial *gymnazie* in Piotrkow know that he had to close the school in Praszka. He was left with only three students and they left the school during the period of the next week. Najfeld alluded to the fact that the Jews of Czenstochow wanted to have him in the city as a teacher.

Najfeld wrote, "The Jews of Czenstochow are, with luck, free of superstitions and, therefore, they have invited me to open a private school in the city for their children."

This time, Najfeld had better luck. It is almost certain that he was indebted to the local people in Piotrkow with whom he had better relations than with those in Warsaw for this permission. The successful permission arrived in July 1851. Najfeld opened his school on Garncarske Street number 23. This was a model school, one of the best in the province. The school had a dormitory because students began to be sent to him from other cities and *shtetlekh.* Josef Szajnhak, an author of a series of works about natural science, taught Hebrew.

Najfeld wanted to expand the curriculum of the school so that the students would be able to enter a *gymnazie* after graduating from his school. In February 1852 he asked for permission to teach French, history and geography. The education trustee immediately realized Najfeld's intentions and, it should be understood, did not give him permission.

Najfeld's school existed until May 1860. In the course of those 10 years, the school graduated a generation that later took a respected place in Jewish life in Czenstochow. We see from biographies of Jewish merchants from Lodz, Wloclawek and Plock that many of them studied in Najfeld's school in Czenstochow. It is difficult to say if he himself was a good pedagogue. However, he had good teachers. There was a time when the school had over 100 students, a quarter of them from outside Czenstochow. The majority of those from outside Czenstochow were from well-to-do homes because it cost a large amount of money to maintain them in Najfeld's dormitory.

[Page 22]

Najfeld was not a practical person. As a matter of course, he did not think of his school or even the dormitory as a business and, therefore, he could not develop his institution of learning according to the model that the German Jews had in Breslau, Kenigsberg [Konigsberg] and where there were many Czenstochow children. Therefore, it is no wonder that this school, not having a good administration, began to lose money. Najfeld was therefore forced to close it. Meanwhile, Orgelbrand invited him to Warsaw to become the director of the Judaistic division of the Great Polish Encyclopedia that he was beginning to publish.

At the end of 1860 Najfeld turned to the education trustee with a request to permit him to move the school to Warsaw. However, two months later he had already withdrawn the request himself.

The further biography of Najfeld has no connection to the history of the Jews of Czenstochow. It is only worthwhile to mention that he took part in the events of the years 1861-1863 and for this he was exiled to Siberia. He came back from there a sick and broken man. For a time, he had a bookstore in Piotrkow. He died in Warsaw in September 1874.

He never broke his connections to Czenstochow. His family continued to live there. His daughter married Leopold Ron, the bookseller, who later became the most successful manufacturer in Czenstochow.

His two sons were doctors. Several members of his brother's family converted. The well-known Polish translator, Bronislawa Najfeld, was his brother's daughter.

But he left many students in Czenstochow, among whom were several who later took part in the Polish-Yiddish press. One of them, Branciki, wrote for *Jutrzenka,* which was edited by Najfeld. In general, Najfeld published many reports from Czenstochow, comparatively many more than from other cities.

A second writer was Shimeon Bergman (the father of the Czenstochow banker, Adam Bergman). He wrote in Hebrew and Polish. Najfeld's most beloved student was Moshe Majman (1812-1874). He was a son of the Dzialoszyn rabbi. Majman graduated from the Warsaw Rabbinical School, worked on *Jutrzenka* and on the *Izraelita.* He died in Czenstochow the same year as Najfeld, his teacher, and he was two years older than him.

As soon as Najfeld's school was shut down, a new pedagogue member of the Enlightenment tried his luck in Czenstochow. The city could not be without a school for Jewish children. True, the very pious Jews did not believe in the school, but the city had too large a number of followers of general education to be able to abandon such an institution through denunciations or simple intrigues.

A Jewish private teacher, who was a fellow townsman of Najfeld, had lived in Czenstochow since 1856. His name was Moshe or Moric Zis. In 1858, Zis turned to the school trustee with a request for permission to open a school. He waited for two years until the school regime decided to accede to his request. Probably because they felt that one school for Najfeld was enough for a city such as Czentochow. The *kehile* managing committee did not want to disturb Najfeld's school and, therefore, did not want to support Zis' request. Only when Najfeld closed his school did the *kehile*, the majority of which consisted of Enlightened leaders, considered it important that Zis receive his permission. On 16 August 1860 the Czenstochow "Leadership Elders" officially certified that Mojrici Zis is a "good and God-fearing teacher" and, therefore, it would be good if he were permitted to open an elementary school for Jewish children. The *kehile*, by means of this declaration, asked that the Jewish population be freed from paying the school tax that was used on behalf of the local Catholic school. Although this school was open to Jewish children, very few parents sent their children to it. This tax amounted to 700 rubles a year. The *kehile* calculated that if this sum were given for the use of a Jewish school, at least 150 children from poor homes would be able to learn without charge and in this way children would be drawn from the religious elementary schools. Meanwhile Zis received agreement to open a school, but the matter did not end with this.

[Page 23]

In January 1861 the education trustee Mukhanow inquired about the sum paid by the Czenstochow Jews on behalf of the local Catholic elementary school. From this he wanted to know "from what source will the loss to the Catholic schools come, if the government should accommodate the request of the *kehile.*"

It became clear that the concession that had been given to Zis had nothing to do with the plan for the school which the *kehile* intended to create. The *kehile* wanted Najfeld as the school-manager and when Najfeld left for Warsaw, it followed that Mojrici Zis should become the school-manager. This was, therefore, the plan that Burszynski had in 1841. That is, not a private school, but a communal one, supported by the *kehile* with the help of the income from the school tax that was used, until then, to support the Catholic school.

The Catholic school was afraid that it would lose a part of its income. The state was not interested in covering the loss of the 700 rubles from its budget. Mukhanow, in general, did not want the Jews to have a Polish school. The uprising moved aside such matters as building a school for the time being. The matter dragged on for so long that a law was enacted about this, that only Russian could be the language of instruction. Thus, the plan for a school was first realized in 1867, this time in Russian. Meanwhile, Zis left for Lodz where he became the manager of the elementary school that the *kehile* there had opened. However, in addition to the Czarist regime, organized Polish society in Czenstochow was against a separate Jewish school. In 1862, thanks to Wielopolski's[5] school policies, a general six grade county school was opened to which everyone was welcomed. At once, 47 Jewish students were registered in the Czenstochow school. Thus, the matter of a special school for Jewish children was no longer relevant. In general, the pious Jews were not interested in this school. They continued to send their children to the *khederim* [religious elementary schools]. In contrast, the very assimilated stratum was not interested in a separate school for Jewish children. For them the question of education was solved individually in accord with their beliefs and incomes.

4. Jews in Czenstochow in the Years 1863–1914

Czenstochow began to play a large role as a new industrial and trade center immediately after the revolt of 1863, when Poland entered the era of "organic work" that was to replace the ideology of national freedom with a program of economic independence. In certain respects Czenstochow even competed with Lodz. But Lodz was given greater opportunities and, therefore, many Jewish industrial pioneers moved there. As, for instance, Ludwig Kon, the large cotton merchant in Lodz, who played a great role in Lodz industry during 1861-1870, who was a Czenstochower Jew.

There is no exact statistical data about the growth of the Jewish population in Czenstochow. It is known only that in 1897 the city numbered 43,863 souls, of them, 11,764 Jews. This means that Jews made up 29.5 percent of the total population. The general population had increased over five times since 1857, while the Jewish population had increased almost six times as much. However, the Jewish share in comparison to the total population decreased. In 1857 Jews made up 34.5 percent of the total population; however, in 1897 only 29.7 percent.[6]

In 1862 the Jewish precincts were abolished. This happened as a result of Wielopolski's Act of Jewish Emancipation. As mentioned, Czenstochow always was proud that the city council there had adopted a resolution concerning the abolition of the Jewish ghetto two years earlier, before this act was proclaimed. The abolition of the precinct meant not only that Jews could live in the entire city, but also that they could settle undisturbed in Czenstochow. Many Jews from the surrounding cities and *shtetlekh* [towns] actually did begin to move there. An interesting migration took place. Many of the first pioneers in industry and trade, who "were the first to suffer" in Czenstochow, migrated to Warsaw and to Lodz, where they could better invest their capital and make use of their experience. Jews with little or no capital began to storm Czenstochow from the surrounding cities and *shtetlekh* and began building new industries and businesses. In such a manner they contributed to the economic growth of the city.

[Page 24]

In 1897 Shmuel Rafal Landau, the founder of "Proletarian Zionism," visited Czenstochow and wrote an interesting report about it. According to his estimate the city numbered 45,000 souls, of them 15,000 Jews. Landau wrote that the greater part of the Jews lived from trade. The frequent mass visits to the "Holy Mary" revived business.[7]

In Czenstochow, he visited the small synagogues and the two Jewish lodging houses.

"An actual Jewish middle class is entirely missing here" – he wrote – "barely 400 people pay *kehile* taxes. Compared to several rich, Jewish manufacturers, there is a large proletarian mass that literally feels itself lucky when it can find a secure income for themselves in these factories."

He further relates that he only visited one factory, where the owner truly strove to have only Jews work for him. This was a factory of needles and sticks for umbrellas. Of the 220 workers, over 100 were Jews, men as well as women. The men earned between four and five rubles a week for an 11 and half hour work day. The young women – between a ruble and 80 *kopekes* to two and a half rubles a week. The very capable even earned three rubles a week. He saw several Jews, many former tavern owners among the workers. The majority of young women were employed with sorting and packing. The work was divided so that Jews did hand work while the Christians worked at the steam machines.

In addition to them, there were Jews employed in paper, celluloid, linen and jute factories.

Landau explains, "A Jewish manufacturer led me into a room where 83 young women pressed colored paper, but there was not one Jewish young woman among them. Therefore, it is curious that this person is recognized as none other than a philanthropist, who was interested in Jewish training, in agricultural work and trade."

In 1902 Khorosz, a Russian-Jewish economist, conducted an investigation into the economic status of the Jews in Czenstochow.

He determined that the Jews in Czenstochow developed a lively and widespread production of toys. The city was given the name of "the Jewish Nirnberg," because just as Nirnberg [Nurnberg, Germany] had acquired a reputation with its production of toys, so had Czenstochow during the 1860's begun to produce "playthings" for children.

Khorosz writes that one Reb Sheya was considered a pioneer of this industry in Czenstochow. He was a lathe turner by trade. First of all, this pious Jew began to make very artistically turned memorial medals with the picture of the "Holy Czenstochower Mother" [The Black Madonna]. These medals were such a success that in time they became an object of collecting on the part of various collectors. The demand for various souvenir medals by the pilgrims to Czenstochow grew so great that it provided the impetus to move toward streamlining the forms of production. Jews, even the very pious, began to fabricate Catholic items that the public gladly bought. However, the Catholic Church could not tolerate this. A series of bans were issued and the pious visitors to Czenstochow, in particular, were warned not to buy these manufactured goods. The Silesian artisans began to inundate the city with their goods. Some of them simply smuggled the goods in and the Russian customs house had to determinedly fight this industrial invasion.

Although the priests admired the "superb wood carving" made by the Jewish craftsmen and every *bec fin* [A person with a "fine palate," therefore, someone with good taste] took pride in his collection of these "devotional items" – the Jews were required to give up their production.

In as much as this decree did not apply to selling the Catholic pictures and carvings – the commerce remained in Jewish hands. Thus, the Jews first switched to making wooden toys; later metal one and others. In the 80's and 90's of the last century [19th century], young people went to Nirnberg, where they learned the craft of making cheap toys. Returning home, they began to produce toys for children in a modest way.

According to Khorosz's calculations, at the end of the 19th century, the production of toys reached approximated 150,000 rubles a year. According to the later reports, this production reached over two million rubles a year in 1908. When one takes into account that Czenstochow produced cheap things, this sum is very large.

[Page 25]

In 1900, Czenstochow possessed 50 percent of the factories making toys for children. Three hundred workers were employed in these factories. Four fifths of them were Jews. The owners of these factories were all Jews. There were many Jews who worked at home. This means they worked for enterprises that would give them the raw materials and the Jews were paid by the piece. However, the majority of these enterprises were the agents for small undertakings. In as much as they had no machines, particularly the small manufacturers, it should be understood that this was hand work. A man was rarely eager to have such work. Therefore, it is understandable as to why young women represented entirely 60 percent of these workers. Their earnings were between 80 *kopekes* and two rubles and 50 *kopekes* a week.

Work in the factories was usually by the piece. A normal work day was then between 12 and 15 hours a day.

The Czenstochower members of the Polish Socialist Party (*P.P.S.*) became interested in the condition of the Jewish workers. Their correspondents in *Robotnik* [*Worker*] and *Przedswit* [*Daybreak*] (published in London) give a clear reflection of the situation in this industry. Alas, it is not known how many efforts were made to organize the workers on the part of the party.

If the Czenstochower Jews were pioneers in this area of the toy industry in Poland, they were also very active in other realms. The manufacture of paper, wallpaper, soap, candles, matches, the five largest frame factories – this was all a Jewish achievement. The large mineral industry, which arose thanks to the exploitation of the natural richness around Czenstochow, developed at the end of the 19th and beginning of the 20th century. Large lime factories and brick-yards were built and, later, iron foundries, metallurgy and textile industries. Large capitalistic enterprises arose and, as a consequence of this, a more solid strata of a well-established Jewish bourgeoisie. Great trade and shipping offices, commission sale houses and various intermediary agents developed around this industry. The role of Czenstochow as a transit point between Russia and abroad greatly raised the economic significance of this city.

Strong anti-Semitism developed as an accompanying phenomenon to the growth of the role of Jews in the economic life of Czenstochow. The inclination to make commerce more Polish was unmistakingly very clear in Czenstochow, much earlier than in other cities. Agitation was present during the processions of the pious pilgrims that took place at the end of the 19th century that these visitors to *Jasna Gora* should not, God forbid, buy from Jews, but should better support the Polish-Catholic merchants and shops. A strong anti-Semitic feeling also began to be felt among the Polish workers. The pogrom that took place in Czenstochow in August 1902 was a volcanic outburst of this feeling. Various strata of the Polish population took part in this pogrom. The victims of the pogrom were in the majority none other than the poor – 120 shops were robbed in the course of one hour. Jews stood up in resistance; the butchers who defended Targowa Street especially excelled, so that the pogrom did not reach there. The military had to be called out. Two fell dead and there were many wounded.

The Polish Socialist Party that held Czenstochow as one if its strongest positions issued an appeal in which it criticized the pogrom.

This pogrom incited Jewish and Polish organized society. The effect of these events was immediately felt in Jewish life. It can be said that since that event, the Jewish bourgeoisie in Czenstochow that had never gathered any money to support Polish artists and writers – began to show signs of a more active interest in Jewish communal life. Since then, Czenstochow records many times where children from deeply assimilated Jewish homes took part in Jewish matters, even of a national character.

About 1899 Jewish communal life in Czenstochow became very poor. No Jewish institutions were active. The *kehile* itself functioned very weakly. The assimilated Jews had the most influence in it. They always were chosen as *dozores* [wardens] because there was no one better, particularly because they permitted themselves to splurge a little.

[Page 26]

Then an agreement came about to look for a place for a cemetery and to build a *mikvah* [ritual bath]. The city really needed both institutions. In March 1899 a Jewish Charity Society was founded that bore the Polish name *Dobroczynnosc* [works of mercy]. The first task of this society was to build a Jewish hospital. The Jewish population grew; the number of Jewish doctors was large enough to be able to serve a small hospital for the Jewish sick.

In September 1900 this society bought a plot on which to build a hospital. But it seemed that the plot was no good. Those involved in the matter remained discouraged. The entire project did not move forward. It was seven years later when the work was renewed. In 1907 the old slaughter house was placed under the jurisdiction of the city. The hospital commission began negotiations with city hall that the spot near the slaughter house should be given for the planned hospital.

In 1908 city hall donated this location and they proceeded to build the hospital.

On 18 Sivan 5669 [7 June 1909], the foundation stone was officially laid with a large parade.

The hospital cost 120,000 rubles. It had 50 beds. Its yearly budget was 30,000 rubles. Part of this sum came from municipal tax payments from the Czenstochower middle class. This income reached 6,000 rubles a year. The remaining monies came from the support of the rich Jews and from income from the patients.

The Polish press strongly praised the organization of the Jewish hospital in Czenstochow and pointed to it as a model of communal energy and organization.

The Jewish hospital greatly increased the prestige of the *kehile*. Little by little, this *kehile* organized a series of institutions that were a model for the other small *kehilus* [plural of *kehile*]. In addition to the handworker's school at the Talmud-Torah [free religious school for poor boys] that was the achievement of the kehile, they built *Hakhnoses-Orkhim* [an organization providing hospitality to guests, most often for *Shabbos*] that numbered 740 supporting members. The Markusfeld family supported the most important communal institutions. Thus, for example, in 1910, a handworker's school was built and named for Adolf and Ernestine Markusfeld, the parents of the rich man, Henrikh Markusfeld. In order to support this school, which had a large staff of teachers, the Markusfeld family participated with large contributions. In addition to this, the *kehile* and also the Jewish Colonization Association (*IKA*) contributed large sums.

In addition to money, Markusfeld also donated a beautiful library to the school. The same Markusfeld contributed money for the library of the Jewish organization, *Lira* [choral society]. The solemn opening of the "Henrikh Markusfeld Library" took place in December 1912. Y.L. Peretz [one of the most important Yiddish writers] was invited as the main speaker. During that time of the boycott movement[8] which was very strong in Czenstochow, it was very interesting to see how assimilated Jews clung to the Jewish *Lira*. Peretz gave a beautiful speech about the sense of Jewish history and developed the idea that Jews in Poland are not "guests," but residents. Markusfeld was very pleased with the speech. It made this institution, which was unquestionably a Jewish national institution, more important to him.

In 1901, the local *Talmud Torah* created a horticultural farm. *IKA* [Jewish Colonization Association] appropriated 18,680 rubles for this purpose. The *kehile* would give 3,000 rubles a year. The farm had 17 acres of land. Its budget reached 10,000 rubles a year. This institution had such a good reputation that in 1907 it received the second prize at the Polish horticultural exhibition.

The following people were on the managing committee of the horticultural farm in 1907: H. Markusfeld, Leopold Werde (1862–1912), Markus Henig, Y. Novinski, Stefan Grosman, Stanislaw Herc, Dr. L. Patawja and M. Frankel.

Leopold Werde was very active in the Jewish charity society and was very interested in Jewish education. The *kehile* supported four elementary schools: two for boys and two for girls. In 1910 these schools were attended by over 300 children. The *kehile* assigned 10,000 rubles a year for these schools. In addition to this there were three *Talmud Torahs*; of them, two were in their own buildings. Sixty students studied in the craftsmen's workshops. Werde secretly covered a large part of the budget that far exceeded the yearly subsidy from the *kehile*.

[Page 27]

In the years 1909–1912, a series of societies and clubs arose in Czenstochow. Passionate, ideological struggles, which alas are little known, took place in many of these societies. In a report about a session of the Jewish Education Society that was held in April 1907, we learn of a language struggle that took place there. It consisted of this, should Yiddish lessons and the possession of Yiddish books by the library of this society be permitted? According to the report of *Goniec* [*Messenger*] *Czenstochowski*, the majority supported permitting Yiddish. Therefore, the anti-Yiddish members resigned from the society. According to this report, the main *jargonistn*[9] were: Kwiatek, Herc and Zigmunt Majorczyk. The last, incidentally, was a follower of [Y.L.] Peretz and a collector of Jewish folklore.

Of the practical societies, the most important was the *gmiles khesed kase* [interest free loan office]. It was partly supported by *IKA*. Henrikh Markusfeld was a member of the chief managing committee of *IKA* and a relative of Hipolit Wawelburg, the famous banker who was the supervisor of the *IKA* fund in Russia and Poland. This is the reason that Czenstochow happened to find favor in the eyes of those in charge of the *IKA* fund more than other Jewish communities in Poland.

Jewish communal life in Czenstochow grew beyond the *kehile* and did not even have much contact with the official representation of the local Jewry. The calcification of the *kehile* in large part caused the weak communal support that its activities had among the Jewish population. All institutions, except perhaps the hospital, were a product of the energy of individuals, mainly those who did not even pay any Jewish communal tax. And inevitably they did not have any influence in the managing committee of the *kehile*. The communal base of these institutions was a democratic one that had nothing to do with the tenure of the *dozores* [council members].These were merchants, storekeepers, intelligent workers, craftsmen from various ideological paths, activists and various legal and illegal circles and groups. Yet Czenstochow excelled among the Polish provincial cities with a lively communal pulse. Many theorists of the new social system in Jewish political thought found their first ideological followers in Czenstochow. There were parties in the Jewish neighborhoods whose chief moral and material support came Czenstochow.

Jewish life was mirrored more in the Lira Society, then, for example, in the activity of the *kehile*. All ideologies from the Jewish neighborhoods were represented in it. The most prominent writers and political activists gave lectures to Lira. Under the conditions of the Czarist regime, Lira succeeded in evoking the ideological programs of various parties. The high level of the discussions that were held there was even echoed in the Warsaw press.

Of all provincial cities in Poland, Lodz and Czenstochow had luck with the press of the country. The detailed reports about the activity of the local Jewish hospital that Polish medical journals published gave evidence as to the high level of this institution.

The same can be said about the old age home. The horticultural farm has already been mentioned.

The conflict between the population and the *kehile* was unavoidable. The restless communal energy sought a concentrated improvement. The moment was ripe for the coordination of the activity of the various groups. The press pointed out the squandering of money because each institution had its own budget, with its own managing committee. There was a demand for the centralization of Jewish communal life. The struggle for democratization of the *kehile* that was then going on in Warsaw had to influence the *kehilus* in the provinces.

It is therefore no wonder that Czenstochow also began to mobilize for an attack that would shatter the old fortress of the *kehile*. The *kehile* was tightly in the hands of several Jewish families that did not want to let out of their control the *placowka* [agency] as the *Izraelita* referred to the *kehile*, coincidentally a powerful card for the assimilated.

The Jewish press in Warsaw often wrote about this and the struggle began in Czenstochow.

This struggle for democratization of the Jewish kehile in Czenstochow began in 1912. A communal campaign by the entire *kehile* was required because the Galveston emigration awoke such wide interest in Czenstochow, where Territorialist[10] sympathies were so strong that many young people left for Galveston.

[Page 28]

The *Czenstochower Tageblat* [*Daily Newspaper*], a newspaper with very lively editing, actually began a campaign for democratizing the *kehile*.

The apathy in relation to *kehile* elections was so great that in 1913 of 1,200 Jewish communal tax payers, only 14 took part in the voting. The Russian regime, it should be understood, had to void the election and set a new one.

That year Jewish Czenstochow began a campaign to build a communal house for all Jewish institutions in the city. Although this campaign did not bring any tangible result in the intervening time, the best communal strengths were mobilized in the city. The assimilated Jews were so drawn into the storm of Jewish life that even during the boycott campaign a plan emerged for the publication of a Polish-Yiddish newspaper. The money was supposed to be given by the Werde and Markusfeld families and the editors were supposed to be the Socialist Yakov Rozenberg and Dr. Zaks. One of the Werdes, Leopold Werde, who died in 1912, was an esteemed communal worker from the assimilationist camp.

During the same year (1913) the Jewish Manufacturers and Merchants Union was founded.

In 1914 on the eve of the First World War, the Jewish press in Czenstochow began a struggle for a Jewish public school. This struggle was supported by all of the Jewish socialist parties and a significant part of the Jewish bourgeoisie.

The *kehile* had already been partly reorganized with a large budget. Its holdings reached a half million rubles. True, its main supporters were still after all the most affluent strata, that is, the assimilated. For now, a democratic *kehile* managing committee that would accommodate the demands of the Jewish community was still far away.

That year the *kehile* numbered 1,145 Jewish community tax payers. Of them, 900 paid on the average 10 rubles a year, while 245 Jewish community tax payers brought in 25, 800 rubles. Thus the main authority was in the hands of the rich Jews, mostly assimilated, although, as was already mentioned, with a much warmer interest in Jewish matters than before. Warsaw, for example, did not have such "assimilated people" who built Jewish libraries, but they were in Czenstochow.

The First World War broke out. On 3 August 1914, the Germans were already in Czenstochow. Jews began to be dragged to forced labor. Several Jews had even been shot. A painful, gray and, sometimes even bloody period in the life of the Czenstochow Jews, began.

The Jews of Czenstochow faced an unknown tomorrow.

5. Rabbis, Scholars, and Writers in Czenstochow

It was mentioned earlier that the city of Czenstochow did not have a Jewish *kehile* until the beginning of the 19th century and was actually a *prikahalok* [provincial *kalal* or community] of Janow. As a matter of course, it did not have a rabbi. During the era of the Duchy of Warsaw, it had religious judges, but still no rabbi. Czenstochow probably had its first rabbi during the time of Congress Poland (1815-1830). In 1821, the *kehile* was abolished in all of Poland and a "synagogue council" (*dozor bóźnici*) was introduced. This meant that the power of the *kehile* as an organization with autonomous functions would be taken over and it would be converted into a managing committee over the synagogues and other institutions that served the Jewish population. As a matter of course, there could not be a chief rabbi who would represent the religious community of the city. It is probable that there were local men who decided matters of religious law. In important matters they turned to the Piotrkow rabbi.

It is difficult to determine who the first rabbi in Czenstochow was.

In the *Sefir Shayles vaTshuves* [book in which a rabbi states his previous *Halachahic* questions and answers to those questions on religious practice] *Brit Avraham* [*Covenant Avraham*] of the Piotrkow rabbi, one Reb Dovid *ABD"K Czenstochow* [*Av Beis Din Kehile Czenstochow* – chairman of the *kehile* court of Czenstochow] is mentioned several times. According to all probabilities, this was Reb Dovid Yitzhak, the author of a commentary on the *Khumish* [Torah] entitled *Beis Dovid* that was published in 5667 (1807). He signed his name *ABD"K* (*Av Beis Din Kehile*) Czenstochow *vaRAB"D* (and head of the religious court) Piotrkow. Reb Dovid Yitzhak died in 5578 (1818). According to other sources, he died in 5581 (1821).

There is, however, information that the first Czenstochower rabbi was the *gaon* [genius] Yissakhar Wajngurt. Alas, there are no facts about him available.

[Page 29]

Among the earlier scholars from Czenstochow is remembered a certain Reb Arya Czenstochow. According to probabilities, this Arya was a *dayan* [religious judge] in Czenstochow. An agreement signed by him is found in the book *Ma'aseh Hoshev* [*Art of Calculation*]. This was a commentary on the tractate *Bove Kame* [*First Gate*] and oaths written by Reb Josef *bar* [son of] Moshe Najminc of Pilce. This book was published in Lemberg in 1796 (5556). This Reb Arya was one of the first scholars who was known in the history of the Jews of Czenstochow.

Dozens of years passed and not one name of a rabbi is found in Czenstochow. This does not mean that the city did not have a rabbi. Simply, that no materials were preserved about this matter. There were probably no great men of their era. They did not write any works and, therefore, any trace of them was lost. There is no indication of bibliographic information about them – as a result a long segment of time was not recorded for history.

Finally, in approximately 1850, a rabbi appeared in Czenstochow who acquired a reputation nor only in his own city but also in Poland and abroad. This was Reb Yitzhak Rabinowicz (1823-1868). We do not know from where he came. We only know that from 1850 until 1868, that is, until his death, he was the Czenstochow rabbi. We also know that he visited Berlin and knew the Rabbi, Dr. Michael Sachs (1808-1864), the well known researcher of Medieval Hebrew poetry and the translator of the *Siddur* [Hebrew prayer book] and *Makhzor* [Hebrew prayer book used on Rosh Hashanah and Yom Kippur] into German. Rabinowicz even corresponded with him. He also knew other German rabbis and preachers. In Prussia, Rabinowicz would buy *seforim* [religious books] and carry out academic debates with these rabbis. However, this does not mean that Rabinowicz was a follower of the German sect. He was a pious rabbi in Poland who had a connection to the German rabbis and who did not see a danger to the foundation of Orthodox Jewry in the Enlightenment.

Rabinowicz was famous as a preacher. In 1863, Moshe Majmon, one of his students and a great Hasid, wrote that Rabinowicz would come to Warsaw and give *droshus* [sermons or speeches] that were successful with the circle of scholarly opponents of Hasidism (*Jutczenka*, 1863, 40).

When Rabinowicz died (in 1868), Shimeon Peltyn, himself a Jew, a scholar, although a *maskil* [follower of the Enlightenment], published a detailed obituary notice in the weekly newspaper, *Izraelita*. It is probable that Peltyn knew the Czenstochower rabbi personally. His description was written with a great deal of warmth.

"He was the only rabbi in our country" – Peltyn wrote – "who combined true piety with free scholarly thought. He was a great scholar in the area of rabbinic literature and no less knowledgeable of worldly matters."

Peltyn further describes how difficult it was for Rabbi Yitzhak Rabinowicz to persuade the *kehile* that worldly studies were in no way in contradiction to piety and learning. True, he was a fierce opponent of Hasidism and passionately fought Hasidus and Hasidim.

The Hasidim denounced him to the regime many times and indicated that he went hand in hand with the heretics. However, the Czenstochow rabbi was goodness itself, without anger, without feelings of revenge. He was a man with a deep feeling for justice and, in general, a very tolerant man.

He believed that one did not have to fear for the pious; they would not become non-believers. It bothered him more that the non-believers not become "entirely gentile." Despite the fact that the Czenstochow *kehile* was in the hands of the "enlightened" rich men, they ran it as the rabbi wished. He gave his sermons in Yiddish. He did not want in any way to permit the smallest reforms. The only one that he brought in was instruction in Polish in the *Talmud Torah* [school for poor young Jewish boys]. Later, Russian, calculations and a little geography.

There was a gathering place for the wise men in his home. The scholars would come together and they would debate the newest research from the German *Hokhmas Yisroel* [Jewish science]. Many Jews heard the names of Yom-Tov Lipman Zunz,[11] Michael Sachs and other scholars from Germany from the mouth of the rabbi. He himself subscribed to the most important periodicals about *Hokhmas Yisroel*.

The most important sermons of Rabbi Yitzhak Rabinowicz were published in 1863 in Berlin under the name, *Nidvot Pi* [The title comes from Psalm 119:108: "Please accept with favor the offerings of my mouth..."] This collection of sermons and subtle argumentations in *halakhah* [religious law] was warmly received by the critics of that time. Moshe Majmon published a detailed review in the weekly newspaper, *Jutczenka*, that Daniel Najfeld, the rabbi's friend, published. In general, Najfeld thought very highly of the Czenstochow rabbi. In his eyes, he was the ideal of a rabbi in Poland. Pious and worldly at the same time.

[Page 30]

Najfeld wrote in an article that "the rabbi of Czenstochow is well known thanks to his tolerance and feel for justice." (*Jutczenka*, 1863, no. 4).

The second section of the sermons was published by the rabbi's son. They were published in Warsaw in 1870.

The sermons of Reb Yitzhak Rabinowicz have not yet been utilized as material to describe the spiritual circumstances of a small *kehile* of that time. The examples and illustrations that the Czenstochow rabbi presents in his sermons are taken from the local reality. There is not present in them exaggerations and also no moralizing tone of reproof. There is a direct turn to commonsense, a truly cautious critique of those bad habits that he wanted to eliminate through quiet means. Questions of Jewish education were very often touched upon in these sermons. In a sermon, the rabbi described how one should raise a child in a rich Jewish home in Czenstochow. The sons go to the public schools as was the custom in those circles. The rabbi suggested that, in the majority of cases, the wife prevailed with the children being sent to the *szkoles* [Polish word for schools]. The father was against them. The child came home from the *szkole*; the mother was full of joy, while the father went through the house and threw curses at the "gentile schools." In another sermon he described an opposite case. The parents sent a young boy to the *Talmud Torah*. But he came home and he found a spirit that was the opposite of that which he was taught in the *Talmud Torah*. Rabinowicz showed the contradictions and warned that such dichotomy is a danger for the survival and unity of the Jewish family.

There was also present in the sermons depictions of the conditions of Jewish life in Czenstochow. For example, in this manner in a sermon, the rabbi describes how the well-to-do families in Czenstochow play cards without end.

In addition to sermons, Rabbi Rabinowicz wrote many letters. It has already been said that he had correspondences with Sachs, Zunz and Kirchheim. He also carried on a correspondence with Polish *maskilim* [followers of the Enlightenment] from Warsaw and Lodz. Alas, many letters were lost and only a few were preserved. So, for example, Josef Graf, a *maskil*, published in a Polish translation two of his interesting Hebrew letters that the Czentochower rabbi had written to the *maskil*, Isidor Kempinski in Lodz (*Izraelita*, 1869, number 8 and 9).

There is present in these two long letters a great deal of homiletic interpretation mixed with good psychological considerations about Tractates of the Sages of blessed memory. We can see from them that Rabinowicz was well versed in Yiddish homiletics that flourished in Germany in his time. At the same time, he was strongly conservative and did not depart from tradition.

On the other hand, his son, Yehuda Rabinowicz, was more a *maskil* than a pious Jew, although he had a reputation as a great scholar. He died a year after his father's death (in 1869) at the age of 24. In 1870, one of his brothers published the second section of his father's sermons under the same name: *Nidvot Pi*.

Between the years 1868 and 1878 we do not hear about a rabbi in Czenstochow. It is probable that after such a sympathetic figure as Rabbi Rabinowicz it was not so easy a thing to find a suitable rabbi who could satisfy both sides, the strongly influential "enlightened" and the majority *minyon* [10 men necessary for prayer] of the pious Jews.

From 1887 to 1894, Gershon Rawinson was the rabbi in Czenstochow. In 1894, Rabbi, Reb Nakhum Asz took his place.

The sudden prosperity of the Czenstochow *kehile* occurred during his time. The most important institutions were built up while Asz was the rabbi. He had a great influence on the *kehile* and was very respected by all of the Jews.

In addition to rabbis, Czenstochow had a series of scholars who were well known throughout Poland and several even outside the country.

Names of Czenstochow Jews are found very often in the lists of subscribers of various Enlightenment and scholarly books of that time. For example, the name of the Openhejm family is repeated very often; three generations of this family were found in such lists from 1850 to 1907. In 1907, a book entitled *Metsudes ben Tzion* [*Fortress of Zion*] was published in Piotrkow. Among the subscribers is found an Openhejm whose grandfather was found in a book by the *maskil*, Mandelsburg, that was published in Warsaw in 1850.

Czenstochow also had private scholars. Thus, for example, Reb Nekhemia Landau, a scholar from Czenstochow, the father of Bernard Landau, the industrialist and wealthy man, one of the pillars of the Enlightenment in Czenstochow, participated with an endorsement of the *Pirke-Oves* [*Ethics of the Fathers*] that was published in Krotoszyn in 1850.

[Page 31]

Among the most important *maskilim* in Czenstochow, whose names are found very often on the lists of subscribers of Hebrew books, it is worthwhile to remember the following: Abele Landa, Aizik Shimeon Ginsberg, Yitzhak Gliksohn, Yitzhak Frajman, Yitzhak Winer, Avraham Sztajnman, Gershon Landa, Dovid Landa, Josef Szmidberg, Yeshayahu Hajman, Josef Zand, Yeshayahu Landa, Mordekhai Kahn, Moshe Lib Wajnberg, Note Rajkher and Fajgenblat.

Moshe Majmon (1812-1874), although born in Dzialoszyce, considered himself a Czenstochower because he spent almost his entire life there. Majmon graduated from the Warsaw Rabbinical School. He was a private teacher of Hebrew, wrote for Polish-Yiddish periodicals and published a great many articles in Polish and Hebrew. Several of these articles have a worth to this day as materials about the Jewish way of life in a series of smaller communities in Poland.

Of the Jews in Czenstochow who wrote in Polish it is worthwhile to remember Adam Wolberg, who wrote in the secular Polish press and also for the *Izraelita*. Particularly important is his work about the architecture of the wooden synagogues in Poland. In 1910 Wolberg created a sensation with his polemical writing: "I Blame the Polish Press," in which he unmasked the degradation of the Polish press that seeks only sensations and demoralizes society and leads it from its path of political activity.

Two Czenstochow Jews wrote novels and short stories in Polish. These were Edward Zaks and Marya Glikson. Zaks even wrote a novel about Jewish life. Glikson was close to the Polish Socialist Party and wrote under the name Marion.

The last of the Mohicans of the former Pleiades [cluster of stars known as the Seven Sisters, here it denotes a group of followers of the Enlightenment] of the Czenstochow *maskilim* died in Czenstochow. This was Tzvi Perla. He was born in 1841. In 1861 he took part in the patriotic demonstrations for which he paid with several months in jail. He knew Hebrew and Polish very well; he educated generations of Jewish youth in Czenstochow and later in Lodz.

During the time of independent Poland, the Rabbi, Dr. Chaim Zeev Hirszberg, a Tarnopoler Jew, represented Jewish science in Czenstochow. A good Orientalist, he published a series of works in various Polish and Hebrew periodicals. However, his political activity did not make him popular. After this, when Dr. Meir Balaban, of blessed memory, who was director of the Jewish *gymnazie* [high school] for a time, left Czenstochow, Hirszberg again carried on the work of cataloguing the Hebrew books of the Czenstochow monastery that Balaban had begun. The Krakow Academy of Science planned to publish the catalogue of the entire library (publications from the 15th to the 18th century) – but the Second World War undid the plan.

Translator's Footnotes

4. False accusation that Jews kill non-Jewish children to obtain their blood for the making of matzoh.

5. Count Aleksander Wielopolski was the head of Civil Administration for Poland under Czar Alexander II. He was instrumental in carrying out educational reforms.

6. The author is inconsistent. In one sentence he writes that in 1897 the Jews were 29.5 percent of the population and in another that they were 29.7 percent.

7. An icon of a "Black Madonna" is found in the Jasna Gora Monastery in Czenstochow and vast numbers of pilgrims visit it each year.

8. In 1912, the Jews supported a socialist candidate in elections to the *Duma*, resulting in a boycott of Jewish businesses by supporters of the National Democrats. Poland was then under Russian control and had representation in the Russian *Duma*.

9. An ironic use of the word *jargon*. Some intellectuals dismissed Yiddish as merely *jargon* – not a real language, but a dialect used by the less educated. In this context, *jargonistn* supported the use of Yiddish.

10. Territorialism was a political movement that called for the creation of a Jewish territory or territories that did not have to be located in Palestine or be fully independent.

11. Yom-Tov Lipman (Leopold) Zunz was a reform rabbi born in Germany who founded the "Science of Judaism" – the study of Jewish literature, religious music and ritual.

[Page 32]

Czenstochow Becomes a City

During the years around 1880 Czenstochow in the main consisted of two parts separated one from the other by large uninhabited stretches. The uppermost part of Czenstochow was lightly populated; the lowermost part was thickly populated and reached to the Warta River. No houses were seen across the river. The old slaughter house had sunk into the river and the new one with a stone building and modern facilities had no fear of the water. Farther along was a meadow that spread out as a green sea without an end. Crossing the second bridge in Zawada, several houses were found near the hilly, stone pits. Near the road lived the only Jewish farmer; on the other side, to the south, was the windmill. The water in the Warta was crystal clear, often visited by women who washed their laundry and even more often by those who filled their wooden ladles and clay pitchers with the "soft" spring water for brewing tea.

There was a Trinity square on the northern side of the lowest part of the city with the three crosses in the middle of a large desert of golden sand. Small wagons from Kalej, Amstow [Msztow] and Wyczerpy would pass here with their village products for the Czenstochow market and with the goods from the city.

Thursdays and Fridays, multitudes of young boys, girls and women appeared at the Trinity with sacks and other containers which they filled with sand to spread over their clay floors and to polish their *Shabbos* candlesticks and the other brass and copper utensils, as their grandmothers and great grandmothers had done before they came to Czenstochow.

On *Shabbos*, the Trinity had a different face. On the "Jewish meadows" near Glowacke, or Shimshe Diabol's mill, lay older Jews, stretched out in the high green grass resting their bones. The young danced and sang:

Sir Ludwig went hunting. Marisha stayed to paint.

The horses of the wagon drivers grazed in the meadows, resting from their heavy burdens, which they pulled during the entire week until late at night. "Aristocratic" horses from Jewish house cabs, which did not pull any heavy burdens, only ferrying "genteel" passengers, grazed separately from them. The "aristocratic" horses were decorated with silver buttons, tassels hanging down from their brows.

The wagon drivers and the horse carriage drivers also lay here with their horses: the hitchmakers, the *Klobucker* [men from Klobuck], the old *dorfsman* [man from a village], the small express train with two vanishing eyes. The "old man," who with his wife, "the old woman" smuggled emigrants and two "Tom cats" who always fought each other because of a passenger.

At that time, the smugglers carried on their business in a systematic manner. One gang carried the emigrants across the border, a second bought fake ships' tickets and exchanged money – so that they were not denounced – and waited for the emigrants in Lublinec.

Grosman's mill, with nearby beautiful gardens, free for everyone to enter, was found on the south side of the lower part of the city on both sides of the river. Several Jews were employed at Grosman's mill; their home was run authentically Jewish and they did not forget the poor.

Markusfeld's Malarnja was found a little higher to the west. The name Markusfeld is remembered as a holy place. True, Jews and Jewish girls did not earn more than the Christians at Malarnja; therefore, Henrikh Markusfeld would not forget to give a few rubles when a young girl got married, to help the Jewish workers on a Jewish holiday, to provide the poor Jewish children with matzohs for Passover and coal during the winter.

Near the Malarnja, on the other side of the paved cobblestone road, lay the old cemetery. Right near the cemetery was Werde's needle factory. Werde was a short Jew with a great deal of wisdom, loved good music, and was a great admirer of Mendelssohn. He also was a bit of a philosopher and smoked a pipe. He was not very loved in the city because he did not go to *daven* [pray].

[Page 33]

A little higher, opposite Stacia Street (later Pilsudski Street), was another Grosman, who provided lime to whiten poor houses for Passover.

We turn back to the *getsewizne* or ghetto, to which peasants came from Czuresk, Miszkow and Janow. The *Ostatni Grosz* ["last penny" – the name of a district southeast of Czenstochow] was also located there. This was the story of the *Ostatni Grosz*: a peasant got very drunk in a tavern in the area. When he realized that he was down to his last *grosn* he began to scream, "*Ostatni grosz… ostatni grosz.*" And the name remained.

Events

A great event in Czenstochow was in 1887 when Russian light cavalry left the city and the dragoons entered. The government building or the police station around Warszawer, Senatorska, Kocza, Czike and Teper Streets was besieged by people. When the parade ended and the crowd dispersed – the fresh, green grass was completely trampled. The young trees barely survived. The green benches were muddied. Only the beautiful green park was saved. In the evening when the buzz of the *chrab¹nszczczes* [beetles] and the playing of the roll call were heard, it was a sign for the soldiers from the dragoon armories to go to sleep – it was lively on the First and Second *Alee*. High officers in light coats, with riding crops in their hand, strolled with powdered women. The covered vehicles were lit with torches. The white blooms of the chestnut trees were spread out on the ground like a white carpet. The ice cream vendor with a white linen robe and a Turkish hat shouted: "Ice cream." And from a distance the *time* (church) shone with thousands of oil wicks, lit in honor of the *Grynem Donershtik* [Green Thursday – Pentecost – 50 days after Easter].

There was much whispering about why the officers of the 7th and 8th Regiments did not go out to greet the dragoons in Czenstochow then…

Above, in the uppermost part of Czenstochow where Czenstochowke [nearby village] and the *Jasna Gora* [mountain on which the monastery containing the Black Madonna is located] are found, from which the church with its tall towers looks down on the city – something was also being prepared. Stone cutters cut high marble stones and laid the foundation for a *pomnik* [memorial] for Aleksander the Second [Russian Czar]. In the city they could barely wait for the event. A large number of Christians waited for the moment to see the Russian Orthodox Czar who would stand at the top of *Jasna Gora*, would look down to the tall poplars that ringed the church. And the holy Mary, the patroness of Poland would look down from her height to the powerful world leader. Finally, everything was completed and the ceremony for the unveiling began. Kith and kin gathered and Jewish fathers and mothers from the back streets led their barefoot children with pocket handkerchiefs from beneath through the dark New Market and *Alees* (all kerosene lamps were turned off) through the forest to see the emperor…

When all the military and religious ceremonies were completed and the sheets that veiled the "monument" were removed – the crowd saw the massive figure of Aleksander the Second on a high marble terrace lit with dozens of bright lights, standing with his face to the city and with his back to the church and the holy mother. Polish patriots, gathered at the opening, left quickly with clenched fists, but the Jews ran home even faster and stayed together. And, indeed, in the morning there was talk that the Jews had given a great deal of money to erect the monument with its face to the city where the *zydes* [Jews] lived. At that time, the wounds from the Warsaw pogrom were fresh and Jews again trembled. As usual, two Czenstochower Jewish communal workers, Markusfeld and Ginsberg, had to do a great deal of work to save the situation. Priests in the churches actually gave reassurances that the Jews were not guilty.

One morning the terraces of the monument were found defiled with garbage. From then on, a military guard was placed at the Czar's statue.

A few weeks later, a new excitement. The *Straz Ogniowa* [firemen] renovated their home on the Pogotka, between Jatke Street and Krakower Street. A fireman with a brass helmet on his head and a trumpet on which he did not stop playing spun on the wooden spire. People said that the tower was the highest in the world... Firemen dragged the new wagon with the rubber hose, quickly hitched up the horses. Here, Poznanski, a Jew in a new hat and a gleaming ax, also busied himself on the side. He was proud of his heroism compared to the Jews gathered on a *Shabbos* afternoon. The wagon moved from its place. The music played and the crowd gave a hoorah.

[Page 34]

On the same night – someone trumpets; something is burning. The bell rings on Senatorske Street; ding-dong. The sky is red. Half naked people run. Where is the fire? Where is the fire? *Tam* (there)! They run breathless up to the firehouse. There a stable is burning. But when the firemen arrived everything was over. In the end, it was a rehearsal by the firefighters.

It was said in the city that Markusfeld had given the new wagon with the hoses. And Szwede's beer factory had given the horses.

A few days later a few comrades arrived in the courtyard opposite from Abele *Shoykhet* [ritual slaughterer] and created their own representation of that fire on Czenstochowke. One of them,

Wigdor Brukacz, sang out in the voice of a tenor:

It's burning... It's burning...
Basses sustained:
Where?... Where?...
Altos and sopranos answered:
At the priest's... At the priest's...

The entire choir:
Bring water... Put it out... Bring water... Put it out...
All of Czenstochow sang the song and enjoyed themselves for a long time.

Jewish Streets

The very poor Jewish population inhabited Czike Street. When the river swelled from the melting ice, it appeared as if the sea would be drawn into Czenstochow and swallow the poor streets. How much lower to the river – how much higher the water stood in the houses. Sometimes up to the beds. There were very few wooden floors in the residences. As the water would recede, they would shovel out the mud and spread sand. On *Shavous*, a great deal of bone meal was spread. There were gardens around the houses. They would be planted with *rosh khodesh* radishes [new moon radishes – radishes that grow quickly, in less than a month], scallions, cucumbers, sunflower seeds and other things.

When a couple got married, the main household worth consisted of two cheap beds, a table with two chairs, a slop pail and a wooden dipper for water. A large share of the household articles came from wedding gifts. The bride brought a green chest with her "wardrobe." A clothes closet was seldom found in a house.

The Teper Street was a little joyful – with Jewish shops, a tavern, covered wagons with bread, common bread, small bagels, smoked herring. But there were not many rich in the street, particularly on the side of the river where one could go through the courtyards from one street to another. Every person arriving came here: organ grinders, fortune tellers, exorcists, jugglers, musicians and ordinary poor people who came to ask for *Rosh Khodesh* [new moon- start of the new Hebrew month] money. Although themselves very poor, the ghetto residents also gave charity, although not an entire *groshn*, but a *prute* [penny] (a fourth of a *groshn*).

Across the street from Frajmark's house up to the *Talmud-Torah* [school for poor children] – was populated with middle class elements from the Jatke [butcher shop] Street, those who were established at the old market. There the mothers gave their children *feshber* (a break between dinner and supper), a roll with a hard egg. Jatke Street was then considered a predatory street. The heroic meat cutters in the butcher shops, the later well known good young men: the Kantors, Avraham-Ber Muczyn, Wolf-Jankl, the Zigases. Well known lads then were also: Avrahamele Klobucker, his brother, Manes, Icik Szlize, Josef Japcak, Hersh-Leib the Jometes (Benimet's), Nuchem-Jankl Frydman, Khenina Lojker, Daniel Bac.

The other side of Czike Street from the synagogue to the government building was populated with wagon drivers, shoemakers, rag traders (Machri was the main buyer), and *feldzers* [barber- surgeons]. A soap factory, a small bead factory was also found there. On the corner, opposite the dragoon barracks was a unkempt cemetery. On the other side of the street, where Teper Street went through the majority of courtyards, the beginnings [of the courtyards] were occupied by the Korpiels or the Dialbols – both with old goods and with the tavern that the old Korpiel, a Jew in a long *arbekanfes* [undergarment worn by pious men with *tsitses* – fringe – at the corner] sold a drink of whiskey for a three *groshn* coin. A little farther was another tavern of a Jew who looked completely different, like a tavern keeper. One spoke to this Jew as if to a rabbi; he would be called by his second name: Dovid Federman. He was a religious Jew, but not a fanatic. All of the weddings of the poor took place here.

[Page 35]

The courtyard was long with a passage from Teper Street to the Czike. Wolf Bom's or Maryem's ("Marjem") son, Itske, drew long wires through an iron press in the courtyard to make brass rings.

A little farther was again a small tavern – Drewniak's. This was the home of the wagon drivers. Farther, a little, Itshe Leib the shoemaker, Arya the shoemaker, Fajertog the shoemaker, down to Spadek – Zalma Zigas the shoemaker, Jached the penny pincher, the Kelbmans, Ceszinski. These were the Czenstochow "400."

Kocze Street was then not populated entirely with Jews. Shepherds grazed cattle in the fields. Fat cows would come onto Kacza Street where women stood ready with pitchers, waiting for the gentile women to milk the cows.

Izrael Win settled there in 1880. He and his wife, Sheyndl, were honest, fine people. He was one of the founders of the group, *Shokher Tov* [Benevolent Friend] with Mordekhai and Jokl Haklmakher, Shimkha Meszngiser, Avraham-Nusen Frydman. Wigder Szwarc was always the *gabbai* [sexton]. Meir Biczner then had a small house on Kocze Alley. Yehiel *Melamed* [teacher] had a small *kheder* [religious elementary school]. The lamplighter lived at the corner. It was frightening to go from Gitl Ester's shop to Golda's house. The deserted houses told the history of the terrible fires in the 1870s. Many people were burned at that time. After the fire, there was a search for gold among the ruins and a weak, burned wall fell in and killed several people. From then on there was fear of going past at night. Many people swore that they themselves saw corpses in white shrouds at exactly midnight. People in white clothing did pass there, but these were the workers in the flour mills.

The Senatorske Alley was completely different. Every newly wed man, Hasidic children in the long coats worn by religious men, merchants, brokers, *shtekdreyers* [good for nothings], lived there. Many *shtreimlekh* [fur trimmed hats worn by some Hasidim], black satin robes with white socks were seen here on *Shabbos*. Most of the Hasidic *shtiblekh* [one room houses of prayer] were concentrated here. The most distinguished site on the alley was the *piantchke* [watering hole – tiny tavern].

Every night it was joyful in the tavern. If a man did not come home, his wife knew where to find him. Scandals took place here often in the middle of the night.

Khederim, Talmud-Torah

[Religious elementary schools and school for poor boys]

Jewish families were settled on Warszawer and Krakower Streets. Most of the children from the streets studied with Yitzhak Kraser – an angry, severe, wide boned teacher. Girls also studied in his *kheder*, but not together [with the boys]. While the young boys learned, the girls sat opposite [the *kheder*] in the courtyard.

The second *kheder* was Moshe *Lerer's* [Moshe the teacher]. A tall Jew, he always suffered from stomach problems and did not sleep. He would go the Rozprozer Rebbe to celebrate the concluding *Shabbos* meal. For the holidays, he would prepare *gregers* [noisemakers traditionally used on Purim], *dreydlekh* [tops traditionally used on Chanukah] and flutes for his students. He would take them on "May picnics." The children of the *Alee* mostly studied with him.

The same year the first *Talmud-Torah* opened on Czike Street. Tovya was the first *melamed*. Many children, from six to seven years old, studied in the *Talmud-Torah* – older youths, mostly from the villages, barefoot, who were just beginning to learn the alphabet. If Tovya had taught each child separately, he would never be finished. The *kheder* closed during the winter because of the snow and frost; the poor children did not have any boots and no capes. The mothers of the children who did have warm clothes were ashamed to send them to the *Talmud-Torah* [which was for poor children].

An historic chapter in the Jewish life in Poland was recorded in the winter of 1899. Jews from various localities, from villages and cities, arrived in the city. In the surrounding localities, the Jews simply died of hunger and cold. So from there they flowed to Czenstochow where charity was given and there was a free *Talmud-Torah*. Many poor houses became crowded with the arriving families. The rich could not bear the knocking on their doors. The *kehile* [organized Jewish community] called for a meeting of the rich businessmen in the city and it was decided to give coal for the poor houses, a few *gildn* a week according to the size of the family, and, in addition, notes for bread and potatoes. It was announced in the synagogues that all of the needy should come to register. The registration lasted for three days and Markusfeld gave a sermon to the assembled Jews and declared that they should not be ashamed to accept charity. Rich women also went from house to house to see who needed clothing. Doctors, the first among them Dr. Rus and Dr. Wasertal, gave free help to the sick.

[Page 36]

Many children died that winter. One, a Lozerl, had to be taken to the cemetery. But instead of taking him to Kucelin, they buried him in the snow. In the springtime, the dead body was found in the middle of the road.

The same year, immediately after Passover, the *Talmud-Torah* was moved from Czike to the Teper Street. A large building with a gate in the front. There were two divisions: one with Tovya for the *alef-beis* [the youngest] children, the second, where the *melamed* was Rabbi (Liulke) Hendl, for *Khumish* [Torah] and Rashi [commentaries].

The *Talmud-Torah* children had a joyous winter in 1890. The city fathers came to the school with shoemakers, took measurements for boots for each child. Many children received warm clothing with *bashlykn* [Russian hoods with long flaps]. They were given candies for Chanukah and several *kopekes* were put in the packages. A few weeks later, the old Gynsberg died. All of the *Talmud-Torah* children marched to the train station, waited for the train to arrive from abroad and the children accompanied the coffin with the respected deceased under a thin, wet snow.

The City Grows

In 1893 several demolished houses were already seen near the Trinity square. Houses appeared on the other side of the city, at Blachownia [town outside of Czenstochow]. On Kocze Street, Meir Biczner erected a large brick building with a courtyard – an entire *shtetl* [town], with shoemakers, tailors, Wolf Kac with a tavern, Kizshe Malarcz with a mangle [wringer, rollers in a frame that extract water from cloth]. In front was the Hasidic *shtibl* [one room house of prayer], and on the second floor the lame shoemaker directed Goldfaden's[1] theater piece. Another large building arrived in Teper Street, across from Drewnjak's tavern, where Izke's daughter, Maryam, remodeled the apartment. The apartment is important because of the later history of Lipe Goldboim. Another new building was erected on Teper Street: the residence of Khasriel Stoldola, the first refuge for our later heroes: Yakov-Ber Zylber (the lame Staluch), Yitzhak Lewi, Josef-Hersh Grejcer, Shaua Glezer, the lame Kopl, Chaim Leibele Szwarc.

New tailors of cheap clothing, shoemakers, fruit sellers, herring and kasha [buckwheat groats] shops were added to the new market. Shaya's son, Hershl, still had his good honest name, as well as Khasriel the *Shenker* [tavern owner] and Meir-Leib Helman. Henekh Lapidus opened a bookshop right after his marriage. His competitor was Emanuel Bejgele. Both supplied reading material for the Yiddish readers which consisted mostly of such stories as: *Di Tsvelf Gazlonim* [*The 12 Thieves*], *Di Farfirtre Kale* [*The Seduced Bride*], *Di Farwunderter Khosn* [*The Astonished Groom*] and so on.

At the corner of Jatke Street opposite the church stood the sellers of lemonade: the *Kopls* [men in hats] in white clothing with tall bonnets on their heads. Sheya Stope with *kvas* [fermented drink made from bread], actually from Petersburg; Nakhum-Yankl Frydman with a keg on his back, a long, tall bird over his head tied with a red turban with two tassels. Nakhum-Yankl was also an "actor." His best role was Hotsmakh [a character in Abraham Goldfaden's *Di Kishef-Makherin –The Sorceress*]. And thus he would offer his lemonade: "As I am Hotsmakh, the devil should take him, buy lemonade, made by the *Bobe Yakhne* [another character – the sorceress - in *Di Kishef-Makherin*], as I am a Jew."

Shlomo Kutner, a good youngish Jew, in a Jewish hat with a large gentile lacquered visor, stood near Nakhum-Yankl and clapped to the beat. Welwele *Dziekan* [dean], a city clown, appeared on the market stage, lifted his thick cane to heaven, declaimed: "I am the king of all the council drivers from Germany... I am the general of the field marshals." The beggars near the wall of the church played their *Jasna Gore* melodies on their fiddles. A second "actor," Hershele Bejtom, a small Jew with a twisted stick, appeared. He sang a song, danced, grabbed a thrown *groshn* and disappeared. Yeshaya Szlitn turned the barrel organ: "Why did my mother give birth to me" and sold *mazel kvitlekh* [lottery coupons], which his caged bird picked out of a box.

Tuesday auction days at the new market were full of other stands and goods: earthen pots, dishes, *koybers* (pillows), trunks, beds, closets, lime, rope, noodle boards, graters and so on, paint businesses, dry goods, haberdashery, Jews with small wagons and package porters. Among the merchants were found such distinguished Jews as the lame Landa with his doll business, Templ, an importer of Russian goods. Avrahamele Suberda, a gentle Jew, would give a great deal of charity. He was the *moyel* [performed circumcisions] for the poor without pay and would in addition give a ruble to the woman who gave birth.

The Ogrodowa Street to the north was lightly settled. Half Jewish, half non-Jewish. Only in 1894, when the Bedzin wood trader, Nomberg, built his large building, did it become equal to the second side of Ogrodowa on the south. Two *malarczes* (painters) lived on both side of Ogrodowa. One was Ahron Goldberg, the first to bring painting into Jewish houses, [paint that] he brought mainly from Lodz and Warsaw. The second, Cymberknop, was a sign painter.

[Page 37]

Most of the businesses were Jewish in the first and second *alees* [alleys]. The first and most esteemed businessman in the second *alee* was Imich and his paint business. Gradsztajn had a bank in the house in which he lived, until he built his new house on Teatralna. Nejgeld had a good reputation; he maintained a warehouse in the first *alee*. He was very respected in Czenstochow.

One often saw a woman in black with a veil over her face running around the alleys with quick steps. She spoke a nobleman's Polish and invited everyone to come to her for a visit because her husband was coming today. This was the crazy Treiza. A second one was the crazy Ruzshe. She gathered small pieces of paper and sang a song:

Pani [Madam] Royze sits in the garden
It rains on her.
When is my groom coming
For a stroll?

It was still empty to the north on Teatralna. A *hrabia* [equivalent to a count] lived there. They went there to skate in winter. Woe to those who greeted the count without his title; they immediately felt the count's whip and the teeth of his wolfhound. The count borrowed money from the Jews and paid back with slaps.

Kohn's factory was located on the other side, to the south. Ginsberg lived across from it. The two manufacturers were different from each other; Ginsberg was a solid Jew and a great philanthropist. Kohn was baptized for spite.

Going on Teatralna, one comes to the two new factories: on one side the "*shpagatchernia*" (*strados* [twine]). On the other side, the Pelcers, both French. New streets with family houses grew up in the fields around them. Work was then cheaper in Poland than in France – the Pelcers built one of the most beautiful palaces in Poland. The palace, three stories high, stood in the middle of a garden decorated with stucco and poured sculptures. In the garden – trees and flowers from all corners of the world. The master craftsmen in the French factory were all French.

Czenstochow spread and grew at a rapid pace and reached Hantke and the swamps. Meanwhile, we will to the Jewish side of the street.

Shabbosdike [Sabbath] Recreation

It was a wintry afternoon. The *Shabbos goyim* [non-Jews who perform tasks forbidden for Jews on the Sabbath] had heated the ovens in the morning, fixed the fires at noon and received their drinks of whisky and a piece of *challah* [*Shabbos* egg bread]. The congregation had finished its prayers, eaten, sung the *Shabbos* songs and rested in enjoyment of *Shabbos*.

However, in several houses such as Jaworski's or Peczke's, *Shabbos* was spent in another manner: servant girls, Jewish soldiers, young cavalrymen came together and they sang Yiddish and Ukrainian songs. It was warm in the room. The sand on the window flowed from the melting frost on the window panes. In the sand – paper funnels filled with cotton and secured with colored paper. The silk shawls and the Petersburg galoshes were removed and the girls told stories about their rich men, of marriage arrangements and of their *shtetlekh* [towns] and villages. Understand that these were poor children from the "outside." But when the girls were included somewhere, the wise guys did not have any influence over them.

Then they began to dance. The girls sang:

Who sewed for you –
Were you yourself capricious
Tra-la-la tra-la-la
Napravo (right).

Who asked you to marry them,
Did you yourself bury your face
Tra-la-la tra-la-la
Nalevo (left).

They became tired and revived themselves with a candy or another snack that the girls had brought with them. Then they began the *broyges-tants* [a dance of anger or offence; a dance done at weddings]:

Are you angry with me – I do not know for what – you go around all day with your nose lowered!

And:

Perhaps you desire a kiss from me
One-two-three-four;

[Page 38]

From someone else, yes – from you, no
La-la-la-la-la.

And they sang further:

Who is the boy who wanted me
Who promised me a kerchief with gold?
There he is standing behind the wall
And holds the kerchief in his hand.

They danced a polka, a *czardas* and a *rach, czach-czach* for going home. These *Shabbos* entertainments lasted until two weeks before Passover, until the beginning of the baking of the matzoh at Elhanu the headstone carver's, Szamper's and others. Young and old boys and girls worked with the matzoh; most of them were rollers, a smaller number were flour mixers, kneaders, hole pokers, scrapers, carriers. They worked from six in the morning until 11 at night, sometimes, in addition, an entire night. They made [the money for preparing for] Passover and sometimes there was [some money] left over for a new calico dress or a hat.

Cholera

The rays of the setting sun fall on the synagogue and on the *Beis-haMedrash* [house of study] at the Warta River on a late summer day and light the large *Mogen Dovid* [Shield or Star of David] on the colored windows that shine out to the world: "East of the sun until His arrival."

But on the streets that encircled the synagogue there was darkness. The entire summer the cholera ate the souls of the small and large. The number of victims was so large, mostly in the small houses on the straw mattresses with rotting straw, full of vermin – that the black coffins in the synagogue courtyard were left to rest and the dead were brought to the Kuceliner cemetery in simple wagons.

In 1894, the cholera was truly fought with better means than the cholera in the 70s. Then Meir Biczner, still a young man, with a few members of the *Khevre-Kadishe* [burial society] put on shrouds and rode white horses through the city waving swords towards heaven, shouting: *Malekh Hamoves* [Angel of Death], get out of our city! Now the city was bigger, with more Jewish doctors who appeared satisfied with a *gildn* or two from a poor man and many times they came without payment and even left a ruble for medicine. The Russian police, the fat *wachmistrz* (*wachtmeister*)[sergeant] Garbarski and the long thin Babrowski went around the city, asking that the gutters be whitewashed with lime and that the sick not be given water that had not been boiled to drink.

The Old Synagogue

A small, white house stood on Warszawer Street, with its face to the government buildings. This was the Jewish hospital. Clean inside, white covered cots, carbolic acid splashed around in all corners. Languid lips drank sterilized water and blessed the city fathers who had quickly put together the Jewish hospital. They were: Gejsler, Markusfeld, Ginsberg, Meir-Leib Helman of the old market, Avrahamele Suberda of the new market, Nejgeld, Imich. Doctors Rus and Waserthal and a few *feldshers* [barber-surgeons] and a poor girl, Gitl Zigas, who came running to the hospital with the first patient, her father Mendl Zigas, and remained there to serve the sick, worked, all doing their work for free.

There was enough work for Meir Biczner: to go the houses to comfort the mourners...

However, the cholera did not stop the work of the small Jewish factories. In Godl Wajnberg's small 10-*groshn* watch factory on Warszawer Street, in a small dark room, they worked from six in the morning until 10 at night. The old marriage age girls worked at the presses. Their harsh lives poured out in the mournful melody of a folksong:

I go out on the small porch
To look over the *shtetele*
A small bird comes flying
And bows to me.

The second manufacturer was Mordekhai Dreksler, also on Warszawer Street, opposite Kotlicki; a small, short Jew with a beard to his navel. His craft was to pour lead roosters. He tried to find a trick so that with one pouring almost 100 roosters would come out. His son helped him in the work and his mother (the *Muter* [mother] – that is how she wanted to be called) said that he had the head of a minister. The *Muter* who was the master of the shop was so bulky that a special soft chair was made for her. Five girls sat around her and decorated the trumpeters, rattles and silver bells. Her mouth never closed; she kept pouring tea into herself. Perhaps she was up to her 30th glass; this was a remedy against the cholera. She said the girls who worked should wait until night, that when they returned home they should cook a large teapot of water and if the did not have any lemon or sour salts, they should use vinegar...

[Page 39]

Konarski's small factory in Golda's house at the old market was a little decent. He paid his workers an entire 60 *kopekes* a week.

There was tumult in the street. A gentile girl fell down in front of Smolek's bakery. One and two – and she was dead. Across was the host of Federman's tavern, a healthy young, tall Jew. He lay down and did not stand up anymore. There was a rumor that he had been buried alive because his grave split; they went to the cemetery, making strenuous efforts at asking forgiveness.

A ruddy preacher came to the city, gave a sermon in the *Beis-heMedrash* that the cholera was a punishment for sin; they must repent, recite psalms and marry off orphans. The orphan who was burned on one cheek was caught and he was matched with an orphan. Women gathered flour, eggs, meat and celebrated a city wedding to chase the cholera.

The city fussed with piety. *Mezuzus* [plural of *mezuzah* – a box placed on the doorpost containing a parchment on which the prayer, *Shema Yisroel* - "Hear O Israel" – prayer that is central to Jewish worship expressing the oneness of God – is inscribed] were checked, the *tzitzis* [fringe on the *tallis* - prayer shawl and *tallis katan* – garment worn next to the body by pious men] were counted; one was prohibited from going out on the tree-lined street without a scarf, servant girls' umbrellas were broken and the children tore out rubber combs from girls heads. This was how it went until the Days of Awe.

Apostates, Dybbuks

There was also excitement in the city because of two new apostates. One was Chaim Leizer (Eliezer), a middle-class man with a wife and grown daughters, who was employed in Kahn's factory on Teatralna. Every morning, his wife saw him kneeling and crossing himself. Then he grabbed his *tallis and tefillin* [prayer shawl and phylacteries], prayed and kissed the *mezuzah* and ran to work. The second was Kopl Moshe, the teacher's son, a *melamed* [religious teacher] who ran to the church every day and cried with bitter tears that he would not be buried on a Jewish cemetery. It was believed in the city that he was the victim of love of a Christian.

Zelkowicz, who stood at the market every day selling pork, was an apostate of an entirely different character. He was a Cantonist. He was caught as a child and became a Nikolajever soldier. He could not bear the torture and surrendered to conversion. But Shmuel Zigas and the old Kelbelman, also Cantonists, risked their lives for *Kiddush ha-Shem*. It was better for them to die than to convert; they came home as Jews.[2]

There were two *dybukim* [plural of dybbuk – a soul who enters the body of a living person] present in the city. One was Golda Dybbuk. A Ludwig spoke from her. The Dybbuk Ludwig shouted: "The Jews, the Jews, they want to kill me." Golda calmed Ludwig: "Do not have any fear, Ludwig." She reminded him of the beer hall in Hamburg where they drank beer, caraway whiskey and Bordeaux wine together. A bright smile stretched over Golda's face. And Ludwig said: "Yes, that time is past ... Oh, the young girl from the beer hall ... blue eyes ... sings and plays ... I was baptized ... I am not a Jew ... no! I am not a Jew! ..." The only one who could calm Golda Dybbuk was Wigder Brukarcz. He would take her by the hands and shout: "Quiet, Ludwig!" – and Golda would swear that she would be quiet.

Wigder Brukarcz said that when he was 16 years old in Germany he had a good friend, Ludwig, who fell in love with a Christian girl, the daughter of the beer hall owner. Because of her he converted. Golda Dybbuk also lived in the same courtyard and it seemed she fell in love with Ludwig. After her wedding to her husband, Aba Sarwer, she became ill with a nervous upset and convinced herself that Ludwig Dybbuk had entered her.

The second was Meir with two dybbuks. One dybbuk was a cantorial dybbuk, who would sing out from [Meir] all of the cantorial pieces, *Shabbos* and holiday prayers. The second dybbuk in him was a Russian guard who would give orders and curse in Russian.

A close neighbor of Wigder Brukacz was Meyta the baker. The aroma from her bread with caraway seeds, which she leavened, kneaded and placed in the oven, was dispersed over the neighboring houses. Meyta (Mayta) the baker's little son, Itsik-Shpitsik, would chase after May bugs and cut the buttons off boys' pants. Wigder demanded that Itsik the buttons; if not he would send him to his father in America.

[Page 40]
Days of Awe

The Days of Awe were coming closer. It was quiet in the Gecewizne [neighborhood of Czenstochow]. The Talmud Torah and the *khederim* were closed. Only the voice of Hendl *melamed* [teacher in a religious primary school] on the topmost story poured out in the spirit of Rosh Hashanah: "A man's origin is from dust and his destiny is back to dust..."

On the other side of the Jewish part of the city at the very tip of the *gubernia* [province] near Reb Shaya Szlitn in bent over little houses in Kocze Alley, they fervently prepared. They dressed up ... and they argued. The holiday guests would allot the places among themselves: who should go to the *shtiblekh* [one room synagogues], who should go to the synagogue, who to the *Beis-heMedrash* - to beg. Meanwhile, they rehearsed how to groan and moan, how to give themselves a hunchback, how to be blind and to sing: My eyes are closed; it is dark for me day and night...

A guest came – Aytsik Szlize, the first one who came out of the Piotrkow jail. The second after Szlize was Josl Yapcak, who murdered his father, Nakhum the shoemaker, and threw him out of bed in honor of Rosh Hashanah. Josl Yapcak was the fear of the Jewish neighborhood because he was as strong as a lion and no one could compete with him. Girls from outside, who came to work as servants in Czentochow, had to pay him a fee.

And it was already Rosh Hashanah. The Jatke [butcher shop] Street and the old market were cleaned up. Only the smell remained that clearly says that last night old fish, rotten cucumbers, spoiled plums and wormy apples were sold here. The peasants from the surrounding villages knew that it was a holy day for the Jews and they did not come to the city with their village produce. Only one gentile moved idly around the street and shouted and cursed. This was Mecner Pajak who would have died from hunger if not for the Jews.

Zelkowicz, the convert, who did not now stand at the market with pork, hung around the *Shul* [synagogue] Street. He would say that his heart drew him to the *Ahron Kodesh* [ark containing the Torah scrolls] and he saw his parents in his dreams. He was nine years old when they tore him away from them.

The barrel organ with the birds that picked out the lottery coupons in Shaya Szlitn's courtyard was at rest. The shutters in Morits's "little house" near the river were closed. The officers would not whip the girls with their riding crops today; the boastful young men would not hit them and the girls would not wink at the passersby from the balconies. Uncle Morits, a short, dark little Jew in dark clothes with a gold chain that was balanced on his fat stomach, held his *talis* bag and a large *Makhzor* [plural *Makhzorim* – Rosh Hashanah and Yom Kippur prayer book] stiffly under his arm and marched to Krakower Street to the leaseholders' *shtibl*.

The Rosh Hashanah sun warmed the Jewish alleys. Men in faded, threadbare, black loose coats – a number an inheritance from the grandfather's wedding clothes – rushed into the synagogue and into the *shtiblekh*. Boys and fathers were dressed in loose cloth coats. The wives wore small Rosh Hashanah bows in their *sheitlen* [wigs worn by pious married women], with padded busts and little pillows underneath; the older ones in headbands, inheritances from mothers and grandmothers and in black dresses.

The women from the boulevard and from the new market were dressed differently, long gold chains around throats, pearls, broaches with diamonds, diamond earrings, rings with diamonds and wide golden bracelets on their hands. The *zogerins* [women who translate the prayers from Hebrew to Yiddish] carried large *Makhzorim* and *Tkhinus* [Yiddish prayer books] to recite for those who did not know Hebrew.

The Old Market

Ayzik Kikele also was all dressed up in a pair of pants from which he fell out, a gift from fat Wolberg and in shoes from which his feet crept out. His left eye was bound with a colored rag, urchins ran after Ayzik, speaking with a twang: *gut yom-tov* [happy holiday], Ayzik, may you obtain a good year.

[Page 41]

The synagogue was lit with a hundred candles. Long streams of water poured from the walls. The fine proprietors with gold and silver *asores* [ornamental pray shawl collars] occupied the middle of the synagogue to the *Ahron Kodesh* [ark with Torah scrolls]. The simple Jews, those who drag sacks and crates, factory workers, bakers, tailors, shoemakers were closer to the anteroom. Outside in front of the synagogue the *ulaner* [an ironic reference to the Polish light cavalry] moved with arrogance: Moshe Pace, the Yomete's Hersh Leib, Avraham Ber Murczyn, Yankl's son, Avraham Wolf, the fast talkers and movers, the boastful ones and their followers.

The gang members were now the heroes of the Jewish neighborhood. They repealed one of the market tax payments, took *pretensja* [demanded or required] money, or they protected the Jews many times from gentile beatings, from gentile attacks and gave blows when it was needed. Sometimes, butcher hatchets, meat cleavers and shafts from wagon wheels were used.

The City Becomes Larger and More Beautiful

Short, bleak days. The deep mud is covered with thin ice. In the Jewish homes, they are talking about the death of Aleksander III. The masses do not read the Polish and Russian newspapers from Warsaw and Petersburg. There is no Jewish newspaper here yet except for the Hebrew *Hamelitz*. Only several large manufacturers, the Grodsztajns and the Kazione Bank make use of the telephone. Yet, the news about the death of Aleksander III spreads quickly and awakes sadness and fear in Jewish hearts. It was said that Czar Aleksander was good to the

Jews and who knows what the new king will be. They consoled themselves that Nikolai II might be good to the Jews because he had a Jewish lover and what a lover!

A soldier who had shot a sergeant-major was then sentenced to death in Czenstochow. *Shabbos* morning, the entire city ran to see how the solider had been shot. But as the body lay in a grave, a telegram arrived that the Czar had forbidden his death sentence...

In 1895, Jews swore their devotion to Nikolai II in the city schools. The city had then grown a great deal. In the First *Alee*, Notl Pankowski erected a new building with stucco on the ceilings and large tiled ovens decorated with ornaments. New houses were built by Kalinski on Teatralne, Winer on the Stacje Street, Kruger on the Blich, the Namberg brothers on Ogrodnowa and Drewniak on Garncarske.

In the middle of the 1890's they began to prepare electrical lighting. The electrical station was built opposite the Russian church, behind the *koze* (jail). The first holes were dug at the new market. It was then learned that the new market was once a large cemetery because many human skulls and bones were dug out. Stories were told that the small building also opposite the church was in the old times a castle of King Zigmunt with an underground passage to the church in which there appeared to be a grave.

The coloring of the first pole for the electrical lighting opposite Imich's dye business was like a great exhibition. People gathered to see the great wonder where they would climb up so high to the tip of the pole with paint and paint brush in the hand. The 13-year old Chaim-Leibele carried this out; he was praised with a bravo and applause from the assembled crowd.

They prepared for the coronation of Nikolai II. The fronts of the houses were colored and covered in lime, the gutters were cleaned, criminals were freed from jail. For the most part, the janitors took part in the holiday. They illuminated the gutters with lanterns and kerosene wicks. The intelligentsia did not take part in the holiday. Jews had not yet forgotten the pogroms in Ukraine after the murder of Aleksander II; in Czenstochow they also sang the song of the Kiev pogrom, "The wild *kacapes* [Great Russians] with their paws, they have corrupted everything..."

The coronation was dominated by drunken scoundrels; beatings took place. Drunk officers tottered in the streets with *Pan* [Mr.] Erlich, the police chief.

Immediately after the coronation, the Czenstochow city fathers decided to introduce sewers into the city.

[Page 41]

Theater, Literature, Movies

The same summer, *Malkha Szwartsnkop [Queen Black Head]* was performed in a summer theater on Teatralne Street. *Shabbas* at night our Jewish guys would drop in there. Whoever did not have a ticket was almost satisfied with looking through the crevices of the boards around the theater. The play was performed in Polish, but one scene was performed by a Yiddish *kheder* in Yiddish. A song that was sung there spread through the Jewish streets. This was:

[Page 42]

"Yonale, Yonale, I want to tell you something.
Here is a young wife but you should not hit her."

The small Jewish guys would also sometimes slip into the theater where Gege, the poster hanger reigned. Also at the expense of Madam Szwarc, the owner of the flower shop in the Second *Alee*, a Jewish child would go up to the gallery. Sometimes a copper ten-piece bribe would be given to the "important one." They performed then, *Gooæeie Przyæodzon (Guests are Coming]* *Gejsha, Halka*. The small Jewish group had become infected with theater fever. Their rebbe was Yakov Ber Zilber or the lame Staluch. He took all of the young children from the old *Talmud-Torah* of Yitzhak Lewi and rehearsed theater there. Yitzhak's father, Mordekhaile, a short Jew with sparkling eyes, and his mother, Beyle, always in a long skirt with a sweet smile on her wide face – would beam with joy at their son and at the entire theater company.

The first presentation, *Kuni-Leml* [a musical written by Abraham Goldfaden] was initiated by Grumen the *melamed* of the *kheder* on Warszawer Street. *Men hot geshtanen oyf kep* [it was very crowded]. Everyone came to see their children, grandchildren and cousins act in the theater. Tickets were not needed. How the small group could carry out such a performance, without any help, without mastery of stagecraft – was God's wonder.

On the second night of Purim, the same piece was performed in Markowicz's house at the old market, in Mordekhai Korek's tavern.

Several weeks later, during *Khol haMoed Pesakh* [intermediate days of Passover], a troupe of actors came from Lodz and performed four plays: *Ahashverosh. Shulamus, Bar Kokhba* and *Kabtsnzon un Hungerman* [*Kabtsnzon and Hungerman*]. Famous actors took part in the troupe: Piurnik, Akselrad, *di gele Tslove* [the blond Tslova]. The theater was fully packed with people for all four nights. Then they were not permitted to perform in Yiddish, only in *Deitsch-Merish* [Germanisms]. Madam Szwarc helped out convincing the police chief that they were acting in "stage German." *Pan* Erlich knew very well that this was not German, but he could not refuse Madam Szwarc, the beauty of the city.

The Jewish neighborhood became richer with new songs. The father absorbed *Khazan* [cantor] Ziskind's beautiful melodies. The girls sang theater songs. Goldfaden's songs were then very popular, particularly *Dos Yidele* [*The Little Jew*]. The Jewish soldiers, entering Jewish homes for *Shabbos* spread Russian and Ukrainian songs.

New Market

The interest in literature in the Jewish neighborhood was also awakened. For the most part, they read Yiddish translations of novels which arrived from America. Shomer [pseudonym of the Yiddish novelist, Nakhum Meir Sheilewitch] was at the head. The young had already begun to thirst for real literature. Books written by Mendele Mocher-Sforim and M. Spektor had started to appear. *Klatshe* [*The Dobbin*] was particularly popular. Shoemaker and tailor apprentices delighted in Tolstoy. Translations of Emil Zola appeared and the young thirsted to absorb the new ideas. Czenstochow began to become a cultural center that influenced the surroundings that was called Zaglembie or Piotrkow *gubernia* [province].

In 1898, the Dreyfus trial resulted in changes in the Jewish street. *Captain Dreyfus*, which was published in pamphlets, became the most popular literature. Anti-Semitism in Poland began to show its teeth.

A Jew appeared at the old market the same summer with a box on his stomach; four white, rubber tubes came out of the box. For three *kopekes* Jews could put the rubber tubes to their ears and hear singing. Posters appeared in the *Alee* that a great world-wonder would be shown in the theater. The wonder was a large chest with a large trumpet on the stage that sang *Bozhe, Tsarya khrani* [*God Save the Czar*] and other songs, and suddenly the room became dark, a white sheet appeared on the stage and two children in two beds threw pillows, feathers flew, people, policemen, firemen ran together.

[Page 43]

People could not understand all of the wonders and assumed it was black magic or delusions, but the young lads from the Jewish street read about Edison in the American publications and knew that the box at the new market and the chest with the large trumpet were gramophones and the black magic on the sheet was called *zywe obrazi* (living pictures).

New streets were cut on the square where the coronation took place, behind the church down to Czenstochowka. A new post office building with a large, wide courtyard, where the highest Russian authorities lived, was erected not far from the church. During the spring and summer days it smelled of greens from the trees and from the open windows pianos played the music of Tchaikovsky, Mozart and Schubert. No wonder that when a child from the Jewish street strayed here and compared everything that he saw and heard with the suffocating poverty of the poor street that sold milk from a farmer for a three-piece coin, chicory for a *kopek* (they did not know about coffee) and two blocks of sugar for two *groshn* – strange thoughts awoke in his head...

The lame Stalich (Yakov Ber Zylber) himself thought about dramatizing and acting in a new play. This was *Shimkha Plakhte*. The presentation took place on Purim in the Pupecki Hall on Tilne Street. Chaim-Leibele made the decorations. After the presentation, a small group began to rehearse *Uriel Akosta*. The daughter of Gradsztajn the banker emulated the children on the Jewish street and founded a theater club for the rich children. The troupe produced one-act Polish plays.

Czenstochow grew like yeast. On *Ostatni Grosz*, Hantke, the converted Jew, began to cover the mud and build an iron factory. At the same time, Leibl Garbinski bought a large house on Tilne Street. Garbinski, who won a great deal of money from Hantke playing cards – later founded a pawnshop where the poor pawned their rings, clocks and overcoats.

In 1899, *A Velt mit Veltelekh* [*A World within a World*] appeared in Czenstochow. This small book spread like a blaze. It fell among the young men in the *yeshiva* and caused real devastation.

New Winds

In 1900 the great Zalel of Piotrkow, Hershele Beker from Lodz, Mordekhai Beker and the lame Kopl came to Czenstochow and they brought plays and new songs. A new star arrived: Lipe Goldbaum, a Lodz turner, who lodged with Izke's daughter, Mariem, or with Wolf Bom. Lipe was the first teacher of science and political enlightenment in the circle to which Chaim Leibele, Josef Hirsh Gricer, the lame Stalukh, Khasriel Totbard (Stadale) belonged. In the circle, they spoke about parliamentarianism, the Czarist government and natural science. During the same year Werde of the gold factory bought the old age home on Ostatni Grosz. At the same time the Czenstochow wagon drivers and porters brought a *sefer-Torah* [Torah scroll] to the synagogue, as was the custom with music, torches and dancing in the street.

During the month of *Tammuz* of that year, three Czenstochower – Chaim Leibele, Josef Hirsh Grajcer and Yakov Ber Zylber – left to wander across the world. Stealing across the

Austrian border, they arrived in the *shtetl*, Teshibin [Teshabin], and rented an inn for two *guldn* to present theater at night. But instead of an audience, a mass of children came with *kreuzers*. The proceeds in the cashbox were one *guldn* and 75 *kreuzers*. The actors jumped out of a window with this sum and went farther on their way.

The group left on foot from Teshibin to Krakow, from Krakow to Chrzanów and Oshpitsin [Oœwiêcin] and from there back to the border near Elkish [Olkusz]. They were again in Czenstochow on Rosh Hashanah.

New winds blew. It was the time of the rise of Zionism. Dr. Herzl's name was well known far and wide. The Czarist government did not disturb the Zionist activity; the Zionist preachers said in the synagogues that salvation was near; they were going to buy *Eretz-Yisroel* from Turkey. The Zionists particularly attracted the middle-class and the young who felt how the ground was sinking under their feet. Young men and girls arranged Zionist balls; poor businessmen saved and bought a *shekel*.[3]

[Page 44]

The resistance to Zionism came from two sides: in addition to the Polanized Jews from "higher" society and a number of the middle class who withdrew from Jewish life in general – the pious Jews, Hasidim and rabbis moved heaven and earth and gave sermons in the synagogues that only *Moshiakh* [Messiah] can redeem Jews from the exile. On the other site, the Socialist agitation among the highest circles in Warsaw, Lodz, Vilna, Bialystok reached Czenstochow. The Socialist Workers Movement began that preached brotherhood and liberation through struggle and revolution.

Little by little the Socialist movement among others also drew in the religious youths; the Enlightenment mainly had an effect on the young men in the *yeshiva*.

Fathers and mothers made fun of their children and others beat their children who wanted to overthrow Nicholai. But there also were fathers and even entire families who assisted the movement.

The struggle between the pious Jews and *Achdusnikes* [Bundists] flared up. An untrue story spread across the city that the *Achdusnikes* in Lodz had dressed a dog in a *talis* [prayer shawl] and *tefilin* [phylacteries] and led it through the streets. *Achdusnikes* became a curse words. The fights and scuffles between the leaders of the *Freiheit* movement and the young rascals often became embittered.

The coming of a new and fresh storm that entered the Jewish streets with a rare zest was strongly felt in 1901. Many new publications from America appeared. New styles for women arose in the winter. The long trains disappeared; the small cushions lay neglected in the street. The short dresses, high heeled shoes, low hats over folded braids, the red capes with the short parasols added a great deal of charm to the working girls. The young men also began to dress up. The caftans became shorter; the hats smaller; they put on paper shirtfronts and paper cuffs. However, the trouble was the shirtfront was nothing short of them creeping out from the undershirt during a "conversation." The cuffs had a habit of falling off the hands. The *spinkes* (studs) broke and the collars opened.

In the evenings we went to the First and Second *Alee* and had discussions. The beloved theme was still: what is heaven, the stars, how large and how far is the sun, what is thunder and lightning and so on. We also spoke about politics. Yiddish love songs and folk songs that had earlier been sung on the *Shabbosim* [Sabbaths] in the squat houses were now sung on the benches in the *Alees* and many new songs were added: *Hatikvah* [*The Hope* – now the national anthem of Israel – was then the anthem of the Zionist movement], *Dort vu di Ceder* [*There Where the Cedars*]. A beloved folk song was:

The clock has already struck 12
Take me home, take me home.
What excuse will I make
For my mother at home?

The first excuse you should give:
You worked late, you worked late.
The second excuse you should give:
You lost your way.

The *lamer kop* [lame head] brought a new song from Lodz copied onto a piece of paper:

It snowed and rained
Sadness in the street.
I met a small girl
Poor, naked and pale.

They did not yet know that this song had been written by Morris Rozenfeld.

Monash Biber brought a song from a workroom in London:

The machines run, the wheels bang,
It is dirty and hot in the workshop.
My head becomes confused,
My eyes become dark,
Dark from tears and sweat.

Things began to stir in the small factories, where adults and children worked. The words bourgeois and proletariat quietly crept into the workers' mouths.

The young group acquired new friends – students and intellectuals. The first were Markus Goldberg, Markus Cymerman, Goldsztajn from the First *Alee*, several girls. A secret meeting took place in an attic in Godl Wajnberg's courtyard on Warsawer Street.

In 1902 in the month of *Shvat*, all of Czenstochow was abuzz. One of the bakers had led a girl named Chanale astray. He gave her drops for an abortion and the girl died. Chaim Leibele then wrote a song named, *Chanale's Toyt* [*Chanale's Death*]. Henekh Lapidus bought this song for five rubles and published it in a booklet. This song reads thus in the Yiddish of that time[4]:

[Page 45]

At three in the afternoon
Whoever was in front of the *shamas's* house,
Began the dark funeral
For the one who saw misfortune.
Running, a shout, a commotion,
A cry among sisters and brothers.
The mother with a muffled voice:
Chanale, where are you being taken?
Oy, Gotenyu [Oh, my God], what has happened to me?
Chanala, I will see you no more. And so on.

This song, *Chanale's Toyt* [*Chanale's Death*] spread not only in Czenstochow, but also in many cities in Poland. Girlish eyes filled with tears while singing and servant girls poured out their bitter hearts with it.

[Page 45]

The Pogrom

The coming of the Days of Awe was already felt in the air. The market was fuller than on all other Thursdays [the days on which people shopped for *Shabbos*]. Ripe fruit was displayed. Plums, red berries, apples and also greens, brought in from the surrounding peasant villages. The peasants knew that the women needed to buy for *Shabbos*; they brought chickens, eggs, ducks. The fishermen displayed the kosher fish, the long pike in Balye's water with swimming carp taken recently from the Warta. The women and their servants, bosses and their apprentices and many, many poor women with baskets would soon come.

Near the fishermen stood the tailors of cheap clothing with their stands: pants, men's jackets, shirts and colored kerchiefs. The wagon drivers and porters waited to earn a few *groshn* for *Shabbos*. Sacks of kasha, beans, peas, broad beans, oatmeal, pieces of salt, soups and barrels of herring stood in front of the shops. The rich bought *shmaltz* herring and roe; the poor – small herrings with a great deal of milk (*mlitsakes*) so that there would be something to chop with onions and vinegar for after the *Shabbos* prayers.

The boastful ones, pickpockets and heroes with knives moved among the carts and fruit sellers.

The quiet, modest Dovid Oderberg also stood with plums among the fruit sellers. Mrs. Teafila, the Polish woman, came to him at nine o'clock in the morning with a basket and asked him to measure several quarts of plums. When the plums were in the basket, she suddenly began to shout that Oderman should give her back her money. She did not want the spoiled Jewish plums. Dovid looked at her astonished and said: "*Pani* [madam], you have not yet paid me for the plums." Teafila began to speak loudly: "*Paskudner Zyd*" [loathsome Jew], give me my money!" The plums were poured out of her basket. Hooligans grew as if from the earth, overturned the troughs of fruits, turned over stands and began beatings. Wagon drivers and fishermen stood in opposition to them with whips and poles, butchers from the butcher street arrived. Nakhum Yankl Frydman, the Yumete's Hirsh Leib, Meir Riz, Melekh Kutner mixed in, brought wagon shafts from the wagons and struck back. However, so many hooligans arrived that could not stand against them.

The wild mob went through Warszawer and Krakower Streets and looted shops, broke window panes. Messengers ran through the factories to stop work because Jews were beating Christians.

A wild mob poured out of all of the factories at twelve o'clock noon. The market was already cleared out, shops shuttered. No Jews were seen in the street. The violent people who later arrived from the distant factories – Hantke's, Pelcer's and Szpogatszarnje's – carried out a pogrom in the Jewish streets in the wildest manner with stones and iron bars. They created the first and largest ruins on Warszawer Street. Pinye Kaminski's barbershop was broken into pieces.

It is clear that the pogrom was well organized earlier by the Polish anti-Semites and scheduled for the time when the military was not in the city. The police also did not appear in the street. A few soldiers were in the city.

Markisfeld[5] sent several telegrams to Warsaw that the military should be sent to Czenstochow before there were mass victims. Warsaw let it be known that it was sending the military immediately. Meanwhile, the pogrom continued undisturbed with the shout of *Bi Zydow* (Beat the Jews). The streets were covered with broken glass and feathers. Jews lay hidden in cellars, in attics, many with Christian neighbors.

Around one at night, Markusfeld was still standing at the new market waiting for the military. The mob had then invaded Tilne and Ogrodowa. Suddenly the military appeared, marching through the First *Alee* to the new market and placed themselves there in straight rows to the church. The pogromists, behind the stone fences of the church, pelted the military with stones and shouted: "Beat the Russian soldiers!" The first salvo came after the military marched into Koszczol's courtyard. The hooligans ran away. Around five in the morning, the military was spread throughout the city. Around six, gentiles with looted goods were being taken to the police station.

[Page 46]

Friday was terrible for Jews. Many Jews scattered to the neighboring cities. It was said that the actual pogrom would begin Friday at night; no Jew would remain from the three crosses to the Gecewizner. Janow, Myszków, ̄arki, Kozieg³owy had guests for *Shabbos*. A dead quiet reigned in the streets. No one dared to sit at the market and in the *Alees*. Military patrols marched back and forth.

Chaim Leibele, the writer of these lines, found himself in the street the entire day and night, many times in the very middle of the wild crowd. In the morning he found the Teper Street covered with feathers and down. In many houses, the little bit of poor furniture was broken; looted stores were sealed with boards. When Chaim Leibele knocked on his parents' door, he did not get any answer. Later, the people came out of their hiding places. *Shabbos*, he traveled to the small towns to calm the Czenstochower Jews there.

The trial of the pogromists that took place in the middle of winter was a tragic farce. Many were entirely freed. Several received a few days in prison and several – six weeks, but actually in the Czenstochow jail so that, God forbid, they would not lack for food and drink.

The Polish Warsaw newspapers wrote that the pogrom was organized by the Jews themselves. The Petersburg *Fraynd [Friend]* was satisfied with just a few lines. Therefore, Chaim Leibele dedicated a song to the pogrom:

Just listen, people, to what has happened.
What has occurred to us in the city.
We Jews have encountered a misfortune:
Burned, beaten and robbed.
There has not yet been such a lament
As there was in Czenstochow,
In the month of Elul, the 9th day,
The misfortune happened to us.
Nine in the morning
A Christian woman came
She ordered plums.
Suddenly she shouted: *Zyd* [Jew],
They are not good,
Give me back my money.
Letters went like telegrams
Into the factories:
When the whistle sounds at 12,
You should go into the streets.
As the 12 o'clock whistle blew
They went out of the factories
With shouts, force and noise,
To the market and the streets
Beat, broke,
Became wilder and wilder,
Goods laid out, shop counters turned over,
Broke into poor houses.
The hooligans' hands
Set fire and burned,
Bedding plucked and torn.

The pogrom song immediately spread across the city. The song was supposed to be sold by the publisher, Benyome (Benyamin) Libeskind in Piotrkow, but Henekh Lapidus anticipated this and paid 10 rubles and published 200 copies. Avraham Hon (Szwarc) went around the market with the song and sang it out loud.

The same year, Josef Hirsh Grajcer was taken into the military. With his departure, the young group lost one of its leaders.

In 1903 the struggles among the various still small party groups began. The Russo-Japanese War broke out and people scattered. The majority to London. The writer of these memories also left his home city then.

Translator's Footnotes

1. Playwright Abraham Goldfaden, considered the founder of Yiddish theater.

2. The term Cantonist is derived from a German term for recruiting district. Jewish boys were drafted into the Russian army for 25 years of military service at age 12 starting in 1827; they were pressured to convert. The length of service eventually decreased to 12 years plus 3 years in the reserve. A Nikolajever soldier served during the reign of Czar Nikolai I. *Kiddush haShem* is the act of sanctifying God's name.

3. Purchasers of a Zionist *shekel* received a yearly membership certificate in the Zionist movement.

4. Until 1908 and the First Yiddish Conference in Czernowitz, Yiddish orthography was not standardized and the song below was written in non-standard Yiddish orthography.

5. This name is spelled elsewhere as Markusfeld.

[Page 47]

Economic Life
Jews in Industry

by D. Bezworodka

The role of Jews in Czenstochow industry was very significant both during the Russian times, when it produced for the wide Russian market and, later, in independent Poland when it adapted to the internal market in the nation itself.

True, the large factories in the city belonged not to the Jews, but to French-Belgian firms such as: Mottes, Czenstochowianke and Gelcers.

They manufactured inexpensive textile goods and employed around 15,000 workers, only Poles, while all of the technical and commercial personnel were French and Belgian. Jewish workers and contractors would be employed there in such work as building, painting, mechanical installations and the like.

With the large factories in Czenstochow can also be included the twine factories that manufactured not only twine, but also sacks which were delivered all over Poland. The most well known were: Szpagaczarnia, Warta, Gnaszyn and Stradom.

Therefore, the middle-sized and small industries in Czenstochow were built almost exclusively by Jewish entrepreneurs and the greatest part also by Jewish workers. Therefore, we have to mention that the Jewish industry in Czenstochow did not benefit from any financial help or economic privileges from the government, not in the Czarist times and also not later in independent Poland. It was entirely the opposite; any connection with the Polish government simply hindered the development of Jewish industrial enterprises. In 1924, that is, still during the "good times" before the open anti-Jewish economic discrimination on the part of the Polish regime, the reporter of the county unambiguously declared to the writer of these lines: The Polish government is not concerned that Czenstochower small industry will suffer; on the contrary, there will be a benefit from this that a small toy industry will develop in Tuszyn, Katowice and in Szczawnica. The Polish economists supported the plans of decentralizing the toy and haberdashery fabrication through the system of the home-worker, who were called *chalupnikes* [a *chalup* is a hut or cottage] in Poland, against the interests of the Czenstochower factory-industry.

The Jewish industry in Czenstochow, particularly the toy and the haberdashery manufacturing, stood on such a high technical level that certain technical systems that were introduced there 20 years ago were still applied in the fabrication of the same articles both in Western Europe (Bohemia, Germany, Belgium, France) and in America. This was even more surprising when it is taken into consideration that these technical methods were devised by people who did not have any technical and theoretical preparation. The Jewish entrepreneurs often began manufacturing almost as soon as they got off the *yeshiva* [religious secondary school] bench, or left the Hasidic *shtibl* [one room prayer house]. A number of them did not later even throw off the long *kapote* [coat worn by religious men]. Their mastery of the trade that they achieved only through experience would be refreshed in such a peculiar manner: they would sometimes take a quick trip to Leipzig or they would visit a German factory and actually only take a quick look, just like a good card player who knows the cards of his partner when he takes a look only at their tops.

Understand that this industry developed from a very small beginning. The "factory" was often arranged in the bedroom of the owner. The relationship between manufacturers and workers was "patriarchal." Even, when a long time later, the factory was built in a modern manner. Several workers from Werder's gold factory, from Jerzy Landau's celluloid factory, from Wajnberg's comb factory, would later tell how they would sometimes interrupt the work at night and go to pray *Minkhah-Maariv* [evening prayers] in the small synagogue that was arranged in the factory itself. The manufacturer would with great effort gather money to pay the workers and they would often wrack their brains over how to collect a commercial debt.[a] A great problem then, too, was how to obtain raw material for the toy manufacturers, as well as celluloid, nickel-tin, mirrors and the like. These reminiscences of the past pioneer era was given to the writer of these lines by the manufacturers Landau, Wajnberg, Zelikson[1], Ringelblum, Hocherman, Rozenberg and others.

[Page 48]

The additional pioneers excelled in the celluloid, toy and haberdashery industries: Jerzy Landau founded his factory at the end of 1900. He manufactured combs, beads, dolls and distributed them in all of Russia through his own commercial salesmen. The Jewish workers in his factory were even more stifled by Christian workers. A number of the former Jewish workers worked their way up to office employment or as technical personnel; a certain number used the experience in order to open their own small factories.

The St. Wajnberg Factory on Wales Street specialized in the production of combs.

Szmulewicz, Ferleger, Brill, Hocherman, Mic produced toys. Rozenberg, on Krutke Street, manufactured combs, dolls and, for the most part, mirrors.

Zeligson, at Ogrodowe 55, had great sales in Russia coming not only from his own manufacturing, but also from the production that he bought from smaller manufacturers.

Ruczewicz manufactured celluloid dolls, combs and mirrors.

Glazer, whose family is now in America, was one of the first manufacturers of rubber clothing, that is collars, cuffs, dickeys of celluloid that were worn then in Poland.

Frydman on Fabryczne Street had a bead and comb factory. In addition there were recorded many more larger and smaller factories of the sort.

Czenstochow Jews also developed large industries for souvenir items that consisted mainly of religious articles, although Jews were officially forbidden to be employed in this. The most important producers in this industry were: Fajgelewicz and Wajnbaum. The latter was a many branched and very skillful family.

The first place in the metal industry was taken by the Spinke factory of the Szaja Brothers. They were known as smart at constructing the complicated stamps. They inherited these abilities from their father. Although each of the brothers worked for himself, they were always connected. The leader was Herman Szaja, not the oldest, but the most intelligent. He would travel to Germany very often. He would also be chosen as an arbiter to settle conflicts between merchants.

As president of the Jewish merchants and factories union in Czenstochow, he would often have the occasion to intervene with the Polish government. In 1920 he led a delegation to the Czenstochow *staroste* [head of county administration] about the Sunday rest law that forced Jewish artisans and manufacturers as well as merchants to rest two days a week (the law was particularly directed against Jewish trade and Jewish artisans).

The Weksler family was known among the pioneers of the toy industry and metal "novelty" (souvenir) articles. The family's father was named Hershl Weksler. His two sons manufactured metal punches for the small factories that did not have their own mechanics. Moshe Weksler, one of the sons, graduated from the artisans' school and became an artist in his trade. He was well paid for his work or professional advice. He was a very dear and good man and was very active in the Socialist Zionist party in 1905 and later.

Czenstochow also possessed heavy iron commodity factories, such as chains for industry, tools for agriculture, hinges and other household articles.

The head in this field was occupied by the manufacturers, Ickowicz and Horowicz. The Ickowicz family consisted of half a dozen brothers. Each had a small factory for himself and each created a different metal article.

[Page 49]

The large gold factory which was assembled in the most modern way, not only according to the ideas of Russia and Poland, but also Western Europe – belonged to Henig and Werde. Both partners were great philanthropists.

Khenenia Goldberg's watch factory was the only one in Poland for a long time. Goldberg's patents were applied to watch fabrication in Switzerland. In , he would receive regular payments (royalties). He also was a good organizer and on a clear day he had time to sit with Blaszczinski and play chess, in which he was a master.

The manufacturing of knives, cheap and better ones, lay mostly in Christian hands. Jews here were suppliers of raw materials and bought the completed goods. The owner of the largest factory was a Jew named Rozencwajg.

The Czenstochower iron foundries had a connection far outside the borders of Poland with pots, ovens, irons and various other household articles. They also produced machine parts for the Czenstochower industries. One of the first was Vulkan, founded by a Russian company. The director of the factory was Engineer Ratner, a well known communal and cultural worker in Czenstochow. Other Jewish employees were Ejznberg, Szwarc, Rysyn, Yakov Rozenberg. After Poland's liberation, the Polish government took over the factory. All of the Jewish clerks were removed. A number of them founded a second iron factory, Metalurgie, with Shmuel Goldsztajn.

The largest iron factory in Rakow, *Huta Hontke*, existed in the merit of Jewish commercial spirit because only Jews delivered and fetched its production.

Czenstochow was famous for its mirror industries in two categories: 1) factories that manufactured mirrors from dark glass; it was cut and delivered unfinished to the factories that framed them in metal, wood and celluloid frames; and 2) factories that produced finished mirrors and brought the goods to all of Russia via agents. Later, after 1918, when the Russian market was lost, the mirrors found a sales market not only in all of Poland, but also in Romania and Bulgaria where they competed with the German products. This was how it was until the Germans brought in the steam system.

The well known mirror factories were:

J. L. Bezbarodko, Stapnicki and Orbach, Grilek, Sercarcz, Waga, Epelbaum, Bridl and Hocherman, Hamburger Hocherman.

One of the largest mirror manufacturers was Josef Bezbarodko. He came from Russia. Being the second generation of mirror manufacturers (in Moscow in 1864), he well knew the taste of the Russian market. Warsaw also had a large mirror industry, but those from Warsaw bought the raw materials in Czenstochow mainly because of the better technical organization and better work system.

Kohn's paper factory was one of the largest paper factories in Russia. Old Jews would call it the mill because it used a great deal of water power from the Warta [River].

Markusfeld's Malarnje spread its wallpapers and colored papers to the farthest corners of Russia. The Kapeluszarnja, a hat and cap factory, and the Klejarnje that produced glue and other chemical products also belonged to Markusfeld.

Czenstochower Jews were also the pioneers of the dye industry. Certain Czenstochower dyers competed with the German A. G. Farben. First of all, we must remember the two large factories – one belonging to Dr. Zaks, a community worker from the assimilated class and Dr. Wolberg, whose children were active in the radical circles in Czenstochow.

Czenstochow factories for wooden pieces for frames developed early in connection with the production of holy pictures. The well known firms were: Kapinski and Szmulewicz.

Another branch of the wood industry, the fabrication of furniture, first developed in later years.

The button industry also belonged to the industries in which Czenstochow played a pioneering role. The button factories in Czenstochow were among the leading ones in Poland and even in all of Russia. The most famous and largest factory in this field was Grosman's. Several of his grandsons had completely left the Jewish people. The first automobile in Czenstochow was bought by one of the Grosmans.

[Page 50]

Czenstochow had the first factory in Russia for leather-glue, the Klejarnie, founded by Henrich Markusfeld. The technical work in the factory was headed by a great man of science in chemistry and an ardent Jew. He was the founder of the Czenstochower garden farm.

Smaller industries in which Jews took part were:

The Rozencwajg firm was mainly known in the manufacturing of brushes made out of imported rice-straw, in addition to an entire series of smaller factories such as Handelman's and others. In the area of the chemical industry must be remembered, Fajge's candle factory, the soap factory of Jubos and Fiszel, Yehezkiel Broniatowski and the German, Kriger.

The Czenstochow bankers were not in the style of the large European banks, but also not usurers. They helped the manufacturers a great deal with their discounted credit. Before the Russian times, the promissory notes were made out for approximately a year. The manufacturers were not able keep up with them.

The most important local banks were:

1) Bergman, 2) Markus Gradsztajn, 3) Zarski, 4) Maszkowski and Pinkus, 5) Warsawski Commercial Bank, founded in Warsaw by the famous Natanson family. Its director was Nowinski. 5) The division of the Petersburger bank in Riga, director – Moritsi Ruf.

One of the large Czenstochow industrialists was Meitlis. He had his own coal pit and provided coal to all of the factories.

The Czenstochow shippers occupied an important place in the trade world. The most well known among them were Ludwig Templ, Dankewicz, Krok and Gradsztajn.

Footnote

a. During the Russian times it was accepted that merchants would arrange an I.O.U. for the manufacturer for a year. This custom even found expression in a joking play on the words: "*God gadud jagodno*[2] and so on." The word play was formed on the word *god*, which means a year in Russian.

Translator's Footnotes

1. This surname is spelled both as Zelikson and Zeligson in the text.

2. It would be paid within a year. God – a Yiddish reference to the "Almighty" – will pay the promissory note within God's year – meaning the debt will not be paid.

———

[Page 50]

Professional Workers Union

by Dr. R. Mahler and Y. Sh. Herc. A. Khrobolowski

The situation of the Jewish worker up to the end of the 19ᵗʰ century and the beginning of the 20ᵗʰ century. – The influences of the political parties. – Reprisals. – The beginning of legal activities. – The crisis during the First World War. – The situation in independent Poland. – The Professional Union and the Worker's Council. – The role of the Central Council and Cultural Office. – The struggle of the young workers. – The role of the Youth Office.

The relatively young Jewish settlement in Czenstochow possessed a very significant worker element at the end of the 19ᵗʰ century. According to the census of 1897 of 12,000 Jews in the city, 2,155 drew their livelihood from industry and trade. Among these categories, there were 801 souls who earned their living from tailoring and 228 from shoemaking. The remaining working elements were in the majority employed in small workshops and factories.

From a report by Shaul Rafal Landau, the well-known Zionist leader who visited Czenstochow in 1898, we hear several important facts about the local Jewish factory workers. There was only one Jewish factory then, which employed a large number of Jewish workers. This was a needle and umbrella factory that counted among 200 workers, more than 100 Jews, both men and young girls.[a] The work day lasted 11 and a half hours. The wages for the work of the adult workers, men, reached from four to five rubles a week. For the young girls – from a ruble 80 *kopikes* to three-quarters of a ruble. In exceptional cases, three rubles... The men would be employed in the production itself, while the girls worked mainly with cutting, sorting and the like. The Jewish workers were active in handwork because they worked Sunday instead of *Shabbos* and on that day the machines were stopped. In the other small Jewish factories, the paper, celluloid, jute and others branches of work only small groups of Jewish workers worked. It is a characteristic fact for the proletarian labors of the Jewish petit bourgeois that among the workers in the needle factory, the giver of the report met a number of former saloon keepers, old Jews, bent and with long disheveled beards.

[Page 51]

The great poverty among Jews in Czenstochow at that time is illustrated by the circumstances of the 708 Jewish families in 1898, that is almost a third of the local Jewish *kehile* [organized Jewish community], who turned to alms for their Passover needs.

During the course of several years, during the beginning of the 20ᵗʰ century, Jewish industry in Czenstochow, as well as the number of Jewish factory workers, grew significantly. The "gathering of material" that *IKO* published in 1904, on the basis of reports from correspondents, provides us with information about Jewish factory workers in Czenstochow:

In the metal industry, the Weinberg and Horowicz factories employed Jewish workers. Fifty people, including 14 locksmiths and blacksmiths worked at Horowicz's, where *tsepes* (threshing boards), locks and metal household items were made.

There were 15 Jewish factories in the toy industry, each of which numbered 15 to 50 employees. All of the factories employed 500 workers in total. Of the 80 percent Jews, the largest number were from the factory of Szaja, the old pioneer of the toy industry, from his five sons, from Hamburger-Hecherman and from Szmuelowicz. The work was exclusively handwork. Only two toy factories possessed motors. The factory buildings were small houses that looked just like residences. The work force in the majority of factories consisted of 60 percent young people and children[b], mainly girls. The work-day lasted for 12-14 hours. The wage system was per piece and, therefore, workers developed such dexterity that one worker alone finished up to 25 gross of toys, that is, 3,600 pieces a day. The norm for piece-work wages varied according to the toy. A foundry pourer of tin rooster heads would receive not more than 4 *kopikes* for a gross

(12 dozen). The norm reached 20-40 for other toys and, even, a ruble and a half for a gross. With this system the weekly wages of children up to 15 years old reached from 80 *kopikes* to a ruble and 20 *kopikes*; young people of 15 years and older, would earn a ruble and 80 *kopikes* a week up to two and a half rubles; adult workers had from three to four and five rubles a week, and those who reached from seven rubles to nine rubles were rare exceptions.

Of the three largest haberdashery factories, such as buttons, needles, pins, cufflinks, metal and celluloid penholders, and the like, the largest one was owned by the Grosman brothers. There were no Jews employed among the 200 workers and there were only four Jews employed in the administration. In contrast, almost all of the workers in Szaja's and Rozensztajn's mother-of-pearl button factory were Jewish, 68 among 70. Jewish workers reached half, 180[11] among the 160, in the needle and umbrella factory of Henig and Partners. In order to keep *Shabbos* the Jewish machine workers would be employed only for five days a week; the Jewish workers, who worked six days a week, were only employed in handwork. The director of this factory, Werde, not only employed the largest number of Jewish locksmiths who had graduated from the Jewish Artisan's School, he also propagated the idea of employing Jews among the local Jewish manufacturers. There were six needle factories with Jewish owners in Czenstochow that did not employ any Jewish workers. The wages of workers in this industrial branch rose very little in relation to its status in 1898. In Henig's factory, young girls earned from 30 to 60 *kopikes* a day; adult men from half a ruble to a ruble 20 *kopikes*. A number of Jewish haberdashery factories such as Szaja and Rozensztajn and, even, Grosman, as well as a number of toy factories gave work to home-workers, exclusively Jewish. Their work consisted of sewing on buttons to cardboard, dressing the toys and the like.

Like a spring wind in a winter-land, the secret and sweet news of freedom and struggle for a better life went through the small factories and workshops. The parties: *S.S.* [Zionist Socialists], Bund, *Paolei-Zion* [Labor Zionists], who spoke to them in the mother-tongue [Yiddish], organized them along lines of factory businesses and trades, leading strikes and achieving shorter work hours and larger salaries.

This was the beginning. In 1906, after the "Constitution" and state of war, the main work of the parties concentrated on the professional [workers] movement. Such trades as *marszantkes*, milliners (women hat decorators), in the shops and in the boulevards were organized and went on strike. Appeals had to be printed in Polish because for the most part they spoke only Polish and elegant young men were designated who would have an effect on them.

[Page 52]

The largest and most difficult struggle between the workers and owners took place among the bakers. The owners did not want to make peace with the idea that the three hours of sleep on the *piekelik* (oven) that the bakery workers had should be [part of] a normal working day of at least 10-12 hours a day. They denounced [the workers], hired men to beat [the workers] and provocateurs. One of them actually was shot and the leaders of the bakery workers sat in jail and were exiled to Siberia or other Russian cities.

We can create an idea of the activity of the Professional Union of Tailors and Dressmakers in Czenstochow from a report that was published in the Bundist, *Folkszeitung* [*People's Newspaper*] of 1 July 1907. The report covers the period from 1 December 1906 to 10 June 1907.

Income (in Rubles and *Kopikes*):

Remaining from Earlier	16.00
Admission and Weekly Money	85.36
Received from a Man's Master Tailor	10.00
Received from a Woman's Master Tailor	5.00
Received from a Master of White Linen	3.00

Received from a Sock Maker	2.50
Received from a Men's Tailor	2.00
Sum total	**123.36**

Expenses

Jobless	2.47
Strikers	5.50
Passing Through	2.35
Stamps	4.00
Quarters	2.05
Writing Implements	0.95
Library	6.00
Folks-Zeitung	3.00
Loans to the Organization	5.00
Admission Booklets and Pads	5.04
Loans to 5 Comrades	15.05
Departing Comrades	10.80
Sum Total	**62.21**
Remaining in the Treasury	**61.65**

*****

Czenstochower Baker's Union with Tsine Arczach (in the middle) as Chairman

The income from individual master tailors, which is included in this interesting report, probably consisted of monetary fines for breaking an agreement, for insults and the like.

With the strengthening of the reactionary forces, the Czarist police also turned to labor's economic organizations, to the professional unions. It would ambush the unions, taking stamps and documents and carrying out persecutions. In the cases where the police took the stamps, the unions reported this publicly and stated that the old stamps were not valid; if, for example, the stamps were round, the new square ones were made in order to easily differentiate them. The police would also carry out searches in the houses of the professional workers and of striking workers.

The searches were not able to disrupt the professional organizations entirely. In 1907 and, even in 1908, when the professional movement in a series of cities and *shtetlekh* [towns] in the Polish provinces were suppressed by the reactionaries, the professional unions in Czenstochow still persevered. At the end of 1908 the professional unions in Czenstochow also almost completely disappeared from the surface, but also then, the Czarist government did not stop suppressing the aspiration for a free and humane life, which the freedom movement awoke in the working masses. Strikes in the large factories even took place the entire time such as at the Mates, Plecer's, at Wajnberg's and so on. And the Jewish workers in the small factories and workshops often arranged secret trade meetings, made collective demands to the owners.

[Page 53]

The "Christian Workers Union" was active among Christian workers in the large factories, an organization founded by the priests to draw them away from the socialist movement. It should be understood that hand in hand with the anti-socialist propaganda went the anti-Semitic agitation of the "Christian" union. In independent Poland, they were known under the name, *Chadekes*, or Christian Democrats, and surpassed the *Endekes* [anti-Semitic Polish National Party] with their reactionary politics and Jew-baiting.

The majority of Polish labor in Czenstochow did not let themselves be fooled by the enemies of the working class.

In 1912, at a set hour of the day, the sirens of most of the factories in Czenstochow gave five signals as a protest against the mass murder of the Lena gold-mine workers in Siberia by the Czarist regime.

* * *

A law was issued in 1913 about bringing sick funds into the factories that employed a large number of workers. What was new in the law was that the workers in each factory could elect their representatives to the managing committee of the sick fund. An energetic agitation among the workers to take part in the elections was carried out in the large factories where only Christian workers were employed. The Jewish workers in the factories and workshops remained indifferent to this in the main.

Therefore, the same year, a widespread movement began among the Jewish workers to create legal professional unions, according to the law that was published then by the Czarist government.

The new law was actually nothing more than the administration of the old *Zubatowszczine* (Zubatov – a gendarme officer who proposed that the workers in Russia have an opportunity to organize in professional unions in order to draw them away from the political struggle), but the Jewish trade workers used the law for their benefit and organized a wide range of professional unions. The initiative came chiefly from Lodz where the central offices were first created. The professional unions in Czenstochow were a division of them.

The first legalized professional union was the wood workers. The founding meeting took place in the premises of the handworkers club on *Shabbos*, 30 November 1913. The chairman was M. Felsensztajn, chairman of the central managing committee in Lodz.

A second representative from Lodz was Dovid Abramson. The speech by Daniel Zaluski had a strong effect on the assembled. H. Fejwlowicz, Sh. Fajnrajch, Z. Tenenberg, Y.F. Guterman and L. Win were elected to the managing committee.

We read about the founding of the Professional Union in the article in the *Czenstochower Woknblat* [*Weekly Newspaper*] of the 13ᵗʰ December 1913:

"The founding of professional unions for the woodworkers branch was a true holiday for the class-conscious workers and their friends.

"There was no trace of apathy and detachment, which we see at the owners' meetings. One after another the workers rose up and showed that the fire of striving for unity in order to lead the struggle for their liberation had not been extinguished in them and one after the other they greeted the newly founded union as a cornerstone of the professional movement in our city."

We read in the *Czentsochower Tageblat* of 13 January 1914, about this, that the movement to organize the professional unions also involved several other branches:

A movement began at that time among the Czenstochower workers to organize professional unions. A short time before, the wood workers branch organized a union. The bakers also organized and now means were employed to organize the small box makers, celluloid workers and other trades. It is superfluous to speak about the importance of professional unions for workers in general and for Jewish workers in particular. The Jewish worker had to endure more than other workers. He did not know of a normal workday. And often it happened that money had to be collected for remedies for a sick worker.

[Page 54]

In 1913-1914 Czenstochower Jewish professional unions of leather workers, tailors, woodworkers, celluloid workers, as well as business employees were active. In 1914 the Society of Business Employees numbered around 300 members. In 1912, this union had an income of 3,822 rubles. In that era a spirit of assimilation held sway over everything in this union.

At that time, the question of the right to work of the Jewish worker was also difficult. A number of large Jewish manufacturers did not let Jews into their factories as workers. One of them, who boycotted Jewish workers, was Landau, the owner of a celluloid factory. He would once employ several dozen Jewish men and women workers. Then he made his factory absolutely *Juden-rein* [free of Jews, the expression the Nazis used during the Holocaust]. Even several Jewish community leaders and pillars of various charitable groups shamefully acted against Jewish workers. Instead of giving the poor, Jewish strata a possibility of earning money for bread through their own work, this strange philanthropy rather wanted to "help" them by throwing them contributions.

During the First World War, under the German occupation, a standstill in economic life began that was particularly difficult for the working population. Many workers emigrated to Germany because of the lack of work. Those who remained in Czenstochow tried to ease their need through self-help. Bakeries and tea-halls for Jewish workers were opened. The professional unions carried out large communal campaigns in connection with the aid work.

The situation of the Jewish workers changed greatly for the worse with the rise of independent Poland.

The greater number of most members of the metal workers union that consisted of Jewish workers in the railroad workshops during the German occupation were replaced with Polish workers. Wajnberg's factory was completely paralyzed and later totally removed to the Soviet Union. Landau's factory stood completely empty. The *Malarnie* and *Kopeluszarnia* and dozens of other large and small factories, which previously worked for the large Russian market, shrunk.

But independent of the negative effects of the political changes, the war itself left economic ruin from which the city of Czenstochow, just as the entire country, could only recover after many years.

The number of divisions of Jewish workers in Czenstochow during the first post-war years is provided in the work, *Jewish Industrial Enterprises in Poland*, that was published in Warsaw in 1923 on the basis of a poll of the year 1921 with the aid of the Joint [Distribution Committee] under the editorship of Engineer E. Heller.

In 1921 there were 1,056 active factories and workshops in Czenstochow, in which Jews were engaged as entrepreneurs or workers.

A series of production trades were only active sometimes, or for the most part inactive: 30 percent in the natural rubber industry, 20 percent in the textile industry, 62½ percent in the metal toy industry. Of all of the enterprises, no undertaking was active in the celluloid comb and the felt hat industry!

The 1,056 active factories and workshops were divided among the separate industrial branches, as a percent of all of the enterprises:

Clothing	58.0
Metal	6.4
Wood	5.8
Construction	3.7
Leather	3.2
Paper	2.6
Textiles	2.3
Machine apparatus	1.8
Cleaning	1.4
Natural Rubber	1.3
Graphics industry	1.2
Stone, lime, glass	.9
Chemical	.9

The characteristic phenomenon is evident that 58 percent, around three-quarters of all enterprises, in which Jews were employed as contractors or workers belonged to the clothing branch.

Of the 1,056 active industrial enterprises, only 588, that is not much more than half (55.7 percent) employed wage earners and the remaining enterprises employed only the owner, sometimes with the help of family members. All 1,056 enterprises employed each season around 4,000 (3,893 people, 26 percent of them owners, seven and a half percent family members and two-thirds (66.5 percent) wage earners.

[Page 55]

Among the 2,643 wage earners were 1,390 Jews, which is around 52 1/2 percent, somewhat more than half.

Jewish workers in the various industry branches reached the following percentages in relation to all of the workers in the branch:

Natural rubber	98.0%
Clothing	95.8%
Cleaning	88.9%
Machine operators	87.1%
Construction	81.3%
Nutrition	77.0%
Paper	36.6%
Textiles	63.0%
Leather	56.2%
Chemicals	51.9%
Wood	45.6%
Graphic Industry	40.5%
Metal	35.8%
Stone, clay, glass	9.0%

However, the participation of Jewish workers was different not only in relation to entire branches of industry but also according to trades in the same branches of industry. Particularly characteristic in this detail is the metal industry branch. This branch employed 508 wage earners, of them, as mentioned, around 36 percent Jews. But in the various trades of the metal industry, the number and percentage of Jewish workers reached:

	General Number of Workers	Jews	%
Foundry	185	5	2.8
Metal buttons	81	31	38.3
Iron chains	64	50	78.1

We see that if even the metal industry as a whole counted Jews as more than a third of its workers, in the foundry trade with the largest number of workers of all the trades in this branch, there were no more than five percent Jewish workers, less than three percent of all workers in this trade.

The fact that in most cases Jewish workers were divided into small enterprises is inferred still clearer in other tables, which gathered the results of the questionnaire. In the stone, clay and glass branches, which employed 699 wage earners, only 9 percent of them were Jewish, amounts to on average more than 79 percent in one enterprise as opposed to 96 percent Jews among the wage earners in the clothing [branches] comes out to not more than two employed persons (2.2) in one enterprise. The enterprises in all other production branches, which mainly employed Jewish workers, were not much larger. In nutrition an average enterprise employed not much more than three (3.3) persons, in construction less than two (1.9), in cleaning something more than two (2.4), in machine operators also approximately that many (2.6). Even in the natural rubber industry, which was considered a manufacturing industry, less than nine people (8.9) on average were employed in one "factory."

The character of production in the Jewish industrial enterprises also meant that Jewish women workers were employed there in the greatest number. In the metal industry, where the general number of Jews reached 144, that means 31 percent of all of the 585 employees, 39 percent were Jewish women compared to 46 non-Jewish women; in the machine industry – 10 Jewish women (no non-Jewish women); in rubber (hard rubber) – 19 Jewish women (two non-Jewish); in the chemical industry – eight Jewish women (not one non-Jewish woman); in clothing – 131 Jewish women (compared to only two non-Jewish women).

Alas, the structure for the Jewish worker in Czenstochow in relation to breaking into small workshops and small factories continued in the later years. The reason was not only the discrimination on the part of the Polish manufacturers, but also on the part of Jewish manufacturers. And Czenstochow then had Jewish men of wealth who played a significant role in local large industry. Warta, the jute factory, which employed a few thousand workers, belonged to Jews; the Jew, Kon, owned a factory with 2,000 workers; several large factories belonged to the well known philanthropist, Henrik Markusfeld; Jews were owners of the textile factory, Gnoshyn. A series of other factories of textile. metal and chemical products belonged to Jews. Among the thousands of workers in all of the factories, Jews could be counted on the fingers. Even during the last few years before the Second World War, when the hearts of some Czenstochower manufacturers became a little softer, they hardly deigned to bring in a few Jews in their offices.

[Page 56]

In light of the divisiveness in the Jewish working class in the small workshops and small factories, we can properly evaluate the immense accomplishments of the Jewish professional unions in organizing the Jewish workers to struggle for better economic conditions, for political class-consciousness and for cultural elevation.

Right after this when independent Poland arose, during the years 1918-1919, the Jewish professional unions played a decisive role in the elections to the local worker council and in the local workers' movement in general. The majority of Jewish professional unions in Czenstochow at that time concentrated around the Educational Union for Jewish Workers. This union was [connected to] socialist Zionism and, then, when the Territorialists united with the Sejmists, it was taken over by *Fareinikte* [united]. New professional unions also arose at this time, such as unions for the [industrial] branches: paper, celluloid and horns, painters, porters and butchers. The greatest number of members in the professional unions, however, were unemployed then.

The number of votes that were given through the various branches and trades during the elections to the workers' council provides an idea about both the organizational strength of the various professional unions and about the number of workers in professions according to their occupations.

Barbers – 55; metal workers – 440; wood branch – 118; celluloid and horn work – 126; needle industries – 410; leather workers – 126; bakers and candy-making workers (cake bakers) – 79; meat workers – 34; paper branch – 62; porters – 174; indeterminate trades – 125; others – 126; Total – 1, 749 votes. A certain number of additional votes came from Jewish workers in small factories.

* * *

In 1920 most of the professional unions were under the leadership of a central council, of which Rafal Federman was the chairman and Yakov Yitzhak Czarnoweicki was the secretary.

The law concerning sick funds did not yet exist in Poland. The Central Council arranged medical help for the members of the organization. Each professional union paid a certain payment for each member to the sick fund of the Central Council.

Because of this, a workers' council aid committee was created with the Central Council that supported the unemployed and their families and took care of the members with medical help.

On *Shabbos*, 19 February 1921, a meeting of the needle workers who had decided to unite the two needle workers union took place at the premises of the Tailors Union at Neyer Mark 2. However, it was a long time before one union was created.

The Professional Union of Needle Workers was not the only one that was divided. The professional movement of the small number of Jewish workers and the still smaller number of the employed constantly suffered from division and splits that the four parties, *Fareinikte* [United], *Bund*, *Poalei-Zion* [Marxist Zionists] and the Communists, led among them, in addition to dozens of "chronic" illnesses, which the Jewish Worker Movement also suffered, such as the insecure boundary between worker, "home worker" and workshop owner, who in the majority was a very poor man. The divisions in the trades into dozens of sections and the struggle of the sections among themselves; the emigration, which each year emptied the ranks of the best professional activists and filled them with young men who immediately went to the workshop after leaving *kheder*.

Founders of the Tailors Union in Czenstochow.

Among others: Tifenberg, Krzepicki, and Rozenblat

[Page 57]

In 1922 the unification of the Jewish and Polish professional unions was carried out in Poland. The Jewish workers being in the vast majority again remained in separate divisions, but formally they were united through their leaders. They took part in the general conventions and in the agencies of the separate industrial unions, or of the national federation.

The unification was stronger in the larger cities because the local Jewish professional unions were connected through a Central Council or Cultural Office and through the mediation of this administrative body were represented in the local *Rade*, that is, in the general municipal central office of all professional unions. This was unification in addition to the connection in the particular trades. Jewish divisions of tailors, shoemakers, textile workers and so on were joined in the general unions of a given trade.

Founders and Leaders of the Tailors' Union under the Influence of the
***SDKPL* [Socialist Democratic Party of the Kingdom of Poland and**
Lithuania] (Communists)

Seated, from the right: Ceszinski, Sobol, Czonszinski, Gonzwa, Rozenblat.
Standing, from the left: D. Richter, Krzepicki, Opatowski, Hirszberg,
Cimberknof, Gonzwa.

The Cultural Office for the most part united the professional unions that stood under the political influence of the *Bund*. Jewish professional unions that were connected to other parties, such as *Poalei-Zion*, the Communists or *Fareinikte*, as in Czenstochow, particularly in the early era, often stood on the side, but were organized in their own central council. The Czenstochow Cultural Office at first only consisted of four professional unions: clothing workers, wood, nourishment and bristle workers. The remaining Jewish professional unions in the city were connected in a central council that was led by *Fareinikte*, later, the Independent Socialist Party. The Cultural Office, which was organized in March 1923, therefore, founded parallel unions under other names. In that way, for example, a splinter of the porters, under the leadership of the Cultural Office, was named the "Transport Workers' Union," from the Meat Workers – "Nourishment Workers," and so on.

Rafal Federman led the Cultural Office that was connected to the Bund and, which earlier as *Fareinikte*, stood at the tip of the central council. Other workers from the Cultural Office were the Bundists Moshe Lederman (leather worker), Avraham Frydman, Avraham Rozenblat, Tsine Orczech (bakery worker), Moshe Berkensztat, Shmuel Rozental, Andje Manowicz, Eliasz Sztajnet, Leibish Kaminski, Josef Kruze, Henekh Fefer, Ziser Cyncynatus and Yitzhak Stopnicer.

Managing Committee of the Professional Union of the Food Industry (Bakers)

Seated, right to left: Mildsztajn Leibl, Grabinski Ludwik, Lebek Leon, Jaronowski Yisroel, Federman Rafal, Altman Betzalel, Zusman Meir.
Standing, right to left: Bajgelman Moshe, Laska Ziskind, Klabisz Stanislaw, Fajtel Feywel, Kolton, Yitzhak, Jakubowicz, Mordekhai, Itskowicz, Avraham.

[Page 58]

In addition to the regular professional work and cultural activities, the Cultural Office also was concerned with help for the unemployed. In March 1926, the Cultural Office divided food among 303 families from the monies it received from the "Country Council" of the Jewish Professional Unions in Poland. During the same month's time, the Cultural Office also divided support among 204 families that it had received from the Czenstochow *kehile* [organized Jewish community]. During the summer of the same year, the Cultural Office divided a larger sum from America among around 500 families of the unemployed. In general, in 1926, 2,390 families, which numbered 6,948 people, took nourishment from the aid actions of the Cultural Office.

In the course of 1926, the four mentioned professional unions joined other unions in the Cultural Office from the branches: chemical industry, metal, leather, transport, butchers, printers and painters. Fifteen professional unions numbering about 1,150 members of the Cultural Office were represented at the conference of 15 January where new leadership of the Cultural Office was elected. At the election the Bund received 36 votes, the Communists – 15 and the Left *Poalei-Zion* – three. The new council consisted of 17 Bundists, seven Communists and one Left *Paolei-Zion*. Resolutions about the right to work of Jewish workers and Jewish workers employed in city institutions and about the right to use the Yiddish language in the general sick office were adopted.

At that time the *stowarzyszenia* (association) of the trade employees, which was transformed into a modern professional union, joined the Cultural Office. This union also ceased to be a fortress of assimilation. The rich union library, with 15,000 books in various languages in addition to Yiddish, later merged with the Medem Library at the Cultural Office, which had only

Yiddish books. The foundation of the Medem Library was laid by Yakov Rozenberg, who upon the death of Wladimir Medem, gave 1,000 *zlotes* to sanctify his name. The first librarian of the Medem librarian was Comrade Andze Muznowicz. The library functioned illegally under the horrible Nazi occupation in the residence of Comrade Rayzele Berkensztat.

Representatives of eight Jewish unions with over 1,000 members were at the conference of the Cultural Office on 5 November 1937.

Up to 1 January 1939, the Cultural Office represented seven professional unions, compiled as such: 1) clothing industry – 438 members; 2) nutrition – 105: 3) leather – 73; 4) trade employees – 200 5) hairdressers – 52; 6) transport – 80; 7) Socialist artisans – 104. Total 1,052 members, of them 766 men, 168 women and 118 young people. In addition to these, 690 Jewish workers were organized in divisions along with Polish workers in the unions of textile, metal, construction and chemicals. 1,472 Jewish workers and employees were organized together since the beginning of 1939 in the professional class unions.

A picture of the working and wage conditions of the Jewish working young can be created on the basis of the correspondence from Czenstochow that was published in *Yungt Werker* [*Young Worker*], 1927, no. 19. There we read:

"The workday for the young workers from the clothing, leather and wood trades is 10-12 hours. Young workers from 11 years old and on are found at work. Their wage is 4-5 *gildn* a week. The situation for the girls, who work with linen, clothing and milliners (hat makers), is particularly difficult. Here children of age 10 can even be found, who work from seven in the morning until 8 at night, with a break of half an hour at noon.

"The majority of young people are not insured by the sick fund. Exceptions are only those who work in workshops with older workers. We meet young people who serve as apprentices over the course of two years and they work entirely without pay.

"The situation for the young in the chemical industry is also difficult. There are 200 young people employed, of them 30 percent Polish. In this industrial branch young people of 10-12 years of age can be found, who work up to 13 hours a day for a wage of an "entire" four *gildn* a week.

"There are cases that when the work inspector comes to visit the small factory, the young workers are locked in the dirty work room in order to prevent a check. The manufacturers even permit the beating of the young workers for such "impertinence" as not wanting to bring water for the owner's wife. About a legal leave (vacation), one can only dream."

[Page 59]

From the same correspondence we also learn about the efforts of the young to organize themselves to fight for better conditions.

"We are now proceeding to create a youth section at the chemical union. The first steps have already been made. Two organizational meetings have taken place and a provisional commission was elected that needs to organize all of the young workers in the chemical industry. The local youth office is carrying out the mentioned work. (The leadership of the youth section of the Cultural Office of the Jewish Professional Unions was founded in 1925.)"

Ten years later the situation of the young Jewish workers in other branches of industry was not very much better than that of the young chemical workers in 1927 and the Jewish Professional Unions proceeded to organize for a struggle. Here we read in *Yungt-Werker* [*Young Worker*] of 1936, number 22, an interesting report about the strike of young Jewish metal workers:

"There are a few dozen metal factories located in Czenstochow that are not yet organized in a metal union. Young Jewish workers for the most part work there, earning 80 *groshn* and one *gildn* for a day of heavy labor. In addition, they work there in the most terrible hygienic conditions. The workers have not even dreamed of leave (vacations). With the help of a group of "futurists," the metal union began a widespread campaign to draw the workers into the union and this succeeded. It was immediately decided to end the terrible exploitation that has been carried on for years. The union presented demands: 1) for a collective agreement; 2) wage supplement; 3) for hygienic working conditions. The negotiations lasted for many weeks and there was no resolution. It is worth mentioning that the Jewish manufacturers chose *Endekes* [members of the nationalist and anti-Semitic Polish political party] as their representatives to negotiate with the workers. On Tuesday, 25 August, the workers proceeded to an occupying strike in 10 factories. Three hundred sixty workers went out on strike, of them 80 percent young..."

Alas, the sad action of the Jewish manufacturers during this strike, their association with the *Endeke* anti-Semites against striking Jewish workers, was not an isolated case. There are still worse examples where Jewish capitalists removed Jewish workers from the factory because they dared to strike and even unbelievable cases where Jewish manufacturers hired *Endeke* hooligans against Jewish strikers. We read here in a report from Czenstochow in the *Folks-Zeitung* of 6 December 1936:

"Jewish and Polish workers work in the Jewish factory of Pol Metal, whose owners are the Misters Yelel and Edelis. The work and wage situation is very bad there. The workers have been trying to organize. This greatly displeased the Jewish manufacturers. As soon as they learned of this, they immediately began to dismiss the few Jewish workers who were employed there. The Jewish workers were paid on the spot for two week's wages and the factory became *Juden-rein*.[2]

And here is a letter published in the *Folks-Zeitung* of 11 April 1938:

"During the occupation strike in the Shaja and Frank factory, Mr. Frank with the help of a band of *Endeke* fighters attempted to drive the strikers from the factory. When this was not successful, he urged the female *Endeke* workers to break the strike and promised to give them work. This actually happened; they broke the strike, left the factory and sent their husbands, *Endekes*, to drive those remaining from the factory. After a 97-day strike in the most terrible conditions, the ostensible democrat (Frank) expelled ten workers from the factory. Everyone else remained."

The same thing happened in Epsztajn's button factory from which the Jewish women workers were expelled.

It is told in a letter about the large Jewish metal factory on Warszawer Street that when several Jewish workers left to serve in the military, *Endekes* were employed in their place. They "present themselves after work for the 'holy trade' of picketing Jewish shops and chorale singing:

"Jews must be in Palestine,
Because they are traitors and pigs."

It is further reported in the same letter about cases where Jewish manufacturers would play both strings of the instrument of Jewish nationalism and of anti-Semitism. During strikes, Jewish manufacturers tried to convince Jewish workers not to go with the *Endekes* and the *Endekes* not to go with the "Jewish good-for-nothings." They tried to persuade the backward Polish worker that it was only a question of throwing out the Jewish workers.

[Page 60]

Jewish capitalists themselves carried wood to the anti-Semitic fire in Czenstochow.

The Jewish professional movement in Czenstochow recorded an outstanding page in the history of the local Jewish settlement.

Footnotes

1. According to the material of *IKO* [Jewish Colonizing Organization] of 1904, we can identify this factory. It belonged to Henig and Partners.

2. According to the memories of Czenstochower in America, many children were so small that they had to be placed on boxes in order for them to reach the table that was in the workshop.

Translator's Footnotes

a. Instead of 80, which is half of 160, the number printed is 180.

b. *Juden-rein* – free of Jews – was a phrase used by the Germans during the Holocaust.

[Page 60]

The Professional Union of Trade Employees

by A. Khrobolowski

The Union of Trade Employees occupies a separate chapter in the history of the professional unions in Czenstochow.

The union was founded in 1907 under the name: Society of Mutual Aid for Trade and Industrial Employees. The majority of the assimilated Jewish workers employed in the large factories belonged to it as well as a few Christians. No one even thought of defending the employees against the owners of the large and smaller factories. One question would appear on the agenda of the annual general meeting: the burial fund: the fund and help for the widows and orphans of the deceased members.

Yakov Rozenberg, A. Crobolowski, R. Federman joined the union in 1913-14 and began a struggle for the union to be concerned with better conditions for the trade employees and that Yiddish should be permitted at general meetings. The fight for Yiddish was then being carried out throughout society and in unions under the assimilated leadership. Rafal Federman describes the spirit of assimilation that reigned in the union in the *Czenstochower Togeblat* [*Czenstochower Daily Newspaper*] of 29 May 1914 with such characteristic facts: "When a member asked permission at a general meeting to present his views in the Yiddish language, he was attacked with abuse for the unheard of nerve… The same member also presumed to demand that the society should provide Yiddish newspapers among all of the other newspapers in the reading room. Hereupon, our well-known community worker, Dr. Zaks, and the director of the Riger Bank argued that if Yiddish newspapers were permitted in the reading room, this would show that the Czenstochower trade employees were on a very low cultural level. It should be understood that the audience was very frightened and rejected the proposal."

The "society" was then located on Dojazd.

During the First World War, under the German occupation, the *S.S.* Party [Territorialists] founded a second professional union of trade employees that had its location in Szlezinger's courtyard on Spadek.

After the First World War, the situation in the "society" immediately began to change after a group of socialist activists and regular socialist members joined it.

In 1919 another long and difficult struggle succeeded in carrying out a decision at a general meeting about changing the "society" into a professional union of trade and office employees. A point was placed in the statute of the union that those who employ those opposed to the union may not belong.

But changing the name of the union did not immediately change the character of the union. Two sides belonged to the union: the "impartial" under the leadership of Kurland, Fogelbaum, Galinski, Foist and others, and the socialist factions, which fought the club character of the union and wanted a true professional union and trade society.

A decisive general meeting of the union took place on 27 November 1921. All of the union groups mobilized their followers and prepared for the "battle." Three candidate lists were presented for the professional elections of the managing committee, which was supposed to consist of 11 people: 1) "impartial" (the old right) with Fogelbaum, Galinski and others, 2) the *Fareinikte* [united] faction with the following candidates: R. Federman, Henekh Nirenberg, Rayzl Berkensztat, Moshe Kremski, Herman Hercberg, Dovid Yelen, Tsesha Alter, Zalman Federman, Jakov Yitzhak Czarnawecki, 3) a combined list of the "Borochov," *Groser* [large or great] and *Royt* [red], with the names: Horowicz, Zilbersztajn, Brum and others.

[Page 61]

The *Fareinikte* faction proposed for the agenda: 1) the question of aid for the hungry in the Soviet Union; 2) to join the union to the central council of the professional unions.

The Red Faction entered a point about fighting for an eight-hour workday.

Mr. Senior, chairman of the union, opened the gathering. Two candidates were placed [in nomination] as chairman: 1) Szpira of the "impartial ones" 2) R. Federman from all of the proletarian factions. The first candidate received 130 plus votes. The second candidate [received 80 plus] votes.

Because of the stir that began when R. Federman began to speak Yiddish, he filed a proposal that everyone could speak in the language that is accessible to him, including Yiddish. For those who do not understand Yiddish, the presidium has to deliver their speeches in Polish.

At the vote on the proposal by name, 146 votes were for and 78 against. With this vote a 16-year old tradition was broken of the union not permitting Yiddish to be spoken at a general meeting.

The vote for the candidates to the managing committee had the following results. List number 1. "impartial" 132 votes – six members, list number 2. *Fareinikte* - 45 votes – two members, list number 3. "Borochov," *Groser* and Red – 49 votes – three members.

In 1926 the union joined the "culture office" of the Jewish Professional Unions.

During the last years, Prikaczszikes Bank belonged to the union and a smaller number of commercial employees from the smaller firms. The more assimilated members (employed in large factories) left the union.

The Bund and the communists had influence over the union. The chairman was Rafal Federman, secretary – Herszlikowicz. The premises of the union and the culture office were located at *Aleja* 20.

After the departure of chairman Rafal Federman for Paris, the party was dominated by the communists. The departure of the secretary, Herszlikowicz, brought the slow dissolution of the union, so that during the last years the union no longer carried out its activities.

———

[Page 61]

The Artisans Union and Guilds

by A. Gotlib

A movement to organize the Jewish artisans in order to elevate their cultural position and to better their economic situation began in Poland in 1912. The initiator of this movement was the engineer, Jan Kirszrot, the founder of the first artisan club in Lodz.

Before the artisan clubs arose, some artisans, such as bakers and carpenters, were organized in *minyonim* [groups of at least 10 men who pray together]. These *minyonim* or artisans' synagogues were also a gathering point where they came together to consider professional questions and where they would also spend time playing a game of chess, dominoes or reading a newspaper.

The initiative to found an artisans club in Czenstochow came from Lodz. Owners and workers were represented at the first meeting, which was occupied with choosing an organizing committee. Among the workers at that meeting were Moshe Weksler, Shimkha Kalka and A. Chrobalowski. Engineer Asorodobraj, Wolf Gostinski, Shlomo Librowicz, Leibush Goldszajder, Ber Balzam, Moshe Tenenbaum, Shlomo Krojskop and A. Chrobalowski joined the organizing committee. Despite the attitude of the owners, the workers' group helped the rise of the artisans' club to a larger degree.

Engineer Asorodobraj and A. Chrobalowski were chosen as delegates to Lodz to communicate with Engineer Kirszrot. The first mass meeting of the artisans, at which the delegates to Lodz gave a report, took place at the *Lira* hall. A large number of artisans joined as members. The session of the organizing committee took place in Sh. Librowicz's house. A group of amateurs, under the leadership of Hershele Feiwlowicz and Dora Szacher, arranged a performance in the *Harmonia* hall, which brought in 150 rubles clear profit. Almost all progressive communal workers and socialists, such as Jakob Rozenberg, Josef Aronowicz, took an active part in the development of the artisans club from the first moment of its founding.

[Page 62]

Engineer F. Ratner, Engineer Asorodobraj, Wolf Gastinski, Artur Braniotowski, Yakov Sztajner, Ludwig Goldberg, Shlomo Librowicz, Shlomo Krojskop, F. Zalcman, Leibush Goldszajder, L. Cymerman, Moshe Tenenbaum. Stanislaw Herc, Moshe Win were found on the first managing committee of the Artisans Club.

Henrik Markusfeld was nominated as chairman.

During the prewar years the Artisans Club mainly was occupied with cultural activities and sociability matters. Family evenings, concerts and readings would be arranged. A library was founded, a reading room. In general, after *Lira*, the Artisans Club was the most active cultural institution.

But in the professional area, the Artisans Club did almost nothing. Several trades, such as carpenters and hat makers, tried to organize actions, but they did not succeed. However, the handworkers union created an important institution that helped improve the situation of its members. This was a second loan and savings fund that was founded in 1913 particularly for artisans, with the help of *IKA* [Jewish Colonization Committee]. The fund was founded by Zigmund Sztiler – chairman, Henrik Markusfeld, Engineer Ratner, Chaim Weksler and W. Gastinski.

The Artisans Club first occupied a large premises on *Aleje* 11, then at *Aleje* 27. In 1913, it moved to Ogrodowa 22. Before the outbreak of the First World War, Engineer Asorodobraj stood at the head of the union as chairman and the vice chairman was – Dr. Hipolit Gajzler, who returned from Germany and practiced medicine in Czenstochow.

From the start of the First World War until 1918, just as with many newly created unions and organizations, the Artisans Club was busy with aid work. An inexpensive kitchen was created, a tea hall that was run by the young people of Czenstochow, with M. Ash, M. Jeshajewicz, D. Krojskop, S. Makrojer and A. Chawtyn at the head. The inexpensive kitchen and tea hall were supported by the *Dobroczynnosc* [charity]. In general a large number of young Jews were organized in sports and music sections around the Artisans Club during the war years. The sport section later was transformed into an independent sport and tour union.

The war years were very difficult for the majority of the artisans. This motivated an entire array of activists to revive the Artisans Club on the basis of a self-help and trade organization. Among the new activists in the union were: Moshe Kac, Shmuel Kac, Yehayshaya Granek, Kopl Orbach, Avraham Frydman, Z. Krug, Dowid Wolfowicz and Hershl Win. Almost all of them were tailors and bakers, because there was comparatively little unemployment among them as there was in other trades. The union organized almost every artisan trade and in 1918, partly thanks to the help of American funds, a fund for widows and orphans was founded. In 1919 the activities of the pre-war loan and savings fund were revived and an entire range of cooperatives was founded, such as the food cooperative, *Zelbsthilf*, and several raw material cooperatives for various trades. A *Patronat* [worker's organization] for professional education for apprentices was created.

In 1919 the artisans club possessed more than 530 members. It also spread its activities across an entire range of neighboring *shtetlekh* [towns], in Klobuck, Kamyk, Koniecpol, and Krzepice where divisions were found.

The Polish regime approved the new statute for the union in 1921. The defense of the interests of the artisans was designated as its main task. According to the statute, only master craftsmen could belong to the union. The official name of the union was changed to "Jewish Artisans Resource." But the union was still called "Artisans Club."

In addition to the earlier mentioned, the following people led the Artisans Club during the years 1917-1923: Dentist M. Grenec, chairman in 1918; Dr. Gajsler, chairman from 1918 on. The vice-chairmen were: Jakov Sztajner, Hershl Wnuk, Avraham Dzialowski. Jakob Fisz, Shmuel Hafnung, Mikhal Ajdelman, Naftali Deresz and Moshe Berman excelled as active members of the union in this period.

In 1924 the Artisans Club came out publicly with its own list for the election. A.Z. Frydman (community managing committee), A. Dzialowski, A. Liberman and Y. Granek. The Artisans Club was represented in the City Council by Dr. H. Gajsler and J. Goldberg. In the bank, *Spoldzielczy* – Dr. Gajsler, B. Sztibl, Sh. Laria. In the council of the Sick Fund – A. Jarkowizna, M. Grenec, M Ejdelman. In *T.O.Z.* [Society for the Protection of Health] – J. Goldberg.

In 1927 the Polish government enacted a guild-law that renewed a series of old authorities for guilds in order to limit Jewish entry to trade. The Artisans Union carried on a difficult struggle to undercut the effect of the edict. For this purpose, the existing sections of the union were transformed into guilds. According to the law, the guilds gave out master certificates, without which one could not open a workshop. The union also organized a convention of all of the Jewish artisans unions in Kielcer province in order to prepare the members for the elections to the artisans' groups.

At that time internal frictions and disputes took place in the Artisans Union, both on the basis of competition between trade groups and because of ideological differences of opinion. In the shoemaker, tailor and carpenter sections, there were struggles among *tandetnikes* [those who made less expensive clothing], *chalupnikes* (those who took the work home) and employees (who work according to the orders they received). The trades divided into separate sections, as for example: employed tailors, tailors who took work home and waist coat makers. Sometimes the Artisans Union succeeded in uniting the break away sections.

Representatives of the Czenstochower Artisans Union and Their Guilds

First row, seated, right to left: J. Fisz, P. Szlezinger, M. Blum, Dr. Ch. Galster, J. Goldberg, J. Granek, and Ch. Frajermojer.
Second row, right to left: T. Braun, A. Grajcki, J. Sztajer, A. Winer, Z. Rozencwajg, A.F. Chidicki and Ch. Kalka.
Third row, right to left: Nafarta, A. Pajem, D. Koniecpoler, M. Zyscholc, Moszkowicz and M. Gelber.
Fourth row, right to left: Ch. Pitel, N. Owieczka, H. Frajman, J. Izraelewicz and L. Kac.

[Page 64]

A sharper struggle took place in the union around the two central offices that were created in Warsaw: the Rosner-Folkist Central on Nalewke and the Zionist Central on Leszna. The Czenstochower Artisans Union stood on the side of the Folkist Central. Later, Czenstochow played a great role in uniting both Centrals in one Central Artisans Union.

The Jewish Guilds, which were created by the guild law, copied the Polish ones, both in the erection of a certain hierarchy of trades and in external symbols. Each trade endeavored to have it own flag and so on.

The celebration of the 15 years of existence of the Czenstochower Artisans Union, in 1928, was very impressive. All of the guilds with their flags took part in the celebration. The union also published an anniversary publication of the history of the union and its activities.

In 1933 a group under the name *Halutz Bale-Melokhe* [artisan pioneers] was create among the Czenstochow Artisans Club. In 1934 the Czenstochow group took part in a convention of all such groups in Poland. The purpose of this movement was to assist the establishment of the Jewish community in *Eretz-Yisroel*. Efforts were made to obtain certificates for artisans and help them emigrate to *Eretz-Yisroel*.

The founding of one Central Artisans Union in Warsaw did not stop the widening embitterment between the two groups (Folkist and Zionist) among the artisans. The fight was strongly felt in the Czenstochower Artisans Union. On 31 May and 1 June 1936, the Fifth Artisans Conference took place, at which Czenstochow was represented by 14 delegates. The congress was a very stormy one. The Czenstochower delegation endeavored to create unity. However, no peace was attained.

With the circumstances in Poland, where the heavy burden of taxes particularly oppressed the Jewish population, the Artisans Union was forced to give massive energy to the tax matter and to pay into the sick fund. Dr. H. Gajsler and J. Goldberg – in city hall and A. Jorkowizne – in the sick fund – were active in this area.

In 1924 the union created two more divisions in Przyrow and Amstow.

In 1928 the union numbered 1,200 members in the following 21 organized sections:

Skilled Tailors Union, Gaitermakers Section, Carpenters Section, Union of Master Bakers, Lathe Operator Section, Master Furriers Section, Shoemakers Section, Locksmith Section, Union of Master Hairdressers, Hatmakers Section, Section for Knitwear, Stocking and Writing Book Branch, Electric-Technicians Section, Watchmakers Section, Goldsmiths and Engravers, Master Small Box Makers Section, Union of Master Tinsmiths, Butchers Section, Cake Bakers Section.

———

HaHalutz Bal Melokhe

by A. Szimeonowicz

The people's pioneer movement *HaHalutz Bal Melokhe* [Pioneer Craftsmen] was created in Vilna in 1933 at the initiative of the Zionist worker, Avraham Kac.

The Czenstochower branch of *HaHalutz Bal Melokhe* was founded in July 1934. It was known for its efficient and intensive work and became one of the most respected and most important branches of the all-Poland *HaHalutz Bal Melokhe* organization.

At the beginning, during the rise of *HaHalutz Bal Melokhe*, a certain antagonism was evident on the part of the general artisan organization, which saw *HaHalutz Bal Melokhe* as a competing organization. However, in time, when they were convinced that *HaHalutz Bal Melokhe* was involved with only cultural and Zionist work, the mood was calmed. And approximately half of its 200 members were members of both organizations. Among the members of *HaHalutz Bal Melokhe* were a series of guild elders as well as the esteemed members of the Artisans Union and they carried out intensive Zionist pioneer work among the wide artisan circles.

[Page 65]

It was a great pleasure to see how each evening, after a difficult work day, the artisan comrades and their wives stormed their Pioneer organization at *Aleje 10*.

There they would learn Hebrew, hear lectures about history, Zionism and general Jewish problems and receive their work assignments for the *Eretz-Yisroel* funds. The comrades fulfilled their Jewish and Zionist community work, which would be arranged for them.

Thanks to the strong pioneer discipline that ruled over the branch, this organization occupied a significant place in communal life in the city.

The organization tried to convince the comrades not only to be prepared spiritually and professionally to emigrate to *Eretz-Yisroel* but also that their wives should adjust to emigration and should be fit to help them in their first steps in the new land. There was also concern in terms of emigration, that the children of the comrades should study Hebrew and study in Zionist educational institutions.

Taking into account the significance of the Czenstochow organization, comrade Szajnfeld and comrade Jakub Lewkowicz were elected to the principal council in Warsaw as representatives from Czenstochow in the central office of *HaHalutz Bal Melokhe*.

It is worthwhile to record the names of the comrades who stood at the head of this organization and helped its development: Szajnfeld, Jakub Lewkowicz, Avraham Gotlib, Moshe Goldberg and Wilinger. Among the Zionist workers who actively helped with their Zionist experience and set the tone with moral support were the well-known community workers, Dr. Bram and Dr. Mering.

At the beginning of 1936 the Czenstochow organization received one or two certificates for each quota for the comrades who excelled in their work and were qualified to prepare for emigration. Thanks to this organization, these comrades emigrated to *Eretz-Yisroel*:

1. Avraham Gotlib. Guild elder and master craftsman in the metal trade in Czenstochow. Good tradesman and specialist in the metal branch; in this special work he was skillful as the master craftsman in one of the largest factories in the country where he did a great deal during the time of the war for state production.

2. Moshe Goldberg, Guild elder of the master bakers, founded a cooperative bakery, *HaAvad* [the worker], now has his own bakery in Ramat-Yitzhak.

3. Wolf Landsman. master locksmith, former instructor at the Artisans School in Czenstochow, owns his own mechanical lock workshop in Jerusalem.

4. Hercberg, shoemaker by trade. After long efforts he acquired his own small shoe factory in the country.

5. Buchman, construction worker in Bnei Brak.

6. Laski, carpentry workshop in Haifa.

7. Szniur, upholstery workshop in Haifa. And other male and female comrades.

8. Comrade Nakhum Szliach, a baker, came to *Eretz-Yisroel* on one of the last ships to appear before the war.

In addition to this, the *HaHalutz Bal Melokhe* obtained certificates for comrades who could show 250 pounds [currency], as well as recommendations.

The number of individual artisans from Czenstochow who came to the land was small in total. But when one takes into consideration that several people came on each certificate, it can certainly be said that in the course of the short existence of the organization, *HaHalutz Bal Melokhe*, several dozen people avoided the fate that so tragically befell the entire Czenstochow Jewry.

In the middle of 1939 the *HaHalutz Bal Melokhe* movement faced the possibility of sending a larger number of comrades to *Eretz-Yisroel*. The cruel war interrupted the life of this young pioneer movement, just as it suffocated the bubbling and effervescent life of Polish Jewry in general.

[Page 66]

Culture and Education
The Gardening School

by A. Buchman

The gardening farm in Czenstochow arose in connection with the trend toward productivity, which was felt more strongly in Poland on the threshold of the 20th century. The first to implement the plan were the well-known community workers, Leopold Werde, Henrik Markusfeld, Grosman and Stanislaw Herc. They bought a piece of land of approximately 20 acres in 1902 for this purpose.

The gardening farm began with ten students in total and at first was satisfied with flowering plants.

A gardening teacher was hired from Germany. The first students were from Czenstochow and its surroundings, aged 12 to 14. The budget was put together from voluntary contributions and subsidies from the Jewish community.

No particular education or qualifications were demanded of the students, except for physical fitness. The manager was a religious Jew and the students had to observe all religious, Jewish laws, such as praying, saying blessings and so on.

The students who did not see any prospects for themselves after two or three years of study in such a school began to demand more secular education and further progress in the trade. But the financial resources of the farm were limited – most of the students dispersed. Only four people remained.

This lasted until 1904. Then the *I.K.A.* [Jewish Colonization Association] became interested in the farm, designated a subsidy and engaged the well-known agronomist, Borukh Sznajerzon, who turned the Czenstochow gardening farm into one of the most blossoming institutions in Poland.

The farm in Czenstochow began to have a good reputation across the entire country. The number of students rose to 30. There they received free: food, a place to live, clothing and they wore special uniforms.

The students who were accepted had to know one of the languages: Polish or Russian and a certain amount of arithmetic. The students received further education in the school from a separate teacher. Sznajerzon, the director, himself taught all special gardening trade subjects: botany, chemistry, physics, zoology and so on. A Polish gardener led the practical work on the farm. All of the accommodations that were needed on the farm, such as the hotbed boxes, beehives and tools were built and created by the students themselves. A library in various languages about everything that had a connection with gardening was also organized on the farm.

Greenhouses were organized. Warm hotbed windows. Plants from various different areas were raised: tropical and sub-tropical, as for example, oranges and figs.

In winter, cucumbers, radishes, lettuce, melons and beans grew in the greenhouses. Henrik Markusfeld bought a large field and donated it to the farm. Various grains were planted in the field.

A varied and large choice of local fruit trees wasplanted. Grafts were taken from them to cultivate more trees. The cultivated trees were sent in the tens of thousands across all of Russian Poland.

A botanical garden was accommodated with hundreds of plantings from various nations.

This all called for more than 6,000 rubles, which *I.K.A.* and the municipality gave. A flower shop was opened in Czenstochow in order to create a new source of income.

The farm became so well known with its practical knowledge in the world of planting that the city decided to create a park: the park in "Ostatni Grosz [district of Czenstochow]." Later, also the city park for the exhibition in 1911.

In 1906 an orchard of hundreds of trees and a rose garden were planted.

[Page 67]

Even a nursery for summer plantings. The farm's *rozarnja* [hot house for roses] made a strong impression among the Christian gardeners in Poland. There was a rose house of thousands of rose bushes of various sorts and blossoming at various times. The roses were sent to the flower shops in Poland and were also transported abroad.

In the month of January during the great frost, the first roses of the Jewish gardening farm appeared in Czenstochow. The cuttings lasted until the month of May when the roses from the open garden began.

There also was a drying room for bulbs of daffodils, tulips, lilies and various other flowers.

In 1911, the Jewish gardening farm in Czenstochow took part in the world exhibition in Czenstochow and received one gold medal and 10 silver medals.

The non-Jewish gardeners were greatly displeased that the actual work on the farm was led by a Christian. Sznajerzon, the director, therefore, sent several of the students to learn about the special ideas of planting in order to be able to carry out the practical work.

General Photograph of the Farm

However, everything began to go downhill when Sznajerzon, the director, left the farm in 1913. Other agronomists, Jews, came, but no one could compare with Director Sznajerzon – in regard to energy, idealism, knowledge and professionalism.

With the outbreak of the First World War, in 1914, many students dispersed. Those who remained worked further with the help of a small subsidy from the community.

The *I.K.A.* committed to its subsidy with the arrival of the director, Dubczinski. However, the farm then took on another character, more of a *halutzish* [offering preparation of pioneers for emigration to *Eretz-Yisroel*]. The main part was taken by agricultural education that was needed in *Eretz-Yisroel*. The pioneer work was carried out until the end of the First World War, when director Dubczinski left the farm, and his place was taken by the agronomist Feldsztajn. Ninety percent of the students who studied under his leadership left for *Eretz-Yisroel*.

Under his leadership the school for girls also was opened and girls came from all over Poland, many of them with a higher education, to learn the gardening trade in order to be able to emigrate to *Eretz-Yisroel*. They adapted well to the physical work in the garden, with the trees, flowers, hotbeds, and also in the cattle stall.

As a result, the prestige of the school began to increase with every Jew, chiefly among the nationalist element. It made a rare impression when young, healthy girls in their farm uniforms stood in the Czenstochow streets with shovels and gathered the manure and threw it in wagons which were driven away to the farm.

A Group of Students with the Director of the Farm

The Czenstochow city hall also began to take an interest in the farm. The farm even was supposed "to receive a gift" of certain rights through the Polish Education Ministry, but just then the agronomist, Feldsztajn, left for America and the entire situation at the farm changed.

The farm was taken over by *Hashomer Hatzair* [Youth Guard – socialist-Zionist youth movement]. Almost all of the trees were cut down. The graftings, the rose garden, hotbeds, decorative planting – all of this was annihilated and the terrain was changed to an agricultural one. Vegetables from the farm were sold in the Czenstochow market. Many male and female pioneers worked outside the farm, waiting for the opportunity to emigrate to *Eretz-Yisroel*.

[Page 68]

After the farm was transferred to *Hashomer Hatzair*, the Jewish community refused to subsidize it. On 2 December 1927, the *Czenstochower Zeitung [Czenstochower Newspaper]* published an article of alarm, demanding that the community provide for the farm under the leadership of *Hashomer Hatzair*.

During the time of its existence until the outbreak of the Second World War in 1939, the Czenstochow farm graduated hundreds of male and female students, who were qualified as gardeners and agricultural workers.

Of the first students, many travelled all over the world: America, Australia, Argentina. But 80 percent of the male and female students are located in *Eretz-Yisroel*, some in *kibbutzim* [collective community], some owning their own farms and in commercial agriculture.

Whoever comes into contact with the male and female students from the gardening farm in Czenstochow in *Eretz-Yisroel* admires their work and activities.

———

[Page 68]

The Artisans School

by A. Gotlib

Graduates of the Cabinetmakers' Division in 1912 with H. Markusfeld,

Engineer Asorodobaj and Jarzembinski, above

The Czenstochower Artisans School was founded in 1898. Its original founder, Henrik Markusfeld, created it as a monument to immortalize the memory of his deceased parents, Adolf and Ernestine Markusfeld.

The importance of the Artisans School can only be appreciated when one remembers that the Jewish artisan or crafts worker still stood at a lower cultural and communal level at that time. A trade went hand-in-hand with ignorance. An apprentice would be given [to an artisan] for several years and he had to do home-work for a long time, while learning the trade. A tailor and a shoemaker were given the title tailoring, shoemaking.

Right from the start, the Artisans School took on the task of uniting a craft with general education.

At first the Artisans School was a division of the *Talmud Torah* [religious school for poor boys] and was officially called: Jewish Artisans School at the *Talmud Torah*. It occupied the three-story building on Garncarska Street.

It included three divisions: 1) Mechanical locksmith division, which until then generally was not available for Jews; 2) Furniture making; 3) Wheelwrights. The director of the divisions were: Szrajber – master locksmith; Akrent – master carpenter. Jarzembinski (a Christian) – wheelwright. The arithmetic teacher was the Zalcman. We should also mention the *shomer hasof* (gate keeper), small Mordekhale.

The School's Mechanical Workshop

[Page 69]

At first, there were few candidates eager to enter the school. If I am not mistaken, at first only those students whose parents could pay 150 rubles for three years in advance were accepted. Later, students from the poorer strata of the Jewish population were also accepted and not only were they free from payment, but each of them received a subsidy from *IKO* [Jewish Colonization Organization] – 10 rubles every three months. Later it was reduced to the sum of seven and a half rubles. The students worked in workshops during the day and studied at the evening courses at night.

Among the students in the first three years were:

The brothers Avraham and Moshe Weksler, Shlomo Dzalaszinski, Shlomo Win, Chaim Win – all of these excelled in their professionalism.

The influx of students increased from year to year. Many young men from the houses of study entered the Artisans School. In the years 1904-1905, when the artisan and the working man organized and showed revolutionary and communal strength – children of more wealthy parents, as well as students from the middle school (*gymnazie*) began to enter the Artisans School.

In the course of time, the directors changed. Jebic took over the office of Director Szrajber. However, he was not successful with the students and he left the school. His place was taken by Gerwicman. Through his initiative the Artisans School began to give guild certificates. In 1912-1913 the director's office at the school was occupied by Engineer Asorodobaj. Under his leadership the Artisans School raised its level to a modern technical school. Studies were held with yearly exams and subsidies were designated for the more capable students to be able to study at a higher technical school.

The institution earned a reputation as a first class school and students began to storm it, not only from Czenstochow, but also from the surrounding cities. With the help of *I.K.O.*, new machines were arranged for and the kerosene motors were changed to electrical.

In 1913 the expenses for the Artisans School reached 11,000 rubles. The income was: 1,500 rubles – from the Jewish community, 500 rubles - the Markusfeld brothers, *IKO* – 4,900 rubles, and 4,000 rubles from school payments and work orders.

A Group of Students with Dr. Josef Markusfeld

and Personnel from the "Farm."

In addition to the above-mentioned people, the school also employed: Oks (Russian, arithmetic and natural science). Awner (Polish and German), Perec Wilenberg (hand drawing), Wajsberg (Hebrew and Jewish history).

In 1913 Henrik and Josef Markusfeld, Engineer Ratner, Stanislaw Herc, Henig Frenkl, Dr. Batawja and director Asorodobaj belonged to the school committee.

With the outbreak of the First World War, when Czenstochow was occupied by the Germans, the subsidy from the *I.K.O.*, the main support for the school budget, ended. The workers could not pay the tuition money and did not continue their studies. Henrik Markusfeld, who refurbished and restored much of the machinery that was damaged during the fire in Malarnja, a short time before the war, again came to help the school. As a result, the Artisans School received the ability to pay the instructors, which lasted until the directors could put together a budget and restore the activities.

After the war, when emigration to *Eretz-Yisroel* began, and there was a demand from there of certain trade preparation – evening courses for the locksmith and carpentry trades, which were needed in *Eretz-Yisroel*, were opened at the Artisans School. Dozens of young people and adults received elementary trade education over the course of several months and with it there was the possibility for many immigrants to arrange for the appropriate work in *Eretz-Yisroel*.

[Page 70]

**A Group of Students with Personnel from the
Artisans School in the School Year of 1930**

In the later years, when the well-known industrial law was given out by the Polish government on 15 December 1929 (it was then called the guild edict) that brought in restrictions for artisans and was aimed against the Jewish artisans – with the cooperation of the artisans club, three year complement courses were opened, in which apprentices received a theoretical trade and elementary mastery that according to the law was necessary for the exams.

The Artisans School did not only train cadres of hundreds of intelligent Jewish artisans, but also created instructors and in general helped to elevate our artisanship to a higher level.

[Page 71]

Worker Nurseries and *Folks-Shul* Named After Y. L. Peretz

by Haya Wage-Ratman

The founding of the nurseries. – The work's program. – The rise of the *Folks-Shuln* [public schools]. – The support from Czenstochower in America. – The founding of *Tsysho* [Central Yiddish School Organization] division. – The solemn welcome for our own school building. – Difficult period in the existence of the school. – Celebrations and holidays.

The beginning of the secular Jewish educational system in Poland was the nurseries that were created during the First World War. Their purpose was to save the homeless children and orphans from hunger and plagues. Y. L. Peretz, [Jakob] Dinezon and, later, Vladimir Medem, the head of the Bund, stood at the head of the first nurseries. However, their basis was the love of the Jewish child, not any philanthropy. Therefore, they blossomed and grew and became the great wonder in the life of the cultural development of the workers and poor masses in Poland.

The first nursery in Czenstochow was founded by the *S.S.* [Socialist-Zionist] party, which immediately was revived with other parties and groups under the German occupation.

The committee that was appointed to carry out the work consisted of: Moshe Weksler, Chaya Waga, Rywca Weksler, Dudek Szlezinger, Rafal Federman, Rayzl Fajertag, Ester Fuks. The first sum of 70 marks was raised from our own comrades. We searched for premises of five light, sunny rooms on Krutke Street 17. This was the most suitable neighborhood for the nursery because it was not far from Warsawer Street that bordered Garncarska, Nadrzeczna, Kozia and Senatarska. The premises were close to the ramparts on the other side and the street itself was clean and sparsely inhabited.

The furniture for the nursery was bought from a liquidated Hebrew nursery that was located in the granaries of Szlezinger's factory. The organizers moved the "furniture" into the freshly painted rooms of the nursery themselves. Comrades chose and donated toys. Comrades created tools for cooking and eating. A piano was found and the joy was indescribable at seeing their own nursery before them.

It was difficult to find the first suitable teacher. However, God helped and sent Yuzshe Stam, who was experienced in the area of a Hebrew nursery. Her folksiness, understanding and deep love for the Jewish child elevated her to the level of an ideal pioneer for the Jewish secular school. In the beginning she herself had to create even the Yiddish pedagogic material from Hebrew and Polish.

[Page 71]

Her assistant, Chaya Waga, was chosen from the committee's own ranks. She initially worked as a helper with Yuzshe Stam and, later, became an independent leader of the nursery, *Fareinikte* [United], which was opened at Strazacka 10.

The children from four to seven came from the poorest levels of the ghetto. They were hungry and physically neglected. They were nourished, the neglected heads were healed, the sick eyes; their hair was cut, washed and they were taught to keep themselves clean. It was necessary to provide doctors and medicines, mainly *lebertron* (cod liver oil), which each child received every day; gatherings of the parents had to be arranged and they were provided with lectures about hygiene for a child. This demanded so much work and devotion that it is hard to describe.

The House at Krutka 17,
Where the First Nursery Was Located

Only those who knew the nurseries from the first day of their creation under the terrible conditions of war and German occupation can evaluate this work. One had to see how the children looked when they arrived with swollen stomachs, bent feet and all of the remaining afflictions that war, hunger and poverty brought to them, in order to later admire their development that came to expression in their dancing, singing, performances and work as children.

The nutrition of the children consisted of a main meal prepared in the kitchen of the nursery and a lunch that at the beginning was brought in large pots from the workers-kitchen on Strazacka Street. The manager, that is, the boss of the nursery, Comrade Fradl, or the "the dark Fradl," was a true, loving mother to the children. Later, lunch was also cooked in the nursery kitchen.

Music occupied a large spot in the nursery. The children carried out their rhythmic exercises, marched, danced, sang and played to the sounds of the piano. Consequently, the music teacher, Terenyela, Mrs. Terena Fajgenblat, was much beloved by the children. Music in the nursery and, later, in the school had the greatest effect on the artistic development of the children.

The songs that the children sang were: children's songs and marches specially written for the nurseries, songs about spring, summer, winter, fall and songs about Jewish holidays: Chanukah songs, Purim songs and other holidays. The singing from the nursery was carried through the poor Jewish homes and streets and brought joy and cheer into the difficult and gloomy life of the poor Jewish masses.

The program of the nurseries consisted of telling stories, of conversations adapted to every opportunity and of practical work with paper, wood, sand and clay. The development of the childish feel and eye for color and painting was one of the most important tasks of the nurseries. Frequent walks in the fields, meadows and parks awakened the love of nature. In summer the children spent time mainly in the garden near the nursery.

The First Group of Children and Their Teachers from the *Fareinikte* Nursery

[Page 72]

The nursery became not only a pedagogic help and cure institution for the children, but a true home. The love of the children for the nursery and for the teachers was indescribable. A number of children did not leave the nursery until it was time to go to sleep.

The nursery was the most beloved institution for the progressive people and workers, without distinction as to party affiliation. The worker-professional unions supported the nursery in every way possible.

At the end of the First World War, after the revolution in Russia and the collapse of Imperial Germany, Poland was resurrected from the dead. Fresh winds of freedom were carried east and west. The workers movement was strengthened and it spread the most beautiful and greatest creation of the Jewish worker and working masses – the nursery and *Folks-Shuln* [public schools].

A second nursery at Strazacka 10 with the name *Fareinikte* Nursery opened immediately after the war. The *S.S.* [Socialist Zionists] then changed its old name from the years 1904-5 to *Fareinikte*. Everything that was created in this period bore the name of the party, just as the Bundist institutions were designated by the name "Medem and the *Paolei-Zionist* – Borochov.*

*[Translator's note: Vladimir Medem was a Bundist leader; Ber Borochov was a founder of the Labor Zionist movement. *Paolei-Zion* – Workers of Zion – was a Marxist Zionist organization.]

The residence for the second nursery was given to the party by Joszek Finkelsztajn. He was a very young member of the *S.S.* [Socialist Zionists] in 1904-5, in a uniform of a Russian *gymnazie* [secondary school] student. Later, he disappeared from Czenstochow like many others and returned after the First World War. His grandmother lived in the residence. After her death, he placed the furniture in the granary warehouse and gave the apartment to the party. This was a very great bargain because there were no empty apartments to be found in Poland.

The House at Strazacka 10, Where the Second Nursery Was Located

The management of the second nursery was taken over by Chayale Waga. One managing committee and pedagogic council, in which Rayzele Fajertag-Berkensztat took an active part, ran both nurseries. The manager of the second nursery was Malka Brat, who died at a very young age.

The place of an aide in the first nursery was taken by Faygele Berliner, a daughter of pious parents, who excelled in her love of children. Under the direction of Jozsa Sztam, she grew into a distinguished pre-school teacher. Later, with Masha Kalabus, a nursery teacher who came to Czenstochow from Vilna, she raised the Czenstochow nurseries as a model for the Jewish nurseries in Poland.

A Group of Children at Play

When the children grew, they opened the first class [of the] *Folks-Shul*, led by Natsha Warsawska and Rayzele Fajertag. Later her place as teacher in the first class was occupied by Rywka Cuker from Siedlce. The second class [of the] *Folks-Shul* was led by one of the sisters, Pola Frydman, also from Siedlce. When Jozsa Sztam left Czenstochow, the other sister, Manya, became the teacher of the nursery at Krutka 17. The first and second classes of the *Folks-Shul* along with Nursery number 2, *Fareinikte*, were located at the house at Strazacka 10.

[Page 73]

A Group of Children Eating

In the summer of 1920, during the very fervor of the Polish War with the Soviet Union, Friend Mendl Szuchter visited Czenstochow. He brought with him help for the schools sent by the Czenstochower Relief in New York and from the Aid Union in Chicago. He brought Rafal Federman's plan to build a house for the nurseries and the *Folks-Shuln* with him.

In 1922 the two delegates from Czenstochower Relief in New York, Louis Szimkowicz and Louis Szwarc came to Czenstochow with instructions to buy their own house for the nurseries and *Folks-Shuln*. Until then, the Jewish schools in Czenstochow were led by three parties: the *Fareinikte* – two separate nurseries and three *Folks-Shul* classes; the *Poalei Zion* or *Borochovtses* [followers of Ber Borochov] – one nursery and one *Folks-Shul* class; the Bund or *groyser klub* [large club] that already arranged for the furniture and was prepared to open a nursery. There were also three separate party libraries. However, a joint distribution committee already was functioning which divided the sum that arrived from America among the cultural and aid institutions of all parties.

Under pressure from the delegates from America a joint management committee was created that administered all of the schools. The management committee consisted of five from *Fareinikte*, two from *Poalei-Zion* and one Bundist. Rafal Federman was the chairman of the management committee.

The delegation from America did not find any suitable house for the schools. Therefore, they decided along with the school management committee to buy the plot with the small house on the courtyard at Krutka 23. The actual house for the school then had to be built. The task of working out the plan to build the house was taken over by Mikhal Alter.

The Children from the Borochov Nursery

On Sunday, 6 July 1924, the solemn dedication of the house took place in Czenstochow. A children's concert took place in the Nowosci Theater, First Aleje 12, on *Shabbos*, 5 July, in honor of the opening of the building. On Sunday at six in the evening a solemn gathering took place with the participation of the leaders of the Central Jewish School Organization in Poland and a banquet took place in the hall of the *Neye Welt* [new world] at night on the same day.

The leaders of the Jewish workers' parties, such as Dr. Josef Kruk, Zerubavel and Beynish Michalowicz came to Czenstochow for the dedication alon g with representatives from many cities and *shtetlekh* in Poland. Greetings arrived from a series of personalities. It was the first house of their own that was erected for Jewish schools in Poland.

The new house had brightly lit corridors, large halls for the school classes with wide windows with Venetian blinds. A garden of various trees and plants was planted near the house in order to acquaint the children with botany, which was completely strange to children from the poor alleys.

The school year 1924 began in their own house in the brightly sunny halls. The nursery at Strazacka 10 also moved.

[Page 74]

The nursery at Krutka 17, in Szmilewicz's (coffee roaster) house, was run in the same house as before.

At the end of 1924, A. Chrabalowski returned from America. The schools already had a large [number] of teaching personnel because with each year a higher grade was added. The financial situation was difficult. The schools suffered a great deal because Rafal Federman left the majority faction, which was called "independent," and joined the Bund. Mikhal Alter ran the school. The chairman of the management committee was Sh. Nirenberg.

The House of the Y. L. Peretz School at Krutka 23

In 1925-1926 the management of the school was taken over by A. Chrablowski [spelled Chrabalowski above]. The beginning of the school year until around the new year of 1926 was very difficult for the schools. The women teachers simply starved and the school was in danger of closing. The Czenstochow city hall – this must be remembered favorably – then voted for a one-time subsidy of a thousand *zlotys*, which was divided among the teachers. Later, help began to come in from Chicago, from Czenstochower Relief and the Ladies Auxiliary in New York. That year the teaching personnel received normal payments of wages. The pedagogic direction of the schools also improved during the year.

At the end of 1926, A. Chrabalowski left Czenstochow forever. The management of the schools was taken over by Avraham Brat, who remained at his work until the Second World War.

The first group of children who spent a total of nine years in the nursery and school graduated from the school in 1928. The names of the children were: Fradela Berkowicz, Shimshon Berkowicz, Gitkela Rozen, Rayzela Kricer, Zlakela.

The completion of the school year in the summer of 1929 was a great event. The celebration was recorded in a film that was sent to Relief in New York and to other cities.

The Parents' Committee of the Y. L. Peretz School
Seated, right to left: Asher Himelman, L. Berkowicz, Avraham Brat, and Others

The First Graduates of the School with Their Teachers

The situation of the schools again worsened from day to day. The depression in America and the struggle between the right and the left stopped the aid en masse that the schools would receive from Czenstochower Relief in New York. At the same time the situation in Poland in general and in Czenstochow in particular became unbearable. The reaction and the dictatorship of the military clique, which seized power, grew. They fired decrees at the schools without stop. All subsidies from city hall were ended even help with coal, which the Y.L. Peretz nursery had received from the city. In addition, there was the danger of the houses being auctioned because of a debt of several hundred dollars that the managing committee had borrowed. The situation also intensified because of the party struggle in the managing committee. Mainly between the Bund and "independents."

[Page 75]

The result was that the Y.L. Peretz *Folks-Shul* with all of its seven classes closed. The residence of the nursery on Krutke 17 was relinquished and the nursery was again located in the house where the school was located before. Because of the difficult situation, a residence in the house in the school courtyard was also rented to a private person. However, the support of the school itself was also difficult because of the meager help from America. In order to create local help, a women's committee was founded in Czenstochow under the leadership of Mrs. Sarna. Mrs. Terenya Fajenblat-Kapinska (wife of Maritz [Moshe] Kapinski), the former music teacher of the nursery, was also active in the committee.

The Teachers and a Group of Students from the Nursery and *Folks-Shul* in 1926–1927

In 1938, the "independent" party was shut down by the Polish government. Several active workers from the schools, such as Avraham Bart and Wolf Fajga, joined the Bund. Changes for the better took place in the managing committee and the leadership of the nursery. The well-known communal workers, Ahron Peretz and Moshe Berkensztat, entered the managing committee. However, it was not long before the Nazi murderers attacked Poland.

After a time under the Nazi occupation, Jewish refugees from Lodz and Krakow were placed in the schoolhouse. Avraham Bart and Wolf Fajga continued to have supervision over the house.

One of the most beautiful accomplishments of the schools and nurseries was the artistic education of the children.

The mandolin orchestra and choir, led by the well-known musician, Zaks of Czenstochow, was one of the most stunning achievements of the school. The choir and mandolin orchestra was founded by A. Chrabalowski in 1926. It was enlarged later by Avraham Brat with the help of 150 dollars, for which the *Czenstochower Arbeter Ring* [Workmen's Circle] branch 211 especially raised money for this purpose. The mandolin orchestra appeared at concerts at various opportunities and was enthusiastically welcomed by its listeners.

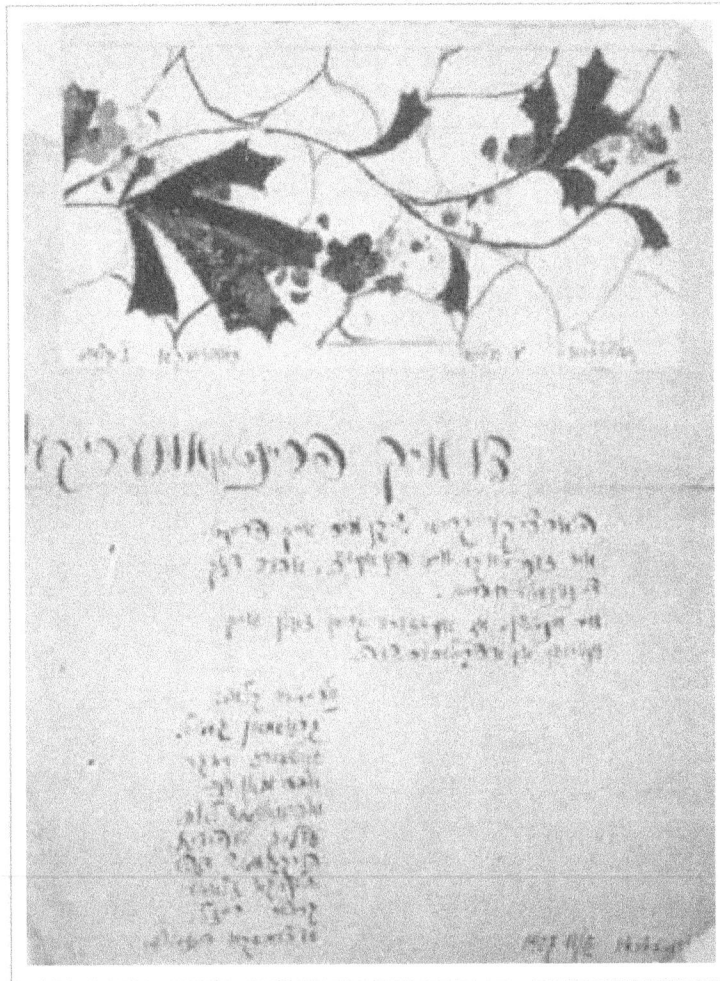

Thank You Letter from a Group of School Children to Czenstochower Relief in New York

The area of the visual arts was not ignored. From 1926 on, the painting teacher in the school was Perec Wilenberg, the well-known Czenstochow artist, who was also a teacher of painting and drawing in the Jewish *gymnazie* at the Artisans School.

[Page 76]

Celebrations of holidays and public performances were the great days for nurseries and *Folks-Shuln*. The traditional Jewish holidays such as Passover, *Shavous*, *Sukkos*, *Chanukah* and Purim were revived in the school in a new form. In addition, literary holidays were added dedicated to Yiddish writers such as: Mendele, Sholem Aleichem, Y.L. Peretz, Avraham Reisen and others. Each year a memorial gathering was arranged for the *yahrzeit* [anniversary of the death] of Y.L. Peretz. They prepared for the performances and holidays for weeks and months. The nurseries and schools educated talent in the areas of singing and dramatic art. Shimson, Dina and Eidele Berkowicz (the children of Leibush Berkowicz), Ruchla Testuler and a whole row of others particularly excelled. A number of them appeared on the stage as children and later as grown-ups with adults and they were the treasure of the Yiddish theater.

The enthusiastic spectators at the presentations mainly were the fathers and mothers of the children. And when the children appeared on the stage with their songs, dances and adaptations of children's stories, there was no strength in the world that could hold the fathers and mothers in their seats.

The children's performances also had a good reputation in the city. Groups of children from other schools in Czenstochow would come to the performances with their teachers.

Innumerable songs were sung in the school. Songs by modern Yiddish poets, children's songs, original and absorbed from other languages: songs of work, of Jewish holidays, of spring, summer, winter and autumn. The songs from the nurseries and schools were spread by the children to the Jewish courtyards and to the workhouses. Entering a courtyard on a Jewish street, one could often hear a circle of children singing and playing the songs, dancing and games from the nurseries.

The hymn of the Y.L. Peretz nurseries and *Folks-Shuln* that was sung at the beginning and end of each celebration and performance was the following:

"Open every door wider –
A good holiday, things are good for us,
We all, all march
Full of courage to our holiday.
We all go in rows
One and two, one and two –
Everyone carries good news
As follows, as follows.
Hand in hand given with joy,
The row is trim, the voices high,
The feet are light; here they soar.
A good holiday, they call."

The Mandolin Orchestra with Zaks, the Director, at the *Folk-Shul*

The slogan of the school was free movement in the free air. During the winter, the children played with snow and with sleds in the courtyard of the school. They also took the sleds along on walks in the alleys during the winter. When spring arrived, the children spent a large part of their school time with nature, at Krutke 17 and later in their own house, in the "small botanical" garden, which Mikhal Alter had so wonderfully arranged. The older children also had a small garden in the courtyard of the new house, which they planted and cultivated themselves.

A Group of Students and Teachers in the Garden of the School Courtyard

[Page 77]

However, the great dream of the students and teachers was for a summer colony outside the city. The best place for such a colony was the Ostrower pine forest that extended for many miles to Herby.

They were successful only once, in 1920, in arranging for a full summer colony in Ostrow for the children.

The children from the nurseries and *Folks-Shuln* were divided into two groups. Each group spent four weeks in the colony. The children's colony consisted of a group of houses with verandas, as summerhouses were built, and with large courtyards. The children mainly spent time in the courtyards and in the forests. They slept in the houses. The children's beds were provided by the school's managing committee. The children brought their own bed linens with them from their homes. Comrades Mikhal Alter and Yehoshua Nirenberg strove to organize the children's colony and provide the food for the children. Comrade Nirenberg was occupied with preparing the food for the children. In general, the summer colony was a difficult and costly undertaking and demanded a great deal of energy and money.

Therefore, the results were splendid. The children, many of them anemic, many with symptoms of other diseases – under the influence of the sun and pine scent from the forest – blossomed and developed their strength.

The teachers at the colony were Yuzsha Sztam, Shoshona Czenstochowska and Chaya Waga. The manager was Malka Brat, with an assistant.

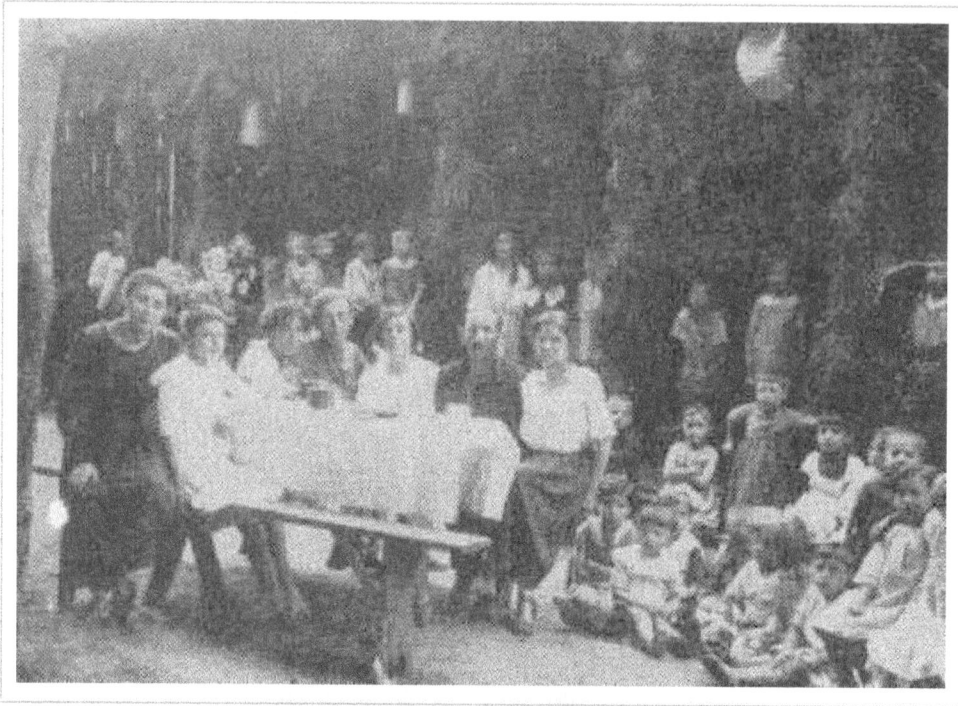

Summer Colony in Ostrow in 1920

*The nurseries and schools were visited by a series of friends and aid workers from America. There were: Friend Pete Owiecki and his wife from Chicago, who brought a larger sum for aid from the Chicago Aid Union. They attended a children's performance in the Straczecki Hall and at a banquet at the close of the 1926 school year. Friend Nirenberg, Friend Gryn, may he rest in peace, Friend Win, may he rest in peace, who on his own accord went to visit a large number of children. Friend Szlingbaum, Friend Szwarcbaum, Friend Yankl Kopin (Kopinsk) and Rose (Rywca) Kuperman.

**American Guests at the School: Y. Kapinski and
R. Kuperman with the Teachers, L. Brener and A. Brat**

Foreign Guests at the School. Seated: Dr. Kruk and Lord Marley

Among the esteemed personalities who visited the schools were: [Dudley Leigh Aman] Lord Marley, a deputy in the English Labor Party, who visited Poland, Sholem Asch, Dr. Chaim Zhitlowski, Dr. [Zemach] Szabad from Vilna.

When the famous singers, Moshe Rudinow and Ruth Leviasz, gave a concert in Czenstochow, they visited the school and sang especially for the children.

[Page 78]

The *Yidishe Gymnazie*

by S. Wirstel

The *Yidishe* [Jewish] *Gymnazie* [secondary school] in Czenstochow was founded in 1917. The opening of the school made a great impression in Czenstochow. At that time interest in Hebrew grew strongly in connection with the Balfour Declaration and with the opportunity for a larger emigration to *Eretz-Yisroel.*

Students from all strata of the Jewish population began to stream into the *gymnazie*: children with Hasidic parents, who had just been studying in a *kheder* [traditional primary school], children of half-assimilated parents who did not know how to read or write Hebrew, had only studied in Polish schools, and, naturally, children of nationalist Jews and Zionists.

The school was called the *Yidishe Gymnazie*, but Yiddish was not taught or spoken there. Both the teachers and the students always used the Polish language, even outside the hours of study. A student was frowned upon even if he was permitted to speak Yiddish during the recess times. Even the Hebrew lessons were limited to a few hours a week. Only the Hebrew teacher and the students who had come from the *kheder* knew Hebrew.

The Hebrew teachers really rejoiced with these students and they achieved the greatest distinction for Hebrew, religion, *Tanakh* [The Five Books of Moses, Prophets and Writings] and Jewish history.

The *gymnazie* was founded on Jasna Street. A year later, it moved to its own spacious building at Szkolna Street 10.

At first, there were only the first, second and third classes, preparatory classes. Then the first and second classes for boys and girls separately. Then a higher class was added every year until the full eight *gymnazie* classes, that qualified [students for] study in the university.

Just like the Polish *gymnazie* in Czenstochow, the c also had its special uniform, in the form of a hat. The hat of a student from the *Yidishe Gymnazie* was of dark blue cloth with a blue-white stripe.

The first director of the *gymnazie* was Dr Shmuel Brisz, a tall man with a short, trimmed beard and a constant smile on his lips. He was beloved by the students because he devotedly felt his duty as director. After a short time, he had to leave his position because of illness. Professor Meir Balaban, now a holy martyr of Polish Jewry, took his place.

Professor Balaban was a very energetic man. He raised the *Yidishe Gymnazie* to a much higher level than before. He hired competent teachers and gave more time for Hebrew instruction. He increased the number of Hebrew teachers and introduced the study of religion and *Tanakh.* The Hebrew teachers of our class were Janowski, Rubinsztajn and Wajnberg. Of Jewish history - Brawer and Miss Stobiecka.

Janowski, our Hebrew teacher, would often invite us to his home and lent us books of modern, Hebrew literature from his valuable library.

Gymnastics at the *Yidishe Gymnazie* were led by the proficient professor, A. Krist. Professor Perec Wilenberg taught drawing.

In addition to the above-mentioned teachers, I remember only Makrojer and Asorodobraj,

Of the women teachers I remember: Werchowska, Gizn, Wolf, Wajs and Latringer. My closest colleagues were: Ahron Luksenburg, Dovid Lewit, Yakov Czeriker, Geniek Zisznicki, Eizner Wolman, Leyzer Rozenberg, Hochman, Lewkowicz (the last two are now in Argentina), Rotbard, Grindman, Kongrecki and Berliner.

[Page 79]

After, Meir Balaban, the director, was invited to Warsaw to the Tachkemoni [Rabbinical] Seminar and his place in the *gymnazie* system was taken by Dr. Dovid Einhorn, a learned man who in the later years occupied an important place in the Jewish literary world.

In his time the *gymnazie* developed with relation to general instruction. However, they adapted so much to the government program for middle schools that the Hebrew subjects were reduced to a minimum.

The Hebrew language was spread outside of the *gymnazie* through Zionist youth organizations, particularly, *Hashomer Hatzair* [The Youth Guard - secular Socialist- Zionists].

A Group of Students from the *Yidishe Gymnazie* with Dr. Dovid Einhorn, the Director

Evening Courses
by A. Khrobolowski

Evening courses for the young workers first were created in 1920 at the workers club, *Fareinikte* [united], later at the central council of the professional unions and in 1926 at the Y. L. Peretz School.

The emergence of the courses was connected with the organization of the youth group, *Shtral* [beam of light]. After the nursery and *Folks-shuln* [people's schools], the youth courses were the best that was done in the realm of the cultural development of the working young. Previously, the young along with the old comrades would pack the clubrooms and workers' meeting places and waste their time doing nothing.

The first organizers of the evening courses were the active workers from *Shtral*: Avraham Brat, S. Wegner, Alek Lewinsztajn, Moshe Lewinhof, Malka Danziger, Gliksman and others.

A group of students from the Hebrew *Yidishe Gymnazie* [Jewish secondary school] also belonged to *Shtral*. Their leaders were Matek Pliwacz and Eksztajn, who later become leading community activists in the workers movement, Matek Pliwacz with the "independents" and Eksztajn with the Bund.

In 1920 the courses were organized in the premises of the nursery number two, at Strazacka 10, with 40 to 50 children taking part, then on Garncarska in the house of the cooperative bakery where there were two divisions, separate for the young and for adults. The number of applicants was large so that there were not enough places for everyone. The premises could only accommodate approximately 90 to 100 students. In the courses emphasis was first given to teaching the young to learn to write, read and speak Yiddish correctly. However, in addition to Yiddish, they also studied: Polish, arithmetic, geography and natural science. During the summer excursions to the surrounding area were arranged almost every *Shabbos* in the morning. Popular talks about literature, history, social science and other topics took place during *Shabbos* afternoons. The evening courses also arranged gymnastic exercises and singing.

Evening Courses for Young People with A. Chrabolowski

A Group of Students from the Evening Courses with Teachers and Managing Committee

[Page 80]

The teacher of Yiddish and general speaking was A. Chrabolowski. The geography and natural science teacher – M. Kanowski, teacher at the gardening farm; Moritz Kremski led the gymnastic exercises.

The greatest benefit of the courses was that the majority of students learned to write Yiddish correctly. The students particularly liked poetry. They were read to aloud and they had a great desire to recite. In general, in Yiddish literature, there was a particularly enthusiastic response to [Y. L.] Peretz's short stories.

The young from various parties took part in the courses, as well many unaffiliated young people.

A number of the students had earlier belonged to the communist movement and a large number of those who belonged to *Shtral* later joined the communists. The majority of them had spent long years in the jails of "independent" Poland.

The Hebrew language was spread outside of the *gymnazie* through Zionist youth organizations, particularly, *Hashomer Hatzair* [The Youth Guard - secular Socialist- Zionists].

Lira and the Jewish Literary Society

by F. Szmulewicz, A. Khrobolowski

Lira, the literary and musical society, was founded in 1908. Its first leaders were Zionists, among whom were found Moshe Zandsztajn and Leon Kopinski. They attracted a number of the assimilated intelligentsia and regular cultural activists to the work.

Avraham Wewiorka, Leon Kopinski, *Khazan* [cantor] Avraham Ber Birnbaum and Zaks took part in the discussion about the name for the society. The Zionist side proposed the name *Hazamir*, the assimilated *Lira*. The latter won.

The assimilated spirit ruled in *Lira* for a long time. The reigning language was Polish. However, the chorus, under the leadership of *Khazan* Avraham Ber Birnbaum, also sang Hebrew songs in addition to the Polish [ones]. Yiddish was foreign to *Lira*. In general, *Lira* had limited influence over a small group during its early years.

Therefore, the "Jewish Literary Society," which was founded in Czenstochow as a division of the Petersburg society under the same name, immediately at the beginning attracted the largest number of Jewish youth and of the Jewish democratic intelligentsia.

Among the initiators were Dovid Borzykowski, A. Chrabalowski, Wolf Lewenhof, Rafal Federman, F. Szmulowicz and Yakov Kapinski.

It is difficult to have access to find the first three responsible people in whose name the society would be legalized. The three, who took upon themselves the liability were: teacher Ufner from the First *Aleje*, Itshe Meir Erlich, who in the evening enjoyed the company of the young people in his wurst business, and Jakob Wajnsztok, an owner of a paper business and an activist in the society.

A Group of *Lira* Chorus Members.
Among them: Warmund, Hercberg, Grabiner, Welgryn, and Oweczka

The managing committee, according to the statute of the society, had to consist of 10 people not younger than 25. Among the members of the managing committee were: Gelbard, Chaim Dawidowicz, Luria, Erlich, Leon Goldberg, dentist Peretz and others.

A. Chrabalowski was chosen for the managing committee from the working class.

Two enthusiastic mass meetings took place in the hall of *Harmonia* [Harmony]. The founding of the society was proclaimed at the first one.

[Page 81]

The managing committee was elected at the second one.

Fervent work began immediately that left even deeper marks in Czenstochow life.

The first evening of the society took place in the *Harmonia* hall. Avraham Wewiorka, among others, presented his two sketches: *Kheykl Shiker* [*Kheykl the Drunk*] and *Der Hoyker* [*The Hunchback*]. The evening brought in a rich income of 25 rubles.

The second undertaking was an entertainment in Walberg's garden, in the First *Aleje* that brought in income of over 100 rubles.

The premises of the society were located at *Aleje* 8. A reading room with newspapers and journals was created. A chorus was founded under the leadership of the director of the choir in the "German Synagogue," as the new synagogue on Dojazd, or Wilson [Street], was called. The soloist with the chorus actually was his small son. The chorus rehearsed Jewish folksongs in Yiddish and Hebrew. One of the classical numbers by the chorus was *Hallelujah...*

The great significance of the "literary society" consisted not only of the fact that a legal cultural center was created for almost all of the young Jews in Czenstochow, but also that all of the parties worked together here for Jewish culture.

In addition to the previously mentioned names, Moshe Weksler, Dwoyra Szicer, Yeta Pokula, Gordin, Yankl Kopinski, Leyzer Berkowicz and Mendlson (now in New Rochelle, New York) were active in the society, either in the chorus or in the dramatic section.

A. Peretz led the dramatic section. Among others taking part in it were: Aronowicz, Szmulewicz, Yeta Pekula, Meir Fajnrejch, Rafael Federman. Approximately 30 people belonged to the section. However, there were few women among them. The dramatic section not only produced acts, but often, mainly on Friday evening, came together in the society room and recited poems by Yiddish poets.

The first presentation of the dramatic section took place on 6 April 1911 in Walberg's garden. They staged *Bokherim* [*Young Men*] by Yitzhak Katzenelson and *Dos Eybiker Lid* [*The Eternal Song*] by Mark Arnsztain.

The great appearance of the "Literary Society" in public was the concert of Jewish folksongs, performed by the Petersburg opera singers Medvedyev, Rozovska, and N. Janowski, accompanist – composer A. Pontoker. Two weeks later, on the 25 of January 1913, *Lira* arranged a concert with the same artists.

At the same time two people came to Czenstochow who excelled in their communal work.

One was Josef Orogonowicz, a student from the famous Vilna Teacher's Institute. He was sent from the Russian public school to Czenstochow by the Russian government as a teacher for Jewish children. He was a Bundist. His first appearance in Czenstochow was a lecture about Lev Tolstoy. This was the time when Tolstoy escaped to a church where he spent the last hours of his life.

The second one was Jakov Rozenberg and his wife, whom we called "Hygenia." He wore a beard and had the stately appearance of a [member of the] intelligentsia. He also was a Bundist. He was from Lodz. He came to Czenstochow from Warsaw, sent by a society as an official of the metallurgical factory Vulkan, where many Jewish officials, among them engineers Ratner, Eiznberg, Kisyn [and] Y. Szwarc were employed.

At the initiative of Lewenhof, Dovid Borzykowski and Hershele Feywelowicz, a group of young people with literary inclinations tried to publish a literary journal in Czenstochow. With the help of Chaim Dawidowicz and other sympathizers, one issue of *Der Folk* [*The People*] was published. The journal was edited by Lazar Kohn in Lodz.

The 70th anniversary of *Zeyde* [grandfather] Mendele[1] was celebrated by the literary society with an informal and intimate banquet. Because of *Zeyde*'s weak condition, the society was not successful in bringing the dear celebrant to Czenstochow. A mimeographic copy of Sh. Niger's treatise about Mendele Moykher Sforim was sent from the Petersburg Central [office]. We sat around covered tables in an elevated mood. Local speakers spoke abut the significance of *Zeyde*. Hershele Feywelowicz, who was a humorist talent and knew how to create rhymes, composed a special song in honor of Mendele, which was sung by a collective chorus.

[Page 82]

The song went this way:

We drink another ladle
In honor of *Zeydn Reb Mendele*
Because it is clear to everyong
That the *Zeyde* is turning 70.

Oy, Reb Mendele, *oy* Reb Mendele,
You still write so beautifully
Oy, Reb Mendele, *oy* Reb Mendele,
You still write so beautifully...

Rafal Federman, being a little tipsy, recited the ode, *Tsu di Shtern* [*To the Stars*] in honor of Grandfather Mendele's great anniversary.

Lectures often took place in the Society, two of them by Rafal Federman. One was on the theme "Yiddish" and the other, "the cross." Both themes were based on the article from Dr. [Chaim] Zhitlovsky's journal, *Dos Naye Lebn* [*The New Life*] that he published in America. A discussion took place at the first reading with the Hebraists represented by Leon Kopinski,. The second reading dealt with the question that Dr. Zhitlovsky raised about a review of the relationship with Christianity.

A smaller audience was drawn to the lecture by Chrabalowksi: "Sholem Asch, the Prophet of the Earth," in which the type of striving by a large number of the young people to to agriculture actually was expressed. This striving was embodied in both Zionism and Territorialism.[2]

The last and greatest achievement of the literary society was the founding of the first legal Jewish library in Czenstochow. The first sum of 100 rubles was donated by 10 members of the managing committee, 10 rubles each. All of their names are found in the minutes-book of the literary society, which remained somewhere in Czenstochow. Only [the names] Erlich, Chaim Dawidowicz, Luria, Gelbard, L. Goldberg remain in my memory.

Rafal Federman and Gelbard were designated to travel to Warsaw to buy books, Yiddish and Hebrew. Another commission had to check the books. The first librarians were Rafal Federman and Yankl Kopinski.

During the course of time Ofner, the first founder of the society and its chairman, resigned from his office. Thanks to the efforts of the managing committee to place at the head well-to-do, middle class and "virtuous" people, the office of chairman was taken by Radoszycki, a well-off wood merchant, and Beser, an owner of a large house in the Second *Aleje*.

At the end of the summer of 1914, the Russian government closed the Jewish Literary Society in Petersburg and all of its divisions. The Czenstochow division received an order to liquidate. The members of the Literary Society had the idea of uniting with *Lira*. The manager of *Lira* then was Josefowicz. It was agreed that all three languages, Yiddish, Hebrew and Polish, would have equal rights and that a managing committee would be elected. A group, with Rafal Federman at its head, was against joining *Lira*. However, the majority, led by A. Chrabalowski, was for it. At the last meeting liquidating the Literary Society in the *Harmonia* Hall, a large majority decided to join *Lira*. With this began the *Lira* epoch of the cultural activity of Jewish Czenstochow.

Elected to the combined managing committee were: Henrik Markusfeld – honorary chairman, A. Peretz – chairman, Alkona Chrabalowski – secretary, Jozefowicz – manager, Markus Herszlikowicz, Rozenberg, Luria, Wajnsztok, Chaim Dawidowicz, Leon Kopinski, Josef Aronowicz, Henrik Szmulewicz – members of the managing committee.

The *Lira* represented a colorful mosaic, the assimilated intelligentsia and the well-known Dr. [Ludwik] Batawia, Zionists and the middle-class youth and with them, all of the Yiddishists [supporters of the Yiddish language and Yiddish literature] of the former Literary Society. Sporadic confrontations, particularly with the manager, Jozefowicz, who represented the assimilated component, did not interfere with working together. The chorus, under the leadership of *Khazan* [cantor] Avraham Ber Birnbaum, sang Polish, Hebrew and Yiddish songs. In Zionist evenings and readings, Yiddishists and Zionists took part in all cultural undertakings in Yiddish.

The most idealistic among the Zionist young was Moshe (Morris) Goldberg, who later left for London. He returned from there after the First World War and arranged a branch office of a bank house in Warsaw, where he died a short time later in his youth.

[Page 83]

Our *Lira* members were: Wajtenfeld, now in Palestine, Moshe Oderberg, an influential *Poalei-Zionist* [Workers of Zion – a Marxist-Zionist organization], now in Chicago, Szferlkas, a sympathizer of the Zionist Socialists, Yankl Kapinski, a *Poalei-Zionist*, now in New York. Also active in *Lira* were: Sh. Chaiutyn and Lutek Gajzler. Two people who ran the buffet at *Lira* and served the members tea and snacks also must be remembered. One of them was Mrs. Frimorgn; the second one – Barensztajn.

Leasha Frimorgn (during the first era of *Lira*), Gutsha Bem, later the wife of Henekh Szmulewicz, Grabiner, Edelist, Moshe Waga and Bem excelled as male and female singers in the chorus.

One of the organizers of the chorus at *Lira* was Berish Dawidowicz, now in New York.

Lira was located on the corner of Dojazd and the First *Alee* over Bloszczinski's candy factory. The windows of the large reading room looked out onto the First *Alee*. The windows of the large theater looked out onto Dojazd or Stancja Street.

The great days of *Lira* were: Y.L. Peretz's three visits to Czenstochow.

The first visit by Y.L. Peretz took place in the spring in 1912. A solemn banquet took place after the reading in *Lira's* large reading room at which he read from his still unpublished folksy history. The "elite" of Czestochow and almost all of the class-conscious Jewish young were gathered at the banquet. Josef Aronowicz greeted the people's poet in the name of the first [group]; Chrobolowski in the name of the second [group]. Josefowicz and Dr. Branitowski (dentist) led the arrangements. They drank champagne. The arrangements were exemplary. The joy and inspiration that also found an expression in song is impossible to describe.

Y.L. Peretz came to Czenstochow for the second time on *Shabbos*, 21 October 1912 to the opening of the Jewish Library in *Lira*. This actually was the library that the liquidated Jewish Literary Society had created. After long preparations and negotiations, the present *Lira* revived the library under the name, Henrik Markusfeld Library, which was led by Faytl Szmulewicz.

The tickets for the evening already had been sold out the day before. High prices were paid to be able to stand on the side.

A cabinet of books encircled with white and blue ribbon was erected on the decorated and richly illuminated platform.

The chairman of the managing committee, Dentist A. Peretz, who gave over the chairmanship to the honorary president, Henrik Markusfeld, opened the evening. Engineer Ratner, Dovid Wolfowicz, Landau and Goldberg were invited into the presidium.

Yosef Aronowicz gave a short review of the history of *Lira* and of the newly founded library in his opening speech. At the end of his speech, he gave a gift to the chairman, Henrik Markusfeld, from the Society: a scrapbook that was symbolic of a Yiddish book, created by the Czenstochow artist, Perec Wilenberg.

Engineer Ratner greeted the opening of the library in the name of the Czenstochower Artisan Club. Greetings also came from the young people of Noworadomsk and Lodz, from the Czenstochower *Reklamen-Blat* [*Advertising Sheet*], from the Bedziner *Anonsn-Blat* [*Announcement Sheet*] and from several *Hazamirs* [the nightingale – possibly theatrical organizations].

Henrik Markusfeld said that of all the institutions that he founded, *Lira* is the most beloved to him because in it the young are found, the source of life.

Y.L. Peretz, who took the floor after him, warmly shook the hand of Henrik Markusfeld, as a sign of approval for his words. About the Yiddish book, Peretz said that it was the duty of the library to obtain even more historical books because we know little of our history... We are spread over the entire world and the entire earth is soaked with our blood and wet with our sweat, and if you knew the history of our people, you would know that here, too, in Poland, every piece of earth, every stone is soaked with our blood and sweat, enriched with our physical and spiritual work and we are not invited guests here. We are equal citizens who have made the country rich with our effort and work and we are entitled to full equal rights as people and Jews.

Y.L. Peretz also was given the honor of carrying out the joyful ceremony of the opening of the library. The librarian gave him a gilded key on a small cushion, made by Moshe Weksler, and a scissors to cut the ribbon.

[Page 84]

In the evening, Y. L. Peretz read two of his unpublished folksy stories: *Shlomo haMelakh* [*King Solomon*] and *Motl Princ* [*Motl the Prince*].

A banquet took place after the [readings] and the crowd enjoyed itself at richly laden tables and with toasts, songs and dance.

Groinem Frank decorated the room and the stage. The lighting was arranged by the electrical technician Landau. The manager of the evening was Henekh Szmulewicz, photographer. The evening made a great impression and left the most beautiful memories with all who took part.

Peretz appeared in Czenstochow for the third time on *Shabbos*, 14 November 1913.

This time his theme was his Yiddish translation of "Song of Songs."

We read in the report of the Czenstochower Woknblat [Czenstochower Weekly Newspaper], number 41:

"The hope of hearing the translation of *Songs of Songs* from the poet's mouth was not fulfilled.

"Our speech is too poor; our ideas are too small for the healthy, physical beauty of the body, separated too much from the wide and free natural life, that one of us – if he is such an artist like Y.L. Peretz, can translate it into Yiddish for us. He has given us the key to *Song of Songs*. Today, the poet is our rebbe.

"And he sat at the table like a rebbe, a teacher and with his clear language and rich ideas, he taught us the literal meaning of *Song of Songs*.

"The evening was a great success and brought a great deal of inspiration into Jewish life in Czenstochow."

Other well-known personalities who appeared in *Lira* were Hillel Zeitlin, Yitzhak Grinbaum and H.D. Nomberg. Grinbaum spoke on the theme: "The sum of Jewish assimilation in Poland." The lecture was very successful and drew a large audience. H.D. Nomberg, who was born in the neighboring city of Nowo-Radomsk, also appeared at *Lira* with a lecture. It was after his visit to America and his theme was: "Our brothers in America." The most important part of his lecture was: "The Jews in America distinguish themselves with their giant organizations and discipline that rules in them, with their industriousness and sobriety and with the physically developed young generation. However, even greater is their success in the general social, communal and cultural life of the country."

Z. Segalowicz, the humorist Josef Tunkl (*der Tunkler* [the dark one]) and the well-known commentator Sh. Rozenfeld also appeared.

There were also readings in *Lira* [by] Muljakowski the Zionist activist, Luria from Lodz, about the poet Sh. Rozenfeld, Zigmund Majorczyk (pioneer from the Zionist Socialists] on the theme: "the Jewish prophets." Y. Abramzon, the editor of the *Czenstochower Togblat* until the First World War, gave several lectures about Dostoyevsky. Engineer Ratner, Leon Kapinski and Josef Aronowicz also gave lectures.

During the course of time *Khazan* [cantor] Birnbaum left Czenstochow and Bensman, the famous musician, took his place.

In addition to classical musical creations, Bensman also was the pioneer of Jewish folk song. He taught several of the folk songs he created, such as *Der Fodom* [*The Thread*], to the *Lira* chorus. Under his leadership the *Lira* chorus changed entirely, becoming more folksy-Jewish.

Among the amateurs who played and the several who distinguished themselves in various performances were: Yeta Pokula, Dara Szacher, Feytl Szmuelwicz, Sh, Frank, Aronowicz, D. Krak, Wener, Pala Mauer (the very talented amateur), Avner, Miss Szapira, Sobol and Kramalowska.

The first sports group also was organized in *Lira*, to which Gonszerowicz, Bram, Krak and such belonged. The group organized a presentation in *Lira* to obtain financial means and endeavored in Piotrkow to legalize a sports union in Czenstochow. As usual, Henrik Markusfeld supported the group.

[Page 85]

The last historic undertaking of *Lira* was the visit of Sholem Aleichem. While the young mainly rejoiced with Peretz, Sholem Aleichem was adored by the entire Jewish neighborhood, by every ordinary Jew. There was no room in the large city theater hall to even stand.

A large mass of Jews gathered at the train station. A downpour began just at the time of his arrival. However, the Jews were not impressed by [the rain]. Sholem Aleichem accompanied by his wife greeted the Jews in the downpour with his customary humor: "Rain means prosperity." – he said.

The mass of Jews accompanied Sholem Aleichem to Behm's Hotel, in which he stayed.

A delegation of the young along with Avraham Wewiorka addressed him in a solemn speech, put together by Avraham Wewoirka.

Warmund, who spoke in Hebrew and for a long time, was also among those offering greetings on the stage. After this speech, Sholem Aleichem told a story of a *khazan* [cantor] who had a very beautiful voice. However, he had one defect, when he began to sing, he forgot to stop...

That same evening a banquet took place in Behm's Hotel. However, because of his stomach illness, Sholem Aleichem could not enjoy the prepared foods and also [made light of this] with a fine joke.

The First World War broke out a short time after this and a new chapter in communal life began in Czenstochow.

––––––––

Translator's footnotes

1. Mendele Moykher Sforim – Sholem Yankev Abramovich – is considered the "grandfather" of Yiddish literature.

2. Territorialism was a Jewish movement working for the creation of a Jewish territory. It sought territory suitable for settlement by Jews, not necessarily in *Eretz Yizroel*.

––––––––

Jewish Libraries

The modern movements in Jewish life and particularly in the workers' movement did not dishonor the name of the old "people of the Book." The Jewish book occupied a place of honor in every organization, in every union and in every party.

After Emanuel Bajgele and Henekh Lapides, the bookbinders and booksellers in Czenstochow, who provided reading books for the Czenstochower Jews, came the illegal libraries of the Jewish workers' parties: *S.Z.* [Socialist Zionists], Bund, *Poalei-Zion* [Workers of Zion – Marxist Zionists]. The first larger Jewish general library with literary works, but by Jewish writers and not Jewish writers in Yiddish translations, was created by the Socialist Zionists. The library was located at the house on Ogrodowa that was one of the locations for Socialist Zionists. There, the comrade from the Social Zionists, Nuta Szwarcbaum, and the Social Zionist sympathizer Berliner had an iron business. Yeshaya Lewenhof also worked there as a bookkeeper. A side room was provided in the house and large crates of books were brought from Warsaw bookstores. The books were registered in a catalogue and distributed throughout the factories, small plants and circles. The designated librarian distributed and received the books according to the requests of the readers through their representatives.

The first legal Jewish library was created by the Petersburg division of the Jewish Literary Society in Petersburg. The library took over *Lira* when the Society was legalized by the Czarist government.

The librarian was Feytl Szmulewicz. More than 2,000 Yiddish books were found in the library and more than 600 in Hebrew. Forty or fifty books were exchanged a day. Seventy-five percent of the works were Yiddish originals. Of the translations into Yiddish, those mainly read were Knut Hamsun [a Norwegian author who won the Nobel Prize for Literature in 1920], Zola, and Victor Hugo. Scientific books, such as natural science, chemistry, biology and so on, were read by 20 percent. Novels – 20 percent, dramas – 10 percent.

[Page 86]

During the time of the German occupation, when *Lira* had collapsed and the members of differing [political] directions took its possessions – the Zionist members took over the library that continued to function in the Zionist premises on Dojazd 19.

However, then the worker movements founded their own parties' tea halls and libraries. A new library was created at the Leather Workers Union with the remaining books from the earlier Socialist-Zionist general library, the first legal professional union under the German occupation. The Socialist-Zionist stood behind this union. Later, the Education Union, which took over the library and enlarged it, was legalized. The librarians were: Chaya Waga, Ester Fuks and Sh. Landau. Smaller libraries existed at *Paolei-Zion* and the Bund.

When the delegates from Czenstochower Relief in New York came to Czenstochow, they brought with them a large sum of money for books. The merger of all worker libraries into one general workers' library took place under their influence. The representatives of *Fareinikte* [United], the Bund and *Poalei-Zion* took part in the managing committee.

The general library was enriched with a great number of books collected by the members of Czenstochower Relief in New York and from the *TSYSHO* [Central Yiddish School Organization] in Warsaw. The city hall, under the influence of the representatives of the Jewish workers in the city council, designated a certain sum of money to buy Polish books for the library. The general library was open to all and everyone who desired to read made use of it.

From its start, the library was located in the house of Nursery 2, Strazacka 10. Later, it moved to the Peretz House of the *Folkshul* [People's School] on Krotka 23.

At first, the librarians were Yakov Yitzhak Czarnowecki and, then, Hershl Lipszic, who was a student in the evening courses and a great lover of the Yiddish book.

On *Shabbosim* [Sabbaths] conversations were held in the general library with readers, particularly with young readers, on themes appropriate for them.

Managing Committee of the Medem Library
Right to left: Y. Rozenfeld, L. Kaminski, Kh. Wilczinski, Kh. Lajzerowicz,
Zamel, R. Federman, A. Perec, Brener and M. Lederman

The report that is given here gives an idea of the activity of the largest and most important library in Czenstochow.

A separate library, not Jewish but only with Polish and Russian books, also existed at the Trade Workers Union. Jewish readers who did not speak or read Yiddish used this library. After a long struggle that lasted for years, the Trade Workers Union became Jewish.

Later, in 1926, the library merged with the Medem Library that was located at the Culture Office. The foundation stone for the Medem Library was laid by Jakov Rozenberg. Immediately after Medem's death, larger sums of money were designated for this purpose.[1] At the end of 1926 the Medem Library possessed over a thousand Yiddish books in addition to those in Polish. In 1927 the library was active every Tuesday, Thursday and *Shabbos* in *Aleje 22* in the premises of the Culture Office.

The registration fee for the library was one *zlote*. A [security] deposit for a book – two *zlotes*. Monthly dues – 50 *groshn*. For young people – registration fee – 50 *groshn*, monthly dues – 25 *groshn*.

[Page 87]

The Medem Library functioned in two rooms of the Trade Employees Union starting in September 1926.

The first librarian was Anja Manowicz. In 1938 the library functioned under the name *Kultura*, and was led by Rayzl Berkensztat. The library functioned illegally under her leadership during the most frightening time of the Gestapo terror during the time of the Nazi occupation of Czenstochow, until the Nazi hangmen tortured her to death. The library had a thousand readers at that time.

The general library later moved to the Second *Aleje* and functioned further under the leadership of Hershl Lipszic.

Hershl Lipszic, the leader of the library, wrote the following in a letter about the role of the library during the difficult years of fascist rule in Poland:

First, the city hall reduced the subsidy for the library from 500 *zlotes* to 200, and yet we succeeded in expanding and beautifying it externally under the most difficult conditions.

Artistic pictures, portraits of Jewish and non-Jewish writers and poets decorated the walls. We created a reading room at the library, where one could find almost all of the periodic publications in the country. From time to time we arranged talks on literary themes. Thus the library became the center, which raised the courage and strengthened the spirit of the masses at a time when apathy and depression planted deep roots.

Thus, with great sacrifice, the Jewish workers and young people held high the flag of the people of the Book until the last breaths of their lives. And Hershl Lipszic, the poorest child of the poorest Jewish masses, who in a cellar home had no more than a bare straw mattress on which to sleep, also perished among all the martyrs of Jewish Czenstochow.

*

To the libraries in Czenstochow should also be added:

The library and reading room at the Artisans' Club, which partly was founded by Henrik Markusfeld.

The library at the Artisans' School named for Adolf Bril.

The library in the gardening farm about botany.

The children at the Y.L. Peretz *Folkshul* [People's School] had their own children's library.

Sections for selling books also existed at the *Fareinikte* [United] cooperative and at the General Workers Cooperative Bund.

Translator's footnote

1. Vladimir Medem was a leader of the Bund. Many institutions in Poland, such as libraries, were named after him.

[Page 87]

Yiddish Theater in Czenstochow
by W. Gliksman, A. Chrabolowski, R. Federman

The Yiddish theater in Czenstochow shared the fate of the Yiddish theater in Russia and Poland on its road of development: it had good and bad times.

In addition to the censor from the czarist regime, which [monitored] each theater piece and gave permission to produce it or forbid performances, theater performances were dependent on the good will of the local official or Russian regional police supervisor. Often it happened that a play was advertised that was being performed with the permission of the regime, either in Warsaw or Lodz, and a different play was performed. In such cases "people" around the theater who also made a living from this assisted in such difficulties.

Our Jewish theater in our city had no greater difficulty than finding an appropriate room with a stage. The performances started in Jewish halls where weddings would take place and in the firemen's hall that was located in the poorest part of the city thickly populated by Jews. In time, however, the Jewish theater performances were moved to the halls of "Lira," "Warta" and even in the building of the Polish Municipal Theater.

Almost all Jewish theater troupes in Poland gave performances in Czenstochow. There was even more material success during the winter months.

However, it was not only the professional theater groups that had an effect on the spreading of Yiddish theater art in our city.

[Page 88]

Amateur circles existing in Czenstochow had a very great part in this. With great strength, devotion and love of Yiddish theater, they gave their successful performances for a number of years and produced several directors and talented [actors] who later took part in professional troupes.

It is worth remembering from which social classes in Jewish Czenstochow the amateur troupes were recruited. It was characteristic for that time of the rising workers movement [for] the Jewish amateur groups to be constituted in great part from the poor Jewish class in general and from the working masses in particular. While the stated purpose for the Jewish amateurs was to spread culture among the Jewish working masses, the Jewish amateurs also wanted to develop their class consciousness through the theater and raise their political and social level of achievement.

Because of the destruction of the Jewish Archive in our city during the Second World War (a greater part was given to the Vilna YIVO [*Yidisher Visnshaftlekher Institut* – Yiddish Scientific Institute]), we are not able to give an exact overview of the development of Yiddish theater in Czenstochow. Because it is worth having a general picture of Yiddish theater in our city, we will provide a chronological report put together on the basis of documents found among those from Czenstochow in America and on their memories.

Professional Acting Troupes and Their Repertoire

One of the first theater troupes that appeared in Czenstochow before the First World War was the cooperative troupe of Kurpinow with Pola Portnoy in the main roles.

The acting troupe of Moshe Zilberkasten under the leadership of Wajshof spent a long time in Czenstochow. Zilberkasten directed several performances and acted himself. One of his productions was Peretz Hirshbein's *Di Neveyle* [*The Carcass*].

On 15 September 1912 a family evening with the participation of Yosef Tunkel (*der tunkeler* – the dark one) was arranged at Lira. Zilberkasten directed Sholem Aleichem's one act play, *Mazel Tov* [*Good Luck*] with Miss Sem, Yeta Pakula, Sh. Frank, F. Szmulewicz, R. and M. Bornsztajn.

On 21 and 22 February 1913, the Jewish troupe under the direction of Madame Triling and Adolf Berman played in the *Lira* hall. The then well–know actors, Fogelnest, Kutner, Lasznowska, Gotfrid, Rozen, Gutherc and others took part. H. L. Czelaza was the director of the troupe. They performed the following three presentations: 1) *Di Eizener Froy* [*The Iron Women*]; 2) *Doktor Zeyfenbloz* [*Doctor Zeyfenbloz* (soap bubble)]; 3)) *Di Amerikanerin* [*The American Woman*]. All three performances were held with great success. On 13 March of the same year, the troupe produced Jacob Gordin's *Di Shvue* [*The Oath*].

In the middle of the days of *Sukkous* [Feast of Tabernacles] of 1913 two Jewish troupes gave performances at *Lira*. One was under the direction of Michalzon, who staged the comic operetta, *Zeyn Weyb's Man* [*His Wife's Husband*]. The second was under the direction of Hendelist with the play *Dora*, a melodrama in four acts and *Der Yidisher Kenig Lir* [*The Jewish King Lear*].

On 14 November of the same year a Jewish troupe presented a joyful four–act operetta, *Der Lustiker Foygl* [*The Cheerful Bird*] at *Lira*.

In 1919 a troupe under the direction and with the participation of the Jewish actor, [Karl] Cymbalist, and with the soubrette soprano, Eizenberg, performed in Czenstochow. Fela Fajnrich–Bira, a Czestochow amateur, took part in this troupe. They performed the plays, *Der Gosn–Zinger* [*The Street Singer*], Zalotarewski's *Der Yeshiva–Bukher* [*The Yeshiva Student*], Z. Libin's *Gebrokhen Hertser* [*Broken Hearts*], *Got Mentsch un Teyvl* [*God, Man and Devil*] and *Der Yidisher Kenig Lir* of Jacob Gordin.

During the first years of liberated Poland we see an entire series of Jewish theater troupes with the most distinguished Jewish actors at the head in Czenstochow. In 1922–23, [Ester Ruchl] Kaminska and her ensemble appeared as guests in the following three performances: *Di*

Zibn Gehangene [The Seven Who Were Hung], *Kritzer Sonata [The Kreutzer Sonata* based on the novella by Leo Tolstoy] and *Mirele Efros*.

The troupe of [Karl] Cymbalist and Regina Cuker played in Czenstochow in 1924. The actors Mikhal Klajn and Blat took part among others. The performances took place in the hall of the Warta sports club in the Second *Aleje*. It is worth mentioning that Moshe Kohn, the Czenstochow amateur who later became a professional actor and passed the exam as an actor at the Artists Union in Warsaw, took part in this troupe. In 1925 Herman's Dramatic Studio visited Czenstochow. Among the then young artistic talents we see Melnik, Pataszinski and Matl Goldblum. They performed Di Greyne Felder [The Green Fields] by Perec Hirshbein and Kwadratur fun Kreyz [Squaring the Circle by Valentin Kataev].

[Page 89]

In 1927, the troupe of Nekhama and Kadisz played in Czenstochow for a long time. Among the series of successfully performed plays and operettas, the greatest success was the play, Der Golem [The Golem], directed by Mark Arnsztajn. The presentations were even attended by the Polish population, which was a rarity in Poland.

These were the first steps toward a continuous Yiddish theater in Czenstochow. R. Federman, the councilman from the Bundist party faction in the city council, passed a resolution with the decision to subsidize the Yiddish theater with 1,000 zlotes. The sum was paid to the Jewish Artists Union in Warsaw.

A committee for Yiddish theater was created among the Jewish population in Czenstochow with the participation of Y. Rozenberg, Ahron Perec, R. Federman, Y. Sak, Z. Sztiler and others. An impressive banquet took place in connection with this. R. Federman was at the time the representative to the Yiddish Artists' Union in Poland for the professional theater troupe that performed in Czenstochow.

These two facts, moreover, explain that Jewish touring troupes began performing in the new building of the Polish State Theater on Kilinski Street. When we think that the first Yiddish productions took place in the firemen's hall, in Lira or even in the "Warta," the fact that the State Theater building was provided for Yiddish performances is a very great achievement.

[Page 90]

During 1928–29 the Vilner Trupe [Vilna Troupe] with Miriam Orleska and [Mordekhai] Mazo visited Czenstochow. They performed Kiddush ha–Shem [Sanctification of the Name] by Sholem Asch with great success. Jakov Wajslic and Josef Kamien were the guests of Czenstochow.

Among the dramatic artists who gave performances in our city as well as appearances by individual actors from the Habima [The Stage, founded in Bialystok, now the national theater of Israel] and the famous Russian artistic cabaret, Der Bloyer Foygl [The Blue Bird], it is worth mentioning Zigmund Turkow and Ida Kaminska, Jonas Turkow and Diana Blumenfeld, Klara Segalowicz, Avraham Morewski, Samberg, Aleksander Granach, Julius Adler, Benny Adler, Hersh Hordt, Viktor Henkin, Brukha Tsfira, Chana Rawina, Herc Grosbard, Ruchl Halcer, Szriftzencer and others.

A Portion of the Actor's Groups Repertoire

They all performed plays from the European and Yiddish repertoire. A short review of the programs shows the interest of the Czenstochow Jewish public: thus, was performed Hinkemann [Expressionist drama by Ernst Toller] with Julius Adler, The Gele Late [Yellow Patch] with Aleksander Granech, Yoshe Kalb with the Morris Schwartz Troupe, Herr Lampertier with Zigmund Turkow and Ida Kaminska in a series of other performances from the artistic repertoire.

It is worth remembering the Ararat, under the direction of Moshe Broderzon with the artists, Gadik, Strugacz, Dzigan, Szumacher (a Czenstochower son–in–law), Ala Lilit, Sheyna Miriam, Goldsztajn and others among the review theater and operetta troupes. The Azazel also visited Czenstochow. The operetta troupe of Herszkowicz with Leibl Winer and Malwina Wajner also guest–starred in our city. The popular M[enakhem] Kipnus and Zimrah Zeligfeld, Winogrodow, Moshe Rudinow and Rut Lewaisz were very often guests in Jewish Czenstochow.

We have little information about the series of performances in Czenstochow that took place shortly before the Nazi occupation.

Amateur Theater Groups and Their Repertoire

According to the description by Chaim–Leib Szwarc, with the Yiddish amateur troupes, "Czenstochow became a city" beginning with the children's troupe of Yakov Ber Silwer. The first play that they produced was Di Tsvey Kuni Lemel [The Two Kuni Lemels]. In 1905, the first theater group was founded from this children's group in which Yakov Ber Silwer, Dovid Zitman, Miss Rubinsztajn, Moshe Sandler, Emanuel Klajnman, Wolf Majarczik and others took part. They then presented Uriel Acosta with great success. Another amateur group with the participation of Nakhum Yankl Fridman, the lame Kopl, Gutsha Ruchl the daughter of the mute one, Hela Bida and Gutsha Montag then took part in the presentations by professional actors from Mrs. Arnsztajn's troupe that appeared in Czenstochow at that time.

A Group of the First Amateur Actors
Standing, right to left: Chaim, the son of
the mute one, D. Zitman
Seated: D. Menlewicz

At the end of 1906 an amateur theater group was organized by S.S. [Socialist Zionists] under the leadership of Comrade Benyamin in which took part: Mendl Szuchter, Meir Fajnrajch, Manya and Hendl Szaferenko, Shimkhah Kalka, Aleksander (Leibush the teacher), Alter Stadole, Laya Herszlikowicz and others. They performed *Jan and Modlen* and the *Yidn* [Jews] by Tshirikower. The performances took place in the Pariski Theater, the main location for theater performances by first class Polish and Yiddish troupes. The performance by the group was a great event in Czenstochow.

[Page 91]

A new chapter of Yiddish theater in Czenstochow began with the rise of the Yiddish Literary Society and its later merger with *Lira* [literary and music society].

The first performance of the amateur drama group at the Yiddish Literary Society took place on Sunday, 16 April 1911, in the Lira hall. Two one–act plays were performed: 1) *Der Eybike Lid* [*The Eternal Song*] by M[ark] Arnsztajn with the participation of M. Fajnrajch, Mrs. Muszinska, Miss Burkan, R. Federman, Gradan, M. Zilberberg, M. Fajnrajch, Miss Muszinska, Miss Burkan, R. Federman and 2) *Bukhirim* [*Young Men*], a comedy in one act by Yitzhak Katsenelson with the participation of: R. Federman, S. Gradan, M. Zilberberg, F. Szmulowicz. Recited the same evening were: *Gezikht* [*Countenance*], by Y. L. Peretz by Miss B. Birkan, Dranow's *Meshugener in Shpitol* [*The Crazy One in the Hospital*] – B. Dawidowicz, *Tsu di Brider* [*To the Brothers*] by Bowzewer – Yeta Pakula. *S'gayt tsu Pesakh* [*Passover Arrives*] by Y.L. Peretz – R. Federman. *Oyfn Buzim fun Yom* [*On the Bosom of the Sea*] by M. Rozenfeld – Dora Szacher. Ahron Peretz directed the performance.

The second dramatic evening of the Yiddish Literary Society took place on Tuesday, 23 May 1911 in the Municipal Theater (Parisian room). Four one–act plays by Y.L. Peretz were presented. 1) *Nokh Kvore* [*After Burial*],– with the participation of Madam Miriam Izraels, Yeta Pakula, Dora Szacher. 2) *A Frimorgn* [*A Morning*] with the participation of Mark Schweid, M. Zilberberg, Miss Y. Aronowicz, Dora Szacher, Miriam Izraels. 3) *S'brent* [*It's Burning*] with the participation of Mark Schweid, M. Zilberberg, Miss Y. Aronowicz, Dora Szacher, Miriam Izraels, R. Federman, Y. Zilberman. 4) *In Polish Oyf der Keyt* [*Chained in the Synagogue Anteroom* by Y.L. Peretz] with the participation of Mark Schweid and Miriam Izraels. The performance was directed by Mark Schweid, who spent some time in Czenstochow because of this.

Miriam Israels also was brought to Czenstochow by Lira where she produced several performances with the help of amateur directors.

On 22 November 1913, an evening of Sholem Aleichem was arranged at *Lira* at which the amateur troupe performed the well–known comedy, *Mentshn* [*People*]. Krak, Aronowicz, Mrs. Sobol, Werner, Miss Kramalowska, Pola Mauer, F. Szmulewicz, Miss Rajchner and Miss Szapira took part in this presentation. This was one of the most successful amateur productions.

Miriam Israels

Two successful amateur performances at *Lira* were arranged at the initiative of the Czenstochower Sports Union. Sholem Aleichem's *Agentn* [*Agents*] was produced for the first time with the participation of D. Krak, Werner, Sziper and Prawer. H. Fajwlowicz and Yosef Aronowicz also took part in the evening, read several monologues. On 15 October 1913, *Der Retenish and di Lezung* [*The Mystery and the Solution*] that was performed as an amateur presentation was staged for the second time, where everyone, the amateur actors, director and prompter, exceeded expectations in their roles. Pola Mauer, Werner and Krak took part in the presentation. Gutshe Bem – the soloist from Lira – also appeared with a Yiddish folksong, *Lebn Tor Men Nit* [*We Are Not Permitted to Live*] – accompanied by H. Makroyer.

On 23 March 1913, the *Lira* society arranged a Purim evening. Mark Arnshteyn's one–act play, *Der Frage Tseykn* [*The Question Mark*].

[Page 92]

The amateur troupes presented a whole series of performances up to the outbreak of the First World War.

An amateur troupe under the name "Lovers of Yiddish Theater Art" was active in Czenstochow at the time of the German occupation of 1914–1918. Taking part in the troupe were: Yakov Yitzhak Czarnowiecki, P. Szmulewicz, Sh. Frank, Gotajner, Dora Szacher, Fela

Rajcher, Cesha Federman, Rubinsztajn, Rafael Federman and Leytsha Gliklich. The director of the troupe was Hershl Gotajner. *Di Meshpoke* [*The Family*] by H.D. Nomberg and *Di Yidn* [*The Jews*] by Cherikower were among a series of plays that they performed then. The success of these presentations in Czenstochow had the result that the *Y.S.K.* [Yiddish Theater Art] had to give a series of performances in the province around Czenstochow. It excelled as the best Jewish amateur troupe in our city.

The Amateur Troupe of Y.S.K. That Presented H. D. Nomberg's *Mishpocha* [*Family*]

The Y.S.K. carried out another cultural presentation on 10 June 1916 in the *Karsa* Theater. This was a memorial dedicated to the recently deceased Sholem Aleichem with the following program:

1. *On the Fresh Grave*, recitation by Cilia Horowicz and illustrated with a living picture by artist Peretz Wilenberg.
2. Yosef Aronowicz spoke about Sholem Aleichem.
3. *Oyf Mayn Kaver* [*On My Grave*] recited by D. Szacher.
4. *Kayn Ein–Hore* [*Without an Evil Eye*] performed by Alter Rotbard.
5. *Di Gimnazie* [*The Secondary School*], read by Y. Aronowicz. Sholem Aleichem's *Mentshn* [*People*] was performed in the second part of the memorial with Y. Aronowicz, Werner, D. Szacher, Polya Mauer, Rotbard, Miss Gela Rozenberg and Fela Rajcher taking part.

The last years of war and the beginning of the new Poland brought a certain suspension of the activity of the Czenstochow amateur groups but on 4 April 1920 the dramatic section of the workers' club, *Fareinikte* [United], revived its cultural work and performed F[ishel] Bimko's play, *Di Ganovim* [*The Thieves*]. The performances took place in the *Polania* Theater with the participation of Moshe Kremski, A. Wenger. Regina Rozengeld (Kuperman), Kh. Bendet, Alek Lewensztajn. Kh. Epsztajn and Pola Kastensztajn. The main role was played by Sh. Frank.

On 22 January, F. Bimko's play, *Di Ganovim*, was performed for the second time in Czenstochow. The entire income was designated for the central council of the professional unions in Czenstochow. *Der Dorfs Yung* [*The Village Youth*] with Lewensztajn and Frank was performed the same year.

A special holiday in the Jewish neighborhood was the children's performances by the Y.L. Peretz *Folks–Shul* [people's school] and children's home. Two of these children, Rukhl Tekstiler and Genya Berkowicz, are mentioned in our report, *Dos Letste Yohr* [The Last Year]. Both of them survived the Nazi hell; the former is in Shanghai and the latter in Czenstochow.

This short summation shows how much understanding Jewish Czenstochow had for Yiddish theater, for Jewish cultural presentations, supporting in full measure its own and foreign talents.

And as the eye delights in seeing how plants and flowers grow in a cemetery, which is the strongest sign of eternity in life, let us again rejoice in hearing about a Yiddish theater in Czenstochow.

————

The Yiddish Press
by A. Khrobolowski, M. Tzeszinski & R. Rederman

The Beginning

Before *Fraynd* [*Friend*] moved to Warsaw from Petersburg and until the publication of *Haynt* [*Today*] and *Moment*, very few Czenstochow Jews read newspapers. *HaMelitz* [*The Morning Star*], *HaTzeifa* [*The Siren*] and *Fraynd* from Petersburg came to Czenstochow to a few subscribers. The two Czenstochow bookbinders and booksellers, Lapides and Bajgele, who provided the Jewish readers with storybooks on loan for a *grosn* also subscribed to the *Fraynd* and one could read their newspaper for one *kopike*. However, one had to wait on line. The line could be ten people or more. The newspaper would become worn out so that the last reader could barely read a sentence.

[Page 93]

Right, top to bottom:
Reklamenblat [*Advertiser*] [The name is spelled differently elsewhere in the original text.]
Vokhnblat [*Weekly Newspaper*]
Togblat [*Daily Newspaper*]
Arbeter–Zeitung [*Workers Newspaper*]
Der Neye Vort [*The New Word*]
Proletarier [*Proletarian*]
Undzer Shtime [*Our Voice*]

Left, top to bottom:
Ekspres Częstochowski
Di Zeit [*The Time*]
Czenstochower Veker [*Czenstochow Alarm*]
Undzer Ekspres [*Our Express*]
Czenstochower Zeitung [*Czenstochow Newspaper*]
Undzer Veg [*Our Way*]

[Translator's note: The photo is of the mastheads of the newspapers published in Czenstochow.]

[Page 94]

The first true newspaper distributors in Czenstochow were the three partners, Moshe Leib Lewensztajn, Heshke Gutfreynd and Shlomo Frankfurter. They were the representatives of Warsaw newspapers, which would usually arrive at noon. There first location for selling newspapers was in the First *Aleje*, at first near Nejfeld's apothecary stockroom, then in the tower of house number 7, where the loan and saving office was located. Masses of people would await the arrival of the newspapers every day. They also had regular customers to whom they delivered the newspaper at home.

The first publication in Czenstochow itself was the proclamations by the parties. Many of the proclamations were printed in Baczan's printing shop, for good or for bad. One of the regular printers of the proclamations was Shimkha Kalka. The Socialist-Zionist organization in Czenstochow later organized its own printing shop.

The first newspaper writer in Czenstochow was Moshe Ceszinski who would write letters with reports about Czenstochow in the Warsaw and other newspapers under the name Moshe Ce. It should be understood that the metropolitan newspapers did not give much space to the provinces. Therefore, local weeklies began to appear in various cities to serve local communal life. The *Bendin* [Bedzin] *Anonsn-Blat* [*Bendin Advertizing Newspaper*] was such a weekly where R. Federman published reports from Czenstochow. This moved the Czenstochow activists to create their own press and the *Czenstochower Reklamen-Blat* [*Czentsochow Advertisement Newspaper*] was founded.

Czenstochower Reklamen-Blat [*Czenstochower Advertiser*]

The first issue of the *Czenstochower Reklamen-Blat* was published on Friday, 6 December 1912, in B. Boczan's printing shop. Signed by B. Boczan as editor-publisher. The founders were A. Chrobolowski, Hershele Fajwlowicz, Moshe Cieszynski and Yakov Rozenberg.

The funds for the first edition of the newspaper were raised by Moshe Ce., who collected [payments] for the first 20 rubles of advertisements. This was not an easy task. He also wrote the local news. Rozenberg, who was then an employee at *Vulkan* (iron foundry), was the financier and the first editor. Hershele Fajwlowicz was the popular columnist and A_ski the feature article writer.

No particular permission to issue the newspaper was required. Permission to print periodic publications then in tsarist Russia only required the signature of the publisher. After publication several copies would be sent to the censor.

The plan to publish a weekly newspaper by a group of amateurs, without financial means was, in general, boldly utopian. However, at the most critical moment, at the publication of the first edition, B. Boczan required that all of the printed material including announcements first be translated into Russian in order to obtain the permission of the local gendarmerie, and Berl Boczan, of blessed memory, was a hard Jew to convince and to force him to relent was difficult. During the revolutionary years even the revolvers of the Socialist-Zionists could not force the publication of illegal proclamations. And the "miracle" of convincing Boczan to allow the printing without Russian translation was greater than the printing of the newspaper itself.

The first issue of *Reklamen-Blat*, price one *kopeke*, contained:

Undzer Tsil [*Our Objective*] that was formulated thus:

"To give every merchant or producer [of goods] the opportunity to make their items and goods known to the wide public and also to show the customer the place and source for where to buy everything that is needed."

Then came the promise: "To report on the activities of communal institutions as for example: Jewish community credit institutions, cultural unions and societies."

Czestochower Neyes [news], two items of news: a) "The *Malbushim Arumin* [society for providing clothes for the poor] will provide 127 pairs of boots and 62 overcoats to poor boys on

Shabbos [Sabbath]; b) "The priest Damazi Matczak was visited in his Piotrkow jail cell by his lawyer Klajn; he should sign the plea to the *Senat* about an appeal. Matczak refused to sign.

[Page 95]

A report from Kielce began on the first page and ended on the second, signed by F. B-O (Fishl Bimko, a report from Noworadomsk by RMI. On the second page, under the feature, was located "The Community's Smart Aleck," assembled by H. Fajwlowicz. On the third page – the light article by A-ski, *Chanukah* – printed in five-point type (the larger type already was being used for the local news and correspondents). There was also a small feature article by Yakov Rozenberg and finally, city news.

Then came announcements from *Uranja*, Second *Aleje* 38 and *Odeon* Second *Aleje* 43. An announcement for a great Chanukah evening in *Lira* with the artist Miriam Izraels, a Chanukah evening at the Artisans Club with a reading by Engineer Ratner about the significance of Chanukah and with the participation of Cantor Z. Rozental and, finally, "Recitations, dance and candy" and three large Chanukah presentations at *Lira* by the comedians Goldberg and Herszkowicz, prima donna Laskowski and light soprano Guczecheter.

The third issue of *Reklamen-Blat* felt as if the child was teething. The article, "The Jewish Anti-Semitism," attacked with strong language the Jews who provided employment who declined to hire Jewish workers in their factories.

A_ski dedicates the feature article in the fourth issue to "A Life's Question," emigration.

The feature article in the fifth issue was dedicated to "Physical Development Among Jews." Two notices in the local news told of the Russian regional police supervior, Denisov, who was convicted in the Piotrkow county court of belonging to the Polish Socialist Party and reported that the Warsaw *Sudebna Palate* [Court of Appeals] convicted the well-known writer Maria Glikson, daughter of the well-known Czenstochow lawyer, of belonging to the Polish Socialist Party and hiding expropriated money. She was sentenced to two years and eight months forced labor.

In the sixth issue, the first article was a call to the Jewish merchants against whom a strong boycott movement had begun after the election for the Fourth Duma, urging them to organize into a merchants' union.

Articles, one in the sixth issue, "*Khoveve Sras Eyver* [Lovers of Hebrew] in *Lira*" by L. K. (Leon Kapinski) and the second in the seventh issue, "The *Khovevim* [Lovers] in *Lira*," by a Yiddishist (A_ski), show that the Hebrew-Yiddish struggle emerged in the split in the Czenstochower press.

In the seventh issue is also found a short opinion article, "With what do Jews rejoice?" by F. Sz___cz (Faytl Szmulewicz). It turns out that these were his first published lines. The issue was published on 17 January 1913.

The *Reklamen-Blat* lasted for nine issues. On 14 February 1913, the *Czenstochower Vokhnblat*, issue 1 was published.

Czenstochower Vokhnblat [*Czenstochower Weekly Newspaper*]

Issue five of the *Czenstochower Vokhnblat* was published in a larger format and began to acquire the appearance of a newspaper. An article, *Vegn Kheder* [*About Kheder* - religious primary schools], was published in the seventh issue that demanded a new secular Jewish *folkshul* [public school]."

The 10ᵗʰ issue – *Vokhnblat – der Pesakh Numer* [the Passover issue] – was almost a "literary one." It contained a feature article by L. (Leon Kapinski), *In der Midbar* ["In the Desert"] signed: a young Jew (A. Ch.), *A Blut Bilbl* [*A Blood Libel*], monologue by a Jewish reporter dedicated to Baylis in Kiev by Ipsolin (H. Fajwlowicz) and *Pesakhdike Kinder-Zkhronus* [*Childhood Passover Memories*] dedicated to my comrade, Meir Hirsh, by Ben Yakov (Moshe Ceszinksi).

In issue 11 Ben Yakov wrote about the emigrants who go across the Czenstochow border and demand that the Jewish community workers open a division of the Petersburg Emigrant Society.

"A member" (A.Ch.) deals with the *Lines Hatsedek* [Poor House]," in a feature in the same issue; he believes that this society needs to care for the physical development of the Jewish child through the founding of a summer colony and the creation of kindergartens in the free air.

[Page 96]

In the 12th issue is found a piece of local news: "Again a Strike in the 'Matta' factory" and a notice with such contents as: "On the First of May in Czenstochow." "A day before 1 May mass arrests and searches took place in Czenstochow. The police also tore down several red flags from the telegraph wires in various parts of the city." This was in 1913.

In the feature article of issue 13, a project was proposed to build a *Folkshoyz* [people's house] in Czenstochow for all societies and unions.

In the 14th issue there was a report by Moshe Ce. about a large group of Czenstochow emigrants who left for Galveston.

Issue 17 and 18 were published under the editing of the young journalist, Y. T. Braun of Warsaw. H. Fajwlowicz again edited issue 19. The main articles were written by A_ski and local writer, Moshe Ce.

Elections of *Dozors* [members of the community synagogue councils] took place in September 1923 in the Jewish community. The *Czenstochower Vokhnblat* carried on a widespread [information campaign] so that the taxpayers would take part in the election and choose *Dozors* who would represent all strata of the Jewish population and not only the "Germans" (the assimilated). A series of communal letters [was published] about the task of the official Jewish community; of the 1,200 taxpayers who had the right to vote in the election only 40 people had taken part. The majority of the votes were received by Dr. Zaks, Ludwig Tempel and Henrik Markusfeld.

Because of a quarrel with the publisher, B. Boczan, the 36th issue was published with Yizroel Placker as the editor. However, the quarrel was resolved quickly and the newspaper was again published with its usual co-workers.

The [Menakhem Mendel] Beilis trial started in Kiev and moved the Jewish press away from other problems. Several issues of the *Vokhnblat* were dedicated to [the issue of] blood libel that was directed against the entire Jewish people. The *Aleje* 6 was flooded with Jews when the sentence of the judges became known. The extra publication was torn from the hands [of those selling it].

Undzer Zeitung [*Our Newspaper*]

In October 1913 a second weekly newspaper began to publish under the name *Czenstochower Zeitung*. The newspaper was published at the printing shop of Lutek Cymerman. The editors were Kronenberg and Lewicz.

During the same year, 1913, two social reforms took place in Russia. One was the workers' sick fund. The second was a law that permitted the founding of professional unions in a limited form. The *Czenstochower Vokhnblat* provided a great deal of space to these questions, particularly the professional unions that were founded during the same period.

In the last issue of *Vokhnblat* (number 46 of 26 December 1913) a report is found that was printed in small type but had a great significance. We learn that the artisans' club organized a solemn meeting in honor of Mr. Henrik Markusfeld in connection with one year of the existence of the loan and saving fund at the club. At the meeting, A. Rotszild, a worker, touched on the question that Jewish workers were not allowed into the factories owned by the Jewish communal workers and philanthropists and those who had been working there earlier were being pushed out little by little. Mr. Markus Win, director of the *kapeluszarnia* [hat factory] where around 140 Jewish girls worked, said that the Jewish Sabbath prevents the Jewish worker from coming to the factory. A great discussion developed. However, there were no great results brought forward. And the *Czenstochower Togblat* that began to publish at the beginning of 1914 again brought up the question several times.

Czenstochower Togblat [Czenstochower Daily Newspaper]

From the beginning the *Czenstochower Togblat* was published by the partnership of B. Boczan and Yakov Rozenberg. However, when the sum of 300 hundred rubles that Rozenberg had invested in it ran out, the result was that B. Boczan himself took over the newspaper.

Y. Abramson was brought from Lodz, where he had worked at a penny newspaper, as the editor of the *Czenstochower Togblat*. He was a good Yiddish writer and had a philosophical head. He belonged to the then penitents who were disappointed by the reactionary years.

[Page 97]

The *Czenstochower Togblat* dealt with the same problems and questions in its features as the *Vokhnblat*. The newspaper came out for reform of the *kheder* [religious primary school] and for creating a Jewish *folks-shul* [public school] and often criticized the attitude toward Yiddish in the communal institutions that mainly were led by the so-called assimilated. The newspaper gave a large place to the election of the *dozors* [members of the synagogue councils] that took place in the summer of 1913. In order to awaken an interest in voting among the Jewish public, the payers of the taxes, articles were published with interviews with Rabbi, Reb Nakhum Asz, Engineer F. Ratner, Herman Szaja, Josef Imich, A. Warszawski, the Wolier Rabbi Iszaiewicz, Leon Kapinski and the lawyer Y. Grinbaum from Warszaw. The conclusion was that the community also needed to be represented by a representative of the orthodox. The candidate was Shmuel Goldsztajn. The candidacy of Engineer Ratner also was made known. The assimilated remained the leaders of the organized community.

Working with Abramzon at the *Togblat* was H. Fajwlowicz, who worked as a proofreader and as a writer of popular columns about city life and about the *shtetlekh* [towns] around Czenstochow. A-ski, who did not agree with Abramzon's tendency to the right, from time to time published articles, mainly about workers' lives.

From time to time R. Federman also published articles about the fight for Yiddish.

The *Czenstochower Togblat* also often published short and longer literary stories from A. Epelbaum and Jack London among others.

With the outbreak of the First World War, the newspaper ceased [to publish]. However, under the German occupation it again published in combination with Lazar Kohn's *Folkszeitung* [*People's Newspaper*] from Lodz. Y. Abramzon, an enemy of the Germans, left Czenstochow at the beginning of the [First] World War. The newspaper, actually the local news, published in Boczan's printing shop, was run by H. Fajwlowicz with the participation of Mendl Asz.

The *Czenstochower Togblat* was again published independently at the end of the war until it ceased entirely in 1919.

Dos Neye Vort [The New Word]

In April 1920, *Dos Neye Vort*, a weekly put out by the communal organization *Fareinikte* [united], dedicated to the worker and communal life in Czenstochow, began to publish. R. Federman was the official editor. A. Chrabalowski led the newspaper and he almost entirely filled it.

Right after the outbreak of the Soviet-Polish War, almost all of the newspapers in Poland that were published by the Bund and *Poalei-Zion* [Workers of Zion – Marxist Zionists] were closed. The majority of labor activists were arrested, among them a large number of Bundist activists from Czenstochow headed by Yosef Aronowicz. *Dos Neye Vort*, which remained almost the only Yiddish workers' newspaper in Poland, recorded the names of the closed newspapers and the arrested communal workers. This news alone would take up several columns.

As compared to other previous Czenstochow Yiddish newspapers, *Dos Neye Vort* gave its main attention, as can be seen in its editorials, to actual political problems. However, Czenstochow communal life also had a large place in the newspaper.

The condition of Jewish life in Czenstochow had changed a great deal during the era of the [First World] War. The assimilated [Jews] were pushed out little by little from the communal positions. A Zionist-Orthodox majority reigned in the Jewish *gmina* [administrative district]. Assimilated Zionists and the Orthodox now were united in one bloc during the various elections and the poor masses stood against them and the organized Jewish workers. *Dos Neye Vort* defended the interests of the poor Jewish population and of the working class. And although the paper was published by a party organization, it avoided narrow partisanship and would therefore be read by workers from all movements and by a large number of the independent young people.

Dos Neye Vort was the party organ of the central committee of *Fareinikte* in Warsaw from 15 October 1920 to 25 February 1921. The editor was M. Mendelsberg of Warsaw. The last two sides [pages] would be dedicated to local life. The number of readers in Czenstochow fell significantly during this time.

[Page 98]

At the end of 1921 the paper again began to publish as a local newspaper. The newspaper became leftist compared to other non-communist worker newspapers in Poland in view of the increased [anti-Jewish] reaction in Poland – *Dos Neye Vort* stood out with its pro-Soviet articles and, therefore, maintained its independence.

Dos Neye Vort paid a great deal of attention to the cultural development of the working masses, particularly of the young workers. At that time a widespread network of worker educational institutions already existed such as worker nurseries, the Y.L. Peretz public school, evening courses for young workers, sports organization and an entire series of young worker institutions. All of this had already been presented in the *Czenstochower Vokhnblat* in 1913.

At the same time, Yiddish also received full civil rights as a language in a series of communal and civic institutions, such as, for example, with the *handlowces* [trademen], in the credit institutions, in retailers' union and so on. This also was in great measure a result of the struggle led by the local Yiddish press.

Thanks to the articles and reports about the local Jewish school system, *Dos Neye Vort* connected Czenstochow with all of its friends in America who supported the local institutions.

The well-known pedagogue, Yisroel Rubin, now in *Eretz-Yisroel*, wrote articles for *Neye Vort* from time to time. Poems by Avraham Zak of Warsaw also would often be published.

At the end of 1922, when R. Federman moved to the Bund, A. Chrabalowski, the actual editor, appeared officially as the editor. A lawsuit was brought against him [A. Chrabalowski] for an article, "The Quiet Murder," against the Polish government closing the schools run in Warsaw and the provinces by the Bundist society, *Undzer Kind* [Our Child]. He then immediately left for America and the editorial board was taken over by Sh. Frank.

Of the articles reprinted from other newspapers, [Moissaye Joseph] Olgin's letters from the Soviet Union printed in the New York *Freiheit* [*Freedom*] occupied the most important place.

Undzer Shtime [*Our Voice*]

In 1928, several issues of *Undzer Shtime*, the central organ of the Jewish section of the "Independent Party" were published in Czenstochow under the editorship of A. Chrabalowski. This was the name of the previous *Fareinikte* that was now united with Boleslaw Drobner's socialist leftist group.

The main articles in *Undzer Shtime* were written by Dr. Josef Kruk. Sh. [Shloyme] Bastomski, the editor of *Grininke Beymelekh* [*Little Green Trees*] in Vilna, published articles here about cultural issues.

Czenstochower Zeitung [Czenstochow Newspaper]

At the same time, Boczan's printing shop again began to publish a periodical under the name *Czenstochower Zeitung*. Yisroel Placker was the editor for a long time. Its [political] orientation was Zionist-Orthodox. Later, the editorship of the newspaper changed often. Sh. Frank worked at the *Czenstochower Zeitung* for a long time, publishing articles about communal life and feature articles. Moshe Leib Lewensztajn, under the name *Levyosn* [Leviathan], wrote weekly reports under the title, "What was heard, what happened." M. Kaufman, a typesetter in Boczan's printing shop, often published topical articles. A. H. Sziper also excelled with his articles.

Neye Zeitung [New Newspaper]

A weekly under the name *Neye Zeitung* was published for a long time in Czenstochow under the editorship of Y. Wajzberg.

Czentochower Ekspres [*Czenstochower Express*] began to publish in 1938, again in collaboration with Lazar Kohan's *Warszawer Ekspres*. News about Czenstochow was printed on the last page.

Undzer Veg [Our Way]

At the same time, the Zionists began to publish their own weekly under the name *Undzer Veg*, under the editorship of M. Tauszkewicz. A. H. Sziper, Dr. A. Bram, C. Rozenwajn, Y. Turner, Y. Klajner and others worked with him.

The Bundist Press
Arbeter Zeitung [Workers Newspaper]

[Page 99]

In 1923 the Bundist organization in Czenstochow began to publish its own weekly organ that announced as its purpose to serve Czenstochow, Zagłębie Dąbrowskie, (Będzin, Sosnowiec and Zawiercie) and the surrounding area. The Bundist weekly newspaper was published with certain breaks until the Second World War under the names *Arbeter Zeitung* and *Czenstochower Veker* [*Czenstochower Alarm*]. It published unceasingly in the printing shops of: B. Boczan, *Aleje* 6, cooperative printing shop, Kultura, A. Helfgot, *Aleje* 23 and M. Rozensztajn in Piotrkow Trybunalski. The first issue of *Arbeter Zeitung* was published on 20 February 1923. The *Arbeter Zeitung* was edited by Rafael Federman (now in America), with the close cooperation of Roza Kantor-Lichtnsztajn (now in America) and Yokheved Zuzman (perished in the Warsaw ghetto), teachers at the Jewish secular school.

Its most important co-workers were:

Yitzhak Pesakhzon (an old acquaintance), a pioneer in the socialist movement in Poland who recently had lived in Będzin and was murdered by the Nazi beasts during the Hilter rule in Będzin in 1943.

His last words to a thousand Jews who were led out of Będzin to the gas chambers were: "Know Jews that there are only a few hours left for you to live. Death awaits you soon. You have nothing to lose. The only thing left for you – resist. Do not let them lead you to the slaughter!"

The 70-year old Pesakhzon, from whose words would usually come wisdom through humor and whose words were loaded with sorrow and steel determination, spoke for seven minutes. The Nazis finally realized what he was saying to the Jews and a Nazi-bullet ended his life.

Yitzhak Samsonowicz and other Bundists stood at the head of the Jewish ghetto during the Hitler years and simultaneously were active in the underground movement. However, when he and others were arrested by the Gestapo, he was successful in saving himself. He was then active for a long time in Warsaw as a member of the central committee of the underground Bund in Poland.

Engineer Kh. Wilczinski and Dr. Emanuel Ringelblum and the lawyer Y. Wilczinski were active in the underground work in the concentration camps in Czenstochow. At the last minute before the liberation he [Kh. Wiczinski] was dragged away to Germany and he perished there.

Lawyer Zigmund Epsztajn (now in America), Yosef Rubinsztajn, Shmuel Frank, Moshe Lederman and other local workers from various trades and workshops.

It is worth remembering that almost all of the above-mentioned co-workers were considered the editors. At first they were dilettantes who took their first steps in journalism at this weekly. However, several of them immediately showed journalistic abilities and in time took part in various Yiddish newspapers in Poland.

Rafael Federman, who wrote under the name "Amicus," mainly handled political, communal and professional questions. He wrote, among others, a longer serial article under the name "The decline of an idea," about the liquidation of the *Fareinikte* party. After 1926, he came out publicly against the Pilsudski government, criticized the ostensible opposition of the Socialist Zionists to the government, spoke about the city economy, *kehile* [organized Jewish community] matters, school questions, the professional movement and issued demands to give amnesty to political arrestees, abolish night work for the bakers and so on. Yitzhak Pesakhzon specialized in themes of socialism and the Bund.

Yitzhak Samsonowicz wrote about various general political, communal and cultural themes.

Engineer Kh. Wilczinski wrote studies on literary themes, such as: about Romain Rolland for his 60th birthday, about Morris Winchevsky for his 70th birthday and others.

Lawyer Zigmund Epsztajn wrote under the name "Arenen" and discussed ideas about socialist problems and socialist economics.

Yosef Rubinsztajn, writing under the name *Mogen Dovid* [Shield of David], and Shmuel Frank wrote columns. Sh. Frank also wrote about the earlier struggles of the Jewish workers movement with rascals such as Moshe Foce and Yitzhak Szlize.

Moshe Lederman – about professional unions.

The *Arbeter Zeitung* also from time to time published articles by the comrades Yosef [Lestschinksy] Chmurner, B. Szefner, Yitzhak Lichtensztajn of Lodz, Arye Naumark. Of the reprinted articles, it is worthwhile to mention a longer article from the *Forverts* [*Forward*] by Sholem Asch about the Bund.

[Page 100]

The *Arbeter Zeitung* ceased to exist after the editors Rafael Federman, Yitzhak Samsonowicz and Wilczinski left Czenstochow.

In 1938 the Bundist organ was revived. Dovid Klin, who came to Czenstochow then, began to publish a weekly newspaper under the name *Czenstochower Veker* [*Czenstochower Alarm*]. He filled the newspaper almost completely with his own articles, in addition to reprinting articles from the extensive Bundist press in Poland. However, Dovid Klin left Czenstochow that same year and moved to Warsaw and the newspaper ceased to be published. During the Hitler rule

Dovid Klin was connected with the underground movement in general and with the Bund in particular. He now occupies an office in the current Polish government. In addition to this, he is a major in the Polish Army. The *Czenstochower Veker* was printed in the printing shop of S. Ofman, *Aleje* 8 and also in the printing shop of M. Rozensztajn and for a time was [a supplement] of the newspaper *Piotrokower Veker* [*Piotrkow Alarm*], which was edited by Yitzhak Samsonowicz. The *Arbeter Zeitung* also was a [supplement] newspaper of the *Piotrokower Veker* for a time when Yitzhak Samsonowicz worked as the secretary of the Presidium of the Piotrkow city hall.

Der Proletarier [*The Proletariat*]

In 1925, after the unification of the proletariat movement in Czenstochow, when the Jewish professional unions organized at the Jewish cultural office were recognized as a national section of the local *rada* [council or committee], an attempt was made to publish a weekly newspaper as an organ of the "Council of the Professional Class Unions" (Jewish cultural office). Only two issues were published. The first – on 4 September 1925 and the second – on 29 September 1926. This publication was printed in the cooperative printing shop *Kultur*, later at A. Helfman in Czenstochow, *Aleje* 23.

This publication was edited by Rafael Federman.

Here is the content of the two issues:

The Jewish worker demands only new elections for the city council (declaration of the Bund faction on the city council); Will we allow the destruction of the Jewish worker schools? – by Y. Samson (Samsonowicz); Should a new *Folks-hoys* [people's house] be built? – by Rafael Federman; Dr Boris Yafa (at his death) – by Rafael; About the local sick fund – by a councilman; About the Jewish cultural office; What is happening in the professional unions?; From the book table – civic and worker sports – by H. Wilczinski, publisher of *Kultur*, Czenstochow 1925; to freedom? – Amicus; A commandment from the time (about the founding schools for adults) – by a worker (Wilczinski); Raise the flag of the professional movement – by Rafael Federman; Who demands an accounting? – by a resident; The work of the aid campaign (statement from the Jewish cultural office in Czenstochow); Public declaration from the professional unions; Beating *Hoshanos* [willows – used during a ritual on *Sukkous* – the Feast of Tabernacles] – feature article by *Heimish* [homey, familiar] (Yosef Rubinsztajn); treasury report from the executive of the Jewish cultural office in Czenstochow.

The Polish and Polish-Yiddish Press

Two Polish daily newspapers were published in Czenstochow: *Goniec Częstochowski* [*Czenstochower Messenger*] and *Gazeta Częstochowska* [*Czenstochower Gazette*]. The editor of *Gazeta*, Adam Peczerkowski, a son of the lawyer, was mentioned in connection with the first pogrom in Czenstochow in 1902 and was the main agitator in the second pogrom in 1923.

Both newspapers were anti-Semitic and yet they were supported by Jewish advertisements and Jewish leaders.

The *Goniec* published a special attack when the news became public that a daily newspaper in Yiddish was beginning to be published in Czenstochow. This frightened the Polish readers that the new *jargonowkes* [those who spoke *jargon* – a negative description of Yiddish] would defend the interests of the Jewish merchants and large industrialists, although the latter only employed Christian workers and their relationship to Yiddish was not any better, but not worse than *Goniec*.

In addition to the constant struggle against Jewish commerce with the slogan, *swoj do swego* [to his own] and their constant agitation – the two Polish newspapers published notices and articles against the performance of Yiddish theater in Czenstochow and in general wrote with hate about every Jewish cultural activity.

In order to counter the poisonous anti-Semitic propaganda of *Goniec*, the Jewish manufacturer, Zigmund Markowicz, co-owner of the Gnashiner factories, undertook an initiative in 1924 to publish a new Polish daily in Czenstochow at his own expense. This newspaper, under the name *Głos Powszechny*. [*Our Universal Voice*], was published for about 10 months, from October 1924 to August 1925, under the editorship of Aleksander Haftka and with the cooperation of the popular columnist Marczin Laski and news writer Yakov Bem. After Markowicz refused to subsidize the newspaper because of large deficits, it was taken over by Sziemjaticki and published under the new name *Ekspres Częstochowski* [*Czenstochower Express*].

———

[Page 101]

Jewish Sports Movement

by W. Gliksman, A. Chrabolowski & R. Federman

The Jewish Sports and Touring Union

The sports movement also arose in Czenstochow as in all of Poland as a result of the upswing in Jewish communal life, which began at the end of the 19ᵗʰ century and found an expression in a Zionist and socialist orientation.

In 1913 under tsarist rule, *Lira* [literary and musical society] formed a group with the purpose of founding a sports union. Belonging to the group, among others, were: Avner, A. Gonszerowicz, M. Brum, A. Chabalowski, D. Krak. A performance was arranged in the *Lira* hall on behalf of the group. A request for permission, signed by Henrik Markusfeld, was given to the Piotrkow governor. Moshe Fajnkind of Piotrkow, who had entry to the powers that be, was the lobbyist, but no permission was received.

However, the idea of the sports movement penetrated even deeper among the Czenstochow young people. In 1915 a group of sportsmen, among whom was the initiator of the sports group at *Lira*, agreed with the managing committee of the Artisans' Club about creating a sports section at the club's premises at Orgodowe Street 22 where there was an inexpensive kitchen.

The first founding meeting had to be postponed for another time because the young people who attended demanded that the deliberations be held in Yiddish.

W. Gostinski, Z. Szlezinger, L. Goldszajder, Engineer M. Milsztajn, Sh. Krauskop, M. Jeszaiewicz, M. Brum, A. Gonszorowicz [spelled Gonszerowicz above], Kh. Kremski, Y. Rozencwajg, H. Lajzerowicz, Sh. Halter, M. Sztajnic belonged to the first managing committee of the Sport and Touring Union. Henrik Markusfeld was elected as the honorary chairman.

The Union became very popular among the young and the number of members immediately reached 500.

The Union joined the Central Federation of Jewish Sports and Touring Unions in Lodz. At the end of 1916 two delegates, Yosef Aronowicz and Maks Brum, represented Czenstochow at the founding conference of the Union in Lodz.

The first appearance of the Sports and Touring Union took place on *Lag B'Omer* [holiday celebrated on the 18ᵗʰ day of Iyar – falling in April, May or June with picnics, outings and bonfires]. Since then the sportsmen have marched through the Czenstochow streets with their flags and orchestra every *Lag B'Omer*. The Jewish population of Czenstochow applauded every appearance of the sportsmen with enthusiasm.

Members of the Sports and Touring Club with the Managing Committee

[Page 102]

On 12 August 1917 a competition between the sports clubs of Czenstochow, Tomaszow, Bedzin, and Sosnowiec took place in Czenstochow. M. Krakowiak received first prize for gymnastics.

H. Halthausn led the sport exercises until the end of 1918. Later Y. Krakowiak, who graduated from an instructor's course at the Central Union in Lodz, was the gymnastics instructor.

In 1916–1917 a dramatic section and a reading foom with the daily newspapers and many periodical sports publications was in existence at the Sports and Touring Union.

The question of whether the management should be carried out in Yiddish or in Hebrew was the sharpest point of conflict in the Union. The majority of the Czenstochower Sports and Touring Union was for Yiddish and therefore the Union refrained from joining the Lodz Central Union for a time.

The activity of the Union was paralyzed during the years 1919-1920 because of the Polish-Soviet War and the requisition of its premises by the Polish regime.

In 1921 the activity was revived. A new managing committee was elected with A. Peretz at its head.

In 1925 the Union decided to join the Bilic *Makabi*[1] Union. The left-Yiddishist members voted against this decision.

From the middle of 1922 to May 1925 the chairman of the Union was Dr. Hipolit Gajsler; from May 1925 until August 1926 – Chaim Dawidowicz.

In 1925 the Union celebrated its 10th anniversary. Delegates from Warsaw, Sosnowiec, Bendin, Zawiercie, Wielun, Bilic, Katowice, Tomaszow and Dziedzice came to the celebration. A parade through the Czenstochow streets took place, a tournament and race for the guests.

The Union also distributed an anniversary publication, edited by Mendel Asz, about the history of sports in Czenstochow.

During the year of the anniversary, the managing committee of the Czenstochow Sports Union consisted of Chaim Dawidowicz, chairman; Sh. Chajutin, vice chairman; A. Peretz, H. Lajzerowicz, H. Tajchner; B. Kurland, L. Kriger, C. Lichensztajn, F. Kirszenblat; M. Kremski, Y. Rozencwajg, M. Sztajnic. The chairman of the anniversary committee was Sh. Czajutin; chairman of the finance committee was Osiasz Win.

A soccer section was in existence at the Union. In 1923 the union opened its own sports area for gymnastic exercises and light athletics.

In 1924 the unification with the "Sport" club took place. The union was connected to the schools and *gymnazies* [secondary schools] with the purpose of drawing the young into the sports movement. At the same time, a musical orchestra was created at the Union and a great national gathering was organized with the participation of Sholem Asch.

In 1928 the Union joined the group, *Yardena* [Jordan], and a division was opened in Krzepic. During the same year a cycling contest was arranged and three representatives of the Union, Sh. Chajutin, L. Wajs and H. Szaja took part in the Krakow conference that created a Jewish council for physical education.

In January 1929 one of the most active workers at the Union, Sh (Shmaryhu) Chajutin, who had occupied the office of chairman from 1926 on, died. His death weakened the activities of the Union for a time.

The Cyclist Group of the Sports and Touring Union

The office of chairman was occupied by the lawyer, Leib Asz, in August 1928. Under his direction the Union again developed widespread activities.

In 1933 the unification of the Warta Sports Club and the Askola Club took place under the name Sport Touring Union *Makabi*. The managing committee, that led the unification consisted of Leib Asz, the lawyer – chairman, Sh. Nemirowski, Dr. D. Kohan, Dr. B. Epsztajn – vice chairmen, engineer S. Kisin, Miss H. Trajman – secretary, A. Szarand – sports director, L. Wajs – manager, R. Bril, M. Horowicz, Y. Fajga and N. Tajchner.

[Page 103]

Askola Sports Club

The Askola Sports Club was founded in 1922 by a group of young people with the name *Hatzvi* [*The Deer*]. C. Fajner, the Trembocki brothers, the Berkowicz brothers, the Miska brothers. H. Koplowicz and M. Tauziewicz were the leaders of the club.

In 1925 the club at first had the name *Makabi*, but according to a directive of the Polish Football [soccer] Union, two sports unions could not have the same name in one county – the name was changed to Askala.

In 1928 a bicycle division was organized by the energetic chairman of the Sports Club, L. Herc, which took part in the race for the championship in Czenstochow in 1930.

At the same time, a dramatic division was created at the club under the leadership of S. Frank and L. Orbach, who carried out the performances.

Askola, which had belonged to the *Makabi* Union since 1931, first proposed the idea of unifying all three sports clubs into *Makabi*.

Jewish Tour and Sports Union – *Makabi*

The negotiations between the two sport clubs and a tour union – Warta – lasted a long time until they united in *Makabi*. The S.T.U. had a folksy, national character from the beginning – Warta was ruled over the years by the assimilated segment [of the population].

The chairman of the Union was Yakov Rozenberg, the chairman of the *kehile* [organized Jewish community]. The vice-chairmen – Dr. L. Goldman and the lawyer, Leib Asz.

In August 1933 the *HaKoyekh* [The Strength] Sports Club, with 23 members, joined *Makabi* Sports Club. The members of the *HaKoyekh* managing committee were: H. Zajdman and W. Owietczko.

The following sections were active at *Makabi*:

Light athletics and boxing, under the leadership of A. Szmarard.

Gymnastics – under the leadership of H. Szaja and Y. Rabinowicz.

Football (soccer) – under the leadership of Ferens and, later, M. Rozencwajg.

Games of sports – under the leadership of G. Epsztajn and later Y. Fajga.

Ping Pong – under the leadership of A. Horowicz.

The most active were the football and gymnastic sections.

Makabi took part in the work in the work of the sports colony, *Kfar Makabi*, in *Eretz-Yisroel*.

In 1934 a ski division was created at *Makabi*.

Binder and Szajn of Czenstochow took part in the boxing exhibition of Polish *Makabi* at the second *Makabi* games in Tel Aviv.

L. Wajz, R. Bril and H. Birnholc – sports workers, Y. Binder, Y. Zilberberg and L. Przyrowski - boxers, Miss E. Sztajer, H. Trajman and H. Goldsztajn – sports games, - A. Kaplan and H. Blausztajn – body exercises, graduated from sports course instructions and various sports camps.

Medical supervision of the athletes was carried out by the doctors, L. Goldman, B. Tenenbaum, D. Kagan, B. Epsztajn and S. Nowak.

Makabi organized a *Makabi* academy in 1934 with the participation of the vice chairman of the *Makabi* Union M. Dikes, a literary evening with Moshe Braderzon and several concert evenings.

In 1935 *Makabi* celebrated the 20ᵗʰ anniversary of Jewish sports in Czenstochow and published an anniversary publication under the editorship of the lawyer, Leib Asz, with pictures of the manager, sports activists and members.

Translator's footnote

1. *Makabi* is a Zionist sports organization that organizes sports competitions for Jewish athletes similar to the Olympics.

The New Synagogue
by A. Koifman

In 1834, 5594, the young Czenstochower *kehile* [organized Jewish community] had only one small synagogue and a small house of prayer in which they prayed during the winter because it was too cold in the synagogue. The population increased over time and the community needed a bigger house of prayer.

[Page 104]

At the initiative of the head of the *kehile* [organized Jewish community], Leibele Kohn, a meeting was called on *Rosh Khodesh* [start of the new month] Adar 5594 in the home of the then *dozor* [member of the synagogue council] Gershon Landau ("the large Gershon") at which it was decided to erect a large synagogue with a women's section. A committee was elected to satisfy the plan consisting of the following people: Gershon Segal Landau (the same Gershon), Yitzhak Leib Bermanski, Yehuda Leib Tenenbaum, Ayzik Shimeon Ginsberg and Meir Majzel.

The same day a call was made through the religious court, which consisted of the judges, Reb Moshe Majzel (Durnfater Rabbi), Reb Nusan Oderberg and Reb Yakov Eli Rozen that all Jews should gather on the 7ᵗʰ of Adar [18 March] in the synagogue for a meeting about the building of new syngagoue.

The second *Shamas* [sexton] Lipman Pukacz, as was the custom at that time, went through the city with a synagogue hammer banging on all of the Jewish doors and windows telling them to [answer the call to] come to the religious court.

The meeting on the designated evening was very impressive; all of the Czenstochow Jews gathered. The religious judges as well as the then well-known rich man and scholar Rabbi Yona Landau (Czenstochower Rabbi) gave warm speeches and all of the Jews were asked to donate for the purpose according to their ability.

The sermons made a strong impression on those gathered. A large number of Jews enrolled as members of the house of prayer and many donations flowed in. The necessary sum was collected over a short time and the house of prayer was built. It existed until the Nazis destroyed it.

Rabbi Moshe Halter, of blessed memory, giving a eulogy at the grave of Rabbi Nukhem Asz, may the memory of a righteous man be blessed

The Meeting to Rebuild the House of Prayer 100 Years Later

A meeting was called at the initiative of Rabbi Reb Nukhush Asz on the 100-year anniversary of the building of the house of prayer in Czenstochow. A gathering was called on Thursday, 25 Adar 5694 [12 March 1934] at which it was decided to rebuild and enlarge the house of prayer.

The Czenstochower Rabbi, Rabbi and Sage Reb Nukhem Asz, may the memory of a righteous man be blessed

The committee that was created for this purpose consisted of:

The Rabbi, the head of the community, may he live a long life.

Honorary chairman – Leib Sojka. Treasurer – Yosef Wajnrib.

Building Commission

Chairman: Henrik Szpalten.

Members: Mendl Kapinski, Yosef Wajnrib, Yitzhak Ber Rotbard, Yosef Krojze, Ahron Berkman.

Publicity Commission:

Shimkha Jubas, Henrik Szpalten, Avraham Gliksman, Yosef Badasz community spokesman, Moshe Asz.

It was decided at the same gathering to turn to the Czenstochower *kehile* [organized Jewish community] about a commission to enlarge the house of prayer, build a second story for a women's section and to build a new hall for study.

It was decided to write a *sefer-Torah* [Torah scroll] with the name *Hatorah Vahamidrash* [*The Torah and the Commentary*] in order to memorialize the hundredth anniversary of the old house of study in which all Czenstochower Jews would have a share.

Two *pinkasim* [register books] were created: one to record the names of those who bought letters in the new Torah scroll; the second with the names of the contributors to the remodeling of the house of prayer.

(Extract from the booklet: Beis-haMedrash 5594-5694 [House of Prayer 1834-1934], published by Avraham Gliksman, Czenstochow, 1934.

[Page 105]

Communal Institutions
Dobroczynnosc

by Dr. Kon-Kolin, F. Szmulewicz

The *Dobroczynność* [charity] in Czenstochow, along with its diversified divisions, celebrated its 25ᵗʰ anniversary in 1926.

The activity of *Dobroczynność* spread into the following areas:

1) Urgent care, 2) hospital, 3) old age and orphan's homes, 4) children's home, 5) supervision of poor pregnant women.

A Group of Women from the Old Age Home

A Group of Jewish Men from the Old Age Home

Jewish Men in the Old Age Home Studying

Children in the Orphans' House with Mrs. P. Sztarke

The founder of the society was Henrik Markusfeld, who also was the chairman of the society throughout his life. After his death in 1920 the office of chairman was taken over by Dr. Edward Kohn. After the death of Dr. Kohn in 1934, the chairmanship went to Dr. Ludwig Batawja.

Under the leadership of Henrik Markusfeld, the mission of providing urgent aid took the form of giving interest-free loans to the needy. During the First World War the activity of the institution was weakened because of inflation and other difficulties and then ceased completely. After the war the division was reorganized under the chairmanship of Advocate Mieczysław Koniarski and, with the assistance of the Joint [Distribution Committee], it carried on widespread aid activity.

[Page 106]

The Jewish hospital was built over many years. The celebratory opening of the hospital took place Tuesday 9 November 1913. The trustees were: from 1913 to 1914 Dr. Jozef Markusfeld, from 1914 to 1918 – Gustav Kohn, from 1918 – Shmuel Goldsztajn.

Children from the Orphans' Home Eating

The Jewish hospital possessed the most modern facilities and divisions for all areas of medicine. Henrik Szpalte directed the construction of the mechanized laundry to which he dedicated a great deal of energy. The first director of the hospital was Dr. Ludwig Batavia who died in 1939. From then on the hospital was directed by Dr. Stefan Kohn-Kolin.

To have an understanding of the activity of the hospital, it is worth mentioning that treatment was given to approximately 2,500 [people] a year just in surgery and gynecology. The yearly volume of business in the last years reached around 250,000 *zlotes*.

Alas, the hospital did not support itself although a large mass of the Czenstochow population, which always generously supported necessary institutions, showed its support with donations. The Czenstochower *landsleit* [people from the same town] in New York supported the hospital through their Czenstochow Aid Union and later through Czenstochow Relief.

Children in the Orphans' House at Practical Work

A Group of Children from the Day Care Center

Children Playing at the Day Care Center

The old age home and the orphans home arose through the efforts of the Werde family in memory of their now deceased only daughter Mina Werde. The Werde family dedicated itself completely to these institutions to which they gave their entire wealth. The institutions had room for 30 old men and old women and 80-90 orphans. Workshops were created there where the children over 16 learned practical work. The leader of the institution was Mrs. Josefa Sztarke.

[Page 107]

Mrs. Izidorowa Wiezszbicka managed the *Dobroczynność* day care center that taught and nourished a large number of the poorest children in the city.

The supervision of the poor pregnant women was in the hands of Mrs. Sarna.

Comments of the editor:

Because of the importance of the institution, we provide a longer report on the history of the Jewish hospital in Czenstochow and on the people who were active in its creation and giving it support.

The Jewish Hospital

On 27 March 1899, when the local society, *Dobroczynność* [charity], was founded, the question of building a Jewish hospital immediately came up at the first general meeting. Elected to the committee were: Henrik Markusfeld, Herman Ginzberg, Dr. Edvard Kohn, Dr. Batawia, as well as the now deceased, Leopold Kohn, Dr. H. Szpigel and Leopold Werda. Henrik Markusfeld was elected as chairman of the committee.

On 5 December 1900 the above-mentioned committee bought Grabowski's lot, which was located on the road to the Jewish cemetery, for 7,600 rubles. However, after much examination, it was shown that this lot was unsuitable for the Jewish hospital for various reasons and the lot had to be sold back and they began to look for another one.

This was a difficult task because the committee wanted the location to be close to the city.

In 1907, when the old slaughterhouse was moved outside the city, the hospital committee began to negotiate with the local city hall about ceding the lot near the slaughterhouse for a Jewish hospital. This lot was particularly suitable for a hospital because the majority of the poor population for which the hospital was designed lived in the area.

Thanks to the intervention of the local city hall, permission to give the plot to the Jewish hospital at absolutely no cost was granted by the high authorities on 28 September 1908.

Receiving the lot, *Dobroczynność* [charity] elected a building committee joined by Dr. Josef Markusfeld, Dr. Batawia, Dr. Aleksander Wohlberg, Herman Ginzberg, Markus Gradsztajn, Engineer Karp, Izidor Frajnd, Ludwig Tempel, Stanislav Herc and Leopold Werda.

The committee energetically took to the work and entrusted to the engineer, Mankowski the working out of the plan for the building. In creating the plan, he took into account that in time it would be possible to enlarge the pavilion.

The society possessed in total 34,000 rubles on 1 January 1908. However, counting on the full donations that various benefactors had announced, the committee immediately negotiated with various firms and finally gave the work to the following enterprises: 1) The construction work was given to the firm Allert and Bule for 84,000 rubles. 2) Central heating, sewer system, plumbing, bathtubs and the like, was given to the firm Lubinus, Sztajn and Company. 3) The drain work was given to Engineer Delof for 600 rubles. 4) Electrical lighting, the firm Szila and Szwiatla for 1,600 rubles. 5) Building a well, the firm Filus for 950 rubles. 6) To erect a fence around the hospital, W. Rozencwajg for 1,200 rubles. This work was to cost 111,130 rubles in total, not considering unforeseen expenses of around 2,000 rubles.

On the 18th of Sivan 5669 [7 June 1909], after closing the contract, the cornerstone was laid, and the construction began immediately.

Large donations immediately began to flow in, as for example:

[Page 108]

Josef W. Landau – 10,000 rubles; the Ginzberg brothers – 10,000 rubles, Henrik Markusfeld, for the completion of the hospital – 10,000 rubles, Pawel Szpigel, for the deceased Garfinkel – 3,225 rubles, Yeshaye Landau – 3,000 rubles, Izidor Gajsler – 3,000 rubles, the inheritance of Leon Aderfeld – 2,500 rubles, the Society for Poor Pregnant Women – 2,100 rubles, Ludwig Tempel – 3,000 rubles, Jan Grosman – 1,000 rubles, the Czenstochower Credit

Society 1,390 rubles, the Strodom factory – 1,400 rubles, Warta – 1,000 rubles, Pelcers – 500 rubles, Rajchman Brothers and Zigman – 500 rubles, the inheritance from Ludwid Mamlak – 500 rubles, the Second Loan and Thrift Fund – 326 rubles, Samuel Maszkowski – 300 rubles, declared donations – 16,399 rubles, smaller donations – 3,128 rubles, from the sale of [the first] location – 8,000 rubles, income from flower [selling] days – 1,500 rubles, from *Dobroczynność* [charity] – 1,800 rubles, interest from capital and coupons from the registers – 12,349 rubles, in total (with still other donations) – 108,749.

In addition, donations from a women's committee were collected for the interior facilities: linen, furniture and the like [worth] 4,741 rubles, Balabonow donated 7,000 rubles for arranging an apothecary in the hospital. Dr. Josef Markusfeld, seeing that the area around the hospital was full of holes and small hills, had the area evened out at his own expense and organized a beautiful park there named for his deceased wife, Emma Markusfeld. This cost 5,000 rubles.

After all of the donations and income had been paid out, there remained in total 20,303 rubles in debts.

The support for the hospital with 50 beds was to cost up to 30,000 rubles a year. For this, there were such legacies: in the name of Yeshaya Landau – 10,000 rubles, Josef and Helena Landau – 1,000 rubles, Wolf and Hinda Landau – 1,000 rubles, Shimeon and Sharlote Bergman – 2,000 rubles, Ludwig Tempel – 2,000 rubles, Lazarus and Rozalie Grosman – 5,000 rubles, Ludwig and Klara Kohn – 3,000 rubles, Adam Bergman – 900 rubles, Moritz Prusicki – 200 rubles, donations, interest and coupons 1,633 rubles. In total, there was present the sum of 26,813 rubles, from which the interest reached 1,411 rubles. The Jewish *gmina* [administrative division] would give 67,000 rubles and the remaining money, which was counted on, came from various donations.

A resolution was adopted at the last meeting of *Dobroczynność* that the main pavilion of the hospital would carry the name of the chairman, Mr. Henrik Markusfeld.

This pavilion consisted of individual rooms, four large general rooms, admission rooms and two large operating halls; 50 beds for the sick were located in the pavilion.

The clinics, several admission rooms, as well as the administrative offices and hospital apothecary were located in the second pavilion.

The third pavilion, which was named after the deceased Leopold Werde, was for infectious diseases.

The laundry and mangle [laundry wringer] of the hospital were located in the fourth pavilion as well as several rooms for the emotionally ill.

The last pavilion served as residences for the hospital officials and for the hospital kitchen.

The following were chosen as doctors for the hospital:

Dr. Batawia would manage the entire hospital; as surgeon – Dr. Broniatowski, as well as the doctors, Edvard Kohn, Stefan Kohn (obstetrician), Waclaw Kohn and Mrs. Dr. Etinger.

As *feldshers* [barber-surgeons]: the Messrs Tarbeczka and S. Zelten.

The newly built Jewish hospital introduced a practical building according to the latest style and the best technical facilities based on the example of foreign hospitals, and the city of Czenstochow could be proud of it.

We received the complete description of the Jewish hospital thanks to the secretaries of the Jewish *gmina* [Jewish community], the Messrs Foist and Markowicz.

(Czenstochower Vokhnblat [Czenstochow Weekly Newspaper], Friday, 31 October 1913)

Sunday, 16 November 1913, the new Jewish hospital was opened. Avraham Ber Birnbaum, the cantor, accompanied by his choir sang *Mizmor Shir Khanukat* [Psalm (30), a Song for the

Inauguration...]. Rabbi Nukhem Asz, Henrik Markusfeld, the city president, H. Glazek, Dr. Batawia and Dr. Zaks spoke.

A banquet was arranged at Jackowski's pastry shop for the invited guests.

[Page 109]

The Popular Bakery

by F. Szmulewicz

Czenstochow was an industrial city. And when the war broke out in 1914 almost all of the wheels in the factories stopped. The entire export market was to Russia. And the war exploded and cut connection to the export market. Need grew in the workers' ranks and among the bourgeois population. In addition, the German occupation took over all of the economic production under the pretext of rationalizing distribution. In truth, food became more expensive from day to day as well more scarce because the occupying regime took the best [products] and sent them to Germany. The worker population did not have the opportunity to buy the needed foods even at high prices. A bite of bread began to be a rarity. The number of bakers also decreased because not all bakers received flour with which to bake. [They received it] only at the discretion of the "authority." So it came about that people would stand at the bakeries in the middle of the night to receive a small loaf of bread. The idea arose to create a bakery to ease the situation for the population and simultaneously actually to create a new workplace for bakery workers.

The dramatic circle under the direction of Hershl Gotajner performed *Di Mishpokhe* [*The Family*] by H. Nomberg to collect the first monetary funds for building a popular bakery. Taking part were: Shmuel Frank, F. Szmulewicz, R. Federman, Czarnowiecki, Dorka Szacher, Fela Rajcher, Miss C. Federman, Miss Leytsha Gliklich and Gotajner.

The evenings brought in the sum of 200 rubles. With this sum, the creation of the "popular bakery" that served the entire city was undertaken.

In order to accumulate the minimal sum that was needed for the founding of the bakery, we asked for the help of the leading citizens of the city. Among those sympathetic to us was Mendl Kaniarski, who was in Russia before the war and studied for the legal profession and had an entry to the better society. We decided to consult with him. The consultation took place at the residence of Rafal Federman and we gave Kaniarski the mission of calling together a larger circle of the elite.

After a short time, a meeting took place in the Kupiecki Hall with Rabbi Asz. As far as I can remember among the assembled were Rabbi Asz, Moshe Asz, Dr. Rus, Dr. Braniatowski and his brother, the dentist, Koniarski, Werde, Dr. Kahn, Markusfeld, Dr. Gajsler, Szpira, Najfeld, Weksler, Goldsztajn and F. Szmulewicz and Czarnowiecki, as representatives of the workers. The chairmanship of the meeting of about 40 people was Rabbi Asz.

The diversity of opinions about the communal character of the bakery was expressed immediately during the discussion of the name of the institution. A number of those taking part proposed the name *Beis Lekhem* [house of bread] as in the example of the Warsaw *Beis Lekhem*, with its similar philanthropic purpose. The worker representative, the writer of these lines, declared that the question of the name was not a trifle because "the garment creates the persona." The name *Beis Lekhem* was not in agreement with the purpose of the initiators who gathered the first sums of money. We did not want to make an error with the name; the bakery had to be a people's bakery both in name and in its character. So the name "Popular Bakery" was adopted.

The next morning the news about the creation of the bakery appeared in the newspaper and there was great satisfaction among the population.

The distribution of the tasks to accomplish the plan were thus:

Bakery workers and local premises: Dentist Braniatowski, Koniarksi and Szmulewicz. The provision of flour: Markusfeld, Dr. Kahn and Werde.

Control of the health and sanitary conditions: Dr. Rus and Werde.

The bakery workers had a professional union under the jurisdiction of the Zionist Socialists. Rafal Federman was chosen as representative of the party to organize the work plan with the bakers.

Meanwhile, there was success in obtaining a bakery.

[Page 110]

This was the Oyerbach bakery on Warszawer Street, which had four ovens, the most suitable and standard for the purpose.

There also was an immediate and great difficulty in obtaining flour. Everything was in operation during the span of one week. The supervision of the bakery was taken on by Szmulewicz and Zarnowiecki. We also turned to *Poalei-Zion* to help us in the work and they sent Avraham Gotlib.

The bakery earned a good reputation in the city. It was decided to open branch locations in various neighborhoods in order to avoid [people] having to stand in line to buy bread. More comrades such as Efroim Meir Fajnrajch, Bem and others were drawn to the work in connection with this.

The character of the bakery changed, but with time in an undesirable direction. This was because the founders had not made sure that the direction [of the bakery] would remain in their hands. Given that they were not represented in the leadership of the business, the direction fell onto individual people who had pure business goals and the system of patronage was steadily [introduced]. People from various strata, who were chasing after a job, began to appear at the bakery. It appeared that Koniarski had betrayed the workers. Instead of protecting the communal purity he was opposed to being philanthropic and he yielded to temptation and the lust for money. The two above-mentioned worker representatives who had custody refused any salary, declaring that the bakery was created as a workers' organization and not for the purpose of business.

After we rejected being paid, the business leader received a free hand and took the supervision away from the workers.

———

TOZ

by F. Szmulewicz

TOZ [Society for the Protection of Health], the society that had its central office in Warsaw, founded a division in Czenstochow in 1923. Its chief leader from its founding on was Stefan Kon-Kolin. The society's divisions were led by the following:

1. Hygiene section was under the leadership of Dr. Leon Gutman.

2. Tuberculosis section with its own infirmary, X-ray office and a bacteriology laboratory was under the leadership of De. Julius Lipinski.

3. Protection for mothers and children, "vitamin-enriched milk" was under the leadership of Mrs. Dr. Orlinski.

4. Dental office was under the leadership of Dr. Perec.

5. Office for physical therapy was under the direction of Dr. Julius Lipinski.

The summer colony that was created in 1930 had its own building in Ostrow and was worth 10,000 *zlotes* and was founded by the family of Dr. Stefan Kon-Kolin and named for Boleslaw Temple. The colony was led by the female Dr. Lipinski with the strong assistance of secretary Yakov Roziner.

Section for feeding of school and *kheder* [religious school] children. Under the direction of female Dr. Lipinski.

Injection campaign against infectious diseases.

Five doctors were employed by *TOZ* and the budget for 1939 reach 120,000 *zlotes*. Approximately 15,000 cases of illness were handled.

The *TOZ* Summer Colony in Amstow

In conclusion it is worth mentioning that the society and its workers and managing committee were of even greater use to the Czenstochow population thanks to Yakov Roziner, the secretary, who had great organization talent.

[Page 111]

Czenstochow, 3 February 1939

To Czenstochower *landsleit* [people from the same town] in New York.

Dear Friends

We acknowledge the receipt of 50 (fifty) dollars for which we have received 263 *gildn* and 50 *groshn* from the Polish State Bank.

At this opportunity it is our purpose to provide you with a short overview of our recent work.

As you know we are carrying out a wide-ranging, widespread activity in the area of health with special adjustments for the prophylactic protection of the health of the Jewish population.

The need of the Jewish masses, which grows from day to day because of the anti-Semitic agitation on one side and driving the Jewish artisans and merchants from the income they had earned until now on the other side, significantly increased the number of families that turned to *TOZ* for assistance.

The also well-known events in the towns around Czenstochow have forced us to expand our activities in the unfortunate and dark *shtetlekh*, such as Klobuck, Krzepice, Truskolaska, Koniecpol, Kamyk, Miedzno, Amstow (Mstów), Przyrów, Janów, Olsztyn and others.

The last months brought [us the need to] care for those deported from Germany. We also needed to provide these unfortunate ones who remained in our city with medical help, children's colonies and so on.

The difficult conditions for the parents had an effect on the health of the children. A colony had to be arranged in Blachownia close to Czenstochow also during the winter months. There we took care of 42 children deported from Germany and 87 children from Czenstochow and the surrounding area.

Today we are carrying out the feeding of 151 children in the schools, *khederim* [religious primary schools] and children's homes.

In Czenstochow itself we are feeding 605 children from the following learning institutions: Peretz Children's Home, *Dobroczyńca* [benefactor's] Children's Home, *Beis-Yakov* School [school for girls], *Mizrakhi* [religious Zionists] *kheder* and *Talmud-Torah* [primary religious school for poor boys]. In the *shtetlekh* in the Czenstochow region:

Town	Children Feeding
Koniecpol	155
Klobuck	96
Krzepice	90
Przyrów	70
Amstow (Mstów)	64
Truskolask	55
Kamyk	36
Miedzno	30
Kuznicki	25
Olsztyn	25
Janów	24
Przystajń	22
Kotczyn	22
Panki	16
Outside Czenstochow	712

However, *TOZ* could not be satisfied with this activity because the need was so great and it also needed to carry out a campaign for clothing and shoes.

All of our activities swallow a large sum of money, strength and energy.

With the minimal help from the official state organs we must work with great deficits. However, we must not consider this and we cannot even decrease the scope of the very urgent and important work for the Jewish population in general and particularly for the Jewish children.

You can learn more about our *TOZ* activities from our annual report that we will send to you that will be completed in the month of April.

With full certainty and belief in your future positive help, we remain

With a fraternal greeting from home,

Chairman Dr. S. Kolin

Secretary Y. Roziner

The Last Report from *TOZ* for Czenstochower Relief in New York

Czenstochower Cooperatives

by A. Khrobolowski

With the rise of independent Poland, the number of cooperatives strongly increased. The Popular Bakery, which baked the so-called *popularke* (with many potato peels and less flour) during the First World War, was the first cooperative in Czenstochow. A nutrition committee then existed here, as in other cities, that had branches all over the city where food products were distributed for coupons according to a designated standard. The nutrition committee ceased to exist after the war and the distribution of food was transferred to the cooperative. Therefore, almost every party and organization founded a cooperative for its members.

The following cooperatives functioned in 1921-22:

Zjednocz (Unite], *Wyzwolenia* [Liberation], *Napszud* [Polish Socialist Party], *Fareinikte* [United], *Self-Help* (Artisans), Workers' Home (*Poalei-Zion* [Labor Zionists]), *Zukunft* [Future] (Bund), Renters, Officials, Traders, *Akhdes* [Unity], Partners (small retailers), *Przyjazn* [Friendship], *Postęp* [Progess], *Robotnik* [Worker].

The cooperatives *Fareinikte* and *Zukunft* later merged. The branches of the two cooperatives were located at the streets – the bakery at Garncarska 32; the first branch at Ogrodowa 27; the second at Senotarska 1; the third at Nadrzeczna 78; the fourth at Starzynska 16 (previously *Zukunft*); the fifth at Pilsudski 19. The cooperative bookkeeping was also there and later the Workers' Emigration Union branch. The central office was located at Spadek [Street] in Szlezinger's house.

In 1927, when the *zlote* had already been established and the crazy jumps in the prices no longer existed, most of the cooperatives mentioned no longer existed, except for *Fareinikte*, which had already liquidated a few branches and led a difficult life. Then a new workers' cooperative headed by the Bund arose with the help of the Joint [Distribution Committee]. During the period of inflation, the cooperatives kept the prices for most of the needed food at a certain level and mainly served the poor population.

———

[Page 112]

Photographs for the article "Worker Nurseries and *Folks-Shul* [Jewish public school] named after Y. L. Peretz

Day Colony in Ostrow

Workers Nursery Named after Y. L. Peretz in Czenstochow in 1922

**Children and Coworkers from the Afternoon School in Czenstochow
during the School Year of 1938–1939**

**Rhythmic Gymnastics by the Children at the
Y. L. Peretz Workers Nursery in Czenstochow, 1928–1929**

**Czenstochow Committee of the *TSYSHO* [*Tsentrale Yidishe Shul-Organizatsye -*
Central Yiddish School Organization], in Poland with the Delegates from
Czenstochower Relief in New York**
Seated, right to left: A. Chrabalowski, L. Szwarc, L. Szimkowicz, R. Federman, Y. Sh.
Nirenberg
Standing, right to left: W. Fajga, N. Wajs. R. Berkensztat, Sh. Wierczbicki, M. Alter

Honorary Member Letter of L. Szimkowicz

[Page 113]

Rescue Committee for Refugees from Germany
by Tz. Szpalten, F. Szmulewicz

Refugee committees to accept and help the refugees were founded in all of the larger cities as soon as the persecutions of Jews in Germany began and, particularly, when they began to deport Jews from there.

Czenstochow, which was almost the first large city near the German border, was the first city to create such a committee.

At the first only individual families were deported from Germany. The pretext was: administrative penalties, as for example, not paying taxes on time or trading without a peddler's license and so on. In such cases a term of 14 days was given to liquidate one's business and leave the country. Those expelled were forced to sell their possessions for the lowest prices and leave the country. The committee tried to make arrangements for the refugees or to send them on to more distant cities or to help them across the ocean.

However, the situation became more tragic when the mass deportations began, when hundreds of Jews were brought together overnight from all corners of Germany and were sent to the border. Since, Czenstochow was located near the German border, we were not forgotten by Nazi Germany and they sent us transports of refugees.

It was *Shabbos* [Sabbath], and in autumn. Jewish Czenstochow, as always, took part in the repose of *Shabbos*. Jews in the synagogues and the houses of prayer had finished praying and were strolling on the *Aleje*. Jews wrapped in *talisim* [prayer shawls] were still standing in the *shtiblekh* [small one-room houses of prayer] and *minyonim* [10 men required for prayer]. Suddenly, [there was a] message, like a storm carried across the city, that the rabbi in Katowice, Handel, had telephoned the director of the Pryzicki Bank that a train with Jews from Germany had arrived. The train, consisting of horse-cars, was sealed and was located on neutral territory between Germany and Poland, that is, in "no-man's land."

The city was in the grip of great excitement. Everyone asked each other many questions: who are they; where are they; were there present acquaintances or relatives; were they sick there? A committee was chosen immediately of the following people: Dr. Hirszberg, Zwi Szpaltman, Szapiro and Neifeld.

The *kehile* [organized Jewish community] immediately designated several people who would leave for Katowice immediately and simultaneously it intervened with the Polish government to allow the refugees into Poland.

When the group headed by Rabbi Hirszberg (now himself a refugee in *Eretz-Yisroel*) arrived in Katowice, they met two representatives from Bytom, Upper Silesia at the [home of the] local [non-Orthodox] rabbi, with the same concern that a train of Jews in the same conditions was at their part of the border. As was learned, such transports of Jews were sent along the length of the German border.

Meanwhile, the "transports" stood in no-man's land and no one was able to contact them. The local authorities argued that they could not let them in without an order from Warsaw. The telephoned appeal to the Polish government in Warsaw lasted an entire day. Night came and the situation remained the same.

The representatives from Czenstochow and Katowice gathered at the border waiting for an answer from the Polish government. Every minute was a year of suffering and worry. Finally, the news arrived that the Polish government would permit the entry of the refugees and that they should be taken to the nearest border city.

The train cars' sealed doors were opened and people began to fall out, one on another. The tears and screams of the unfortunate ones tore the heart. We remained uncomprehending, not knowing where to start. Women in nightclothes, men in pajamas and slippers and men in black suit jackets, just coming from an orchestral concert, and naked and barefoot children appeared before our eyes. One person did not know the other one; all of the people had been taken, some from their homes, bedrooms and beds; some from the streets and others from theaters, restaurants and other premises. This happened at the same time in various cities in Germany. The arrested Jews were packed in groups in the trains' horse cars and sent to various borders. Women were torn from their husbands, children from their parents, brothers from sisters. One did not know where the other had gone

[Page 114]

After the people were a little calmer, we entered Katowice with a transport of 600 Jews, where the refugees were registered. Communal premises had been prepared earlier with places to sleep and everyone received something to eat. The most difficult task was to calm the agitated mood. However, this was not easy for us. Everyone groaned and cried over their hardship: "Where is my husband, where is my wife, where are my children?"

Tired and broken, one by one they fell asleep.

There were also comic moments in the tragedy.

In one of the corridors a young man in his twenties dressed in an overcoat walked among the sleeping refugees and grumbled to himself. When we asked him why he was not sleeping, he answered that he did not have a toothbrush and did not know what to do. We provided him with a toothbrush and he went to sleep.

In the morning there was the question for us of what now? What would happen when another such transport came today or tomorrow? Therefore, we decided to take all of the refugees to Czenstochow so that Katowice would eventually be free for another transport. The decision was given to the Czenstochow *kehile* [organized Jewish community] and vehicles arrived immediately that took us to Czenstochow.

Czenstochow already had prepared food and beds. The entire Jewish population had taken part in the aid work. The young gathered straw sacks for sleeping, the older ones, food and clothing. Women sewed linens; a kitchen was organized. Women cooked; men served.

The *kehile* registered the refugees and communicated with other cities and over time they were successful in bringing together many dispersed families.

Later the aid work was organized in a more constructive manner. A number of the refugees were provided with work. A number received weekly support. Tradesmen were given the opportunity to be employed in their trade. Spots for singers and musicians were created in orchestras; tailors and shoemakers and other artisans were provided with machines and tools. Emigrants were provided with certificates. We did everything in our power to create a homey atmosphere for the refugees so they would feel like brothers among brothers. They, themselves, arranged a Chanukah gathering. Presents were distributed that evening and there were appropriate words of consolation. We assured the refugees that what we did not think that what we were doing for them was a favor, but our fraternal duty. In general, the aid work for the Jewish refugees from Germany did not have a philanthropic character. It was more the consciousness that what happened to them [the refugees] could happen to us tomorrow. It is a fact that many of those who took part then in caring for the refugees are today spread across the four corners of the world, some in *Eretz-Yisroel*, some in Teheran, or more widely dispersed. However, the majority of the members of the rescue committee for refugees shared the cruel fate of the Czenstochow *kehile* and of all of Polish Jewry.

* * *

Several People from the Yiddish Press in Czenstochow (for the article "Yiddish Press")

A. Chrabolowski

W. Lewenhof   **R. Federman**

M. Ceszenski

[Page 115]

The Jewish Workers Movement

S.S. (Zionist-Socialist Workers Party), "*Fareinikte*" (United), "Independent"

by Yitzhak Gurski, S. Feinreikh, Feitl Shmulewicz, and A. Khrobolowski

The beginning of the Zionist-Socialists in Czenstochow can be dated to the year 1902. The first group of Labor-Zionists already had arisen in Minsk and Dr. Nakhman] Syrkin had founded the first Zionist-Socialist group, *Heyrut* [Freedom] abroad.

The first Zionist workers group in Czenstochow was organized under the leadership of Josef Kruk (Josef "Number One"). Dovid Molarski and Meir Fajnrajch were the first in the group and Mendl Szuchter joined them. Yitzhak Gurski, Alek Templ, Hela Birman, Bronka Koniarski, Mendl Koniarski, Maks Dankowicz, Matvey Dawidowicz (engineer on the Herby train) were intellectuals in the first group. Later, Nukhem Singalowski, came to Czenstochow to teach in the trade school. Mikhal Alter, Hershl Gotajner, Kuba Goldberg, Kac from Warszawer Street studied in the same school. They all joined the Zionist-Socialist movement.

**Standing, right to left: D. Oberman, Y. Goldsztajn, Dovid Szelkowicz
Seated, right to left: Gurski, Leibush Lehrer (Aleksander), Y. Lewenhof**

The first area of agitation by the group was at the elections. One of the first meeting places was in the house of the teacher, Zigmund Majerczik at Strazacka [Street]. They would also meet at the *Talmud-Torah* [school for poor boys] at Garncarska [Street] and at the Artisans' School. The meeting place for the intellectual group was in Josef Kruk's house.

In the summer of 1903, after the split in Zionism into *Tzioni Tzion* [Zionists of Zion] and "Ugandists" – the group broke away from the Zionists. The first group of middle school young also was founded as a division of the Labor Zionist Union.

After the conference in Świder, near Warsaw, and then in Odessa, the group took the name Zionist-Socialists.

In 1904 the Zionist-Socialist organization in Czenstochow led a widespread campaign for the founding of a self-defense [organization]. This was after the Kishinev pogrom. Mass gatherings were organized. Speakers appeared in the synagogues and money collections were carried out for this purpose in Czenstochow and its surroundings.

[Page 116]

The Czenstochow organization also took part in buying weapons abroad in southern Russia for the self-defense organization. These weapons were smuggled through the Herby border with the aid of Engineer Matvey Dawidowicz.

In 1904 a eulogy took place in the Czenstochow synagogue for [Theodor] Herzl. Among the organizers of the gathering were: Makrojer, general Zionists, Natan Gerichter and Khemia Fiszman – *Mizrakhists* [religious Zionists]. The Zionist-Socialists demanded that their speaker should have permission to appear at the gathering. Yitzhak Gurski, the representative of the Zionist-Socialists, went up to the *bimah* [platform from which the Torah is read] against the will of the leading Zionists and stated his position toward Herzl and to the Zionist movement. After the eulogy a large Zionist-Socialist demonstration was organized in the street.

The first illegal appeal from the Zionist-Socialists was published at that time. The appeal was mimeographed in Alek Templ's residence.

Ahron Singalowski, Nukhem's brother, came to Czenstochow at the beginning of 1905. With his oratorical abilities, he helped a great deal to create the Zionist-Socialist mass movement in Czenstochow that was sustained by the objective conditions of Jewish working life in the city. Many small and a few larger Jewish factories existed in Czenstochow and the Zionist-Socialists organized the local Jewish workers to fight for better economic conditions.

The fact that Czenstochow was an emigration point [helped with] the development of the Zionist-Socialist movement. Masses of Jewish emigrants, helpless, exposed to the mercy of smugglers and swindlers, streamed through Czenstochow seeking new homes. This was a stimulus for the local Jewish intelligentsia and working class to think about an organized systematic solution to the Jewish emigration problem.

The Odessa Declaration of the Zionist-Socialists in 1905 was celebrated in Czenstochow at a large gathering in the Olsztyn forest. The brochures with the Declaration, printed abroad, were smuggled across the Czenstochow border and sent throughout Russia.

The Zionist-Socialist organization became the strongest factor in Jewish life in Czenstochow.

Owners and their employees and workers turned to the organization to reconcile conflicts.

The work in the professional area encompassed the celluloid branch, with Wajnberg's celluloid factory at the head, the metal branch with Rozensztajn and Szaja's small factories, the bakery workers, tailors, shoemakers, hat makers, clerks, female hat makers and so on.

The organization had a large number of bourgeois sympathizers in addition to the group of intellectuals who took part in the leadership. One of them was Moritz Najfeld.

Large mass gatherings in the Olsztyn forest, behind Shimshon Diabal's mill or at the cemetery grew from the small gathering that began at Shmuel Szuster's [home] at Jatka Street. Discussions with other parties, principally with the Bund, often were arranged. They would take place under the open sky, in locked premises and in the factories. A number of these discussions would last the entire day. One discussion with a member of the Polish Socialist Party took place in Wajnberg's factory. The Jewish speaker from the Polish Socialist Party was, I think, Feliks Perl from Krakow. He was later one of the leaders of the Polish Socialist Party in independent Poland.

One who also was very admired by the Zionist-Socialist workers in Czenstochow was Sh. Niger, who appeared at a giant mass gathering arranged at the cemetery.

With the help of the cantor from the "German Synagogue" (synagogue on Dojazdowa Street), a Zionist-Socialist gathering was organized in the synagogue at which L. Pines appeared, who later received the title, doctor, for his *Geshikte fun der Yidisher Literature* [*History of Jewish Literature*].

The most beloved speaker at the mass gatherings was "Comrade Ahron," (Dr. A. Singalowski). His effect on the masses was simply hypnotic. He also had great importance among the intelligentsia and when he would appear at the synagogue during prayers, the crowd would listen to him breathlessly.

Josef Number Two (Josef Rabinowicz from Warsaw) was also among the leaders of the Czenstochow organization. One of the most active intellectuals was Moritz Grinbaum, at that time still a student.

Standing out with their activism then among the so-called half-intellectuals were:

[Page 117]

Mikhal Alter, Yusik Finkelsztajn, Gutek and Anya Bornsztajn (both from Zawiercie), Kuba Goldberg and Yakov Goldsztajn.

J. J. Kruk and N. Bornsztajn

Among the women, Hela Birman was the most active. In addition to her clandestine tasks, she also directed the information work among the women and ran a secret school åwhere girls were taught to read and write.

An entire group of heroes and active workers also emerged from the awakened Jewish masses. In addition to those in the first group already mentioned earlier, a significant role was played in the Czenstochow organization of the Zionist-Socialists by Kopl Gerichter, Moshe Welkser, Dovid Akerman, Yitzhak Zarnowecki, Shaya Yakov (Sh. Minkof), Mendl and Yosl Berliner, Owieczki, Fradl Brat, Skharye Lewensztajn, Faytl Szmulewicz, Mordekhai Altman,

"Kostek," Aizik Szloser. Shmuel Eizner was active among the trade employees (the merchants' clerks).

An important place in the organization was occupied by Dovid Guterman (Jaicarcz) and Mendl Szwarcbaum.

In 1905 the location [for the trading of ideas] of the Zionist-Socialists was at the New Market, to the rear of Strazacka Street. The meeting place was at Golda's tea hall, in the very center of the Jewish neighborhood. It always swarmed with people there like in a beehive. Workers from other parties who came to discussions with the Zionist-Socialists also visited Golda's tea hall. One of them, at that time, was Mendl Molarcz (Mendl Wolf), the fervid Bundist.

The two great events in the history of the organization in the summer of 1905 were: the fight with the brawlers who were driven from the Jewish neighborhood by the Zionist-Socialists and the tragedy at Lerner's celluloid factory, where five or six Jewish girls were burned during a fire. The Zionist-Socialist organization stopped work in all of the factories and workshops with Jewish workers and arranged a funeral for the victims at the cemetery. Ahron Singalowski gave one of his passionate speeches there.

* * *

The winter of 1905-1906 was a difficult one. Golda's tea hall was attacked often by the dragoons who hacked at it with rifle butts as if it was cabbage. The "white headbands" rampaged in the streets. The intelligentsia escaped. Ahron Singalowski also left Czenstochow. His last appearance in Czenstochow was at a mass gathering at Wajnberg's factory, which was arranged on the most difficult days of the state of war with great danger. The work that winter was carried out in the economic area by people who the masses themselves had generated. There were also those activists who arrived from outside [Czenstochow]. One of them, who was beloved by the masses, was Comrade "Jan," who came from Paris. He always was poorly dressed. He did not agree with the means used against the owners and entrepreneurs because he was inclined toward anarchism.

In the spring of 1906 the freedom movement, newly revived, but with fewer mass gatherings and more groups and illegal gatherings during the summer was joined in their work by two members of the intelligentsia: "Yakov" and "Avraham," who both were from the Pinsk area.

The [female] Comrade "Basha," with her very folksy speech, was particularly beloved by the workers. She came from the Bobruisk area and worked throughout the Zagłębie region.

"Ruwin," who worked as a pharmacist in Najfeld's apothecary warehouse, and "Dan," a pensive and quiet person who was like dozens of others, traveled through Czenstochow on their way to America and have earned the right to be remembered.

The tragedy of that summer was the fall of three comrades: Dovid Lewenhof, Dovid Fajnrajch and Yosl Berliner who were sent to the provinces to collect money and used revolvers for that purpose. Yosl Berliner got away with a short term in jail. Dovid Lewenhof and Dovid Fajnrajch were sentenced to six years in jail. The first one died in prison and the second was freed in 1912, spiritually dejected.

[Page 118]

Comrade "Aleksander" (Leibush Lerer[1]) arrived in Czenstochow in the middle of the summer of 1906. As someone from Warsaw, he was close to those from Czenstochow in his speech and his spirit. In addition to his spiritual influence on the workers, Comrade Aleksander devoted himself to organizing the trades.

Mikhal Alter, Yusik Finkelsztajn, Gutek and Anya Bornsztajn (both from Zawiercie), Kuba Goldberg and Yakov Goldsztajn.

Standing, right to left: N. Bornsztajn, Binyamin, and M. Altman
Seated, right to left: M. Fajnrajch, and Y. Y. Zarnowecki
Middle: Sh. Minkof

The leadership of the Zionist-Socialist's Czenstochow organization was then taken over by Dovid Lewin from Homel, known as Comrade "Binyamin." He was a person with a great deal of knowledge and organizational capabilities. He was the founder of the self-defense [organization] in Homel. Because of his head of dark hair and dark beard, he was called *Święty Ojciec* [the Holy Father] in bourgeois circles. He had a great deal of authority in the organization and a great influence on the comrades.

The library opened by the Zionist-Socialists the same summer had great significance for the movement.

Self-defense against the pogroms that were expected in Czenstochow several times occupied an important place in the activity of the organization. Self- defense groups also were sent out to the *shtetlekh* [towns] around Czenstochow where rumors of pogroms had spread. However, no pogroms or attacks against the Jews occurred at that time.

That summer an assassination attempt that the Zionist-Socialists carried out on Warszawer Street against one of the worst regional police superintendents shocked Czenstochow. The Zionist-Socialists meeting point was then in Kahn's garden on the Second *Aleje*.

At the end of the summer a dramatic society that performed a series of plays began to function under the leadership of Comrade "Binyamin." The rehearsals took place in Kopl Gerichter's house on Krotka Street.

In 1908, Comrade Mendl Szuchter was exiled to Siberia for his activity in the Zionist-Socialist organization.

In 1910, "Marx" and R. Federman, who came to the Zionist-Socialists from the *S.D.K.P.L.* [Social Democracy of the Kingdom of Poland and Lithuania] stood at the head of the Zionist-Socialist group. Faytl Szmulewicz, Simkha Kalka, Moshe Weklser and Yakov Yitzhak Zarnowecki also were active in the Zionist-Socialist organization in Czenstochow.

Until the First World War no regular organization existed in Czenstochow. However, there was a large group, in which [the following] took part: A. Chrabalowski, Simkha Kalka, Meir Fajnrajch, Faytl Szmulewicz, Gradon, Kon, [female] Comrade Aronowicz, [female] Comrade Fefer. The group would come together from time to time and arrange activities, mainly with the purpose of gathering monetary means. "Berl" Gutman, the only member of the central committee, often would come to Czenstochow. Moshe Litvakov once also traveled through Czenstochow. The gathering at which he then appeared was arranged in the lower room of the *kawiarnia* [café] at the Third *Aleje*.

Appeals came on every 1 May, addressed to the office of the *Malarnia* [paint factory], where A. Ch[rabalowski] was employed. The attendants in the office would receive them from the post office and bring them with all of the packages. Moshe Weksler, the cashier, was the distributor of the appeals and would lay out his own money when it was necessary.

[Page 119]

The Zionist-Socialists played an important role in the Literary Society, in *Lira* [literary and music society] and in the founding of the Artisans Club, in the creation of the Yiddish press and the fight for Yiddish among the traders and in other societies, such as in the founding of the legal professional unions. They all were workers, such as Faytl Szmulewicz, Simkha Kalka, Gradon, Kon and others, or trade employees, such as A. Chrabalowski, Federman and the Zionist-Socialist sympathizer Sziperblat.

The Zionist-Socialist organization again grew as a mass movement during the First World War. The most important leaders then were R. Federman, Hershl Gotajner, Mikhal Alter, Shaya Nirenberg, Yakov Yitzhak Zarnowecki and Abe Wegner. The very capable Dudek Szlezinger particularly distinguished himself. Directly or indirectly, the Popular Bakery, the educational union for Jewish workers, the workers kitchen, the Y.L. Peretz children's home and a series of professional unions were created then by the organization.

The Zionist-Socialists were represented in the provisional workers council by 11 delegates, (Bund - 4, *Poalei-Zion* – 6 [of the total delegates]), in the executive by three (Bund - 1, *Poalei-Zion* – 1 [of the total delegates]).

The Czenstochow Zionist-Socialist organization issued a protest appeal against the then People's Government headed by Ignatz Daszynski in connection with the bloody pogrom in Lemberg that was organized by the Polish legionnaires.

On *Shabbos*, 4 August 1919 a solemn meeting took place at which the Zionist-Socialists changed its name to *Fareinikte* in accordance with a decision of the conference in Warsaw.

Despite the system of electoral selections, during the election to the city council under the German occupation, the organization elected four councilmen: Shaya Nirenberg, Tarbetszka, Shlomo Horowicz and A. Lipszic.

In the declaration read by the councilmen at the city council there were such statements for which the German occupation regime would exile [someone] to the Modlin [Fortress]. One of the sentences was: "The light comes from the east." It was after the revolution in Russia.

Coworkers from the *Fareinikte* Cooperative

Picture from the Election Campaign for the City Council

At the end of the [First] World War, A. Chrabalowski returned from imprisonment in Austria and Juczek Finkelsztajn from the Soviet Union and placed themselves at the disposal of the organization.

During the first days of independent Poland the Zionist-Socialist militia helped to disarm the Germans and brought weapons (rifles) to the premises of the club, *Aleje* 43.

אַרבײַטער-דעלעגאַטן-ראַט טשענסטאָכאַוער

לעגיטימאַציע פֿון ראַחל-קאַמיסאַר

געפֿן,פֿריַיַען געדול
פֿאַרײ'-אַנעהרערינגקײַיא יעזעלי'-צײַון

טשענסטאָכאָוו, ד. 27 דעצעמבער,   1918

פֿאַר'ן דײַיִסוײַיליגען בוײַפֿאַרהוגבאַ-ראַפֿ'מײַ

פֿאָרזיצער   סעקרעטער
ראָול פֿעדערמאָן   י.שײ אַרזנואּװעצי

טעפֿיטיק דורצזאָיהערן ר'
וואַהלען אין אַרבײַטער-ראַט
צווריַיאַן די יעדדעז
אַרבײַטער אין טשענסטאָכאַוו

[Czenstochow Worker Delegates Council]

[Page 120]

A total of 1,786 votes were returned in the elections to the workers council from the [different] lines [of work]; *Fareinikte* received 941 with 19 delegates (*Poalei-Zion* – 256 votes and 6 delgeates, the Bund – 277 votes and 5 delegates).

The most active members of the executive of the workers council were Juczek Finkelsztajn and Dudek Szlezinger. R. Federman was the vice-chariman of the workers council.

The first elections to the city council in independent Poland took place on Sunday, 6 March 1919. *Fareinikte* received 2,259 votes out of the 6,417 votes that were submitted for the Jewish lists and four councilmen were elected: Rafael Federman, Shaya Nirenberg, Juczek Finkelsztajn, Hershl Gotajner (*Poalei-Zion* – two councilmen and Bund – one councilman).

The Czenstochow organization presented Dr. Josef Kruk as one of the candidates from the Czenstochow district to the Polish Constituent Assembly. The election was [fair], but the large number of votes was not enough to elect the candidate.

The Czenstochow organization, *Fareinikte*, branched out and grew every day. It headed most of the professional unions that were organized in a central office where Abe Wenger and Yakov Yitzhak Zarnowecki were employed. And Shaya Nirenberg was busy with the economic work such as the workers' kitchen, workers' restaurant. Hershl Gotajner managed the bakery and the cooperative. Rafael Federman was the head of the schools. A. Chrabalowski, the chairman, who held the reins of the entire organization in his hands, was the secretary and mainly was concerned with cultural work that was organized in *Shtral* [light beam], stood at the head of the evening courses for the working young and edited the weekly newspapers: *Undzer Vort* [*Our Word*] and *Dos Neye Vort* [*The New Word*].

The center of the activity of the organization was the hall at the workers' kitchen at Straczecke 11, in Garbinski's house, which was changed to the name: *Zal Neye Velt* [New World Room]. All of the mass meetings, party gatherings, banquets, dance evenings, literary evening and so on took place there. The Bund also organized the memorial service after the death of Vladimir Medem there.

The *Fareinikte* faction at the city council, led by R. Federman, who also was the secretary of the city council for a time, actually was the only one that spoke sharply against the anti-Semitic politics of the *Endekes* [anti-Semitic Polish National Party] majority and against all injustices that were committed against the Jewish population. The faction and the Polish Socialist Party protested against the arrest of Bundist city councilman Yosef Aronowicz and demanded that the city council intercede and bravely denounced the pogrom of 1919, of which many of its [the pogrom's] spiritual leaders sat in the city council. It also protested against quartering the headquarters of bloody [Ukrainian politician Symon Vasylyovych] Petliura in Czenstochow.

Persecutions and repressions, which came both from the government in Warsaw and from the local rulers, including the city hall, poured on the organization.

[Our candidates for the city council are ...]

In 1920 the premises of the club, *Fareinikte*, at *Aleje* 43 was confiscated and the club was liquidated by the police. Later the premises of all of the professional unions were requisitioned. Great efforts were made to arrange readings and concerts at which the police often did not permit speaking or singing in Yiddish (everything as in the Tsarist day and much worse)

[Page 121]

The organization endured everything and tried to rebuild.

In 1921-1922 a division of the "Workers Emigration Union" finally was opened at *Fareinikte* in Warsaw. Rayzele Fajertag [Berkensztat] was employed at the office of the division at Dojazdowa 19. Emigration to America was already limited then. However, brothers, sisters, children and wives still could go to their family members with affidavits. Help from the office was particularly important in receiving foreign permits for the emigrants because this demanded so many formalities, papers and other notes from the dozens of consulates in the manner of the Polish bureaucracy.

At that time, Berl Gutman, Yitzhak Gordin, Pinya Bukshorn, Sh. Gilinski, Yakov Pat, L. Pines, M. Mandelsberg, Dr. Eiger of Lodz and Friszman gave readings or made appearances at mass meetings of *Fareinikte*.

Pinya Bukshorn also was a poet. His song *Farloste Fabrikn* [*Deserted Factories*] based on a motif of Maria Konopnicka's *Rota* [*Oath*] at first was sung at all mass gatherings. He became ill with influenza in Czenstochow and lay in the Czenstochow hospital for a time.

Shlomo Zisman participated in a series of lectures for a chosen circle to raise the Jewish socialist consciousness of the politically active workers.

In 1922, *Fareinikte* began to go downhill in Czenstochow. This happened for several reasons: the emigration that emptied the ranks of the most active ones; the split and the movement of a large number of workers, the activists and the young to the communists as well as the economic crisis from which the economic institutions suffered. However, the greatest trouble came from the leaders in Warsaw who mostly were dispersed, some to the Bund and some to the communists.

At the end of the summer 1922 a unification conference took place in Czenstochow in the *Neye Vort* [New Word] hall with Bolesław Drobner's socialist group under the name "Independent Socialist Party." The Jewish workers in the party were concentrated in a special section. The party as a whole recognized the necessity of intense emigration, industrialization and organization of Jewish workers.

Elections to the Polish *Sejm* [parliament] took place in October 1922. The Czenstochow organization, now [named] "Independent," again presented the candidacy of Dr. Josef Kruk for the Czenstochow district and then also carried out an election campaign among Polish workers.

**A Group of Czenstochower Zionist-Socialists before
Their Emigration
— M. Alter, H. Gotajner, R. Federman, and D.
Gebirter**

However, connections were created then with the Zionist-Socialists. Several worker activists and leaders of the Polish Socialist Party joined "Independent." One of the most well-known among them was Antony Domanski, a worker at Warta who was very admired by the Polish workers in Czenstochow.

[Page 122]

In 1925 he was elected as a councilman from "Independent" and returned to the Zionist=Socialists with Drobner.

The Czenstochow organization "Independent" still carried out vigorous activities for a number of years among both the Jewish and the Polish workers. *Dos Neye Vort* [*The New Word*] published during the entire winter of 1923 at the *Kultura* printing press that the organization had founded with three partners. Mass meetings and readings in Polish and Yiddish took place in the hall of the *Neye Vort*. In general, the "Independent" organization in Czenstochow participated a great deal in bringing the Jewish and Polish workers closer together.

The Independent Socialist Party was from the start involved with the Vienna "Two and a Half" International [The International Working Union of Socialist Parties]. In 1923 when the Vienna International was liquidated and joined the Second Socialist International, the party as a whole also joined the same International. The majority in the Czenstochow organization, under the leadership of A. Chrabalowski, voted against the decision of the party.

Many communists worked under the legal protection of "Independent." This brought severe repression against the leader of the organization by the "defense" (secret police) and police. Frequent searches and confiscations of all of the papers took place in the hall and private residences of the leaders.

In 1925 the Czenstochow *starostwa* [administrator] forbid "Independent' from demonstrating with the other parties on 1 May.

The Committee of "Independent"

Seated, right to left: D. Szlezinger, M. Weksler, Dr. J. Kruk, Y.Y. Zarnowecki,
A. Chrabalowski, and Sh. Nirenberg
Standing, right to left: M. Alter, Win, A. Brat, Sh. Frank, and L. Berkowicz

Dr. Josef Kruk, who often appeared in Czenstochow, was accused in court and sat in Piotrkow and Czenstochow jails for a time.

Before the beginning of the Second World War, the Polish government liquidated the party completely and sent Dr. Kruk to the sadly well-known Kartuz-Bereza [concentration camp], from which after great efforts, particularly from abroad, he was released. He emerged from the concentration camp with a serious illness.

When the last group of "Independent" with Dr. Kruk at the head joined *Poalei-Zion* [Workers of Zion – Marxist-Zionist party] in Warsaw, those in Czenstochow, as was explained, went with them, as well as the old members of the Zionist-Socialists who had gone through all of the transformations of the party. One of the first martyrs who was murdered by the Nazi murderers was Yakov Yitzhak Zarnowecki.

After R. Federman moved to the Bund and A. Chrabalowski left for America, Dudek Szlezinger took over the leadership of the organization. He was admired by the Polish as well as the Jewish workers. He had the help of active comrades such as Shaya Nirenberg, Wolf Fajga, Avraham Brat, Leibush Berkowicz and for a time, Matek Pliwacz.

Translator's Footnote

1. The name Leibush Lerer was previously spelled as Leibush Lehrer.

The Zionist Socialists in Conflict with the Scoundrels

by M. Feinreikh

Before the revolution of 1905 a band of scoundrels reigned in Czenstochow that terrorized the Jewish population. The leaders of the band were: Aizik Szlize, his brother, Yekl, Moshe Pace, Meir Hudies and others. With the rise of the revolutionary movement, several members of the band moved to our side and became devoted fighters in the ranks of the Zionist Socialists. The remaining saw in us a danger to their rule; they joined the Russian police, served as spies and helped persecute the workers movement.

[Page 123]

Among the victims were Comrade Shimeon Beker and large group of bakery workers who were denounced to the police and were sentenced to six months in jail. With their help, Comrade Kopl Gerichter also was arrested and beaten on a *Shabbos* [Sabbath].

Right after this, on a Sunday in May 1905, the Zionist Socialists mobilized several groups of workers, mainly from Wajnberg's and Itsikl Szaja's factories, armed them with revolvers, sticks, stones and even dippers of petrol and surrounded the old market, the main spot where the band operated. They were employed by the fruit-sellers at that time. These were the Jews and peasants from the surrounding *shtetlekh* [towns] and villages who brought their fruit to the city. The band had a "monopoly" on many small merchants and took a payment from each of them [for protection]. Then the group began to disperse. The group waited on every street corner for them. Moshe Pace went home in the direction of Tendler's house. Two workers with revolvers let him pass by and at the same time let him have it with two bullets. One hit his hand, the second – his chest. He tried to escape to Lichter's leather shop and fell down. A worker with a ladle of petrol gave him a little "water" to drink and he died.

The remaining group concentrated itself around the milk wagons, where Aizik Szlize, the leader of the band, hid under a wagon. Police arrived and took Szlize under their protection. He walked around the *shtetl* with a police guard for a time. Later, he ran away to Upper Silesia. A few weeks later he returned to Czenstochow and immediately fell dead from a bullet shot by a Zionist Socialist. However, the rule of the scoundrels ended on the day in May 1905 when the band was annihilated. The old and the new market, the Jewish market-sellers and small merchants breathed freely.

[Page 123]

The General Jewish Workers Bund

by Sh. Y. Herc

The Rise of the Bund

The Jewish socialist movement in Congress Poland arose later than in Lithuania and White Russia [Belarus]. Jewish wage–workers already were in many Polish cities during the last decade of the 19th century, but they were not yet politically organized. With the exception of Warsaw and some other cities where the Bund was active at the end of the 19th century, the Jewish socialist movement in Congress Poland spread out a few years later, mainly during the first five years of this century [20th century] when the waves of revolution reached all corners of the country.

One of the reasons for the late arrival of the Jewish workers movement in Congress Poland was without a doubt the fact that the traditional, pious life of the masses was strongly rooted in the life of the Polish Jews and lasted longer. The old Sephardic[1] Jewish life in Poland first began to change greatly in the epoch of 1905.

The rise of the Bund in Czenstochow also occurred during this time.

In 1902 the Bund made contact with the city for the first time. The pogrom took place that year during the summer. In addition, the Bund sent one its most important activists, the later well–known leader of the Bund during the Russian Revolution in 1917 – Mark Liber. After thoroughly investigating the events, Liber published a detailed description of the Czenstochow pogrom in the overseas organ of the Bund, *Poslednie Izvestia [Latest News]* (no. 92, 30 October 1902). With the severe Tsarist censorship and a [failure by] the usual Jewish press, Liber's printed report that brought out the truth about the pogrom was of great importance.

[Page 124]

In the Revolutionary Period

The Bundist movement in Czenstochow grew widely starting in 1905. Large strikes, demonstrations and other important actions were carried out during that revolutionary year.

It is worth mentioning a few of them.

In August 1905 the Bund in Czenstochow took part in carrying out a three–day political strike.

At about the same time the local Bundist organization carried out widespread activity in connection with the great misfortune that occurred in Landau's factory. Five female workers and three male workers were burned during a fire in August 1905. In addition, several people received severe burns.

The Bund called a general strike on the day of the funeral. None of the Jewish workers appeared at work. From morning on, a great mass began to flow to Garncarska Street where a deceased worker, a victim of the fire, lay. A crowd of 6,000 men came together. The windows, balconies and roofs were covered with people.

The Bundist speakers, who were lifted up onto the shoulders of their comrades, spoke before the thousands assembled. There were sharp words, loaded with immense bitterness and rage that was felt in everyone's heart. There were nine speeches. The typical funeral gathering in front of the house of a worker–victim lasted 12 hours.

**A group of Bundists in 1905 in
Czenstochow**
Standing on the ladder: Avraham
Goldsztajn; near him: Mendl Braun;
standing from the left: Grajcel

The burial took place at the cemetery at one o'clock where speeches again were given before the excited masses.

The Bund also issued 2,000 copies of an illegal appeal. The appeal, which began with the words, "In the name of the victims," made a strong impression.

An interesting financial account of the Czenstochow Bund organization for the half–year from 1 September 1905 to 1 March 1906 gives us an idea of the scope of the Bundist work at that time.

Income: Literature 21 rubles and 14 kopekes; Zawierce 83 r. 50 k.; Noworadomsk 30 r. 20 k.; lottery 10 r. collected 450 r. 20 k.; remaining 59 r. 39 k.; Sosnowiec 9 r. 70 k.; tailor 2 r. 72 k.; carpenter 3 r. 5 k.; baker 20 k.; clerks 95 k.; *feldsher* [barber–surgeon] 10 k.; watchmaker 10 k.; tinsmith 2 r. 72 k.; cabinetmaker 3 r. 5 k.; baker 20 k.; painter 5 k.; lathe operator 35 k.; lost pamphlet 50 k.; for A.R. 4 r.; wood pile 2 rubles 15 k.; through birth – 6 r.; Blond 50 k.; legal literature 9 r. 98 k.; pictures 7 r. 40 k.; received 30 r.; for a special purpose 300 r.; from the striker's aid committee 29 r. 38 k.; borrowed 12 r. 59 k.; intelligentsia 5 r. 45 k.; receipts 5 r.; through H. 10 r.; through H. 7r.; through Sh. 5 r.; a worker 1 r.; number 10 – 40 k.; number 2 – 4 r. 50 k.; various 22 rubles; from the regional committee of the Bund 160 rubles; from committee abroad 73 rubles 50 k.; "small Bund" 50 kopekes.

Total 1,329 rubles 77 kopekes.

Expenses: region 98 rubles 7 kopekes; travel costs 54 r. 75 k.; support for workers 41 r. 72 k.; technical 62 r. 3 k.; arrestees 49 r. 30 k.; the Polish regional committee of the Bund 366 r. 46 k.; providing loans 110 r. k.; apartments 60 r. 75 k.; mail 13 r. 45 k.; for special purposes

394 r. 15 k.; meetings35 r.; passages 34 r. 20 k.; permits 2 r. unemployed 166 r.; strikes 85 r. 28 k.; for legal literature 25 r. 60 k. binding 12 r. 25 k.; miscellaneous 7 r. 85 k.

[Page 125]

Total 1,619 rubles 2 kopekes.

Deficit of 289 rubles 2 kopekes.

With the then poor conditions, the expenditure of 1,619 rubles for a half–year was a considerable sum and showed the scope of the movement. It is conspicuous that there was no payment for salaries; all of the diversified work in the ghetto was done voluntarily by members. It can be seen from the income and expenses that the Czenstochower organization also served the surrounding cities. Only three cities were mentioned in the financial account. However, the number of surrounding cities actually helped by Czenstochow was a lot larger.

The connection to Noworadomsk, which is mentioned in the financial report, was that very lively activity took place there. In a report published in the *Folks–Zeitung* no. 49 of 8 May 1906, we read:

"There are present here about 400 Jewish workers who stand mainly under the influence of the local Bund group. The group carried out its work with great energy and its influence grew even more and more in the city and in the surrounding shtetlekh [towns] of Plawno, Przedborz and others.

The working masses still related to their bosses as in the old patriarchal times. The salaries were very low; their needs even smaller. It was even worse for the Christian masses. They were sympathetic to the *Narodowa Demokraczja* – [anti–Semitic, Polish Nationalist Democratic Party].

Despite the backwardness of both the Jewish and the Polish neighborhoods, the Noworadomsk Bundists carried on strong revolutionary activity. Their work among the large military garrison was particularly done with self–sacrifice. They made a connection with many soldiers in the military division and other formations. In 1906, the Noworadomsk organization of the Bund, among others, distributed military proclamations, which the military–revolutionary organization had published about the Bialystok pogrom carried out by the garrison there [in Bialystok].

It can be seen from the treasurer's report that there was close contact between Czenstochow and the Polish regional committee of the Bund. A series of Bundist activists, who helped to better establish the work and gave speeches at gatherings, came on assignment from the regional committee. Among others, Eidl Motalski and Alter Epsztajn, activists from the Polish regional committee, came to visit Czenstochow many times. A. Litwak and B. Wladek, well-known Bundist leaders, came.

One entry in the cashbook demands a clarification: both in the income and in the expenses there is an entry "for a special purpose." The income is 300 rubles, the expense is 394 rubles 15 *kopikes*. The "special purpose" was weapons.

Special fighting divisions or *B.O.* [Battle Organization, known in Polish as *Organizacja Bojowa*] existed then among local Bundist organizations. Their tasks were to support the movement against police spying and to support the Jewish population against pogroms. Such a *B.O.* existed at the Czenstochow organization of the Bund. In his memoirs, *In Loyf fun Yorn* [*Through the Years*], Leibeczke Berman explains that in 1906 the important Bundist activist, Dovid Kac (Toras), came to Czenstochow regarding this matter. He came here as a representative of the "Mim" commission, which existed at the central committee of the Bund and which had the task of organizing the instruction and arming of the *B.O.* on the ground.

For example, about the work of the *B.O.* in Czenstochow:

In June 1906 a frightening pogrom was organized in Bialystok by the Tsarist regime. They thought about doing something similar in other cities. Then, the *B.O.* appeared on the scene, which organized special self–defense divisions. In a letter about Czenstochow that was published in the Bundist daily newspaper, *Folks–Zeitung* [*People's Newspaper*], no. 109 of 20 July 1906:

"Recently the mood here was uneasy. The Bialystok pogrom brought fear to the entire area and even more to Czenstochow, which had tasted the flavor of a pogrom several years ago.

"The Polish and Jewish revolutionary parties (Bund, *P.S.D.* and *P.P.S.* [Polish Social Democrats and Polish Socialist Party]) began to carry out energetic propaganda activity among the working masses. They also prepared for self–defense and they divided the city into various sectors. A number of the self–defense groups also were prepared for the region, but they were not needed there.

[Page 126]

"The local Jewish community is nonchalant toward the self–defense groups. Of course, it is no wonder now that a large number of the Jewish population believes little in self–defense because everyone knows that the police carry out the pogrom with the help of the soldiers and one cannot do anything against Browning guns. Yet one did not have to wait with indifference, because even the Bialystok pogrom showed the usefulness of the self–defense groups.

"An outrageous movement against self–defense must be noted among most Jewish manufacturers. They wanted to take revenge on their workers for the days in which they had to take part in the self–defense groups and could not work. One local rich man, Mr. W., closed the doors of his house and would not allow a division of the self–defense group to enter, which wanted to make use of the apartment for a few hours until the procession ended."

"Polish society did not protest and did not adopt any resolutions about the Bialystok pogrom. They only had a ball and the income from it went to those [who experienced destruction]. It is also a wonder that the local Polish society, in general, said nothing. They believe, it seems, that the tactic of the "successful" is to be quiet. But the proletariat is not quiet. Many mass meetings took place then, where they spoke about the Bialystok pogrom and about other political questions of the present moment. The organization of the Bund also held two such meetings. There were more than 600 people at each meeting."

We see cited here the indifference to self–defense on the part of the "community," that is, the rich strata and the intelligentsia.

In a series of places, the *B.O.* actively fought not only against the police and pogromists, but also against the Jewish hooligans who aided the Tsarists in their fight against the revolutionary *Akhdesnikes* [members of the association of Jewish workers] with the blessing of the middle class and the rabbi.

The *B.O.* used weapons against the Jewish hooligans who had serious crimes on their consciences. During the second half of 1905, the middle–class in Piotrkow and Czentochow hired "brawlers" who attacked the workers under the protection of the police, brutally beat them and turned them over to the Tsarist police. Armed Jewish workers answered them by shooting a number of organizers and those taking part in the reactionary, anti–Semitic attack on the socialists in Piotrkow and Czenstochow.

The Internal Party Life

At the end of 1905, the committee of the Bund in Czenstochow consisted of the comrades Avraham Lipnik. Aleksander Golde, Uriel Flajsher, Ester Alter, Henya Garelik and Anjute.

Lipnik was the chairman of the committee (he later was known as an eminent Bundist activist and medical doctor in Grodno). In independent Poland, Ester Alter (a sister of the later Bundist leader, Viktor Alter) was active as lawyer Ester Iwinska in Warsaw where she was a well–known Bundist activist and councilman in the Warsaw city council.

The Czenstochow organization took an active part in the internal life of the Bund, debated and decided upon a series of questions that were on the agenda then.

On 8 October 1905 a gathering of 200 Bundists took place in honor of the 8th anniversary of the Bund. After the speeches, the party meeting adopted a resolution, which expressed satisfaction with the successful struggles and activities of the Bund. The success of the struggle against all bourgeois political leanings among the Jewish people themselves and the determination and struggle of the Jewish proletariat, who were found in the front ranks of the worker–fighters in the entire country, were underlined separately.

The gathering expressed its thank you to the 6th Conference of the Bund for accepting the decision to found a Polish regional committee in the Central Committee and for quickly making the decision a reality.

The accepted resolution of the gathering of the Bundist organization ended with the following words:

"We Czenstochower Jewish workers celebrating the 8th anniversary of the Bund express our full readiness to fight against the existing political and social order for full political and social liberation, never ceasing to make any sacrifices. We also promise to carry on a constant ideological fight against those who want to use the energy and readiness to fight of the Jewish proletariat for ideas that are foreign to them.

[Page 127]

"Acknowledging the importance of the organization and strategy of the fight, we commit ourselves to be ready at every call of the Czenstochow organization of the Bund and support its successful activities with all our strength."

Those assembled voting for the resolution considered it an oath, as a sacred commitment, which they had taken upon themselves.

We will mention a few more of the various Bundist party meetings during that period: a holiday gathering took place on Purim 1906 dedicated to 1 March. A series of speakers spoke on various themes and particularly about 1 March. (This date was celebrated as the holiday anniversary of the murder of the Russian Tsar Aleksander II). The previous Haman was connected to the tsarist Haman in the speeches.

Of very important significance was the Bundist party gathering in the summer of 1906. The question of the Bund rejoining the Russian Social–Democratic Workers Party was considered then. Fervent debates about the circumstances of the reunification took place in all of the Bund organizations in the country [Poland]. Two main schools of thought were cultivated that were known as "hard" and "soft," that is more and less flexible. The Czenstochow organization sided with "hard." The general meeting of the council in Czenstochow (that is, the leaders of the separate Bundist groups – the central municipal meeting) debated passionately, accepting the resolution of the "hard," with 16 votes for, seven abstentions. The most important points of the resolution were:

1. The Bund is the social–democratic organization of the Jewish proletariat, unlimited in its activity by any regional forces.

2. No other organization that joins the Russian Social–Democratic Party beside the Bund can have as its purpose leading the social democratic activity among the Jewish masses.

3. The Bund has representatives in the Central Committee of the Russian S.D. Party.

4. The program of the Russian S.D. Party is the program of the Bund, but the Bund maintains the right to retain its program on the national question that was adopted at the 6th Conference of the Bund.

5. The Bund has the right to raise money independently for all matters of their organization.

6. The Bund organization will send its representatives to all general congresses and conferences of the Russian Social–Democratic Party on the same basis as the organizations of the Russian party.

7. The basic points can be changed at the general conference of the Russian Social–Democratic Party, only with the consent of the Bund.

On 27 and 28 March 1907, a conference of representatives of the Bundist organizations in Poland took place to elect delegates to the 5th conference of the Russian Social–Democratic Party, which took place in London. The Czenstochow area also was represented at the election conference of the Bundist organizations.

Like many other cities, a "small Bund" also existed in Czenstochow – today, a legendary revolutionary children's organization, which excells in its naïveté, heroic excitement and devotion. The later well–known lawyer, Stanislaw Nojfeld, and Shlamek Birnbaum, the son of the well–known *khazan* [cantor], Avraham Ber, among others, were in the Czenstochow "small Bund."

The Fight to Improve Economic Situation of the Jewish Workers

The political fight of the awakening Jewish worker went hand in hand with the fight to improve their terrible economic situation. The professional unions in various trades were active along with the political organization. The unions, which were led by the political organization, carried out both large and small strikes. A managing committee stood at the head of each union, which was concerned with the interests of the workers in its trade. At first there was a tendency among the workers to use very primitive fighting means, such as making use of economic terror, threats and such methods. The Bund organization tried to combat this atmosphere and carried on widespread educational work as to why such methods could not be effective and were inappropriate for an aware worker. It was not easy work to eliminate the wild fighting methods. However, the workers themselves finally were persuaded with their own successes that the road that the Bund recommended was much better and more secure, that with a stronger, disciplined organization one could reach more permanent success than by applying blows at the boss or destroying goods.

[Page 128]

At that time the professional unions were party ones. The Bund was involved with the metal and construction trades, leather trades, tailor and other trade unions. The Bund was involved with five local professional unions in 1906.

The Bund began activity to create a central office for Czenstochow and the region that would take in all professional unions of both Jewish and Polish workers. A conference of the managing committees of the Jewish professional unions was called for this purpose at the end of 1906 and it was decided to turn to the *P.S.D.* (Social–Democratic [Party] of Poland and Lithuania) with a proposal about unification. Lively professional activity was carried out at that time and many strikes were won.

The Last Revolutionary Chords

Tsarism mobilized all the dark strength of its giant empire and all of the organs of its power to suffocate the revolution. Weariness and despair began to dominate the ranks of the workers. The large number of victims, the overflowing jails, the shootings and hangings broke the fighting spirit. The revolutionary wave began to abate and the workers carried out a long rearguard campaign, fighting in groups that met under the pressure of decisive–aggressive strength. New tasks emerged everywhere then that the Czenstochow Bund organization had to fulfill.

One of the most important tasks at that time was to help the victims of the revolution, the imprisoned fighters in the jails. The work was carried out by the so–called "red circle" of the Bundist organization.

In a letter from the "red circle" of the Bund, printed in the daily Bundist *Folks–Zeitung* [*People's Newspaper*] (20 November 1906), we read:

"The situation for the arrestees and suppressed gets even worse and more severe from day to day. The various measures, which once would support those exiled and were never sufficient, are of almost no significance now with such frightfully [large] numbers of arrestees and exiled. It is absolutely necessary that every sympathetic person, to whom the fate of the unfortunate victims is dear, set aside [money] from their own use, to help the forlorn exiled to the distant deserts.

"The sacred duty to use all means to gather money for them particularly lies with our comrades. If every city or shtetl [town] would send something, this would become a great sum. We can imagine that this would only be a drop in the ocean. However, we cannot say that this will not be of help.

"The old appeal should be spread everywhere: "Help the arrestees and exiled!" And help will come from all sides.

"Meanwhile, 28 rubles and 50 *kopikes* have been collected in Czenstochow from a number of Bundist comrades for this purpose.

"May this letter by a signal for an active collection for our languishing comrades in distant Siberia..."

We did not have to be occupied only with help for the arrestees and exiles. The local Bund organization also had the occasion to help Jewish workers who stopped in the city before emigrating abroad and illegally crossing the border. It should be understood that the organization did not possess the necessary finances for this. At most, they could give a little monetary support. Often, people were left on the long road [of emigration] without the necessary financial means and required more help. The only effective help that we could give and we did give to the emigrants was making sure they did not fall into the hands of the swindlers who promised [help in] crossing the border and cheated and swindled the emigrants. Therefore, the local organization published warnings in the labor press. Here is an extract from one such warning (end of summer 1906):

"The Czenstochower Bund organization reported that many workers arrive to cross the border. The organization does not have enough financial means and therefore those arriving wander around through the streets and are dying of hunger. Therefore, the organization warns that no one should rely on it for support. Only those should come who have the necessary [financial] means. The organization will help them, so that they do not fall into the hands of swindlers."

[Page 129]

However, it would be an error to think that the Bundist movement was only involved with aid activity during the period of the decline of the revolution. Despite the increasing apathy, fear and even hate from the surrounding bourgeois environment, the Bund tried to maintain the fighting spirit of the Jewish worker.

Before the elections to the Russian Duma [parliament] at the end of 1906, the Bundist organization, ignoring the strong apathy, endeavored to awake the far–reaching masses. A total of 3,398 voters were registered in Czenstochow during the *Duma* elections; of them not more than 1,000 Poles. The majority of the registered consisted of Jews. The Bund carried out its campaigning among the working strata. The Bundists arranged a series of meetings of various trades and several in factories in connection with the election campaign. Then the Bundists carried out self–taxation of one day's wages for the fund of the central committee of the Bund.

So the work was carried out under a hail of repressions. The police even stopped passers–by in the street and searched their pockets and patted their bodies. House searches were a frequent phenomena. Arrestees were beaten.

Despite the repressions, the Polish and Jewish worker organizations issued an appeal for 1 May. Red flags had been hung out on the telegraph lines and on the chimneys of the factories in honor of the international workers holiday. On 1 May, all of the police were on foot and they had difficult work removing the red flags. Almost all of the workers were on strike from the workshops and factories. Only two factories were not on strike because the majority [of workers] there consisted of *Endekes* [members of the anti–Semitic Polish National Party].

The picture would not be complete if we did not remember the sharp, idealistic fighters (who did not always take on purely ideological identities) among the Bund and Zionist–Socialists. Czenstochow was one of the few cities where the Zionist–Socialists were strong. Here the Zionist–Socialist movement began earlier and lasted the longest while it declined everywhere else. The *P.S.D.* [Polish Social Democrats] also had a certain effect on the Jewish street, although it was very small. The majority of the Jewish intelligentsia was assimilated or supported [Jewish] nationalism. Therefore, it was mainly distant from the Jewish workers movement.

In the Yoke of Heavy Reaction

The reaction that came after the revolutionary period of 1905 hit the workers movement in the Tsarist Empire hard. The masses were terrorized and apathetic. A large number of activists were held in jails and in Siberia; the organizations collapsed. Only here and there, in a small number of cities, groups of devoted and tireless, small remnants of the previously powerful organizations held together, carried out a conspiratorial life deeply underground. They were like rare oases in a giant desert. All of the revolutionary parties lived through such conditions, although not all in the same measure. The Bund in this regard was no exception, although, perhaps more than others it was rescued from the reactionary catastrophe. This was thanks to its massive size and the deep roots it had struck in Jewish life.

One of these cases was Czenstochow. The city belonged to the fortunate exceptions where the Bundist movement was not interrupted even in the difficult years of the reaction. Once it took root in the earth of the Jewish workers life in Czenstochow, it was impossible to pull it out even in the darkest cloudburst of reaction.

It should be understood that the activity of the years 1908–1915 had to be limited due to general conditions in the country. However, it is important [to know] that the organization constantly functioned and, in the frame of limited possibilities, kept on supporting the beliefs and the strivings of the Jewish worker.

As has been said, the work had to be very conspiratorial; only in very rare cases were signs of life shown in public. One of these cases was after the death of Bronislaw Grosser, the leader of the Bund. A short announcement was printed in *Di Zeit* [*The Time*], no. 2, which was published in Petersburg:

"Czenstochow. A group of Czenstochow friends expresses its sympathy on the untimely death of Bronislaw Grosser."

[Page 130]

The same year, on *Shabbos* [Sabbath], 2 October 1913, a mass arrest of Bundists took place in Czenstochow. A meeting took place at the field near the *klejarnia* [adhesive factory]. Many police and gendarmes with the chief of the gendarmes and the regional police superintendent Arbuzow at the head surrounded the meeting and arrested around 60 people.

The majority of the arrestees consisted of tailors, among whom were young people. All were taken to the police station under heavy guard and from there to jail. The following people were arrested then:

Avraham Rotbard, Avraham Granek, Yakov Laska, Avraham Kaczka, Tovya Mas, Icek Gelbard, Avraham Walman, Yosef Rozenblat, Benyamin Rozenblat, Ruwin Luks, Leibele [diminutive of Leibl] Rajzblat, Shlomo Haneman, Chaim Buchalter, Yakov Dlugonogi, Leyzer Berkensztat, Moshe Grinberg, Avraham Tovya Frajermauer, Mordekhai Wajsfelner, Nakhman Epsztajn, Yosef Izraelowicz, Wolf Tapenberg, Leibish Dilewski, Dovid Panriser, Kalman Gelber, Shlomo Markowicz, Kalman Szklarcz, Wolf Wien, Yakov Kogun, Yonatan Gutman, Henekh

Feldman, Hershl Wargan, Yehuda Frajermauer, Y. Jadnur, Mordekhai Wajntraub, Yisroel Gutfrajnd, Avraham Ferenger, Daniel Goldberg, Kopel Tajchner, Daniel Chlapak, G. Drajzner, Ayzyk Libgut, Yudl Lipszuc, Ahron Niedziela, Shmuel Enzl, Perec Fintowicz, Yehuda Kernik, Faygel Fridman, Nakha Szturkman, Meir Golach, Avraham Fridman, Chaim Grinblat, Shlomo Buchner, Dovid Futerhendler, Moshe Pedszt, Yisroel Lublinski, Shlomo Lewkowicz, Leibish Zajdman, Yisroel Iman, Yakov Kagut, Marian Staszkowski and Wladislaw Szuster (the last two were Poles).

Sixty–one people in total were arrested. The arrestees were sentenced administratively to three months in jail. Twenty–five of them were sent to Piotrków in a procession under escort; the remainder sat in the Czenstochow jail. Only one, Leibl Rajzblat, was freed.

This was a meeting of Bundist workers. The arrest made a great impression in the city. The police and gendarmerie, which undertook to eradicate sedition from the soil of Czenstochow, were not satisfied by the large [number of] arrests and carried out another series of searches and arrests.

In connection with the strong persecutions at the beginning of 1914, the Bund organization in Czenstochow sent an appeal to the Socialist Democratic faction in the Russian Duma [parliament] to deliver to the government an interpellation [parliamentary maneuver demanding an official explanation for a government policy or act] and thereby bring the matter before a wider public. Because of the interpellation, the press in Russia wrote about the searches and arrests among the Jewish workers and socialists in Czenstochow.

The majority of the arrestees consisted of members of professional unions, which existed despite the great interference of the tsarist regime.

A short time before the outbreak of the First World War, summer 1914, Wiktor Szulman, the Bundist activist, came to Czenstochow in connection with the 8th Congress of the Bund that was supposed to take place in 1914 in Vienna and was called off because of the outbreak of war. Czenstochow and Noworadomsk had to send delegates together. In addition, Szulman had to set up contact in Czenstochow, Bedzin and Sosnowiec for bringing the delegates across the border.

During the Years of the First World War

Czenstochow was taken by German troops right at the beginning of the First World War. The Germans exhibited brutality in various ways then, but in general their behavior was more civilized than the previous Russian satrap. Therefore, a communal revival began with the arrival of the Germans.

The Bund organization often arranged public readings that drew a large crowd. Among those who held gatherings in Czenstochow was the famous leader of the Bund, Vladimir Medem. The room was overflowing with an audience of 800 men, who listened to his report with keen interest during his appearance on 17 January 1917. Not only workers, but people of various other Jewish political beliefs came to hear Medem's speeches about "the communal strivings of Jews." An important means then for spreading the word among Jewish workers was the only Yiddish workers newspaper in occupied Poland – the Bundist weekly *Lebns Fragn* [*Life Questions*] that was published in Warsaw under the editor, Vladimir Medem. In Czenstochow in 1916 100 copies of *Lebns Fragn* were sold weekly. The newspaper was spread among the workers of the wood, leather, paper, garment, celluloid and other trades. In 1917 the number of each issue of *Lebns Fragn* sold in Czenstochow exceeded 200 copies. At the end of 1916 the Bundists founded a club named for the deceased Bundist leader, Bronislaw Grosser. Bundists and sympathizers gathered at the club. The club was not only a home in which one enjoyed a comradely environment, but was also a center of cultural activities. In 1917 the club received great monetary support from Bundists from outside [Poland]. In its first three months of existence, the club carried out nine readings and gatherings with 1,800 attendees.

[Page 131]

At the time of the German occupation during the First World War, members of the Czenstochow Bund committee were: Yakov Rozenberg – chairman, Yosef Aronowicz – secretary, Hershl Frajman, Avraham Rotbard and others. Comrade Straus, known as A. Galicianer, later a Bundist activist in Lemberg and correspondent for the Bundist *Folks–Zeitung* [*People's Newspaper*], was among the active Bundist community workers at that time.

The most esteemed leader for the local Bundist organization at that time was Yosef Aronowicz. With his readings he helped break the communal influence of the former assimilated circles in the city.

The election campaign for the city council occupied a significant place in communal life at the time of the First World War. The election ordinances, which the German occupying regime established, were not very favorable for the poor classes of the population. There were six curiae and they left just one mandate [seat] in the sixth *curia* for the workers.[2] The Bund voted independently and it contested the bloc of the Jewish bourgeois parties. In one of the Bundist appeals at the end of 1916, it said:

"The Poles of Moses' belief [the Jews], the Zionists, the Hasids – all of those who during the war speculated with our *groshns* hard–earned with our sweat and blood and with the outbreak of the war threw out the workers and trade employees from their factories and businesses – have united in a bloc, They speak now of the interests of the Jewish people. We, workers, do not believe their beautiful phrases.

"We know what is hidden under the words of peace and unity.

"The truth of the words was confirmed by the action of the Jewish–bourgeois bloc, which joined in unity with the Polish bourgeois parties about dividing among themselves the mandates in the first six election curiae.

"During the election campaign, the Jewish group of the Polish Socialist–Democratic Party (*P.S.D.*, later the Communist Party) split off. The splinter group joined the Bund. In a public declaration those who had left [the *P.S.D.* party] emphasized that they consider the Bund as a Socialist–Democratic Party and their demands for national equal rights as an expression of the demands of the Jewish proletariat. Considering the national program of the Bund – the declaration further states – we have come to the belief that the demands are just and the Jewish workers need to say this often and loudly."

There was a transition in Jewish life during the fourth year of the First World War, a transfer from tsarist rule to the changed conditions of independent Poland. A new era began that was the most intensive and most colorful in the history of the Jewish community in Czenstochow.

In Independent Poland

The Bundist movement constantly grew and strengthened during the 20 years between the two world wars. New fields of activity arrived – in the city council, *kehile* [organized Jewish community], sick fund. The party professional and cultural work was expanded. New branches of the movement joined in, such as a Youth Bund, *Zukunft* [Future]; the children's organization, *SKIF* [*Sotsyalistishe Kinder Farband* – Socialist Children's Union]; the sports organization, *Morgnshtern* [Morning Star], the women's organization; *YAF* [*Yidisher Arbeter Froy* – Jewish Women Workers]; the school organization, *Undzer Kinder* [Our Children]; the general workers' cooperative and the publishing cooperative, *Kultura* [Culture].

New, young people from the generation that grew up after the First World War joined the old activists and members. The former possessed tradition, experience, class–consciousness; the later, enthusiasm, daring, dynamism; and both groups, the old and the new, were fused into a unity through their idealism and unlimited devotion.

[Page 132]

On a New Foundation

The Bund approached widespread, challenging work in independent Poland with different conditions, a new communal atmosphere [and] with an influx of young strength.

The first, broader activity was connected to the rise of a workers council. All of the worker movements in the city belonged to it. From the Poles – the Polish Socialist Party (P.P.S.), communist party, the nationalist grouping, *Narodowy Związek Robotniczy* (*N.Z.R.*) [National Workers' Union], the Christian Democrats (C.D.); from the Jewish workers – the Bund, *Fareinikte* (*Z.S.*) [United] and *Poalei–Zion* [Workers of Zion]. Yosef Aronowciz, Zalman Tenenberg, Maks Brum, the baker–worker Avraham Rozenblat and others belonged to the Bund faction.

The speeches by Yosef Aronowicz, particularly his appearances against the anti–Semitic proposals of the *Cadekes* [Christian Democrats], made a strong impression. The *Cadekes* proposed among other [resolutions] that Jews could not belong to the workers council. The *Cadekes* remained alone. All of the other groupings rejected the arrogant, anti–Semitic proposal.

In addition to the workers council, which was the expression of the revolutionary mood in the work force during the first years after the [First] World War, a people's militia also existed for a few weeks. Many Jewish workers participated in it. Jewish workers armed with rifles stood guard, patrolled the streets or carried out other police functions. However, the people's militia, as is said, lived even a shorter time than the workers council.

The city council remained a lasting institution of main significance to the city. Its significance was great, as was its competence as a communal self–managing organ. It simultaneously became a political tribunal.

The Bund had its representative there elected by the Jewish workers. Yosef Aronowicz, the Bundist representative to the first city council of independent Poland that was elected in 1919, in principled declarations and speeches expressed the stand of the Bund on a series of political and social questions in the city and in the country. The Bundist representative also made a strong declaration against the Polish–Soviet War.

A series of repressions against the Bund began in connection with the strong declaration (the same thing happened in the entire country). The Polish regime arrested the Bund's entire Czenstochow committee headed by Mr. Yosef Aronowicz. In later years Aronowicz moved to Vilna where he was an esteemed worker in the Bund, in the professional unions and in the Jewish–World School–Organization (*TS.B.K.* [*Tsentraler Bildungs Komitet* – Central Education Committee]). After occupying Vilna in October 1939, the Soviet regime arrested him along with a group of other Bundist workers and all traces of him disappeared.

The following Bundist workers were arrested in Czenstochow with Aronowicz in 1920: Zalman Tenenberg (later a Bundist worker and head of the *kehile* [organized Jewish community] in Piotrkow; perished during the Second World War in the Auschwitz death camp after a sweeping arrest of Piotrkow Bundists, when a transport of illegal literature was seized); Grinbaum, Chencinski, and Chaim Dovid Wolhendler. They then also came to arrest the Bund activist and leader of the baker–workers, Tsine Orczech (now in Canada). As he was then a convalescent after [suffering from] typhus, he was left alone. Orczech threw himself into the aid work for his arrested comrades. He founded an inter–party aid committee (with *Fareinikte* [United] and *Poaeli–Zion* [Workers of Zion]). Then, he, himself, was arrested in Krakow when he went there with help for the arrestees who were being held in a camp in Dąbie, near Krakow.

The first committee of the Bund in Czenstochow in independent Poland consisted of the following comrades: Yosef Aronowicz, Zalman Tenenberg, Moshe Lederman, Tsine Orczech, Yosef Izraelewicz, Avraham Fridman, Avraham Rotbard and M. Borzykowski. Some were taken into the military at the time when a number of the committee members were confined at the camp in Dąbie. Of the committee members, only Tsine Orczech was left to [continue the] work.

When he needed to decide important questions, the remaining committee member went to the military barracks and conversed with comrades Moshe Lederman, Avraham Fridman and Moshe Tuchmajer through the barbed wire. "Meetings" of the committee were held in that way then.

[Page 133]

The arrested Bundist activists were held at the Dąbie concentration camp until the end of the Polish–Soviet War. In connection with the arrest of the councilman, Yosef Aronowicz, the representative of *Fareinikte*, Rafal Federman, brought a proposal that the city council demands the freeing of the arrestees in order to provide an opportunity for him [Aronowicz] to continue to fulfill his functions as an elected representative of the population. The *P.P.S.* [Polish Socialist Party] councilmen also supported the proposal and it was adopted by the city council.

Of the appearances at the city council at the beginning it is particularly worthwhile to remember the declarations and resolutions proposed by the socialist councilmen in connection with the pogrom of 1919, which ostensibly broke out because a Jew had thrown a stone at a soldier in Haller's Army.[3] The speeches by Yosef Aronowicz, the Bundist representative, made a great impression at the time.

The Bund also joined the Jewish kehile [organized community] several years later. The Bundist *parnosim* [elected heads of the community] led a fight for the *kehile* to take on a worldly character. At every opportunity they raised political questions that had a connection to the condition of the Jewish population. The principal fight with the civil majority was held in considering ethics. The Bundist representatives demanded that no taxes be placed on the poorer population and using the expenditures mainly to satisfy the needs of the poor, to raise the social and spiritual conditions of the poorest, underprivileged strata.

The Bundist movement in Czenstochow vastly expanded in the first few years of Polish independence. The number of organized Bundists and their influence among the Jewish workers, in general, grew in the professional movement, which found itself under Bundist influence, such as the unions of garment workers, woodworkers, bakers and others. The influence of the Bund rose in the large organization of trade workers. In the assimilated *stowarzyszenia* [association], the Bundists headed by Yosef Aronowicz and Yakov Rozenberg (later head of the Czenstochow kehile) led a fight against the ruling assimilationist group and for a Jewish proletarian character of the union.

A group of new activists joined, who had an influence in the various areas of Jewish life in Czenstochow. From time to time eminent leaders and members of the central committee would arrive from Warsaw.

Fareinikte [United] Joins the Bund

The Zionist–Socialists, who had been called *Fareinikte* since 1919, was one of the oldest and strongest organizations in Czenstochow. The process of decline, which seized this movement everywhere, did not by–pass Czenstochow. Although here, *Fareinikte* hung on the longest. The first great crisis came in 1922 when a significant number, headed by Rafal Federman, the chairman of the city committee and councilman at the city council, moved to the Bund.

A short time later (February 1923), a public gathering of the Bund took place in Czenstochow at which, in addition to Federman, Ahron Singalowski (Ahron Czenstochower), one of the most eminent founders and leaders of the Zionist–Socialists, appeared as a speaker.

In addition, disappointment in the founding principles of *Fareinikte* was another reason for a large group leaving this party. It actually dissolved and joined with smaller, splinter group of the P.P.S. [Polish Socialist Party] under the leadership of Dr. Drobner. Together, they built a so–called independent socialist party.

Its Own Newspaper

In February 1923, the Bundist organization began to publish its own newspaper, which served Czenstochow and the surrounding area. Its name was *Arbeter–Zeitung* [*Workers Newspaper*] (see more in the article, "Yiddish Press in Czenstochow").

Work for the Jewish Secular School

In June 1922, the unification of the secular Jewish schools created by each party came about as a result of the demands of the Central Jewish School Organization in Poland. Three movements entered the general Czenstochow organization: *Fareinikte*, the Bund and the left *Paolei–Zion* [Marxist–Zionists].

[Page 134]

In February 1923, a division of the *Undzer Kinder* [Our Children] society was founded in Czenstochow through which the local Bundist organization carried out its educational work. At the founding meeting, where the tasks and obligations of the Jewish working class in relation to the Jewish secular schools was widely discussed, the actions at that time of the bourgeois Jewish deputies in the *Sejm* [Polish parliament] were heatedly criticized. The Jewish *Kolo* ["circle" – faction in parliament), the union of the Jewish deputies and Senators, voted against the secular schools [using] the Yiddish language. The gathering accepted the following resolution about this:

"By voting against the Jewish schools, the Jewish *Kolo*, which consists of Zionist and Orthodox deputies, has shown to the entire world that it stands in the camp of hate of the Jewish schools and strives toward its collapse. The Jewish *Kolo* indirectly took under its protection all repressions against the Jewish school system and gave the government a certain justification to continue with the repressions. The Jewish masses branded this action as a criminal one. The gathering asked that the Jewish working masses stand guard over their schools and to support them with ever more energy against the reactionary wave.

"The representatives of the professional unions of the garment workers, the wood workers, the nutrition workers and the paper [workers], as well as the delegation of the young Bund, *Zukunft*, delivered declarations that their organizations join in the protest."

The Bundist organization surrounded the Jewish secular schools with love and warmth and did everything to strengthen their position. In 1925 the Bundist faction in the city council led a campaign for the city to help the Jewish secular schools through the giving of subsidies. The campaign also was supported by the *rada* [council] of the professional unions (Polish and Jewish). The campaign and efforts of the Bundist city council faction was crowned with success. City hall decided to give subsidies to the Jewish worker schools.

According to the proposal of the Bundist councilman, Rafal Federman, the city council, in December 1926, decided to raise the subsidy of the Jewish secular schools, 4,000 *zlotes* instead of the previous 1,500. The Bundist weekly newspaper in Czenstochow, *Arbeter–Zeitung*, (24 December 1926) wrote about the decision:

"This time the Jewish bourgeois councilmen, such as Goldsztajn and others who would always abstain from voting on such a question or would leave the room, also voted for the proposal. (This time) the avowed *Endekes* [members of the anti–Semitic Polish National Party], such as Dr. Nowak and friends who always voted against, abstained. Only four *Cadekes* [Christian Democrats] voted against.

At that time there was a well–established six–grade public school and a children's nursery in Czenstochow, which was led by the Jewish School Organization. The public school bore the name of the great Yiddish writer, Y.L. Peretz.

In 1936, the government powers disbanded the Czenstochow division of the Jewish School Organization (*Tsysho* □[*Tsentrale Yidishe Shul–Organizatsye* – Central Yiddish School

Organization]). At the initiative of the Bund, the division was reopened in 1938. There was a new managing committee, which consisted of A. Peretz, M. Berkensztat, Y. Jaronowski, W. Fajga, Sh. Yakukowicz, A. Brat, G. Prenski, Y. Kaufman and Y. Yakubowicz. At the beginning of 1939, the new division of *Tsysho* opened an afternoon school, *Powszechny* [public] school for the children of the Polish state. They taught Yiddish and Jewish history in the afternoon school.

Struggle in the City Council

The Socialist faction at the Czenstochow city council, Jewish and Polish, fought an embittered fight against the municipal majority. The city council lengthened the period of its existence for a few years after its term of office had been supposed to end. Finally, in 1925, the Socialist faction decided to leave and in this way force elections to be held for a new city council.

On 24 June 1925, a declaration in connection with this was read in the name of the Bundist faction at a meeting of the city council that provided a picture of the bad municipal economy and of the struggle of the Bundist councilmen, among others. Among other things, the declaration said:

"The politics of the city council in the course of its six–year existence was supported by a majority of the Polish–Jewish bourgeois and capitalist elements that were supported by the ostensible representatives of the *Cadekes* [Christian Democrats] and *Enprowces* [National Party]. The latter went hand and hand with the rightist groups against the interests of the working class.

[Page 135]

"Our faction at every opportunity in considering the budget or through urgent proposals tried to unmask the politics hostile to workers and at least to partly alleviate the situation for the working masses who always carried the entire load of conditions of war or industrial crises in the form of unemployment.

"Only for belonging to the Bundist city council faction and for his open activity in the area was the councilman, Yosef Aronowicz, interned in a concentration camp and only after eight months, under the pressure of the Socialist councilmen, did the city council decide to accept a proposal to free him. He was finally, in general, forced to leave our city.

"The proposal about distributing subsides for the Jewish public schools that carry on the work and in which up to 200 children from the poorest strata of the population study was presented several times.

"The enthusiasm of the city council and city hall clearly shows their position toward the excesses of 27 May 1919, as well as the fact that until this day no Jewish worker or official has been employed in the city hall.

On the question of the continued existence of the old city council and city hall, just as in the other important cases, one group of the socialist councilmen, Polish and Jewish, was fostered against the united front of the bourgeois and reactionary councilmen of both nationalities.

A short [term of office] came after the long city council, which contrinued its existence for one and a half years and in May 1927 was dissolved. At the last meeting, before the dissolution a declaration from the Bundist faction was read in which among other things it was shown that although the working class had a majority in the city council, the city hall served the interests of the owner classes. This was possible because the non–socialist workers movement, mainly the *Cadekes*, had reached an agreement with the representatives of the capitalists. The *Cadekes* (Christian Democrats) went hand and hand with the Jewish and Polish bourgeois in all economic questions with harm to the working masses.

The Fight for Democratizing and Secularizing the Jewish Kehile

There were several more public–legal institutions on the soil of Czenstochow in which the Jewish workers took part through their elected representatives.

One of these was the Jewish *kehile* [organized Jewish community] leadership. The Bundists always attempted to raise the state of the institution. They therefore fought the disorder and negligence, the influence and bias and other bad qualities, which were so characteristic of many *kehilus* [plural of *kehile*] in Poland. The Bundist representatives tried to transform the *kehilus* into institutions that would serve the poor strata of the people, help their cultural development and also satisfy their other needs, such as the health system, help when in need and the like.

A bitter struggle about this was carried out with the Orthodox, who wanted the kehile to mainly to take care of the religious needs, as well as with the powerful men who wanted to dominate with a strong hand, with their own strength and with the strength of their protectors, the regime representatives.

The Bundist *parnosim* [elected members of the *kehile*] also attempted, at appropriate opportunities, to deal with the question of general Jewish interests. One such case was during the well–known pogrom in Romania. On 9 January 1927, at a meeting of the kehile council, a representative of the Bund made such a proposal:

"The Czenstochow *kehile* council protests in an energetic manner against the continuing politics of the Romanian reaction that found its most recent expression in the bloody anti–Jewish pogroms in a series of Romanian cities. The Czenstochow *kehile* council protests against the shameful politics of the bourgeois reactionary Jewish parties in Romania that support the anti–Semitic Romanian government and, during the last elections to the Romanian parliament, worked hand in hand with the anti–Semitic reaction."

The bourgeois majority of the *kehile* council rejected the Bundist proposal and adopted its own text of the protest resolution.

[Page 136]

Therefore, the Bund, in general, fought so that the *kehile* managing committee would be democratized and [would] listen to the needs of the wider, Jewish masses and not become a tool in the hands of the clergy.

The Bund received 478 votes and two mandates [seats] during the election, which took place in September 1936. The elected Bundist *parnosim* then were Ahron Peretz and Yisroel Jaronowski.

The activists Rafal Federman, Ahron Peretz, Yisroel Jaronowski and Moshe Berkensztat were Bund representatives at the Czenstochow *kehile* at various times. The last head of the *kehile* was Yakov Rozenberg, a former Bundist.

In addition to the *kehile*, the Bund also represented the Jewish worker at the sick fund – an obligatory institution, which needed to provide medical aid to all workers and employees. The Bundist faction with other worker representatives carried on a struggle for improving the institution on behalf of the working class. The Bundist faction particularly fought so that the Jewish workers and employees would not be wronged. They also demanded in connection with this the right to use the Yiddish language at the sick fund and also to carry out the educational work in Yiddish.

May 1st

The international workers holiday – 1 May – evolved into a firmly rooted tradition among the Jewish workers in Poland. They did not work on the day. An account of the previous year was made at meetings and demonstrations in many cities together with the Polish workers and the recent and continuing work was recorded. The spiritual appraisal made by every worker – the young as well as the old – was more important than the dry examination of their conscience. It was a day of total celebration in the socialist sense.

The Czenstochow Jewish workers were no exception in this regard. They celebrated the day of 1 May every year. The *Arbeter–Zeitung* [*The Workers Newspaper*], the Bundist weekly in Czenstochow of 6 May, wrote about the celebration in 1927:

"The Jewish masses poured out of their lairs, crowded cellars and attic rooms. There were the tailors, shoemakers and other workers with their callused hands. The porters came in their *Shabbos* [Sabbath] garments.

"The educational work of the Bund brought the appropriate results. New people came from everywhere to the ranks of the socialist camp. Innumerable workers placed themselves in the jurisdiction of their party and were required to lead them in the streets. The bourgeois watched with envy and wonder as the Jewish workers marched in closed ranks, soaked by rain, which had fallen the entire morning.

"The Bund can take pride with great satisfaction that their crowds grow from year to year. The cadres, which gather under their wing, grow still larger. This was seen in this year's demonstration in Czenstochow where the entire organized Jewish working class demonstrated under the banner of the Bund."

The demonstration itself was described in the *Arbeter–Zeitung* in this way:

"The magnificent Bundist flag was carried first, then the flag of the Jewish cultural office, then the flag of the Youth Bund, *Zukunft*, the flags of the professional unions of garment, wood, meat, transport (which marched for the first time with the Bund), nutrition, chemical [workers]. The members of the professional unions walked under the flags. Banners were carried in the demonstration with the inscriptions, "We demand political amnesty! Let the worker and peasant government live! Let live the national–cultural autonomy! Let live the eight–hour work–day! Down with night work in the bakeries!" and others.

Seven hundred workers took part in the Bundist demonstration procession. Several meetings took place in addition to the demonstration.

The 1 May demonstrations looked the same in later years. Not only the adult young people marched in the demonstrations, but also several elderly workers, a number of whom had been active fighters against Russian Tsarism.

The Bund almost always demonstrated with the Polish worker organizations on 1 May. The Jewish workers were attacked several times by the anti–Semitic hooligans during joint demonstrations with the Polish workers. In several cases, the well–organized militia of the Polish Socialist Party came to help and helped the Jewish workers drive away the hooligan attackers.

[Page 137]

During the last years before the Second World War, the Polish government, which became more and more anti–Semitic, did not permit joint demonstrations by Polish and Jewish workers in a series of cities. It was the same in Czenstochow. And above all, the regime did not permit any separate street demonstrations by Jewish workers. Therefore, they had to come together only at meetings, which drew large crowds (up to 1,000 men), which expressed their anger and protest against the action of the government powers. Thus it was, for example, in 1937 and in the later years.

Youth Bund – *Zukunft*

From the first moment on, during the time of the First World War and in the years after it, the Bund had a large youth movement across the entire nation. When the revived Bundist youth movement took shape, the young workers in Czenstochow also began to gather under the flag of the Bund. As in other cities, they also linked the torn threads of the former "small Bund" and, in 1919, created *Zukunft* [Future], a youth organization.

Youth sections were created in the professional unions (in 1922), which had the task of caring for the economic interests of the young workers. Three youth sections existed at the beginning of 1925, in the garment, wood and brushmaker trades. *Zukunft*, the Youth Bund, educated the Jewish working young people politically, raised their cultural level, created a communal home for them and included them in the fight carried on by the entire working class. For the children of the poor Jewish streets, the self–education circles of the Youth Bund's *Zukunft* were like the university for the rich sons and daughters. From time to time, the youth organization also arranged public meetings and gatherings to which large crowds of young people came. Among others was the undertaking under the name, *Yugnt Zeitung in Lebedikn Wort* [*Youth Newspaper in Living Word*]. The speakers and activists came from the youth masses themselves. More than one Czenstochow Jewish worker–activist had his first communal school in the Youth Bund, *Zukunft*.

A Bundist children's organization, *SKIF* [*Sotsyalistishe Kinder Farband* – Socialist Children's Union] and *Morgnstern* [Morning Star], a sports organization, arose in later years.

The Bundist youth were in contact with the Polish socialist youth [organization] and at times arranged joint appearances with it, such as, for example, a joint meeting dedicated to the struggle against nationalism took place on 17 June 1933. A large crowd of young people came; all were dressed in blue shirts and red ties, which was the uniform of the socialist youth. The young people waved red flags over their heads. The speeches were delivered in two languages – Polish and Yiddish. The young people sang the Polish workers' hymn, *Czwewoni Sztandar* (*The Red Flag*) and the Jewish workers' hymn, *Di Shuve* [*The Oath*] of the Bund. This demonstration of Polish–Jewish fraternity and of international workers solidarity took place in the residence of Polish clericalism, where for years, hundreds of thousands of pilgrims from all corners of the land came to the miracle–working picture in the church at Jasna Gora.

There also were camps and excursions among the various activities carried out by the Bund. There is a description of one such summer camp in the Warsaw *Folks–Zeitung* [*People's Newspaper*] of 23 August 1936:

"The Youth Bund, *Zukunft*, as every year, this year, too, organized its own summer camp in the beautiful area of Cszanstow outside Czenstochow. The necessary sum was collected from savings and voluntary taxation of comrades and friends. Our young people joyfully spent time in a Bundist, comradely environment in their own camp, which was led by the comrades M. Lederman and M. Kuszir. Our *Zukunftists* returned cheerful and ready for combat and they took part in our work with new fervor.

Youth Bund, *Zukunft*
The Excursion in the City Park

The Czenstochow *Zukunftists* took part in a series of excursions organized by the Youth Bund on the staff's quarter acre of land or in the region.

One such excursion – in 1935 – took place in Czenstochow itself. In addition to those from Czenstochow, *Zukunftists* from Zaglembie (Bedzin and Sosnowiec, Dambrowa Gonica), Piotrkow, Radomsk and other neighboring shtetlekh [towns] took part in the excursion. The excursion made a great impression in the city. The socialist city hall provided the city park for the arrangement of a a parade. The Polish socialist movement took part with a delegation.

[Page 138]

Morgnshtern [Morning Star], the Bundist sports organization in Czenstochow, was founded in 1937. Its achievements could already by seen in the summer of 1938, at the anniversary of *Morgnshtern*. A tour–fest took place in the *Makkabi*'s hall. Its success was so great that it had to be repeated a short time later. The second time, the tour–fest took place in the firemen's hall and Zalman Fridrich, the representative of the central managing committee of *Morgnshtern* in Poland, also gave a report then about the significance of sports for the Jewish workers and young people. (Zalman Fridrich later played a great role in the underground movement and in the Warsaw ghetto uprising of April–May 1943 and he perished at that time.)

In 1939 the Czenstochow *Morgnshtern* organization had hundreds of members. Its activists also established organizations in neighboring cities such as Sosnowiec, Radomsk, Zawiercie, Klobuck and others.

Yitzhak Stopnicer, Zisa Cincinatus, Hershl Prozwer, Motl Kusznir, Yadza Stopnicer, Shimshon Jakubowicz, Eliash Sztajgic, Simkha Zilberberg and others stood at the head of the Bundist Youth organization through the years. They were all activists from the young themselves. Ahron Peretz, the old Bundist activist, Henrik Lajzerowicz, the former Zionist-Socialist activist who moved to the Bund, Gerszonowicz, Kusznir and others stood at the head of the sports organization, *Morgnshtern*. The teacher, Liber Brener, Melman, Krul, Moshe Lederman, the Bundist activist, Itka Lazar (murdered by the Nazis in Warsaw during the Second World War) and others led the Bundist children's Organization SKIF.

Anti–Semitism and Boycott

The bacillus of anti–Semitism found a suitable place to fertilize itself in the thick Catholic atmosphere of the city where great fanatics were clouded by glorification and superstitions. Czenstochow was one of those Polish cities where anti–Semitism was intensive and aggressive. The *Endekes* [members of the *Endecja – Narodowa Demokraczja* – anti–Semitic, Polish Nationalist Democratic Party] and the *Nara*–followers (Polish fascists) led strong boycott campaigns and organized various anti–Jewish excesses during the last years before the Second World War.

Thus, in 1937, a week before *Shavous* [spring holiday celebrating the "Giving of the Torah"], they proclaimed a propaganda campaign for the Polish merchants and artisans. An extensive boycott campaign was carried out during the week of 2 to 9 May. Special calls for boycotts and placards were printed. Pickets in green armbands stood in front of Jewish businesses and shops and did not allow any Polish customers to enter. The slogans were: "Do not be a fool; buy only from Poles." "You do not want to destroy Poland, buy only from Poles."

From time to time, the *Endekes* carried out anti–Jewish demonstrations. On 15 August 1938, during one street appearance of this kind, they shouted the chorus: "*Żydzi na latarniach, niech zginą marnie*" (Jewish are hanging on the lamppost, may they die in loneliness). The Endeke demonstrators also attacked Jews and began to break windowpanes. When they entered the Jewish neighborhoods, groups of Bundists came out into the street and chased the hooligans. Several were bloodied. Many police arrived and "restored order."

[Page 139]

The Bundist Militia in Czenstochow
Seated, first from right to left: in the second row – Y. Pendrak

At the end of 1937 the Polish workers, socialist Pepesowces [members of the Polish Socialist Party], organized groups to fight against the Endeke pickets and drive them from the street.

The Polish Socialist Movement and Its Solidarity with the Jewish Workers

The Polish Socialist Party (*P.P.S.*) was strong in Czenstochow. Its great influence was expressed in various elections and during meetings and street demonstrations. It was strongly represented in the city managing committee sick fund and other institutions.

The Bund stood in friendly contact with the Polish workers movement. There were many cases in which Polish socialists actively appeared against the anti–Semitic rampaging.

Czenstochow was a nest of Catholic clericalism and this could not remain this way without the influence of a certain part of the working class. The city was relatively greatly influenced by the power of the C.D. (Christian Democrats) and *N.P.R.* (National Workers Party) – both nationalist, anti–Semitic workers organizations. The majority of the Polish workers did not go with them. They mainly belonged to the Socialist Party and a much smaller number, to the communist movement. The P.P.S. always had a large faction in the city council, although not a majority. *Pepesowces* were elected president or vice president of the city with the votes of the Jewish socialist and bourgeois councilmen.

During the years when the *Sanacja* ["healing" – an authoritarian political movement] government had a strong policy against the opposition, the repression also began to be felt in Czenstochow. There was a time when the followers of the government regime began to mimic the methods of Rome and Berlin. They then removed all socialist employees from city hall and from the sick fund. There also were repressions against the Bund because the Bundist organization refused to give a declaration of loyalty to the government. The Bundist activist, Rafal Federman, who was the only Jewish employee at the sick fund, was removed from his job. He was told he could remain if he would resign from his opposition position in the government.

The repression reached its highpoint when a band of senators (followers of the government camp) attacked the party premises of the *P.P.S.* They took out the red flags and publicly burned them. As an answer to this, Jan Kosczewo, an old *Pepesowce* fighter, an official at the city council, attempted an assassination of activists of the *Sanacja* (government camp) and shot six men. In the end, Jan Kosczewo ended his own life. Thus, an old Polish revolutionary erased the shame of the burning of the flags of his party.

The Polish worker movement not only carried out a bitter fight with the *Sanacja*. It also did the same with the *Endekes*. The Polish socialists often had direct confrontations with the *Endekes*. One of the bloodiest confrontations with the *Endekes* took place on 1 May 1937. The *P.P.S.* led 12,000 workers under its flags into the street. Bottles of poisoned liquid were thrown out of the *Endekes* hall and shooting began when the procession marched past. The *Pepesowces* strongly resisted. They attacked the *Endekes* hall and made a ruin of it. One of the *Endekes* was killed and 11 lay wounded. Two *Pepesowces* were lightly wounded and two were heavily wounded.

In an earlier chapter, we mentioned the active appearance of the Polish socialists against the picketers who carried out the boycott actions against the Jews. They fought the anti–Semitic actions in other ways, too. It was described in the Warsaw *Folks–Zeitung* [*People's Newspaper*] of 13 August 1938:

"Factory meetings recently took place in a series of large factories in the Czenstochow region at which representatives of the *rada* [council] distributed the appeals of the national council about the struggle against anti–Semitism and the rights of the Jewish masses." (The *rada* was the central municipal administration of the professional unions, Polish and Jewish, in Czenstochow: the national council was the highest administration of the Jewish professional unions in Poland. A series of Polish workers organizations also spread the appeals of the national council against anti–Semitism.)

[Page 140]

The Polish and Jewish workers showed their international solidarity more than once in the Polish capital of Catholicism, in the fortress of clericalism and hatred of Jews. One of the last acts of this kind, before the catastrophe of September 1939, was the yearly municipal conference of the professional unions, which took place on 2 April 1939. Rafal Federman was elected a representative of the Jewish workers on the presidium along with representatives of the Polish workers. Among the 134 delegates from the 29 professional unions were 23 delegates who represented the professional unions of the Jewish workers. Three representatives of the Jewish workers, the Bundists – Yisroel Jaronowski, Moshe Berkensztat and Motl Kusznir – were elected to the *rada* of the new city central administration.

The Bundist Organization and Its People

The Bund in Poland grew enormously in the last five years before the Second World War. It extended its influence to all corners of the country and drew in the largest number [of members] from the Jewish masses.

The growth and the spread of the Bundist movement also were noticed in Czenstochow. The party organization of the Bund grew with its various institutions that had as their purpose to satisfy a series of needs of the working strata and to serve their need in every way possible. The Bundist organization, itself a justification of the progressive and [class] conscious part of the Jewish working class and people's institutions, simultaneously was a servant and guide for the most inclusive strata of the people.

The Jewish masses answered warmly when the Bund called them to political actions and appearances. In the last year before 1939, the Bund itself called or was the initiator of large political strikes against the anti–Semitic rampages in the country. It called on the entire Jewish population to come out and it carried out protest strikes with extraordinary solidarity. Czenstochow was no exception is this regard.

One of these strikes, on 19 October 1927, a half–day protest strike against the installation of ghetto benches[4] at the college, appeared this way:

All Jewish workshops, all Jewish businesses were closed. The Jewish workers in all trades, without exception, went on strike. In the factories and workshops in which mixed personnel of Polish and Jewish workers worked, the Polish workers also went on strike as a sign of solidarity with their Jewish comrades. The Polish workers in a series of other factories went on strike for an hour. The following factories with Polish workers went on strike: Horowicz, Vulkan, Kosmos 1 and 2, Stal. Polish workers in these factories gave short speeches about the significance of the protest strike. Despite the fact that meetings of the Bund were forbidden, thousands of striking workers stormed the courtyard of the party hall. The surrounding streets were dark with the giant mass of people. Police surrounded the courtyard and did not let anyone enter. Yet the crowd gathered in the nearby streets. The police arrested several young people while dispersing those gathered. The arrestees were later freed. More than 15,000 people took part in the strike. The children in all "public" state *Folks–Shuln* [public schools] for Jewish children as well as the *khederim* [religious primary schools] went on strike. Large placards hung in front of four schools with the inscription, "We protest against the ghetto benches." (*Neie Folks–Zeitung* [*New People's Newspaper*], 20 October 1937).

During the same year, at the end of 1937, the 40–year anniversary of the Bund was celebrated in an impassioned way. Five hundred people came to the ceremonial meeting.

Sitting on the presidium during the meeting were Ahron Peretz, the veteran of the Bundist movement in Czenstochow, Engineer Avraham Blum, the emissary of the Central Committee of the Bund in Poland (he was a legendary figure in the Warsaw ghetto during the Second World War, one of the pillars of the underground movement – he perished after the Warsaw Ghetto Uprising [1943], in which he played a leading role). Representatives of various Polish Workers

(Polish Socialist Party and the *rada* [council] of the professional unions) also sat on the presidium.

In the name of the regional committee of the Polish Socialist Party, the well–known Socialist activist, Yosef Kaczierczak, greeted [the meeting and] in a sharp speech described the situation in the country and declared that the Polish worker would not remain aloof in the fight against anti–Semitism.

[Page 142]

Motl Kusznir spoke in the name of the Youth Bund, *Zukunft*. He had brought a gift for the Bund on its anniversary – 25 members of the Youth Bund, *Zukunft*, joined the party.

Yisroel Jaronowski spoke in the name of the Central Committee of the Professional Unions of the Jewish Workers. There were speeches and greetings from still more Jewish and Polish organizations, among them as well, from the *rada* [council] of the professional unions, from the Polish Socialist Cultural Organization, *Tur*, and from the Polish Socialist Party women's organization.

The most solemn act was giving an anniversary flag to the Czenstochow organization of the Bund. The act of giving the flag was carried out by an emissary from the Central Committee. Taking the flag from Ch. Blum, Yisroel Jaronowski declared that the Czenstochow Bundists would devotedly serve the ideals of the Bund and would not let the red flag out of their hands.

"Hundreds of young boys and girls from the Youth Bund, *Zukunft*, marched in, dressed in blue blouses and red ties. Twenty–five of them joined the party ranks and Liber Segal spoke in their name. He took an oath of unlimited devotion to the Bund. Avraham Blum, the representative from the central committee, then gave a spirited speech about the 40 years of the Bund."

The years of work and struggle, the effort and the victims were not fruitless. The Jewish workers became powerful, a class–conscious, creative collective that looked with a clear vision and went with a sure step toward their goal.

The people who represented the Bundist movement in Czenstochow were diverse: from those with university degrees to the porter, from the effervescent young people to the old man with a grey head [of hair], from the highly educated to the illiterate, sons of illustrious–descended families to children of the back alleys. However, they all were united in the same ideal; they were forged in the movement, and from themselves they created a harmonious unity, the Bund in Czenstochow. Hundreds and hundreds built the movement year in and year out in the course of 40 years and developed it further. It is impossible to list everyone; we will remember a few here.

Ahron Peretz, a relative of the great Jewish writer, Y.L. Peretz. He already was active in the Bund in 1905 and devotedly served the Jewish workers movement without interruption. He represented the Bund at the *kehile* during the last years before the war. He worked a great deal to elevate the cultural level of the Jewish masses in Czenstochow. He was greatly loved in the city. He was a dentist by trade. He always was ready to help the needy. He was the Bundist city councilman in the city council and chairman of the school organization during the last years before the Second World War. He continues to be active in the Bund.

Moshe Lederman. A specialty shoemaker by trade. He already was active in the Bund at the time of the First World War. He was a member of the Bundist committee and an important worker in the professional [union] movement for many years. Starting in 1935, he was active in Lodz with the garment workers among whom he was very beloved. He was a member of the Lodz underground committee of the Bund during the years of the Second World War. He spent the entire time in the Lodz ghetto and now is again active in the Bundist movement in Czenstochow.

Yitzhak Stopnicer. A hat maker. He was active in *Zukunft* [Future], the Bundist youth [organization]. He was chairman of the *Zukunft* organization for many years and the main leader of the youth faction of the clothing union. He also had great stature with the Bundist youth movement in the *shtetlekh* [towns] of the Czenstochow region. He served the *Zukunft* organizations of the surrounding area with advice and action. He moved to Bedzin before the Second World War where he was an esteemed activist for the party and the youth organization. His further fate is unknown.

Motl Kusznir. A clothing worker. He was an activist in the Bundist youth organization for many years. He was a good speaker. He later was the secretary of the garment union. He went through all of the pain in the ghetto during the last war [Second World War] and finally was taken to the German concentration camp, Bergen–Belzen. After the liberation, he returned to Bundist work in Czenstochow.

"Karl Marx" – thus we called him because of his outward appearance, because of his head of hair and beard that made him look very similar to the face of Karl Marx. This was an older man who excelled with his extraordinary devotion and attachment to the party. Although he was poor, he always was the first to pay into any assessments carried out. He never missed any Bundist meeting or demonstration, as a fervidly pious Jew cannot fail to pray in a *minyon* [10 men needed for prayer].

[Page 142]

Wolfowicz. An older man, a baker–worker. He showed a strong connection to the Bund and to the professional unions. He was a religious Jew and he really showed a religious relationship to the organization to which he belonged. To him a strike was a sacred object and he related to a strike–breaker as to one who was a blasphemer. He could not understand how one could break from unity. Wolfowicz was burdened with nine children. During a strike there was hunger in his home. His wife and children tormented him and demanded food. The old baker–worker was afraid that, God forbid, he would not be able to resist the temptation and break down. In such cases, he would not go home and spent the night at the Bund meeting hall.

Avraham Rozenblat. Also a baker–worker. He was active in the Bund starting in 1905. He belonged to the "Iron Guard" of the Bund. He came from the lowest strata. Refined and uplifting, he devoted his entire soul to the Jewish workers movement. He was very beloved among the workers and would often be sent to party or professional union congresses in Warsaw.

Yisroel Jaronowski. A meat worker. He also came to the workers' movement from the lower strata and raised himself to a moral height from which he never descended. The meat trade, and particularly employment with kosher meat, provided an opportunity for lucrative non-kosher earnings. As a leader of a professional union, he was a guard of purity and honesty. He became an active worker–activist and, finally, chairman of the Bundist organization and *parnes* [an elected head of the Jewish community] at the *kehile* [organized Jewish community] in Czenstochow. The Jewish and Polish food workers in the city elected him many times as their delegate to the national congresses of the professional unions of the food workers. He showed strength of character during various difficult situations and justified the trust in him. He also was among the leaders of the secret underground movement in the ghetto during the terrible [rule] of the Nazi murderers. He also took part in preparing to arm the uprising. When the Nazis came to arrest him he jumped out of the second story and broke a leg. He fell into their hands and perished.

Moshe and Rayzele Berkensztat. Husband and wife. He a leather worker, she a teacher. Both joined the Zionist Socialist organization during the First World War. And from 1922 on they were active workers in the Bund. Moshe was a child of poor parents. A vision of a better life always shone in him. Despite the difficult circumstances, this man who excelled with his simplicity and gentleness, never lost the pleasant smile on his lips. He was the secretary of the local Bundist organization for many years. He was a member of the committee of the underground Bund during the Second World War. The Gestapo arrested him and his wife on 6 June 1941 and they were terribly tortured during the investigation. Moshe Berkensztat was sent to Auschwitz where he perished.

Rayzele Fajertag–Berkensztat was a child of the *Yatke–Gas* [the street of butchers], the daughter of a butcher. Her environment of toiling people did not prevent her from acquiring a great deal of knowledge and great intelligence. In the best way possible, she found herself in the world of thought and books. She became a Fröbelist[5] and was one of the founders of the Y.L. Peretz Workers Nursery. In later years she was the librarian at the Medem Library, the same function she also carried out for almost two years under the Nazi rule. Twenty–thousand books were brought to her house and over 1,000 people secretly took books to read from her. She was arrested with her husband and tortured. In the end, the Czenstochower Bundists worked to extract her from the nails of the Gestapo. She later perished.

The Bund was a real cross–section of the Jewish masses in Czenstochow, a meeting place for all who wanted to join forces in the duty of serving in the freeing of all oppressed and underprivileged.

[Page 143]

A. Peretz and His Family

The Vilner Committee of the Bund with Yosef Aronowicz
(standing in the middle)

Hershl Frajman and His Family

Moshe Lederman

Rajzele Berkensztat

Moshe Berkensztat

Henokh Fefer

Zalman Tenenberg

Motil[6] Kusznir

[Page 144]

The last committee of the Bund of September 1939 consisted of the following comrades: Yisroel Jaronowski – chairman; Moshe Berkensztat – secretary. The other members of the committee were: Moshe Tuchmajer, Motl Kusznir, Rayzele Berkensztat, Avraham Rozenblat, Yitzhak Rozenfeld and L. Brener.

In various years, the comrades Yosef Aronowicz, Rafal Federman, Avraham Fridman, Hershl Frajman (fell in the fight with the Nazis on 4 January 1943), Henekh Fefer (secretary for many years), Moshe Lederman, Dovid Klin and a series of others were on the committee.

The Czenstochow Committee of the Bund in 1929
Standing, right to left: Moshe Tuchmajer, Z. Cincinatus, B. Cincinatus, L. Kaminski, A.
Rozenblat, Zilberberg
Seated, right to left: The wife of Z. Cincinatus, R. Federman, H. Halberg–Cincinatus, Moshe
Lederman, H. Lederman
Near the photograph of B[einish] Michalewicz on the right: Shimshon Jakubowicz; on the
left: Yitzhak Stopnicer

The majority of activists and members, who in life and death connected themselves with the ideals of the Bund, perished in the Czenstochow ghetto and in various other ghettos or in concentration camps. Only a small group succeeded in weathering the difficulties of the seven gates of the Nazi hell and continuing their work in the new, liberated Poland.

Translator's Footnotes

1. The term "Sephardic" is used in a very broad sense. It possibly refers to the *nusakh* or liturgical tradition of the prayer book and religious traditions used in a synagogue. Many Hasidim and other pious Jews used the Sephardic *nusakh* even though they were of Ashkenazi origin.

2. The *curiae* system of voting divided voters into electoral groups designated by class.

3. A military contingent led by General Jozef Haller during the First World War. The soldiers in Haller's Army often held anti–Semitic beliefs and participated in anti–Jewish actions.

4. "Ghetto benches" were used at Polish universities starting in 1935 to keep Jewish students segregated from the general student population. The ghetto benches occupied a side section in the lecture halls.

5. Friedrich Fröbel was a founder of kindergartens and gave them the name.

6. Spelled Motl in the text of this article.

Left *Poalei-Zion*

by Yakov Kener

The beginning of the activity of a *Poalei-Zion* [Workers of Zion – Marxist-Zionists] organization in Czenstochow occurred in the summer of 1904. Its activists were: Shimeon Waldfogel, a tailor, who came from the village of Krzywanice, near the neighboring *shtetl* [town] Sulmierzyce; Meir, a local tailor journeyman, who worked in the same workshop with Shimeon and Moshe Ceszinski, a son of middle-class parents who, as was expressed then, "supported the workers."

However, Shimeon Waldfogel, who conspiratorially was known as "*Feigele,*"[1] was the soul of this set of triplets. Shimeon had previously devoured many illegal brochures and he was very drawn to the workers' movement. However, he had no desire to join the Bund nor the *S.Z.* (Territorialist Zionists) because both Jewish workers' parties, which had existed in Czenstochow previously, did not support *Eretz-Yisroel*, but he, Shimeon, as a 14-year old boy, working in Radomsk and a member of the Zionist library, already dreamed of going to Zion.

In groups of three, the above-mentioned *Poalei-Zion* pioneers in Czenstochow began to spread the ideas of the party at the workers exchange until they created three such small groups of 10 men and each of them led such secret groups. The Czenstochow *Poalei-Zion* organization, which already numbered over a hundred male and female workers, grew out of the separate small groups.

[Page 145]

As the youngest organization, it could not be compared in strength with the two older and already strong Czenstochow institutions – but it was taken into account in the city and at political strikes, in street demonstrations that often took place in that era, *Poalei-Zion* had its representation in the general strike committees. Hundreds of Jewish workers marched in the large street demonstrations of 1905 under the *Poalei-Zion* flag through the streets of Czenstochow with Shimeon Waldfogel in the lead as flag bearer.

A Group of the First *Poalei-Zionists*
Standing, right to left: Dovid Borszykowski, M. Berman, Z. Warszawski
Seated, right to left: Moshe Ceszinski, M. Montag

During the Period of Reaction

The failure of the first Russian Revolution in 1905 brought with it persecutions of the workers movement by the Tsarist regime and the best known communal workers of all political beliefs had to escape abroad. Moshe Censzinski left for Vienna (Austria) and from there to America. Shimeon Waldfogel left for Germany and from there for Paris, where he worked as a tailor and was active in the local trade union movement.

Meanwhile, the workers movement lived through an era of suspension, in Czenstochow, as in all other cities in Poland. The Tsarist reaction rampaged and the working masses rolled up their flags, postponing their open struggle for another time.

In particular, the Jewish workers movement, which did not have any large factories as its base of activity, shrank. Organizations that numbered in the thousands were reduced at that time to several dozen and hundreds became smaller groups. The Czenstochow *Poalei-Zion*, which was strongly reduced, also had the same fate; yet it was active under the leadership of the young Moshe Oderberg. In the end, he also had to escape abroad.

Comrade Yeta Graj, who in now active in the *Poalei-Zion* organization in Los Angeles, California, also immediately left for America.

Comrade Moshe Oderberg in now in Chicago and had been the leader of the local left *Poalei-Zion* organization for dozens of years. Before escaping from Czenstochow, he succeeded in strengthening and assuring that the organizational and ideological nucleus of *Poalei-Zionism* would take root, so that when Shimeon Waldfogel retuned to Czenstochow from Paris in 1913, it was possible for him to transfer his experience in the West European workers movement and further build a strong *Poalei-Zion* organization.

He was deeply involved in the founding of the illegal professional worker unions and, simultaneously, in the professional movement, re-erecting the political party groups. Shimeon Waldfogel again became the former "*Feigele*" in Czenstochow, who flew from one meeting to another, from one city to another and everywhere encouraged and awoke the masses to professional organizing and to political activity. He sought the "enlightened" and assembled those returning from Tsarist exile and gathered the battle-ready around him. Thus things proceeded until 1 August 1914, when the First World War broke out and the political-social life again suffered a blow.

Under the German Occupation during the First World War

When Poland was occupied by German and Austrian troops in 1915, the communal strength quickly recovered from the sudden blow it had received at the outbreak of war. The most urgent task at that time was the fight against hunger and epidemics that were spread by the war. Shimeon Waldfogel then devoted all his energy to organizing the aid institutions for the Jewish masses and, with the support of the remaining *Poalei-Zion* comrades in Czenstochow, a work home that functioned the entire day as a free-of-charge tea hall and inexpensive people's kitchen was created immediately that, incidentally, was the first Jewish work home in all of Poland. The tea hall and the people's kitchen were a great deal more than a hall for the provision of food. They were transformed into political and cultural clubs for the local Jewish labor force and they also served as a model for the remaining Polish provinces. The workers gathered there and discussed the latest war news and the post-war problems among themselves. There was support for the lost and homeless Jewish families from the small, surrounding *shtetlekh* [towns]. There, in the *Poalei-Zion* workers home, the political consciousness of the Jewish masses was forged daily. Thus, was the soil prepared for the later blossoming of the Jewish workers movement! When the German occupiers were driven from Polish soil, the Jewish workers and folk-masses immediately swam to the communal surface with their various kinds of political, economic and cultural organizations.

[Page 146]

Managing Committee of the *Poalei-Zion* Cooperative
Standing, right to left: A. Gotlib, L. Zajdman, Y. Gotlib, W. Landsman, S. Szaja
Seated, right to left: Mrs. Koniecpoler, G. Frajman, Y. Berman, A. Berkowicz

The *Poalei-Zion* organization, just like other parties, quickly grew into a mass organization with widespread economic and cultural institutions. During the first post-war years, the *Poalei-Zion* organization in Czenstochow had a good reputation for its products-cooperative and consumer shops. Of particular great significance was the bakers cooperative, in which were employed dozens of workers and employees. The *Poalei-Zion* bakers cooperative was a blessing for the poor population during the constantly growing scarcities. The bakeries not only gave employment to the workers for normal wages, but it also made it possible for the members of all cooperative stores to receive the appropriate quantity of bread for a normal price every day and thus created an effective resistance to the illegal bread trade on the black market that was spreading greatly then.

The bakers cooperative that was founded with the financial help of the "Joint" [Distribution Committee] had its own horses and wagons, with which the bread was taken to the cooperative shops every morning so that the member-customers would not need to stand in long lines.

However, the Czenstochower *Poalei-Zion* was not satisfied with only providing the Jewish population with bread. The organization also founded a library, a children's home, a dramatic circle, an evening school, a youth club and, simultaneously, was active in the political and professional (trade unionists) area.

In 1920, when typhus was raging in Poland, Shimeon Waldfogel died in Sosnowiec as a victim of this illness and his death strongly affected the further activity of the Czenstochower *Poalei-Zion* organization.

New activists did appear, but *Feigele*'s enthusiasm was missing. Shimeon's widespread range was missing and the orphaned Czenstochow *Poalei-Zion* organization found it difficult to take its place in Jewish life, for which the deceased Waldfogel had wanted to fight.

The Czenstochow *Poalei-Zion* organization consisted entirely of workers and toilers.

A Group of *Poalei-Zionists*

Standing, right to left: Kotlarcz, A. Wajs, Goldberg, Zajdman, G. Frajtag
Seated, right to left: Turner, P. Tuchmajer, R. Sajadczik, S. Szaja, and A.
Litman

[Page 147]

It did not possess – not then and not in the later years – any professional intelligentsia or determined young people and this also made its struggle for ruling positions in Jewish workers' life more difficult. Therefore, the Czenstochow *Poalei-Zion* organization always was for workers' unity and when the parallel worker institutions actually were united, as for example, the libraries, the children's homes and the professional unions, this desire for workers' unity found favorable grounds in the ranks of *Poalei-Zion*.

In the autumn of 1920, when the *Poalei-Zion* movement split into right and left, the entire Czenstochower organization and all of its institutions remained in the ranks of the left *Poalei-Zion* movement. The left *Poalei-Zion* never relinquished certain privileges that came to it by right to be able to more quickly take a stand for worker unity.

The library, the professional unions and the children's homes were united under a general joint management committee in which left *Poalei-Zion* received its representation and they loyally worked there until the outbreak of the second world slaughter. However, in general, this meant that they did not at all relinquish their ideology or their political positions. [The work of] peace and war was to be kept separate – this was the motto of their daily work.

United in the professional area, however, they did not permit any political action at which they did not appear independently with their own voting list or with their own political slogans, even when they had no certain prospect of a concrete victory. United in the school system or in the area of the library they, however, simultaneously on their own led the struggle against clericalism, against illiteracy, against fascism and for Palestinism [support for *Eretz-Yisroel*].

While the older party comrades, under the leadership of A. Pregski, Kh. Birencwajg, Leibus Tenenbaum and, later, M. Szwarc and the councilman, Avraham Blum, were mainly active in the joint managing committee of the trade unions, in the library and in the school system, the "young" were active in the area of cultural activity, sports, summer camps, anti-clericalism and in various other areas.

The writer of these lines had the occasion several times to be the speaker from the Czenstochow *Poalei-Zion* young people at various public undertakings and I always left [these undertakings] with a feeling of deep spiritual satisfaction from the enthusiasm and with the deep seriousness with which our local youth organization breathed.

In the early 1920s, the *Poalei-Zion* young people were under the leadership of the Comrades Baremhercik and Jozefowicz, teacher-workers, who then emigrated to Paris and, finally at the end of the 1920s, Sholem Kalberg was the leader, who then emigrated to Canada. Later, the youth work was led by Avraham Blum, the baker-worker, who in 1939 was saved by escaping to the Soviet Union and is now active in Moscow in the ranks of the Polish Jews, the tailor-worker, Yisroel Szimanowicz, who perished in a Nazi concentration camp, in Mauthausen (Austria), and Dovid Jakubowicz, who survived and is active in the camp of the liberated Jews in Feldafing (Bayern).

Let us be permitted to remember here in only a few lines just a small part of the lively and exuberant activity of our Czenstochower *Yugnt* [Youth] on the basis of my observations during my visit there:

In April 1926, a public protest of the young workers in connection with a draft law that the Polish reaction had introduced in the *Sejm* to take the right to assemble from the young. Four or five hundred young male and female workers filled the large meeting hall. The entrance to the hall was besieged by agents of the secret police. The young activists also distributed reproduced leaflets in the street in which they called on the young to protest against the assassination attempt on the rights of the young.

In December 1927 a large public memorial for the 10th *yohrzeit* [anniversary of a death] of Ber Borochov [took place] which was transformed into to a beautiful demonstration for proletarian Palestinism.

In the autumn of 1928 [there was] a public demonstration against the fact that in the Soviet Union the party of left *Poalei-Zion* was dissolved.

[Page 148]

In September 1929, when the organization had its own premises, a celebration [was held] in honor of the international youth day in the forest outside the city and after, dozens of young people marched into the city singing revolutionary songs.

Particularly during the year 1929, the Czenstochow *Poalei-Zion Yugnt* and the party excelled in selling thousands of declaration cards for the Pre-Palestine Workers Congress that took place in Warsaw and sent an appropriate number of delegates.

The Czenstochow *Poalei-Zion* – the party and *Yugnt* – would demonstrate under their own flags in the general workers procession every 1 May and in the evening hold their own May assemblies.

Cultural Activity

The *Poalei-Zion* Cultural Society, Evening Courses for Workers, would arrange public lectures every year during the winter months on various themes and almost every week brought speakers from either Warsaw or Krakow. The Messrs Dr. Borukh Eizensztat, Dr. Rafal Mahler, Mina Abelman and Dr. Emanuel Ringelblum, may he rest in peace, often came to Czenstochow to give lectures. The Messrs Avigdor Bursztyn and Lubek Szmerler, about whom there has been a lack of signs of whether they are still alive, would often come from Krakow. During the various election campaigns, the Lodz Messrs Chaim Brand, Yisroel Stolarski, Moshe Citrinowski would come as speakers and to public celebrations. The Messrs [Yakov] Zrubavel, Y. Lew, N. Buksbaum, the author of this article and still others often came there [Czenstochow] with political readings. The Jewish masses in Czenstochow were always ready to listen to the *Poalei-Zion* speakers and they always responded with sympathy to every political or financial action carried out by the Czenstochow organization.

In the ranks of Czenstochow *Poalei-Zion Yugnt* an event took place that made a strong impression at that time and it is worthwhile here to remember this event because it was very characteristic of the spirit of the Jewish working class in Poland. A young locksmith-worker, Eliezer Wajs, a child from a poor working family, belonged to the *Yugnt* organization. At the readings and at private, internal educational circles, the young Wajs heard his fill of the necessity of education and about the lack of our own intelligentsia so he decided to stop working in a workshop and begin to study. This was very difficult to carry out in the economic conditions of that time. His plan sounded like a fantasy and his parents, because of economic need, were against this fantasy. However, Eliezer Wajs was encouraged by the organization and his older brother, who was earning a little bit, promised to support him financially. Wajs began to study with stubbornness and he finished his *gymnazie* [secondary school] courses in a relatively short time, or as was said in Poland, he received his *matura* [secondary school certificate]. He then left for Krakow where he, under the most difficult financial conditions, studied at the law faculty in the local university, until he received the title, "Doctor of Law." During all of the time of his studies, he did not break with the organization. In the evening hours in Czenstochow, and then in Krakow, he carried out educational work at the *Yugnt* organizations of the cities mentioned. He led elementary courses for the young people who came from small *shtetlekh* [towns], or from the villages, and had not had any education. He devoted himself to the work of the *Yugnt* organization libraries with special love and energy. Later, he even wrote a large brochure about how the libraries needed to be led and the secretariat for library education at the Central Office of the communal evening courses in Warsaw had 5,000 copies of his booklet published.

In Krakow itself he was the chairman of the famous Y.L. Peretz Library that belonged to the left *Poalei-Zion* organization and, under his leadership, this library blossomed as one of the nicest and largest Jewish libraries in Poland. The Central Committee of the Society of Evening Courses for Workers also organized a special four-week course for librarians which Dr. Eliezer Wajs led and at which he was one of the most important lecturers. In order to lead these courses, Wajs had to free himself for a month at a time from the private work that he did in Krakow as an assistant to a lawyer there. However, he did not let any obstacle stop him from realizing his dream, the desire to spread education among the working young people and to strengthen the Jewish library system.

[Page 149]

The Czenstochow *Poalei-Zion* organization and the local Jewish working class in general was proud of its *landsman* [person from the same town], with its Eliezer Wajs, who in a short time was transformed from a locksmith apprentice into a lawyer with the title doctor. And he would sometimes come home to his parents for several days; this visit was always a celebration for the organization with his readings, conversations and reports.

However, this joy did not last long because he became very, very sick with the flu in the month of November 1930, and on 10 November, he died in the very bloom of life at age 30 of complications of an inflamed kidney.

The Krakow comrades immediately sent telegrams to Czenstochow about this and in the morning when the funeral was to take place, a delegation arrived from Czenstochow, which consisted of his brother and two other comrades who demanded that Eliezer Wajs be brought to his home city for burial. Those in Krakow bent to the desire of his family. They wrapped the body in a red flag and brought him to Czenstochow where, on Wednesday, 12 November, a giant funeral demonstration took place. Hundreds and hundreds of comrades left work and came to give their last respect to the only intelligent and important cultural worker who grew out of their own ranks. At the opening of the grave, he was eulogized by both his own comrades and representatives of all of the other political groups in Czenstochow and the left *Poalei-Zion* then observed every *yohrzeit* [anniversary of a death], always remembering him with respect and with veneration.

However, Dr. Eliezer Wajs was not the only esteemed *Poalei-Zion* activist who rests or has rested at the Czenstochow Jewish cemetery. Next to Comrade Wajs, the grave of the Sosnowiec councilman Moshe Judenherc is located or was located – who in 1924 was murdered in the very bloom of life at the age of 36 when entering a train at the Czenstochow train station.

Over the course of eight years, Moshe Judenherc was a representative of the Jewish workers at the Sosnowiec City Council, chosen by the left *Poalei-Zion*. He fought with great bravery from the city hall dais against anti-Semitism and because of this was much admired and beloved among the Jewish masses in all of Zaglembie and its surroundings. Therefore, it is no wonder that the Czenstochow Jewish worker and common people and the Sosnowiec *Poalei-Zion*, erected a magnificent marble headstone over his grave after his tragic death, while in Sosnowiec itself a people's library was built in his name, which functioned until the outbreak of the war.

Under German Occupation in the Years 1939–1945

We do not as yet know what happened to the Czenstochower Jewish cemetery during the Hilterist occupation. We do not know if, perhaps by chance, the German people and cemetery defilers took care of the generations-old cemeteries of Sosnowiec and Czenstochow where the bones of Shimeon Waldfogel, Eliezer Wajs and Moshe Judenherc among others rest. However, we know that the young Jews in general and, particularly, the *Poalei-Zion* comrades from these two cities did not only in the pre-war times regard the memory of our guides who perished with reverence and respect, but during the war in the most difficult ghetto conditions, they also were devoted and carried out the unwritten testaments of their above-mentioned three deceased comrades.

Here, let only one fact be mentioned about the desire to fight and about the readiness to fight of the Czenstochow left *Poalei-Zion*, of the melancholy but simultaneously heroic, ghetto era of 1943.

When the Warsaw ghetto prepared for its famous Uprising against the Nazi murderers, the Czenstochower *Poalei-Zion* organization, through the secret underground channels, received from Warsaw, from the leader of the left *Poalei-Zion* – from Dr. Adolf Berman – a call to come immediately to Warsaw with weapons in their hands to help the success of the Uprising.

[Page 150]

A group of 10 young, courageous and physically powerful comrades, under the leadership of the above-mentioned comrades, Dovid Jakubowicz and Yisroel Szimanowicz, sneaked out of the Czenstochow ghetto and over a day and night they finally smuggled themselves to Warsaw with the help of the left Polish underground movement. However, upon reaching a suburb of Warsaw, it was impossible to enter the Warsaw ghetto, which already stood in flames and was surrounded on all sides by the bands of German murderers.

The 10 brave heroes, for lack of a choice, had to go to Czenstochow in sorrow and pain where they met the same fate as the entire Jewish population: deportation, active resistance, and death. Yisroel Szimanowicz was tortured in the Mauthausen slave labor camp; Dovid Jakubowicz survived and is now in Feldafing [Displaced Persons Camp], where he is active as the secretary of the left *Poalei-Zion* in Bayern [Bavaria] and, simultaneously its representative in the Munich central committee of the liberated Jews in the American zone in Germany.

Meanwhile, what happened to the remaining eight as, in general, with all of the other older and younger *Poalei-Zion* comrades, is unknown to us. However, it is known to us from the first issue of the *Arbeter-Zeitung* [*Workers Newspaper*], the organ of left *Poalei-Zion* in Poland, which is now published in Lodz, that the left *Poalei-Zion* has been revived now in Czenstochow, and it again is carrying on vigorous activity among and on behalf of Jewish survivors in Czenstochow.

————

Translator's Footnote

1. A *feigele* is a small bird; the surname Waldfogel means "forest bird."

————

[Page 150]

HaShomer HaTzair

HaShomer HaTzair [The Youth Guard – Socialist Zionists] occupied a very honored place in the social life of Jewish Czenstochow. The Jewish youth movement arose in several large cities in western Poland at the start of the First World War. Under the influence of the German *Wandervogel* [can mean hiking or wandering bird] movement, of the Polish scout movement and of the *HaShomer* in Israel, the young people began to gather and organize in scout groups, which over time developed and crystallized ideologically. Driven by the longing to live independently and to be active, and as a reaction to the one-sided, exclusively spiritual education of the Jewish young, the Jewish youth movement embraced the scout form. The Jewish scout groups arose at almost the same time in several large cities in Poland.

The Czenstochow group belonged to this first scout organization. It was founded by young gymnasts, workers and those employed in trade. During its first years, when the movement still carried the clear scout character, it was received with great sympathy in the Zionist circles. They found a patron in the well-known Czenstochow community worker, Henrik Markusfeld, who offered a comfortable apartment for the use of the organization, a large place in his house on Kościuszka Street (later Aleja Wolności).

A short time after its rise, a large number of the young Jews in Czenstochow belonged to the scout organization.

[Page 151]

In 1917 the first conference of the scout organization in Poland took place in Czenstochow. Representatives of the Jewish scout organizations from Warsaw, Lodz, Piotrokov, Bedzin and other cities came together at the premises that later were taken over by the Jewish Sports and Touring Union. It was decided here to create a general national organization. A constitutional conference was called and it proposed adopting the name *HaShomer HaTzair*.

In later years until the outbreak of the Second World War, *HaShomer HaTzair* occupied an important place in the life of the young Jews in Czenstochow. Its members stood out with their special scout clothing. For years *HaShomer HaTzair* demonstrated on *Lag B'Omer*,[1] marching in closed ranks under their flags and to the sounds of their own so-called field orchestra. From time to time, it arranged beautifully prepared evenings and amateur presentation for the public. However, the outward appearances were only accompanying manifestations of an intensive work that was carried out daily in the "*ken*" (ken – nest; that is what the premises of the organization were called). Here, life boiled in the *ken*. Young people from 12 to 20 gathered daily. Group after group trained in various physical and scout exercises or studied. Important educational work was carried out in physical and spiritual areas. The character of the Jewish generation, the generation that provided the builders of *Eretz-Yisorel* and the ghetto fighters, was forged here. Here in the *ken* the young people built a worldly outlook. Here, the young searched for a way in life.

HaShomer HaTzair produced the type of Jewish intelligent young people for whom spiritual creation was not unfamiliar, that could not be indifferent to communal problems, who were active in the ranks of all progressive communal movements. Yermiyahu Gitler, who stood at the head of the Czenstochow Jews during the last tragic years – in the years of the ghetto – was one of the builders of Czenstochow *HaShomer HaTzair*.

However, this is not the main point. Over the years *HaShomer HaTzair* crystallized and adopted concrete goals, drawing in the new Jews, the young Jewish generation, by building a normal Jewish life in *Eretz-Yisroel*. The most concrete educational purpose was – to make real the Zionist and socialist ideal in the *kibbutz* [communal settlement], in *Eretz-Yisroel*. And from the first years of its existence, there was a continuous emigration of Czenstochow Young Guards to *Eretz-Yisroel* and to the *kibbutz*.

A Group from *HaShomer HaTzair*

Here in *Eretz-Yisroel*, you will find them all over and above all in a *kibbutz*. Czenstochower Guards are in the following *kibbutzim* [plural of *kibbutz*]: Beit Alfa, Mishmar HaEmek, Ein HaHoresh, Ein Shemer, Gan Shmuel, Mesilot, Negba, Ein HaShofet, Mitzpe Hayam and in the youth *kibbutz* Gal On near Ness Ziona. In addition to the *Hashomer HaTzair kibbutzim* mentioned, a group is located in Kibbutz HaMeukhad in Beis Oren. [There was] a long chain of emigration from 1920 to 1939.

In addition to the intensive educational work, the nest also actively took part in various comprehensive communal movements and undertakings.

The nest excelled in the work of *Keren Kayamet L'Yisroel* [*K.K.L.* – The Jewish National Fund]. It stood in the first rank [of support] for many years. Let us again remember the name of Shmuel Horowicz (Kuc), who worked with *K.K.L.* for many years up to the last minute in the ghetto. The nest was active in the *Tarbot* [network of secular Hebrew schools] movement. They lived in the nest as in the atmosphere of *Eretz-Yisroel*; the Hebrew language sounded alive here. *HaShomer HaTzair* took an active part in all of the *Tarbot* endeavors.

HaShomer HaTzair held a special place in *HaHalutz* [Zionist pioneer movement]. The *bogerim* [adults] (the older strata, aged 18-20) joined *HaHalutz* in 1923. *HaHalutz* immediately was revived in Czenstochow. *Shomrim* [Guards] stood at the head of the work, as well as in the League for Working *Eretz-Yisroel*.

There were good relations between *HaShomer HaTzair* and *TOZ* [Society for the Protection of Health]. The well-known health society found a devoted friend in the *Shomrim*. *HaShomer HaTzair* carried on collections of money. The *HaShomer HaTzair* organization appreciated the worth of a healthy body. Year after year, the *Shomrim*, with the support of *TOZ*, went to the village to their colony during the summer.

Shomrim workers were found in the professional unions, in the workers' library (led by the Independent Socialist Workers Party, under the leadership of Lipszic). The general national and international *Shomrim* movement took an active part in the Czenstochow nest.

Czenstochower *Shomrim* took an active part from the above-mentioned first preliminary conference in 1917 to the active fight in the ghetto-war at various significant moments in the national movement. Here is a list of Czenstochower members: Iszojewicz (or Ishi in Tel Aviv), Yermiyahu Gilter, Yosef Heyman, Bolek Fajglowicz (now Gan-Shmuel), Shimeon Wajntraub (now Beit Alfa), Chaim Landau (now Mesilot), Moshe Klarman (now in the Jewish Brigade) comrade of Kibbutz Mitzpe Hayam and others.

[Page 152]

Czenstochow also was the center of the Keliec-Zaglembie Galilie (region). The above-mentioned comrades carried on the work. Regional conferences and meetings took place here.

Czenstochow became an important place in the general *Shomrim* movement in 1928 when the Czenstochow garden farm moved to the authority of the *Shomrim* world movement. *Hakshore* (preparation) [agricultural training for potential emigrants to *Eretz-Yisroel*] *Shomrim* from various areas in Poland and Galicia were concentrated here [in Czenstochow]. The primary leadership (the national center) of Poland, of Galicia, the top leadership (main leaders of the world movement), Yitzhak Birnbaum, Avraham Hercfeld, representatives of the press took part in the harvest festival (the celebration of the harvest) of 1928. Meetings of the central committee took place here from time to time. The farm also was a central place for the nest. The Czenstochow *shomrim* met there with *shomrim* from other areas in Poland. The *Shomrim* from Lithuania and from the border areas (Kresen [western Ukraine]) influenced the Czenstochow *Shomrim*, bringing in much liveliness, strengthening the feeling of membership in one large family.

A *hakshore kibbutz* [settlement] was concentrated on the farm starting in 1932, which penetrated into various working places in the city, into factories. Comrades from the farm were active in the city and in the nest.

The *hakshore* settlement aroused sympathy in the best circles. *HaShomer HaTzair* was seen here in its reality, a kind of miniature of a *kibbutz* in *Eretz-Yisroel*. Visitors from various circles were carried away, seeing a new type of Jew. I remember two facts. Dr. Szobad, a well-known non-Zionist activist from Vilna, visited Czenstochow as a guest of *TSYSHO* [*Tsentrale Yidishe Shul Organizatsye* – Central Jewish School Organization; a system of schools organized by the Bund]. He also visited the farm. In the evening during his reading arranged by the Jewish School Organization, he spoke about the great impression the *Shomrim* at the farm had made on him.

Dr. Josef Kruk, of the Independent Workers' Party, visited the farm during Passover 1934 – [he was] not yet a Zionist. He also was impressed by the lively collective of the *Shomrim* youth and from then on, he was a friend of the *Shomrim* farm.

During the last tragic and heroic years, the Czenstochow *HaShomer HaTzair* continued its work. During the first years of the ghetto, before the total annihilation, it brought young people the belief in an ideal that did not let the young people despair, become broken; it tempered its character and made it capable of revolt.

A heroic chapter that still needs to be written is the last days in the ghetto. Here, too, the *Shomrim* were in the first row.

Translator's Footnote

1. Holiday celebrated in the spring, during which it is customary to go on outings and to light bonfires.

Political Persecutions and Trials

by A. Khrobolowski and H. Zigas

Political Persecutions in Tsarist Times

As one of the first well-known political trials in Czenstochow, the trial that took place in connection with the Polish demonstration in 1874 at the opening of the *Pravoslavna* [Russian Orthodox] church Magistratski Square was a symbol of Russian rule.

In 1906 a trial of a group of Russian soldiers from the Czenstochow garrison who belonged to a branch of the Russian *S.S.* (Socialist Revolutionaries) took place in Czenstochow.

Leaving aside all of the arrests, political and military terror actions in 1904-1906 that are mentioned in other articles, we will only record the political persecutions, murders and trials that that took place after the liberation movement was suppressed.

At the end of 1906 several workers from the hat-makers' union were shot during a dispute. The charges against them were difficult to learn. They only knew that they [the workers] had been on strike and had gone to pick blackberries in the woods. According to Stalipin's account, they were arrested and were sentenced to be shot as bandits.

[Page 153]

The trial of Private Vasili Denisov, who was accused of belonging the *P.P.S.* [*Polska Partia Socjalistyczna* – Polish Socialist Party] was supposed to take place in Piotrkow Court in1913. The trial was postponed for several days because of his health. Vasili Denisov was betrayed to the police along with other members of the fighting division of the *P.P.S.* by the arrested Sukenik.

In May of the same year several workers at *Czenstochowianka* [a factory] were arrested in connection with a strike of 5,000 workers. The strike took place because the master craftsman Ejchler insulted a worker. The master craftsman was thrown out of the factory by the worker.

In July 1912 a trial took place in Czenstochow of a large group of "revolutionary avengers," under the leadership of Dluczewski. The lawyers Szumanski, Berson and Medalus appeared as defenders. Five of the judged were sentenced to hanging, but because of a demonstration the sentence was changed to 20 years of hard labor. Others were sentenced to various terms of hard labor and external exile.

On *Shabbos* [Sabbath], 4 October 1913, at one in the afternoon, the police and gendarmes with the *Pristov* [police commissioner] Abruzow at the head, surrounded and arrested everyone taking part in the Bundist gathering near the *Klejarnia* [adhesives factory]. Approximately 60 people, mainly tailors were arrested (see the article "The General Jewish Workers Bund" by Sholem Herc for details about this arrest).

Moshe Ceszinski and the entire managing committee of the then legally registered bakery workers professional union were arrested at midnight on Friday, 23 January 1914. The arrests took place as a result of a denunciation by a bakery owner.

Moshe Ceszinski had visited [was brought to] the gendarmerie because of a series of articles about the professional unions and the sick funds that had been published by A.C. in the *Czenstochower Wokhnblat* [*Czenstochow Weekly Newspaper*] under the pseudonym, "a worker." The direct cause of his arrest along with the bakery workers was that he, as coworker at the *Czenstochower Wokhnblat*, had been invited by the presidium to a legal meeting of the managing committee of the bakery workers in the *Harmonia* hall. Therefore police spies included him in the list of the leaders. He was in the Czenstochow jail for a few months.

Under German Occupation during the First World War

Mass political arrests and expulsions took place at the time of the German occupation. The arrestees mainly were sent to the Modlin Fortress, near Warsaw. Among those sent to Modlin were: Shimeon and Fela Biro (Birencwajg), arrested in Germany for anti-war activities in the Independent Socialist Party. And Kaneman was arrested in Czenstochow for his activities in the Social Democratic Party of the Kingdom of Poland and Lithuania.

In Independent Poland

In August 1920 a search was carried out at the *Wiedza Robotnicza* [Workers Knowledge] Society, previously the Kasprzak Club[1], and a group of its members were arrested. The society was a legal one and all of its members were registered. Poles and Jews as well as a number of women belonged to the society.

Anshel Judkewicz was sentenced in October 1920 for belonging to the *Kompartei* [Communist Party] and for spreading literature. The judges were: Kaczarewski, City Councilmen Januszewski and Gawendzki. The lawyer Rumszewicz defended the accused. Judkewicz was sentenced to one year in jail and the loss of all his rights.

A new series of political persecutions and trials began with the rise of "independent" Poland.

The first large political trial in Czenstochow took place in 1922. The Polish "Defensive" ruled then instead of the Russian gendarmes and police. Its leader was Janusz, a former member of the Polish Socialist Party who founded and led the provisional workers council in the name of the Polish Socialist Party. His helpers were: Zdanowicz – the overseer who tortured the arrestees, Hibner – a German and "Squirmer," who could read and write Yiddish, which helped him a great deal in his espionage work. Later came "Janek," a former Social Democrat.

[Page 154]

A regional conference of the *ZM'K* (*Zwiazek Mlodczeczi Komunistycznej* [Young Communist League]) then took place in Zawade that was denounced to the police by one of the Poles taking part. About 17 people were arrested, among them: Bayla Temerowicz, Maks Opatowski, Alya Lewensztajn, Salek Zilbersztajn, Borukh Brakman, Sholem Tobiasz, Shlomo Librowicz, Herman Zigos and Koniarski. Bayla Temerowicz was broken under torture and gave the names of the leaders of the conference.

The trial took place in Czenstochow in September. It lasted four days. Appearing as witnesses for the accused were Dr. Markusfeld, Dr. Gajzler, Dudek Szlezinger, A. Chrabalowski, R. Federman, Aleksander Ben, Shaya Nirenberg, Josef Kazmierczak, Shmuel Goldsztajn, Mendl Asz, Dr. Bram and Jan Hempel, publisher of *Książka* [The Book – a communist publications cooperative].

The lawyers defending the accused were: Honigwil, Dudacz, Dombrowski, and Brajter from Warsaw, M. Koniarski from Czenstochow and Wuczinski from Piotrkow.

Opatowski, Lewensztajn and Zilbersztajn were sentenced to 15 months in prison. All of the rest were freed.

Dembal, the communist deputy in the Polish *Sejm* [parliament], brought a parliamentary question in connection with the trial, protesting against the fact that the act of accusation began with the words, "A band of criminals came together in the holy Czenstochow to undermine the foundation of the Catholic Church and of the social order."

Wolf Zlatnik was one of the most active among the communist young people. He led the student group and wrote in the journal, *Swiatlo* [*Light*]. He was sentenced to two years in prison.

In May 1926, the "Revolution" of Pilsudski still ruled the government of the Chjeno-Piast [coalition of Polish political parties]. The communists took part in the general demonstration on

1 May. On Teatralna Street the police on horseback waited for those who stood at the gates and they made many arrests. Among the arrestees were Opatowski, Lewensztajn, Zilbersztajn, Brakman, Tobiasz, Librowicz, Ruczka Rozenfeld, Shlomo Kaneman, Moshe Richter, Krimolowski – student, Wolf Zlatnik, Leaszka Kachman, Leon Tenenberg – a student, Yitzhak Tenenberg, Moshe Shuchter, Ester Zbarowska, Feygl Zbarowska, Zigas and Szajnwald.

They spent seven months in the jail. A number of them were freed. Opatowski, Lewensztajn, Zilbersztajn, Zlatnik and Zigas were accused of "state treason, according to article 102 of the Russian Codex." Others were accused under article 126 of agitating against the government. With the help of Lawyer Wuczinski from Piotrkow, all of the testimony was [thrown out] and the trial was annulled.

A trial took place again in 1927 and W. Zlatnik, Ester Zbarowska and Ruczka Rozenfeld were sentenced to 4 years in prison. Tenenberg and several others in the area received two years in prison.

In 1928, in the county court in Piotrkow, Laya Szwierczewska of Krzepice and a group of communists were sentenced. She succeeded in escaping when she was being taken to a dentist to heal a tooth and she became one of the leading people in the communist organization in Berlin.

Later, Wolf Zlatnik resumed his political activity and became the director of the *Bank Kupiecki* [Merchant Bank] in Krakow.

The students Perec, Bem and Pruszicki, also were among those who were sentenced for taking part in the communist movement. It is characteristic that their parents belonged to various political movements in 1905. A. Perec was a Bundist, Bronya Bem was an *S.S.* [Zionist Socialists] member and Pruszicki, a brother-in-law of Adolf Bril, was considered a Social Democrat sympathizer.

Leaszka Kachman, Krimolowski and Elek Lewensztajn were sentenced a second time to four years in prison in 1928.

During the same year in Lodz, Dovid Richter also was sentenced to four years in prison. Previously, he had been arrested often and was tortured.

In 1935, Yitzhak Tenenberg was sentenced to four years in prison. Ruczka Rozenfeld was sentenced in 1937 to four years of serious imprisonment in Warsaw.

Laya Tenenberg, a nurse, was sentenced with a group of arrestees in Warsaw to eight years in prison for activity in the military division of the communist party.

[Page 155]

Two Czenstochow provocateurs, Moshe Szuchter and Herszlikowicz, were shot as a result of a sentence from the communist party. Because of Herszlikowicz, many communist activists were arrested all over Poland.

Our party in Czenstochow also suffered from police terror and persecutions, although not in as great a measure as the communists.

In 1920 the entire Bund committee was arrested. Among the arrestees were Yosef Aronowicz, Bundist city councilman at the Czenstochow city council, Yosef Izraelowicz, Zalman Tenenberg (perished at Auschwitz), Mendl Braun, Grinbaum, Czanszinski and Chaim Dovid Wolhendler. The arrestees were held at the Dombier prison camp, the first concentration camp for political arrestees. There is more precise information about this arrest in the article, "General Jewish Workers Bund," by Sh. Herc.

In 1920, the *Fareinikte* [United] club at *Aleje* 43 was liquidated through a decree by the Czenstochow *starosta* [senior official]. In connection with this, the Czenstochow city hall requisitioned the hall of the club and gave it to the police who installed their branch there. Later, the same hall was transferred to Christian officials as a private residence. The halls of many groups of professional unions located at the club also were requisitioned. The two Polish

Endekes [*"Endecja"* – *"Narodowa Demokraczja"* – anti-Semitic, Polish Nationalist Democratic Party] newspapers in Czenstochow agitated for a long time against the *Fareinikte* club, saying it was a communist nest in the very center of the city. Denouncers went to the government in Warsaw and, at the order of the government, the club was liquidated and the hall was requisitioned.

The trial of Rafal Federman, who was accused in court by *starosta* Griboszinski of insulting him as a state official, took place the same year. The quarrel between the *starosta* and R. Federman took place because of the ban on giving a speech in Yiddish. R. Federman argued that the ban was against the constitution, which protected the rights of national minorities. From that time on, the edict about Yiddish was annulled in Czenstochow. As revenge, the *starosta* accused Federman in court.

The lawyer, Mieczysław Kaniarski, defended the accused. R. Federman was sentenced to three months in prison. However, a general amnesty freed him from the sentence.

In 1923, during the election to the *Sejm*, the police and the National Defense carried out a police raid at all institutions and offices of the Independent Socialist Workers Party, which had presented Dr. Josef Kruk as its candidate for the *Sejm*. In connection with this, house searches took place of the private residences of all of the people who were on the party's candidate list. Many party documents and private writings were taken during the searches.

On 5 October 1926, the trial took place of the editor of the Czenstochower *Dos Neie Wort* [*The New Word*], A. Chrabalowski, for an article published in 1923 entitled "The Quiet Murder," which protested against closing the Bundist society, Our Children and the dozens of schools administered by the society. The court consisted of the judges: Walaszinski, chairman; Kamienbrodski and Keler. Lawyer Mencznicki defended the accused. Dr. Moric Grinbaum, Dr. Josef Kruk and Josef Stanisz appeared as witnesses called by the accused. The trial lasted all-day and ended with the release of the accused.

On 19 November 1926, the trial took place of Dr. Josef Kruk who was accused of treason against the state for his appearance at a mass meeting in Czenstochow that the foreign minister of the Soviet Union, [Georgy] Chicherin, held in honor of the prime minister of Poland, [Aleksander] Skrzyński, where in a toast he [Kruk] referred to *"kochajmy się"* (Let us love each other), and called on the Polish workers to follow the example from above.

The main witness against the accused was Commissar Kulinski (a former worker from Rakow). The witnesses for the accused were Dudek Szlesinger, chairman of the meeting, and Bialek and Antony Domanski. The defender was the lawyer Botner from Warsaw.

Dr. Josek Kruk was sentenced to a year and a half in prison. He was held in the Czenstochow and Piotrkow prisons for a long time.

[Page 156]

Later, he was freed by the court of appeals in Warsaw.

A great deal has been written in the country and abroad about the sadism and torturing of the political arrestees in Poland. In a letter from the Czenstochow political arrestees to their friends in America, dated 6 April 1929, we read:

"We, Czenstochow political arrestees, finding ourselves behind the bars of Polish prisons for many years, being by chance (now) in the Czenstochow prison, turn to you. Comrades, with a call that you come to help us in our situation.

"For our fight in the ranks of the revolutionary proletariat, for our devotion to the ideals of the working class, for our devotion to the cause of the worker and peasant state, for our striving for a better and brighter morning, for our fathers and mothers, brothers and sisters whom we cannot nonchalantly observe living in need and fear for the insecure morning, for this, we have declared a fight [against] our local clerical-nationalistic rulers, because we will be free people in a freer system – the executioner and blood-thirsty fascism has thrown us in Polish jails for many years, wanting to crush in us the will to fight, to suppress the revolutionary idea.

"You have certainly heard how we 'live' here. It is difficult to describe what we go through here daily. We suffer from hunger, need and cold. The prison regime feeds us with spoiled, frozen potatoes, smelly, filthy soup and dark, muddy 'bread.' It nauseates us when we take it in our mouths. Our relatives have no way to help us because many of us were their only providers. Hunger tortures us so much that we faint and during the long winter nights we toss on the plank beds not able to sleep because of hunger.

"There are comrades here among us who have found themselves in prison several times and struggle with their remaining strength.

"Therefore, it is no wonder that many of us suffer from tuberculosis. We have no medical help, except iodine and ... powders.

"The prison regime, which is composed of inhuman creatures, observe that hunger does not break us, so they turn to every means to suppress us physically and spiritually. We have fought daily with the jailers and various prison dignitaries and high officials. We are thrown into dark cells for the smallest rebellion.

**Signatures of the Polish Arrestees on a Letter Sent
Secretly from the Prison**

"This all makes our life unbearable. At every step and stride we have had to defend the honor of the revolutionary and class-conscious proletariat.

"However, we can affirm to you with pride that no persecutions, cruelties or suffering weakens our will to fight for the cause, which is the purpose of our lives. No prison, no dungeons, no legal penalties will suppress the fighting spirit in us. We use the time that we spend here to increase our knowledge so that we are able, when we leave prison, to again stand in the ranks from which we were torn away."

––––––––––

Translator's Footnote

1. Marcin Kasprzak was a Polish Socialist and a member of the Social Democracy of the Kingdom of Poland and Lithuania Party. He was executed for participating in resistance against the Russian rulers of Poland.

[Page 157]

Jewish Fighters on the Fields of Spain

(Dedicated to the illustrious memorial of the Czenstochow heroes: Adam Dawidowicz, Heniek Guterman, Leon Inzelsztajn and Godet)

> "... If I had the strength
> I would have taught the stones
> To block the road of tyranny ..."
>
> — Lord Byron

The Civil War in Spain was the laboratory of world fascisim, where Hitler with the aid of his partners, Mussolini and Francisco Franco, prepared the world slaughter of 1939–1945.

The bloody attack of the hangman did not come suddenly.

The European people from a series of nations bravely and stubbornly stood against the fascist dictators. For example, against [Pierre] Laval in France, against [Józef] Pilsudski in Poland, against Prince Starhemberg in Austria, against the Spanish Falangists [Alejandro] Lerroux and Antonio Maura, against the Belgian, Swedish and Finnish fascists...

It began with uprisings in 1934: the days in February in Vienna, Graz and Linz, the uprising of the masses under the slogan of the *Einheitsfront* [United Front]. As always, the bourgeoisie helped the fascists strangle the uprising and hanged the leader from Graz, Koloman Wallisch [and] the leader from Linz, Reichelberger. The enraged French workers and the progressive members of the intelligentsia with battles in the streets of Paris, Marseilles and Lille answered the provocations of the "crosses of fire" of Dario [Fo] and [Léon] Degrelle and signed their victory over fascism with their blood. The 400 great capitalist French families, led by Petain, threatened to turn the people over to Hitler.

In Spain, the land of great poverty and of the great luxury of feudalism in which the 13 richest families possessed 67 percent of the entire Spanish soil, the government of the "Popular Front," which at the time came out with the slogans popular for hundreds of years of land reform for the landless peasants and land workers, of labor legislation and a minimum wage for the municipal workers and artisans, for social support and public education, won [the election] in February 1936.

The spring for the Spanish people began: schools, hospitals for the poor, the division of aristocratic land under the direction of the Agricultural Minister, Vincente Urime [Uribe] is the correct surname], medical care for children and mothers – this all was like a dream come true for the enslaved, starving Spanish people, over whom the Catholic Church has ruled for hundreds of years, the hated *Guardia Civil* [civil guard] (the police) and the brutal exploiters – the grandees and marquises of the Spanish court, such as: Marquis de Espinos, Prince Oliva and the like.

On a warm day, in the summer of 1936, 18 July, the Workers' Olympiad, the proletariat sports competition, to which hundreds of foreigners were invited was supposed to begin in Barcelona. Among them also came a group of Jewish children from working Paris, children from our cultural institutions in France. Everything was prepared so that the Olympiad would be transformed into a holiday of international sports competition for the working masses in the progressive countries in Europe, as a means of opposition against the Nazi Olympiad, which workers did not attend. But instead of songs and a march with flags through the "Avenida Catalunya," at seven o'clock in the morning shots came from the barracks of the Spanish Army whose officers in Madrid, Valencia, Barcelona and Malaga gave the signal to rise up against the new democratic government of the Popular Front.

[Page 158]

This was on 18 July 1936. A date that will remain in our memory forever, because it also signified the end of a new revival in Spain for thousands of Jews who had come to Spain at the call of Spanish Foreign Minister de los Rios[1]. These were the great grandchildren of Sephardic Jews from Turkey, Greece, Macedonia and *Eretz Yisroel*, who had been driven out during the Inquisition as well as the new immigrant Jews from Poland, Germany, Austria and France whom anti-Semitism had driven in search of new homes and whom the Spanish Popular Front government had widely and sincerely welcomed to Spain after 1936.

Jewish Fighters on the Fields of Spain
(a Czenstochower is marked with an X)

The date was the chasm that opened years later for the millions of Jews of east and west Europe when Hitler, with the quiet agreement of the great democracies, enslaved Spain and began to burn the nations south and east of Spain.

We will not forget the date because of the thousands of Jewish fighters from all over the world covered in glory and we will recognize the Jewish names because they covered with their blood the old Spanish homeland from which the brutal feudal Catholic Church drove their great grandfathers and grandmothers 600 years before.

This fact explains that in February 1936, when the Popular Front government won, Jews began to to Spain...from Tarnopol and Tel Aviv, from Berlin and Rome, from Athens and Lodz, from Constantinople and Trieste.

And when, at dawn, the shot from the barracks was heard in Barcelona and Madrid, the Jewish gymnasts, sportsmen and teachers who were heading for the French border, turned around – to fight against the officers of the Francoists and the officers of the Franco clique, against officers of the richest Spanish families. At the same time, soldiers did not take part in the uprising in the three largest cities in Spain; they were against Franco, for freedom, for land, for bread, for the Spanish people.

Spain was the center of the world's attention. A bloc of states was organized that consciously and consistently helped Franco with all of their terrible means of power: weapons, money, propaganda and legions of aid...

It clearly came to expression in France, Spain's bordering nation and the only country whose masses proclaimed without preconditions support for the Loyalists in Spain. From there, from the small border town of Serber between France and Spain, small lines of people, who came from 28 nations, began going across the rocks, the boulders of the Pyrenees Mountains at night to help the people of Spain in their heroic struggle against Franco. They walked with enthusiasm and self-sacrifice, young and middle aged, not speaking a work of Spanish, people from all professions, education and religions, with only one wish: not to let Franco and world fascism defeat the people of Spain because behind the people of Spain stood the families of people from all of Europe and with beating hearts they thought about the path of their own fascists at home.

They went against cannons, machine guns, against Nazi airplanes that spread death and ruin. Not having any military training themselves, the majority had been in fascist jails and concentration camps at home for many years.

Serber, the border town, saw thousands of young men and women who entered Spain and placed themselves under the jurisdiction of the Loyalists, forming the famous and glorious "International Brigades." There were five "International Brigades" on the battlefields of Spain: the 11th Thalmann Brigade, the 12th Garibaldi Brigade, the 13th Polish Brigade named after Jaroslaw Dabrowski, the 14th French *La Marseillaise* Brigade and the 15th Abraham Lincoln Brigade – the Americans.

In 1937, while the Polish 13th Brigade fought on the front at Aragon, the Jewish workers and artisans from Polish cities and *shtetlekh* [towns], from the emigrants in Paris, Brussels and Antwerp, from Holland and Czechoslavakia, from Austria and *Eretz Yisroel* organized a Jewish unit based on the decision of the headquarters of the 45th Division, where the commandant was the Polish General Walter, today's hero of the fight for Warsaw and Silesia in the Soviet-equipped and armed Kosciuszko division that marched through Poland with the Red Army on the victory march to Berlin. The Jewish company in the Palafox Battalion was grouped under the name of the Jewish worker Naftali Botwin who was shot in Lemberg in 1929]...[2]

[Page 159]

The company was named in honor of Botwin, the martyred hero who shot the Polish spy and traitor [Josef] Cechnowski. In the trenches of Aragon, the historically first Jewish fighting unit in Spain was organized by dim light, face to face with the enemy, which was only about 30 feet from the Polish fighters. The company had its own commander and a battlefront journal, *Botwin*, which would appear every month in the Yiddish language.

For the first time in 500 years, Yiddish sentences were sent from Paris to be printed in Albacete, not far from the old university city of Murcia [in Spain], where the anti-Jewish laws of the Spanish monarch were once printed – a Jewish newspaper, *Der Freiheit Kemfer* [*The Freedom Fighter*].

Hundreds of young and middle-aged fighters passed before my eyes and before my heart. My arrival in Madrid as a member of the Anti-fascist Writers Congress in June 1937 was fascinating as an episode that no director of a modern film could stage.

Riding on the largest and widest street in Madrid, Avenida Prado, the column of automobiles with the participants of the Congress (we traveled from Barcelona and from Valencia to Madrid in a total of 84 vehicles) stopped on a side [of the road] to meet with the representatives of General [José] Miaja, the commandant of Madrid and of the Madrid Front. A young, excited blond solider ran along the column and held a *Neye Prese* [*New Press*], a Yiddish newspaper from Paris in his hand. He waved the newspaper like a flag, waiting until the members of the writers' congress would declare themselves as Jews and would stop him...I actually did this and the young soldier's joy was indescribable...He knew that the congress was supposed to open in the evening; he had taken a furlough from the front, which, as has already been said, was 20 minutes by tramway from the center of the city, and had gone to look for a Jewish writer. When I asked his name and told him mine, he became even redder, blushing more... "Gina Medem! My comrades from *Feunte Franseze* [French Source] will not believe me that I have seen you..." Therefore, I wrote my name and the date on the same newspaper as a joke.

We came to an agreement that at the congress in the morning several of his friends from his battalion would come to the official greetings from the writers to the Congress. He then told me how to say his name: Feldman – then I started the car and he left, running, as he had come, and waving the newspaper. I did not see him again because, on the same evening, the fascists set off one of their explosions under the house where they had dug a tunnel to our lines and he was injured along with a group of Spaniards...

Several Polish-Jewish Front fighters came on another day to greet us: Sewik, Yosek Mazel and Benyamin Lipszic, known under the name Barcelo Lorento, a member of the Bundist youth organization *Tsukunft* [future] in Warsaw who came to fight in Spain.

Yosek Mazel (Sulinski) born in Russia and educated in Warsaw, was later an editorial member of the Polish Brigade weekly *Dąbrowszczak*. He was the inspiration and the most unaffected, tireless archivist who helped me in the publication of my book in Madrid: *Yidn – Freiheit-Kempfer* [Jews – Freedom Fighters]. He gave me unlimited interesting details and dates about the 13th Brigade where he later organized the Naftali Botwin Company. With pride he related the fact that our Gershon Szur and Captain Elbaum, the first commandant of the Botwin [Brigade], fought the Spaniards, [along with] Greeks and Jews from many nations, [including] Matias Kac from Hungary, Yona Brodski from *Eretz-Yisroel*, Efroim Wauzek, Shlomole Feldman, Rotenberg and more and more.

Polish Jews were represented in the Spanish battalions in the largest number because the greatest percent of the emigrants would come from Poland, the first fascist country, with an outspoken fascist *Sanacja* [Pilsudski's political movement, whose slogan was "moral cleansing" - sanitation] government in Eastern Europe.

It is not important that every young Polish man came from Paris, Brussels, Argentina, *Eretz-Yisroel* or Austria; their motherland was Poland. The very first Jew who fell at the gates of Madrid, immediately after his arrival in Spain and a few hours after being on the battlefield, was Albert Nakhomi Wajz, a young fighter from Poland, a resident of *Eretz-Yisroel*. His memorial was dedicated in Jewish Paris, which in 1937 organized a historic museum of documents from the Spanish people's fight in the name of the first hero, Albert Nakhomi Wajz. Right afterwards, the Jewish fighter, Landau, fell, then Kirszenbaum and Natan Czak, the author of the battle hymn of the *Dąbrowszczak* Brigade that was sung by all of the anti-fascist Poles and the fighters on the [battle]field.

[Page 160]

It is difficult to write about the glorious lives and struggle of the Spanish people and not mention the glorious, unassuming and heroic figure of Bobrush Nussbaum, the working child of Warsaw, whose older brother was murdered at age 20 by the Warsaw "Defensive" in 1934 during a metal workers strike in Warsaw, and who, at age 16, was the only support and provider of food for his mother and five younger children. He threw himself into the fight against fascism in Poland with all his young fervor and immediately was thrown into the Polish fascist murder pit of Kartuz-Bereza, the concentration camp that did not have to feel shame when compared to Dachau, Belzec and the later Majdanek... Kartuz-Bereza, where people became crippled overnight by murderous blows with rubber clubs, became tubercular from sleeping naked on asphalt in winter, where young men left with white hair after the Inquisition-like investigations of [Colonel Waclaw] Kostek-Biernacki and [Tadeusz] Wojciechowski...

And Bobrush Nussbaum bore everything, counting the days until his departure and studying a map of Spain copied from memory from his meager months in school as a child by a weak, flickering lamp and hidden from the prison guards under the lice-covered straw mattress. Bobrush prepared for his legendary journey to Spain where he dreamed of taking revenge for all of the blows, all of the persecutions of his mother at the prison walls by the gendarmes and for the death of his beloved brother...

His trip, without papers, without money and without knowledge of a foreign language, of the five countries of which he had to sneak across the border: Czechoslovakia, Austria, Switzerland and France, in addition to the Polish and Spanish borders, rings like a legend: arrests, hunger, sleeping on benches in Prater Park in Vienna, going on "a leg of the journey" from one jail to another until the Jewish community in Geneva gave him clothing and a little bit of money and he arrived in Paris. Here he was fortunate: he left for Spain... After a short education in Albacete, the site of the instruction courses for the International Brigades, Bobrush went to the Polish Palafox Company at the front at Huesca where he took part in the battle of Zaragoza.

The battalion went first. They drove out the fascists. Bobrush was in a machine-gun group. His only love was his "Maxim," the heavy machine-gun. He cleaned and oiled it like a beloved toy; he sent out piles of bullets to the fascist murderers; for the brothers in Kartusz-Bereza, for the murder of Naftali Botwin, for the gallows of Cáceres where General [Antonio] Aranda machine-gunned 1,800 Spanish workers for their refusal to fight against the Republic.

The battalion left for the distant fascist hinterland. They went ahead for three days. The Moroccan cavalry surrounded the battalion – the group was too far away and had no cover from the artillery – it was a heroic advance-march, but they were alone. The order was given to retreat to their own lines. And Bobrush and a small group of machine gunners covered the path of the battalion back to the Loyalist lines. They were so close to the city of Zaragoza that the lights of the city could be seen. Mowing down the Moroccans, Bobrush sang *Dambrowski's Hymn*, "We shall ; not one of us will be missing." The battalion broke through. The group of machine gunners grew smaller; only Bobrush remained. And here, in Villamayor de Gallego, sending out the last ribbon of bullets, Bobrush, with a song on his lips, was felled by a fascist bullet from a sniper not far from the first line of our trenches...

Bobrush, the child from Żelazna Street, the young, strong-as-iron martyr of the Polish prisons, his mother's beloved son, the defender of the Spanish people and its best defender, the best shot in "Worinski," his company, the founder of the battlefront newspaper *Adelante* (*Forward*) was no more.

*

[Page 161]

Every city in Poland left a son under an old olive tree or in the vineyard: both a Pole and a Jew. Names that were legendary, names of pioneers in the fight against Hitler and against Hitlerism, names that will be sanctified for as long as even one progressive person remains in the world, because they were our first teachers on the battlefield, who did not separate a word from a fact, a slogan from an action, because they were the inspiration for the *Waldbrüder* [forest brothers – partisans] who fought four years later, in 1941-1944, on the roads of Kielce, Lublin, Czenstochow, Warsaw, Tarnow, Lemberg and Lodz against the same Hitler and Franco, who could not take Madrid with the weapons they had in hand.

Every city in Poland had a dear name on the cemetery in the area of Madrid. There is a special cemetery for the International Brigades and it is a passionate, but proud accident that we read the first name on the first grave: Izzy Kupczik, Brooklyn, New York... and Kupczik is a lucky one; he died in a hospital among witnesses, a nurse held his hand, a doctor gave him medicine and did not betray with a look that [Kupczik's] death was near.

But [for] Albert Nakhomi Wajc, the Polish Palestine emigrant Jungkraut and Moshe Landau and Chaim Elkan and Warszawski and the Czenstochow hero, Captain Adam Dawidowicz and his *landsman* [person from the same town], the very talented soldier and painter, the child of workers, Heniek Guterman?

Where is their last rest? Under which tree, under which pile of ruins do their exploded bodies lie? The sanitary groups had to dig feverishly, laying Flaczik like a worm, to bring the dying hero to our lines to protect him against the defilers on the side of the wild Moroccans.

*

My first meeting with Heniek Guterman took place in Madrid at the editorial offices of *Dąbrowszczak*. I saw a young, very pale soldier on whom the uniform lay wide and crumpled, not sewn for him. He noticed my gaze and said with a smile, "I am not elegant, I know; the responsibility falls on the Polish judicial system." He had the fine, ashamed smile of a person who rarely smiled. However, then his small face with gray-blue eyes and thin nose suddenly would become young and handsome. It usually was worried and old. It was autumn, 1937, after the battles in Kichorna and Brunete, when the wounded returned to the front and new groups voluntarily arrived from Figeroa near the French border.

I learned from Yusek Mazel, the editor of *Dąbrowszczak* that Heniek Guterman had just spent four years in the Kielce jail, that he was 26 years old and that he had great talent: a sculptor and illustrator. I understood why he always sat in the coldest, darkest corner of the large hall, where five national groups worked at five journals. He was so extremely modest that he did not permit anyone to look at his work. He had just come from the front for a few weeks of rest because he had lost weight and his commandant, Zigmund Moliec, had sent him to Madrid to work on a magnificent marble figure, which represented the struggle and the death of the first Polish commandant of the Polish battalion, Mickiewicz, a coal miner from France, born in Sosnowiec, named Antonio Kochanek. He fell near Madrid, defending the famous Casa Blanco, The White House that the fascists set on fire and where the heroic Leon Inzelsztajn, a Czenstochow shoe-worker also fell.

As Heniek Guterman kept coughing, we, the Polish group, got together at an hour when the fascists were not bombing the city and went to look for a small electric oven to warm the room.

This did not help Heniek. He argued that, "Man must harden himself, only with you in America is there such dissoluteness that you must have steam and central heating. We are front soldiers – and Madrid is the front."

However, the Italians, the Americans and the French editorial staffs fervidly supported the Yiddish project – and we went to search for an oven. A crafty 14-year-old Spanish boy, Mario, sniffed out as if from the earth a hidden small oven in a half-empty shop. The merchant did not want to sell it to us on the pretext that he only had things for the front. However, Mario told him that when the front was heated by electric ovens Franco could, God forbid, enter Madrid. We bought the oven for 180 pesos and laughter reigned in the large hall of the commandant of the brigades when the oven on a very long cord went from one editorial table to the next. The only one who did not warm himself was Heniek Guterman...

[Page 162]

The young man was one of rare consistency. When he said something it was a law for him and his neighbor. When he finished the sculpture and sent it to France, as a means of gathering aid for the Army in Spain, Heniek was given a second mission: to illustrate the Polish brochure, written for the Third Brigade for the mothers and sisters in Poland that was called, *Di Biks un Dos Harts* [*The Gun and the Heart*]. Heniek asked me to find for him to draw [various] types of people among our Spanish and Polish nurses and employees of the childrens' homes. We would sit in the kitchen of the commandant in the evening where it was warm because we had coal from Asturias and while the women either knitted or sewed or prepared packages for the front, I spoke to them and asked them to pose for Heniek. When he needed male types, we would go through the streets of dark, clouded-over Madrid in the evening with a *salvaconducto* [safe passage document], permission from headquarters, and enter a small *bodega* [cellar] where we would sit with a small glass of wine with old militiamen (*luftschutz* [air protection]) waiting for an alarm. Heniek would quietly and seriously sit down at the table, ask me to carry on a conversation with the residents of Madrid (He only knew one word in Spanish: "*Fuego al enemigo!*" [Fire on the enemy!]) and not look to his side. The old bakers and carpenters from the suburb immediately grasped [what he wanted] and wanted to take him to the commandant: "Why are you drawing our faces: who ordered this?"

However, [with] the military [identification] card with General Mejacho's name, a few declarations and the "*hermano foloko*" [brother folk], the Polish brother continued to draw. I saved the album when leaving Catalonia and I found another small picture in it that he had drawn of me when he needed to illustrate a woman who was writing a letter to her son in Spain. Heniek Guterman only once spoke about himself when he again left for the front in the direction of Lérida, after the breakthrough of the fascists at the ocean in 1938.

Heniek Guterman
(a self-portrait)

He lost his parents very early. His family members each took a child. Thus, Heniek was raised by his uncle, his brother by another uncle and his sisters by an aunt. The children were torn apart and Heniek became lonely early on. He studied at the Czenstochow *ezkola powszechna* [elementary school]. At 14 he became a tailor's apprentice in Czenstochow, first with an uncle and then he left to work in Warsaw. There, the real school of life opened for him. He became acquainted with young, Polish professional workers and he attended evening courses to learn the language and history of Poland, as well as other subjects that the four years of elementary school could not give him. He went on the road of a class-conscious worker, took part in organizing widespread anti-fascist work among Polish and Jewish workers in Warsaw and returned to Czenstochow as a mature, capable young man with a desire to fight for a free Poland and with the dream of developing his artistic abilities in the area of sculpture. However, he was arrested in Czenstochow in connection with the wave of protests against the bloody oppression of the peasant strike in Poland. His arrest brought a sentence of four years in prison.

He used the four years to educate himself even more, as far as possible within the framework of a Polish prison, the location of the same bloody attacks as the murdering of political prisoners during a hunger strike, as Heniek related the tragic events in the Kielce prison, when after serving four years, he came to see his relatives and immediately left for Spain.

A restrained, but tenacious and courageous fighter, he voluntarily reported to an intelligence group at night, during the battle for the city of Lérida [Lleida].

He left his trench in the morning – and never returned. No trace was found of him when they went to search for him. The thought was that the fascists caught him at his task and tortured him to death because Heniek would have let himself by hacked to pieces and would not have talked...

[Page 163]

His smile and the gleam in his eye remain with me. When I asked him to create the title page for my Spanish book about the Jewish fighters, he drew his own face in big grotesque, bold lines. His steel helmet was clasped tenderly to his gun... and both were symbols of his militant worker's nature...

Heniek Guterman! We will search for your grave in free Spain, which we will once again help liberate. This we promise you today, in Autumn 1945, when the dead in Spain cannot sleep...while a new war rages in Asia against a colonial people.

Heniek Guterman only spoke about his family once: his sister was somewhere in Czenstochow and his brother, whom I met in Amsterdam in 1939 and told him about his quiet, strong brother. And he said to me: "When he was still a child, Heniek showed his strength. He never complained about anything. He wanted to study, more than anything, and he never asked for anything."

His personal life was short, too, cut off. Prison had separated him from his dearest [woman] friend: both of them had to pay with their best years for wanting a free Poland and their short encounter in Spain was cut short by death.

Leon Inzelsztajn was a worker from Czenstochow, a shoemaker by trade. He left for Belgium in about 1934, when the Polish "defensive" chased after him, because he was known as an organizer of the shoemaker trade.[3] He was among the group of "French-Belgian" volunteers who came to Spain. He was assigned to a machine-gun company of the Dabrowski Battalion. As a politically responsible volunteer, with great courage and discipline, he always was there where the danger was the greatest, where the young, inexperienced, volunteers face to face with the murderous fire of the enemy, could have fallen in panic – then his brave, high voice would be heard and his machine gun would mow the ranks of the attacking fascists. Thus, when his company was surrounded on all sides, he alone with his machine gun created a path for his comrades and made it possible for them to return to an olive tree grove.

"The White House, the Casa de Campo," became the victim of the beast. The most dedicated volunteers of the International Brigades felt with every nerve that the entire world was looking at them. As the short, feverous news in the Spanish newspapers aroused a storm of enthusiasm among the people, that their actions, their heroism, their deaths would feed the cause of the Spanish people and it would protect against defeat...

The enemy moved to the "White House," a stronghold of the Loyalists, which could not be taken. The Moroccans threw grenades into the house and it was ignited. A group of French-Polish volunteers was inside, among them Leon Inzelsztajn. It was fated to be his tragedy to be in this very fire...

Leon Inzelsztajn

**Leon Inzelsztajn Examining an
Enemy Grenade**

When the top floors were barricaded and the house was in flames, several people tried to jump out of the windows – into the arms of the Moroccans, who were already sure of victory over the hated *Rocos* – as they called the Republicans. However, Leon did not lose himself. He proposed that he go onto a gutter of the roof: four jumped down easily to the ground, as they slid down on the gutter. Leon's plan succeeded. He also came down. Two groups went to search for their battalion in two directions. The Moroccans shot after them! Two of the four fell: Leon Inzelsztajn was the second one!

[Page 164]

A daring heart was released from suffering. The blood-soaked ground of Madrid swallowed the young man from Czenstochow...

*

He was a captain on the battlefield of Spain. His name? Adam Dawidowicz. His profession? A painter [artist]. He spoke very little about himself. We only knew that he came to Spain, interrupting his studies in painting, which he went through in Paris, later in Brussels.

At the beginning, Adam Dawidowicz was in the "General [Walery Antoni] Wroblewski" company, named in honor of the hero of the Paris Commune in 1871. Then the company became the Jaroslaw Dabrowski Battalion, named in memory of the Polish fighter against Tsarism and against the Prussians at the barricades of the "Paris Commune." He was a rigorous disciplinarian and systematic soldier, who immediately began to move forward during the first battles at the Madrid front, in the Jarama mountains, where he rose in the ranks from a soldier to be a *teniente* (lieutenant) and, later, a captain. At the headquarters of the division, the commandant was Walter (Karol Swierczewski, a Polish general, the leader of the Kosciuszko Brigade near Warsaw in 1942, with the Soviet Army), who took an interest in the young fighter-artist. He [Dawidowicz] moved ahead on the front of Huesca, where he led a machine-gun battalion. This was one of the most difficult and bloodiest battles for the road to Zaragosa and several assaults were repelled by the fascists, who had a tremendous preponderance of material and men. The battalion lost a great number of experienced veterans, trained fighters from the winter victory at Guadalajara. The battle near Huesca was sung about by the Jewish worker poet and soldier from the Warsaw front, Olek Nuss [Hershl Orzech], who developed a talent for poetry at the front. He became the author of the best fighting songs of the 13th Polish Brigade.

Captain Adam Dawidowicz met an enemy bullet and fell on 20 June 1937, covering the retreat of the battalion with his machine gun, going last in the ranks of the rearguard.

At his grave, the battalion swore to take revenge for its most beloved commander and later distinguished itself gloriously at the battles of Quijorna, Belchite and Brunete – another heart stopped beating, the modest, proud and courageous heart of a Jew, a patriot of the tradition of freedom, of an artist, of a child of Czenstochow.

A few months later, a second Czenstochow fighter, also an artist, Alfred Nadet, fell at the battle for Tajuña.

He also was in the machine-gun division and annihilated fascist nests sitting in the rocky lairs of Morata de Tajuña. At the last ribbon-cartridge, when he was crawling near a machine gun of a dead comrade, a sniper-bullet hit him. A few days later, a *"łącznikowi"* [liaison], a liaison-soldier, brought a simple soldier's rucksack to the editorial room of the Polish newspaper: a few letters from those closest to him, a toothbrush, several photographs and a booklet with front-essays – a sign that the position was held by us and that the body had been brought to us to bury [behind] our lines.

*

Among the few documents that were successfully saved from the archives of the aid committee for Spanish fighters in the French concentration camps in 1940, when Paris already was occupied, I found a list of Jewish and Polish names from Camp Vernet in southern France. The following fighters from Czenstochow there were:

[Page 165]

**A Group of Czenstochowers in the Republican Army during the Civil War
in Spain**

Rozental Moric Born 21 May 1910. Mechanic.

Bronitowski Mieczysław Born 9 April 1912. Student.

Lubczik Aloizi. Born 9 September 1909. Metalist.

Rozen Wiktor. Born 15 June 1903. Artisan.

Kuper Shmuel. Born 17 October 1917. Tailor.

Wajman Yakov. Born the 24 January 1910. Tailor.

This is only from one concentration camp, in 1940, when I was still in France and while we still had contact with the camps and could support them with the help of the French people and of the Botwin Committee in New York and Paris (before Hitler captured Paris, it should be understood).

When the Nazis drew closer to the southwest of France, where the camps of the Spanish fighters were located (about a quarter of a million Spaniards from Catalonia left [Spain] in March 1939, among them army units that had protected the evacuation of the sick, the wounded and the archives and who had carried out the "withdrawal" combat against Franco's fascist armies), the fighters broke the gates and wire obstructions of their camps and left [to join] the underground, to the French partisans who carried on a stubborn fight against the Nazis up to the day when they united with the first American troop landings in the fortresses of the Atlantic.

Many of the Jewish fighters perished in the battles against the Nazis. Many were guillotined by the Petain regime for fighting against the Nazis. Among them we have the names of Y. Jungerman, Majerowicz, Bursztajn, Kutner and Zachariasz (the last two had been imprisoned in the Polish concentration camp in Kartuz-Bereza and were very sick when they came to France, not long before the outbreak of the war). Mendl Langer was guillotined in Toulouse on 23 July 1943 – in the same city, eight fighters fell in the battle against fascism. Fell by death sentence...

One wants to hope that there will be success in finding the above-mentioned Czenstochow *landsleit* [people from the same town] who were still in Camp Vernet at the beginning of 1940 among the hundreds of surviving men and women, some in Algiers, Africa. Searching for them will be the task of the activists and friends of the large Czenstochow family, which is spread across America and takes such a generous and heartfelt part in creating aid for the already liberated community institutions in the home city. The tradition of the earlier work for the victims of Polish fascism that was expressed in *Patronat*: the aid through the former "People's Relief" and of the *landsmanschaftn* [organizations of people from the same town] has been revived again, in the largest Jewish tragedy of all times. With the united strength of world Jewry, it is coming back to life – we give our word!

The work of laying a foundation for the rebuilding of our lives must be done with unity. The remainder of Polish Jewry is waiting for this.

Translator's Footnotes

1. Bernardo Giner de los Rios was not the foreign minister. He served the Republican government as the Minister of Communications, Transport and Public Works in the cabinet.

2. He actually was shot in 1925.

3. The "defensive" consisted of a government-initiated boycott of Jewish businesses as a "defense" against Jewish "exploitation" of the Polish population.

[Page 165]

Pogroms
Forward

Dr. Rafal Sohler

The Jewish community in Czenstochow experienced three pogroms from the beginning of the 20th century, pogroms that marked with blood the road of reaction in Poland and cast a dark shadow in advance of the dark night of Hitlerism that annihilated this community along with the entire Jewish community in this country. All three pogroms against the Jews in Czenstochow, under various political regimes, essentially were organized by the same dark reactionary forces with the same political purpose – to drown the striving for freedom by the Polish masses in the blood of Jewish victims, just as the determined stand of organized Polish labor in each of the pogroms is mirrored in the growth of the political consciousness of the workers movement in the city and the entire country.

The pogrom in 1902 was organized by the Polish *Endekes* [anti–Semitic Polish National Party] in alliance with clergy under the Black Wing of the Tsarist administration, although without its initiative, as a means of staving off the masses of the newly arising socialist movement that kept spreading over the country. The young and persecuted Polish socialist movement did not do more than demonstrate its protest against pogroms in appeals that it tried to spread in Czenstochow, Lodz and other worker centers (see the footnote of Shimkha Lev to the report of the *Arbeter–Shtime* [*Voice of the Worker*]).

[Page 166]

The pogrom in 1919 in "liberated" Poland was much bloodier and more tragic than the first pogrom 17 years earlier. The reactionary [forces] in Poland were stronger and more widespread among the ruling classes and more brutal than in the Tsarist times because there was much more at stake than there was then [in Tsarist times]. The Polish reactionaries stood face to face against the direct danger of a social revolution that was victoriously carried out in neighboring Russia. The slogan of the pogromists – fight against "Bolsheviks" and Jews – already had the full support not only of the *Endekes* Party and the clergy, but of the Polish military and state apparatus, including the majority of the *Sejm* [Polish parliament] and the city administration and city council. The Polish and Jewish workers parties, organized in a local workers' council, appeared against the pogrom, but the weak results of the intervention of the workers' council were proof alone that this initiative that arose in the early revolutionary excitement among the working masses in Poland had already lost all its tangible political significance.

The third Czenstochow pogrom in 1937, took place in the era of the frightening intensification of fascism in Poland that was a link in the bloody chain of pogroms that extended from Przytyk, to Minsk Mazowiecki and Brisk, and was one of the terrible culminations of the cold economic pogrom that intolerably oppressed the Jewish population in the country. Both camps of the Polish reactionary bourgeoisie, the ruling *Sanacia* [Jozef Pilsudski's political movement] camp and the sullen opposition *Endekes* struck their hands over the heads of the Jews. The Black Wing of "home–grown" Polish Hitlerism already waved over the country like a portent of the black swastika that in the course of two years came to Poland on the German bombers. Organized Polish workers already clearly understood then how when anti–Semitism appeared in the history of Poland, it was a poisoned weapon that recently has been aimed exclusively against the workers' movement. Polish workers in Czenstochow protested, sent delegations to the regime, split into [factions] and severed connections among themselves. But the Polish workers' movement in Poland, just as others in other nations, did not succeed in defeating fascism. The foundation of the misfortune of Polish Jewry and of the later extraordinary catastrophe lay in the tragedy of the Polish worker class.

———

The "Rabinek" – the Pogrom in 1902

by Mark Liber, Supplemented by Shimkha Lev

The first pogrom against the Jews in Czenstochow broke out on Monday, 11 August 1902 (*Erev Tisha B'Av* [the eve of the Ninth of Av – fast day commemorating the destruction of the First and Second Temple in Jerusalem] (5662). We were then still ashamed of the word "pogrom," so we called it a *rabinek* [from the Yiddish word, *rabiner*, to loot or plunder].

This *rabinek* was described at that time in the illegal *Arbeter Shtime* [*Voice of the Worker*], number 30 (of October 1902). We provide this report here word for word:

"Three days earlier, before the pogrom took place, there was a parade in Czenstochow in honor of the new church that had opened that day. On the morning of that day, the police overseer and the president of the city (*gorodskoy golowva* – mayor) informed several Jews (unofficially) that a pogrom was being prepared in the city and they warned the Jews that they should not appear near the new "shrine." Those taking part in the pogrom themselves said later that they had not made the pogrom on 8 August as was planned because they 'did not want to disturb the holiday'... It was obvious that it only was a coincidence that a spark had fallen into a box of gunpowder at the market. Several Jews had fought and come to blows with a Christian woman at the market. The Jews as well as the Christian woman were professional thieves. The Jewish leadership had for a long time asked the police to send these Jews from the city, but the bribed Czenstochow police let these Jews remain in the city to spite those [who had made the request]. The Christian woman who the Jews had beaten already had been sentenced three times as a thief. And the Russian government and Polish 'society' gave the fighting among thieves as the main reason for the 'unrest'...

[Page 167]

"The beaten Christian woman was not even badly wounded and on the same day she signed herself out of the hospital. But, despite this, everyone, even the doctors in the hospital, spread a rumor that the Christian woman had died.

"On 11 August, at half past 12 in the afternoon, at the time when they left for the factories to eat lunch, a mob of brickworkers (*mulaczes*), factory workers and young gentile boys began to throw stones into Jewish shops at the 'old market.' No police were seen there; there were no soldiers in Czenstochow. They had been sent away on maneuvers. The Jews began to close their shops. Then several policemen and a commissioner (*pristov*) and a gendarme officer appeared. The workers dispersed, beating every Jew in a long kaftan on the way. The 'old market,' the center of Jewish trade, was calm then. However, at the same time, a 'pogrom' began in the poor streets. A group that consisted of workers, artisans and the unemployed, who were then many in Czenstochow because of the [economic] crisis, began to break windowpanes in the Jewish warehouses and pillage the goods. They broke into the houses, broke furniture, tore the bedding, and the feathers from the Jewish pillows flew far. The Jewish shops on Krakower Street, in which more Christians than Jews lived, had particularly bad damage. [Some] did not allow their warehouses in the Christian courtyards to be looted, as for example, Kriger, who defended his property with a revolver in his hand. There were no police at the beginning and afterward they were afraid of what to do because there were too few [of them]. Then when patrols arrived of a few soldiers, who remained in the city. they began to arrest individually the most stubborn rioters and led them to the police station (*utshastok* – police). Several of the arrestees also fought the police. At five o'clock, it became a little quieter for a while, but Krakower Street already was completely looted. Everyone waited in fear for the pogrom to begin again around seven o'clock when the factory workers left work. A deadly fear spread among the Jewish population and the rich Jews began to run from Czenstochow.

At one o'clock on the next day, the police sent a telegram to the Piotrokow governor. Afterward, when the mob broke the windowpanes in the Jewish synagogue where Jews were gathered in honor of *Tisha B'Av*, the Jewish community turned to the high ranking *nachalnik* [commander] for help. But he hid and did not even go out to the Jews... Then the community sent a telegram to the governor and the general governor. The police created patrols of soldiers who had remained in the city and of the *tamazhne straznikes* [customs guards] (soldiers who guard against contraband). Among the soldiers who had remained in the city were many Jews, and the Polish anti-Semites then spread a rumor that only because of this had the soldiers not refused to shoot into the crowd.

The police turned its entire attention to protecting the main street in the city, the remarkable *Alejes* on which were located the branch of the *Gosudarstvennyi* [State] Bank, several bankers' offices and various government facilities... The surrounding areas remained, as is said, "in God's care." No one protected them. Therefore, they were badly looted. Various distinguished people began to appear at the First *Aleje* at close to seven o'clock... Everyone waited in fear for what would happen at seven o'clock... And actually, right at seven, the factories began to release masses of workers who joined with those who already were waiting at the boulevard. With shouts of "Hurray! Let's get the Jews!" And with terrible whistling from whistles, the mob went to the Second *Aleje*. The soldiers drove the mob and beat [the mob] with the butts of their rifles. The mob dispersed, came together again, but the soldiers finally were successful in driving them completely from the *Alejes*. The masses then assailed anew at the "old market" and in the Czenstochowka [area of Czenstochow].

Meanwhile, despite this, the police protected the rich quarter and didnot let anyone approach it. The entire city looked as it did during the time of the [First World] war and in the poor quarters, meanwhile, the mob, not meeting any opposition, rampaged widely. They robbed and destroyed all of the Jewish warehouses, beginning with the small shops and ending with the large, rich department stores, which had placed "icons" and candles in the windows. In addition to this, only the Jewish street, Targowa, escaped, where the Jewish butchers had promised that they would lay down on the spot anyone who dared to loot [the Jewish shops].

[Page 168]

The mob broke into several parts, one of them attacked Mejtkowicz's grocery store, broke off the doors and stole the goods, despite the fact that the vice governor and prosecutor who had come to Czenstochow at seven o'clock with a few soldiers were nearby. They began to convince those taking part in the pogrom that they should disperse. But this did not help and they did not stop their looting. The mob was warned twice that it should disperse; twice bullets were fired in vain, but this only provoked the mob more and they began to throw stones at the soldiers. Then there was substantial gunfire; two were left dead on the spot and several were seriously wounded... It is interesting that there were several Jews among the wounded. Therefore, it should be assumed that the soldiers shot not only at the aggressors but also at those who were attacked.

It was quiet after the massacre, but the looters did not stop in the surrounding streets. There was particularly severe looting on Warszawer Street and in Czenstochowka; here, several from the mob [of people] threw several stones at the Tsar Aleksander II memorial. And the singing of the Polish national song, *Jeszcze Polska nie zginela* [*Poland Has Not Yet Perished*], was heard. Because of this, several later spread a rumor that the pogrom ostensibly carried a political character...

They wanted to set fire to several places during the pogrom (such as, for example, Helman's warehouses were doused with kerosene). But they were not successful. They succeeded in setting fire to only one house near the old synagogue. The pogrom stopped at 11 o'clock at night and at 12 o'clock, when the mob had robbed almost everything, 60 *stojkowes* (*gorodovyyes* [policemen]) from Lodz and 100 Cossacks from Bendin arrived. The governor and the prosecutor from Warsaw *Okruzhnoy Sud* [District Court] also came and the arrests started: stolen goods also were found among the arrestees.

In total, the pogrom left 120 stores looted, two dead and masses of wounded people [and] dozens entirely impoverished, who were sentenced to go to beg for donations. But this was only the material damage brought by the "Rabinek." This damage was not as terrible as was the spiritual and moral damage. The abyss that divided the Jewish and Polish populations deepened. The separation and the hate between them became sharper. Only those in the Russian regime won.

Such a situation was terrifying for the Tsarist regime when the Jews were so persecuted and oppressed that they had to find their only help from the bullets of soldiers and the whips of the Cossacks against the wild violence of another people, of the Poles, who also were trampled under the feet of the Tsarist regime. These are the facts. However, what was their cause? Who is responsible for this terrible war between two people whose historical destiny itself, it seems, calls for a fraternal bond against the common enemy? At each new chance, this question appears for us and it is necessary to reflect on it...

The Czenstochow data did not come unexpectedly for anyone who was acquainted with Jewish life in Poland. What we were accustomed to encountering in our everyday life was just sharply expressed in this pogrom. This was the deeply rooted anti-Semitism of the Polish nobility (*szlachta* [nobility], *dvoryanstvo* [gentry]), of the small and great Bolsheviks and of all of the strata of the Polish people who had not yet been freed from their destructive influence. In order to characterize the relationship between the Polish and Jewish population in Czenstochow, it is enough to provide several facts from the lives of the higher strata of the society (the Jewish working masses in Czenstochow at that time were still ignorant and still lived completely apart from the Polish workers); the principal maxim of this relationship was "Down with the Jews!" They [the Jews] were not assured by such a relationship, not even the

"Poles of Mosaic belief" (as the Jewish intelligentsia and bourgeoisie of Poland called themselves), who were always ready as a result of a merciful look from someone, from a *wielmożni pan* [great gentleman], to reject solidarity with the Jewish people... A constant struggle against the Jews was carried out in all temples, starting at the temple of Hermes (the god of trade) and ending with the temple of Melpomene (the goddess of theater art), not to mention the Roman Catholic temples where the "holy fathers" constantly provoked the fanatical masses against the "non-believers" for "God's honor."

[Page 169]

There is in Czenstochow, for example, a "credit society" that was founded with the help of the Jewish bourgeoisie. The majority of members of this society are Jews. Jews also are a third of the board of directors of this society. Christians are in two higher positions in the society. And when there was a vacancy for a third position, an intelligent Jewish woman was proposed. The judgment was that she had proved that she knew the work well and that she could take this position, but only under the [guidance] of the Polish members of the society. The woman refused [to accept] this condition and they openly made the declaration that if this position were to given to a Jewish woman, they could not be completely sure that the society would remain "a truly Christian one"... This referred to the Jews in the Temple of the Golden Calf [worship of money]. But there is no surprise here. It is known that where money was dealt with, where the road had to be cleared of competition, there one could use all means. But we saw the same attitudes in the temple of "pure" art, [no Jews] in the musical society *Lutnia*, [no Jews] in the "Society of Lovers of Dramatic Art." They did not admit Jews... and we could provide hundreds of such examples.

The relationship of the Polish "intelligentsia" to the Jews in Czenstochow was particularly clearly expressed at the time of the last pogrom itself. There was no one among the entire "intelligentsia" who tried to have an effect on the mob, to hold it back. On the contrary, everyone openly sympathized with taking part in the pogrom. A regret was often expressed that they had not slaughtered all of the Jews. We provide only a few facts.

Wigowski (his father was a seller at a "government" warehouse), a sixth class *gymnazie* [secondary school] student, sold whiskey to the neighboring crowd and bartered it for bottles of wine stolen from a Jewish wine cellar all evening despite the fact that that day the police had forbidden the sale of spirits later than seven o'clock (this fact was known in court). Not very far from this "civilized" savage, his "elders" – people who had graduated from the university – also left [without interfering]. On the street they [the Jews] turned to the well-known Dr. Bieganski, the author of an article about medical ethics (morals) and asked that he give medical aid to the Jews wounded [during the pogrom]. Doctor Bieganski refused to do so. He left the sick in the hands of the police. He turned around and walked calmly further on his way. His colleague, Dr. Wczesnieski, also did the same thing. A Jewish woman with a broken bone was brought to him so that he could provide medical help; he drove her away with laughter. The lawyer, Paciorkowski, encountering one of his Jewish acquaintances on the street, said to him in a satisfied voice, "Aha, ours are beating yours!" The beer manufacturer, Karl Szwede, stood with several of his brew-masters and watched several healthy young men beat a Jewish boy; he very much enjoyed the deed and laughed uncontrollably... (The Jews then initiated a boycott of his beer.) I believe that the facts speak clearly... They provide an understanding of the sources of the pogroms.

I only have to add that in Włocławek (Warsaw *gubernia* [province]) there was a proclamation not long ago that called for "murdering the Jews." There also were such rumors about Warsaw and other cities. Understand that not all of this news needed to be believed, but in any case, they showed us again that the Czenstochow pogrom did not take place for local reasons. The sources lie a great deal deeper – in general in the relations between the Jewish and Polish populations.

On the question of the relationship of the Christian population in general to the Jews, I cite particularly the question of Jewish-Polish relations in general for several reasons. First of all, the history of the Jews in Poland is in the full sense different from the Jews in Lithuania and Russia. This was one side. On the other side, anti-Semitism was stronger, without a doubt, among the Polish population that among the Russians. Anti-Semitism was absorbed by the majority of the Polish society and was also characteristic of the *zagenanta* [informed] "intellegentsia." The press is also full of him [the member of the intelligentsia]. Even such a respectable organ as I believe *Pravda* to be did not renounce him when long ago he appeared against Zionism from a pure anti-Semitic standpoint, expressing its solidarity with the Jew Orensztajn who prostituted himself for the anti-Semitic gang – and with the newspaper, *Gazeta Polska* [*Polish Newspaper*], which bribed him. We must here quickly mention that we were principally opponents of the Zionists and we welcomed every struggle with them, both legal and illegal, that was led from a socialist-progressive basis. Yet we must with all of our strength fight with the gentlemen who want "to throw out the baby with the water," who think that with the destruction of Zionism, the Jewish question itself would be eliminated. Of the entire Polish press, only one, *Golos* (under its then editor), was a genuinely progressive newspaper, also in its connection to the Jewish press.

[Page 170]

I end my correspondence with a call to the Polish comrades, that they seriously (earnestly – editors) respond to the Czenstochow drama and see how much it is possible for them to not repeat such phenomena that can lead to an alienation and mistrust between the Jewish and Polish proletariat. It is still laughable that until now there is no socialist brochure against anti-Semitism in Polish; the *P.P.S* [Polish Socialist Party], which is always connected with the Bund, has not developed any feeling of solidarity with the Jewish proletariat and with the proletariat of other ethnic groups.

Remarks by Shimkha Lew

According to information from "Help from the Warsaw General Government for the Police Division" (chief of the gendarmerie in Poland), written to the Warsaw General Governor on 13 November 1902 (old style, according to the old Russian calendar), there appeared in Lodz an appeal about the "anti-Jewish unrest" in Czenstochow (that is how the Czenstochow pogrom was known in Tsarist administrative language). The appeal was distributed to the Lodz group of the *P.P.S.* by the intellectual, "Boloslav." The police could not find out who "Boloslav" was. The police seized 43 copies of this appeal. The same appeal was found in Czenstochow and Sosnowiec on 6 October 1902. 6 October old style is 19 October new style, the accepted [calendar] style in Europe in general and Poland in particular. Thus there was no discrepancy in the dates. Alas, we do not have the full text of the appeal, which was not filed away. However, we have a little content from the proclamation that the gendarmerie chief gave to the General Governor and for a lack of a choice, we will have to be satisfied with it.

This is the content in a word by word translation from Russian:

"The appeal condemns the anti-Jewish unrest in Czenstochow and advises the [class] conscious workers, worn out by toil in the revolutionary struggle, in case such kinds of disorder were repeated, to make use of them on behalf of the worker's cause: because this is necessary, to make use of the situation created to convert the senseless anti-Jewish appearance into a [class] conscious demonstration against exploitation and against each sort of violation."

(Archive of the Warsaw General Governor. General number 101.654, number 8 of 1902, page 190 of the first director, second commission).

Naturally it is difficult to draw a general conclusion from a summary. The style, the language that speaks about the mood and spirit of the writer, is important in a proclamation. Relying on the dry administrative language of the Tsarist gendarme managing committee is impossible. At least it can be noted that although we do not know how strong and open the *P.P.S.* [Polish Socialist Party] reaction was to the Czenstochow pogrom, we do know that the

P.P.S. did not remain indifferent. And this must count for the sake of historical truth, so as not to be misled by the party passion in the struggle of that time and of which the correspondent of the *Arbeter Shtime* [*Workers Voice*] is probably not free.

———

The Second Pogrom

by H. Feiwelowicz, A. Khrobolowski

The second Czenstochow pogrom took place on Tuesday, 27 May 1919. A. Kh., writes about it in detail in his article in the *Czenstochower Togblat* [*Czenstochow Daily Newspaper*] of Monday, 2 June 1919, under the title, "The Guilty."

The black heroes of liberated Poland were finally here in Czenstochow – in the holy residence that carries the godly mother, the patroness of Poland and a symbol of human love – and they generously harvested the fruit of their long, difficult work: the murder of five people in a terrible manner. Dozens beaten to death. An entire row of houses burned. Many widows and orphans, hundreds of bloodied bodies and thousands of bloody wounds in the souls of the entire Jewish population.

[Page 171]

This happened on the eve of the holy Christian holiday of *Himlgang* [Feast of the Ascension – 29 May 1919].

They had the full right to take pride in their own work... The massacres, the cruelty of wild mobs, which carried the dead by the feet until the entrails of the dead came out; who so cruelly did not respect the young and old, no man or woman; the carousing and frolicking and dancing by the children around the bodies of those murdered; the great participation of the Polish school youths in robbing and murdering, showed very clearly how their work was to poison the souls of the masses completely with human hate and ferocious blood thirstiness.

It is no surprise. But it is a surprise that we escaped, although we had victims. Certainly, reading all the notes, articles and appeals in *Goniec Częstochowski* [political, social, economic and literary journal] and *Kurier Częstochow* [*Częstochow Courier*] (two Polish newspapers that were published in Czenstochow), one could look carefully at the consistency with which the agitation work was carried out. Every day there was more news about how Jewish Bolsheviks ruined Poland, [about] attacks in Lemberg, Pinsk, Vilna, on the Polish military, [about] shooting at them from the corners, trying with all their strength so that Poland would not impede them at the Paris Peace Conference [Versailles Peace Conference], [about] carrying out Bolshevik propaganda and, chiefly, starving Poland and causing large price increases – and you will understand how they turned people into blood–thirsty animals.

The trainers themselves were afraid of calling out the animals in their most terrifying form. And several priests who had for so long preached from the pulpit about the true "love of man," of hate of the Jews, tried to restrain the infuriated mob in several cases.

However, it already was late. "You called me here and I am here," the animal argued in the language of Balaam's ass. "You have incited us against the Jews until now and now you yourself want to defend him" – the wild masses shouted. "You prostituted yourself for money to the Holy Father with this thing."

The *Kurier* actually wrote correctly that the bloody unrest had been invited by the secret, hidden enemy of Poland. But it is not true that they were secret and unknown. Not true! The true enemy of Poland was well known. Yes, well known! However, no one disturbed them in their work; their newspapers were not closed; their appeals were completely legal; their clubs did not endure a pogrom. No one made a move to lay their hands on them, certainly not all of the representatives of the people, from the highest *Sejm* [parliament] to the city council...

The chronicle of that horrible day for the Jews of Czenstochow was as follows:

Poland was in the middle of ardor over the military conflict that began right at [Poland's] liberation. Among the various military formations quartered in Czenstochow, as a city near Upper Silesia, where the fight against the Germans took place, were the Hallercziks [followers of the anti–Semitic Lieutenant General Jozef Haller] – the legion that Haller, a former teacher of gymnastics at the Lemberger School, organized in France and *Poznanczykes*, Germanized Poles mobilized in the Poznan area, which was given to Poland after the First World War. They were not able to speak Polish. Therefore, they knew well the trade of cutting Jewish beards and banging Jewish heads. This happened every day all over Poland and also in the streets of Czenstochow.

Unemployment and hunger were rampant among the masses. The factories stood empty. The poor masses maintained themselves through "charity" with the help that mainly came from America. Demonstrations by the unemployed, who demanded work, would often take place in front of the city council. The bitterness among the masses grew and with it the agitation. The city hall organized a little public work to pave the streets. A majority of the workers worked with spades and hatchets on the Second *Aleje*.

A lighted match was thrown accidentally or on purpose into the embittered and agitated atmosphere as into a cask of gunpowder. There was a rumor that a Jew had shot a Hallerczik. In truth, no one was shot. Later, an investigation showed that a soldier, not a Hallerczik, had received some sort of blow on the head, but with what or how could not be determined.

Almost at the same time – this was at noon – two policemen went to a Jewish *feldsher* [barber–surgeon], Moshe Nasanowicz, who had a hair establishment at the Second Aleje and told him to provide aid to the wounded. Nasanowicz took his tools and went with the policemen. A rumor spread among some of the city workers on the street that the Jew who had shot the Hallerczik had been arrested and he was being led [by the policemen]. They immediately attacked Moshe Nasanowicz, the *feldsher*, who was walking, accompanied by two policemen. They murdered him on the spot with spades and hatchets. Other hooligans, soldiers and schoolboys immediately joined the city workers. The mob went to the poor Jewish streets and began their bloody work.

[Page 172]

The pogrom in general was murderous and cruel. The mob was brutal and wild. Each Jew they found in the street was beaten mercilessly. A large number of Jewish shops and homes were robbed. A large number of the military from various formations took part in the pogrom. The pogrom lasted all of Tuesday and persisted through Tuesday night into Wednesday.

On Wednesday morning a horrible picture of the destruction was revealed to the Czenstochow Jewish population. The four who were murdered lay in the morgue of the Jewish hospital (the fifth, Nasanowicz, was at the Hospital Ste. Maria at the Second *Aleje*) as dead evidence of savagery and brutality that had very few equals in history.

The Attack on the *Shoykhetim*

The *shoykhetim* [ritual slaughterers], Nakhemia Gotlib, Yehezkiel Bergman and Moshe Dzialowski, were in the slaughterhouse in the synagogue courtyard. They heard the approach of a mob of Hallerczikes; they hid in the residence of the Christian janitor. The mob entered the house; first they dragged the *shoykhet* Gotlib out to the courtyard and beat him for a long time with crowbars and stones until he lay dead. The other two succeeded in escaping. On the way, they [the mob] attacked *shoykhet* Yehezkiel Bergman and beat him so badly that he had to be taken to the Jewish hospital.

While murdering *shoykhet* Gotlib, they [the mob] stole 1,200 marks and his slaughtering knives. The murdered one left a wife and six children. A coat and 500 marks were taken from *shoykhet* Moshe Dzialowski.

Then the hooligans entered the residence of the synagogue *shamas* [sexton], Makhel Rauzenberg, and severely beat his wife and his son, Malekh, who was taken to the Jewish hospital.

The Attack on the Synagogue

The pogromists then left for the synagogue, tore off the door and the gate, tore open closets and the *Aron–Kodesh* [ark in which the Torah scrolls are kept] and searched everywhere. A Torah scroll was later found lying on the floor.

On Garncarska Street

The pogromists broke open the gate at Garncarska 34, knocked out almost all of the house's windowpanes, tore out the window frames, broke off the doors in the residence of the baker, Yekl Gelbard, stole all of the clothing from the closets and about 700 marks. The young Avraham Shimeon Gelbard was severely beaten.

At house number 38, the pogromists tore off the doors from the Finklsztajn's residence where they only found his sick wife and a daughter. The mob overturned everything in the house, broke open a small safe. In the same house, they broke open the doors of the Jewish residents, Itshe Mendl Dukat, Itshe Meir Tuchmajer and Itshe Kantor. They searched for weapons everywhere and they took a hatchet from one house.

On Mostowa Street

Shlomo Brakman's shop and house at Mostowa 11 was a terrible ruin. The mob broke everything they found there, not leaving any unbroken windowpanes. Most of the Brakman family suffered. In addition to their murdered son, Moshe Brakman, the hooligans also badly beat the shop owner, Shlomo, who had to be taken to the hospital. His two daughters were wounded and his second son, Leizer, had a broken leg.

When the hooligans broke into the Rajnman's residence on the same street, the latter grabbed a hatchet to defend himself. The pogromists called the police for help in disarming the Jew. The policemen saved Rajnman and gave him back the money that had been taken from him.

The Train from Kielce

[Page 173]

A mob of hooligans waited for the train that arrived from Kielce and with the shout, "*Hura Na Żydow*" [Let's hurry, get the Jew], they attacked the arriving Jewish passengers and badly beat them. The [army] recruit, Meir Werthajm, from Włoszczowa, who had come to present himself to the military, was beaten so badly that he fainted. Mrs. Sziper and Helberg, the student, who took him into their residence, saved him. They [the mob] also stole his gold watch. M. Faktor of Piotrkow, who arrived on the train, was attacked by a group of Polish students who took a bread and other things he was carrying with him. The Christian owners of the Hotel Kaliski on Dojazd Street did not permit the Jews who escaped from the mob to spend the night [in the hotel]. He told the Jews that it was completely proper that there was a pogrom against them.

Mostly young people and students took part in the action. The Jewish residents at house number 9 on Dojazd Street saw their janitor's son leading a group of young hooligans who attacked the arriving passengers with sticks and beat them mercilessly.

Other Details

Mordekhai Apelbaum and his wife and children [living at] Warszawer 39 arrived from Kielce at nine–thirty. His 18–year old son, Yehiel, received a heavy blow of a fist in his eyes, which blinded him. Apelbaum himself was attacked by a student from Sudajka's *gymnazie* [secondary school]. A Jewish girl from Dojazd 13 ran to him, protected Apelbaum with her elbows and began to shout at the hooligan that he better kill her rather than her father... That moved a priest and an officer to save Apelbaum and take him to the Hotel Angelski. Mrs. Tamczik, the owner of the hotel, helped the Jews take him to her house.

Alta Nakha Zajdman, 15 years old, Nadrzeczna 41, was attacked in the synagogue courtyard by the pogromists who cut her severely in the head and the face. The girl became deranged.

Shmuel Fridman, who arrived on the Kielce train, was attacked by Hallercziks who beat him in the face and blackened his eyes. All the linen, furniture, shoes and other things worth several thousand marks were stolen from Mordekhai Sznajer, the factory owner. The hooligans chopped up the door, chopped the cabinets, the beds and stole money totaling 600 marks from the residence of Josef Broniatowski, at Nadrzeczna 46. Moshe Grinberg, Garncarska 70, was severely beaten in the head and on the sides.

A mob, among whom were the students from Kaszminski's *gymnazie*, attacked Moshe Buchner, Warszawer 35, and began to beat him with sticks. Buchner wanted to save himself in house number 37 on the same street. The Christian neighbors in the house began to hit him from all sides. He fainted. Standing up, he dragged himself to a house that belonged to a Christian, Kapolski. But the neighbors in the house again barred the gate and would not let him in.

On Ogrodowa Street, two Christians attacked Shmuel Mendl Pajsak, Krakower 23, and beat him over the head with sticks. When he fainted, the hooligans, thinking he was dead, left him alone.

Other victims of the pogrom were:

Meir Berkowicz, Senatorska 20; Borukh Briliant, Wielun; Ahron Fajerman, Nadrzeczna 2; Ludwik Montag, Ostatni Grosz; Ahron Dovid Goldberg, Warszawer 28; Yakov Szpalten, the widow Praszkewicz, Moshe Dawidowicz, Avraham Finkelsztajn, Nadrzeczna 38.

The Police

In general, the police did not get involved and did not use the necessary means to stop the pogrom. Individual policemen who tried to stop the raging mob were shouted at by the hooligans with the words, *pachołek żydowska* [Jewish stooge]. The mob threw the police commandant, Proczmawski, from his horse when he tried to chase the pogromists. However, in general, the police remained "neutral" for the entire time of the frightening events and did not use the appropriate means to defend the lives and property of the Jewish population.

The Funeral

The funeral of the martyrs took place on Thursday, 29 May. Thousands of Jews began to assemble at nine o'clock in the morning at the municipal hospital. An honorary guard stood on both sides of the hospital. At around noon, the body of Nasanowicz, the murdered *feldsher* [barber–surgeon], was taken out of the hospital. A guard of young Jewish men walked on both sides of the casket. The members of the synagogue council of the Jewish community, the Jewish councilmen from the Czenstochow city council, a delegation from the Jewish press, among whom was found the editor of the *Lodzer Togenblat* [*Lodz Daily Newspaper*], Y. Unger, a delegation from the Jewish *gymnazie*, with the director, Prof. Balaban at the head and representatives of all Czenstochow Jewish societies and professional uniuns, walked at the head of the magnificent funeral. Dr. Rozenblat, the Lodz deputy at the Sejm [Polish parliament], took part in the funeral.

[Page 174]
At the Jewish Hospital

The funeral [procession] stopped in front of the Jewish Hospital, from which the remaining four martyrs were taken out. The coffins were carried to the cemetery by the friends and comrades of those murdered. One of the [pallbearers] was the deputy, Dr. Rozenblat.

With the appearance of the coffins of the four martyrs through the gate of the Jewish Hospital, a terrible lament broke out among the many thousands in the crowd. Everyone, without exception, cried bitterly. Even the policemen who were maintaining order could not hold in the tears and wiped them.

Even more terrible were the voices of lamentation at the cemetery where the martyrs were buried in one large mass grave, one next to the other. The voices were indescribable each time the *khazan* [cantor] recited the *El Maleh Rahamim* [God full of compassion – the mourner's prayer recited at a funeral] and called out the names of the fallen victims.

There were no eulogies. It was quiet, but there was a demonstration against the glaring injustice that none of those present will ever be able to forget.

The Czenstochower Pogrom in the Polish *Sejm*

At the meeting of the Polish *Sejm* on Friday, 30 May, Hartglas, the Jewish deputy, brought an urgent proposal about the pogrom in Czenstochow. The deputy Oszecki answered that there was no special information about such a pogrom. The urgency of the proposal consequently was rejected. The *Dwa Grosza* [*Two Groshen*], the anti–Semitic Warsaw newspaper, reporting about the proposal of the Deputy Hartglas, wrote that the entire story about the pogrom was a fiction...

The Funeral Procession

In Czenstochow City Council

A meeting of the Czenstochow City Council took place on Wednesday, 28 May. The chairman of the city council was Dr. Nowak, a well–known Czenstochow anti–Semite. The Jewish councilmen entered the hall with downcast heads and did not greet anyone. The first item of the meeting was to send a condolence telegram to the Čečin Polish workers who perished in a catastrophe in a coalmine (Čečin belonged to Czechoslovakia).

The president [mayor] of Czenstochow, Bandtke Stenczinski, read a declaration about the pogrom in which it was said: At a time when we stand a total of 22 *viorst* [.62 of a mile or a little over a kilometer] from the enemy's border and the unity of all residents is necessary, there are provocateurs and Bolsheviks[11]) who agitate for one part of the population against the other and unrest breaks out that is so harmful for the fatherland. The president expressed regret for the sad events and hoped that it would not happen again.

The *Fareinikte* [United] faction, through its councilman, Rafal Federman, put forward an urgent proposal undersigned by all of the Jewish councilmen and Polish Socialists (P.P.S. – Polish Socialist Party), which demanded that the city council publicly condemn the brutal murder and attack against the Jewish population, designate a commission that would search for the reasons for yesterday's pogrom, establish the extent of the harm of the sufferers and take steps to turn over the guilty to the hands of justice.

[Page 175]

A separate urgent proposal was made by the *P.P.S.* in which it was demanded that the military units that took part in the pogrom be removed from Czenstochow immediately, that an investigating commission be created with the participation of the Jewish community and that the interior ministry should designate a sum of state money to support the families of the victims of the pogrom.

Councilman Yosef Aronowicz (Bund) declared in the name of all of the Jewish councilmen that the urgency of the proposal did not need to be justified. The city council only accepted the urgency of the proposal but did not permit the proposal itself to be discussed and did not bring it to a vote, only turning it over to the municipal authorities. Councilman Federman and other Jewish councilmen protested against this and left the hall.

At the second meeting of the city council on 5 June, Councilman Aleksander Bem (*Poalei–Zion* [Marxist–Zionists]) inquired of the city council why there was no answer to the question about the pogrom that had been handed over to the city council the week before.

The president declared that he had given all of the material about the matter to the interior ministry. Councilmen Sztiler, Zandsztajn (Zionist) and Helman appeared against the president. Then a proposal was entered to interrupt the discussion. Councilman Federman protested sharply against this and said: "At the last meeting our mouths were shut through a maneuver and again they want to keep us quiet. The city council sends sympathetic telegrams to the Polish workers in other lands, but will not condemn the brutal murder of innocent people who appear before their eyes." We cannot remain calm when we see how the murderers who commit the horrible murders walk through the streets freely." The anti–Semitic majority of the city council decided to end the discussion.

Investigations

On 1 June a coalition commission arrived in Czenstochow to investigate the pogrom. The commission consisted of two Americans, two from England and two from France. The commission convened with various members of the Jewish community, Nakhum Asz the rabbi, Shmuel Goldsztajn, Glikson the lawyer, Leon Wajnberg, Dr. Kahn and Dr. Wolberg. The Jewish representatives informed the mission about the entire flow of the events and the reasons that led to the pogrom.

Bek, the vice minister, came to Czenstochow to investigate the pogrom and as a result of a conference with the editors of the two Polish newspapers in Czenstochow, *Goniec and Kurier*, which the Jewish population had accused of being the main agitators and most responsible for the pogrom, he [the vice minister] demanded that the editors not write anything against the Jews for 10 days...

Thousand Mark Reward

The police published an appeal in connection with the pogrom, which offered 1,000 marks to those who would find out who had wounded the Hallerczik, which led to the outbreak of the pogrom. A delegation of Jewish recruits who appeared before the police commandant asked the commandant why no reward had been published for those who found the murderers of the five Jewish victims, who still were walking around the streets of Czenstochow freely.

A Document of Accusation

A delegation from the Czenstochow Worker Delegates Council gave the interior minister in Warsaw the following memorandum:

Czenstochow, 27 May 1919

To the Interior Ministry

On 27 May, this year, the executive committee of the Czenstochow Worker Delegates Council sent the following telegram:

We have learned that the People's Militia is leaving Czenstochow. Because of the agitated mood and the possibility of anti–Semitic unrest, we ask for a halt to the departure of the militia in which the population has trust. The ministry disparaged our warning. Today a pogrom took place against the Jews in which the Hallercziks and *Poznanczykes*, street youths and dark powers took part.

The police command, the city command and military leadership showed a powerlessness and helplessness in relation to the mob.

[Page 176]

The blood of the three victims fell on the consciences of those who could have prevented the events by leaving the militia in Czenstochow and who did not consider it appropriate to fulfill our request.

The Czenstochower Worker Delegates Council

Chairman, Josef Dzobo.

Josef Dzobo

The murdered:

Moshe Nasanowicz, a *feldsher* [barber surgeon], Second *Aleje* 20, murdered by a mob when he went to bandage a wounded person accompanied by two policemen.

Hershl Dzialoszynski, 54 years old, a broker, beaten with sticks and hatchets by hooligans at the old market until he fell unconscious on the ground and his brains left his head. He was brought dying to the hospital where he died immediately.

Nakhemia Gotlib, First *Aleje* 2, a *shoykhet* [ritual slaughterer], 45 years old, murdered in the synagogue courtyard by the hooligans. He was brought dying to the hospital where he died immediately.

Nakhemia Gotlib

Moshe Brakman, Mostowa 11, 26 years old, attacked by the murderers when he wanted to enter the gate of his house. He was brought in dying condition to the hospital where he died immediately.

Anshil Cymerman

Anshil Cymerman, 20 years old, a bakery worker, Garncarska 14, attacked by the murderers when he wanted to enter the gate of his house. He was brought in dying condition to the hospital where he suffered terribly and died on Wednesday morning.

Severely Wounded:

Binem Wajnrit, 37 years old, Targowa 5, terribly beaten in the face and hands. He was standing at the market with goods; the murderers attacked him, throwing him in the gutter and they stabbed him until he lay unconscious.

Mordekhai Czeszniewski: 63 years old, a Jewish janitor at the *Talmud–Torah* [primary school for poor boys]. He wanted to close the gate to protect the children; the murderers attacked him and beat him severely.

[Page 177]

Other severely wounded who were at home and in hotels were:

Meir Kalman Kaminski, Fabryczna 7 (robbed of money, linen and the like).

Gedalia Perlman, (his wife and daughter were stabbed).

Elihu Biber, 57 years old, Koszarowa 28.

Yehoshua Himelman, 24 years old, Garncarska 66.

Hershl Pacanowski, Czelona 7.

Hershl Szwarin, Yisroel Kamelher, Dovid Szwarin, Garncarska 74.

Avraham Glik and **Moshe Leib Glik**, Krotka 21 (a large amount of goods was stolen from them).

Lightly Wounded:

Yehezkiel Bergman; Moshe Szmahl; Gitl Szwarcbaum; Shlomo and Leizer Brakman (relatives of the murdered Moshe Brakman); Yehiel Klajnman; Yoskha Rozenberg; Shimkha Rajch; Moshe Goldberg; Meir Werthajm (Wloszczowa); M. Faktor (Pitrokow); Nakhemia Munowicz; Yakov Moshe Himelman; Chana Gold; Chana Morgensztern; Yitzhak Kaliszer, Straszica 16; Mrs. Gutman from Zawodzie; A. Bekerin; Avraham Gotajner, Krakower 10; Shmuel Kuperman of Wloszczowa (two officers saved him); Moshe Wajsberg from Wloszczowa, they took 500 kron and 60 marks from him; Shraga Slomnicki, Spadek 13; Shmuel Szapczak, Krakower 11; Henekh Fefer, Garncarski 59; Y. Sztajer and his wife, Fabryczna 5; Mrs. Goldberg, Fabryczna 9; Grajcer, Fabryczna 8; Yekl and Dovid Glik, Krotka 21; Maurici Najfeld, standing on a balcony, was hit in the head with a stone. Yeshaya Maszkowicz and Birnholc were wounded on Warszawer Street by Polish soldiers.

Hershl Birnbaun, 56 years old, Garncarska 65, broke a leg when the hooligans chased and beat him.

Dovid Poslaniec, Nadrzeczna 88, a hairdresser, 17 years old. The hooligans stole two haircutting machines, a scissors, a razor and 250 marks from him and murderously beat him.

Itzek Szpisman, 16 years old, Torowa 16, remained unconscious from the blows he received.

Mendl Majtles, 19 years old, Krakower 31. **Shmuel Englender**, 65 years old, Ogrodowa 27.

Josef Zalcberg, 56 years old, came from Zawierice to bring his son for his military service in the Polish Army. The hooligans attacked and severely beat him.

Editor's Footnote

1. Compare the agitation of *Kurier* against the "Secret Bolsheviks" – Editor.

The Third Pogrom

Polish fascism began to arrogantly show its claws during the last years before the war. Polish fascists devotedly followed the German Hitlerists, although they themselves were threatened from there [Germany] with great danger, which carried with it the catastrophe of 1 September 1939. The hate for Jews was as strong as in the stronghold of the fascist regime. If the sincere voice of a Professor [Tadeusz] Kotarbinski was heard or of other sincere democrats, it was a voice in the desert. The *Prystorowes*[1], the dukes, the [Lucjan] Żeligowskis all had a say about what happened then in Poland and they agreed with the Premier–General [Flelcjan Sławoj] Składkowski: *Owszem* [yes]...

Then the [pogroms] really did happen in Przytyk, in Minsk–Mazowiecki, Brisk and Czenstochow and on and on.

It was in the morning on *Shabbos* [the Sabbath] on 19 June 1937. Stefan Baran, a train porter, a Polish acquaintance of Yosl[2] Pendrak, approached him not far from Maria *Aleje* and demanded money for whiskey from him. Pendrak refused. They began to argue and a fight immediately started. Then Pendrak drew his revolver and shot twice at Baran, who fell seriously wounded. Baran immediately died in the hospital. Pendrak was arrested and the police carried out an investigation.

At a quiet time the incident would have ended with this, but not in the heated atmosphere of hatred toward Jews encouraged and tolerated by the Polish government.

[Page 178]

At once, at a secret call, secret groups began to gather, young Polish boys led by the *Endeke* [anti–Semitic Polish National Party] intelligentsia, which showed them where the Jews lived, and a pogrom began with all its manifestations, which had been developed in Tsarist Russian and improved upon in Poland. They began to break windowpanes, to break doors and windows, to break into shops and steal the goods, to cut open bedding and spread the feathers in the streets and to split Jewish heads. The pogrom lasted four days with little intervention from Składkowski's police. Twenty large Jewish businesses and dozens of Jewish shops were thus completely destroyed.

During the course of the events, according to the newspaper *Tog* [*Day*] (New York) and *Folks–Zeitung* [*People's Newspaper*] (Warsaw):

It began in Czenstochow on *Shabbos*, 19 June at 9:30 in the morning. The Jew, Avraham Zelwer, noticed that thieves wanted to rob his iron warehouse. He chased the thieves. Then [Zelwer] immediately was provoked by Stefan Baran, the porter, himself a member of the underworld and an adventurer who already had been to jail several times for criminal offenses. It also could be that Baran had a connection to the thieves who had been chased.

During the dispute between Zelwer and Baran, the 36–year old meat wagon driver Yosef Pendrak walked by. He intervened and defended the provoked Jew. During the fight, Pendrak shot his revolver twice and Baran was killed.

The incident took place in the morning and yet, according to plan, the pogrom did not break out until about 10 hours later, around six in the evening. During these 10 hours, the *Endeke* Party organized the ostensibly "spontaneous" turmoil of *folkstsorn* [popular fury]. Special couriers were sent out on motorcycles to the surrounding *shtetlekh* and villages by *Endeke* headquarters and mobilized the dark comrades who filled the streets of Czenstochow that evening. Mobs of local members of the underworld as well as the young students and part of the intelligentsia went out together to demonstrate and throw stones at the windows of the Jews. Signs appeared on Polish shops: Catholic. The Christians placed religious pictures and crosses in their windows.

When the pogrom already had started, the local police informed the central power in Warsaw that the incident did not have any serious character and that they would cope with it without any special police reinforcements. The "neutral" position of the police increased the fury of the hooligans and the pogrom flared up with wild enthusiasm.

The rest of the night passed in relative calm after a row of shops was demolished on the evening of *Shabbos* (19 June) and the windowpanes of Jewish residences and shops were knocked out in a number of streets.

Meanwhile, the wild Christian mob began to rage against Jewish houses on the periphery of the city, robbing and demolishing Jewish houses and everything that came into their hands.

Thus was a row of Jewish shops demolished in Czenstochowka (a suburb); everything was stolen or destroyed. Whatever had any value. The residence of the bakery owner Urner was shattered in this way. A terrible assault also took place at Warszawska 338, at the residence of Kopl Haberman, whose entire furniture and bedding were destroyed. In addition, 150 *gildn* were stolen from him and he was severely wounded and his wife also was beaten.

This all happened on the day of *Shabbos* (we will later give the names of the wounded and the list of streets where the attacks in Czenstochow took place). On Sunday the hooligans were still aggressive. While on *Shabbos* they had waited for it to get dark, they did their fine pogrom work in the clear daylight on Sunday.

All told, the second day of the pogrom (Sunday) was a terrible one. Pieces of glass protruded from the beautiful exhibition show windows of the businesses. Broken shelves, pieces of goods lay around on the sidewalks in front of the shops. Metal venetian blinds split under the heavy blows of benches, which usually stood arranged in the *Aleje*s [wide boulevards of Czenstochow]. It wasn't enough that the band of hooligans was armed with hatchets, knives, hammers and iron bars; they also made use of city benches on the streets.

Even the *powszechna* school (public school) was not treated with respect. However, this all occurred according to a plan: children were sent to the children's school.

[Page 179]

Fourteen and 15–year old children broke the windowpanes of the school with stones and chopped up the seats and all of the furniture inside.

For example, the hooligans committed such thing as: Wajnberg's house was being built on Jasnogorska Street. It was not yet entirely finished – they carried it away, not leaving even a small piece of wood.

A series of witnesses said that esteemed Christian merchants showed the hooligans which businesses were Jewish, what needed to be destroyed. A certain Zigmund Orlowski of the Third *Aleje* 36 led an entire band, commanding with a hatchet in his hand.

A large number of members of the mob carried valises and briefcases so they would be able to take the stolen goods with them. A number of women entered the city barefooted to work and, while robbing a shop, they chose a pair of shoes for themselves there.

There were cases in which the hooligans beat several Christians thinking they were Jews based on their appearance. A comical fact is that nothing helped the convert, Dr. Wajnblum, who hung holy pictures in his windows – all of his windowpanes were knocked out.

Word came that there was concern that order be restored after the intervention with the *starosta* [a city official] by a group of communal workers. Szczodrowski, the city president, also intervened with the *starosta* at the start of the unrest and he himself put out a call to the population [about ending the unrest].

The vice president, Professor [Josef] Dzobo (P.P.S. [Polish Socialist Party]), himself confirmed that he had seen how the hooligans had [committed] robberies undisturbed. The hooligans had thrown stones after him when he had driven by in an auto from the *magistrat* (city hall).

The situation worsened even more after the meeting on Sunday, the second day of the pogrom. The Jewish *kehile* [organized Jewish community] had held a special meeting and as a result dispatches were sent to the First Minister Gen. Składkowski, Kielce *Voivode* [province] and to the prosecutor of the county court. The content of the telegrams was that the situation in Czenstochow was dangerous and that the Jewish population was not receiving the proper protection.

On Sunday evening a rumor spread that the true slaughter of the Jews would take place on Monday. Police telephoned the *kehile* chairman, Yakov Rozenberg, and warned him that they had information that an attack was being prepared on the *kehile* premises. Therefore, the police asked that when the attack occurred they should call immediately. However, an hour later the telephone at the *kehile* premises "suddenly" was disconnected. When they [the *kehile*] turned to the main post office about having the telephone repaired, an excuse was ready: The telephone could not be repaired given that today was Sunday. Thus the *kehile* remained without a telephone.

All of the anti–Semitic workers were brought in methodically according to the precisely worked out plan from the headquarters of the *Endeke*s. It is enough to remember that when the pogrom was in full force, the local *Endeke* newspaper, *Goniec Czenstochowski* [*Czenstochowa Messenger*] published an exact list of the streets in which the Jews had not yet been robbed... The pogromists had precise information about which house, which business and even which apartment in a house belonged to Jews.

The situation became tense with the fall of night. The mob, which had gathered in various parts of the city, became larger and took on a provocative attitude, making open threats that the real "scene" would take place at night (Sunday).

Meanwhile, information was obtained that a decree had arrived from the central regime in which it came out publically with complete intensity against the pogromists and for this purpose a special messenger from the Interior Ministry was to come. At approximately nine o'clock in the evening an energetic posture by the police could be seen and all of the streets were cleaned up in a short time. Seeing that it was difficult to do anything on Warszawer Street, the band of young hooligans left for Garncarska Street with the purpose of "carousing." However, they ran away after seeing that a larger group of Jewish workers had assembled there. Thus Sunday night passed peacefully.

Early Monday (12 June), movement in the city was very animated. However, all of the Jewish shops remained closed and heavy police patrols stood on the street corners. At around three o'clock [in the afternoon], the funeral of the murdered Baran took place under heavy police guard. Jews stormed the offices of the *kehile* all day to submit [information] about the losses they had suffered.

[Page 180]

Monday at noon, when it was learned that the funeral of the murdered Baran was taking place [in the afternoon], a mob of several thousand men gathered around the hospital and demanded that they release the body of the murdered one. The mood was red hot. Individual attacks against Jews began again. A stronger police patrol arrived after the intervention of the *kehile* and drove away the giant, agitated mob, which ran to the nearby alleys.

At around six in the evening the news arrived that it again was turbulent in a series of streets. There were cases in which they tried to set houses on fire. A band broke into the house of prayer and destroyed everything there. A fire was started at the corner of Mirowska and Garncarska. The firemen who were called out extinguished the fire. A band of Christian women attacked the emotionally disturbed girl, Kurland, at the old market and beat her murderously. The cigarette kiosk at the First *Aleje* belonging to the Jewish war veteran, Avraham Kawon, was set on fire.

The appeals for calm by the city president were constantly torn down. An illegal appeal by the *Endeke*s filled with agitation and venomous provocation appeared in the city. A few thousand people had assembled at the grave of the stabbed Baran a day earlier. There were speeches [in accordance with the mood].

The provincial governor, [Waldyslaw] Dziadosz, arrived from Kielce on Tuesday (22 June) and took over the command of Czenstochow. Bishop [Teodoro] Kubina turned to all Catholics with an appeal and demanded that they remain calm.

However, the same "spiritual shepherd" simultaneously assured them that he understood the just irritation of the Polish masses and that he also believed that Baran's spilled blood demanded revenge. The anti–Semitic press actually published only the part of the bishop's letter in which he spoke of just revenge...

A delegation of the *P.P.S.* [Polish Socialist Party] visited the provincial governor on Tuesday and conferred with him about the situation in the city. The provincial governor promised that the calm would not be disturbed in any way. On the same day, the work in the factories stopped for a short time and a delegation was sent to the provincial governor from every factory. The latter again gave assurances that no excesses would be permitted. The mounted police constantly patrolled the streets.

Monday night, groups of workers chased away a band of hooligans who were just about to attack on Nadrzeczna, Garncarska and Senatorska Streets. However, the workers were driven away by the arriving police.

On Tuesday many telegrams arrived in Czenstochow from relatives from abroad asking about the health of their closest relatives. The telegrams arrived from America, *Eretz–Yisroel* and France and England. The American citizen, Nakhum Kot, just happened to be in Czenstochow then. He sent a telegram to the American Consul about the events. Therefore, the Czenstochow police questioned him for many hours.

On Tuesday evening, delegations of Jewish and Polish workers from a series of factories went to the provincial governor, Dr. Dziadocz, the *starosta* [senior official] and labor inspector. The factory workers, the comrades Kozlowski, Liberman, Baluszkewicz and Entelis, told the mentioned representatives of the regime that they were solemnly protesting against anti–Semitic hooligans who were still rampaging in various parts of the city. The delegation spoke in the name of the workers from the following factories: Metros 1 and Metros 2, Deres, Zylbersztajn and others.

Market day fell on the same day, but the police did not permit the peasants to enter the city for security reasons.

It was characteristic that the Polish anti–Semitic press defended the pogrom and spoke of the appearance of the hooligans with great joy. They tried to show with all of their power that they had destroyed Jewish goods, but that they had not stolen anything. The Socialist *Robotnik* [*Worker*] did report that they had stolen things.

Such a mood of terror reigned in the city that no lawyer wanted to take on the defense of Yosef Pendrak.

The bloody total of the pogrom was: around 75 wounded Jews; of them, several had serious wounds. The material damage to Jewish possessions reached around 200,000 *gildn*. About 150 Jewish shops were damaged; of them, around 30 were completely looted. The large Jewish shops on the main streets emerged with less damage because there the police guard was stronger. Understand that the poor Jewish shopkeeper suffered the most and especially the stall–keepers who did not dare open their small stalls in non–Jewish areas in the post–pogrom atmosphere. Approximately 40 Jewish families remained completely without food and had to ask for charity.

[Page 181]

Partial Estimate of Material Damages for the Czenstochow Jews After the Pogrom in 1937

(According to the list sent to the Joint [Distribution Committee] on 6 July 1937)

Damages in Polish *gildn*.

Ninety–five shops partially destroyed: destroyed windows and furnishings – 15,300; goods destroyed – 42,800.

Twenty–eight shops completely destroyed: destroyed windows and furnishings – 9,000; goods destroyed – 22,000.

Two artisans' workshops destroyed: destroyed furnishings – 1,500; destroyed goods – 1,000.

Approximately 25–30 completely destroyed apartments – 10,000.

Destroyed farms and gardens – 500.

Jewish *kehile* [organized Jewish community] property destroyed; synagogues, houses of prayer, *mikvah* [ritual bathhouse], slaughter house – 10,000.

Destruction at new synagogue – 1,000.

In addition, 15,000 window panes broken – 30,000.

Total sum of the destruction: 142,350 *gildn*.

The Victims of the Pogrom in 1937

Murdered:
Natan Lipowski.

Wounded:
Avraham Plowner
Malekh Szapiro
Yosef Czenstochowski
Grilak
Dr. Ignaci Szrajber (gymanazie [secondary school] teacher)
Leib Birenbaum
Avraham Czarni
Yitzhak Czarni
Mrs. Abramowicz

Looted and Demolished Jewish Institutions, Residences, Shops, Synagogues, Houses of Prayer, and Communal Institutions:
House of Prayer – Nadrzeczna Street
The Old Synagogue – Nadrzeczna Street
The New Synagogue (all of the windows knocked out) – Wilson Street
Jewish Gymnazie – Dambrowski Street
People's Bank – Aleje 7
Artisans' Union – Aleje 12
OZA [organization offering medical care] Center – at Kaminski near Czenstochow.

Residences:
Kopl Hoberman, shopkeeper
Hajlenberg, baker
Wajsnberg, carpenter
Dr. Leopold Kohn, industrialist (a bomb was thrown at his house)
Daniel Dzalowicz – Jasnogorska Street
Redlegski – Narutowicza Street
Kusznir – Narutowicza Street Galster – 3rd Aleje
Dr. Torbeczka – Katedralna Street
Avraham Czarni – Warszawer Street
Khone Maiorczik – Warszawer Street
Yosef Ber Nactigal – Nadrzeczna 2
Hercka Dilewski – Mirowska 10–12.

Businesses and Industrial Enterprises:
Klinber – wood warehouse, set on fire.
Kaminer – wood warehouse, set on fire.
Avraham Brajtler – mill.
Brekler – mill.
Frug – furniture factory.
Rolnicki – bookkeeper.
Wajnrib – grocery business.
Czanczinski – haberdashery business.
"Plumas" – chocolate business.
Langer – shoe business.
"Rai Dzieczinczi" (toy business).
Rozencwajg – candy shop.
Najman – photographic institution.
Strug – factory for wood finishing, Strazcka Street.
Prelman – hat business – Ogrodowa [Street].
Farberg Kaler – butcher.
Mali Berg (convert) – Kino "Luna."
Biber – whiskey business – Natutowicza [Street].

[Page 182]

Spigelman – glass business – 1st Aleje.
Altman – food shop – Dambrowski [Street].
Bruszaki – frame factory – Sulkowski [Sreet].
"Sztuka" – photographic institution.
Epsztajn – fruit shop – Pilsudski 17.

Businesses (type of business not provided):

Granek
Lenczicki
Ratmil
Erner
"Helena"
Josefowicz
Kroza
Librowicz
Fiszman
Galster
Estrajch.

Quickly, several court trials, which had a connection to the events, took place after the pogrom. Of the arrested pogromists, 60 of the 300 imprisoned hooligans remained under arrest – a number were sentenced and got away with small punishments of several months in prison, as opposed to the severe trial of Yosef Pendrak for whom the prosecutor demanded the death penalty.

His trial was prepared lightning fast – on the 13th day after the shooting. He was brought to the court with chains on his hands. The defendant, Yosef Pendrak, described the course of the tragic incident at the trial this way:

He met three young Christians at Wal Dwernicki's who were talking to the son of Zelwer, the owner of the iron warehouse. Simultaneously, Stefan Baran, who was driving a wagon, arrived. Baran came at him with a wagon shaft with the clear intention of giving him a blow. Zelwer was supposed to go into the city and was afraid. He, Pendrak, proposed that he would accompany [Zelwer] to the city.

The arriving Baran (a 25–year old giant) threw himself at Pendrak and said: "What do you want, mangy Jew? You are such a strong fighter!"

At the same time Baran threw off his jacket, grabbed a stone and threw it at Pendrak. The latter warned that he would shoot if the stone were thrown. Baran drew back a little, stood behind the three boys and began throwing stones. Pendrak withdrew and shouted to the boys that they should move to the wall. Pendrak then shot his revolver and hit Baran.

Ludwig Honigwil (a Bundist), the well–known Warsaw lawyer, and Jan Dambrowski (Polish Socialist) defended the accused at the first court judicial division. While the prosecutor wanted the death sentence, the investigating judge worked in court for a lighter sentence. When the lawyer Honigwil came to Czenstochow, the investigating judge reached out to him and advised him to carry out the defense on the grounds that the defendant had only crossed the boundary of necessary defense when in danger.

During the trial, the prosecutor demanded the death penalty. During the deliberation by the three judges, the chairman of the court supported the demand of the prosecutor. However, the other two judges decided to oppose it and thus the final sentence was life imprisonment.

On 26 October 1937 Pendrak's trial took place for the second time at the Warsaw Appeals Court. The defending lawyers appealed to accomplish two goals: decrease the sentence and change the grounds for the sentence. A third lawyer, the famous lawyer, Leon Berenson, was added to the previous two defense lawyers.

The course of the appeals trial was favorable for the defendant. The speaker, Judge Kramer, in his speech emphasized that the course of the trial at the first judicial court, at the county court in Czenstochow, did not provide any proof that the accused, Pendrak, had carried out the murder because of racial hatred, which was the grounds in the sentence by the county court. He also showed that Yosef Pendrak was known as an honest man, while Baran had been sentenced many times and punished for drunkenness and resisting the police.

The appeals court did not recognize the motive of racial hate and decreased the sentence to 13 years in jail. The decreased sentence was motivated by the fact that Pendrak had a connection to Baran as to a type from the underworld (in the first instance the motive of race–hatred was based on Pendrak's question to Zelwer at the beginning of the incident: "What does the gentile want from you?").

[Page 183]

Both the prosecutor and the defending lawyer were not happy with the sentence by the appeals court and requested an annulment [of the sentence] from the highest court. Both of their requests were denied and the sentence went into effect.

Yosef Pendrak was released by the Polish prison regime in Piotrków in September 1939, a few days after the outbreak of the Second World War. The liberated one then came to Warsaw.

Earlier Yosef Pendrak had become a member of the S.S.–Fareinekte [Socialist–Zionists–United]. During the split in this party in 1922, he and those who split joined the Bund. He also belonged to the Bundist Party Militia.

————

Translator's Footnote

1. In 1935, Janina Prystor, a deputy in the *Sejm* – Polish Parliament – introduced a bill that would affect the ritual slaughter of animals by the Jews. Her followers were called *Prystorowes. Składkowski*, speaking in the *Sejm* – Polish parliament – used the word *owszem* referring to an economic struggle against the Jews. This led to an economic boycott of Jewish businesses.

2. The names Yosl and Yosef are used interchangeably in the narrative about Pendrak.

[Page 183]

The Last Year

(The year 1939 in Czenstochow. A short chronicle from the Czenstochower Zeitung *[Czenstochower Newspaper])*

The shadows of Hilterism hung like a Sword of Damocles over the Jewish population. The vanguards of the incoming storm of death were the refugees who arrived naked and barefoot in Czenstochow from Zbaszyn.

In an article: S.O.S. from M. Ruczewicz in the *Czenstochower Zeitung* of Friday, 17 February 1939, the Jewish population was enjoined to support the refugees numbering 130 souls who stood at the edge of hunger and death if further, increased aid action was not urgently organized.

Measures were undertaken to save the existence of the Jewish hospital that found itself in a very critical situation at a conference in the hall of the Merchants' Union where the communal activists, Boleslaw Helman, Lawyer M. Hasenfeld and M. Kapinski, appeared.

An afternoon school for the children from the public school was opened at the Y.L. Peretz School for them to study Yiddish, literature and history. The number enrolled reached over fifty children.

The "refugee" committee arranged a performance. It staged Leonid Andrejev's *Der Groyser Gedank [The Great Idea]*.

Two performances from [Abraham] Goldfaden's repertoire, *Bar Kokhba* and *Shulamith*, were presented on Sunday the 19th and Monday 20 February in the firemen's hall. The leading artists were: Liza Szlosberg and Dovid Zajderman.

The "Knowledge and Improvement" Society arranged a reading by Dr. Oksar entitled, "Total war and the air defense of the civilian population."

The death of Josef Szlezinger, administrative member of the Merchants' Union, of Achiezer [organization to help the poor], of the Jewish *gymnazie* [secondary school] and of the Zionist organization was reported in the newspaper of Monday, 3 March.

R. Zaczecki, the chairman of the *Endekes [Endecja – Narodowa Demokraczja* – anti-Semitic, Polish Nationalist Democratic Party] club at the city council delivered an anti-Semitic declaration rejecting the Jewish state and people's farm and demanded that no Jewish help be accepted for the defense of the state. He was answered by City Councilman Dr. Arnold Bram.

Yakov Roziner, secretary of *TOZ* [*Towarzystwo Ochrony Zdrowia Ludności Żydowskiej* – Society for Safeguarding the Health of the Jewish Population], in an article, "*Keyn eyn groshn far Yidishe Institutsies*" ["Not one *groshn* for Jewish institutions"], records the sad fact that the city hall in its budget crossed out the sum for *TOZ* and the old age home and the orphans' home.

The 20th anniversary of the youth association, *Poalei-Zion* [Workers of Zion – Marxist-Zionists] was celebrated on Tuesday, 4 April.

Clothing, linens, sugar, eggs and milk were distributed to the needy by Ezra, the women's association at Katedralne 11, on 30 and 31 March. One hundred sixty-six families made use of the Passover arrangements made by Ezra, mainly the poor and sick.

Picketing in the streets near the Jewish shops by the Polish anti-Semites was revived.

Two American actors, Jennie Lewitz and Haimy Stern, appeared in the operetta, *Der Rebitzen's Nekht* [*The Rabbi's Wife's Night*] during the week of Passover.

[Page 184]

The chorus of the Sports and Tour Union, *Makkabi*, under the leadership of the conductor, Professor Y. Rozenwajn, appeared in a concert on *Shabbos* [Sabbath] evening, 15 April. Wolf Szmid, the student of Cantor Birnbaum and well-known singer, wrote a professional and warm critique about the concert.

Shabbos, 22 April, Leib Shniurson, an emissary from *Eretz-Yisroel*, appeared at the *Makkabi* hall and spoke about *Irgun Tzva Leumi* [National Military Organization].

A unified Jewish block was created for the election to the city council that took place at that time. The Bund and the retailers presented separate lists.

The sum contributed by Czenstochow Jews to the air defense loan came to one million, seven hundred thousand *zlotes*.

Tuesday, 9 May, a solemn memorial service took place on the third *yahrzeit* [anniversary of a death] at the grave of the Rabbi, Reb Nakhum Asz. Moshe Handler gave a eulogy. Chalewa, the city *khazan* [cantor], recited the memorial prayer and the choir under the direction of director Rosenberg sang a chapter of Psalms.

The second anniversary of *Morgnstern* [Morning Star], the Czenstochower sports club, was celebrated on 27 and 28 May.

The general meeting of *TOZ* took place on *Shabbos*, 27 May. The meeting was opened by Dr. Stefan Kahn. They honored the memory of Zigmund Markowicz, one of the most active *TOZ* managing committee members. The budget adopted came to 122,000 *zlotes*.

Two performances by the Y.L. Peretz dramatic circle under the direction of Ahron Peretz took place on *Shabbos* and Sunday, 3 and 4 June, at the *Makkabi* hall. A series of scenes and tableaus were presented from [the works of] M[oishe] Broderzon, M[oishe] Nadir, *Der Tunkler* [Yosef Tunkel, known as *Der Tunkler* – the dark one], B. Szefner, Broyder and others. Among those taking part in the performance of the various pieces were: Genya Berkowicz, Herszlikowicz, Testiler, Bornsztajn, Dimant, Orbach, Bornsztajn, Yarasz, Dzialowski, Rubinsztajn, Gebirtik. The decorations were planned and painted by L. Kusznir with the help of D. Ripsztajn. The recitations for the performances were written to the point and with talent by M. Kaufman, a former apprentice, and later a printer at Baczan's print shop.

It was reported in the *Czenstochower Zeitung*, no. 23, of 9 June:

The yearly meeting of the *Beis Lekhem* [bread for the needy] took place in the new synagogue; according to the report, the women's section of the society and *TOZ* together feed 400 children every day at the *Machzikei HaDas* [Those who reinforce the Law][1] and municipal *Talmud Torah* [a free religious primary school for poor boys]. Y. Imich, M. Rozencwajg, D. Dobczinski, B. Rubin, D. Markowicz, G. Deres, Y. Sojka, Y. Manhejt, M. Epsztajn, M. Kazak, Y. Sztausberg, Y. Kahn, A. Winer, K. Rajcher, A. Szumaber, Weltman, M. Jakubowicz, Y.D.

Potaszewicz, M. Goldsztajn, Y. Koplewicz, L. Jakubowicz, H. Czitnicki, A, Gitler, Weksztajn and Ufner were elected to the managing committee. Inspection committee: B. Grinlak, D. Win and Sh. Glewicki.

Laying of the Foundation Stone for the New House of Prayer

A gathering of the newly elected Jewish councilmen took place at the Artisans' Club. Communal questions were discussed. Councilmen Goldberg, Koniecpoler, Lawyer L. Asz, Lawyer Markowicz, W. Czeriker, Y. Rozenberg (chairman of the Jewish community), Dr. Bram, Sh. Frank (editor of *Czenstochower Zeitung*), Wajs, Fajgenblat, A. Ickowicz, Professor Janowski, Y. Gerichter, Dzialowski, Gerszonowicz, Grica, Kaufman, Epsztajn, Rotbard, Raziger and others. Dr. Gajsler, the chairman of the Artisans' Union, was chairman of the meeting.

The children at the day care center at *Dobroczynno??* [charity] at Przemyslowa 6 arranged a performance in their own hall.

A reading on the theme of "*Eretz-Yisroel* in the year 1939" by Dr. Josef Kruk took place on *Shabbos*, 10 June, in the large hall of the Baltik cinema.

In the *Czenstochower Zeitung* of 23 June:

The annual general meeting of the *Machzikei Hadas* took place. The chairman, Mr. Krel, opened the meeting. Chairman: Yeshokhar Moszkowicz. Members of the presidium: Dovid Pelc, Avrahamtshe Czenstochowski, secretary Yehoshia Zeligman. The new members of the managing committee: Yehiel Landau, Manasha Marglius, Dovid Kahn and Hirshl Wajnbaum.

[Page 185]

In connection with the death of B[erl] Baczan, the *Temokhi Aneim* [Supporters of the Poor] Society (of which the deceased had been the chairman) arranged a memorial event at which his memory was honored.

The Jewish students at Dr. Oksar's *gymnazie* arranged a theater performance. The old historic, literary work, *Antigone*, was peformed.

The following Czenstochower students graduated from the Artisans' School: Yitzhak Czarni, Moshe Brokman, Pinkhas Edelist, Chaim Fajerman, Mendl Perlbril, Dovid Ginsberg, Wolf Garfinkel, Ziskind Gelber, Yosef Haftka, Yisroel Kifer, Mordekhai Krakauer, Sholem Lajzerowicz, Stefan Montag, Yitzhak Hirsh Majlich, Henya Girenberg, Mendl Rotholc, Dovid Brojner, Dovid Hauptman.

The Managing Committee of *Temokhi Aneim*

A conference with the participation of Dr. E. Ringelblum about the publication of a monograph about Jewish Czenstochow took place in the hall of the Jewish community.

Dr. Ludwig Batawia, who from 1913 on was the chief doctor at the Jewish hospital and chairman of a series of charitable and scientific societies in Czenstochow, died.

In the *Czenstochower Zeitung* of 30 June:

A solemn graduation from the Y.L. Peretz children's home and the afternoon Yiddish courses took place. Ahron Peretz opened the celebration. Avraham Brat and the [female] teacher, Jacheles, gave the reports. The greetings were given by A. Brum, Sh. Frank, Mlodinow, Miss Berkowicz, Kh. Kaufman and others. Seventy children graduated from the day and night school.

The children appeared with songs and recitations. At the end, a small banquet took place for the children. The three [female] teachers, Jacheles, Y. Guterman and S. Ginsberg were presented with flowers.

The *Powszechne* [public] school for Jewish children, number 13, led by Miss N. Szacher, received an award for their work for the Red Cross.

The Polish film, *Der Shatn iber Europe* [*The Shadow over Europe*], was shown at the Lura cinema.

In the *Czenstochower Zeitung* of 14 July:

The annual meeting of the interest-free loan fund took place in its own hall at Pilsudski 31. The chairman was Mr. Grin, attendees were Szumacher and A. Rubinski, secretary Haftka.

The memory of the two deceased managing committee members, B. Brener and B. Sojka, was honored.

Lawyer Goldberg, Szumacher, Grin, Warmund and Szajnweksler were elected to the managing committee.

The *Folk-shul* [public school] of Jewish Children Headed by Ms. Szaber

A meeting of the interest free loan fund, *Ahavas Akhim* [Brotherly Love], took place. Chaim Wajnholc, Chaim Lancman, Chaim Yitzhak Pacanowski, Avraham Grinszpan, Yakov Rozenberg, Meir Szmulewicz and Josef Zajman were elected to the managing committee. Representatives: Ejzensztajn, Fajer, Frank and Przedborski. To the review committee: Zinger, Kolin and Szternberg.

The Yiddish film by Yakov Gordin, *Un a Heym* [Homeless], was exhibited at the Eden cinema. The artists Ida Kaminska, [Shimen] Dzigan and [Yisroel] Szumacher took part in the film.

In the *Czenstochower Zeitung* of 21 July:

Levyoshn [Leviathan] (Lewensztajn), in his weekly feature article, "*Vos gehert, vos gezen*" ["What was heard, what happened"], greatly praises the *TOZ* colonies, where 180 children from the poorest houses and with the greatest need are found. Mordekhai Kaufman in an article "*Kinderland*" [Children's Land] also praises the wonderful effect of the colonies on the children. The *TOZ* children colonies that in 1939 were led jointly with *Dobroczynno??* were located in Amstov, Przyrów, Chzszanstow, Krzepice, Janowa, Olsztyn, Klobuck, and Bliachownia.

[Page 186]

The Yiddish film *Der Dybuk* [The Dybbuk] was shown in the Baltik cinema.

In the *Czenstochower Zeitung* of 21 July:

A memorial service took place for the deceased Artisans Union activist, Daniel Dzialowicz, at his grave, and his headstone was unveiled.

A flood occurred in Czenstochow after the greatest heat. The Warta and the Kucelinka [Rivers] spilled over their banks and the Zawadcza area, the Naturowicz market and the Stradom [railway station] were flooded. The cellars and ground floors of the houses were inundated with water.

The same thing happened in Krzepice, where *TOZ* ran a children's colony. The teaching personnel heroically saved the children from the flood.

The American actors, Pesakhke Burstein and Lillian Lux, staged two performances, *Der Komediant* [*The Comedian*] and *Zeyn Sheyner Kholem* [*His Beautiful Dream*], at the firemen's hall.

The Yiddish film, *Dem Khazan's Zundl* [*The Cantor's Young Son*], with Moshe Oysher, was shown at the Eden Cinema.

In the *Czenstochower Zeitung* of 25 August:

The *Makhzikei Hadas Talmud Torah* undertook a campaign to protect the institution, so that an auction would not take place because of its debts.

The completion of the summer season took place at the *TOZ* colony at Bliachownia and at the half [day] colony in Czenstochow with a children's performance. The director of the colony was L. Brener.

―――――――

Translator's Footnote

1. *Machzikei HaDas* was an organization of synagogues and religious secondary schools whose goal was to improve both education and religious observance.

Several Coworkers from the Jewish Press in Czenstochow
(for the article "Jewish Press")

Y. Rozenberg

Sh. Frank

M. Asz

Y. Pesakhzon

Translator's Footnotes

1. (Shmuel) Artur Zygielbojm was a Bundist leader and a member of the National Council of the Polish Government in exile. He committed suicide to protest the indifference of the Allied nations to the plight of the Polish Jews. He left a very moving letter explaining his suicide.

[Page 187]

Czentochow Holocaust

[Page 188]

The Catastrophe of the Community

by L. Brener

Czenstochow numbered 29,000 Jewish residents at the outbreak of the war in 1939. The first hundred Jewish victims fell on "Bloody Monday," 4 September 1939, when the Germans carried out the first pacification in Czenstochow. Then the permanent torture of the Jews began. Groups of Jews were driven daily to work and, under the blows of rifle butts, women and men, children and young people were forced to fill air-raid trenches, carry bricks from place to place without purpose and carry out other physical labor. Krieger, the then chief of the Gestapo, excelled the most in this work of torture.

On 16 September 1939, at the order of the city chief Wendler, the *Judenrat* [Jewish council] of six men, was created, which was to be involved with the creation free kitchens for the poor.

On 15 November a [compulsory] contribution of a million marks was placed on the Jewish population. Under the threat of hundreds of Jews being shot, the contribution was to be paid over the course of 10 days. After bribing the city chief with hundreds of thousands of marks, the contribution was reduced to 400,000 marks.

At the end of December 1939, a small pogrom against the Jewish population was carried out under the direction of the gendarmes, which ended with the burning of the new so-called German synagogue.

**Front Cover of the 1940 Statistical Yearbook Published by
the *Judenrat***

The Back Cover

On a certain Friday in the middle of the night in January 1940, thousands of men, women and mainly young girls, half naked, were driven from their residences. After detaining them for long hours in the snowy frost, the wounded and seriously beaten ones were freed. Those remaining were driven together to one designated point. There, everyone had to undress completely naked. The German officers and soldiers tortured them in a sadistic manner. A number of young girls were raped and then sent to various kinds of labor. In addition to forcing the Jews to work in Czenstochow itself, many were sent out to work camps in unfamiliar places that devoured many victims.

[Page 189]

Deportations from the entire ghetto began quickly, as well as from individual houses. No one was sure if he would still be where he had created his new home in the morning. After each removal [of Jews], the Germans looted for their furniture treasury, but even more – for themselves privately. All Jewish possessions were confiscated. The Jews became poorer and the need deeper every day.

From March 1940 on, the Jewish population kept increasing with thousands of refugees from the surrounding cities and *shtetlekh* [towns], which were annexed to the Reich. At the beginning of April 1941, the Jewish community in Czenstochow numbered 48,000 residents.

On 23 April, there arose the large ghetto. While the 29,000 Jews in Czenstochow had inhabited 9,000 houses before the war, now the 48,000 were pressed into 4,529 houses. Infectious diseases began to spread. Typhus and dysentery had their lucrative harvest, mainly among the mass of refugees. The blows were frequent and increased. They consoled themselves even more after each blow and continued to drag the heavy weight of life, awaiting new blows.

[Page 190]

There also were some bright rays in the dark life: under the wing of *TOZ* [*Towarzystwo Ochrony Zdrowia Ludności Żydowskiej* – the Society for Safeguarding the Health of the Jewish Population], which carried on intensive activity from the start of the war. Two hundred newly educated medics threw themselves with great fervor into the fight again contagious diseases. Thanks to the devoted and passionate young people, the feeding-location (*œwietlices* – lounges) that *TOZ* ran for 2,000 starving children, quickly was transformed into a warm and bright home for all of the children in the ghetto. The young people with their passionate hearts lit and warmed the life and mood of the poor and lonely children. A choir and a dramatic circle of adults also were active at *TOZ*. TOZ also published an illegal periodical publication, *Rasta* (shortening of *Rada Starszycz* [council of elders]), under the leadership of the lawyer, Koniarski, Y. Roziner, L. Brener, and R. Fobel, as well as with the technical help of L. Kusznir and M. Kusznir, in which were presented the life of the Jews in the ghetto, the activities of the German government organs and of the *Judenrat*.

[Page 191]

The political parties also showed animated activity. The Bund illegally maintained the Medem Library for the entire time, as well as spread illegal literature that was published by the Central Committee of the Bund in Warsaw. On 16 July 1941, the work of the Bund was interrupted because of the failure of the illegal printing shop in Piotrków. Several Bundists paid with their lives (Moshe Berkensztat and others). Only two of the arrestees succeeded in slipping out of prison thanks to the help of the Central Committee. The communists also carried on intensive activity the entire time. However, their work was interrupted for a time because of the large [number of] arrests on 29 April, when many of them and their families were deported to Ocewiêcim [Auschwitz]. *Hanoar Hatzioni* [the Zionist Youth] also carried on some organizational and political work.

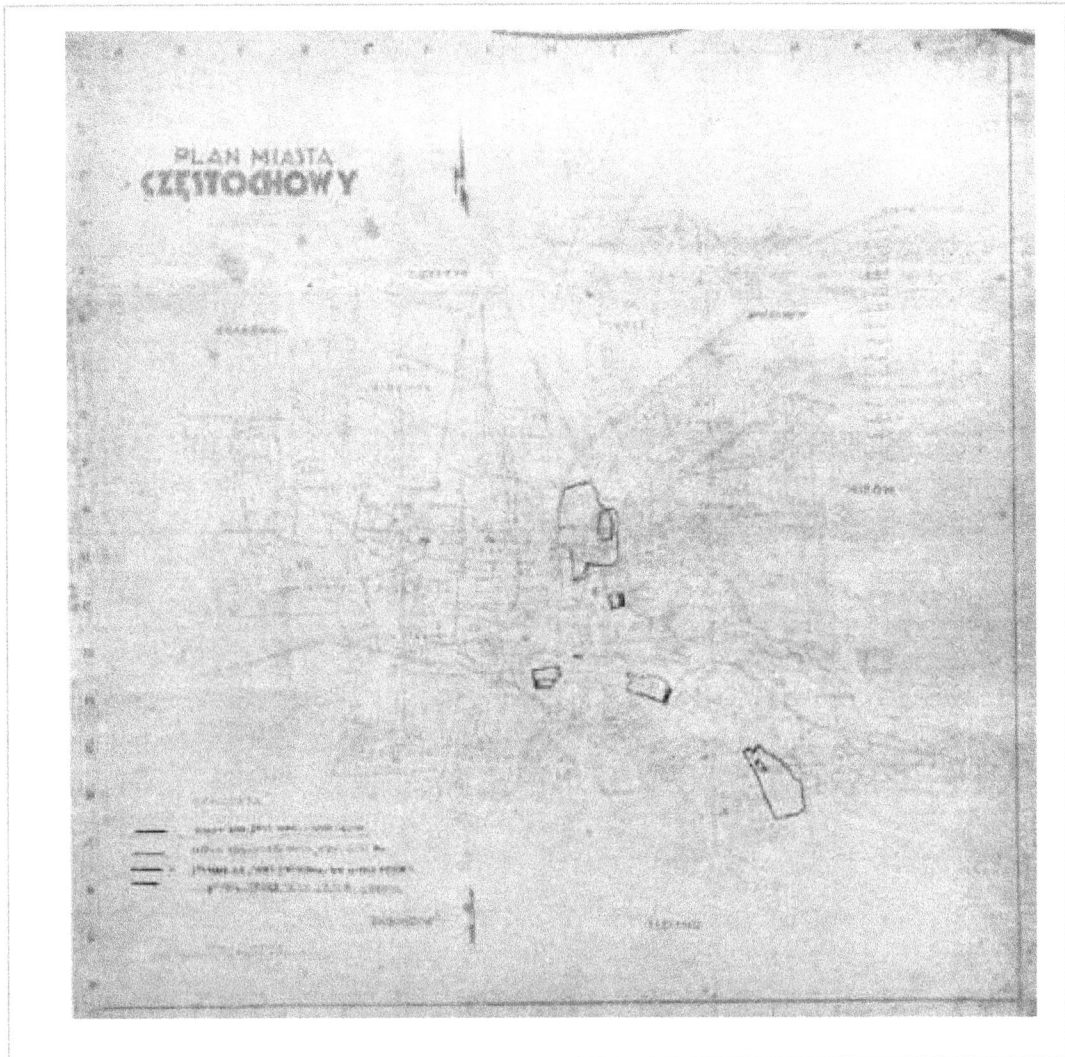

Map of the City with the Ghéttos and Camps Outlined

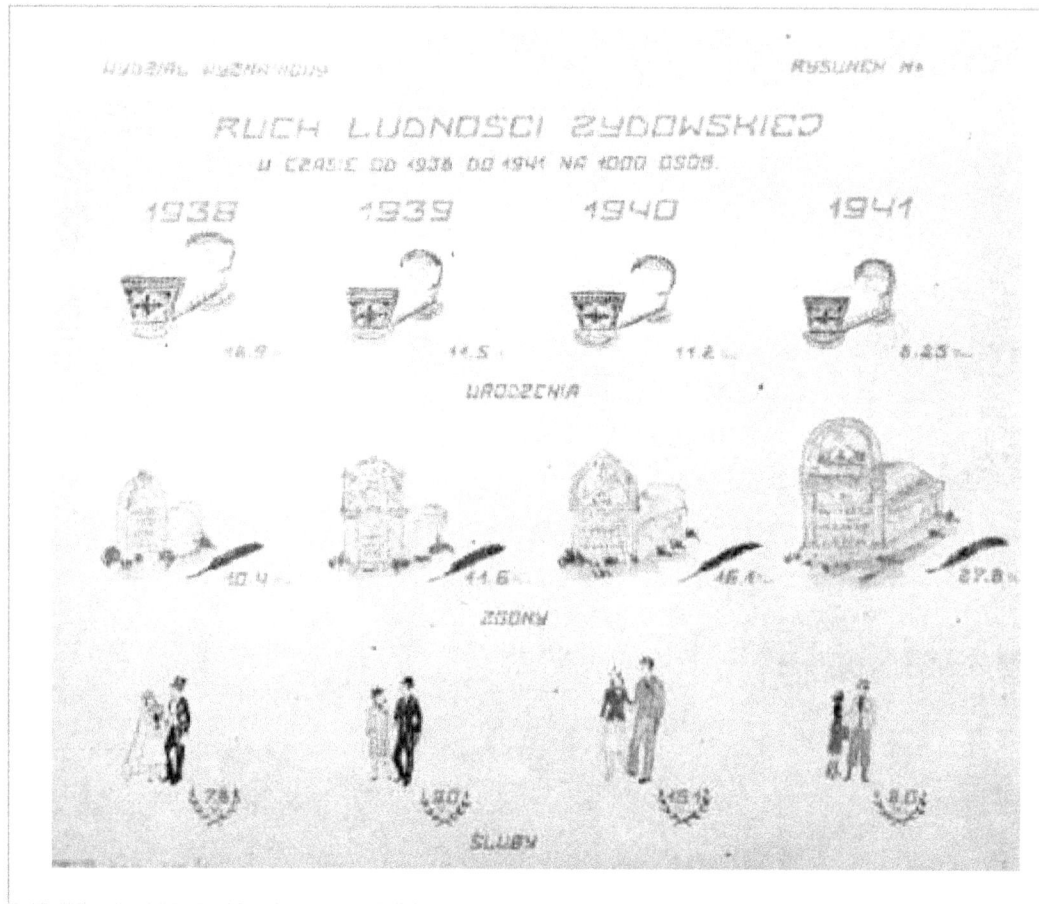

Movements of the Jewish Population from 1938–1940 (percentages for each 1,000 people)

The leftist parties also organized a professional union that took care of the work and demanded that *Judenrat* to pay better wages and feed and clothe the workers, who would by sent by it [the *Judenrat*] to various German workplaces. Quiet strikes took place and more than once the premises of the *Judenrat* were demolished when the demands of the worker delegation were not filled.

In the spring of 1942, news about the Lublin expulsion tore into the ghetto like lightening and in the summer came the news of the Warsaw explusion. Unease enveloped everyone like an electrical storm. But the unease increased when the *German Sondergerichten* [special courts] instituted prison sentences to be served until deportation for leaving the ghetto or for a similar "sin" instead of the death penalty. Everyone's hope turned to the "shops" (identification cards from the shops were to serve as certificates confirming that those possessing them were useful workers); these included the thousands of starving, exhausted Jews driven out of cities and *shtetlekh* and now located at the refugee areas. To all of those considered useless [the shops] were supposed to be everyone's redeemer...

Second Count of the Jewish Population in 1940

Statistics on the Number and Percent of Those Married

[Page 192]

The lines at the labor office grew longer from day to day. Doctors, lawyers, professors, students; directors, merchants and just ordinary traders were transformed into shoemakers, tailors, locksmiths and brushmakers.

There were also giant lines at the premises of the *Judenrat*. Here thousands of forlorn skeletons wrapped in rags with hands eaten by leprosy pushed toward the windows and tried to convince the officials that they were well-to-do and needed no one's help, that they could work, too, and as useful elements they also had full rights to further remain in Czenstochow.

The political parties began to negotiate about a joint armed appearance in case of some sort of "action" on the part of the occupiers. The most decisive conference in connection with this was supposed to take place on 21 September with the participation of a messenger from the Warsaw ⁻OB [*ʒydowska Organizacja Bojowa* – Jewish Combat Organization] and a local Jewish captain, Dr. A. Walberg, but itdid not come about. Several delegates from the political parties, who were supposed to take part in the conference, were held by the gendarmes. The same day the unease grew from hour to hour. The police chief, the murderer Degenhart, threatened the strongest repression for spreading false rumors and demanded that the *Judenrat* and the Jewish *ordnungsdient* [Jewish police force – order police] end the spreading of rumors. On 21 September, at three o'clock at night, Ukrainian and Lithuanian auxiliary police were placed in the streets of the ghetto. Everyone saw that obviously the *aktsia* [action – usually a deportation] was beginning.

B.

The *aktsia* began on 22 September, early at five o'clock. Thousands of people ran from room to room, from house to house and from street to street like frightened ants whose anthill had been stepped on. One person dragged a backpack, another a pack of linen and another a few utensils. Everywhere they came up against gendarmes and Ukrainian auxiliary police armed from head to foot. Under a hail of blows, everyone was chased to the metal factory where the "shops" were located. Wives were torn from husbands, children from mothers and woe to those who dared to say goodbye to a wife or a child. Notable among the great mass of those chased were several with hatchets in their hands; others had their fists in the air; as well as those who knelt and begged for pity from the murderers. However, everyone's end was the same – death...

The German hangmen marched them to their annihilation and death among hundreds of murdered bodies. The old, the weak, children and also those who dared not be torn from their wife and child paid with their lives. The streets were full of frightened, wailing masses. Crazy with despair they called their children who had been lost and fell with shattered skulls. The cries and shouts of hundreds of children, who were searching for their mothers, tore through the air and tore at the heart. The contagiously ill escaped from the hospital and fell at the gate. Human shadows with small red books in their hands that should have confirmed the usefulness of their [owners] stood in front of the of the gates to the metal factory and moved along in front, dark in giant rows one pressed against the other. Degenhart, the cruel police dog, the chief murderer, strolled here calmly and indicated with his walking stick: "You to the right! You to the left!" and so on.

The small red books actually traveled to the trash basket and the people to the cattle cars where the packs were taken from everyone, their shoes were removed and they waited to push up to 120 people into a train wagon. Only a small number were successful in being accepted in the "shops," where a number of members of the *Judenrat* already were working.

The day ended with 6,000 sent out and several hundred murdered on the spot.

In the morning – all of the ghetto streets were heavily guarded. There was heavy gunfire in the area from which Jews already had been sent out. Jews here who tried to hide were murdered. Shots that ended the lives of those who dared to look out through a window or to appear on a balcony also reverberated in the still occupied streets.

They found themselves tensely waiting for four days. Thoughts of hope flew through many: perhaps, perhaps nothing more would happen! Four days – the worried waiting lasted for [what seemed like] four long, terrible years. On the fifth day, 27 September, the news that more Jews were being driven from a certain number of streets arrived like frightening thunder. All were chased to the large square at the New Market where "selections" were taking place. Thousands of Jews were arranged in two dense, long rows. Dozens of gendarmes and members of the Gestapo and hundreds of Ukrainians surrounded the square. There was a deadly silence. Only the stuttering voice of the cruel police chief was heard: "What is your profession?" and not waiting for an answer, he pointed with his cane over the head. With his characteristic, "you to the right, you to the left!" – he determined life or death for everyone.

[Page 193]

The day also resulted in 6,000 deportees and many dead on the spot. Suddenly, a ray of hope: gendarmes brought a group of Jews who had been ransomed for goods, money and diamonds to the "shops." Based on this, the Jews began to collect ransom money for the security police. Jews parted with their last possessions. They paid in everything they had, even jewelry that had been inherited generation after generation, if only to save their closest relatives, sacks of gold, jewelry and precious stones traveled to the gendarmes and the fooled Jews – to the cattle cars to Treblinka.

A wild hunt began for spoils. The living were cheated out of everything; golden teeth were pulled and fingers with golden rings were cut off the dead. Wagons of Jewish residents' possessions were drawn through the street to the storehouses of the security police. The Jewish *gwardia* [guards] from the "furniture camp" under the leadership of hard-working and bold Makhl Birencwajg carried secretive cabinets, china cabinets and coal boxes – this was not very easy. Mothers and children were smuggled in these pieces of furniture to the bunkers in the "furniture camp" that had been prepared under the noses of the Germans. Seventy-three children and their mothers were saved in such a manner.

The murderous "action dance" lasted for six weeks. Hunger and death reigned without end. About 41,000 Jews were sent to Treblinka and perished there. Six and a half thousand remained in the "shops" and at temporary labor camps and about a thousand – hidden in cellars and in various bunkers.

The ghetto had been cleaned out. A deadly silence. The widespread, frightening melody of death and destruction was the only thing that carried through the doors and windows. The walls of the day rooms that over the course of 19 months absorbed the soulful warmth of the young people and the cheerful sounds of 2,000 children who had their bright home here cried. The orphan's house that in the course of 19 months fed, supported and warmed 150 young orphans and was now itself orphaned, cried.

The situation for the survivors was cruel. The suffering was most terrible for those who were sent to the *HASAG* [*H.A.S.A.G.* is the acronym for a German metal goods manufacturer, Hugo Schneider Metallwarenfabrik Aktiengesellschaft] ammunition factory.

Suffering from hunger and filth was the daily bread here. Only those who had the strength to save a little coffee from their daily half-liter portion could wash their face a bit.

The policemen were triumphant. They completely accomplished their duty in regard to the "Great Reich." Now they were the true sons of the true "master race."

The *aktsias* ended on 1 November. Six and a half thousand surviving Jews were taken from the "shops" and from the temporary work camps to the small ghetto in continuing deadly fear and to further "selections."

View of the *HASAG*

C.

The "small ghetto" – three small, filthy, parallel-laying, narrow alleys, fenced in with barbed wire, guarded day and night by the security police and the Ukrainians. Six and a half thousand sad shadows that by chance had stolen a little bit of life were locked into a suffocating cage. Six and a half thousand deprived slaves were pressed into 1,200 narrow, small rooms. Those sentenced to life were forced to build their new home here. There were no households of one's own. Everyone had to work and draw their means of support from the kitchen run by the *Judenrat*.

Everyone was on their feet in groups at five o'clock in the morning, under guard, marching to their designated workplaces outside the ghetto where they experienced pain, jokes and mockery. At nine in the evening, the sad melody of the trumpet spread, ordering them to sleep.

[Page 194]

A melancholy mood hung like a heavy cloud in the sky. Everyone had lost everything and everyone. Mothers, dying of grief, were cheered up by their children's bright, laughing eyes. Charming Jewish children, saved by a miracle, lay in dark bunkers and cried their eyes out, longing for their mothers' gentle hand.

Every group was counted precisely and verified when marching out to work and coming back. The mood then was quiet and serious. Yet, a powerful song from a group of workers was heard from time to time at the marching into the ghetto. This was not a song of intoxication and joy. Thus 200 workers from the "furniture camp" deafened the cries of the surviving children, who were being smuggled in large bread sacks from bunkers outside the ghetto into the ghetto where new bunkers had been prepared for them.

The camp leader – the executioner Ibersher – stood at the well-known small Warszawer market square almost every day during the marching out to work and with the bent handle of his cane he caught one here, here another one by the throat like a pugnacious dog and dragged him into the "butcher-shop." From there large groups were sent to Skarzysko and Blizyn. Entire groups of workers often were taken from the workplaces and sent away. Each "whistle" was accompanied by victims: several fell because slaves needed to be taught a little respect and several [were murdered] when they jumped from autos or from the cattle cars.

There were more frequent conversations about a new deadline for complete liquidation. The nerves could not stand the constant unease and uncertainty. The physical threat to life grew stronger from day to day and hour to hour. Striving to make a fortune to be able to escape from the ghetto grew more strained. Entire packs were stolen from the police storehouses where the looted Jewish property was stored and they were sold. The uncertainty for the next morning grew enormously. One was rich and wanted to drive away one's own suffering from the night and today. Life became wanton. Gorging oneself and debauchery were transformed into a cult. There was the impression of living in a thick, dark jungle.

A second life developed at the same time, a life in bunkers and in deep cellars. Here sat young men and women, without concern for political differences and their feeling for revenge hardened. The heavy burden of ghetto life was loathsome to them. Those sentenced to death threw off the yoke of suffering and doubt and strengthened their will to fight. Young boys and girls, almost still children, transformed these cellars into a wonderful "enchanted land." The sadness here was overshadowed with gentle love and the despair with hate. Love and hate. Love for the memory of the so tragically murdered and hate for the German hangmen. They worked tirelessly day and night. They bought a revolver and in deadly danger smuggled in bullets that were stolen from the German ammunition factory for dynamite. They made their own grenades with almost no experience, with their bare hands. A large tunnel also was prepared that was to serve in case they would need to withdraw from the fight. They collected money from the rich Jews for weapons and they eliminated traitors. The mood in the ghetto changed little by little, mainly after the great defeat of the German army at Stalingrad. The number of fighters grew from day to day and the work more intensive.

The security police carried out further annihilation work. New edicts kept coming. It became forbidden for men and women to live on the same street. Every day brought new victims. Those on whose cheeks burned a tubercular fever were shot. Men were shot who dared to cross the threshold of their sister who lived on the women's street and the reverse. Those who "hid" in the ghetto and did not go to work were shot. Mothers who lost their minds were shot. Fourteen year old children who did not go to work because they wanted to protect their insane mothers from committing suicide and so on were shot.

[Page 195]

At 10 o'clock in the morning on 3 January the ghetto was surrounded from the outside by fully armed Ukrainians and gendarmes. The ghetto was shaken. There was murmuring as in a beehive. The people ran from place to place. They looked at each other with eyes full of fear. The question: "What more would happen?" did not leave anyone's mouth. The ghetto was full of unease. The gendarmes in helmets strolled calmly outside, right near the barbed wire, and looked nonchalantly at what now was happening in the ghetto. Suddenly the ghetto was full of Ukrainians, *granat* police [Blue Police – Polish police in the Nazi-occupied area], gendarmes and Jewish *ordnungsdienst* [Jewish policemen]. Terrifying voices and screams carried from one corner of the ghetto to another. Old people, fathers with children were dragged out of the houses, from the cellars and the attics. Several let themselves be led indifferently; others threw themselves to the ground and defended themselves with teeth and nails. People's blood froze in their veins watching this tragic struggle. The *aktsia* was halted at night, but not ended. The *aktsia* was continued early in the morning. They again dragged entire groups of mothers and children from hiding places. Terrible despairing voices drifted with the almost constant shooting. Everyone in the ghetto was driven out to the well-known market square. A new "selection" took place. The fighters from the "enchanted" land participated in their first test: Mendl Fiszelewicz shot at the gendarmes. Twenty-five Jews then paid with their lives, among them Fiszelewicz's closest comrade, Y. Fajner, the old Bundist *bojowec* [fighter] Hershl Frajman and the lawyer, Rozensztajn, the member of the League for Working *Eretz-Yisroel* [a Zionist organization]. More than 300 men, women and mainly children, as well as young fighters were sent to Radomsk under heavy guard to complete the transport from there to Treblinka.

The ghetto received another appearance. People prepared feverishly to escape from the bunkers that had been prepared earlier at great expense. Grey-haired women and men had received pitch-black hair overnight. Young, darkly cute girls and boys were suddenly blond. They escaped to the Polish side with false passports and smuggled themselves to Germany to work with false identification cards. Many of them were identified or accidentally recognized and perished. The impulse to escape did not decrease.

The young did not rest and prepared feverishly. Groups went into the forests. Groups left for various diversionary work. Many of them also perished taking additional victims with them.

February 1943. It was passed from ear to ear that Jews who had relatives in Palestine would be exchanged for Germans who were in England. A new ray of hope began to lighten the mood of hundreds of unfortunate ones. The *Judenrat* carried out the registration. Those who did not have family in Palestine "borrowed" such from acquaintances and registered themselves, too. The registration ran for two weeks and was interrupted. Hundreds of slaves lived through another disappointment.

20 March 1943, Purim. A beautiful, sunny day. It felt a little like a holiday in the ghetto. It was particularly like a holiday among the doctors' families, who today were celebrating the birthday of the most beautiful child in the ghetto – of the small Lili Winer. All of the doctors and their families were assembled now at Doctor Winer's house. The men carried out animated conversations: Dr. Winer told how he, as a transport worker, in the very fervor of the deportation action on 27 September 1942, managed to get into quarantine and there with great self-sacrifice was also able to bring in his wife and their two children. Dr. Blumenfeld drew a pessimistic conclusion about the further fate of the few remaining Jews. The young Dr. Lipinski tried to persuade everyone that the Jewish doctors in Czenstochow would survive the war because the hangman Degenhart had a special weakness for doctors and Dr. Kiak amused the group with his humorous description of the appearance of Germany after the war. However, the majority of the guests were engrossed with the few dozen children entertaining them. Everyone's attention was now riveted on the dance that the children were doing. The children were radiant. The small Lili was particularly radiant. The black velvet little dress, the white anklets on her slender legs, the large snow- white ribbon on her head in her thick black hair gave her a special charm. Lili was now completely aglow. This day was her holiday. This day we celebrated her 7th birthday. The guests could not tear away their eyes from the delicate, beautiful and gorgeous child.

Memorial Tablet at the Grave of Six Shot Fighters from the Jewish Fighting Organization (19 March 1943)

[Page 196]

Suddenly a new order from the city chief spread: the *Judenrat*, all doctors and the intelligentsia in general, needed to appear with their families at the sadly famous market square. The ghetto again became agitated. The square was full of men, women and children. The chief declared that they were being sent to Palestine. Large trucks had been prepared and stood unguarded. Everyone had to climb into the vehicles. The vehicles moved slowly. The vehicles stopped on Warsawer Street. Armed gendarmes jumped out of various hiding places. More vehicles with gendarmes arrived. The vehicles then moved quickly in the direction of the Jewish cemetery. The victims felt threatened with danger. The 20-year old W. Kopinski, a member of the Jewish Fighting Organization was the first one to jump from the speeding vehicle. Others jumped after him, of whom only six were successful in escaping from death. The remaining 127 men – the remainder of the professional Jewish intelligentsia – were brought to the Jewish cemetery. The entire cemetery was surrounded by security guards and Ukrainian auxiliary police. The victims were forced to take off their clothes and one by one they were shot. The gendarmerie alone was involved in this "holy" worship. The oldest were shot first. The German hangmen still had time for the children. They had a desire to play a little with the children. They themselves were fathers and there were still children present... With one hand they lifted the children by strands of hair or by their small feet into the air and with the other took aim at their hearts or their bodies. There was no harm in that all of the children did not immediately exhale their souls. It did not matter that the earth was covering those who could still shouted out their last Ma...

The small Lili was the last one. All her [clothes] were removed. Only the white ribbon in her hair – a memory of her holiday – was left. The small one stood in all her beauty and her large black eyes wandered from one murderer to another. It is difficult to characterize what was mirrored in the eyes of the small, delicate child. The gendarmes, already satisfied with enough blood, did not move to lift their hands to shoot. Each one wanted another one to end the bloody game. [There was] a long pause... The tall, broad-boned camp leader Ibershter interrupted his comrades prolonging this. With the call: "For the Fatherland," he aimed at the chest of the small Lili, who closed the chain of the 127 victims on the 7th anniversary of her birth.

One hundred and twenty-seven men filled a new mass grave, where an unknown hand erected a broken stone from a desecrated *matzeveh* [headstone] on which was engraved: Czenstochower Jewish Intelligentsia, Purim, 20 March 1943.

Memorial Plaque on the Mass Grave of Those who Fell on 3 January 1943

The Headstone on the Mass Grave of the Czenstochower Intelligentsia

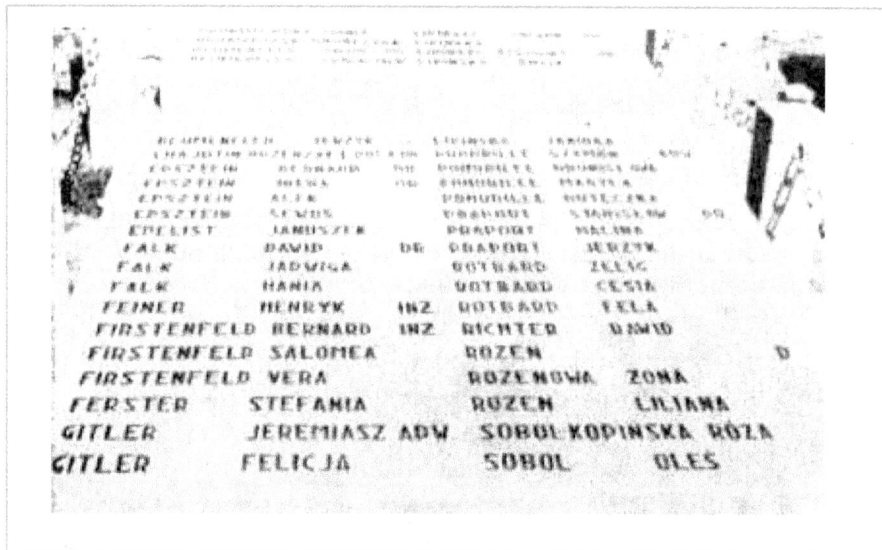

Some of the Names on the Headstone on the Mass Grave

[Page 197]

The ghetto was closed from the 1 to 4 May 1943. No one was allowed out for any work. No workplace was active. *"Dos Juden-problem is über alles!"* [The Jewish problem is above all else!] The mood in the ghetto was dejected. Various people made comments. Several believed that this was the arrival of the total liquidation of the ghetto. Others interpreted it as a means of protection, that the Jews would not meet with any Poles at the workplaces on the holiday of 1 and 3 May [Constitution Day in Poland]. Meanwhile, there was hunger in the ghetto. The filth was great. People were smuggled out in barrels of filth and bread was smuggled in in the same barrels. On the morning of 5 May the trumpet that called us to work was heard again. The mood calmed a little.

A few weeks of a "normal" and tragic life dragged on.

In the second half of June 1943 there was an attack by the security police on the Jewish workers in the furniture camp. There were victims. All small workplaces were liquidated a few days later. The above-mentioned active Dr. A. Walberg was dragged and murdered. Two-dozen workers who were employed in the police storehouses also were murdered. Those in the ghetto sentenced to hard labor understood that the last and decisive action in the ghetto was approaching.

The small ghetto was surrounded and fired upon in the afternoon of 25 June 1943. The bunkers of weapons were discovered and the fighters in the bunkers perished. Night fell and the *aktsia* was suspended.

On 26 June at 10 o'clock in the morning, all the men were driven out to the well-known market square, which was surrounded with gendarmes, members of the Gestapo, security police and soldiers. There were wagons [filled] with dead bodies in the center of the square. Under the threat of death, whoever had money and jewelry had to give it to the gendarmes. Those who lived in the houses in which bunkers of weapons were found were dragged from the rows. Older Jews and fathers with children also were dragged from the rows. They were loaded onto large trucks under blows from rifle butts. The cries and the frightening laments from the women in the ghetto who were watching and understood what was happening were unbearable. The packed vehicles left in the direction of the Jewish cemetery and the remaining men were led away to the nearby *HASAG* ammunition factory

A Delegation from the Czenstochower Fighting Organization and Members of the Fighting Organization in Warsaw Lay Flowers on the Mass Graves in the Small Ghetto (June 1945)

Fragment of the Destroyed Cemetery

At the same time, the security guards and Gestapo attacked the exit from the tunnel outside the ghetto. A short and determined fight. All of the young fighters fell, but the security police and the Gestapo also were victims.

The rows of women arrived, mothers with children were packed into the trucks and driven away to death accompanied by the wailing of the remaining women. The remaining women who had no children with them were led away to the ammunition factory like the men had been earlier. On the morning of 27 June, the chief hangman, Degenhardt, declared an amnesty for all of those who still were lying hidden in bunkers in the ghetto. The Jewish *ordnungsdienst* [ghetto police] carried the "news" of the amnesty throughout the ghetto. Eighty-four men, 60 fathers with children and approximately 100 children crawled out of their hiding places. They were permitted to console themselves with belief in the amnesty for two days. On the third day their hopes were broken forever... Mothers with children increased the number of mass graves in Czenstochow.

[Page 198]

House after house was exploded with dynamite. Hundreds of those hiding perished under the ruins. Dozens who left the bunkers after the "amnesty" [was announced] were shot on the spot and burned. Many were thrown into the fire while alive. Magnificent dreams were turned into smoke.

Place Where the Old Synagogue Once Stood

Human torches were carried with tongues of flame to the sky and German murderers – the sons of the *herren-volk* [master race] – danced their cruel annihilation dance in honor of the "Third Reich" in the glow of the flames.

D.

HASAG [*H.A.S.A.G.* is the acronym for a German metal goods manufacturer, Hugo Schneider Metallwarenfabrik Aktiengesellschaft] - two ammunition factories, *Pelcery* and *Rakow*. Here now was the concentration camp for 3,990 still-living Jews in Czenstochow. Meanwhile the security police borrowed for their disposition 230 men from [the factories]. The mood of the survivors was crushed. Some had lost their last child, some their last friend. Each was unfamiliar with the other. Everyone felt lonely. They talked to each other with bitterness about those who had been preparing to fight and had hastened the new misfortune. The small number of remaining fighters felt a little guilty and strange. Guilty – perhaps they really did hasten the misfortune. And strange because they read painful resentment in the looks from several [people]. The hunger was strongly felt. Twenty deca [numerical value of 10] of bread and a little watery soup from dried beets (*viln zup* in the language of the *HASAG*) that was given out daily per man could not satisfy anyone. Yet, they began to accustom themselves to this. The thought sneaked in that perhaps they would at least remain alive here. It was an ammunition factory and they still needed hands to work! Hungry, broken, but with a new light of hope, they lived for three weeks and two days. They starved for three weeks and two days, eaten by lice and for three weeks and two days they believed that they would remain alive because the labor force of slaves now was necessary for "victory."

On 19 July 1943, at 11 o'clock at night, everyone was driven out onto the street. Everyone had to march through a small alley where a new "selection" took place. This time, the "selection" was made by the master craftsmen from the factory and by the leaders of the security guards. The security police only assisted. They looked into each face separately and evaluated each one separately as to who, according to their opinion, was too old or too young. Each master craftsman also indicated which of their slaves who were "slaggards" needed to perish. A horrible lament carried through the entire factory. Those who remained alive for now did not cry any less. They were all now convinced that the ammunition factory was less important than the "Jewish problem."

Two hundred and sixty were thrown into a dark cellar and then experienced their last night of a frightening nightmare. Two hundred and sixty men were waiting for their final redemption – for death. Early in the morning, 20 July, the entire *ordnungsdienst* [Jewish police force – order police] and their families were thrown into the same cellar. The security police also made a donation of 130 men from its slaves for this "holy" purpose. On the same day at 11 o'clock in the morning, a terrible struggle took place in the cellar. More than 400 of those sentenced to death fought with the master craftsmen who dazed each victim with hammers before throwing them into the vehicles. This time the German hangmen again were victorious.

Fragments of the Destroyed Small Ghetto

[Page 199]

The survivors were still crying and the dark cellar walls were filled with inscriptions of those who just had perished cried with them:

"Ruwinku Feldman. I part with you son. Keep well!" – Your mother Ch. Feldman.

Inscriptions from those murdered to their relatives scratched by the hands of the martyrs on the walls of the cellars in the *HASAG* and of the ruins of the arrest house of the Jewish police in the small ghetto before they went to their deaths

"Dear Ruwin, I leave calmly. I kiss you." – Your mother Chana.

"Dear daughter Yadza, I go to my death calmly. Do not lose hope! I kiss you." – Your mother Moszkowicz.

"I leave calmly." – Yuzik Yung.

"Zasha Winder says goodbye to her husband Kalman. I leave calmly." – Zasha Winder.

"I am already tired of constantly running from death. I leave calmly. How will my children live? What will become of them?" – Kh. Sh.

The Jewish cemetery grew larger with a large mass grave of more than 400 men. The master craftsmen, the lame security guard Klem and his accomplice, the 140-centimeter [four foot 6 inches] cripple Sztiglic had shown that they could do the "holy" work just as well as the security police.

Wooden barracks were built quickly in the area of a scant square kilometer surrounded by barbed wire, heavily armed on all sides with security guards. Here was the living place for 3,000 men. Every day had its number of victims: someone was shot by a security guard just like that, another by the Gestapo for a transgression of some kind, someone for an attempt to escape and someone by a master craftsman as a "slaggard." A child was born; it immediately had to be murdered. If someone was seriously ill, there was also a solution for him…

Resident Barracks in *HASAG*

Resident Barracks in *HASAG*

A Fragment of the *HASAG*

[Page 200]

The days in the camp were monotonous. Every day at 5 o'clock in the morning everyone had to be ready for the count. The cripple Sztiglic then created a circus: for being late for the count, he forced old women to kiss young boys, and young girls to kiss old Jews [men]. He gave 10-20 or more lashes as a penalty for the same transgression. Every day entire groups were led by the master craftsmen under the watch of the security guards to receive their lashes for not working up to their standard. Some died only with a *kratke* [Polish – grille shape] (marks only on the lower part of the body in "*HASAG* language"). Others traveled from the guards straight to the hospital.

The few Jews here were turned into a large, numbed, melancholy mass. The hard labor, between grey factory walls, murderous master craftsmen and heavy machines at which they had to work up to 12-14 or more hours a day standing and the hunger brought the result that one met dried out men whose skin barely kept their bones from collapsing. One also met those who could barely drag their feet, which were swollen by hunger. Typhus and tuberculosis had a rich harvest here. Clothes of rags and wooden shoes brought from various camps that had been closed were the usual clothing here. Apathy and resignation began to spread even more and wider.

However, the political parties began to revive again. Cells were created by: members of the Polish Workers Party, the Bund, left *Poalei-Zion* [Marxist Zionist] and other Zionist groupings. They came to an understanding with political workers, who smuggled food for the Jews and various legal and illegal newspapers for the cells. The comrades outside made contact with us. They sent in letters, bulletins and brochures. (*A Year in Treblinka*; by [Jankiel] Wiernik, bulletins from the Bund with the last letter from Artur Zygielbojm[1] and so on). They also sent literature and letters from abroad. We also began to receive help in the same way. Two illegal kitchens immediately were created: one for the sick and the second for children and young people. Individual help also was organized for everyone about whom we could be certain. The comrades on the outside informed us abut the liquidations of various concentration camps (Trawnik, Pianko and so on) and warned us against having illusions. A second party commission of five men arose that concentrated in its hands the organization of all of the activities. Plans for revolt were prepared in case of an *aktsia*. Three plans were prepared: 1. Organize groupings in the barracks that would prepare the tools that they would need to begin a fight, 2. Blow up the factory by igniting the dynamite warehouse, 3. Organize 125 men who would be ready to sacrifice their lives and attack the security guards, disarm them, control the factory for a time in order for a larger number to be able to escape. The masses in the barracks began to come to life again. The cells increased from day to day. On 22 July 1944, a separate revival was noticed when the press brought the news about the assassination attempt on Hitler. The Peoples Workers Party and Bund cells were particularly active.

One day the security guards attacked the bunkers and confiscated all of the collected tools. The workers' plan failed. The dynamite warehouse was ignited twice. However, the firemen were successful in keeping the fire from spreading both times. However, courage did not fail in anyone. The victorious march forward of the Red Army strengthened the will to fight. Therefore, they prepared their third and [most] determined appearance. The group of 125 was doubled.

Meanwhile the number of Jews in the Czenstochow camps kept increasing. Jews were brought from Lodz, Skarzysko and Plaszow. The Czenstochow camps numbered 11,000 men. The mood imroved and little by little began to change. The constant assuring, "I will not go into the forest anymore," was no longer heard. The majority was convinced that if people were being sent to Czenstochow from other camps and [not killed], then they would not exterminate the Jews in Czenstochow. The will of the people to fight lessened. The interparty commission came to the conclusion that in such a situation an attack would result in certain failure. However, the aid work was carried out further. The comrades from Warsaw and Krakow did not remain aloof and, after a short interruption because of the Warsaw Uprising, made use of every opportunity to continue to help us. They also demanded that the active comrades escape if we did not fight because the danger now was no less threatening than before. The activists from all parties decided not to escape, to not cause danger to the lives of everyone in the camp.

[Page 201]

The mood in the camp kept changing. The daily news about the victories of the Red Army from the smuggled in press encouraged everyone and strengthened the belief that everyone would soon be liberated.

On 15 January 1945, when the Red Army began to approach the gates of Czenstochow, the members of the *S.S.* and the security guards succeeded in evacuating almost 6,000 men from the Czenstochow camp. The evacuation of the remaining 5,200 men by the security guards and the *S.S.* members was not successful. The majority escaped from the barracks and left the factory. The directors, the master craftsmen, members of the *S.S.* and the security guards began to withdraw from the factory, dragging only a few dozen Jews with them. On the morning of 17 January 1945, 5,200 men opened the gates of the camp and went out to freedom.

Five thousand two hundred slaves with death sentences in their pockets. Of them, 1,518 were Czenstochow residents; 1,240 born in Czenstochow and the remainder were from various cities and *shtetlekh* [towns] won back their lives in freedom.

Five thousand two hundred were liberated – 5,200 living headstones in an endless cemetery of our tragic reality.

Translator's Footnotes

1. (Shmuel) Artur Zygielbojm was a Bundist leader and a member of the National Council of the Polish Government in exile. He committed suicide to protest the indifference of the Allied nations to the plight of the Polish Jews. He left a very moving letter explaining his suicide.

[Page 201]

Testimony

[Testimony] taken in Jerusalem with A. (Haran) and B. (Randes) who were in Poland until 1943

When the war broke out I was in Żarki (Zhurik), my city of birth, near Czenstochow. The Germans entered the city on 2 September at nine o'clock in the evening, on *Shabbos* [Sabbath]. The Nazis bombed the city on 2 September in air attacks. One hundred Jewish victims fell. Many houses were destroyed. Entire families with children were murdered. A terrible panic arose. There were civilians as well as the surrounding peasants who escaped with their families from Żarki itself. However, the Germans traveled more quickly and wherever one went, the Germans already were there. The Germans distributed bread and small candies among the refugees on the road and asked of them one thing: they should all return home. And so everyone returned to Żarki.

On 4 September the Germans set fire to the old synagogue in the city and burned it. When the young Jews saw that things were turbulent and insecure, the majority left for the nearest forest. The Germans suddenly declared that the civilian population, including the Jews, had shot at the German military and had killed a number of soldiers. And the repressions were because of this. They took hostages (esteemed Jews) and brought them to the church and threatened that they would be shot. Later we returned from the forests. The Germans began to grab Jews and send them to Germany. I myself was in a camp in Nirenberg. There were 3,000 Jews there, mainly from Kalicz and Lodz and 17,000 Poles. After a month's time, I was sent to a Nazi camp in Krakow. The 3,000 Jews were freed three weeks later. We suffered from hunger the entire time. We were beaten and they also shot at us. Later, we were helped by the Jewish community.

I returned to Żarki. The situation in the *shtetl* [town] had grown worse. The Nazi leader was a savage man. The Jews were dragged to work; they were beaten and so on. Once they gathered all the Jews, men, in the synagogue and told them they would be finished with them. The panic grew, but they were freed after several days.

Later, another German leader came, a bit of a better person, and although the situation was difficult, we still went on with life in the *shtetl* and people worked. Three thousand two hundred refugees from Polck were in Żarki, among them 300 Jews. There also were those from Lodz there who had escaped to Żarki from their city. In Żarki, the leather industry had particularly evolved (the manufacture of boots, coats and so on). The decrees from the General Government, as for example, the yellow patch and others were not applied in Żarki. All of this was at the beginning, but later when Żarki was joined to the Radomsker District (summer 1940), all kinds of edicts were issued in regard to us. We were not allowed to trade. Work was restricted. Every Jew had to wear a white patch. However, there was no official ghetto. The Germans created the *Judenrat* [Jewish council] that took on all formalities. The Germans would take bribes and many of them were bribed and thus we coped for a time.

[Page 202]

In 1941 a group of about 50 young people (a number of them came from Warsaw) organized an agricultural farm [in Żarki], as a part of *hahalutz* [pioneers preparing for emigration to *Eretz-Yisroel*] and the *Hashomer HaTzair* [The Youth Guard – Socialist Zionists] movement. We worked on the land that had previously belonged to us. The *Judenrat* leased it from the Germans and it was given to us to work on. The Germans checked our farm and many among them, particularly those among them who had lived in villages, strongly praised our "exemplary work." There were also Jewish representatives from Warsaw and they helped us (the Joint [Distribution Committee] and others).

The large expulsions began in September 1942. The German "Committee for the Annihilation of Jews" arrived in Czenstochow on 22 September 1942 and the terrible days began for all of the Czenstochow area.

The expulsion began in Żarki on 6 October 1942. We learned a day earlier that there would be expulsions. A number of Jews escaped to the fields and forests and to the surrounding villages as well as the neighboring *shtetl* [town] of Piltz (Pilica). Expulsions had been carried out in Pilica months earlier and some Jews there escaped to us and lived in Żarki. When the expulsions arrived in Żarki, the Pilica Jews and some of the Jews from Żarki escaped to Pilica (which already was *Juden-rein* [cleansed of Jews]) and they hid there.

One hundred Germans and Ukrainians arrived in vehicles on 6 October. In addition, they gathered the local Nazi police as well as the "border guards." The Germans ordered all of the Jews to gather at the market. They went from house to house and chased the Jews to the market. Whoever was found hiding in a cellar or anywhere was shot on the spot. Those sick in bed also were shot. Only 30 Jews were left alone to clear the Jewish possessions.

Thus, the Nazis assembled 780 Jews at the market (they immediately shot 23 Jews). Every one of those assembled (men, women and children) was permitted to tale a small package with them. All of the Jews were led to the Zlati-Potok train station. There, they were treated with the greatest savagery. They were all packed into trucks. When mothers did not want to give up their children, they were shot on the spot along with their children. Young people who wanted to escape also were shot.

The Jews who had escaped to the forests began to return to Żarki, unable to endure in the hiding places. Many of them were arrested and, when a group of 40-50 Jews were assembled, they were sent to Czenstochow (later to Piotrkow) because groups of deported Jews went on from there.

I, myself, escaped to Pilica. I was there for three weeks, along with a group of 25 comrades. We worked there with the Polish partisans. Together we filled various functions, went on attacks in the forests, shot at Germans and made assassination attempts on them. The partisan movement had just started there at that time. With weapons in their hands, the young Jews organized attacks against the Germans.

I have to add that before the expulsion from Żarki took place, a group of young Jews, particularly the *halutzim* [those training for agricultural work and emigration to *Eretz-Yisroel*] and *Hashomer HaTzair* [the Young Guard – Socialist Zionists] organized self-defense group. We worked out detailed plans of how to cut the telephone lines, attack the Germans and so on. However, we could not carry out the plan because the Germans issued a rule that if a shot was heard they would murder the entire Jewish population around them, as well as the women and children. Because of this we did not want to take away the last hope of the Jews of saving themselves and, without a doubt, their children.

The second expulsion in Pilica, of the entire Krakow district, took place three weeks later. After the edict, if a Jew was found in the region (Pilica, Wolbórz, Miechow), he would be shot on the spot. We, who had hidden in Pilica, ran back to Żarki. We were not supposed to appear in the streets because every Jew was being arrested. The Jews entered sealed houses. They hid in the attics and in the bunkers. There was no food. In the evening we went to the 30 Jews (whom the Germans had left [here]) and received food products from them. There were heavy frosts then and it was difficult to endure the conditions.

[Page 203]

As the Germans knew that there were many Jews still hidden, they issued an order that the Jews should enter a ghetto by 30 November 1942 and they would be permitted to live and work there. The Nazis declared that the "record of the expulsions already had ended."

Sixteen new ghettos were created then in the four districts: Warsaw, Krakow, Radom, Lublin. The nearest newly created ghetto to Żarki was in Radomsk (in Czenstochow there was only a labor camp, but no ghetto. There the Jews worked in factories important for the war).

Those hidden had no way out and remaining in the forest longer was impossible – they presented themselves and left for the ghetto in Radomsk. Among them were the Pilica Jews and the Wolbórz Jews. In this manner, a group of 5,000 Jews was created in the Radomsk ghetto. There were up to 10,000 in Radomsk until the first expulsion. They then were all sent away. Only 200 Jews were left to liquidate the Jewish possessions.

I was among those who went to Radomsk. The Germans concentrated all 5,000 Jews in seven large houses. One can imagine the kind of cramped conditions found there. There were 30 people in one room: [including] women and children. The conditions were terrible. Food was only available from Poles for large sums of money.

We were in Radomsk until 6 January 1943. Jews worked in only one wood factory (300 Jews), making sleds and wagons for the Germans. The Nazis gave assurances that "nothing bad would happen to all of the Jews because they were working for the Germans."

We sent a messenger to the Pilica forest to the partisans and we brought a Polish partisan from there to help us with the work because we, ourselves, had organized Jewish partisan groups of five people (*finferlekh* – fives). They, the Poles, needed to send us armed vehicles to take us to the forests, where the Polish partisans were found. However, before the Polish partisan leader arrived, another expulsion occurred in Radomsk (6 January 1943) and we no longer could reach the forests.

Three days before the expulsion, 3 January 1943, the Gestapo informed the *Judenrat* [Jewish council created by the Germans] that there was an opportunity to travel to *Eretz-Yisroel*. They created three categories: 1) citizens of *Eretz-Yisroel* and those who had passports from *Eretz-Yisroel*. 2) those who had close relatives who were residents of *Eretz-Yisroel*. 3) those who had more distant relatives in *Eretz-Yisroel*. The *kehile* [organized Jewish community] began to register Jews. The number of people was extraordinary. They stood in long lines until they could enter the office. Three thousand Jews registered. Later, the Nazis told the *Judenrat*, ostensibly "in secret," that they could only take 300 Jews. A new selection was made and a new list. Everyone had to give the exact address of his relative in *Eretz-Yisroel*. The mood improved a little. They hoped with enthusiasm and longing for *Eretz-Yisroel*.

Later, there was the thought that if a new expulsion occurred, they would not run. Running was beyond their strength. Constant running there and back, again a new place, again hunger, cold. It was decided what ever is, will be. They had no more strength to run again. In the meantime, the Germans added a few more houses to the ghetto and brought the Czenstochow Jewish doctors. They wanted to create a "ghetto atmosphere."

On 6 January 1943, the new expulsion took place. The German police along with Ukrainian and Polish police surrounded the ghetto and began the liquidation. I was in Radomsk then. All of the Jews were assembled at the *Judenrat* early in the morning. The Jews still remained in Radomsk that day. They were deported the next day. I myself saw all of the Jews taken out. Everyone was told to take along a small package of 10-15 kilos. Three hundred young, healthy Jews were chosen from the 5,000 Jews and sent to the labor camp in Skarzysko near Radom and Kielce. The remaining [Jews] were taken to railroad cars near the train. Their packages were taken from them and many of them (particularly those who were a little better dressed) had their clothing removed and they were packed into the railroad cars in their shirts. This picture was horrible. The crying and shouting went toward heaven because the Jews knew what awaited them. There were those among them who had escaped several times from various places. Among the deported were many women and children. Everyone was packed into the railroad cars and the railroad cars were sent to Treblinka that same day. Twenty-three Jews were left by the Germans to take care of the possessions [taken from the Jews].

[Page 204]

A few Jews succeeded in hiding in the bunkers, but after eight to 10 days, the Germans searched every house. Their number was then 350. They were taken outside the city; Poles were brought to dig pits. These Jews were shot and buried in a mass grave. Two boys (one 15-years old and one 13-years old) of the 350 Jews succeeded in escaping, because when the Germans told the Poles to dig the pits, the two boys moved closer, took spades and later left with the Poles. These two boys later came to Bedzin.

The final end of the Radomsk ghetto and the Jews in the surrounding *shtetlekh* [towns] came in that way.

I personally succeeded in escaping with 11 comrades. We bribed the German with a large sum of money. It was very dangerous to travel because the Nazi headquarters and all sorts of policemen were very strict. They often checked the identity of those passing by. Four of us finally arrived outside of the city. We hid in the house of a worker, rented a sled and went to Czenstochow.

The liquidation of the "large ghetto" in Czenstochow, in which there had been over 6,000 Jews, among them many from Lodz, Warsaw and Plock, had already taken place. Officially, there still remained 5,500 Jews as "working Jews," who worked in the labor camps in the city and in the area (Rakow *HASAG* [labor camp operated by the German company Hugo Schneider Aktiengesellschaft Metalwarenfabrik AG]), who worked on German armaments.

The large Czenstochow ghetto, which was created in 1942, took in the first *Aleje* [inclusive], the new market, Nadrzeczna, Kocza and the surrounding streets. At the liquidation of the "large ghetto" – on 22 September 1942 – the "small ghetto" remained which was located on Nadrzeczna, Garncarska and Kocza. The old and new markets no longer belonged to the ghetto. No one was permitted to live there; not the Poles, either. Whoever was found there was threatened with receiving the death penalty. Later, eight months after the expulsion, after a rigorous check, Poles were permitted to live there.

We did not see any children when we arrived in Czenstochow because the Germans only permitted those who worked to remain (only a few children remained who succeeded in hiding in bunkers). Men and women were not permitted to live in the same streets. Men were in one street, women in the other.

In many places, all of the Jews were gathered in one place and sent away. It was different in Czenstochow: the Germans, Ukrainians, Latvian and Polish police went from house to house. Leading out Jews, they were taken to the train station where the boxcars were; the Gestapo stood there. It did not make any difference if someone was working or not, who he was, what he was, age, gender and so on. The Nazi chief of the department also was there and he designated which of the Jews would remain and which not. The majority of the Jews was packed into the railroad cars and sent to Treblinka.

Five thousand five hundred Jews were left[1], designated by chance, mostly young people. Some [members of the] *Judenrat* also were deported. The expulsion lasted three weeks because there was a lack of boxcars in which to send out the Jews. The boxcars were brought again every other day to take the Jews. The expulsion was accompanied by a terrible quiet: the masses were subdued by desperation and exhaustion. They knew that there was no rescue and there was no way out.

One hundred and fifty Jews would be packed into a boxcar and the door would be closed. There were cases in which half of the passengers suffocated because of the lack of air. Everyone stood in the crammed boxcars, then in death itself.

[Page 205]

Many children were among those who suffocated. The Germans threw the children into the wagons like balls, playing with them savagely. Many children were killed during the "devil play." Many Jews committed suicide in their homes when the Germans came to take them. A large number of members of the intelligentsia were among those who committed suicide.

"This is our fate," many said in despair.

On 4 January, on the eve of the liquidation of the Radomsk ghetto, the Germans decided to assemble the 300 Jews who were not working just then and declared that they would be sent to Radomsk[2]. The revolt started then. The first incident was when a *halutz* [pioneer – one training for emigration to *Eretz-Yisroel*] took out a revolver and tried to shoot a Nazi. However, the Nazis around him threw themselves on him. He wrestled with a German policeman and severely wounded him. However, they [the Germans] got control of the Jew and as a punishment for daring to do such a thing, the Nazis shot every tenth Jew in a row. Twenty-one Jews were shot then. The remainder were sent to Radomsk and, from there, they were sent to Treblinka with the remaining [Jews in Radomsk].

I was in Czenstochow for several days. Every Jew in the ghetto wore not only a white patch, but also a number made of tin. The number meant that the Jews were allocated for designated work.

The Germans would remove a certain number of Jews (200 or 300) from the "small ghetto" every week and send them to the labor camp in Skarzysko where there existed terrible conditions, where they worked at hard labor for 16 to 18 hours a day and for which the Jews received 15 or 20 decagrams [five to seven ounces] of bread. Naturally, this did not sustain the majority [of Jews] and many died. Typhus also broke out immediately.

The *halutzim* young people decided to organize a defensive fight. The most important problem was collecting weapons and dynamite. They succeeded only in part. They obtained with great effort about 45 revolvers (they mainly were bought on the Polish side and also brought from other comrades in Warsaw). They organized a warehouse of weapons. They dug a tunnel of tens of meters that led from the "small ghetto" to the Polish side.

However, the Germans discovered the bunker when the master craftsmen were still at work. Before they looked around, the bunker already was surrounded by Nazis and the Jews could not make use of the weapons. The Germans immediately shot 30 comrades from our *kibbutz* [group] (who were located in Nadrzeczna Street). The remaining Jews were taken to two factories outside the city and they were not permitted to leave that place.

A number of *halutz* young people had left earlier for the forests of Koniecpol and Zlati-Potok to [join] the partisan fight. It was difficult to make contact with the Polish partisans and, therefore, we created an independent Jewish partisan division. They carried out various actions against the Germans in the area. We taxed the Jewish population to buy weapons. The Jewish partisans carried out actions against the Germans at the Ost railroad, where they destroyed the rails and blew up the rail switches. They carried out various acts of sabotage at the factories where the Jews worked.

At the beginning of 1943, Degenhart, the German leader of the Jewish ghetto, came to the chairman of the *Judenrat* and said to him that there was permission for 150 Jews to travel to *Eretz-Yisroel* and he should register the Jewish intelligentsia who would travel there. One hundred and fifty, who had already prepared to take their things with them, actually were registered. They were led out of the ghetto. Two trucks were waiting for them. They began to drive them to Olsztyn. As they were being driven, they already knew that they would be shot because the Nazis would bring the Jews and Poles on whom they had carried out a death sentence to the Olsztyn forest. Twenty-nine Jews from this group succeeded in escaping (among them Kapinski's son). The remaining 131 were shot in the forest and buried there[3]. It was later learned that this was a special action against the Jewish intelligentsia.

[Page 206]

I will add only that before the expulsion took place there was intensive productivity by the Jewish population. Each Jew tried to work in a factory or workshop that was led by the Germans in the hope that in this way they would save their lives. Almost 96 percent of the adult Jews worked in the factory, also in the very large one. They wanted to reestablish the large Jewish agricultural communal farm and Dr. Wendler, the German city chief, even agreed to it. The *Judenrat* declared its readiness to help. A Jewish delegation came there, but the Germans drove them out because the Poles also wanted to live there. The farm was settled by the Germans, who carried on their own agricultural activity there.

Footnotes

1. According to the report by A. Izbicki, the number reached 7,000. L. Berner said 6,500. (Editor)

2. According to a report by A. Izbicki, the Germans received an order to provide 100 Jews for Skarzysko.

3. According to the report by L. Brener, the mass murder of the Jewish intelligentsia took place at the Jewish cemetery.

Testimony

[Testimony] given (in Kiryat Anavim, in July 1944) by Avraham Izbicki, who came to *Eretz Yisroel* in May 1944

I left Poland at the start of 1944. I was in Czenstochow the entire time since the [start of] the World War and I experienced the persecutions and "resettlements" there. Later, I was forced to escape from Czenstochow and to hide in other Polish cities.

German Panzer troops occupied Czenstochow on Sunday, 3 September 1939. The entire Jewish population was in hiding. The first day after they took the city, the German soldiers behaved decently enough: they would enter the Jewish streets because they could communicate more easily with the Jews. They would shop in the Jewish stores and pay the exact amount. Many of them would come to Jewish houses and distribute chocolate among the children. And when individual anti-Semites would shout, "These are Jews," the soldiers would answer, "This is not important." The Jews were a little assured by this and left the cellars and hiding places. They then began to open the closed businesses and prepared for a more normal life.

This was the first day. However, immediately on the second day, Monday 4 September 1939, the situation changed radically. Monday, right at 12:30 in the afternoon, as if by order, every German soldier, wherever he was located, began shooting at the civilian population, at the women and children. In the course of just five minutes all of the streets – both where the Jews lived and where Poles were located – were covered with dead bodies. This was, ass it is well known to us, "Bloody Monday." The Germans, wanting to find a pretext, created a false accusation that they had been shot at. After this first mass murder, the Germans ordered the entire civilian population to leave their apartments for the street with up-raised hands; they were searched. Whoever moved from the spot or wanted to go to a child during the search was shot on the spot. The Jewish and Polish population was taken to four points: into two barracks and a church and to the jail (on Zawodzha [Street]). There was such crowding that in a small cell in which six arrestees normally were held, there were more than 140 people. We were held there for three days, without food and without anything to drink. Nine people died immediately by the second day. Many died later (after they were freed) from exhaustion.

The majority of Jews mainly were concentrated in the large Catholic cathedral (near the brewery), because they lived in the neighboring streets (Garncarska, Ogrodawa, Berka Joselewicza), New Market. The Germans shot into the church and a terrible panic arose. Many Jews were murdered then. The entire area of the church was in a pool of blood.

At freeing (after three days) the population, the Germans ordered everyone to to their employment, declaring: "From now on, everything will be in order." During the three days, while the population had been held by the Germans at separate points, the Nazis carried out searches of all the houses and they just carried out a pogrom: they stole everything that had some value. During the course of three days many people were murdered in the various parts of the city.

[Page 207]

A little while later, the Germans began to persecute, in particular, the politically engaged people, both the Poles and Jews. The intelligentsia, the workers and the communal workers suffered severely. Among the first Jewish martyrs who fell were Yitzhak Yakob Zarnowiecki, the leader of the former "Independent Socialists Workers Party," who was the secretary of the Czenstochow committee of *Poalei-Zion* [Workers of Zion] (Zionist Socialists) after the unification with *Poalei-Zion* (Zionist Socialists). Zarnowiecki organized the first Jewish kitchens, various cooperative institutions and heroically would help the Jewish masses during the worst times. He would restore everyone's courage and energy. The Germans arrested him and sent him to a concentration camp, actually a death camp in Auschwitz, where he was murdered after long torturing. Later, his wife in Czenstochow received an envelope with a small amount of ashes from Auschwitz... The same happened to Moshe Berkensztat, the Bundist activist and member of the community managing committee. The Revisionist activist, Shmuel Nemirowski, also suffered the same fate.

However, in comparison with other cities, the situation in Czenstochow was much better. We continuously convinced ourselves of this because many refugees would come to us, at first from other Polish *shtetlekh* [towns], which were absorbed into the Third Reich (Lodz and its surroundings, Wielun, Krzepice, Kolbuck, Pajęczno).

Thus was the situation until the summer of 1941 when the Germans entered the war with Russia. Then, the era of "resettlements" began, that is, the Jews were told to leave various *shtetlekh* and to go where they wanted to go. Then, the Plock Jewish population, among others, who also suffered the same fate, came to Czenstochow. The Czenstochow Jews welcomed the Plock Jews with extraordinary sincerity and warmth. They were given clothing and apartments. The small children were taken and given care. But despite all of this, the mortality of the Plock Jews was extraordinarily great (because of exhaustion and the suffering that they had been through). Dozens of funerals for the Plock Jews would take place every day.

The Statutory Residence Question

The matter of residential rights was bizarre and changed several times, however, for the worse.

a) At first, Jews had to live in a designated quarter that, however, was very large and encompassed most of the streets where Jews had lived earlier. Beginning from the train bridge in the First *Aleje*, across the old and new markets up to the prison bridge at Zaworcze [Street] on one side and from the bridge to Mate's factory across Krakower [Street] and Warszawer Street to "Three Crosses" Street. Totaling some 60 streets.

Jews could also own shops and places of employment outside the mentioned streets and the Jews could go freely through the city. There was no walled-in ghetto here. The Germans even forbid that the Jewish streets be referred to as a "ghetto." It was called *"dos Juden Wohn Firtil"* [the Jewish residence quarter]. The Christians had the right to enter [this area] and they traded with the Jews in the then self-evident pitiful conditions, when earrings or a wedding ring or a small watch would be sold for a small amount of beans, flour and other foods.

[Page 208]

b) In the second era (from 1941 on), the Jews no long were permitted to have shops and places of employment in the general part of the city, only in the *"Juden Wohn Firtil,"* where they had lived. Yet, Christians still had the right to come there. Jews could go to the Christian part of the city only with special permission. All of the large Jewish businesses and enterprises were completely taken over by the Germans. Or they remained under the Jewish firm but with a German commissar. The Jewish owners had to work there as employees. Also employed there as commissars were various people (Poles) who became "Germans" just at the start of the German occupation, as for example, Leszicki (a large merchant), Woloszcik (grocery wholesaler, earlier a *narodowiec* [nationalist] and Wladislaw Bonczek (previously a large coal merchant, activist with the *Sanacia* [Polish: "cleansing" political life of factionalism and corruption, a movement led by Marshal Josef Pilsudski]). When the Jewish workers, who carried out various work according to the orders of the Nazis, turned to them the last time for bread or a little water (if the Nazi controllers were not nearby) they answered that they knew no Polish. In addition, they threatened us with "consequences" if we turned to them again.

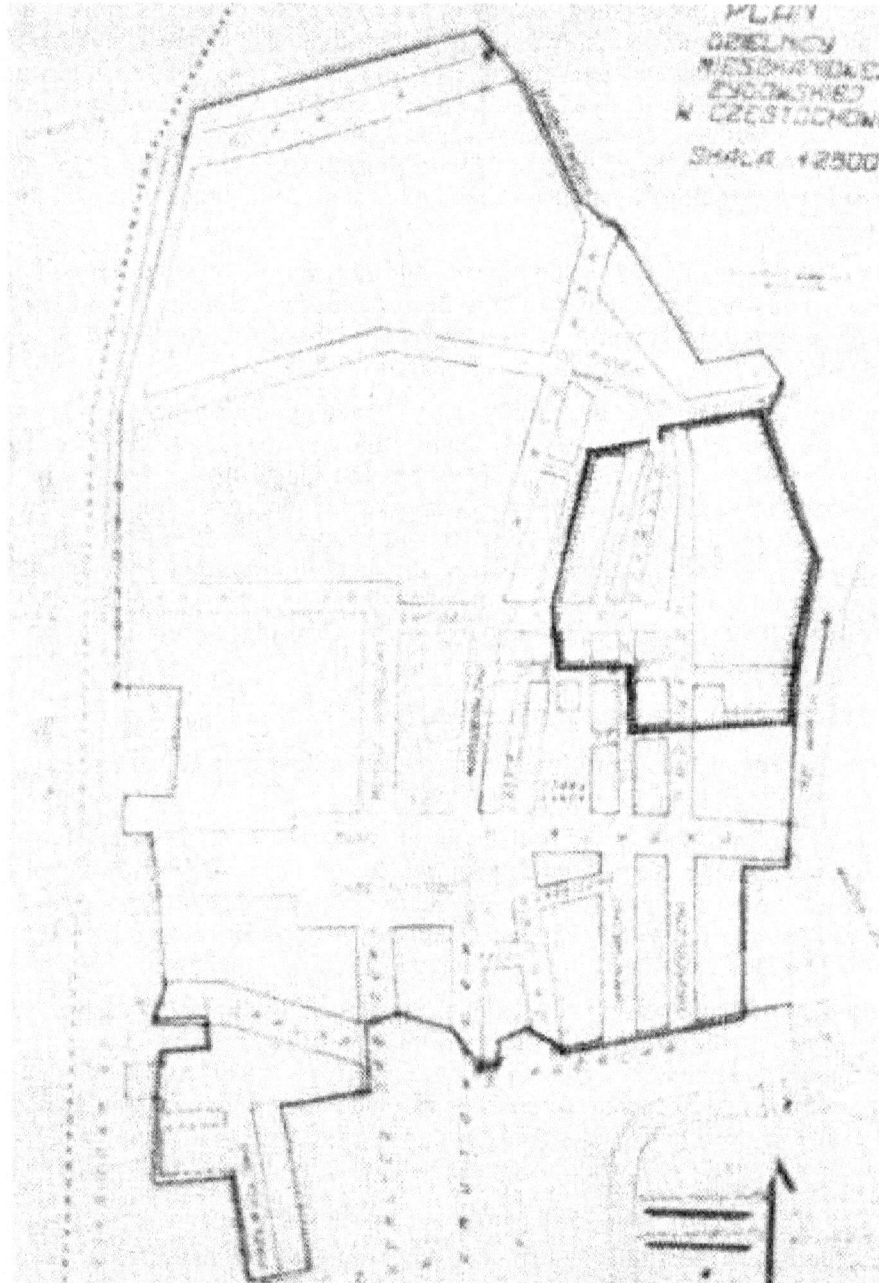

Map of the Large and Small Ghettos

A Ration Card

c) The third era began in March-April 1942. The ghetto was greatly decreased [in size]. Under the threat of death, the Christians were no longer permitted to enter the Jewish streets, which, incidentally, had already received the designation of ghetto.

Hunger was felt strongly then. Black bread cost 36 *zlotes* (two kilo of potatoes – four *zlotes*). Despite this, hundreds of Jews still left the ghetto for the Christian streets to buy a roll. They were shot on the spot when they were caught or denounced. However, the need was so terrible that immediately on the day after someone was shot for such a "sin," other Jews left the ghetto.

Parallel with this, forced labor increased. All Jews, men and women from the age of 15 to 55, daily (seven times a week) went to work at the Oest trains, to the power station, the water management of regulating the rivers, hotel service, army construction jobs, as well as at the heavy war industry and the important war industries, such as at the large Czenstochowianka, Mates and Enro (the Rotsztajn brothers' large Jewish iron factory). Many Jews would specially be sent to the two large factories, first Rakow and Pelcery which were now combined into an "arms factory" under the name *HASAG* [Hugo Schneider AG – a German metal goods manufacturer that ran a forced labor ammunitions factory].

d) The ghetto was decreased in size even more during the 4th era and all of the streets that cut a path through the Christian neighborhood were divided (for example, Tartakowa Street, Krakower, Strazacka, Wilson). The ghetto became "round" and was strategically prepared, particularly for the coming persecutions and murders.

The Liquidation

The situation for the Jews became constantly more frightening and grew worse. Young men from age 16 to 30 were sent away to various labor camps outside Czenstochow on special trains, as for example to Skarcziska in the Lublin area, then to the Radomsko area (Tapisz, Gidle). Day in and day out we would receive more terrifying news from them. Their mortality grew. They were brought back to Czenstochow shortly before the destruction (September 1942). We were very happy [about their return]. We did not know that they had been brought to Czenstochow in order for them to go with everyone to the most terrifying death.

At the beginning of September 1942 rumors began to spread that the liquidation of Czenstochower Jewry would begin on 22 September. Everyone trembled in fear because the earlier rumors about the liquidation of the *shtetl* of Włoszczowa (a neighboring *shtetl*) had come true. Therefore, the panic grew even greater. Jews took their best possessions to Christians, goods, jewelry, money, whatever they had so that – when it came to misfortune – they would be able to hide with the Poles or save themselves in any possible manner.

[Page 209]

Erev Yom Kippur [on the eve of Yom Kippur], the captain of the security police, Major in the *S.S.* [Paul] Degenhardt, called the chairman of the *Judenrat*, Y. L. Kapinski. Degenhardt had lived in Dąbrowa Górnicza before the war where he had his possessions. He was a man of 60, with a higher education, with outwardly good manners and thought of himself as a great intellectual and aristocrat. (He had a scar on his right cheek, evidentially from a duel.) He played a bloody role in the murder of the Jews in Czenstochow and in the neighboring cities. He was the commissar of the special *S.S.* Division 7 ("Jews Division").

Degenhardt called the chairman of the *Judenrat* and had him give holiday wishes to the entire Czenstochow Jewish population. He said that he knew of the mood of panic among the Czenstochow Jews, but that it was completely groundless. He knew that the Czenstochow Jews had the best reputation with the German regime; that they worked in the factories and that large military orders had just arrived for that branch of the industry in which the Jews worked. Finally, he asked Kapinski to calm the Jews and said they should always be devoted to him, adding: "I am their father and care about them." He said to Kapinski very secretly that on the 27th of the month [something] new would happen in Czenstochow, but not with regard to the Jews. Ten thousand Christians would be sent to Germany to work at digging potatoes. Thousands of young *S.S.* men arrived at the same time, but many people interpreted this as, Poles would be sent to Germany to work because Degenhardt had assured this [would happen].

The Jews went to *Kol Nidre* [prayer opening Yom Kippur services] with a heavy heart. My mother said to me, "Let us even have worse times next year for Yom Kippur, but let us be alive, let us just remain alive." The Jews walked with the *talisim* [prayer shawls] into the hidden houses of prayer. They cried terribly, like small children, raising their hands to heaven in the houses of prayer, asking for mercy. After having a good cry, the congregation went back to their rooms after *Neilah* [final Yom Kippur prayer]. They all kissed each other and with tears wished each other a better year, at least a year of life. The congregation, exhausted from fasting, went to sleep. The young people stood in groups and spoke late into the night, [saying] that they should not believe Nazi assurances.

The fate of the Czenstochow *Judenrat* was sealed on the same night. The ghetto was surrounded by several rings of hooligans at three o'clock at night, first by the Ukrainians, the murderers specially trained for this purpose (these were young people of 16 to 25 years of age). The German gendarmes stood near them; further on stood the Polish police, still further the Nazi police with heavy machine guns stood in a thick circle. Between these three rings swarmed Gestapo agents. A large number had come from neighboring cities (Kielce, Radomsko, Radom). They rode through the streets on motorcycles and made sure that everything was in order and according to orders.

The news about this spread among the population. We felt death hovering in the air; desperate scenes played out. We wrung our hands. We could not breathe. A devastating chapter of suicides began. The first took the life of Zalman Windman (Zalman the baker) from Garncarska Street, number 22. When someone tried to escape from the ghetto he was shot on the spot by a Ukrainian. However, a number of Jews succeeded in going through the "Ukrainian line" and they thought that they had been saved. But, immediately, they hit against the "second line," where the Germans stood, who fired machine guns. And in this way, hundreds of Jews were killed on this night.

At seven o'clock in the morning, all of the Jews were ordered to leave their apartments and to stand in the street in rows. Everyone was permitted to take a pack weighing 10 kilos. They were led to the marketplace (New Market) according to houses and blocks. There stood the Gestapo divisions with the above-mentioned Degenhardt at the head. He decided the fate of each individual Jew: with his walking stick, he indicated who should go to the left – these were those who were taken directly to the railroad cars at the Towarowa station "Warta" or he indicated going straight in the direction of the *Aleje*. These were taken through Wilson Street to Landau's factory building and to *Metalurgia*. I was designated for this group. These Jews, almost exclusively young people, were designated to remain in the city to carry out the liquidation of the ghetto. Degenhardt did not consider any criteria, if one had a trade and had a work card or not. He arbitrarily told someone to go to the left and another one straight. When members of a family did not want to separate, and many of those whom Degenhardt had told to go "straight" (that is to remain in the city), wanted to go to the left with their families (that is to death) rather than separating from the children and wives, the Nazi leader, laughing cynically, just told such a Jew to remain. He ridiculed people who were being transported, saying, "Do not be afraid; he will come to you later. You will all meet on a nice street in heaven."

[Page 210]

Those sick in the hospital were shot immediately on the first morning. The old and children who were in their homes and could not leave their residences were later shot on the spot. The small children, who were in the orphans' home, were murdered on the spot together with the old.

Every group that was transported to death consisted of 7,000 people who were packed into 60 transport railroad cars. Then the Germans paused for two days until the railroad cars turned around and came back and another 7,000 Jews were again packed. Thus did go such transports for four weeks.

After the first month, the transports left frequently and in smaller groups because these were Jews who had hidden in the cellars, in attics and so on. The Germans discovered them, searching everywhere with the help of trained police dogs. Groups were put together of these people and they assembled in the courtyard of Katedralna Street number 11 and they were deported later.

The Remaining

Those remaining at *Metalurgia* (7,000 Jews) were divided into various groups and sent to various *Metalurgia* offices, some to the "air force," "army service positions." They worked there and also slept there at night, always being heavily guarded by the German gendarmerie. Degenhardt or his representative, Master Rahn, would come there. They again "sifted through" the Jews and, of the 7,000, left only 4,000. Degenhardt would thus deliberately divide the family members, sending one to death. Telling the other one to remain alive. Although the unfortunate Jew in question wanted to go to death with his entire family.

The Germans created a new ghetto for the remaining Jews, a much smaller one fenced in with barbed wire and heavily armed by Ukrainians, Germans and Poles. The ghetto consisted of the streets: Nadrzeczna from number 48 to 90; from Garncarska Street (Straus's house) to the end of the street and Kaczka Street (Fajga's candle factory to the Warszawer market). The Jews were brought there every day. Every morning they were taken to work under police supervision, mainly to liquidate the previous ghetto. Seeing that Jews were living here, the Jews who had hidden in the streets of the newly designated ghetto crawled out of their hiding places. The Gestapo did nothing to them. Just the opposite – Degenhardt declared that he was very happy that there were still Jews. He ordered that they be treated well, especially the old and the children. Individual Jews from surrounding *shtetlekh* who had hidden in the forests reported to the new, smaller Czenstochower ghetto. If the Germans had until then shot on the spot every hidden Jews they had found or who had been denounced, now it was the opposite; now they did nothing to these Jews. They only brought them into the ghetto. Hundreds of Jews who had hidden in the forests and particularly in the burned and abandoned houses or who wanted to save themselves by jumping out of trains were denounced to the Gestapo agents by various Poles. The number of Jews reported in such a way reached 7,000. In addition to them, a certain number of the old and children, whose relatives did not want "to report" that they were hidden with them, would be given bread and water at night.

One morning Degenhardt came, asked that the Jew, Galster (from the *aprowizacja* [provision of food division] of the *Judenrat*) be brought and told him with a revolver in his hand: "If the poor Jewish children continued to be so badly supervised and cared for, he [Galster] would be shot... How are the small children guilty of the war, which is a misfortune from God?!" Galster answered that he had no way to give them more food. Degenhardt answered this: "Yes, you are correct," and ordered that Galster now receive special portions of milk and eggs for the children.

[Page 211]

People began to register the children, who had been hidden when the news about this spread in the ghetto. From then on, day in and day out, the children did receive special portions of milk and eggs. A short time later, Degenhardt came to the ghetto and said that, "If he had the assurance that several women would take good care of the children, they (the women) would be freed from work in order for them to only be concerned with the children." A special residence on Kacza Street was designated for the young children, numbering over 100. The children were treated well there. Degenhardt would go there every day; he would bring the children gifts and pat their heads.

A while later (in December 1942), on an extraordinarily frosty day, Degenhardt came to the children's house and ordered the gendarmerie to bring the children to the police station where the city hall was located at Warszawer market. Seeing that a certain number of children who had been registered were missing from the list, he ordered the *Judenrat* to bring the remaining children in two hours or, if not, they would be shot.

The children were brought. They immediately were thrown like stones into the garbage wagons and they were sent away to their death.

Before this, the children were undressed half naked and their clothing was taken. Many children began to freeze on the wagons because there was one of the strongest frosts. And Degenhardt personally stood nearby and his face beamed with joy that this time was distinguished with "success."

At the beginning of January 1943, 10 o'clock in the morning, when the Jews were outside the ghetto, Rahn, Degenhardt's representative, came and told everyone who remained in the ghetto doing various household work (cooking, peeling potatoes, transporting garbage, bringing coal for the cellars, and so on) to appear in rows. I was among them along with my younger brother. Soldiers arrived. Individual people among us were told to leave the autos. Later, it appeared that the Germans had received an order to provide 100 Jews for the labor camp at Skarcziska. However, standing in a rows, we began to think that they would send us to Treblinka.

At that moment, a young man from Radomsko, Mendl Fiszelewicz, left one of the rows. He was a *haHalutz* [member of the pioneers], belonged to the local group that had begun to arm itself and planned an armed struggle. Fiszelewicz came out with a revolver in his hand and with several others, threw himself at the Nazi representative Rahn, wanting to shoot him. However, the revolver jammed. A second comrade did shoot, but missed Rahn. The gendarmerie shot this comrade on the spot. Then Fiszelewicz threw himself at Rahn, threw him down on the ground, beat him over the head with the revolver and bloodied him. When Rahn tore himself away from Fiszelewicz, Fiszelewicz hid among the crowd. The gendarmerie ordered that the guilty one be given to them. When this was not done, the soldiers began to raise their rifles in our direction.

Then, Fiszelewicz himself stepped out and said, "Here I am, you dirty dog." Rahn and the other Nazis shot Fiszelewicz on the spot.

A division of gendarmes and Gestapo members arrived immediately and, as a punishment, decided to shoot every tenth Jew on the spot. My brother and I deliberately stood next to each other, so that if one of us were shot as the tenth in the row, at least the other one would remain alive. I was one of the 23 chosen to be shot.

We, the 23, were divided into two groups. The first group of 11 men were placed at the wall at the Warszawer market. Soldiers stood opposite them. We still thought that maybe they would not be shot. However, the soldiers received the order, "Shoot!" and all 11 fell. Those who were still breathing were shot a second time. Among them were the lawyer Rozensztajn, Leizer Trembacki and the baker Wernik.

Then the second group was told to go to the wall. I was among them, but none of us wanted to go voluntarily. One threw himself to the ground, another was pulled to the wall by his hair, two of us began to run and jumped over the wires. The Germans shot after them.

[Page 212]

And when all of the attention had turned to those escaping in their direction, I began to move toward the group of Jews that was on the square and was forced to watch the execution. I succeeded in doing this in such a way that I was saved from death. We were taken back into the ghetto and a number of us were sent to the labor camp at Skarcziska.

Several hours later rumors reached me that Rahn had counted those murdered and saw that one was missing and he knew [the person's] name. Because of this, I no longer went to work, but hid in a stall full of sacks and old things for several days. Later I learned that the rumors were false. However, because of my long absence, I had become "unclean" to the Germans. As a result I decided to get through the ghetto wires, although I knew that the chances [of success] were 99 percent against me. However, I was successful.

Jews Driven to Germany Through Czenstochow
by Shimeon Gotayner

The arrestees were driven from Tomaszow to Radomsk and from Radomsk to Czenstochow. The road to Radomsk was a good one; it was said to be even a happy one. The skies brightened. There was the smell of plants, forests and orchards and there was a more easy feeling about the experiences through which they had gone. There also was food to eat that day because the Tomaszow Bundist women had brought so much to eat that there also was enough to take with them.

Radomsk was the first city that had been almost completely destroyed. In the road: sprayed with gunfire and knocked down houses and entire streets, smoldering piles of ash and bricks. Our hearts again were saddened. The feeling of one's own loneliness was mixed with sadness because of the surrounding devastation. However, this was not thought of for long because the vehicle went further – to Czenstochow.

Were the Jews here tortured? The refined pain that was caused for them was so slyly thought out that it seemed that they had caused it themselves. The participation of the Hitlerist beasts in the torturing, in the painful "accidents" was absolutely clear: The accidents, it should be understood, were not accidents, but a precise, system of torture. Moreover, there was no lack of open torture.

Czenstochow appeared almost normal; the proletarian suburbs had mostly suffered from the bombardments and the center of the city through which the arrestees were taken barely had any signs of the bombardments.

It appeared that giant groups of prisoners and civilian prisoners had gone through Czenstochow because a Christian aid committee was working very actively on the main street of the city, distributing bread, wurst and tea to all passersby. Hundreds of old and young Christians were standing on the sidewalks, working very actively at distributing the food. Polish girls went from person to person, from vehicle to vehicle, not making any differentiation between Jews and Christians, giving everyone their portion of food. They did it with a full heart, but almost without speaking. Only a few of them spoke halting, interrupted words, full of pain and compassion. Everyone raised a hand to another's face to wipe a tear that rolled down the girlish cheeks.

The Polish girls and the Polish women really did not create a difference between Jews and Christians although it was rare that Jews received something to eat. The angry Hitlerist hands that guarded the arrestees did make a difference. As soon as the girls approached a group of Jews, such a hand began to chase [them] with words and if the words were no help – with a rifle.

[Page 213]

– Not allowed...

– They are Jews.

It was *erev* [the eve of] Rosh Hashanah (14 September) according to the Jewish calendar, but even the pious Jews among the arrestees had not calculated the days [and did not know what day it was]. Several Jews remembered that it was *erev* Rosh Hashanah when they were imprisoned in a kind of dark, underground hole in a kind of damp, musty cellar.

Several hundred Jews, who were sentenced to spend two entire days here together, were stuffed into this cellar. There probably was enough room for 200 people to stand. However, this was too great a luxury for the "accursed" Jews, as was said, so several hundred people were packed in. No one knew exactly how many people were in this cellar in the course of two days. It was impossible to count and no one thought to do so. What the hundreds of Jews survived during these two days was a true hell.

At first, no one understood what had been prepared for them. Everyone felt the restrictions from the first minute on. However, an hour passed and a second and it appeared that they had been pushed in not for minutes or hours but for a longer time and everyone was enveloped by terror. They thought: do not stand, do not sit, do not extend a hand. It became so suffocating in the cellar after two hours of confinement that there was [no air] to breathe. The perspiration poured off everyone, but even removing their clothing was impossible because people were so pressed together that they could not move their arms.

People covered in sweat stood pressed together like herring in a cask for the entire night. The hope smoldered in everyone that the situation would change in the morning and they would be taken on their distant way. People can never know what will turn into their greatest hope. That night the several hundred Jews had such an elementary thing as a little fresh air as their ideal. That night no one thought about the fact that he was hungry. Everyone was thirsty, but no one said anything about it – the most terrible thing that night was the feeling that everyone had been confined in the cellar so that they would lack air and that they would die.

Several people succeeded with the application of a series of gymnastic movements to take off their jackets and shirts. By touching each other, one bathed the other in sweat, which ran from the body. They spoke very little to each other. However, the little bit of conversation that was expressed whirled around only one question: a little air.

Weary, tired, several men fell asleep on the sweaty shoulders of each other – it should be understood – while standing. A middle-aged Hasidic Jew in a distant corner, it seems, remembered that it was Rosh Hashanah and he quietly and sadly began to murmur melodies from the Days of Awe. All of the wells opened at once. Crying broke out in the cellar, like in the woman's section of a synagogue. At first, individuals sobbed, then it became a general cry...

Thus passed this terrible night. But the new day did not bring any salvation. Hour after hour passed. The sunny day outside was seen through the small, four-corned cellar windows. However, no one thought to open the door and set free those imprisoned. They had ceased talking about eating and drinking - they had not been given [food or drink] on the entire way here [to the cellar].

Open talk about the Bund began among the arrestees. The men breathed with their last strength. In such moments, a strange, unlimited stubbornness to live, to persevere, to spite the oppressor awakens in the most tortured people. They did talk among themselves in the cellar that they must do something, that they must not let themselves be tortured.

– Let happen what ever does – individuals among the arrestees said in desperation. – but the Hitlerists must learn that we will defend ourselves.

A fog lay in their brains. The idea worked slowly with everyone. No one even tried to control his thoughts of the feasibility of any stand they would take. Thus, suddenly a roar arose from several dozen voices:

[Page 214]

– Water!...

– Water!...

– We are dying!...

The face of a young German Hitlerist appeared in one of the small windows.

– *Was los*? [What is happening?]

He asked as if he did not understand what was happening here. Several dozen voices suddenly rushed up to the window. One rang with supplications, another with anger. There was no differentiation in the words. Everything was mixed in one great shout:

– Air!...

– Air!...

– Air!...

– Water!... We are dying!...

The Hitlerist did not answer at all. The face disappeared from the small window. For a while it was quiet both in the cellar and outside. However, for only a short time – a few seconds. The laughter of several voices echoed outside. It appears that the Hitlerist told his comrades there what was happening in the cellar and they, the human beasts of the 20th century, reacted to it with laughter...

Again, some time passed, this time longer and, in the suspenseful quiet that reigned over the cellar, it could be heard that the Hitlerists were driving by outside the window. Suddenly, a flood of water flowed through the little window. It came over the heads of those standing closest [to the window] with a reinvigorating freshness as if someone had created the greatest pleasure. A shout of pleasure came from everyone:

– Ah, ah, ah!...

There was a commotion in the cellar. They began to push towards the small window; we began shouting out to the Hitlerists that they should let the water flow in through the other window.

The Hitlerists did wait for us to ask; they showed their "mercy" – they permitted water to flow in through all the windows without end. Everyone was up to their ankles in water, but everyone asked that the water be permitted to continue to pour in. The hydrant outside worked obediently. Everyone stood soaked like cats; their clothes were pasted to their bodies and moistened to the last thread. At first, it did not bother anyone. There were those in the cellar who gathered the water with their hands in the air and brought it to their lips. A kind of mania reigned over the cellar.

The madness withdrew when the hydrant was shut off. First, everyone began to feel the curse that had come with the relief; everyone was standing in water up to their ankles. Those among the imprisoned who were still wearing shoes felt the torment less. But quickly it was felt by everyone that the Hitlerists had favored them with a little water that had been turned into a curse.

However, a new hope suddenly flashed. The door to the cellar opened and two young, smiling Hitlerists appeared on the threshold.

– Are you labor Jews?...

– Labor Jews out!...

A flow of fresh air invaded [the cellar] when the door opened. A burning eagerness was awakened to leave the cellar at any price. Almost without exception, there was a rush to the door; everyone shouted that they were labor Jews. Only individual, stubborn religious men did not try to leave because they did not want to desecrate the God-fearing day of Rosh Hashanah. However, many of them did rush to the door, but had to remain inside because the Hitlerists counted several dozen men and took them outside.

When they returned two hours later, they were a group of broken men. They had been a little refreshed outside, but what they described in broken voices was terrifying: they had been tortured outside with refined sadism.

One group had been led deep into a courtyard to some sort of toilet, which was not only full of excrement from the inside, but also on the outside. It appears that on their last day, large masses of people had relieved themselves here and no one had cleared away the excrement. Large mounds of excrement even lay around the wooden toilet building and the stink, which was everywhere. was unbearable.

[Page 215]

The Jews were forced to clear away the excrement with their hands. The Hitler-beasts stood from afar and mocked them. During the "work," they [the Germans] thought of other things [for the Jews to do]. For example, one moment, they forced the Jews to "play-act" in a bakery of sweets: they had to form small cakes from the excrement! Later, they were forced to taste the "baked goods." Others were forced to smear their faces with excrement. The beasts beamed with delight at all of this that they had thought up and when the tortured men began to vomit, the Hitlerists gave out such joyful whinnying, like African cannibals.

Another group was taken somewhere else to another corner of the courtyard and they had to exercise murderously! They were forced to run at superhuman speed, kneel and use their feet like speed racers on bicycles and so on.

It was not so easy for the bicycle riders. First, the groups were lined up and they were asked who among you knows how to ride a bicycle and then, when dozens of young men had announced voluntarily that they could, they had to do these "exercises."

Finally, everyone was placed in a line and one had to hit another one. First, one just hit the other, then the one who had been hit had to hit back the other because he had dared to hit him and after all of this, the Hitlerists battered both as a punishment because they had not hit each other hard enough...

The two days that the Jews spent in the Czenstochow cellar and in the torture yard that were described here were truly Days of Awe [the High Holy Days – Rosh Hashanah through Yom Kippur] for them. No one wanted to go to work in the morning, but they were driven with rubber clubs. Men could barely stand on their feet because of hunger and lack of air. They fainted en masse. They begged for death a thousand times.

However, death did not come. The reserves of the human organism were exhausted. However, the group was still on its feet after the two terrifying days.

When everyone was led out of the cellar on Rosh Hashanah and taken to the train, they dragged themselves like shadows. However, no one lagged behind. They were no longer men, but a weak people.

They did not know yet that they were very, very far from the end...

The Destruction of the Synagogue
(New Synagogue)
by L. Brener

It was on the night of 24 December 1939, barely four months after the Germans occupied Czenstochow.

On this night when the Christian world celebrates the birthday of the creator of their religion who preaches love of people, brotherhood and tolerance, the German Christians with the aid of dark elements in the Polish population did one of their most shameful deeds in our city. They burned and destroyed the Czenstochow synagogue, known to us in the city as the "new synagogue."

The writer of these lines lived close to the synagogue so that he had the opportunity to observe this shameful act happening in the street although I did not want to see it.

Even in pre-war Poland, Jews avoided appearing in the street on the night of *Boże Narodzenie* [Christmas], not wanting based on their understanding of the anti-Semites, to provoke the religious feelings of the Polish population. Because our familiar Polish anti-Semites wanted to make use of every feeling of the Polish masses against the Jews. During the war years when we were under German rule, if such irrational impulses broke out on the part of the Polish population, they would bring sadder consequences.

[Page 216]

Because of the usual fear that the Germans had provoked, we confined ourselves to our residences. We did not even come together often with neighbors so that we would not be accused of holding a meeting and speaking about politics and against the Germans.

Therefore, on 24 December 1939 the Jewish population in Czenstochow withdrew to their residences and rooms with the fall of night, although they were still permitted to appear in the streets under the police curfew.

Suddenly the wild screaming of Polish young people mixed with German exhortations was heard on Garibaldi Street (once Spadek Street), and the throwing of stones at the windows of Jewish residences began immediately. This was the first portent of something bad.

The Main Entrance to the Synagogue

And several minutes later it could be seen how the German and Polish hooligans threw incendiary bombs into the synagogue.

The fire quickly engulfed the innermost facilities of the synagogue. The chairs, the Torah reading lectern, the Torah ark and the Torahs, candelabras and all other parts of the house of prayer were destroyed by fire that spread further.

The synagogue in which Jewish Czenstochow took pride, the place where we would come together for every celebration, the house which had had H.N. Bialik, of blessed memory, as a guest. Here where the musician, singer and composer, Avraham Ber Birnbaum had an effect and created, this building ceased to exist.

The cry of Fishel the *khazan* [cantor] of this synagogue, may he rest in peace (perished during the deportations in September 1942), when the flames of the fire chased him and his family from the residence he occupied near the synagogue, still rings in my ears. A cry of grief and rage tore from his chest. He cried over the destruction of the Czenstochow synagogue.

But not only the most internal facilities of the synagogue were burned then.

Like the example of the Judaistic Library at the Warsaw synagogue, such a library also existed at our synagogue in which was found religious and secular literature. Czenstochow Jews, pious and liberal, old and young, would come there every evening to read, to do research, to study and to learn. We had a spiritual rest there after a difficult workday. Treasures from Yiddish literature, religious books, manuscripts collected and donated by Jews from all over the world were found in the library. The cantorial literature, melodies written by Avraham Ber

Birnbaum, may he rest in peace, were the only copies or one of a few copies of a kind, a thing that can no longer be printed.

They [the Germans] annihilated the written Jewish word with a kind of wild, sadistic joy. It was reminiscent of the *auto-da-fé* of Caliph Omar, who in Cairo burned everything that was against the Koran, [but here] everything that was against *Mein Kampf.*

It should be understood that the fire, the god of destruction, continued to be victorious, as if living people had spit out the flames into the sky. It seemed as if they were screaming and asking why?... There was the danger that the flames would carry over to the neighboring houses.

But the Germans "took care" that the fire would not spread. So the firemen arrived with their equipment and tools. However, their role was to make sure that the fire would not spread and encompass houses neighboring the synagogue. The synagogue itself had to burn. The large tower of the synagogue with the *Mogen Dovid* [Shield of David – the Jewish star] at its top fell down at exactly midnight (a symbolic hour). At three at night the fire was extinguished, grew weaker, a small fire smoldering here and there and burned the remainder of the former large synagogue.

[Page 217]

Interior of the Synagogue during the 150ᵗʰ Anniversary of the Independence of the United States, 1776–1926

[Page 218]

External Appearance of the Synagogue after it Burned

Czenstochow Jews assembled around the burned synagogue early in the morning, marveled at the cruel action of the German murderers and mourned its former magnificence.

During the years 1941–1942, the writer of these lines, along with the *gabbaim* [sextons] Markowicz, Manhajt, Dawidowicz, and Mic had the honor through various ways and means to save the synagogue from complete destruction. Because the Germans were not satisfied with burning the synagogue; they wanted to destroy the brick walls completely, to destroy the Jewish sanctuary.

But through the material efforts of the above-mentioned Jews with several members of the middle class for whom the synagogue was dear and loved and through the devotion of the writer of these lines, the complete destruction of the synagogue was successfully avoided.

Today, its walls stand as a memorial to the former magnificence of the Czenstochow *kehile* [organized Jewish community] and as a stain of German barbarism.

A Night in the Czenstochow Ghetto
by A. Izbicki

Everything I have written until now had been about my life in the bunkers. And this was in Bedzin, in Upper Silesia, but not in Czenstochow. I pose the question many times as to why it is easier for me to write about my underground life in other places and avoid the horrible tragedy of my own city? Is it that I am unconsciously afraid that my heart will burst or that only when I think about something else am I successful in freeing myself from the terrible images that always appear before my eyes and accompany me every step of the way?

And how can one write something about Czenstochow? My entire life would be too short to completely describe even one street, one alley, Garncarska, for example! Where will I find the words and the years to describe how our alley looked on the day of destruction? I will now try to describe one house. Let this house be 23 Garncarska.

It was a house like all of the houses on Garncarska, Mostowa, Korczaka, Senatorske or Kaza. Three tailors, two quilters, a glazier, a carpenter, a tinsmith, hat maker, bakery, a dairy, three market sellers, a *dayan* [religious judge], a house of prayer – actually an entire *shtetl* [town]. Almost all of the girls went to the factories. The boys all went to *kheder* [religious primary school]. However, everyone learned something different. One was a fervid Zionist, another a leader of the young Bundists, a third was a leader of the communist movement. And not only did they study in the same *kheder*, but they played in the same sand in the courtyard, just as their fathers and grandfathers had done before them. And there would have been more generations in the same corner playing in the same sand. But I remember, yes, I remember very well that on the day, on the last day, that children, the last children played in the same corner...

Everyone was in the courtyard that day. Everyone, everyone, women, children, young and old. Children from other houses came here with their fathers and mothers. The fathers and the mothers came to the old courtyard of their youth, to the house of their youth, to their parents' house. And everyone was in the courtyard! As the finale of a horrible play.

Half of the Jews already had been taken away from the city. Street after street, house after house.

[Page 219]

It was already the 10ᵗʰ day that the ghetto had been surrounded. Today was again a quiet day. While last night, 60 wagons had gone to Treblinka. They would not return until the morning. There was no doubt that in the morning it would be our turn. And everyone in the courtyard was silent and if a word was spoken it would be heard clearly by all. And every word cut like a knife:

– A girl said, "My young years, alas, my young years, woe is me."

– And a grey grandmother said, "And for what have I lived to be so old, for what has God given me so many years!"

And the children play in the sand, weak, tired, pale. The day before yesterday, the housing committee had divided the last food that was made from the dirt that was scraped off the ground in the bakery. Everyone received a spoonful of soup. It was already three weeks since the ghetto was surrounded with murder, so that a cat could not worm its way outside. Night was falling, the last night. Everyone knew it. Clearly! The question that the small children, the adults asked suffocated them, "Why? Why?"...

And yet a little joy appeared that went from house to house. The little bit of joy on the last evening before annihilation. It was thus:

A son could not watch the grief of his old mother and he told a lie taken from thin air that in another courtyard there were signs that the extermination had ended... that an order had arrived from Berlin... and that the last transport had been sent back home... and we had been helped. And believing it recklessly like children, one told the other. Everyone believed it because they wanted to believe it... There immediately was great joy. We had new strength. We jumped with joy, wished each other *mazel–tov* [good luck, a wish of congratulations], kissed each other and cried with joy.

Anyone with doubts immediately saw that this was the truth... Because one could see that they were dancing with joy in the neighboring courtyard and they were shouting over to us, *mazel–tov, mazel–tov*!

We talked and tried to learn what had brought the help until the grey day. One said that it had been ordered from Berlin because the Jews were needed for work. Another said that the same would be done to the Germans in America, so they [the Germans] were afraid.

– "But why was the entire guard still standing around the ghetto," someone asked.

– "Why? Because they had not received the order," another one answered immediately.

They wanted to interpret everything for the good; they believed until the last minute, hoped, wanted to live. But...

A few hundred wagons on carriage springs drove into the ghetto at six o'clock in the morning. The same wagons as would appear before in order to take away the old and the children to train cars and to gather the dead. (The old and the children who could not come out to the street were shot in the houses and their bodies were carried out on stretchers. It was not necessary to wait for long this time. Let it already end... Survive it... It already was good for those who had gone with an earlier transport... They had already survived...

Thus appeared the last day and the last night in the house on Garncarska in which I was born. I had seen everything myself and still do not believe it all myself that it is no longer there... Although I was one of the last who left the house to be taken to the wagons. Later, I was taken with many other young people to make order in the houses (we were left for a short time for this purpose) and I was in my house, too. We did not see any living people, many dead. Walls were sprayed with blood, windowpanes were broken. And everything was so black, so dark. I saw everything myself, but when I think about my house on Garncarska today, I still see the courtyard of the past, entirely as it once was. I also see the children like me... and the same corner in which I played...

[Page 220]

The Last 24 Hours in *HASAG*

by D. Koniecpoler

1.

On the morning of Tuesday, 16 January 1945, the *HASAG* [*H.A.S.A.G.* is the acronym for a German metal goods manufacturer, *Hugo Schneider Metallwarenfabrik Aktiengesellschaft* – ammunition factory] construction system did not have the same face as the day before.

Early Monday, at five o'clock, we were awoken as usual by the trumpet; everyone went outside for the roll call. The *S.S.* man and the Jewish camp leader, Goldsztajn, who had been brought here from the liquidated Plaszow-Krakow Jewish concentration camp, still slapped and kicked people for not reporting exactly how many prisoners the *kapowa* (group leader) was taking out of the camp to work or for not marching straight and the like. Thus would the day begin in the newly led "Jewish Concentration Camp Czenstochow," as our factory camp had been called since 1 January 1945. The groups of workers who worked in the city were let out of the camp. It could have been thought that the day was going its normal way. Later, it first appeared that the number of Jews in the four ammunition factories in Czenstochow had decreased by 4,000 souls.

In the evening, coming back to the city from the work, we found a different camp, where everything was packed, the fear and panic indescribable. In the morning, Tuesday, all of the women were supposed to be sent away from the camp. This meant that a new *aktsia* [action, usually a deportation], a fresh "segregation" and the result – fresh Jewish mass graves somewhere in a collection camp. It was particularly suffocating for the few Jewish couples who despite the hardships and pain were still together. They understood that their last hour of their life together, which consisted of seeing each other from time to time, had arrived. Who could express the deep sorrow of these [couples]? None of them dreamed that they would see each other again in this life. The same tragedy was lived by the individual Jewish mothers, who had their young or older children with them. They waited in deadly fear that in a few hours they would be torn from their dearest and holiest possessions. But the hand falls. A number of men ignored the prohibition of being in the women's barracks and remained with their wives and mothers during the last hours and heart-wrenching, choking cries and heartbreaking sighs were the chorus of this sleepless night.

The great and cruel helplessness against the refined murderer of the Jews hung over everyone like a heavy black cloud. Around one at night, the guard, the cripple Sztiglic, arrived and announced that the women were not going and in the morning it would be a normal workday. But who believed him?

2.

Tuesday morning, 5 o'clock. We assembled at the camp square. There was no roll call. The *S.S.* man came and left. It appeared that he did not have any precise instructions. Their Jew, Goldsztajn, who had his large canine paws ready to beat the "*hunde*" [dogs] and "*schweine*" [pigs], as he called the Jews, had to have a little patience. Meanwhile he struck out his swinish chest and shouted and shrieked at us, the tortured and dejected. Thus was the nightmare of 15 and 16 January 1945.

The moon was slowly extinguished. The clear rays [of the sun] from the east broke through. The day woke up, but who among we slaves watched this magnificent game of nature? We did not even feel the cold in our bones after standing in the frost half naked for two hours. We were dominated by fear: what would the ray of the sun bring us? What had the evil devil known as Germans prepared for us?

Only the bakers, who baked bread for us in the city, were let out of the camp. Everything was in tense expectation. The labor camp was almost empty when daylight spread over the horizon. Everyone entered the barracks to warm their limbs a little. Suddenly an order: The mass murderers were all fastidious about "tidy and clean."

The director of the factory, Mr. Lit, came with all of the factory foremen. The square quickly became filled with the Jewish slaves, who were driven out of the barracks. Each carried his small bundle. It seemed that the factory was being reorganized with a smaller "number of workers." Laborers from the "human material" were taken from the various divisions at the large ammunition factory. It was a strange picture of human shadows who had had all of the sap of life extracted by the hunger and cold, by nakedness and resignation, who strove to work in the munitions affiliate. What is remarkable? If one lost their workplace, it meant being sent away on a "transport."

[Page 221]

The German foremen drove away. They each had chosen their number of workers. Those remaining immediately were surrounded by the "factory security" (factory police) and large rows of women formed who were taken right to the train station. Our group was reduced in number. The night before, 1,800 men left the camp, today approximately 1,300 women. They were sent with a little bread, canned food; and then Jewish children left. Perhaps, perhaps you will yet see a free world. Meanwhile, you traveled to the Auschwitz death camp. And the hangmen already prepared for the [arrival of] their victims.

3.

For a while a thought flashed in the mind of a *HASAG* Jew who lived in a constant nightmare. He asked himself:

The great Russian offensive had begun. There were rumors that Kielce and Włoszczowa have been taken; the victorious Russian army of liberators was marching a few kilometers from the city. The bandits truly did not have any important work. How should they deal with the Jews? The train cars, which were needed to "roll to victory," were being used for the hated Jews. What was actually happening here? However, there was no time to reflect.

The divided workers dispersed to their work; there was no time even to cry for our sisters and brothers who had been torn away. Yesterday in the factory we had been more than 4,000 Jews; today not even 2,000. But who thought about this. Those hidden again created workplaces to be able to receive a portion of bread and soup.

The mood was very oppressive. No bread had been distributed today. In trading, two kilos (five pounds) of dark bread that the Polish workers smuggled in cost 100 *zlotes*. But who would allow themselves to indulge? Therefore, we rejoiced at the news that at noon, the kitchen would distribute [food]. The wooden boxes were carried through the factory. And the worker-slaves, starved, tired, weary from pain and worry, devoured the soup. Suddenly: Bang! Bang! A pilot was attacking the city. So unexpected. Bombs flew in the air. They exploded with a primordial roar. The air literally shook. We felt the entire horizon move. A fire bomb exploded not far from the factory and the just built barracks stood in flames. Everyone was confused. The factory [work] stopped immediately. Rumors spread that the German foremen were leaving the factory; that the director, Lit, and the major, Zauer, the chief of the *S.S.* and of the concentration camp, stood ready with small packages in their hands and were waiting for means of communication. What had happened? Had the mass murderers been frightened by the bombardments or was the liberation really so close that they all had to escape? Who could know? Of course, we under threat knew nothing. We simply rejoiced at the frightening explosions, at the giant flames that we observed. All of us were tortured in the same way. Each of us wanted to die quickly from a bomb rather than to continue to live such a life. We were sure that the mass murderers would not release us from their paws. Therefore, the strong explosions had absolutely no effect on us. Just the opposite, we were ruled by a strong desire for the explosions to be stronger and more resounding and that we would perish.

The train line to Germany ran not far from the factory. We observed the German soldiers running to it and stopping a locomotive and jumping onto it in a terrible panic. We did not believe our eyes. The German Army was truly in flight?

Alas, a *HASAG* Jew could not think about this for long, even on the historic day of 16 January when a new world was arriving to replace everything bad and frightening that had been on the rampage until then. Those enslaved here, realized that the large and small murderers were being pushed out. The *werkschutz* [factory security] leader, Herman, his representative, Sztiglic, and the entire mob of *werkschutz* drove all of us Jews into the camp. It became clear to us that the last act was approaching. Everyone searched for those closest to them to be together during the last hours or minutes. We repacked the knapsacks and took only what was most needed. Others did not want to take any pack at all, for what? A second passed and we all stood arranged on the camp square.

[Page 222]

The day passed. The sky was covered with a dark-blue color. We had the impression that nature did not have the boldness to illuminate so much grief and pain. Everything became grey from the oncoming, difficult night, from this night that was to bring us so many surprises. We, who had gone through so many tortures. Our dearest and closest had been taken away and shot before out eyes. Forty thousand Czenstochow Jews. We watched, on 3 January 1943, how the two heroic Jewish young people, Isha Fajner and Fiszelewicz, who, with weapons in their hands, threw themselves at the murderer, Rahn. This was the moment when Rahn wanted again to send hundreds of Jews to Treblinka and had shot 25 Jews on the square. On 20 March 1943, the *Judenrat* [Jewish council], all the doctors and, in general, those members of the intelligentsia and their families who remained, were shot, among them 40 small children. We were witnesses on 26 June 1943 to how at the liquidation of the small ghetto, the mass murderers shot approximately 800 Jewish and then, again, on 25 July, the same number. At the same time, Laszinki and Kestner, the two camp leaders, the German security policemen daily shot and burned Jews at the stake.

And here we stood again and looked at our murderers in the eyes and quietly asked ourselves: What had they again devised for us? What refined torture or means of death had they thought up for us on this night? Who knew?

4.

An order came "to start." My eyes met Dr. Szperling. Was this our last act! We all stood arranged among our bundles and waited for further orders.

Suddenly the moon rose in her complete splendor and illuminated we human children. We did not know what this meant. Was it her [the moon's] last parting with us or an omen of something new, something unexpected for us?

Meanwhile, another order thundered:

– March ! ! !

We bowed our heads. Everyone took a quick look at the square. We would not see it again. How sad life here was for us. Would it be more difficult there in the new, unknown camp?

Not reaching the exit gate – Back in the barracks! – thundered another order. We went like driven sheep.

Rumors reached us that street fighting with the liberating Red Army was taking place in the city. A Jewish wagon driver said: he himself had seen Russian tanks, had traveled with Germans himself – over dead Germans. And all of this was happening while we were under the threat at the very end of the city, guarded by the greatest murderers, by the vilest hangmen.

At around nine o'clock the *werkschutz* [factory security] leader, Herman, an *S.S.* man and the *werkschutz* Daraszenka entered the camp and ordered: "Everyone out on the square and march with them." Everyone assembled on the square, but no one wanted to go to the exit gate. Anyone who did not see this could not imagine how human instinct dictated that a mass [of people] would defend themselves in a time of danger.

The Germans roared wildly:

– This way, left to the gate!!!

They beat and pushed and it did not help. The mass [of people] drew back from the tower, swirled together. The security men pleaded:

– Children, for your good!

– This way, left to the gate!

The instinct to fight among those tortured by the torturer was wonderful. There was no possibility of any sensible calculation at this moment; we struggled against leaving the ghetto driven only by the instinct to survive.

5.

Suddenly, bursts of fire and explosions that shook the air cut through the dark horizon. Without stop, there was a thunder of bangs, the echo of the first explosion had not been stilled and a second and third already had come. We looked at it. We did not hear and did not see the Germans. It appeared that they had left. However, our group had also decreased. The devils had still succeeded in tearing away several hundred Jews. Those remaining were uneasy: What if they [the Germans] returned?

The bombardment did not stop. We already recognized the distinct artillery shooting. Intense flames had appeared in the city, which tore into the extreme darkness like guides for the unfortunate, as if they were crying out:

Rip apart the wire!!!

Go free!!

We, fiery columns, will lead you, enslaved, people to your freedom!

And thus as if pushed by the cry, a group of "prisoners" decided to break out from the *HASAG* and go to welcome freedom.

[Page 223]

The Activity of the Jewish *Ordnungsdienst* (Jewish Police)

(Excerpt from the Statistic Book Published by the *Judenrat* [Jewish Council] in 1940)

As has been deduced from the attached copy, the *ordnungsdienst* [Jewish ghetto police] had another name at its beginning. Several members of the leadership were quickly arrested by the *schutz-polizei* [security police] under various charges and abuses of their power. A new leadership was designated. Starting in April 1941, the *IRU* [*Inspekcja Ruchu Ulicznego* – traffic inspection] received the name, Jewish *ordnungsdienst*.

Although in comparison to the Jewish police in other cities, the *ordnungsdienst* in Czenstochow behaved tolerably, it did carry out its sad role [here], serving the German government organs. The Jewish policemen were sure that in this way they would save themselves and their families from death. For the entire time of its existence it most energetically provided assistance with all of the decrees from the German government organs so that they could be carried out in full by the Jews in the ghetto: they grabbed [Jews] for work; searched for those who hid from work, guarded the transports that were to be sent to various labor camps. Particularly sad was their role at the time when the "resettlements" began. It was they who had to call out in the courtyards where Jews lived that the Jews had to appear for the *aktsia* [action, usually a deportation]. They called out that the Jews who were hiding in various bunkers should come out because the *aktsia* had ended and hundreds of Jews, believing them, paid with their lives in Treblinka.

A Type of Jewish Policeman

The saddest was the role of the Jewish police in the small ghetto. Their power was unlimited here and they made use of it to the full extent possible. They worked to reveal thefts, except those in which they themselves were involved, and they punished the criminals, chasing them to work and uncovering those who turned away from work. The played the main role in discovering bunkers with hidden Jewish property. Each *ordnungsdienst* was required to present a certain number of older people, or mothers and children at each resettlement action and they fulfilled this perfectly. In all of the hiding places, where there were large numbers of children and which the Germans and the Polish *granat* police [Blue police – Polish police in the Nazi-occupied area of Poland known as the General Government] could not find or were afraid to search, the Jewish policemen found [them] and with their active help, the Germans could locate and annihilate the majority of the remnant of survivors and families hidden with great self sacrifice. Their sad role ended on 20 July 1943 when they and their wives and children endured the same fate as more than 400 victims, who were killed then in the Czenstochow *HASAG* [a slave labor camp of *H.A.S.A.G.*, the acronym for the German metal goods manufacturer, Hugo Schneider Metallwarenfabrik Aktiengesellschaft] concentration camp.

L. Brener

Official Report

Six and a half thousand Jews, who were enclosed in a small ghetto, remained in Czenstochow after the deportation of the Jews. At the initiative of the Bund, an interparty conference to create a resistance movement was called at the hall in which the Zionist young people lived (later this became the collective). Taking part in the conference were the Bund, the left *Poalei-Zion* [Workers of Zion – Marxist-Zionists], communists, *HaShomer* [the guard – Socialist Zionist youth movement], Gordinia [Zionist youth movement] and regular Zionists.

A fighting organization was created as a result of the conference, which took for itself as a task to defend the ghetto in case the ghetto were to be liquidated by the Germans. A defense committee of 10 men was trained, which was joined by Comrades L. Berner, M. Kusznir, H. Prozer – Bund; A. Szimanowicz – left *Poalei-Zion*; S. Abramowicz – communists; Yehuda, R. Glanc, Gewercman, Kantor – Zionist groupings and Mendl Fiszelewicz – Group Nadrzeczna 66. The military leadership was taken over by independent Jewish captain, Dr. A. Walberg.

[Page 224]

They began to acquire weapons and a plan of resistance in case an *aktsia* was planned. Gasoline [petrol] and other incendiary fuels also were prepared to set the ghetto on fire. Comrade Fiszelewicz was given the leadership of this action. The comrades Frajman and Jachimek took over the getting through the [barbed] wire and various other points in the ghetto. The camp organization was divided into *drużynas* [squads] according to the party membership and also mixed squads according to their workplaces.

The work was carried on in this way as a deep conspiracy until 4 January 1943. On 4 January, when a small number of fighters remained in the ghetto – all of the others were at work outside the ghetto – the Germans carried out a "selection" among those who were employed in the ghetto. The group of fighters who were still in the ghetto could not decide how to act. Then Mendl Fiszelewicz on his own began to shoot at the gendarmes and wounded one gendarme. Twenty-five victims fell, among them the members of the fighting organization: Mendl Fiszelewicz, Itsha Fajner – Group Nadrzeczna 66; Hershl Frajman – Bund.

After this failure, the differences of opinion became stronger and led to a split in the camp organization.

The Bund and the left *Poalei-Zion* believed in avoiding the taking of individual stands [against the Germans] and that all of their attention should turn to defending the ghetto in case of an *aktsia*. All of the other groupings believed that they had to give up the idea of defending the ghetto and make every effort to reach the forest.

The two parallel movements with two separate purposes began to have an impact in the ghetto. On one side, the Bund and left *Poalei-Zion* with a fighting organization of more than 150 men under the military leadership of Captain Dr. A. Waldberg and on the other side all of the other groupings of more than 200 men under the leadership of "Mojtek" – Zionist; R. Glanc, Henriek Pesak, Y. Kantor, Gewercman, "Yehuda" – *HaShomer* and Gordinia; Mutek Abramowicz – communist. However, both movements maintained contact through liaisons: from the Bund and left *Poalei-Zion* – L. Brener and from the so-called *kibbutz*[11] Pesak. Despite the split, the Bund and *Poalei-Zion* did not withdraw its members from the combined fighting groups.

Thus the two movements carried on their work, on one side cold, calculating fighters under seasoned leadership and on the other side, young people full of fervor, devotion and spirit. Both movements had various methods of work. The first had carried out their work in a very conspiratorial manner. They robbed the German warehouses and sold the materials. They bought weapons with the money they received [for the materials]. Money also was collected from well- situated and safe people for the same purpose. The second [group] began to confiscate money and clothing, boots, sewing machines and other things from the Jews, which demoralized the camp movements. This exaggerated the differences even more. Various underworld members also made use of the situation and with guns in their hands began to eat away money from the Jews in the name of the fighting organization. These people were eliminated by the *kibbutz*. The *kibbutz* began to send out people to make contact with the non-Jewish underground fighting organizations. This was the most difficult and most dangerous work. "Riwke (Rywka Glanc) led this work. The group of five left the ghetto for the forest as a result of the contact that was made. However, they perished in a fight with a larger *A.K.* [*Armia Krajowa* – Home Army] band. Among those who perished were: Ramek Fajgenblat – *HaShomer*; Moshe Rozenberg – Bund and three communists. I do not remember their names.

It seemed that it was very difficult to make contact and it was not only the *A.L.* but also the *A.K.* that were prevailing in the forest.

Of the 10 groups of five men in a group sent out later, four men remained alive who had hidden in a bunker in the *shtetl* of Koniecpol. Among those who perished was Yehuda, the leader of the *HaShomer*.

We then began to pay more attention to ghetto defense. We began to build underground tunnels. Three giant tunnels, of which the best construction engineers would not have been ashamed, were built over three months, with primitive tools, without suitable craftsmen. The first tunnel was at Nadrzeczna 80/82. The entrance was through an ordinary, well disguised cooking oven and led to the storm sewers. The exit [was] at the end of Jaskrowska [Street] in the middle of a field. The second and most important tunnel extended from Garncarska 42 up to the old market where it exited on the Aryan side. Hundreds of men worked daily in two shifts in the building of the tunnels. The men did not go to work and were provided with *ausweisen* [identity cards] indicating that they were working the night shift and thus they received the food cards and were not tormented by the camp leaders. Mazej Krause, who was employed by the labor group, distributed the *ausweisen* to the members of the fighting organization. Kantor of *HaShomer* led the building of the tunnels. The lack of success in making contacts demoralized the entire action to a certain extent; after coming to an understanding with the underground organization about providing weapons, the delegation from the fighting organization, Comrades "Mojtek," H. Kantor and Renia Lenczner, left for Kaminka to receive a transport of short guns for 250,000 *zlotes*. They were surrounded by members of the Gestapo and gendarmes when they left with the weapons. They began to shoot at each other. Several gendarmes fell. "Mojtek" and Kantor successfully broke through and escaped. Comrage Renia Lenczner was wounded, but she fired at the gendarmes for as long as her bullets lasted. She was captured alive with a weapon in her hand. However, she did not reveal [the names of her comrades] and she perished at the Gestapo headquarters during an investigation. The Gestapo was certain then that something was happening in the ghetto. They undertook measures to counter this. They changed the camp leadership and in their place assigned the dogs to two other gendarmes and spread a net of collaborators.

It was established that "Makl Kilabajka" Herman was in contact with the Gestapo. He was eliminated immediately by the fighting organization. A rumor was spread in the ghetto that he had escaped from the ghetto with a member of the Gestapo. It was learned later that a Jewish *orduningdienst*Rozenberg, who had provided the Gestapo with information about the fighting organization, had been arrested at night. A trial took place. He was stubborn and did not want to answer the questions he was asked. A sentence of death was issued that was carried out immediately. The provocateur was buried with the judgment. The judgment was placed in a bottle. Among the survivors who took part in the court, Avraham Czarni, secretary of the Jewish Regional Committee, is today in Czenstochow.

When the collection of weapons became more difficult from day to day, a workshop were created in the ghetto in which primitive grenades of great explosive power was produced. The necessary tools and explosive material was smuggled out of the *HASAG*, Enro and Vulcan ammunition factories and the furniture camp where the Jews were employed. "Jacek" (Heniek Wiernik) led the workshop. The grenades made in the workshop were of a high level. When the Comrades Marek and Wladek visited the workshop they decided to move it outside the ghetto and expand it in order to make grenades not only for Czenstowchow. This did not happen because the ghetto was liquidated two days later.

Two more cases, which they did not expect at all, accelerated the liquidation of the ghetto and the attack on the fighting organizations. A group of five men who belonged to the Nadrzeczna 66 group went to carry out diversion work at the Ost [east] train. They were caught at their work. Four men perished and of the 50 Jews who were employed at Ost train, 25 were shot as a reprisal.

[Page 226]

The second case was: a delegation of three men, "Riwke," "Hipek" and "Lolka," was traveling to Warsaw to buy weapons. However, there was not enough money for the expedition. "Hipek" returned alone late in the evening and he entered the ghetto with the workers from Enro. By chance there was a search at the entrance and ration cards were found on him. He was arrested and he was held under arrest by the Jewish *Ordnungsdienst*. The commandant was not in the ghetto and the fighters did not have any weapons. They brought weapons from the Bund with which they terrorized the entire commissariat and freed "Hipek." This caused great anger among the Germans.

Two proclamations were published in the Yiddish and Polish languages during the existence of the ghetto. One was a 1 May call and the second turned to the Polish working class about help for the fighting organizations.

On 23 June the commandant of the Bundist fighting organization, Captain Dr. Walberg, was unexpectedly dragged and murdered by the *schutz-polizei* [security police]. The fighting organization suddenly found itself without a military leader and became entirely disoriented. Two days later, on 25 June 1943, the Gestapo gendarmes attacked the weapons bunkers and tunnels. A tragic struggle took place in which almost all of the fighters fell and among them, "Mojtek," "Riwke" and other Zionists and Pola Szczekac, P. Lewensztajn – the Bund. The commandant and representatives of the communists perished several days later outside the ghetto. However, many gendarmes and members of the Gestapo fell. The ghetto was liquidated and more than 5,000 Jews perished during the liquidation.

Signed:
L. Brener
A. Czarna
M. Krojze

Assembled by M. Kuszner

Translator's note:

1. A *kibbutz* is a collective community in Israel, often involved in agriculture. In the ghetto, it was a group
    of people organized to fight against the Germans.

———

Activities of the Bund
under the Hitler Occupation
by M. Kushner

The outbreak of war. A few people remained of the party committee. The outbreak of the war found the chairman of the committee, Comrade L. Brener, in the province at the liquidation of the *TOZ* [the Society for the Protection of Health] children's colonies; some comrades on the committee were mobilized. Therefore, hiding the party archive fell only on two comrades, on my comrade, Rozenfeld and on me. The flags, party publications and other important party documents were given to us to bury in the garden of *Aleje* 20, where the Medem Library had previously been hidden. We did not succeed in cleaning up the archive of the professional unions and of the school organization on that day. The same day, 1 September, Comrade Peretz (Bundist councilman and chairman of the school organization) turned to me to clean out the material from the Jewish school organization, while he left Czenstochow. On 4 September, Czenstochow already was ruled by the Germans, who began to rampage, as was their way. Comrade Szimkowicz and a small group of members of *Zukunft* [Future – the Youth Bund] decided to save the archive of the professional unions and of the school organization, which was then located at our hall at Pilsudski 17. We placed a guard of young comrades in front of the gate and the older ones entered the hall and began to work. Half an hour later, the hall was sprayed with a hail of bullets. Our guard warned that the situation was threatening. After a short deliberation among all of those taking part, we decided not to take a risk and to set the hall on fire so that the archive would not fall into the hands of the murderers and to make our escape. When the hall already was in flames, we left the courtyard and and we went off in separate directions. However, not everyone was successful in reaching home. The so-called "Bloody Monday" already was in effect in the streets. The majority of comrades of the party committee returned to Czenstochow on 18 September. We came together in the hall of the Jewish council and deliberated about how to carry on our party work and how to help the Jewish workers who were now in extreme need. We decided to work with *TOZ* [Society for the Protection of Health], which had begun aid work in all areas and one of whose leaders was our Brener, our comrade. We set this [*TOZ*] as the address of our conspiratorial party work. We also brought help from there to all cellars and all attic rooms and everywhere that help was needed. Therefore, a struggle against *TOZ* began by a small clique at the Jewish council.

[Page 227]

We had no contact with the Central Committee [of the Bund] until 1940. At the beginning of 1940, thanks to Comrade Falk, we made contact with our Central Committee. We also received food packages from abroad, which Comrade Rafal Federman sent from America through Portugal to the addresses of several comrades. The food packages were valuable; therefore, we exchanged them for bread and other needed food items and thus stilled the hunger of many Bundist families.

The first party meeting was held at the grave of our fallen comrade, Mikhal Szimkowicz (member of the *Zukunft* committee). The funeral of this comrade was a demonstration by Bundists, *Zukunftists* and *Skifists* [members of *Sotsyalistishe Kinder Farband* – Socialist Children's Union] in Czenstochow. The second meeting took place during the month of February 1940, three months after the fall of Comrade Mikhal, when the party erected a modest headstone for him.

At the beginning only two comrades, L. Brener and I, did all of the work. The Comrades Shimshl Jakubowicz, Moshe Berkensztat and Moshel Tuchmajer were the leaders after making contact with the Central Committee. All of the members of the *Zukunft* Party and *SKIF* were divided into groups of five, whom were made use of by the members of the committee. The Medem Library, which numbered 20,000 books, was smuggled over to the house of Comrade Moshe Berkensztat and it was given to Comrade Rayzele Berkensztat to run the library illegally. More than a thousand readers made use of the library.

The Comrades Falk, Celemenski, Frajnd, Samsanowicz, Kaufman and Lazar provided us with instructions and literature from the Central Committee. The energetic distributor of the illegal literature among us in the city was Comrade Alebarde (Alfa), who later perished in Warsaw.

In June 1940, the party committee in Krakow sent a group of party comrades to us, for whom we made accommodations and provided with work. Among them were the well-known Bundist activists in Sosnowiec, Bela Szczekacz and her family, Saski and Nasek and their families.

After the outbreak of the war between Germany and the Soviet Union, mass arrests began of political and communal activists. The Gestapo kept looking for Comrades Federman, Klin, Peretz and Prozer.

The Comrades Moshe and Rayzele Berkensztat were arrested here because of the failure in Piotrkow of the courier with the illegal literature from the Central Committee, who would stay with them. This was on 6 July 1941. The entire party became involved and made contact with comrades from various cities who informed us of the arrests that were taking place everywhere in connection with this failure. They [the Gestapo] began again to search for the old Bundist activist. Comrade Prozer succeeded in making himself "ill" and was taken to the hospital for contagious diseases. In the time that he lay in the hospital we were able to bribe the chief of the Gestapo and draw Comrade Prozer from danger. We also were entrusted with hiding Comrade Dr. Fensterblau of Krakow in Czenstochow for three weeks and then taking him to Warsaw. Comrade Fensterblau was hidden by the dentist, Mrs. Markowicz, a regular reader of our illegal literature.

On 16 July 1941, when I sat with my office work at *TOZ*, a comrade with our guard shouted to me through the window that the Gestapo was coming. I immediately left through the same door through which the Gestapo entered. As revenge that I had escaped from their hands, they arrested five co-workers at TOZ, my mother and brother, whom they threatened to shoot if I did not appear. I appeared at the disposal of the party committee, which decided that I should not leave the city and wait until the situation became clear. When the situation for the arrestees became dangerous, the majority of the committee decided that only we were obliged to carry the responsibility for our deeds and despite the fact that I was going to a certain death, I must appear to extract the innocent from the talons of death. I was in agreement with the majority; I said goodbye to those closest to me and to the comrades and went to the Gestapo. I was sure, as were all of the comrades, that the road to the Gestapo was my life's last journey.

[Page 228]

I was taken to the jail right from the Gestapo, without an investigation. There they stood me with my face to the wall, brought in [Moshe] Berkensztat and asked him if he knew me. I did not hear his answer. Then they led us to separate cells. In the morning, at nine o'clock, I stood at a hearing at the Gestapo with my hands in handcuffs. Five members of the Gestapo investigated me; they simultaneously also investigated the Comrades Berkensztat. They murderously tortured us and we fainted many times. The worst pain was for Comrade Rayzele Berkensztat when the Gestapo clamped her breast in the door of a cabinet. They lay me down with my head under a faucet with drops of water dripping in the very middle of my head. They also did the same to Comrade Moshe Berkensztat. Thus they tormented us from nine in the morning until late at night. Then they sent us back to the jail. After the investigation, I lay two weeks without moving. The arrested Polish teacher who sat with me in the same cell took care of me until I regained my strength.

The comrades outside, as well as my family, did not rest. Although the efforts to free us looked like a hopeless struggle for a lost cause, they did everything to remove us from the hands of the murderers. After nine nightmarish weeks, after nine weeks of constant pain, the comrades outside managed to sneak me out of the jail. However, Comrade Brener was not satisfied with this and a new "offensive" was started to free Comrades Moshe and Rayzele Berkensztat. He succeeded in this only partly. There was success in freeing Comrade [Rayzele] Berkensztat, but alas, Comrade Moshe Berkensztat perished in Auschwitz.

The contact with the Central Committee had not been broken during the course of our arrests. However, it was as if party work had ceased because everything was brought to a head to arranging bribes to free us and to erase the traces [of the bribery]. A month after [my] release, in the second half of October 1941, a [female] comrade from Tomaszów Mazowiecki came to us as an emissary from the Central Committee (I do not remember her name) and brought a package of literature from the Central Committee. She left the package in Comrade Brener's house. Before we could remove the package, the entire house was surrounded by gendarmes. Because Comrade Brener was not in the house, we were afraid that the package would fall into the hands of the gendarmes and then there would be a new misfortune. We decided to enter the residence at any price. We made use of various means and various ways and everything was unsuccessful. We were sure that a catastrophe awaited us. However, we were not yet defeated. Finally, Comrade Brener succeeded in entering the residence and removing the package, thanks to a comrade who was employed at the gendarmerie.

This was the last package of literature that we received from the Central Committee, and contact with the Central Committee was interrupted. We only received messages from Comrade Klin about the persecutions of the Bund in Warsaw. We also began to receive news about "resettlements" of Jews in a series of cities. Without waiting for instructions from the Central Committee, we called an interparty conference to organize a larger resistance movement. A large group of fighters made up of members from all of the political parties was organized under the leadership of an independent Jewish captain, Dr. A. Wolberg. A plan of resistance was prepared. However, alas, we could not collect any weapons and we were powerless at the *aktsia* [action, often a deportation] that began in Czenstochow on 22 September 1942. The *aktsia* lasted five weeks. The destruction was indescribably great. Only a small handful of our large group of party comrades remained.

[Page 229]

The six and a half thousand Jews who remained in Czenstochow were driven into a small ghetto. We also began to organize a resistance movement there. We made contact with all of the political parties and we began to collect weapons, tools for cutting through the wires and benzene for igniting the ghetto in the event of an *aktsia*. The command was taken over by the Jewish captain, Dr. A. Wolberg. Our Comrades, Frajman and Jachimek, were in charge of the group cutting the wires and M. Fiszelewicz, a young fighter, led the group that would have to set fire to the ghetto. The entire command was in the hands of an interparty commission that consisted of 10 men. The number of fighters kept growing. All were subdivided into camp *drużynas* [fellowships]. Our group consisted of 125 men, in addition to a group of comrades who were in the combined-camp groups. Dividing the fighting groups into such a manner was necessary because the fighters were located in various workplaces.

On 4 January 1943, when there were only a small number of our fighters in the ghetto, the Germans carried out a "selection" among those who worked in the ghetto. Mendl Fiszelewicz on his own initiative began to shoot at the gendarmes. The fight was a short one, but tragic. Twenty-five victims fell, among them our old Bundist *bojowiec* [fighter], Comrade Hershel Frajman. Only one of the gendarmes was wounded.

After this event there were strong differences of opinion among the representatives of the Bund, left *Poalei-Zion* and the remaining political groupings represented in the fighting organization. We and the left *Poalei-Zion* took the viewpoint of defending the ghetto and avoiding individual actions and the remaining groups believed in sending groups to the forests and giving up the idea of defending the ghetto. The differences of opinion led to a split. Two parallel movements with two separate purposes began to prevail in the ghetto. Both movements still kept in contact with each other through liaisons for a certain time – Comrade Brener on our side and Comrade Pesak on their side. Frequent conferences took place to reunite both fighting organizations. However, our different opinions sharpened and we could not come to any understanding because they [the other movement – not the Bund and left *Poalei-Zion*] had begun to confiscate boots and other clothing in addition to money for weapons that we believed would expose our entire activity. Yet we did not withdraw our comrades from the combined fighting groups. The first group, which left for the forest to join the other partisan groups, perished in a fight with the *A.K.* [*Armia Krajowa* – Home Army – the largest Polish resistance group]. Among those who perished then was our Comrade, Moshe Rozenberg, the chairman of the Bundist youth organization in Radomsk.

On 25 June 1943 the activity of the fighting groups was discovered because of the betrayal by one of the Jewish *ordnungsdienst* [Jewish ghetto police]. The *Schutzpolizei* [protection police – uniformed police] captured the weapons bunkers and rampaged with impunity the entire day, murdering the large and the small, young and old. In the morning, a small remnant of the fighters still defended the exit of the tunnel on the Aryan side. All of the fighters in the tunnel perished. However, gendarmes and members of the Gestapo also fell. Among the fighters who perished then were our two members of *Zukunft* [Future – the Bundist youth organization] from Sosnowiec, Pola and Dazja Szczekacz and Comrade Pinkhus Lewenstajn.

After the action, we found ourselves in the concentration camps in Czenstochow where the ammunition factories *H.A.S.A.G.* Pelzery and Rakow were located. At first it was impossible to do any organizational work. Many of us perished during the previous event and the few survivors were divided into two [different labor] camps. Comrade L. Brener, the chairman of the party committee, and I were in the same camp. Little by little we began to make contact with our surviving comrades. Thanks to the help of Polish workers, we also made contact with Comrade-Lawyer Wilczinski, who was in the other camp. Here and [in the other camp] we began anew to organize our remnants. With the help of Polish workers, the comrades from the Central Committee in Warsaw and Krakow made contact with us. We received letters with the signatures of Comrades Fajner, Henrik, Samsonowicz, Marek and Wladka. We also received bulletins from the party, brochures and money. We immediately organized aid for the comrades, for the sick (a typhus epidemic was raging), for children and the young people. We organized two illegal kitchens with the active participation of all the other political groupings. In general the work in the camp of all political groupings was coordinated. After we received the news from our comrades outside about the liquidation of a series of camps, an interparty committee arose that worked out three plans of resistance actions.

[Page 230]

The first plan: organize small cells in the barracks with an appropriate number of tools, which would start a resistance in the case of an *aktsia*. The second plan: attack the guard of the *Schutzpolizei*, gain control of the factory and free the Jews enclosed in the factory. The third plan was to blow up the factory by igniting the dynamite storehouse. We prepared for all of the plans in a rigorously conspiratorial earnestness. The ignition of the dynamite storehouse was planned by our comrades. The storehouse was ignited twice, but the firemen came both times and after great effort succeeded in controlling the situation. We in the first camp kept in constant contact with comrades outside, as well as with Comrade Wilczinski in the second camp. One Polish worker who brought us what had been sent by our comrades outside fell as a victim when he smuggled in a small package of money and letters. The money was seized from him, but at the last minute he succeeded in swallowing the letters before he was shot. For an unknown reason, our Comrade Brener (the ideal of conspiracy) had a failure, which ended in good fortune. On 26 December 1944, two members of the *S.S.* immediately arrived after a courier had left after giving him [Brener] a large sum of money from our Central Committee.

They searched him and found the money because he had not yet been able to hide it. Comrade Brener was arrested immediately, beaten murderously for an entire day and tortured so that he would reveal from where the money had come. Comrade Brener stubbornly insisted that the money was his own. After an entire day of pain, he was successful in persuading the members of the *S.S.* that they could take the money for themselves privately and free him. The two *S.S.* men let him "convince" them and Comrade Brener was finally freed. That evening was a great holiday for everyone without regard to their political leanings.

Despite the fact that after these events all of the Jews in the camp learned of everything that was being done by us, we did not end our work until the Red Army liberated Czenstochow from the Hitlerist murderers.

The few comrades who were liberated immediately began their party work. Many comrades had been dragged to Germany, to Buchenwald and other concentration camps by the *S.S.* and among them were the comrades: Wilczinski, Yankl Fajga and me. Comrades Wilczinski and Fajga perished there. The group of comrades and I who survived returned to Czenstochow and again stand at our Bundist posts devotedly as before.

The Activities of the *Kibbutz* [Community] during the German Occupation

by L. Yurikhte

In the morning of 1 September 1939, the noise of airplanes interrupted sleep. Strong detonations were heard several minutes later. There was no longer any doubt – the war had begun. The Germans occupied our city and the entire area on the fourth day and we immediately felt what German occupation meant. When Warsaw fell and all of Poland already had been occupied and the Gestapo began to rage in the city, the committees of the *Poalei-Zion* [Marxist-Zionist], *Yugnt* [Youth – *Poalei-Zion* youth movement], *Freiheit*,] Freedom], *HaHalutz* [organization of young people training for emigration to *Eretz Yisroel*] came together with the leaders of the *kibbutz* [community]. They all came to an agreement that the work must be concentrated. The committees were dissolved and a commission of five comrades was chosen. Their task was, first, aid activity. Actually, the majority of factory worker comrades remained unemployed and without the means of support. Secondly, maintaining contact with the central institutions in Warsaw. It was decided to hide the party flags and the party archives. A discussion brought out the question of whether the group should be dissolved or whether it should continue to exist illegally. With a majority of the votes, it was decided that the group must continue to be supported in all circumstances. The group did exist until the last minute, that is, until the complete liquidation of the small ghetto.

[Page 231]

Political activists began to be arrested at the beginning of 1940, and among others sent away to concentration camps was our former councilman, Comrade Zarnowiecki. The remaining influential comrades hid and the aid work for the comrades was carried out the entire time. They received money from Warsaw and from several well-to-do comrades. Comrade Zarnowiecki had sent out 100 *zlotes* every month because it was only permitted to send that amount. They counseled the refugees! Those such as [the refugees] were particularly devoted to carrying out the half-legal activity. The *Judenrat* [Jewish council] knew exactly what Zionist work was being done there and Leon Kopinski, the chairman of the council, and the presidium members, Bernard Kurland, lawyer Yeremihu Gitler, helped the *kibbutz* a great deal. The *kibbutz* numbered 160 to 200 comrades – refugees from various cities or those for whom the ground had burned under their feet. They were drawn to our city to the *kibbutz*. They were provided with documents and food. On 22 September 1942, when the liquidation of Czenstochower

Jewry began, the *kibbutz* had 208 comrades. Seventy comrades were successful in sneaking across to the Aryan side past the Ukrainian guards. And the rest went to the *aktsia* [action, usually a deportation]; of them, only some 40 comrades remained.

The *kibbutz* again immediately organized in the small ghetto and put itself in contact with Warsaw. Among the first fighters in the Jewish Fighting Organization were comrades from the Czenstochow *kibbutz*. The first grenades and other kinds of ammunition also were produced in the *kibbutz*. The entire ghetto knew what was happening in the *kibbutz* and all of the Jews related to it with sympathy and respect for the heroic fight. News arrived immediately that the small ghetto would be liquidated, that is, that some would be sent to work and the rest would be annihilated. A discussion was held about whether to defend the ghetto or whether as many of the comrades as possible should leave the ghetto and go to the partisans in the forests. The majority decided to defend the ghetto and, in addition, Jewish honor, fight like heroes and fall in battle. We heard resolute talk: "So many weapons were not brought into the ghetto with so much effort and sacrifices to leave it and let the survivors be exterminated without resistance!" In particular, this idea was fervently defended by the leader of the *kibbutz*, Comrade Rywka Glanc, who incidentally after her death was awarded a medal of one of the highest military orders by Polish Marshal [Michał] Rola-Żymierski for her heroic deeds.

There were hidden storehouses with weapons concealed in several houses and in sewers and everything was prepared for the fight. However, the storehouses were discovered by accident or through a denunciation and dozens of comrades immediately paid for this with their lives. Yakov Potaszewicz, one of the best comrades in the *kibbutz*, perished in an admirably heroic way. He was taken to the Gestapo and beaten murderously with sticks and iron bars over two days and two nights. Then he was brought back into the ghetto, where everyone had to march by him for him to say who belonged to the *kibbutz* and to the Jewish Fighting Organization. He no longer had a human face; he was completely swollen from the blows. Suddenly he stood up with his last strength and began to run and shout: "Down with the Hitlerist murderers! May the Jewish people live!" Several strong blows from the murderous gang ended his young, fighting life. Honor his memory!

Comrade Leibush Tenenbaum was one of those who maintained contact with the Aryan side and organized the sending of partisans to the forests. Wanting to evacuate another [group] of comrades to the partisans, he contacted a German chauffeur who presented himself as a socialist and already had taken out several groups. Taking the group then, it appeared that his German conscience overcame his "socialism" and instead of leading them to the woods, he took them to the Gestapo and denounced them to the leader.

The ghetto was surrounded by the gendarmerie on the same day. Everyone had to go out to the ghetto square. In this way, they [the gendarmes] wanted to catch Comrade Tenenbaum, but they were not successful then. They promised large bonuses for bringing in Comrade Tenenbaum alive. When Comrade Tenenbaum succeeded in worming his way out of the *HASAG* [a slave labor camp of *H.A.S.A.G.,* the acronym for the German metal goods manufacturer, Hugo Schneider Metallwarenfabrik Aktiengesellschaft] with the rest of the comrades during the liquidation of the small ghetto, he was recognized by the German master craftsmen and he was shot in front of everyone.

The discovery of the weapons storehouse brought about the earlier liquidation of the ghetto.

[Page 232]

At first there was confusion among the German villains.

When a number of Jews from the ghetto had been taken to the *HASAG* ammunition factory and the rest were supposed to be shot, the comrades from the *kibbutz* opened fire on the gendarmerie. Wanting to avoid their own casualties, the Germans began to shoot house by house with dynamite. When all was clear and the fight ended, Zilberberg (Moitek), the commandant of the *kibbutz*, committed suicide. When Comrade Rywka Glanc, the leader of the kibbutz, and the Slomnicki brothers already had fired all of their bullets, they tried to move to the Aryan side through the sewers. However, they fell, seriously wounded under a salvo of bullets. Their hearts stopped beating on the threshold of the ghetto.

They strove their entire life to revive the Jewish people and *Eretz-Yisroel* and when the hour struck, they threw themselves into the fight for the honor of the Jewish people. The fight they launched will continue on.

Honor their memory!

———

How the Party Flags of Left Poalei-Zion[1] Were Hidden

by Yehezkeil Brzezinski

Monday, 4 September 1939, the "Bloody Monday," when all the adult men from the city assembled at designated places under the threat of death according to the order of the German military regime – a group of comrades risked their lives to go to the party premises to hide the party and youth flags.

When gunshots from rifles and machine guns echoed in the streets of Czenstochow and dozens of people fell at the assembly spots in the streets, the comrades gathered in the upper story room at the Old Market 18, knocked out holes in a wall, wrapped the flags in the last edition of the *Arbeter-Zeitung* [*Workers Newspaper*] and bricked-up the wall.

During the liquidation of the Jewish community in Czenstochow in September 1942, on the way to the train-cars to Treblinka, dozens of comrades took a glance, taking leave of the place where their flags were hidden. Most them said goodbye for eternity.

At Treblinka, before going to the gas chamber, the last call of Comrade Gershon Prentki to Comrade Gelbart, who escaped from Treblinka, was: "Ahron, do not forget the flags!"

In the small ghetto, we, a group of comrades, came together every evening after the heavy labor to tell each other of the suffering and pain of the day and talk about the political situation as well about our part in the preparation for armed resistance.

Before the liquidation of the small ghetto, we often went to the barbed wire of the ghetto fence and looked at the wall where our flags were bricked in and found in this consolation and hope.

When the dying comrade, Yisroel Szimonowicz, lay on his deathbed at the Mathausen camp (Austria) and I said goodbye to him, he told me which was "the location of the window" where the flags were bricked in.

Immediately after the liberation, we, four comrades, left for the former party premises to take out the flags, but we could not find them. In September 1945 when Comrade Ahron Gelbart returned from the camp at Theresienstadt and Comrade Ratholc was demobilized from the Red Army, we found the spot in the wall with the flags. With grieving hearts, the few comrades who had survived, unwrapped the unsoiled flags and gave honor to all who were no longer alive.

According to a decision from the central committee of the Left *Poalei-Zion* in Poland, the flags, as the only remaining ones of all Jewish and Polish workers' flags in Poland, were turned over to the central committee. During a visit to Poland by Comrade [Yakov] Zrubavel, the flag from 1928 was given to him as a gift for our national union office as a symbol of Jewish struggle and death.

Translator's footnote:

1. *Poalei-Zion* – a Marxist-Zionist political party.

[Page 233]

The Artisans and the Devastation
by D. Koniecpoler

At the beginning of the Second World War, under the rule of German barbarians, the artisans in Czenstochow did everything possible to help their comrades maintain their workbenches when they were driven from their residences into the ghetto. We organized a juridical office that, as far as possible, legally supported the Jewish artisans, created the opportunities for them to buy licenses and so on.

In June 1942 we received an announcement: "Any Jewish artisan who has not paid the necessary sum for his examinations and contribution will be sent out of the city." We then collected the difficult thousands of *zlotes* so as to not give the Nazis a pretext [to say] that the Jewish artisans are illegal. However, none of this helped. On 22 September, both the Jewish artisans who worked in the specially created workplaces and the other Jews, were all sent to the gas chambers at Treblinka.

It is impossible to list the names of the thousands of Jewish artisan-martyrs who perished with the 40,000 Jewish martyrs from Czenstochow. Here we can only record the names of the individual activist artisans who miraculously survived.

Yeshaya Granik, Samuel Kac – tailor group; Goldberg – hairdresser group; Dovid Koniecpoler, Yosef Izraelewicz (returned from the Soviet Union) – carpenter group; Avraham Grajcer – painter group; Ahron Dorfgang – shoemaker group.

Orders from the German Regime
Copy of the original notice

CALL TO THE JEWISH POPULATION

On the basis of the 3rd section of the second implementing rule to the ordinance of 26 October 1939 on the introduction of the labor force for the Jewish population of the General Government (Ordinance sheet G.G. P. page 246) I decree:

The Jewish males who are compelled to work, as well as the baptized Jews in Czestochowa from the year of birth 1914 up to and including 1923, must report to the *Ältestenrat* [Council of Elders] in Czestochowa, Marienalle, no. 9 during the office hours 9-15 for the purpose of enrollment for a work card in the following order:

on 9 March 1940 with initial letters A–H.

on 10 March 1940 with initial letters I–R.

on 11 March 1940 with initial letters S–Z.

Noncompliance with this order will be punished with imprisonment for up to 10 years. In addition, property may be confiscated.

> City Captain
> (–) *Dr. Wendler*
> Czestochowa, 8 March
> 1940

CALL to the Jewish Population

On the basis of section 3 of the Second discussion paper of the Ordinance of the 26th October 1939 on the incarceration of the labor force of the Jewish population of the General Government (ordinance sheet G.G.P. page 246), I decree the registration of all male and female Jews who are forced to work *as well as the baptized Jews in Czenstochowa with birth years 1879 to 1913 inclusive as well as 1924 to 1927 inclusive.*

Registration for cards to enter the workforce will take place during the office hours 9–15 at the Council of Elders in Czestochowa, Katedralna 7 reporting in the following order:

[Page 234]

on 18 March 1940 the years 1910, 1911, 1912, 1913;

on 10 April 1940 the years 1900, 1901, 1902;

on 11 April 1940 the years 1897, 1898, 1899;

on 12 April 1940 the years 1894, 1895, 1895;

on 19 March 1940 the years 1906, 1907, 1908, 1909;

on 20 March 1940 the years 1902, 1903, 1904, 1905;;

on 21 March 1940 the years 1898, 1899, 1900, 1901;

on 22 March 1940 the years 1894, 1895, 1896, 1897;

on 23 March 1940 the years 1891, 1892, 1893.

The registration dates for the years 1879 to 1890 inclusive as well as the years 1924 to 1927 inclusive will be announced separately.

The dates are to be observed punctually. Identity cards are required.

The nonobservance of this order will be punished with prison for up to 10 years. In addition, the total assets could be confiscated.

> The City Captain
> [–] *Dr. Wendler*
> Czestochowa, 16 March
> 1940.

* * *

Copy of the original notice

CALL to the Jewish Population

With reference to my call of 16 March 1940 concerning the compulsory work, I have the following:

I.   The further registration for the years 1881–1913 inclusive and in particular:

    a.   Commercial craftsmen and technical workers (e.g. particularly bakers, butchers, tailors, shoemakers, locksmiths, mechanics, electricians and the like);

b.   [Registration of] the liberal professions and of the chemists takes place in the following order:

on 6 April 1940 the years 1910, 1911, 1912, 1913;

on 8 April 1940 the years 1906, 1907, 1908, 1909;

on 9 April 1940 the years 1903, 1904, 1905;

on 10 April 1940 the years 1900, 1901, 1902;

on 11 April 1940 the years 1897, 1898, 1899;

on 12 April 1940 the years 1894, 1895, 1896;

on 13 April 1940 the years 1891, 1892, 1893.

II. Registration for the years 1880-1890 inclusive, as well as the years 1924-1927 inclusive, occurs in the following order:

on 15 April 1940 the years 1889, 1890;

on 16 April 1940 the years 1887, 1888;

on 17 April 1940 the years 1885,1886;

on 18 April 1940 the years 1883, 1884;

on 19 April 1940 the years 1881, 1882.

on 20 April 1940 the years 1880, 1924;

on 21 April 1940 the years 1935, 1936;

on 22 April 1940 the years 1927.

III.   The enumeration applies to male Jews, *including baptized Jews.*

IV.   The application for registration will take place at the Council of Elders, Katedralna 7, during the office hours from 9 to 14.

V.   Those who must register [born in] the years 1924-1927 inclusive must appear accompanied by a father or mother.

VI.   The appointed dates are to be observed on time.

VII.   Identification cards are required.

VIII.   All male Jews, as well as baptized Jews, [born in] the years 1880 to 1927 inclusive, who will, after the termination of registration, continue to be transferred to Czestochowa, are obliged to report immediately after their arrival at the Council of Elders in Czestochowa in order to register for a workforce card.

IX.   Noncompliance with this order will be punished with prison for up to 10 years.

[Page 235]

In addition, it should be understood that all of their property will be confiscated.

The City Captain
(–) i. V. Kadner
Czestochowa, 3 April
1940

Note: Baptized Jews are those who were baptized themselves as well as those whose Jewish parents or grandparents were baptized.

Copy of the original notice

NOTICE

On the Subject of Metal Collection

A metal collection will be carried out in the city of Czestochowa. Every household is obligated [to provide] during the period from 15 to 30 June of this year three kilograms of metal (copper, brass, tombac, silver, nickel, nickel silver, lead or tin) in the form of shapeless objects. The supplier will be issued a receipt. Light metals such as aluminum, zinc and iron will not be accepted. The weight of the objects made of tin will be doubled.

Anyone who intentionally retains metal will be punished with imprisonment.

The metal collection from the Jewish population will be carried out by the Judenrat [Jewish council].

This order does not apply to the *Volksdeutschen* [those considered "Germans in terms of people or race" by the Nazis] in the city of Czestochowa, those who are in possession of an identity document or to the Ukrainian population.

> The City Captain
> *Dr. Wender*
> Czestochowa, 14 June 1940
> Through: *Kurjer Czestochowski*
> [*Czentochowa Courier* –
> Polish-language newspaper issued by the German General Government]

On the basis of the housing ordinance of 3 March 1941, I decree the following for the municipality:

1. Empty, vacated or newly created residential and commercial premises (these are: residential premises, warehouses, office space, garages, etc.) are to be reported by the owner, the beneficiaries of owners within one day:

    a. Insofar as housing and premises are concerned, which are occupied by German (as well as *Volksdeutschen*), with my housing office,

    b. Insofar as they are located outside the Jewish quarter of the Polish city administration in the town hall,

    c. Insofar as they are within the Jewish quarter of Jewish residences.

2. Residential and commercial premises may only be rented with the permission of my housing office.

The rental of residential and commercial premises can only be carried out if a written request with the corresponding substantiation of the vacancy is present. This application must be submitted:

    a. By the German population at my housing office directly.

    b. By the Polish population at the Polish city administration (Town Hall).

    c. By the Jewish population at the Council of Elders.

3. Rental and leasing conditions may only be concluded and canceled with the prior consent of the landlord and the owner.

4. Rooms designed or intended for residential use may only be used or altered with the approval of my housing authorities.

5. Vacant residential or commercial premises may not be publicly advertised.

6. Borrowed items of furniture may only be removed with the approval of my housing office.

7. On the basis of my announcement of 12 September 1940, furniture and household items may only be transported with the permission of my housing office in the district of Czestochowa.

[Page 236]

8. A separate announcement is made on the rental of residential and commercial premises. My announcement of 2 June 1940, concerning the residence permit, is overridden effective from 4 April 1941.

9. According to the 8th section of the ordinance on housing by the administration of the labor division of the General Government, certain buildings, residential and utility areas, with the exception of numbers 6 and 7, do not fall under this announcement.

10. My notice of 15 July 1940 concerning the registration of all vacant dwellings in Polish buildings is herewith repealed.

11. Cases of violation of these regulations will be subject to mandatory punitive measures according to sections 10 and 11 of the ordinance on housing of 3 March 1941.

> The City Chief
> *Dr. Wendler*
> Czestochowa, 30 August 1941.
> Through: *Kurjer Czestochowski*

DECREE

On the basis of the ordinance of the general governors (VOBL. GG. page 8), all inhabitants of the city, who have completed their 15th year, with the exception of the Germans of the Reich, the German people and foreigners, *are obligated* to obtain an identification card issued by my office.

Jews and gypsies are required to possess an identification card even if they have German nationality.

The identification cards are to be requested personally on official form sheets from 8 am -15 pm:

a. for the non-Jews in the office on Wolnoscistrasse no. 12.

b. for Jews in the office on N. Marii Pennystrasse no. 12.

The application requires a proof of identity (birth certificate, certificate of marriage, official ID and the like) as well 2 unretouched photographs of a required size.

A fee of 4 *zlotes* is payable at the time of the application.

The acceptance of the application for identity card will take place according to the following plan:

Residents with the initials:

A, B, C, D, E, F, G, H, I, J.
Sign in daily (except on Sundays and holidays)
from 1 December until 31 December 1941

K, L, Ł, M, N, O, P.
from 1 January until 31 January 1942.

R, S, Sz, T, U, W, Z. Ż,
from 1 February to 28 February 1924.

The issuance of the identity cards will be announced.

The City Chief
Czestochowa, 18
November 1941.
Through: *Kurjer
Czestochowski*

* * *

NOTICE

Concerning:

Change in the Curfew Hours

For the period from 20 June 1942 to 31 August 1942, the curfew hours for the city of Czestochowa is fixed.

1. For Poles from 23 to 5 [11 pm to 5 am].
2. For Jews from 21 to 5 [9 pm to 5 am].

Whoever is in the city area during the curfew without a pass will be punished.

Simultaneously, a curfew is imposed on the Polish population in the Polish-occupied areas starting at 10:30 pm.

Czestochowa, 16
June 1942.
The City Chief
Dr. Franke

* * *

Copy of the original notice

NOTICE

In accordance with the instructions of the Department of Labor in the Government of the General Government, Cracow, all male Jews aged 12 to 60 years [must] immediately report to the registration office for the purpose of reregistering and signing the card at the special bureau for Jewish labor at Lindenstrasse (formerly Wilson) with a photo 4.5x4.5 and identity card.

[Page 237]

The Jews have to appear as follows:

On 22 June 1942 from 7:30 to 12:30 letter A.

On 22 June 1942 from 14:30 to 17:30 letter B-Bd.

On 23 June 1942 from 7:30 to 12:30 letter Be-Bek.

On 23 June 1942 from 14:30 to 17:30 letter Bel-Br.

On 24 June 1942 from 7:30 to 12:30 letter Bs-Ce.

On 24 June 1942 from 14:30 to 17:30 letter Cf- Cz.

On 25 June 1942 from 7:30 = to 12:30 letter D-Dy.

On 25 June 1942 from 14:30 to 17:30 letter Dz-Ep.

On 26 June 1942 from 7:30 to 12:30 letter Er-Fh.

On 26 June 1942 from 14:30 to 17:30 letter Fi-Frej.

On 27 June 1942 from 7:30 to 12:30 letter Ga-Geb.

On 29 June 1942 from 7:30 to 12:30 letter Gec-Gn.

On 29 June 1942 from 14:30 to 17:30 letter Go-Grh.

On 30 June 1942 from 7:30 to 12:30 letter Go-Grh.

On 30 June 1942 from 14:30 to 17:30 letter Hi-Hil.

On 1 July 1942 from 7:30 to 12:30 letter Him-J.

On 1 July 1942 from 14:30 to 17:30 letter Jak-Jel.

On 2 July 1942 from 7:30 to 12:30 letter Jem, K-Kat.

On 2 June 1942 from 14:30 to 17:30 letter Kaw-Kl.

On 3 July 1942 from 7:30 to 12:30 letter Km-Kr.

On 3 July 1942 from 14:30 to 17:30 letter Ks -Kup.

On 4 July 1942 from 7:30 to 12:30 letter Kur-Lib.

On 6 July 1942 from 7:30 to 12:30 letter Lich-Mak.

On 6 July 1942 from 14:30 to 17:30 letter Mal-Mich.

On 7 July 1942 from 7:30 to 12:30 letter Mk-Nek.

On 7 July 1942 from 14:30 to 17:30 letter Nel-Oj.

On 8 July 1942 from 7:30 to 12:30 letter Ok-Pik.

On 8 July 1942 from 14:30 to 17:30 letter Pil-Pz.

On 9 July 1942 from 7:30 to 12:30 letter Ra-Rn.

On 9 July 1942 from 14:30 to 17:30 letter Ro-Ros.

On 10 July 1942 from 7:30 to 12:30 letter Tot-Ryz.*

*[Translator's note: this seems to be a typographical error. It most likely should be Rot-Ryz.]

On 10 July 1942 from 14:30 to 17:30 letter S-Sy.

On 11 July 1942 from 7:30 to 12:30 letter Sz-Szo.

On 13 July 1942 from 7:30 to 12:30 letter Szw-Szz.

On 13 July 1942 from 14:30 to 17:30 letter T-U-V.

On 14 July 1942 from 7:30 to 12:30 letter Wajs-Wil.

On 14 July 1942 from 14:30 to 17:30 letter Wilm-Woz.

On 15 July 1942 from 7:30 to 12:30 letter Wr-Zaj.

On 15 July 1942 from 14:30 to 17:30 letter Zaks-Zom.

On 16 July 1942 from 7:30 to 12:30 letter Zon-Zy.

On 16 July 1942 from14:30 to 17:30 letter ZZ.

Whoever does not obey the notification to report will be strictly punished.

                                                    Czestochowa, 17
                                                    June 1942.
                                                    The City Chief
                                                    Dr. Franke

[Page 238]

Concerning:

Changes in Street Names

In effect from today, the Marienalle will be designated as

ADOLF-HITLER-ALLEE.

                                                    Czestochowa, 28
                                                    November 1942.
                                                    The City Chief
                                                    Dr. Franke

Copy of the original notice

Report about the health conditions for the German Regime

Monthly Report: Health Care

In the month of July, 8,172 [people were] treated, many of whom [had injuries of] a serious nature. There were some serious cases treated such as amputations of fingers, injuries of the eye and wounds on the face.

**Poster for an Exhibition about Jews
[Text on poster: "Exhibition of the
Jewish World Plague"]**

In the internal outpatient clinic, medical assistance was provided in 2,183 cases. 1,429 people received dental treatment. 194 people were treated in the surgical department. Of 59 operations, 17 were stomach operations.

[Information about] deaths after surgery was not available. One hundred and two people were treated in the isolation hospital. One person died of lung tuberculosis.

There was one case of abdominal typhus, but not a single case of spotted fever. The medicine we received from the JUS [Jewish Aid Center] was of tremendous importance to us.

Such remedies as calcium-sandoz in all forms and glucose were irreplaceable when treating our infectious patients.

The salves and compounds from JUS were excellent.

Tin Emblem, Worn in Small Ghetto

Wounds healed very well with these salves, and the people quickly became able to work.

The food from JUS was very good.

The general nutrition and bread distribution was adequate.

(signature)
/–/Dr. I. Szperling

Copy of the original notice

Monthly Report: Health Care

In the month of September, 8,872 [people were] treated, many of whom [had injuries of] a serious nature.

[Page 239]

There were some misfortunes like amputation of fingers and wounds treated on the face.

Medical assistance was provided in 2,978 cases in the internal outpatient clinic. Dental care was provided for 1,477 people.

108 people were taken care of in the surgical division.

Of 56 operations, 19 were stomach operations (very serious cases).

Information about death after surgery is not available. One hundred ninety-two people were treated in the isolation hospital. Two people died of tuberculosis.

There were no cases of spotted fever. The medicine we received from JUS was of immense importance to us.

Such remedies as calcium-sandoz in all forms and glucose were irreplaceable when treating our infectious patients.

The wounds healed well with the use of these salves and the people quickly became able to work.

The food from JUS was very good. The general food and bread supply was adequate.

[–] Dr. I. Szperling.
Hasag, 1 October
1944.[1]

Copy of the original notice

Translator's footnote:

1. Hugo Schneider AG, a German company that operated a factory in Czenstochow using Jewish slave labor.

———

The End...

by Dr. Josef Kruk (Jerusalem)

Generations and generations of Jews worked, fought hard and often voluntarily dedicated themselves so that "their city," our unforgettable, dear Czenstochow would develop progressively, would constantly be enriched with all of the new spiritual treasures, would be free, would be beautified and refined.

Dr. Josef Kruk and [Yakov] Zrubavel

For this purpose they united directly and indirectly with the best and most progressive elements of the Polish population because they understood that despite all of the differences this still was a joint matter in the city for all of its citizens and inhabitants. They were often – too often! – oppressed and maltreated but they fought with dignity and boldly for universal and Jewish national equality and liberation. Therefore, the Czenstochow Jewish masses always supported every useful and progressive city institution and helped them to carry out [their work]. Much of Czenstochow had Jewish support, help and even Jewish initiative to thank – but it was not appreciated. And parallel with the work on behalf of the general institutions, the Jews created a series of exemplary Jewish institutions in all areas of economic, social and cultural life.

Every class, every group, every party evaluated its institutions with pride: children's homes, national progressive schools, the exemplary artisans school, the famous "farm" that later became one of the best, not only in Poland, but also in Europe, in regard to preparing idealistic pioneers [for emigration to *Eretz-Yisroel*] – *hakhshare* [Zionist agricultural training]. And the large Jewish *gymnazie* [secondary school], orphans' houses, the old age home, the new Jewish hospital, artisans unions and a network of powerful professional unions.

[Page 240]

And the party life: they often fought ideologically against each other. But, how great was the self-sacrifice, idealism and refinement they placed in the parties, Zionists of all leanings: Territorialists, Folkists; socialists of every shade and nuance: the Zionist-Socialist Workers party (*S.S.* and *Y.S.* [Jewish Socialists]), communists, *Hashomer HaTzair* [The Young Guard – Zionist-Socialist youth], Independent Socialist Workers Party, even the anarchists for a time.

The old generation still remembered the active participation of the Jews in the Polish Uprising (my grandfather was one of its leaders in the Czenstochow forest). And how great was the support given for the Polish and the Russian Revolutions! How many Czenstochow Jews, workers and members of the intelligentsia, old and young, went to jail and to prison, to Siberia on forced labor, from which some did not return.

And how many were wounded and shot on the streets of Czenstochow when they devotedly and courageously demonstrated under the red flag of social justice, political freedom, human brotherhood and international peace, for unity among people and nations?

And how many – older and younger – had to leave the home city, their families, comrades and friends and leave to wander over distant lands, often working at hard labor in sweat conditions…? They knew what awaited them, but they voluntarily and consciously went on the thorny path so as not to renounce their ideals, which had grown organically in their souls.

And even in the distant cities and nations, in the peaceful Swiss Zurich, in the noisy Paris and romantic Amsterdam, in the "diamond" Antwerp, in the exotic Argentina, in tropical Australia and South Africa and first of all, in the various large and small cities of the United States of North America and Canada and in Jerusalem, Tel Aviv, Haifa, in the various *kibbutzim* of *Eretz-Yisroel* – the Czenstochow Jews everywhere often remembered their young years and youthful struggles "there."

There – at the old or new market, in the First or Second *Aleje*, on Warszawska Street, Nadrzeczna, Strazacka, Ogrodowa, at the "Three Crosses," at "Fuszin," on the Czenstochowka, on Krotka Street, near the old or new synagogue, "Tilna" or "Teatralna," in the park near the quiet shore of the familiar Warta [River] or near the green walls.

And even a cemetery outside the city, across the old bridge – where their closest ones lay, parents or intimate comrades and friends.

With love and devotion, the Czenstochower, in their new homes, supported all kinds of communal institutions. [These included] the library, the children's homes and schools in their old home [Czenstochow] so that those remaining in the old home would be free to develop a dignified, happy life.

And with warm love, the Czenstochow Jews answered the love of their *landsleit* [people from the same town] across the sea. And thus the threads of Czenstochow were stretched across the entire world. These characteristic and remarkable threads gave encouragement to the general Jewish population during the frequently very difficult living conditions and increased the strength for a further struggle against the general dark reactionaries, anti-Semitic counter-revolutionary power.

All of this is now gone!

Jewish Czenstochow was completely destroyed. The entire Jewish population – men, women, children – all were murdered by the Hitlerist hangmen.

"Wanting is the father of an idea." And, therefore, there was the wish not to believe that all of the Jews were murdered. We knew that Adolf Hitler, Heinrich Himmler, Dr. Goebbels, Göring and the anti-Semites, the German Aryan [Alfred] Rosenberg were murderers. We prepared for terrible times. We knew that many would fall. However, that the entire Jewish population could be slaughtered – this we could not, did not want to believe.

I was in Warsaw at the beginning of the war, when many Czenstochow Jews arrived there. A number of them [came] on foot, carrying children in their arms. Approximately 6,000 Jews, women and men, children and old people "filed by" the clique of blood hounds, snakes and locusts, who lay in wait over our lives. We knew that Czenstochow, near the border, would be one of the first cities the Nazis would occupy. The Czenstochow refugees hoped that in Warsaw they would be able to save themselves and "wait."

[Page 241]

They all survived a frightful time with us when the Warsaw civilian population with almost no help from the central government heroically defended itself for weeks. Hitler's heaviest cannons fired at the civilian population the entire day without stop. And at night Göring's airplanes [Hermann Göring was head of the Luftwaffe] with black swastika systematically, with Aryan precision, constantly burned the suburbs and the cities with their unprotected populations. Not one Czenstochow Jew perished there.

I remember two moving moments connected with Czenstochow.

When the German airplanes murderously bombed the small but well-known peaceful sanitarium in Otwock and Świder (near Warsaw), they reached a row of small houses and villas and killed defenseless people and small children. During one such airplane raid, Mrs. Renia Kempinska (previously a music teacher for many years at the Czenstochow Y.L. Peretz *Folks-Shul* [public school] and children's home) ran to the small villa in which we lived then. With tears in her eyes, she asked my wife, a doctor, to save her severely ill child.

The Kempinskis lived in Czenstochow. When the German military neared the city, they grabbed their child and escaped from Czenstochow with a group of Jews. She lost her husband on the road. Finally, she successfully arrived in Warsaw. Many streets were burning when they entered the city.

She again grabbed her child and escaped to Świder-Otwock. Her child caught a cold on the way and was very sick. Świder was almost without a population. Just then I destroyed my archive and I was just about to to Warsaw. But how does one not help a desperate mother?

Her villa was far away, deep in the pine forest. Her child lay with a high temperature. It already was empty and unoccupied all around them. Even the apothecary already was closed. "What should I do? Where should I go? Can I remain here? And how can I go with such a sick child? And where is my husband? Will he yet be found?"

At that moment there was no one in the entire large villa, as well as in the neighboring villas and sanatoria. The tall pine trees stood in the late, cold autumn wind. The desperate mother and her sick child were helped with whatever we could. We remained with her for several hours. She lamented, "Why did I unluckily come here? It would have been better to remain in Czenstochow. Even death would have been better there!"

Later I left for Warsaw on foot where we survived the entire time of siege and fire.

And I remember one of the most genteel Czenstochower young women, Helencia Fliwacz, who for a long time devoted herself to the Jewish and general working class, to their struggle and cultural striving.

When the official war operations ended in Poland and both Czenstochow and Warsaw lay in Hitler's hands, [Helencia] Fliwacz came to Warsaw from Czenstochow under the greatest difficulties to find out how her sister, a young student at Warsaw University, was.

She was so shocked when she saw that the house in which her dear sister lived was a complete ruin and when she learned that her sister was there when all of the residents were burned alive.

I spent a long time with her, but we were quiet because what could we say in such circumstances? And we knew that now the true bloody war against the unprotected Jewish population was beginning. I helped Fliwacz to Czenstochow. And such a trip was a difficult and dangerous undertaking then. In parting we warmly and in a friendly way shook hands. "A greeting to all of the comrades and friends; we must remain brave and perhaps we will see each other again in better times!" She had tears in her eyes. I looked at her quiet steps for a long time as this genteel, intelligent girl left Leszna Street for Czenstochow. "Will we see each other again?" She was one of the last people from Czenstochow whom I had seen in Warsaw, since they returned to our city of birth.

We helped a group of people from Czenstochow return to Czenstochow. Warsaw was the most destroyed and most burned city in Poland. Perhaps, we thought, it would be easier to live [in Czenstochow] through the difficult times.

[Page 242]

And the small, always quiet Hershele Erlich of Kamik-Czenstochow (the *Bontshe Shvayg* [*Bontshe the Silent*][11]) whose room was destroyed and who by a miracle survived with one shirt, saved from an explosion, yet in Warsaw he gave ration cards for midday meals at a workers' kitchen to several of the Czenstochow refugees, often formerly rich people or eminent intellectuals. A "midday meal" meant a little soup and a piece of dark bread.

The first kitchen in Warsaw that provided bread for lunch was on Pawia Street and, in part, this was thanks to Hershele Erlich's help. He found an acquaintance in a bakery, a baker from Czenstochow, and through a series of illegal ruses, we received the first 200 rolls for those eating at the kitchen. What a sensation and what pride this gave us that a Kamik-Czenstochower was the first to decide upon hazardous illegal measures and made a fool of the murderous Hitler administration.

* * *

Later, bad news would arrive from Czenstochow, but then in comparison with other cities the situation there was a little more bearable. News of murders came less often than from other cities. And most important: the Jews in Czenstochow were not sent away as in hundreds of other cities. On the contrary, Jews from a series of Jewish cities were sent to Czenstochow where they worked hard, but still were alive. Therefore, we hoped...

However, at the end, what happened to all of Jewry in Poland and the captured areas of the Soviet Union happened to the Czenstochower Jewish population.

Murder, murder, constantly murder – of men, women, the old, the sick and children.

In the summer of 1943 a group of (exchanged) Jewish women arrived in *Eretz-Yisroel* with a well-known community worker from Piotrkow, H. Kurc. He brought us terrible news from Poland about the Nazi "annihilation commission," which principally was traveling through the Jewish cities and murdering the Jews en masse. He told us about Piotrkow and Radomsk and also gave us terrible greetings from Czenstochow from which many trains filled with Jews already had been sent to Treblinka. We first learned, thanks to a young Czenstochower tailor whom the Nazis had transported with thousands of other Czenstochow Jews, that Treblinka was a death factory in Poland. At the last moment, he succeeded in escaping from there and he told the terrible, deadly truth, which he knew face to face.

Kurc's stories shocked everyone to the very depths of their souls. A protest day was declared then in all of *Eretz-Yisroel*, a *tanes-tsiber* [a communal fast day] and a general strike, with an appeal to the free world, to the parliaments, governments, churches, universities, professional unions, parties – to save the remnant of our unfortunate people.

In the late summer and beginning of fall 1944, two young fighters who had been in Czenstochow and the surrounding areas, such as Zarki, Radomsk. Zawiercze and Bedzin, arrived in *Eretz-Yisroel* after an extraordinary effort and brought the last greeting from Czenstochow.

They were, Ahron Brandes and Avraham Izbicki. I knew both of them from Czenstochow. They visited me several times and told me...this was the last greeting from the last Czenstochow Jews!

It was not easy for them to talk about what they had experienced. And with great effort they told me one episode after another about the worst hell.

We bit our lips listening to them; our hearts cried and bled. Our fingers twisted together into fists. It was difficult to listen, but we wanted to know more and more, all of the new facts, just as after the death of someone close and dear to one, one wants to know how they lived in their last minutes, what they thought, said and felt, what sort of testament they left for us.

Brandes (now over 30 years old) belonged to the young people of leftist socialistic *halutzim* [pioneers], *Hashomer Hatzair* [socialist-Zionist youth movement] and also was active in the movement during Hilter's time. His brother belonged to the general main headquarters of the Warsaw Uprising and fell in an extraordinarily brave manner. Ahron Brandes also took part in underground work and participated in the Jewish anti-Hitlerist uprising actions. He was in Czenstochow, Zarki and Radomsk several times and as he traveled back and forth and again back and forth and back, it was an epic for him of the hopes and experiences of the masses of Jews sentenced to death.

[Page 243]

Izbicki, the 28-year old, lived in Czenstochow the entire time. He was raised from childhood on in a combative group, in a radical family. His mother belonged to the United Jewish Socialist Workers Party (Zionist-Socialists and Jewish Socialists) and later to the Independent Socialist Party. He, himself, belonged to the Zionist-Socialists, the *Poalei-Zion* Association [Workers of Zion]. His education helped him to maintain himself longer and, finally, through a series of perilous steps, to visit Bedzin-Sosnowiec where there still were Jews, after the Jews in Czenstochow and the other cities already had been murdered. He and Brandes fought in the Jewish uprising in Bedzin.

When it already was after "everything," they literally, through a miracle, wandered through villages, cities, borders and regimes and finally came to *Eretz-Yisroel.*

Both Brandes and Izbicki lost the many branches of their families and all of their friends and those closest to them. It was difficult for them to tell us, but it also was not easy to write about this. I wrote everything verbatim as they related it.[2] I had to interrupt my writing several times because it was beyond my power to keep from crying. I met with them in Jerusalem and Tel Aviv, in the mountainous *kibbutz* [communal settlement], Kiryat Anavim, and in the well-fortified young *kibbutz*, Ma'ale Hahamisha (where mostly Lodz *halutzim* [pioneers] live) and wrote the official report. It took several weeks until I could finish the writing and they, themselves, signed their historical statements about how the end came to the Jews of Czenstochow, Radomsk and Zarki.

This is their statement at the end of the report: "Thus came the end of the Czenstochow Jews after generations of work, struggle and self sacrifice, of whom only a small remnant remained."

And just as has happened often at the grave of our closest fallen comrades, swearing devotion to the liberation and revolutionary fight – today we give a threefold oath: not to rest until we take revenge against all Nazi-fascist murderers of our dear martyrs.

Footnotes:

1. Translator's note: *Bontshe Shvayg* is the name of a story by Y.L. Peretz.*****

2. Compare the reports by Brandes and Izbicki.

Revenge Is Sweet

(How I caught the murderer and liquidator of the Czenstochow small ghetto and turned him over to the hands of justice)

The feeling of revenge is foreign to us Jews. In the course of our long exile we always venerated anyone who possessed strength. Forgiving all the crimes our enemies committed against us and still commit to this day entered our blood and formed our exile character, our exile psychology.

We, the weakest of the weak, have always looked for a way to live, to continue to survive. We have stifled every felling of revenge in ourselves.

However, when we remember our recent past, those nightmarish days when our most bloody enemy of all times, the Hitlerist angel of death, brandished fire and sword over every

Jewish community, over every Jewish home, seeing the life of all of European Jewry abandoned, how elevated, how ethical, how sweet the feeling of revenge became to every Jew who was overlooked by the eye of the reaper, like individual stalks during the harvest of a field.

In those nightmarish days, each of us had one plea, one desire: "to survive." Not just as a desire to live but so that we could take revenge, Revenge for our parents, revenge for sisters and brothers, revenge for our children, revenge for the prematurely cut lives of our dearest and best.

At the beginning of war time, I, like other Jews from my *shtetl* [town], turned up in Czenstochow, marching through all the seven divisions of hell of the local Jewish community.

[Page 244]

At that time, Czenstochow was the place of refuge for "resettled" Jews from all of the cities that belonged to the so-called "Third Reich." The Jewish community in Czenstochow grew to approximately 16,000 Jews with the newly arrived Jews. The Jews said among themselves that here, in Czenstochow, they could somehow survive...

The time of the ghetto arrived. Life became worse. The Germans took the Jews for various work, as well as constantly taking large tributes [of money]. Even a small child was shot for crossing the designated border of the ghetto. No one spoke of the daily "deportations" of Jews.

However, all of this "was not yet" the most terrifying. They could still "survive" somehow. The saddest news about an *aktsia* [action, usually a deportation] in Warsaw reached us. The specter of fear and terror began to create pressure in our heads. Jews began to sign up for various work en masse, hoping in this way to save their lives.

Until – until the frightening news of Yom Kippur 1942 arrived, when the Jews felt that their fate had been sealed.[1]

During the morning after Yom Kippur, we saw the strength of hordes of S.S. members and Ukrainians. The *aktsia* [action, usually a deportation] in Czenstochow had begun. The tragic masquerade lasted for three weeks. Degenhardt, the well-known bloodhound, waved his "famous walking stick" – right and left. This meant: who would live and who would die...

Approximately 16,000 Jews, women and men, children and old people were then "paraded past" for a clique of bloodhounds, snakes and locusts who lay in wait for our lives. We felt powerless. It appeared as if heaven and earth were united against us...

Thus going to the slaughter, I looked into the eyes of the murderers that burned with a passion to destroy us, and from the depths of my heart I whispered a quiet prayer: *Raboynu shel olam* [Master of the Universe], give me the great privilege to take revenge against these bloodhounds...

Approximately 5,000 Jews, whom the German rulers made slaves, remained alive after the "action harvest." This was the time of the so-called "small ghetto."

Every day the Jews went from the small ghetto, which was fenced in with barbed wire and guarded by the Ukrainians day and night, to various factories and other work.

"Selections" took place from time to the time. A few Jews were shot then. The entire professional intelligentsia was taken to the cemetery then; every last one was shot. The Jews in the small ghetto felt that this was not the last word from the German rulers. The Jews felt that something still hung in the air; that there were difficult tests ahead for us.

There were some Jews who organized, prepared a desperate revolt. However, the situation did not last long. Because of a Jewish informer and partly because of the irresponsibility of the young people, of the so-called partisans, the matter of a Jewish revolt reached the ears of the Germans and, as always in such cases, we felt the consequences.

A stronger course came with regard to the Jews. In place of "eschewing" and "tolerance," immediately came the "well-known" two murderers, Leszinski and Kestner.

We have spoken about Leszinski, that he was a "proper butcher." We spoke among ourselves in Hebrew that for the smallest sin, he "exploded."

A number of Jews knew that Kestner, his right hand, a few days before he was designated to take over our guardianship, had changed into old civilian clothes like a Jew in a camp and come with a sack for coal to the coal camp of H. Zajdman. Kestner came secretly to Zajdman, who more or less knew him since childhood. Therefore, he [Zajdman] asked him who the coal was for; Kestner, who spoke Polish well, presented him with a note from the Jewish worker group and, in addition, complained about the Jewish police who denounced the Jews to the Germans, adding that he alone also had had to flee from another camp because of harassment on the part of the Jewish police. Kestner turned to the Jews at the ghetto kitchen, who had just taken coal, wondering why the Jews did not create a partisan group as had been done in other camps. The Jews, not knowing to whom they were speaking, assured Kestner that there also were active Jewish partisans in Czestochow.

[Page 245]

Sodom's judgment arrived: the small ghetto was bloodily liquidated; a few hundred Jews were shot by the murderers. All of the Jews who lived in the three houses at Nadrzeczna 84, 86 and 88 were shot on the pretext that there was a nest of revolt located there; the three mentioned houses were blown up with dynamite. Many Jewish children and old people mostly were harmed in the bunkers that had been constructed and in the hiding places in the ground.

Approximately 3,500 Jews, whom the Germans had shut in within the walls of three Czenstochow factories, "survived" the bloody harvest, where naked and barefoot the Jews had to do difficult and bitter work in dog-like conditions, receiving their frequent murderous beatings. Every one, at the edge of despair, gripped at the naked, worthless life, with teeth and nails, with the hope of taking revenge against the greatest barbarians of all times.

After the liberation, I was in Breslau several times. Walking, fortuitously, on one of the most beloved streets, on Matias Street, the appearance of a passerby who was strolling accompanied by an unfamiliar woman suddenly [figuratively] slapped me in the face. We were walking and met face to face. [Our gazes] met. Instantly, the thought flashed in my brain, this is he! I did not spare any effort; I ran after him in order to again be face to face with him and I was certain that my visual memory had not fooled me: walking by I had recognized – Kestner. I almost had an attack of madness. I really could not contain myself. A flood of thoughts flashed through my brain. Yes, this is he. Yes, this is me who recognized him. This was my dream, our dream, this was our highest vow, the holiest oath; this was our most fervent, most incandescent desire: revenge!

These were not abstract words; this was not a pious wish. We were no longer under a fearful fear of death by the German boot. How strong the experience was, a one-time experience!

And he, the person in question, did not know who was walking with him, going along Matias Street, as if nothing had happened, accompanied by a woman.

Simultaneously I observed him [Kestner] and a Jewish acquaintance, who could help me detain Kestner. I found out that this was a Jew, Baczan, who was in the small ghetto in Czenstochow and escaped from there. He knew Kestner well. Seeing Kestner, Baczan got excited and I had a partner.

After everything, we did not want to risk approaching Kestner. We were afraid that he could, God forbid, escape. We divided the roles. I watched and Baczan ran for other Jews, from Czenstochow, who lived on this same Matias Street. When I saw Baczan coming with the Jew, Layzer Rozencwajg, who I knew from the Czenstochow ghetto, it was clear that my fate was sealed.

I went over to Kestner and asked him if he was a German. Kestner, not suspecting the worst, said that yes, he was. When I asked him if he had been in Czentochow, his ability to speak actually was taken from him. He lost the ground under his feet as if a deep abyss had opened for him. After a moment, he regained his senses and wanted to escape. Then Layzer Rozencwajg and others came and detained Kestner.

We gave him into the hands of justice. The woman accompanying him, seeing that Kestner was going to be arrested, made use of the tumult and disappeared. Arrested and seeing that his fate was sealed, Kestner wanted to make use of a moment and spring from the window. This was noticed. Kestner was bound by the hands and feet.

I looked then in the green eyes of the dull German simpleton, in which I again saw the sadly well-known bloodhound, the liquidator of the small Czenstochow ghetto. I saw before my eyes on [the day of] the new accomplishment that fearful day with all of its cruelties and atrocities. I recognized in Kestner the murderer of our children, this insane bloodhound who had with special joy held them by the hair of their small heads and shot them.

There ignited and burned in me the feeling of unlimited revenge against this evil-doer! Revenge for the martyred death of our dearest, best, and most beautiful. Revenge for insulting the human family, the image of God.

[Page 246]

I lived through the strongest emotions of my life. I became drunk with good fortune. It seemed to me that this fact would, to a certain extent, improve the chances of my survival of the terrible storm.

Revenge is sweet...

Translator's Footnote:

1. Yom Kippur, the Day of Atonement, is the holiest day in the Jewish calendar. A person's fate for the coming year is believed to be sealed in heaven.

The Hitlerist Bandit Will Hang on the Gallows
(Reprinted from the Czenstochower *Glos Narodu* [*Voice of the Nation*])

[Heinrich] Kestner was a typical German gendarme, who voluntarily reported to serve in 1931. Born in Mazaniec, Silesia, he spoke Polish fluently. Like all renegades, he excelled with his German obedience and heartlessness. Well-known as a sadist, he was chosen along with another Hitler bandit, Laszynski, to liquidate the so-called small ghetto. His and his comrade's qualifications of cruelty and bestiality exceeded that of Zapart, the until then commandant of the ghetto. When the German regime learned in the summer of 1943 that the Jewish Fighting Organization was preparing for a military revolt, it found it necessary to delegate Kestner and Laszynski, as especially qualified murderers, to "liquidate" the remainder of the Jewish population that had been squeezed into several small alleys of the eastern part of the city. Kestner carried out his task splendidly... In his testimony he declared that he did not exactly remember how many people he had murdered with his own hands. It could be 300 and perhaps altogether 800 people. He was a little modest at the trial and insisted that he had slaughtered "only" 22 people. However, during the course of the trial, it was shown that his modesty did not match the terrible reality. We heard the statements and accusations of people who went through the entire hell of the ghetto, the bestial terror of liquidating thousands of brothers and sisters. Iwietszka, Koniecpolski, Szpits, Kramalowski, Delkowicz spoke about the events that they witnessed and experienced with tears in their eyes. They had to watch how Kestner cold-bloodily shot minor children and helpless old people: how the heartless bandit lifted a little girl by her hair and holding her thus, shot several bullets into her heart. However, all of these events were "unimportant" fragments of Kestner's "activities." Kaszinski, the prosecutor, brought out in its horrible totality his [Kestner's] true appearance and his bloody role. He characterized the entire German people as "slavish cattle" who, without thought, carried out every order inhumanly and bestially, whatever it was. Hitler knew best the psyche of the German people. He, the [worst] criminal in the history of humanity, only continued the doctrine of Friedrich Wilhelm, who believed that the German people could only be raised with a cane. Among the entire German people not even one voice of protest was heard against all of the orders from Hitler, orders that were a contradiction of what constitutes a humane way of [waging] war, if war in general can be humane. One such as Kestner and his countrymen did not even think about not carrying out the orders from their leader, because mainly then there would not have been a war. Everything that served the German people according to the precepts of Hans Frank who was sentenced by the International Tribunal to be hung in Nuremberg (1946) was legal to them.

The Murderer Kestner before the Court

In the Courtroom during Kestner's Trial.
The Witnesses and Victims

The Holy Bible of the German people was Hitler's *Mein Kampf* [*My Struggle*], the book that is a synthesis of hate and murder. Hitler began to build the German *Reich* [realm] that would last a thousand years on these precepts. With luck, he did not succeed in this, even with the help of such as Kestner, who without a conscience, murdered hundreds of people whose only guilt was that they belonged to the Jewish people.

If the principles of humanity and humanitarianism have any significance, such murderers, whose entire activity was so terrible, so inhuman, must receive a punishment of elimination from human society – the sentence of death.

After the prosecutor, the lawyer, Idzkowski, whom the court had officially designated to defend the accused, took the floor. He declared that the accused was only a small screw in the heartless Hitler machine that had without scruples murdered millions of innocent people. He firmly stated that the entire world carries the guilt for not stopping in time the gangrene of Hitler's plague in Germany. And also not later when it spread through the world.

Kestner was sentenced to death.

[Page 247]

On the Third Anniversary of the First Jewish Revolt in the Czenstochower Ghetto
(Printed in *Głos Narodu* [*Voice of the Nation*] of 3 December 1945)
by L. Brener

Today is three years since the heroic death of the victims of the openly armed uprising against the savage occupier. Today is the third *yahrzeit* [anniversary of a death] of the day on which the Jewish fighters took their historic test.

In order to hone the memory of the tragically fallen and clearly provide the facts of the last days of their lives, I will give a short portrait of the "small ghetto."

The "small ghetto" consisted of three parallel, small, dirty and narrow streets in the poorest part of our city – Nadrzeczna, Garncarska and Kozia – fenced in with barbed wire and always guarded by the gendarmes and Ukrainian fascists.

Six and a half thousand tragic shadows of people who succeeded in grabbing another little bit of time from their tragic fate were held under lock in a crowded cage. Six and a half thousand slaves from whom everything had been taken were packed into 1,200 crowded rooms without any sewer system. Here, the condemned had to build their new lives.

The day in the ghetto began at five in the morning. Everyone had to be ready then to leave the ghetto in groups for their designated workplaces where they had to go through the terrible procedures of torture, degradation and mockery. At nine o'clock at night the bugle to go to sleep sounded sadly. The streets were as if dead.

The melancholy mood hung like a heavy, lead cloud over the ghetto. Everyone here had lost everything; those closest to them and everything that gave significance, worth and content to their lives. Mothers grown lonely lost themselves in their sorrow, thinking about the bright, laughing eyes of their slaughtered children. [Some children] saved by a miracle, lying in a dark bunker, longing for their mother's tenderness and bursting into heartbreaking sobbing, they called their mothers who would never again come to them...

[Page 248]

Almost every day during the march out to work, the chief murderer, Iberszer, stood at the "workplaces," at the sadly famous Warsaw Market. He grabbed individual people from the group by the throat with the bent handle of his cane and dragged them like dogs to the so-called *yatke* [butcher shop]. Entire groups were sent to Skarżysko and Bliżyn [forced labor camps] from the "workplaces." Each deportation brought victims. People were murdered for attempting to escape or from the bullets of the gendarmes who shot into the packed vehicles for no particular reason: to amuse themselves or to evoke fear and for discipline. The idea of total liquidation lay over the ghetto like a nightmare. It was a constant theme in all conversations. We speculated about the time of the end. Our nerves could not handle the constant strain and the next day's insecurities.

However, there were also those who did not wait passively with folded arms. These were the young from the fighting organization who were carrying on underground work in the bunkers and cellars. Here were young girls and boys, with no consideration of political beliefs and hardened in their hate. The terrible [feeling of] vegetating in the ghetto oppressed them. However, they, the condemned, hurled away their helplessness, despair and pain and with a powerful will strengthened their actions. Girls and boys, almost children, created an enchanted world in the dark cellars and holes.

The gloom changed to a clear, deep love and the desperation into a boundless hate.

Love and hate! Love of those who had fallen so tragically; hate for the German murderers and bandits. The work was carried out day and night: they buried revolvers and in deadly danger smuggled bullets and dynamite that was stolen from the German ammunition factories into the ghetto. Inexperienced young men experimented clumsily with making grenades under the constant shadow of death. A tunnel was dug with an exit far outside the ghetto to provide an opportunity for escaping to those who were forced to pull back from the fight.

The mood in the ghetto gradually changed, particularly after the great defeat of the German Army at Stalingrad. The number of fighters grew day by day. The underground activities became more active, more intensive. The gendarmerie continued its extermination work. New contacts appeared more often, [there were] more severe restrictions. As, for example, women and men were not permitted to live in the same street. Every day brought fresh victims. The sick, anyone whose face carried a trace of tuberculosis, were shot. Men were shot for visiting their sisters. Mothers, who went insane under the pressure of the events and misfortunes, were shot. Thirteen-year-old girls who did not go to work to prevent their mothers from committing suicide [were shot]. We paid with our lives for remaining in the ghetto for even one day [and not reporting for work], for leaving work and so on.

At 10 in the morning on 3 January, the ghetto was surrounded by a large division of gendarmes and Ukrainian fascists. The ghetto was agitated. It hummed like a beehive. The situation was feverish and despair escaped from everyone's eyes: what was going to happen? What kind of devilish plan did they have for us now?

The gendarmes, prepared in iron helmets, strolled calmly near the wires and simultaneously they looked at what was happening in the ghetto.

Suddenly a division of gendarmes and Ukrainian fascists invaded the ghetto. *Gevald!* [a statement of alarm], and shouting filled the air. From the cellars and attics they dragged out old people, mothers with small children. Several, resigned, let themselves be led without any resistance. Others fought bitterly and defended themselves with all of their strength against annihilation. The blood congealed in the veins and in view of the tragic struggle.

The hell on the streets of the ghetto lasted for an entire day. The *aktsia* [action, often a deportation] was suspended at night, but not ended.

The morning brought a continuation. And again they dragged mothers and children from hiding places and again heart-rending screams came from almost every house. The moaning, the screaming, the lamenting and crying were accompanied by heavy gunfire. All residents of the ghetto were driven to the market where they were segregated.

The fighters of "the enchanted world" took their first exam.

Fiszelewicz shot his revolver at the gendarmes. Fajner, a very young one, threw himself at the murderers. The others followed him. After a short struggle, 27 Jews paid with their lives in the defense of their human worth.

[Page 249]

The young did not rest. They left the ghetto in groups and took part in various acts of sabotage and fighting. The youngest group of fighters as well as 25 Jewish workers was annihilated when taking part in the actions near the so-called *Ost-Ban* [East train]. The second diversion group, which fought near the area of Wilson Street 32, fell. The partisan group in the Olsztiner forest was slaughtered. Of the 15 partisan groups in the Olsztiner forest, only seven remained.

The remaining fighters in the ghetto carried on their intense work and prepared for their final armed appearance on 22 June 1943. The majority of them fell in the cruel, uneven fight.

Now, on the day of the third *yahrzeit* [anniversary of a death] of the first armed fight against the Hitler bandits, when we bring the 27 fighters to their graves, we stand, a handful of survivors, with aching hearts and bow our heads in reverence in sacred memory of the fallen heroes.

The New Czenstochow

by W. Gliksman

A new era of reconstruction began in Czenstochow during the month of January 1945 as it did for all of the remaining Polish Jewry.

The fact that on the day of the liberation, 16 January 1945, 5,200 Jews saved from the four labor camps were in Czenstochow, motivated several people with initiative to immediately create an administrative body that would stand the survivors back on their feet.

Cut off from the outside world by the long, dark war years, without the prospect of quick help from the *landmanschaftn* [organizations of people from the same town] in America or *Eretz-Yisroel*, the refugees in Czenstochow rose to their difficult task.

On the ruins of the former homes, on the ground soaked in the blood of those closest to them, morally beaten, the Jews of Czenstochow brought courage and energy to undertake the organization of immediate and rapid aid activity.

Several months passed after the war and an administrative body of the surviving Jews in Poland first was created in the West.

And yet a small group headed by L. Brener took upon itself the sacred duty of doing what life demanded.

The idea that in time *landsleit* [people from the same town] who had been in the Soviet Union during wartime would return strengthened even more the decision to create a Jewish committee in Czenstochow. In addition to this, there were approximately 100 children, either completely or half orphans, among the 5,200 surviving Jews, who during the time of the war were in the bunkers, with Christians and those who survived through a miracle. An urgent problem also was the approximately 200 young people without protection or support, dozens of invalids and hundreds of sick who came marching in with the Soviet Army. They all were in even more need of practical aid work.

The first news about Czenstochow came to America to the United Czenstochower Relief in New York from the then Polish ambassador in Moscow, [Zygmunt] Modzelewski. We provide the full text of the letter in another part of this book.

Further news came directly from Czenstochow and a regular exchange of letters then began between the Czenstochow *landsleit* in America and our home city.

[Page 250]

The Jewish committee in Czenstochow assembled of people from various political directions developed widespread activities with a responsible consciousness but with limited means.

A house was created for the homeless, for invalids, for orphans, a reading room just for the young and a preparatory school. Children and young people received instruction and full nourishment.

And although the number of Jews in Czenstochow decreased for a short time and in May of the same year the number in the Jewish community was counted as 2,000 souls, in July the number reached 6,000 with those returning to Czenstochow from various camps.

The Jewish Committee in Czenstochow 1945–1946
Standing, right to left: M. Lederman, Brzezinski, Birnholc, L. Baum, L. Jurista, Nirnsztajn
Seated, right to left: Eiznberg, Czarne, M. Hasenfeld, L. Brener, Y. Goldberg, D. Koniecpoler and Z. Weksztajn

New tactics were presented to the Jewish *kehile* [organized Jewish community].

Cooperatives were organized for shoemakers, tailors, cabinetmakers, locksmiths and hairdressers. [This was] in connection with the emergence of certain difficulties, such as receiving [the required] cards certifying one as an artisan. However, with great effort the committee succeeded in overcoming the difficulties.

A small community began to be built, but on a healthy basis. The Jewish population in Czenstochow began to work, trade and arrange its daily life.

It was very difficult to solve the problems of the Jewish children: after many years of being in the camps, in the bunkers, with "Aryan papers" among Christians or in the bunkers, churches, they required a basic, new education. Several showed nervous agitation, a number were afraid to be recognized as Jews and there were even those who showed a relationship of hatred to Jews and *Yidishkeit* [a Jewish way of life]. There were children who did not understand any Yiddish.

Much energy and work was required to these children to Jewish society.

The Jewish committee organized the entire intelligentsia, the best pedagogical expertise, and they threw themselves into the work with enthusiasm and heart and soul. The fruits of this undertaking could be seen a short time later. The children began to learn Yiddish, to play, to dance and from time to time gave performances, in time, larger and more beautiful. Torn from their parents and those closest to them, they again became Jewish children who mastered the Yiddish language in speaking and writing.

However, the hostile appearance of the Polish population, individual murders of Jews in Czenstochow and other cities, as well as the pogrom in Krakow led to further emigration of the Czenstochow Jews and, at the end of 1945, the Jewish community in Czenstochow amounted to 3,000 souls. In March the number fell to 1,200 heads. This also removed some of the courage among the leaders of the small Czenstochow *kehile*. The work of the cooperatives, workshops decreased and commerce by the Jews fell, but with good fortune, only for a short time.

Repatriation began from the Soviet Union. The number of Jews in Czenstochow began to grow and again the handful began to build and strengthen the Jewish community.

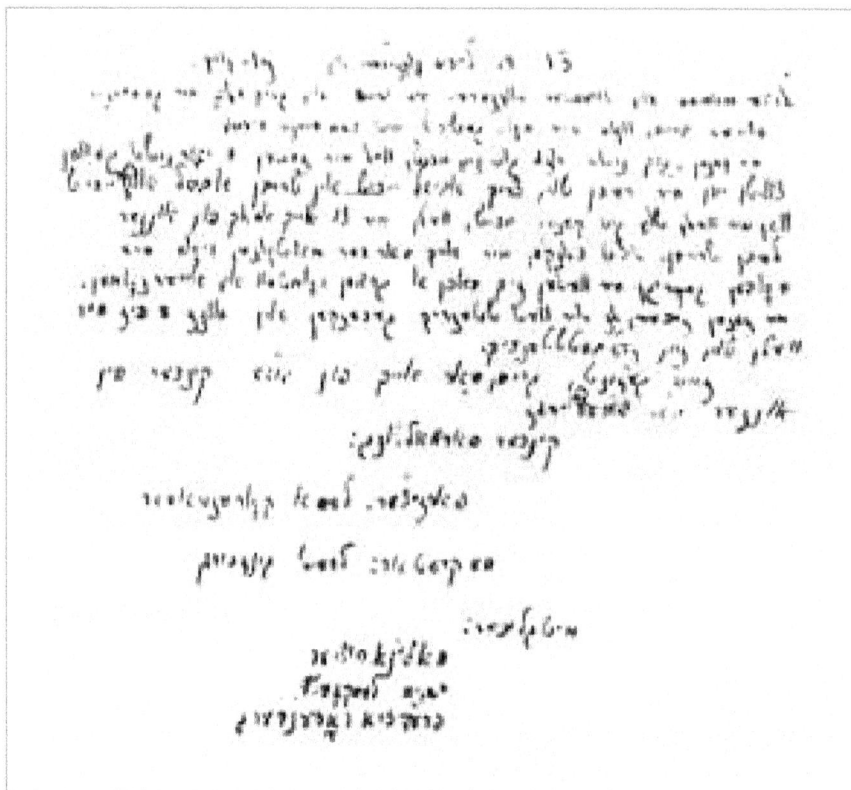

**A Thank You Letter from the Children in the Y. L. Peretz
School to the Ladies Auxiliary**
[Summer 1946]

The activities of the communal institutions, of the labor workshops again were expanded. The cultural work also was strengthened. In May 1946 the number of souls reached 2,500. The belief in Jewish community grew and provided strength for the work.

However, in July 1946 a new wave of anti-Jewish excesses went through Poland. The blood libel about ritual murder was spread. The horrible pogrom in Kielce took place; the result was a further decrease in the Jewish population of Czenstochow. And, although the mood slowly eased, this led to the partial liquidation of the private residences, businesses and workshops. A new emigration began.

[Page 251]

And yet while the Jewish community in Czenstochow is small, it lives.

It is worth providing a number summary in order to have a picture of the achievements of building a new Jewish Czenstochow.

a. About 200 children went through the children's home. Their parents were found for many of them who had been torn from them at the time of the war. More than 100 children were brought back to their own homes [through] relatives or guardianships.

b. Dozens of invalids received prosthetic feet and hands and thus were capable of taking part in some work. Some actually became independent.

c. Hundreds of the sick were taken care of in the hospital and supported by the Jewish Committee until they became completely well. Now they are under the supervision of *TOZ* [Society for the Protection of Jewish Health in Poland].

d. A special house was arranged for the homeless.

e. Old men, the poor and those who were weak as well as workers received lunches, dry groceries, etc.

f. A house to care for those with lung diseases was arranged and the majority [of the patients] were healed.

g. A kindergarten was founded where children from three to seven were educated with the Jewish spirit.

h. Approximately 70 young people are studying in the supplementary schools.

i. In addition, those repatriated received a one-time payment of support of 2,000 *gildn* [as well as] a monthly allocation of dry food products and lunch for 10 days a month.

A number of enumerated institutions were closed because of the improving condition and because of immigration. Yet several cooperatives still exist today and the aid work for individuals continues in full measure.

We are also active in the area of cultural work in the new Czenstochow. Large memorial evenings were arranged at the anniversaries of the liberation in the month of January in 1946 and 1947.

Technical Workshop of the Artisans School at the Jewish Committee

Opening of the Zionist Premises *Ikhod* [Unity] (December 1945)

Personnel of Workers Restaurant at the Bund

In March 1946 a memorial service took place for the 3rd *yahrzeit* of the annihilation of the Jewish intelligentsia. A solemn ceremony at the unveiling of a giant *matzevah* [headstone] at their mass grave took place at the Czenstochow cemetery.

A memorial to Y L. Peretz took place in April 1946, the first after the war. This was a great holiday for Jewish Czenstochow.

[Page 252]

A large event in Czenstochow was the visit of Yakov Pat, as a representative of the Jewish Workers Committee in New York. The hall in the Hotel Polonia, where a lunch took place, was filled to the edges by the entire Jewish population of Czenstochow.

Excavation of Those Who Perished at the Small Ghetto Liquidation

Transfer of Victims of 4 January 1943 from the Small Ghetto to the Cemetery

A beautiful chapter in the history of new Czenstochow is being written by the religious community. It runs a communal kitchen from which 100 lunches are given out daily. It supports a *mikvah* [ritual bath] with a hygienic bathing facility, a school for children, a *yeshiva* [religious secondary school], a rabbi, a *shoykhet* [ritual slaughterer] and, in general, takes care of the religious needs of Jewish Czenstochow. It also provides doctors and medicine for a number of sick people.

In conclusion it is worth remembering that the Jewish Committee provided social help of one million *gildn* in the first half of 1946. Five million *zlotes* was for the cost of fencing in and restoring the destroyed Jewish cemetery.

The Jewish Religious Kitchen

The Jewish Religious Kitchen

The Jewish Religious Community
Seated, from the right: Y. Landau, A. Zander, A. Darfgang, L. Rajcher, N.
Edelist, M. Goldberg, the Rabbi E. Wajsler, H. Rajbman, Sh. Granek, D.
Koniecpoler and Ch. Sztibel

The Jewish community in Czentochow stands together with the [other] Jews in Poland today in the fight for its existence. We believe that on the ruins of the former great Jewish Czenstochow will again sprout a pulsing and vibrant Jewish life in our city.

[Page 253]

The Children's House in Czenstochow

by Ida Merczin

It was not long ago that the children's home received a new two-story, light-filled building at Yasnogorske 36 surrounding a garden, hothouses, cages for doves, chicken and rabbits.

Forty children aged 3 to 15 are found in the house. The youngest attend the trade school on the premises. The older ones [attend] the *gymnazie* [secondary school] and *folks-shuln* [Jewish public schools] in the city.

The children sleep in large, bright bedrooms. They have a large dining room, magnificent bathrooms, a room in which to learn and to play.

The supervisor-children serves the food beautifully and esthetically at the table.

The food is nutritious and tasty.

The children are dressed with charm. The clothing is suitable to their size, to their face. The Czenstochow children's collective is one large family; there is the atmosphere of home. After breakfast they disperse, the young ones to the pre-school, the older ones to school, but they spend the [early] mornings and the evenings together. The older girls find time not only to prepare their lesions in school and to do their own hairdos (all are beautifully combed and stylish), but also to be busy with clothes. They put them on; they wash them. They learn to keep order, clean and the like.

It also is joyful with the boys. The oldest study electrical assembly. They like their trade and constantly make new attempts. They had already made a night-light for their bedroom, now they would make a projector, a stand. I cannot analyze their project, but the comrade is delighted. The older one helps. The young ones look on in awe and with envy at such wonders and when the lamps were lit, the older one smiled with satisfaction and the young ones shouted with ecstasy.

However, now in autumn, the children go to school. The time must be planned. The participation of each child in homework must be limited and calculated and, therefore, the children now have tours of duty. The work is divided. The children exchange their work. Quietly and calmly they hand a tour of duty to one another.

In the Children's Club at the Children's House of the Jewish Committee

A joyful phenomenon for us educators also is the mood of joy of the children. We have come to a performance. All of the children are busy. They sew; they wash. They prepare decorations. Entire days are occupied with rehearsals. There is absolutely no time for us guests. They do not look at us at all and therefore we feel the joy that fills the hearts of the children. They sing in the Children's House; they sing a great deal. They sing waiting for soup. They hum when they iron a dress. And the small children!! Another one always runs to the middle of the room and sings along to the dance he is dancing. Sometimes I recognize a fragment from the performance; sometimes it is a free improvisation.

The Children's House has the face of our Jewish secular schools. And it is not accidental. The [female] Comrade Brener (the consultant for child protection at the *województwo* [province] committee) is an old, experienced Jewish teacher who spends all of her free time in the Children's House. The work hours are divided so the greatest amount of her time is at the Children's House.

Y. Pat visiting the Children's House, February 1946
Seated, right to left: M. Lederman, Y. Weksztajn, Y. Pat, L. Brener, S. Edelman
[guest from Lodz], Y. Ejzenberg and Ita Brener)

Comrade Brener (a teacher), the chairman of the committee, comes to the House often. He knows all of the children; he lives with them through everything that happens in the house.

The program is varied, Jewish issues and work. This is felt in the conversations of the youngest in the bedroom (what kind of work does a cat have and why does she have four feet?) and the conversations of the older ones, 'We strive to be the best students in school.' I was there for two days and except for a girl who was suffering from a tooth-ache, I did not see any idleness or a child longing [for someone]. When they have no work, are not preparing for a class, they read a book.

The program is diverse, Jewish issues with Polish ones, but the leitmotif is identical:

"Let the hands be healthy with calluses; sweat should pour from the forehead."

The words of the hymn, "Sing a praise and song for the toil and work. Greet from the heart with love and hate," with which the children left the building of the Czenstochow theater, rang in my ears for a long time. And perhaps not only the words, but actually the comprehension, the deep beliefs of the children, the feeling and enthusiasm of them for the work and to work.

The collective of Czenstochow Children's House succeeded in redressing another important educational problem – this is the problem of the connection of the [Children's] House to the city.

This was one of our most vexing problems until 1939.

The doctors forbid contact for health reasons. They trembled about influences from the street and the house on the souls of the child. The children in our "orphan houses" before the [Second World] War were withdrawn from life, all of its manifestations.

The Children's House in Czenstochow boldly broke with the old traditions of locking guests out of the house. Every Sunday a small holiday for children from the school and other children from the city takes place. We drink tea and cookies with them. We read the court newspaper. The children do a few numbers from their artistic-amateur activities.

The guests, the school and city children come very eagerly to the entertainments.

(*Dos Neye Lebn* [*The New Life*], number 23 from Lodz, 12 January 1945)

Czentochower in America

[Page 256]
Documents for the Article "General Overview of Fraternal Help"

A School Certificate for the Y. L. Peretz *Folks-Shul*

Report of the Division of American Monetary Aid

A Letter from the Jewish Hospital to Czenstochower Relief in New York

[Page 257]

General Overview of Fraternal Help
by A. Khrobolowski

Alas, we do not have any exact statistics as to the number of Czenstochowers in America. The three large organizations in New York: the Czenstochower Young Men, Czenstochower *Arbeter Ring* [Workman's Circle] branch 261 and Czenstochower branch 11 of the Jewish People's Order (International Worker's Order) – together number between six and seven hundred members. However, this is only a small part of the Czenstochower in New York. It surely would not be an exaggeration to say that the number of Czenstochower and their many branched families in New York, Philadelphia, Detroit, Chicago, Los Angeles and other cities now reaches to over 10,000. The number itself shows how large is the contribution of Czenstochowers to the country in general and in particular to the Jewish community in the country.

Three Main Waves of Emigration

The first pioneers from Czenstochow came here [to the United States] in the 1880s. Among them were the well-known relief workers Louis Szimkowicz, Sam Goldberg, Max Karpiel and Jacob Zeidman.

The second great wave of emigration to America began in the years 1905-6. Among the emigrants of that era were the new generation of socialists and worker-fighters such as Mendl Szuchter, Dovid Malarski, Skharye Lewensztajn, Mordekhai Altman, Kopl Gerichter, Khona Gliksman, Moshe Censzinski, Yeshaya Yakov Minkov, Shimkha Grilak, Yeta Grilak, Max Berliner, Yosl Berliner, Lou Ufner, Abe Kaufman, Yosef Kaufman, Yakov Ber Silver, Avraham Yakov Senzer.

The third wave of emigration began after the First World War. This wave carried with it in great mass the social waves that the Russian revolution and the founding of the Soviet Union evoked in the world. Among them were found Yehiel Lewensztajn, Dovid Tanski, the Wajz brothers in Chicago, Abe Wenger, Sam Wenger, Rose Rozenfeld-Kaufman, Fradl Brat-Gliksman, Chayala Waga-Rojtman, the Holbergs in Canada, Fayga Ajzner, the Wilingers, the Senzer brothers and so on.

From 1924, because of the quota, emigration ceased except for a very limited number of wives and children of citizens. The last Czenstochower emigrants were refugees who survived Hitler's bloody nails. They can be counted on the fingers. They are Dr. Grinbaum and his wife and son, Dovid Guterman, who came to the World's Fair, Yitzhak Gurski and his wife and two children, who survived in Vienna, M. Kelcziglowski, Zundl Starozum, Rafal Federman, Dr. Lazarowicz, A. Haptka, Herman Zigas, the lawyer, Zigmund Epsztajn, Andja Munawicz, who had survived [going] through the Soviet Union and came here across Japan.

The First Pioneers

In 1923 an emigrant from Czenstochow on a ship met a Jewish emigrant who had come to America 30 years earlier and they carried on a conversation. The emigrant from 1923 traveled as a second-class passenger. The Jew was returning from a visit home, also in second-class. The old emigrant described his trip to America 30 years earlier.

"We traveled without external passports," the old emigrant said – without external passes. Smugglers brought us across the border on a dark night and robbed us from head to foot. Then the ship agents packed us in a horse wagon and brought us to the ship like a herd of cattle. On the ship we lay around on the lower deck, were fed potatoes and herring and treated like animals.

And when we arrived in America, no dear homes of parents, brothers and sisters waited for us. Our "homes" were the dark shops where we worked up to 16 hours a day.

And they also had no unions that could support them and there also were no *landsmanschaft* organizations where they could meet a friend from the city. "The small number of Czenstochower *landsleit*" [people from the same country] – writes Friend Yosef Kaufman about the pioneers of the Young Men – "would come together every evening on Delancey [Street] at the corner of Norfolk after a difficult day of work and the first Czenstochower Society in America was born there.

[Page 258]

However, the path of the emigrants who left later was in no way spread with flowers. They also endured enough hardships from the smugglers, Prussian gendarmes, ship agents and ship companies. True, during the years 1911-14 there was an organized immigration to Galvaston (Yankl Kopinski was one of those in such a group). H.I.A.S. [Hebrew Immigrant Aid Society] was active in Poland during the years after the First World War and at that time a division of the Workers Emigration Union was active in Czenstochow, which helped many Czenstochow emigrants of that time get their passports and visas. However, this help did not have great meaning. In general, Jewish emigration to America, which created the largest and strongest Jewish community in the world, was abandoned, unorganized, unsupported and left in God's care. No matter how much we shouted or wrote in the Czenstochow press and in other cities about the need for an emigration society to provide help and support for the Jewish emigrant – the appeal remained in the desert. In 1912 the communal workers in Czenstochow wanted to legalize an emigration division. They needed for this the signatures of 10 respected and "virtuous" people. They went from house to house asking for these signatures and did not get them...

Jews Go to America

However, Jews did not wait for an emigration society to be created for them, did not wait for the "territory" and were not afraid of "emigrationism," but traveled to America. However, not alone. Jews took Czenstochow with them to America – all of Czenstochow: Warszawer and Jesienna Streets, Kacze and Yatke Streets, the old and the new markets, the *Alejes*, Drozdowa, Walowa, Spadek, Krutke Street, the old *shul* [synagogue], the new synagogue, the Yiddish Literary Society, *Lira* [literary and music society], the schools, the party clubs, everything with which the people had lived in their old home they took with them to America, carried and remained attached with the unbroken and strongest connection of the soul.

How great their love and connection to Czenstochow was is shown in the aid activity of the Czenstochow *landsleit* in almost every city in America over the course of 25-30 years.

Brothers in Joy and Suffering

In the Czenstochow weekly newspaper, *Dos Neye Vort* [*The New Word*] of 3 September 1920, there is an estimate of the aid that was received by Czenstochow from America:

"In our history the expression of the most beautiful pages will be that everyone – and with a few exceptions, these individuals include almost everyone – received support during these bitter times from their friends, relatives, sisters and brothers and children. Not only this, but the hopes of thousands were lit to be able to leave the swamp of need in which they were sinking deeper and deeper for the past seven years (since the First World War began) to leave sooner or later. Not only this, but a series of institutions and modern schools exist with the help of our friends in America. Obviously these are very important things that cannot be swept away with the hand. But the nicest and brightest remains the humane consciousness, that all of the American aid activity and great fraternal love that flows to us speaks to us with clear language and awakes in us a feeling that we are not alone, that we possess in the world a loyal, devoted connection with our friends through life and death.

"During the war we, a group from Czenstochow, were in a prisoner [of war] camp in Austria. We were just a day's trip from home, but an entire year passed before we lived to receive a letter from there [home]. On the contrary, letters without end flowed from America. Everyone who knew us well or distantly wrote, consoled us and sent money. In addition to our brothers and sisters, Moshe Ce. wrote continuously. Yankl Kopinski, Hela Sercacz, Yetsha Grilak, Shimkha Kalka and Czenstochower Relief in New York sent money several times for the Czenstochow prisoners of war and asked how things were in Czenstochow."

Jewish Czenstochow, in great need that began with the First World War and grew greater with each year found its consolation in America, with aid and hope. A letter from America in a Jewish house in the Jewish quarter of Czenstochow [brought] a holiday, particularly when the letter never arrived "empty." America was not content with hollow words. Its help was always tangible. In many cases, America helped carry the heavy load of the thousand and one taxes that were one of the extermination methods used against the Jewish population by reactionary Poland.

[Page 259]

At the time of the First World War, organized help from America through the Aid Union and then through Czenstochower Relief in New York reached Czenstochow in various ways. Most of the aid was sent to the organized Jewish community in the name of Rabbi, Reb Nakhum Asz. After the [First] World War a workers distribution committee for American aid for workers institutions was founded in Czenstochow. And this is a report from the committee about the sums that arrived from America in 1922.

The income of the committee arrived from New York Relief – 1,100 dollars and 100,000 marks, together – 855,300 marks; from Chicago Relief – 244 dollars or 905,240 marks. From Toronto, Canada, 52,000 marks, total – 1,812,540 marks. In addition to this the committee was supported by the Central Dinezon Committee[1] in Warsaw and by the Jewish school organization.

The committee in Czenstochow divided the monetary aid among the following institutions: the children's homes and *folkshuln* [Jewish public schools], evening courses for the working young, reading rooms and libraries, workers' Red Cross and Workers' Rescue Committee at the central council of the professional unions, workers' kitchen and tea halls.

In addition great sums [of money] arrived from America in the name of the general American committee, which consisted of representatives of the organized Jewish community, the Jewish hospital, *Dobroczynnoœæ* [charity], and so on. Alas, we do not have any numbers indicating the size of the sums, but it is assumed that they were not smaller that those sent to the workers' institutions.

The following sums from America appear in a report from the Y.L. Peretz children's homes and *folkshuln* for the 1925–1926 school year:

From Czenstochower Relief in New York	$400.
From Czenstochower Ladies Auxiliary in New York	$600.
Chicago Relief Committee	$251.
From Aid Union in Detroit	$100.
From Youth Club in New York	$20.

In a report from the Workers' Distribution Committee a sum is found designated for the evening courses. They are described separately in an article about the schools, but the great moral and spiritual effect that they had on the young students in the workshops is shown among those who survived Hitler's murders and today are helping to rebuild the life of our so few surviving brothers in Poland.

The children's homes and *folkshuln* that were built and supported with so much self-sacrifice were so beloved in distant America as in Czenstochow. Immediately after the First World War, a large number of friends in New York organized a separate group that supported the children's homes. With unlimited work, fraternal sacrifice and sincerity, those from Czenstochow in America gave so much to support and develop the children's homes and schools. A letter from that time provided evidence about how much effort and work it cost to erect the massive Y.L. Peretz house for the children's homes and schools:

"After Comrade Mendl Szuckter returned from his visit to Czenstochow, with doubled energy we undertook the carrying out of the plan to buy our own house for the workers' school. We exerted all of our strength. Days and weeks were devoted to this purpose; we did not even take the time to spend with our families. Theater presentations and friendly amusements were organized.

When the large number of books that were collected by all of the Czenstochower organizations in New York for the new library arrived in Czenstochow it was a great holiday for the Czenstochowers who were lovers of books – and who among the Jewish workers and men of the people did not love books! One had to be in the library in the evening when the books were exchanged and see the gleam in the eyes of our dear young men, girls and older people from all strata of the Jewish population who took the heavy books to their poor homes. They read by [the light] of oil lamps and they thought of them and lived with them as if they were their closest friends."

[Page 260]

The German murderers at the time of their bloody rule corrupted everything, killed everyone; no one and nothing was respected: old and young, old people and children – the hand of the Jewish brother and sister in America was stretched out to the brother, to his child and to the old home across the distant seas and lands but did not reach them. The fire of fraternal love that was ignited in every heart during its thousand-year history of martyrdom could not extinguish the Hitler murderers.

The Czenstochower *Landsmanschaftn* and Jewish Life

From the short or long descriptions of the Czenstochower *landsmanschaftn* organizations that were published in this book, such as Young Men's, *Arbeter Ring*, Jewish-National Workers Union and later the International Workers Order, we see clearly that here in America, too, the Jewish masses grouped together according to certain idealistic movements in Jewish life, even if not according to strongly divided party lines. Without a doubt each organization did a great deal to support Jewish life here, to raise the communal consciousness and the cultural development of their members to a higher lever. In addition to this, that these organizations provided the members with certain insurance in case of illness or other cases of need and joined the thousands of individuals and associations and did not permit the Jewish masses in America to be transformed into human dust.

The history of the activity and meetings of all of the organizations is so rich that we can in no way describe them all in this article. At the time before the split, 400 people would attend the readings at the Czenstochow *Arbeter Ring* branch. There were large and important gatherings where we felt pride and elevated by the old friends and the young. At a meeting of Young Men's we always felt that we were in an earnest, pragmatic and always fraternal environment. It was felt at a meeting at the Czenstochow branch of the Jewish National Workers Union (when it existed) that a great national idea lives here and has an effect. The social and cultural struggle of our time was felt in the Czenstochower branch of the Jewish Fraternal Order (International Workers Order), the youngest *landsmanschaft* organization in New York. The most important thing with which it distinguished itself was in the supervision of the Jewish school, an area that was so badly neglected by the leaders of the Jewish masses in America. The same spirit reigned in the unions in Detroit, Chicago, Toronto and Los Angeles. The younger Independent Union in Chicago brought something new and very important into the lives of the *landsmanschaftn*. Namely, it underlined the need to work for the culture of the Jewish masses in America itself. In addition to this a large number of Czenstochower were spread over other not-Czenstochow *landsmanschaftn* and lodges such as the *Zaloshiner* [Dzialoszyn] *Chevra Anshei Bnei Achim*, the Masons and Odd Fellows.

However, in the aid work carried out by the Czenstochower Relief in New York, by the Ladies Auxiliary and, later, by United Czenstochower Relief in New York – they were united for one purpose under one roof – all of the Czenstochower organizations that were spread across the breadth and width of the world, which means New York, as well as Chicago and those in other cities. All those from Czenstochow, no matter their political leanings or the order to which they belonged, were above all connected by the strongest threads of their souls to their home city where they had lived through so much and lost so much...

After the great destruction of the Jewish cities and *shtetlekh* in Poland became known, many false prophets predicted the end of the *landsmanschaftn* organizations here in America, particularly the aid organizations: "Your cities were brought to ruin; there is no one to help." They did not grasp and did not understand that, after the horrible destruction of our Jewish cities in Europe, the cry, "O Israel! Now see to your own house..." [II Chronicles 10:16] now meant: Let us each approach in our own way the treason against our people and Hitler's accursed work of extermination. Surely, now the wonderful strength of the *landsmanschaft* that binds together thousands of individuals from a city in one fraternal union is needed to extend the golden chain from past generations further and from the millions of annihilated martyrs. The greatest duty rests on us here in America where we remain the largest and strongest Jewish community.

[Page 261]

     * [[****]]

The aid work for Czenstochow demanded very great sacrifices, but also brought a great deal of joy and festivity to the usual grey and difficult life in America. The annual balls during the first years of the aid work actually were Czenstochow holidays. We came together from all of the corners of the city. We came from the suburbs, from the surrounding towns. Grandfathers and grandmothers who had been brought from Czenstochow came. The fathers and mothers came and grandchildren came.

At the balls, first the young people danced. "The children first." Incidentally, at the home of a wedding – and every ball here was a true Jewish wedding – the young people would also dance first. Then the old danced a dance of the bride and groom. When the young emptied the place, the old began a *sher* [lively dance] and *hopke* [Russian dance] and *karahad* [circle dance] and everyone danced what was danced in Czenstochow at joyous occasions.

And a "finance" took place after every ball – that meant an accounting in the house of one of the relief workers. They again made a "supper," drank a *l'chaim* [a toast to life], celebrated that they were in America and they could aid Czenstochow and they increased the income from the ball. They did not come together in America without a purpose...

In addition to the balls, banquets took place not only with all of the good things that America possessed, but also with Jewish joy, enthusiasm and the confidence that was brought from the home [Czenstochow]. The young pioneers of Yiddish theater in Czenstochow and old, eternal aid worker, Yakov Ber Silwer, his friend Leon Teich and other singers filled the room with Yiddish melodies and we held inspired talks and collected money and, still more, gathered strength to be a Jew and we did not surrender to the riches of America.

Income	Sum *zl. gr.*[2]
Balance to 1 September 1925	548/70
From Czenstochower Relief in New York $400	3,615/-
From Czenstochower Ladies Auxiliary in N.Y. $600	4,858
Czenstochower Chicago Relief Committee $251	2,254/10
Czenstochower Aid Society in Detroit $100	980
Czenstochower Youth Club in New York $20	181/60
[Assistance] through Dr. Peter Awicki $25	227.50
Subsidy from city hall for the children's homes	4,800
Subsidy from city hall for the schools	2,100
Subsidy from the Jewish community	275
Subsidy from the Central Jewish School Organization in Warsaw	1,777/70
Tuition	1,297/49
Projects	547/96
Saving actions for the meeting places	205/65
Objects sold	140
From the children for breakfasts	40/23
Loan of $100	980
Rent from the premises at Stroczacke 10	144
Total	24,972/93

Expenses	Sum zl. gr.
Teaching personnel salaries	13,146/59
Servant personnel salaries	1,519/50
Administration (managing committee and managing committee expenditures)	1,686/84
Management of the schools	435/85
Management of the children's homes	337/75
Inventory	383/60
Heating and lighting	613/17

Premises [at] Strazynskiego 10 (residences for the teachers and premises)	1,320/30
Premises for the children's home	701/-
Teaching tools	117/28
School materials	17/55
General Worker Library	12/-
Rescue actions for the premises	15/-
Debts	1,764/20
Events	603/60
Food for the children	608/84
Sick fund	300/-
Repairs	1,160/30
Total	24,743/37

Balance to 1 September 1926	229/56

Chairman Sz. Nirenberg; Secretary Y. Jurista; Treasurer W. Fajga; Manager A. Chrabolowski; Members: Avraham Brat, Leon Zajdman, R. Federman, M. Alter, M. Weksler

Document accompanying "General Survey of Fraternal Aid" Article

[Page 262]

When the opening of the Y.L. Peretz house was celebrated in Czenstochow, a magnificent banquet took place in New York at Beethoven Hall. The Czenstochowers in America certainly had the right to celebrate after such work was done in erecting a beautiful house that cost 10,000 dollars. The heroes at the banquet really were the two delegates to Czenstochow, Louis Shimkowicz and Chaim Leib Szwarc. Abe Kaufman was chairman of the banquet. The toastmaster was Friend Jacob Zeidman who spoke English, but who possessed more Jewish humor and more of a devoted Jewish heart than anyone else. At the banquet, friends Chaim Leib Szwarc, Louis Szimkowicz, Kopl Gerichter, H. Win, Abe Kaufman and Mrs. Samuels, the then chairwoman of the Ladies Auxiliary, recognized the great achievements of the Czenstochowers in America, who erected the first house in Poland for the Y.L. Peretz School. Finally at the banquet appeared Friend Mendl Szuchter, who had proposed the idea of the house in Czenstochow and the hundreds of friends at the banquet celebrated with him.

Two great holidays for the Czenstochowers were two local people's banquets.

One took place in honor of Friend Yosef Kaufman, long-time secretary-treasurer of United Czenstochower Relief, and his wife, Rachel Kaufman, a devoted activist for Relief and of the Ladies Auxiliary. The love and respect of all of the Czenstochower friends for two of their best and most devoted members was expressed at the meeting by the greeters, who represented all of the Czenstochower organizations in New York and by many personal friends.

The second banquet took place at the departure to California of the president of United Czenstochower Relief in New York to improve his health. With the large number of those assembled and with the collection of a large sum of money for Relief, the Czenstochower *landsmanschaft* showed how he was valued and esteemed as one of its best men of the people, who carried on himself the burden of responsibility and difficult leadership of fraternal aid activity.

A very enthusiastic gathering took place when the Ladies Auxiliary unveiled a tablet with the names of the children of American *landsleit* in the American army.

There was also a great holiday for the Czenstochowers in New York when the publishing of a sample (model) of the book *Czenstochower Yidn* [*Jews of Czenstochow*] was celebrated, which tangibly showed the thousand Czenstochowers in America how the book would look.

As at every enumerated holiday and celebration, as well as at many others, as at a welcome for those who were saved from the Hitler destruction, or at the of Federman from his tour through several American cities to organize the National conference and so on, Yiddish song, Yiddish poetry and Yiddish humor recited by our own Czenstochower artist, Fela Fajnrajch-Bira and our artists and singers illuminated and enthralled the gathering and connected those taking part with the greater Jewish life that flows everywhere like an eternal spring wherever the Jewish people live or will live.

War Time, Destruction of Czenstochow and Aid for the Survivors

Normal contact with Czenstochow was interrupted with the start of the Second World War. However, our hearts did not cease to ache for the Czenstochower, fathers and mothers, sisters and brothers. From the scant information that arrived, we only knew about individual arrestees, such as Rayzele and Moshe Berkensztat, about the ghetto into which the Jewish population had been forced and of the great need that reigned there.

צום „טשענסטאכאװער רעליעף" און „לײדיס־עקזילערי" אין נױ־יארק!

צו די טשענסטאכאװער הילפס־פאריינען אין שיקאגא, דעטראיט, טאראנטא א. א.!

צו אלע טשענסטאכאװער לאנדסלײט און קרובים אין אמעריקע!

To Czenstochower Relief and Ladies Auxiliary in New York!
To the Czenstochower Aid Unions in Chicago, Detroit and Toronto and So On!
To all Czenstochower *Landsleit* and Relatives in America!

[Page 263]

Document from United Czenstochower Relief

Comrades and friends!

We turn to you in our present appeal with a strong cry of pain that comes from the hearts of hundreds of children, parents, friends and comrades:

Our children's home and *folks-shul* [people's school] [in Czenstochow] has existed for 13 years. It is only thanks to your great fraternal help as well as the constant care and the self-sacrificing work of the dedicated men and women volunteers of the Aid Union in America that these institutions were supported, where our children – the children of our relatives and friends and hundreds of children from the poorest strata of the Jewish population – received light, education and a healthy upbringing, thus bringing such joy and light to the corners of their warm and dear homes. However, now the cherished institutions [in Czenstochow], which were built with great effort and hardship by all of our devoted friends, are in danger because there is no help from anyone.

No government in Poland has ever supported our schools. Just the opposite, the Polish government wants to annihilate our children's home and *folks-shul* because they educate our children in the living people's language of the Jewish masses – in Yiddish – and because our school is educating a new, healthy generation that will truly be capable of fighting every flagrant injustice being done to us and [to meet the] needs of the Jewish masses. At this moment it is even worse; the dictators in Poland suppress with their brutal hands and destroy everything that has been built by the working masses with blood and sweat and they do not exclude our children's homes and *folks-shuln* that were created with so much sacrifice and devotion.

The city hall, which during the course of recent years did subsidize our institutions, now under the influence of the government commissar took away this long fought for subsidy (over 10,000 *zlotes*) that the school received until now and they have refused to support the children's home and *folks-shul* in the future.

At the same time, there is terrible need in the land, hovering unemployment. The need and poverty of the Jewish masses is even greater. The poverty of our parents, who because of their own critical situation cannot pay tuition and [are unable] to support the school, is particularly obvious and our beautiful school building in Czenstochow is in danger.

Over 200 of our poor workers remain in the streets without education and schooling and [in danger] of losing their warm places if immediate help does not arrive, to the delight of our enemies.

Can we let that happen?

Mendl and Chaya Bat
Mordekhai and Miriam Bernard
Shlomo and Fanya Borzykowski
Leib And Sura Grinsztajn
Yokim and Ester Grinszpan
Gershon and Fradl Gliksman
Shlomo and Ester Dilewski
Mordekhai and Sura Herszlikowicz
Hersh and Mirl Wiewiorowski
Ayzik and Leah Zajfert
Avraham and Dobra Zajdenknopf
Yisroel and Zlata Jaranowski
Ziskind and Zisl Laska
Meir & Rayzl Zusman
Meir and Chaya Sura Mitelman
Aba and Mirl Michlasz
Alta and Fradl Naparta
Itshe and Ester Poslaniec
Mordekhai and Yeta Flachte
Avraham Foringer
Yehiel and Pesa Szarf
Zalman and Chana Richter
Hercka Fiszbajn
Yehezkiel and Dwoyra Frajmowicz
Moshe and Perl Krawczyk
Yankl and Ester Kaczka
Meir and Sura Kupfer
Shayndl Rajber
Avraham and Franya Rozental
Hinda Ruszin
Moshe and Leah Rajnharc
Dovid and Ruchl Rotensztajn
Hershl and Golda Szwarc
Yeshaya and Shifra Szpic
Yosef and Chana Szwider
Shlomo and Manua Szmulewicz
Yitzhak and Gitl Moszkowicz

Moshe Braun
Moshe Leib and Rywka Szimkowicz
Avraham and Rywka Lubinski
Eliyahu and Brukha Fawlowicz
Moshe and Mariem Gobrowski
Moshe and Rayzl Berkensztat
Berl and Sura Berkowicz
Zalman and Sura Bulwik
Makhl and Pesa Beser
Avrahm and Leah Berman
Dwoyra Teper
Liba Jakubowicz
Borukh Shimeon and Chava Jakubowicz
Hershl and Bulove Lewkowicz
Arin and Royza Lewkowicz
Moshe and Chava Lederman
Zalman Lederman
Hershl and Ruchl Markowicz
Pinkhus and Perl Secemski
Yankl and Sura Ester Poslanec
Yankl and Sura Cygler
Dovid and Dwoyra Rotensztajn
Leibl and Fradl Rozenstajn
Moshe and Royza Sztarlman
Ahron and Rywka Opoczinski
Fajnski
Mabinc Balzam
Berl and Mindl Dorfman
Chaim and Eidl Ezring
Ahron Furberg
Mirl Grinbaum
Shayndl Jakubowicz
Shlomo and Chaya Krakowski
Kopl and Faygl Poslanec
Golda Szliwka

Brothers and Sisters!

You know well that with our own poor strength we cannot support our school ourselves without your support. When we, on our side, exert ourselves and do everything we possibly can, this is not enough because the school is in need, particularly now – due to the catastrophic situation created – [we need] your great fraternal help. We also know very well about the great crisis now reigning in America, but despite this, we strongly believe that you will make every effort so that our children's homes, which are dear and precious to you, will continue to exist and work normally.

Therefore, we appeal to you:

Save our educational institutions that have been supported by you until now! Send your fraternal support quickly!

Save our consolation – our children! Do not let our children be thrown out into the street ... without education and have them suffer from hunger and the cold!

Create a large rescue fund that will make possible the existence of our school!

Support the rescue campaign with whatever you can! Convince your friends and acquaintances to also give their fraternal support. You will do a great thing, thus fulfilling your fraternal and human duty to the children of your old home.

Help further to support the only warm and bright children's homes!

Care for the further existence of all of our beautiful work – the Jewish school!

With a comradely and fraternal greeting

The Managing Committee of the Workers Children's Homes and *Folks-Shuln* named for Y. L. Peretz in Czenstochow

Sh. Girenberg, A. Brat, R. Federman, Z. Krakower,

M. Szlezinger, L. Berkowicz, D. Jakubowicz, W. Fajnc,

M. Lederman, M. Entelis, L. Tenenbaum, H. Zawadski.

*

The Parents of the Children

Leibush and Yentl Berkowicz
Szaya and Yoska Makowski
Mordekhai and Faygl Figlasz
Berl and Shifra Sticki
Leib and Liba Rozenberg
Avraham and Shprintsa Litewski
Meir and Dora Zeligman
Leibush and Fradl Kayzer
Elihu, Manya Czerwonajagoda
Shlomo and Fradl Richtiger
Arin and Zisl Altman
Yitzhak and Ester Bendit
Eidl and Leah Bomba
Mordekhai and Rayzl Buchwalter
Yosef and Miriam Berkensztadt
Shlomo and Sura Wajnbaum
Mendl and Frimet Wajs
Shmuel and Sura Czarny
Melekh and Hendl Chlewicki
Melekh and Nakha Lublinski
Meir and Rodl Merin
Pinkhus and Chana Markowicz
Meir and Chaya Sura Mitelman
Mordekhai Dovid and Hela Salem
Arin Friberg
Henekh and Leah Frajermauer
Luzer and Rayzl Eizner
Yitzhak and Manya Eisner
Yisroel and Leah Orbach
(illegible)
Moshe and Royze Warszawski
Shajndl Jakubowicz
Yisroel and Tsirl Unglik
Yitzhak and Chena Lubinski
Avraham and Faygl Libeskind
Khonen and Ruchl Majerczyk
Asher and Brayndl Szklarz
Leib and Tauba Erlich
Kopl and Faygl Poslaniec
Zelig Piatigorski
Rajzl Pramisel

Yosef and Chava Furberg
Yakov and Dwoyra Fraylech
Dwoyra Ruszecka
Shlomo and Manya Sztarkman
Mendl and Tauba Babrowski
Yankil and Brayndl Brat
Nakhman and Chaya Gutman
Mordekhai and Sura Herszlikowicz
Yitzhak and Tauba Wolski
Avraham Ber and Leah Oberman
Zalman and Leah Brat
Chaim and Chana Bendet
Avraham and Royza Brat
Shaya and Rayzl Wajntraub
Mendl and Fraydl Wajs
Ester Leah Wroclawska
Moshe and Manya Zonensztajn
Yehezkeil and Shayndl Jakubowicz
Fishl and Manya Lederman
Gershon and Yakhet Krakowski
Shaya and Chaya Erlich
Hershl and Rywka Frajman
Mindl Salomonowicz
Yisroel and Chava Dorfman
Berish and Chava Jablonkewicz
Rafal and Ruchl Dimant
Yankil and Liba Wasilewicz
Hersh Leib and Dina Szeradski
Zisman and Yente Zilberszac
Mendl and Rywka Krakowski

Czenstochow, February 1930.

The United Czenstochower Relief supported the Joint [Distribution Committee], the ORT [Society for Trades and Agricultural Labor], HIAS [Hebrew Immigrant Aid Society], Workers' Committee, the Russian War Relief, the Red Cross and other state aid organizations.

America had entered the war. The contact with Czenstochow ceased completely. Horrible, terrifying, unbelievable information and reports tore through the walls of fire and iron that surrounded all of Europe. The children of our aid workers and *landsleit* went to the front. However, the fraternal hand was not lowered in despair. We must be ready for when the hour of liberation comes became the slogan of aid work.

[Page 264]

The victory of our armies, along with our allies: the Soviet Union and England who liberated the world from the fear of the Nazi barbarians, also exposed the horror and terror of the Jewish destruction. Czenstochow, like hundreds of other cities and *shtetlekh* [towns] in Poland is no more, except for a small number of survivors on the spot and in the extermination camps in Germany. It was six months after the liberation until it was clear that we had to gather all our strength for those who were saved earlier and later in America, *Eretz-Yisroel* and other nations in order to help the surviving brothers in Czenstochow and unite in the reconstruction after the largest Jewish annihilation since the destruction of the Temple.

A national conference was called of all of the Czenstochow *landsmanschaftn* in America and Canada. A central office of all aid unions was created. The conference itself, at which representatives assembled from all of the cities in America and Canada with the greatest number of Czenstochower *landsmanschaftn*, was a historic event.

It was the first expression of a deep consciousness that awoke in the masses of Jewish people in America that in view of the immense, terrible destruction, we could not and must not be divided into separate local groups. The aid work, as well as our entire continuing struggle for survival must be done as one, with united strength, no matter how difficult this will be and no matter what interferences there will be on our road. In this sense, the Czenstochower *landsmanschaftn* in America showed the road to others. They must not stray from this road. This was of the greatest importance in the current perilous hour of our history.

However, the connection with Czenstochowers in other countries also had a very great significance. In the first place was our connection with the *landsmanschaft* in *Eretz-Yisroel*, from which we were separated for so long. The contact that was made with our *landsmanschaftn* in Argentina, Mexico, Australia, England (London), France, Belgium, Sweden and China (Shanghai) was also important and as much as was possible with the camps of the uprooted people in Germany and Austria. Czenstochower *Landsman-schaftn* organizations even were created in a number of camps.

United Czenstochow Relief together with the central office of the Aid Unions in America and Canada was in constant contact with the Jewish regional committee in Czenstochow and provided it with large sums of money and goods. Packages of food products were also sent everywhere where there were Czenstochower refugees and those saved from the lime ovens as long as it was possible to reach them.

Czenstochow, Jewish Czenstochow, where generations of Jews lived is a ruin, destroyed to its foundations by the German blackguards. Only a small number survived. However, the children who were raised by Jewish Czenstochow and who are now spread all across the wide oceans and [in many] countries remain and will remain its children. And their parental home city will never be extinguished in their hearts. A friend from Chicago spoke before them from the depths of his heart and said: "If, God forbid, there had not been a living soul remaining there, we would have sanctified the stones on which our parents, our brothers and sisters had walked."

With a flaming love in our hearts for our city, for our Czenstochower survivors, we will live, work, begin anew to come together from all corners of the world, unite like brothers to help them, to help ourselves, to continue to draw the golden chain of Jewish generations and of Jewish survival.

Translator's Footnotes

1. The Dinezon Committee was composed of both Bundists and others who supported the creation of secular Yiddish schools in Poland. The committee was named for Yankev Dinezon, who worked with Y.L. Peretz to create children's homes and schools for Jewish children orphaned during the First World War.

2. *Zlotes* and *groshn*

[Page 265]
Czenstochower Aid Society and Czenstochower Relief Committee in New York
A. Koifman

The idea of founding a Czenstochower Aid Society was born in Tompkins Square Park, Seventh Street and Avenue B in New York at the beginning of the summer of 1914.

Czenstochower *landsleit* [people from the same town] would come together there and share the news from their old home city and learn what was happening among the *landsleit* here in New York. The purpose of the society was to be a frequent gathering of the *landsleit* who were divided and separated from one another and to support the needy in case of illness, unemployment or other cases of misfortune.

The first gathering of a large group of *landsleit* took place on 2 July 1914 at the synagogue of the Belchatower Society, Sixth Street, between Avenue B and C in New York. Everyone present agreed to create an organization to which all *landsleit* could belong without any distinction due to age, religious or social beliefs.

It was decided that the organization would be called "Czenstochower Aid Society."

The purpose of the society was established thus:

1. to help every *landsman* or *landsfroy* [man or woman from the same town] at times of need or illness.

2. to create work among our *landsleit* for the unemployed *landsleit*.

3. if either a *landsman* or *landsfroy* cannot remain in America for certain reasons, to help them with financial means to return home.

4. everyone can become a member without distinction as to party and organization.

Officials and an executive member were elected to lead the organization.

Friend Chaim–Leib Swarc was elected as the first president.

It was decided that the meetings of the society would take place every Monday.

New members came to each meeting.

At one meeting, on the last Monday in August 1914, we learned that the First World War had broken out and Czenstochow was taken by the Germans on *Shabbos* [Sabbath] night (the Germans occupied Czenstochow on the morning of 3 August – ed.) We rejoiced that we had become "Germans"... we did not understand then that the world war meant death for us and for the entire world.

On a Sunday in September, the Aid Society had its first picnic in Glendale Schuetzen Park, in Brooklyn. Several hundred people came together and had a good time together.

Several hundred flags with the inscription "Czenstochower Aid Society" were sold at the picnic.

It was decided later to arrange a picnic every year and this did indeed happen continuously for several years. The *landsleit* knew that we would come together for a picnic in the summer and spend the entire day among *landsleit*, family, friends and acquaintances.

In those years, two *landsleit*, Simkha Kalka and Joseph Kaufman, had their printing shop at 154 Delancey Street, where many friends and acquaintances would meet. The news arrived then that our friend, Elkone Chrabalowski, was in a prisoner–of–war camp in Austria. It was decided immediately to send him several dollars and when we received an answer, to send [money] again. Thus was help sent several times.

The Aid Society became very well–known among our *landsleit*. Everyone who needed help was supported by the society. After the First World War, the Aid Society helped several friends who could not remain here [in New York] return home.

The first ball took place at Avenue A between 4th and 5th Streets, in New York, in 1915. Around 550 people came together. The ball was a success. The next year, the ball was arranged in Tammany Hall on 14th Street, then one of the most beautiful locations in New York. Our balls took place there several years in a row. Later, a larger place was needed; the balls took place in various hotels. Over a thousand people would come to the ball.

[Page 266]

The balls were a tradition for the *landsleit,* just as the yearly picnic.

At the beginning, the society supported the sick and the needy in New York with the income brought in by these undertakings; later, large sums were sent to Czenstochow every year.

At the beginning, the aid money for Czenstochow was sent to the address of the Rabbi, Reb Nakhum Asz for him to divide the support among the institutions of the *kehile* [organized Jewish community], such as, for example, the old age home, the Jewish hospital and so on, according to our instructions. Right after the First World War, the Aid Society joined the workers organization that carried on aid activities among the workers and poor masses, such as the workers kitchen, children's home and so on and with other general charity institutions and the aid money was sent directly to them.

At any opportunity at a get–together, the friends and activists of the Aid Society did not forget the society, as, for example, a large sum [of money] was collected in 1917 at the wedding of Friend Joseph Kaufman and Rachel Szaja.

The society also undertook theater benefits many times. The members took part in committees, visited *landsleit* and sold theater tickets. In general, the active members of the Aid Society and, later, the Czenstochower Relief in New York gave a great deal of time and energy for the benefit of the society.

Each undertaking demanded a great deal of effort and work. The *landsleit* had to be visited, one had to climb to the fifth or sixth floor and sometimes higher. However, no sacrifice was too difficult for the holy work of aid for the brothers and sisters in the old home.

The famous, popular speaker, Joseph Barondess, appeared at a theater undertaking of the Czenstochower Aid Society and appealed to those in the theater to support the war victims in Czenstochow. His appeal made a strong impression and several hundred dollars were collected then.

The executive would come together at the house of a member after each function and make an accounting (financial) of the expenses and income. The member at whose home they would come together, as was the way, would arrange a nice meal for those assembled. A large sum of money always would be collected and this money would increase the amount made from the function.

In 1920, the writer of these lines was sent on a tour of America. He visited Chicago, Detroit, Toronto, Pittsburgh, Cleveland and Philadelphia, spent around three months in all of the cities and collected several hundred dollars in aid for the war victims.

The main income of the society, and, later, Relief, however, was from the balls, actually from the journal that was printed at this opportunity. The friends and *landsleit* gave their greetings (complements), printed advertisements and also gathered [greetings and advertisements] from their acquaintances who were not from Czenstochow. Each year, the journal brought in hundreds and many times thousands of dollars of profit.

There were many *landsleit* who donated 50 dollars and more every year. Among those who stood out was Friend Jakob Rechnitz, who contributed 100 dollars to the ball every year and, in addition, bought tickets for 25 dollars.

The need of our brothers and sisters in Czenstochow grew even more than the work of the Aid Society did. The idea arose of bringing to the aid work the existing organizations in New York, which at first consisted of the *Arbeter Ring* branch no. 261, Czenstochower Young Men and the Czenstochower branch of the Jewish National Workers' Union. The organizations agreed and elected their representatives. At one of the meetings of the Aid Society with the representatives of other Czenstochow organizations in New York, it was decided that the name "Aid Society" would be changed to the Czenstochower Relief Committee. The committee would have the separate task of collecting aid for the war victims in Czenstochow. The annual ball for 1921 had already been arranged through the Czenstochower Relief Committee.

In 1921, Friend Mendl Szuchter, one of the leaders of the workers movement in Czenstochow, esteemed communal worker in Chicago and member of the then People's Relief Committee in America [P.R.C.] was sent as a delegate of the P.R.C. to a conference in Europe. He also was supposed to visit Poland and give a certain sum of money for aid purposes. The Czenstochower Relief Committee voted to send several hundred dollars through Comrade Szuchter for the local [Czenstochow] aid organizations and also called a special meeting to say goodbye to Friend Szuchter before he departed. At this opportunity, Friend Szuchter was asked to investigate the condition of the Jews in Czenstochow and to find out which institutions there were the most useful and the most in need.

[Page 267]

When Friend Szuchter returned from his trip, the Czenstochower Relief Committee again arranged a meeting to hear his report. He described the terrible situation for the Jews in Poland, which meant [the need] of help for them from America. He particularly emphasized the important work of the Jewish children's homes and *folks–shuln* [public schools] in Czenstochow in which several 100 poor workers' children were fed, studied and raised. He declared that if the Czenstochow *landsleit* [people from the same town] in America wanted to do something useful and substantial for their home city that would remain a permanent memorial for their brothers on the other side of the sea, they should help erect their own house for the children's homes and *folks–shuln*.

Friend Szuchter's proposal inspired everyone. It immediately was decided that from then and into the future we would do everything that was in our power to accomplish this magnificent plan.

An appeal that we were preparing to create our own house for Jewish children's homes in Czenstochow was printed in the journal that was published for the annual ball in 1922. The *landsleit* accepted the idea with inspiration and the ball that year had the greatest success.

In addition to these undertakings, the friends at the various organizations contributed certain sums for the purpose of building the house. Thus, the members of Czenstochower Young Men taxed themselves five dollars each. The Czenstochower *Arbeter Ring* [Workman's Circle] branch 261 and the Czenstochower branch of the Jewish National Workers' Union also contributed their portions of money.

The Czenstochower Relief held a series of meeting after the sum of several thousand dollars was collected and discussed the question of sending a delegation to Czenstochow to purchase the house. The two Relief activists, Friend Louis Szimkowicz and Chaim Leib Szwarc were elected. They traveled to Czenstochow and spent several weeks there.

During [their visit] they held a large number of conferences and meetings with representatives of various classes of the Czenstochow population, heard about a large number of plans about how to accomplish the idea of creating a house and after much deliberation, decided to buy the house located at Krutka 23 for the sum of 3,700 dollars. The disadvantage was that the actual house for the children's home and school had first to be built because the house that was on the property was too small for a school. The situation had a great attribute that in building a new house, it could be planned specially in a way so that it was suitable for a children's home and school.

The Relief delegates in Czenstochow who bought the house also carried out the unification of several children's homes and schools under the joint managing committee in which three political group, *Fareinikte* [United], *Poalei–Zion* [Marxist Zionists] and the Bund were represented. In addition, a general library was created out of the three separate libraries that existed then in Czenstochow. The delegates designated a sum of money for new books and for the general library and also designated certain sums of money for other worthwhile institutions.

When the delegates returned to New York they gave a full report at a large meeting about everything that they had done in Czenstochow. The entire Relief Committee took note of the report with great satisfaction and thanked them for their great work.

Relief began energetic and feverish activity to collect the money to build the house.

The ball organized in 1923 was dedicated to this purpose and in the journal published on 17 November 1923 they [the Relief Committee] made use of the opportunity to issue a call in with the title:

The Czenstochow Relief in New York is buying house for the children's home and *Folkshul* [public school] in Czenstochow.

From then on, the income from all undertakings increased, averaging around 2,000 dollars a year. Most of the money was utilized for the Y.L. Peretz Children's Home and *Folkshul* in Czenstochow.

[Page 268]

The Ladies Auxiliary, which was founded by Friend Szimkowicz before he left for Czenstochow, helped Relief in its work to finish the house and sent the first 500 dollars to Czenstochow. The decision was made at a meeting at Friend Yisroelka Brader's house in March 1923.

In April 1923, Relief undertook the collection of books for the general Czenstochow library. The branch of the Jewish National Workers' Union contributed 130 books to the activity. The number of books collected by Relief and sent to Czenstochow reached several hundred.

On 13 January 1924 the worker leader and emissary from *Tsysho* (Central Jewish School Organization) in Warsaw – Beinish Michalewicz – visited the meeting of Czenstochower Relief and gave a report about the situation for the Jewish masses in Poland and about the problems of the Jewish schools all over Poland and in Czenstochow.

In June 1924 Relief received a report from Czenstochow that the official dedication of the house for the children's homes and *folkshul* would take place on 5 July.

In December 1924 Friend Chrabalowski returned to Czenstochow after being in Chicago for a year and brought 600 dollars with him for the schools. Two hundred dollars [were from] Chicago, 200 dollars from Czenstochower Relief in New York and 200 dollars from the Ladies Auxiliary. In addition, Relief sent 100 dollars with him for the Jewish hospital and 100 dollars for the old age home. He also was authorized to be the official representative of Relief in the managing committee of the children's home and *folkshul* in Czenstochow. The committee also called for the house to be named after Y.L. Peretz.

Relief and all of the other Czenstochow organizations collected the sum of 1,000 dollars in 1926 because of the great need among the general Jewish population in Czenstochow, which was expressed in an urgent call for help, and sent it to Rabbi Nakhum Asz and to the chairman of the school managing committee, Shaya Nirenberg. Instructions were sent with the money to create a joint committee that would distribute the money among the general philanthropic and worker organizations.

The same year, Relief carried out activities to install a marble plaque with the name of the organizations and people who had taken part in the campaign to build the Y.L. Peretz House in Czenstochow.

In addition to the annual balls, theater undertakings and other gatherings organized by Relief, yearly banquets and meetings took place. The largest and most impressive banquet took place in 1926 at the Beethoven Hall that brought in the sum of around 1,200 dollars.

In December 1926 Friend Chrabalowski came to New York for the second time. He gave a report at a Relief meeting on 13 December about the terrible situation of the Jewish masses in Poland in general and about the schools in Czenstochow in particular. Mr. Chrabalowski remained active in Relief from then on as a contact–correspondent with Czenstochow and as secretary.

On 6 April 1928 Friend Zilber organized a theater performance with the help of the actor Leon Reich who appeared at Relief banquets several times. The performance brought in over 200 dollars in income.

On 27 May 1928 a Relief and Ladies Auxiliary banquet took place. Friend Chayala Waga-Rojtman, one of the first children's home teachers who had come to New York that year, appeared.

At a meeting on 14 May 1928 it was decided that Relief would arrange its activities jointly with the Ladies Auxiliary and the income would be evenly divided between both organizations.

On 4 February 1929 Relief decided to call a conference of all Czenstochower organizations to consider the question of aid for the political arrestees after Friend Szlingbaum, who had visited Czenstochow, gave a report about the political persecutions and arrests in Poland.

On 4 March 1929 Relief decided to begin the work of publishing a book about the history of Czenstochow with the name, *Czenstochower Album*. A committee was elected that began the work, but the work ceased because of a series of difficulties.

In April 1930 Czenstochower Relief in New York arranged a concert and a film about the children's home and *folkshul* in Czenstochow. A film made in New York of the activists from Relief and the Ladies Auxiliary was shown with the film that was sent from Czenstochow. Relief also organized such film–concerts in Detroit and Chicago. Friend Karl Gerichter was the delegate of Relief who organized the concerts in the two above–mentioned cities. The income from the film reached over 500 dollars.

[Page 269]

At that time the financial situation of the school in Czenstochow became worse from day to day. The [donations] from Relief became smaller because of the rising depression in America. The managing committee of the school mortgaged the house for a sum of 600 dollars and rented out a part of the house as private residences. Seeing that if things continued in this way they would lose the school and the house, Relief decided to send demands to the managing committee that the school abandon the seven classes, maintain the children's home and arrange afternoon classes for the older children.

A number of active members declared on 11 May 1930 that they were leaving Relief because differences of opinion among the so–called right and left had became stronger at that time. A meeting of Relief activists was held at the home of Friend Fridman at the end of summer of that same year. It was decided to end the work of Relief as a separate organization and to work with the Ladies Auxiliary as much as possible to support the children's home in Czenstochow. Thus closed a beautiful chapter of fraternal aid and self–sacrificing work done by the Czenstochower *landsleit* in New York for their brothers and sisters on the other side of the ocean.

                    * * *

The first chairman of the Aid Society and, later, Czenstochower Relief in New York was Friend Louis Szwarc. Friend Silwer took over the chairmanship in December 1925. And the chairmanship during the last months of Relief was taken by Friend Szimkowicz and by Friend Kolin. Over the course of time, Friend Fajertag took the chairmanship many times.

Friend Y. Win was the secretary of Relief until June 1926. The secretaries from 28 June until January 1928 were Friend Karl Gerichter and Abe Kaufman. From 1928 on – Friend A. Chrabalowski.

Friend Fajersztajn was the finance secretary until the last day of his life. After him – Friend Fridman.

Most of the meetings of Relief would be held at 276 Houston Street and then at 305 East 6th Street.

─────────

The United Czenstochower Relief Committee in New York

A. Khrobolowski, A. Koifman

The position of the Jewish masses in Poland already was unbearable in 1935. The government of the *polkownikes* [colonels], the so–called *Sanacja* [sanitation in Polish, a Polish political movement led by Marshal Josef Pilsudski], with the help of all the reactionary powers in the country, barred the Jewish population from the main sources of income through laws and restrictions. Hunger and need reigned everywhere. Several *landsleit* [people from the same town] received letters from Czenstochow, which described the terrible situation and asked for help. It was before Passover and there was an urgent need to provide matzos for the needy Czenstochow Jews. The question was considered at a meeting of the Young Men and it was decided that help would be sent. A committee was founded, which collected 400 dollars. The Young Men contributed 100 dollars. This money was telegraphed immediately to Czenstochow in the name of Rabbi Nakhum Asz.

On 29 May 1935, the committee called a special meeting of the Czenstochow organizations in New York with the purpose of reviving the aid committee. Taking part in the meeting were the Young Men, *First Zaloshiner* [Dzialoszyn] *Chevra Anshei Bnei Achim*, branch 261 of the *Arbeter Ring* [Workman's Circle]. Several weeks later, a revived aid committee also became involved in the Czenstochower branch 11 of the United National Workers Order.

[Page 270]

The meeting decided that the new aid committee would be called United Czenstochower Relief.

Elected as officials were:

Natan (Nisen) Cymerman, president.

Avraham Yakov Senzer, vice president.

Louis Szimkowicz, finance secretary.

Joseph Kaufman, secretary.

Over the summer of 1935, the renewed "Relief" organized and recruited members for the organization.

The first ball of the United Relief Committee took place on 25 January 1936 in Webster Hall, which brought in a net income of 1,422 dollars.

The following unions and institutions in Czenstochow were supported with this sum:

1. Y. L. Peretz children's home.
2. the Jewish hospital.
3. the unemployed in the professional unions.
4. *Beis Lekhem* [bread for the poor].
5. *Tomkhai Ani–im* [support for the poor].
6. *Moyshev skeynim* [old age home].
7. *TOZ* (Society for Medical Help).
8. *Patronat* (society in New York to help the political arrestees in Poland).

Seated, right to left: G. Lewi, S. Korpiel, J. Kaufman, H. Fajerstein, Y. Kopin
and A. Kaufman
1st row standing, right to left: R. Federman, Kh. Gliksman, M. Kepp, M.
Gelber, Frajermojer, G. Jacobs and T. Lenczner
2nd row standing, right to left: M. Fajner, Y. B. Silwer, D. Zitman and Y. Kiel
[Kelciglowski]

In April 1936 the elections of officials took place for the second time and elected were:

Louis Szimkowicz, president.

Yeta Lenszner, vice president.

Joseph Kaufman, secretary.

Itshe Zelkowicz, treasurer.

In February 1937 the woman's organization, the Ladies Auxiliary, was newly founded at United Czenstochower Relief.

The new officials [of United Czenstochower Relief] elected in 1937 were:

Avraham Yakov Senzer – president.

Abe Herszkowicz – vice president.

Sam Oberman – treasurer.

Charlie (Skharye) Lewenstein – recording secretary.

In 1937 the Czenstochow *landsmanschaft* [organization of people from the same town] was shocked by the news that pogroms (the third pogrom) had again taken place in Czenstochow. This was in addition to the need and bitter despair that reigned there.

Relief designated the sum of 500 dollars for aid for those suffering. One thousand dollars was sent, including 500 dollars donated by the Union of Polish Jews. The money was sent to the dentist, Ahron Peretz.

Relief called a *Patronat* meeting in connection with the pogrom at the Czenstochower *Chasam Sopher* synagogue under the chairmanship of president Avraham Yakov Senzer, at which the representatives of the "Joint" [Joint Distribution Committee] – Kilimowski, a representative of *ORT*[*Obchestvo Remesienogo Truda* – Association for the Promotion of Skilled Trades], Sister Yeta Lenczner, Morris Szwarc – from Noworadosmk, Y. Frajd of the *Morgn Freiheit* [*Morning Freedom*], Comrade Mordekhai Zelig Hoyrish of the Dzialoszyner Society and others appeared.

The annual ball in 1938 took place on 8 January at the Edison Hotel. The net income reached 2,800 dollars.

The officials elected in 1938 were:

Avraham Senzer, president.

Izzy Berger, vice president.

Joseph Kaufman, finance secretary.

Charlie Lewenstein, recording secretary.

Yankl Kapin (Kapinski), treasurer.

The annual ball in 1939 took place at the Manhattan Center. The officials remained the same for that year.

Relief organized a mass meeting on Sunday, 22 October, the same year at the *Chasam Sopher* synagogue, Clinton Street. Avraham Yakov Senzer (president of Relief] was the chairman of the meeting. Comrade Mordekhai Zelig Hoyrish and Friend Yitzhak Kurski, among others, appeared at the meeting.

The sum of 3,100 dollars was collected by Relief in the year 1939.

The Second World War broke out. The Hitler bands occupied Czenstochow. However, the aid work for Czenstochow did not stop. It was carried out through the intervention of the national organizations, such as the "Joint," ORT and others.

The ball in 1940, which took place on 6 January at the Manhattan Center, was not a joyful one that year. Firstly, Czenstochow already was squirming in the bloody hands of the Nazi murderers; secondly, that evening, the Czenstochow *landsleit* learned of the sudden death of Charlie Lewenstein, who was beloved by everyone who knew him. His funeral took place on 7 January. A large number of *landsleit* and friends accompanied him to his eternal rest.

A memorial evening was organized by United Czenstochower Relief several days later, on Wednesday, 10 January, dedicated to the memory of Charlie Lewenstein.

Friend Max Kaminski was elected as the new recording secretary.

Several friends from Czenstochow arrived in New York during the winter 1940–41, who had succeeded in saving themselves from Hitler's devils via the Soviet Union. They were Rafal Federman, the lawyer Zigmunt Epsztajn, Aleksander Haptka, Herman Zigas and Chana Munawicz. Dr. Lazerowicz came later.

Dr. Moritz Grinbaum and his wife and son, who had come here to the World's Fair, already were in New York.

Friend Rafal Federman was welcomed by United Czenstochower Relief as a leader of a wide series of worker undertakings in Czenstochow and for many years a fighter for the rights of the Jewish masses in Czenstochow. Friends Dr. Lazarowicz, Aleksander Haptka, Zigas and Chana Munawicz also appeared at the meeting of Relief and were welcomed by the president, Friend Senzer, and their Czenstochower friends.

In May 1940 Friend Harry Fajerstein was elected as vice president. The remaining officials remained the same.

[Page 272]

Relief collected the sum of 2,400 dollars during 1940.

The annual Relief and Ladies Auxiliary ball took place in January 1941 at Manhattan Center. There were up to 700 people present.

According to an earlier decision by Relief, a welcoming banquet for Friends R. Federman, Yitzhak and Hela Gurski, Dr. Moritz Grinbaum and his wife, Gertrude, the lawyer Zigmund Epsztajn, Herman Zigas and Chana Munawicz took place on Sunday, 2 March 1941. The banquet was one of Relief's most beautiful undertakings. A large number of guests and representatives from national organizations took part. Friend Joseph Kaufman, finance secretary of Relief, opened the gathering and turned the leadership over to the president of Relief, Friend Avraham Yakov Senzer. Friend A. Chrabalowski greeted the honored guests, who had played a significant role in the life of modern, Jewish Czenstochow, on behalf of United Czenstochower Relief and the Ladies Auxiliary. Friend Tabaczinski, the representative of the Jewish Workers' Committee and the well–known socialist leader of *Freiland* [Freeland] in America, Ben Adir (Dr. Rozin) also appeared. Friend Rambach spoke in the name of the Czenstochower *Arbeter Ring* branch 261. Telegrams and written greetings arrived from Cina Ozszech in Toronto, Canada, Grilak, Epsztajn and Menkof in Los Angeles, Mr. and Mrs. Cincinatus in Toronto, Fanny and Sam Chablow in Chicago.

Finally, Friends R. Federman and Yitzhak Gurski responded to the greetings.

The banquet left a deep impression on those gathered.

At the end of 1941, Friend Abe Kaufman was elected as recording secretary. The remaining Relief officials remained the same.

The income in 1941 was 1,990 dollars.

[During its existence] Czenstochower Relief collected 15,798 dollars. The aid institutions in Czenstochow have already been mentioned. When contact with Czenstochow was interrupted during the war, Relief carried out its aid work through the Joint [Distribution Committee].

Landsleit and Guests at the Banquet Arranged for the Arrival in America of the First Czenstochow Refugees in 1941

Relief decided to support the Workers Committee in New York in connection with the fact that it helped to save several friends from Czenstochow and brought them to New York (R. Federman, Epsztajn, Zigas, Andzsha [Chana] Munawicz.

[Page 273]

At the same time, Relief also supported *ORT* in America and HIAS [Hebrew Immigrant Aid Society].

Relief organized an information bureau after the outbreak of the Second World War that had a great significance as long as there still was a mail connection with Czenstochow, under the direction of R. Federman. The information bureau connected many Czenstochow families and people with their friends in America and dozens of packages of clothing and food were sent with the help of the bureau.

The four issues of the *Bulletin of the United Czenstochower Relief and Ladies Auxiliary in New York* (edited by R. Federman and A. Chrabalowski) had a great significance for the relief work during wartime.

*

On 7 December 1941 our country was shaken by the Japanese attack on Pearl Harbor. America entered the Second World War and new tasks arose for United Czenstochower Relief and the Ladies Auxiliary. Special meetings of the executive and membership of Relief took place. Friends Senzer, Federman and Wajsberg were given the task of drafting a resolution. Such a resolution was adopted:

"United Czenstochower Relief in New York, still remaining devoted to its fundamental position as an aid organization for Czenstochow, considers it as its civic duty with the entry of America into the Second World War, to increase its activity for the essentials of life and to adapt to the needs of our country at a time of war.

"Therefore, we have decided:

1. To recommend to the Ladies Auxiliary that it join the American Red Cross as an organization, help in all of their activities and influence our *landsleit* to join.

2. According to the decision by Relief, a certain sum that our undertaking, the ball, will bring in will be designated for medical and war aid for America and its allies.

[Page 274]

1. United Czenstochower Relief and the Ladies Auxiliary will organize, as far as possible, special undertakings for the same purpose."

On *Shabbos* [Sabbath], 7 February 1942, the annual Czenstochower Ball took place at Central Plaza. This was the last ball arranged by United Czenstochower Relief and the Ladies Auxiliary.

According to a previous decision, part of the income from the ball was designated for the Jewish council of Russian War Relief, for the American Red Cross and New York War Relief.

At a special meeting of the executive on 22 March 1942 it was decided to call a conference of representatives of the Czenstochower organizations in New York to discuss the question of publishing a Czenstochower Almanac. Thus began new, important work for United Czenstochower Relief.

In connection with this, it was decided to collect a fund of 10,000 dollars as a construction fund and for the first aid for Czenstochow and its neighboring *shtetlekh* [towns].

In the call that was printed in connection with the decision, it was said:

"Brothers and sisters:

"The bloody fight with the Nazi beasts is now in full fervor. We know that still more blood – dear blood from the best children of humanity in all corners of the world – will continue to be spilled and great sacrifices will be made by each of us until the horrible, cruel Nazi beasts will finally be beaten.

**Representatives of the Jewish Community with Rabbi Reb Nakhum Asz
at Entrance to the Synagogue after the Celebration of the 150th Rear of
Independence of the United States. Among others, Y. Kopin and A.
Sigman, the delegates from United Czenstochower Relief Committee**

"However as certain as we know that the night must end and the day will come – just as certainly must come the end of the Nazi murderers and now today we must prepare for that day.

"And when the great day comes, dear brothers and sisters, let us remember that what remains of our brothers and sisters after the slaughters, atrocities, torture in the ghettos and concentration camps, will be those gravely tortured, starved, naked, barefoot and without a place to lay one's head.

"The cry to us for help by the individuals who survived the Nazi hell will reach to heaven and woe to us and woe to them, to our unfortunate brothers, if we are not ready to answer their call and give them their first help."

The first sum for this designated purpose was collected on *Shabbos*, 20 June 1942 at St. Marks Place at the inauguration of Relief and the Ladies Auxiliary.

Over 1,000 dollars was collected on *Shabbos*, 19 June 1943 at the celebration in honor of the publishing of a sample of the book, *Czenstochower Yidn* at the Academy Hall.

A farewell banquet at Academy Hall at the departure for Los Angeles, California of Friend Avraham Yakob Senzer, president of United Czenstochower Relief, to improve his health, and around 1,000 was collected.

Friend Harry Fajerstein represented him as chairman and Friend Sam Korpiel as vice chairman during his absence.

Friend Senzer returned from Los Angeles at the end of March 1944 and again took his office as president.

Thursday, 15 May 1944, Relief arranged a special gathering in honor of Friend Izzy Berger, former vice president and executive member of Relief – at the departure of he and his family for Los Angeles, California. A large group of members of Relief and their families and of friends of I. Berger attended the meeting.

Reports began to arrive about the extermination of our brothers and sister in Poland. At first only the names of individual martyrs was known.

Dr. [Emanuel] Ringelblum (well–known historian, who took part in the founding of the committee for a Czenstochower *pinkes* [book of records and history of a community], created in Czenstochow) was honored at one of the meetings of Relief, as well as Ch. Wilczinski, who perished with him at the hands of the Nazi murderers.

On 13 October 1944 a meeting of Relief decided to turn to all *landsleit* in the United States and Canada to send representatives to a national conference with the purpose of coordinating the aid activity for Czenstochow and mobilize all of the *landsmanschaftn* for the book, *Czenstochower Yidn.*

After the victorious entry into Poland of the Soviet Army, when the Jewish Central Committee was founded in Lublin, it was decided to send a transport of food packages through the Polish Union in the name of Dr. Zomersztajn.

[Page 275]

At the same meeting the assembled Relief members donated a large number of food packages.

When the sad news arrived about the martyrs' death of Moshe and Rayzele Berkensztat, Relief arranged a memorial evening at which Friends A. Chrabalowski and Rafal Federman spoke about the idealistic activity of the two martyrs. Avraham Yakov Senzer was the chairman of the meeting.

Friend R. Federman was sent on a tour to visit the cities of Detroit, Chicago and Toronto as was decided earlier by Relief. He also visited Los Angeles and he returned at the end of December.

On Sunday 17 January 1945, under the chairmanship of President Avraham Yakov Senzer, Relief arranged a welcome for Friend Federman, who gave a report of his trip. Those assembled for the evening donated 1,468 dollars.

Friend Nisen Cymerman, first president and founder of United Czenstochower Relief, also sat at the president's table that evening. He died suddenly on his way home.

On Wednesday, 24 January 1945, Relief, under the chairmanship of President Avraham Yakov Senzer, held a memorial gathering in honor of the memory of Nisen Cymerman. The speakers were: Max Jacobs, Joe Jacobs, Max Rabinowicz, Dr. Wajskop. Emanuel Wargon, Sziper, Federman, Charbalowski, Willy Nachtigal, Joseph and Abe Kaufman. In accordance with a proposal by Friend Silver, those assembled honored his memory with the collection of a large sum of money for food packages for the Jewish Central Committee.

It also was decided to accept the proposal of Dr. Wajskop that Relief should arrange a memorial meeting every year on Friend Cymerman's *yarhrzeit* [anniversary of a death].

Czentochow and almost all of Poland was liberated from the Nazis on 16 January 1945. Reports had already come in about the extermination of the Jewish population of our home city from Izbicki and Brandes, who had succeeded in saving themselves in *Eretz Yisroel.* The reports were published in the Jewish newspapers in New York.

Relief organized a mass meeting on Sunday, 25 February 1945. It was a meeting of joy mixed with grief and pain. Czenstochow was liberated from the Nazi murderers. But it already was clear that with the exception of several hundred people, the entire Jewish population – the fathers, the mothers, brothers, sisters and friends of those assembled – had been annihilated. The speakers choked with tears. Those assembled cried. A declaration was accepted at the meeting to erect an eternal light for those who had perished and to arrange an annual memorial day that would be held by all Czenstochower around the world.

A letter came to Relief from the Polish Ambassador in Moscow, Zigmunt Madzelewski. He said that he came from Czenstochow and had learned about our [organization] Relief. He asked that we maintain contact with him.

On Saturday and Sunday, 23 and 24 June 1945, the national conference of the Czenstochower *landsmanschaftn* in America and Canada took place in Beethoven Hall.

A celebration banquet in honor of the delegates to the conference took place on Sunday evening in the same hall. A large group of New York *landsleit* took part. Three thousand four hundred dollars was donated. The Czenstochower Young Men donated 500 dollars from their treasury, 1,000 dollars collected from their members; totaling 1,500 dollars. The Ladies Auxiliary donated 500 dollars and the Czenstochower branch 11 of the Jewish Fraternal People's Order – 200 dollars.

Ambassador Madzelewski's Letter

[Page 276]

The following telegram arrived from Czenstochow several days after the conference:

"A hearty greeting from the children of Y.L. Peretz house."

Signed: Brener, Lederman, Hasenfeld, Weksztajn. Czarni, Yosef Goldberg – Jewish Committee – Aleje number 7.

It was decided on 11 July 1945 in connection with the decision to publish the book, *Czenstochower Yidn*, that 1,500 books would be printed.

Food packages were sent to *landsleit* in various countries whose addresses we had received. It also was decided to send support to the Jewish community in Czenstochow to rebuild the cemetery.

Two thousand dollars were sent to Czenstochow through the Joint and 500 dollars through TOZ.

There was a convention in Detroit on 24 and 25 November 1945.

A mass meeting took place on Sunday, 9 December 1945, at Manhattan Center at which over 3,300 dollars was collected.

On Wednesday, 9 January 1946, a memorial meeting for the deceased president, Nisen Cymerman, took place. Around 500 dollars for matzos for Czenstochow was collected. The Ladies Auxiliary donated 100 dollars.

Five thousand pounds of matzos costing 835 dollars was sent through *Agudas Yisroel*.

A relief committee was founded in Montreal. Friend Federman was at the founding as a delegate of the United Czenstochower Relief Committee.

Five hundred dollars was sent to Paris and 300 dollars to Sweden.

There was a mass meeting at Irving Plaza on 19 May 1946. Yakov Pat reported about his visit to Czenstochow and to Poland in general. Various photographs of Czenstochow were shown. One thousand three hundred and twenty–two dollars was collected.

Friends Senzer and Federman were delegates to Chicago; they brought the sum of 1,800 dollars to send to Czenstochow.

On Wednesday, 12 June 1946, Friend Wolf Gliksman, who had not long ago returned from Europe, was present at the Relief meeting. He gave his greetings to Relief. It was decided to place the full text of his speech in the minutes as well as to print them in the book, *Czenstochower Yidn*, which we provide here:

The Speech by W. Gliksman

Gathered Friends.

When, during the time of the large ghetto, later in the small ghetto and finally in the concentration camps of Auschwitz and Dachau, I would sometimes dream about a land where I could build my old–new life, I had before my eyes *Eretz–Yisroel* and the United States.

In addition to purely personal reasons that drew me and brought me to this land and drive me on to *Eretz–Yisroel*, I had as a purpose coming to a Jewish center in a Jewish environment.

After the destruction of the large Jewish community in Poland, we the survivors wanted to make contact with Jews, draw strength from them for our future life.

True, we tried to live in exclusively Jewish groups in Germany or Poland, Hungary or Lithuania after the liberation, in order to refresh ourselves together and fight for our own new existence.

Alas, we in Europe ran into hatred on the part of the non–Jewish population. Now, all the more so, we do not want to remain in Germany.

I was one of the fortunate ones who had the opportunity to leave Germany on the first transport and go to America.

We, those saved after the destruction, mainly come here with the help of our sisters, brothers or close relatives. But the strength that draws us here is the great Jewish community and in the first ranks are our *landsmanschaftn*.

Dear *landsleit*: It is a great honor for me to be present this evening and to remember a little about our old home. I already have had the opportunity to become acquainted with some of you. I will mention the name of Rafal Federman with whom I have discussed various questions concerning our city. I must here express my thanks to Mr. Federman for the great work he performed for our city, while still in Czenstochow and, particularly, here in America. His work is inestimable.

[Page 277]

I had a warm reception at the meeting in the house of Mr. Chrabalowski, where I could meet *landsleit* such as Mr. Silver and A. Kaufman; incidentally, the latter was a *yeshiva–bukher* [*yeshiva* – religious secondary school – student] of my father, may he rest in peace.

I also want to meet our *landsleit* and to work with them in every way for our brothers in Czenstochow.

And although I do not come directly from Czenstochow and do not have the right to speak in their name, I want to express my thanks here to everyone for everything you have done so far for all of them.

I also had the opportunity to read various letters from our *landsleit* from all over the world to Mr. Y. Kaufman and to Relief in which they say thank you for the help, which had been sent.

I see the good will, effort and sacrifice and that you remember your old home in the work of the secretariat of our Relief [organization], in which I have been active since a few days after my arrival here and where I work with Mr. Federman in the great work.

I must greet your institution with a particular joy and honor at the publication of the book, *Czenstochower Yidn*. Mr. Federman played an important part here.

While in Munich I brought to the historical commission at the central committee, which had the task of gathering the historical material, documents, photographs, writings, which concerned the Jews during 1933 – 1945.

It is not yet possible to evaluate the great work that the historical commission in Germany and in Poland has achieved. It is not only material for our future historians who will write the sad history of European Jewry, but also the most beautiful headstone for our martyrs.

Our book also will be a part of the great historical material. A monument for us, a remembrance for all of the Czenstochow martyrs.

As I said earlier, I do not have the right to speak in the name of the Czenstochow *kehile* [organized Jewish community]. I also will not speak about what we already know, although each of us lived through something different. It would only cause renewed pain and rip open our wounds. I will not speak about them or for them. I will speak to them for you.

In the great aid work by American Jewry for the small Jewish community in Poland, Czenstochow was a link in the great chain that consisted of aid for the repressed, poor, sick children repatriated from Soviet Russia who had survived by a miracle.

Remaining alive does not mean living. Living means building, creating, working. We must help our brothers. I ask of and desire from you additional help and support and I am certain that you will continue to do your work, your best to support our *landsleit* and I wish you success in this work.

Five Hundred dollars were sent to Rome, Italy.

A Czenstochower Relief Committee was founded in Melbourne, Australia. They collected 1,200 pounds at two meetings.

———

Czenstochower Relief Workers in New York

A. Khrobolowski

The organizations of Czenstochow *landsmanschaftn* [organizations of people from the same town] in general and the aid organization in particular during their existence did a world of work. The work is described in the reports about the particular organizations. Here we will give a picture of the activities of several people who can serve as an example.

It is not yet possible to evaluate all of the meetings of Relief and the Ladies Auxiliary as to whether he was president or not, [but] the oldest, most devoted and most loyal among the Relief Workers [was] Friend **Louis Szimowicz**.

He was the first president of Young Men and, later, one of the pillars of Czenstochower Relief in New York and he traveled with Louis Szwarc to Czenstochow as a delegate in 1922.

Seeing everything with his own eyes while in Czenstochow, not only the dark, black times: the need and suffering of Jewish life, but also the light: the inspiration and will to fight of the young and the joy of the children in their own, free, bright children's home – he was strongly influenced by the new, young Czenstochow. Returning to America with renewed strength, he began the aid work for his brothers and their children in Czenstochow and has not given up the work even today.

[Page 278]

Along with him, we need to remember those from the older generation of Relief workers for whom not their age, not their time, not their conditions in life tore them away from helping the aid work, from taking part in assisting with every undertaking, with every meeting starting with the first years, 30 years ago, until today. They are:

Itshe Zelkowicz, who remains so connected to the aid work, so rooted in Czenstochow, like a tree with the strongest roots so that no winds or storms can tear it out. And:

Sam Korpiel, who always was here and we hope will be the representative for many, many years, who represents and welcomes the Czenstochower *landsleit* [people from the same town] to their meetings, prepares and himself serves the food and draws pride and joy from every gathering, from every meeting.

One who had carried first the Aid Union and then Czenstochower Relief in New York on his strong shoulders is Friend **Louis Szwarc**. He, along with Friend Louis Szimkowicz, was one of the delegates to Czenstochow. He carried out the magnificent plan to erect the Y.L. Peretz house with iron strength and unbroken will. That the living wellspring of a poet and writer beat in him is shown by his folksy poems from his young years in Czenstochow, riper poems published in the Yiddish press in America and his work, *Czenstochow Wert a Shtot* [Czenstochow Becomes a City], written for the Czenstochow book and also printed in the *YIVO Bleter* [*YIVO Pages* – Jewish Scientific Institute].

Kopl Gerichter is one who embodies the strength, heroism and unlimited energy and will of the new generation of Jewish workers. He was the first one to connect the aid work in America with Czenstochow after the First World War. He was the fighting spirit at Relief, one of the most active workers in the Czenstochower *Arbeter* Ring [Workman's Circle] branch, later at the Jewish Peoples Order, in addition to his activity in the painters' union and other activities. Years ago a serious illness tore him away from communal life. His work will never be forgotten.

One of the most devoted aid workers from the first day of the Aid Union until today is **Itsik Dikman**. He was described as a child in the chapter, *Czenstochow Wert a Shtot*. Czenstochow certainly did not give him much luck, like many children from the ghetto. However, he repaid Czenstochow with unlimited devotion.

Khone Gliksman has always been devoted, always infatuated with the work, since the first years until now. [His wife], the *shwartse* [dark] Fradl, does not lag behind [in her devotion to the work].

Dovid Zisman occupies a singular and esteemed place in the aid work just as in Young Men, where he was elected president several times. He was always original, exceptional, matter-of-fact and earnest. He was and remains one of the pillars of the aid work for Czenstochow.

Sholem Oberman is a devoted aid worker who occupies a respected place in the aid work. His presence and appearance at a Relief meeting always brings pragmatism to the work.

I think that one who did not miss even one meeting of the Czenstochower *landsmanschaft* is the dear Friend **Yisroelke Broder**, who should be called Zigas because two brothers, great grandfathers of the Zigas family, were listed with two different names: Zigas and Broder. Yisroelke Broder can serve as an example of a aid worker for many of those younger than he who came to America many years later.

One who provided a great deal of work and energy to the aid relief work was **Yehezkal Win**. Over the course of several years, he was the secretary of Czenstochower Relief in New York and an official of the Czenstochower branch of the Jewish National Workers Union.

Abe Kaufman, the scholar of old *Yidishkeit* [Jewish way of life] and devoted comrade of the new movements, gave more years of work than anyone for Czenstochow. He was always the secretary of Relief. We cannot imagine that any undertaking, any meeting would have happened without him, without his work, without the information he possessed about the *landsleit*. As a member of the editorial committee of the book, *Czenstochower Yidn*, he contributed a great deal to collecting the historical material and, in general, helped in great measure to accomplish the great ideal of memorializing Czenstochow in a book.

[Page 279]

The last, the most beloved is the old–young **Yakov-Ber Silwer**. His personality is the best evidence of the great strength of life of the Jewish folk–masses. His energy and devotion to his brothers, to whom he dedicated his entire life, merits that his name be written in golden letters in the history of our family. He was president of Czenstochower Relief in New York for several years, chairman of the executive of United Czenstochower Relief and chairman of the publication committee for the book, *Czenstochower Yidn*. As such, he greatly helped with the work of the editorial committee and led the work. His character is such that he has pushed forward everything in which he takes part.

*

With the founding of United Czenstochower Relief along with the previously mentioned workers, an entire group of new friends joined who excelled in the aid work.

The office of president ha been occupied by Friend **Avraham Yakov Senzer** since 1928. It was decided and carried out under his leadership to collect a fund of 10,000 dollars and to publish the book, *Czenstochower Yidn*. With his iron energy and wisdom he led Relief through the frightening times of the destruction of the Second World [War] when we were completely separated from Czenstochow and when the horrible news of the destruction of Czenstochow arrived. He held together the Czenstochower Jewish community in America at all times to be ready when the call for help would come from across the ocean. It was not an easy thing to carry out all of this, particularly for a workingman. In addition, great perseverance and tact and inborn wisdom was demanded and Avraham Senzer was blessed with it in very great measure.

Joseph Kaufman who occupied the office of finance secretary [created] very large earnings for the Czenstochow aid work in New York. A son of the Czenstochow scholar, Reb Berish

Dayan [religious judge], he serves his Czenstochow community of Jews in America from the old and new home with objective advice and actions. He provided years of arduous work to Relief. He would do the work at night after a day of difficult work in his printing shop. He would often close the shop and go to a Relief meeting. But nothing was too difficult for him when it came to fulfilling the *mitzvah* [commandment] of fraternal aid.

Jack Kopin or **Yankl Kapinski** in the old home, the good comrade at *Poalei–Zion* [Workers of Zion – Marxist–Zionist party], of the Literary Society and *Lira* [literary and musical society], whom everyone loved – is the treasurer. He is the busiest relief worker at the undertakings of Relief, collecting the money for the Czenstochower Fund.

The vice president, **Harry Fajerstein**, together with them devoted long years of work to United Czenstochower Relief. He occupies the leadership of the work, not only with his office, but more with his generous contributions at every collection.

Max Kaminski represented the young generation in America in the aid work for Czenstochow as recording secretary. He already was president of Young Men.

A. Chrabalowski carried out the missions that the leaders, teachers and most of the children and their fathers and mothers gave him at Czenstochower Relief in New York, at the Ladies Auxiliary and in United Czenstochower Relief. He spoke, asked and demanded in their name. Now in the horrible time of the destruction of Czenstochow – the only hope and consolation that remains for all of the workers for Czenstochower fraternal aid is that Jewish children will again live there and their Yiddish language and song again will echo there and their lives will be better and nicer than [it was] for those who perished in such a terrible manner.

One of the youngest Relief workers in America is **Rafal Federman**. He came to America at the beginning of the Second World War and helped work on the call for aid, the cry of pain and despair from our brothers who already were squirming in the murderous teeth of Germany's murder machine. He gave a great deal of energy to the relief work as leader of the information bureau, at preparing the material for the bulletins of United Czenstochower Relief and Ladies Auxiliary, at preparing the national conference and every conference that took place over recent years; as secretary for the publication of the book and member of the editorial committee, he joined together the Czenstochower *landsmanschaftn* in America, in Eretz Yisroel and in other countries and in a very great measure contributed to the completion of the idea of a memorial book, *Czenstochower Yidn*.

[Page 280]

*

The youngest of the Relief workers, **Wolf Gliksman**, shared in all of the horrors of Nazi rule, lived through the exterminations of Jewish Czenstochow and was saved from the lime ovens of Auschwitz and Dachau with the survivors. After coming to New York, he immediately became active in United Czenstochower Relief where he took over the work as secretary and in great measure the burden of the widespread activity demanded by Relief. He took on the leadership of the information bureau and press division of the United Czenstochower Relief Committee. Wolf Gliksman gave a great deal of energy and effort to help complete the book, *Czenstochower Yidn*, as a member of the editorial committee.

* * *

Dozens of more people who were active in Relief as officials and in the executive of Relief at various times deserve to be mentioned with honor. Among those who excelled are:

Izzy Berger, Morris Gelber, Joe Jacobs, Max Jacobs, Emanuel Wargon, Natan Wajsberg, Jack Liwy, Avraham Fridman, Dovid Fridman, Meir Fajner, Frajermojer, Max Kuszminski, Max Kepp, Joe Rozenblat.

* * *

Those Who Were Torn Away from Us (Our Deceased Workers)

Our sacred duty is first of all to remember those who have left us, whom death prematurely tore away from us. May these lines in their memory be the expression of the great love and esteem felt by the entire Czenstochower family.

Harry Fajerstein died in 1936. He gave all of his free days and hours to the Czenstochower branch 261 of the *Arbeter Ring*, the Czenstochower Aid Union and Czenstochower Relief in New York after the difficult work in his shop. He was the treasurer of Relief until the last day of his life.

Max Korpiel died in 1936. Representative of the Young Men and Czenstochower Relief in New York and active coworker in the work of the Ladies Auxiliary. He was one of the most beloved figures among the Czenstochower *landsleit*. He was a sincere, good person, with a great deal of faithful devotion and connection to his brothers. The sums [of money] sent by the Ladies Auxiliary for the children's homes and other institutions would arrive under his name. And his name will always be blessed!

William Sobol died in 1936. He did a great deal of work for and was devoted to Young Men and the relief work, both at Czenstochower Relief and at the Ladies Auxiliary. He did not get tired, did not stop the work at his shop and the work for his brothers here and in Czenstochow until the last day of his life. There were differences of opinion in Czenstochower Relief in New York and every other organization, but Sobol, with his true, honest talk always calmed the mood, smoothed [things out], united us like brothers. We are all working for the same purpose; to help our brothers, he would say. And his words always worked. No one was provoked because they [his words] came from a good, Jewish heart and feeling soul...

Kay Sobol, his wife, died in 1936. Her dear face with its good–hearted smile, which was like a warm, bright fire, illuminated all Czenstochower meetings, remains so alive and shines in the hearts of everyone who knew her and it will always do so...

Skharye Lewensztajn. He died in 1936. He was a worker in Wajnberg's factory at home [in Czenstochow] and was beloved and honored by the Jewish workers as one of the leaders of the freedom movement in 1905. He also suffered a great deal in America and he left the world when he still was very young. He was active at the Young Men as finance secretary and as recording secretary at United Czenstochower Relief. Just as at home [in Czenstochow], his thoughts here were sharp, clear and intelligent. And he was listened to. His death caused a great shock for all Czenstochower *landsleit*. His memory will live for a long time.

Nisen Cymerman died in 1936. He sat as always at the head with his dignified persona at a meeting of Relief, stood up, pressed the hands of the friends sitting near him and left... left forever. He died on the way home. He also worked until his last day in his shop and was one of the younger (one of those from 1905) presidents of Young Men, the first president at the Dzialoszyner [Dzialoszyn] *landmanschaft* [organization of people from the same town] and the first president of the organization, United Czenstochower Relief. He possessed a great deal of wisdom and the dignity of a leader. His words were weighed and measured and, therefore, always achieved their purpose. The Czenstochower *landmanschaft* honors his memory every year with a meeting and he well deserves it.

[Page 281]

Rose Dichter died in 1936. She was an active worker at the *Arbeter Ring* branch 261 and vice chairlady of the Ladies Auxiliary.

Meir Dembak died in 1936, also suddenly left this world [while still] young. He was a respected member and activist at the *Czenstochower Arbeter–Ring* branch 261 and often appeared in the name of the branch at Czenstochow meetings. His last appearance at a Relief banquet was symbolic. The danger of a fascist attack in New York had passed and the "dim–out" (dark lighting) had ended and all of the lights were turned on for the first time on the "train" [subway] on which he traveled to the banquet. He saw in this, the rise of light for the world. The soul of this dear person and comrade, like those lights, never stops shining.

———————

The Czenstochower Synagogue in New York

Y. Kirshenbaum

All Czenstochower *landsleit* [people from the same town] from New York and other cities gathered together around the United Czenstochower Relief and Ladies Auxiliary. One of the addresses of the Czenstochower Jews is the "Chasam Sopher Synagogue," 8 and 10 Clinton Street, New York in the very heart of the Galicianer neighborhood – the well known Jewish philanthropists, Jacob Schiff and Lewisohn, helped to build the synagogue.

The Czenstochower Chasam Sopher synagogue on Clinton Street is now a Galicianer synagogue. It is among the oldest synagogues in New York. The synagogue was once almost like a reform synagogue. Dr. Stephen S. Wise's father was the rabbi and Dr. Stephen Wise had his *Bar Mitzvah* in the synagogue. The rabbi of the synagogue is now the Rabbi, Reb Mordekhai Meyer, a student from the *Chachmei Lublin Yeshiva* [center of Torah study in Lublin, Poland], where the Piotrkower Rabbi, the Rabbi Szapira, was the head of the *yeshiva* [secondary religious school].

The officials of the school tell us the history of the Chasam Sopher Synagogue in simple words. Mr. Lieber Grill tells us that in 1886 a small synagogue with the name Chasam Sopher existed on Columbia Street that mostly was supported by Hungarian *landsleit* – in memory of the great Hungarian *gaon* [sage] of the Chasam Sopher *Yeshiva*. The synagogue had 200 members. And when the synagogue [building] became too small, they began to look for a larger house of prayer. And they found favor at 8-10 Clinton Street. The then named Rodeph Sholom – a real reformed synagogue in the proper manner: Jews and their wives came in "carriages" on *Shabbos* [Sabbath] and an organ played, accompanied by the "boys" and girls in the "choir" and so on. And even a younger Jew, did not dare to enter there and pour out his heart for God Almighty in a Jewish way. The house was bought after full negotiations and with luck renovated and immediately transformed into a real orthodox synagogue. But in the course of only two years the group split, not being able to support the great operating costs that a synagogue needs to have. More than 150 members left the synagogue and founded a lodge under the same name, Chasam Sopher Lodge. In 1890, the handful of members did everything to support the synagogue. However, it was impossible to honor the debt of the mortgage and the interest. The mortgaged was "foreclosed" on the house and Jews remained almost as if on the street without a synagogue. As in all other societies, there also were good-hearted members who carried more responsibilities than others. When ex-president, Sh. Glik who already is in the world of truth [died], saw that the house had been sold to speculators and they already had begun to pull the bricks from the walls to transform the house into a theater or cinema, he went to work and went into the street to the societies to look for partners for the broken building. In four weeks, he succeeded in saving the synagogue.

It is necessary to say that the congregation then only had 40 members.

[Page 282]

On a secluded corner on Sherriff Street existed a society with the name *Czenstochower Khevre* [Czenstochower Society], which consisted of 15 members. Two of them, the brothers[1] D. Geizler and Yisroelke Broder, may they live long, had already been members of the society for 50 years. Despite the fact that Hungarians and Poles were never suitable in-laws, the match took place. The above-mentioned came to an understanding after several conferences with a few Jewish communal workers, such as the ex-presidents, the deceased Sh. Goldberg, H. Wilczinski and D. Geizler, may they live long; they are still members. Both societies merged.

With united strength they immediately threw themselves into worship and in addition to the joint assets, capital of thousands, they also collected contributions. As all of this was not enough, they went to Jakob H. Schiff and Lewisohn and they both donated up to 1,000 [dollars] on the condition that the society collect 25,000 dollars. They gathered penny to penny, even went through the streets with a handkerchief and visited "societies" and unions, which not only did not give anything, but they even, according to the old way in New York, did not even let the committee enter. The "soldier with the bolt [of the door]", the "inner guard" said, "No." The general, the president with the hammer commanded no. Even the eulogies that were given in the synagogue on *Shabbosim* were of little help. However, after much effort the few members gathered the sum of 18,000 dollars and the remainder was covered with mortgages. They immediately began to rebuild almost the entire synagogue, which was broken into pieces and looked like a real ruin.

Now the synagogue is one of the most beautiful and oldest synagogues in the Galicianer neighborhood.

Translator's Footnote

1. It is probable that the use of the word "brothers" is in the sense that it was used for members of the same organization.

———

[Page 282]

Czenstochower Young Men

by Y. Kirshenbaum

The Czenstochower Young Men's Society was founded in 1888 by 18 young men, all from Czenstochow.

Not being in America for long and being small in number – there were several dozen *landsleit* in the entire country – they would come together every evening, after a difficult day of work, on the corner of Delancey and Norfolk Street and there the first Czenstochower Society in America was born.

Of the first founders, Joseph Hofnung, who was the recording secretary for many years and Louis Szimkowicz, who was president 30 years ago as well as at the 50th anniversary, are the most active members until this day.

And here let us remember the remaining pioneer-founders who, alas, are no longer found among the living but who will always be remembered with honor. They are:

Berl Bratman
Max Karpiel
Sam Goldberg
L. Gotayner
M. Rozenthal
V. Sobol
Sholem Cohen
Leyzer Wilinger

During the early years the members taxed themselves 10 cents a week, but without any benefits.

In 1889 the organization arranged its first theater benefit in the then great Oriental Theater. The theater activities were organized over a number of years. The income from the activities was used to support the members in case of illness.

It was not so easy to obtain support for the society. At that time the Jewish immigrant element was very different than in the later years. The Jewish immigrants of that time had not gone through the school of communal work at home. Here they knew very little about the country and its language. However, the strong will and stubbornness of the first pioneers surmounted everything.

Czenstochower Young Men became a model, not only for the later emerging organizations from Czenstochow in its area, but also for other cities. Today the Young Men is one of the oldest Jewish societies in the country.

[Page 283]

Its first constitution was adopted in 1891.

The society paid its members five dollars a week sick benefits for the first 15 years. Later the benefit was raised to eight dollars a week. A *shiva* [period of mourning] benefit also was introduced.

Several names need to be recorded of the oldest members who have belonged to the society for over 49 years and today are active in its leadership. They are:

Jack Zajdman
Samuel Karpiel
Itshe Zelkowicz
A. Rikman
Gronem Szimkowicz

In 1900 the Society bought its first burial plot at Mount Zion Cemetery. In 1920 – its second plot at Mount Judah. In 1929 – its third plot at Beth David (*Beis Dovid*). The [cost of the] three plots at the cemetery reached over 30,000 dollars.

The loan fund that gave loans of up to 25 dollars without interest was founded in 1903.

[Page 284]

The Aid Fund was founded in 1907 to support members in case of need.

Czenstochower Young Men has supported all of the national organizations since the first year of its existence. They were one of the first to join and support the Union of Polish Jews. Young Men has paid the Polish Union one dollar a year per member for many years.

Many members of Young Men served in the American Army during the First World War. Seventy members of the Society and 24 children of members were in the American Army during the Second World War.

* * *

During the First World War, when Czenstochower Relief was created in New York, Young Men as an organization and its individual members supported Relief in a very big way with the greatest fraternal love and devotion. They carried upon themselves the heavy load of aid work for the old home.

In 1919 Young Men organized support for Relief with 300 dollars. From then on, Young Men supported the undertakings of Relief every year with large sums of money. The sum reached 500 dollars in 1922.

The participation of Young Men in the construction of the Y. L. Peretz House in Czenstochow was important and substantial. The members of the Society taxed themselves five dollars each especially for this purpose.

The following members of Young Men are found on the memorial tablet placed into the wall of the Y.L. Peretz House with the name of those who helped to build it:

Buchner William
Zajdman Jack
Zelkowicz Itshe
Teper Izzy
Mentkow Abe

Sobol W.
Karpiel Max
Rikman Izy
Szimkowicz Louis

The Ladies Auxiliary, which occupies the most magnificent place in the history of Czenstochower fraternal aid, was originally founded by Young Men. In 1922 when Czestochower Relief decided to erect the Y. L. Peretz House in Czenstochow and it demanded limitless work, the Ladies Auxiliary joined with Relief to aid in this gigantic undertaking. However, Young Men remained the leaders and co-workers of the Ladies Auxiliary.

The Czenstochower Young Men

Seated, right to left: Mike Weiskopf, Sam Karpiel, vice president Jack Jacobs, president Al Jacobs, finance secretary Max Kaminski, treasurer Abe Pinkus, recording secretary Joe Nowak.
Standing, right to left: ex-president Karl Buchner, ex-president Robert Weinstein, ex-president Max Jacobs, membership chairman Sam Zeligman, loan-fund chairman Morris Gelber, cemetery chairman Joe Kaufman, ex-president Dave Zitman.)

Generation after Generation

As with an entire people, an organization also shows its ability not only in that it ages, but also in that it becomes rejuvenated. This happened during the last 15 to 20 years with Czenstochower Young Men. A new, younger generation, children born here and a younger group that came later from Czenstochow, grew up and partly took over the leadership. Thus we see for example that the people who were the officials at the 30th anniversary of the organization that was celebrated on 7 December 1918 at the Royal Lyceum consisted of the following:

Ex-presidents:

L. Szimkowicz, H. Wilczinski, M. Rozental, G. Szimkowicz, B. Bratman, L. Wilinger, S. Goldberg, B. Gotajner, J. Zajdman, W. Sobol, M. Karpiel, I. Zelkowicz.

Officials for 1919:

President – S. Goldberg, vice-president – W. Sobol, recording secretary – J. Hafnung, finance secretary – T. Kohen, treasurer – I. Zelkowicz, first trustee – L. Wilinger, marshall – I. Zelkowicz.

However, at the 40th anniversary celebrated on 9 December 1928 in the Park Palace, there were several young members among the officials, such as Jack Jacobs – ex-president, Davi Zitman – second trustee and Nisen Cymerman, may he rest in peace, M. Weiskopf, A. Nirenberg, D. Wajskop, Morris Weiskopf – and the arrangements committee of the anniversary.

At the 45th anniversary held on 24 December 1933 in Central Plaza, David Zitman was found on the list of the ex-presidents and S. Rabinowicz, born here [in the United States] was president, Skharye Lewenstein – finance secretary, Wolf Buchner – trustee and Max Jacobs – chairman of the Aid Fund.

Other ex-presidents among the new communal workers were: Nisen Cymerman, may he rest in peace, Robert Weinstein and Max Jacobs. A series of younger members were active in the committees.

[Page 285]

At the celebration of the 50th anniversary that was held on 25 December 1938 in the Manhattan Center, with the participation of 400 people – the honor of being president and recording secretary was given to the founders and oldest members of the Society – Louis Szimkowicz (president) and J. Hofnung (rec. secretary).

The other officials that year were:

Joseph Kaufman – vice-president, Skharye Lewensztajn – finance secretary, M. Weiskopf – treasurer, W. Sobol – trustee, Sam Karpiel – trustee, Sam Goldberg – cemetery chairman, Jack Jacobs – chairman of entertainment, Max Glikson, of blessed memory – chairman of the Aid Fund, Robert Weinstein – chairman of the Old Age Fund, Dave Sheier – sergeant at arms.

A group of members from the young generation took part in the arrangements committee for the 50th anniversary. Among those who took an esteemed place in the leadership of the Society were: Max Zeligman, Max Kaminski, J. Nowak, Abe Pinkus and Al Jacobs.

The leadership was transferred completely to the younger generation during the past eight years after the 50th anniversary. Most recently the leaders of the Society were: Max Jacobs, he was president for two years; Max Zeligman – two years as president; Max Kaminski – three years as president.

The officials in 1945 were:

Karl Buchner – president, M. Weiskopf – vice president, J. Nowak – recording secretary, J. Jacobs – finance secretary, D. Zitman – treasurer, J. Zajdman – trustee, S. Karpiel – trustee, R. Weinstein – chairman of the aid committee, J. Kaufman – cemetery chairman, M. Gelber – chairman of the loan fund, Max Kaminski – chairman of entertainment, Abe Pinkus – chairman of Old Jewish Fund, J. Jacobs – membership.

Newly elected officials for 1946:

Al Jacobs – president, M. Blitz – vice president, Max Kaminski – secretary, A. Pinkus – treasurer. The other officials remained the same as in 1945.

Czenstochower Young Men and United Czenstochower Relief

In another place, it has already been mentioned that United Czenstochower Relief was founded at the initiative of Young Men. Three of the first officials of U. Cz. R. were Nisen Cymerman – president, Louis Szimkowicz – treasurer, Joseph Kaufman – secretary. At the same time they were also the leaders of Young Men. Like Czenstochower Relief in New York, the same for United Czenstochower Relief; it received the greatest and strongest support both morally and materially, that is, the largest sums of money from Young Men.

The fact that Friend Joseph Kaufman in the name of Young Men contributed the sum of 1,500 dollars to the collection for Relief at the mass meeting on 27 May 1945 at Manhattan Center shows how great was the support of Young Men for United Czenstochower Relief. This sum was collected by an especially created committee that collected 1,000 dollars from the members and the organization allocated 500 dollars from its own treasury.

The committee consisted of the following members:
Joe Kaufman, treasurer
Max Kaminski, secretary
Karl Buchner
Morris Gelber
Al Jacobs
Joe Jacobs
Jack Jacobs
Max Jacobs
Robert Weinstein
Michael Weiskopf
David Zitman
Jack Zajdman
Abe Pinkus
Joe Nowak
Sam Karpiel

[Page 286]

Czenstochower Young Ladies Auxiliary in New York

by A. Litman

The women took a large part in the work of the Help Union and Czenstochower Relief in New York the entire time. No ball, no other undertaking took place without their work and help.

In 1922, through the initiative of Friend Louis Szimkowicz and other friends of the Young Men, a separate women's organization was started under the name – Czenstochower Young Ladies Auxiliary, with the goal of supporting the war orphans and poor children in Czenstochow with food and clothing.

The petition for a charter was signed by: Louis Szimkowicz, Bertha Bratman, Anna Wajskop, Zelkowicz, Katy Jackson and Rae Sobol.

The composition of the first Board of Directors consisted of: Celia Szimkowicz, Rose Wajskop, Dora Rozen, Helen Fridman, Anna Zelkowicz, Helen Lajcher, Ruth Hiler, Celia Jacobs, Rose Goldberg, Beatrice Zajdman, Gussie Jacobs, Rebecca Skowornek.

Later others joined: Lena Win, Yetta Korpiel, Anna Rips, Rose Adler, S. Foist, Minnie Korpiel, and Samuels, Gussie Lewensztajn, Wajnstajn.

Friend Louis Szimkowicz was elected the first President of the Czenstochower Young Ladies Auxiliary; Lina Win as Vice-President; Recording Secretary – Rose Adler; Finance-Secretary – Katy Jackson; Treasurer – Rae Sobel; Representative - Anna Wajskop.

Their first large undertaking was the ball that took place on the night after *Shabbos* [Sabbath] on 14 January 1923 in the Park Palace, New York.

The second chairwoman of the Czenstochower Young Ladies Auxiliary was Mrs. Anna Samuels.

Mrs. Yetta Lenczer was elected chairwoman in 1924. Vice-chairwoman - Martha Korpiel; Recording Secretary – Yetta Korpiel; Representative – Broder; Finance- Secretary and Treasurer remained the same.

Starting in 1928, the Ladies Auxiliary organized the yearly balls in partnership with Czenstochower Aid in New York.

In 1928 Mrs. Anna Samuels was elected as chairwoman, Anna Broder as vice chairman.

The arrangements committee consisted of the following ladies: Anna Nirenberg, Celia Szimkowicz, Yetta Lenczer, Martha Korpiel, Molly Gotlib, R. Moskowicz, Malka Fridman, Celia Lewental, Chana Fajersztajn, Fanny Fajersztajn, Mary Lefkowicz.

Anna Wajskop – chairwoman, Molly Gotlib – vice chairwoman, Katy Jackson – recording secretary, representatives – Florence Nirenberg, Celia Szimkowicz, Anna Broders [previously recorded as Broder] were elected as officers in 1929.

Yetta Lenczer – Chairwoman, Rebecca Skwornek [previously recorded as Skowornek] – Vice Chairwoman were elected in 1931. The remaining officers were the same.

The organizing committee consisted of Chana Manuszewicz, Anna Samuels, Sara Singer, Celia Lewental, Mary Lefkowicz, M. Hiller, Martha Korpiel, Gussie Pitman, L. Skowronek, Chana Fajersztajn.

After Czenstochower Relief in New York ceased to exist, the Ladies Auxiliary for a long time alone carried on the aid work for Czenstochow, first in order to support the Y. L. Peretz Library. Friends Louis Szimkowicz, Sam Korpiel, Sobol and Charlie Lenczer always worked with the Ladies Auxiliary. In the end, the Ladies Auxiliary, too, ceased its activities and was reorganized into a new organization with United Czenstochower Aid in New York.

The renewed Ladies Auxiliary in United Czenstochower Relief began its activities in 1936.

Until now the ladies have worked together with Relief and had their representative, Yetta Lenczer, as vice-chairwoman.

[Page 287]

The first officers were:

Yetta Lenczer, Chairwoman; Fanny Fajersztajn, Vice-Chairwoman; Celia Jacobs – Finance-Secretary, Sura Senzer, Recording-Secretary; Glantz, Treasurer; Gussie Gelber, Chairwoman of the Activities Committee; Rae Kaufman – Treasurer of the Activities Committee; Martha Korpiel, First Representative; Kep, Second Representative.

*

The founding of the Ladies Auxiliary in 1922 begins its history in the Czentochower *Landsmanschaft*. Many wives whose husbands were members of various organizations belonged to the Woman's organization. The Ladies meetings often were larger than the meetings of Aid. The leaders of the Young Men participated in large numbers in the meetings of the Ladies: Friend Louis Szimkowicz, Marks Korpiel, of blessed memory, Sam Korpiel, W. Sobol, of blessed memory, Charlie Lenczer.

Ladies Auxiliary at the United Czenstochower Relief Committee
Seated, right to left: Gutsha Gelber, Sadie Senzer, Celia Jacobs, Yetta Lenczer. Fanny Fajersztajn, Martha Korpiel. Standing, right to left: Reila Frajmoyer, Esther Kep, Celia Levy.)

[Page 288]

The most important work of the women's organization is shown by the monies sent to Czenstochow for the children's homes and folks schools that were raised by the Ladies Auxiliary itself, besides the sums that were transferred to the Aid for the building of a house and other purposes:

1925	$1,095
1926	$850
1927	$1,150
1928	$1,150
1929	$700

In the course of just five years a total sum of 4,945 dollars was sent.

The women and friends of Young Men who worked with the Ladies Auxiliary during the time when no aid organizations existed deserve separate recognition. The remaining members of Czenstochower Aid in New York had partly abandoned their activities because they had the ability to work together with the Ladies Auxiliary. The Ladies Auxiliary remained the only aid organization in New York that not pay attention to the severe Depression in America and the discord in the Czenstochower organization in New York and continued to perform aid work.

The newly reformed women's organization was already more closely connected to United Czenstochower Relief than before. The meetings took place in the same hall on the same evening. The Ladies Auxiliary must be recorded as doing the larger part of the work for Relief, even as both organizations jointly carried on the undertakings.

Often the joys and sufferings in the lives of Czenstochower *landsleit* found reverberations at the meetings and get-togethers of the Ladies Auxiliary, just as with Relief. If a member of Relief or the Ladies Auxiliary had a wedding for a child, a certain sum was spent by Relief and whiskey and hors d'oeuvres were brought to the meeting, and there was rejoicing and the parents were wished *mazel-tov* [good luck]. The same when a child or a grandchild was born. Just as on such an occasion, the fathers and mothers in the old home treated those praying in the synagogue or Hasidic *shtibl* [one-room synagogue] with cake and whiskey. If someone got sick, or God forbid, left this world – the sisters and brothers visited the mourner in his house and mourned along with him and suffered the misfortune that had been met by the Czenstochower family.

The Ladies Auxiliary also directed aid work among the *landsleit* in New York who found themselves in need.

*

Mrs. Anna Samuels was the first president of the Ladies Auxiliary. In later years she was again elected as president and to other offices. She was born in America, but was always ready to do everything in her power for the aid work for Czenstochow.

Yetta Lenczner, today as 30 years ago, is the most active and energetic Relief worker. She surpassed everyone with the number of years as president of the Ladies Auxiliary and there is no equal to her in the work that she gave for Czenstochow and harmony among the Czenstochower *landsleit* in America.

Katy Jackson, the English-speaking recording secretary, in the course of many years, always added charm and energized the members of the Ladies Auxiliary.

Helen Fridman, the financial secretary of the First Ladies Auxiliary for the entire time of its existence, is the best heir of our old mothers who embodied the maternal love and goodness of the entire world.

Let us also remember the active and devoted activity of Anna Broder, as vice president and in other offices. Among the officials of the Ladies Auxiliary during recent years, Sara Senzer, recording secretary, is particularly worthy of being remembered. She excelled with her folksy Yiddish, which she brought with her from Czenstochow.

Celia Jacobs, finance secretary, Celia Szimkowicz, trustee, Anna Wajskop, chairwoman in 1929, Florence Nirenberg, trustee, Anna Nirenberg, Gussie Gelber, chairwoman of the enterprise, Rae Kaufman, treasurer of the enterprise, Kop, trustee, gave much energy and life to the aid work.

[Page 289]

Czenstochower Br. 261 *Arbeter Ring* [Workman's Circle] in New York

by A. Litman

Thirty-seven years ago (in 1909) a group of 28 Czenstochower young people, who had settled in chaotic New York, founded a branch of the then still young workers' organization – the *Arbeter Ring*.

These young people were the children of the poor streets of Czenstochow, whose parents toiled in the workshops or traded in the market. The fathers and mothers dreamed that their children would, perhaps, find something better and with broken hearts they said goodbye to their children and accompanied them to the train station, from which they traveled beyond the sea, to the end of the world – to the unknown, distant America...

On arrival in the giant city of New York, the young Czenstochowers searched for a corner in which to pass the time, to come together and discuss the problems of home and the world.

True, they had then already heard that here all sorts of organizations and societies exist where *landsleit* [people from the same city or *shtetl*] come together and one feels at home. The religious Jews built synagogues in which to pray and to study a chapter of the *Mishnah*. The ordinary non-religious Jews founded "lodges," "societies," "groups of friends" that were concerned with help for the sick, preparing a grave after over 120 years [Translator's note: It is customary to wish that someone live "until 120"]... These groups of friends grew like mushrooms after a rain and they confused the circles of newly arrived immigrants in New York.

What did the new immigrant who in Czenstochow had been an artisan – a tailor, a cabinetmaker, a hat maker, an upholsterer, a baker – think of this? Here he fell into a "sweatshop" where they suffered and slaved from morning until late in the night, lived in the "tenement" districts, in the crowded, stuffy little rooms, without air and sun. Strikes would break out. The strikes would be bloody and long. The workers often lost the strike. Returning to the shops, they did not lose their courage and they did not give up hope of bettering their bitter condition.

Then the Czenstochower immigrant workers in noisy New York came to the decision that an organization must be created that would be interested in their condition, help the workers organize unions, defend their interests; at the same time, they were looking for a progressive, friendly environment. They heard the song of the poet Y. Adler (B. Kovner) who had published the song about the founding of the *Arbeter Ring* that was then only nine years old. This song resounded in the Jewish workers' neighborhoods with a fiery enthusiasm. The song was entitled *Undzer Boim* [*Our Tree*] and was sung as follows:

"In a winter night, a grey one,
No stars shone,
Then good people
Planted a small tree for us..."

*

The following twenty-eight young people were the first ones to conceive [of the idea] of founding a Czenstochower branch of the *Arbeter Ring*: Leon Fridlender, Avraham Montag, Morris Rozencwajg, Harry Szerman, Harry Frejman, Dovid Faucht, Louis Goldman, Ruwin Fajerman, Yisroel Inzelsztajn, Pinkhus Gotlib, Max Szajer, Sidney Glazner, Heimy Gotajner, Moshe Bornsztajn, Sam Silversztajn, Louis Besser, Avraham Warmund, Louis Eizner, Louis Rafalowicz, Harry Brzezinski, Shmuel Lewkowicz, William Grin, Moshe Kraus, Louis Upner and Aba Kaufman.

They came together on 8 February 1909 in Mrs. Szajer's house at 712 East 6th Street, New York, where the founding meeting was held.

The history of the *Arbeter Ring* Czenstochower branch 261 is actually the history of each branch of the *Arbeter Ring* in general.

The founders of our branch, 36[1] years ago, were influenced by the same ideals and dealt with the same problems as our mother organization that was then already in existence for nine years.

[Page 290]

The *Arbeter Ring* and Branch 261

There was a time when our branch breathed with communal life. There was a time when the branch carried out various plans whose purpose was to better the material condition of the members at a time of economic need and in case of an illness. A fund was created for local health benefits that paid three dollars a week at the start and later was raised to four dollars a week. We also created a "loan fund" and a fund to pay the bills of such members who could not do so because of need; a fund for the old that was to pay the bills of members who could no longer work. In general, the democratic spirit rules in the branch and friendship of one member with the other and everyone was one family...

Czenstochower Branch 261 *Arbeter Ring*
Seated, right to left: Av. Litman, S. Richter, Y. Szubin, M. Fajner, A. Goldfinger, H. Brzezinski.
Standing, right to left: M. Wilinger, M. Sztern, P. Szwajcer, A. Kap, M. Kap and M. Gotlib

A Civil War Breaks Out in Our Branch

Every dispute in an organization has a destructive effect: its growth stops; it cripples its activity; it demoralizes the members and the hand of destruction gets the upper-hand...

When the branch split, 36 members officially left it. However, the storm carried away a greater number of members who were lost to the *Arbeter Ring* and fell into bourgeois societies.

The branch would, perhaps, have gone into a state of complete helplessness and feeling of loss if it had not found several of the older active members and the younger members who stood on the side and were not active in the branch at the time of the dispute, but after the split again became active with the wish to revitalize the branch and renew its activities. However, they were greatly hindered by the economic crisis that then began to be rampant in the country.

[Page 291]

The Branch Begins to Revive

We began several plans in order to revive our branch. Two of the plans were: first, that our meeting place would move to the Bronx instead of downtown because two-thirds of the members lived there; the second plan was – to merge with another branch of the *Arbeter Ring*. The first was done immediately. The second – was postponed until later...

As is evident, the "changes" worked. The members began to attend the meetings; we took in a number of new members; we also took a number of wives of our members into the branch. With joy, we record that they do good work for the branch. During the course of the past few years, the branch has carried on cultural work and holds lectures on various problems. The branch has a theater undertaking for the benefit of the sick fund and finally the branch is again in the position to pay local sick benefits. Three years ago, the branch moved into a downtown apartment, on 14th Street and Broadway.

The Branch Supports All Worker and People's Organizations

During the course of 36 years the branch supported the following institutions and organizations: Jewish Children Schools; *Arbeter-Ring* branches; Young Circle League; unions and strikes; orphanages; sanitaria; convalescent homes; Old Jewish Homes; day nurseries and hospitals; Socialist Party and its press, both in America and in Europe; the *Yidisher Visnshaftleker Institut* [Jewish Scientific Institute – YIVO]; ORT; the Jewish Worker Committee; HIAS [Hebrew Immigrant Aid Society]; orphanage in Czenstochow; political prisoners in America and Europe; Bund in Poland; Romanian workers; Spanish People's Front; Czenstochower Relief; Jewish children's schools in Poland; cooperatives; worker *lyceums*; Young People's Socialist League; Deb's Fund and yet more organizations.

*

There was a bakery worker in Czenstochow who emigrated to England and lived there for 10 years. He helped found the baker's union in London. He came to America in 1907, immediately joined the local bakery union local 305 where he was active for many years and a delegate for the union. He was respected and valued by the members for his idealism and readiness to struggle for the masses. He fought for unionism, picketed and went on strike, although there was no bread in his house for his wife and children ... he was torn away from his activities in the workers movement at the age of 54 and died at his post in the fight for bakery workers.

Our Branch in the Struggle against Fascism

A long time before the world was ignited by the Nazi barbarians in 1939, our members understood that the Fascists across the world were gathering to drown the workers movement in blood. We, therefore, supported the underground struggle against both Fascism in Italy and the half-Fascists in Poland. And when the bloody struggle broke out in Spain, our members supported the Loyalist struggle with life and soul.

When the world conflict with Fascism broke out in 1939, our branch immediately threw itself into the struggle. Our branch can with pride show that although we were only a small family of 78 households, we gave the American Army and Navy 80 young fighters on all fronts and bought war bonds for 50,000 dollars.

[Page 292]

The members of the Czenstochower Branch 261 have inscribed a beautiful chapter in the activities for the old home – for Czenstochow. Our members were the founders and builders of Relief. All of the great work for Relief were successful thanks to the fact that the members of our branch did their part.

Arbeter Ring Branch 261 did not only give financial support to Czenstochower Relief, but also leaders and guides. The secretary-treasurer of Relief, Josef Kaufman who served the organization these past years with devotion and loyalty, is a member of *Arbeter Ring* Branch 261. Rafael Federman, the secretary of the book committee and editorial member for the book, *Czenstochower Yidn* [*Czenstochower Jews*] – has been a member of our branch since 1941. A series of other workers for Relief, such M. Fajner, Max Wilinger, Sam Richter, M. Gotlib. Av.

Hershkowicz, the late Meir Rembach and others also worked with Relief. The present finance-secretary of the branch, M. Sztern, although not a Czenstochow *landsleit* [person from the same town] (he is from Tomaszow), in the course of the six years he has been in office, has helped everyone in the work of Czenstochower Relief. The writer of these lines, Avraham Litman, who has been active in Relief since arriving in America, also took on the special task of waking the *landsleit* through the press that they should not forget Czenstochow, their home city.

When sorrowful reports arrived from Czenstochow – in 1937 – that hooligans rampaged and carried out a pogrom on the poor Jewish population, murdered five Jews and wounded several hundred, our member, Avraham Litman, appealed to the Jewish Workers' Committee in the name of Czenstochower Relief, that it should come to the aid of the victims. The Jewish Workers' Committee then granted the sum of 500 dollars for the suffering Jews in Czenstochow.

It should also be recorded here that Branch 262 of the *Arbeter Ring* also particularly helped the orphan's home in Czenstochow and virtually financed the orchestra of the school in Czenstochow.

*

In the present historic hour the Czenstochower Branch 261 *Arbeter Ring*, of course, does everything it can to help in the sacred work of revival of the survivors from Jewish Czenstochow.

Translator's Footnote

1. In the first paragraph the number of years since the founding of the organization is given as 37.

[Page 292]

Czenstochower Branch 11 of the Jewish Fraternal People's Order

by D. Tanksi

Introduction

The official birthday of our order and branch is 1930, but unofficially the seeds for the new order were planted years earlier.

We will not go into the facts about the reasons that brought the rise of the new order. However, it is worthwhile to establish a few facts.

The outbreak of the October revolution brought strong differences and splintered Jewish society. The two workers orders – the *Arbeter Ring* [Workman's Circle] and the National Workers Union – were drawn into this conflict.

The struggle between left and right took on a sharper form. The Czenstochow branch 111 was dissolved by the National Workers Union. Over 70 percent of the members were excluded from Workers branch 261.

It was clear that the further coexistence of the various movements and groups was impossible and, in any case, they could not live harmoniously together. This created a necessity to found a new order for those excluded and those who could not find a homey atmosphere in the existing orders.

When a test of fire was presented to those from Czenstochow they acted like Czenstochowers: they took up the challenge and created their own organization. Those excluded from the *Arbeter Ring* branch 261 and the dissolved branch 111 of the National Workers Union created the Workers Order in March 1930.

[Page 293]

Among the dozens of pioneers and charter members who joined the new organization, at least some of the most active should be mentioned here: Yakov Ber Silver, Abe Kaufman, Pinkhas Gotlib, Dovid Gotlib, Morris Szwarc, Yasker, Max Rozenblat, Benny Rozenblat, Benyamin Rozenblat, Mordekhai Altman, Willy Wilinger, Sam Wilinger, Ruwin Berger, Izzy Berger, Khona Gliksman, Max Wajnrit and his brother, Szlingbaum, Karl Gerichter, D. Tanski, Max Kuczminski, Hershl Grosberg, Avraham Grosberg, Frajlich, Frajman and others.

The Internal Life and the Character of the Branch 11

Born at a time of the most difficult crisis in the history of the country, when unemployment spread across the country lightning fast and the masses lived in poverty; our branch encountered a great deal of difficulty and disruptions. But thanks to the untiring work of our union and certainly more because of the necessity of having a progressive order, our branch quickly grew and expanded. The branch and the order increased the total number of members and began to play an important role in the communal life of our city.

Our branch avoided the mistakes of becoming a partisan organization. Therefore, we established a wide base. Not considering the larger or smaller number of branch members, the branch was always the place of great, effervescent communal activities, a concentration point of progressive workers, united around the struggle in our country and united in the concern for its allies. Immediately at the start, the branch opened its door wide for everyone who wanted to belong. Each member, no matter their [political] beliefs, had their place and their value in our branch. Every fight by the masses was supported with a generous hand; every action for the Jewish people was supported and shared with other organizations.

[Page 294]

The internal life of the branch was established so that every old or new member would feel comfortable and would find a friendly atmosphere and a fraternal atmosphere. The absolute tolerance of the various factions, the interest and the welfare of the members, the right of everyone to decide the character and course of our activities – the collective leadership – these and other not less important traits led the members to be active and to care about the growth and existence of the branch. Here they became familiar with all communal questions; here they found an echo of all struggles carried out by the masses; here they lived culturally and communally; here they joined the Jewish people; here they found mutual aid and all benefits that a fraternal organization must provide.

The Aid Fund that was led then by the Seidur Society and the Rozenblat Society, took care of aid for the sick and needy members. With their tactful approach, with their understanding and devotion to their work, the members of the Seidur and Rozenblat Societies established the fund on a basis of self-help, as an expression of friendship and concern of the branch for its members. The branch did not lose any member because of unpaid bills through all of the years of its existence.

Our branch also deserves praise that it led the wives of our members out of the kitchen and interested them in communal activities and in the problems of the branch.

A women's club with its own autonomy and its own area of work was created with the participation of the female comrades Frajlich, Minnie Rubinsztajn, Frida Najberg, Annie Goldberg, Ester Kaczminski, Wladimir, Haursh and Tanski. Through the club many women came in contact with problems that were once foreign to them. They were drawn into all of the battles carried out by the branch, helped the branch in its activities and developed very important work among the women of their neighborhoods. They evolved socially and culturally in the club, became activists and leaders and worked with their comrades in every area. Today, many of them still play a leading role in the branch. Thus the comrade Frajlich is a permanent member of the executive, a tested campaigner for Jewish rights, a builder of the Jewish school, a communal worker and leader in several organizations.

Czenstochower Branch 11 of the Jewish People's Order

The "covered tables" [tables covered with food] at the branch became widely known. At the *laMelekh* [*belonging to the King*][1] that the branch organized very often, the members had a good and enjoyable time and benefited from the cultural undertakings. The summer excursion also would draw a crowd because the branch, under the capable leadership of Comrade Silver, always found means to entertain its members in a cultural-communal manner.

Today we have 250 members, not all from Czenstochow. So, for example, Kh. Brodski, from Odessa, who is one of the most active members of our branch and for many years has been more concerned with our assistance program than many from Czenstochow.

Branch 11 is now one of the best branches in the Bronx district in New York.

The Cultural Work

We excelled especially in the area of cultural work. We carried on a widespread and serious campaign for the necessity of cultural work, to acquaint ourselves with our culture and to spread it in depth throughout our membership. We encouraged self-education on a great scale. Many of those students then continued their studies in advanced schools. Dozens of them are active today on the cultural front. We have trained a number of speakers, workers, intelligent workers, who today occupy prominent places in our order.

Every meeting was transformed into a cultural undertaking. An introduction, a lecture, a discussion, literary evening, musical concert, recitations, cultural holidays dedicated to our classics and to the new literature, the celebration of historical events – all of these were opportunities to acquaint our members with the cultural achievements of our people. We distributed various Jewish journals, pamphlets, books, newspapers and other publications. The question of selling literature was taken up at every meeting and widely discussed. Our literary agent, Comrade Silverman, did his work with dedication and self-sacrifice.

It is understandable that the branch heartily supported the Jewish Cultural Union, *I.K.O.R.* and its journal *Yidishe Kultur* [*Yiddish Culture*].

[Page 295]

Therefore, our interest in cultural work influenced our branch to give the greatest attention to the school.

From the first day we had supervision over a school that we supported morally and materially. Hundreds of children were recruited for the school by the branch. The majority of them then continued their education in the Order's higher schools. We created a special group of school workers who specialized in their areas, prepared with enough knowledge and understanding of the Yiddish proletarian school. Such old school workers from the branch such as the comrades Kaczminski, Nayberg, Silwer, Sadie Berger, Louis Goldberg, [female] Comrade Freylich, [female] Comrade Nayberg and others may really be proud of their work.

We distributed thousands of pamphlets about the Yiddish school, attracted a wide strata from the area in the struggle for its existence and development. Through the school we gained influence on the parents, who not long ago had had a negative, or in the best case, a passive attitude toward Yiddish and to Yiddish literature.

Today the parents are drawn into the fight against national nihilism and against assimilation. Today our school is School 5. It serves over 50 children. Comrades Lou Goldberg, Sadie Berger, Frajlich and Nayberg represent the branch there and work tirelessly for the school. The branch is proud of School 5 and with the very large contribution of our comrades to the school.

The earnest relationship to the Yiddish school and to Jewish culture and the concern for the young generation placed the branch at the head of the front ranks of Jewish cultural institutions in our city.

Communal and Political Activities

Our branch carried out a broad campaign for unemployment insurance. We distributed thousands and thousands of leaflets, collected thousands of signatures, sent speakers to the neighboring organizations and called large mass meetings under our banner at which our members spoke.

We took part in the march to Washington and were represented there by Comrade Abe Kaufman.

This action is only an example of the hundreds of actions that the branch carried out and of the manner in which it took part in the actions with its members and money. The popularity of the branch grew thanks to these activities. Our branch was automatically included among the endorsers when an area committee to fight the anti-Semitic [*New York*] *Daily News* was organized in 1945.

Our branch always took part as an organization in all of the local and national elections. Special meetings were dedicated to the analysis of the candidates' programs. We carried on a widespread campaign to take part in the election, supported the progressive candidates and unmasked the reactionary ones. Street meetings organized by the branch often were mobilization points for the great masses in the area.

The branch delegated its best workers, such as the comrades Silver, Szlingbaum, Abe Kaufman, D. Tanski, Rubin Berger, Izzy Berger, Kaczminski, Lou Goldberg, the female comrades Frajlich, Wladimer, Annie Goldberg, Ellen Tanski. Khona and Fradl Gliksman, Handlesman and his wife, Joseph Rozenblat, Willy Wilinger, Sam Wilinger and others.

As an anti-fascist organization, our branch supported the Anti-Nazi Council right from the first day of its existence. It took part in its activities both as an organization and with its members. The branch called a boycott of Nazi goods, picketed the businesses where they were sold and distributed large numbers of copies of anti-Nazi literature. The branch was a member of the Anti-Nazi Council through its delegate Comrade Louis Goldberg.

Branch 11 also warmly supported the activities of *I.K.O.R.* – the Society for Jewish Colonization in the Soviet Union. We energetically took part in the campaign to popularize the resolution of the Jewish and national question in the Soviet Union, where anti-Semitism was declared a crime against the law.

We supported materially and morally the Jewish territory in Birobidzhan where the Jews of the Soviet Union will be put on a normal footing as a people with their culture, language and political and economic independence.

[Page 296]

Our comrade, Abe Kaufman, was a member of the central committee of *I.K.O.R.*

We held it as our great duty to defend the Jewish settlement in Palestine against the imperialist machinations of the English government, for its peaceful development, for a free Palestine [Israel], built on Jewish worker cooperation, for a Jewish national home. We held dozens of meetings dedicated to the struggle against the "White Paper," sent protest telegrams to members of Congress and called upon our members to take part in every action to abolish this criminal discrimination against Jews.

Branch 11 grew as a consistent organization struggling against reaction and anti-Semitism, for Jewish rights in every nation.

When the war broke out our branch quickly took its place among all of the party organizations and supported our government with all its strength. We carried on true anti-fascist and party work simultaneously to clarify the purpose of the war and the task of everyone to do his duty in the sacred war against the Nazi beast. Dozens of our members left for the front. We supported them for the entire time, kept them as members and encouraged them in the bitter fight against the enemy of humanity.

On the battlefield during the war, we lost our comrade soldiers: L. Nestin, Friend Rubinstein and Lou Lefkowitz.

We bought bonds for tens of thousands of dollars and the branch was thanked by the Treasury Department. Our contribution to the U.S.A. Ration War Relief and other war aid agencies also was significant.

Our meeting when the returning soldiers visited the branch was a true holiday. The closeness, the camaraderie that the branch brought out among its members was felt. It was a triumphant holiday and a celebration for greeting our brave soldiers returning to their home, to their branch.

After the war our branch took part with all our strength in the great national task of strengthening the survivors of the Jewish people in Europe.

Our Order issued an appeal to collect a quarter million dollars in 1944 and a million dollars in 1945 to help the Jews in every nation and our branch reached the quota assigned to it for both appeals.

We carry out widespread work focused on the condition of the Jews in the suffering nations and call on every member to contribute more than they can.

Our aid actions will not end until Jewish life is normalized and we, as individuals and as an organization, will do its duty! We will help create the necessary unity of the American Jews for a widespread democratic program of aid work, for the solution of the Jewish question in the world, for the eradication of fascism and anti-Semitism, for insuring the rights and lives of the Jews.

The Branch and Relief

Branch 11 wrote an important chapter in the history of Czenstochower Relief and its very selfless work.

As a *landsmanschaft* branch, a Czenstochower organization, it also had local problems to solve. These were the problems of our home city where we had left our closest ones and friends. And we never forgot them. Czenstochow stood first in all of the money campaigns that we carried out.

Immediately at its founding the branch connected to the Relief [organization] organically and worked harmoniously with it. We helped work out the guidelines for Relief, carried out its work and widened its field of activities.

Our members of Relief took a distinguished position and thanks to their devotion to it, they obtained the recognition of all of the *landsleit*. Mr. Yakov Ber Silver, the chairman of the executive of Relief and also the chairman of the *Czenstochower Yidn* book committee, is certainly considered one of Relief's best activists. His own large monetary contributions, his extraordinary capabilities in leading Relief had a great significance in creating a "United Relief" that could become a meeting point for all *landsleit* without distinction as to the political beliefs of groupings. Abe Kaufman, editorial member of the *Czenstochower Yidn* book, was connected to Relief from the first day of its existence. His contribution also is considerable. Alkana Crabalowski, an old member of our branch, is now one of the editors of the *Czenstochower Yidn* book, a worker widely known for his cultural and communal activities even in the old home, who greatly aided Relief with his work and particularly in the planning, publishing and editing of the book.

[Page 297]

And we certainly cannot undervalue the work of such branch comrades as Joseph Rozenblat, Kaczminski, Gliksman.

As an organization, the branch always supported Relief materially and morally. It arranged several lectures about Relief and its activities. It called a special campaign for Relief in 1945. Although a large number of members were not from Czenstochow, each one answered the appeal. The branch brought 1,000 dollars to Relief, not counting the personal, individual contributions of our members.

This campaign was carried out by the entire executive with complete devotion and full responsibility, particularly by Comrades Brodski (himself not from Czenstochow) and Tanski.

Branch 11 will always cooperate with Relief and use every opportunity to support it in its sacred work on behalf of our brothers and sisters on the other side of the ocean.

Conclusion

The Czenstochower Branch 11 of the Jewish Fraternal People's Order can be proud of its 16-year existence, with its contribution to Jewish life and to the building of Jewish culture here in this country; with its contributions to the suffering Jews in Europe; for its enduring struggle for progress and against fascism and anti-Semitism; for its work with Czenstochower Relief.

The entire branch is not isolated by boundaries of narrow fraternalism, but is connected with every movement and with every camp that bears a progressive character, here in this country and in the life of the Jewish people.

The branch works with all organizations that will make Jewish life more secure and healthy, such as the American Jewish Congress and others. We are represented in the Federation of Polish Jews by Comrades Kaczminski and Louis Goldberg and we cooperate with the Federation in every area.

Greeting to Czenstochow

Through the mediation of the book, *Czenstochower Jews*, the Czenstochower branch 11 sends its hearty greeting to its brothers and sisters in Czenstochow with an encouragement in their difficult situation and promises every possible help for the building of Jewish life in our home city.

Branch 11 is certain that the Jewish community in Czenstochow will become even more vested, as before the war, because those from Czenstochow were always tested fighters for a new and more beautiful life, because a new day will sprout with hope in the lives of the entire Jewish people.

Committee of Czenstochower Branch 11 of the Jewish
Fraternal People's Order in the United States of America:

Brothers Silver, Tanski, Wargon and A. Grosberg

Officials of Branch 11 in 1964

President	Yehiel Brat;
Vice president	Carl Wargon;
Finance secretary	A. Grosberg;
Cultural director	Yakov Ber Silver;
Treasurer	Berl Erlich;
Publicity and press	Dovid Tanski;
District delegate	Ruwin Berger;

[Page 298]

Recording secretary	M. Nafman;
Hospitality	Abe Kaufman;
Fund for Needy	Joseph Rozenblat;
School Volunteers	[female] Comrade Frajlich, [female] Comrade Sadie Berger, [female] [sic] Comrade Louie Goldberg.
Representatives to the Polish Federation	Max Kaczminsi, Louie Goldberg.

Members of the Executive:

In addition to the above-mentioned officials the following people are members of the Executive:

Louis Brodski, Ellen Tanski, Sara Gliksman, [female] Comrade Rose Mandel, Comrade Willy Wilinger, Comrade Max Wajnrit.

Translator's Footnote

1. *Shiru laMelekh – Praise to the King –* is a song often sung at gatherings; the Order used *laMelekh* as the name of its celebrations.

Czenstochower Branch
of the Jewish National Workers Union
by J. Wein

The idea of organizing a Czenstochower branch of the Jewish National Workers Union arose among a group of Czenstochower *landsleit* [people from the same town] in New York who were members of the *Poalei-Zion* [Workers of Zion – Marxist-Zionist] party. The initiators were H. Grosberg, Sh. Szlingbaum (Harlem branch), Moshe Censzinski and H. Win (branch 6). After the organizing of the Czenstochower branch, the four Wajnrit brothers and R. Berger, and later Avraham Litman, joined the *Poalei-Zion* party.

The founding meeting of the branch took place in 1917 on Ludlow Street, in the hall of the Jewish National-Radical People's School. Comrade Mitchel, the organizer of the Union, declared the principles and purposes of the New Worker's Order (the Union was founded in 1913). The first ones to join the Czenstochower branch were: Sh. Szlingbaum, R. Berger, the four Wajnrit brothers, S. Wilinger, A. Wilinger, H. Frajman, Grajcer, H. Win, Moshe Censzinski. H. Grosberg, the Wenglinski brothers, M. Szapira, L. Katel, A. Fridman. Later A. Birnbaum, Kh. Gliksman, Y. Gliksman, Izzy Haber (Radomski) and L. Litman joined.

The branch was officially installed on 17 April 1917 with a literary-musical evening. The chairman was Moshe Cenczinski. A banquet took place in the evening with H. Win as chairman.

The first finance secretary of the branch was Sh. Szlingbaum; the recording secretary – Y. Grajcer. Our officials were: H. Win, R. Berger and H. Grosberg.

The Czenstochower branch of the union took an active part in the work of People's Aid that was created after the First World War, supported strikes by the Jewish workers, which were frequent then, and organized open-air meetings to support the candidates of the Socialist Party in Congress and the City Council.

The Czenstochower branch as a whole and all of its members dedicated themselves to the work of Czenstochower Relief in New York with the greatest devotion. They helped a great deal with the creation of the fund for the Y.L. Peretz house in Czenstochow. The branch and its members collected a large number of books for the general workers' library in Czenstochow. H. Win was the secretary of Czenstochower Relief for a long time.

The branch also was involved in cultural work and often arranged talks and readings about Jewish literature.

Several members of the branch attended the courses on political economy, Jewish history and the history of socialism that were given in 1919 by the party school of branch 6 of the *Poalei-Zion* party. Several of those members are now active in various areas of Jewish communal life.

*

With the issuing of the Balfour Declaration at the end of the First World War the Zionist idea strengthened in the Jewish neighborhoods and influences large masses of Jewish workers. The "trade union campaign" for *Eretz-Yisroel* was created, led by the secretary of the "United Trade Unions" and by the energetic socialist fighter [Abraham Isaac] Shiplacoff, who had already collected several million dollars.

[Page 299]

The Bolshevik Revolution that came as a result of the First World War shocked the worker masses of the world like a hurricane. The results of a passionate struggle between Zionism and communism were also felt in Czenstochower Branch 11 of the Jewish National Workers Union.

There were members who tried to hold together the 100 members of the branch by a synthesis between maximum and minimum (Bolshevik and Menshevik) socialism and the strivings of Zionism. However, they did not succeed in this. Like many other organization, the branch split. The great majority joined the International Workers Order. A minority remained in the Union and it was reorganized as the Yitzhak Ayzik Hurwicz Branch 10, to immortalize the name of the Jewish-educated theorist of the socialist movement in America and expert on immigration matters.

This ended the chapter of the Czenstochower Branch 11 of the Jewish National Workers Union.

The Czenstochower *Patronat* in New York
(Committee to Aid Political Arrestees in Poland – 1931-1939)
by D. Tanksi

During the 1930's bleak information began to arrive from Poland. The fascist regime, which held the country as if in iron pliers, robbed the masses of every right and every possibility of existence. There remained no trace of freedom. Only fascism reigned free. The *pogromshtshikes* [those carrying out pogroms] frolicked freely; anti-Semitism was free. The ruling clique wanted to save itself from the rage of the people by throwing blame for all of the anguish, pain and suffering of the masses onto the Jews, by inciting pogroms, by crushing democracy in the country. However, the masses did not let themselves be deluded by false, fascistic slogans and struggled bitterly against the regime. The struggle brought many victims.

However, the Polish guard was not satisfied with torturing the arrestees. They would shoot worker activists in the street, without any trial or warning. Adek Landau, the well known Czenstochower activist, was murdered in this way. The police shot him in the street, quietly buried his body and did not even tell his family about this. Jail terms were dispensed with a generous hand. Here a sentence was given against a group of Czenstochower: Frenkl – 15 years in jail, Knapik – 15 years, Brajtman – 12 years and Olszewski – five years. The Polish civil press furnished the following terrible statistics: From 1 May 1926 to 1 May 1936, 1,534 anti-Fascists were murdered without a trial; 2,400 – were wounded and 125,000 sentenced to jail. During that time the courts gave sentences overall in the amount of 50,000 years.

It was not a surprise that Jews, the most persecuted, also provided the largest number of political arrestees. The Jewish arrestees also suffered more than others: they were tortured as Jews and as political [activists]. The Jewish masses in Poland sought help for their struggle and turned more than once to organized Jewish society all over the world. They demanded that we, immigrants from Poland, stand up publicly to the Polish government, provide actions of moral support and financial help for the victims of fascism. "Why are you silent?" – the American Jews were often asked.

B. Smoliar, the correspondent from the New York *Tog* [*Day* – a Yiddish newspaper], openly warned that if American Jewry did not force the Polish Panske government to restrain the appetites of anti-Semitism, the Polish Jews would be doomed. It was a question of simple human feeling to extend a fraternal hand of anti-fascist solidarity to the masses in Poland and our national debt to help the Polish Jews in their struggle. Support for the political victims of Polish fascism was the commandment of the hour.

[Page 300]

Patronat was created in 1931 in order to organize the recommended help.

At first, the *Patronat* emerged to fight against the atmosphere of indifference that reigned in the *landsmanschaftn* [organizations of people from the same town]. If the interest in the old home found a reverberation among the local *landsleit* [people from the same town], it was expressed in philanthropic relief work. But this work, too, was carried out on a very small scale. Splits and divisions made each vigorous action more difficult. The news from Poland was not brought to the attention of the Jews in America. The wide public was not angered and seized with the events in Poland because the leaders of American Jewry did not find it necessary to arouse the Jewish masses against fascism in Poland. When persecutions against the Jews in Poland took on such proportions that a broad strata of the *landsleit* began to demand action, a conference was called together, wrote a resolution in chosen words and the matter ended with this. Even in the later years, when fascism threw off the mask of democracy and freely threw itself into action on the backs of the Jews of Poland, here, in America, concern for the most part was expressed with words and not with deeds. Only the Jews of Poland boldly and spiritedly expressed their protest against the Polish hangman like the free Jews in America. In 1936, Dr. Margoshes, the editor of *Tog*, had to warn the local *landsleit* that the relief work must take form and that "the moral aid that was strongly neglected until now, is of tremendous value and must be given much faster..."

The work of *Patronat* was very difficult under these conditions. A great deal of effort, energy, consistency and patience was demanded in order to cultivate the *landsmanschaftn* to eliminate all prejudices and win the trust and support of the *landsleit*. They had to be interested in the bloody struggle in Poland, in the ruthlessness of Polish fascism, in the need and in the suffering of the Polish martyrs.

On the other side [of the ocean] connections had to be established with the arrestees in the Polish barracks, maintain contacts, send the assembled money, receive authentic reports from there, despite persecutions and disturbances by the Polish guard.

But the work was crowned with success. A small group of founders of *Patronat* was created of not widely known people, simple workers, without high social positions, without bags of money, but to whom the struggle against fascism was close. In time the *Patronat* became strong, won prestige, weightiness and recognition by the *landsleit*. Even the stubborn opponents had to change their opinions and took a positive stand to the devoted work and self sacrifice of the *Patronat* workers. In the end they had to understand the necessity of fighting Polish fascism. One had to agree with the historically important purpose of the *Patronat*.

To implement its program, the *Patronat* turned its entire energy to acquaint the *landsleit* with the terrible terror that reigned in Poland and with the struggle that was being carried out by the masses. The *Patronat* spread all of the news from the old home, collected money for the political arrestees and helped to create the so much needed unity among the *landsleit* of various directions for the struggle against the political Sanacia regime. We must underline with pride that the *landsleit* reacted well to the appeal by *Patronat* and supported it generously. All *landsmanschaftn* organizations, such as the Young Men's Association, the Ladies' Auxilary, the *Arbeter-Ring* [Workman's Circle] branch 261 and the International Worker's Order branch 11, were always represented in all undertakings of *Patronat* and supported its work. There were very close connections with the relief organization. It is really hard to show where the relief work began and where the work of *Patronat* ended. Both worked for the welfare and freedom of our brothers and sisters in the old home. As the relief was impartial and progressive, *Patronat* also became a center for all progressive Czenstochower who were interested in overthrowing Polish fascism. Each action on behalf of the Jews in Poland was recognized and actively supported by *Patronat*, no matter who took the initiative in the action. Each arrestee was given help, as much as was possible, regardless of his or her party membership. The *Patronat* was an integral part of *landsmanschaft* life and a stronger instrument to forge the *landsmanschaft* unity. Whoever was present at the well-attended *Patronat* meetings and banquets truly felt the joy that unity can create and the sympathy that the *Patronat* engendered for the political arrestees.

[Page 301]

Since 1936, both organizations – Relief and *Patronat* – have carried out joint balls each year and a portion of the income has been designated for the political arrestees. Each ball has been a manifestation against Polish fascism and an expression of love for the brothers in Poland.

The *Czenstochower Patronat* in New York organized a division in Los Angeles, California, that in time became an important factor in the life of the *landsleit* there. It organized public protest meetings against Polish fascism and also various undertakings on behalf of the political arrestees. Groups were also created in Detroit, Canada and South America. At the initiative of the Czenstochowers, a *Noworadomsker Patronat* was created which became a respected member of the *Patronat* family. In praise of the *Czenstochower Patronat*, the fact must be underlined that it was among one of the most important instigators of the central *Patronat* organization. Among other accomplishments, it succeeded in persuading the already existing two *Patronats*, Nowodworer and Bialystoker, to unite all their strengths to found the central organization, which would have the task of building new *Patronats*, and in general spreading the struggle against Polish fascism.

The rise of the central organization was of very great significance. The struggle again Polish fascism took on a broad national character. The central organization was able to popularize the *Patronat* among the *landsleit*, undertook various activities on behalf of the political arrestees in Poland, deepening the work and preparing the soil for joint appearances [with other organizations].

In a short time the central organization created 35 *Patronats* in which all of the important *landsmanschaftn* participated. Each *Patronat* had autonomy, but all worked together under the leadership of the central organization. *Tsu Hilf* [*To* Help], the journal published by the central organization, on average had a circulation of 5,000 copies. The *Czenstochower Patronat* sent its best workers to the central organization and, in general, was responsible for a large amount of the work.

1936 was a year of great, intensive activity. That year a new wave of anti-Semitism flooded Poland. Pogroms against Jews were a daily phenomenon. The *reaktsie* [right wing reaction] raged unbearably and the number of arrestees rose immensely. Official Poland threw away the pretense of democracy and rolled into the arms of Hitler, both in its external and its internal politics. The Polish regime shamelessly ascended completely on the road of open and brutal fascism.

In the summer of 1936 the *Czenstochower Patronat* took an active part in the creation of the "People's Committee to Combat the Pogroms on the Jews in Poland" that undertook a number of actions. Thousands of signatures with protests against the wave of pogroms were sent to the Polish ambassador in Washington.

The *Patronat* also participated in the large and impressive street demonstration organized by the People's Committee against Anti-Semitism and was represented in the delegation that was sent to the Polish Consul in New York.

The impressive historic march on Washington, organized by the same People's Committee against Anti-Semitism must also be mentioned. Thousands of delegates who represented around a quarter million Jews, 30,000 Ukrainians and hundreds of *landsmanschaft* organizations took part. Our *Patronat* was also represented with a delegate. Senators, members of Congress, writers and communal workers, Jewish and non-Jewish, endorsed the march. Senator Thomas led the delegation to the President who was presented with a detailed memorandum. This was the first time that official Washington heard the cry of pain of Polish Jewry.

On 11 July, 1937, our Relief, with strong assistance from *Patronat* called a meeting against the pogroms in our home city. This was a great demonstration of our *landsleit*. All *landmanschaft* organizations were represented. The speakers denounced the Panske government in the strongest manner and demanded immediate abolition of every discrimination and persecution against the Jews. Each action, each event in Poland, in general, and in Czenstochow, in particular, found an echo in the activities of *Patronat*.

[Page 302]

The *Czenstochower Patronat* declared in its last report to the central organization:

"...we had great difficulties reaching the *landsleit* who belong to various organizations. Many misunderstandings and denunciations reigned among the organizations. But thanks to our untiring work and efforts, we succeeded in convincing the *landsleit* that it is necessary to unite all forces for the struggle against Polish fascism, which is the father of the pogroms against Jews. Today we have united Relief, which raises aid for those suffering from need in Czenstochow and also for the political arrestees…"

Understand, since the war, *Patronat* no longer exists. Only Relief remains. As earlier, all former *Patronat* workers are active in it. They remain devoted to their sisters and brothers in Czenstochow who need more help now than when [*Patronat* existed].

The *Patronat* wrote an impressive page in the struggle against Polish fascism. Many of the former Polish arrestees, whom *Patronat* supported, fell as heroes on the barricades of the ghettos; many were partisans, and those, who survived are helping to build a new Poland that will no longer need any *Patronats* for political arrestees.

The following *landsleit* and friends were member of the *Czenstochower Patronat*:

Altman, Rose and Max
Berger, Izzy and Eva
Berger, Rubin and Bela
Buchner, Morris and Sophie
Beira, Shimeon and Fela
Beser, Leizer
Bobrowski, Rose
Brat, Yehiel
Gliksman, Khone and Fradl
Gliksman, Sara
Gerichter, Karl and Regina
Gotlib, Pinkhas and Mali
Gerichter, Abe
Grauman, Irving
Grauman, Sam
Grosberg, Avraham
Goldberg, Lou and Annie
Gotlib, Dovid, may he rest in peace
Handelsman, Lou and Rose
Wilinger, Sam and Gussy
Wilinger, Willie and Blanch
Wargan, Karl and Helen
Tenski, Dovid and Ellen
Treger, Dovid
Lewensztajn, Yehiel
Lewkowicz, Morris
Monowicz, Shlomo, may he rest in peace
Frajman, Hershl and Leah
Cuker, Yehoshaya
Kinstler, Zishke
Kraus, Joe
Kraus, Morris
Kuczminski, Max and Ester
Kaufman, Abe
Rozenblat, John and Bela
Rubinsztajn, Joe and Minnie
Richter, Dovid
Ruk, Shlomo, may he rest in peace
Szlingbaum, Shlomo and Miriam
Szwarcbaum, Avraham and Leah
Szwarcensztajn, Gabriel
Szaja, Morris

[Page 303]

**The following *landsleit* and friends were founders and supporters
of the Czenstochower Aid Union and the Czenstochower Relief
Committee. The two organizations were supported through their
help and devotion:**

Oberman, Sholem
Ajzner, Lou
Izrael, Harris
Broder, Yisroelke
Brzezinski, Harry
Bialik, Gershon
Buchner, Willy
Brokman, Max
Benker, Henry
Bajro, Shimeon
Brat, Yoshke
Brat, Yehile
Balzam, Jacob
Balzam, Joe
Bratman, Berl
Granek, Leibish
Gerichter, Karl
Gliksman, Khone
Gryn, Samuel
Grynberg, Sol
Goldberg, Feitl
Goldberg, Yehoshaya
Grosberg, Mendl
Glater, Max
Gotlib, Pinkhas
Gotajner, Haimy
Gelibeter, Abie
Grauman, Harry
Gerszonowicz, Dovid Leib*
Goldberg, Sam*
Glater, Max*
Gliksman, Josl*
Gliksman, Mendl*
Gerichter, Willy*
Gotlib, Dovid*
Davis, Harris*
Herzlikowicz, Barnet*
Hoyrszman, Wolf*
Wilinger, Mordekhai
Win, Yehezkiel
Wargaon, Emanuel
Winger, Morris
Wajsberg, Shlomo
Wajskopf, Aleks
Wajskopf, Samuel

Wilinger, Max
Waserman, Abe
Wolf, Mendl
Wenger, Abe
Wenger, Sam
Wajnrib, Max
Win, Hershl*
Wajsblum, Abraham*
Waserman, Jack
Wajnrit, Henry
Zelikowicz, Itshe
Zajdman, Jack
Zitman, Dovid
Zelikowicz, Morris
Zigas, Yisroel'ke
Zigas, Harry
Zigas, Sam
Zilberberg, Moshe'le*
Teper, Izzy
Jaffe, Sam
Chrobolowski, Alkana
Lefkowicz, Shmuel
Lefkowicz, Yisroel
Lefkowicz, Leibl
Lewi, Izidor
Lenczner, Charlie
Lajcher, Yehoshaya
Litman, Jack
Litman, Avraham
Libowicz, Charlie
Lewensztajn, Yehiel
Lewensztajn, Zakharye
Lewensztajn, Saul
Mientkowicz, Aba
Mendelson, Yakov
Munowicz, Shlomo*
Nirenberg, Abe
Nirenberg, William
Nirenberg, Julius
Nachtygal, Willy
Silver, Yehoshaya Eliezer
Silver, Yakov Ber
Senzer, Abie
Sercardz, Julius
Sercardz, Charlie
Storozum, Mikhal
Sobol, Avigdor*
Skowronek, Rafal*
Epsztajn, Bernard
Eberman, Judl
Eksztajn, Chaim*
Fajertog, Yehuda Hirsh
Frajman, Hershl
Frydman, Dovid
Fajersztajn, Harry

Frydman, Avraham
Fajner, Meir
Finkler, Dovid
Finkler, Jack
Fajersztajn, Hershl
Ceszynski, Moshe
Cymerman, Nisen
Cuker, Yehoshaya
Kaufman, Aba
Kenigsberg, Shlomo
Kopinsky, Yankl
Kaufman, Joe
Kremsdorf, Irving
Kaminski, Arush
Kaminski, Folek
Kohen, Lou,
Kuczminski, Max
Kinstler, Zishke
Kohn, Chaim*
Karpiel, Max
Kalka, Shimkha*
Rikman, Icek
Rechnic, Jacob
Rabinowicz, S.
Rozenblat, Max
Rozenblat, Joe
Ruk, Shlomo*
Rembak, Meir*
Swarc, Chaim Leib
Szimkowicz, Lou
Szlingbaum, Shlomo
Swarcbaum, Mendl
Szpicer, Shlomo
Szimkowicz, George
Szajer, Khananye
Szajer, Max
Szajer, Dovid
Sztencl, Mordekhai
Sztencl, Kopl
Szmidt, Leon
Szaja, K.
Szaja, Morris
Sztajnhaus, Yoal'ke
Szimkowicz, Ahron*
Szmulewicz, Shlomo*

*Deceased

Czenstochower and Vicinity Educational Organization in Chicago

by R. Pozner

We remember our city with its trees and grass, paved streets and muddy streets. We remember the synagogue and house of prayer where our fathers went to pray, carried on conversations and studied. We also had poor people and those who gave charity and even a municipal crazy one like all other cities. And there were the doctor, the *feldsher* [barber-surgeon], the apothecary and the respected aristocratic Jews and there was the market with male and female peasants who brought all the good things to sell and Reb Haim who purchased a calf for a *zlote* more or less and clapped the peasant's hand.

And there is the *salia* [hall] to which the young people went to dance. And we also remember the *Aleje* [boulevard] where we strolled and romanced. And there is the church and the *Yasna Gora* [monastery famous for its Black Madonna]. And there is Jotka Street with young men and women. Revelries, beatings. This was a life!

And how beautiful the city looked on *Shabbos* [Sabbath] after the *cholent* [stew cooked overnight for the Sabbath meal]. How idyllic the Friday night appeared after the blessing of the candles when the mothers put on their bonnets and shone like the bright sun.

We also had an intelligentsia who turned up their noses and did not want to be friends with simple artisans. It was a colorful life with rain and storms, with sunshine and darkness, with richness and poverty and yet interesting and original and this is how it eternally remains in our memories.

Life in Czenstochow, our city of birth, is now crushed, burned and annihilated by the Nazi dogs. They defiled every sacred object, looted and destroyed and murdered our fathers and mothers, brothers, sisters, comrades and friends and all of Jewish Czenstochow, turning it into one large cemetery. Our tragedy was wider than the sea. The ache and pain in our hearts cannot be told in words. No living person has created the words to mark them But as always we again stand ready to fulfill our debt to the city where we were born that will always remain in our hearts.

[Page 304]

We will never forget the city where our parents were born and where we spent our childhood and young years. And even if, God forbid, no Jews remain living on Czenstochow soil, we will sanctify the stones on which we and our own walked.

*

The first immigrants from Czenstochow settled in Chicago in 1898. When the tsarist persecutions increased in 1905, many of the workers in Czenstochow were forced to leave their old home city because of their revolutionary activity and a large group of *landsleit* [people from the same town] settled in Chicago. In 1913 our *landsleit* began to think about organizing help in case of illness or death, first for our *landsleit* in Chicago itself. The unofficial union that was founded for this purpose that later also was occupied with sending aid to Czenstochow continued this way until 1919. At that time we founded the Czenstochower *Arbeter Ring* [Workmen's Circle] branch 459. The branch existed for only a short time. The general office dissolved it because it was too far to the left. We again were an unofficial organization until 1927 and continued to do relief work.

The branch also took part in cultural work and very often arranged talks and readings about Yiddish literature.

In 1924, in the presence of Friend A. Chrabolowski in Chicago, a Czenstochower Aid Union was created here to support the children's homes and *Folkshuln* [People's Schools] in Czenstochow. The most active workers in the Union were the Miskis, the Malarskis, Friend

Weiss, Gotajner, Max Kabinski, Warszawski and a large group of the current Educational Union. The meeting of the Aid Union took place in Moshe Ceszinski's store (bookstore). That year several large undertakings were organized and larger sums [of money] were sent to Czenstochow.

In 1927 a group of *landsleit* came together in Friend Max Weiss's house at 3261 Armitage Avenue on the occasion of the 15th wedding anniversary of Leah and Louis Solomon. Among the 40 *landsleit* there were: Albert Astor, Morris Solomon and his wife, Miski and his family, the Federman family, Hymie Wolkow and a number of others.

It was a Sunday and after the wishes of *Mazel Tov* [good luck, often translated as "congratulations"], we talked about the city in which we were born. We decided then to lay a cornerstone for our Union. At the founding it was decided that the main work would be to support the Yitzhak Leibush Peretz *Folkshul*, which had a good reputation in Czenstochow and among the *landsleit* in America. It should be understood that those *grine* [greenhorns; new immigrants] just arriving influenced the undertaking of support for the *folkshul*.

The first organizational meeting was held in Parkway Hall on 23 January 1927. At the meeting, Abe Miski was elected as the first secretary and A. Wolkow as chairman. And thus little by little our Union began to take a respected place among the Czenstochower *landsleit* in Chicago.

With pride we want to record here that in the first years of our existence we sent five to six hundred dollars each year to the Y.L. Peretz *Folkshul*. Thus we carried on the aid work until the Nazi scoundrels made a ruin of our home city and all the Jewish communities in Poland.

In the course of a year after the founding we enacted a sick benefit and the membership of the Czenstochower Union grew to around 200. Both the meetings and the work were always carried out in a homey and familiar manner. We also made an earnest attempt to draw our children into the Union. They actually were with us for a short time, did good work, but as it appears, the young people could not adjust [to working in the society].

We also created an aid fund in addition to the benefits for the members. This is a fund founded in the name of Saul Baum in in 1920 in his house. We support every needy member from the fund. Very few of them have left the union in the course of its existence thanks to our contact with the members and *landsleit*.

[Page 305]

We also want to record that we have paid out 9,000 dollars for a cemetery lot. Our members should live to be 120, but it is good sometimes to think of what will happen in the future...

It should be understood that we take part in the activities of Jewish communal life. We support all of the important national organizations. We joined the Jewish Congress, support the trade union campaign for *Eretz-Yisroel*, Russian War Relief, the Red Cross as well as many other institutions.

In the present war [World War II] we can note with pride that we took part in every activity to help defeat the bloody enemy of the Jewish people and of all freedom-loving humanity. Although our organization is not one of the largest, we collectively, together with individual members, bought war bonds for 25,000 dollars.

We say with pride that 35 children of our members serve in the American army. The Czenstochower Union as a whole maintained contact with these children-soldiers through letters and gifts that we sent to them. We received many thank you letters that were read by our members.

We want to remember with respect and thanks all of the presidents, who faithfully served our Union with heart, soul and dedication, for their devoted work: Emil Wolkow, Izzy Miski, Dr. F. Owiecki, Abe Miski, Morris Solomon, Rubin Warszawski, Zelig Gotayner, Jack Levant, Saul Baum, Louis Gross, Louis Winer, Dr. Lou Gotayner and the current president, Max Wajs. We particularly recognize George Fisher, the former secretary who occupied his post for over 10 years and did his work with great conscientiousness and dignity.

We believe that each member who worked with us from the first day on is worthy of being mentioned in acknowledgement [of their work]. However, only those who occupied high office have been recorded at various opportunities and we will not break with tradition. However, let us say that the contribution of our members to the Czenstochower and Vicinity Education Organization and its services have not diminished. Such dedicated *landsleit* will never be forgotten.

The Czenstochower and Vicinity Educational Organization in Chicago took part in the conference of all of the *landsmanschaftn* in America and Canada, which took place in New York in the summer of 1945 with a large number of delegates. The delegates from the organization took an active part in the conference and excelled in revising the resolutions. The union joined the central executive of all of the *landsmanschaftn* in America, supported the undertaking to publish the book *Czenstochower Yidn* that needs to immortalize the past life of our home city and with all of the Czestochow *landsleit* is ready to extend its fraternal hand to the survivors on the other side and to help them build and reestablish their lives.

In conclusion, in the name of all of our members, *landsleit* friends and comrades in Chicago, we want to send a fraternal greeting to all of the surviving brothers and sisters in our home city and all of the Jews who were saved from the bloody claws of the Nazi cannibals. Our great sorrow and sadness because of all of our dear ones who tragically perished is mixed with pride for our heroes who fell in an unequal titanic struggle with the hangmen.

May these Jewish heroes in the Warsaw Ghetto, who like the Maccabees sanctified the name of the Jewish people, be blessed. May those who carried on the struggle against the bloody hangmen of the Jewish people in the Polish forests be blessed.

The courage of our heroes will strengthen us and give us new strength to continue our work and to fight for the future and earthly good fortune of the Jewish people.

[Page 306]

Czenstochower Independent Union in Chicago

The Czenstochower Independent Union in Chicago was founded on Sunday, 23 October 1938.

The founding meeting of our new union was held in the house of the well-known *landsleit* [people from the same town], Sister and Brother Cwirn, 3336 Potomac Avenue.

The new union arose at a time when the flow of immigration from the other side of the ocean almost ceased and no new *landsleit* emigrants arrived. Many *landsleit* previously had been united in a Czenstochower organization that we ourselves had earlier helped founded and built.

Landsleit friends, Lesser, Hercki, Warszawski, Ahron Eizensztajn, Moshe Ceszinski and the Cwirn family came to our first deliberations. At the meeting, it was decided to found a new Czenstochower Independent Union in Chicago to give us the possibility of carrying out various communal and cultural work in our own way.

The name, "Independent," was needed to express the independence of our organization.

A certain sum was collected right at the first meeting for carrying on the work. Everyone was unanimous about this, that the new organization needed to excel with good cultural work and with a comradely and friendly environment.

Moshe Ceszinski then was elected as secretary and treasurer.

The second meeting of the newly organized Union was held on 30 October 1938 in the house of the well-known *landsleit*, Leib Lesser and Mrs. Lesser, 1924 South Harding Avenue. Several members joined at the meeting. It also was decided to send out a call to acquaintances and *landsleit* to join our Union and to give notices to the Chicago Jewish newspapers. Friend Moshe Oderberg, the well-known *landsman* and *Paoeli-Zion* [Workers of Zion, a Marxist Zionist organization] worker came to the third meeting and joined as a member of the Union.

Little by little we began to win more members and we became even more accepted in Chicago.

The first literary-musical undertaking by the Czenstochower Independent Union was arranged on Sunday, 11 December 1929. The beloved cantor, Avraham Kuper and Miss Prawalski, a member of the union and the well-known pianist, took part in the program. Cantor Kuper sang a series of interesting folksongs with the piano accompaniment of Miss Prawalski. This first event in public made a good impression and was a big hit with the gathered guests and members.

The beloved Cwirn family also took part in the evening. The entire family together illuminated the holiday with their faithful singing of old Jewish folksongs, duets and couplets, mixed with joy and sorrow.

Many new members enrolled at the literary evening, among them, Mrs. Rose and Dave Hofman, Mrs. Khaya Zewin, the Gotajners, Mrs. Danciger, Yisroelke and Eva Warszawski, Dave Richtiger, Haimy Szternberg, Dr. Peter Awieczki, and later, Berta Warszawski and a group of others also became members. The Lesser family, the Cwirn family, Rose and Dave Hoffman, Chaya Zewin-Oderberg excelled as tireless workers for the Union, as well as later the newly arrived beloved members, Mrs. Fanny and Adolf Wilinger. They are all still at work today for the Union.

In 1940 the Czenstochower Independent Union already had a good organizational apparatus, with responsible officials: M. Oderberg as president, Mrs. Rose Hofman – vice president, M. Ceszinski – recording secretary, S. Cwirn – finance secretary and Friend Leib Lesser as treasurer, as well as executive members.

On 24 March 1940 we carried out our first Purim ball in the Homboldt Boulevard Temple. At this opportunity we published our first souvenir book, which differed from our publications of this sort in that in addition to an English section, there were several pages in Yiddish.

[Page 307]

The money that our Union began to receive would immediately be divided for various communal purposes. Thus we supported the Chicago Polish Union and the trade union campaign for workers in *Eretz-Yisroel* with significant sums. Our members were executives in both organizations. Support also was distributed for *folks-shuln* [people's schools], needy members and non-members, as well as for matzos for the poor, orphan institutions and cultural institutions.

The Czenstochower Independent Union stood and remains in contact with *landsleit* in various nations. In contrast with other *landsmanschaftn* [organizations of people from the same town], our meetings were held often, with free entry for members from other organizations.

In 1941 our union took out a charter. Signing the charter were the Friends: Leib Lesser, Sam Cwirn, Moshe Ceszinski, Mrs. Rose Hofman, Moshe Oderberg, Ahron Eizensztajn and Mrs. Aida Zevin. We organized a banquet in honor of the charter to which a large number of members, friends and guests came. The toastmaster at the banquet was Friend Dr. Peter Owieczki, known by all of us.

The terrible catastrophe in Europe caused our union members to respond with even more warmth to the aid appeals from various kinds of Chicago aid organizations.

In 1943 our union bought its own cemetery. Friend Dave Shelwin, now administrator of the cemetery, and Friend Leib Lesser, the then secretary of the cemetery division, carried out the purchase.

It is worthwhile to mention that our Union bought "Liberty Bonds" for several hundred dollars and supported the Red Cross with $160 as our taxes for winning the war.

HIAS [Hebrew Immigrant Aid Society] – 150 dollars; American Federation of Polish Jews – 250 dollars; Jewish Charities – 75 dollars; for the underground movement in Europe – 50 dollars; for the building committee to create a home for the Jewish blind – 40 dollars; the trade union campaign for the workers in *Eretz-Yisroel* – 100 dollars. We also supported other institutions with smaller sums.

Friend Rafal Federman, the emissary from New York for the book, *Czenstochower Yidn*, was welcomed by us with joy and received our help in his important work. The Union gave $50 as a donation for the book. A meeting with Friend Rafal Federman took place at the home of *landsleit*, Mr. and Mrs. Lesser of the active members of our Union. At a table set in a holiday mood, Friend Rafal Federman described the purpose and tasks of the book and also gave greetings from landsleit from New York and elsewhere. Over 200 dollars was collected by our small organization for the book. Before Friend Federman departed, a banquet took place in honor of our guest. Chairman Friend Moshe Oderberg was present at the evening. Among others, Moshe Ceszinski, the secretary of the Union, said goodbye to our guest.

[Page 308]

In 1944 many new members again joined, mainly thanks to the efforts of Friend Shelwin.

The fifth banquet of the Czenstochower Independent Union took place the 27 February 1944. At that opportunity, the Union published a printed souvenir book of 60 pages. Our Union numbers 65 male members today, as well as their wives.

A Group of Founders of the Czenstochower Independent Union in Chicago
Seated, right to left: Moshe Oderberg (president), Chaya Zewin (hospitality), Moshe Ceszinski (secretary)
Standing, right to left: Gutsha Zwirin, Sam Zwirin (treasurer), Adolf Wilinger and Fanny Wilinger

Among the founders of the Czenstochower Independent Union in Chicago it is worthwhile to note the following people: Bessie and Louis Lesser, Dave and Rose Hofman (current vice president).

This time at the election for officers of the Czenstochower Independent Union that took place in the organization at the end of 1945, almost a majority of those elected were from Czenstochow: Moshe Oderberg, again as president; treasurer – Sam Cwern; vice president – Rose Hofman; recording secretary – Moshe Ceszinski; hospitality – Chaya Zewin; to the executive – Adolf and Fanny Wilinger; finance secretary – Ben Arkin; director of the cemetery – Dave Shelwin.

The newly elected officers began to take on and carry out both communal and cultural work with special closeness and kinship and with special interest in listening to everyone who had a connection to our old home-city Czenstochow.

The Union was represented at the first United Czenstochower Relief Conference that took place in New York on 23 July 1945 by the especially sent delegate Moshe Ceszinski.

A Banquet of the Czenstochower Independent Union in Chicago

[Page 309]

In 1946 the Union supported various Chicago communal institutions as well as [those] in Czenstochow and *Eretz-Yisroel* with the following sums:

One hundred dollars for those working in *Eretz-Yisroel*; 100 dollars to the Czenstochower New York United Relief; 25 dollars for HIAS [Hebrew Immigrant Aid Society]; 25 dollars for Jewish Workers Committee; 25 dollars for a place for the sick poor to rest; 10 dollars for a greeting to the 20th anniversary of the Chicago Sholem Aleichem Institute; 10 dollars for the Society for Incurable Sick Jews; 10 dollars to the Rescue Fund for Jewish Refugees.

The Union contributed a designated sum for the Czenstochower sisters' Ladies Aid Society, bought tickets for several dollars to the fish dinner, donated several dollars for a greeting in a souvenir journal of the Czenstochower Regional Education Union and many other contributions for other organizations and committees that came to the meetings of the Union to ask for help.

Czenstochower Women's Aid Society in Chicago
by J. Gliksman

Nine energetic women decided to have a Czenstochower Women's Aid Society in Chicago. They held their first meeting on 29 January 1937 in the home of Friend Bessie Winer, 1401 Tripp Avenue.

The pioneers of the organization were: Bessie Winer, Rena Gotajner, Roza Glikerman, Shirley Paul, Tilly Biter, Dora Warszawski, Helen Szlezinger, Kate Ansel and Edith Warszawski. They immediately undertook a campaign to recruit members among the Czenstochower women and temporarily held their meetings in the homes of the initiators. Membership quickly increased and they had to rent public rooms for the meetings.

The first officials of the organization were:
First chairwoman: Bessie Winer
Vice chairwoman: Roza Lewkowicz
Treasurer: Kate Ansel
Recording and corresponding secretary: Rena Gotajner
Members of the Executive: Tilly Biter and Roza Glikerman.

The young organization had to overcome many difficulties. First of all, the Czenstochower Union that had been organized for a long time did not want another Czenstochow organization out of fear of competition. However, it was shown that the women' club would have many uses and would help the Union. Disruptions of a personal character were worse. In time, the organization under the energetic leadership of its founders strengthened and became popular among the Czenstochower women. It took out a charter and in 1939 adopted a constitution for the new organization that gave it the official name: Czenstochower Women's Aid Society. The Society has its regular meeting place and came together the first and third Mondays of the month.

We support the following organizations: day and night children's nurseries, American Red Cross, Los Angeles Sanatorium, Chicago Center for Soldiers, Jewish Philanthropic Fund in Chicago, organization to help tuberculosis patients, war aid for the Soviet Union (Russian War Relief), General Jewish Fund for the Needy, Jewish *Folksheym* [people's home] for the Sick, Trade Unions Campaign and still more smaller organizations that come to us for help.

It is worthwhile mentioning that although our membership consists of only 40 women, our assessments for various philanthropic institutions reached a sum of $5,227.

The main purpose for which we organized is, after all the same, that is to help those suffering from need in our home city. We designated a special fund that we invested in bonds for this purpose.

[Page 310]

We have many members who are not from Czenstochow, who help us in our work. Our president, Bessie Winer, who is not from Czenstochow, has held the office for seven years and is very energetic in the work of spreading and strengthening our organization. Friends Tilly Biter, Roza Glikerman, Gertrude Fox and Shirley Paul have been in their offices without interruption.

We want to continue our work to help those suffering from need. Now, after the war, we also can benefit from the sociability that our organization can offer.

Czenstochower Women's Aid Society in Chicago
Seated, right to left: Gertrude Fox (corr. and fin. sec.), Helen Szlezinger (treasurer),
Rose Hofman (vice president), Betty[1] Winer-Pradel (president), Shirley Paul (record.
sec.), Sura Helberg (1st trustee)
Second row, right to left: R. Glikerman, H. Zewin, D. Warszawski, R. Federman, C.
Warszawski, T. Biter, B. Warszawski, A. Szwarc
Third row, right to left: R. Lefkowicz, A. Poper, M. Trembot, A. Gibrik, L. Lesser

Translator's Footnote

1. The name of the president of the group is given both as Bessie and Betty

---

Czenstochower Regional Union in Detroit

by J. Gliksman

The founding committee came together in the house of Friend Y. Gliksman on 25 December 1925. Taking part in the deliberations were Y. Gliksman, F. Fajertag, N. Richter, M. Starszum, H. Yoskowitz, Max Grosberg and A. Grosberg.

A mass meeting took place on 1 January 1926 at the home of Friend H. Yoskowitz and 30 members joined.

The following officers were elected:

M. Fradelski, chairman, M. Grosberg, vice chairman, P. Gliksman – secretary; M. Starozum – recording secretary, H. Shumer (Szmulewicz) – treasurer; executive: M. Fradel (Fradelski), T. Halberg, Y. Gliksman, A. Birnholc, H. Yoskowicz, H. Shumer, M. Starozum, A. Grosberg, A. Jacobs, A. Fefer.

[Page 311]

During the existence of the Union, it supported the nursery and the Professional Unions in Czenstochow, as well as *TOZ* [Society for the Protection of Health], with considerable sums of money and we also helped a number of national and local organizations here in this country [the United States].

The Union was dissolved on 14 October 1928.

Czenstochower Regional Union

The Czenstochower Regional Union in Detroit was organized on 23 February 1935. The organizing committee held its first meeting in the house of Friend Sam Halberg, with the participation of: Y. Gliksman, N. Richter, S. Halberg, R. Luks, B. Kalin, T. Halberg, A. Winter, Haimy Yoskowicz (deceased), A. Birnholc, H. Halberg.

The mass meeting was held in the assembly hall.

The following officials were elected:

Chairman – S. Halberg, vice-chairman – Haimy Yoskowicz, finance-secretary – Y. Gliksman, recording-secretary – A. Winter, treasurer – B. Kalin.

Executive – T. Halberg, R. Luks, A. Birnholc, A. Leser.

During the 10 years of its existence, we supported the following organizations with a sum or $14,263:

Czenstochower children's homes, cultural office of the professional unions, and divisions of *TOZ* in Czenstochow, the Federation of Polish Jews, Allied Joint Campaign, H.I.A.S., *IKOR* [Organization for Jewish Colonization in Russia], trade union campaign, National Fund, *Khesed Shel Emes* [Good Deed of Faith – organization for arranging burials in the Orthodox tradition], the Red Cross, War Chest, Los Angeles Sanatorium (Detroit division), Denver Sanatorium, USO, Russian War Relief, Chinese War Relief and dozens of other organizations.

During the course of six war loans, the members of Czenstochower Union bought 65,000 dollars worth of bonds through the organization.

Our members have 38 children in the American Army. During the three years of war, we were in constant contact with the children in the army and each was sent a package every three months.

[Page 312]

We worked with all members of the Federation of Polish Jews and sent a large number of packages to Lublin.

Even in the past, the Czenstochower Regional Union in Detroit took an interest in our old home city, Czenstochow. We had collected a large fund for this purpose. The income from the banquet in honor of its 10th anniversary that took place on 25 February 1945 was designated for this fund.

The Czenstochower Regional Union in Detroit celebrated the second annual anniversary with a beautiful concert and banquet on Sunday, the 22nd of January 1938, in Carpenter's Hall.

For the short time of its existence, the Czenstochower Union managed to develop energetic activity in various areas, which was expressed in the tasks the Union set for itself at its founding.

The Union also stood on watch and did everything possible to help its own members who at times were in need of fraternal help.

The Executive of the Czenstochower Regional Union in Detroit
First row, seated, right to left: Mrs. A. Birnholc, Mrs. A Zbarow, Mrs. M. Richter, Mrs. M. Fein, Mrs. J. Holcberg
Second row, seated, right to left: S. Zbarow, B. Wratslowski, M. Fein, R. Federman, J. Halberg, T. Halberg, N. Richter
Standing, right to left: J. Wiatrok, S. Richtman, A. Birnholc, Ch. Halberg, A. Goldsztajn

The fact also should be recorded that the Union did not remain indifferent to the local city communal life and took an appropriate part in the large people's movement to build a house in the Los Angeles sanatorium in the name of Detroit Jewry and also joined in several national and state administrative bodies with annual contributions. In general, the Union answered very fraternally every appeal of our friendly organizations.

Simultaneously, the Union took care of its cultural tasks, so that in the course of two very successful years, concerts, literary family evenings and other similar cultural ventures were carried out.

All of the important tasks that the Union seriously and sincerely endeavored to serve made the Union a communal factor in Jewish life in Detroit and also drew the attention of many non-*landsleit* [people from the same town] who volunteered their help to the Union in order that the work be more successful. The result of this was that several important people joined as members.

Understand that all of this was in great measure thanks to the deep devotion and self-sacrifice of a very large number of active members, who brought life and activity into the work and into the tasks of the Union.

The charter was given to the organization as a gift from Eleizer Gliksman.

The following officials left their offices in 1944. Chairman – Fine, vice chairman – A. Halberg, finance secretary – B. Wiatrak, recording secretary – a. Birnholtz, treasurer – B. Wraclowski, hospitality (men) – J. Wiatrak, hospitality (women) – R. Halberg, executive – N. Richter, Sister[1] G. Richter, Sister Helen Sbarow, T. Halberg.

Newly elected officials for the year 1945:

Chairman – Isidor Gliksman, vice chairman – S. Rechtman, finance secretary – B. Wiatrak, recording secretary – J. Czudnow, treasurer – B. Wraclowski, hospitality (men) – J. Wiatrak, hospitality (women) – Jenny Wiatrak.

Executive – A. Birnholc, T. Halberg, Lizzy Halberg, S. Halberg, A. Winter, Helen Sbarow, N. Richter and Sister G. Bajtner.

The Czenstochower Regional Union opened its activities with a banquet on 14 October at the Jewish Culture Center, 2705 Joy Road.

The banquet was dedicated to the 50th anniversary of the long time [greeter] and esteemed worker, Joe Wiatrak. The campaign for the "Victory Loan" also was opened that evening.

Thanks to the capable leadership of the Czenstochower Union in Detroit, there were significant results in all relief and communal undertakings of the Union during the course of the last years.

The Czenstochower Union excelled in the sale of War Bonds and received a "citation" from the War Department in Washington that was reported on the radio.

The Detroit Union delivered the sum of one thousand dollars to Czenstochower Relief in New York for aid purposes.

The Union took an active part in the campaign of the Jewish Committee for Russian Relief, collecting a significant sum of money. The leaders of the Czenstochower Union in Detroit produced a series of plans for communal actions.

[Page 313]

*

The Czenstochower branch 620 *Arbeter Ring* [Workman's Circle] was installed on 23 December 1928.

The following officials were nominated:
R. Luks – finance secretary.
Y. Gliksman – recording secretary.
W. Yoskowicz – treasurer (died).
B. Kalin – hospitality.
Executive: Panksi, Kenigsberg, F. Fajertag, Willis, Abe Wenger, N. Richter, Y. Gliksman and R. Luks.

The branch led cultural work and supported many local and national bodies.

The branch was dissolved on 30 July 1932.

*

The founding meeting of the Czenstochower Patronat [organization that supported Jewish political victims in 1930's Poland] in Detroit took place in the home of Friend Y. Gliksman on 18 November 1937. In attendance were: Y. Gliksman, B. Wraclowski, S. Rechtman, Fajerman, Ritsh, B. Kalin, N. Richter. Chosen were: provisional chairman – B. Wraclowski; Y. Gliksman – finance secretary.

During the six months that the Patronat existed, we succeeded in carrying out several undertakings, supported the Patronats with a sum of more than $150 as well as distributed the Patronat publications in great numbers.

Translator's Footnote

1. Members of *landmanschaftn* – organizations of people from the same town – often addressed each other with the honorific "brother" or "sister."

————

The Czenstochower Aid Union in Los Angeles

The Czenstochower Union in Los Angeles was organized with the help of the president of the Joint Czenstochower Relief in New York, Friend Avraham Senzer, who spent several months here and with the participation of Friend Rafal Federman during his trip through the larger cities of the United States.

Yeta Grey (Grilak), H. Epsztajn, Harry Grauman joined the temporary committee that was founded in December 1944.

The committee immediately began its activities and their work was crowned with great success.

Shabbos [Sabbath], the 22nd of December 1944, the first meeting took place in the Park Manor Hall.[1] The appeal to all Czenstochower *landsleit* [people from the same town] had an appropriate success. Everyone gathered with warm fraternal readiness to help carry out the task that we stated as our purpose.

Friend Rafal Federman spoke before a meeting about the Jewish situation in Poland before and after the war. He particularly emphasized the situation of the Jews in Czenstochow that moved the gathering to tears.

After a short discussion, a temporary committee was chosen of Friends: Epsztajn, Grauman and Federman with the task of preparing a large meeting of all Czenstochower in Los Angeles and its vicinity.

The founding meeting of the Czenstochower Aid Committee took place at Clifton's Restaurant in Los Angeles on *Shabbos*, 9 December 1944.

The chairman of the meeting, Friend H. Epsztajn presented to the gathered *landsleit* the guest, Friend Rafal Federman, who described the destruction of Jewish life in Poland and explained the difficult task that stood in front of the Jews, in general, and our *landsleit* in particular, concerning their Czenstochower brothers whose hour of liberation and the throwing off of the Nazi yoke was approaching.

Gina Medem, the well-known journalist and lecturer, also greeted those assembled.

The following managing committee was elected at the founding meeting:
Chairman: Max Pepper
Secretary: Harry Grauman
Finance Secretary: Izzy Berger.

Elected to the executive were:

[Page 314]

Max Pepper, Izzy Berger, Harry Grauman, Philip Grosberg, Ahron Grosberg, Mendl Grosberg, Yosl Berliner, Dovid Miller (Malarski), Sheyndl Szuchter.

How much energy and how intensively the Czenstochower Relief in Los Angeles worked is seen by the undertakings and sums of the receipts for six months of activity.

At her own initiative Mrs. Rose Klein also arranged a gathering that brought in the sum of 60 dollars.

Mrs. Marvin Gelber organized a lunch at which 195 dollars was collected.

The Czenstochower Relief in Los Angeles used every additional opportunity to strengthen the activity of Czenstochowers in Los Angeles. The liberation of Czenstochow by the victorious Russian armies provided such an opportunity. Seven thousand Jews in Czenstochow were saved from certain death thanks to the rapid march of the Red Army.

An event was organized in the home of Mr. and Mrs. Philip and Ester Grosberg on 18 February 1945 at which 187 dollars was collected. The president of Czenstochower Relief in Los Angeles, who began the collections, had entirely separate earnings. Mrs. Rose Klein had the opportunity to give the 60 dollars that she collected in her home at a lunch. The actress, Dekla Kapulasz, lent beauty to the evening with appropriate folksy readings and recitations.

On 29 April 1945, a meeting of all Czenstochower *landsleit* was organized in the house of the Berger family. A plan of constructive aid for the Czenstochow Jews surviving the Nazi-hell was worked out at this meeting. At this occasion 120 dollars was collected.

At this opportunity, Max Pepper, the president, introduced his son, Sheldon, who had returned from Italy where he fought as an American soldier against Nazi Germany.

The assembled greeted him heartily and in order to honor the young hero, 183 dollars was collected for Czenstochow at the initiative of Mr. Grauman. The first to respond was Friend Yosl Berliner.

The Czenstochower Aid Union in Los Angeles, California
Seated, right to left: Dovid Malarski [Miller], Yitzhak Berger, Yitzhak Hersh Grauman, Meir Pieprz [Pepper], Yosf Berliner
Standing, right to left: Hershl Epsztajn, Adolf Landau, Chaya Berger, Yeshaya Yakov Menkof, Gitl Menkof, Philip Grosberg, Ester Grosberg, Toba Pieprz (Pepper), Ahron Grosberg

[Page 315]

The last gathering brought the opportunity to send 500 dollars with the money from the previous collection for food packages through Czenstochower Relief in New York.

Not quite a month passed and there again was an opportunity to help our Czenstochower *landsleit.*

Friend Yosl Berliner celebrated the *Bar-Mitzvah* of his son Saran in a very inspired manner. Czenstochower and Radomsker *landsleit* met there and they sang old folksongs that reminded them of their old home. Friend Epsztajn, himself a Radomsker, called everyone to further aid work. Friends Davidson and Grauman greeted the group. Two hundred dollars was collected, which was divided among the Czenstochow and Radomsk *landsleit*.

[The idea of] immediate help penetrated the deep consciousness and the minds of all Czenstochower *landsleit*.

On Sunday, 15 August, the families *shtibl* [one room synagogue] in Van Nuys near Los Angeles arranged a picnic. On this occasion, 320 dollars was collected that was divided among the Czenstochower and Radomsker Jews.

On the 2nd of September 1945, Friend Berliner organized a victory party in his house in honor of the ending of the Second World War.

One hundred thirty-four dollars was collected and distributed equally among Radomsker and Czentochower Relief.

Relief also bought War Bonds for 50 dollars and had income from them of 100 dollars.

Sunday, 18 November, the Czenstochower Aid Union called a mass meeting in the Park Ville Manor at which Max Pepper, the chairman, pointed out the great task that now stood before American Jewry to help rebuild Jewish life in Poland.

Friend Grauman gave a report of the activity to that time and read a letter from the Czenstochower AJA committee that arrived in Los Angeles.

Three hundred dollars was collected to which Friends Berliner and Berkowicz added 100 dollars.

However, this is not everything the Czenstochower Relief in Los Angeles did. The plans for the near future show that Czenstochower Relief in Los Angeles has assumed the task of energetically helping our *landsleit*.

Relief reorganized with the following people:
President: Max Pepper
Secretary: Harry Grauman
Financial Secretary: Dovid Borzykowski
Treasurer: Yosl Berliner

Executive:
  Yitzhak Berger
  Ester Grosberg
  Fishel Grosberg
  Mendl Grosberg
  Ahron Grosberg
  Dovid Malarski

Report from the Treasury:

Since 17 December $1,858.65 was collected; $1,240.11 was paid out; $618.54 remains in the treasury.

Translator's Footnote

1. The correct date is probably *Shabbos*, 2 December 1944.

[Page 315]

The Czenstochower *Patronat* in Los Angeles

In 1933, when the dark clouds of the coming fascist terror in Europe encouraged the dark powers in Poland to carry out pogroms, there awoke in us, the Czenstochower in Los Angeles, the feeling of responsibility for our brothers and sisters in Poland who struggled with pride for their equal rights.

At the beginning of 1933, we, a group of Czenstochower *landsleit* [people from the same town] (Max and Tessie Feffer, Shirley and Jack Sztibl, Leah and Chaim Leib Szwarc, comrades Israel, May and Harry Grauman) founded the first *Patronat* [group to provide assistance to political prisoners] on the shores of the Pacific Ocean. We received the trust and encouragement of our sister organization in New York. We had functioned for more than a year as a Czenstochower aid organization for political arrestees in Czenstochow and its surrounding areas (*Patronat*).

[Page 316]

Whereas there were not many Czenstochower *landsleit* then in Los Angeles, it later was decided to become a territorial *Patronat* that encompassed *landsleit* from various cities and towns in Poland. Therefore, we changed the name of our committee to Los Angeles Aid Committee for Political Arrestees in Poland (*Patronat*).

The central committee of the Polish *Patronats* in New York gave us the great honor of assuming the care of the two prisons in Poland, Fardan and Rawicz, where the majority of the female political arrestees were held. With pride and honor, we carried out our humanitarian aid work on behalf of the fighters [against] and [those martyred to] Polish fascism.

In 1938 our *Patronat* helped found the Novi Dvor and Vilna *Patronat* in Los Angeles and together we carried out a series of undertakings and several *Patronat* meetings against the wild murderers of the Jews in Poland.

Our organization was involved with the important aid work until August 1939 when the Nazi beasts attacked Poland.

The writer of these lines is proud that he was the co-founder and secretary of Czenstochower *Patronat* and later the general secretary of the General *Patronat*.

Let us hope that for the so heavily tested Polish Jewry, along with all of humanity, a new epoch of good fortune begins.

[Page 317]

Rozenblat–Dykerman Circle in New York

While still living, Sol Dykerman and Chaya Rozenblat expressed a wish to create a circle for the Dykerman, Kuperman and Tanski families. The purpose of the circle was that the members of the families should stay together.

———

For various reasons, the circle was founded after their deaths. Its founders were Benjamin Rozenblat, Max Dykerman, Benny, Harry and Morris Kuperman, as well as Dovid Tanski.

Almost all the members of the mentioned families belong to the circle, which numbers over 100 members. Its task is to bring the three families closer together, for them to know each other better, to spend time together and to help everyone who is in need.

Bulletins and Announcements from Czenstochower Organizations in America

The circle comes together once a month and interesting evenings are presented. The atmosphere is a very joyful, intimate one. Meeting each other on one platform, the thread of family that until now had been almost torn becomes connected and stronger.

The circle has a special fund from which gifts are given to members at various opportunities, as well as support for the needy. A committee of two members allocates the support and the question does not have to be brought before the wider membership. This is so as not to embarrass the needy.

The circle had 25 members in the army, among them: Major Hyman Ditman, doctor of medicine; Lieutenant Hyman Rozenblat, in the navy, doctor of philosophy, and Lieutenant Sol Morey. The circle maintained close contact with the members in the army and navy. Packages were sent regularly to every one of them. War Bonds were bought for 100,000 dollars. The circle supported various institutions such as the Red Cross, hospitals and so on. The circle is doing its duty now in the campaign for the Jews in Poland.

The circle plans to strengthen its existence through the creation of medical help in every form for its members.

A Meeting of the Members of the Rozenblat–Dykerman Circle

[Page 318]

National Conference of the *Czenstochower Landsmanschaftn* in America and Canada

by R. Federman

A certain connection of the New York Czenstochower Relief Committee and the United Czenstochower Relief and Ladies Auxiliary with the Czenstochower *landsmanschaftn* [societies of people from the same town] and aid organizations in other cities in America has existed at almost all times since the aid work for Czenstochow has been carried out. Thus, for example, the Czenstochower Relief Committee in New York helped the organizations in Detroit and Chicago to organize film presentations from the Y.L. Peretz children's home and Jewish public school in Czenstochow.

At the start of the Second World War, when the horrible news arrived about the destruction of our brothers on the other side of the ocean, it became clear that the aid work for Czenstochow would demand such great sums of money and such great effort that it would need to be done in partnership with all friends in America and in other nations. The connection among the Czenstochower *landsmanschaftn* in America, *Eretz-Yisroel* and other nations was particularly timely after the decision to publish the book, *Czenstochower Yidn*. Such a large publication could not be accomplished by a *landmanschaft* in one city, even as large as New York.

On 13 October 1944 at a meeting of the United Czenstochower Relief, it was decided to turn to all of the Czenstochower *landsmanschaftn* in America and Canada about sending representatives to a national conference to coordinate the aid activities for Czenstochow and to bring about the publication of the book, *Czenstochower Yidn*.

On 25 April 1945 the organizing committee of United Czenstochower Relief led by R. Federman, according to an earlier communication with Chicago and Detroit, sent out an appeal to all of the Czenstochower *landsmanschaftn* in America and Canada to send delegates to the national consultations (conference) in New York on Saturdayand Sunday, 23 and 24 June 1945.

The conference was held at the designated time in the Beethoven Hall, 201 East Fifth Street, New York.

The delegates taking part in the conference were: from Chicago – S. A. Fridman and Mrs. Louis Gras and Mrs. A. Wilinger, A.S. Miska and Mrs. Sam Szlezinger and Mrs. Saul Baum; from the Czenstochower Independent Union in Chicago – Moshe Ceszinski; from the Czenstochower Ladies Aid Society in Chicago – Mrs. Rose Hofman; Czenstochower Aid Union in Toronto and its surroundings – Kenigsberg, Mr. Goldberg and Tsina Arczech.

Czenstochower branch 11 United People's Order (International Workers Order) – R. Berger, D. Tanski.

First Zaloshiner Chevra Anshei Bnei Achim – William Najtigal, Emanuel Wargan; Czentochower Young Men – Karl Buchner, Max Kaminski, Jack Jacobs, Jack Zeidman.

Detroit – Isidor Gliksman.

Czenstochower branch 262 *Arbeter Ring*, New York – M. Feiner, Y. Szubin.

United Czenstochower Relief in New York.

Here are the greetings from United Czenstochower Relief and Ladies Auxiliary that was shared with the delegates, along with the agenda of the conference, the program of the book, *Czenstochower Yidn* and projects of the resolutions:

Greetings

Dear Assembled Delegates and Guests,

The Nazi beast was annihilated with the blood of millions of victims from all people of the world and the entire world can breathe easier with us.

Most of the victims of the devastation and genocide that the German-Nazi beasts carried out during the time of their rule were Jews, who the barbaric murderers annihilated and tore out by the roots, leaving small remnants who survived through a miracle.

[Page 319]

Coming together today for the conference to consider the best means and ways to help our surviving brothers and sisters in our home-city, our first thought and feeling is for those who gave their lives in the fight with the German murderers, and let us today remember in the front ranks, the Jewish martyrs of our city and of all the Jewish communities who perished at the hands of the cruelest human-animals.

Their pain and suffering, their sacred memory will strengthen us to carry out the work that we have undertaken:

To help the survivors repair their lives and build up the Jewish community and Jewish life in our home city.

We hope to reach our goal with new courage and old beliefs that sustained our people during the course of thousands of years, with the united and shared strength of those gathered here and those who are located in other parts of the world.

Welcome, assembled delegate friends and guests!

United Czenstochower Aid
Committee in New York
President: A. Y. Senzer

Czenstochower Ladies Auxiliary,
New York
Chairlady: Yeta Lenczner

The conference opened at 9 o'clock in the evening in a very solemn and earnest mood. There were a large number of guests present in addition to the delegates.

The stage of the presidium was decorated with the American Stars and Stripes on one side and the [Zionist] blue and white flag on the other side. A picture of the not long dead president, Franklin Delano Roosevelt, looked down on the assembled from above. Lit candles burned in a Jewish menorah in sacred remembrance of the martyrs from Czenstochow and the hundreds of other cities and *shtetlekh* [towns] in Poland.

The following inscriptions were found on the stage: "*Brukhim habaim*" – "Welcome, delegates and guests, to the first National Conference of the Czenstochower in America!" "Building Jewish National Life Everywhere!" "Ten Jews are a *minyon*; hundreds – a community, thousands – a tribe, 12 tribes – a people."

There was a general impression that this was an earnest meeting of men of the people for a great thing for the people.

Friend Yakov Ber Silver, chairman of the organizing committee, opened the conference.

Among other things in his opening speech, he said:

The catastrophe of the Jews in the countries under the Nazi authority already was clear to us when we decided to call together a conference of the national Czenstochower organizations and the frightening picture of the Jewish destruction already hovered before our eyes.

National Conference of the Czenstochower *Landsmanschaftn* in America and Canada

[Page 320]

We felt that it was our elementary duty to organize aid for our surviving brothers and sisters. Today, we already know that humanity is not in a state to absorb the great misfortune that befell our people. We know today that our own indifference and the indifference of the entire ostensibly civilized world bear the complicity for the great crime that was committed against our people.

The answer of the Czenstochower *landsmanschaftn* to our appeal, the numerous delegates who arrived today, did not disappoint us.

Dear friends, delegates and guests, accept in my name, in the name of our secretary, Rafal Federman, and of our entire organizing committee, our hearty thank you and welcome.

He then gave over the chair to the president of United Czenstochower Relief, Friend Abraham Senzer, who announced the names of the delegates and the organizations taking part and whom the delegates represented. He established that 36 designated delegates were authorized to take part in the conference.

At the assembling of the presidium, the president declared that during the course of the discussions all of the delegates would be represented in the presidium. The following friends were invited to the first meeting: Josef Kaufman, Harry Feierstein, Rafal Federman, Yeta Lenczner, Gussie Gelbard, Karpiel, Moshe Censzinski, Rose Hofman, Sol Baum, Fridman, Isidor Gliksman, Tsina Arczech.

A. Chrabalowski, Abe Kaufman and Chaya Waga-Rautman were chosen as secretaries.

Dr. Rafal Mahler, editor of the book, *Czenstochower Yidn*, was also invited to join the presidium.

After taking care of all formalities, the chairman gave a bang with his gavel, a sign for everyone assembled to stand up. Miss F. Czarny played the American hymn, *Star Spangled Banner*, and then *Hatikvah* on the piano. Then came the words of Friend A. Chrabalowski who honored the memory of those who fell in the fight against Fascist Nazism and the annihilation of millions of Jewish martyrs with the following words:

Our first word and our first thought belongs to our children, our brothers and the children and brothers of all of the people in the world who fell on the battlefields, in the Warsaw, Czenstochow and other ghettos, in the partisan divisions, in the death camps in the fight against the German Nazi murderers – we bow our heads for them with reverence, in deep sadness.

Honor all of their memories!

We Jews took first place among the [victims of the] outrages and hurricanes of death and annihilation carried out by the Nazi murderers. Thousand-year old rooted communities were erased from the earth. Among them was also our home city, our old birthplace, Czenstochow.

We are speaking in human language too weak and too poor, crying out our hearts, suffering painful sorrow for the tens of thousands of brothers and sisters, fathers and mothers, young people and children who perished. Sh[imon] Frug's *Shtormen Blut un Taykhn Trern* [*Streams of Blood and Rivers of Tears – written about the pogroms of 1881-1882*] will not suffice and no human heart and human feeling can absorb so much ache and pain.

Our great misfortune, our unheard of tragedy, the sorrow and pain of millions perishing from hunger and cold, horrible cruelty and mass murder in the gas chambers – became a thousand times greater in that it remained a quiet tragedy [about which] we ourselves were incapable of shouting out, crying out and suffered the pain.

The world remained deaf and dumb when for many years the calls for help came from the ghettos and death camps and it also is silent now.

The Czechoslovak Lidice is remembered thousands of times and has been written about before and now. Our tragedy – millions of times larger – was passed over in silence. The Nazi robbery, murder and annihilation was done to Jews. To the demand to be paid for all the crimes, we were French, Poles, Belgians, Dutch and so on. The suffering and torture and the heroic fight of the martyrs of all peoples against the Nazis has been presented in dozens of films but as of now no films have been shown about our martyrs and holy ones, our heroes in the ghettos

Generations of us created and developed Jewish life in Czenstochow, built up the first streets of the Gecewizne [neighborhood in Czenstochow]: the Nadrzeczna, Garncarska, Senatorska, Teper and Yatke Streets. Then the old market, the new market, the Ogrodowa, Tilna. Then the First *Aleje* was established. The Second *Aleje*. the Spadek, the Wales, the Dojazdowa Street and so on. Vast stretches were changed into a wide cultural community, institution after institution that were the pride of Poland, such as the Artisans' School, the gardening farm. The new Jewish hospital was erected and an extensive social life sprouted and blossomed in Czenstochow.

[Page 321]

The liberation movement in the arena of our lives at the beginning of the 20th century was carried out by a new and young generation that began a fight for a new and freer life. And new institutions, new cultural institutions arose. The Yiddish language, Yiddish songs that were spoken and sung before only in the cellars and poor houses of Gecewizne rang out free and proud from the wide and beautiful rooms of the Literary Society, *Lira*, Sport and the touring union created by the new Jewish young. They created their own Yiddish press as a beautiful dream amidst the reality. The Y.L. Peretz children's home and *folkshul* created by our brothers and sisters in America was erected at Krotka 23 as a living legend.

Thousands of our Czenstochower brothers – old and young – emigrated to America, *Eretz-Yisroel* and other nations and with their effort and work helped to build new Jewish communities and they occupy a respected place everywhere.

The death storm of Nazi annihilation arrived and eradicated, devastated and destroyed everything.

In the ruins, the tragedy of death and annihilation, even just in our city, is so great that the human heart stops and the ability to speak disappears.

Who can describe the fear and pain of a city that night after night, week after week waited for death in the wagons or the gas chambers that would bring an end to their suffering?

Who can describe the outrageousness of the murderers who fooled the remaining tortured ones through dozens of tricks?

Let us, dear friends, engrave this in our minds and in our hearts and never forget it.

Let us give it to our children so that they will remember it!

Let us not forget our brothers and sisters who perished and never forget or forgive their murderers!

Let us erect an eternal light for them not only in Czenstochow, but in the home, in every heart and soul so that its fire of love and sorrow for our martyrs will always glow.

Let us sanctify their memory with our work to help the survivors rebuild their lives for which we have come together today.

The first word, the first thought of our conference we dedicated to those, our martyrs and holy ones.

Let us all stand up, bow our heads in deep grief and sorrow and sanctify and honor their memory!

With tears in our eyes we, the assembled, stand to honor the memory of our brothers and sisters who perished. Mrs. F. Czarny played Chopin's *Funeral March.*

After this, Friend Avraham Yakov Senser turned to the delegates in the name of United Czenstochower Relief and the Ladies Auxiliary with the following greeting:

Honored delegates and guests. Honored conference:

The settling of Czenstochower Jews in America is probably as old as Jewish immigration to America in general. After half a century, the largest number of Czenstochower Jews live in America. Over time, the Czentochowers have created their schools, societies and unions across America. They also never forgot their old home where they left those closest to them and their friends. They always felt their sufferings and joys and always helped to make their lives easier, which always was difficult enough. This is the first time that a conference of Czenstochower organizations in America has come together in which delegates from 13 organizations from various cities in America and Canada are taking part. It is certainly an important event in the life of the Czenstochower Jews here.

What gave rise to the calling of such a conference and that it is taking take place?

A great misfortune, the greatest misfortune in the history of the Jews, had befallen our people. A third of the entire Jewish people has been annihilated in a shameful manner by Hitlerist criminal fascism. All nations had victims in the war, but no other people suffered a loss like the Jewish people.

[Page 322]

The great disaster and misfortune brought forth our conference.

Honored delegates and guests, let us keep this in mind during the entire time of our negotiations.

Therefore, because our misfortune is so large, we do not want the remaining fragment of our people to be ground among the wheels of the further evolution of human society. We must gather all of our strength, all of our remaining strength and say: we will live! And we will live equal to all of the nations! We must intercede for our further existence with deeds, just as our brothers and sisters, our closest and dearest in the Warsaw and Czenstochow ghettos did. We must gather together all of our material and spiritual strength, everyone in his area and further advance our people's life, not as individuals, but as a nation.

Let us have this in mind during our dealings.

Our conference was small at first, but it was very large in substance if we take into account that the focus of our activities is in only one city, one Jewish community, our home city, the city of our parents – Czenstochow.

I want to believe and I am certain of this that our conference will be permeated with the great will to help our surviving brothers and sisters in their present difficult situation and in their further existence and will obtain the most successful results with God's help.

I heartily greet you friend delegates and guests in my name and in the name of all our the members of the United Czenstochower Relief Committee in New York with an enthusiastic welcome and wish you and us fruitful work in the deliberations of the conference and successful results.

Welcome!

Friend Sol Baum, on behalf of the Educational Union in Chicago, Friend Moshe Ceszinski – Independent Union in Chicago, Friend Harry Goldberg – Czenstochower Aid Union in Toronto, [female] Friend Rose Hofman – Aid Society in Chicago, Friend Isidor Gliksman – Czenstochower Aid Union in Detroit. A telegraphic greeting from Friend Harry Grauman in the name of the Aid Union in Los Angeles also was read. The feeling of the delegates at the conference toward the greeting was most clearly expressed by Friend Moshe Ceszinski from which we here present several excerpts:

"I have traveled almost a thousand miles in order to meet with you again. Like many of you, hundreds of times I have dreamed, fantasized and looked for ways as to how and when to meet with you face to face and to share the grief of our large catastrophe and organize the work for our refugees.

"I have two strong contradictory feelings of joy and grief. I cannot hold back the tears at the horrible Jewish destruction in general and of Czenstochow in particular.

"However, here at the meeting, may the evil eye spare us, there is such a large number of friends whom the 'sword of Damocles' of the murderers did not reach and we represent a Czenstochower Jewish organized community of many thousand Jews who were brought here by the wave of immigration before the Nazi hangmen began the bloody task of murdering and annihilating our most beautiful, most beloved and dearest whom we left in our old home. We cannot suppress the feeling that this was lucky not only for us personally, but for the entire Jewish people.

We here, on American soil, over time grew strong, matured socially, nationally, and in many ways. This is seen at today's conference and in that we have set as a goal the publication of the book, *Czenstochower Yidn.*

"Many years ago, in 1923, there already were plans in Czenstochow to publish a *pinkas* [record book, often containing Jewish community records] under the name, *On Both Sides of the Ocean.* It was then no more than a dream. Now the dream will be brought to fruition. This is the achievement that makes us proud, although we now live after our most horrible tragedy through all of the Jewish generations."

[Page 323]

* * *

The last point on the agenda for the evening meeting was the report by Dr. Rafal Mahler on the theme, "the future of the Jews in Poland." The most important passages of his content-rich lecture were:

The great trouble of "independent" Poland was the unanswered agricultural question that half of all of the land ownership belonged to a handful of lords. Because of the large mass of poor peasants, trade and industry shrank. Instead of work and land, the reactionaries fed the masses with anti-Semitism and they agitated for pogroms.

The fundamental social reforms that the democratic government of liberated Poland is carrying out, such as the division of the land among the peasants and socializing the heavy industries as well as the Soviet-friendly policies, will create the soil for true democratic and economic development of the land.

The present circumstances of the small number of those rescued Jews is a great deal worse than that of the larger Polish population because they [the Jews] remained literally naked and barefoot. However, the worst is the pogroms organized by the local fascists. Therefore, a large number of the surviving Jews in Poland yearn to emigrate, particularly to *Eretz-Yisroel.* We are fighting for them so the door of the Jewish homeland will be opened. But Jewish communities in Poland still wish to remain and Jews, as equal citizens of the new Poland, have the possibility of taking part in the building of a new Poland. We must extend our fraternal hand to them and do everything in our power to help them build and reestablish their lives.

The second meeting of the conference took place Sunday, 24 June at 12:30 in the morning.[1]

President Avraham Ber Senzer opened the meeting and invited Friends Louis Szimkowicz, Ruwin Berger, M. Kep, Yitzhak Gurski and Harry Feierstein, vice president of United Czenstochower Relief, which led the meeting, to join the Presidium.

The proposed agenda was accepted.

Friend R. Federman read the greetings that were received from the United Jewish Appeal, the Joint, ORT, the American Federation of Polish Jews, Russian War Relief, the Jewish Workers' Committee, the Czenstochower Central Committee in *Eretz-Yisroel,* the Czenstochower

Society in Buenos Aires, Dovid Akerman in London, Ivan Ganz, Melbourne, Australia, Godl Fajertag, Tel Aviv, Louis Szwarc, Seattle, Washington. The greetings were received with heavy applause.

Friend Josef Kaufman, finance secretary of United Czenstochow Relief gave a detailed report of the immense aid work in New York and illustrated his presentation with a series of numbers.

Friend Sadie Senzer gave a report from the Ladies Auxiliary in New York.

The delegates reported on the situation of their organizations:

Moshe Ceszinski, Rose Hofman, Harry Goldberg – Toronto; Mrs. Winkler – from the Zaloshiner [Dzialoszyner] Ladies Auxiliary in New York – submitted a check of $100.

A break took place for a snack. The evening meeting began at 3:30 in the afternoon.

Vice president Harry Feierstein turned over the running of the meeting to the president, Friend Avraham Yakov Senzer.

The two most important reports were read – one by Friend Yitzhak Gurski on the theme, "On why and how the construction fund must be transformed." The second, by Dr. Leon Lajzerowicz, [was] about medical aid for the survivors in Czenstochow. The reports were a great success with their earnestness and thoroughness.

A discussion occurred about the form and character of the national organization that needed to be created by the conference. Taking part were friends: Berger – New York; Kenigberg – Toronto; Tanski – New York.

A resolutions committee was elected consisting of:

Harry Feierstein, Joseph Kaufman, Louis Szimkowicz, Isidor Gliksman, Fajner.

The commission held its meeting in a separate room and came to a unanimous decision about all of the points of the proposed resolutions.

The closing meeting began at seven in the evening under the chairmanship of Friend Josef Kaufman. Friend A. Chrabolowski read the following resolutions that were unanimously accepted by the conference.

[Page 324]

I

The delegates gathered in New York at the national conference of the Czenstochower organizations in America and Canada on 23 and 24 June 1945 have become completely aware of the thoughts expressed at the presentations and discussions and have recognized that:

1. The reconstruction and the revival of the physical and spiritual circumstances of the Jewish population in Poland is the most important task at the present moment for all Jewish national organizations throughout the world.

2. The possibility of providing urgent aid for the surviving Jewish population in our home city of Czenstochow needs to be created within the framework of activity of the Czenstochower Aid Organization, such as:

    a. Medical aid, food items and clothing.

    b. Care for orphans and children and the focusing of attention on their education and development.

    c. Constructive aid (craftsmen's tools, machines, production workshops).

    d. Jewish cultural institutions and religious teaching establishments.

    e. Help for the refugees and those deported who are in various nations temporarily.

3. The aid needs to be provided first directly to the leading Jewish institutions in Czenstochow or through existing Jewish national organizations that are active in Poland in general and in Czenstochow in particular, with the agreement of the executive in each case.

4. These tasks apply to all existing Czenstochower organizations wherever they are that have collected and are collecting aid funds.

II

Therefore, the conference decided:

1. In order to collect funds through the organizations in the most expedient, most productive and most rational way, a joint agreement of all of the organizations taking part in the conference is created.

2. To train an executive committee that was created by the plenipotentiary representatives of the existing organizations who are meeting [because of the present needs], with the purpose of bringing to realization the decisions adopted by the conference.

3. An elected secretary of the executive committee located in New York leads the work of the executive.

4. Until the meeting of the executive committee, the work will be carried out by Rafal Federman, the elected secretary of the conference, in agreement with the executive committee of United Czenstochower Relief in New York.

III

The executive committee is empowered by the conference to carry out the following tasks:

1. To come to an agreement with the Czenstochower aid organizations in other cities in America, Canada and other nations.

2. To aid the organizations to increase their aid funds systematically.

3. To designate the manner and way that all collected funds will be used in agreement with above mentioned adopted decisions.

IV

Bureau for Contact with Relatives

The conference decides, because of the great importance of individual contact among the surviving Jewish brothers and sisters, many of whom are spread throughout the cities and camps in all of the European nations and even in China with their relatives in America, that the bureau of United Czenstochower Relief that will have the task of searching for and connecting all surviving brothers and sisters with their relatives in all of the cities in America should be reestablished.

V

Bulletin

In order to inform the Czenstochower *landsleit* [people from the same town] in New York, in other cities in America and in other nations with the deliberations and decisions of the conference, in order to record the historical work of our conference, which is the first national conference of Jewish *landsmanschaftn* in America – the conference decided that it would publish a bulletin with the most important material from the conference.

[Page 325]

VI

Thanks to the Jewish Press

The National Conference of the Czenstochower *Landsmanschaftn* in America and Canada that came together to consider the means with which to successfully help to repair and rebuild the Jewish life of the surviving brothers and sisters in our hometown, Czenstochow, thanks the

Jewish press: *Forvets*, *Morgn Freiheit*, *Tog* and *Morgn Zurnal* for their assistance in the work of United Czenstochower Relief in the organizing of the conference.

VII

Acknowledging the Relief Committee

The Conference heartily thanks United Czenstochower Relief for organizing and successfully leading the national conference.

VIII

Resolution About the Book *Czenstochower Yidn*

The Conference decided:

1. Each *landsman* from Czenstochow is obliged to buy the book, keeping in mind that the profit increases the construction fund for a new Jewish life in the old home.

2. To give the Jewish representation created in Czenstochow as a voluntary gift the necessary copies of the book, *Czentochower Yidn*.

3. The organization will use every means so that the book will reach every Czenstochower *landsman* wherever he lives.

4. All organizations commit themselves to collaborate so that the book will be published without fail not later than the end of 1946.

5. The organization commits itself to carry out a campaign among the Czenstochower who are not yet represented in the book with their assessments, biographies, biographies of their children in the army and, in the memorial section, those deceased who are closest to them and to have them do this as quickly as possible.

6. With the publication of the book, let special celebrations be arranged with the help of the executive in every city by Czenstochower organizations for all Czenstochower *landsleit*. Selling the book should bring in larger sums of money from individuals for the construction fund.

7. All sums received by the organizations from the sale of the book will remain in the treasury of the organization receiving them. Obviously, after the subtraction of the actual costs of the book and this undertaking.

8. Each city accepts for itself a task and takes upon itself the responsibility to sell a minimum of as many books as amounts to half the number of *landsleit* in the city.

Because of a lack time, the resolutions by A. Chrabalowski about the necessity of contact among the Czenstochower organizations in all parts of the world and by Abe Kaufman about a perpetual flame were not considered. They were added to the minutes of the conference. The resolutions by Friend Tanski about the rights for the surviving Jews in Czenstochow also were not considered.

Friend R. Federman was elected as secretary to carry out the work of the national organization until a national executive is created that would lead the work in accord with the Czenstochower Relief in New York.

After the conference a supper and departure evening took place for the delegates. A large group of Czenstochower *landsleit* in New York took part. The president Avraham Yakov Senzer took on the chairmanship of the evening. Stella Glazer, the singer, appeared with a series of Yiddish and Hebrew songs which were a great hit with the attendees.

Those assembled responded warmly to the appeal by Friend Yakov Ber Silver and the sum of over 4,000 dollars flowed in.

* * *

The provisional central committee that was created in accord with the decision of the conference consisted of the chairman, Friend Avraham Yakov Senzer and secretary – R. Federman.

Copies of the decisions enacted were sent with the first circular to all of the organizations, which were invited to approve and appoint responsible people to the executive at once.

[Page 326]

The provisional central committee made known in the third circular its decision to call the first meeting of the central executive committee in Detroit.

The plenary meeting of the central executive committee of the Czenstochower Aid Union in America and Canada took place on 24 November 1945 in Detroit in the ballroom of the Jewish Cultural Center. They thanked the delegates and guests for the great honor that was granted to the Czenstochower *landsmanschaft* in Detroit that the first meeting of the central committee to help the surviving brothers in Czenstochow was taking place in their city.

(Photo, caption: Conference of the Central Executive of the Czenstochower *Landsmanscaftn* in America and Canada, in Detroit.)

The agenda was: 1) minutes of the conference; 2) report of the secretariat of New York Relief; 3) reports from Chicago, Detroit, Toronto and Los Angeles; 4) help for Czenstochow; 5) help for Czenstochowers in France, Belgium and other nations; 6) company for publication of the book, *Czenstochower Yidn*; 7) resolution and further directives.

There were those authorized from three cities: New York – Avraham Yakov Senzer, R. Federman, Silver, Cap and wife, Lenczner and wife, Frajermojer and wife, Gelber and wife: Chicago – representative Mrs. Fradel [and] guests, Leser and Wilinger; Detroit: Friend Izidor Gliksman, Rechtman, Birnholc and a large number of guests.

The meeting was opened by Friend Avraham Ber Senzer who invited Friend Winter to be secretary. Friend Gliksman greeted [everyone].

The chairman, Friend Senzer, greeted the delegates and guests. He asserted that the Czenstochower Aid Union in America and Canada was the first to unite into a central [organization] that coordinated the aid work. The national Jewish aid organizations, such as the Joint [Distribution Committee], American Federation of Polish Jews, ORT [Organization for Rehabilitation through Training] and the Jewish Workers' Committee recognized the great importance of our pioneering work.

Rafal Federman read the minutes of the historic conference in New York, which were heard with great interest and attention.

[Page 327]

Reports from the cities were given: Friend Senzer – from New York; Friend Federman – from the provisional central committee: Friend Silver also reported about the agreement with the "Joint" to send clothing and food worth 2,000 dollars to Czenstochow and with "*OZA*" to send medicine worth a thousand dollars. Friend Fox read the written agreement with the above-mentioned organizations. They were acknowledged and praised by the conference for their good work.

Friend Gliksman read the telegram from the Independent Union in Chicago.

Photographs were taken of the meeting.

A banquet for the members of the central executive and a large number of friends from Detroit took place in the evening.

The second meeting took place on Sunday, 25 November.

Friend Rechtman opened the meeting and handed over the chair to Friend Avraham Yakov Senzer.

A report from the friends in Los Angeles was read that they regret that they were not in a position to send a delegate to the meeting. They sent greeting to the meeting and committed themselves to carry out the decisions [made at the meeting].

Friend Isidor Gliksman, in the name of those from Detroit, was in agreement that the central committee should by located in New York. He also reported that the Aid Union in Detroit possesses over $500.

Friend Federman spoke about the names of surviving Jews in Czenstochow, about the connection of the regional committee to the Central Committee in Czenstochow and with the aid committee of the religious community and asked that the representatives of the aid organizations carry out unified aid work and to prevail upon the Czenstochower Union in Toronto to join the Central Committee.

Mrs. Fradel of the Czenstochower Ladies Aid Society in Chicago gave assurances about the support from the group that she represented.

According to the proposal by Friend Gliksman, it was decided to allocate $500 as aid for the Czenstochower *landsleit* in Paris.

After Friend Silver gave his report about the coming publication of the book, *Czenstochower Yidn* and Friend Senzer talked about how important it was that the organization determine the number of books they would order, a Central Executive was elected with Friend Avraham Yakov Senzer as president, Friend R. Federman as secretary and one representative from each city where there was a Czenstochow organization.

The greetings to the meeting from the Toronto *landsleit* were heard and the first meeting of the Central Executive of the Czenstochower organizations and Aid Unions in America was closed.

* * *

Declarations Attached to the Official Minutes

We Czenstochower *landsleit*, assembled Sunday, 24 June 1945, the 13th of Tevat, 7005, in Beethoven Hall, New York, give a sacred oath:

We will never forget the destruction and annihilation of our brothers and sisters in our old home city; the extermination of tens of thousands of lives of several generations at once and will always remember the thousands of martyrs and holy men whom the bloody German murderers killed.

We will never forget, never forgive and we will not cease to demand revenge against the German murderers for their scandalous murders, limitless cruelties, the annihilation of Jews from entire cities – of an entire people. May the creators and leaders of Treblinka, Majdanek, Auschwitz and other torture camps and ghettos and the accursed land in which they were born be eternally cursed.

We will never forget the indifference and the silence and keeping silent of the entire so-called civilized world that remained deaf to the desperate cries for help and calls for rescue that came through the years from the ghettos and killing camps where our brothers and sisters and their families were annihilated en masse.

We will erect in Czenstochow, as an eternal monument, an eternal light for the souls of our martyred known and unknown brother victims.

With heads bent in deep sadness and pain, we stand at the graves of our martyrs and swear a holy oath, to never tire, to never let down our hands in despair, but with all of our strength to continue to help the survivors reestablish their lives and further extend the links of the golden chain of existence of our eternal Jewish people.

Translator's Footnote

1. It is more likely the meeting took place in the afternoon.

[Page 328]

Neighboring Landsmanschaften
There Once Was a *Shtetl* [Town] Dzialoszyn

Mary Rozen

The *shtetl* Działoszyn near Czenstochow lies in a valley, ringed by fields and tall, green mountains. A clear river flows past the city and divides it in two. One part of the river is called the Court River. The women would bathe there. In the second part – near the bridge – the men would bathe. The river flows into the Warta, which flows by Czenstochow. The center of the city consists of a large four-sided market with many side alleys. In each corner of the market are found wells and the *shtetl* took its water from the four wells.

In the middle of the market stands the house of the firemen and during a fire the bell on the high wooden tower sounds. The sounding of the bell brought panic to the *shtetl* each time.

During a fire they would grab the horses from the arriving peasants or from local businessmen and harness them to the firemen's equipment.

The firemen's house also had a meeting hall where theater presentations and dance evenings took place. The firemen's equipment was taken out of the meeting hall for the presentations of dance evenings.

Theater presentations took place in Polish and also in Yiddish, most by arriving actor troupes. The firemen's building was called the *vog* [scales]. No one knew the significance of this name.

A large chestnut tree ringed with a flower fence was the ornament of the Christian population. The greatest pride of the Jews in Działoszyn was the synagogue. They would boast that this was one of the most beautiful synagogues in Poland. It was a tradition that this synagogue was built in the 18th century by the same Jewish master architect who had erected the gorgeous synagogue in Przedborz and, it was assumed, also in Pińczów. The *khazan* [cantor] of the synagogue, who was called "the Litvak," prayed with a choir of choir boys. When a guest would come to the *shtetl*, he was taken to see the synagogue. When the *aron kodesh* [ark containing the Torah scrolls] was opened, birds with which it was adorned, gave out musical notes. It was said that only two such synagogues were found in Poland, built by a German master.

Jewish Subsistence

A large number of Jews had small shops of various goods. A similar number were artisans: tailors, shoemakers, cabinetmakers, tinsmiths, hatmakers and others. There were also those who were involved with black market goods from Germany. There were also women among them. When a woman would be sentenced to several months in jail, a sister or a relative would often spend the night with her so that it would be homey.

[Page 329]

Działoszyn also possessed a watermill and a sawmill that belonged to a Christian family of three people: the old unmarried Fildowski and his two sisters. From the beginning he traded with Jews. When anti-Semitism strengthened, he made his own butter from his milk and sold it in the larger cities. After the First World War with the help of his mill he brought electric lighting to the city and was the master of light and darkness. He provided light when the sun set and turned it off late at night. When there was a celebration in the *shtetl* one paid for an entire night of electricity and one had to sleep with electric lights.

There was also in Działoszyn:

Several weaving workshops where woolen cloth was made. The most important of them belonged to Moishe Zalman Rusak, Hershl Weber, Yehuda Leibush Gnaslaw. Each weaving workshop consisted of two or three weaving machines and employed several workers.

Two sock factories with hand machines that employed Jewish girls belonged to the Rusak family, to Shloma Sztemplers and Zelikowicz.

About 10 girls worked in the two straw hat factories of Alka Barnsztajn and Hershl Kutlak.

Dozens of workers, Jewish and Polish, were employed in the two Jewish tanneries.

The finished goods were sent by wagon to Warsaw, Lodz and other cities.

Every two weeks a fair took place in Działoszyn. Peasants from the villages and Jews from the surrounding *shtetlekh* arrived with their products and goods.

*

Działoszyn couples loved to stroll in an informal garden that were called *lipkes* because of the *lipove* [linden] trees. The gardens belonged to Tovya Jakubowicz, the Hasid. However, Reb Tovya strolled here after his *Shabbos* nap and the young people moved to the Czenstochower road at the bridge.

The group *Shomrei Shabbos* [Shabbos Guardians], which did not permit girls to stroll together with boys, often disturbed the strolling of the young couples in order to protect the city from illnesses...

Two *feldshers* [providers of medical care, often referred to as barber-surgeons], Yehuda Hersh and Itshe Meir, who also served as doctors and dentists, also protected Działoszyn from illnesses. Their wives were midwives, delivering the children for the women in childbirth.

*

The *malamdim* [teachers in religious schools] in Działoszyn: the lame Leib, Moshe P.... Mendl Trene and Motl Sz...

Zalme Didje taught the children of well-to-do parents how to read and write in Yiddish, Polish, Russian and German.

The young left the *shtetl* at 15 or 16. They mainly went to Lodz or Czenstochow. Then when they needed to serve *Fonya* [Russia – service in the Russian army] – they left for America.

Chaim Szilit was the *uszony yevrei* [learned Jew]. He reported the births of children, wrote petitions and when necessary defended Jews – he was also an *advokat* [laywer].

*

Nakhman Blander was the poor man of the *shtetl*, had a dozen children who helped him earn his living. With even more children – more pity and donations. The *brisn* [ritual circumcisions for his sons] were paid for by the city. There was no name for the child at the last *bris*. At that time, the rabbi said that he had seen various poor people, but this was the first time that he had seen that a poor person did not possess a name.

Działoszyn had several charity societies, such as the *hakhnoses orkhim* [provides hospitality to visitors], *hakhnoses kalah* [assistance for poor brides], *gmiles khesidim* [interest free loan societies] and *bikur-khoylim* [society to visit the sick].

The poor house was near the cemetery. Visitors from elsewhere went through the *shtetl* collecting donations. City Jews took home visitors for *Shabbos*.

When the *hakhnoses kalah* married off Binele the hunchback of Działoszyn to Zelik the water carrier from Pajczeno – the *shtetl* was joyful. The wedding took place in the house of the *gabbai* [synagogue trustee], Moishe Zalman Rusak, and all of the Jews in the *shtetl* were in-laws. The groom and the bride were led to the *khupah* [wedding canopy] in the synagogue courtyard as in all of the weddings in the *shtetl*. Household utensils for the couple tumbled from the wedding presents that all of the Jews of the *shtetl* had given.

[Page 330]

The main water carrier was Itsik the *goylem*.[1] Once, during the winter, he slipped and fell down. A crowd of Jews saved him. His first words were: "*Gevald* [Yiddish word meaning violence, but used as an exclamation when seeking help], Jews, look, I am still alive!"

*

There were no fights between the Jews and Christians. Jews were only cursed with the word, *Zydze*. At *kol nidre* [prayer recited at the start of the Yom Kippur – Day of Atonement - evening service annulling all vows] on Yom Kippur, the intelligent Christians, such as the *rejent* [notary public], the *sędzia* [judge], the *sołtys* [village head] and the scribe for the government office came to the synagogue.

It occurred that the Jewish judge's daughter came from Wielun with a groom – a Russian soldier.[2] The *shtetl* learned of this, went to the father's house and poured tar on the daughter's head. The groom ran away. The bride had to shave the hair on her head and remained a Jewish daughter.

A Jew in the *shtetl* had a carousel.

Before leaving to be conscripted, recruits having a fling removed the horses from the carousel at night and carried them through the entire city. At every house stood a little horse. The Jew had enough work gathering the horses and restoring his income.

Działoszyn suffered from a storm 40 years ago.

After a severe winter, when the snow on the surrounding hills melted, water flooded the *shtetl* and transformed all of Działoszyn into a giant river in which various tools, cattle and even people floated around.

It was necessary to go by boat in order to from one corner of the city to the other.

The city became severely impoverished then because the people could not work for two weeks and could not carry on any commerce.

But Jewish Działoszyn again lived, worked, bought and sold and increased its size. Until the bloody flood of Nazi-German murderers wiped it from the earth like hundreds of other *shtetlekh*.

Only a memory remains: There once was a shtetl Działoszyn.

Translator's Footnotes

1. A *goylem* in Yiddish refers to someone who is slow or clumsy. A *golem*, from which the Yiddish word is derived, is a man-like figure shaped from clay. Rabbi Judah Lowe of Prague (the *Maharal*) is supposed to have created a *golem* to defend the Jews of Prague from anti-Semitic attacks.

2. The implication here is that the soldier was not Jewish.

———————

[Page 330]

First Zaloshiner [Dzialoszyn]

Chevra Anshei Bnei Achim in New York

[Translator's note: The Yiddish text of excerpts from the constitution is written in phonetic English, German, and Yiddish. Three dots replace unrecognizable words.]

The founding of the Dzialoszyn *landsmanschaft* [organization of people from the same town] organization took place on 9 August 1897. Several Dzialoszyn *landsleit* [people from the same town] came together then in New York. Among them were: Ahron Hillel [Aaron Hill], Leib Kuper [Cooper], Mendl Libowicz [Max Leibowitz], Chaim Lewy [Levy], Jacob Mitchell, Mendl Pelta, Moshe Rot [Roth], Moshe Mikhal Stawski [Morris Stofsky], Zalman Sinet and Moshe Szilit [Morris Schillet]. They were the organizers and the founders of the society.

In 1910 the "Constitution of the *First Zaloshiner Chevra Anshei Bnei Achim*" was published in book form in the Yiddish language. This constitution of the society was unanimously accepted at a meeting on 24 April 1909.

The name of the society was established, as the city is named in Yiddish, Zaloshin, although in Polish the name of the *shtetl* [town] is Dzialoszyn.

The constitution, which was preserved in book form, was put together by a "law committee" that consisted of the following people: Herman Kohn, chairman, Moshe Stawski, Herman Szilit, Moric Szilit, Jacob Mitchell, Leib Cooper, Yoal Steinhaus, Leib Lefkowicz, Yehuda Hirsh Fajertag [Harry Fiertag], Moshe Gelbart and Shimshon Yakov Horowicz.

According to the original constitution, the society was called *Chevra* [society, association or friends] and its purpose was "mutual support in need, sickness and death."

It is said in the further paragraphs of the constitution: "When for various reasons ... members voluntarily leave or the society excludes them, the society will retain its name and the assets it possesses as long as there are seven members in good standing."

[Page 331]

"When another society wants to join our society it can do so only after accepting the name and laws of our society.

"The language at the gatherings, meetings, in the minutes, accounting, notices and so on will be carried out in Yiddish."

Every member who belongs to the society among other things:

"Must have been in the country for at least one year, be moral, physically and spiritually healthy. Must believe in the Jewish religion. When he marries, he must marry a Jewish woman in a Jewish ceremony according to the laws of Moses and Israel; and his son must be circumcised. He must show the society's doctor that he and his wife are healthy and he must uphold the position of his family."

The incomes of the society are:

"Proposed monies," "initiation monies," "regular contributions," "fines," "promised donations," "synagogue tickets," "Four Gates Acres" (cemetery) and so on."

"Every new candidate must pay five dollars for the Four Gates Acres."

The managing committee of the Society consists of: president, vice president, recording and finance secretaries, treasurer and three trustees. "They must at least be able to sign their names. Each official must pay all of his debts to the Society before he is installed."

The exact duties and activities of the officials were given precisely in 13 paragraphs.

Here is the wording of a number of these paragraphs:

"Every member is obligated to pay donations and other contributions to the Society. [Every member should] be present at all general and special meetings, [visit] the home of a deceased brother or his wife, God help us, on the authorization of the secretary and provide the costs for the deceased and from there accompany the deceased to a designated place. At the death of a member or his wife, God help us, or [during] *shiva* [period of morning], brothers [society members] will [provide] a *minyon* [10 men needed for prayer]. The society must provide a *minyon* for the mourners every morning and evening and the costs will be divided evenly among the brothers. When a brother is very sick, God help us, a guardian [must be provided] at night. The finance secretary should in turn send two brothers every night. The brother in question must appear himself [or provide a substitute] no later than 10 o'clock in the evening and must not leave the house before six in the morning. When a member or his wife, God help us, is dying, the *gabbai* [sexton] of the burial society needs to make sure that those present remain with the deceased until the burial. When one brother or his wife, God help us, dies and is buried at the cemetery, the society should take care of the preparations of the cemetery plot: provide a wagon or two carriages for the family and without cost. At [a member's] death, a tax of one dollar should be placed on each member and the money should be given to the widow or to the next member of the family. At the death of a member or of his wife or children, [they will be] buried at our cemetery; the society will [take care of] the stone.

The *shiva* [seven days of mourning], sick benefits and support for members and their families were [controlled by the rules] in 14 paragraphs.

The assignments and rights of the *khevre kadishe* [burial society] or the funeral committee are given in eight paragraphs. Paragraph seven reads as such:

"Regarding the burial of a body, no one is to send word except the *gabbai* of the *khevre kadishe* and the president."

Paragraph 8 reads:

"The *gabbai* of the *khevre kadishe* or any office of the society has the right to sell or give away cemetery plots to one of our members ... the agreement of all brothers."

The *khevre kadishe* ... "a first *gabbai* and second *gabbai*"I and can have its own fund. The income and expenses of the *khevre kadishe* are regulated by paragraphs five and six. The paragraph defines:

"All [previously] unspecified expenses by the *gabbai* of the burial committee of the Society, for example, [used for] arrangements for a deceased [member] will be paid by the society."

Paragraph 6:

The *tzedakah* [charity] money from accompanying the casket of the deceased as well as the revenue from the *aliyahs* [being called up to read a portion of the Torah] and the *Shemini Atzeret* [holiday following the Feast of Tabernacles on which the prayer for rain is started, to be repeated until Passover] vows and the eighth day of Passover will belong to the *khevre kadishe*.

"The *khevre kadishe* also is authorized to take five dollars each year from the society's treasury for one banquet..."

[Page 332]

The task of the *gabbai* of the *khevre kadishe* according to paragraph 3:

"At the death, God help us, of a brother or his wife, the *gabbai* must go to the house of mourning and verify that the purity and clothing according to Orthodox ritual [has been observed]."

In accordance with paragraph 4:

"When the deceased is a male, the [head of the household] must take care of him; however, when the deceased is a woman, two women must be provided by the *khevre kadishe* and the [preparation of the body] and clothing will be taken care of under the *khevre's* direction.

Brothers from the *khevre* can be punished with a fine, according to this constitution, for not coming to a funeral or for not performing any duty and they can be removed from the *khevre* for not behaving properly or for a criminal offense.

Changes in the constitution can be made with a majority of two-thirds votes and when the change has been considered at two meetings.

When the constitution of the society was adopted, the officials were:

Former presidents: Zalman Sinat, Moshe Pinkus and Moshe Granek.

President: Moshe Mikhal Stawski; vice president: Yoal Sztajnhaus; recording secretary: Hersh Meir Szerade; finance secretary: Yitzhak Zelkowicz; treasurer: Moshe Szalit; first managing committee member (trustee): H. Szilit; second: Leib Kuper; third: Sam Stawski.

There is no doubt that most Dzialoszyn *landsleit* were grouped around the *First Zaloshiner Khevra Anshei Bnai Akhim* in New York. A large number of Czenstochow *landsleit* also joined this society. The number of members grew from day to day and the society carried out the task of bringing help to the needy and, first of all, to the newly arriving Dzialoszyn immigrants. The constitution cited developed as a result of the daily needs of the members. The communal significance of the Society grew greatly from 1905-1907 when a large number of immigrants arrived and still more during the First World War.

Immediately after the First World War, the Society introduced new important tasks to help the remaining *landsleit* and families in the old home, Dzialoszyn and the Dzialoszyn Aid Committee, about which we write separately, was founded.

In 1932 the new charter was published in book form with 112 pages in Yiddish as well as in the English language. The new charter of the Society was adapted to the requirements of the time, under the heading "Constitution – *First Zaloshiner Khevra Anshei Bnai Akhim*." The emblem symbolized "welcoming hands."

As is mentioned in article 11, paragraph 15, "This constitution was completed and read to the brothers three times and accepted by the officers and the brothers on the 2nd of August 1931 in New York." All of the offices and committees of that time are stated in this constitution.

Ex-presidents: Moshe Granek, Yehuda Hirsh Fajertag, Moshe Mikhal Stapski, Yudl Stapski, Chaim Kohn, Leibish Granek, Yoal Sztajnhaus, Emanuel Wargon, Nisen Cymerman, Willy Nachtigal, Sam Kolin.

Willy Nachtigal, ex president; Avraham Senzer, president; Sidney Kessel, vice president; Yakov Brzezinski, recording secretary; Yakov Zaks, finance secretary; Nisen Cymerman, treasurer; Avraham Senzer, first trustee; Emanuel Wargon, second trustee; Harry Gold, third trustee; Yehuda Hirsh Fajertag, chairman of the loan fund; Sam Kalin, treasurer of the loan fund; Emanuel Wargon, chairman of the ... fund; Sam Wien, doctor; Irving Kleinman, doctor; Nisen Cymerman, chairman of the cemetery fund.

Khevre Kadishe:

Mikhal Stapski, first *gabbai*; A. Nachtigal, second *gabbai*.

Constitution Committee:

Nisen Cymerman, chairman; Moshe Granek, secretary; Yehuda Hirsh Fajertag, Harry Fajersztajn, Emanuel Wargon, Yudl Stapski, Yakov Miczel, Willy Nachtigal, Joe Markowicz, Yakov Zaks, Avraham Senzer, Yakov Brzezinski, Leibish Peltc, Zakan Rozenthal, Philip Lazarow, Leibish Lefkowicz, Moshe Gold, Sam Kessel, Morris Lesser, Izzy Epsztajn, Harry Gold, Sam Kalin and Yoskowicz.

Again it stipulated the society with the name of its home city. Article 1, paragraphs 1 and 2 of the Constitution states: "As long as there are seven members in good standing, the name *First Zaloshiner Khevra Anshei Bnai Akhim* will remain, the name of the Society cannot be changed." Conversely, the first constitution in which it is stated that the Yiddish language is the only official language of the Society, in article 1, paragraph 4 of the new constitution, English is given equality: "All dealings of the Society, as well as the books, shall be carried in the Yiddish or English languages." The constitution itself was published in both languages, in Yiddish and English.

[Page 333]

Article 1, paragraph 5 of the Constitution establishes: "The laws of the United States of America, as well as the laws of the State of New York and the laws of the Jewish religion, will be the basic law of the Society and will be carried out according to parliamentary rules."

In short, the membership of the Society felt established in this country and the American laws and the democratic customs became a part of their communal consciousness. But, the religious basis of the Society remained untouched. The warning about relationships from the old Constitution were repeated in article 3, paragragh 2: "Each candidate must have been in the country for six months and must be healthy. When he marries he must do so according to Jewish law. He must have his sons circumcised and ... and feed his family. When one is married and wants to join alone, he may not enter the Society. When a single man belongs to the Society and marries not according to Jewish law, he will be legally stricken from the Society."

In article 7, paragraph 17, it also is said that, "When a brother does not sit *shiva* for a full week, he is not entitled to any *shiva* money."

First Zaloshiner *Khevra Anshei Bnai Akhim*

Seated, right to left: Emanuel Wargon, Yehuda Hirsh Fajertag, Moshe Meyers, Willy Nachtigal, Joe Lewin, Hymie Epsztajn, Yakov Brzezinski, Avraham Szifer.
First row, standing, right to left: Itshe Epsztajn, Philip Winkler, Avraham Yakov Senzer, Leibl Lefkowicz, Benny Pelcz, Dovid Rozensztajn
Second row, right to left: Harry Fajersztajn, Yitzhak Rozen, Morris Swetlow, Charlie Lenczner, Joe Markowicz

[Page 334]

All the other articles and paragraphs from the Constitution also did not create any substantial changes in the basis and character of the Society.

The Society numbered 232 members (222 men and 10 women) in 1932; the majority of the members of the Society were Dzialoszyn *landsleit* and from a number of surrounding *shtetlekh* [towns]. A considerable number of Czenstochow *landsleit* belonged to the Society.

Today the Society numbers 190 members (180 men and 10 women). It has four cemeteries valued at $20,000. Thirteen members took part in the Second World War in the American Army. The Society bought War Bonds [worth] $7,000. The benefits of the Society are:

Sick benefits, *Shiva-minyon* [10 men to pray at the home of those in mourning], old age, aid and loan benefit. During the last three and a half years – from 1942-1945 – 250 dollars were paid to members as sick benefits; *shiva* benefits – 200 dollars. Aid benefits [were paid of] 175 dollars and 2,500 dollars.

The income at the same time reached approximately 14,000 dollars and the expenses – 12,000 dollars.

The Society supported the following communal institutions in their campaigns: United Joint Appeal, American Jewish Congress, New York and Brooklyn Federations, HIAS, American Federation of Polish Jews, United Chinese Relief, Russian War Relief, New York War Fund, American Red Cross, Deborah Sanatorium, Saratoga Springs House, National Association of the Jewish Blind.

Officials for 1945 were:

Joe Lewin, ex-president; Wm. Nachtigal, president; Morris Meyers, vice president; Joe Lewin, treasurer; Hyman Epsztajn, finance secretary; Jacob Brzezinski, recording secretary.

Chairman of Funds:

Benj. Peltc, Endowment; Charlie Lenczner, Old Yiddish; Avraham Yakov Senzer, Cemetery; Joe Markowicz, Loan; Morris Swetlow, Treasurer of Loans; Philip Winkler, Aid.

Chairman of Cemetery:

Avraham Y. Senzer, 1030 Bryant Avenue, Bronx, N.Y. Telephone: Dayton 3-8908.

Trustees: L. Lefkowicz, Y. Epsztajn, D. Rozensztajn.

In the year in which these lines are published in the book, *Czenstochower Yidn*, the *First Zaloshiner Khevra Anshei Bnai Akhim* will celebrate its 60th anniversary. This alone gives witness to the share this Society has in the history of Jewish communal life in America.

The Aid Work for the Old Home, Dzialoszyn

The aid work for the old home, Zaloshin (Dzialoszyn) takes up a separate chapter in the history of the Society.

Immediately after the First World War, in 1919, letters began to arrive from relatives and friends from Dzialoszyn, the old home, and from *landsleit* who lived in the surrounding *shtetlekh*, such as: Kielczyglow, Krzepice, Truskolasy and in the city, Czenstochow. The letters told about the great need of the local Jewish population, about the difficult problems of earning a living and about the ruins created by the war. The letters from the Zaloshiner Rabbi and *Khazan* [cantor] were extremely heart-rending. His call for help resonated with the catastrophic situation of the Jewish community in Dzialoszyn. The Society then decided to dedicate all of its energy to help for the brothers on the other side of the sea and called upon its members to found a Dzialoszyn Relief Committee.

The founding meeting of the Relief Committee took place in Mendl Pelta's house on 10 August 1919. Nusan Cymerman, Mendl Pelta, Moshe Stafski, Philip Lajzerowicz, Morris Lajzerowicz, Shmuel Shaya Szilit, Jacob Mitchell, Moshe Gold, Zokn Rozental and Lou Cymerman came to the meeting. It was decided to found the First Zaloshiner Relief Committee. Elected were: chairman – Nusan Cymerman; secretary – Zokn Rozental; treasurer – Mendl Pelta. A committee that established contact with the *landsleit* in Paterson was also established and a printed letter was sent to all Dzialoszyn *landsleit* about the founding of the Relief Committee. Forty-two dollars were collected immediately on the spot.

The activity of the Relief Committee lasted until February 1931. During this time, in addition to those mentioned above, those active were: Kalman Samsonowicz, Morris Meyers, Hymie Fox, Feywish Markowicz, Willy Nactigal, Mishe Pinkus, Dave Zlatnik, Sam Szilit, Max Meyers, Joe Stone, Jack Szlezinger, Urbach, Abe Hayden, Max Hayden, Joe Markowicz, Demsy, Landau, F. Stone, Zigman Frydman, Yisroel Pinkus, Isidore Rozen, Leser and Sztajnhaus.

[Page 335]

The majority of the dozens of meetings of the Relief Committee took place in the residences of the aid workers. And at every meeting, there would be collections for the Relief Fund among the members themselves and, when it was necessary, loans were made by those taking part, starting at five up to 100 dollars. The chairmen of the committee over the course of time were: Nusan Cymerman, Moshe Stafski, Yudl Stafski and Morris Lajzerowicz, secretary: Zokn Rozental, treasurers – Mendl Pelta, Yisroel Pinkus.

The Women's Committee that helped with the activity consisted of Pinkus, chairwoman, Samsonowicz, Szlezinger, Stafski, Markowicz and Ticzberg.

Mass meeting took place at which reports were given about the activities and collections were made. Theater performances also were undertaken that brought very large sums of from 300 to 500 dollars at one time into the treasury.

Pushkes [cans] were also divided among the *landsleit* to collect money at every opportunity.

First of all, every time aid was sent, the Society sent not less than 100 dollars from its treasury. In total, the Society paid 600-700 dollars into the Relief Fund. Several hundred dollars came into the Relief Fund from the *pushkes*. The member of Relief paid their voluntary assessment every time and each of them gave an on-going monthly payment for a time.

To Whom the Aid Was Allocated

Because of the drop in the [value] of the Polish currency immediately after the First World War, the dollar would mostly be exchanged for Polish money and Polish marks[1] were sent to Dzialoszyn. At first the aid was sent individually to the needy. Each request that arrived from the needy was accepted, even from *landsleit* [outside of] Dzialoszyn, such as from Krzepice, Kielczyglów, Truskolasy, Czenstochow and others. Later, help was sent for every holiday, particularly for Passover. Communications were established with the committee, which often changed its composition, under the chairmanship of the Dzialoszyn rabbi. The committee would receive instructions as to how to divide the aid and would send a receipt signed by everyone who received the support. In 1919, 153 people in Dzialoszyn received support of up to 200 marks each. In the year 1920 a sum of 159,325 marks was sent. In 1921 – 5,000,000 marks and support of 1,500, 2,000 and 3,000 marks was distributed per person. In 1922 the total support reached 300,000 marks and it was decided to invest a million marks in a *gmiles khesed* [interest free loan] fund. In 1924 – five million marks for 82 people.

The idea of creating a *gmiles khesed* fund arose because of the frequent conflicts that occurred over the division of support. It was decided that the *gmiles khesed* fund would give loans of 10 to 15 thousand marks without interest to everyone who was in need of support. Relief in New York created a statute for the fund with 13 points. It was decided in connection with this plan to recruit members with dues of 50 cents specifically for the fund. On 25 June 1922, 82 dollars arrived for the fund from members' dues. The founding of the interest-free loan fund met legal difficulties from the Polish administration and the matter was delayed. When Brothers Lajzerowicz went to Dzialoszyn for a visit in 1922, Relief authorized them to found the interest-free loan fund and take 75 dollars with them for this purpose. A banquet was held at their departure.

The loan fund in Dzialoszyn finally opened in 1924. This took place in the presence of the aid workers Sam Szilit and Mrs. Rozen, who had then come to visit their home city. A managing committee for the fund was designated with a paid official, who took over the conduct of the business. The fund also received the support of the Joint [Distribution Committee]. At the departure banquet Friend Szilit and Mrs. Rozen were given 300 dollars for the Fund and the authorization to take an additional 200 dollars from the Joint if it would be necessary.

On 26 October 1924 Friend Sam Szilit and Mrs. Rozen gave a report about the fortunately established fund. The managing committee of the fund voted to give loans up to 25 *zlotes* to be paid back one *zlote* a week. In 1926 Relief sent 400 dollars for Passover. Two hundred fifteen people benefited from the support and 42 received it in the form of money. [They also] received matzos. In 1930, 300 dollars was sent through HIAS [Hebrew Immigrant Aid Society] and 150 dollars in 1931 for potatoes and matzos.

[Page 336]

In total, during the course of the time mentioned, Relief supported the needy in the home city with a sum of over 2,000 dollars. In addition to this, Relief also supported the firemen in Dzialoszyn with a one-time sum and helped to repair the community buildings.

At the conclusion, let us remember the *landsleit* in Dzialoszyn who helped to distribute the support and lead the interest-free loan fund. These are the esteemed people who were chosen by the Relief Committee in New York.

The Rabbi, Reb Benyamin Elia, chairman.
Avraham Meir Szilit.
Gershon Lajzerowicz.
Yankl Meierowicz.
Mikhal Warszawski.
Yakov Nusan.
Feywl Widawski.
Dovid Kaplowicz.
Leyzer Sholem Lipszic.
Fewysh Lapides.
Hershl Lajzerowicz.
Wolf Zisking, chairman.
Wolf Chaim Till, treasurer.
Josef Chwat, secretary.
Sholem Hersh Markowicz.
Josef Szilit, chairman.
Sheptel Bornsztajn, vice chairman.
Khaskel Apelsztajn.
Avraham Hersh Szilit.
Yudl Kupper.
Ahron Szilit.
Avraham Bendes.
Yosl Szmulewicz.
Ahron Pancz.
Yuda Hersh Izbicki.
Berish Szilit.
Wolf Cymerman

The First Zaloshiner Ladies Auxiliary

Seated, right to left: Masha Zelkowicz, Dora Nachtigal, Mary Lefkowicz, Fanny Winkler, Chaya Ruchl Wargon, Mary Rozen.
Standing, right to left: Dorothy Epsztajn, Sadie Senzer, Becky Meyers, Ita Leah Lenczner, Ray Gold, Fryda Fajersztajn, Helen Markowicz

[Page 337]

The Renewal of Aid Work in 1936

On Sunday, 1 November, Dzialoszyn *landsleit* came together and it was decided to revive Dzialoszyn Relief to be in a position to help the needy in Dzialoszyn. The stimulus was the fact that at the time very sad reports arrived from the *shtetl*. A meeting was held immediately under the chairmanship of Brother Nisen Cymerman and the following officials were elected:

Abe Menzer, chairman.
Nelson, recording secretary.
Dovid Dresler, financial secretary.
Philip Lazarow, treasurer.

The following people immediately joined as members with the commitment to pay weekly dues of 10 cents:

Chaim Yehuda Fox, Markowicz, Swiatlow, Lefkowicz, Morris Leser, Avraham Lazarow, Kalman Samsonowicz, Shmuel Yeshaya Szilit, Yoal Szteinholc, Philip Lazarow, Dave Dresler, Brzezinski, Willy Nachtigal, Mordekhai Meyers. Warszowski, Joe Star, Sam Pelta, Moshe Gold, Moshe Roed, Emanuel Wargon, Rozen, Abe Senzer, Nisen Cymerman, Nelson, Jay Winer, Mosher Liker.

The First Zaloshiner Ladies Auxiliary

The First Zaloshiner Ladies Auxiliary was founded on 16 September 1932. The founders were the Sisters: Mary Rozen, Yetty Lenczner, Sadie Senzer, Mary Lefkowicz, Ruchl Wargon, Fanny Winkler, Lizzy Sziman, Jenny Lesser, Sister Lazarow, Becky Meyers, Rachel Gold, Helen Markowicz, Rozy Meyers, Fryda Feierstone, Sadie Stone, Gussy Szilit, Dora Nightingal.

In 1945 the managing committee consisted of: ex-chairwoman – Sadie Senzer, chairwoman – Fanny Winkler, vice chairwoman – Mary Lefkowicz, finance secretary – Dody Epsztajn, finance secretary – Dora Nightingal, recording secretary – Dora Nightingal, treasurer – Ruchl Wargon.

Managing committee members: Ruchl Gold,[2] Lizzy Sziman, Helen Markowicz, Yetty Lenczner and Masha Zelkowicz.

Translator's Footnotes

1. The Polish mark was a currency created by the German regime during their occupation of Polish territory during the First World War.

2. The name is given as both Rachel and Ruchl in the printed text.

[Page 337]

Nowo-Radomsk

In the Jewish world the city should have been named *Nei-Radomko* [New Radomsk]. However, it would be better to call it Young Radomsk because Radomsk near Czenstochow distinguished itself with its youthful fire, hot temperament, lust for life and enthusiasm – for both old and new ideas.

Radomsk is like a suburb of Czenstochow. One sits oneself on the Warsaw-Vienna railroad and in half an hour one is in Radomsk.

There were many Nowo-Radomsker Hasidim in Czenstochow. However, there were more Czenstochower "Hasidim" [followers] of other movements in Radomsk. There was the entire young generation of Zionists, *Poalei-Zion* [Workers of Zion – Marxist Socialists], *S.S.-ovekes* [Zionist Socialists], *Fareinikte* [United- Socialist Workers Party], Bundists, who were under the influence of Czenstochow.

However, many young men in Czenstochow also were influenced by Nowo-Radomsk… More accurately, by the Radomsker girls who had a good reputation for their beauty.

The well-known musician, Mikhal Gelbart, director of the *Arbeter-Ring* [Workman's Circle] choir, who was the director of *Hazamir* [a youth choir] in Radomsk, writes about the city in the *Nowo-Radomsker Almanac* this way:

"Nowo-Radomsk belongs to the category of Jewish cities in Poland that never remained backward in any area. When the Enlightenment and, later socialism, began to penetrate the Jewish neighborhood – Radomsk was one of the first where these ideas were adopted.

"When the *Hazimir* Choir blossomed in Poland – Nowo-Radomsk was one of the first to organize such a *Hazimir* and if Nowo-Radomsk did something, it had to be better and more far-reaching than somewhere else.

"I see before my eyes the magnificent *Hazimir* premises with its large, beautiful concert hall and its own library – a spiritual and communal home for the young."

[Page 338]

The *Hazimir* possessed not only a good choir but also a dramatic section that performed dramas by Yiddish writers, such as *Mitn Strom* ["With the Storm"] by Sholem Asch. They read and discussed Yiddish literary works. They organized literary evenings.

According to the memories of Maks Szpiro about Nowo-Radomsker *Hazimir* in the same *Almanak*, the *Hazimir* was founded in 1909. *Hazimir* reached the highest boost to its development when the famous composer, Matisyahu Bensman, was hired as the director of the choir. In addition to arranging Yiddish concerts of classical and folk music, the opera, *Yidn* [Jews], with words by [Evegnii Nikolaevich] Chirikov and music by M. Bensman was performed in Hebrew.

Years later, at the time of the First World War, the union, *Kultura*, arose, thanks to *Hazimir*, which carried on widespread cultural activities among the young.

After his from *Eretz-Yisroel*, Moshe Szwarc became an active worker for *Hazimir*. He would lecture and organize theatrical presentations. He also would bring his friend, Shmuel Frank, and the dramatic section from Czenstochow, which presented [Yakov] Gordin's *Der Yidisher Kenig Lear* [The Jewish King Lear] and other plays.

Under Austrian Occupation during the First World War

The occupation by the Austrians during the First World War was in all respects a great deal milder than the occupation of a series of other cities by the Germans.

The economic and communal life in the city more or less stabilized. The pre-war industry had been completely paralyzed; the large furniture factories and the smaller factories ceased to operate. Therefore, new wartime sources of income developed, such as taking the necessities or other goods from one city to another. This was the main source of livelihood for the general Jewish as well as the non-Jewish population. Everyone [was involved with] trade and commerce. The true name for this was – smuggling.

However, right at that time, in Radomsk, as in most cities in Poland, exciting communal and cultural activity began. The young had awakened as if from a long, lethargic sleep and with its hot Radomsk temperament threw itself at the fresh spring of life that was called culture. The poorest strata like the rich, the tailors and the shoemakers as well as the intellectuals – all were influenced by the cultural storm.

The institution around which everyone grouped themselves was the famous *Kultura* [culture], with its library and reading room. Every evening the young invaded the library and the reading room like hungry locusts and the books were taken outside, as if Radomsk had been turned into a university city.

Rich cultural evenings with musical programs were arranged. Each cultural evening was prepared as if it was a great holiday. The leader of the Jewish bourgeois and of the worker parties in Warsaw often came to agitate for their programs and ideas. Heshl Farbsztajn, the Zionist leader, the leaders of the *S.S.* [Zionist Socialists], Dr. Josef Kruk and Pinya Bukshorn, the Bundist leader Vladimir Medem, the *Poale-Zionist* leaders, [Yakov] Zerubavel, Dua [D. Bogen] came.

Under the influence and leadership of the party center in Warsaw and also of the neighboring city, Czenstochow, the organizations of the Jewish Workers Parties in Poland formed in Radomsk. The organization of *S.S.* arose, later *Fareinikte* [united] which, following after Czenstochow, took first place in Radomsk. After them came the *Poalei-Zion* and the Bund. *Fareinikte* and the Bund led the professional unions that were created later. A consumer-cooperative was created later that was led by *Fareinikte* and *Poalei-Zion*. A workers' nursery was created, the most modern and prettiest that was created in the Jewish neighborhood. A new, great epoch of the Russian Revolution arrived that revolutionized the great majority of working masses. This was not very well "liked" by even the occupying regime of the "dear" Austrian power.

However, the war also endowed Radomsk with other events that interrupted both the "cultural idyll" and the struggle of the political parties.

A train of the homeless from the war front in White Russia and Lithuania arrived in Radomsk. The homeless, mainly Jews with several of their Christian neighbors, had traveled by train for several weeks until they were brought to Radomsk. The youth of Radomsk, blessed may they be, ceased their party struggles for a while, rolled up their sleeves and with the usual Radomsker fervor and enthusiasm, threw themselves into the work of giving the first assistance to the unfortunate Jewish war victims.

[Page 339]

Young, energetic hands carried the old broken bodies of the refugees and dragged their bundles, which they had been able to save along with themselves from the war's destruction. The temporary home for them was organized in Kohn's factory. Immediately after, groups were organized to collect food, to obtain beds and everything that the homeless needed. This was not a one-time kind of work, but was on-going, daily, devoted concern, and work that was connected to the difficult struggle with the Austrian city officials. It was possible to obtain warm food and other necessities from the Jewish population, but obtaining such luxuries as sugar and coal had to be fought out with the Austrian "rulers." But this, too, was done. The brilliant communal workers, Fishl Gliksman and Leyzer Bajgelman, excelled particularly in this area. Fishl Gliksman, particularly with his folksy soulfulness and humor, encouraged and cheered the spirits of the dejected homeless.

The brotherly love and friendship that Radomsk showed for the homeless evoked a warm feeling for the city and its Jews. They idolized Fishl and Leyzer. Many of the homeless later moved to America and here showed their gratitude to Radomsk through their help to and interest in our old hometown.

It should be understood that this is only a short and incomplete picture of Radomsk during the time of war.

A City of Torah and Hasidim

However, Nowo-Radomsk also had a reputation for its rabbis, pious Jews and Hasidim. The names of the most famous rabbis remain immortalized in the religious books that they created: *Tiferes Shlomo* [Splendid Shlomo] and *Khesed L'Avraham* [Kindness of Avraham]. Many folk legends are spun around them, which are transmitted from generation to generation.

The Nowo-Radomsk Hasidic rebbes had great number of followers in Poland and in Galicia. The *shtetl* [town] was full of them during the Days of Awe.

From the beginning of the 18th century when the Jews began to settle in Radomsk until the 1930's, the Jewish population there reached over 11,000 souls.

Trade and Craft

The trade and the crafts-work lay mostly in Jewish hands. The wide four-cornered market consisted of the nicest buildings and was like a large exhibition of Jewish businesses. Every Thursday was a market day. The peasants from the surrounding *shtetlekh* and villages would bring their village products to sell and to exchange for the city's goods.

Radomsk also possessed a large button factory, where many Jewish workers were employed. The owners of the factories were the well-known Fajerman family.

There was also a large cigarette paper factory there, under the name Gronis.

Jews also played a dominant role in the shoemaking, tailoring and carpentry trades.

The city had a series of professional unions established by the parties: *S.S.* [Zionist Socialist], P.Tz. [*Paole Tzion* – Workers of Zion] Bund and communists.

When the workers council arose immediately after the First World War, the P.P.S. [*Polska Partia Socjalistyczna* – Polish Socialist Party] and the N.Z.R. (*Narodawy Zwiazek Robotniczy* [National Union of Workers]) created a workers council without the participation of the Jewish worker. Later, one representative from each socialists faction was admitted: the only representative on the executive committee of the provisional workers committee was Hirshl Kroyze of *Fareinikte*.

There were six Jewish and three Polish candidates' lists during the voting for the city council in 1919. The following were elected as councilmen: three *Fareinikte*, three *Poale Tzion*, two from the artisans-*Mizrakhists* [religious Zionists] and Zionist list, two *Shlomi Emuni Yisroel* [Faithful in Israel]. The P.P.S. elected seven, N.Z.R. three, the *Endekes* [National Democrats – an anti-Semitic party] four, the Bund and the *Tseiri-Zion* [Zionist youth] received up to 70 votes. One hundred sixty-five votes were required to elect a candidate. The city council, which consisted of 24 councilmen, had a socialist majority of 13 to 11.

Religious Life

The religious Jews were also divided into various groups. On the *Shabbosim* [Sabbaths] and holidays, the shoemakers, tailors and other trades formed into groups in the city synagogue.

The new house of prayer was the meeting place of the middle class, quiet business owners. The bakers and retailers also prayed there. The Jewish porters had their own *minyon* [group of 10 or more men praying together].

Hasidic groupings, such as the Gerer, Aleksander, Rozprzer, Amshinower and others had their separate Hasidic *shtiblekh* [small, one-room synagogues].

[Page 340]

The old house of prayer belonged to the Radomsker rebbe's courtyard by inheritance. The Radomsker Hasidim would come together there on *Shabbosim* and holidays to celebrate Hasidism. It was like this for many years. The last rebbe was Rebbe Avrhamele, the son of the Amshinower Rebbe, who married the daughter of the Radomsker Rebbe, Reb Yehezkiel. He had many followers among the retailers and artisans. He fit in with the progressive world and was very beloved in Radomsk.

The Hitler murderers cut the chain of the Radomsker Rabbinical Court with [the murder of] him.

The Destruction of Nowo-Radomsk

The destruction of the Jewish population in Nowo-Radomsk was carried out by the German-Nazi murderers in the same manner, and according to the same system, as in a series of other Jewish cities. In many cases the German murderers applied the same methods as in Czenstochow. Both cities, which were so closely connected in their lives and development, suffered the same fate in their collapse.

The innocent blood should never be forgotten. We will never forgive the murderers!

Nowo-Radomsker *Landsmanschaft*
in New York

by P. Kalka

The Nowo-Radomsker Society in New York has existed for close to 50 years. The founding meeting of the first group of Nowo-Radomsker *landsleit* [people from the same town] took place in 1898. In the course of time, it was shown to be an important factor both in Jewish life in America itself and in the area of aid activities for our brothers and sisters on the other side of the ocean:

The Nowo-Radomsker Society was and remains an exemplary, progressive *landsmanschaft* [organization of people from the same town] organization in America.

From the first day of its existence, the *landsmanschaft* was the center where all Nowo-Radomskers came together without differentiation as to belief. Rich, middle-class people and workers belonged to the society. Many of them were American born. The atmosphere of unity and tolerant attitudes towards each other gave the society the opportunity to develop widespread activities.

The membership of the Nowo-Radomsker Society was never content with just benefits and "cemetery insurance," but was always also aware of all Jewish national problems, cooperating in the implementation [of solutions to these problems] and, in general, took part in the struggle for human rights.

After the First World War, the Nowo-Radomsker Society was one of the first organizations to help the Jewish settlement in *Eretz-Yisroel* and voted 1,200 dollars for the purpose.

When the movement here [in America] began to create *Patronats* [organizations that supported Jewish political victims in 1930's Poland], which would come to the aid of victims of the militaristic-fascistic cliques in Poland – the society was one of the first to create a Now0-Radomsker *Patronat* and to support it very generously.

The Nowo-Radomsker Society was one of the initiators and founders of the Jewish People's Committee in 1936 which, with all anti-Fascist elements here in [America], organized a series of public appearances and street demonstrations against anti-Semitism and Fascism.

The society published a very well edited *Almanac* of 160 pages at the 40th anniversary of the society, in 1939. The *Alamanc* was edited by the long time Nowo-Radomsker Society worker, Moshe Schwartz, with the help of Pinye Kalka.

The *Nowo-Radomsker Almanac* described the history of the society and the aid work that the Nowo-Radomsker *landsleit* had done in such great magnitude for their brothers in their old home city. Reports about Jewish institutions in Nowo-Radomsk and biographies of many personalities, both from the old generation and the younger generation, were published in it.

The book was received with enthusiasm by all Nowo-Radomsker *landsleit* and recognized by the public as a great contribution to the rich history of the Jewish *landsmanschaftn* in America.

[Page 341]

Now, after the catastrophic destruction of the Jewish population in Nowo-Radomsk, the only clear memorial for the content rich and full-blooded life of a beautiful Jewish community that was named Nowo-Radomsk, remains for the present in the *Nowo-Radomsker Almanac.*

30 Years of Nowo-Radomsker Relief

The Nowo-Radomsker Relief is, like a series of other institutions, a branch of the Nowo-Radomsker Society. With the greatest love and devotion, the friends and members of the society are dedicated to the work. The Nowo-Radomsker Relief had fraternally supported and helped create in Nowo-Radomsk such institutions as: *Linas haTzedik* [society for visiting the sick], *Gemiles Khesed* [interest free loan] Fund, secular children's homes and public schools, *Talmud Torah Malbish Arumim* [organization to clothe the needy] and a series of institutions that have eased the need of the poor Jewish population. The aid work has particularly been distinguished by the great contribution from our beloved *landsman,* Sol Grynberg.

At the time of the Second World War, when the news about the dreadful catastrophe of the Jewish people under the reign of the Nazi cannibals began to arrive, the aid work became much more intense. In the first year of Hitler's rule in Poland, the Nowo-Radomsker Relief sent food products in the amount of 600 dollars through Christian aid organizations. Confirmation from those to whom the packages had been mailed came for many of the sent packages. The Nowo-Radomsker Relief undertook the creation of a fund of 10,000 dollars to help the surviving brothers rebuild their ruined home. Relief made contact with the Nowo-Radomsker *landsleit* in the liberated nations such as France, Belgium, the Soviet Union and sent them aid through packages of food products.

A separate Orphan's Fund was created by Nowo-Radomsker Relief named for Manny Shapiro, the deeply beloved son of the devoted Relief workers Mote and Leyke Shapiro, who fell in Burma as a fighter in the American Army. His father, Mote Shapiro, on his own initiative, had undertaken to create the Fund, contributed the sum of 200 dollars and himself collected the greater part of the remaining 400 dollars.

The Relief, too, as the entire Nowo-Radomsker *landsmanschaft*, did not forget the children of its members who were in the American Army in all parts of the world. The Relief provided 900 dollars for packages that would be sent periodically to each one as an encouragement in the struggle against our bloody enemies and the foe of all humanity. Half of this sum that was provided for this purpose was donated by brother, Sol Grynberg.

The further sums that the Nowo-Radomsker *Landsmanschaft* Union and Relief donated during the war years for various purposes show the wide scope of the aid work.

Help for Nowo-Radomsk in 1939 – $600 sent to the Joint [Joint Distribution Committee], Children's Fund and Matzo Fund from 1939 to 1945 - $1,200; for Russian Relief – $1,000; for *Eretz-Yisroel*, Labor Union campaign and *Histadrut* – $400; for Red *Mogen-Dovid,* American Red Cross and British War Relief – $200.

                    * * *

Most recently, a Nowo-Radomsker Relief was organized in Los Angeles that sent the sum of $300 to New York and also sent $100 for the Manny Shapiro Orphan's Fund.

The Nowo-Radomsker *landsleit* organized two Relief organizations in *Eretz-Yisroel*, one in Tel Aviv and the second in Haifa. The Relief organizations in *Eretz-Yisroel* carry out widespread aid activities.

The Victory Committee, which during the war endeavored to sell still more war bonds, now undertook raising money for two Victory Bonds for each member's son returning from the war. Alas, six children from the *Landmanschaft* would not . They fell in battle against the Nazi and Japanese enemies.

A Grynberg Loan Fund also exists with the Nowo-Radomsker *landsmanschaft*, where each member has the right to borrow the sum of 35 dollars. The fund gives the loans without any interest.

[Page 342]

Society Officials in 1945

Dovid Lefkowicz – President.
Sam Epsztajn – Ex-President.
Max Golden – Vice President.
Shirley Vitrofski – Finance Secretary.
Leon Ellenberg – Protocol Secretary.
A. Haber – Treasurer.
Mote Shapiro – Hospitality
Ahron Gliksman – Funeral Director
Max Itzkowicz – Auditor
Trustees: S. Krauz, M. Zelkowicz, Avraham Brakman.

Grynberg-Loan Fund Officals

Chairman – A. Zoberman.
Secretary – D. Feder.
Treasurer – Jack Almar.

Relief Officials

Sol Grynberg – Honorary Chairman.
Pinye Kalka – Chairman.
Harry Szedlecki – Vice Chairman.
Harry Fiszman – Aid Chairman.
Chaskl Pazanowski – Finance Secretary.

Relief Committee

Jack Almer, Lou Beserman, Philip Knapf, H. B. Israel, L. Brakman, F. Frisz, A. Lefkowicz, M. Itzkowicz, M. Brader, Ahron Gliksman, Harry Oberman, Shimeon Medwedow, Sam Dikerman, Sam Ickowicz, Avraham Haber, Chaskel Rudnicki, Lou Dikerman, H. Kasoy, H. Rosztajn, Morris Szwarc, Jack Dikerman, A. Krauz, S. Szolom, Abe Soberman, Karl Ellenberg.

Greetings from the Nowo-Radomsker *Landsmanschaft* in New York

The Nowo-Radomsker *landsmanschaft* gladly accepts the invitation of the neighboring Czenstochower *landsmanschaft* to take part in the historic book, *Czenstochower Yidn* that will be published by the United Czenstochower Relief Committee in New York.

This book will remain the greatest historical document of a *landsmanschaft*, a book of blood and tears.

This will be a valuable book for the remaining *landsleit* from Czenstochow and its surroundings that will spread over all parts of the world.

We, Nowo-Radomsker *landsleit*, will help with the work, so that the book, *Czenstochower Yidn*, will reach these thousands of *landsleit* across the entire world.

We give our warm greetings from the Nowo-Radomsker who are so close to you. We will energetically disseminate the work on behalf of the Jews here in America, and especially on behalf of the dear survivors on the other side of the ocean.

[Page 342]

Kamyk

(Kamyk, Poland)

50°54' 19°02'

Kamyk was almost the smallest of the *shtetlekh* [towns] around Czenstochow, but it distinguished itself with its rich history and with lively young people.

The Jewish quarter of Kamyk was separated from the Polish one by flowing water. This division was planned – the one God knows by whom. However, the Kamyk Jews, it appears, did not want to be suspected of having created a "ghetto" for the Gentiles – so they placed the religious officials, the synagogue, the rabbi, the *mikvah* [ritual bath], the *Shamas* [man who assists in the running of the synagogue] in the Polish quarter.

The Jewish population of Kamyk consisted of 100 families, the majority cattle traders and butchers. They would go to the surrounding villages to buy something or go to a market in other *shtetlekh.*

Understand that Kamyk also had several Jewish shops, several teachers, a few shoemakers and tailors who clothed the Kamyk population.

Almost every family had its own piece of field that was seeded with a small amount of potatoes, rye, wheat and this was a contribution to their livelihood.

In the old times the young people would, immediately after being let out of *kheder* [religious primary school], go with their fathers to a village or travel with them to the market and, in time, become "perfect" merchants. However, with the arrival of new times, this changed. The young began to be drawn to the large city, Czenstochow, a journey of two hours walking. The first step was taken by the young shoemakers and tailors. Thoughts about becoming better shoemakers or tailors than their fathers arose in their heads. In addition, the large city, where one lived differently, one spent time differently and one grew up differently than in the *shtetl*, drew them like a magnet. Small groups of young people began to leave for the larger city of Czenstochow; they worked there, they grew there in a city atmosphere, met new people, new friends and comrades. In 1905, the Kamykers in Czenstochow took an active part in the freedom movement or, as it was called, *Akhdes* [unity].

[Page 343]

Kamyk also had its own industry: tanning. At the beginning, thick leather (*konine – kon* is the Polish word for horse] was produced. Several factories were erected; professionals were brought from the larger cities; a better sort of leather was produced and the entire industry took on a broader public scope.

Kamyk was also known for its fires. They called: "Kamyk is on fire." Frequently, a fire would devastate an entire street or several streets at once. For weeks and months, families with eight or 10 children would wander around in barns and stalls with the cattle and poultry and were frightened of another fire.

Kamyk believed that the fires were God's punishment, until it was shown that it was the handiwork of the local hooligans.

Zandsztajn, a Jewish dignitary, resided in Kamyk. He conducted himself like all of the Polish noblemen in the area. He had a courtyard almost like a palace, surrounded by a fruit and flower garden, with many fields, meadows, forests, cattle, horses, with a sawmill and a steam mill. The mill and the sawmill brought life to Kamyk. Wagons carried wood from the forest; the sawmill cut boards and sent them to the city and Kamyk had income.

The Kamyk Jews, as is customary, were proud of the Jewish lord in the *shtetl*, although they felt wronged and insulted that the Jewish landowner held himself strictly separated from the poor Jewish population and the estate guards, who carefully guarded everything that belong to the estate, looked at everyone with angry eyes.

Many times the Jewish lord distributed potatoes. This would take place during winter at the time of great need.

Kamyk would celebrate dedications in a local manner. Mainly, it was the *Khevra Tehilim* [Psalm Society], which celebrated *siems* [celebrations for the completion of the writing of a new Torah scroll] for several Torah scrolls. Each dedication was a true holiday in the *shtetl* that would last several days. Young and old would take part in the great celebration, with musical orchestras, food, drink, song and dance.

The solemn holiday spirit of the dedications would leave a deep longing for them when everything returned to weekday life.

The *Khevra Tehilim* also would often celebrate the end of *Shabbos* and would end *Simkhas Torah* [fall holiday celebrating the completion of the year-long Torah reading and the start of the new year of Torah readings] with dance and song. The *hakofes* [procession with the Torah scrolls] would be accompanied by illumination.

Natural beauty also was found around Kamyk. The most beautiful was the famous *Nisn Barg* [Nut Hill]. The young, who would come home during the summertime for *Shabbos* after working in Czenstochow during the week, would refresh themselves in a sea of green in which the entire *shtetl* and its fields, forests, waters and meadows were submerged.

However, the *Nisn Barg* was more beloved than anything else. After [eating the] *cholent* [Sabbath stew], we were drawn to it. When the over-worked *shtetl* became absorbed by sleep, the young would go to the *Nisn Barg* with a newspaper, with a book, with an illustrated journal, to lie and feel as if in an enchanted palace . . . when they reached the top of the hill it seemed as if not only did Czenstochow lay at their feet, but that the entire world could actually be reached with their hands.

Two people in the first ranks of the Kamyk youth distinguished themselves: Berl (Beny) Yelen and Hershele Erlich. They had two separate bodies with one soul. They were the "dreamers of Kamyk." Yet despite their limited possibilities, through their actions they accomplished their dreams.

First of all they created a young circle among themselves and endeavored to create reading material for themselves, from a newspaper and journal to philosophical works. When the circle grew larger they undertook the creation of a youth organization with the name *Khevra Bokhurim* [society of young men], with its own *minyon* [prayer group] and own Torah scroll.

[Page 343]

However, the Kamyk zealots sensed that something else was hidden under the *Khevra Bokhurim*, with its own *minyon* and a conflict flared up in all of the corners of the *shtetl*, in the street, in the synagogue, in the *shtibl* [one-room prayer house] and even in the *mikvah* [ritual bath] – everywhere they spoke of the misfortune that had appeared in Kamyk.

However, the young won. The *Khevra Bokhurim* became a reality with its own *minyon*. The first *Shimkhas-Torah* [the autumn holiday celebrating the completion of the yearly Torah reading] that the young men celebrated surpassed the *Khevra Tehilim* [Psalm Society]. When the society arranged a "march" in the street with candles and song, candles were lit in every window for their sake. Kamyk had not seen such a picture before. Even the gentile neighbors celebrated the holiday with them.

With the outbreak of the First World War all of the factories and workshops closed in the cities and *shtetlekh*. The Kamyk young returned to their fathers and mothers from the cities for financial support. The young circle with its two leaders did not neglect the opportunity and often arranged gatherings and meetings that held together the young and developed their feeling for communal questions and interest in literature. Representatives of the workers movement would often be brought from Czenstochow, such as Rafal Federman, Shmuel Frank, A. Chrabalowski, Hershl Gotayner, Moshe Berkensztat and others.

With the end of the First World War, the economic situation in Kamyk did not improve, nor get worse.

The greatest part of the Jewish population was hungry. Children walked around naked and barefoot. Thanks to the efforts of the influential group of the young who were connected to the Czenstochower *S.S.* [Socialist Zionists], later *Fareinikte* [united], Kamyk received help with food that America had sent for Poland. A kitchen for children was opened where they received several meals a day, they were provided with a little clothing and finally a nursery was created named for Y. L. Peretz, with which all of Kamyk found joy and pride.

It should be understood that without the help from Czenstochow, from the *Tsysho* (Central Jewish School Organization) and from friends in America, this would have been impossible. The soul of the nursery was Faygele Berliner, the first teacher, who with her deep love for the children and self-sacrificing dedication raised the nursery to a very beautiful level. The Kamyk children, as well as the entire population of Kamyk, paid her with love and respect.

The first class of the *folks-shul* [Jewish public school] opened during the second school year. Friend Berl Yelen was already in American then and he supported the work with all of his strength.

When the delegates from Czenstochower Relief in New York came to Czenstochow to create the Y.L. Peretz house, they also visited Kamyk and gave the Kamyk school 100 dollars.

With the help of the Czenstochower Dramatic Circle, performances, readings and dance evenings also were arranged that would bring in financial help.

A parents committee also existed at the nursery and it would often arrange parents gatherings. Orthodox Jews were represented in the parents committee who understood that their children were better educated in a modern school than in the old-style *kheder*.

Kamyk also took part in the election struggles in independent Poland and a great number of Jewish voters supported the progressive socialist candidates.

In general, Kamyk moved forward at the head among the *shtetlekh* around Czenstochow with its activist youth who struggled for a better life and carried along the *shtetele* [small town] with it. We must not forget Kamyk.

For the "Kamyk" article

[Page 345]

Czenstochower
in *Eretz-Yisroel*

Czenstochower in *Eretz-Yisroel*

Around 2,000 people from Czenstochow are located in *Eretz-Yisroel* [the land of Israel] today. The first group of pioneers came in 1919. They took part in all branches of work and went through all of the difficulties demanded in building *Eretz-Yisroel*.

In 1925 the storm of emigration from Poland to *Eretz-Yisroel* increased and many Czenstochower also left for *Eretz-Yisroel* with the so-called Grabski *Aliyah* [the fourth wave of emigration, named for the Polish Minister of Finance, Wladyslaw Grabski who introduced an anti-Jewish tax policy]. The Czenstochow emigrants, who stayed together the entire time and when possible helped one another, met together for the first time at the home of Leib Asher (Umglik [when he lived in Czenstochow]), then in Reb Moshe Halter's café. The Czenstochower Union was born at this meeting and its first chairman was Comrade Eisajewicz (the Wolier Rabbi).

Aba Lubrowicz, a Zionist activist from Czenstochow, was among the first who built his own house here. Working on the construction were only those from Czenstochow. The *Histadrut* [organization of trade unions in Israel] organized a group of five Czenstochow workers under the leadership of Godl Frajtag, one of the active *Poalei-Zionists* [Marxist-Zionists] from Czenstochow and called it the "Frajtag *Kibbutz* [group]." The other comrades from the *Kibbutz* were: Pik, Oderberg, Kaminski, Benclowicz. The additional workers also were Czenstochower.

Helmund Buchenhaim, a construction entrepreneur in Czenstochow, a German, lived among the Czenstochower group then. He also came to work in the *kibbutz*. The same Helmund Buchenhaim became the commissar over all of the factories in Czenstochow when the Nazis occupied Poland in 1939.

In 1927 a crisis began in the country. Construction work had ceased and many in the group, particularly those who were well-to-do, began to to Poland. The Czenstochower Union then organized mutual aid for its members. A new committee was created under the chairmanship of Gamalinski. The committee turned to Czenstochow, to the Czenstochower in America for support. An aid committee was created in Czenstochow and help arrived twice. Worker groups and collectives of various trades were founded: a group of carpenters with Moshe Zilberszac at the head; a group of galoshes makers who repaired galoshes; a group of unskilled laborers and so on. Little by little conditions got better. From workers arose clerks and small entrepreneurs. Larger workshops developed out of artisan cooperatives. More wealthy entrepreneurs became industrialists. A celluloid factory also was created here with the participation of Sztencl, Yakov Fefer, Handlsman, Gotlib and others.

It is worth recording those enterprises that had a certain significance for the *Eretz-Yisroel* industry: Karp's factory that produced agricultural tools and during the war its work for military purposes. Up to 44 workers were employed in the factory, a large number of them from Czenstochow. The haberdashery factory of Yakov Gotlib, a locksmith and mechanic by trade, a graduate of the Czenstochow Artisans' School. He also employed many from Czenstochow and himself gave a great deal of time to the Czenstochower *landsmanschaft* [organization of people from the same town]. His wife, Chava, née Richter, helped him in the communal activity.

Recently, weaving and knitwear industries developed in *Eretz-Yisroel* in which Czenstochower are represented in large numbers.

In addition to the small workshops that work alone or with individual helpers, there also are present a few large enterprises, for example the factory of Tzwi Szpalten, a good organizer and also active in other areas, who came here during the war, as well as: Lewit, Mendl Gilbert and others.

[Page 346]

Moshe Zilberszac (carpentry shop), Sztibl, Henekh Kalka from Radomsko, a brother of Shimkha Kalka from Czenstochow acquired good reputations among the artisan enterprises. Landsman, a graduate of the Artisans' School in Czenstochow, is known for his mechanical locksmith shop in Jerusalem. He is the chairman of the Czenstochower Union in Jerusalem and a member of the national committee. The Sosowski brothers, also activists in the Czenstochower Union, worked in the carpentry branch in Jerusalem. Meir Fajnrajch, a former member of the Socialist-Zionists and a graduate of the Czenstochower Artisans' School, has a mechanical locksmith shop in Haifa. The artisans Blum and Amsterdam from Czenstochow also are in Haifa. Yehoshua Kalka is among the entrepreneurs. The Kalka brothers also employ many Czenstochower at various sections of their trade. Ariali, [known as] Kaluszinski [in Czenstochow], occupies an esteemed place in the printing section.

Simkha Rajch, an active member of the *Poalei-Zion* [Marxist-Zionists] in Czenstochow, is known for the manufacture of stone and marble, which developed a widespread market here.

Represented in trade are: Mos, Kohn, Gewercman, Hacherman and others. Godl Fajertag also founded the first tea factory, Kras. Before the First World War, his tea factory sent tea to America and to other nations. His firm carries the names Kras number 72 or Kras number 93.

More than in all other areas, the Czenstochower excelled in agriculture and gardening and this was thanks to the Czenstochow gardening farm that graduated many tradesmen in whom Czenstochow could take pride. Buchman, a student of the gardening school, is the only gardener in Tel Aviv. Many Czenstochower, students from the gardening school also are found as members of the *moyshavus* [cooperative agricultural communities] and *kibbutzim* [collective communities, often agricultural] or *Halutzim* [pioneers]. The Czenstochower who are involved with planting orange groves are Wolfowicz, Szacher, Lipski, Kongreci, Zaksonhaus, Pik, Goldsztajn, Gewercman and others. Shoshona Czenstochowska is well-known for her magnificent and theoretical knowledge in the area of tropical plants.

Many Czenstochower who could not get used to agricultural work, learned trades and were employed independently or worked in small enterprises. A number with energy reached the universities in Jerusalem and Haifa and continued their studies and received diplomas under the most difficult conditions. The Haifa engineers who graduated in this way were: Lipinski, a son of Dr. Lipinski, and Wilinger. Both served in the ranks of the allied armies as engineers.

Thus one meets Czenstochower all over, in the leading institutions, in agriculture, building the most beautiful houses in Tel Aviv, at office work and so on. Shimkha Rajch, well-known to all, could be found decorating houses with marble, Feitl Szmulewicz – installing glass in houses, Sztibel – finishing with the carving work, such as doors and windows. Many sides [of paper] could be filled out with the names of Czenstochower who built and are building the community in *Eretz Yisroel*.

Three rabbis in Tel Aviv were from Czentochow: Rabbi Szaiewicz, of blessed memory (he died in 1941), Rabbi Sztencel [and] Rabbi Tamar. In the course of years a Czenstochower: Klajnman (Pesl the flour merchant's grandson) was the chief of police. Yakov (Krimalowski's grandson] also was a sergeant in the same police force. Other policemen from Czenstochow were Adler, Fridman, Asher Szwarcbaum (Yehiel Szwarcbaum's son, First *Aleye*), Zilbersztajn and others.

Wolhendler, a Czenstochower, fell in Haifa in 1939 in a heroic fight against the attacking Arabs. Two from Czenstochow still stand at the head of the *Poalei-Mizrakhi* [social democratic organization] today: Shragi, Feiwelowicz [in Czenstochow] and Leslau Roizen. Shragi is also in the executive of the Jewish Agency in Jerusalem. Szajewicz is a representative of the Agency in Teheran, Persia [Iran]. Today he is called Dr. Moshe Yashi (son of the Woler rabbi).

Czenstochower Jewry gave great respect to Bronislaw Huberman, who created the symphonic orchestra [now the Israeli Philharmonic Orchestra] with a magnificent building in Tel Aviv. It is the most beautiful that has been created in the entire Near East.

At the outbreak of the war, many Czenstochower among many thousands of others, voluntarily reported for Palestinian military service, such as Potaszewicz, Kartuz, Jakubowicz, Bril. Yitzhak Zelkowic, born in Czentochow in 1898, entered the French Foreign Legion. When France fell, he returned to *Eretz Yisroel* and belonged to De Gaulle's faction.

[Page 347]

When the Australians came to *Eretz Yisroel*, Sztajnic, the youngest son of Sztajnic the leather merchant at the new market came, with them. Berkowicz (Layzer Berkowicz is his father) came with the South Africans. Many Czenstochower members of the military came with the Polish military from Soviet Russia, among them several officers, such as Dr. Kon, Dr. Fajnman, Bochenek and others.

Godl Frajtag, Yakov Jaskel, Fajtl Szmulewicz, Szczekacz and others took an active part in the land distribution organization that was created during war time under the name, *Mishmar Ezrahi* [Civil Guard].

The Czenstochower *Irgun* (branch) of the Association of Immigrants from Poland (Association of Polish Jews in *Eretz Yisroel*) was the first and the strongest (now there are 40 divisions). Dr. Hurwicz, a son of the Czenstochow chain manufacturer, stands at the head of the general organization. Szmulewicz is vice-chairman. Others who occupy esteemed places in the leadership and in the council of the organization are: Szpalten, Wajdenfeld. Yehuda, Fejwelowicz, Efriam Shmuel, Yakov Gotlib, Mrs. Rozencwajg, Dovid Gruszka, Trajman, Karp, Arieli (Kalaszynski), Lewit [and] Henekh Girenberg.

Dawidowicz is on the *iriya* (city council) of Tel Aviv. Shmuel Efriam [in the previous paragraph his name is given as Efriam Shmuel] is in *Histadrut* [General Organization of Workers]. Feitl Szmulewicz joined the artisan organizations. He also took part in the Hebrew and Yiddish press (*Neie Welt* [*New World*]) with articles about artisans.

The Czenstochower also occupied an active and influential place during the Passover activities (contributions to the poor for Passover) – Godl Frajtag, Dr. Hurwicz, Mrs. Hurwicz, Mrs. Rajngold, Tzwi Szpalten.

In 1939 the Association of Immigrants from Poland founded a division under the name *Vaad HaMochod* [Council of Unity] whose task was to help the Jews from Poland who survived Hitler's gangsters in the nations where help could reach and, particularly, to give the first help and provide work for those who survived [and came to] *Eretz Yisroel*. Dr. Hurwicz is the leader of *Vaad HaMochod*. Feitl Szmulewicz leads the Czenstochower division. Others from Czenstochow who help with this work are Shmuel Efriam, Wajdenfeld, Kon, Szpalten, Frajtag, Yakov Jaskel, Dovid Gruszka [and] Lewit. With their help there was success in collecting the addresses of Czenstochower in the Soviet Union. About 85 such addresses have been collected so far. The Czenstochower *Irgun* sent a large number of packages with food and clothing. Those who themselves contributed large sums of money for this purpose were Karp, Frajtag, Jaskel, Avraham Gotlib, Yakov Gotlib, Ahron Mas, the Kon brothers and their father, Chaim.

The "Czenstochower Day" was a large undertaking to help the Czenstochower victims of Hitlerism. That evening, a sum of 75 pounds was collected and in addition 200 packages were sent to those who did not have any relatives in *Eretz Yisroel*.

"Czenstochower Day" in Jerusalem was arranged with the participation of Dr. Hirshberg, Dr. Josef Kruk and Avraham Izbicki. A large sum of money also was collected there for the purpose.

Every anniversary of the outbreak of the war, 1 September, the *Vaad HaMochod* arranges a flower day under the name *Yom Yaades Polin* (a day for the Jews from Poland). Women play the main role and, in general, surpass the men in the matter of collecting money. The names of the Czenstochower women who take part in the flower day every year are Mrs. Grinberg, Szegin, Gotlib, Frajlech, Moszkowicz, Blechsztajn, Herszlikowicz, Wajcenblat, Leslau, Rajch, Szczekacz, Hocherman, Marczun, Lewit, Bornsztajn, Rozencwajg, Rywka Fajnrajch, Zajdman, Kalka, Izenberg, Prajs, Yekl, Bornsztajn, Chana-Tzwi-Chaim, Propenatur, Podamski and others.

When Dr. Kruk arrived in *Eretz Yisroel*, the Czenstochower in Tel Aviv arranged a gathering for him and he was elected honorary chairman of the Czenstochower *Irgun* (division). Representatives from various other divisions of the Association of Immigrants from Poland also were represented at the gathering. Jerusalem and Haifa were represented by Wolf Landsman and Wzowski. Dr. Kruk described his experiences of his last days in Poland and presented memories of the years of his youth in Czenstochow. The evening made a deep impression on everyone. Later, more evenings with Dr. Kruk took place.

[Page 348]

A Meeting of Czenstochower in Tel Aviv

by M. Smulewicz, G. Freitag

Sunday, 3 March 1946, a mass meeting of the Czenstochower *landsleit* [people from the same town] took place in Tel Aviv.

The meeting was arranged in one of the largest premises in the city, the Habima Society; the hall was fully packed with people. Several hundred *landsleit* took part in the meeting.

The hall presented an interesting picture that mirrored the former Czenstochow, grey–haired heads, old Jews who had been here in Palestine for many years, people from all strata of the population, workers, employees and manufacturers (yes, we also had "our own" manufacturers in Tel Aviv). Everyone came to hear the reports about the condition of our brothers and sister there in distant Czenstochow. There was enormous interest. Everyone was thirsty to receive news about those who survived through chance.

And therefore, many *landsleit* could be found in the hall who live in the provinces [countryside] and gave their time to the meeting. Before the meeting began one could encounter scenes where people actually cried with great joy that after so many years of not seeing each other, they had met again. At this opportunity, everyone poured out their bitter heart and tears ran when an old woman said that, alas, of her eight children in Czenstochow no one survived. A young halutz [pioneer], who arrived in *Eretz–Yisroel* just before the outbreak of the war, said that he remains alone and lonely like a stone. No one survived from his large family. And thus, they shared the appalling news until a ring from the chairman, who called on all those assembled to take their seat.

Managing Committee Members of the Czenstochower Union in Tel Aviv

(*Khavri Heuer Czenstochowim b'Tel Aviv*)

Seated, right to left: Y. Yeshkol, E. Szpalten, N. Frajtag, Sz. Rajnwald

Standing, right to left: Dr. A. Horowicz, Re. Lesloi, A. Gotlib, Czecmer, F. Szmulewicz

The First Group of Czenstochower in Tel Aviv [1919]

Among others: Gerichter, F. Wajcblat, Dr. Horowicz, Gamulinki, Rajchman, Horowiczik

The meeting was opened by Mr. Lewit (a son–in–law of the *Magid* [preacher] of Klobuck); he greeted those assembled and read a heartbreaking letter, which had just arrived from the Czenstochower Jewish Committee.

The first speaker was Dr. Hirszberg, the former preacher and rabbi at the New Synagogue [in Czenstochow]. He spoke about the tragedy of the refugees, because not long ago he found himself in the same situation, and he appealed on behalf of our brothers and sisters in Czenstochow for support for the charity activities that were being carried out by the local committee.

Dr. Josef Kruk also spoke to the same matter. He read several letters that recently were received at his address. He turned to those assembled to spread [the news about] the *Czenstochower Almanac* that would soon be published in America.

The last [speaker] was a soldier from the Jewish Brigade, Ezriel Jakubowicz, who visited Czenstochow in December 1945. He brought a living greeting from the remnant of Jewry of the great Jewish community that still remained there. He spoke precisely about how Czenstochow looked after the "liberation." He spoke of the institutions that still existed there and about communal life in general. The greeting, in general, was a sad one, more terrible and more frightening than had been imagined.

[Page 349]

Managing Committee Members of the Czenstochower Union in Jerusalem
(***Khavri Heuer Czenstchowim b'Yerushalayim***)
Seated, right to left: F. Zuzowski, Dr. Josef Kruk, W. Landman
Standing, right to left: Sh. Zuzowski, N. Beserglik, A. Zuzowski, D. Zuzowski

National Committee of Czenstochower in *Eretz–Yisroel*

Standing, right to left: Dr. Y. Horowicz, Y. Gotlib, C. Spalten, F. Szmulewicz, P. Zubski
Seated, right to left: W. Landman, Dr. J. Kruk and Y. Danciger

**Representatives of the *Irgoen Olei Czenstochow*
[Organization of Immigrants from Czenstochow] in Haifa**
Seated, right to left: Blum, Danciger, Fajnreich
Standing, right to left: Y. Goldberg, Windman, Borzykowski

A Glass of Tea with Czenstochower in Haifa

A Group of Czenstochower in *Eretz Yisroel* in 1926

The First Group of Czenstochower in Haifa in 1926

Among others: Y. Danciger and his wife, A. Szwarcbaum and his wife,

Meir Fajnrajch and his wife, the brothers Yehiel and Yakov Klajner, Windman

[Page 350]

Jakubowicz also spoke about the hundreds of Czenstochower whom he met during his sojourn in Europe, in various countries and camps. The situation was in most parts difficult; there were many present who were very hungry for bread and were without shoes and clothing during the winter. Their only hope was to emigrate to *Eretz-Yisroel* or other countries, because there was no way back to Poland. Previously they were murdered by the Nazis and now the same appears before them at the hands of the Poles.

The meeting was ended with warm greetings being sent to our brothers in Czenstochow and all over the world.

A great deal of money was collected on the spot for this purpose [aiding the survivors]. The meeting left a strong impression on all participants.

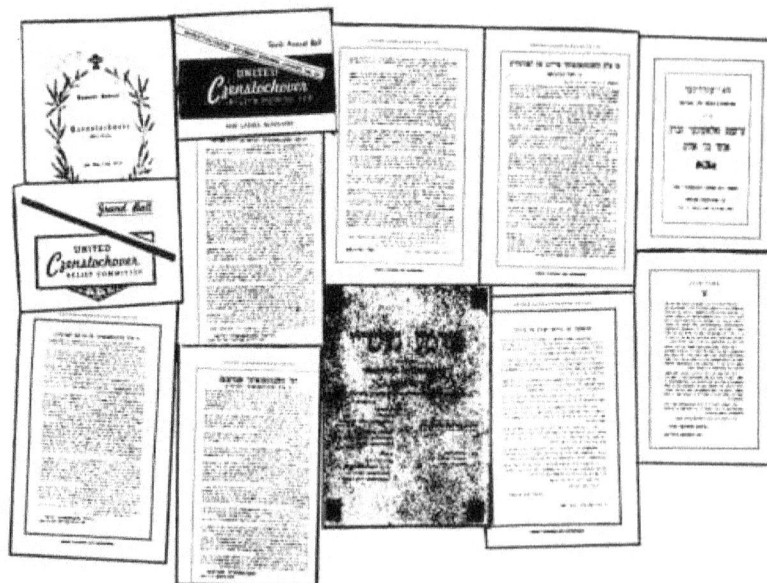

Documents from Czenstochower Organizations in America and Canada

[Page 350]

Czenstochower in Canada

[Page 351]

Czenstochower Area Aid Society in Toronto (Canada)

by W. Glicksman

The first meeting to found the Czestochower *landsmanschaft* [society] in Toronto took place on 8 January 1943 with the participation of the following people: C. Orzech, Sh. Kaminkowski and B. Cyncynatus.

A short time later, a second gathering of the following people took place on 29 March 1943: Dovid Berenholc, C. Orzech. Sh. Kaminkowski, B. Cyncynatus and Moshe Pinkus. [It was decided at the gathering] to call the first founding meeting and create a permanent Czenstochower Union in Toronto. The deadline was set for 4 April 1943 in the home of Friend D. Berenholc.

On that the day, a group of *landsleit* [people from the same town] came together at [the home of] Friend D. Berenholc and a presidium was created with the following composition:

C. Orzech – provisional chairman.
Shimshon Lichter – provisional secretary.
Dovid Berenholc – provisional treasurer.

A provisional executive [committee] also was created of the following people:

Moshe Tarnowski, Sh. Lichter, B. Wocznica, A. Dalman and Sh. Kaminkowski.

The elected members of the presidium and executive [committee] approached their work with great energy and immediately collected the first monetary funds from the members attending the meeting. D. Berenholc particularly excelled in this area.

It also was decided at this meeting to give the Czenstochow Society in Toronto the name "Czenstochower Area Aid Union" in Toronto.

How devotedly and loyally the members of the presidium and the executive [committee] worked is shown by the fact that they succeeded in winning over approximately 100 new members by the 2nd of May 1943, in gathering a large sum of money and also calling a general meeting on that day.

The meeting held on the 2nd of May 1943 elected the following officers:
Moshe Tarnowski – chairman.[1]
Yehiel Goldberg – vice chairman.
Hershl Goldberg – vice chairman.
B. Wocznica – vice chairman.
Shimshon Lichter – finance secretary.
Sh. Kaminkowski – recording secretary.
Dovid Berenholc – treasurer.

Executive [committee]:
M. Berenholc, B. Kalchory, B. Wocznica, Y. Czapnik, S. Wocznica, Kh. Goldberg, Y. Goldsztajn, H. Landau, H. Starr, Mrs. M. Berenholc. Mrs. B. Kalchory, Mrs. S. Lichter, Mrs. Wocznica, Mrs. Kh. Goldberg, Mrs. Lazarus and F. Kenigsberg.

It is worth mentioning that under the leadership of Friend Moshe Tarnowski, the Czenstochower Aid Union had great success. The families Berenholc, Wocznica and Eltster stood out in their activities with the Union.

The wives of the Czenstochower *landsleit* [people from the same town] took a very large role in the work of the Czenstochower Aid Union. They excelled in collecting great sums of money and helped their husbands in their intense aid work.

In order to collect larger sums of money, the first larger undertaking of the Czenstochower Aid Union in Toronto took place in 1944.

[Page 352]

Through the initiative of several people a banquet took place at which a souvenir book was given out. The banquet was attended by a large number of *landsleit* and with their contributions they strengthened the money fund of the *landsmanschaft*.

Managing Committee of the Czenstochower Area Aid Union in Toronto [Canada]

Seated, right to left: D. Berenholc (treasurer), Sh. Alster, M. Tarnowski (president), H.
Goldberg (vice president), Sh. Lichter (fin. sec.).
First row, standing, right to left: A. Winter, E. Szwicer, F. Kenigsberg, B. Wocznica, Y.
Freyermoyer, Y. Goldberg.
Second row, standing, right to left: Sh. Kaminkowski (rec. sec.), M. Berenholc, C. Orczech, H.
Starr, Y. Czapnik

A second banquet with a souvenir book that had a great success took place on 28 January
1945.

A summary of activity of the Czenstochower Area Aid Union in Toronto shows the following
numbers:

Fifty food packages to Czenstochow, 500 dollars in cash through Dr. Tenenbaum, president
of the Federation of Polish Jews, an active participation in all aid institutions, as well as in the
moes–khitim [money to provide Passover foods to the poor] campaign, a part in the United
Palestine Appeal and others.

The above–mentioned was created through the work of the local friends and through the
moral support of the United Czenstochower Relief in New York that sent its representative,
Friend R. Federman, for this purpose.

The Czenstochower Aid Union in Toronto has not ended its work. Conscious of its purpose
and tasks, it continues to stand in the ranks of builders of a new Jewry in general and
Czenstochow in particular.

Translator's Footnote

1. The officers are referred to as chairman and vice chairman above and then as president and vice president in the photo caption below

————

[Page 353]
Czenstochower Area Aid Union in Montreal (Canada)

by W. Gliksman

The first founding meeting of the Czenstochower *landsmanschaft* [organization of people from the same town] in Montreal took place on 16 December 1945 at the initiative and in the house of Mr. Merowicz-Wajcman. Present were: Mr. Nathan Gelber, Mr. Borzykowski and his wife, and Mr. Silver Berkowicz.

The main question at this meeting was how to help the survivors in Czenstochow.

The assembled *landsleit* [countrymen] at the first opportunity of meeting each other greeted the initiative of Friend Merowicz with enthusiasm and decided unanimously to take on actively the aid work for Czenstochow.

Elected on the spot as temporary president – Mr. Berkowicz, vice president – Nathan Gelber, treasurer – Dovid Gelberg, campaign manager – Borszkofsk, campaign chairman – A. Merowicz and as temporary secretary – Philip Merowicz.

The president, Mr Berkowicz, opened a general meeting and gave the first 25 dollars; further donations were brought: Mr. Nathan Gelber – 25 dollars, Mr. Markowicz – 25 dollars; Mr. Borszkofski – 10 dol.; Mr. Silver – 10 dol; Mrs. Juris and Mrs. Bels – up to five dollars. One hundred dollars was collected during the same month. The first meeting was closed with the decision to call a second meeting on the 30th of the same month.

A larger endeavor by Czenstochowers in Montreal dedicated to the martyrs in Czenstochow took place on Sunday, 17 February 1946, at a memorial meeting in the *Arbeter-Ring* [Workman's Circle] hall.

Managing Committee of the Czenstochower Area Aid Union in Montreal (Canada)

Seated, right to left: Dovid Gelber, R. Federman, H. Berkowicz, A. Majerowicz
Standing: H. Zablonkewicz, Y. Klajn, N. Gelber, T. Zilberberg, A. Wajskof)

[Page 354]

The stage was decorated with pictures from the Holocaust time and of present Czenstochow.

Chairman, Mr. M. Merowicz, introduced to those assembled the president, H. Berkowicz, who acquainted the attendees with the purpose of the day's meeting. The memory of the female member of the Czenstochower Aid Union in Montreal, Mrs. Nora Klein, was sanctified. Speeches were given about the prematurely deceased by Mr. M. Merowicz and Shlomo Grunt.

After the greetings from two delegate-*landlsleit* from Toronto, Mr. D. Klein, Rabbi H. Denenberg and lawyer Leon Kristal, national chairman, gave speeches about those arriving and about the purposes and tasks of American Jewry on behalf of their brothers and sisters across the sea.

The cantor, Avraham Matz recited *El Male Rakhamim* [*God, Full of Mercy* – prayer for the deceased].

The guest speaker, Rafal Federman, gave a picture of the destruction in Czenstochow and about the present conditions in our home city in an impressive speech. He called upon those gathered to further help those remaining in our old home.

The money collection that was carried out brought in over 800 dollars.

President H. Berkowicz closed the meeting with a further appeal to join the Czenstochower Aid Union.

A banquet took place on the anniversary of the existence of the Czenstochower Area Aid Union in Montreal on Thursday, 26 December 1946, at which the honorary president, George Klein, thanked those assembled for the good work and presented to them the newly arrived two young children of Czenstochow, the Wajskop brothers.

Chairman, Friend M. Merowicz, gave a report about the activities up to then: 1,700 dollars in cash was sent to Czenstochow along with 1,200 pounds of clothing, as well as a large number of private packages.

The appeal by the chairman at the banquet collected 1,140 dollars from the 35 guests attending, which was designated for Czenstochow.

The society displayed strong activity in the field of internal organization. The monthly meetings and the strenuous work by individual members was a further guarantee of the existence of the Czenstochower Society in Montreal and that would continue to help their old home city.

[Page 354]

Czenstochower in Argentina
Union of Czenstochower *Landsleit* in Argentina

The Union of Czenstochower *Landsleit* [people from the same town] in Buenos-Aires was founded in 1929. It introduced as its main task to provide material help for the needy *landsleit* here and for loans with easy conditions for payment. The number of members was small then because the Czenstochower *landsleit* did not show any interest in the Union.

The leadership of the Union consisted of a committee of seven men. The income of the Union came from tea-entertainments, when the group would come together and speak with [other] *landsleit* whom they had not seen for a long time. At this opportunity, they listened to a few words from the leaders about the need to support the Union.

We must confess that the principles of the Union were not upheld. The Union carried a bourgeois character through and through and, therefore, did not receive the appropriate support of the Czenstochower who had a different approach to the communal question.

The activity of the Union stopped a short time later.

In March 1943, when the terrible news from Czenstochow and from all of Poland reached us here in Argentina, we saw that we needed to exert all of our strength to create help for our unfortunate sisters and brothers. The Czenstochwer *Landsleit* Union reorganized with enthusiasm. Many members contributed large sums, others undertook paying [their contribution in installments] until such time as they would receive an exact address in Czenstochow to which to send the collected money.

[Page 355]

The work of us in the Czenstochower *Landsleit* Union was energetic, just as in other *landsleit* organizations, a number of which had only recently been organized. All *landsleit* organizations now concentrated on one task – help for the old home.

The address of the Czenstochower *Landsleit* Union in Argentina is: Buenos Aires, Junin 122.

Czenstochower Union in Argentina

Spanish heading on photo: Society of Residents of Czenstochow and
Its Surroundings in Buenos Aires in 1945

[Page 355]

Czentochower in Paris

A large number of people from Czenstochow and its environs now live in Paris. It is difficult to provide an exact number. We counted around 300 people. The number before the Second World War was a great deal higher. More than half were deported and perished in the German death camps.

A larger emigration from Czenstochow to Paris began in 1919, right after the First World War. Those who were in Argentina at Buenos Aires, Junin 122, were forced through coercion to emigrate to Germany. From there, they came to Paris[1]

All emigrants from Poland and from other lands, generally faced loneliness, unfamiliarity with the language and the strangeness of the way of life of the country, longing for a familiar environment and helplessness in cases of need and at times of sickness. All of this drove Jewish emigrants in Paris to create the *Landsmanschaft Farband* [union of people from the same town] and led in 1928 to the creation of the society, Friends of Czenstochow.

It is hard to describe the activity of the Society during the 20 years in a short article. We will only underline that our work was almost the same as all of the emigrant societies in France. At first the work was carried out in a limited amount. Several young people took part in it. The main emphasis was placed on creating a memorial for the dead in a small cemetery plot. There also was some monetary support for times of need and medical help for members and their families. Visits also were made to sick members and they were helped with whatever they needed. The Society was apolitical and carried on its activities within the limits of its circle.

[Page 356]

The situation changed with the coming to power of Hitlerism in 1933. The first deportations of the Jews from Germany to Zbaszyn (Poland) in 1934 shook the Jewish consciousness in the world. Also, we Czenstochower in Paris levied upon ourselves our portion, collecting money and clothing for the first Jewish victims. When a large number of refugees began to stream to Paris, we worked together in the creation of a people's kitchen, which at that time fed thousands of the hungry. When the fascist revolt in Spain broke out in 1936 and thousands of Jews fought in the ranks of the Spanish Loyalists, Czenstochowers, who fought and fell in the war against fascism, also were represented among them.

A great change to our Czenstochower Society took place in 1938 before the outbreak of the Second World War.

Our Society developed a new face with the arrival of younger emigrants from Poland who already had gone through the fire of struggle with home-grown fascism and anti-Semitism there. The "Jewish cemetery" ceased to occupy the main concern of the work of the society. The gathering became lively. Cultural conversations took place. Our society supported *TOZ* [Society for the Protection of Jewish Health in Poland], which took care of the sick and weak children from our home city and worked with the existing Czenstochow *Patronat* [committee to aid political prisoner in Poland] in Paris, which supported the arrestees in the Polish jails. Our society also helped create the Jewish People's Clinic in Paris, which gave medical help to thousands of Jews in Paris. Understandably, the eternal struggle between old and young also existed, but the course of events led to the reconciliation of all difficulties. The society endeavored to assemble all of the *landsleit* [people from the same town] from the *shtetlekh* [towns] surrounding Czenstochow, such as Klobuck, Krzepice and others.

The Second World War

With the outbreak of the Second World War in 1930, the majority of *landsleit* were mobilized or volunteered to join the French Army. The contours of Auschwitz, Majdanek and Treblinka already were seen on the horizon. There was paralysis in the activity of the society. However, the small number of members who were not mobilized were busy with sending financial support to the members in the army and in several cases to support their wives and children. The work of our society ceased completely with the arrival of the sad day of 14 June 1940, when the Hitlerist army marched into Paris. However, our members, as individuals, worked with the general aid organization that supported the victims of barbaric fascism and the first Jews imprisoned in the death camp, Drancy, near Paris. The work grew more difficult from day to day. The dark clouds in the Jewish sky became darker every hour. Grief and pain filled every Jewish soul and blood dripped from every Jewish heart. Men were torn away from their wives and children, women with tiny children in their arms were deported, Jewish possessions were looted and stolen by German bandits and French collaborators. Every few days [train] wagons were packed with Jewish men, women and children and sent away to the death camps in Poland and Germany. A large number of Czenstochowers were among them. It was impossible under such circumstances to do any organized work, but a large number of *landsleit* took part in the resistance movement and stood out with their heroic courage. It is impossible to spend more time on this within the framework of this article.

After the Storm

We first saw the destruction after the Nazi flood, when the sky began to clear. Our best and most active members were missing. [There was] sadness and grief in the hearts of the survivors but mixed with joy that we had lived for the defeat of the largest and most horrible murder of Jews in our history. And we were as if we had risen from the dead! The individual survivors began to look for and search through the ruins to find every surviving soul from our Czenstochow family in Paris. Our president, Wroclawski and the remaining members of the committee who did everything within their power to reestablish our society should be praised and thanked here. When the first deported Czenstochow Jews began to , everyone, members and non-members, began to receive a thousand francs as their first assistance. The fund was almost empty, but the committee worked beyond its strength to give the survivors even a little material and moral help.

[Page 357]

Czenstochower Committee in Paris

Seated, right to left: Tenenbaum (general secretary), Levy (vice-president), Wroclawski (president), Dawidowicz (vice president)
Standing, right to left: Wajnman (treasurer), Firstenfeld, Krzepicki, Ruman, Landau, Pankulowski)

* * *

Our communal work now is with the Union of Jewish Societies in France for the general aid committee to support the children of those who perished in the German death camps, with the People's Clinic and with the loan fund. Our ranks have slowly begun to increase, but we are still not able to help everyone who is in need. There remain a number of people whom we must help. These are women with children who although they are working are not able to support their children. Our society is strengthening. On 12 January 1946 we arranged an evening ball and a large concert. We came together in joy mixed with sorrow. But life is still stronger than death and being sad and we rise to a new life.

We Czenstochower in Paris received with joy the happy news that you have decided to publish the book, *Czenstochow*.

We send you the short history of Czenstochower in Paris with our sincere greetings to the *landsleit* in America from Czenstochow and its surroundings.

* * *

Shortly after the end of the war, United Czenstochower Relief in New York began intensive aid activity for the Czenstochower in Paris. A large number of food packages, money and other help were sent. United Czenstochower Relief in New York has not ended its help for the Czenstochower in Paris, as well as for the Czenstochower in other nations.

[Page 358]

* * *

We want to record the names of the founders of our society along with our report. They are:

Blum, Artman, A. Perleger, the Wrublewski brothers, A. Slobiak, the Gutman brothers, B. Kopinski, Wajsbard, Cimberknop, Kamelgarn, Pankowski, A. Kapinski, Y. Lewkowicz.

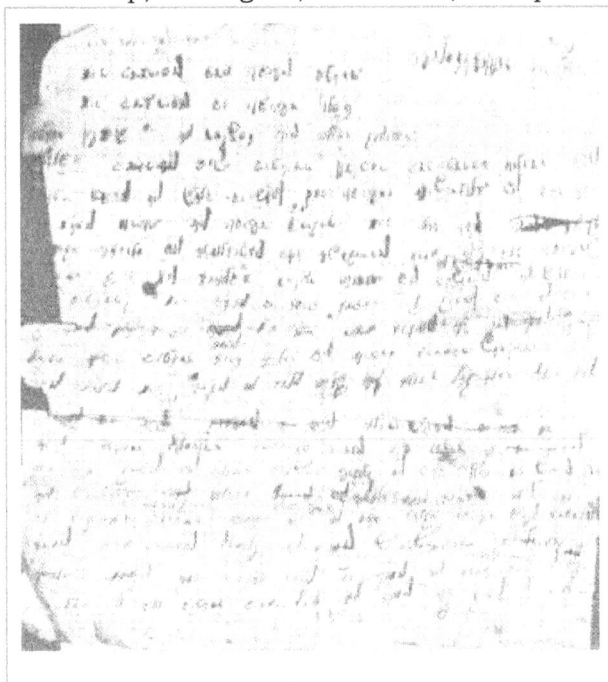

A Manuscript by Avraham Wiewiorka.
Lived in Czenstochow. Died in Moscow. The
brother of Wowtshe Wiewiorka of Paris (the
latter perished in Auschwitz

Translator's note:

1. The address of the Czenstochower *Landsleit* Union in Argentina was Buenos Aires, Junin 122.

[Page 359]

Memories and Photographs

A Day in Czenstochow

by Avraham Reisen

(A fragment from Epizodn fun Mayn Lebn [Episodes from My Life])

It already was difficult for me to remain in Krakow where I published *Dos Yidishe Vort* [*The Yiddish Word*]... The leaders of the *S.S.* [Socialist Zionists] – Zalmen Meisner and Julius Golde, who were then visiting Krakow for party reasons, told me "what was happening" in Warsaw and took upon themselves to take me to the border through Czenstochow. I immediately decided to go to Warsaw... and a week later, after their arrival, all three of us traveled from Krakow to Warsaw.

Zalmen Meisner paid for my expenses. He, the financier for the *S.S.* publication, wanted a story from me for the periodical, which the *S.S.* then published. Sholem Asch was then a regular coworker of theirs. In one issue of the periodical *Der Neyer Veg* [*The New Way*], Sholem Asch already had an article about the 40 times 40 churches in Moscow. I do not know if he wrote it from his head or he had already visited the city of Moscow because of his drama, *Meshiekh's Tsaytn* [*The Time of the Messiah*] or *Der Kholem fun Mayn Folk* [*The Dream of My People*], which [Fyodor Fyodorovich] Komissarzhevsky was supposed to present, and later, did present at the Art Theater in Petersburg. However, I think the article was written with a naïve, revolutionary tone. Sholem Asch celebrated the revolution then and expressed in song, the new bells that were ringing in Moscow... Nevertheless, he also gave me several compliments... However, it was only for the sake of appearances. Possibly because he already was under the influence of Shmuel Niger who was then a young man – however, already had as a member of the Socialist Zionists taken shape as a future critic...

Julius Golde, I think, read little Yiddish and if he even spoke Yiddish, it was the Yiddish of an intellectual who had "just" learned to speak. However, he related to me with great respect and even with friendship.

It happened that we spent the night near the border in a small hotel somewhere in a German *shtetl* [town]. They both, Zalmen Meisner and Julius Golde, were in the best mood. As party people they had the most important plans and the most far-reaching objectives... And Meisner and his then nickname, "Zalmen Bourgeois," because of his father's wealth, was, in general, a dreamer ... I, for whom the ideals of the Zionist Socialists were distant, looked at them philosophically and did not then even discuss [the ideals] with them ... As they were socialists, what kind of complaints could I have about them ... particularly when my fate lay in their hands and they were to lead me to the border or obtain the right agent for me, or such a Jew from Czenstochow with influence with the border guards...

I crossed the border peacefully with a "full belt" ... The soldier only searched my bags "courteously" and let me go through first ... They both, Zalmen Meisner and Julius Golde, already were visible, often crossing [the border] and they had regular passports. Without a doubt they had crossed. Although their trip to Krakow was with illegal literature. The publication of certain brochures was not permitted then in Russia.

[Page 360]

And thus we arrived in Czenstochow and I felt on more secure ground. The greeting that I received there from important personalities, among them a brother of M. Litvakov, whose family or a part of the family then lived in Czenstochow, made me comfortable and helped me forget my "desolation..." I spent the night with a rich engineer whose name I have forgotten. However, I remember exactly the room in which they had prepared a bed for me, as if for a great guest. I ate a magnificent breakfast in the morning and the young, handsome host, the engineer, actually a member of the Zionist Socialists, served me himself...

I also had a strong impression of the city of Czenstochow itself. I particularly liked the main street, a wide and long one that reminded me of Warsaw's Marszalkowska. Its noise was half business and half holiday-like. Something about this street seemed as if it was *khalemoyed* [intervening days of holidays], like the first day after a holiday and the holiday would again resume... Young men from all of the movements and parties, with all kinds of slogans in their inflamed eyes, met each other, greeted each other, stopped and had vigorous discussions... the district and the regional police superintendent, who glanced at them, appeared half-confident and half dispirited. They themselves did not know how great or how little their power was. In any case, I, without a passport and in addition a fighter for freedom, certainly was a little afraid of them, although I knew that they would not dare stop me in the street and ask me for a passport...

Spending two days in Czenstochow, I already, as if I had rehearsed, learned that one also can live without a passport. And surer, full of hopes and expectations, I left Czenstochow where I had spent a few days among dear people and traveled to Warsaw.

And my impression of Czenstochow is of this dear city with an animated Jewish population, from which come several significant Jewish cultural workers and socialist spokespeople who still remain dear and sacred to me. And when I think with pain of the fate of many Jewish destroyed cities, Czenstochow also comes to mind and it ignites in me the belief that it will be repaired and rebuilt as all of the cities that our enemy devastated with such cruelty. And the survivors who are spread all over the world will once more delight in its construction and revival.

Czenstochow, My Czenstochow

by Leibish Lehrer

I was in Czenstochow a very long time ago, in 1906-1907, and yet there are few other details from earlier and later in my life that reflect such lively memories. In total, I was in Czenstochow less than a year. And yet I feel as if I had been intoxicated there with the wine of warm friendship and the ecstasy of a new revelation. In that short time I was connected to only one group, to only one circle, to the Socialist-Zionist Party. And yet there has remained in me the Czenstochow echo of a large city's waving multitude that rocked and rose, permeated and enchanted and extended, extended as wide as the physical and spiritual eye could reach. My illegal functions in Czenstochow also forced a hidden name upon me – Aleksander, a name with which I identified my life for only a few months. And yet I feel as if someone quietly had pasted this name on me at my birth. I feel in this name such a deep sense, such fascinating afterimages that its light had forced its way through the edges of all further times of my life.

Czenstochow, my Czenstochow, in a café, or at the Socialist-Zionist *bourse*[1] where I learned to play *kręgle* [bowling], or at a meeting of party committees, while strolling alone or with friends through the *Alejes* [boulevards] that beautify and add charm to the center of the city – from everywhere echoed the secret of intensive life that with such internal pride celebrated in song even in moments of sadness or grief. For me the city for did not remain as a point on a map, but a symbol of a transformed life, one of those symbols that sings out from each of us during quiet moments of spiritual appraisal.

[Page 361]

Czenstochow, my Czenstochow, in the dreadful tragedy that now streams over you, over my dear and precious ones who have remained in you, I cry with all of your mourners at your great catastrophe. I strive with my last strength to maintain the hope that happy news will yet come from you.

Translator's footnote

1. The *bourse* is the French stock exchange – it is used here to mean a place for exchanging ideas.

––––––

In and around the Workers Club
(a picture of workers clubs after the First World War)

by A. Chrobalowski

The memories that we present here encompass only one facet of the Czenstochower Workers Movement – the *Fareinikte*. In essence, however, in large part this is also representative of the other two worker clubs in Czenstochow – the Borochov Club, at the First *Aleje* 12 and the Medem Club at the Second *Aleje* 40.[1]

The Workers Club – *Fareinikte*

It now numbers up to 700 members. Its bright halls and rooms are filled daily with hundreds of workers who find here a friendly home, their fraternal environment.

Here there is a quiet, calm reading room with all newspapers and journals. A rich library in Yiddish and in other languages is connected to the reading room. Here there is a tea hall where one can get an inexpensive evening meal. Here also is the office that provides medical help.

Dozens of professional unions, united in one central office that encompass all Jewish trades in the city, are concentrated around the workers' club.

Whatever evening one enters the club, there is the hum of the work of the central committees, managing committees, general and trade unions.

In the Meat Workers

Exemplary comradely life reigns in the professional unions. The meat workers have a general fund into which go the general weekly earnings. Every Sunday the members come together and divide the wages according to three categories. The conflicts and incidents with the butcher shop owners do not need to be straightened out by the power of the state. There also is a union with a secretary and it is enough to end a quarrel with an announcement, a letter.

In the Needle Branch

The majority of the members of this union are women (sewers of undergarments, milliners, seamstresses and so on). Therefore, the managing committee consists mostly of women comrades; the only male comrade who is found here (the deceased Comrade Szliwinski) gives the impression of [being] "the last of the Mohicans." However, he is not marginalized... On the contrary, they relate to him with great tolerance. The managing committee sits around a table with the chairwoman, Comrade Halberg, at the head. They deal with the question of an eight-hour working day and of higher wages in several workshops. Here they do not speak at all about equal rights for women.

Professional Union of Metal Workers

The union numbers more than 400 members. The managing committee does not have any great business to carry out because almost all of the members are unemployed. However, there are old accounts here with the factory owners. They closed the small factories, so they would not have to pay the 14–day compensation that was required by law. They do not want to meet their obligations to the workers because they feel that the musician [and Polish Prime Minister Ignacy Jan] Paderewski now plays their music [agrees with their position]. However, the workers already have their union, their central office, their delegates in the workers' councils and not matter what they would be consulted...

[Page 362]

Porter Workers

Older Jews with beards sit around the managing committee's table with hardened faces and hardened hands. They have left their porter's fur pelts and torn, short street jackets at home. They have to change [their clothes] at the union. Bent backs are straightened out and their faces show the facial features with human dignity. In *Bontshe Shvayg*[2] the person who had suffocated for so long under the heavy load of sacks and packs woke up. They [the porters] begin to understand that a better life is one of comradeship, not a competitive one, but of supporting one another.

Various Activities

Here in a room sits the economic committee, listening to reports from widespread institutions. In a second room sits the literary committee, which is concerned with the spread of literature. In a nearby room, identification is given out to the unemployed who are authorized to make use of the free food. In a side room a group is being led and in a large meeting room the general meeting of this or that professional union is taking place.

In the Workers Kitchen

A gigantically large room with many large pictures of Y.L. Peretz, Mendele [Sholem Yakov Abramowich, known as *Mendele Mocher Sforim* or Mendele the Book Peddler], [Ferdinand] Lassalle and Karl Marx. The latter is the largest picture.

The two tables that take up the entire length of the room are covered from end to end. The lunch consists of soup with a piece of bread. A majority of the "consumers" are children whose heads barely reach the plates and could comfortably walk under the table. There are also many small children who eat in the laps of their parents. After the children have eaten their portion, [the parents] sit them on the bench near them and they eat.

Kitchen Number Two

This kitchen shows an ideal picture of class equality and interparty cooperation. The Bundists and *Fareinikte* [United] make peace here. The "bourgeois" and the proletariat forget about class struggle here – all are equal and friendly at lunch. Whoever is not so well off is able to pay 10 marks for lunch – coming here. It should be understood that lunch here is not a sumptuous one.

Y. L. Peretz Children's Home

The workers' Children's Home is ventilated, warm and gleams with children's pictures and with white, clean children's furniture. The intimate relationship for the teachers to the children, the expression of satisfaction and joy in the eyes of the small ones, the playing, dancing and singing brings to the visitor's mind his own childhood years in the *kheder* [religious primary school] with the teacher and his whip, when we played under the table, on the ground and the floor...

The children sing:
Little fish play in the river,
It is joyful, only a treat.
Or:
Eylu, liylu, eylu, liylu
Sleep, my dear one and rest.
Someone who has a mother is happy
And a cradle, too...

And I think like this:

– Sing, children, dance, jump! May your eyes shine, your faces laugh! Perhaps your childhood, your future will be more beautiful, better than ours.

The *Neye Welt* [New World] Hall of *Fareinikte*, Strazacka 11

Translator's footnotes

1. *Fareinikte* (United) was the club of the Zionist Socialist Workers Party; the Borochov Club was named after Ber Borochov, a Marxist Zionist, and the Medem Club after Vladimir Medem, a Bundist.

2. *Bontshe Shvayg – Bontshe the Silent* is a story by Y.L. Peretz, a story interpreted as depicting the suffering caused by poverty and meant to teach the need for political organization.

[Page 363]

Czenstochower Coalminers

by Shimeon Biro

The tsar's Cossacks escaped and the Germans entered Czenstochow on a hot August day in 1914. The factories ceased working. The workers wandered through the streets.

The first week of the First World War brought a half-carnival mood to Czenstochow.

Both the Jews and the Poles were delighted with the defeat of "Nikolai" [Tsar Nicholas II]. We waited to see if the cultured German people would reopen the factories, bringing bread and freedom. A trifle – Germany with its cultural treasures, inventions, Reichstag, social democracy...

It did not take long until a notice appeared in the streets as follows:

"Requesting 2,000 workers as well as tradesmen to work in Silesia. Good conditions, good and inexpensive food. Report at Dojazd Street, opposite the train station."

There was excitement for working Czenstochow over the course of two hours. This was what they had waited for: work, money and bread.

The requested number was filled in one day and one group after the other left to work in Germany.

Another thousand, to whom the news arrived too late, did not have the good fortune of going to Germany and remained in Czenstochow to continue starving, walking around at loose ends. They were envious of the lucky ones who were taken to work and looked at the "dead" chimneys of the tar works, adhesive factories, hat factories and dozens of other smaller workshops and small factories. In about a week, the news began to arrive from the "lucky golden ones" in Germany: instead of human work – slavery, instead of an apartment to live in – barracks with Prussian discipline, instead of freedom – captivity.

Notices for workers again appeared in the streets, but everyone had decided that it was better to eat a piece of dry *popularke* [small, round breads] than to take up Prussian labor.

So the Germans took off their "cultured gloves" and started on their work. They closed off streets and grabbed people, 50-100 at a time, packed them into horse wagons and sent them to work.

There is a *shtetl* [town] in Upper Silesia – Chorzów. This *shtetl* was suddenly a part of Czenstochow.

Czenstochow workers, the young who came voluntarily and those grabbed from the streets, were drawn into the earth two and three hundred meters [about 656 to 984 feet] deep. There, under force and threats from the Prussian overseers, they dug coal in the old, dark coalmines by the light of small, carbide lamps [acetylene gas lamps].

Men who had been hat makers, gaiter quilters, celluloid workers, tailors the night before were transformed into coalminers by Prussian militarism through hunger, whips and blows.

Tired, broken, barely dragging their feet, they left the coalmine late at night to go home – to the "sleep house," where the food consisted of one small piece of German sprouted bread and a watery soup for which they were enrolled [in a book] for a good [high] price.

"Pay day" was at the end of the month, for which everyone waited in order to be able to send home a few marks to their hungry wives, children and parents in Czenstochow.

What a great surprise when instead of money they received this kind of an account:

20 days of work at 4-50 marks	90 marks
30 days of food at 2 marks	60 marks
1 coalminer's lamp	5 marks
1 shovel	4 marks
Sick fund	4 marks
Insurance in case of death	3 marks
Penalty for not filling the quota	5 marks
Sleep house	15 marks
Taxes	2 marks
Total	98 marks

Remains owed to the Chorzów *Bergwerk* [mine]

8 Reich's marks

A piece of coal fell off a beam. Perhaps the beam was rotten. Perhaps gas seeped through– who could know. However, a victim fell; Yelen, a Czenstochow Jewish worker, was crushed to death somewhere in a mine in Upper Silesia.

[Page 364]

Like lost sheep, the Czenstochow workers – coalminers – gathered around the body. Not knowing what to do, how to bury him. Late at night, the Chorzów *Bergwerk* sent some little German who presented himself as a rabbi. Ten men were permitted to go along to the cemetery. The rabbi changed into a black robe and a high, black *yarmulke* [cap worn by religious Jews] and a large white necktie and sang the *Adonoi natan, vadonoi lakakh* [God has given, God has taken] with a gentile accent. Ten grown men cried like children. The Chorzów mine sent a letter of condolence to Gancarska Street and 50 marks for "death insurance" for the murdered father.

Doctors

by Dr. L. Lazarowicz

I see before me in my memory my birth city – Czenstochow, with its small, long streets that then in my young eyes seemed as large as Broadway in New York. Appearing before my eyes as if alive, the old and the new markets that on market days – Tuesday – were noisy and rustling, no less than Times Square. So I saw in reality the three boulevards with trees planted on both sides that were dearer to my heart and were no less beautiful than all of the boulevards of the rest of the world, such as the famous Champs-Élysées in Paris.

And last but not least – the Czenstochow park – the old one that went to the right and the new one that rose a little to the left – how dear and close they were to me, in my memory with all of the memories of my time spent there in my childhood years.

Today, after years of separation from my city of birth, being transplanted first to Warsaw and then to New York, pictures often come to my mind of those distant, good times and among them images and silhouettes of the Jewish doctors in Czenstochow who I knew and who played such an esteemed role in Jewish life in Czenstochow.

How different the relationship to doctors was in those years! When the floor of a Jewish house was washed on a weekday and the threshold and entry was spread with yellow sand, it was clear indication that they were waiting for the arrival of a doctor.

Your father, walking in the street, gave you a jab in the side – he let you know that you needed to move to the side, because ... the doctor was walking.

We stepped aside for the doctors everywhere, on the road, in the street or in a shop, in a wagon or in a cinema. No one dared to sit, to speak loudly or wear his hat on his head in the presence of a doctor. A doctor never put his coat on by himself. Usually he would just put his hand in a sleeve of his coat or fur coat, which someone handed to him.

Such doctors were the old Russians who would stroll on the boulevards alone in a top hat and with their dogs on a leather leash. Dr. Wasertal and his heavy cane in his hand; Dr. Edvard Kon with his golden chain on his fat stomach, the oldest of the Kon family of doctors – Waclaw and Stefan, the latter survived [by moving] from Poland to *Eretz Yisroel*.

Dr. Finkelsztajn was to the sort of doctor who would never refuse to come to a sick person both during the day and the night – and thinking about his patients and their illnesses, he would love to stroke his short beard and whiskers as if this would help him determine how to help the patient get better. Dr. Batawia, the throat specialist and director of the Jewish hospital at Zawodzia, also occupied a respected place in Czenstochow.

In those days, the doctor would be viewed as representing his good name. He would not ask for payment before. He wrote prescriptions, had designated fees [and] maintained an office with a secretary. He would go alone to visit the sick and took as payment however much he was given or simply however much was placed in his hand. It would be said, "Let *Hashem* [God] add to the remainder."

[Page 365]

Those times have passed. A new generation of young doctors arose that were less assimilated and closer to the Jewish masses. Dr. Koniecpolski, the leader of the Hospital for Infectious Diseases, who was very active during the years 1916-1921, when severe epidemics reigned in Czenstochow that took many victims, belonged to this group. Dr. Koniecpolski died of a heart attack not long after the [First] World War. Dr. Bram, an esteemed radiologist and leader of the Zionists, also belonged to this group. During the war, he ended up in Kowel, where he worked in a local hospital and what happened to him later I do not know.

Mrs. Kiak

Dr. Kon-Kolin [now in *Eretz-Yisroel*]

The above-mentioned doctors were different from their colleagues from the older generation. They were not so arrogant and self-important. They tried to be closer to the Jewish masses, work with them, help them to organize and spoke to them in their language – in Yiddish.

The newer generation of Czenstochow doctors from the years 1920-1930 went even a step further. These doctors were completely with the Jewish masses and struggled together with them – each in his area according to his ideals. True, there were still a few Jewish doctors who were known as assimilated, but their number and influence in the Jewish neighborhoods was very small.

Of the doctors of this era whom I knew in Czenstochow, I will mention Frankenberg, Goldman, Lewin, Mokrauker, Walberg, Nowak, Gutman, Rozen, Lewkowicz, Epsztajn, Helman, Szperling, Glater, Grunwald, Mrs. Wiesberg and Tarbaczko. Many of them were exceptional doctors with a good reputation among Jewish and Christian patients.

Kiak with Several Members of His Family

Above all, Dr. Tarbaczko must be remembered. At first, he was only a good *feldsher* [old fashioned barber-surgeon] and worked at the Jewish hospital. I met him there in 1918 when I came to the hospital to practice as a medical student. This good *feldsher* later decided to give up his large practice and to study medicine to become a doctor. He left his wife and two children with his father-in-law – also a *feldsher* named Kiak from Krakowski Street – and left for Warsaw where he lived in a small room and worked hard – working during the day to earn his means of support and studying medicine at night. Years passed. His children grew up and they themselves began to study at the university – until he finally reached his goal and became a medical doctor. It is interesting that he received his diploma at the same time as his oldest son who caught up with his father in his medical studies.

In addition to his medical practice, Dr. Tarbaczko also was active communally and for a time was a councilman at the city council in Czenstochow.

Dr. Tarbaczko was not the only former *feldsher* who excelled in medical practice. Czenstochow had a series of old, experienced *feldshers*, each of whom had a reputation in a particular specialty. Who *hot geshtelt bankes* very well [was good at "cupping"], as did Tajchner; who had a light hand at *shteln pijawkes* [placing leeches], as did Kiak and who could so easily provide enemas as did Dovid Yosl Epsztajn; and who could precisely and quickly coat [a patient's] throat with medicine, as did Herc or Fiszman?

[Page 366]

They were a distinctive cast of medical specialists of a characteristic stature! A generation, who little by little disappeared and who left no offspring.

In addition to medical doctors in Czenstochow, there also were many teeth-doctors or dentists of whom I remember: Artur Broniatowski, the son of the *feldsher* Broniatowski and brother of two doctors; Ahron Perc, the esteemed Bundist activist; Grin, Lewkowicz, Lajzerowicz, Eidelman, Krauskopf, Nowak and Miszinska – a female dentist. They all arrived in the later years and earned their place in the communal life in Czenstochow.

Thus, I see the former Czenstochow before my eyes as a kaleidoscope.

Jews of Czenstochow! You have not disappeared from our memories! We will remember you day in and day out and night after night – for as long as our memories are alert and alive and for as long as we breathe!

———

A Bouquet of Flowers

by F. Gerbowski

I traveled to Czenstochow for 10 years without stop as a messenger for *Keren- Hayesod* [central financial organization of the Zionist movement; it is now the Jewish Agency]. Every year I happened to meet and work with many people. I acquired great love for two of them and my esteem for them strengthened from year to year. They were:

Yehiel Jachimowicz – a well-to-do brick manufacturer. He was fluent in Hebrew, often read a religious book and wrote well in Hebrew. He was the chairman of *Keren-Hayesod* in Czenstochow and carried out the daily work as if he were a paid official. He gave attention to payments of promissory notes that donors took out and went around demanding the sums from those who did not pay on time. At the time of the *Keren-Hayesod* campaign he was as "swift as a deer" from morning until night to raise pledges for *Keren-Hayosed*.

However, he had a fierce competitor [who shared] his ideals and would always try to do better than he did. This was Avraham Gerszonowicz, the well-known Zionist worker in Czenstochow. When he would see that Jachimowicz had already collected a respectful number of declarations [of support], he would become "as strong as a lion" and turn his extraordinary energy to surpass the other one. Their "competition" was well known in Zionist circles. They were called the "competitors" in the manner of Czenstochow, the factory city. Such idealistic competition was truly rare.

Shmuel Horowicz – a son of a Czenstochow manufacturer, an engineer by trade, was the permanent secretary of the *Keren-Hayesod* campaign. When the *Keren-Hayesod* collection would begin, the managing committee of Horowicz and Partners knew that he ceased to be the boss of the young engineers and he had completely become the envoy for *Keren-Hayesod*. He would carry out his secretarial abilities with extraordinary accuracy.

Yehuda Engel, chairman of the *Mizrakhi* [religious Zionists] in Czenstochow, was an older man and it was not very easy for him to climb flights of stairs. However, he disregarded the weakness caused by his weak heart

Two Zionist workers were called "the pair" in Zionist circles. They were a rare, blessed pair, really a match made in heaven. They would travel and work successfully and fruitfully together at every *Keren-Hayesod* campaign.

[Page 367]

They existed two separate worlds with separate world outlooks. They would merge their work for *Eretz Yisroel* with one aspiration and desire – to collect even more for the construction of *Eretz Yisroel*.

The well known *Mizrakhi* worker Belchsztajn was a pious Jew with a beard, dressed like a Hasid. His second half was Doctor Rozen, a European-educated man and, in addition, a follower of the Enlightenment. They were "as if kneaded out of one dough" at their work for *Eretz Yisroel* and by day and late in the evening they were always seen walking together out of one house into another. Then it was known in Czenstochow that the "pair" was at work.

The frost burned and seared; a blizzard would cover the street – the "pair" did not see it and did not feel it, but went about their service with enthusiasm.

They and dozens of others dreamed about *Eretz Yisroel* for many years and did not live to save themselves in its lap and find rest on its earth. There in the hell of Hilterism they remained, sharing the gruesome fate of their brothers.

I do not know what happened to each of them, but they breathed out their souls in the multifarious inhuman suffering and shared in the fate of the millions of martyrs in Poland – may my modest words about them serve as a bouquet of flowers on their unknown graves.

Honor their memory!   **Tel Aviv, May 1944**

* One of the Zionist workers who saved himself in time in *Eretz Yisroel* was Yakov Yehoshua Kohn.

Anonymous *Landsleit*[1]

by Bela Goldwirt

I became acquainted in the Belgian capital of Brussels with three people from Czenstochow who made a deep impression on me. Such people remain in one's memory for a long time.

Faygele Berliner

They were Faygele Berliner, Leon the shoemaker and his friend Sala. No one knew the family names of the last two. They registered with the Belgian police with various names, but none were the correct ones.

I was told that Sala's father was a well-to-do person in Czenstochow. He had a dried fruit business there. Sala graduated from a *gymnazie* (high school) at home [in Czenstochow].

She was small and silent like a quiet chick, but she quietly spread illegal literature, recruited members for *Patronat* [assistance for political activists in Poland] and collected money for the Red Aid [International Red Aid – an organization that provided aid to political prisoners].

She and Leon were arrested and deported from the country many times, but they always stole across the border again, returning to Brussels and continuing their work.

Leon saved himself from police hands in Poland and left. Sala went with him. They still had money for expenses until [they reached] Czechoslovakia. They could not remain there, so they left on foot for Belgium.

They arrived in one German state with a few *pfennigs* in their pockets – it was before Hitler came to power – enough to buy a quarter of a pound of bread. It was more than a few days since they had eaten. They entered a bakery and showed the German woman the few *pfennigs* – all that they possessed. They told her that they were very hungry. The German woman was not ashamed, she cut a thin, small slice of bread, weighed it, not a hair more than for the few *pfennigs*. Leon and Sala looked despairingly at the thin, small slice of bread; who would take a bite of it first and how would it satisfy them?

[Page 368]

They walked for several weeks. It was summertime; they fed themselves with greens from the fields. They gathered wood, made a fire and roasted potatoes.

They arrived in Brussels with swollen feet. There, too, they were threatened with arrest and being deported every day. However, this did not stop them from carrying out their work.

Leon was a little taller than average, broad boned, in his 30s. The look in his eyes was of calm goodness. On his earnest face with its pointed jaw, with his strong flattened nose and with his wrinkled brow lay his firm determined character. He was not a big talker but the words he did say were reasonably thought through and consistent.

Leon the Shoemaker (*Inzelsztajn*) (the first one from the left in Brussels, Belgium) with a Group of Comrades

When the Civil War in Spain broke out in 1936 he was one of the very first to go to fight against Fascism. He distinguished himself greatly and fell in battle.

Faygele Berliner was no less interesting. The first time I entered her small room under a roof with the bent walls made an unforgettable impression on me. The only little window lay in the ceiling and looked straight into the sky. The cleanliness shone from every corner. The walls were decorated with small and large pictures. There was a cabinet in a corner on which stood amateurish knick-knacks. Faygele was just finishing her dinner. Her face appeared delicate and full of love of the world in the light from a small lamp.

Her pitch-dark hair was divided in the middle by a part; on the sides lay still, docile waves like in a calm river. Her cheeks – like red blossoms. There was a deep goodness in her charming eyes and there was a dear smile on her lips.

She did not expect anyone that evening, but how beautifully and exact she had set the table for herself! A plate with a piece of cheese, a glass butter dish with butter, a flowered serving dish of sardines and a salt-box stood on a clean, pressed colored tablecloth. A piece of bread lay in a pretty, wicker basket. On the side lay a napkin of the same color as the tablecloth. A small vase of flowers stood in the middle of the table. Her patience and care in beautifying and preparing the table for herself alone evoked [my] delight and admiration of her.

Faygele took the burden of communal work on herself so precisely and patiently. She was quietly and modestly devoted to the progressive workers movement with her whole heart. She went to the meetings and carried out her duties with deep devotion.

Translator's footnote

1. *Landsleit* is the Yiddish word for people from the same town.

The Malarskis
The History of a Czenstochower Family
A. Chrobolowski

Avraham Malarski, the father, was born in the *shtetl* [town] Sejny, Suwalki *gubernia* [province]. His mother was the daughter of a religious judge, his father, Zelig, the son of a blacksmith who was known in the entire Suwalki area because he once had the opportunity to shoe the horses of Nikolai the First. For his good work he was freed from paying taxes.

[Page 369]

At age three, Avraham was left without a mother. He was raised in the home of his grandfather, the religious judge, until he took him with him to Nowy Dwór, Warsaw *gubernia* [province]. He became an apprentice to a rope maker, worked at a spinning wheel 14 hours a day and suffered from hunger and cold.

At age 21, he married Sheyndl Tac, a daughter of Eliezer and Bluma Tac in Nowy Dwór. Sheyndl's parents, her grandfather and grandmother of the Czenstochower Malarskis, traded with orchards and meadows around the Vistula [River] and ran a diary farm.

Avraham Malarski left the rope maker and became a harness maker. At the time his father Zelig, who had previously been an employee in the Nowy Dwór fortress, became the owner of several buses that took passengers and goods to Warsaw and back.

The first two children in the family, Yudl and Royza, were born in the house of their grandfather, Eliezer. Sheyndl, the mother of the Malarskis, being a mother of two children [Yudl and Royza] and still only 20 years old, had not yet made peace with her place in her parents' house. She was drawn to another life.

Leibush Berman, a son-in-law in her extensive family, was a model for her. The grandmother Yokheved, who took care of orphans and abandoned children in the city, had found him near the bathhouse driven from his house by his step-parents. She raised and educated him, married him off to her daughter and had great pleasure from him. At first he became a bookkeeper, then became a supplier of food to the military at the fortress. His children studied in Warsaw. One of his daughters took part in the First Zionist Congress in Basel. She [the daughter] would tell her cousin Sheyndl of her experiences in the wider world. This made a strong impression on Sheyndl who was more of a *dorfs-maidel* [a girl from a village].

In time, however, Sheyndl, in devotion to her husband, the modest rope-maker, Avraham Malarski, brought an entire generation of ten children into the world. Four sons and six daughters. They moved to Czenstochow, then to America. They acquired a good reputation among the Czenstochow Jews.

The Malarskis in Czenstochow

Of the 10 Malarskis, only one, Moshe (Morris), was born in Czenstochow. The remaining, Eidl, Royza, Dovid, Chaim Shlomo, Chaya Ruchl, Hodes, Yeta and Leah (Lina), were born in Nowy Dwór. With the help of their grandfather Eliezer and particularly from their grandmother Bluma who had an ingenuous way of helping to count the money that came in payment in the hundreds for the winter fruits... The family, which then already consisted of 11 souls, the parents and nine children, succeeded in moving to Czenstochow. Dovid became a locksmith. The remaining older children went to work in the factories and workshops where the poor children of Czenstochow were employed. In 1901 Eidl Malarski, a tinsmith by trade, married a Czenstochow girl and settled there. A little later he found a position for his father, Avraham, at the harness-making division of the artisans school.

Their first experience in Czenstochow was the pogrom of 1902. The family lived then in a house at the *Talmud-Torah* [religious school for needy boys] and they hid with all of their neighbors on the fourth floor of the brick house where the pogromists' stones did not reach. The father was in Radomsk then. When he returned home the pogrom has passed.

They moved to the old market in the courtyard of the Sheiketes' house in the same year, late in the autumn. The new apartment had two entrances; one from the courtyard through the old market; the other (the ceremonial...) through the window and alley to Warszawer Street, or through Horowicz's coal warehouse.

The residence was a dark one. The sun never reached it. The walls never dried from the dampness. The workshop with all kinds of leather goods on the walls filled the house with the smell of raw leather. However, with the beginning of the liberation movement in 1904-1905, a great light of hope and struggle for a better life arose from the house and spread through all of the corners of the Jewish neighborhood in Czenstochow. The Malarski's house was the center of the Socialist-Zionist movement, which enveloped Czenstochow like a forest fire.

The dark attic over the residence neighboring Bluma the "filthy one," always noisy and full of rags, was the warehouse for weapons and the place to hide oneself. Various frames trimmed with colorful paper laces hung in the house and behind them hidden with bricks were hidden packs of literature. Red flags were hidden in an entirely different hiding place near the oven. There were two ovens in the house, one made of tin for cooking. The other one was brick. And the second one was never heated. It served for important purposes...

[Page 370]

The [sound of the] crack of a revolver shot often carried from the house. The revolvers were being tested in the dark attic. The revolvers often fired when they were being greased with oil and when there were being cleaned. Once the bullet flew by a group of children in the house who were eager to watch what the adults were doing. The children fell in fear like dolls.

One of the couriers who would bring the weapons to where they were needed was the red-haired, quiet but fearless Hodes (Safa). She would place half a dozen revolvers in her apron, throw on a kerchief and leave for the designated place.

A wagon often would arrive at night at the "ceremonial" entrance, that is, through the alley to the window near the coal warehouse, and off-load sacks and packs just then smuggled through the heavily patrolled border. The father, Avraham Malarski, would hide them in holes under the floor and cover them with dirt.

In the morning, the mother, Shayndl, would drag two baskets of fresh rolls for the rich middle class in the city. This was of help because of the poor earnings of her husband. However, there were other things in the baskets under the rolls...

Eidl lived in Blachownia [a town 10 kilometers from Czenstochow] and worked in a factory there. It was only seven miles from there to the heavily patrolled border, through which went transports of arms and literature. He would come to the city [Czenstochow] on Sunday. Then the Malarski's house would be very crowded with people who would come together to discuss very important things...

The police attacked the house very often at night, searched and rummaged in every corner and usually found nothing. They would turn over the wardrobes and throw the children out of the beds. Shayndl already was accustomed to this and had her method of how to open the suitcases that had been left by comrades who passed through and show the boxes full of old pieces of leather from her husband's work.

We could write many, many pages demonstrating the unassuming heroism and martyrdom of one of the Jewish mothers of a revolutionary family of that time. Shayndl, the mother of the Marlaskis, was an example.

One of the louts, who demanded "payment" for a place at the old market, honored her with such a slap in the face that no one dared to intervene. She very often had to fight with the police chief and his assistants on behalf of her arrested children and she turned to another method: diplomacy. There were several Malarskis, *kein ayin hore* [no evil eye – said to ward off an evil eye]. For example, once when Eidl was arrested after the explosion of a bomb at Stancia Streeet, they reasoned with the police chief that Marlarski-the-revolutionary was abroad and the arrested Malarski was completely innocent. He was a married man and led a quiet life with his wife and child. (Eidl, the "quiet one," as a tinsmith prepared things that exploded with such a boom that it shook the entire city.) When Eidl already was in America, she turned her "diplomacy" to another side and defended Dovid.

In addition to her children, she was the mother to dozens of other revolutionary activists who hid in the attic in her house. Many had to be sneaked across the border. Many needed to receive *ful-paskes* (certificates to cross the border). One of those, who often looked for protection from her, was Ahron the red-haired one (Ahron Singalowski). Once he arrived unexpectedly at the house on Friday, right at the time to light the candles, pursued by the police. Shayndl interrupted the candle lighting and hid Ahron somewhere.

The greatest misfortune occurred when she was running around, fell and broke a leg. She walked with crutches for a long time. Her leg healed badly and she suffered terrible pains. During the same winter, Dovid, who worked illegally in another city, was arrested and was brought to Czenstochow in a procession of prisoners under escort. With the help of the crutches, Shayndl went to the barracks in a horse-drawn carriage to see Dovid. Mass arrests had taken place after the bomb explosion on Warszawer [Street] in the summer of 1906. A large number of visitors came to [visit] the arrestees, among them Shayndl. During the great tumult, she and Dovid mixed in among the visitors and left in freedom. After this, she, with the help of Eidl, who was sending money from America, went to Breslau to have an operation on her foot. After the operation, she went to her father at the orchards near the Wisla [Vistula River].

[Page 371]

They could not rest completely there. Dovid, who was supposed to be abroad, was caught at a Socialist Zionist printing shop on the first floor [in European usage, this was the second story] of a house on Krutka Street. He and the printer jumped out of the window. The police shot after them. Both successfully escaped. The news reached Shayndl. She already was suffering from diabetes as a result of a difficult and troubled life. Dovid left for America the same summer and settled in Chicago.

Dovid Malarski

Dovid Malarski belongs among those whose names become legends.

He was a locksmith by trade. His entire learning both in *kheder* [religious primary school] and as a locksmith took place in Nowy Dwór. He came to Czenstochow in 1902 and immediately after his arrival he joined the first working group organized by the Socialist Zionists. The workers movement in general and the Socialist Zionists in particular then consisted of a few individuals. Dovid Malarski really was the one who led the masses with the stubbornness of a pioneer, the fearlessness of a revolutionary and the enthusiasm of a child for whom a new world and a new ideal of life are revealed.

His great virtues as a revolutionary did not consist of words but of deeds. The most difficult and most dangerous work was entrusted to him: taking illegal literature across the borders; sending the literature to other places; organizing self defense [groups]; protecting the group with espionage; support for the Jewish population against pogroms; the organization of printing shops and the terrible work in the printing shops. Dovid Malarski's hand was in all of them.

Watched and chased by Tsarist spies and police in Czenstochow, he would disappear over the horizon for a while and then immediately appear again when a printing press failed or another extraordinary event happened.

He was there with the typesetter from Piotrkow when the police uncovered the Socialist Zionist printing shop on the first floor of the house on Krutka Street. Dovid jumped down unhurt from the window onto Krutka Street. However, the "one chosen from all people" sprained an ankle jumping and could not run. Under the fire of the police, Dovid ran back to the spot where his comrade lay and carried him away to a safe place.

In America he tried to extinguish his fiery temperament with education. He studied, went to college. He also was active in the Socialist Zionists and in the school movement.

A serious illness that had attacked him years earlier tore him away from communal work where he is now greatly missed.

Leah (Lina) Malarski

She came to Czenstochow while still a child, but brought with her the strong impression of her birth city of Nowy Dwór which was as large as a walk from one grandfather to another; [memories] of a visit to her Grandmother Bluma who lived on the Piasek [street name] and always served sour milk and sweet *challah* [Sabbath bread]; [it was] quite separate from her grandfather's orchard where one could eat the most beautiful fruits that fell from the trees and where the entire family – large and small – which consisted of some seventy grandchildren would gather on *Shabbos* [the Sabbath].

Leah received her first education in Moshe Mordekhai's *kheder* [religious primary school]. The *rebbitzen* [rabbi or teacher's wife] taught Hebrew from a *Siddur* [prayer book] with a pointer and helped [the students] recite the Hebrew words. Tuition was five *gildn* a month. The *rebbitzen* rewarded [the students] with a small candy for bringing the few *gildn*.

Then she studied writing and reading and she carried a notebook and story book, *Russkaja Rech* [Russian] with her.

Later her father himself, because of the poverty in the home, taught her while he worked.

In 1904-1905 the intelligentsia in Czenstochow from the *Freiheit* [Freedom] movement organized small educational groups in private houses. Leah studied in a small group at the house of a dentist. The poor children would be treated with tea and *ciates* (small cakes) in the wealthy house. This was a kind of earthly heaven for the children...

Leah helped her mother earn a living while still a very young child, carrying the baked goods to the rich middle-class women. She would usually carry a small basket. When her mother broke a leg, she [Leah] and another sister dragged the large baskets that might have been bigger than she was.

[Page 372]

She was often sent with a basket of food to Eidl in Blachownia. She would carry back baskets of things that were a secret to her. [She took] the road to the train that was then a little outside the city, then [she took] the train itself to Ostrow and from Ostrow [she went] in the forest to Blachownia, which was a powerful experience of joy and fear for her.

Once her father waited for her at the train and with a horse drawn coach. This was a great mystery to her... A few days later a bomb was thrown on Warszawer Street.

The Constitution of October 1905 was for her as if a great holiday had fallen from heaven. Therefore, the winter with house-searches and arrests, which increased right after this [the issuance of the Constitution], was doubly difficult for her. The mother and her daughter [Leah] often would be stopped in the street by the military police and searched...

It must be added that these were the experiences of a child of eight to 10 years old.

The Malarskis in America

The family's emigration to America began in 1906. Eidl left first, then Dovid. The third to go was Avraham Malarski himself, then already an upholsterer. Chaim Shlomo, the third son, who had just returned from military service and brought along a wife, came next. Then three sisters came: Chaya Ruchl, Hodes and Chana. After them came the oldest sister, Royza, and her two small children, Meir and Zelda. The two youngest children in the family, Yenta and Moshe, came with her. The last to go were Shayndl, the mother, and Leah (Lina). This was in 1910.

Everyone settled in Chicago. This was the happiest meeting of the entire family, which had been for years scattered and spread; some in military service, some in prison and some in America.

Their house was always full. Two sisters got married during the year of their arrival. All of the other children had friends. The house was always open to everybody. The dining room looked like a familiar inn. Sadly, it did not last l ong. The diabetes that Shayndl, the mother, had beaten back at home (in Poland) came to America with her. She left this world on 18 May 1913, leaving a deep melancholy over a previously lively house and Moshe, an 11-year old child.

Avraham Malarski lost his job and moved to a small town in Indiana with his two youngest children.

Eidl died in 1925. And Chaim Shlomo died in 1931. However, the large Malarski family in America branched out further, increased [in size] and continued the work here with devotion to the ideals brought from the old home.

Eidl had organized the landsleit [people from the same town] here and was the first chairman of the Nowy Dwór Aid Union.

For many years, Dovid was the most active Socialist Zionist worker here – later he was active in IKOR [Organization for Jewish Colonization in Russia] and in the Sholem Aleichem Institute.

Royza, Chaya Ruchl and Hodes were active in the parents' union of the Sholem Aleichem School and in the Nowy Dwór Aid Union.

Leah (Lina) belonged to the left Poalei-Zion [Workers of Zion] in Chicago, was active in IKOR and was one of the first members of the Czenstochower Patronat [organization to aid political arrestees in Czenstochow] for the political arrestees and also was the provisional secretary of the organization when Graman left for New York. She belonged to the Fraternal People's Order and was active in the parents' committee of the Order's schools.

The third and fourth generations of the Malarski family here consists of 23 grandchildren and seven great grandchildren. Almost all have studied in Yiddish secular schools. Royza's children, Max and Zelda, the oldest grandchildren, studied at the first National-Radical School of the Socialist Zionists in America, of which Dovid was one of the original founders. The younger ones studied at the Arbeter-Ring [Workman's Circle] Schools. Dovid's and Chaya Ruchl's children studied at the Sholem Aleichem Schools. Beverly, Lina's daughter, studied at a People's Order School.

All of the Malarskis without exception have taken part in the aid work for Czentochow. Malarski's grandchildren also have taken part in this work. One of them is Zelda, Eidl's daughter.

In 1923, a banquet was organized with the help of Lina, Dovid, Hodes (Safa) Royza and Zelda at the departure of Friend Chrabalowski for Czenstochow. And with Dovid the toastmaster they succeeded with his extraordinary energy to collect $200 for the Y.L. Peretz Folks-School in Czenstochow.

The family chronicle of the Malarskis would not be complete without the history of the youngest son, Moshe (Morris).

[Page 373]

Morris Miller

The "unease" of the Malarskis would not let him rest. [He lived] in a small town in Indiana with his father. He joined the American Army at the age of 16 during the First World War under the name Morris Miller.

After the war he joined the Navy, became a sailor and sent letters to his father from distant places with the signatures of rabbis [testifying] that he had not forgotten to recite *Kaddish* [memorial prayer] for his mother. When he returned home after a long time of wandering, he was like a stranger among the family. He had almost forgotten the Yiddish language. The only Yiddish words he still remembered were: "*Veyst Tata*" ["Do you know, father?"]. He did not know any more. His father, Avraham, would answer him: "*Ikh veys, ikh veys*" ["I know, I know"]. He meant: "You are lost among the family."

However, he returned... This was during the years of the Depression. The Malarskis were active in the ranks of the left. He [Morris] was drawn to the movement. He began to study in the workers' schools. He studied political economy, Marxism and so on. He appeared at the mass meetings and inspired his listeners.

He also was active in the workers' theater and had great success in the sketch, "Waiting for Lefty." He won a scholarship (stipend) to study dramatic arts and became very popular with his character roles.

He took part in the March on Washington as a veteran of the First World War and was the leader of a column. The newspapers gave him a great deal of publicity then and Morris Miller rose to leadership.

He changed completely and married and became attached to the family. He worked as a fireman at the Inland Steel Company in Indiana during the Second World War and is now involved in theater and communal activity.

The Malarskis took part in the Second World War with a grandson, Joe (Zelig) Malarski-Goodman, Clara's son (he is in the photograph with his son, a great grandson of the Malarskis).

However, during the prelude to the Second World War, in the Spanish Civil War, Chaim Miller, Dovid Malarski's son, left his university where he was studying chemistry and left for Spain to join the Loyalists.

The Malarski family is described here, not as an exception, but as an example of the life of our people.

Shayndl Malarski

Avraham Malarski

Chaim Shlomo Malarski

Hodes Malarski

Morris Malarski

Eidl Malarski

[Page 374]

From My Life

by Rafal Federman

My environment, Czenstochow, my home city, was savagely annihilated by the German beasts; all of my closest family members, hundreds of friends and comrades with whom I lived and struggled for a better and more humane world, did not even obtain any kind of burial place on this earth. Therefore, let my memories serve as a *Kaddish* [memorial prayer].

My Childhood

In general, I did not know my grandfathers. I only knew my Grandmother Rywka on my mother's side. Her maiden name was Rudnik. She lived with my parents for many years and helped in the work of earning a living.

My father, Dovid, was employed in the whiskey warehouse of Kruk, the father of the well-known socialist activist, Dr. Josef Kruk. The whiskey warehouse was located in Kruk's own house on Tilne Street (later Straczacke).

My father was dressed long [he wore a traditional kaftan], but already wore a stiff collar [was more modern]. He trimmed his beard. He prayed in the Rozprza *shtibl* [one-room house of prayer, usually associated with a Hasidic rebbe] and traveled to the Rozprza Rebbe for advice when he found himself in a critical situation. My mother, Gitl, ran a tavern on Garncarska Street in German Holer's house.

I was born in the house where the tavern was located. The records of birth dates for all of the children were written into some sort of Yiddish book. The exact hour was even shown. The book no longer exists and I take my birth date according to the official Russian and, later, according to the Polish passport: 24 March 1892. It appears that I was not entered correctly. My father later reminded me that he had done it because of my older brother, Zalman, for whom he thought that in order to have definite relief from the draft he should be too many years older than me.

When a law was issued that Jews could not own taverns with whiskey, we moved to the other corner of Garncarska Street, near the old market, near the old synagogue and *beis-hamedrash* [house of prayer], in Bentkowska's house. My father lost his long-time position with Kruk because of the whiskey monopoly, but because he had Kruk's protection, he received permission to open a beer tavern (without whiskey). This tavern was found in Bentkowska's house.

My Mother, Gitl

The struggle for income was difficult. My mother; Hinda, my older sister; Fraydl, my youngest sister; and even my grandmother Rywka; worked hard in order to earn a livelihood for the entire household. My brother, Yeshayahu, studied in the *beis-hamedrash* and my brother, Zalman went to school and was preparing to enter Retke's *pro-gymnazie* [preparatory school for entry into secondary school]. I, the youngest of the sons, went to the *kheder* [primary religious school] of Yehiel Sh... (this was how we referred to him) and later to Meir Gliksman on Warszawer Street in Goldman's house and still later to Feywl Avigdor, who prayed in the same *shtibl* [one-room prayer house] as my father.

Rafal Federman

There in the *kheder*, which consisted of only a few students, I became friends with Leyzer Berkowicz, with whom my friendship endured until the ripest youth. The *kheder* was located on Garjeszne Street not far from the crates near the "Warta." During the winter I would go to *kheder* with a lit lantern in the morning when it was still dark.

I was very obedient and pious as a child. When my mother did not have time to say a blessing with me, I would run in to our neighbor, Reb Itamar Joskowicz, a Jew with a white beard, with large eyeglasses on his nose; he looked like a rabbi. He said the blessing with me. Otherwise, I did not want to taste anything. He loved me very much and had a great influence on me.

[Page 375]

I went with my father to pray in the Rozprza *shtibl* and often also went to the rebbe in Rozprza. Of the men in the *shtibl*, those who remain in my memory are the men who recited the prayers on the holidays, Yekl Kelcziglowski, Reb Itshe Meir Frank – the father of my friend, Shmuel Frank – Moshe Shabtai, the usual *gabbai* [assistant to rabbi], with whom the rebbe lived when he came to Czenstochow. I most strongly remember Reb Itshe Meir Frank, a tall Jew, always with a pipe in his mouth. His business was selling hides and he recited the prayers in the *shtibl*, which was located in his own house. He would pray *musaf* [supplementary *Shabbos* and holiday prayer] and he also blew the *shofar* [ram's horn]. His sons, Josef and Shmuel helped him as choirboys.

I remember a case when his oldest son, with a fine, long face and curled *peyos* [side curls], who was then a grown man, did not obey him and he received a slap. One of his teeth fell out. From then on I was very afraid of Reb Itshe Meir. Reb Yekl was a wide Jew, happy, a singer and good-natured. I remember him best from his *Shimkhas-Torah* [autumn holiday celebrating the completion of the annual Torah reading] dance; his ecstasy transported me. As young as I was, I was also well known for my *Shimkhas-Torah* dance, a *kozak* [Cossack dance]. Year in, year out, the finale of the Hasidim's dancing in the *shtibl* was: "Fulthsa (that is what I was called) will dance a *kozak*!"

All of the children from the *shtibl*, as well as Shmuel Frank, befriended me because of my dancing success. He stuck to me although he was more of a scholar than me. Perhaps I was popular because the barrels of beer were bought from us for all of the meals concluding *Shabbos* and we often dragged the barrels of beer from the tavern into the *shtibl*.

After me were two more sisters, Tsirl and Rayzele. I do not exactly remember their births; I remember them only as something foggy, where my mother lay in childbirth with the youngest, with Rayzele. Therefore, I remember very well when Rayzele, a gorgeous little girl of 4 or 5, suddenly became ill with scarlet fever and died immediately after. This was a great misfortune in the house. My mother and father did not permit me to go to the funeral. I remember that for years my father and particularly my mother did not go to sleep until they had had a good cry over the great misfortune. I remember how I would go to the old cemetery and would look for hours at the small headstone on which was written, "Here lies Rayzele Federman" and the dates of her birth and death. Therefore I had even stronger love for my younger sister, Tsirl.

Our material situation was not great. Although we had a tavern, even a piece of herring was something important for us. My mother would divide only the leftover head or tail of the herring for us. We had to eat a roll without butter. The usual fear of the *smotshikes* (inspectors) was great. Whiskey was also sold secretly in our tavern. My mother or my oldest sister would carry the bottle of whiskey under their aprons and it was sold only to Jews or well-acquainted Christians. The inspectors often sniffed the glasses, wanting to find out if there was whiskey in them. And it happened that bribes would cost a considerable amount to have "the sin erased."

My father despised the constant fear with this situation and in every way he looked for a new, more respectable income.

My Father Wins the Lottery

Once, on a winter morning, when I arrived at *kheder*, my rabbi, Feywl Avigdor, greeted me with an expansive "Good morning and gave me a *Mazel Tov* [congratulations]. I did not understand what this meant and thought that the teacher was making fun of me, but the rabbi and the *rebbitzen* [rabbi's wife] told me earnestly that my father had won the grand prize in the lottery. I did not want to believe this, but they assured me that it was true because the shoemaker who lived in the cellar of the same house had also won with the same lottery ticket that was divided among a group of neighbors.

I got up immediately and ran home at full speed, telling my parents the good news. Arriving at home, I found my mother fixing the oven in the kitchen and my father was getting ready to go down to the tavern (we lived over the tavern, on the first floor). My father listened to me and said to me the words: "Go my child, back to *kheder*. If it was true that I won the grand prize in the lottery, I would have been told, and, in addition, I do not have any receipt. I play there at Yehoshaya Leyzer's on a note something like a half ruble. He was here with me last night and said nothing to me about it. Evidently, the 'stake' was won (the amount invested), so people are saying, the grand prize!"

[Page 376]

Mournfully I returned to *kheder* with my heart embittered by the rabbi because he had fooled me. However, the rabbi again assured me that he had not made any kind of joke and that people knew better, that if it was being said, then it was true. He just suspected that perhaps my father would not admit it about his grand prize, not to be arrogant about it.

I went home with my friend, Leyzer Berkowicz, after studying lessons for several hours to grab something to eat. Getting closer to the house, I noticed that the tavern was closed. I understood that something had happened and I had the idea that it was true, that my father had won the grand prize.

I found my mother tearful at home and my father occupied as if he were preparing for something. To my question of whether the news I brought in the morning was true, my mother's crying grew louder and my father came to me and with wet, teary eyes, he hugged me and kissed my head saying to me: "It is true, Fultshe, you were the first to tell us the joyful news!" And I, myself, also broke out in a loud cry and I, therewith, expressed my resentment that they did not want to believe me earlier. "I immediately knew that the rabbi would not fool me!" – I cried out.

This was the only kiss that I remember my father giving me, although he loved my very much. He always was delighted with me, when I danced the *kozak* in the *shtibl* on *Shimkhas-Torah*.

I did not return to *kheder* that day. I only ran back to the rabbi to tell him it was true. We were partners in a grand prize, that my father had a receipt for an entire ruble. The rabbi again wished me *mazel-tov* and told me to bring cake and whiskey to *kheder* the next day.

There was turmoil in the house as in a kettle. People came; they talked secretly and spoke loudly; my father was congratulated and negotiations began about the size of my father's portion of the winnings. A long time passed until an understanding was reached about how much was in our portion. I only remember that my father took me along to the negotiations and made calculations with me. My father's portion was supposed to be more than 3,000 rubles, but they did not want to give more than 2,000 rubles. I only remember that I made a "speech" at the "meeting" (my first speech) and with my calculations showed that much more was coming to us and I protested against the sin (my first protest against sins) that they wanted to do to my father. My words helped because we were paid a hundred rubles more. Yehoshaya Leyzer said later to my father that he only gave the hundred rubles because of me and he asked that the remaining partners should learn of this.

Dozens of Jews were comforted by the grand prize. They all took part in the same ticket. These were the largest winnings with a prize from the Braunschweiger Lottery that fell on Czenstochow. I still remember the number of the ticket – 52935.

The winnings brought joy and great hope in our house. My father paid debts and thought about ways to put away a dowry and make a match for my oldest sister, Hinda, and about ways to better our income.

The conduct in relation to the education of the children changed a little in our home. My older brother, Zalman, who had earlier studied with Zlatnik, entered Retke's *pro-gymnazie* and I again took after my friend, Leyzer Berkowicz and entered the *Narodnoje Ucziliszcze* (People's School), directed by Leder – the teacher for many years.

During the several weeks I went to the school in the *Wstepne* (initial training), I had to endure much trouble from my friends in the *shtibl* [one room prayer house]. When I came to pray with my father on *Shabbos*, they accused me of becoming a "gentile." I took off my short jacket, my cap with the shiny visor and put back on my long kaftan and again began to study with Feywl Avigdor with great zeal. Every *Shabbos* morning I studied a bit of *Gemara* at home; *Maariv* [afternoon service], it was the Torah portion and my parents beamed with joy and bragged about me, saying that I was growing to be a young genius.

The Pogrom

The pogrom in our city in 1902 was a shock for my childish soul.

[Page 377]

I was then around nine years old. Even today, frightening images float before my eyes: all of the shops were closed at night. Windowpanes were knocked out of Jewish windows. The neighbors and the mistress of the house, Bentkowska, who was acquainted with us, calmed all of us. Suddenly a large stone hit the window of our house and the windowpane was broken into small pieces. We began to move along the wall. The mistress of the house lit candles and put crosses in the windows. Each time, the master of the house, Bentkowska's husband, ran into the street and brought back the news from there. However, I had the impression that he himself was helping with the pogrom and, ostensibly, from time to time, came to calm us. Several hours later, opposite our house, on the next corner, in the coffee-roaster Szmulewicz-Hasenfeld's house, a band of gentile boys ran in and looted the store and set it on fire. Through a window in our house we saw a red glare and the grieving among us became greater.

In the middle of the night we heard several shots. It was calm in the city. Bentkowski, the master of the house, came running breathlessly and told us that we should sit calmly; the Russian soldiers were shooting. There were wounded in the streets. I took my youngest sister, Tsyrl, with me and went to Piotrkow to my Aunt Hinde Staszewski, my mother's sister. Several days later in Piotrkow, my sister became sick with scarlet fever and had a high fever. I felt guilty because I had taken her away from home. My father and mother came quickly to Piotrkow and wanted to send me home so that I would not be infected. However, in no way did I want to leave my sick little sister's bedside. I finally returned to Czenstochow when my little sister could get up from her bed.

Several days later there was again talk about a pogrom in the city. I was so afraid that I began to beg my parents to send me away somewhere.

Tsyrl. my little sister, later we called her Tsheshe, went to Wolf Yakov Szacher's school as a child. [He was] a tall, wide Jew with a long, wide, beautifully cared for beard. My mother had also studied with this teacher.

The Fire in Landau's Factory

A giant fire in Landau's celluloid factory made a great impression in our city. Around five to six girls were burned there, a number of them from Garncarska Street where we lived. The funerals took place from there in which thousands of people took part. Speakers stood on the shoulders of the surrounding people. I swallowed every word. I went to the cemetery in secret, without the knowledge of my parents, along with the thousand-headed multitude and there cried along during the burial.

The flaming gold young man with the long face still stands alive before me and his Lithuanian Yiddish speech still rings in my ears. This was Ahron Czenstochower (the blond Ahron), today Dr. Ahron Singalowski, the general secretary of ORT [*Obshestvo Remeslenofo zemledelcheskofo Truda*– Society for Trades and Agricultural Labor]. His words reached my soul and my brain.

I no longer went to *kheder*. I benefited from my brother Zalman, who went to the *progymnazie*, with a little Russian and arithmetic, and I attempted to to Leder's *Narodnoje Ucziliszcze*. I entered the second class. My teachers were Leder and Abner...

I Make Demands

Josef Zajdman and Lajzer Genendelman, my school friends, lived in the house at Dojazd 30, not far from Herczn's barracks. Our favorite pastime is school was playing soldiers. We drew almost all of the classes of the school into this play. We carried out wars and we gave gifts to those taking part. Everyone received a small book that cost from one to five *kopekes*. It was inscribed in the books that it was being given to him and him for good achievements in the battle. It was signed General Josef Zajdman and Colonel Rafal Federman. Zajdman was the practical one, because he knew the drills and I was the theoretical one.

We persuaded all of the students in the second division of the above-mentioned school that the black caps with the shiny peaks that we, the students wore were plain compared to the caps worn by the *gymnazie* students. Each would wear various colored ribbons and stars in the front of the cap. Therefore, we turned to the school inspector and asked that the students in the *Folks-Shul* [public school] also receive other uniforms and caps.

[Page 378]

The demand of the students was filled after long negotiations and after a personal visit by the school inspector to the school and several weeks later we all paraded in the *tabelny dens* [red-letter days] or in the *galuwkes* [celebration of a Czar's birthday or anniversary of his death] in caps of dark blue cloth circled in green. The form of hat also spread to the *Folks-Shuln* [public schools] in other cities.

I graduated from the second class with distinction. We desired greater things in the third class and I was always the organizer. The new request was that we learn Polish and Russian in school. In order to achieve this, I recorded all of the students in the class as "on duty," that they had done wrong and I also included I, myself. When the teacher entered the class and saw my report on the blackboard about the guiltiness of the students, he punished us with everyone having to stay in class after the lecture.

We were happy with this, because we then had the opportunity to issue our demands. The main one for us was Polish, the language of the country that the Russians had oppressed. We proposed German as a camouflage, giving as the reason that whereas we lived not far from the German border we needed to know the language of our neighboring country.

The teacher understood that this was an organized "mutiny" by the students and that the demands had a political component. This was at the time when student strikes took place in universities. The teacher punished us and reproached us over the course of two days. He reminded us that we were receiving our education entirely without cost; that we were poor people's children and if we did not calm down and give up our demands, the school would be closed.

He also sent for the children's parents and reported to them about this. The meeting was fatal; several students cried and the entire class gave up the demands.

I no longer appeared at the school after losing the strike. However, I did appear for the exams and graduated from the school with an award that consisted of some sort of small red Russian book. I explained not coming to school for a few months with the fact that my father was sick and I had to help in the house.

I Speak to the Governor

My father suffered from an illness for a long time and I helped earn income in the soda factory that my father ran at that time.

In order to open a soda-water factory, it was necessary to have special permission from the Piotrkow governor. My father had to present the best certificates of integrity and had to bear various denunciations on the part of the existing soda-water manufacturers. The highest local police official had to be *untershmirn mit "opsmen"* [smeared with "poison" – in other words, bribed], as the Jews said, so that all of the denunciations were removed. The police also constantly let my father know where the matter stood with higher authorities. My father squandered a great deal in order to receive permission for this undertaking on which he built his entire future. He was refused several times and he had great heartache because of this. His illness came from this.

The last hope to receive the permission was connected to me. I was sent to Piotrkow to my aunt and I, personally, went with her to the governor and asked for an audience with him. I stood with a *proszenia* (request) in my hand before the governor and asked that he grant us permission for the soda-water factory. I told him in Russian that I had come because my father was ill. When my aunt quietly advised that I should kiss the governor's hand I cried in front of him. The governor patted me on the head and said to me: "I would receive an answer in three days; all will be fine."

When I left the governor with my aunt, she said to me: "I have the impression that you have succeeded and let God help with what remains." And in three days, this was in the morning on *Shabbos*, the police commissioner of our street called to my father through the window and told him the joyful news that permission for him for the soda-water factory had come. My father left to pray with a beaming face of joy and in the belief that this was my good luck.

[Page 379]

We arranged the soda-water factory in the same courtyard in which we had the beer tavern, in the house of the Bentkowska. We carried the siphons of soda-water in a hand cart to the shops in the nearby streets. I helped my father instead of going to school. I learned how to make the gas with great interest. One had to be very careful at this work. A bottle could explode if the gas was not precisely made.

I was trained in the trade and it was left for me to do more than once. From time to time I also helped to push the hand wagon with the siphons of soda-water and to collect the money.

In time a law was issued that the soda-water factories could not be located in any inhabited houses. Our factory was moved to a neighboring house owned by Yankl Dawidowicz, who built a special small house with several rooms for the factory. According to the regulations, Jacob Ber Silver's *tshaynik* (tea house) was also located in the same house, where the Bundists would come together.

I Enter the Movement

In my free time, after work, I read a great deal. I read Russian, Polish and Yiddish. When the Russo-Japanese War began I devoured the newspapers with the news. From time to time I began to bring into the house the thin books, published on Bible paper [thin, lightweight paper], that I received from *kheder* friend Leyzer Berkowicz.

I began to go to the *birzshe*[1] that was located on Ogrodowa Street on the corner of the new market up to the *Kapeluszarnia* [hat factory]. The agitators at the *birzshe* were: "Mordekhai Kopertszki," Dilewski, a shoemaker with long hair and a fine intelligent countenance, "Ira," Dora Warszawski, Avraham Lemanski, Dzialowski, Avraham Kawa, Jarkowizne, quilter, "Doctor" Itshe Czanszinski and others. This was the *birzshe* of the *S.D.K.P.L* [Polish socialist party] (later communists), the Jewish group under the name "Czargonowo [*czargon* or jargon is a derogatory term for Yiddish] group." I was accepted in the organization and became an active member of it. The organization was divided into *dzielnicas* (quarters). There was also a Jewish quarter to which I did belong. Each quarter had its committee. From time to time conferences of all of the quarters took place. Koperczuk was the representative of the "Czargonowa group."

The Jewish *dzielnica* had its group gatherings from time to time. Kuperczuk (now in America, a union leader in the leftist movement) and Ira led the group. *Masuvkes* (mass meetings) would also often take place at which a delegate from the central committee appeared. The *masuvkes* took place in the Polish language and also in Yiddish, although very rarely. The more evolved workers were taught the Polish language. Several groups studied with Miss Bril (later the wife of Stanislaw Przicki, director of the Merchants and Manufacturers' Bank). Adolf Bril, who gave lectures of a higher level in the Polish language, was popular among the Jewish workers. He was famous as a theoretician of the party. Ira also very often taught and gave various readings in Polish. Leon Kapinski, who had just come from Germany, once held a *masuvke* in the forest in the Yiddish language. At that time a second *dzielnica* member conference took place to which comrade "Josef" Feliks Dzerzhinsky (famous after the Bolshevik Revolution as the head of the *Cheka* [secret police]) of the central committee came. A heated discussion took place at this conference about the above-mentioned *dzielnica* groups. I defended, and only in the Polish language, the point of national independence of the organization and the publication of literature in Yiddish against a series of other Jewish members of the intelligentsia.

Kuperczik was elected as a delegate to the first national conference of the Jewish group. After this conference, the publication began of *Di Royter Fan* [*The Red Flag*] and the brochure, *What Do We Want?* by Rosa Luxemburg and others.

Large discussion gatherings were also held very often in Wajnberg's celluloid factory where the representatives of various workers unions would appear. These gatherings remain very much in my memories. Ruwin Rubinsztajn of the *S.D.K.P.L.,* Ahron Signalowski (today the ORT worker, Dr. Signalowski), Benyamin, Golda, Litwakow – of the *S.S* [Zionist Socialists], Oril Flaszer, Lasal-Wladek – of the Bund, also took part. The gatherings were entirely instructive, interesting and were visited by hundreds of workers.

[Page 380]

As for my activity, I was the contact person with one of the Polish *dzielnicas* where I received the literature for the Jewish *dzielnica*, the newspapers, *Czerwony Sztandar* [*Red Banner*], *Przeglad Spoleczny* [*Social Review*] and the various proclamations for the Jewish *dzielnica*. It often happened that I also brought the literature from Warsaw for the entire region, that is, for Czenstochow and Zaglembie-Dambrowskie.

Here I will describe one such trip that was, incidentally, my first trip to Warsaw:

I changed into the clothing of my friend Leyzer Berkowicz, who dressed in a short jacket and a hat; I also took his passport and left on the trip. Arriving in Warsaw I went to an address that I had been given. From there I was taken to a confectioner's shop where a student was waiting for me. It should be understood that I did not know his name. He spoke to me briefly, and convinced that I was "kosher," he gave me another address where I went to receive literature. A Polish worker lived at this address. This was somewhere in the Wolya (a Polish working area in Warsaw). They drank a considerable amount there and I was also treated to a glass of whiskey and snacks. I barely tasted the whiskey because I was afraid of becoming drunk, jeopardizing my entire trip, which was complicated enough.

In my young brain, I remember, an unpleasant thought then sneaked in: how could I drink during such important and responsible illegal work? But I did not say anything, and took my "goods" that were packed in an elegant valise. I entered a *droshky* [open carriage] and went to the Warsaw–Vienna train station. On the way, a young man with a package had been stopped and from the *droshky* I saw how the police officer cut open the package with his sword and the entire package of literature was lost. A large crowd of eager people gathered around them and watched the incident. Possibly as a result, I escaped with my package of "goods."

The danger from this was not yet past. Police and gendarmes stood at the entrance of the train station as usual and they searched everyone the packages of everyone on whom fell a bit of suspicion. Therefore, when I arrived at the train station I spoke loudly, like a rich man, called a *nosilsacaik*(porter) to take my package from the *droshky* and in a loud voice I also ordered him to buy a second-class ticket on the "courier." First of all, I was freed from the package. Understand that if the porter was stopped I would not be.

I also moved away from the package in the train wagon. I sat on another seat and lay the package on a distant shelf. The careful action was not excessive because searches were often carried out in the train wagons. Thus I arrived in Czenstochow. The same procedure happened there: I took a porter, asked him to take the package to a *droshky* with which I rode in the direction of Stradom. Descending from the *droshky*, I left on foot for a nearby field as had been previously arranged and there placed the valise among the wheat. Several comrades arrived at a designated hour, took the valise and carried it to a house of a Polish worker. On the road, they had to avoid the border guards who often looked for contraband, because Czenstochow was close to the German border. They organized their own guard who went in front and when they noticed a patrol of border guards approaching, we were given a sign and we hid in a courtyard until the patrol passed.

After much hardship and gambling my freedom, the valise finally arrived at the designated address.

In addition to the local workers in the various factories, among whom I knew: Roman Wowczinski, Pietrek, Domanski and the intelligent Josef Olszewski, the sons and daughters of the assimilated Jewish intelligentsia also took part in the workers movement: the daughters of Yokhl Lerner, the Szwarces, Dadek Szajnweksler, Momloks, Senjar, Birnbaum, the German Khun's son. Of those from the intelligentsia sent from the central office, who would appear at the various mass meetings in the Czenstochow factories, I was acquainted with: Adam Kanrach, Bashke (Sholem Asch's sister-in-law, today a high official in the government in Moscow), Janek and Ksower.

[Page 381]

The storehouse of illegal literature could not be kept in the Polish areas. They were raided too often. The storehouse was moved to the Jewish quarter where it was quiet for over a year. A room at a Jewish baker was found across the bridge over the Warta in the so-called *Zawoja*. Leyzer Berkowicz was registered in this "cavalry residence." He did live there at first, but later the room was packed with various illegal publications, even several guns that the organization had the opportunity to acquire during an attack. Only a few comrades knew about this illegal book storehouse; the designated managers from the central office, Leyzer Berkowicz, Zelik Rotbard (the son of Itshe the stable owner) and me. From there, the illegal literature was divided among all of the Czenstochower factories and throughout the area.

However, finally the owner of the bakery, a Jew whose son, incidentally, was also in the movement, sensed what was happening in the rented room. However, he already was mixed up in the matter, was afraid for himself and he had to be quiet. But in time the police discovered the traces of the storehouse. They knew that the illegal literature that was found so often during searches and the proclamations came from *Zawoja*, but they did not yet know from which house. And they began tracking. They even once made a raid in the entire area and carried out searches of houses, but they searched the lime ovens that were next door.

In time the storehouse had to be liquidated by the organization. On a beautiful clear day, with the help of Nekhemia Warszawski, a Jewish worker from the Djubos soap factory, who drove up with a horse and wagon from the factory, all of the archives were taken and they moved them to the Pelcer and Son factory. A comrade of the organization worked there and he took it under his protection. The rest of the material that was not very needed was burned on the fields near the lime ovens during the course of two nights and a red glow covered the quiet sky. Only the Jewish organized workers of the *S.D.K.P.L.* knew about this.

There was also a case of a failed storehouse of illegal literature that has a connection to me:

My Failure and My Mother Is Arrested

In 1904-1905 I was strongly engaged in the illegal movement, although I simultaneously was the wage earner for my family. In 1905 my father died of stomach cancer at the age of 42 after a long illness that swallowed much money. My mother cried for years about his premature death. She would always say, "Thus the lottery money runs out..."

I became the wage earner and worked in the soda-water factory. There was a Polish worker there Pietrek. He was the main master craftsman in the factory and, under my influence, he became a member of the *S.D.* Party.

The Bundist "teahouse" was also in the courtyard of our factory, as mentioned above. I sat in the teahouse and was busier with party agitation and singing revolutionary songs than with working in the factory. In the attic over the factory, to which there was no staircase, but one needed to place a ladder, lay the balloons [gas containers] and broken soda water siphons and there I found the most appropriate place to hide the illegal literature. Several issues of *Der Royter Fon* [*The Red Flag*], the organ of the Social Democratic Party, the brochure, *Wos Wiln Mir?* [*What Do We Want?*] by Rosa Luxemburg and dozens of packs of other "unkosher goods" lay there. A number of these books were bound with the same binding as my legal books at home. If the police found both libraries they would immediately know who was their actual owner...

Once, on a cold, frosty winter night our factory was attacked by the police and a military division with the then police commissioner, Abruzow, in the lead, and they began a thorough search. They woke up our entire family (we lived in the neighboring house) and demanded the keys to the soda-water factory from us. The search also had to concern my mother; she was certain that she was responsible to God and calmly went along with the police. She laughed to herself at their foolishness: found a spot to look for illegal literature...

[Page 382]

But my soul almost rose [I almost died] from fear and dread. I went along to the factory. The police carefully went through all of the corners and did not find anything; Abruzow, the police commissioner, asked where is the ascent to the attic. It all became dark for me and I felt as if my feet were breaking under me out of fear.

– The entry to the attic is from the courtyard! – my mother calmly answered.

The police placed a ladder and several seconds later – they did not have to look for long – the commanding voice of the police commissioner was heard:

– *Vsiech arestovat!* (arrest everyone).

My mother began to lament and cry and she expressed her innocence, that the attic is open. There was not even a lock for it. She did not know about anything... and this was true. She really did not know about anything. I was the only one in our entire family who knew.

In the blink of an eye a flash came into my head; the remaining legal books at our home that were bound with the same binding as the illegal ones still could carry the particular traces. I decided that my books at home must be destroyed at any cost... But how?...

As the books from the attic began to fall down like rain and as the order came from the police commissioner: Arrest everyone, I maintained an innocent facial expression and moved closer to the police commissioner, who had come down from the attic with a triumphant look, and asked him, "Me, too?..."

– *Poshol van!* [go about your business] – the police commissioner shouted at me and gave me a resounding slap in the face.

I took the slap as an earned gift and quickly ran home. When I came into the house breathlessly, I gave a choked shout to my sister: "Take out all of the books!" My entire library collected with so much effort was immediately thrown into the toilet and – no more library!

My mother and Dawidowicz, the owner of the house, were taken to a small church. The entire city was electrified by this arrest. Everyone made a false accusation against the Bundist teahouse. Only I, unfortunately, knew the entire truth.

After several days in jail and after strong efforts, the governor punished my mother as well as the host of the house in an administrative manner with three months of arrest for having kept the attic open and, therefore, allowing it to become a nest of seditious literature. A sufficient sum of money was collected with great effort to pay for my mother's penalty so that my mother would not have to go to jail.

For many years, my sister and brothers blamed me at every opportunity: "This was your bit of work, Fultshe!…" However, they were not certain about this accusation. I confessed to them for the first time when Poland became independent and there was no longer any trace of the Tsarist gendarmes.

As I assumed then, Pietrek, the worker in the factory, had revealed the warehouse with illegal literature to a policeman while having a glass of whisky in the tavern. However, during the investigation, he did not say who had placed the packages of literature there. This saved me from years in prison.

[Page 384]

During the Reactionary Years

I returned home when the repressions in Czenstochow had quieted down a little. I obtained work in Moris Najfeld's pharmacy warehouse as an employee. My friend "Ira" (Doro Warszawska) worked there as a higher official; I felt a great deal of sympathy toward her. This was the time when the movement was dead. We read books, were embraced by a romantic mood. Dwoyra (Dorke Szacher), the daughter of my mother's teacher, Wolf Yankl Szacher, had a large place in my heart then. I gave her a great deal of time and energy so that she could climb the ladder of life and go along with the spirit of that time. I drew her into the communal life of the Jewish Literary Society, *Lira*. I interested her in the Yiddish theatrical art. Under my influence, she performed with success, in declamations and in theatrical pieces, but she had an inclination toward fantastic exaggeration and wanted to impress me with it. However, this had the opposite effect on me and I withdrew from her. Later, she was the wife of my party comrade, Yakov Yitzhak Czarnowiecki, who perished at Auschwitz.

[Page 385]

During our friendship, she was certain to be part of my life. At the same time, I also had a friend named Yetshe Pakula who went along our youthful path with our group. We often came together in her house. Her room was a modest one; her father, Mendl *Kowal* [the blacksmith], with his great love for his wife and children, created a warm atmosphere of love and friendship in his house. Mendl *Kowal* was the *Yekl der Shmid*[2] type. Ideas, feelings for a new life, were born in this house. Many friends and comrade came through this house, such as Mendl Szuchter (became the husband of his [Mendl *Kowal's*] daughter, Sheindl), Yehoshua Jakov Mientkewicz, Jakov Yitzhak Czarnowiecki, Elkone Chrachalawski and others. When Mendl *Kowal* died after an operation in a Warsaw hospital, his death left a deep tear in my soul. I felt as if I had lost my second home.

During the Time of the Renaissance of Jewish Literature

That was the time of the renaissance of Jewish literature. The Jewish Literary Society was founded as a contradiction to the existing assimilationist-Hebraic *Lira* [cultural group]. Sharp fights for Yiddish took place then. Then I also gave my first lecture about the Yiddish language and I even remember how I ended with a citation from a brochure that was written by the writer Sh. L. Kawa and how *toykhekhe* [chapter of Biblical curses] was heaped on those who were ashamed of Yiddish. A second lecture by Leon Kapinski, who defended Hebrew as the national language of Jews, took place as an answer to my lecture.

Mark Szweid and Miryam Izraels then came to Czenstochow. She was the wife of [Szymon] Kratka, the artist. This was a holiday time for us. I took part in several one-act plays by Peretz with them and under their direction. I looked at Miryam Izraels then as a biblical figure. She spent several months with small interruptions in our city. She was a visitor to Ahron Perec's house. I remember when she had to come from Warsaw for the second time. I already had a feeling of great sympathy for her at that time, but I never said anything to her about it. I waited for her at the train with a bouquet of flowers, but to my great despair she did not come that day. However I hid the flowers and I brought them to her at Ahron Perec's house.

It was warm in her company. She sincerely interpreted songs, playing on a box with metal plates and rhythmically dancing to the sound of the music. At the same time that she performed one-act plays in Yiddish, *Lira* invited her to perform [Gerhart] Hauptmann's *Khanusia* in Polish with Kuszminski as a partner.

My telling her the truth greatly irked her then. Yes, why was she performing in Polish and, yes, why was she giving more attention to the Polish partner than to me... Two photographs of her remain a keepsake for me. In one is seen her genteel biblical face in profile in a hat with a large original feather and in the second one she is sitting in a sports costume and Kuszminski is standing in front of her declaiming. I saved these photographs in my archive until the last day I was in Poland. Years later I met her by chance in Warsaw on the tramway as Maria Arciszewska. We spoke Polish to each other. Mendl Kowal's [a *kowal* is a blacksmith) son-in-law, Mendl Szuchter, and his wife and, later, Yecze Pakula left for America. A deep longing for a warm house that reminded me of the struggles of my youth remained.

I met Yeta[3] Pakula, a sincere and unforgettable comrade, years later when I came to America. She was very active in Los Angeles in the *Poalei-Zion* movement. I also met her 82-year old mother with her. I again felt the warmth of my youth in Czenstochow in her house. The love and humane warmth of Mendl Kowal floated in her house.

I Travel to Vienna to the Territorialist Conference

At a time when the reaction began to ease its restraint, Comrade Berl Gutman appeared as an emissary from the Central Committee of the Socialist-Zionist party and a group of Socialist-Zionist followers was called together. The gathering took place in the hair salon of Wolf Pakula (Mendl Kowal's son). The emissary spoke about the conference of the Territorialist organization that would take place in Vienna and about the conference of the Socialist-Zionists that would be held there at that opportunity. Three comrades traveled as guests to the conference from Czenstochow on their own accord: Pinkhas Kalka, my humble self and my brother, Zalman.

[Page 386]

There were then in Vienna the Czenstochower activists, Dr. Josef Kruk, Meir Fajnrajch and Yitzhak Gurski, who was one of the organizers of the conference and the convention.

After returning from the Vienna conference, we no longer had the soda water factory. The factory was operated by our first son-in-law, the husband of my oldest sister, Hinda, Mates Fuks. We lived together with my mother and my youngest sister, Tsirl, on Ogradowe Street in Tenenbaum's house. We lived a little quieter because I, my brother and sisters were all suitably employed and materially it was not bad for us.

A Search of Our House

Our house was attacked one night by gendarmes and police and they carried out a search. They did not find any illegal things. During the search, several books from the library were taken, but no one was arrested. We did not know who they were looking for with this search, my brother or me. Later, when I was called to the gendarmerie for an investigation, I sensed that the search had a connection to the Vienna conference.

How My Brother Was Freed from Military Service

My brother, Zalman, had to appear for military service. He then was working for Dr. Walberg in the paint factory and his earnings were not bad. The problem was how to save him "from the gentile hands," because if he had to serve in the military we would lose our family's main wage earner . He made a few mistakes, but even with the mistakes they took him. In time, he was freed through a *makher* [fixer] from Lublin and in his place an "angel" began to serve... (It was referred to as an angel when a person was sent to the military in the place of the one called to serve).

Zalman Federman

The problem of income changed when my brother safely returned home from "military service." But two years later, the question of me appearing for military service arose.

I Write the Articles of Engagement According to the Laws of Moses and Israel and Go to "Serve" *Fonye*[4]

Until the draft I normally worked for Moric Najfeld in the apothecary warehouse as an assistant bookkeeper. Najfeld, my boss, as well as his wife Klara, Polishized Jews, had the best relationship with me. Moric Najfeld, himself, also was a radical man and he had been exiled abroad because of his political beliefs. He lived in German Herby[5] near Czenstochow and carried out his business from there. In 1905 he took part in the large demonstrations. When Tsar Nikolai gave the "Constitution," he carried a Torah ark curtain embroidered with a Polish eagle from Napoleon's time. He was punished for this sin. His daughter, Wanda, a musician, had married a Czech named Kapezk. Also a musician, he would give concerts from time to time for charitable purposes. In her youth, Wanda belonged to the Bund and the home of her parents was the place for various socialist gatherings.

His second daughter, Dr. Natalia Najfeld, fell a victim of the typhus epidemic that reigned over Czenstochow during the First World War. Having sat for three days with a person sick with typhus, a worker from the Rakower factory, not permitting anyone to take her place, she became infected with this illness and in the course of a week left the world. She gave her life in the struggle against the epidemic. Moric Najfeld lived his last years alone (his son and daughters all died tragically) and only his daughter Wanda remained, whose husband, the Czech, had left. He died a normal death under the Nazi rule.

There was a silence in communal life. The young danced, I survived certain disappointments. I lacked someone close with whom I could share my joy and suffering.

[Page 387]

At this time I became acquainted with a girl named Hela. She was the daughter of my mother's friend, the lame Gitl Hasenfeld. I thought I had found [someone with whom to share my joy and suffering] in this girl. She was an intelligent girl, always walked around with a book under her arm. An emaciated daughter of her very wealthy parents, a small, dainty face, her constant laughter, purity and proficiency in literature drew me and I fell in love with her. I acquainted her with Yiddish literature, about which she had no knowledge. I read to her often. In time we signed an engagement agreement according to the laws of Moses and Israel, even though her parents were against it because I did not earn enough of an income. There could not yet be talk of marriage because I was not then free of the draft.

In 1913 I finally reported for the draft and at the first evaluation I was sent to Piotrkow for a *gubernia* [administrative division] evaluation and there I was recognized as *godien*, that is, as capable of military service. It should be understood that I did not desire to serve *Fonye* and I searched for various ways to escape from it. Meanwhile, one night the gendarmerie came and I was arrested and placed in the Czenstochow jail. I was again investigated in connection with my trip to Vienna to the convention of the Socialist Zionists; I was in jail for four weeks until I was informed that the case against me was void. But I was immediately sent to military service in a special convoy to the *zborni-punkt* [meeting place]. I was successful in extracting myself from there. I was helped by Baum, the military tailor from Czenstochow, who then lived in Piotrkow. I then appeared together with the *makher*, a Hasidic Jew from Lublin, who had freed my brother Zalman. First of all, he tried to have the additional paper that I was a political suspect removed from my military papers. He came to Piotrkow from Lublin especially because of this. Then I received the paper in my own hands and had to report myself to Yuryew (Dorpat [Tartu, Estonia]) to my designated *pulk* [regiment], where I started to carry out my military service.

The *makher* stipulated that for 1,000 rubles he would free me completely. He would take 500 rubles in cash and the other 500 rubles in a promissory note that was given to him by my employer, Moric Najfeld.

I traveled to Winice with my papers. The *makher* waited for me there in a hotel. He took the papers from me and asked me to travel to Lublin or another city and to wait there until he would let me know that I was free. A so-called "angel" went to serve in my place... I never learned his name. I saw him only once in Winice in the corridor of the hotel. Later, several Czenstochower, who served in Yuryew, told me that they served with a certain Rafal Federman who was a slight cripple and was immediately freed from the regiment.

I Become My Mother's *Shadkhen* (marriage broker)

During the time that my "angel" was supposed to serve, I had to hide in a strange city where I was not known. I spent a little time in Warsaw, but I could not remain there for long because Czenstochowers came there; several times I was with the *makher* in his house in Lublin. Until I got the idea to visit one of my great-uncles, who I did not know at all but who I often heard discussed in our home. This was my father's uncle, Dovid Federman. He was a Nikolajevska soldier [soldier in the army of Tsar Nikolai] and had been married in Russia. Because of this he became estranged from his family and he never came to visit us. He settled in Augustow and was a *feldsher* [barber-surgeon] there.

After being with him for several days, I told him of the untimely death of my father, about the surviving children and about the material situation of our family. He also complained to me about his loneliness. His wife had died not long ago. His two daughters were married; one was in America and the second one in Charkow. However, he explained that his income was good. He had plenty of good things. The peasants considered him a doctor and the Jews thought highly of him, too. I felt a longing in his words for a family life and instantly had the thought: my lonely, crying mother ... what would be the result for her? ... Perhaps I am the emissary ... perhaps my mother would no longer be a widow ... My uncle had the same name ... Yes, it was an idea.

Before leaving my uncle, I spoke openly with him about this, of what had occurred to me and we agreed that after I had spoken to my mother, I would send him a telegram and he would come to Czenstochow.

[Page 388]

Several days later, when I received a telegram that I should come to Winice, I understood that my "military service" had ended and I was a free man. I received my liberation ticket in Winice and I was shorn like a true Russian soldier, grew a moustache, put on a pair of boots and traveled with my soldier's pack to Czenstochow. When all of my friends and acquaintances saw me they said: "Look at what several weeks of service as a soldier can make of a man! The barracks lay a stamp on the face..."

This was in January 1914.

I returned home from the military a freed man and with the mission to have my mother married. I immediately interested the entire family in this matter, had, so to say, a "family conference." I assembled my sister, brothers, my Aunt Hinde Staszewska, my mother's sister from Piotrkow, my Uncle Sholem Federman, my father's brother. I discussed the match for my mother with everyone and everyone was in agreement that it was a good thing. Several weeks later, after receiving my telegraph, my uncle, Dovid Federman, came to Czenstochow. And – my mother married with luck for the second time. It is interesting that my mother never called her second husband by his name, but "uncle." She spoke to him in the third person, *"Zol der feter geyn,"* *"Zol der feter tuen,"* [Let the uncle go, let the uncle do] and so on.[6]

My mother left Czenstochow and only my brother, Zalman, my sister, Tsirl, and I remained in our house. Several months later came the outbreak of the First World War.

Under German Occupation

Czenstochow was occupied immediately by the Germans. We remained in our workplaces for the entire duration of the war. My sister, Tsirl, ran our household. Life became more difficult from week to week. The workers in the city began to organize and professional unions arose. The existing, rickety professional unions at the time of tsarism also began to exhibit lively activity. Certain aid work, such as a tea-house for workers, was organized around the unions and, simultaneously with this, the political life began to sprout. I took part in the organization of this work. Although separated from the rest of the world, we, however, hoped for the revolution that would come after the defeat of tsarism.

A library and an educational union were founded for Jewish workers. The dispersed former Socialist-Zionists came together and the organization was revived. When Warsaw was taken by the Germans, we sought contact and with an entry pass from a suburb of Warsaw, I arrived there and immediately established a connection with Comrade Shlomo Zisman, who then stood at the head of the Social-Zionist Party in Warsaw.

Elections to the city council took place at that time in Czenstochow according to a curia system [reserved political seats]. The Social-Zionist organization decided to take part in the elections. The candidates had to be not younger than 30 and since it was difficult to find such comrades we had to join those who were sympathetic to or those who once had some connection with the party. We then carried all four candidates to the curia: Shlomo Horowicz, a former trade employee; Dovid Tobeczko, a *feldsher* [barber-surgeon] who never belonged to the party; Yeshaya Nirenberg and Lipszic were once Territorialists. Approaching the municipal elections it was very difficult to create a platform with which we could go to the masses because we were not connected to Warsaw. Therefore, we took the platform of the Lodz Bund and added a point about immigration and colonization and this became the platform of the Socialist-Zionists.

The history of the Socialist-Zionists in Czenstochow is rich in interesting episodes. At the end of the war, when the news reached us that Wilhelm II had abdicated, I quickly called together all of those active in the Socialist-Zionist organization and also advised all of the other organizations, such as the Bund and *Paolei-Zion*. I proposed having a joint demonstration across the city. The proposal was accepted. It was in the evening. The Jewish workers were the first who went out into the street with red flags and demonstrated for the victory of the German revolution and for an independent Poland.

The German patrols that still strolled through the streets did not react immediately with great surprise; on the contrary – they saluted with great respect and honored the demonstration. However, the Polish hooligan-students, who attacked the Jewish demonstrators with great hate, could not bear this and disbursed them. The red flags were saved with great self-sacrifice; several male and female comrades were very badly beaten. The next morning, the German secret police searched for the leaders of the organizations.

[Page 389]

Being committed to the communal work that was so important at that moment, under the influence of Dr. Josef Kruk, I left my position in the apothecary warehouse and took over the leadership of the widespread activity of the movement. The communal work became the content of my life and I completely abandoned the idea of family life. My new employment did not please the parents of my fiancée and on my side I, too, was afraid of the duties of a family man. On a beautiful, clear day I sent back the engagement agreement. In a short time my fiancée married and moved to Piotrkow. On the day of her wedding, she came to say goodbye to me. We parted very friendly. I was accompanied out of the house with a bouquet of flowers and we remained good friends. We met each other again after 30 years in Boston. She is the mother of three successful grown children. She recently became a widow.

In Independent Poland

After the First World War, my mother and her husband, Dovid Federman, who had gone with the Russian Army deep into Russia, returned to Augustow. They had gone through the Russian Revolution, suffered a great deal, but finally, returned to the *shtetl* in independent Poland.

I was absorbed in the turbulence of Jewish communal life in newly independent Poland. I carried out my party duties with intense energy. The Social-Zionist organization in Czenstochow and its branch institutions grew robustly. It fell upon me to be the chairman of the organization representatives in the city council, councilman and secretary in the city council. As representative in the main commissions at the city hall, I would appear at many meetings and I took part in various campaigns.

The Social Zionist organization in our city or, as it was later called, *di Fareinikte* [the United], was the liveliest division of the party in the nation. Therefore, the representatives of the Central Committee willingly came to Czenstochow. Everyone, without exception, visited our city and found the warmest atmosphere there. At that time we were visited by: Sh. Zisman, Gilinski, Jakov Pat, Yitzhak Gordin, Berl Gutman, Leon Fajgenbaum, Dr. Josek Kruk, Pinye Bukshorn, Mendlsberg, Wiktor Fiszman, Gute Margolis, Dr Ejger, Izer Goldberg, Sh. Bastomski, Jankele Danciger, Halpern, Chaim Rozenbest, Gajst and others. The first school convention occurred during the flourishing period of the party, at which *Fareinikte* took part with a conspicuous faction. A considerable number of delegates came from Czenstochow. When the party experienced its ideological crisis, many left for the Communist Party, for the Bund. However, Czenstochow stood firm and this was thanks to the personal influence of Dr. Josef Kruk, "the Czenstochower"... The discussions about the crisis were very fervid.

For example, good friends were enamored with Czenstochow; that is, in the people in the Czenstochower organizations. When they wanted to rest and draw courage, they came to Czenstochow. They lived intimately with the Czenstochow comrades. I was then against joining the Bund and I expressed this in a discussion, that the Bund was an ideological matter. A good comrade then sprung up and, with a bang on the table, called me to order. "You have to have respect for the party that has such a rich past behind it," she cried out.

The Faction, *Fareinikte*, at the First Conference in Warsaw

[Page 390]

If the word "luck" is a reality, this was the lucky period of my life. I found complete satisfaction in my communal work, in the worthwhile struggle for human rights for my people.

The movement continued and grew and advanced and I with it. We had need of new, young people; we needed to have teachers for our schools, professional workers in the unions. We looked for these people everywhere among the studying young, among the workers at the machines. And many of them were drawn into the work. One of them was a young, blooming girl. Her name was Chaya Waga.

Chaya Waga took upon herself an internal, deep devotion to learn and simultaneously to take this to a children's home or colony that was created and into every other branch of the movement. To the children, Chayele [diminutive of Chaya] was the teacher "Wagele" [diminutive of Waga]. If music was needed for the children for their rhythmic dancing and singing, she learned music, if the organization needed a female speaker for a women's meeting, she was the speaker, when the organization arranged a masked ball for economic purposes, she was at the masked ball in a mask and helped with the success of the evening. When the opposition spoke and she found what he said incorrect, she would innocently add a heckler's interjection and if we needed to demonstrate, she summoned everyone, but she was in the first ranks. She received the devotion of the children and of the adults. She was beloved by everyone. Everyone knew that she was honest and devoted to the general thing in which she believed and that she was unequivocal. When Chayele was given a compliment, she accepted it with pleasure, but she blushed and lowered her eyes. If someone did an injustice to her, more than once she went to the side and cried. The important thing was to ignite her belief and this was not difficult – Chayele undertook work with her entire soul, not saying one word about it.

Right to left: Rafal Federman, Gute Margulis, Ester Fuks, Shmuel Landau, Chaya Waga, Rayzele Fajertag Berkensztat

In the confusion of the whirling life I often felt that I was alone; Zalman, my older brother, was married; my youngest sister, Tsirl (Tseshe), who understood me best and was proud of my activity and to whom I was bound with all the threads of family feeling, also found a young man and married him. This was Mikhal Alter, for many years a devoted worker in the Socialist Zionist movement. I suddenly felt all alone. My loneliness began to disappear with my close friendship with Chayele.

The movement *Fareinikte* grew. The Jewish *Folkes-Shul* [public school] was located in Krotka and Strazacka Streets. The teaching personnel consisted of several teachers who had been sent by *TSHISHO* [acronym for Central Yiddish Schools Organization – secular Yiddish schools]. Among them were: Jozsha Stam, Terenya Fajenblat, Rayzele Berkensztat, Yokhoved Zisman, Roza Kantor-Lichtensztajn, Mashe Kolobus and Manya Frydman, Rywka Cuker and others.

The personnel employed by all of the existing *Fareinikte* economic and cultural institutions numbered from 25 to 30 people. A Jewish secular environment was created. The male and female teachers, who were young and gifted, created a warm family atmosphere and participated in general communal life despite the difficult economic situation.

I was sick then. I was operated on and my life hung by a hair. My male and female comrades, particularly Chayele and Rywka Cuker; – both comrades nursed me and did not leave my bedside.

When I became healthy, I had to rest for a long time and was not supposed to take part in any communal work. I then became close friends with Rywka and we got married in Warsaw in 1922.

Rywka Cuker

[Page 391]
I Enter the Bund

Important events took place in party life during the same year. The *Fareinikte* had united with Drobner's socialist group and formed the Independent Socialistic Party. The unification conference took place in Czenstochow. I took part in all conferences that took place after the unification. Elections also took place then to the *Sejm* [lower house of Polish parliament] and we were all certain that the Czenstochow region would carry Dr. Josef Kruk, who was the first candidate on the list.

The result was that Kruk did not succeed. Therefore, the tense mood in the Czenstochow area led to the candidacy of the Jewish *kolo* [faction], Professor Meir Balaban. Later, Czulowski, a worker for the Polish Socialist Party, told a joke at a meeting about the failure of the "independents," that "if only those who loved him would have voted for him he would have won, he would have drawn more votes than the entire 'independent' party."

During the unification with the Drobnerowtses [followers of the Polish socialist, Boleslaw Drobner], I represented the viewpoint that the aim of Dr. Kruk [a leader of the territorialist Zionist Socialist Workers Party] and his followers, "centralized emigration and concentrated colonization – "territorialism," was not the principle point of the unification project. During the election campaign itself, I had to appear before a large audience in Krakow where the main speech was given in Polish by Dr. Drobner. In his formulation of the election platform, he showed how very little he was versed in the Jewish question. Comrade Dembicer answered him very successfully. His [Drobner's] speech was so crushed that I was forced to go up to the dais and give a statement that the formulation by Dr. Drobner was not exact and that this was the result of not being proficient in the Jewish question.

I was still more convinced that the unification actually only had an organizational purpose, far from which was the Territorialist ideology.

For me personally, this was an interruption in my idealistic development which led me to enter the Bund.

I traveled home from this meeting in an depressed mood. I immediately saw the comrades in Czenstochow and I told them that I had decided to leave the party.

At an official meeting of the municipal collective of the independent organization that last several hours, I gave a detailed declaration about my departure from the party and my transfer to the Bund. Several active comrades, such as Rayzl and Moshe Berkensztat and others, went with me. It was a painful moment in my life. It took several months until I became active in the Bund. The comrades with whom I was bound and connected in this work tried to convince me that I should not join the Bund and remain at my work in the cultural institutions.

My first appearance for the Bund was at a meeting of the Professional Unions together with Comrade Berl Gutman, who had joined the Bund even earlier. My declaration about joining the Bund took place at a banquet at which Comrad Henrik Erlich was present. For me it was one of the most elevated moments in my life. I felt that I had been liberated from the utopian idea of the so-called Territorialists, who did not match the idea of socialism.

However, when it delivered credentials to everyone, the "independent" party did not ask me to give up my mandate as councilman in the city council. I gave a declaration about this in the city council and I immediately joined the Bund faction.

My second public appearance was with Dr. Ahron Singalowski, who came especially from Berlin to the memorial for Comrade Vladimir Medem. Working in the party was elevating for me. The organization grew. Several intellectual powers joined the party, such as Yitzhak Samsonowicz, Zigmund Epsztajn, Kh. Wilczinski and sympathizers, such as the teachers from the schools.

The *Arbeiter Zeitung* [*Workers Newspaper*] began to be published. Readings and meetings took place often. The party workers passed through my house.

[Page 392]

Arczech, Sura Szweber, Wiktor Szulman, Jakob Pat. Sz. Gilinski, the Misters Henrikh Erlich, Wiktor Alter, Chaim Waser, Gershon Zibert, Artur Zigelboim, Maniek, female comrade Dina, female comrade Hister, Dr. Aleksandrowicz, Baum, Dr. Emanuel Szerer, Zigmunt Muczkat. Comrade Moshe Lederman returned from Berlin then with his wife Chaya. He was a shoemaker worker at a workshop. An example of a Bundist. His devotion to the Bund was really "without limits." His house breathed Bundism. We became very good friends and we were always seen together. As comrades we often exchanged names: I was called Lederman and he – Federman. Therefore, they began to call us by our first names: I, comrade Rafael and he, comrade Moshe.

The meat worker, Yisroel Jaronowski, also joined the party. An esteemed member of the *Fareinikte* independents, despite his trade, he grew into one of the most class-conscious workers. He was honest in his work and devoted to worker matters with his entire soul. In later years, he was elected as *parnes* [elected member] of the *kehile* [organized Jewish community] and took my place as chairman of the Czenstochow Bund organization.

I took part in all central conferences of the party and in all branches of the movement. At the election to the *kehilus* [organized Jewish communities], the organization voted in two councilmen, Ahron Perc and me. Our appearance in the *kehile* placed the organization face to face in a struggle with the Jewish clergy. We brought in dozens of proposals and we acquired great sympathy among the Jewish population. The elected *kehile* representatives of the opposing parties received our speeches with great respect, although the struggle was embittered. In the *kehile* I met with Shmuel Goldsztajn, Viktor Alter was his father, a Jew, a scholar, smart. He represented *Mizrakhi* [religious Zionists], which stubbornly struggled against all parties, but most sharply against the Bund. The Rabbi, Reb Nakhum Asz, a man of stately appearance, who attended the sessions of the *kehile*council, principally fought the Bund, however, in the highest cultural manner. And I must confess that although I fought against the budget for religious needs, I could never prevail upon myself to not stand up with all of the representatives at his entrance to the session. When we said goodbye before I left Czenstochow for Paris, he felt it necessary to give me his book with an appropriate written educational inscription. All Jewish parties, such as *Mizrakhi, Agudas Yisroel* were represented in the *kehile*. Their leaders were Kac and Nimierowski; the artisans – the leader was Avraham Dzialowski, the former *Esdek* [Social Democrat].

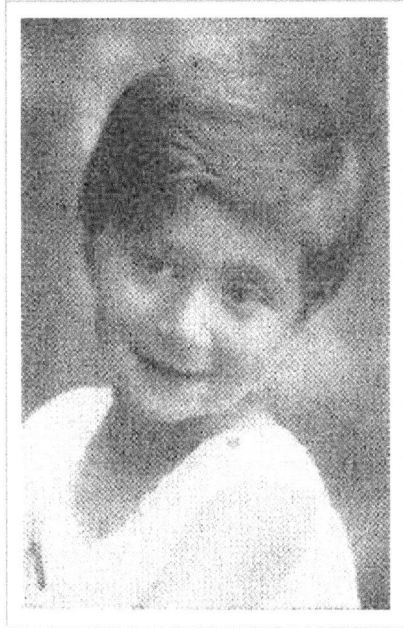

Chaya-Surale Federman

Elections took place both to the city council and to the *kehile* several times before the independence of Poland. The Bundist organization received the largest number of votes each time.

In spite of the growth of the organization, my material situation was not satisfactory. My only child, Chaya-Surale, who was raised in the Peretz nursery, was a very bright child and was the joy in the lives of her parents.

Every comrade who visited Czenstochow fell in love with her. There was never a time that I arrived in Warsaw that Berish Michalewicz or Henrik Erlich would not remind me of a song of my dear daughter with whom they had sincere fun.

When my wife's sister Tirtsa came as a guest to Czenstochow from Paris and saw our battle and struggle for existence, she strongly urged that we move to Paris.

Pilsudski's Party Takes Over the Health Fund and I Am Forced to Leave Czenstochow

For two years I was working then at an office of the Health Fund in the "insurance for the spiritual worker" (employee) division. My office became the office of the organization. When the so-called *Sanacja* [Polish word for purification – a political movement] came to power, all socialist elements were removed from there in a real way. I also fell a victim because I refused to sign a loyalty declaration to the Pilsudski regime. I became unemployed and was forced to send my wife and child to Paris.

My little daughter Chaya-Surale began to attend school in Paris and her mother did not want to separate from the child. I had to begin to think of leaving Poland and settling in Paris.

[Page 394]

A few months later Comrade Mirski and several other activists were arrested and they were exiled to Kartus-Bereza [Byaroza, Belarus] and Hershlikowicz was shot by his own comrades, about which they themselves reported. It was revealed that he had served in the Polish secret police.

I Become Secretary of the Printers Union

With the departure from Poland to Australia of Comrade Bunem Warsawski, the secretary of the Printers Union, the national council of the Professional Unions nominated me for the office of secretary of the Central Managing Committee of the Printers Union in Poland. I held this office from 1935 until the outbreak of the Second World War.

As the secretary of the Printers Union, I carried out several successful strikes in the Oksidenc Printing Press as well as at a series of newspapers. The last strike at *Moment* even took on a political character. I was arrested twice; once at a strike at the Warsaw Polish-Yiddish newspaper, *5-to Rano* [*Five This Morning*], which agreed to the arrest of the delegates of the union in a provocative manner. The publisher and editor of the newspaper was the well-known Zionist Swislocki. However, under the pressure of the union, he himself had to try to obtain our freedom. I was arrested a second time during an ambush of the union by the police when a lecture by Comrade Sh. Mendelson took place. Dozens of Jewish workers then fought and were arrested My wife, Rywka, who had returned from Paris, my sister Tsirl Alter, who was then visiting us in Warsaw, and another friend, Pala Kesterszztajn, also were arrested with me. All of the arrestees were released after the investigation that lasted several days. I was held the longest because during the investigation I was questioned forcefully in connection with the shooting of the provocateur, Herszlikowicz. The suspicion resulted from the fact that they had a report that I had fought with him in the Trade Employees Union in Czenstochow and because he had been killed. I went straight to Paris for a short time.

My Daughter Chaya-Surale Dies

My departure for Paris was connected with the most tragic event in my life. My daughter, Chaya-Surale was in Paris with her mother and went to school there. In 1936, at age 14, she came to Poland with her mother on a visit. After several months spent in Poland on vacation, she traveled back to Paris alone. My wife remained with me in Warsaw. Surale arrived in Paris safely. She suddenly became ill with appendicitis right at the beginning of the school year and despite an operation by the greatest professors she did not survive. My wife arrived in Paris and found her fully conscious. Her last words said to her mother before breathing out her soul were: "I have two mothers, you and Aunt Tirtsa." She asked about me, but when I came to Paris, I found only a grave. She died on 24 October 1936.

This great misfortune brought gloom to my personal life and even more to the life of my wife. A deep sadness covered both of our lives.

I showed police documentation for the cause of my sudden departure to Paris and this time it probably had an effect, the investigation against me was ended.

Returning to Warsaw with my wife, I continued the work in the printers union. I must add that only thanks to the comradely environment that reigned around the printers union was I able to more lightly bear the personal tragic loss of my only child, Chaya-Surale.

We cannot go without remembering the superb figure of the dear, sincere and always optimistic smiling chairman of the Printers Union, Klog. Lozer Klog, with whom we worked and lived communally as with a sincere devoted father in an exemplary family. Birthdays for communal workers very rarely were celebrated in Poland. However, it was not without reason that we celebrated the 50th birthday of Comrade Lozer Klog with so much joy and real enthusiasm. Not only the members of the Printers Union, but all of Jewish proletarian Warsaw. All of our activists from the Bund and all of the printing workers without difference as to parties, who were capable and had something to say or to write, took part in the book compellation in honor of Comrade Klog's birthday. He was one of the most active workers in the underground work of the Warsaw Ghetto and perished there with his large family to which he was so paternally bound. As long as my eyes are open and my memory works I will see his image and remember him with exaltation and respect.

[Page 395]

The Printers Union was an exemplary union for all of Poland. There were never any splits. All factions of the proletarian movements worked together in it. In May 1939 the fourth conference took place in Warsaw and a plenary meeting of the central managing committee in Vilna. I aided this work with all of my strength. Only two to three weeks before the outbreak of the war I represented the Printers Union at a conference of the Polish print workers in Katowice. The frightening picture of the war stood before my eyes. I appeared with the then *Sejm* deputy, Stonczik (now Minister in Poland), and spoke about the importance of solidarity in the struggle for a new Poland, for a Poland led by the representatives of the peasants and workers.

When I returned from the conference the union already had organized work battalions at the request of the party to dig trenches around Warsaw. Every day the Printers Union voluntarily marched to work to help in the war against Hitler. Bundists, *Paolei-Zion*, communists, unaffiliated – young and old – appeared for the work.

Right on that day, on the very eve of the war, my wife left Warsaw. She wanted to see our closest family in Paris and she also intended to extend her consular passport whose validity was about to expire. She could not manage to return because several days later, 1 September 1939, the war broke out.

The Second World War and My Refugee Road

The military events ran lightning quick. Bombs over Warsaw, thousands wounded and dead, military itineraries, refugees from cities and *shtetlekh*. The war approached the gates of Warsaw with giant steps. It became clear on the 4th and 5th day of the war that Warsaw would fall into the hands of the Germans. On the order of the party authorities, all of the important documents and the membership books for the party were removed so that they would not fall into the hands of the Hitlerists.

The leadership of the party decided that whichever party members wanted should leave Warsaw and that they should go to the other side of the Vistula River where it was hoped to stage a resistance. The party leaders decided that they were leaving on 6 September at 10 o'clock in the morning and we all had to meet at the Vilna train station.

This moment was more than painfully difficult. It was very difficult for me to decide to leave Warsaw; I was then in Comrade Midler's house.

The leadership of the party left Warsaw at 10 in the morning and we had to meet at the Vilna train station. When we arrived at the designated time at the Vilna train station, we found groups of comrades here and there. We were supposed to take the train. However, the hail of bombs from incoming German airplanes scattered us to all sides.

There was no longer any talk of traveling by train and we, a group of comrades, decided to march on foot. The march route was through Minsk-Mazowiecki, Kaluszyn, Siedlec, Mezrich [Miedzyrzec Podlask], Biala Padolska, Janow, Wysoko-Litwesk, Kamieniec, Pruszani, Kartuz-Bereska, Drohiczyn, Pinsk and we were chased by German airplanes in every *shtetl* and city in which we arrived. Burning cities, piles of dead and wounded, roads clogged with autos and people. A group came walking from Siedlec in which were found Henrik Erlich and his wife and their son, Shlomo Mendelson, Emanuel Szerer and his wife, Chaim Waser and others.

Thus we reached Pinsk. Who knows if we would have reached there if not for the devotion of the Bundist comrades who met me on our wandering road? I drew a great deal of strength from Comrade Erlich's example. We had to throw ourselves to the ground dozens of times because of the incoming German airplanes. Comrade Erlich with his dignified figure and self-control and his firm step and smart smile magnetically gave over to us his will to go farther and farther and he strengthened everyone.

We heard the last blast of the German bombs when we arrived in Pinsk in the morning of 17 September. Several of the local Pinsk residents fell dead and several were wounded. In Pinsk, we learned that we did not have to go farther because the Red Army was coming from the other side. We waited two days for the Red Army.

[Page 396]

On 20 September 1939 the Red Army marched into Pinsk. I remained in this city until 13 October. Then, still other comrades arrived, such as: Noach, Sura Szweber and others. The material situation was very difficult. I presented myself to the professional union of trade employees, which was organized then, and asked for work. They took my entire pedigree, both personal and political. I did not receive any work. Meanwhile, news arrived from the entire area that my party comrades were being arrested in a series of cities and among the arrestees also was Comrade Wiktor Alter. The last time I saw Wiktor Alter in Mezrich was at a conference and he then was chosen to go to Lublin with a group and to set up his work there and to start a fight against the Hitlerist invasion. I shook his hand for the last time there, in Mezrich.

After hearing the disturbing news about the attitude to Bundists on the part of the Soviet regime, it was decided that Comrade Henrik Erlich should leave Pinsk. The moment of leave-taking was moving and tragic for everyone. I remember how we kissed him with stinging tears and it is certain that everyone had the thought that this was the last *bleib gezunt* [remain healthy – a parting statement] to our leader and teacher.

Of course, it was a great disappointment for me when I learned several days later that Comrade Erlich was arrested in Brisk and under what circumstances.

When it was learned that Vilna would be returned to Lithuania and there was also no work, a group and I decided to move to Vilna. On 14 October 1939, the group of comrades, Szerer, Chaim Waser, Andje Monowicz and I left Pinsk. We arrived in Vilna on 15 October. The news reached us while we were still at the railroad station that my dear Comrade, Josef Aronowicz, who worked so much in the development of the workers movement in Czenstochow, was arrested the night before in Vilna by the Soviet regime along with all of the remaining members of the Bundist committee. It was another tear in the soul: Why? and dozens of times: Why? Who could give me answer to this?...

When Vilna was given to Lithuania, the situation changed again. Thousands of refugees arrived in Vilna, Jews and Christians. A refugee committee was created. Comrade Andje Monowicz and I were among the first who began to organize a kitchen for the Jewish refugees. Comrade Giterman from the Joint [Distribution Committee] helped me a great deal in supplying the kitchen. The local comrades from the Bund also worked, particularly Kac the teacher and her husband, who with self sacrifice and great effort provided the first food products for the kitchen and showed great friendliness and devotion to our work. I took part in the newly created worker aid committee the entire time of its existence. A strong connection was established with the outside world. Letters from Poland, France began to arrive as soon as the Lithuanians took over the regime. However, we also were not spared from a small pogrom by Lithuanians and Poles. In this area, two enemies made peace. They broke windowpanes and beat Jews.

After several months the work of the aid committee had strengthened so much and spread – arranging dormitories for the night and distributing clothing – that it also began to establish cultural activities connected with the kitchen in which over 500 lunches a day were given out.

However, the Lithuanian regime was envious of the workers refugee committee and cast an evil eye on it. Once the police attacked the premises, arrested a few dozen people and many were forced to leave Vilna and they were forced to settle in other Lithuanian cities, such as Panevezys and Ukemerge and other *shtetlekh*. It was our fate to travel to Ukemerge. There I received letters from my wife in Paris and from my sister in Czenstochow. I also received a letter from America. My friend, Chayale Waga-Rotman, heard of my existence and how great was my joy and how encouraged I was when I received her first letter and the first 15 dollars. This was already during the beginning of 1940.

A normal life was established in Lithuania under a provisional Lithuanian regime.

[Page 397]

Politics was interpreted in various ways at that time. When I had the opportunity in 1940 to be present in Vilna for a glass of tea among our own comrades, on 1 May, where we spoke about the situation, I remember only that I said the following in my speech: "I am not a mathematician with numbers in my hand to show what will happen, but I have a deep belief that salvation in the war will come from the Soviet Union."

The arrest of the Bundists still continued. The persecutions against our comrades threw fear into the ranks of the mass of Bundist refugees in Lithuania. The connections that were established with America awoke the hope of leaving Lithuania for America. It even appeared as a fantastic dream. But what fantasy did a person not carry with him them!

In time I received the news from my friend, Chayale Waga-Rotman, that the Jewish Labor Committee in New York during the time of the war was making efforts to save the worker activists who were in Lithuania. In short, the fantasy looked as if it was no longer a fantasy; it could become a reality. Chayale also wrote that she would hurry and make possible my coming.

Meanwhile the situation on the battlefields became worse and worse. The Germans went from victory to victory. The consulates of the lands where it was possible to save one's self began to close little by little. Therefore, it was self-evident that when I entered the American consulate and the consul said to me that he was ready to give me a visa to America, I did not believe my own ears. He asked me if I knew who William Green was in America. My answer was that I knew who William Green was, that he was the president of the American Federation of Labor and that I had the opportunity to see him once at a convention of the Professional Unions in Poland. "This is enough!" – the consul answered me – "Try to obtain the visa more quickly, because the consulate is about to close."

After I received the American visa, actually several days before the close of the consulate, the rush and the bustle to receive transit visas through the Soviet Union and Japan first began. This was the only way to go to America. After several weeks of efforts, fear and heart palpitations every time I needed to obtain a paper, a document, I finally left Lithuania on 22 September 1940.

Our comrade, Rywka Pat, the wife of Jakob Pat, also had an American visa as I did. However, she did not live to obtain a Soviet transit visa; she died of a heart attack and I was one of the few comrades who accompanied her to the Vilna cemetery. This was my last funeral for a close comrade in Poland.

In America

I went through the following main cities during my trip: Minsk, Moscow, Sverdlov, Birsk, Tatarsk, Krasnoyarsk, Bajkal, Irkutsk, Tchita, Kuybyshev, Biro-Bidzhan, and others. I was in Vladivostok on Rosh Hashanah. On 7 October I was placed on a Japanese ship in Vladivostok along with the entire group of 30 people who were the first to be saved by the Jewish Labor Committee and on 9 October we arrived in Tsuruga, on the 10th in Kobe. We left Kobe on the ship Heian Maru on 16 October 1940. We were in Yokohama on 30 October. We traveled through to Vancouver on 31 October, and on 31 October we got off the ship in Seattle, Washington. Comrade Minkof, the representative of the Labor Committee, met us.

The first encounter with the American friends took place in Chicago and the next day I went to see my Czenstochower *landsman* [person from the same town], the well-known Jewish publisher, Moshe Ceszinski. On 5 November we finally arrived in New York, the worldly city I had dreamed of visiting and which I had almost visited before the war as a delegate of Czenstochow organized labor, but because of obstacles I did not come. Now I came here as a refugee.

I did not have family or relatives in America, but I knew that I possessed comrades and friends and even intimate friends here. However, I had almost never corresponded with them.

New York did not make any special impression on me, not even the skyscrapers. The greatest wonder for me was the greenery, the parks that I found. I always imagined that America was one big factory and in the end I saw grass, actually green grass, trees and heard the singing of birds.

[Page 398]

At encounters with friends and acquaintances, they often asked me, "How do you like America?" I shrugged my soldiers and did not have an answer and not waiting for my answer, they immediately said that "I would make a living and I would be alright in America." This stuck me in my heart; my answer was, "I did not come to America to make a living, I have only come for the time being..." I could not make peace in any way with the idea that I was already someone from here. I still thought only of "there." And with my entire soul and being I went to great lengths to be active and serve the "there."

My desire to work for my *landsleit* [people from the same town] remaining there became stronger. In addition, the arrival in America of Comrade Artur Zigelboim brought a living greeting from the tortured and struggling Jewish masses to whom I felt such a deep and devoted closeness; I believed that all of the saved Bundist comrades who had been brought all the way to New York by the tide of war would themselves build a voluntary camp and we would live on bread and salt and experience "here" the martyr-filled roads of those who remained "there" devoted to our ideas, the ideas of the Bund. How could it then be different! However, who should we lean upon? In the Jewish working neighborhood enmity reigned, civil war instead of international solidarity!

Weeks, months flew by. I looked around: the majority of my comrades were consumed in the shops. They carried on a normal life. "They made a living." "They were alright..." They spoke of a great longing for the old home. They wrote letters and received bad news and worse, they sent aid and they felt that they were slipping into the small circle of American life.

In order to be able to exist, I had to go to work in a shop and my communal activity was connected to the Czenstochower Relief Committee. I set as a goal for myself to weave together and connect the simple Jews, *landsleit*, without distinction to persuade them that when the bright hour came we would be able to take over the role of the annihilated *kehile* [organized Jewish community] of the old home, Czenstochow.

During the entire time that I was in America I thought of myself as a member of the party of the Polish Bund. I searched for ways to physically rejoin it. Alas, meanwhile, I was powerless to achieve this and I relive this painfully.

I made the activity I did for the United Czenstochower Relief Committee my main goal. Here, working with Czenstochower *landsleit* from all factions, beginning with religious people and ending with communists, I tried to strengthen the warm atmosphere and to spread the idea for which the Relief worked. The idea emerged of publishing a book, *Czenstochower Yidn* [*The Jews of Czenstochow*]; the idea was cemented.

In connection with this activity, I came in personal contact with hundreds and even thousands of *landsleit* in New York, Detroit, Chicago, Los Angeles, Toronto, Montreal – all without exception, party comrades and party opponents, all gave me a friendly and comradely welcome and reacted with devotion to the thing with which I had come to them. I felt understanding among them, a deep feeling of love for their *landsleit* in the old home, for their sisters and brothers on the other side of the ocean who survived our bloody enemy. May their hand be strengthened!

**Rywka Federman [came to America from Paris on
9 September 1946], the wife of R. Federman**

As I finish writing these words I am just 55 years old. I find myself satisfied in rich, large America. However, I am still in exile. I remained the only one of my family, the inheritance of my family – the ash dispersed over the world, that is a part of the six million annihilated Jewry. I absorb this. I will carry this for as long as my eyes see the world. I will dedicate my further strength to this, that the ash shall go and demand that the earth, which was fertilized by the ashes of ours sisters and brothers, will be able to bear on itself only a world of fairness and justice and humane love of one to the other, of people to people and my Jewish people shall be among them.

Translator's Footnotes

a. A *birzshe* is an exchange, in this case a place for the exchange of ideas.

b. Yekl the blacksmith – Yekl is a diminutive of Jakov, as is Yankl. David Pinski wrote a play, *Yankl der Shmid*, which became a popular Yiddish movie in 1938.

c. Yeta is likely a diminutive of Yecze.

d. *Fonye* is the name Jews gave to Russia.

e. Herby is a town about eight miles (almost 12 kilometers) from Czenstochow. It was located on the border of Russian Poland and Upper Silesia.

f. In Yiddish, the third person is used in formal speech.

[Page 399]

The History of the Book
Czenstochower Yidn [Czenstochow Jews]
by Editorial Colleagues

Without a doubt the idea that the history of Jewish Czenstochow should be immortalized in a printed edition (book) was alive for a long a time before the history of the book *Czenstochower Yidn* began.

However, it came to expression in published form once in the publication *Dos Neye Wort* [*The New Word*] of Tuesday, 18 July 1922 published by the district division of *TSYSHO* [*Tsentrale Yidishe Shul-Organizatsye* – Central Yiddish School Organization] and during a visit to Czenstochow by the two delegates, Louis Szimkowicz and H. L. Szwarc, the following was published on the last page of an issue of *Dos Neye Wort*:

The idea of the book resulted from the contact of the Czenstochower *landsleit* [people from the same town] on both sides of the ocean that also came to expression in the creation of the house for the Y.L. Peretz children's homes and *folks-shuln* [public schools] in Czenstochow.

It was a long time from then until the decision by United Czenstochower Relief to publish a book, *Twenty-five Years of Fraternal Aid*. However, the idea already was alive in a certain form. An attempt also was made to bring about a book during that time.

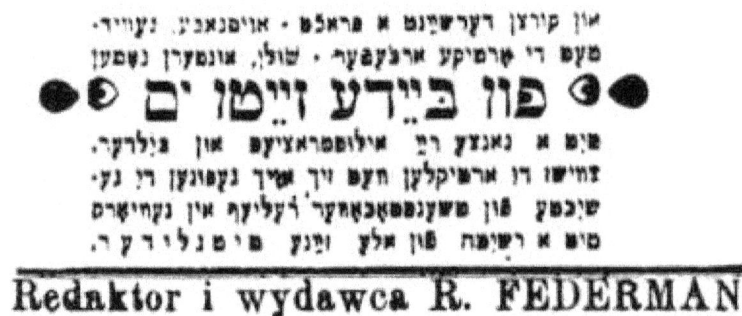

In October 1924, E. Ch., being in America, published an article in *Dos Neye Wort*, dedicated to the golden book, *Fun Beide Zeitn Yam* [*From Both Sides of the Sea*].

On 4 March 1929, Czenstochower Relief in New York decided to begin the work of publishing a book of the history of Czenstochow under the title, *Czenstochower Album*. Szimlowicz. Litman, Charbalowski, Lewensztajn, Rok, Win, A. Kaufman, Gerter, Silver and Rikman were elected to a committee. The committee made contact with Chicago and Czenstochow. However, Czenstochower Relief in New York was weakened and the plan again only remained on paper.

The idea to publish an historical book was stronger in Czenstochow itself than in America. Engineer H. Wilczinski (perished in Warsaw), one of the main initiators, gave a great deal of time and work for this purpose. At his own initiative, he researched the old documents of the old *kehile* [organized Jewish community], gathered material and even published a series of articles about individuals in the *Czenstochower Zeitung* [*Czenstochow Newspaper*] and in other Yiddish publications. Through his initiative, an historic commission to publish a monograph of the history of the Jews in Czenstochow was created at YIVO [*Yidisher Visnshaftlekher Institut* – Yiddish Scientific Institute, now the Institute for Jewish Research] in Warsaw. Moshe Asz, the son of Rabbi Nakhem Asz, also gathered material from the Czenstochow *pinkasim* [registration books] and published it in the *Czenstochower Zeitung*.

In 1932, the Friends of Jewish History in Czenstochow Society was founded at the initiative of R. Federman. Found in the presidium of the managing committee [of the society] were: Dr. Al. Walberg, chairman; Yakov Rosenberg, vice chairman; Z. Markowicz, treasurer, Engineer H. Wilczinski, secretary.

The Society printed and sent a communiqué to a wide group of people in Czenstochow and other cities in Poland and America in which among other things was said:

"In the projected monograph, the economic and cultural development of the Jewish population in Czenstochow will be expressed in words and pictures."

The communiqué called for help from "the widest circle of the Jewish population in our city," using their "shared efforts and strengths to create the history of the Czenstochow Jewish settlement, from its start to the present day, for today and the future generation."

As a result of the appeal of the committee in Czenstochow and from Mr. Wilczinski of Warsaw to Moshe Ceszinki in Chicago, who was then a member of the Educational Union, Moshe Ceszinki led a broad campaign in the union for the plan, and gave a long lecture at a members meeting about the history of the Jews in Czenstochow and of the importance of publishing a history book. The Chicago Educational Union elected a committee with Moshe Ceszinki as chairman, which held a meeting. However, a members meeting later rejected the project.

[Page 400]

There was no relief organization in New York then. The Czenstochow committee, therefore, made contact with individual people to help with the work.

Seven years passed. In that time, Yakov Rozenberg became chairman of the Jewish community in Czenstochow and at his initiative, on *Shabbos* [Sabbath], 24 June 1939, a large conference with the participation of the historian Dr. E. Ringelblum (perished during the years 1939-1945) from Warsaw took place in the hall of the Jewish community in Czenstochow, at which a local committee was created that would work with an already existing committee in Warsaw.

The initiative group, which called the conference, published the following appeal in the *Czenstochower Zeitung* [*Czenstochower Newspaper*] of Friday, 23 June 1939:

History of Jews in Czenstochow

The initiative group for publishing the history of Jews in Czenstochow, which was created by the historical committee for Poland at the Jewish Scientific Institute, turned to all Czenstochower with the following appeal:

The Jewish community in Czenstochow has existed for approximate 250 years. The special laws that were applied to Czenstochow, as to a spiritual city, made it impossible that previously a Jewish community would arise here. In the course of the 250 years that Jews have lived in Czenstochow, they have contributed a great deal to the development of the city. With their initiatives and capabilities, Jewish entrepreneurs developed a series of branches of production, such as the metal industry, toys, the haberdashery industry and so on, and then created the ability to work for thousands of workers, Jews and Christians.

Czenstochow also played a great role in Jewish life. The various currents that were active in Czenstochow created a series of institutions and establishments that were jewels for Czenstochow.

It is the obligation of today's generation to give honor to the past generations. It is our duty to summarize what has been done until now by the Czenstochow Jews in the areas of the economy, culture and so on. For this purpose a committee to organize the publication of a monograph about the Jews in Czenstochow was created by a group of Czenstochower under the protectorate of the Historical Committee of Poland at the Jewish Scientific Institute [*YIVO - Yidisher Visnshaftlekher Institut*].

The Czenstochower committee turned to all Czenstochower in Poland and in other nations to make contact with the committee and to provide all materials in their possession (photographs, documents, periodicals and so on) as well as [providing] financial help for implementing the planned publication. Address of the committee:

Historical Committee at *YIVO*
Warsaw, Bladna 2.
For Czenstochower Committee

Or:

Jewish Community in Czenstochow for the Monograph Committee.

A special meeting of the executive [committee] of United Czenstochower Relief on 22 March 1942 decided to call a conference of representatives of Czenstochow organizations in New York to approve the decision to publish a Czenstochower Almanac in connection with the 25 years of help activity by the *landsmanschaft* [organization of people from the same town]. The book was to be called: "Twenty-five Years of Fraternal Aid."

The conference took place on 23 May 1942. In truth, a great number of devoted communal workers remained unenthusiastic about the idea of publishing a book. Above all, a great sum was collected as the first aid for rebuilding Czenstochow. Both items, both the sum of $10,000, which we decided to collect, and the publication of the book appeared more fantasy than reality.

A separate administrative body under the name, "Committee for 25 Years of Czenstochower Fraternal Aid," was established as follows at its first meeting, Wednesday, 8 July 1942:

Chairman: Yakov Ber Silver.
Vice-chairmen: Louis Szimkowicz, Nisen Cymerman, Harry Fajersztajn, Mrs. Yetta Lentszner.
Treasurer: Yosef Kaufman, Secretary: R. Federman.
Editorial Committee: E. Chrabalowski, R. Federman, Abe Kaufman.

[Page 401]

Elkone Chrabalowski

Rafal Federman

Dr. Rafal Mahler

Wolf Gliksman

Abe Kaufman

Editorial Colleagues for the Book *Czenstochower Yidn*

Executive members (alphabetically):

Isidor Berger, Samuel Karpiel, Mrs. Rose Kuperman, Zigmund Epsztajn, Mrs. F. Fajersztajn, M. Fajner, Mrs. R. Frajermojer, Morris Gelber, Khona Gliksman, Yitzhak Gurski, R. Grodzenski, D. Guterman, Joseph Jacobs, Mrs. Ray Kaufman, Jacob Kapin (Kapinski), Jacob Lewi, Mrs. C. Lewi, Simon Lipszuc, Abraham Litman, Andza Monowicz, Samuel Oberman, Isidor Rikman, Chaya Waga-Rotman, Joseph Rozenblat, Itshe Zelkowicz, Abraham Senzer, Mrs. Sadie Senzer, Mrs. Ray Sobol, N. Wajsberg, Max Wilinber, H. Wajn, Emanuel Wargon, Michal Wajskop, David Zitman, Herman Zigas.

The committee held a series of meetings, sent circulars with a questionnaire to all *landsleit* [people from the same town] to collect material for the parts of the book, "biographies and memoirs," and established a connection with Chicago, Los Angeles, Detroit and with groups of *landsleit* in other cities in other countries.

A letter from the Organization of Czenstochower *Landsleit* in *Eretz-Yisroel* was read at one of the meetings of United Czenstochower Relief in New York in which it was reported that they would take part in the work of the construction fund and with the publication of the Czenstochower Almanac. The first letter from *Eretz-Yisroel*, where the largest number of Czenstochower *landsleit* live after America, brought joy and elevated the mood at the gathering.

In addition to *Eretz-Yisroel*, connections were made with Czenstochower organizations and people from Buenos Aires (Argentina), Melbourne (Australia) and London.

Material and Editing of the Book *Czentochower Yidn*

In 1942, when the actual work of the book, *Czenstochower Yidn*, began, the editors were cut off from Czenstochow and [they] had almost no material in their possession besides an incomplete set of *Dos Neye Vort* [*The New Word*] of several years, which Louis Schwartz had taken with him to America after his visit to Czenstochow, a full set of the *Czenstochower Reklamen-Blat* [*Czenstochow Advetiser*] and *Czenstochower Vokhnblat* [*Czenstochow Weekly*] and a large number of *Czenstochower Togeblat* [*Czenstochow Daily Newspaper*], which Moshe Ceszinski (Chicago) had provided, a number of issues of *Arbeter-Zeitung* [*Workers Newspaper*], which Friend Rubin Luks from Detroit had collected and a number of issues of *Czenstochower Zeitung* [*Czenstochower Newspaper*], which were in the possession of the chairman of United Czenstochower Relief in New York, Friend Avraham Ber Senzer.

[Page 402]

The materials and articles that were collected, mainly written and revised by Feitl Szmulewicz, and sent from *Eretz Yisroeli*, were a great help to the editorial staff of the book.

In addition to him, Godl Fajertag provided a large mass of the gathered material from *Eretz Yisroel* that was used for the article, "Czenstochower in *Erstz Yisroel*."

The first two reports of the destruction of Czenstochow, put together by Dr. Josef Kruk according to the testimony of the two Czenstochow refugees, Avraham Izbicki and Brandes, also came from *Eretz Yisroel*.

The publication of the book was delayed in order to provide a more detailed picture about the destruction of Czenstochow and to obtain more material about the Nazi times, directly from Czenstochow. The war had just ended, contact with the old home was established and it would have been a great loss for the entirety of the book if the time of the destruction did not appear in the book. The material had to be written as an eternal memorial for our martyrs. The completion of various articles resulted in the book needing to carry the title, *Czenstochower Yidn*.

Taking part in the editorial staff, which planned the compilation of the book and arranged the content of the articles were: E. Chrabalowski, Rafal Federman, Abe Kaufman and Yakov Ber Silver.

As a result of the decision of the editorial staff, the well-known historian, Dr. Rafal Mahler, who himself revised and completed a large number of articles, was invited to become the editor of the book. Most of the material for the book was revised by E. Chrabalowski.

After the arrival in New York of Friend Wolf Gliksman, the editorial committee designated him as a member. In addition to the preparatory work that he carried out for the book, Friend Gliksman was very useful in compiling the material from the time of the destruction, which to a great extent he himself lived through in Czenstochow.

Friend Wolf Gliksman and Friend Rafal Federman took over the technical work of compiling all of the material for the book, preparing it for printing and a great deal of other work.

18 May 1947 was designated as the day on which the book would be made public.

Gathering Dedicated to the Forthcoming Publication of the Book

[Page 403]

Administrative Committee of the *Czenstochower Yidn* Book

Yosef Kaufman

Avraham Yakov Tenzer

Yankl Kapinski (Kapin)

Yakov Ber Silver

[Page 404]

Dr. Raphael Mahler

He was born on 15 August 1899 in Sondz (western Galicia). He studied in a *yeshiva* [religious secondary school] until he was 15 and in 1918 graduated from the *gymnasia* [secular secondary school] in Krakow. He studied history and philosophy in Vienna and there received the title of doctor in 1922. After returning to Poland he taught general and Jewish history, first in the *Yavne* [religious Zionist] Hebrew *gymnazie* in Lodz, then in the Lyceum Askala in Warsaw. Here he began to research the history of the Jews, in general, and of the Jews in Poland, in particular. He belonged to the left *Poalei-Zion* [Marxist-Zionists] movement from his youth on. He published articles in the weekly, *Arbeter Zeitung* [*Workers Newspaper*], and in *Fraye Yungt* [*Free/Secular Youth*] and was active in the youth and student movements.

He was connected with *YIVO* [*Yidisher Visnshaftlekher Institut* - Yiddish Scientific Institute] with his scientific work from its beginning in 1925 and was nominated there as a member of the history section.

He came to America at the end of 1937 and settled in New York. He was hired as a teacher at the seminary of the Jewish National Labor Alliance, at the Jefferson School for Social Studies and at the newly founded School of Jewish Studies.

In America he did his scientific work with *YIVO*. In his communal work he was active in the Committee of Jewish Writers, Artists and Scientists (founded in 1941 to unite the Jewish communities around the world) and in *IKOR* [*Yidishe Kolonizatsie Organizatsie in Rusland* – Organization for Jewish Colonization in Russia].

He published articles in Der Zukufnt [The Future], Yidishe Kultur, [Jewish Culture], Eynikeyt [Unity] and in the Tog [Day]. In his special area of scientific work are: Di Geshikte fun Yidn in Poyln [The History of the Jews in Poland], Di Ekonomish Ontviklung fun Yidishn Folk [The Economic Development of the Jewish People], Religiez-Tsociale Bavaygungen bei Yidn [Religious-Social Movements among Jews] (Karaite-Hasidim) and Di Ontviklung fun der Yidisher Historographie [The Development of Jewish Historiography].

In Poland, he was the editor of: Yunger Historiker [Young Historian], Bleter far Geshikter [Pages for History], Dos Visnshaftlekhe Lebn [The Scientific Life].

Dr. Mahler published dozens of treatises in the *YIVO Bleter* [*YIVO Pages*], historical writings at *YIVO* [and in]

Jewish Quarterly Review
Miesięcznik Żydowski [Jewish Monthly]
Encyclopedia Judaica
Jewish Social Studies, History, Judaica

Dr. Mahler's published works:
Mekoyrim tsu der Geshikte fun Yidn in Poyln in der Tseit fun Mitl-Alter ["Sources for the History of Jews in Poland during the Middle Ages"], Warsaw, 1930 (with Dr. Emanuel Ringelblum);
Der Kamf Tsuvishn Haskalah un Hasidus in Galicia ["The Fight Between the Enlightenment and Hasidus in Galicia"], Library of YIVO, New York, 1942;
Jewish Emancipation: A Selection of Documents, publication of the American Jewish Committee, New York, 1942;
Jews in Public Service and Liberal Professions in Poland 1918–1939, publication of the American Jewish Committee;
Geshikte fun Yidn in Poyln ["History of the Jews in Poland"] (up to the 19th century), published in Eretz-Yisroel in Hebrew by Sifriat Poalim Publishing Company, 1946; to be published soon in Yiddish by IKUF [Yidisher Kultur Farband – Yiddish Cultural Union] Publishing House.

Dr. Mahler's most recent publication: Karaimer: a Yidishe Geule-Bavaygung in Mitlalter [Karaites: a Jewish Redemptive Movement in the Middle Ages] (Eliyahu Shulman, New York).

**Dr. Emanuel Ringelblum, one of the
initiators of an historical book about
Czenstochow**

Some Co-Workers

Several co-workers on the book
***Czenstochower Yidn* [*Czenstochower Jews*]**

Gina Medem

Y. Sh. Herc

[Page I]

Who and Where
Biographies

Alef א

Samuel Oberman

Born in Czenstsochow on 6 July 1898. Came to America from Germany in 1913. He was a member of the Czenstochow branch 261 of the *Arbeter Ring* [Workman's Circle] in New York. His son, Gustav, served as a sergeant in the American Army.

Moshe Oderberg

The Oderbergs had a Czenstochower lineage. Moshe, one of their sons, was born in 1891. He received a traditional and *frume* [pious] Jewish upbringing in his parents' house, later in the Krimalowner *yeshiva* in Czenstochow.

In 1904/5, the freedom movement, which penetrated the *yeshiva* and the *shtibl* [small prayer house], carried him away. Against the tradition of his home, he put on a worker's shirt at age 14 and began to work as an apprentice with a locksmith.

Welwel, the *Bundist* who worked with him in the locksmith shop, made a strong attempt to get M.O. to join the "*Bund* Youth." However, this idea had no impact on him. He was drawn to *Poalei-Zionism*; particularly, because several of his *yeshiva* friends has already joined the movement.

He was called "*Ben Akiva*" in the *Poalei-Zion* organization. He decided to open a locksmith shop in his home, in order to serve the party better, which was in need of weapons that were brought in from out of the country and often needed many repairs. His carried out his plan together with Meir Grajcer – a good lock worker.

The second location of his locksmithy was in a cellar in Josef Oderberg's house on Warsawer Street. This house adjoined Marcusfeld's men's hat store. Once the police surrounded the house where the lock workshop was located and carried out a rigorous search. At that time, not only were revolvers and revolutionary [literature] in the cellar, but also two soldiers, *pepesovtzes* [members of the illegal Polish Socialist Party] who had run away, one of whom had shot his officer; the second escaped from a military prison where he was imprisoned for spreading literature that called for an uprising. With luck, the police did not find the cellar. However, after the sudden attack of the police, the "workshop" was no more.

Later, Moshe was forced to escape to Germany. The police arrested his brother Nusen as a hostage. His parents succeeded in ransoming him with a large sum of money.

After a time he returned to Czenstochow and, in order not to be arrested, he left for Lodz. He remained there from 1908 to 1913. He mostly gave up party and cultural work. During this period, underground party workers made use of the cultural unions as a legal means for their activity.

Moshe Oderberg returned to Czenstochow in 1913 and was elected with Moshe Ceszynski as a delegate to the third *Poalei-Zion* convention in Krakow.

He left for America a short time after the convention. Here he did not find in either the *landsmanschaft* organization or in his own *Poalei-Zion* party the lively fire that burned and glowed in the Jewish masses in his birthplace. He decided to found party organizations for the young that would become the pillars of fire for socialism and Jewish liberation.

While in Chicago, together with a group of comrades he founded the *Poalei-Zion* Social-Democratic Branch 2, a union of true Borokhovist [followers of Ber Borokhov, a Russian Socialist-Zionist labor movement leader] with Borokhovism as its slogan. He was also the co-founder of Social-Democratic Br. 3 in Chicago, taking in a wide range of young people.

[Page II]

When *Poalei-Zion*'s school movement begins, he finds himself in the front ranks. He becomes the administrator of the Maccabi schools in Chicago. Also active in the aid work for our old home. He becomes an active co-worker in "People's Relief" and when Mendl Szukhter resigns his office as administrator in Chicago – takes his place.

At the same time, he is also district-secretary of *Poalei-Zion* and co-editor of the Chicago edition of "*Yidishn Kempfer*" [*Jewish Fighter*], under the editor Dovid Pinski. Later under the Borokhov-Zbubovl [Jacob Zerubovel, Leftist *Poalei-Zion* leader] editor.

In 1921, when there is a split in the *Poalei-Zion* World Movement – he participates in the founding meeting of the Leftist *P.Z.*, becomes a member of the central committee and co-editor of the central party organ. He moves to New York. He writes articles for many years under the pen name M. Neyman, and publishes articles under the names M. Berglson and Josif Neyman in the Argentinean *Yiddishe Prese*, in the *Arbeter Welt* [*Workers' World*] in Warsaw, in the *Nei-Welt* [*New World*] in *Eretz-Yisroel* and in *Proletarishn Gedank* [*Proletarian Thought*] in New York.

When the movement for the Borokhov Children's Schools comes to America, Chicago founds two schools – and Moshe Oderberg is their administrator.

In the late years he is active in the *P.Z.* party in addition in the Jewish Workers' Committee in the union's *Histadrut* campaign, in the *Arbeter Ring* and in the Czenstochower *landmanschaft* organization.

Moshe Oderberg was one of the founders of the Czenstochower Independent Union in Chicago; was chairman for three years and actively assisted in all of its undertakings.

Morris Owetzki (Awietszke)

Chicago

(photograph)

Son of Josif and Margula. Born in Czenstochow in January 1890. He married Ceshe Konicepolski. Came to America on 2 July 1913. He is a member of the Czenstochower Educational Alliance in Chicago. His sons Willy and Martin and his son-in-law, Morris Ginsberg, have served in the American Army.

Yankl Owetzki

Son of Pinkhas and Yentl. Born in Czenstochow on 15 March 1886. Came to America on 9 January 1909. He is a member of Branch 295 of the *Arbeter Ring*. His son Saul served as a sergeant in the American Army.

(photograph)
The parents of Yankl Owetzki

Efrom Auslander Chicago

Son of Josef and Chana. Born in New York on 15th January 1903. He is an executive member of the Czenstochower Aid Society in Chicago. His son, Leibl, served in the American Army.

Isidor Izbitzki

Son of Haim and Rifka. Born in Czenstochow, April 1895. Came to America in 1923. He is a member of the First *Dzialoszyner Khevra Anshei Bnei Achim* in New York.

Abraham Izbitzki

Tel Aviv

(photograph)

The son of Wolf and Ester. Born in 1915. His received his social education in the Zionist-Socialist youth organization, *Freiheit* [freedom] and in *Gordonia* [Zionist pioneer youth movement]. In 1932 he became secretary of the Zionist-Socialist Workers' party, *Histadrut*. Later a member of the party council. After the deportation of the Czenstochower Jews, he fled to Bedzin and joined the ranks of the underground struggle that was mainly made up of the young; he saved himself in dozens of cities and *shtetlekh* in Poland. Later, the underground effort carried him to Upper Silesia.

He succeeded in assignments by the movement in saving many young people from concentration camps and ghettos and hid them in the bunkers (popular name for a hiding place). He traveled with the false papers of a *volksdeutsch* [ethnic Germans living in another country]. He helped with smuggling across the Polish-Slovak border and, later, the Slovak-Hungarian border.

In Budapest he was again active in organizing the young. He was a member of the *Haganah* [defense] council and *Hatzalah* (self-defense and rescue committee). In May 1944, he was the first to cross the Hungarian-Romanian border and arrived in Bucharest. Later, hundreds of refugees went the same way. A large number of them reached Bucharest. Subsequently, he legally left Constanza for *Eretz-Yisroel* where he arrived on 25 May 1944.

[Page III]

Yokheved Israel

(neé Rubel)

Chicago

(photograph)

Daughter of Moshe and Feiga Rubel; born on 25 July 1894 in Piotrkow. At age 9, her mother gave her to a woman tailor where she worked for two years. Her older sister, Rifka, who works in Czenstochow then takes her with her to Czenstochow where she works with her sister making cheap clothing. At 12, Yokheved Israel enters the *Bund* and takes part in the strike that the *Bund* leads among the tailor workers. In 1913 she marries Itzhe Dovid, a grandson of the Kraserkes, and, with her husband and her sister, she comes to America.

Harris (Israelowicz) Israel
(photograph)

Son of Dovid and Jean. Born in 1867 in Czenstochow. He came to America in 1888. Was a director and member of 22 organizations in New York, as well as the United Czenstochower Relief in New York. Died in June 1941.

Charles Eisner

Son of Moishe and Malka. Born in Czenstochow on 2 January 1892. Came to America on 4 October 1910.

Icek (Yitzhak) Eisner

(photograph)

Born in Plomieniec near Krzepice (Poland), husband of Mindl Eisner and the father of Lemel, Pinkhus, Leibish, Willy, Harold, Mary, Beatrice and Frances. Died in New York on 30 July 1940 at age 90.

William Eisner

Son of Isidor and Mina. Born on 7 March 1892 in Czenstochow. Came to America in 1907.

Pinkhas Eisner

(photograph)

Son of Mordekhai and Sara. Died at 79 in Czenstochow in 1937.

Henry Altman

New Rochelle, NY

Son of Kopel and Feigel. Born in Przyrow in March 1887. Came to America in July 1920.

Benimin Amsterdam

Philadelphia

The son of Abraham and Guea. Born in 1903 in Amstow near Czenstochow. Member of the *B'nai-Brith Shalom Sofer*. His son Gustav is a major in the American Army.

Charles Luay (?) Amsterdam

Philadelphia

The son of Abraham and Gwendolyn. Born June 1890 in Czenstochow. Came to America in 1902.

Shlomoh Amsterdam

Philadelphia

The son of Yoel and Perl. Born on 20 May 1881 in Czenstochow. Came to America in 1905. Member of the Warsaw *Socjal*.

Alter Astor (Ast)

Chicago

(photograph)

The son of Yehoshua and Mindel. Born in Lelew (Poland) on 15 September 1888. He married Haya Weisfelner and came to America in April 1913 from Czenstochow. Is a member of the Bendiner Society, Hebrew Progress and the Czenstochow Educational Society in Chicago.

Dovid and Hana Akerman London

Born in 1882 in Lublin of *frume* [pious] parents. At 14 he became an apprentice in bronze work and at 16 he left for Warsaw, from which he returned to Czentochow in 1903.

While in Warsaw he had already joined the *Bund*. In Czenstochow, he became acquainted with Dovid Malarski, Mendl Szukhster, Meir Fajnreikh and Kopl Gerikhter and became one of the most active wokers in the *S.S.* [Zionist-Socialist Workers' Party) workers organization. During a strike in Wajnberg's factory, he met Josif Number 1 (Dr. Josif Kruk) who in Dovid Akerman recognized the type of Jewish class conscious worker and harnessed him in party work, Together With Ahron and Nukhmen Singalowski, they helped build the *S.S.* organization in Czenstochow.

[Page IV]

When Dovid Malarski was arrested in 1905, Dovid Akerman was sent to Warsaw to *"Zalman Burszu"* who familiarized him with a "technique" that would help free Malarski from prison.

During the workers' strike in 1905, Dovid Akerman, as committee representative, ran the supplying of food to the striking Jewish workers in Golda's teahouse.

In 1906 he married Hana Eichl from Lublin.

In 1909 he left Czestochow for Warsaw. A year later – to London. There he first worked as a silversmith, then arranged for a stall with costume jewelry. In time he developed an export and import business with costume jewelry and various haberdashery articles with which he is active to this day.

Until 1924-25, he was connected with the *S.S.* group which Dr. Josif Kruk led at the time of the First World War. Akerman, along with D. Dawidowicz, took part in the founding of *ORT* in London and took part in a whole range of communal and aid activities.

His house in Stepford Hill was the place where Dr. Josif Kruk and a full range of leaders of communal organizations would live when they visited London.

In the summer of 1946, Dovid and Hana Akerman visited New York. Their reception was at a meeting of United Czenstochower Relief and and contributed to the Aid Fund for Czenstochow.

Dovid and Hana Akerman are active to this day in various communal organizations in London. They have three sons: Jerome (in the R.A.F. during the war), Henry and Mory.

(photograph, caption: The father of Zine Orszek)
Orszek Zine
(photograph)

Son of Aba and Feigl. Born on 4 June 1893 in Czenstochow, came to Canada on 26 January 1926. Member of the *Arbeter Ring*; founder of the *Bundist* Branch; founder of the Czenstochower Aid Society; and of the Aid Union of the Bakers' Union.

Orszek Zine, a baker by profession, became an active worker in the Prof. Union in Czenstochow, an old *Bundist* worker even in the Czarist period. Also a co-worker in the Czenstochower *Arbeter-Zeitung* [*Workers' Newspaper*].

In 1938, Orszek visits his birthplace, Czenstochow, where he is solemnly received by his former comrades.

Bet ב

[Page IV]

Max Kh. Baron

(Czenstochowski)

(photograph)

The son of Yitzhak and Beila. Born in 1891. He lost his mother at age 5 and was raised by his grandmother. He went to *kheder* until he was 12, then began working in Feiga's candle factory at Kasze Street 5. He was already working as a hairdresser with Isidor Pola (Iser Pakula) in 1910-11. He left for London in 1912, and in April 1913, he left from there and came to America, where he settled in Chicago. In June 1914, he graduated from an English primary school and entered John Marshall Middle School. He later studied at the Lewis Institute, the University of Chicago and in 1921 received his philosophy diploma, after further studies.

In 1924 he studied in Paris at the Sorbonne and visited a wide range of countries in Europe. In June of the same year, he married Felicia Rubinec of Warsaw. Their daughter Guta is 16 years old. In America, he took his mother's childhood family name: Baron. He was a French and Spanish teacher for a time in various Chicago primary and middle schools and now is a teacher of the same languages at the De Paul Academy.

Yakov Balzam

Son of Haim and Hana. Born on 18 December 1877 in Czenstochow. Came from Warsaw to America on 7 September 1909. Member of the Czenstochow Branch 260 of the *Arbeter Ring* in New York.

[Page V]

Mendel Borzykowski

(photograph)

Son of Yitzhak and Frimet. Born in Pilicia (Poland). He died in Czenstochow in 1918 at age 39.

Feiga Haja Borzykowski

(photograph)

Daughter of Yehoshua and Mindel Szercz. Born in Lelew in 1879.

Karl Buchner

Son of Haim and Ita. Born on 16 August 1901. He left Czenstochow in 1914 and came to America in 1919. Married Ester Wajsholc. He is an active member of the Czenstochower Young Men's Society in New York and finally occupied the office of president.

Meir Boim

(Meir Biszner)

(photograph)

The son of Leibl and Leah. Was born in Czenstochow. He was one of the oldest and best-known members of the *Khevra Kadishe* [burial society] and was active there until the last years of his life. He also took an active part in the groups *Hakhnoses Orkhim* [to provide hospitality to poor visitors on *Shabbos*] and *Malbesh-Arimim* [to clothe the poor].

Died on 19 March 1938 in Czenstochow at age 102.

Ita Boim

(neé Windman)

The daughter of Fishel and Chana. Known in the city as a righteous woman. She died in 1916 in Czenstochow at age 70.

Sholom Boim

Chicago

(photograph)

Son of Meir and Ita. Born in Czenstochow on 10 December 1883. In 1903, he left Czenstochow and came to England. He came to America in 1907. He is an active member of the *Arbeter Ring*, former president of the Czenstochower Educational Society in Chicago and the secretary of the Relief Committee of the Aid Fund under the name Saul Boim.

Edna Boim

(neé Hantwerker)

Chicago

Daughter of Naftali and Sara. Born in Czenstochow in 1885. She came to America in 1905. She is active in the communal field in a series of women's institutions, such as the Federation of Polish Jews, *Hadassah*, *Ezra* and the Czenstochower Aid Society in Chicago.

Israel Yitzhak Boim Chicago

(photograph)

Son of Wolf and Devojra. Born in Czenstochow on 15 July 1898. Came to America on 15 November 1913. Member of the Zionist organization and of the Czenstochower Educational Society in Chicago.

Toba Bitter
Chicago

Daughter of Berl and Haya Bromberg. Born in Grojec. Came to America on 11 June 1911. Her son Herman served in the American Army.

Gershon (George) Bialik

(photograph)

Son of Mendel and Miriam. Born in Czenstochow on 10 June 1893. Came to America on 13 November 1913. He is a member of Czenstochower Young Men in New York and vice president of the Federation of Kosher Butchers.

[Page VI]

Hilel (Herman) Bialek

Son of Daniel and Eidl. Born in Pajeczno (Poland) on 10 July 1881. Lived in Strasbourg, France. Came to America on 9 September 1939. He has two sons in the French army.

Ruchl Bialek

The wife of Hilel, she has been in France since 1939.

Helen Bida

(photograph)

The daughter of Avraham and Yente. Born on 21 May 1898 in Czenstochow. Having an inclination toward scenic art, she left Czenstochow and traveled to London in 1912. There she met Rusze Szklarz, the wife of actor Max Brin who engaged her as an actress in the Yiddish Pavilion Theater. The first role she played together with Jakob Zilbert – then a guest player from America – in *Tzinele Di Blinde* [*Tzinele the Blind*] and in *Yeshiva Bukher* [*Yeshiva Boy*]. In 1913 she performed in Paris with Jakob Libers, under the direction of Akselrod, in various melodramas. She also performed in Antwerp. During the First World War, she played in Denmark and Sweden with a group of wandering actors, among them Mr. and Mrs. Bielawski, Rotsztein and others.

(photograph, caption: Avraham Bida)

(photograph, caption: Yente Bida)

In 1916 Helen Bida came to America. The first season she performed in the theater under the direction of Shor and Lipman at the Lyric Theater. Later she played in Chicago, St. Louis, Cleveland, Detroit, Winnipeg. The last years – in Brooklyn, in Parkview and in the Hopkinson Theater. She also appeared at the Bronx Art Theater in the last season.

She also appeared as Rifkele in *God of Vengeance* with Joseph Schildkraut as Lancelot in *Shylock*. She also played with Joseph Scheingold, Boris Thomashefsky, Leon Blank, Bertha Kalisch, Jacob Ben-Ami (*The Deserted Inn*); also as Maita in *Di Grine Felder* [*The Green Fields*]. Also with Ludwig Satz and Celia Adler in *Gozlin* [Thief].

Her father, Avraham Bida, the son of Reuwin and Haya, was born in Dzialoszyn. In 1930, at age 78, he died in Czenstochow.

Her mother, Yente Bida, daughter of Noakh and Breindl Szapranski, was born in Dzialoszyn; in 1937, she, too, died at the age of 85.

Shimeon Biro

(photograph)

Son of Yitzhak and Beila Birencwajg. Born on 1 May 1900 in Czenstochow. His parents, middle class people, tried to give their three sons and a daughter a good education. In the conflict at that time between the *haskhala* [enlightenment] and *hasidism*, Shimeon, like all other Jewish children in their bright youth, lapsed in *kheder*. With luck, his *kheder* rabbi was Tanski, a modern type of teacher and he taught the children without a whip, as was the habit with other teachers in those years. His received his first worldly education from the teacher Edelist.

When Shimeon was 10, he entered the Polish *gymnazie*, Mickiewicz. Here he made his first acquaintance with anti-Semitism. The Polish students had the Jews at their mercy: the abusive word "Beilis" [Mendel Beilis was accused by the Russians of having murdered a young Christian boy to obtain his blood for ritual purposes]. The Jewish students had a bigger "card" against them: "Macoch." And "Damazy Macoch" [a priest in the Czenstochow area accused of murdering a married woman with whom he was romantically involved] was indeed a good answer.

At the outbreak of the First World War in 1914, the schools were closed, and the Germans began catching young men to work in the ironworks and coal mines in Germany. Shimeon, with a group of Czenstochowers, was brought to Konigshutte, an Upper Silesian coal mine. The German foreman was brutal, the hunger great; many of the captured Czenstochower workers escaped to other cities in Germany, without papers and without money, to look for a piece of bread.

[Page VII]

In 1917, Shimeon succeeded in returning to Czenstochow. During that time, the workers unions – S.S., *Bund*, *Poalei-Zion* and the Social Democrats – managed to build up a half legal workers' movement and conducted many-faceted cultural activities. He then joined a "larger club." This was the *Bundist* cultural institute that stood under the leadership of the teacher from the Czenstochower artisan's school, Josef Aronowicz.

Shimeon Biro could not remain in Czenstochow for long. He again left for Berlin. There he joined the then Independent Social Democratic Party.

There was then a group of Czenstochowers in Berlin, one a leftist *Bundist* leader "Leibel," Dr. Ahron Singalowski, Feigele Fajnrajch and others. Almost all carried on anti-war activities. At the beginning of 1918, Shimeon was arrested by the German military secret police. He sat in the

Berlin military prison for 6 weeks; then, he was sent to the Modliner Fortress near Warsaw, where about 150 political arrestees, men and women, were held. Among the women political prisoners were: Madam Groser, the wife of Bronislaw Groser, and Feigele Fajnrajch of Czenstochow. Later the Czenstochower *S.S.* [Social Zionists] member Kaneman was brought, too. With the end of the war, after a 5-day revolt in the Modliner prison, they were freed.

Shimeon returned to Czenstochow and he again began to be active in the workers' movement and was elected to the local *rada rabotnicza* (workers' council) that was short-lived because of the upper-hand of the reaction. He again traveled to Berlin where he met Mendl Szukhter, who helped Shimeon come to America.

In America, Shimeon Biro was sometimes more, sometimes less, active in Czenstochower organizations; at first in *A.R.* [*Arbeter Ring*] Branch 261, later in *A.A.O. Czenstochower* Br. 11, and in the Czenstochower division for the aid of political victims in Poland and in Czenstochower Relief.

Fela Biro-Fajnrajch

(photograph)

Her family lived at Warsawer 72, near the "three crosses." There were ten children. Her father Moshe Josef came from Lelow. He was a *frumer* [pious] Jew and a scholar. His income came from buying dairy goods from the non-Jews in the surrounding villages. Her mother, Haya, came from a Hasidic, aristocratic family. Her mother's father, Ziskind Zigelboim, had a watermill with a large estate near Klobuck. One of Fela Fajnrajch's uncles, Moshe Zigelboim, had a mill on Dombiye near which illegal meetings would take place.

In the years of the liberation movement, heated discussions took place in the home of the Fajnrajchs between Meir and Dovid – members of the Social Zionists – and Shimeon – a *Bundist*. Later, Meir and Dovid were arrested. Dovid was imprisoned together with Dovid Lewenhof (died in prison) and Josl Berliner for six years. His mother cried many nights, took food to Meir and brought packages to Dovid.

In contrast with her father, her mother was "enlightened" and quietly supported the liberation movement. Fela Fajnrajch's parents died before the Second World War. The rest of the family was spread over the entire world." Meir (Meir Fajnrajch) and Shimkhah are in *Eretz-Yisroel*; Avraham – in the Soviet Union, one in Argentina and Izak, Dovid, Yankl and Ruchl (lived in Lodz) and Sara, with the greatest bad luck, remained in Poland.

Fela studied *davnen* [praying] and Yiddish in a *kheder* [religious school]; other languages in a private school on Garncarska. She began to work in Wajnberg's factory at a very young age; then for a short time she studied corsetry at "Hygiene" (the wife of Yakov Rozenberg). She also learned sewing with Waldfogl.

Meir was a lover of literature and theater and he, himself, took part in amateur performances. The rehearsals took place in the home of Fela's parents. Preparations were taking place for the play, *Di Tzvei Kuni Lemels* [*The Two Simpletons*]... The performance took place in the large ballroom of the Bem Hotel on Second Avenue. Manya Szaferanko played the beautiful Karolina. This play was Fela's first encounter with the theater. From then on she did not miss any Yiddish performance in Czenstochow.

Shmuel Frank brought her on stage. Her first role was Teibele in *Yidishn Kenig Lir* [*The Yiddish King Lear*]. The play was staged in Noworadomsk *Hazamir* [choir group; the name is Hebrew for nightingale]. She played with the amateur troupe in Lodz; Zimbalist, Madam Glikman, Waksman, Ajzenberg and others under the direction of Wajsberg. Later she joined the amateur troupe of *Lira*. This was at the time of the First World War. Then, the popular movie theater, Odeon, in Czenstochow presented a supplement of vaudeville, in addition to movies. A

Yiddish supplement was presented for several weeks in which she took part under the direction of the well known actor Zimbalist. The Yiddish vaudeville was a great success.

[Page VIII]

Fela joined the *Groser Klub* that was directed by Josef Aronowicz, Jakub Rozenberg, Avraham Yehoshua Sztorim, Lederman, etc. In 1918, she left for Berlin where a large number of Polish refugees from the Czarist times still lived. She was arrested in the spring of 1918 for taking part in the anti-war movement. After two months in the women's prison, she was sent to Modlin. Among the arrestees in the Modliner fortress, she met Mrs. Slava Groser and the *Bundist* Manya, Emanuel Novogrudski's wife. In 1918, she again left for Berlin. There she joined the Yiddish theater under the management of Herr Schudlower. Aleksander Granak, who would later become famous, was also a player in the troupe. In 1923, with the help of her friend Mendl Szukhter, she came to Montreal, Canada and there performed in the Monument National Theater.

Fela came to New York in 1924. When the *Vilner Troupe* came here, she joined it and performed in a wide range of plays. With the *Vilner*, she learned to pay attention to and maintain the clarity of the language. Later the *Freiheit* Dramatic Studio was founded that was transformed into *Artef*. Under the direction of famous professionals, they first studied theater arts, staged a wide array of plays and tried to uphold the best type of Yiddish theater.

Fela also took part in Maurice Schwartz's Art Theater, playing in a wide variety of plays in New York and in the provinces and enjoyed the great creative joy that the art theater gave their performers and spectators.

Fela Biro dedicated these last years to the great purpose of bringing the creative Yiddish word to the wide masses at their meetings and gatherings. Appearing on stage in solo recitations of classic and modern Yiddish poetry and with songs and poetry of the Jewish catastrophe in Europe, she expresses in an artistic form the great silent grief that presses heavy stones on the spirit of hundreds of *landsmanschaftn* [organizations whose members were born in the same city or town], whose fathers and mothers, brothers and sisters were annihilated by German cruelty.

Today Fela Fajnrajch lives in New York.

Yitzhak-Mendel Birnholz

(photograph)

Son of Avraham Dovid and Malka. Born in Szczekociny (Poland). He died on the first day of the Second World War [September 1] in 1939 in Czenstochow, at the age of 93.

Avraham (Abe) Birnholz

Detroit

(photograph)

Son of Yitzhak Mendel. Born on 7 November 1896 in Czenstochow. Came to America in February 1920. One of the founders and active members and secretary of the Czenstochower Regional Union of Detroit.

Manya Birnholz

Detroit

(photograph)

Daughter of Moshe Shmuel and Pesel. Born in Sosnowiec in June 1907. Came to America on 15 July 1920. Active in the Brandeis Club in Detroit and in the Women's Pioneer Organization.

Manashe Birman

Born in Kleczew (Poland) in 1886. Always lived in Czenstochow and where he was a well-known merchant. He and his wife Hana Birman, born in 1888, and their children – Dorcia (27), Miriam and Hershl (22) – shared the fate of the Jews of Czenstochow during the deportations. Manashe and Hana's youngest daughter, Blima, survived the Nazi *gehenim* [hell] and the ghettoes and concentration camps of Czenstochow and Bergen-Belzen. She lost her husband, Elihu Barewietzki (also from Czenstochow), because he was sent away from Czenstochow in a transport to Germany.

(photograph, caption: Blima Birman)

Blima Birman is now in New York with her uncle and aunt, Max and Jenny Grosman. She is a member of United Czenstochower Relief.

Tuvya Beitner

Detroit

Son of Moshe and Leah. Born in Sosnowiec on 30 December 1876. Came to America in 1913. Member of the Czenstochower Regional Union in Detroit.

Bajla Beitner

(neé Starozum)

Daughter of Yakov Hersh and Perel. Born in Czenstochow. Came to America in 1920. Was a member of the Czenstochower Regional Union in Detroit. Died 10 October 1932 in Detroit as the age of 50.

[Page IX]

Leizer Bajgelman

(photograph)

(photograph, caption: Leizer Bajgelman with his wife and daughter)

Son of Tzaduk and Ruchl. Born on 18 May 1896 in Radomsk of Hasidic parents. His father died when he was 10. His closest relative, the Amshinower [Mszczonow] rebbe, wanted to take him under his guardianship; however, he refused this and became a hat maker. Being under the influence of the socialist agitation, he joined the *S.S.* [Social Zionist] Party where, in a short time, he became a leading person. Led a strike of the hat makers. Later, he gave up his vocation and together with Hershl Kraus, led an *S.S.* cooperative children's home. Became a member of the committee to distribute aid after the First World War. The homeless arrived in the city. He married one of the homeless women. His father-in-law then sent him the required papers and he came to America in 1921.

Here he again became a hat maker. Became acquainted with a group of workers in the same occupation, led "enlightenment" work among them. After carrying out a successful strike, he was ejected from the hat making trade because of a denunciation and threw himself into communal work, becoming a representative of the *Morgn-Freiheit* [*Morning Freedom*] in Rochester, N.Y., where he lives to this day.

During the war, Bajgelman took part in the sale of war bonds and reached a sum of three hundred thousand dollars. Therefore, he received an award from the Treasury Department. He also took an active part in the clothing campaign for the needy, suffering Jewish war victims.

Y. Beser

(photograph)

Born in Czenstochow in 1892. Came to America in 1907. He is a member of the Knights of Pythias.

Josef Bezborodko

(photograph)

Josef Bezborodko, one of the pioneers of the mirror industry in Czenstochow, was expelled by the Czarist government from his residence in Russia that was outside the Pale of Jewish Settlement. He settled in Czenstochow in 1907 when he was already 40 years old. He became rooted in and bound to his new hometown, so that later when he had the opportunity to settle legally in Petersburg, where his brother lived, he refused, placing the Jewish environment and education of his children above material privileges.

Born in Slutzk, a city in Belarus known for its learning, with a father who was a glass-maker, he migrated with his parents to Moscow where he attended a Russian *gymnazie* [secondary school]. Not having the standing to enter a university because of a quota, at age 20 he began to work with his older brother in the mirror factory that his father had founded in 1891.

With the expulsion from Moscow, he had to leave the city within 8 days, while his older brother could remain for another year in order to liquidate their assets. He settled in Orsha, which was located within the Pale of Jewish Settlement; founded a mirror factory there, but it was not successful. He was then 24 years old. He gave up the factory and together with his brother founded a little factory in Praga near Warsaw. When it was not successful, he left for Lodz, where the stream of Russian Jews from Moscow went. Here, he founded a textile factory (of Polish quilts) with his brother, but the factory was also quickly liquidated. He married a daughter of an estate owner from Nezwich, not far from his home and himself became a landowner in Andrzejow near Lodz. Several years later, he decided to to his trade – mirror fabrication. Meanwhile his brother had set up a mirror factory in Petersburg and communicated with Czenstochow. This led Bezborodko to the idea of founding a mirror factory in Czenstochow.

At that time, in 1907, the entire mirror industry in Czenstochow produced 2-3 crates of mirror glass a week. However, Bezborodko foresaw that Czenstochow could become a better place for mirror fabrication than Moscow because Germany and its modern methods of production were next door and because of the rapid development of industry in Czenstochow in general.

Being acquainted with the demands of the Russian market, he appropriately advised his customers, the small manufacturers of celluloid and metal frames. Thanks to this, their production grew and more mirrors were used. The mirror industry in Czenstochow grew from 2-3 crates to 30 crates a week in the Bezborodko factory alone, in addition to around 6 in the remaining mirror factories.

[Page X]

Bezborodko was a man of stately appearance and a sage. In addition he was also a person with a good Jewish soul and a great philanthropist. He was both *frum* [pious] and worldly. He permitted his children to study in the Polish and Russian *gymnazies* and also was concerned with their Jewish education. As a Russian Jew, a "Litvak," a *misnagid* [opponent of Hasidism], he was viewed with great sympathy by the diverse Hasidim, who by nature did not think highly of Litvaks. He made his entire home Jewish at Dojazd 21 (where he established his factory and also his residence), which was previously a Christian neighborhood. He founded a *shul* for praying in the courtyard of the house and for a time, gave his own apartment for that purpose. He was one of the founders of an interest-free loan fund and often he himself helped with interest-free loans. He worked in the *Makhziki haDas* [Supporters of the Faith] *Talmud Torah* together with the Gerer and Pilcer Hasidim. As a longtime worker with *ORT* in Russia, he helped the Czenstochower Artisan's *shul* and the gardner's farm. He belonged to the founders of the communal *Tevunah* [Understanding] which was led by the Grajewer Rebbe, a *Mizrakhi* leader, who had the goal of teaching *yeshiva-bohkerim* (students) worldly subjects and a trade. He was also active in the Lodz *Hazamir* [choir].

During the pogrom of 1919, the Christian workers from his factory came running from Stradom and Rakow to protect his house and family.

Although he suffered from a weak heart the entire time and had frequent heart attacks, his illness grew greater during the pogrom. He died in 1922 at age 55, leaving a wife with 10 children. [Translator's note: It is stated that he had 10 children, but below the names of 11 are given.]

The Jewish *kehile* [community] in Czenstochow gave him the best [burial] place near the *ohel* of the Pilcer Rebbes, although he was a Slutzker *misnagid*.

Josef Bezborodko's children, 4 sons and 6 daughters – Hilel, Bashka, Asnakh, Dovid, Miriam, Perl, Haya, Israel, Sara, Ryfka and Boris (the last 4 born in Czenstochow) – all settled in France. A number of them created mirror and glass industries there.

The pioneer among them was Dovid (Dave) Brezborodsko, who went abroad on business in 1924 and, by chance, became ill and as a Russian citizen found that his visa had expired and he remained abroad. After wandering, he settled in France, created several important inventions in the pharmaceutical field, mirrors for instruments, and founded two mirror factories there – one in Saverne and later a second in Paris. In 1929, with his assistance, his entire family came to France.

The mother and all of her children, sons-in-law and grandchildren survived the tragedy of the Hitler occupation. Three sons and two sons-in-law served in the French army. The youngest son, Boris, who graduated from a *lyceum* [secondary school] and was an officer and two sons-in-law were in German captivity, one of them wounded. However, they successfully escaped from the prison camps and came home, then to Lyon, in the so-called "free zone." The family stayed together and survived with the help of a Christian friend. The sons were active in the armed underground. Boris, in particular, excelled as a leader of a Jewish group. A scout leader as a youth and knowing the paths in the Alps, his assignment was to smuggle Jewish children across to Switzerland. He was arrested and terribly tortured by the Gestapo. However, he successfully escaped and continued further his rescue work. He was arrested a second time and sent to Oswiecim [Auschwitz]. Through a miracle, he saved himself from the lime kiln. He came home after Hitler's defeat – a skeleton with sunken eye sockets; several months passed before his strength and human appearance returned.

A second victim was the son-in-law Ginsburg, an agronomist, who was occupied in providing food for the underground fighters. He was arrested by the Gestapo several days before Paris was liberated and until now has not returned.

(photograph, caption: Dovid Bezborodko)

The only one who left France was Dovid (Dave Bezborodko). He came to New York with the help of the French League of Human Rights, in which he was active. He experienced all of the difficulties of a refugee, particularly because of his Bezborodker stubbornness in keeping *Shabbos*. Later he founded a mirror factory, Mechanical Mirror Works, where up to one hundred workers are employed. As a *Poale-Mizrakhi*, his ideal was to create a cooperative glass and mirror factory in *Eretz-Yisroel* and to develop the glass and mirror industry there.

Izzy Berger

Son of Shlomoh (Pultrok) and Sheindel; born in Czentochow on 10 November 1911. Came to America on 4 August 1911. Member of the Czenstochower Branch 22 of *Int. Arbeter Ring* and executive member of the Czenstochower Relief Committee in Los Angeles.

His two sons, Jack and Seymour, served in the American army.

Izzy Berger was one of the first founders of the *Patronet* to help political prisoner arrestees in Poland and the first meeting took place in his apartment. He was the treasurer of *Patronet*. He also helped to organize the Nowaradomsk *Patronet*; in addition, he helped create 22 *Patronets* that did their important work for several years.

[Page XI]

During the war, he worked very hard with Czenstochower Relief.

(photograph, caption: Izzy and Eva Berger)

Eva Berger

Born in Wolbrom on 20 October 1893. Came to America in 1912. Married in 1915. Member of Br. 11 Int. *Arbeter Ring* and in the Czenstochower Ladies Auxilary.

She died in 1946.

Bronislaw Bergman

The well known banker Bronislaw Berkman occupied a very distinguished place among the personalities and communal workers in Czenstochow.

Born on 20 December 1861 in Boczkowice (near Czenstochow), he showed great capabilities in his youth while still a student in a *gymnazie*. His father, Shimeon Berman, a *maskhil* [enlightened] Hebraic writer and a co-worker at the journal *Yudshenko*, wanted to give his son an academic education in addition to a national-progressive upbringing. However, the weak condition of Bronislaw Bergman's eyes caused him to end his studies and enter the world of trade and industry.

He worked a short time outside Czenstochow and in 1890 came back and took over the management of his brother's bank business, where he later became a partner.

In addition to the field of banking, he also excelled as a founder of various industrial undertakings that played a role in Polish industry. He was also one of the founders of the Czenstochower Credit Society.

The years of crisis after the revolution of 1905, as well as the state of health of B.B.'s eyes forced him to reduce his social and commercial activities. In 1923, he completely lost his sight and, on 29 December 1929, he died.

Bronislaw Bergman was also very knowledgeable about the law. Often, even lawyers would turn to him for advice and he always showed them how to emerge from difficult entanglements.

He participated in the social work of our city in *Dobroczynnosc* [charity] and also with the creation of the Czenstochower synagogoue. As a great philanthropist, he and his wife, Tekla, aided many of the poor of our city.

(photograph, caption: Tekla Bergman)

Tekla Bergman (née Herc – of the well know family Poznanski in Lodz – her father graduated from rabbinical school in Warsaw and was a community worker in Lodz) also participated on her own in aid work for Jewish Czenstochow...

(photograph, caption: Anna Bergman)

Bronislaw Bergman left three children: one son – Dr. Stephan Bergman, today a lecturer at Harvard University in Cambridge, Mass., and two daughters, Anka and Marta; the latter was a practicing lawyer in our city before the war. Both perished during the German occupation.

s

Marta Bergman

(photograph)

Daughter of Bronislaw and Tekla. Born on 2 February 1904 in Czentochow. After finishing *gymnazie* in Czenstochow, studied at Warsaw University and graduated as a lawyer.

After practicing in various cities in Poland, Lodz and Piotrkow, she settled in Czenstochow where she was active as a lawyer. In 1935, she married Engineer Haltrekht of Lodz and because of this moved there, where she was further active as a lawyer.

Shared the fate of the martyrs in the years 1939-1945.

Yosel Berliner

(photograph)

Born in 1887 in Czenstochow. In 1903 he came to Lodz to work as a tailor for 80 *rubles* a year. The work hours were from 6 in the morning until 12 at night.

In 1904 Yosel Berliner took part for the first time in a meeting in the woods around Lodz. After the meeting, a demonstration took place that led to mass arrests. He was one of those arrested and he served three months in jail. After, he came back to Czenstochow. He joined the S.S. [Social Zionists] and worked for the liberation movement, where he excelled in his boldness and heroism. Once he was wounded in a clash with the police and Yankl the cane maker took him home to Warsaw. After two months, he returned to Czenstochow and his friends sent him to rest in a village. A friend went along to help him. The friend had a revolver with him and it fired unintentionally. The police came and began to shoot at them. They shot back and the police ran away. He and his companion had to go to a safer place.

[Page XII]

Once, the committee sent Berliner to Klobuck to prevent a pogrom organized by the *Endekes* [anti-Semitic nationalist party]. According to the information, the pogrom was supposed to start after the mob left the church. He took a group of firemen in Klobuck with him and left them at the entrance to the church. He went inside alone and warned those assembled that if a pogrom took place, much blood would flow. The leaders became frightened and promised that no pogrom would take place and at that time they kept their word.

He was arrested in the summer of 1906, with Dovid Fajnrajch and Dovid Tavenhof, while collecting money for the party in the provinces and served three years in the Kelce prison. One of the many prison episodes was when he was locked up in a dungeon. The political prisoners all protested, broke everything in the prison and declared a hunger strike.

After being freed from Kelce prison, he left for America. At the Austrian border, he was arrested because he had a letter from the party with various addresses with him. The gendarmes beat him murderously in order to extract the names of his friends.

In America, he joined the International Ladies Garment Workers Union and helped the organizational campaign of that time. Later he moved to the Cloak Makers Union. The working conditions were then terrible. The workers were not easy to organize. They would throw bottles and stones and poured water through the windows of the shops on the organizers. It was difficult and bitter work to convince the workers that the union would better their situation. It was a long time until success in creating one of the best unions in America.

Yosel Berliner can be recorded as one of the fighters for workers' rights in his birthplace and in America.

———

Harry Bernstein

Son of Milton and Rose. Born in Brody (Austria) on 18 November 1902. Came to America in 1919.

———

Harry (Yeheil) Bratt

Norfolk

Born in Czenstochow. After serving for a year and a half in the Polish army, he left Czenstochow and settled in Berlin where he lived until 1923. In 1923, he moved to England and remained there until 1926. From England he came to America in 1926. Member of Branch 13 of A.F.F.A. in Norfolk. Also a member of Branch 11.

———

Moshe Dovid Brat

Son of Abraham and Fradel. Born in Kamyk (Poland). Died in Czenstochow in 1932 at the age of 76.

(photograph, caption: Moshe Dovid Brat and Zelda)

Zelda Brat

Daughter of Zelig and Hana Ita Helfgot. Died in Czenstochow, January 1941 at the age of 80.

Malka Brat

Daughter of Moshe Dovid and Zelda. Born in Czenstochow in 1895. A co-worker in the Y. L. Peretz School in Czenstochow starting in 1920. She died in Czenstochow.

Shaya Bratman

He was born as his parents' oldest son. After his father died, Shaya became the money earner for his family. This strongly affected his weak health and as a result he became ill. Despite the efforts of his comrades (he belonged to *Poale-Zion*) a cure did not succeed and in 1920 he died at the age of 22.

Max Brody (Berliner)

Chicago

Born in Lelew (near Czenstochow) in 1891. He belonged to the *S.S.* organization in Czenstochow during the years of the liberation movement and, was one of its active workers. He took a strong part in the organization of self-defense and directed its sections when a pogrom was expected in Czenstochow or when the sections were sent out to the *shtetlekh* around Czenstochow. A large number of revolutionary and conspiratorial undertakings were carried on with him taking part. He was recognized by the leaders of the party and beloved among the large number of party comrades. He was known in the party under the name "the dark Mendl."

He came to America in 1908.

Max Brody was a member of the Order of B'nai Brith and was also one of the founders and first president of the Czenstochower Educational Union in Chicago.

[Page XIII]

Yisroelke Broder

(photograph)

Son of Mordekhai and Rakhel. Born in Czenstochow in 1864. Came to America in 1884. Married in 1888 and has 5 grandchildren in the American army. Is a member of the Czenstochower *Chasam Sopher shul* [located at 8 Clinton Street in NYC], Bnai Israel Society. Was also a founder and treasurer of the Czenstochower Aid Society in New York. Today, a member of the United Czenstochower Relief in New York.

Ahron Broslowski

Fond du Lac, Wisc.

(photograph)

Son of Feiwel and Gitel. Born on the 20th July 1904 in Kamyk. Came from Czenstochow to America on 23 November 1922.

Max Brokman

Son of Wolf and Miriam. Born on the 16th August 1878 in Czenstochow. Came to America in June 1913. Married Minnie Lajpciger. Their sons, Louis and William, served in the American army. The first with the rank of captain and the second, a corporal.

Minnie Brokman

(photograph)

Daughter of Ahron Wolf and Tema Lajpciger. Born in Dzialoszyn. Was a member of the Ladies Auxiliary of the first *Dzialoszyner Khevra Anshei Bnei Achim.* Died on 4 December 1943 in New York at age 62.

Liber Brener

Czenstochow

(photograph)

Chairman of the Jewish regional committee in Czenstochow, member of the C.C [Central Committee] of the *Bund* in Poland. Born in Turyisk on Wolin of Hasidic parents who were intimates of the Trisker rabbinical court. He studied until age 13 in *khederim* [religious primary schools] and *yeshivus* [religious secondary schools] and teaching courses. Was one of the builders of the Jewish school systems in Wolin and pedagogues of the peoples' schools in Wolin, Lublin and in the Peretz school in Czenstochow. In 1925 lost the right as a teacher and educator because of his public political appearances. In 1936, he took over the management of children's insurance of *TOZ* [Society for the Protection of Health] in Czenstochow and in the entire Czenstochow area. Carried out this work until the outbreak of the Second World War. During the war until the liquidation of the Jews in Czenstochow, was one of the chief individuals with *TOZ* in Czenstochow, which carried on widespread activity. In the course of the German occupation until the deportation of the Jews, carried on an illegal children's club (*Swietlica*), where two thousand children received instruction, education and complete support. Ran a similar *Swietlica* illegal underground school] for 120 surviving children in the small ghetto. At the order of the Bund, during the entire occupation, he carried on conspiratorial work for the party in Czenstochow. While in the concentration camp of the *HASAG* [private German company *Hugo Schneider Aktiengesellschaft-Mentalwarenfabrik* that used concentration camp inmates for arms production] in Czenstochow, carried on constant contact with party and with the aid organization in Warsaw and Krakow. On 17 January 1945 when Czenstochow were liberated, he stood at the head of the Jewish regional committee in Czenstochow.

[Page XIII]

Gimel ג

Hirsh (Euzial Tzvi) Gancwajch

(photo)

Son of Mordekhai Gancwajch of Zawiercie, grandson of the famous rabbi Reb Yisroel Leib Gancwajch. Descended from many generations of rabbis. He received a religious education as a child, studied in the Ostrowcer *yeshiva*, and was the beloved student of the Ostrowcer Rebbe.

In 1893 he married Rywka Breindl, the only daughter of Henekh and Esther Yasower of Czenstochow and for many years he lived at his father-in-law's and studied *Torah* [*hut gegesn kest*]. At the same time, he studied in secret and graduated as an official rabbi. His youngest son, Abraham Gancwajch, was a Yiddish journalist in Lodz.

(photo, caption: Daughter of Hirsh Gancwajch)

[Page XIV]

He remained in Czenstochow at the outbreak of the Second World War and suffered the fate of the martyrs.

Yisroel Leib Gancwajch
Melbourne (Australia)
(photo)

Oldest son of Hirsh Gancrajch, also known under the name Ivan Ganc. He received a religious upbringing in the home of his parents. At age 13, he entered a *gymnazium*. He became a fervid Zionist under the influence of the literature of the Enlightenment. His friends were: Eliezer Plotzker, secretary of the Zionist organization in Czenstochow, and Wowche Wiewiorke, well known writer, who at the end lived in Paris and perished in the gas chamber at Auschwitz during the Nazi occupation.

In 1919, he came to Berlin where he continued his studies, then left for Antwerp, Belgium, where he lived until 1924. In that year he gave up his studies and began to trade in diamonds. He again became involved in his Zionist activities, such as working with Dr. Kubowitzki and Dr. Pruczanski, was active as a commissar of the Jewish National Fund and wrote articles in the Belgian Zionist publication, *Hatikwah*. In 1924 he left for Australia where he has a fur business and where he has remained to this day.

Moshe Dovid Gotajner

(photo)

Father of Hershl, Chaim, Yisroel, Saltshe and Abraham. Died on 16 November 1941 in Czenstochow.

Rojza Gotajner

(photo)

Daughter of Shimshon Horowicz. Perished in 1942 during the deportations together with her son Hershl and his wife, and her daughter Sara Gruntsztajn and her child.

Moshe Gotlib

(photo)

He was called Moishele Gotlib in Czenstochow. His father, the *shoykhet* (ritual slaughterer) Nekhemia Gotlib, was murdered during the pogrom of 1919. Moishele belonged to the rightest *Poalei-Zion* and, although he was the youngest of his comrades, he became the chairman of the group. The struggle for Yiddish and Yiddish culture was at the head of his social activities. [His articles often appeared] in *the Czenstochower New Word* and in the *Czenstochower Zeitung* (newspaper). However, he suffered from lung disease and died at 30 years of age. In the last years of his life, he knew that the end of his life was near, but he did not stop his social activities and he never lost the smile on his face. He died in 1930.

Yisroel Goldsztajn
(Srolke the sugar baker [baker of cakes as opposed to bread])

(photograph)

Born in Piotrkow in 1873; came to Czenstochow in 1900. He married Hena Jakubowicz of Czenstochow and had a bakery there. Came to America in 1920; in the beginning he lived in Detroit. Later, in 1932, he came to New York. However, not being able to grow accustomed to the New York environment, he returned to Detroit, where he opened a bakery.

(photo, caption: Hena Goldsztajn)

Yisroel came to America with eight children (seven sons and one daughter). Joe and Arthur Goldsztajn today work in the bakery, under the name "Goldstein Brothers"; Seymour Morton (changed his name) is a pharmacist; David G. Morton - a doctor (served in the American army); Herman Goldstein – a mechanic; Karl and Morris Goldstein – pharmacists. The daughter, Rose, married Harry Jacobs (in Czenstochow, Yakubowicz). Born in Czenstochow, a son of Moshe Ahron Yakubowicz.

[Page XV]

(photo, caption: Arthur Goldstein with his wife and son)

Hena Goldstein died in Detroit on 19 May 1940 and Yisroel, 14 September 1934. Yisroel and Hena Goldstein belonged to the *Arbeter Ring* Branch 111 and to the Czenstochower Society.

Jonah Goldstein
Detroit

Son of Yisroel and Hena. Born in Czenstochow on 27 February 1903. Married Ester Litwonowicz. Came to America in 1921. In Czenstochowa was active in the *Fareinikte* [United] Party. He was a member of Bakers' Union, local 78 and in the Czenstochower Regional Union in Detroit.

Shlomoh and Ester Goldberg

(photo)

Son of Meir and Sara. Born in Noworadomsk (Poland) in 1870. He married Ester Gliksman. Came to America in 1922. Was a member of the Jewish National Union, Branch 10, in New York. Today he is a member of a family society; also belongs to the Melcer synagogue.

Jack Goldman

Son of Tuvya and Laya. Born in Czenstochow on 16 February 1899. Came to America in 1920.

David Guterman

(Photo)

Son of Zundl and Ruta. Born in Czenstochow in July 1908. Came to America in 1939. He is a member of United Czenstochower Relief in New York.

Wladislaw Gurski

Born in 1879 in Czenstochow.

Olga Lipska-Gurski

Daughter of Mauricy and Felicia Lipska. Born on 20 March 1884; the wife of Wladislaw Gurski.

Yitzhak Gurski

(photo)

The house in the neighborhood where he grew up can be designated as Orthodox-*Maskil* [enlightened] - assimilated. His grandfather, Hersh Gurski, founder of the first weaving factory in Dzialoszyn, near Czenstochow, himself a *frumer* [pious], a *mishnagid* [opponent of Hasidism], had a French governess for his daughters. They spoke French among themselves. The son, however, Yitzhak's father, Abraham, or Abremele (as the city called him), received a national-Jewish education. *Hatzfire* and *Di Izraelita* were read in his house. In general, he was only Polish on the outside, internally, Jewish.

Yitzhak Gurski, the youngest son of 4 brothers (8 children), studied in a *kheyder*, in Edelist's *folks* school and later took an examination to enter a *gymnazie*. Because of the restrictions for Jews, he went to Pabiance where the first commercial school was located with a 40-percent quota for Jews. He came to Czenstochow for vacations and maintained ties with his friends – Josef Kruk, Leizer Broniaslawski, Shimek Pruszicki, Alek Templ, Aizek Szwarc, Hela Birman, Matwei Dawidowicz and all of the others, who later belonged to the managing intelligencia of the *S.S.* [Zionist Social] Party.

In 1902, he, like all of his friends, was influenced by the Zionist organization. However, simultaneously, the revolutionary and social political ideas being carried like storm winds over Russia also had an impact.

He was one of the leaders of the *S.S.* Party and distinguished himself with his idealism, extraordinary energy and practical sense. And he was also the closest co-worker of Josef Number One (Dr. Josef Kruk).

Yitzhak Gurski was one of those who immediately began to plan and push the Czenstochower *S.S.* organization to organize the Jewish workers in Wajnberg's factory and in all the smaller factories, in order to obtain for them better working conditions and higher wages. He appeared on stage at the party mass meetings, taught political economy and other sciences to groups of people and campaigned among individual workers during the elections. He spoke in the schools when they came out openly against the Zionists and when the Jewish population was called to help with self-defense.

In February 1906 he was arrested and sentenced to exile in Siberia. However, he became ill and spent time in the city hospital, *Swenta Marya* [St. Mary]. The meetings of the leadership took place in the room where he lay and there was also storage of illegal literature.

In May 1906, because of the birth of the *Czarovitch* (Russian crown prince), an amnesty was issued. Yitzhak Gurski was then freed from prison.

[Page XVI]

On the same evening on which he was freed, an important party conference took place. Military and political police surrounded the house and arrested many participants. Gurski was successful in jumping out of a window and escaping.

In prison, where he served for three months, he became acquainted with several *pepesovtzes* [name derived from initials *P.P.S.* – Polish Socialist party] – clerks with the Herber Railroad. Through their patronage and acquaintance with the chief accountant, Grigory Cwietayev, a socialist, he was hired as an employee – almost the first Polish Jew, as a railroad clerk. The Polish anti-Semitic weekly, *Der Bocian* [*The Stork*], could not bear this and published his caricature with a long Jewish nose and bent shoulders on the first page.

The *P.P.S.* comrades assigned him to organize a professional union of the railroad workers. He carried out the assignment with great success. He was immediately fired from his position. The railroad workers and clerks presented him with a gift with the inscription, "in union there is strength."

Party work in Czenstochow was impossible for him. The Central Committee of *S.S.* appointed him and the *S.S.* member Dovid Pinski (shot on Piotrkow Street in a demonstration) to work in the Lodz organization.

Yitzhak Gurski was already a law student at Dorpat University then. In Lodz, he was occupied with giving private lectures. He devoted all of his free time to the *S.S.* movement.

In 1909, he left for Vienna because of police persecution. There he continued his studies as a legal scholar.

Yitzhak Gurski organized an *S.S.* group there, together with [Wolf] Latzki-Bertoldi, Dawidowicz, Anin, Chernikhov and other *S.S.* leaders who later came to Vienna, took part in publishing the journal *Freiland* [*Freeland*] and helped organize the Territorialist Congress in 1912 with Israel Zangwill at the head. He was also elected as president of the "Jewish Students from Russia," which counted around one thousand members; the second candidate for this position was the *S.S.* member, Moshe Raskin.

As president of the Russian students in Vienna, he was chairman of the international meeting to protest against the mass murder of the Lena gold miners in Siberia. Viktor Adler, Bertoldi, Daszinski, Borokhow, Tratzki, Levintzki, Anin, Ratner and many others appeared at the meeting. The protest meeting made a great impression abroad, such as in Russia.

During the First World War, Yitzhak Gurski was mobilized as a censor of the correspondence of prisoners of war because of his linguistic ability. He became chief of the division and received a silver medal from the Austrian government, although he was considered an "enemy foreigner."

His position as censor gave him the ability to connect with the Jewish war prisoners in the camps. He had a close connection to the group of Czenstochower war prisoners in the camp near Lintz, supported them and bonded with Czenstochow. He also helped organize a library and supported other cultural activities for the Jewish and non-Jewish prisoners in the camps.

At the same time he worked with the Austrian group of the *Zimmerwalder* (socialists who were against supporting their government in the war), led by Freidrich Adler, who shot the then Austrian Councilor, Count Sturgkh. From then on, he devoted his energy and ability to the Austrian workers' movement. He was the co-founder of the unions, *Freie Shul* [Free School] and *Kinder-Freint* [Children-Friends], and then helped both merge. He took an active part in the cooperative movement, was an instructor of rational conduct in cooperatives and a member of the managing committee of the "bulk purchase unions." During that time, he was a delegate to the Socialist International Congress 3 or 4 times.

As a close co-worker of Dr. Karl Renner, he led the Society for Russian-Austrian Exchange of Goods with great success and worked in all of the economic institutions of the workers' bank.

After the Dolfus-Schuschnigg putsch in 1934 in Vienna, he was arrested along with a series of socialist leaders, such as Dr. Karl Renner, Seitz – *Burgermeister* [mayor] of Vienna and many others.

He was one of the active workers when the *Freiland* movement was reorganized in 1936-1938, along with Dr. A. Singalowiski, Dawidowicz, Fajnleb, Dr. Kruk and others. Then he organized a large Territorialist organization in Vienna that counted thousands of members and published its own journal – *Freiland* – in German.

He also supported the Jewish children's homes in Czenstochow. The pharmacy there was set up with the financial resources that Yitzhak Gurski sent from Vienna.

In March 1939, Hilter annexed Austria. At the end of June of the same year, [Yitzhak Gurski] together with his wife, Hela (née Hela Birman) and their two children were successful in coming to America.

His son, Joslan, born in Vienna, graduated from the University of Technology as an electrical engineer and also studied the English language at the University of London.

His daughter, Irene, also born in Vienna, studied medicine in the universities in Vienna, Rome and in America – at Philadelphia's Woman's Medical College. She practices now as a physician [in a] post graduate hospital and specializes in heart ailments.

In New York, where Yitzhak Gurski settled, he is active in the *Freiland* movement, in the Austrian Socialist Group and in the aid work for Czenstochow.

At the time of the Second World War, his pharmaceutical corporation, which he founded, produced important articles for the war industries. His son, Joslan, engineer and manager of the factory, also created several important inventions in the field.

[Page XVII]

Yitzhak Gurski left the following family members in Czentochow: sisters – Rywkale and her husband, Yakov Dawidowicz, Cesha and her husband, Dovid Leizerowicz, Ester and her husband, Henek Krawizki, Wola-Krisztoforga, Toyba and her husband, Yakov Kroskalowski.

Brothers – Wladek Gurski and his wife Olga Lipska and Bernard Gurski.

(photo, caption: Wladislaw Gurski)

The only ones who survived were Adek and Henya Kromalowski, children of Yakov Kromalowski – now in Czenstochow; Henya and Branislaw Leizerowicz (brother of Dr. Leon Leizerowicz, now in New York, practices as a medical doctor) – both in the Soviet Union, and awaited in Poland; Nadja Gurski, a daughter of Bernard Gurski, a dentist in *Eretz Yisroel*; Manka Gurski, a daughter of Wladek Gurski – should be found in the Soviet Union.

Hela Birman-Gurski

Her mother, Szlezinger, was a Czenstochower. Her father came from Nowo-Radomsk. The Birman family lived in Czenstochow until 1901, then they moved

(photo, caption: Hela Gurski and Madja Zalcman)

to Sosnowiec and there founded an exchange house. They were well-to-do, middle class and progressive. In addition to a worldly education, her brothers studied Hebrew. Hela studied only Polish and other languages. Her brother Ludwig Berman was one of the pioneers in the *S.S.* Party and took part in the Congress in Swider, where the middle school youth organization of the Worker-Zionists was founded. He was a great influence on his sister, Hela. At the same time, Hela was under the influence of Adolf Bril and Senjar, who worked together with her in Markusfeld's office at *Malarnja* and they both were leaders of the *S.D.K.F.L.*

Senjar (a brother-in-law of Radek) was one of the pillars of the S.D. Party. The center of Social Democratic literature was in his house – *Iskra* [*Spark*], which was published abroad, was sent from his house to all of the cities of Russia.

The main place in her consciousness was won by the program of the *S.S.* because it matched the facts of life which she saw around her such as, for example, how the Jewish workers were ejected from a factory such as *Malarnja*. The same as in all other factories, Jews were directors and bookkeepers and the non-Jews were at the machines in the factory. On the contrary, she saw the great Jewish masses as poor merchants and market stall keepers and the Jewish peasants carried their baskets around to the houses.

Hela Birman – quiet, modest, withdrawn from the noisy life – quietly carried out responsible secret party work, such as forwarding illegal literature, transferring weapons and similar missions.

One of her most daring assignments was once to clean out the quarters of Ahron Singalowski, who was "exiled." She had to take with her a mass of weapons and literature which was beyond her physical abilities. And to cross several streets.

When her brother, Ludwik, was in the Piotrkow prison and later sentenced to hard labor, she smuggled literature to him and maintained his party connections.

She and Bronya Koniarski led organizing work among the peasants. Hela also ran a secret school where girls were taught to read and write. The "dark" Frandl was one of her pupils.

She met Yitzhak Gurski in 1903 through her brother, Ludwik. He, along with Yitzhak Gurski and Josef Kruk, influenced her in favor of the *S.S.* Party, for which she was a great prize. However, the prize was even greater for Yitzhak Gurski himself, because on 31 December 1911, they were married in Sosnowiec and, in January 1912, they were already in Vienna.

In Vienna, she helped Yitzhak Gurski in his community work, particularly in the education and organizing work among the masses

"What I dislike the most is the lack of understanding among the masses," she would say. And she tried to fight the lack of understanding.

In New York, Hela Birman is active in the women's group of the *Freiland* League.

Hersh Ber Gimpel
Chicago

Son of Yitzhak Yona and Chana. Born in Koniecpol (Poland) on 26 August 1878. He married Ruchl Berkensztat. Came from Czenstochow to America on 6 August 1906. Is a member of the Hebrew Progressive and Czenstochower Educational Union in Chicago.

Abraham Meir Glater
and Freidl Glater – Vienna

Son of Mordekhai and Ryfka. Died in Czenstochow at age 56 in Czenstochow.

(photo)

[Page XVIII]

Max Glater

(photo)

Son of Avraham Meir and Franya. Born in Czenstochow on 24 December 1886. Lived for a time in Germany and, from there, came to America on 4 June 1906. He married Millie Silberberg. Was president for 5 years of the Eva Magnes Memorial Family Society, president of the Educational Industrial League in New York and member of *B'nai Brith*. His son Sidney served in the American army.

Millie Glater

(photo)

Daughter of Hershl and Liba. Born in Lodz. Came from Germany to America on 4 June 1906. Married Max Glater.

Ruchl Gliksman

Daughter of Abvraham and Miriam Gliksman. Born in Czenstochow in 1911. Graduated from the Jewish *gymnazium* in Czenstochow. Now in New York. Member of United Czenstochower Relief. Married Ari Fogel, son of Reb Akiba Fogel, may he rest in peace.

Reb Abraham Gliksman, may he rest in peace

(photo)

Born in Czenstochow in 1885. The son of Dov-Berl (known under the name the *groiser* [big] Berl) and Hinda Gliksman. He studied in a *kheyder* from his early years on with the Amstower rabbi, with the *gaon* (Reb Avraham'la, of blessed memory) and later studied independently in the city *beis-hamedrish* [house of study].

Along with his Jewish studies, he simultaneously had a worldly education and this enabled him to become an independent merchant. He became well known as an honest and solid merchant in the world of trade in and outside of Czenstochow. He excelled with good virtues in his private and family life, too.

He took part in the communal life of Czenstochow for a time as a managing committee member of the *beis-lekhem* [bread for the needy – organization to help the poor] and for the Jewish *gymnazie*. He was also one of the co-founders of the new *beis hamedrish, Ohel Nahum* and published a special brochure about them. In addition to his usual offices in the above mentioned organizations, he assisted with every activity for the poor in our city

He suffered the fate of the martyrs in the years 1939-1945.

May his soul be bound up in the bond of eternal life

Sheva Gliksman

The daughter of Abraham and Miriam Gliksman. Born in 1908 in Czenstochow. Graduated from the Jewish *gymnazium* in Czenstochow. Married Yitzhak Horowicz (son of the well-known industrialist Dov Ber Horowicz). Suffered the fate of the martyrs in the years 1939-1945.

May her soul be bound up in the bond of eternal life.

Miriam Gliksman, may she rest in peace

(photo)

The wife of Abraham Gliksman, may he rest in peace. She was born in Czenstochow in 1885 as a daughter of Reb Nusen-Yakov and Feigel Klajner (née Grylak). She took part in the communal life of our city as vice-chairman and member of the managing committee of the woman's aid organization, *Ezra*, and also as a member of the *Dobroczynnosc* [group that gave aid to the poor]. In addition to this, she was active in every aid activity for the poor and needy and gave a great deal of effort and strength to them. Her house in Czentochow was the location where every poor man found help and support. Year in and year out, every winter she herself would organize a clothing collection for the naked and barefoot.

In private life she was *frum* [pious] and traditional.

Suffered the fate of the martyrs in the years 1939-1945.

May her soul by bound up in the bond of eternal life.

Abraham and Miriam Gliksman had five children: Wolf Gliksman, secretary and executive member of United Czenstochow Relief, now in New York.

Sheva Gliksman-Horowicz – suffered the fate of the martyrs in the years 1939-1945.

Rukhl Gliksman-Fogel – now in New York.

Dr. Engineer Josef Gliksman – now in Tel Aviv.

Dov-Berl Gliksman – died in 1930.

Clare Barenboim-Gliksman

Daughter of Avraham and Sonya Barenboim. Born on the 4th February 1914 in Odessa. The second wife of Wolf Gliksman.

[Page XIX]

Dr. Engineer Josef Gliksman
Tel Aviv

Son of Abraham and Miriam Gliksman. Born in Czenstochow in 1913. He, like every Jewish child of the Jewish middle class, studied for a time in a *kheyder*, private school, until *gymnazie*. After being a student in a Jewish *gymnazie*, he had taken part in a wide range of activities among the Jewish youth, spreading Zionist ideas as one of the organizers of *Betar* [militant Zionist youth organization] in Czenstochow, where he later became head of the youth branch.

In 1933 he received a certificate of university admission from the Jewish *gymnazium* in Czenstochow and the same year went to study in Italy. After attending universities in Genoa and Milan (Italy), he ended his studies in 1939 with the title Dr. of Civil Engineering.

After a short visit with his parents, in July 1939, he traveled as an "illegal" immigrant to *Eretz Yisroel* on a ship which carried the name *Pirata*, which sailed around the Mediterranean Sea for seven weeks. The occasion arose for him to play a significant role. The immigrants decided on a certain day to arrest the captain and the sailors because they refused to bring the ship to Tel Aviv. A committee was organized that took the ship into their hands. Dr. Eng. Josef Gliksman managed the machine room and brought the ship *Pirata* under the white and blue flag into Tel Aviv opposite the Ritz Hotel on 22 August 1939.

In the years 1939-1942 he worked in Syria, Trans-Jordan and Lebanon.

Today he lives in Tel Aviv, as an independent construction engineer, with his wife, Frida (born in Vienna, Austria), also an illegal immigrant, and their son, Gabriel.

Itmar Gliksman

Son of Wolf and Sofia Gliksman. Born on 10 January 1939. Suffered the fate of the martyrs in the years 1939-1945.

Master of *Phil.* Sofia Minc-Gliksman

The first wife of W. Gliksman, daughter of Yitzhak-Meir and Sara Minc. Born in Czentochow in 1907. After graduating from the Jewish *gymnazium* in Czenstochow, she studied at Warsaw University and graduated from the Philosophy-Humanistic faculty (history) with the title Master of Philosophy, with a description about the city of Sireadz (Poland).Coming back to Czenstochow, she taught general and Polish history in the first state *gymnazie* (Pladowski) in Czenstochow. Sofia Minc later officially became the vice director and teacher at the government *folk*-school no. 13 on Krakower Street, where she held the position together with Miss Natalya Szakhner until the outbreak of the Second World War.

Suffered the fate of the martyrs during the years 1939-1942.

Elfrida Shimerling-Gliksman
Tel Aviv

Daughter of Otto and Ernestina Shimerling. Born on 8 January 1918 in Vienna (Austria). The wife of Dr. Eng. Josef Gliksman.

Reb Josef Gliksman,
may his soul be bound in the bond of eternal life

Son of Dov Berl and Hinda Gliksman. Born in Czentochow. Studied with the Czenstochower *gaon*, Reb Abraham'le, of blessed memory and there received his rabbinical diploma. Was known in Czentochow as a prodigy and one of the few scholars.

Suffered the fate of the Martyrs in the years 1939-1945.

Isidor Gliksman
Detroit

(photo)

Son of Meir and Sara Genendel. Born in Czenstochow on 5 March 1892. Worked in Czentochow in the celluloid trade and there was active in the sections of the professional unions. He was also active in the *S.S.* [Zionist Socialist] party. He left Czentochow in 1912 and emigrated to Galveston with the 67th group [Translator's note; numbering system used by the Jewish Immigrant Information Bureau to identify shiploads of immigrants coming to Galveston, Texas]. Came to America (New York) in 1913. He was a member of the *Arbeter Ring* Branch 261. He participated in the work of the Czenstochower Relief Committee. He served in the American army during the First World War. In 1919 he married Rosy Wegner and settled in Detroit. There he was one of the founders of the Czenstochower Union and is still active in the organization. He was also one of the founders of Czentochower *Arbeter Ring* Branch 620 in Detroit. His son, Meir, served in the American army.

Fishel Gliksman
Los Angeles

Son of Yitzhak and Hudes. Born in Noworadomsk on 3 February 1893. He married Gitl Birn-

(photo)

boim. Came to America on 10 December 1921. He was a member of the *Arbeter Ring*, executive member of the Jewish Workers' Committee in Los Angeles, and was also active in the Welfare Fund. His son Sidney served in the American Army. Died in 1946.

Gitl Gliksman
Los Angeles

Daughter of Shmuel Yakov and Beila. Born in Noworadomsk on 24 November 1897. She married Fishel Gliksman. In Noworadomsk she was active in the party of the left *Poalei-Zion*... also participated in the dramatic section under the of Artist Lesman. Came to America on 20 February 1935 with her son. She was a member of the the *Arbeter Ring*, active in the *Arbeter Ring* school union, Jewish Workers' Committee, *Arbeter Ring* chorus and with the Ladies' Auxiliary.

[Page XX]

Eliezer Gliksman

Son of Berl and Frimet. Born in Noworadmsk. The father of Elihu Ber, Ruchl, Moshe, Shlomoh, Bluma, Khona, Yosel and Nekhemia.

He died on *Lag b'Omer* 1921 in Krakow.

(photo, caption: Eliezer and Miriam Gliksman)

Miriam Gliksman

The wife of Eliezer Gliksman. Daughter of Khona and Sara Kalekhare. Born in Czenstochow. She died in Czenstochow in 1935.

Josel Gliksman

(photo)

Son of Eliezer and Miriam. Born in Czenstochow in 1891. He was a member of the Jewish National Workers' Union in New York. Died on 15 October 1918 in New York.

Nekhemia Gliksman

(photo)

Son of Eliezer and Miriam Gliksman. Born in Czenstochow. Married Sera Borszikowski. He died at the age of 47, on 2 August 1941 in New York.

Lipush Gliksman

(photo)

Son of Shlomoh and Dworya. Born in Czenstochow in 1910.

Khona Gliksman

(photo)

Born in 1889. Son of Eliezer (known under the name Eliezer's Khona) and Miriam. Being very *frum* [pious], they raised their children, 6 sons and 2 daughters, in a spirit of religion.

Khona Gliksman went to *khedorim* [religious schools] until 1905. That year, he started to work in Wajnberg's factory, where he was drawn into the *S.S.* [Zionist Socialist] party.

He was arrested in the factory on 23 January 1906. This was the day after the strike in connection with the *yahrzeit* [anniversary of the death] of Gabon who had led the Petersburg workers to the slaughter. Wajnberg, the manufacturers, incited the Christian workers against the Jewish ones. A fight broke out between them. Khona Gliksman said to the bosses – if they are interested in a pogrom, he would be the first one to make one on them. This led to his arrest. He was in the Czenstochower and Piotrkower prisons for 15 weeks and on 6 May, he came home to Czenstochow and became active in the revolutionary movement.

Realizing that they could not keep him away from the struggle, Khona's parents decided to send him to America. In July 1906, they sent him with the Bakheneks, family acquaintances (neighbors), to Toronto, Canada. He was there until December 1906. Later he arrived in New York to the Kremsdorf family (copper workers) who took him in. They are the best of friends to this day.

He was in New York until 18 December 1907, but because of economic and physical circumstances, he was forced to to Czenstochow.

Although he was at home for five years, he was very dissatisfied. He left Czenstochow for the second time in 1913 and, in February of the same year, he came to New York. He learned the presser trade where he works to this day.

In 1914, he helped create the Czenstochower Relief Organization, later the Czenstochower Relief Committee. He was very active in the organization. He was a member of the Czenstochower branch 111 of the Jewish National Workers' Union, and when the branch was united with a group of members of branch 261 of the *Arbeter Ring*. He was later a member of branch 11 of the International Workers Order, where he is a member to this day.

In 1920, he brought from the old home, Fradel Brat, now his wife, who the *landsleit* would call "the dark Fradl" and in April of the same year married her. A daughter – Chana – was born to them in August 1921. In March 1941, their daughter married Harry Singer, who volunteered to join the American army in 1942.

[Page sXXI]

Fradl Gliksman also worked in Wajnberg's factory. Was active in the revolutionary movement. Belonged to the *S.S.* party. Was one of the founders of the children's home, worked there at first as a volunteer for several months, later was paid – was hired officially to take care of the children and run the household. She worked with the teachers, Yusha Sztam and Haja'le Waga, who is now in New York.

Fradl Gliksman

Her childhood name was Fradl Brat. She was popularly known as "the dark Fradl."

Grew up in a poor house (her father, Moshe Dovid and her mother, Zelda), with seven children. She had to begin work at age 9 in a small toy factory. Later, in the years 1904-05, she worked in Wajnberg's comb factory.

In the years of the freedom movement, she was in the *S.S.* party and later was an example of self-sacrifice and devotion to the ideals of the party. She took part in the most dangerous secret undertakings, such as arranging for secret publications and never missed the stormy meetings, the mass meetings and street demonstrations.

In 1906, she was expelled from Wajnberg's factory with Khona Gliksman, as leaders of a strike. It was impossible for her to find work for a long time. In order to be in constant contact with party work and avoid arrest, she worked as a "cook" in Golda's teahouse. Later, she succeeded in getting work in Werde's needle factory. She threw herself again into the work, first in the years of the First World War, when the Education Union was founded. Later, in 1917, without any education, she began to work in the Y.L. Peretz Children's Home that was her ideal. In her free time, she devoted herself to organizing work among the masses of children. She left Czenstochow in 1920. She came to America that same year and married her young friend, Khona Gliksman.

In New York, she first joined a Jewish National Workers' Organization; now, she is a member of the Czenstochower branch 11 of the Jewish Peoples Order (International Workers Order).

She was an active worker in aid work for Czenstochow for the entire time, where her name will never be forgotten.

Yitzhak Gliksman

Son of Rubin and Ruchl Leah. Born in Czenstochow in 1901. When Czenstochow was occupied by the Germans during the First World War, he worked as a railroad worker and perished as a result of a tragic accident.

Sera Gliksman

(photo)

The daughter of Mendl and Feiga Haya Borszikowski. Born in Piltz [Pilica] (Poland). Lived in Czenstochow. Married Nehemya Gliksman. Came to America on 20 March 1921. She is an executive member of the *A.F.F* Order and a member of the Czenstochower Ladies Auxiliary in New York.

Efriom Glikerman

(photo)

Son of Yankel and Esther. Born in June 1883 in Czenstochow. Came to America in 1916. He was an active member and, for many years, treasurer of the Czenstochower Neighborhood Educational Union in Chicago. Died on 20 January 1938 in Chicago.

Haya Ruchl (Rose) Glikerman
Chicago

Daughter of Shmuel and Esther Sheindel. Born in Czenstochow on the 10 of July 1887. Came to America on 18 August 1920. Is a member of the Czenstochower Educational Union and Czestochower Aid Society in Chicago and the 1st Trustee of the Aid Society. After 18 months in the American army, her son, Sam, perished in a heroic death on the battlefield in France in the fight against Fascism.

Moshe Gebrowicz

(photo)

[Page XXII]

Born in Czenstochow in 1891, to poor parents. In 1904 his father died and this forced him to work and to alone feed himself. At this time he became a member of the small *Bund* and of its *boyuvke* [armed bands] and he took part in various actions until the party sent him to Piotrkow with two comrades. There he took part in freeing several arrested party comrades from prison. Approximately 30 men took part in this work. This happened at around 10 or 11 at night in the following manner: The guards that protected the prison on the street side were each attacked by 4 men from the *boyuvke* at a particular moment. They were rendered harmless by having sacks put over their head and they were taken away. The place of the guards was taken by [the attackers] and with a given signal, a thin string was lowered from a window to which Moshe Gebrowicz attached a thick one. Then the fences around the windows were removed and approximately 12 men began to lower themselves through the windows. They were immediately driven away in specially arranged horse cabs. After the "work," the participants and Moshe, too, were provided with a small sum of money and special letter and were driven to Lodz. There they were supported in a "teahouse," supported by the unemployed themselves, but simultaneously active in the party.

Once Moshe G. and several men were sent with party representatives to a wedding to collect money. It was then winter and the streets were full of snow. Around 2 o'clock at night they were attacked by the police and soldiers. It was clear that they had been denounced and the older ones who had weapons had just been able to give the weapons to Moshe the youngest of them. However, as he was unable to "legitimize" himself, he was arrested with the others. On the way to the arrest, he succeeded at a particular moment in diverting the attention of the police and he jumped into a pile of snow. He remained there until the frost drove him out. Meanwhile, the other detainees were led further away and seeing that the street was empty of people, he quickly returned to the wedding hall. There he met the representative and he was able to present himself as a server and in this way avoided arrest. Moshe G. devoted himself to everything. In such a manner, he saved the arrestees, because they did not find any weapons on them.

Moshe Gebrowicz lived for a time in Belgium and then in *Eretz-Yisroel*. A short time before the outbreak of the Second World War, he came to America and now lives in New York.

Itshe Gelber

Son of Dovid and Esther. Father of Morris. Died in 1924 at age 77 in Czenstochow.

(photo)

Malka (Dimant) Gelber

Daughter of Josef and Ruchl. Mother of Morris. Died in 1909 at the age of 60 in Czenstochow.

Morris Gelber

Son of Itshe and Malka. Born in Czenstochow on 10 December 1890. He married Gutshe Granek. Came to America on 17 December 1912. Gelber is an active member of the Czenstochower Young Men – chairman of the Loan Fund; is very active in United Czenstochower Relief in New York and, also, in the "Czenstochow" Book Committee. His son, David, and grandson, Saul Inerfeld, served in the American army.

(photo)

Gutshe Gelber

Daughter of Mikhal and Esther Granek. Born in Czenstochow on 2 May 1892. Came to America on 17 December 1912. She is one of the founders and most active members of the Czenstochower Ladies Auxiliary in New York and held the office of vice-chairlady for several years. Now chairlady of the relief undertaking. She is also a member of the "Czenstochow" Book Committee.

Leonard Gelber

Son of Morris and Gutshe Gelber. Born on 15 October 1914 in Pittsburg, Pa.

Merkin Gelber
Los Angeles

(photo)

Son of Shmuel and Liba. Born in on 5 May 1902 in Czenstochow. Came from Germany to America in January 1920. He married Fanny Akerfeld. Is a member of the Relief Committee of the Czenstochower in Los Angeles.

Khasrial Gelber

(photo)

Son of Yitzhak Leib and Shprinca. Born in Czenstochow in 1871. Came to America on 4 September 1929. Belonged to Cong. *Bnei Yakov*. Died in Montreal, Canada on 20 September 1934.

[Page XXIII]

Sara Gelber

(photo)

Daughter of Avraham and Chana Reizl. Born in Czenstochow on 20 March 1879. Came to America on 4 December 1929. Belonged to *Hadassah* and to Congregation *B'nei Jakob*. Died in Montreal, Canada on 27 October 1943.

Shimeon Gelber

(photo, caption: the father of Merkin Gelber)

Lipsze Gelber

(photo, caption: The mother of Merkin Gelber)

Died at age 40 in Czenstochow in 1906.

Avraham Gelber

Son of Lipsze Gelber. Born in 1883 in Czenstochow. Married Toyba, the daughter of Eli and Malka Wenger. Came to America in 1905. He is a member of the *Dzialoszyner Khevra Anshei Bnei Achim* in New York.

Abe Gerikhter

Son of Dovid and Reizl. Born in Czenstochow on 17 March 1894. Came to America in December 1909. Took part in the First World War as a soldier. He is a member of Jewish War Veterans and Branch 86 of A.F.F.A.

Kopl (Karl) Gerikhter

Son of Dovid (the big Dovid) and Relya Gerikhter. Born in Czestochow in 1885.

He studied in *kheyder* [religious school] and in Leder's school until age 14. Later, he worked in Tartak with the pious Reikhman and Rozencwajg. At age 16 he joined the *S.S.* [Socialist-Zionist Workers] Party. Later he was exiled to Wiotk *gubernya* [province], from where he successfully escaped and returned to Czenstochow.

Karl Gerikhter came to America in 1909, became a house painter and took a very active part in the Painters' Union local 1011. In 1910 he became a member of the Czenstochow Branch 261 *Arbeter Ring* and was secretary there for several years. In 1921 he married Regina Shmid. Gerikhter was always active in the Czenstochow Aid Union. When the Czenstochower Br. 11 of the Jewish National Workers' Union was founded, he became secretary of the branch and is a member to this day.

Because of his health, he cannot take part in communal activities.

Shlomoh Ahron German

(photo)

Father of Avraham Hershl, Helen, Ester and Israel. Died in Czenstochow in 1935.

Avraham German

Son of Shlomoh and Sheindl. Born in Czenstochow on 12 October 1900. Came to America on 10 November 1913. His is a member of the Czenstochower Young Men's Society in New York.

Mikhal Granek

(photo)

Son of Itshe Ber and Kreindl. Died at age 67 in 1930 in Czenstochow.

Makhshe Granek

(photo)

Daughter of Mikhal and Ester, sister of Gisze Gelber. Born in Czentochow on 10 June 1900. She was a victim of the First World War. Died on 15 September 1920 in Czenstochow.

[Page XXIV]

Esther (Lewkowicz) Granek

Daughter of Mikhal and Leah, died at age 68 in 1932 in Czenstochow.

Yehuda Leib Gruman

(photo)

Born in Janow (Poland) in 1859. Died in Czenstochow on 26 January 1935.

Perl Gruman

(photo)

Born in Janow (Poland) in 1868. Died in Czenstochow on 20 September 1929.

Rywka Gruman

(photo)

Daughter of Yehuda Lieb and Perl. Born in Czenstochow on 15 August 1908. Came to America in 1928.

Harry Gruman
Los Angeles

(photo)

Born in Czenstochow in 1898 into a poor home; the family consisted of 7 people (father, mother and 5 children). Lived in a room on Cicha Street in Meir Bem's house. His father, Leibush, was a shoemaeker, who earned from five to seven *gilden* a week. His childhood was a chain of hunger and need. He received his first "education" in a "day nursery" that was supported by charitable women. He did not spend a long time in *kheder* [religious elementary school]. He was more involved there with sewing buttons on panels for Grosman's button factory than with learning.

At age ten, he started to work at Koniarski's toy factory. At twelve his father offered him as an apprentice to his uncle, a tailor. However, he could not endure it for more than a year and then obtained work with the Marczak family, which treated him well.

In 1914, during the First World War when the Germans occupied Czenstochow, and hunger, cold and typhus were rampant in the poor neighborhoods, he worked for the Germans digging trenches in Biala Gora for a little warm soup and then went to Germany to work in the coal mines in the Rhineland. After working for six months in the coal mines under the most terrible conditions, he and a group of comrades escaped to Berlin, found work in a factory and later were active in a German theater.

In 1918 he took part in the revolutionary events of the German workers. In 1923 he came to New York and was active in the aid work for Czenstochow. In 1928 he moved to Los Angeles, Cal. and there became active with the progressive German workers. He was one of the organizers of Czenstochower *Patronet* in Los Angeles, which supported the political arrestees and their families in Poland. In 1940 he organized the "Naftali Botwin [Translator's note: Polish-Jewish Communist executed in Poland in 1925] Committee that seeks aid for the former Jewish volunteer fighters in Spain. In 1942 he was elected as Financial-Secretary of the city committee of ICOR. Always supported and was an active coworker in the work of Czenstochower Relief.

Moshe Gruman

(photo)

Son of Leibush and Perl Gruman. Born in Czenstochow on 4 February 1909.

In 1919 he went to Germany, where he settled in Berlin. When the Nazis came to power, he went to Belgium – from there to France. After the occupation of France, he entered the underground movement and thereby avoided deportation to Poland.

After everything, Moshe Gruman is now still in France.

Ruchl Grobowski
Chicago

Daughter of Moshe and Feigl Rubel. Born in Piotrkow. Came to America from Czenstochow on 9 May 1914. She was a member of the *Bund* in Poland.

[Page XXV]

Hersh Kalman Grosberg

(photo)

Son of Fishl and Dwoyra. Born in 1859 in Noworadomsk. Came to America in 1923. He was a very *frum* [pious] Jew until the end of his life. Died in 1944 in Los Angeles.

Ahron Grosberg (photo)

Son of Kalman and Chana. Born in Czenstochow, 1893; came to American on 11 September 1913. He belongs to the following organizations: Hotel and Restaurant Union, Am. Fed. of Labor, Jewish Fraternal Order, American Red Cross and Czenstochower Aid Organization in Los Angeles, where he is an executive member. He lives at 2516 Kent Street, Los Angeles, Cal.

Ahron Grosberg was of six children of Kalman the baker. His religious father placed great hopes on him and waited for him to become a religious scholar. His two older brothers already belonged to the Czenstochower workers movement. However, the stormy days of that time did not pass him by. After the premature death of his mother, he joined *Poalei-Zioni* under the influence of his friend, Moshe Censhinski. He became very devoted to the workers' movement, when a fire broke out in Landau's solenoid [coil of wire with an electric current and magnetic properties] factory where 7 young girls, workers, were burned. Instead of going to school as usual, on that day, he followed the funeral for the seven girls who perished. There was then a large demonstration in Czenstochow. All the factory workers stopped their work as a protest.

Here in America, he settled into further activities as a fighter in the workers' movement for a better world.

Mendl Grosberg
(known under the name: Mendl Kalman the baker's

[the son of Mendl Kalman])
(photo)

Son of Kalman and Chana. Born in Czenstochow in 1892. Came to America in 1912. He belongs to the Czentochower Aid Organization, Jewish Fraternal Order, American Red Cross. Is an executive member of the Czentochower Organization. Mendl ended his studies at the Czentochower *yeshiva* and went to work as a gaiter stitcher. He belonged to the *S.S.* [Zionist-Socialist] Party until leaving for America. Here he settled in Detroit. Worked with shoes and in Pensy Leather Goods. Finally he settled in Los Angeles, Cal., 2516 Kent Street. Mendl Grosberg is active in the progressive movement.

Fishl Yakov Grosberg

(photo)

Son of Kalman the baker and Chana. Born in Czenstochow in 1890. He became an orphan at age 11 and began to work in Wajnberg's comb factory and then became a member of a small covert group that was created there and from which the *S.S.* (Zionist-Socialist) movement later grew, to which he belonged.

Later he went abroad, where he wandered for several years. After returning home, he married Esther Peisak, known in Czenstochow as Esther the *Yaneverin* [woman from Yanev/Jonava, Lithuania] or Esterka, an employee in Erlich's sausage business.

Fishl Yakov Grosberg came to America in 1920 and settled in Detroit. In 1939 he moved to Los Angeles.

He has two sons. The oldest, Morris, has a wife and two little children; the second son, Eli, was a lieutenant in the army and served in the Hawaiian Islands.

Belongs to Czentochower Aid Organization; also takes part in the progressive movement.

Louis Jay Gross (Gric)
Chicago

(photo)

Son of Josef Hersh and Brandl. Born in Czenstochow on 5 May 1893. He married Netty Feldman. Came to America on 12 December 1911.

He is a member of *B'nai Brith*, American Jewish Congress, Zionist organizations and is one of the most active members of the Czenstochower Educational Organization in Chicago; executive member for many years and was president of the organization for two terms. He is also active in the Relief Committee in Chicago.

[Page XXVI]

His son, William, served in the American army.

Chantsha Grosman

She died in Philadelphia in 1941. Was an active worker for many years with Czenstochower Relief.

Y. Grosman (photo)

Died in 1941 in Philadelphia. Was an active worker for many years with Czenstochower Relief.

Yakov and Beila Grilak

(photo, caption: Yakov Grilak)

Son of Josef Grilak. Born in Krzepice (near Czenstochow). Was a member of the *Kherva Kadishe* [burial society] and *Gemilas Khesed* fund [interest-free loan fund]. One of the best Jews in Czenstochow.

Died in Czenstochow at the age of 75 in 1935.

(photo, caption: Beila Grilak)

Beila Grilak suffered the fate of the martyrs in the years 1939-1045.

They were the parents of Shimkhah Grey of Los Angeles, Cal.

Shimkhah and Yetta Grey (Grilak)

(photo, caption: Shimkhah Grey)
(photo, caption: the mother of Yetta Grey)
(photo, caption: Yetta Grey)

The Grilaks of Czenstochow were considered one of the aristocratic families. Yakov Grilak, Shimkhah's father, was a distinguished businessman, a *frumer* [pious] Jew and a member of the *Khevra Kadishe*, of the *Gemilas Khesed* and several other groups.

Shimkhah Grilak studied in the Czenstochower artisans' school; he was a student in a Warsaw technical high school.

In his early youth, he joined the *Poalei-Zion* movement and remains loyal to the idea and the party to this day.

As a student in the artisans' school, where Mendl Pakula was a master, he became acquainted with his daughter, Yetta Pakula, and married her before he left for America in 1912.

Yetta Grey, née Pakula, is the youngest daughter of Mendl and Reizl. The family consisted of two sisters and two brothers – Iser, Wolf, Sheindl (Szuchter) and Yetta. During the revolutionary years, the party workers would come into their house and later the *literatn* (workers of the Jewish literary society) and lyricists. Yetta took an active part in both – cultural and musical societies and excelled as an amateur in the dramatic section.

In 1913, she came to America and settled in Chicago. For a long time, the conditions in America were not easy for Shimkhah and Yetta. However, Yetta, a child of a toiling family, herself a tailor at home, with her work and, even more, with her natural cheerful good spirits, managed to lighten their life. Shimkhah and Yetta raised 2 children in America – Dan and Ruth. Both received a nationalist-Jewish education in the spirit of their parents.

Their house in Chicago was like the Pakula's in Czenstochow – one of the centers of *Poalei-Zion* and Jewish cultural activity. She was one of the first of a group who supported the children's homes in Czenstochow.

Under the pressure of difficult conditions, they left Chicago for Los Angeles, Cal., and, although, alone at first, she created, with her usual energy, a group of *Poalei-Zion* sympathizers around her and developed strong social activity.

Yetta Grey is active today, too, in the aid work for Czenstoochow.

Her mother, Reizl Pakula (her childhood name – Kwort), lives with her in Los Angeles. She is now 85 years old.

[Page XXVII]

Efriom Greitzer
Los Angeles

(photo)

Son of Shmuel and Toba. Born in Rudnik (Poland) on 25 August 1889. Married Feigl Birnboim. Came to America in 1912. Died on Wednesday, 16 January 1946. His sons, Melvin and Sam, served as officers in the American army.

(photo)
Feigl Greitzer

Meir Greitzer
Los Angeles

(photo)

Son of Shmuel and Toba. Born in Noworadomsk on 12 November 1887. Married Frimet Teneberg. Came to America from Czenstochow in June 1912. Is a member of *B'nai Brith*, Gardians and the Old Home for the Aged in Los Angeles. His son, Nathan, served in the American army.

(photo)

Frimet Greitzer

Mildred Gred

(photo)

Daughter of Isidor and Mary Rozen. Born August 1919 in New York. She married Stanley Gred on 31 January 1942. Their daughter, Joyce Ellen, was born on 23 December 1944.

Meir Grinberg
Detroit

(photo)

Son of Tuvya and Feige. Born in Czenstochow on 30 October 1898. He married Ita Balanski. Came to America on 12 May 1913. An active member of the Czenstochower Regional Union in Detroit.

[Page XXVII]

Dalet ד
Yehuda Danciger
Eretz Yisroel
(photo)

At age 15 his parents apprenticed him to a *tzuker-beker* [baker of cakes and pastries]. Later he left Czenstochow for Lodz and joined the *Poalei-Zion* party. He carried out conspiratorial work for it and was active in the professional movement, too, and took part in "self defense." One of his closest friends in Lodz was Holoderski, who fell in the struggle with the Nazis in the Lodz Ghetto.

In 1906 he was arrested and spent a year in the Sieradz prison. A year later he was exiled to the Tomsk region in Siberia for three years. Yisroel Warszawski, who is now in America, was exiled with him.

Upon his to Czenstochow, he was taken into the military in the Czarist army and took part in the First World War where he was captured [by the enemy].

After the war he returned to Czenstochow and, under the leadership of Shimeon Waldfogel, he again became active in the *P.Z.* party. He was a party candidate for Czenstochower City Council and after the death of Shimeon Waldfogel succeeded him.

He arrived in *Eretz Yisroel* in 1925. Here, too, he took an active part in the workers' movement. Led his trade section and was a member of the city managing committee for the *Vaad Hacarmel* in Haifa.

[Page XXVIII]

He was the founder of the Czenstochower *landsmanschaft* society in Haifa and is a member of *Vaad Hartzi* of the Czenstochower *landsmanschaft* in *Eretz Yisroel*. He is the founder and chairman of the interest-free loan fund in Haifa, where Czenstochower *landsleit* [people with a connection to a town] receive loans.

He did not stand alone in his work during the entire time of his communal activities. His life's companion, his wife, always helped him in the work and together with him led the struggle for a better future for our people.

Esther Danski
Detroit
(photo, caption: née Krakowski)

Daughter of Moshe and Dwojra. Born in Czenstochow in 1923. She is a member of *B'nai Brith* and the Jewish Center in Detroit.

Berl and Rywka Ducon
Newark, N.J.
(photo)

Son of Shmuel and Chaja Sura. Born on 5 May 1890 in Czenstochow. Came to America in 1912. Member of the Tarnopoler Society in Newark, N.J.

Moshe Jalowski
(photo)

Born 1870, died 1936. He was a distinguished merchant and shoe manufacturer. He received a bronze medal at the exhibition in Czenstochow in 1909 as an award. His product: a pair of boots – stood in water for the entire time of the exhibition and did not allow any dampness to penetrate inside.

His daughter, Feiga Hirszberg, in now in *Eretz Yisroel* and made a contribution to the Czenstochower Aid Fund in his name.

Hershl Dukat
Chicago
(photo)

Son of Eliezer and Yocheved (Yachet). Born in Witkowic (Poland) on 25 May 1892. He married Sura Cwajgenboim. Came to America on 29 August 1913. Their sons, Leizer and Naftali, and sons-in-law, Arthur Schapiro and Irving Zeidman, served in the American army.

Hershl Dukat is a member of the Mount Sinai Synagogue, *Bikur Cholim* [group for visiting the sick] and of the Czenstochower Educational Society in Chicago.

Wolf and Miriam Diamond
(photo)

Wolf Diamond was born in Czenstochow, January 1867. Came to America – New York – in 1904. He is a member of Czenstochower Chasam Sopher Synagogue, New York.

Philip Jacobs
Philadelphia

Rose Jabobs
(née Goldsztajn)
Detroit
(photo)

Daughter of Israel and Hena Goldsztajn. Born on 23 February 1912 in Czenstochow. Came to America in 1921. She is a member of *B'nai Brith*.

Hersh (Jakubowicz) Jacobs
Detroit
(photo)

Son of Moshe Ahron and Liba, born on 8 June 1904 in Czenstochow. Came to America on 2 July 1921. He is a member of *B'nai Brith*.

[Page XXIX]

Joe Jacobs
(photo)

Son of Hersh Leib and Chana. Born in Proskau (Poland) on 15 April 1890. Came to America on 10 November 1906. He is a member and active worker of the Czenstochower Young Men's Society and executive member of United Czenstochower Relief. His son, Irving, served in the American army.

Gussy Jacobs

Daughter of Isidor and Dorothy. Born in Vilna on 28 September 1893. Came to America in May 1906. She is the wife of Joe Jacobs. Is a member of the Czenstochower Ladies Auxiliary in New York.

Annie Druz

The daughter of Mr. and Mrs. Druz. Married Jack Rozen, son of Izidor and Mary Rozen.

Max (Kupersztok) Delow
(photo)

Born in July 1889. 14 years later he was already in *Achdus* [Unity] in Lodz and a year later, a member of the *S.D.K.P.L.* (Social Democracy of Poland and Lithuania) in Czenstochow.

The number of members of the Czenstochower organization at that time consisted of about 50 people – 20 intellectuals and 30 workers. The names of several intellectuals were: Magdeline, a bookkeeper with the Czenstochowa-Vianke, Karl Olszewski, bookkeeper with Szpagaczarnja, Wirgorowski, a pharmacist with Malarnja, and our Rubinsztajn, beloved by everyone (Rubin), Doctor of Philosophy, member of the Central Committee, who traveled from city to city and, therefore, was rarely in Czenstochow.

A mass movement grew out of the small group that was spread through all the large factories.

The most difficult struggle that the party carried on was with the *P.P.S.* [Polish Socialist Party] that was more popular and more established among the Polish masses. A Jewish group also arose in the organization that was called *Zargonowa* [ironic name, taken from the word used to describe Yiddish in a derogatory manner, as German jargon] with about 25 members.

In the course of a few weeks, Delow stood between life and death. After 17 weeks in the hospital, he left crushed and without the means to live. A few weeks later, a fire broke out in the old market. His good friend, Dovid Gotlib, ran to see what was burning and came back with a pot full of money (the fire was at his grandfather's and that which he had taken was his portion of his inheritance...). With the money, Dovid Gotlib bought clothing for himself and for Delow and, later, he left for Paris. Years later, Delow met his friend Dovid Gotlib in New York as a member of the leftist movement, where he [Gotlib] died a violent death. Honor his memory!

The revolutionary movement spread over all of Russia and grew from day to day. Czenstochow was in the first ranks of the struggle for freedom. There was a great deal of work – meetings, small covert groups, discussions, proclamations. On a certain night, Delow was arrested after spreading an appeal and spent 4 months in Piotrkow prison. There he perfected his Polish and learned much from the discussions with the prisoners who knew more than him. The prison was a good university for many other political prisoners. He emerged from there more mature, more class conscious and with an eagerness for work in the movement.

[Page XXX]

Many strikes took place at that time in the small Jewish factories in which Jewish and non-Jewish workers took part. Very often the *S.D.* [Social Democrats] took part in the strikes together with the *S.S* [Zionist Socialists].

The most famous general strike began in October 1905. All of the factories and railroads in Czenstochow stood still. Only "doormats" worked. The factory was besieged by the military. At a meeting of the council of that area, 8 volunteers appeared to close the factory. One of the eight was Yoszak. They went into the factory. Yoszak climbed onto the boiler oven to the little pipe (siren) and gave the strike signal. The factory came to a halt, but only Yoszak did not appear together with the rest to leave the factory. He was killed when he came down from the boiler in a shooting by the police and soldiers.

Delow, also one of the eight, scrambled up on a high fence around the factory. The soldiers quietly helped him climb up on the fence with the butt end of their guns. However, he fell into a pit of garbage and waste on the other side of the fence. Several workers pulled him out of there.

The *S.D.* arranged a funeral for Yoszak, the fallen comrade. The demonstration was the largest that Czenstochow had seen. All of the Polish and Jewish worker parties took part.

Coming back from the funeral, they encountered a large meeting at the new market where the speaker criticized the just conferred constitution.

In the few days of holiday, the party came out from underground. The *S.D.* party opened a club where Adolf Bril gave the first report on the subject: "The Erfurth [city in eastern Germany] Program of Karl Kautski [leader of the German Social Democrats]."

Immediately, a worse reaction began with blood baths, arrests and exile. Delow was then again arrested, spent 4 months in jail and was exiled to Vilna.

The *S.D.* party was very active in Vilna among the Polish speaking workers. There was a lack of people who could speak Polish. Delow, knowing the language well, was of great use to the party and took a large part in the work.

In 1909, he returned to Poland and, being again in Czenstochow, was again arrested. He served two weeks in Czenstochow, one month in Piotrkow, two months in Lodz, two months in Sieradz and then was exiled to Archangelsk. After three weeks, he was freed from there by an amnesty. He was sent back to Vilna where he became ill and gave up his party activity for a time.

Finding his *besherte* [predestined partner], they settled down to a life in a small *shtetl* near Vilna. Two weeks later, Delow received a message from Czenstochow that the police were looking for him. He left his wife with two children and departed for Germany. From there he left for America with the help of the party.

"The world, life goes constantly forward. The masses do not notice the process. Only when one looks back to the time when the history begins, approximately forty something years ago, is it seen how the life and the people have changed. History is progress and progress brings new times and new requests from the people who live now. Our present society demands new laws conforming to the time in which we live; that which was good 40 years ago, is old and backwards in the new times."

And that is how Delow finds himself in America. He belongs to the leftist movement of the *S.P.*

Delow works in a shop that also employs people who, in the old country, were bosses in shops where strikes were led. His shop, here, went out on strike too, during which he was arrested and received the opportunity to become acquainted with an American prison.

Delow has remained devoted to the same idealism as 40 years ago and, after everything, still hopes to live until the time when those ideals will be fulfilled.

[Page XXX]

Hey ה

Tuvya Halberg
Detroit

Son of Sholem and Chaya. Born in Czenstochow on 15 April 1885. Left Czenstochow in 1913. Came to America from Canada in 1914. He is a member of the Jewish-Folk Union and the Czenstochower Regional Union in Detroit where he is one of the active members. Was president for a time.

Abraham Shlomoh Halberg
Detroit

Son of Yehoshua Dovid and Feiga Dwoyra. Born in Czenstochow on 25 December 1896. Came to America in 1920. In Czenstochow, was a member of the Left *Poalei-Zion* organization; managing committee member of the workers' home and of the co-operative. In Detroit he is a member of the Jewish Folk-Union and of the Czenstochower Regional Union.

[Page XXXI]

Issy Halberg
Detroit

Son of Yehoshua Dovid and Feiga Dwoyra. Born in Czenstochow on 22 April 1892. He left Czenstochow in 1913. Came to America in 1914. He is an active member of the Czenstochower Regional Union. His two sons – Berl and Yeheil – served in the American army.

Sarah Hamer-Jacklin
(photo)

Born in Noworadomsk to well-to-do parents of Hasidic background. Her father, Josel Hamer, had a sock factory in quiet partnership with Shlomoh Henekh Rabinowicz, the son of *Khesed l'Abraham*.

At the time of the First World War, Shlomoh Henekh Rabinowicz was one of the most famous rabbis in Poland. He was also famous as a great merchant. He amassed a fortune and with it helped impoverished Hasidim. He built Noworadomsker *shtiblekh* [small houses of prayer] all over Poland and Galicia. Later he moved to Sosnowiec and left the partnership. However, Sarah's father continued with the trade. He traveled widely to the large cities in Poland and, on one such trip, took Sarah with him, traveling to Czenstochow where a part of their family lived.

Czenstochow engraved itself on Sarah's childhood memories and she did not want to go home. She remained with her uncle who had come with her father as a salesperson.

After a few days in Czenstochow, Sarah's uncle loaded her up with many good things and sent her to Radomsk on the pretext that because of business matters, he, the uncle, must remain in Czenstochow.

From that first trip to Czenstochow, as Sarah's father would prepare to go to Lodz, Warsaw, Piotrkow or Czenstochow, without asking, Sarah would immediately pack her small valise and was ready to go with him... However, her father did not want to take her along. Her mother would say one word: "*Aha, Czenstochow!*"...

(photo, caption: Josel Hamer with his children [sitting – Sarah Hamer])

A lot of water has flowed since then; bloody wars and revolutions have taken place; kings have attacked; the largest villain of all times – Hitler *yemakh-shmoy* [may his name be erased] arose and made an end of our hometown and murdered our closest and dearest. However, Sarah's memories of her birthplace, Noworadomsk, have remained dear; Czenstochow stands clearly before her eyes. Przedborz, the small *shtetl*, where her illustrious mother, Frajda, was born is beloved to her. Sarah would travel there, too.

Her father's business grew worse and worse. And suddenly her mother became ill and, just before a doctor arrived, she died at the age of 28.

Her father married a woman from Lodz 6 months after her mother's death, to whom Sarah remained strange and cold... It turned out that her father, too, was not jubilant... Because he suddenly decided to go to America.

They left Radomsk and spent some time in Antwerp, where her father's Gutsha (the step-mother) had family who were large diamond merchants, and in Antwerp the "*Mume-chi*" [literally "little aunt," but Radomsker Jews referred to a step-mother as "*Mume*"] decided that she was not going further – she wanted us to settle in Antwerp. She did not want to travel to a strange, *treif* [non-kosher, i.e. irreligious] land. Either Antwerp or back home!... Seeing that she meant it earnestly, Sarah's father then divorced her, gave her 1,000 rubles and she went back to Lodz.

[Page XXXII]

The father with his three young girls continued the trip and they went to Toronto, Canada, to an uncle. In the course of five years her father became a little Americanized and began to build up a knitting factory. He became very ill because of a neglected cold and after several days in bed, he died at the age of 39.

As the oldest of the three girls, Sarah learned the millinery trade (ladies hats). However, during the entire time, some latent restlessness drew her and demanded "something" that was not clear to her – to travel? To wander? The "something" remained very foggy, until she saw Yiddish theater for the first time – Jakob Gordon's "*Slaughter*" was being presented at that time. She began looking for a way to join the Yiddish theater. Sarah actually had two "loves" – 1) acting and 2) writing. In the first "love" she found her solution – in Toronto, she joined a dramatic group and performed with amateurs and played great roles. This, however, did not satisfy her – she was drawn further to the wider Yiddish theater.

Sarah left Toronto and came to New York to become an actress. After strenuous effort and long hardship she reached the professional theater where for 7 years she played with various companies in America and Canada. She performed with Boris Tomashevsky, Regina Prager and

J. Adler when they were already in their last years of glory. She also performed with various companies. She played all kinds of roles: dramatic, comedic and also frivolous young women. She had very good reviews. However, the life of wandering, the theater politics – this all undermined her health and a doctor told her to give them up for a little while – perhaps a year or two more.

While she performed in the provinces, she wrote a "diary" that described the whole gypsy life… the behind-the-scenes politics… the jealousy and hate that eventually undermines the soil of the Yiddish theater. It also included pictures of the cities and towns with various occurrences.

In the days that were sad and heavy on her heart, she would find comfort and relief in the pen.

When she remained in New York after a long tour, she read her diary again and again and it showed her that it was not badly written. She decided to take it to the editor of the *Tog* [*Day*] and she waited with a pounding heart for an answer. The answer was that "The Diary of An Actress" is extraordinarily interesting and written with talent; alas, the diary could not be published as it was written because it would result in the closing of all of the Yiddish theaters… The editor is of the opinion, however, that she should be sure to write because the diary shows a talent for fiction and she should write a story and send it to the editor… She then wrote her first story: "Florence – the Shop Girl" and again sent it to the editor of the *Tog* and with a pounding heart waited for an answer. And the answer came quickly with a check for 40 dollars. And immediately, it was widely announced on the first page of the *Tog* that this week publication begins of a story by a new talented story teller – Sarah Jacklin, entitled "Florence," which will run from *Shabbos* to *Shabbos*. The story began publication on 20 April 1934. Since then, her stories and novels have been published, in addition to the *Tog*, in [*Undzer*] *Weg* [*Our Way*] in Mexico, in *Amerikaner* [*American*], in the *New Yorker Wokhnblat* [*New York Weekly*], in *Kinder Zhurnal* [*Children's Journal*], and in the Toronto daily newspaper, *Der Yidisher Zhurnal* [*The Yiddish Journal*], in *Zhurnal Chicago*, in the *Yidisher Welt* [*Jewish World*] of Cleveland. Many of her writings were re-published in South America, as well as in the Lodz and Warsaw Yiddish newspapers, before the last horrible world war broke out.

Now her first book has come out – *Lives and Images*, published by the Noworadomsker Society. This book was warmly received by the critics and received a warm response from writers as well as readers across the country. However, she was not content to sit and rest and to be satisfied with her previous creations. She is now busy with writing a larger novella, but her greatest dream was always to return home in order to see and to absorb and, later to write. However, as there is no longer any home… it is only to look at the city where her cradle stood and to be at her mother's grave; to travel to Czenstochow where among the survivors remain the last threads of her large family, a look at Przedborz, where her mother was born, whose bright memory she carries with her always.

Itche Handwerker
Chicago
(photo)

Son of Naftali and Sara. Born in Amstow on 27 September 1888. Came to America on 21 May 1921. In Czenstochow, he took an active part in the work of the *S.S.* [Zionist Socialist] party. He, also, spent 6 months in prison as a result of the struggle with the so-called "nice fellows." In Chicago, he is an executive member of the Czenstochower Educational Union.

[Page XXXIII]

Naftali Handwerker
(photo)

Son of Berl and Ruchl. Born in Amstow (Poland). He died in 1936 in Czenstochow at the age of 75. The father of Itche and Benny Handwerker.

Benny Handwerker
Chicago
(photo)

Son of Naftali and Sara. Born in Amstow on 15 August 1885. He married Chaya (Annie) Moskowski. Came to America in 1905. He is a member of the *Arbeter Ring* [Workman's Circle] and of the Czenstochower Educational Union in Chicago. His son, Harry, served in the American army.

Golda Handwerker
(Née Napartei)
(photo)

Daughter of Yisroel and Chana Beila. Born in Czenstochow. Came to America in 1922. She died on 17 September 1941 in Chicago.

Moshe Hopman
Detroit
(photo)

Son of Zalman and Yentl. Born in Janow (Poland) in 1892. He married Sara Fajner. Came to America in 1922. He is a member of the Sosnowicer and Bedziner Society where he is a *hospiteler* [*landsmanschaft* member who visits the sick in hospitals].

Dovid Berish Horowicz, may he rest in peace

Born in 1869 into a family of *misnagdim* [opponents of Hasidism] and raised in a traditional religious spirit. Himself a *maskil* [adherent of the Enlightenment], he mastered the Hebrew language and also the new literature, as well as foreign languages. With the founding of political Zionism, he belonged to the Zionist movement. He was one of the founders of the first Jewish Zionist clubs in Czenstochow (in the time of the Czar when all political organizations were banned). In 1916, he entered the city council as a councilman representing the Zionists; One of the co-founders of the Jewish *gymnazium* [high school] in Czenstochow and a longtime member of the managing committee. He was also a member of the Jewish artisan's *shul* in Czenstochow and of the Zionist organization; he also was the synagogue warden of the Czenstochower *kehile* [Jewish community]. He was one of the Czenstochower industrialists. He died in 1924.

Shlomoh Horowicz
Toronto, Canada

Born in Szerew [?] in 1876. At age 11 he began to work in a bakery in Zanew [Janow] for 11 rubles a year with food and board. The work began *Shabbos* at night after *havdalah* [closing *Shabbos* prayer] and ended Friday at the candle lighting. At age 12, he came to Czenstochow and, until he was 21, he worked for Lozer Wilinger on the Blich. He served in the Russian army for 5 years. After this he married Yentl Szlumer. In 1902, he was mobilized as a result of the outbreak of the Russo-Japanese War. Leaving his wife and child, he was sent to Brest-Litovsk. On the way east, he traveled with a Greek Orthodox priest, who agitated for the revolutionary movement.

In 1905, Shlomoh Horowitz returned to Czenstochow and joined the *S.S.* [Zionist Socialist] party. He was then working for Moshe Funtowicz and Kopl Auerbach. In 1907, when a difficult struggle began between the bakery workers and the owners, Feivish Jakubowicz, who led the struggle against the workers, was shot and several [workers] such as Shimeon Siditzki were arrested through denunciations. Shlomoh Horowicz was also arrested in Orbach's bakery at Warszawer 11. Shlomoh Krasziner, the *groiser* [large] Leib and the *gruber* [fat] Berish were arrested before him. Later, Yehezkeil Litwak and the two apprentices who were called the "black monkeys" were arrested. We sat in the Piotrkow prison for three months, then received "*freie vysykla*" [free deportation – travel from place to place to complete a sentence].

"*Gruber*" Berish, Shlomoh Krasziner, "*groiser*" Leib and the "monkeys" were exiled to Vilna and Shlomoh Horowicz was sent to Smolensk, from there to Homel, Kiev, Kishinev, Argeyev, Bessarbia – all in a "procession of convicts." The trip lasted three months. Then he wandered from *shtetl* to *shtetl*, over a part of Russia, going as far as Odessa. From there, Sh. H. returned to Minsk; across the Kaliszer border, he arrived in German Ostrow and from there was sent back to Kalisz. Here he again spent three months in prison and again – on a *vysylka* – through Warsaw and Brisk to Vilna. He was in Vilna for 9 months and brought his wife there. In 1911, he returned to Czenstochow.

[Page XXXIV]

The bakery owners did not permit him to work. He joined a baker's *minyon* [prayer group] and after *davnen* [praying], he agitated among the workers to organize a union, which was later legalized by the Czarist government. The leaders of the union were Abraham Munowicz, Shlomoh Horowicz, Chaskl Baklasz, Avraham Rozenblat, the *shwartze* [dark] Moshe and Rafal Wolman.

Two members of the intelligencia worked with the union: Frida and Ganzwa.

In 1912, due to a denunciation by the bakery bosses, Sh. H. and a group of bakery workers were again arrested and served for 3 months.

In 1919, in now independent Poland, the union declared a strike of the bakery workers and the entire management committee was tried for alleged terrorism.

The representative of the Prof. Class Unions, Antony Kermaz, gave evidence at the trial that the *starost* [village chief] had been bribed by the owners. The accused were defended by Ludwig Honigwil (now in America). All of the accused were freed.

Sh. H. was a member of the managing committee of the bakers union until he left Czenstochow in 1930.

In Toronto, Canada, where he settled, he works as a baker.

Sara Hantwerker
(née Wajsberg)

Daughter of Elya and Ruchl Wajsberg. Born in Amstow (Poland). She died at the age of 53 in 1922 in Czenstochow.

Roza Hopman
Chicago

Daughter of Ahron and Yachet Gwercman. Born in Czenstochow on 25 October 1907. She is socially active in a series of institutions and takes an eminent part. She is a member of the

Czenstochower Independent Union in Chicago and of the Aid Society where she is Vice Chair Lady. Her two sons, Yenkl Josef and John, served in the American army.

Abraham Hoiptman
Detroit

Son of Zalman and Yentl. Born in Janow (Poland) on 25 October 1890. Came to America in 1913. His two sons – Joe and David – served in the American army.

Chana Sara Hershlikowicz
(photo)

Daughter of Avraham and Dwoyra Ester Essig. She died at the ago of 62 in Czenstochow in 1910. She was the mother of Ita Lenczner.

Feiwel Hershlikowicz
(photo)

Son of Mordechai and Miriam. He died at the age of 74 in Czenstochow in 1924. The father of Ita Lenczner, New York.

Berl Hershlikowicz

Son of Yankl and Fradl. Born on 28 February 1887 in Czenstochow. Came to America in 1906 from England. He left Czenstochow in 1900. Belonged to the *P.P.S.* and was active among the Polish workers. In London he was again connected to the party, came

(photo)

into contact with Pilsudski and Wasilewski. Returned to Poland for 7 months and there organized the general strike. In 1905 he was a delegate of the London *P.P.S* [Polish Socialist Party] group to the Socialist International in Amsterdam.

Here in America, he is a presser and is a member of Local 3.

Abraham (Abe) Hershlikowicz
(photo)

Son of Henech and Sara Leah. Born in Czenstochow in 1890. Came to America in 1906. He married Yetta Finkler in 1919. Is one of the founders and former secretary of Czenstochower Branch 261 of the *Arbeter Ring* in New York and also a member of the Wieluner Society in New York. Was one of the founders and secretary of Czenstochower Aid Society in New York and today he is a member of United Czenstochower Relief in New York. His two sons – Irving and Bernard – served in the American army.

[Page XXXV]

Vav ו
Shimeon Waldfogel
(photo)
Born 1887 – died 11 February 1920

This is the history of a typical worker's child who, thanks to his inborn abilities and diligence, rises to be a leader and fighter for the working masses. Shimeon Waldfogel was born in 1887 in the village of Krzywanice (Radomsko County) to a Jewish farmer. His childhood was spent in the village environment. When he turned 5, his father hired a teacher for him in a neighboring town, Sulmierzyce, and early every morning the small Shimeon had to run two kilometers to the town to study Hebrew. He learned quickly and showed a great deal of understanding.

The *kheder* did not satisfy him for long. The village was too confined for him. His father also saw no practical purpose for him to remain in the village. He apprenticed him to a tailor in Sulmierszyce – a small nearby *shtetele*.

Shimeon's rare abilities, his healthy commonsense helped him and even in difficult circumstances, he was successful in learning something. He started to read a book, a small brochure and thought through various questions. He also progressed in his work, became a considerable journeyman and in 1903 traveled to Czenstochow where he received a first class work position.

One of the first *Poalei-Zion* organizations was in Czenstochow. In 1904, right at the start of its creation, Shimeon became one of its most devoted members. He won the trust of all of his comrades with his devotion to and love of the ideal of the working class and he quickly became one of the most agile and most efficient propagandist-organizers. When the first wave of strikes broke out, young Shimeon stood at the head of a group of comrades in organizing a tea hall and low-cost canteens. One large tea hall was organized by *Poalei-Zion* in the summer restaurant in the "Tivoli" garden.

After the failure of the revolution, Shimeon was strongly persecuted by the Russian police, until he was forced to emigrate abroad, at first to Germany, then to Switzerland and later to Paris, where he remained for a few years and was active as a managing member in the German speaking section of the Tailor's Syndicate in Paris. Throughout his immigrant life, Shimeon maintained close contact with *Poalei-Zion* abroad.

Czenstochow was occupied by the German military regime during the first weeks of the First World War and the first victims of the war – the working masses – were thrown out of the workshops and factories into the street. Self help institutions became necessary; Shimeon was here. He organized a tea hall, a low cost canteen and created the "worker's home" of that time. He organized a professional union, a children's home, a dramatic circle and evening courses for adult workers.

In 1918 he organized the first regional conference of the Zaglebier region. The political work greatly increased and Shimeon was elected as a councilman on the Czenstochower city council and he was beloved by the entire Jewish population in the city, thanks to his devoted activities. Shimeon was a delegate to the first meeting of the *Poalei Zion* party in September 1918.

He neglected his private life and in 1919 he went to Sosnowiec to work. Here, too, he took an active part in the party work, traveling around the region. At the beginning of 1920, he became ill with typhus and died in his bloom of youth, in the middle of his work for his great ideal – for *Poalei-Zionism*.

Kopl Wargon

Son of Shmuel and Chava. Born in Czenstochow on 8 August 1904. He began his first steps in the workers' movement with the *Bundist* youth organization *Tzukunft* [Future]. There were about ten young members in the youth organization during the years 1921-22, among them Comrade Mendl Wilinger, a bakery worker. They did not show any great activity at that time. From Warsaw, only the *Yugnt-Werker* [*Young Worker*] – the weekly newspaper for the working young – was received. Activity first increased when a teacher from the Y.L Peretz School in Czenstochow came to help. On the agenda of the first meeting in which she took part was the item "reorganization." Wargon was the secretary for the meeting.

A large number of new members came from the youth sections of the professional unions that were under the influence of the *Bund*. One of the new comrades was Yitzhak Stopnicer of the Tailor's Union who later grew to be the leader of the *Bund* youth [organization], *Tzukunft*.

On several ocassions joint May celebrations by the entire worker youth of the city took place. Wargon appeared as a representative of *Tzukunft* at one of these May celebrations.

He and Mendl Wilinger were delegates to a regional meeting of the Czenstochower area.

At a demonstration for 1 May, he observed who were the railroad workers, the coal miners, the thousands of workers in the steel factories and who were the tailors, shoemakers, bakers and workers in small factories. The former were almost all not Jews and the latter – all Jews. This thought led him to the idea of a homeland in *Eretz-Yisroel*. He left the *Bund* and joined the Left *Poalei Zion.* He did not remain there for long.

He joined the leftist movement, although it was illegal and everyone who took part in independent Poland was persecuted and tortured in prison.

[Page XXXVI]

In 1921, at age 17, he was drawn into the Prof. Union of the Clothing Industry by his cousin, Chaim Erlikh of Kamyk. He lived at Second Street 40 and was under the influence of the *Bund.*

At the time, a youth section was organized in the union. There he received his first enlightenment as a worker. He was elected as chairman of the youth section.

A second Prof. Tailor's Union existed at that time – New Market 2, which was under the influence of the left and a youth section existed in this union, too.

The existence of two prof. unions in the same trade had a largely bad effect on the condition of the tailors. Understand that this was the result of party struggles between the *Bund* and the left. It lasted for years until they were merged.

Just then Wargon came to America. This was May 1928. Today, his membership book remains as a reminder, with the following signatures: Dreksler, Tobiash Wargon, Meler, Sticki, Goldberg.

Kopl (Karl) Wargon is a member of the A.F.F. Order Br. 11 and executive member of the Y.L. Peretz School in New York.

He married Hudes Wargon in 1928.

Emanuel Wargon
(photo)

Son of Shmuel Dovid and Chaya Tzipora. Born in Czenstochow on 18 July 1878. Member and former president of the First *Dzialoszyner Khevra Anshei Bnei Achim, gabay* of the *Khevre Kadishe* [burial society], co-founder and active member of the Czentochower Aid Organization and Relief Committee in New York.

His son-in-law, Sam Wein, was a doctor in the American army and died on 10 July 1943. His son, Seymour served in the American army.

The Warszawski Family
Our Last House

Our last house was the house we inherited on Garncarske or Teper Street 77.

From our house to the government buildings and to the river, where we swam during the summer and spent time at the marshy shore, was a few minutes walk. The fate of the house was, perhaps, the same as all of the Jewish houses in the ghetto. However, the red brick two-story house will always remain in our memory – our dwelling in Czenstochow from which we parted forever when we left for America.

Our Brother Meir and His Wife Lina (née Szusterman)

He was the first to leave. This was before the First World War. After the war, with the greatest difficulty, he brought all of us – our father, may he rest in peace, our mother and five brothers – to America and in that way saved several generations of our family from doom. He and his wife Lina, who devotedly helped with the difficult task, should be inscribed in eternal memory and appreciation by us, our children and future generations.

(photo, caption: The memory of our father Mendl, may he rest in peace)

He lived in Czenstochow, from which it was difficult to part, for most of his life. Here in America, he always remembered his birthplace with affection.

He was a religious Jew. The *shul* and the *beis-midrash* were bound with his spiritual life, although he was a modern – according to European concepts – person.

He died in Chicago at the age of over sixty and was buried in the Czenstochower cemetery in Chicago.

His will be remembered always by his wife, children and all who knew him.

Through these lines we greet and send a heartfelt greeting to all the surviving brothers and sisters in our birthplace, Czenstochow, where several generations of our family lived out their years and, also, all Czenstochower *landsleit* in America and in all the world.

Our bitter fate is that in our time, Jewish Czenstochow, which generation after generation built and created, was almost entirely annihilated. However, as long as our eyes are open, we will remain bound to our birthplace and brotherly bound with all of our *landsleit* wherever they find themselves and who we will remember when reading this book, *Czentochower Yidn.*

(photo, caption: Tzviah Warszawski)

Our mother, Tzviah Warszawski, née Blajweis. Born in Czenstochow in 1870. Her father's name – Hershl, her mother's Tzirl. She was and is one of the most active women in the aid work of the Czenstochower Educational Union in Chicago and the Ladies Aid Society.

[Page XXXVII]

(photo, caption: David Warszawski)

David Warszawski, born in 1899, and his wife, Annie (née Fajnarc). Live now in Oklahoma.

(photo, caption: Abraham Warszawski)

(photo)

Abraham Warszawski, born 1908, and his wife, Shirley (née Fen). Came to America in October 1922.

(photo, caption: Meir Warszawski)

Meir Warszawski, born 1895, and his wife, Lina (née Szusterman). Lives in Columbus, O.

The Warszawski family together in America consists of six families, twelve grandchildren and one great grandchild. In addition to the two brothers in Oklahoma and Columbus, all of those remaining live in Chicago.

(Photo, caption: Reuven Warszawski)

Reuven Warszawski, born in 1896, and his wife, Ita (née Weisfelner). Former president and vice president of the Czenstochower Educational Union in Chicago.

(photo, caption: Ahron Warszawski)

Ahron Warszawski, born in 1893, and his wife, Dwoyra (née Grojman). Member of the Czenstochower Educational Union in Chicago and of the Brzeziny Society.

(photo, caption: Hercke Warszawski)

Hercke Warszawski, born 1901, and his wife, Klara (née Grynberg). Came to America 1920. Belongs to the International Worker's Order and to *ICOR* [organization of Yiddish speaking working class immigrants].

Mary Waron
Detroit

Daughter of Heimy and Fanny Yoskowicz. Born in Czenstochow in 1909. Came to America in 1920. She is a member of *B'nai Brith* and of the Jewish Congress in Detroit.

Mendl Wulf

Like all Jewish children, he spent his childhood in *kheder*. His father, a tailor, wanted him to be a *beis-midrash bokher* [prayer house young man – i.e. wanted him to study]. Although only 13, Mendl understood that this was not practical and he became a painter.

He worked very hard, from early to late at night and remained religious.

In 1905 he was drawn into the *Bund*. He read much revolutionary literature and became an active party worker. His new belief was in socialism and the Jewish worker under the flag of the *Bund* as its *avant-garde*.

When the reaction again lifted its head, he was not surprised. There was no work then and in 1908 he had to emigrate to America, although the *Bund* appealed to its members that they should not leave the place of struggle.

His spiritual thirst was quieted in America through Josef Szlosberg's and Dovid Pinski's lectures. Later he moved to Pittsburgh and joined the Jewish branch of the Socialist Party.

He was with the pro-German side in the S. P. at the beginning of the First World War. However, the Kerensky revolution in Russia and Wilson's 14 Points completely changed his views. He left the party after the pro-German declaration of the S. P. at the St. Louis convention.

In the end, Bolshevism in the Soviet Union, the demoralizing struggle between the right and the left in the workers' ranks in America, led to his complete disappointment in socialism and, in the end, led to his to religion and into a believer.

[Page XXXVIII]

He became united with the Zionist movement and joined the Revisionists.

Shlomoh and Tzirl Wolkowicz
(photo)

Son of Aba and Frajdl. Born in Czenstochow on 25 May 1877. Came to America in 1920. His three sons – Avraham, Willy and Jakov served in the American army; Avraham had the rank of captain.

Aba Wolkowicz

Born in Radomsk; died August 1919 in Czenstochow.

Frajdl Wolkowicz

Daughter of Yitzhak Meir and Gala-Hinda. Born in Czenstochow and died there in April 1895.

Josef Wiatrak
Detroit
(photo)

Son of Yitzhak Shlomoh and Tauba Gitl. Born in Dombrowa [Dabrowa Gornicza] on 20 February 1895. He marred Dobra Szinjawski. Came to America December 1912. Is one of the founders and most active members of the Czenstochower Regional Union in Detroit for the entire time of its existence. His son – Morton – served as a corporal in the American army.

Eliezer Wilinger
(photo)

Born in Czenstochow and died there in October 1922 at the age of 64.

Mordekhai Wilinger
(photo)

Son of Eliezer and Chaya Rywka. Born on 28 April 1883 in Czenstochow. He marred Minnie Weksztajn. Came to America December 1904. His son, Henry Ruwin, and his daughter served in the American army. He is a member of the Czenstochower Society of Young Men in New York and the "Masons."

Abraham Wilinger
Chicago
(photo)

Son of Eliezer and Chaya Rywka. Born in Czenstochow on 5 June 1895. He married Fanny Klajnman. Came to America on 15 July 1913. Is a member of Czentochower Educational Society, Czenstochower Independent Union and of the Jewish National Worker's Union. He and his wife, Fanny, are the most active in all of the above mentioned institutions. They are always executive officers and trustees.

Morris Wilinger
(photo)

Son of Zalman and Golda. Born in Czenstochow on 25 October 1888. Came to America on 12 August 1912. Is a member of the Czenstochower branch 261 *Arbeter Ring* in New York.

Abraham Mordekhai Wilinger

Son of Zalman and Golda. Born in Czenstochow on 1 July 1884. Came to America on 6 September 1906. He is a member of the Czenstochower branch 261 of the *Arbeter Ring* committee to visit the sick in New York; one of the founders and active workers of the Czenstochower Aid Union and also a member of United Czenstochower Relief in New York and of the book committee for *Czenstochower Yidn.*

Benny Wilinger
Cleveland

Son of Abraham and Bayla. Born in Czenstochow. Came to America on the 22nd June 1912.

[Page XXXIX]

Yehezkeil (Henry) Win
(photo)

Son of Grunem and Ruchl'e (died in New York and buried at the cemetery of the Czenstochower *shul* in Elmont, L.I.). Yehezkeil was born in 1896 in Czentochow. Came to America in 1913. He was drawn into the famous Branch 6 of the *Poalei-Zion* party and was a member until his departure in 1920.

Yehezkeil Win was secretary of Czenstochower Relief during the years 1918 – 1922 and, with a number of other *landsleit*, founded the Czenstochower branch 111 of the Jewish National Workers Union where he was secretary for many years. He was also a member of the city committee of the union and of the general executive. Right after the First World War, he and Moshe Z. sent a library to the Workers' Home of *Paolei-Zion* in Czenstochow.

In 1924, he married Yeta Glater of Czenstochow. They have two children.

Yehezkeil Win is still an active member of the National Workers Union, branch 10, which is not a Czenstochower *landsleit* branch, but consists of Jews from all over, but united in the idea of a free world and the restoration of the Jewish people as members of the family of man with equal rights.

Shlomoh Winter

Son of Shmuel Josl and Ruchl. Born on 28 December 1890 in Czenstochow. Married Celia Enzel. Came to America on 15 January 1913. Is a member of the Hungarian Society. His son, Julius, served in the American army as a sergeant.

Leibus Win
with Family
(photo)

Son of Shmuel and Ester Sheindl. Born in Czenstochow. Came to America in March 1915. He was one of the most active members of the Czenstochower Neighborhood Educational Society in Chicago, executive member for many years and former president of the society. He was active with Aid until the last minutes of his life. He died at age 52 on 14 July 1943.

Louis Winter

Son of Shmuel Josl and Ruchl. Born on 24 April 1892 in Czenstochow. Came to America on 14 July 1914.

Sidney Weis
Jacksonville
(photo)

Son of Dovid and Ita. Born on 8 June 1899 in Czenstochow. He married Chana Lustigman. Came to America in 1920. His son, Isidor, served in the American army.

Yakob Weisbard
Chicago

Son of Yitzhak and Shifra. Born in Czenstochow on 9 May 1888. He married Gitl Hantwerker. Came to America in 1920. He is a member of Czenstochower Educational Society in Chicago. His son, Heimy, served in the American army.

Naftali Wajsberg

Son of Israel Sholem and Chana. Born in Czenstochow on 30 April 1891. Came to America from London on 2 October 1913. He is an active member of Branch 581 *Arbeter Ring* [Workman's Circle] in New York, of the Labor Party, Finance Secretary of the Bronx *Arbeter Ring* School 2. He is also a member of United Czenstochower Relief in New York. His son, Arnold, served in the American army.

Abo Wajsberg
Norfolk

Son of Sam and Bertha. Born in Czenstochow.

Moshe Weisfelner
(photo)

Son of Hershl and Reizl. Born in Polamaniec (Poland); he died there in 1915 at the age of 66.

[Page XL]

Rudel Weisfelner
(photo)

Daughter of Leizer and Rywka. Died at the age of 68 in Chicago on 13 April 1926.

Ahron Weisfelner
(photo)

Son of Moshe and Rudel. Born in Polamaniec (Poland) in 1886. He died on 25 May 1918 in Chicago.

Mordekhai Weisfelner (Max Weis)
Chicago

Son of Moshe and Rudel. Born in 1889 in Polamaniec (Poland). Came to America in 1906. He is one of the most active members and president of the Czenstochower Educational Society in Chicago.

Emanuel Wajsberg
(photo)

Son of Shaul and Chana Laya. Born in Czenstochow on 8 November 1909. Lives in Aruba, Dutch West Indies. Came to Aruba in 1933. Belongs to the Jewish Aid Society.

Max Winuk
Pittsburgh
(photo)

Son of Leizer and Ester Malka. Born August 1882 in Koniecpol. He lived in Czenstochow and came from there to America in May 1907 together with his wife Gutshe (née Planszinska), born in Czenstochow in March 1876.

Max Wunik belongs to the *Arbeter Ring*; member of the Faternal Order; ICOR; *Morgn Freiheit* [*Morning Freedom*] Association, President of the Warsaw Support Union.

Yitzhak Winuk

Son of Mordekhai and Faygl. Born in Koniecpol (Poland). Came to America in 1912. He died at age 82 in Chicago in 1937.

Chana Winuk
(née Gimpl)

Born in Lelew (Poland). Came to America in 1912. She died in 1938 in Chicago at the age of 84.

Mikhal Weiskopf

Born in Czenstochow on 26 December 1882. Came to America in 1890. He married Rose Weiskopf. Is a member of the Czenstochower Young Men in New York. Now lives in Saratoga Springs, N.Y. His son, Melvin, served as a staff sargeant in the American army.

Mike Weiskopf
(photo)

Came to America in 1906. Here he married a woman from his birthplace. He is occupied with communal work. Active in Czenstochower Relief. Now is Vice President of Czenstochower Young Men

Mozes Wenglinski
Stamford

Son of Avraham and Ester. Born in May 1890 in Czenstochow. Came to America on 3 November 1920.

Abraham (Abe) Wenger
(photo)

Son of Elihu and Malka. Born in Czenstochow on 4 July 1897.

[Page XLI]

In July 1914, he graduated from the Artisan's school in Czenstochow. When the First World War broke out, Czenstochow was occupied by the Germans; he had to find a means to support himself. At that time, the German regime was looking for locksmiths and mechanics to work in Germany in the ammunition factories. He left for Cologne together with several friends, also locksmiths like Wenger – Gotlib, Rizenzan, Najman and Lancman. However, they were not there for long because they were going to be forced to remain there until the end of the war. They decided to escape to Upper Silesia. Wenger and Lancman left first, after them the rest. Wenger and his friend were successful in reaching Glewitz. However, Najman and Gotlib were caught and they were sentenced to six months hard labor in a German prison. The last two remained in Cologne. Wenger often traveled to Czenstochow from Glewitz. Through a bribe, he received a job as a locksmith in the train workshop and right after took part in the first train strike. They issued a demand for better working conditions and higher wages. As an answer, the German officers threatened each striker with arrest. They left the workshop immediately. On the same day they held a meeting at the Polish cemetery. The *Social Democrats* (*S.D.K.P.L.* [Polish Social Democratic Party]) led the strike, but there were also traitors. Luckily, the Germans arrived at the meeting place after those at the meeting had left. Many were arrested in their homes. After several days they went back to work with the old conditions. However, the Germans later granted many concessions to the workers. This led Wenger to the idea of founding a metal

union. He turned to Moshe Weksler and they brought together all of the locksmiths in
Czenstochow. A metal workers union was founded at the meeting. Moshe Weksler was the first
chairman and secretary. The newly founded union carried out a whole series of strikes in Shaya
Rozensztajn's factory and others.

At the end of the First World War, when the Germans were ready to leave Czenstochow, a
group of Jewish workers noticed that the Germans were making preparations to take away the
locomotives. The group rendered these plans harmless and the locomotives remained on the
spot. The next day the railroads were already under Polish management. However, when the
Jewish workers came to work, the found an inscription near the entrance that the Jewish
workers were not permitted to enter. This was the first act of freed Poland. The same thing
happened in other cities.

A. Wenger joined the *S.S.* [Zionist Socialist] Party, later – *Fareinikte* [United] and was a
member of the party council and later was elected as a delegate of the metal union to the
workers council. At the time, he was completely devoted to the professional movement and
helped to organize the Polish union, union of hairdressers and bakery workers. His hardest
assignment was to organize the porters.

The porters and their union, which consisted of several hundred people, was divided into
several sections: those who have the packages in baskets and carry them on their own backs,
often with the help of their wives, and those who worked with horses and wagons and can, in
general, be compared with the Chinese rickshaw.

Wenger was the secretary of the porters union for a long time. It not only bettered their
material condition, but the union also awoke in them the feeling of human worth and social
responsibility. They were devoted to the union with life and soul.

In order to avoid competition, there was a system of equal shares of the daily earnings for
the porters with horses and wagons. All worked the same number of hours. This required much
energy and patience. However, it was a great success. The porters were very disciplined and
carried out the decisions of the union.

When the cooperative was founded, Wenger was hired as the paid manager of the
cooperative store on Nadrzeczna Street, in Esig's house. Comrades Feigele Frank and Helenche
Pliwacz worked with him.

However hard it was to organize the porters was not even equal to what the employees of the
cooperative had to bear from their consumers. First, they wanted to receive their products at
once, which were assigned by the city provision office for an entire month. Secondly, the
cooperative did not receive enough *"popularke*-bread" [small round breads] for all of the
consumers. An *"oganek"* (a line) of 300 people would stand and wait, but there were only a
hundred little breads a day to distribute.

Wegner left Czenstochow in 1920. He was aided greatly by Comrade Dovid Szlesinger, who
helped him obtain an external passport through his unusual energy and acquaintance in the
"offices."

In New York, he was a member of the Czenstochower *Arbeter Ring* branch 261 and when, in
1926, he moved to Detroit, he was one of the founders there of the Czentochower Aid Union in
Detroit that would send help from there to Czentochow and also helped the work of Relief in
New York.

He is a member and President of the Manhattan Lodge number 473 and of the Independent
Order of Odd Fellows.

Sam Wenger

Born in Koniecpol. He was one year old when his family moved to Czentochow. He studied in
a *kheder* until his bar mitzvah, then in the elementary school with Aronowicz, Szekher, Avner
and Leder. During the German occupation of Czenstochow, he obtained work in the train

workshop. As soon as the railways were again under Polish management, he was dismissed together with the entire group of Jewish workers. With the help of Comrade Dudek Szlezinger, he obtained employment in public work, digging sewers far under the city.

His attachment to the *S.S.* [Zionist Socialist] Party began through the metal union where the Jewish railway workers were organized. He was then around 15 years old. When Comrade Khrabalowski began to organize the youth in *Shtral* [Ray or Beam of Light], he was the first to join the organization with Avraham Brat, Motek Fliwacz and Yoal Wajs and take an active part in the work and also helped organize evening courses. Sam Wenger and Motek Fliwacz represented *Shtral* in the party ranks.

He left Czenstochow in 1920 at age 17. In New York, he was active in the Czenstochower *Arbeter Ring* branch 261 until the split. From then on, he belonged to the Odd Fellows.

The first years in New York, he was employed in Morris Lipman's "cloak shop" and joined the International Ladies Garment Workers' Union, to which he belongs until today. He was also active in Czenstochower Relief in New York for as long as it existed.

In 1933 in New York, he married a Czenstochower girl, Sheindl Fajersztajn, daughter of Bruchia Feiersztajn. In Czenstochow, he was an active member of the sports club, "Warta."

Sam Wenger, with thousands of friends, will keep sacred the oath: never to forget the Czenstochow of their young years, to help the survivors build their lives in a new and free Poland and always honor the memory of the annihilated brothers, sisters, comrades and friends, the casualties of savagery, of Polish anti-Semitism and German cruel murder.

He helped publish the book, *Czentochower Yidn*, by collecting money. He is a devoted *landsleit* and contributes according to his abilities to the aid work for his birthplace.

[Page XLII]

Josef Ahron Wenger

Born in Koniecpol (Poland) in 1889. Settled in Czenstochow with his parents in 1903. He took part in the revolutionary movement. Came to America in 1913. He was a member of the Czenstochower branch 261 of the *Arbeter Ring*. Now he is a member of the Odd Fellows. His son, Albert, served in the American army.

Shimkhah and Chava Wraclawski
(photo)

The only surviving brother and sister of the Wraclawski family in Czenstochow. Their parents perished in Czenstochow during the years 1939-1945. Shimkhah and Chava Wraclawski were in the concentration camps of Czenstochow and Buchenwald. They came to America in 1946. Today they are in Philadelphia.

[Page XLII]

Zayin ז
Abo Zaluski

Son of Moshe Yitzhak and Malka. Born in Konske (Poland). Died at age 90 in Czenstochow in July 1914.

(photo, caption: The parents of Daniel Zaluski)

Leah Zaluski

Daughter of Josef and Chana Gryn. Born in Brzeznica (Poland). Came to America in 1920. She died in 1921 in Chicago.

Daniel Zaluski

Born in Czenstochow in 1887. His father was called Abo, his mother, Leah. He became a cabinet maker after ending his school years. He would work from 6 in the morning until 10 at night for three rubles a week. On Thursday, work would last the whole night until Friday at noon. The boss was very poor. Life was unbearable.

Lipa Goldman, who came from Lodz and was a member of the Polish *S.D.* (Social Democrats), was the first one with whom Zaluski became acquainted in the movement for freedom. Zaluski also met Josef and Abraham Grajcer and they all would gather at Avraham Malarcz's on Nikolajevski Street. They tried to collect money in order to improve conditions through a strike; however, they did not succeed at first due to Czarist terror and worker backwardness. Zaluski worked very hard in very difficult conditions and looked

(photo)

for further ways to participate in the workers movement. Once on a *shabbos*, a mass meeting of the Bund took place in a forest. This was a protest meeting against the beating of arrested workers. The police and Cossacks arrived and they dispersed the meeting.

[Page XLIII]

On a Sunday afternoon, when Zaluski went to work, he met a demonstration of a great mass of workers with a red flag on Piotrokower Street. "Down with self rule," was shouted. The Cossacks came and immediately began hitting with blackjacks. The street was sprayed with blood. This was his first revolutionary experience. He was forced to leave Lodz because of a threat by his boss that he would give him to the police and he went to Stara Wiece. He came back to Czenstochow six months later, more class conscious and full of courage. He met new comrades. One of them was a Jewish soldier from the Dragoon regiment in Czenstochow – Edelman from Vitebsk. Zaluski and Edelman joined with a representative of the Czenstochow *S.D.* [Social Democrats] – Olkhowski. The meetings took place at night in the city hall where several Polish comrades were employed. The work among the Jewish workers was difficult, because besides *Czerwoni Standar* [*Red Banner*] (Polish organ of the *S.D.*), there was no Jewish literature. There was no connection to the Bund. Dovid, the Jewish soldier from the Dragoon regiment, introduced Zaluski and his comrades to a Polish non-commissioned officer, Szmiglewski, who was also a member of the *S.D.* group. However, he was a provocateur. Because of this, Zaluski, Abraham Malarsz and two more comrades were arrested at a meeting. Zaluski's hands were tied; he was beaten with rifle butts and taken to the jail in the city hall. They were transferred to the Piotrkow jail at three o'clock in the afternoon. There they sat in separate cells; they were taken together only for walks. Zaluski took full responsibility at an inquiry. Therefore, he was held in jail together with a Polish comrade for 8 months (all of the others were freed). There were points in the indictment for which he was threatened with exile at hard labor. However, the "Constitution" of 1905 freed him.

They walked from Piotrkow to Radomsk because of the general railway strike, then took a wagon to Czenstochow.

A state of war was declared immediately and repression began again. The police began to search for him and he lived illegally on a false passport. Once, in 1907, his father was arrested because of Zaluski. He was taken out of the *sukkah* on Garncarske Street [structure built for the holiday of *Sukkos* in which meals are eaten] while he was eating. However, he was later freed. Zaluski was again betrayed by a provocateur and he was recognized by one of the policemen who came to arrest him. This happened on Teper Street at Szkapen. Zaluski succeeded in leaping from a window and ran to the old market. There he was detained by

Fremer's band of provocateurs. The *pristov* [Czarist Russian police commissioner], Arvuzov, who was there, ordered the beating of him to stop. Later, after the wounds in his head were bandaged, he was again thrown in jail. A military judge sentenced him to 4 months in jail. After jail, he went to military service in Kovkoz. He was home for 6 months after military service, helped the organization of the professional unions and artisans' clubs, until he was again arrested and received a *vysylka* [banishment] until the First World War.

Now he is in Chicago. He belongs to the Carpenters' Union and here raised two sons – Max and Lawrence; both have served in the American army.

Shmuel Zborowski
(photo)

Son of Khanina and Feigl. Born in Myszkow (Poland). He died at age 69 in 1933 in Czenstochow.

Gitl Zborowski

Daughter of Avraham and Teltzl Rinsky. She died at age 40 in Czenstochow.

Shimeon (Zborowski) Zborow
Detroit
(Photo)

Son of Shmuel and Gitl. Born in Walbrom on 2 October 1892. Came to America from Czenstochow on 8 July 1913. He married Hena Bluma Szikman. In Czenstochow, he belonged to the *S.D.K.F.L.* [Social Democratic Party of Royal Poland and Lithuania], later to the *S.S.* [Zionist Socialists] In Detroit, he was a member of the *Arbeter Ring* branch 156. Now he is active in the Czenstochower Regional Union and a member of the Revision Commission.

Hena Bluma Zborow
Detroit
(photo)

Daughter of Dovid Leib and Feigl Szykman. Born in Czenstochow on 14 April 1897. Came to America on 29 March 1913. She is an executive member of the Peoples' Committee of Russian War Relief, Young Women's Trustee in Mizrachi, European Welfare Fund, Mount Sinai Hospital, *Keren Hayesod*, Jewish Old Folks Home, War Chest, Red Cross and of the Czenstochower Regional Union in Detroit. She is one of the most devoted and most active workers in all areas of Jewish and general American communal life.

[Page XLIV]

(photo, caption: Malka Szykman with children, the mother of Hena Bluma Zborow [Translator's note: the above text gives her mother's name as Feigl])

Benny and Harry Zigas

Harry, the son of Shmuel and Leitshe Zigas, was born on the April 1892 in Czenstochow. Came to America in September 1907. His two sons – Seymour and Irving – served in the American army.

Sam Zigas
(photo)

Son of Shmuel and Leah. Born in Czenstochow on 15 April 1898. Came to America in 1908. He married Szprinza Stal in 1921. Was a member of the National Workers' Union and of the Czenstochower Aid Union. Now he is a member of the Czenstochower Young Men's Society in New York. His sons – Seymour and Isidor – served in the American army.

Yisroel'ke Zigas

Born in Czenstochow. Died on October 26, 1945.

Szprinza Zigas

Daughter of Itshe and Rive Stal. Born in Czenstochow in 1901. Came to America in 1914. She married Sam Zigas. She is a member of the Czenstochower Ladies Auxiliary in New York.

Dovid Zitman

(photo)

Son of Wolf and Sheindl. Born in Czenstochow on 4 June 1891. A child of poor working people. At age 12 or 13, he had already joined the socialist party, Bund, and was one of the dozens of leaders of "combat sections" helping to lead strikes and organize various trades, such as: the tailors, the painters, carpenters, linen sewers, housekeepers and others. He worked with the well known Bundists in Czenstochow – Hershl Blobarsz-Frajman, Rywka from Piotrkow, Yankl Blakharsz and others. He led a number of fighters at the time of the tendency toward pogroms in Czenstochow and had a seat in the city's Center, with Dr. Bronjatowski. He stopped work at the Zapalszarnje factory and others during the general strikes. Distributed illegal literature in the *shtetlekh* surrounding Czenstochow. He was also arrested by the Czarist police several times.

At the same time, he showed a great love for the stage and acted in the play, "Urial Acosta" with Jakub Ber Silver that was performed with great success in Czenstochow for the benefit of the Bund. He appeared in the role of Ruwin.

After the revolutionary period of 1905, he took part in the creation of an amateur troupe that toured a series of cities such as Zaglembia, Dombrowska, Radomsk, Piotrkow, Tomaszow and others.

He came to America with great difficulty. On the way, he performed on the Jewish stage in Paris, from which he came to America in 1909. Here he lived a difficult life doing various work.

In 1912 he went back to his birthplace, Czenstochow, where he spent 7 months. When he returned to America, he settled in New York and joined the Czenstochower Society of Young Men and there became one of the most efficient members. He was president of the society for a time, member of the Czenstochower Relief in New York. Now he is the treasurer of Czenstochower Young Men and an active member of Czenstochower Relief and the *Czenstochower Yidn* book committee. His son – Willy – served in the American army.

———

Sara Zitman

Daughter of Hilel and Dreiza Jakubson. Born on 12 August 1890 in Riga. Came to America in 1905. She is the wife of Dovid Zitman.

———

Sam Ziser

Detroit

Son of Wolf Leib and Rojza. Born in Czenstochow on 15 November 1888. Came to Galveston in 1912. He has been in America since 1919. [Translator's note: The dates 1912 and 1919 are as published.] He is a member of the F.F. Order and of the Czenstochower Regional Union in Detroit.

(photo, caption: Miljen Zitenfeld)

[Page XLV]

Wowa and Miljen Zitenfled
Chicago
(photo)

Son of Mordekhai and Feiga. Born in Rozprza (Poland) on 15 December 1888. Came to America from Paris in 1915.

Anna and Morris Zitman
Philadelphia

Morris was born in Czenstochow in 1888. Came to America from Paris in 1915.

Meir Dovid and Sheindl Zajdman
Philadelphia

Son of Jakov and Chaya Rywka. Born on 28 December 1888 in Zawiercie. Came to America in 1913. He is a member of *Machzikei Hadas*.

Yitzhak Zandsztajn

Son of Wowa and Macha Zandsztajn. Born in 1890 inCzenstochow. Spent the First World War as a soldier in the Russian army. Was a member of *Achiezer* [organization to help the poor], *Beis-Lekhem* [bread for the needy] and *TOZ* [Society for the Protection of Health] in Czenstochow.

(photo)

———

Daughter of Perec Goldsztajn. Born in 1900 in Kanyev, Ukraine.

These were the parents of Aryeh Leib Zandsztajn, who perished in the years 1939-1945. Their second son, Eliezer Zandsztajn, perished with them.

———

M. and Mrs. Zilberberg
Philadelphia

Aryeh Leib (Lutek) Zandsztajn
(photo)

Son of Yitzhak and Miriam Golda Zandsztajn (née Goldsztajn). Born in Czenstochow on 13 August 1926. Former member of the Polish Workers' Party and officer in the Polish army. He is now in New York.

———

M. and D. Zajdman
Philadelphia

———

Chaya Zewin
Chicago

Daughter of Moshe and Feiga. Born in Piotrkow on 25 December 1884. Came to America on 4 July 1913. She is a member of the Czenstochower Educational Union and of the Aid Society in Chicago.

[Page XLV]

Tet ט

[Translator's note: The names that appear below begin with a *tes* (*tet* in Hebrew) when written in Yiddish. They are transliterated with the spellings as they appear on Polish vital records.]

Yakov Dovid and Sara Czarny

(photo)

(Née Szerman).Well known Czenstochower residents. Suffered the fate of the martyrs in the years 1939-1945. Their children met the same fate – Rojza Czarny-Salamanowicz and her husband, Pesa Czarny-Kuperszmid and her husband and child, Shmuel Czarny and his wife and two children, as well as Freidl and Grinya Czarny.

Honor their memory!

Avraham Czarny

Died in Czenstochow in 1938.

(photo)

Chana Reizl Czarny

Died in Czenstochow in 1932.

Nokhem Czarny

(photo)

Son of Avraham and Chana Reizl. Born in Czenstochow in 1900. He died on 1 January 1938 in New York.

Yakov (Jack) Czarny

Son of Avraham and Chana Reizl, born in Czenstochow on 11 October 1893. He married Andja Goldberg. Came to America in 1920.

[Page XLVI]

Andja Czarny

(photo, caption: Yakov and Andja Czarny)

Daughter of Sholomh and Ester Goldberg. Born in Czenstochow on 5 April 1899. Came to America in 1920. She was active in the *S.S.* [Zionist Socialist] party and the educational union for Jewish workers in Czenstochow.

Fay (Feigl) Czarny

Daughter of Yakov and Andja. Born in New York on 16 September 1924. She is a student at Hunter College in New York.

Yitzhak Czarny

Chicago

Son of Yakov Moshe and Miriam. Born in Czenstochow on 7 March 1888. He married Manja Zobszajn. Came to America on 13 September 1913. He is a member of the Czenstochower Educational Union in Chicago; holds the office of treasurer there. His son, Philip, served in the American army.

Shimkhah Czenstochowski

Son of Kalman. Born in Czentochow in 1860. Died there in 1941.

Mendl Czenstochowski (Kalmens)

Paterson, N.J.

Son of Kalman and Ruchl. Born in Czenstochow. Came to America in 1904. He is an executive member of the Lodz branch 140 *Arbeter Ring* in Paterson, N.J.

Feigl Czenstochowski

Daughter of Ruwin and Gela Abusz. She was a righteous woman and a worker for the poor. Died at age 52 in Czenstochow.

Her mother went to Jerusalem to die and died the same year in which she arrived there.

Abraham Czenstochowski (Kalmens)

(photo)

Son of Mendl and Feiga. Born in Paterson, N.J. on 15 August 1910. Was a member of the Young Men's Hebrew Association and other Jewish communal organizations. Died in an accident on 6 February 1940.

Shoshona Czenstochowska

Tel Aviv

(photo)

Daughter of Eige of the most aristocratic Hasidic family in Czenstochow. The spirit of a poet was awakened in her soul from her earliest youth and she began to write touching and popular songs. As a result, she quickly acquired a good reputation and was beloved by a widespread reading public. Her first songs were published in *Czenstochower Tageblot*. One of her songs was published in every Friday edition of this newspaper and always provoked interest and sympathy among the public. With their publication in the *Czenstochower Tageblot*, her songs became known in the entire Jewish press in Poland and even in America and she began to receive invitations to contribute to various literary and artistic journals. Her songs were also published, among others, in a special edition that came out in New York, in which only women poets took part.

Together with a proclivity to poetry, an inclination to pedagogy and children's education awoke in her and she began an interest – at the beginning of the First World War – in the then newly founded workers children's homes, children's schools, educational courses and was very close to the central Jewish school organization *Tzisho* and worked for a time in its institutions.

However, her parents did not see any great "practical purpose" in both of the "trades" and, according to the advice of their rebbe, they decided to marry her off to a respectable Hasidic young man, who the rebbe himself had seen as a true match.

Not being able to bear the stress and sorrow of her parents, whom, incidentally, she loved and respected very much, she decided to leave her home and went to Lodz. There she received immediate access to the Jewish literary and social circles, became a frequent visitor of Yitzhak Katzenelson, Tabenkin, Miriam Ulinower and other Yiddish writers, poets and teachers who befriended her. She began to diligently study the Hebrew language and in a very short time she acquired a reputation as a first-class teacher and children's educator.

[Page XLVII]

When the well-known Jewish scholar and historian, Prof. Meir Balaban was given the position as director of the Jewish *gymnazie* in Czenstochow, he immediately hired Shoshona Czenstochowska as a teacher and as a nanny for his own children.

She worked at the Czenstochowa *gymnazie* for several years with great success and was very beloved by the children, as well as by the parents and the director and all of the teaching personnel who were first class educators, a number of whom are today found in *Eretz-Yisroel*, such as Yitzhak Szweiger, Dr. Szwarcbard, Perelka and others.

Her reputation as a teacher was widespread in Poland and she began to receive invitations from various cities describing their good conditions.

However, as a fervent Zionist from her earliest youth, she decided to go to *Eretz-Yisroel*, in order to plant her life and her work in the field of pedagogy and the education of children.

In 1924 she traveled to *Eretz-Yisroel* and immediately found a place at the largest *kibbutz* in the country, in Ein Harod. She was welcomed to Ein Harod with open arms and became one of the builders and founders of the children's educational institutions and schools in Ein Harod that later served as a models for all worker-settlement *kibbutzim* and collective agricultural settlements throughout the country.

She worked at Ein Harod for several years with great success, was sent to Western Europe in order to learn the newest methods and achievements in the field of pedagogic and childhood education. She spent several months there and collected new materials and fresh materials for her further activities in *Eretz-Yisroel*.

Returning from abroad, Shoshona Czentochowska regularly contributed to the various pedagogic journals in the country and joined the pedagogic council of the country's United *Kibbutzim.*

Today she holds the position of instructor of all the schools of *Kibbutz* HaMeuhad and travels around the entire country and gives lectures and lesson to teachers and kindergarten personnel and is considered one of the most distinguished pedagogic experts in *Eretz-Yisroel.*

*

Here is added that her parents, Reb Berish Czenstochowski and his wife, who were not pleased by the career of their daughter in Poland, today also live in Ein Harod. Reb Berish continues as the leader of prayer and Torah reader and lives in peace and at rest at the collective together with the community of Jews, *kein ein hora* [Translater's note: literally, no evil eye, said after something positive to prevent something bad from happening.], pious and Hasidic people, all parents of the comrades of the *kibbutz,* who live their characteristic independent life, free and undisturbed at Ein Harod. And not long ago, he, Reb Berish Czenstochowski, was delegated by his friends at Ein Harod to go to Jerusalem to have a *sefer-Torah* written for the synagogue of the pious Jews who live at Ein Harod, the largest Jewish socialist workers' *kibbutz* in *Eretz-Yisroel.*

_____

[Page XLVII]

Yod י

Yakob Joselowicz (Salamon)

(photo)

Son of Zwi Hersh and Feiga. Born in Kozienice (Poland). Came to America in 1921. Worked in the "Vulcan" foundry. His father, Hersh, was a soldier in Nicholas's army and served in the military for 25 years, beginning his service at age 12. He is descended from the family of Berek Joselowicz, the hero of the Polish rebellion in 1863. He was a very religious Jew until the end of his life. He died at age 76 on 4 October 1943 in Chicago.

_____

Ester Joselowicz (Salamon)

(photo)

Daughter of Shimeon and Perl Majerczak. Came to America in 1921. She was very religious. Charity was one of the chief *mitzvus* [good deeds] for her. She gave birth to and raised 10 children. Died at age 76 on 29 January 1943 in Chicago.

_____

Larry and Simon Yelin

[Translator's note: Although two separate names are given above, only the following biography appears and there is no indication whether it is for Larry or Simon Yelin.]

Son of Ahron Shlomoh and Chaya. Born in Czenstochow on 27 August 1886. Came to America on the 20 August 1902.

_____

Lipman Yellen

(photo)

Died at the age of 74 in Kamyk, in 1936.

Ester Yellen

(Née Yakubowicz)

Born in Witkowice (near Klomnice, Poland). Died at the age of 70 in Kamyk in 1934.

[Page XLVIII]

Ester Yellen

(photo)

Daughter of Avraham and Chava Pantofel. Born in Kamyk on 24 May 1907. She was active with the Jewish school system in Kamyk. Came to America on 9 April 1929.

Harry Yellen

Son of Lipman and Ester. Born in Kamyk (near Czenstochow) November 1898. He belonged to the Jewish socialist party, *Fareinikte* [United], in Poland. One of the founders of the Jewish school system in Kamyk. He married Ester Pantofel. Came to America on 18 April 1927.

Benny Yellen

(photo)

Son of Lipman and Ester Yellen. Born in Kamyk in 1892.

Freidl Joskowicz

Detroit

Daughter of Yosef and Feigl Landau. Born in Czenstochow in May 1885. Came to America in 1920. One of the active members of Czenstochower Regional Union and vice president of the Ladies Auxiliary of the Jewish Folks Union in Detroit.

Itmar Joskowicz

Son of Eliezer Lipman and Mindl. Born in Czenstochow. He belonged to various Czenstochower organizations. Died at age 78.

Moshe Joskowicz

Son of Itmar and Ruchl. Born in 1884 in Dzialoszyn. He lived in Czenstochow before coming to America in 1913. Now belongs to the Jewish National Workers' Union and Right *Poalei-Zion*.

Moshe Joskowicz is a distinguished member of *Farband*. He helped to organized branch 15 and has been involved with its work from the first day on. Since the founding of the branch, he has been one of the organizers of A.N.A.F. and a representative of the *Farband* on the general executive and on the New York State committee.

In 1945 branch 15 celebrated Moshe Joskowicz's 60th birthday and published a special book in his honor in which the most distinguished *Farband* workers took part.

Samuel (Joskierowicz) Josker

(photo)

Born on the August 1893 in Sosnowiec. Came to America from Czenstochow on 5 August 1913. He is a member of the Jewish Fraternal Order in New York. His son-in-law, George Kaufman, served as a sergeant in the American army.

Samuel Josker was one of the founders of the Czenstochower branch 11 of A.F.P.A. in New York.

The Rabbi Meir Henokh Iszajwicz, of blessed memory

(photo)

Born in Szrensk in 1872. At age 18, he married a niece of the Czenstochower Rabbi – Reb Nakhum Ash, of blessed memory. He became a rabbi in Czenstochow.

In 1924, he settled in *Eretz-Yisroel* with his family, where he died in 1940. He published many *seforim* [religious books], such as *Ma'or Hadesh*, also a thousand year calendar. At the time of the *Beilis Proces* [trial], he took part in debates against the blood libel baiters. He published an open letter in *Freint*, then published in Warsaw, in which he came out strongly against the Black Hundred that had instigated the *Proces*.

Comrade Iszajwicz was known as the child prodigy from Szrensk, where he took a significant part in Jewish education, founding a *yeshiva* that existed for two years and had to close due to a shortage of funds.

(photo, caption: Dr. Moshe Iszy [Iszajwicz)

In Tel Aviv, he continued to work in the scientific field; wrote a commentary on *Berashis Raba*; successfully publishing the first volume of the manuscript.

[Page XLIX]

His children – sons and daughters – are spread all over the world. His oldest son lives in New York, as does a daughter. A second son – in Paris. Three sons and a daughter – in *Eretz-Yisroel* and two daughters – in the Soviet Union.

[Page XLIX]

Kaf כ

Sara Ruchl Chlopak

(photo)

Daughter of Yakov Dovid and Rywa Laya Fiszman. Born in Czenstochow in 1871. Came to America in 1920. Lives with her children.

Dovid Chlopak

(photo)

Son of Leib and Sara. Born on 9 July 1882 in Czenstochow. He married Malka Frydman in 1908. Came to America in 1913.

Leib Chlopak

Father of Dovid. Son of Dovid and Rokhma (née Frenkel). Died in 1909 in Czenstochow.

Alkhana Chrabalowski

Our Family

(photo, caption: Yosef Yitzhak Chrabalowski)

(photo, caption: Alkhana Chrabalowski)

(photo, caption: Lou Chrabalow)

The grandfather was named Zwi-Hirsh Charbolowski. The family name comes from a residence that is the village Charbalowki. He was a fisherman and ran an inn. Later, he lived in Belsk, Grodno *gubernia*. He had three sons and one daughter: the oldest – Yosef Yitzhak (Alkhana's father), Alkhana, Shmuel and Malka. Yosef Yitzhak was the educated one among them; the other two sons were blacksmiths.

Alkhana's father, whose name was shortened to Yoslitche, married Rywka (Alkhana's mother) of Zembrow. Her family name was Akselrod. Her parents were chandlers (made tallow *Shabbos* candles) and settled in a small *shtetl* –Janiszewo, Lomza *gubernia*. The children were born there, spent their childhood and matured, like birds in a nest they flew to all corners of the world.

In addition to their main source of income – teaching, Alkhana's parents were also chandlers and cigarette makers. This would be done in the early mornings or late at night, before and after *kheder*.

The family consisted of four brothers and three sisters, in addition to two who died as children. One sister, Chava, a grown girl, died in Bialystok. Those still living are, according to age: Yankl, Fanny (Slava-Feigl), Alkhana, Annie (Chava), Louis (Leima), Sam (Shmuelke). All, except Alkhana, live in Chicago.

Alkhana, his father and his grandfather

The oldest brother, Yankl, was a *Beis-Midrash* boy [Translator's note: he spent his time studying in the synagogue or house of study]. Alkhana stayed near his father; he helped him teach the *kheder* boys during the day and, at night, Alkhana taught the girls of Janiszewo to write in Yiddish and to do arithmetic. He was then about 9 or 10 years old. He also helped the *kheder* boys learn to write Yiddish and Russian. Alkhana knew almost the entire *Tanakh* [*Torah* plus the Writings and Prophets] by heart and, *lehavdil* [word used to separate the sacred from the profane], *Russkaya Ryetch* [*Russian Speech*]. He dictated or wrote down letters for girls from Blosztajn's letter almanac.

In addition to teaching and other trades, Alkhana's father was also a letter writer. He would compose letters for brides and grooms and write letters for women whose husbands were in America. When Alkhana's oldest brother, Yankl, was a groom in Ostrowe, his father wrote the love letters to his bride for him.

When the Jews lost the right to operate inns, great poverty descended on the *shtetl*, which drove Alkhana's father to seek teaching positions in other cities. At age 12, Alkhana left with his father for Lapes, near Bialystok where his father, Shmuli, had a cousin. Later, the grandfather also joined Shmuli and he and Alkhana – the grandfather and grandchild – slept together in the attic. The grandfather was in his 70's. He died at age 106. His eyes were undimmed and his hand did not shake; as in his youth, his handwriting was curved in old age.

[Page L]

Alkhana was already a rebel at eighteen and struggled against his father's old-fashioned *Yiddishkeit* [Jewishness]. And yet, of the entire family, Alkhana was the grandfather's and father's heir. He had the same ardor for his new *Yiddishkeit* as his father for his old beliefs. Of all of the sisters and brothers, he was the last to remain with his father in Czenstochow. The father died two weeks after Alkhana left for America.

From Janiszewo to Czenstochow

Alkhana was about 15 when his father took him to the Szczawa train station and traveled to Sonspow, a forest near the Krakow border where a relative – Yehuda Leib Landau – was a *wald-schreiber* [person who keep the register of the trees cut down]. This was Alkhana's first trip alone on the railroad. The trip took around three days. He traveled without a train ticket. He spent a couple of years in the gorgeous mountainous area around Ojcow, which is a branch of the Carpathian Mountains. Later he was in Olkusz, Krimolow, Zawiercie and Kaminsk. He taught Jewish children everywhere: Hebrew, *khumish* with Rashi, writing in Yiddish and other languages. This happened against his will – in his heart he hated it – he wanted to study in an artisan's school in Bialystok, but his father was afraid that he would become a non-believer... One summer he was in Warsaw as an employee in a shop. He lived there for the entire time without a passport that was impossible for him to obtain until he completed military service.

Alkhana's father came to Zarwiercze later and there was a *malamed* again. The whole family came to Zarwiercze together. In the summer of 1905, they moved to Czenstochow. The parents were died there and all of the children emigrated to America.

The Sister Fanny – The Mother's Representative

In 1908, Fanny was the first to emigrate from Czenstochow to America. To her came, later: Annie, Lou, Sam; then, Alkhana. From the time the family came to Zarwiercze, Fanny substituted for her always ill mother. In America, her house was the family home for a long time. In addition to the worries and the joys of peace time – she had to bear two world wars. The two brothers, Lou and Sam served in the American army during the First World War, and Alkhana in the Russian. All of Annie's three sons served in "Uncle Sam's" army during the Second World War, and Fanny had enough worry and enough work baking "cookies" and sending "packages."

(photo, caption: Sam Chrabalow)

The father, it seems, placed great hope on Alkhana and Fanny... He would wake them at dawn and study with them...

Fanny – now Fanny Schwartz – also was active in aid work for Czenstochow. She was in the first group in Chicago that supported the children's homes after the First World War.

Reuniting of the Family in America

Alkhana traveled to America twice – once in 1923 when he remained in Chicago for a year and then returned [to Poland]; the second time – in 1926, he remained in New York in the large Jewish "exile community." A large Czenstochower family is found here; the friends and comrades of 1905, from 1911 and younger friends and comrades from the First World War; friends and comrades from Bialystok, from Warsaw, from Noworadomsk; here are the *kheder* friends from Janiszewo, with whom Alkhana played at hobbies during the summer evenings, here are also the "further" family, his Uncle Alkhana's and Aunt Malka's children from Wysoka whom he did not even know at home.

His uncle, Alkhana, who took the family name Kaplan because of military conscription, brought 14 children into the world, sons and daughters. Five of the sons are in New York, one in South America. His Aunt Malka's three daughters – Etl, Friedka and Chaya are also in America, two of them in New York and the third, Chaya, in Los Angeles.

Who knows if any of the grandfather, Tzvi Hersh's generation survived there. However, here, in New York and in Chicago, his family grows, *kein ein hora* [Translator's note: may no evil eye occur, usually said after something positive to prevent something bad from interfering], and often celebrates weddings, at a *bris* [ritual circumcision], and at a *bar-mitzvah*. The entire family comes together at a celebration, they sit around the table with lots of good things, they drink a *LaChaim* [a toast to life], the music plays, "Star Spangled Banner" and the "*Hatikvah*" [Israeli national anthem]. "Barbaretto" and other jazz is played for the young generation. Then comes the *mitzvah tenzl* [traditional dance with a bride and groom], the *sher* [usually a dance tune played by *klezmorim*] and the *hopke* [circle dance]; then the Jews stand up from the tables – men and women – from Wysoka, Bialystok, Zembrowa, Zaromb, make a circle, lay hands on shoulders, lift a foot, clap with the hands, forget the broken English and again become Jews, like their fathers, mothers, grandfathers, grandmothers were. The children, the grandchildren, the great grandchildren are drawn into the *freilekh* [circle dance] and everyone hops happily.

No matter, Tzvi Hersh's great grandchildren in America will not know any Yiddish. However, they will long, long dance a Jewish circle dance, a *mitzvah tenzl*, a *freilekh*.

[Page LI]

Tet ט

Helen Tempelhof-Chrabolowski

Max Tempelhof
(photo)

Heniek Tempelhof
(photo)

The Tempelhof family comes from Ozorkow. It then settled in Lodz. They were an extensive family consisting of about 200 people. In Lodz, they lived on Piotrkower Street, number 24. Helen's father, Shimkhah Tempelhof, may he rest in peace, ran a men's clothing workshop in Lodz. [The clothing] was sent to Russia. They moved to Czenstochow in 1913. There were four brothers and three sisters. In time they came to love Czenstochow more than Lodz. Helen's closest friends were: Heltche Pelc, who lived in Belgium and now in London, Andje and Gutsche Win, Ramek Szwarcboim and Szmulewicz. She married Alkhana Chrabolowski in 1923. In 1929, she came to America with her then one-year old daughter, Chavele.

(photo, caption: the parents and brother and sister of Helen Tempelhof)

In 1932, her father died at the age of 83. Her two brothers – Max and Heniek – emigrated to Belgium. Her youngest brother, Pinkhus, took part in the march of the *halutzim* [pioneers] who wished to reach *Eretz-Yisroel* through Romania. At the start of the Second World War, he and his wife remained in Baranowicz. He became a tractor operator there and nothing has since been heard from him.

Her brother Heniek escaped to France during the Nazi occupation of Belgium. He later returned to Liege, Belgium, was dragged away by the Nazis to a concentration camp and perished there, leaving a wife Chavche (née Broder) from Czenstochow and a daughter. Her brother Max jumped from a train that was carrying him to his death and survived. The oldest brother, Moshe, married Dora Lederman and had four grown children. None of them survived. Her sister, Ita, lived in Lodz with her husband, Zelig Rapuk. During the German invasion, they escaped to Czenstochow. Of there children, four sons and one daughter, two sons – Dudek and Itzik and the daughter, Sonja, survived and are now in Bergen-Belsen [Translator's note: There was a displaced persons' camp in Bergen–Belsen after WWII]. Her [Helen's] youngest sister, Chava, stayed with their mother in Czenstochow and they both perished.

Of the large Tempelhof family in Lodz, almost no one survived.

May their sacred memory remain for all Jewish generations and their untimely, innocent death never be forgotten.

Lamed ל

Charlie (Zechariah) Lewensztajn
(photo)

One of the first original founders of the *S.S.* [Zionist Socialist] party in Czenstochow. Led the struggle against the Czarist order for freedom, for a more beautiful and better life for the Jewish masses. He was and remained beloved by all of his friends and comrades.

He came to America right after 1905. Here he continued his work in the struggle that he had begun in the old home. He was the secretary of the Czenstochower Young Men, also the recording secretary of Czenstochower Relief and the Ladies Auxiliary.

He died at age 50 on 5 January 1940.

Chone Lewensztajn

(photo)

Born in Czenstochow in 1902. His mother died when he was two years old. His father, a Jew, a *maskil* [follower of the Enlightenment], was a correspondent for the Warsaw newspaper, Heint [Today], Moment and others.

[Page LII]

At age 14, Lewenstzajn graduated from the Artisan's School in Czenstochow. A Yiddish professional theater group appeared in Czenstochow at that time. Because his father was a newspaper correspondent, he had free entry to the theater; Lewensztajn could attend presentations almost every day. This had a great influence on him and he began to dream about performing in the Yiddish theater. However, he first realized his dream in 1920. As a soldier in the Polish army, he became a Russian prisoner in 1920/21. Here he attempted to enter enroll in the dramatic studio that existed at that time in Leningrad under the leadership of Aleksander Kugel (Homo Nuvos). His first appearance was in the role of Holophernes in the play *Yehudit* by Hebel.

In 1922, he returned to Poland where he began appearing with professional troupes. He appeared in a series of roles such as: Yankl Chapshawicz in *Gut fun Nakumahi* [*God of Revenge*], Mishka Cyganiak in *Di Zibn Gehangene* [*The Seven Who Were Hanged*], Jean Valjean in *Gbur in Keitn* [*Conquered in Chains*].In 1930 he was hired by the Vilner Troupe and appeared as Yankl Boile in *Dorfs-Yung* [*Village Youth*] and in the role of the *golem* in *Golem* [a human-like creature made of clay].

He was successful in escaping to Russian territory in 1939 and reached Tarnopol and, here, he was hired by the Jewish State Theater. He appeared in the role of *Tevye* in *Tevye der Milkhiker* [*Tevye the Milkman*] and in the role of the landowner in *Oifstand* [*Uprising*] by Dr. Ciper. Here he received an award for playing various roles.

With the outbreak of the Russian-German War in 1941, he escaped to far Russia. Since he knew the Russian language, he was employed in one of the best Russian theaters, played important roles in many Soviet plays and received the Stalin Award.

He appeared in a series of Soviet films, among them: *Against the Darkness*, *Revenge Taker* and *Riga Ghetto.*

He returned to Poland in 1946. Today he appears in the Yiddish Theater in Lower Silesia.

Yeheil Lewensztajn

(photo)

Born on 8 July 1900 in Czenstochow. Son of Moshe Leib and Dwoyra Danciger-Lewensztajn. He studied in a *kheder* until age 13, as well as in a Polish elementary school. At 15, he began acting with the famous character actor Shlomoh Hershkowitz, with Zhelazo and so on. 1919/20, he acted in Germany. Came to America in 1920. In 1923 he joined the Yiddish Theater Society under the name *Undzer Teater* [Our Theater], under the leadership of M. Elkin, Peretz Hirshbein, Dovid Pinsky and the famous German-Jewish actor, Egon Brecher. In 1928 he joined *Artef* [acronym for Arbeter Teater Farband or Worker's Theatrical Alliance]. Later, he appeared in concerts in various characterizations. In 1944, he began to appear with the Yiddish Theater Ensemble under the leadership of the famous director, Benimin Zemakh.

Yakov Lewit
Eretz-Yisroel

Born in 1888. He was one of the most famous manufacturers in the textile industry, one of the first in this field in Poland.

He worked with the Jewish *kehile* [religious community], was one of the founders of the Manufacturers and Merchants Bank, co-founder of the Jewish *gymnazie* that in recognition of his contribution named a room for him and his wife. He took part in almost every communal undertaking and aid activity that was organized in Czenstochow.

He came to *Eretz-Yisroel* in 1939. Here, he and his son founded a factory for spinning and weaving wool in Ramat Gan, a division of Zwirn-Rey.

Here he remained the same communal worker and donor as he was in Czenstochow and there he spent the greater part of his life.

Bernard Lewkowicz

Son of Yakov and Dora. Born on 22 September 1921 in Boston, Mass. He died on 18 November 1944.

Sam (Shmuel) Lewkowicz

Son of Pinkhas and Nakha. Born 1857. The family consisted of nine children – five sons and four daughters. He was the oldest of the sons. He studied to be a tailor. After he returned from the military, he married Perl Libgot. Then emigrated to Paris; he was there for four years and then came to America.

At the founding of the cloakmaker's union, he was one of the first members. The same for Czenstochower branch 261 of the *Arbeter Ring*; there he held several offices. He was also a member of the Czenstochower Aid Union and Relief Committee and did good work.

His three sons and two grandsons served in the American army.

[Page LIII]

Meir Yona Litman, may he rest in peace

(photo)

Born in Moscow in 1860 and brought home to Noworadomsk as a young man by his father, Reb Zawel (a soldier in Nicholai's army, who was caught as a child in Noworadomsk and served Czar Nicholai for the entire 25 years) home to Noworadomsk as a young man. In 1880 he married Beila, the daughter of Nisen Zelik Kalka of Noworadomsk, with whom he lived for 50 years and who bore him four daughters and four sons. In 1900 he moved to Czenstochow, where he lived until he emigrated to America in 1920, right after the First World War.

In his youth, Reb Meier Yona Litman was carried away by the Hasidic movement that enveloped the Jewish masses in East Europe. He became an enthusiastic Hasid and follower of Hasidic rebbes. In Czenstochow, he was the *shamas* for Reb Avigdor Szapira whom our *landsleit* remember well.

(photo, caption: Reb Avigdor Szapira, May the memory of a righteous person be blessed)

While in the Rabbi's court, where the poor Jewish masses would come to tell about their problems and "pour out their bitter hearts," Meir Yona became a great lover of the poor people, of the suffering Jews who searched for help when in need and for consolation in time of trouble.

When he emigrated to America with his family in 1920, he did not forget the poor masses who remained in the old home, Czenstochow. Not for one minute did he break the thread connecting him to those in need of help. He constantly stood bound to the Czenstochower Rebbe, Reb Nukhum Asz, may the memory of a righteous person be blessed, with the Jewish hospital, with the *Linat Hazadek* [medical aid society], *Beis Lekhem* [bread for the needy organization] and with the *Talmud Torah Machzikei Hadas* [Translator's note: traditionally, a *Talmud Torah* is a tuition-free school for needy children]. Not only did he collect money from his children, *landsleit* acquaintances and friends, but he even interested other Jews – Lithuanians, Russian and Galicianers – in the needy in the city of Czenstochow.

It can truly be said about Meir Yona Litman "that he himself was an aid committee." Every year he would arrange a concert in a *shul* and the receipts would be sent to Czenstochow for the institutions that were dear to him. When the *khazan* in the *shul* (a fervid Litvak), who would give a concert without cost, complained that he is not a Czenstochower and he does not even know where the city is located, "So why should I abuse my throat without payment?" Reb Meir Yona, with a good-natured smile, answered: "The poor little children in Czenstochow need food and shoes..." The *khazan* immediately became softer and replied: "If you are the 'ambassador' of the poor little Jewish children in your Polish city, Czenstochow, I cannot refuse and I will sing with great heart and without a *groshn* payment..."

That is how our distinguished *landsman* Meir Yona Litman tirelessly worked for our birthplace Czenstochow. He had the suffering luckless Jews in Poland and in the ghettos in his mind until his last breath and did everything that he could to help them. In his home, there was always talk about how to help those suffering in Czenstochow. He, himself, collected clothing and shoes, made small packages and sent them to Poland. His rooms were always filled with packages, things, about which he would say with pride: "They will keep the people at home alive..." This was all done quietly, without noise and without asking for recognition.

In America, too, in the *shul* at which he was the *shamas*, he was beloved and respected by everyone. When he turned 80, the *shul* gave a banquet in honor of his 80th birthday. The banquet was a great success and brought in over two hundred dollars in cash. The *shul* decided to give the money to Reb Meir Yona as a gift. However, he did not want to accept the gift. "It is better to give it to a *Talmud Torah*, for the poor little children," he answered and this was actually done.

The orthodox *Morgen Zhurnal* [*Morning Journal*] in New York wrote the following about our *landman*, Reb Meir Yona, after his funeral:

"Reb Meir Yona Litman, may he rest in peace, one of the nicest types of the old generation, died on Tuesday, 17 November 1942 at the age of 83.

"Immediately after his arrival from Czenstochow twenty-two years ago, he joined the Young Men's Hebrew Association Synagogue, Fulton Avenue and 171st St., the Bronx, where he was the *shamas* until the last day of his life.

"Reb Meir Yona Litman was beloved and popular in all of the Crotona Park neighborhood in the Bronx. He made himself beloved with his good heartedness and charity. Every morning after praying, he would give loans to dozens of people who would turn to him for help and no one left empty-handed. He regularly supported dozens of rabbinical families in America and in Poland with money and packages.

"He was also the founder of an interest-free loan fund and dozens of businessmen and workers were helped by it.

"The funeral took place Wednesday and the large *shul* was overflowing with hundreds of men and women.

"Eulogies were given by Rabbi Zalman Reikhman, Rabbi A. Y. Khatowicz and by a young friend of the deceased, Rabbi Wajntroib.

[Page LIV]

"All of the rabbis spoke about the rare personality of the respected deceased and about his extraordinary virtue and honesty."

Beila Litman
(photo)

Born in 1861; died in 1931.

Dovid Litman

Son of Meir Yona and Beila. Born in Czenstochow on 15 June 1894. Came to America in July 1913. He is a member of the Noworadomsker Society. His son Wolf served in the American army.

———

Shmuel Linch

(photo)

(photo, caption: Asher Linszicki, the father of Shmuel Linsch)

Son of Asher and Ruchl. Born in Czenstochow on 5 August 1892. Before coming to America, he lived in Tashkent, Astrakhan, Persia and Bukhara. Came to America in 1906.

———

Ruchl Linszicki

Daughter of Leibish and Chaya. Born in Czenstochow in 1907; died there.

———

Sam Lash Chicago

Born on 1 March 1873 in Piotrkow. Came to America in 1913.

(photo)

(photo, caption: the Levys parents)sd

———

Yakob (Jacob) Levy

Son of Mordekhai and Ester Cesznjewski. Born in Przedborz (Poland) on 15 April 1886 and came to Czenstochow as a child with his parents. Here he studied carpentry at the artisan's school and he studied at the *Talmud Torah*. At that time, he studied together with Khone Kalekharje, Shmuel Noren, Avraham Apter, Haim Win and Yankl Wajsbard. The first director of the school was Menachem Josef Szrajber; he was also the one who opened evening courses for adults and every *Shabbos* afternoon also gave various lessons in the form of lectures that were very interesting and were heard with great thoughtfulness by the students. The first carpentry *meister* [master] was Eliezer Bimka.

Later Levy was active in the *Bund* until leaving for America in 1906. Here he was one of the organizers of the organization, Progressive Young Men, and in 1908, with his friends Meir Gleber, Moritz Kyak and Benyimin Wolhendler, he returned to Czenstochow. During the time he spent there, he was a member of the artisan's club and of the library.

In 1913, he came to America for the second time. He was then a member of the Czenstochower *Arbeter Ring* branch 261 and, also, of the Cz. Aid Union. He was also a member of the organization, Adler's Young Men; he was one of the most active members of United Czenstochower Relief in New York and of the *Czenstochower Yidn* book committee.

Yitzhak (Isidor) Levy

(photo)

Son of Mordekhai and Ester Cesznjewski. Born in Przedborz (Poland) on 15 July 1882. He came to Czenstochow at age 13 to study as a painter with an uncle. In his youth, during the summer months, he helped his uncle – the *meister* [master]. During the winter months when there was no painting work, he worked in various little factories, such as with Godl Wajnberg in the chair back factory and so forth. He *hut gegesn teg* [Translator's note: literally, "he ate days" – ate with families that provided him with free meals] at the home of the *meister* and, finally, had to to his family in Przedborz. After a certain time, Yitzhak returned to Czenstochow because he felt that he had capabilities for painting and entered the employment of the famous sign painter, Haim Josef Cimberknopf, who was probably the first sign painter in Czenstochow. He took on Yitzhak for a year and paid him thirty rubles a term. Later, [Yitzhak] brought his parents to Czenstochow, where they settled and they took over the work in the *Talmud Torah*.

[Page LV]

Yitzhak Levy became a friend of Yakob Silver and the latter began to come to visit him in his room. They even began to dress alike. After a year or two, they began to think about working in the theater because Yakov Ber was a great reader of books. They decided to revise and stage the story, *Shimkhah Plakhte*. They produced *Shimkhah Plakhte* together with other colleagues, Haim Leib Szwarc, Josef Hirsh Grajcer and Kasriel Rotbard (*Stadole*). Yitzhak painted the scenery and played the role of Shimkhah Plakhte's wife himself, a comic role. He was then 18 years old and the greatest tragedy for him then was that he had to shave his whiskers and later was ashamed to be seen on the street without them. The theater piece was staged by Yankl Sibirski in Winer Hall. The presentation was a great success. He was freed from Czarist military conscription and decided to enter the world.

He worked for Cimberknopf for a year and a half; he then worked as a painter for Okrent and Gastinski. On his way to America, he also worked for Gastinski's brother in London. He brought his brother, Yankl, and he worked as a painter.

He married Chana Fiszkowicz in New York in 1907. Six years ago, he began to attend the Art Students League in New York and today he paints various nature landscapes such as flowers and fruits. He has painted several oil paintings and with watercolors. He has not given up the abilities of his youth.

Yitzhak Levy is a member of the Cz. Br. 261 *Arbeter Ring*, the Vilner Society, United Czenst. Relief Committee and of the *Czenstochower Yidn* book committee. His son, Benjamin, served in the American army.

Leibl Landau

(photo)

He was known in Czenstochow as a *malamed*, warden and *gabay* in the synagogue. Died in 1936 at the age of 75 in Czenstochow.

Chana Gitl Landau

Wife of Leibl Landau. Born in Czenstochow; died there at age 60 in 1929.

Rajzl Lakhman
(née Rajzl Rikhter)

(photo)

When the rooms of the Workers' Home in Czenstochow were filled with young, self confident song – it was known that this was Ruszke's voice. However, in life and in party work, she was earnest, loyal and devoted with her whole heart. For all of her years, she worked at home and when she came to *Eretz-Yisroel* with her husband and two children, she became ill and the last two years of her life, she lay in the hospital or at home. Her comrades and friends – Abraham Gotlib, Shimkhah Rajkh, Yudl Dancijger, Yakov Gotlib (her brother-in-law), Godl Frajtag and others – stood watch at her bed in the last weeks before her death. During the last days of her life she would say: "I have suffered to live and thus I suffer to die."

She died in 1942 at the age of 42.

Dr. Leopold Lazarowicz

(photo)

Son of Dovid and Tziviah (née Gurski). Born in Czenstochow in 1895. He graduated from the Rusita *gymnazie* in Czenstochow in 1914 and later studied medicine in Warsaw. He received a degree as a medical doctor in 1922. As a student he was a managing committee member of the Jewish Academic Circle in Czenstochow.

From 1922 until 1939 he practiced in Warsaw as an independent specialist of in internal medicine; he also worked in the Jewish hospital in Warsaw and was a member of the chief managing committee and vice president of the Warsaw division of *TOZ* in Poland. Later, he occupied the office of secretary of the Jewish medical society in Warsaw.

Came to America in 1941. Passed the medical exams and opened an office in Manhattan as a doctor of internal medicine.

Associated as a staff member of the hospitals: New York Postgraduate School and Hospital; Metropolitan City Hospital.

Also active here in New York in the communal realm: 1) Executive member of the American "*OZA*;"; 2) delegate to the American Council of Voluntary Agencies for United Service; 3) Veteran Service – member of medical staff; 4) medical advisor to the relief committee of Polish Embassy; 5) secretary of the American-Polish Medical Alliance.

[Page LIV]

Simon Lipszic

(photo)

Son of Moshe Meir and Pesa. Born in Praszka (Poland) on 14 June 1885. Came to America in June 1902. During his time in America, he visited Poland and the Soviet Union twice. He is a member of the Czenstochower branch 11 of the Jewish Fraternal Order in New York.

Mauricy Lipski

Son of Wolf and Stefa. Born in Piotrkow. He was one of the largest wood merchants in Czenstochow. Died at the age of 83 in 1936 in Czenstochow.

Felicia Lipski

(photo)

Daughter of Bernard and Chana Hamburger. Born in Czenstochow. She was the wife of Mauricy Lipski. Died in Czenstochow at the age of 72 in 1929.

Ludwig Lipski

Son of Mauricy and Felicia. Lipski was born in Czenstochow in 1885.

Kopl Lederman

(photo)

Born on 7 May 1915 in Czenstochow. His father, Fishl Lederman, was a shoemaker, just like his grandfather, Shimeon Lederman and his grandfather's brother, Moshe. Shoemaking was then an occupation that went from generation to generation. His mother, Manya, (n"Manya (née Szwarcboim), was a simple, honest woman. Her two main goals in life were: to raise her children to a better life than she had (a goal that she only partly achieved) and to help her husband in earning a living. The Ledermans saw meat in their home only twice a week; fish – only to brighten the *Shabbas* table. Now, Kopl is in America and when he thinks of his deceased mother, she appears before his eyes as a symbol of Jewish women, ignoring the heavy burden that they had to bear, they always dreamed about a better life, if not for themselves, then at least for their children. And they looked to the bright little corner that is named America.

Like all Jewish boys, at the age of four, Kopl began to study in a *kheder*. There he learned Hebrew, Rashi-*Khumish* and *Gemara*. Many times, Kopl's rebbe explained a portion of the *Khumish* by hitting him on his full bottom. Kopl's grandfather, Reb Mendil, hoped to see his grandson as a teacher of the very young boys or, perhaps, even a *shoykhet* [ritual slaughterer].

In 1921/22 new winds began to blow in Czenstochow. The secular Jewish Folk School was born on Krutka Street that was one of the most beautiful chapters of Jewish life in Czentochow. Kopl remembers with pride the Jewish school where he and other Jewish children were raised as class conscious Jews, who knew to struggle for their rights and never bowed under the Fascist rod.

In remembering the Czenstochower Jewish Folk School, K.L. does not forget to give honor to all of those who helped to build the school.

However, more than anyone else, he remembers the workers and teachers who worked and struggled for the Folk School in Czenstochow itself – Comrade Rafael Federman, Comrade Brat,

Waga the teacher (now Mrs. Rotman), Comrade Leibush Berkowicz, Moshe Lederman and many other dazzling personalities from Czenstochow who devoted their time and health to our school.

After graduating from the Folk School, K.L. began to work as an apprentice to a tailor, in order to learn the trade. The Czenstochower garment workers union was founded then. The purpose was – to demand an eight-hour workday and that the owners should treat the journeymen and apprentices better. The struggle for an eight-hour workday was very difficult. However, thanks to the unity in the ranks of the workers, the struggle was won. Thus, the life of the poor tailors became a little easier.

With the outbreak of the Second World War in 1939, K.L. was lucky to come to America. After a very great effort and much work, his two uncles in New York succeeded in bringing him over, for which he is thankful to this day.

It was difficult for him to find a job in the first months because he was not a member of a union and he had to be satisfied with 12-15 dollars a week. Ignoring this, he worked diligently and he was happy to be in America. He remembered the Czenstochower *landsleit* who had come to America 20-30 years ago and who had worse conditions to fight.

When the war broke out in Europe, the terrible news reached him that his father, Fishel Lederman, was one of the first victims of the Nazi beast.

[Page LVII]

The attack on Pearl Harbor came two years after his arrival in America. Lederman entered the American army. Three months later he was sent to the South Seas. He was in Australia, New Caledonia, in the Fiji Islands and he took part in the difficult battle of Guadalcanal in 1942/43. The six months on Guadalcanal were the worst that he lived through and he remembers them often with pride. Kopl L., a young man from Czenstochow, took part in the most beautiful chapter of the struggle of the American army – that was the first victory of the Second World War.

Now he is back in America. His health has been undermined by tropical malaria, but the spirit of freedom and brotherhood, the willingness to help create a freer world, a world for which we, the Czenstochower youth and the fallen heroes of Guadalcanal, fought is not broken.

K.L. lived to see the complete defeat of the yellow, brown and black beasts, but at the same time, the extermination and annihilation of all of the Jewish communities in Poland, the deaths of our fathers, mothers, brothers, sisters and friends. This places on us, those saved from doom, a heavy debt to work together to help the surviving remnant of brothers on the other side and not to despair, not to tire of working further and to struggle for the survival of our people.

Yisroel and Ester Lenczer

(photo)

Born in Lelew (Poland). They died in 1914.

Parents of Yeshayahu (Charles) Lenczer.

Yeshayahu Lenczer

(photo, caption: Yeshayahu and Ita Lenczer in their youth)

(photo, caption: Yeshayahu and Ita Lenczer in their middle years)

Son of Yisroel and Ester. Born in Lelew (Poland) on 18 November 1881. Came from Czenstochow to America on 13 April 1906. He is a member of the *Zaloshiner* (Dzialoszyn) *Erste Chevra Anshei Bnei Achim* and the chairman of its loan fund. Also a member of the Williams Avenue Synagogue. Very active in United Czenstochower Relief Committee in New York.

Ita Lenczer

(photo)

Daughter of Feiwel and Chana Herszlikowicz. Born in Czenstochow in 1885. Came to America in 1906. Married Yeshayahu Lenczer.

Belonged to the following organizations: New Lots Ladies Aid Society (former president); New Lots Pennsylvania *Talmud Torah* (former trustee); *Ezrat Yetomim* [orphan's aid organization] in Brownsville (former vice-president), Beth-El Hospital Auxiliary (former chair-lady); Jefferson Nursing Home (member); East New York Y (member); American Jewish Women Volunteers (member); *Zaloshiner Chevra Anshei Bnei Achim* Ladies Auxiliary (one of the founders, now chairlady); Hadassah in East New York (member); Czenstochower Ladies Auxiliary (chairlady); Czenstochower Relief Committee (vice president); book committee, *Czenstochower Yidn* (executive member).

Her children are: Moshe Lenczer and Perl Lenczer, married to Mory Shatz, a lawyer.

Frances Lederberg

Born in Czenstochow. Married Harry Lederberg in New York. Living in Lindenhurst, Long Island.

Yitzhak Lesser

Son of Anshel and Matl. Died at age 70 on 10 April 1925 in Czenstochow.

(photo, caption: Yitzhak and Zelda Lesser with family)

Zelda Lesser

Daughter of Efroim and Chaya Reizl Garbinski. Born in 1863 in Praszka (Poland). Came to America on 18 September 1923. She was a member of the Czenstochower Regional Union in Detroit. Died on 19 October 1938 in Detroit.

[Page LVIII]

Benny Lesser

Detroit

(photo)

Son of Yitzhak and Zelda. Born in Czenstochow in 1894. Came to America in 1922. His son, Sidney, served as a sergeant in the American army.

Leib Lesser

(photo)

Son of Yitzhak and Zelda. Born in Czenstochow on 17 March 1883. Came to America in 1914. At first, he lived in Galveston (Texas), then in Detroit. He has been in Chicago for twenty years.

Leib Lesser was one of the members of the Czenstochower Independent Union that was organized in Chicago in 1938. He always took part in all of the important work that was carried out by the Czenstochower Independent Union; he also was secretary of the cemetery committee of the Czenstochower Independent Union. He also belongs to the Czenstochower Educational Union and to various other charitable community organizations.

[Page LVIII]

Mem מ

Chana Monowicz

(photo)

Daughter of Henekh and Ruchl Beila. Born in Pilica. Came to Czenstochow as a child and graduated here from Madam Kyak's Folk School. Belonged to the *Bund*. Was active for several terms as a committee member of the Bundist organization in Czenstochow. She was the treasurer of the Professional Union of the Clothing Industry for a few years; one of the founders of the Medem Library and its first librarian. Was an executive member of the cultural office of the professional unions and took part as a delegate in meetings "for the right to work" of the Jewish workers in Poland.

In the many faceted activity of communal life, she became known as a modest and conscientious comrade.

In 1933, she moved to Warsaw and was active in the *Bund* there and in the professional movement, etc.

At the outbreak of the Second World War in 1939, she left Warsaw and made her way through Pinsk, Vilna, Moscow, Vladivostok, through Iran, to America where she arrived in New York at the end of 1940 with the help of the Jewish Workers Committee.

Gershon Monowicz

(photo)

A gaiter maker by trade. Belonged to the United *S.S.* Was one of the founders and, later, managing committee member of the Leather Union. In later years, belonged to the *Bund* and was active in the Jewish secular school system.

Died during the Second World War in the *Hasag* concentration camp in Czenstochowa.

Leon Monowicz
(photo)

Son of Henekh and Ruchl Beila. Born in Pilica (Poland) on 21 August 1906. Came to America from Paris on 30 July 1942.

Nekhemia (Harry) Monowicz

Born in 1895 in Pilica. Lived in Czenstochow from childhood. Was a member of the professional union of the nutrition industries and active in the *Bund*. He was deported to Germany for forced labor during the First World War. On his return to Czenstochow, he was badly wounded during the 1919 pogrom. Came to America in 1923. Supports the aid work of the Czenstochower Relief Committee.

Chava Manishewicz

Daughter of Yitzhak and Pesl Zharkowski. Born in Czenstochow on 20 July 1885. Came to America on 15 June 1904. She is a member of the Kamenets Podolsker [Kam"yanets'-Podil'skyy] Society and of the Czenstochower Ladies Auxiliary in New York where she was vice chairlady for a time.

[Page LIX]

Zigmund (Shlomoh Zalman) Markowicz

Son of Mordekhai and Salomea. Born in Czenstochow. Was in America as a visitor in 1928. He was the chairman of the managing committee of the three Gnasziner factories of the Gnasziner Manufacturing Action Society in Czenstochow, member of *B'nai Brith*, managing committee member of the Jewish *gymnazie* in Czenstochow, member of the managing committee of the New Synagogue in Czenstochow, of the council of the Jewish *kehile* [communal organization] in Czenstochow, council of the *województwo* [province] in Kielce, managing committee member of the merchants and manufacturers union in Czenstochow, managing committee member of the Jewish sports organization, *Makabi* and of a whole series of secular organizations in Czenstochow.

He died on 17 February 1939 in Otwosk and was buried in the Czenstochower cemetery.

He was the son-in-law of Isidor Sigman.

Anna Markowicz

Daughter of Isidor and Regina Sigman. Born on 15 September 1892 in Strzemieszyce (Poland). She was the wife of Zigmund Markowicz of Czenstochow. Came to American from Poland through England in May 1943.

An active member of all worthy active Jewish organizations in Czenstochow, such as: orphan's house, old age house, and so on.

Her son, Morris, served as an engineer in the Polish army.

Helena Markowicz

Daughter of Zigmund and Anna. Born on 24 May 1925 in Czenstochow. Came to America from Poland through England, May 1943.

Moshe Makrojer

(photo)

Born 1869 in Czenstochow. Comes from a family that lived there for 200 years. He was one of the first Zionist leaders in our city and distinguished himself with his communal activities. He helped considerably in spreading the Zionist ideas in Czenstochow. He was chairman of the Zionist Committee for many years and delegate to the Fourth Zionist Congress in London. He worked in the *kehile* as a consulting member, was a managing committee member of the *Talmud Torah* and artisan's school. Councilman in the Czenstochow city council from 1917-1920; one of the founders of the Jewish *gymnazie* and chairman of the managing committee.

In private life, he was the director of Grosman's button factory for many years. In 1924, he and his family emigrated to *Eretz-Yisroel* and settled in Tel Aviv.

He was the honorary chairman of the Czenstochower Union in Tel Aviv.

Recently, he is busy writing a history of the Zionist movement and activities in Czenstochow.

Yitzhak Meir Minc, may he rest in peace

Born in Czenstochow in 1867. Distinguished himself with *tzadekah* [charity] and help for the poor. Was a member of the managing committee of the New Synagogue. Known as an industrialist in the celluloid industry.

Died in Czenstochow on 28 June 1942.

Louis Miller

Chicago

Son of Henekh and Beila. Born in Koniecpol (Poland). Came to America on 30 June 1914. He is a member of *B'nai Brith*, Zionist organization, *Anshei Emes* Synagogue and is active in the Czenstochower Educational Union in Chicago. His son Barton served in the American army.

Abraham Shlomoh Miska

Chicago

Son of Shmuel Wolf and Leah. Born in Czenstochow on 16 December 1891. Came to America on 26 February 1907. He married Ita (Edna) Hantwerker. Is a member of *B'nai Brith* and one of the most active members, former president and secretary of the Czenstochower Educational Union in Chicago. He is also an active member of the Relief Committee. His son, William, served in the American army.

Leibl Miska

Son of Shmuel Wolf and Leah. Born in Kamik. Came to America in 1905 from Czenstochow. He is a member of the Czenstochower Educational Union in Chicago. His son-in-law, Heimy Lebicki, served as a sergeant in the American army.

Abraham Mentkow

(photo)

Son of Yeshayahu and Shifra Mientkowicz. Born on 1 November 1882 in Czenstochow. Came to America on 18 December 1903. His sons-in-law, David Roshef, a lieutenant, and Dr. Stefan Levy Weis, a captain, were in the American army.

[Page LX]

Zisman Miska

(photo)

Son of Shmuel Wolf and Leah. Born in Kamyk (Poland) 1888. Came to America 1906. One of the founders and former president and active member of the Czenstochower Neighborhood Educational Union in Chicago.

He died on 16 October 1946 in Chicago.

Sara Hinda Miska

(photo)

Daughter of Meir and Malka Szilit. Born in Kamyk on 23 February 1888. Came to America 1905. She is second vice-president of the Czenstochower Educational Union in Chicago; member of the Czenstochower Aid Society; trustee of the *shul* and a series of other humanitarian organizations. Her son, Milton, served in the American army.

Yeshayahu Ber Mientkowicz

Died in Czenstochow 1930.

Shifra Mientkowicz

Died in Czenstochow 1929.

Yeshayahu Yakov Menkow

Los Angeles

(photo)

(photo, caption: the mother of Yeshayahu Yakov Menkow)

(photo, caption: Mrs. Menkow)

Son of Yitzhak Aizik and Chaja Ester. Born in Klojnz? (Miebawer? *Powiat*). The brother-in-law of the Gerer Rebbes was his *sandek* [man holding baby during circumcision]. When Menkow grew up, he studied with his *sandek* in the *yeshiva* and ate his meals at his home. After his father's death in 1903, Menkow came to Czenstochow. At the beginning, he strove to study further for half a day and simultaneously to be an assistant in a wine business at the old market (the owner, I think, was named Reb Yeshayahu). However, the needs of his family, a mother and three sisters, forced him to be a worker in Wajnberg's factory.

In 1905, he joined the *S.S.* party. His teachers were Ahron Singalowski, his brother Nakhum, later – Josef Number Two and Aleksander (Leibush the teacher).

[Page LXI]

He again had to leave Czenstochow in the summer of 1908 and to emigrate to Vienna, then to Zurich (Switzerland) where an *S.S.* group was located with Dr. Josef Kruk at the head. He returned to Krakow in March 1909 and there married his acquaintance from his young years, Gutshe Granek. They then, with the help of the ITO [Jewish Territorial Organization] Emigration Committee traveled to Galveston (America) and arrived in Lincoln, Neb., where his wife gave birth to two sons. Later, they moved to Chicago, then to Los Angeles where a daughter was born.

In America, he joined the Jewish Socialist Union, *Arbeter Ring* International, Ladies Garment Workers Union, Independent Order of Foresters [a fraternal organization] and the Jewish Workers Committee.

He is vice president of the district committee of the Southern California *Arbeter Ring* and secretary of the Los Angeles Workers Committee.

Kalman Merkazin

Son of Shlomoh Meir and Sura. Born in Koniecpol in 1908. He has been in *Eretz-Yisroel* since 1932. Served in the army since 1940. He is a son-in-law of Berl Pataszewicz of Czenstochow, may he rest in peace.

Jay Mendelson

New Rochelle, N.Y.

(photo)

Born in Warsaw in 1886. His mother died when he was 10 and his father handed him over to a purse maker (handbag worker) as an apprentice. At 12, a Czenstochower manufacturer brought him to Czentochow. At 16, he was already a member of the *Bund* and carried on a struggle against the terrible exploitation. At 18, he joined the *S.S.* [Social Zionists] and was active in the transporting propaganda literature and as an agitator in the "arena of ideas."

In 1908, after the suppression of the Russian revolution, he was one of the active workers in the Czenstochower division of the "Literary Society" and in 1910, he co-founded *Linat-HaTzedekh* [hostel-like institution] in Czenstochow. Mendelson was also involved with community work such as creating kitchens to feed the poor and organizing bazaars whose income went to the needy. In 1911, he left for Germany and, later, from there to London where he founded his own factory and employed many *landsleit* [people from the same city], taught them the trade and helped them in every feasible way. In 1914, after the outbreak of the First World War, he came to America. At first, he spent his time in Boston. In 1916 he came to Chicago and there joined the Czenstochower branch 261 of the *Arbeter Ring* with others, to which he belongs to this day. Together with other *landsleit*, among them Moshe C., he founded the Czenstochower Aid Union, of which he was the first president. His lucky marriage to a wife who bore him a son took place there; his son is a college student studying accounting and law.

In 1918 he and his family returned to New York and in 1923 he settled in New Rochelle, N.Y., where he still lives as an independent leather goods manufacturer. He has remained a devoted helper in the aid work for Czestochow the entire time. He has given material and moral support and he has remained an idealist who strives for a more beautiful and better life for the Jewish masses and is bound to his birthplace, Czenstochow.

Abraham Merowicz

Montreal, Canada

(photo, caption: Abraham Merowicz with his family)

Born in Przyrow near Czenstochow. He received his education from his uncle, Reb Shlomoh Wajcman, known as a *moyel* [ritual circumciser] in Czenstochow. Abraham Merowicz studied in *Makhzikei Hadas* and during his childhood he would assist his aunt in helping the sick in the Jewish hospital in Czenstochow.

Now he lives in Montreal, Canada. He is a founder of the Czenstochower Society in Montreal and one of its most active members.

Berl Mertz

Son of Grunim and Fradl. Born in Rudnik (Kalisz *gubernia,* Poland). He married Ruchl Slawni. Came from Czentochow to America on 5 June 1914. He is a member of the Polish Synagogue and of the Interest Free Loan Union in Detroit.

[Page LXII]

Nun ב

Sara Nakhtigal

Born in Plawno in 1866. Died on 30 October 1939.

(Photo)

Abo Nakhtigal

Son of Wolf and Leah. Born in Krzepice near Czenstochow in 1857. He married Sara Epsztajn. Came to America in 1902. He is a member of the First *Zaloshiner Chevra Anshei Bnei Achim* in New York.

Moshe Nakhtigal

Son of Abo and Sara. Born in Czenstochow 1888. He perished during the First World War as an American soldier in France on 30 September 1918.

(Photo)

Yitzhak Wolf Nakhtigal

(Photo)

Son of Abo and Sara. Born in Czenstochow in 1885. Came to America in 1903. He married Doba Lazarus of Czenstochow. He is president of the First *Zaloshiner Chevra Anshei Bnei Achim* in New York.

Shimeon Nidjinski

(Photo)

(Photo, caption: Josef Nidjinski)

Son of Josef and Reizl. Born in Radoszyce on 16 May 1887. Was one of the organizers of the illegal bakers union in Czenstochow that was founded by both Polish and Jewish workers. He belonged to the *S.S.* party. Was placed in prison due to the denunciation of the bosses: Auerbakh, Itshe Khusz Kozewoda, Pontshe Beker and Aupner. He was exiled to Piotrkow. In 1907 Pontshe Beker was shot. Nidjinski served a year and in 1908 he was exiled to Siberia, where he served three years, until 1911. He returned to Czenstochow and again began party work. In the same year, 1911, the 19 September, he came to America.

Here he belongs to the bakers union, is a member of People's Order br. 307 (bakers branch). He is an executive member of the union and treasurer of his branch.

His son, Harry, born on 9 February 1916 in New York, served as a sergeant in the American army.

Lola Nidjinski

Daughter of Pinkhas and Riva Ejzner. Born in Czenstochow on 15 May, 1897. She is a member of the Jewish Fraternal People's Order.

Melekh Nidjinski

(Photo; caption: San Jose, Costa Rica, Central America)

Son of Shmuel and Rywka. Born on 1 January 1908 in Czentochow. Came from Belgium to Central America in 1933. A member of the Jewish Center in Costa Rica. Former managing member of the Center and of the synagogue committee. Married Masha Liberman.

Masha Nidjinski

Daughter of Leib and Miryam Liberman. Born on 16 March 1911 in Czenstochow. Came to Central America from Belgium in 1933. She is active in and was the secretary of the women's committee of the Jewish Center in Costa Rica.

William Nirenberg

Son of Josef and Nakha. Born in Czenstochow on 14 July 1887. Came to America in 1905. He is a member of the Czenstochower Young Men's Society in New York.

[Page LXII]

Julian Nirenberg

Son of Josef and Nakha. Born in Czentochow on 31 March 1894. Came to America on 18 June 1913. He is a member of the Czenstochower Young Men's Society in New York.

Abo Nirenberg

Son of Josef and Nakha. Born on 18 July 1891 in Czenstochow. Came to America in 1905. He is a member of the Czenstochower Young Men's Society in New York.

[Page LXIII]

Samech ‎ס
Kalman Samsonowicz

Son of Yehezkeil and Sara Ita. Born in Dzialoszyn (Poland) on 12 April 1887. Came to America on 15 August 1913. He is a member of the First *Zaloshiner Chevra Anshei Bnei Achim* in New York.

Ray Sobel
(Photo)

Daughter of Aizik and Chana. Married William Sobel, who was one of the founders and active workers of the Czenstochower Young Men's Society in New York.

Ray Sobel was one of the founders of the Ladies Auxiliary and of late held the office of treasurer of the organization. She died at the age of 65 on 2 August 1943.

William Sobel
(Photo)

Born in Szeps (Poland). Was an active comrade and an executive member of the Czentochower Young Men. Also, a member and one of the founders of the Czenstochower Relief Committee. He died at the age of 67.

Peretz Salomon (Waszilewicz)

Son of Leibl and Laja. Born in Derby, Conn., on 6 February 1913. He died in Chicago on 4 July 1922. He was his parents' only son.

Ruda Staszewski
(Photo)

Daughter of Ruwen and Miriam Kokocinski. Born in Brzeznica (Poland).

Isidor (Yisroel Jona) Sigman

Son of Israel and Hinda. Born in Kunov (Poland in 1868. Came to America in May 1915. He was a member of the *B'nai Brith*. He was the founder and president of the action society of the Gnosziner Factory in Czentochow.

Abe (Abraham) Sigman

Son of Isidor (Israel) and Regina. Born in Czenstochow. He came to America twice; the first time in 1915 and the second time in 1938. He was a member of the Masonic Lodge, of the managing committee of the Jewish *gymnazie* in Czenstochow, of the managing committee of the Czenstochowa manufacturers union, of the managing committee of the sports' union, *Makabi* in Czenstochow and of the managing committee of the Gnosziner action society in Czentochow.

He died on 19 July 1940 in Buffalo, N.Y.

Stanley (Stanislaw) Sigman
(Photo)

Son of Isidor and Regina (née Herc). Born on 3 August 1898 in Piotrkow. Came to America for the first time in 1915, returned and again came in 1940. Belonged to various organizations such as: Mason Lodge, American Legion, member of the Czenstochower Industrial Union and of several charitable and cultural organizations. He now lives at 249 St. James Place, Chicago 14, Illinois.

Stanley Sigman is, both at home in Czenstochow and in America, a community worker; he helped greatly with the book, *Czenstochower Yidn*, with the various material and photographs that he provided.

[Page LXIV]

Edmund Sigman
(Photo)

Born in Czenstochow January 1888. At age 10 he began to attend Lamparski's school, studying while simultaneously learning to play the violin with Balsam.

In 1905 he began to study in the Leipzer Conservatory and the same year, he and Wanda Nojfeld gave a chamber music concert in Czenstochow, in which the noted *khazan* [cantor] Birenboim also took part. The receipts from this concert were donated to a workers' bakery.

After a year of study in Petersburg, Sigman moved to Warsaw where he played with the Philharmonic as a violinist for two years under the direction of Fitelberg and Birnboim; at the same time, he perfected his music in Borcewicz's Conservatory and privately with the famous violinist, Isidor Loto.

In 1911/12 he became a violin teacher in the music school in Poltava.

After the outbreak of the First World War, he gave several concerts with Wanda Nojfeld Kopecka in Czenstochow. The proceeds were given for various charitable purposes.

In 1915, he came to America with his father and brother. First, he settled in Chicago. He was a teacher and, simultaneously, he organized a cooperative symphonic orchestra with which he gave a series of concerts.

In 1926, he moved to Philadelphia, gave lessons in the Settlement Music School, often appeared as a soloist on the radio and, also, organized a chamber orchestra with which he appeared in the Labor Institute.

In 1930, he traveled to Paris, appeared as a guest director of the Warsaw Philharmonic on the radio and with the Lodz Philharmonic.

In 1934, he directed a Chopin concert in Carlsbad. Later, he appeared in a series of concerts in Leningrad, Tel Aviv and Jerusalem.

In 1938, he returned to America. He settled in New York where he appeared as a guest director of the Federal Symphonic Orchestra.

Recently, he has given private lessons, created compositions that are often played on the radio.

(Photo, caption: Edmund Sigman conducts the Philharmonic Orchestra in Tel Aviv)

Tamara Sigman
Chicago
(Photo)

Daughter of Robert and Jadwiga (Yeta) Svitgal. Born on 3 October 1906 in Lodz. Came to America in 1937. A member of all of the Jewish charitable and communal organizations in Czenstochow and of American ORT.

Yosef Staszewski
(Photo)

Son of Moshe and Leah. Born in Piotrkow. Died at the age of 60 in Dzialoszyn in 1932.

Hershl Silver
(Photo)

(Known by the name – Hershl Namerower), father of Yeshayahu Leizer Silver and grandfather of Yakov Ber Silver. Died at the age of 88.

Ruchl Silver
(Photo)

Mother of Yeshayahu Leizer and grandmother of Yakov Silver. Died at the age of 90.

Yeshayahu Leizer Silver
(Photo)

Son of Hershl and Ruchl. Born in Dvinsk, December 1859. He came to Czenstochow as a child, at the age of five. He married Chana Birman of Noworadomsk in 1880.

He came to America for the first time in 1889; he was here for a year and a half. The second time in 1906, he remained until the present.

He is a member of the *Bnei Yisroel* Society, of the *Zaloshiner Chevra Anshei Bnei Achim* and of Czenstochower Relief; one of the founders and first trustee of the Czenstochower Aid Union.

His five grandsons served in the American army.

————

Chana Silver (Photo)

Wife of Yeshayahu Leizer and mother of Yakov Ber, Cyrl, Reila, Sara Sprintza, Leibish and Toba.

She died in New York.

————

Yakov Ber Silver
(Photo)

Born in 1882. His father, Yeshayahu Leizer was a hat maker. His mother, Chana (née Birman), comes from a village near Radomsk. Yakov Ber is the oldest son of his family of eight children – two sons and six girls. The incident of his lame foot greatly influenced his entire life. It was on a *Tisha b'Av* when the old Jews go to the visit the graves of their parents and the children make a ruin of the cemetery. Because of this, the cemetery man locked the gate. However, Yakov Ber, the small *mazek* [mischievous child], wanted to show his friends how to jump over the fence. That is how he banged his knee; he lay in the hospital and could not go to *kheder* nor to school. His father taught him a little Hebrew at home. He received the nickname, *Lamer* [lame] *Staluk* because there was a gentile in Czentochow who was called the *Lamer Stelmak*.

From childhood on, until 1901, he worked in the small factories in Czenstochow where the "earnings" then were 20 *kopikes* a week. They lived in Bajer's house, which was called "Bajer's Hotel" on Nadjeczna. At that time, he had organized a troupe of *Purim-shpeilers* that was the first baby step of a Jewish theater in Czenstochow.

He left for London, became a presser and returned to Czenstochow in 1904. Here he opened a "teahouse" in Yankl Klajnhandler's house (entered through a small alley), that became the quarters of the Bundist organization. He became the scapegoat for everything that happened then. If the *S.S.* [Zionist Socialists] set fire to Aizik Szliz's house – Yakov Ber was blamed; if a bomb was thrown somewhere – the police looked for Yakov Ber. However, between one arrest and the second – Yakov Ber did his part – organized, agitated and turned the world upside down.

As it happened, the Bund was too reserved for Yakov Ber's temperament. Learning of the activity of the anarchist group under the leadership of Yankl the *kamashn-makher* [gaiter maker], he made a short visit to Warsaw to see him. However, Yankl the *kamashn-makher* had already been arrested after an attempted bombing. Yakov Ber was watched by spies, who followed him to Czenstochow. He was immediately arrested on the charge of anarchistic activity in connection with the bombing attempt. He served a year in jail, from which he escaped to Berlin. After a time, he returned, joined a traveling acting troupe, then a professional troupe and acted in the Czenstochower area.

During a performance of *Uriel Acosta* in Radomsk, the theater manager began to marvel that so many unknown and "uninvited" guests were in the theater. Yakov Ber, who played the main role wanted to run away after the first act. However, all exits were occupied by spies and gendarmes. He was arrested in the middle of acting and his role was taken over by Dovid Zitman. The performance was not interrupted. Yakov Ber was accompanied by a large parade of Noworadomsker Jews. He was in prison for six months and was convicted only of distributing anarchistic literature [and sentenced] to one year in jail – the time he had already served up to the trial. Later, he again acted in the theater, until he left for London in 1909 and after three months for New York.

Here he joined the Czenstochower *Arbeter Ring* branch 261. Working the entire time in a shop, he took part in various amateur and professional theater troupes, until he took over the leadership of Czenstochower Relief in New York. He remained chairman of Relief for several years.

[Page LXVI]

He has been a member of Czenstochower branch 11 of the Jewish People's Order (International Workers' Order) since 1930. He was one of the founders and most active workers of Czenstochower Patronet; chairman and executive of United Czenstochower Relief and chairman of the committee and its representative on the editorial board of the book, *Czenstochower Yidn.*

Katy Slawina
Detroit

Daughter of Yudl and Gitl. Born in Slomnik (Poland) on 25 May 1887. Came to America in 1912. She is a member of the Western Ladies Aid Society in Detroit.

Eida Slowik

Born 1884, died on 13 September 1933.

(Photo)

Morris Slowik

Born 1882, died on 5 August 1945.

In memory

The children:
Tila Rubin
Dora Lopaty
Max Slowik
Abo Slowik
Ana Slowik

Carl Seltzer

Son of Aizik and Chana. Born in Czenstochow on 10 April 1894. Came to America on 4 October 1912. He is a member of the Zionist Organization, *Bnei Brith* and of the Jewish National Workers Union. Lives in Houston, Texas. His two sons – Irving and Arthur – served in the American army.

H. Slowik
(photo, caption: Meir Goldberg)

Daughter of Meir Goldberg (Meir Zabiak), who was well known in Czenstochow and was a friend of everyone.

He greatly aided the sick and fed the poor during the First World War.

His children in America and in Canada always remember his name with great reverence.

[Translator's note: The above biographical sketch describes the life of H. Slowik in the first paragraph. The two remaining paragraphs seem to refer to Meir Goldberg.]

————

Nakhum (Cyncynatus) Senzer
(Photo)

Son of Hershl and Chaya Sara. Born in Krzepice (Poland) December 1867. He married Dwoyra Ester Kremski. Came to America on 10 June 1914. He was active in the First *Zaloshiner Chevra Anshei Bnei Achim* in New York and was the treasurer of its loan fund.

Nakhum Senzer died on 5 February 1944 and was buried in the cemetery of the First *Zaloshiner Chevra Anshei Bnei Achim*. He left eight children (three daughters and five sons), 15 grandchildren and one great-grandchild.

His daughter, Lili and her husband, Ruwin Baker, Aida and her husband, Lou Meizlin (live in New York), and Minnie and her husband, Faska Doimaz (live in France).

————

Dwoyra Ester (Cyncynatus) Senzer

Daughter of Mordekhai and Pese Kremski. Born 1872 in Czentochow. The wife of Nakhum Senzer. Came to America on 12 October 1920. She died on 20 March 1945 in New York. Is buried in the cemetery of the First *Zaloshiner Chevra Anshei Bnei Achim*.

————

Abraham J. (Cyncynatus) Senzer
(Photo)

Son of Nakhum and Dwoyra Ester. Born in Czenstochow on 30 January 1894. In his young years, in Europe, as a trade employee, he showed his activism with the founding of the illegal trade employees union of the *S.S* organization [Zionist Socialists]. He came to America on 7 July 1913.

He occupies a distinguished place in Jewish communal life in New York. For the past 25 years, he has been one of the most active members of the First *Zaloshiner Chevra Anshei Bnei Achim*. During this time, he held the office of president, vice president, finance secretary and now he is its chairman for the cemetery. He was president of the Dzialoszyner Relief Committee in New York for 10 years, after the First World War. He is a member of the Czenstochower *Arbeter Ring* branch 261 and one of the founders of *Arbeter Ring* branch 324, as well as the Czenstochower Aid Union in New York and he was one of the founders and first vice president of the United Czenstochower Relief Committee in New York. He is now and has been president of the United Czenstochower Relief Committee for nine years. He is an active member of the *Czenstochower Yidn* book committee. Thanks to his activity, he has appeared on the administrative board of the American Federation of Polish Jews for 10 years; on the administrative board of the Joint Distribution Committee for the last six years, on the administrative board of the ORT society for the last eight years, executive member of the Manhattan division of the American Jewish Congress, executive committee member of the World Jewish Congress and on the administrative committee of the Jewish Council of Russian War Relief in New York from its creation on.

[Page LXVII]

(photo, caption: Kremski Family – sitting from right to left: A.J. Senzer [President of Relief])
[Translator's note: Only one name is listed]

(photo, caption: Mordekhai and Pesa Kremski)

He married Sadie Yakubowicz (Jacobs) in New York on 5 August 1917. They have three children: Israel – served in the American army, and daughters, Chaya Sara and Malka.

Sadie (Cyncynatus) Senzer

Daughter of Israel and Perl Yakubowicz (Jacobs). Born in Czenstochow on 28 March 1896. Came to America on 20 December 1912. She is the wife of Abraham Jakov Senzer.

Sadie Senzer is one of the most active women in Jewish communal life in New York. She is one of the founders of the Zialoshiner Ladies Auxiliary of the First *Zaloshiner Chevra Anshei Bnei Achim* – was chairlady and vice president for a long time, and now executive member. She is one of the founders of the Czenstochower Aid Union and Czenstochower Ladies Auxiliary – was chairlady and now the secretary for many years; one of the most active members of the David Mayes *malbesh-erumim* [provides free clothes to the needy] – former vice president and Exec. Member; one of the founders of the Star Charity Sisters – was vice president, president and now treasurer and executive member. She is active on the *Czenstochower Yidn* book committee.

Irving (Iser Cyncynatus) Senzer
(Photo)

Son of Nakhum and Dwoyra. Born in Czenstochow on 17 January 1901. He married Gitl Senzer. Came to America from Germany on 23 January 1923. He a member of the Dzialoszyner Society, *Zaloshiner Chevra Anshei Bnei Achim* and of the Czenstochower branch 11 of the Jewish Fraternal People's Order in New York.

Gitl (Gussy) (Cyncynatus) Senzer

Daughter of Abraham and Ita. Born on 27 March 1901 in Czenstochow. Came to America in June 1913. She was the wife of Irving Senzer. Was a member of the Zaloshiner Ladies Auxiliary and of the Jewish Fraternal People's Order.

Gitl Senzer died on 2 June 1943 in New York.

Hershl Skowronek
(Photo)

Died in Czenstochow in 1918 at the age of 55.

Reizl Skowronek
(Photo)

Daughter of Berl and Chana Mass. Died in New York at the age of 61, April 1931.

Rafal Skowronek

Son of Hershl and Reizl. Died on 12 November 1936 in New York at the age of 44.

[Page LXVIII]

Isidor Skowronek
(Photo)

Son of Hershl and Reizl. Died on 2 March 1943 in New York at the age of 48.

Yeheil (Skowronek) Skowron

Son of Hershl and Reizl. Born on 10 June 1898 in Klobuck. Came to America on 23 December 1921. He married Ester Cymerman. Is a member of the Czenstochower Young Men's Society in New York.

Aleks (Skowronek) Skowron

Son of Hersl and Reizl. Born in Klobuck on 23 December 1899. Came to America on 5 August 1920. He married Gitl Drilings. He is a member of Czenstochower Young Men's Society in New York.

Jack (Skowronek) Skowron

Son of Hershl and Reizl. Born in Klobuck in 1902. He married Leah Klajn. Came to America on 10 December 1920. His son Harry served in the American army.

Joe (Josl) Litman
(Photo)

Son of Reb Meir Yonah and Beila. Born in Czenstochow on 18 April 1898. Came to America in 1912. Married in London (England) in 1925. Vice President of the Lodz Organization in London.

Josef Nijinski

Son of Abraham and Sara. Father of Shimon. Born in Radoszyce (Poland). Died at the age of 92 in Przedborz (Poland) in 1915.

[Page LXVIII]

Ayin ע

Wolf Enzel
Chicago

Yudl Ebersman
Piermont, N.Y.
(Photo)

Son of Mordekhai Josef and Rudl-Mindl. Born on 28 October 1880. Came to America in 1920.

Chana Evenson
Los Angeles, Cal.

Daughter of Abraham and Sheindl Malarski. Born in Novy Dvor on the 10 1892. Came to America on 24 November 1908. Is active in Russian War Relief. She is a member of the Fraternal People's Order in Los Angeles.

Haim Enzel

(Photo)

Son of Asher and Chana. Born in Czenstochow, December 1890. Came to America in 1911. He was a member of the Czenstochower Young Men's Society in New York. Died in New York on 23 June 1941.

Chana Enzel

(Photo)

Mother of Mikhal Wolf, Chena, Kreindl, Nakhman, Haim and Feigl. She died in Czenstochow in 1913.

Max Enzel

(Photo)

Son of Asher and Chana. Born on 5 August 1896 in Czenstochow. Came to America in 1912. He is a member of the Czenstochower Young Men's Society in New York.

[Page LXIX]

Asher Enzel

Father of Mikhal, Wolf, Chena, Kriendl, Nakhman, Haim and Feigl. He died in Czenstochow in 1917.

Lena Enzel

New York

Nathan Enzel

Chicago

Son of Israel and Chana. Born in Czenstochow on 25 October 1894. He married Lilia Szipper. Came to America in 1914. He is a member of the Czenstochower Educational Society in Chicago.

Abraham Essig

Died in 1908 in Czenstochow at the age of 85.

The grandfather of Ita Lentsher, N.Y.

(Photo)

Dwoyra Ester Essig
(née Sztrojm)

Died in 1906 in Czenstochow at the age of 80.

The grandmother of Ita Lentsher, N.Y.

Samuel Essig

Son of Hershl and Ruchl. Born in Czenstochow on 16 August 1892. Came to America on 10 September 1911. He is a member of the American Legion, Jewish War Veterans, Zionist Organization, *B'nai B'rith* and United Czenstochower Relief in New York.

His two sons served in the American Navy.

Shlomoh Yitzhak Epsztajn
(Photo)

Son of Ahron and Toba. Died at the age of 70 in 1932 in Noworadomsk.

Hershl Epsztajn
Los Angeles, Cal.
(Photo, caption: Hershl Epsztajn and R. Federman)

Son of Shlomoh Yitzhak and Tema. Born on 27 September 1888 in Noworadomsk. From 1903 to 1913, he was one of the most active members of the *S.S.* [Zionist Socialist] Party in Poland. In 1913, he came to America and joined *Poalei-Zion* and a Jewish Socialist Union. He is a member of the *Arbeter Ring* and the secretary of his branch for many years and he is active in the Jewish Workers Committee, the Unions Campaign, *Histadrut* and is one of the founders of Noworadomsker and Czenstochower Help Unions in Los Angeles. He is a devoted and responsible worker who draws appreciation and respect to himself. He married Sara Szarigrad. Their son served in the American navy.

Sara Epsztajn
Los Angeles, Cal.
(Photo)

Daughter of Israel Iser and Laya Szarigard. Born on 17 June 1891 in Noworadomsk. From 1903 to 1913 she belonged to the *S.S.* Party in Poland. Came to America in 1912.

Sara Epsztajn is a member of the *Arbeter Ring*, Rozenblat Loan Circle and *Histadrut*; she is also active in the Jewish Worker's Committee. She is one of the founders of the Noworadomsker and Czenstochower Help Unions.

Feigele Epsztajn
Los Angeles, Cal.
(Photo)

Daughter of Hershl and Sara. Born on 19 July 1926 in San Gabriel, California.

Israel Yitzhak Epsztajn

Son of Yehezkeil and Reizl. Born October 1881 in Czenstochow. Came to America in 1903. He is a member of the First *Zaloshiner Chevra Anshei Bnei Achim* in New York and is an active executive member there. His son, Feiwl, served as a sergeant in the American army.

[Page LXX]

Pch פ
Leibl and Mrs. Pakela
(Photo)

Iser (Pakula) Paul
Chicago

(Photo)

Son of Mendl and Reizl. Born in Tomaszow Mazowiecki on 5 October 1885. He married Chana Welner. Came to America on 4 May 1914. In Czenstochow he was active in the *S.S.* Party for years. He is a member of the Czenstochower Educational Union in Chicago, treasurer of an institution for the care of children in Chicago.

Welwl (Pakula) Paul
Chicago

(Photo, caption: the children of Welwl Pakula, Mendl and Ruchl)

Son of Mendl and Reizl. Born in Tomaszow Mazowiecki on 1 May 1888. He married Sheindl Grosman. Came to America on 25 March 1922. He and his wife are active members of the Czenstochower Educational Union and Aid Society in Chicago. Executive member for many years and active in the Relief Committee.

Their son, Mendl, served in the American army.

Abraham Pieprz

(Photo)

Son of Yitzhak Shlomoh and Freidl. Born in Koniecpol (Poland) in 1870. He died in Czenstochow in 1935.

Tessie (Toyba) and Max (Meir) Peper

(Photo)

Son of Abraham and Rina Pieprz. Born on 14 April 1900 in Czenstochow. He lived in Germany and France for many years. Came to America in 1919. He once belonged to the *Arbeter Ring*, then to the International Workers Order. Fifteen years ago, he was active in the Czenstochow Union in Detroit, was also active in the Fraternal Order in Los Angeles, Cal.; held various communal offices, now chairman of the Czenstochower Aid Union in Los Angeles.

His son, Sheldon Sam, born on 14 November 1920, served in the American army.

Max Peper now lives at 224 S. Poinsettia Place, Los Angeles, Cal.

Chaya Sara Pozner

Daughter of Yakov and Ester. Born in Czenstochow in 1902. Came to America in 1920. Belonged to the International Order, *ICOR*, the Garelik loan circle, *ICUF*. Occupies the office of secretary of the Garelik loan circle. She is the wife of Rafal Pozner.

Rafal Pozner

Son of Yeheil Yitzhak and Perl Yehudis. Born in Litomiersk in 1898. Lived in France, Germany, Belgium, Cuba, Mexico and Guatemala in South America before coming to America. Came to North America in 1926.

Reb Josef Prokosz, may he rest in peace
(Josele Kir'a)

He was known as Reb Josele Kir'a in Czenstochow. He was one of the genuine Jews who are now almost impossible to find.

Modest, calm by nature, he only had good friends in Czenstochow and there was no one in the city who would speak a bad word about him. He decided matters of rabbinical laws and was a member of the Czenstochower rabbinate.

Reb Josele was one of the greatest scholars in Czenstochow, sitting day and night in the study of rabbinical law. Often he had to be reminded of meals – he was so absorbed in study. His house was always a meeting place in which the learned came together. People from the entire city came to him to ask questions and to study, and to seek his advice in various matters, such as lawsuits before the rabbinical court. And he was a "loose constructionist" in deciding questions of *kashrus* [the laws of what is kosher]. It was very hard for him to utter the word *treif* [not kosher].

[Page LXXI]

Reb Josef Prokosz was born in 1872 in Galicia. He was brought to Czenstochow by the wealthy man, Reb Notl Pankowski, who was well known in our city, to teach his children and sons-in-law. He lived in Czenstochow from that time on and married the daughter of Reb Hersh Yoal Amstower.

The entire Jewish population loved and valued him regardless of their political persuasion; Reb Josele Kir'a was one of the Czenstochower middle class in whom Czenstochower prided itself. He suffered the fate of the martyrs in 1939-1945.

May his soul be bound up in the bond of eternal life!

Gershon Preger, may he rest in peace

(Photo)

Came to Czenstochower from Brisk in 1911. Became known as a Zionist and communal worker in our city. Took part in the development of the Jewish metal industry in Czenstochow.

Died in Czenstochow in 1942.

Yudl Pittel
Chicago

Son of Shlomoh Meir and Gitl. Born in Czenstochow on 18 July 1889. Came to America on 26 July 1912. He is a member of the Czenstochower Aid Society in Chicago.

Binyamin Pinkus

Son of Ahron and Genendl. Born on 1 July 1880 in Czenstochow.

Polya Pilin

(Photo)

Born in Czenstochow. Attended the Czenstochower Y.L. Peretz School. Came to America in 1930 and here she became famous as a painter. She had exhibits in New York, Chicago and in other places and was warmly received everywhere.

(Photos of painting, captions:
"Chicago Side Street" by Polya Pilin
"New Mexico Life" by Polya Pilin)

———

[Page LXXII]

Leizer Pajnski
Detroit

Son of Izrael Moshe and Chava. Born in Czenstochow on 5 December 1900. He married Chaya Szuldinger. Came to America on 18 February 1921. In Czenstochow, he was active in the United *S.S.* organization. He is president of the Sosnowicer and Bendiner [Bedzin] Society and was president of and an active member of the Czenstochower Regional Union. His son, Max, and his son-in-law, Saul Fiszman, served in the American army.

———

Pesi Prodel Chicago

(Photo, caption: Pesi Prodel with her family)

Daughter of Hershl and Chaya Kaplan. Born in Lubin* (Lublin County) on 10 March 1905. Came to America on 12 May 1914. She is the chairlady of the Czenstochower Aid Society and Vice President of the Czenstochower Educational Union in Chicago. She is one of the most devoted and active workers of the Czenstochower organizations in Chicago; she is active in all of the campaigns carried out by the organizations.

[*Translator's note: the town is given as Lubin, the county as Lublin.]

———

Perl Pelc

(Photo, caption: Oren Pelc with his wife, Perl)

Daughter of Yitzhak and Malka Gelber. Born in Czenstochow in 1872.

———

[Page LXXII]

Feh פ
Dobra Feiwlowicz
(Photo)

Daughter of Nakhum and Miriam. Died at age 89 in Czenstochow.

———

Toba Feiwlowicz
Chicago
(Photo)

Daughter of Abo and Dobra. Born in Czenstochow in 1886. Came to America in 1913.

———

Meir Feiwlowicz
(Photo)

Born in Czenstochow in 1888. He worked in Werde's needle factory (Igliarnia) where a large number of Jewish workers were employed (approximately 30 percent). Meir belonged to the *Poalei-Zion* Party and was a member of the city committee. In 1904 he helped to organize the workers in the needle factory and founded the illegal metal industry union.

He left for Lodz because of the persecution of his family. There he was active in the *Bund* under the pseudonym, "the dark Meir." In 1905 he returned to Czenstochow after the "bloody Wednesday" in Lodz and again joined *Poalei-Zion.*

Once he was chosen to transport a May 1st appeal. He was arrested with another comrade, Yakov Wajgensburg (now in Philadelphia). He passed himself off as a lace maker, taking the entire responsibility on himself and served 11½ months in prison. He was arrested again in 1906 and escaped from the barracks in which he was held. The soldiers shot at him and a bullet hit his foot. He was caught because he left traces of blood and was taken to the hospital. Again he escaped from there and stayed in Vienna for a time and came back to Czenstochow.

He was again arrested with 38 people in an ambush of the *S.S.* Party's "Golda's Teahouse." And again – trial and prison.

After his release from prison, he again left for Vienna where he worked in a factory and was active in the *Poalei-Zion* Party.

[Page LXXIII]

He came to America in 1914 and was active in the *Poalei-Zion* Party and in the Czenstochower *Arbeter Ring* branch in Chicago. Later, he joined the leftist movement and joined the International Workers Order. He was also active in *ICOR* from the start and very actively took part in Czenstochow aid work.

Godl Frajtag
(Photo)

Born in 1895 in Czenstochow. His father – Yitzhak Moshe – was a tailor. His first childhood experience was the pogrom of 1902. He was then studying in Hercka the *malamed*'s *kheder* [in a teacher's religious school]. On the day of the pogrom, his mother, Khasha, disguised as a Christian, came to take him home. At that time they lived in Weksler's house at Alee 6 – one of the largest houses in Czenstochow, with two courtyards and two iron gates. Many Jews hid their "bag and baggage" here.

During the October strike and the proclamation of the Czarist Constitution of 1905, Godl Frajtag led a procession of children with a red paper flag that his father had made for him.

At age 13, he began as an employee at a colonial business and in 1912 he joined the *Poalei-Zion* Party. Hipek Gajzler (later Dr. Hipolit Gajzler), who lived with his parents at Alee 4 and there created a learning circle for children [whose parents were] not well-to-do, taught him in the evening.

In 1914, during the First World War, he lived with his parents on Pilsudski (earlier Dajazd) 27. *Poalei-Zion* began to organize like the other parties. The first meetings took place in Avraham Gotlib's house and in Shimeon Waldfogl's small room. When the workers house was created, he was working at "Fridn's Hute," near Boitin, in Germany. There, he took an active part in the creation of a cultural and support union. The following Czenstochowers were elected to the managing committee of the union: Brakman, Lewenhof, Fajerman, Feldman, Godl Frajtog and Berl (his family name is forgotten).

In 1917 Godl Frajtag returned to Czenstochow, was a railroad worker, joined the metal union that was organized by the *S.S.* [Zionist Socialists]; he was elected as a member of the managing committee. He and his partner, Comrade Rinya Gros, later Mr. Szlezinger, won first prize during a "flower day" [a fundraising event].

In 1918 the creation of cooperatives began. Godl Frajtag became an employee at the "Workers Home" cooperative (of *P.Z.*) and one of the most active *Poalei-Zion* workers in Czenstochow. He was elected as a delegate to the workers council of the trade employees; he took an active part with Shimkhah Rajkh in the election to the first City Council to which *P.Z.* elected two councilmen. He helped create the "Borokow Children's Home" and the low-priced kitchen at the children's home and was active in the trade workers union. His party membership did not prevent him from working with other parties in wide-ranging communal undertakings.

During the split in the *P.Z.* Party in 1921 into Rightist – under the leadership of Dr. Sziper, and Leftist – under the guidance of Zerubavel, Godl Frajtag remained with the Rightists who occupied the workers' home meeting hall. However, they were a minority and were excluded from the party. They organized themselves into a separate party, using the residence of Comrade Wajn as a meeting place.

G. F. took part in the Palestine office in 1923/24, as the representative of the Rightist *Poalei-Zion* and with emigration to *Eretz-Yisroel*. He was a supporter of *haksharah* [agricultural training for those preparing to emigrate to Palestine] and *Hahalutz* [the pioneer movement] in Linkawa, near Piotrkow, created by the Czenstochower *P.Z.*

At his departure from Czenstochow for *Eretz-Yisroel* in 1925, the Right as well as the Left *Poalei-Zion* took part in the banquet in his honor. Leon Zajdman, leader of the Left *P.Z.*, dedicated a song to him and Shimkhah Rajkh gave him a memento for his devoted work in the name of the party.

His organizational activity in *Eretz-Yisroel* began with the creation of *Kvutse Frajtag* [Frajtag Collective]. There was a group of Czenstochowers who worked, with the support of *Histadrut*, building houses as a collective group. Their first work was building Abo Librowicz's house. When the Czenstochower immigrants to *Eretz-Yisroel* organized a separate *landsmanschaftn* union and, later, when the organization, *Olei Czenstochow* [Czenstochow Immigrants], was created, he was the first to help with the organizational work and was elected to the managing committee of *Olei Polnia* [Polish Immigrants] with Moshe Zilberszac. In 1929 he was elected Chairman of the Czenstochower *Landmanschaft* Union in Tel Aviv and Rabbi Yeshai (the Walner Rabbi) – Honorary President. In 1931 he took part in creating a bank for Polish Jews in *Eretz-Yisroel*.

After the house building work ended, the Czenstochower group, *Kvutse Frajtag*, built roads (highway work), then G.F. created a tea packing business and exported his tea to various parts of the world: Africa, America, Canada, France, etc. His tea firm received awards at the world exhibition in Tel Aviv in 1929 and in Paris – in 1931. In 1932 he visited France, Belgium and Poland and organized the export of an entire series of manufactured goods to *Eretz-Yisroel*. His fervent love for Jewish Czenstochow never ended. He visited Czenstochow twice, the last time in 1937. He wrote for the *Czenstochower Zeitung* and for *Undzer Weg* [*Our Way*] (Zionist weekly in Czenstochow] and spread the Czenstochower Yiddish newspapers to *Eretz-Yisroel*. He met many Czenstochower *landsleit* [countryman] on his trips through various countries and he campaigned for the idea of creating Czenstochower colony in *Eretz-Yisroel* and a world union of Czenstochower *landsleit* from all parts of the world.

[Page LXXIV]

During the Second World War, he did everything possible to organize aid campaigns for Czenstochowers and to help the Czenstochower refugees in the Soviet Union and in other nations. He greatly helped with the publication of the historical book, *Czenstochower Yidn*, with collections of money and reports about the lives of the Czenstochower *landsleit* in *Eretz-Yisroel*.

In 1939, when the militia, *Mishmar Ezrahi* [National Guard], was created, Godl Frajtag was one of the founders and members. Now he has received an award for his five years of service. His daughter is one of *Mishmar Ezrahi's* youngest officers.

Reb Akiva Fogel, of blessed memory
(Photo)

He came to Czenstochow from Lask, near Lodz. He studied in Amstow near Czenstochow and in his youth he had a reputation as a child prodigy. He was involved with charity and good deeds for the poor in our city and always was studying. He was also a founder of the first manufacturing business in Czenstochow.

He died in Czenstochow in 1940 and was buried there.

May his soul be bound up in the bond of eternal life.

Mendl Fogel

Born in Lask in 1880 (near Lodz). Took an active part in the communal life of Czenstochow; was president of *Agudas Yisroel* and the synagogue warden for the Jewish community.

Suffered the fate of the martyrs in 1939-1945.

Abraham Fox
Detroit

Son of Akiva and Leah. Born in Czenstochow in 1893. He married Jenny Krakowski. Came to America in 1921. He was the manager of the Left *Poalei-Zion* cooperative in Czenstochow. He was also one of the founders of the Czenstochower Regional Union in Detroit. He was the secretary of the Union until 1938. His wife, Jenny, is active in the Ladies Circle of the Jewish People's Order and in the Yiddish schools of the People's Order in Detroit.

Sam Finkel
(Photo)

Son of Yehuda Moshe and Ita Beila. Born on 22 December 1882 in Zawiercie; later, he lived in Czenstochow. Came to America on 16 November 1906. Belonged to branch 90 of the International Workers Order, co-founder of the Federation of Polish Jews and on the administrative committee of the Jewish Congress, as well as the United Jewish Appeal; one of the founders of the Jewish section of Russian War Relief; former active worker in the bakers union; co-founder of the Bendin [Bedzin]-Sosnowiecer Society and Fraternal Order of Bendin-Sosnowiec.

In 1938, Sam Finkel traveled to the Soviet Union (he won the cost of the trip in the campaign for the *Morgn-Freiheit* [*Morning Freedom*]).

Sam Finkel (Shmelke the baker) married Malka Urman of Bedzin. He was a baker for 12 years, helped to organize the bakers union in Bedzin, Dombrowa [Dabrowa Gornicza], Sosnowiec and Czenstochow; belonged to the central managing committee; first he was a member of the *Bund*, later – of the S.D.K.P.L. [Social Democracy of the Kingdom of Poland and Lithuania]; he was arrested in Bedzin in 1905 and spent 22 weeks in jail, then was exiled to Minsk. After returning to Czenstochow, he left for America. Here he was a member of branch 261 of the *Arbeter Ring*. During the split – he left for the International Workers Order.

Berl Finkel

Son of Shmuel and Rywka Finkel. Born in Czenstochow. His father was a Hebrew teacher in the *Talmud Torah* there. In 1924, he went to *Eretz-Yisroel* and there he worked in the Easterner's Arya Yehuda Collective. He came to America in 1928 where he worked with ladies' belts in New York.

Dave Finkel

Son of Yitzhak Meir and Chaya. Born in 1879. The family consisted of eight children – five daughters and three sons. Dave was the oldest. He studied sign painting. Worked with the famous painters, Cymberknop and Zalcman. Came to America in 1900. Here he married Josie Levit of Wielun in 1915. He is an active member of the Wieluner Society. He was president a few times and also held other offices. He is also a member of the Czenstochower Relief Committee and always helps with the work. His son-in-law, Willie Goldberg, was a lieutenant in the American army.

Sadie Fishel

Daughter of Nukham and Miriam. Died born* in Kamik in 1913. [*Translator's note: both the words "died" and "born" appear at the beginning of the sentence.] Belonged to the Szczekociner Society.

Her son and son-in-law – both officers – served in the American army.

[Page LXXV]

Zalman Fajner
(Photo)

Son of Yakov Meir and Odel; the father of Meir. Born in Amstow. He died at age 42, March 1904 in Czenstochow.

Beila (Kantor) Fajner
(Photo)

Daughter of Aitche and Chena; mother of Meir. She died at the age of 63, in 1931 in Czenstochow.

Meir Fajner

Son of Zalman and Beila. Born in Czenstochow on 15 May 1895. He marred Royza Wisocki. He was in London and in Canada before coming to America on 4 September 1916. He is an active executive member of the Czenstochower br. 261 of the *Arbeter Ring* and active member of United Czenstochower Relief in New York.

Meir Fajner

Son of Yakov Meir and Odel; born in Wielun. His wife, Feigel Fajner, and their children perished in Treblinka as martyrs in the sanctification of God's name.

Cudek Fajner
(Photo)

Born in Czenstochow in 1902. He and his wife and children perished in 1945 in a concentration camp in Germany at the hands of the German barbarians.

Philip Fajertag
Detroit
(Photo)

Son of Nota and Sarah. Born in Czenstochow, December 1886. Came to America in 1913. He is a member of the *Arbeter Ring* in Detroit. His son, Max, served in the American army.

Ruchl Fajersztajn
(Photo)

Daughter of Moshe and Sheindl Grinberg and wife of Avraham Zalman Fajersztajn. Died at the age of 58 in 1921, in Amstow.

Avraham Zalman Fajersztajn

Born in Olsztin. Died at the age of 32 in 1882, in Czenstochow.

Brukhia Fajersztajn
(Photo)

Son of Avraham and Ruchl. Died in Czenstochow.

Harry Fajersztajn
(Photo)

Son of Avraham Zalman and Ruchl. He was born in Amstow on 6 May 1881. He lived in Lodz. He married Frida Szpic of Czenstochow in 1907. Came to America on 4 July 1909. He is an executive member of the First *Zaloshiner Chevra Anshei Bnei Achim*, member of the Dzialoszyner Relief Committee, Zionist Organization, Young Israel, of the Czenstochower Aid Union, of United Czenstochower Relief Committee, of which he is vice president and of the *Czenstochower Yidn* book committee.

His family consists of three children. His son, Sidney, married Sybil Seiman; his daughter, Rose, married Sam Bagatel and his son, Joe, married Minnie Szeftel. Joe was a lieutenant in the American army.

[Page LXXVI]

Fanny Fajersztajn
(Photo)

Daughter of Yeheil and Rotza Szpic. Born on 15 April 1887 in Czenstochow. She married Harry Fajersztajn on 25 December 1907 and came to America in June 1910. She is a member of the Ladies Auxiliary of the *Zaloshiner Chevra Anshei Bnei Achim*, Hospital for Incurable Diseases in Brooklyn, Rouz-Rubel Society in Flatbush and of the Ladies Auxiliary of Czenstochower Relief, as well as the *Czenstochower Yidn* book committee. For several years, she has held the office of vice president of the Ladies Auxiliary and is one of its most active women who does work for the old home [Czenstochow].

Moshe Leib Fajersztajn
(Photo)

Son of Hershl and Feigl. Born on 10 March 1890 in Czenstochow. Came to America in 1925. He is a member of the Jewish National Workers Union in Omaha, Hebrew Club and the Zionist Organization of America.

Hershl Fajersztajn
(Photo)

Born in Czenstochow in 1878. Was one of the founders and treasurer of Czenstochower branch 261 of the *Arbeter Ring*; also a member and one of the founders of Czenstochower Relief.

Died on 31 October 1938.

Chana Fajersztajn
(Photo)

Daughter of Yankl Kremski. Born in Czenstochow. She married Hershl Fajersztajn and came with him to America in 1906. The family consisted of six children.

The first executive meetings of the Aid Union and of Relief were held in Chana Fajersztajn's home. She is also a member of the Czenstochower Ladies Auxiliary in New York.

Zalman Frydman
(Photo)

Son of Avraham. Died in Czenstochow.

Samuel Fajerman
Detroit
(Photo)

Son of Meir and Feigl. Born in Zarki (Poland) on 17 May 1894. He married Esther Fajerman. Came to America from England on 7 February 1922. He is a member of the Jewish Fraternal Peoples Order, branch 42, in Detroit.

(Photo, caption: Esther Fajerman)

Heinrikh Frojlich
St. Louis, Missouri
(Photo)

Son of Yitzhak and Nisel. Born in Czenstochow on 25 September 1884. Came to America on 21 December 1904. Member of the *B'nai Brit* organization. Was one of the founders of the Czenstochower Union in New York, was also the secretary of the Czenstochower branch 261 of the *Arbeter Ring*.

[Page LXXVII]

Gela Hinda Frydman
(Photo)

Born in Czenstochow; died there January 1904.

Feigl Frydman
(Photo)

Daughter of Shlomoh and Ester Goldberg. Born 1893 in Czenstochow. She came to America in 1917. She died in a tragic accident on 3 January 1922 in New York.

Zisl Frydman
Chicago
(Photo)

Daughter of Itche and Cyrl Kusi. Born in Gorzkowice in 1873. Came to America from Czenstochow in 1927. She is a member of the Czenstochower Educational Society and of the Aid Society in Chicago.

Sarah Ruchl Frydman

Daughter of Yitzhak Jakov and Leah Kozak. Died at the age of 47, in 1904, in Czenstochow.

Abraham Frydman

Son of Zalman and Sarah Ruchl. Born on 4 July 1878 in Czenstochow. He married Helen Kremsdorf. Came to America in August 1903. He is a member of the Czenstochower Young Men's Society and of United Czenstochower Relief in New York. His son, Harry, served in the American army.

(Photo)

Helen Frydman

Daughter of Yudl and Chava Kremsdorf. Born in Czenstochow on 15 January 1886. Came to America on 22 September 1902. She is very active in communal life – in the Woman's Division of HIAS, treasurer of the general board of the Kremsdorf Family Circle and [active] in the activities of the Czenstochower Ladies Auxiliary; member of the *Czenstochower Yidn* book committee and of the Concourse Center Sisterhood.

Helen Frydman is one of the founders of the Czenstochower Ladies Auxiliary in New York.

Nusan Avigdor Federman

Son of Itche and Pesa Tzitl. Born in Przyrow (Poland). He died at the age of 70, 1914, in Czenstochow.

Meir Shimon (Sam) Federman
Chicago

Son of Nusan Avigdor and Toba. Born in Przyrow in 1885. Came to America from Czenstochow in 1906. He is a member of Hebrew Progressive and the Czenstochower Educational Society in Chicago. His son, Nathan, served in the American army.

Dovid Zalman Federman
Chicago
(Photo)

Son of Nusan Avigdor and Toba Hinda. Born in Przyrow (Poland) 1884. He married Ruchl Saks and came to America in 1910. He is a member of the Bendiner [Bedzin] Society, Hebrew Progressive and of the Czenstochower Educational Society in Chicago.

Nakhum Yankl Frydman
(Photo)

Son of Abraham Nusan and Freidl. Born in Warsaw in 1870. He married Zisl Kisy. Came to America in 1920. He was a member of the Czenstochower Neighborhood Society in Chicago; died there in 1940

Moshe Frejlech

Father of Shlomoh, Zisl, Joe, Etl, Emanual, Chava and Avraham Hirsh.

Ruchl Mitler and Leah Garber.

He died in 1907 in Czenstochow.

[Page LXXVIII]

Joe Frejlech

Son of Moshe and Chaya. Born in Czenstochow in 1891. He married Etl Pieprz in 1912. Came to America in 1912. He is a member of the Bakers Union, local 169 and executive member of branch 307 of the Jewish Fraternal People's Order.

Emanuel Frejlech

Son of Moshe and Chaya. Born in Czenstochow in 1895. He married Chaya Frejlech in 1920. Came to America in 1923. His son, Morris, was a volunteer soldier in the American army.

Abraham Hersh Frejlech

[Translator's note: his given names are spelled as Avraham Hirsh in the biography of his father and as Abraham Hersh in his biography.)

Son of Dovid and Sarah. Born in Czenstochow in 1904. He came to America in 1920 and is a member of the Czenstochower branch 11 of the Jewish Fraternal People's Order.

Abraham Fefer
(Photo)

Son of Moshe and Ester. Born in Czenstochow on 1 May 1888. Came to America in December 1911. He is a member of the Czenstochower Young Men's Society in New York.

Yakov Frajermauer

Died in 1918 in Czenstochow at the age of 85.

Relia and Tuvya Frajmor
(Photo)

Son of Yakov and Riva. Born in Czenstochow in 1897. Came to America in 1914. He belongs to the Wloszczower Society. He is a dress operator.

Relia Frajmor was born in a small *shtetl* near Czenstochow. At the age of 9, she came to Czenstochow where she was drawn into communal work and joined the *S.S.* [Socialist Zionist] Party whose leader there was Rafal Federman. Reila, under the influence of Federman, who had gone over to the *Bund*, also joined this party. In 1924 she came to America. Due to family matters, she withdrew from communal work. She raised her children as a member of a Jewish socialist party should; they went to a Yiddish school. She, herself, is a member of *Arbeter Ring* School. For a time she was the chairlady there.

When R. Federman came to America and began his activities, Relia was again drawn into the work. She became a member of Czenstochower Relief, where she is an executive member. She is also a member of the Czenstochower Ladies Auxiliary.

Leib and Lina Frajermauer

Son of Yokl and Frayda. Born on 20 October 1885 in Czenstochow. Came to America in 1906. Member of Young Men's. His two sons, Max and Abe, served in the American army.

Hershl Frajtag
(Photo)

Reb Hershl Frajtag was a well-known name in Czenstochow. He was the *shamas* in the "German Synagogue" for five years. But before the synagogue was built, he was the *shamas* for a *minyon* that was called "Reikher's [rich man's] *minyon*" on First Avenue 10, to which the Czenstochower aristocracy belonged, such as Rajkher, Weirnik, Henig, Werda, Herc, Grosman, Markusfeld, Grodsztajn, Frojnd, Imik and others. This *minyon* built the "German Synagogue" (New Synagogue) in 1894. The land for the synagogue was donated by Henig.

Reb Hershl Frajtag died in 1935 at the age of 107. Godl Frajtag, his grandson, is in *Eretz-Yisroel*

[Page LXXVIII]

Tsadek צ
Aizik Cymerman
Australia

Born in Czenstochow. He graduated from the *Folks-Shul* [secular, public school], attended the Mickiewicz and Szudejka *gymnazie* and studied jurisprudence at the Warsaw and Krakow Universities. He was active in Jewish academic circles during his last 15 years as a student and in building a Jewish academic home in Warsaw.

(Photo)

He settled in Lodz in 1924. He practiced as an attorney. He was active in communal life as vice president of the Central Artisans Union (Poludniowa 4) in Lodz; worked in the academic council of the Jewish World Congress under Dr. Tartakower; co-founder of the club for Jewish intelligenica and founder of the Jewish Lawyers Union in Lodz and the first president; where in 1933, Dr. Comersztajn founded an all Polish Council for Jewish Lawyers in order to help to defend the position of Jewish lawyers in the *Sejm*. Cymerman was the representative on the council from Lodz. In Lodz he was also active as a writer on current public matters.

[Page LXXIX]

As a refugee in Vilna, Lawyer Cymerman was one of the founders of the home for the intelligencia.

In 1941, he came to Japan through Russia and there worked on the Jewish Refugee Committee as the administrative director. In August 1941, he came to Australia, where he occupies a distinguished position in Jewish communal life.

He is the co-editor of the only Jewish newspaper, *Sidney Jewish News*, and was the honorary secretary of the Jewish World Congress for four years. He founded the Federation of Polish Jews in Australia and is a member of the Board of Deputies. He is one of the founders of the Aid Fund for European Jews.

Lawyer Cymerman's articles and columns of a political, social and literary character were constantly published in the Australian press.

Isidor Cwern
Chicago
(Photo)

Son of Josef and Chaya. Born in Czenstochow on 16 October 1888. He married Gitl Kirszenboim. Came to America from Belgium on 10 April 1909. He is one of the founders and a member of the Czenstochower Independent Union in Chicago and was Finance Secretary for four years.

Mordekhai Ceszniewski

Died at age 77 in 1928 in Czenstochow.

Ester Ceszniewski

Died at age 76 in 1927 in Czenstochow.

Bluma Ceszynski
(Photo)

Born in Komarna, Galicia in the month of Chesvan. Her father, Reb Yitzhak Lemberg, was a Hasid of the Belzer Rebbe. Bluma was raised in a very *frum* [pious] house. In 1914 she left her home at a very young age and lived, worked and studied in Paris and in Berlin. Came to America in 1923, settled in New York. She now lives in Chicago. She is the wife of Moshe Ceszinki.

Moshe (Moshe C.) Ceszynski
(Photo)

His parents, observant Jewish people, who lived at Garncarska 58 – belonged to the luminous Jewish figures, who in the greatest poverty – did not renounce the privilege of paying tuition for their children. Therefore, Moshe, one of three brothers and one sister, went to a *kheder* [religious school], not to the *Talmud Torah* [religious school for poor children]. And tuition was also paid for the *yom-tovim* [religious holidays], because just like every Jew – his father, Yakov Ceszynski, reasoned with his mother, Ester Feigl – the teacher also has to celebrate *yom-tov*.

(Photo, caption: Yakov and Ester Feigl Ceszynski)

In addition to studying in a kheder, Moshe studied Russian, Polish and a little German in a city Folks-shul [public school]. At 15, he began to work. Thanks to his father, who was a Mizrakhi [a member of the Orthodox Zionist group] and took his son to Zionist meetings – he already knew about Dr. Herzl and his ideal, Zionism. However, more than Di Velt [The World] from Vienna, Der Yid [The Jew] from Krakow and other Zionist pamphlets that he read – the Dreyfus trial and the pogroms on the Jews in Russia and Poland had an effect on him.

(Photo, caption: Moshe Ceszynski's brother)

In 1904 Moshe Ceszynski joined the *Poalei-Zion* Party and took part in all of the struggles and dangers of the revolutionary movement of that time. He remained active and devoted to his idea for all of the time he was in Czenstochow and also now in America.

In 1910 he was the Czenstochower correspondent for the Warsaw *Moment* under the editorship of Zwi Prilucki. Even earlier, he was a correspondent for the Warsaw newspapers, *Der Weg* [*The* Way] and *Undzer Lebn* [*Our Life*]. His pseudonym, Moshe C., comes from these reports.

[Page LXXX]

Carrying out educational work in the *Poalei-Zionist* circles during the revolutionary years – he later took part in the cultural work of the Jewish Literary Society and supported every cultural undertaking.

From 1912, Moshe Ceszynski was one of the first pioneers and most important co-workers in the Jewish press in Czenstochow, beginning with the *Czenstochower Reklamen-Blat* [*Advertising* (*News*)*paper*], *Woknblat* [*Weekly* (*News*)*paper*] and *Togeblat* [*Daily* (*News*)*paper*]. He helped in the greatest measure its rise with his terrific energy and bursting momentum and planted his roots in the Jewish life of Czenstochow. He ignored the great difficulties that stood in its way. After the First World War, he also supported the Czenstochower Yiddish press morally and materially.

In America, he collected, took care of and gave special attention to the publications of the weekly and daily editions of the Yiddish newspapers in Czenstochow. An entire series of material for the book, *Czenstochower Yidn*, was taken from the newspapers that Moshe Ceszynski collected.

In 1913 he took part in the World *Poalei-Zion* Conference in Krakow as the delegate from Czenstochow.

The Russian gendarmerie kept an eye on him, particularly because of the many published newspaper statements about workers' lives. In 1914 he was arrested with the managing committee of the Professional Union of Bakers for his public appearance at one of their meetings and served several months in jail.

Moshe Ceszynski left for America in 1914, on the eve of the First World War. He immediately found a wide-ranging field for his communal activities in New York and was one of the founders of the Czenstochower branch 11 of the Jewish National Workers Union.

In 1915, his brochure, *Prison Memories*, was published in New York. His main employment at the time he was in New York was traveling agent for various Yiddish book publishing houses and newspaper distributors. He traveled through cities and towns and filled homes with classic books: Mendele, Sholom Aleichem, Peretz and young Yiddish poets.

(Photo, caption: Hinda Rajch, wife of Elkhanan, Moshe Ceszynski 's sister. Died in Czenstochow.)

(Photo, caption: Elkhanan Rajch, brother-in-law of Moshe Ceszynski. Died in Warsaw.)

In 1922, Moshe Ceszynski settled in Chicago. There he was bound with Bina Ceszynski. She came from Kremenitz. She was raised in her birthplace more in Russian than in Yiddish. Upon coming to Chicago in 1914, she learned a juicy Yiddish and took part in the work of the National Workers Circle. She was particularly devoted to the Jewish Children's School. Bina Ceszynski was one of the founders of the Macabee School in Chicago; she assisted in the creation of the Sholom Aleichem branch of the Jewish National Workers Union, where she was the executive member and was also an aid worker. Politically, she was a sympathizer of the Left *Poalei-Zion* movement.

The same year in Chicago, Moshe Ceszynski 's bookstore was established, which was the center in Chicago for Jewish readers, writers and intelligencia from all directions.

Discussions never stopped in Moshe Ceszynski 's bookstore – they took place from early morning to late in the night. Poets corrected their manuscripts, painters sketched their illustrations, plans for literary works were made, meetings were held, for among others, the Czenstochower Aid Union in Chicago.

At the same time, Moshe Ceszynski 's bookstore was also a world center for writers and book publishers from all over the world; writers from Poland, *Eretz-Yisroel*, Mexico and Argentina, who visited America, did not fail to pay a visit to M.C.'s bookshop – to learn world literary news, make plans and buy rare bargains. M.C.'s bookstore also stood in an authorial relationship with Yiddish writers, publishers and cultural institution across the entire world.

Moshe Ceszynski himself published articles covering political, communal and literary matters in a wide range of newspapers and journals in Chicago, New York, Philadelphia, Toronto, Buenos Aires and so on.

*

In 1931, he started a new period of his life. He started a publishing house and published Yiddish books – "Moshe Ceszynski's Book Publishing House in Chicago." With the large number of published books, the publishing house occupied a treasured place on the literary world map. Due to the circumstances in America, he spent a lot of money on it. However, the Ceszynskis were not disappointed by it and did not remain detached from the work.

From 1931 to 1942, his publishing house published around 50 books by European and American writers. Among the more well-known editions, Leivik's song, *From the Garden of Eden*; Fishl Bimko's nine volumes of dramas; Rywka Kalin's song, *Teibele*; Sholom Szwarcbord's two volumes of memoirs; Dr. Poliszik's two volume, *The Development of Consciousness and the Process of Knowledge*; Dr. Israel Marcus's *Chosen Pearls of Our Cultural Treasures* and others.

[Page LXXXI]

Ceszynski's book editions were sent to all of the Jewish centers in Europe. The publications were sent to many European cultural institutions free of charge. All that was needed was a request and the desire to read and support the Yiddish word.

In general, Moshe Ceszynski's innumerable activities with Yiddish books and for the Yiddish word were too many to enumerate – but one of them must be remembered here – because it does not have a connection to Jews living in various countries, but to Jews on their way – Jewish emigrants. M.C. contacted the ship companies in many nations with a circular asking that they establish Yiddish sections in their ship libraries for the large number of Jewish passengers they carry. His message should be an example for our large and influential Jewish organizations.

*

In Chicago, Max Ceszynski was one of the first members of YIVO (Institute for Jewish Research). Earlier, he had sent an entire series of books and material and a small amount of money to YIVO in Vilna to support Jewish writers, although because of this he had to forgo many personal needs.

He was active in the Chicago Cultural Society and helped create the Society for Jewish Culture; is a member of the Sholom Aleichem branch of the Jewish National Workers Union; is a member of the Sholom Aleichem Institute; assists in the work of the various types of Yiddish schools, such as: Sholom Aleichem schools, *Arbeter Ring* schools, *Farband* schools and others. He took an active part in the Chicago division of the American Federation of Polish Jews, where he was an executive member for several years; he is one of the founders and the secretary of the Czenstochower Independent Union and was active in the aid work for Czenstochow during his entire time in Chicago.

M. Ceszynski was the executive of the *landsmanschaftn* for workers in *Eretz-Yisroel* for several years.

*

In addition to the founding of their book selling business, the Ceszynskis, Moshe and Bina, began collecting books and rare editions for their private library. His agents in Europe bought the best cultural treasures for him. Over the years, he successfully collected a giant library that was well known in Chicago. Many writers would come to their house, where the library occupied a separate room, to search for information for their literary work.

The good and patient Bina Ceszynski gave the library her unlimited effort and attention; even when she was sick, day in and day out, she dusted the thousands of books and publications and kept them in order.

In December 1934, a banquet for the Sholom Aleichem Institute was arranged by a large group of friends, writers and cultural workers with the Ceszynskis as the main luminaries. A large number of friends, readers, writers and cultural workers took part in the banquet. The large number of greetings from distinguished personalities, writers and cultural workers from America and from other countries showed the Yiddish literary world's appreciation for the devotion of the Ceszynskis.

Bina Ceszynski died of a heart ailment in December 1936. Moshe Ceszynski lost his wife, most faithful friend and colleague in all of his undertakings.

Even more than Moshe Ceszynski, their home library remained an orphan after her death and it remained in a storage house for many years. Nothing came of the negotiations with the Sholom Aleichem Institute in Chicago, with the *Beis Hamidresh L'Torah* Library and other institutions to include the library on their premises. It was through the initial mediation of Mendl Elkin that the library found a place at the Institute for Jewish Research (YIVO), 535 West 135th Street in New York (YIVO). The "Bina Ceszynski Library" is located in the YIVO building together with the library of Kalmen Marmor. There are many interesting old manuscripts, fine art pictures, statues and the like among the books. There is in the same room a fine art portrait of Bina Ceszynski painted by the Chicago Jewish artist, Sam Beyer, in memory of the deceased.

In 1942, Moshe Ceszynski married his second wife – Bluma Weiner, who comes from a Hasidic family from Komarno (Galicia). Her father was called Mirel Leah's Reb Itsik [Mirel Leah's son]. The Yiddish language and culture and other European languages are strangers to Bluma Weiner Ceszynski.

To everything that has been said about Moshe Ceszynski, or his popular name, "Moshe C," must be added one quality, perhaps the greatest and most beautiful compliment for a person: He never – in his youth, or now, in his older years –politically, socially and personally – was embittered, did not carry out plots against anyone. He was always everyone's friend and everyone's comrade.

Ceszynski Collection in the Central Library and Archive of YIVO
(Photo, Bina Ceszynski)

The Central Library and Archive of YIVO was enriched with an important book and periodical collection. This book treasury that consists of approximately two thousand pieces was brought in by the Chicago cultural worker and publisher Moshe Ceszynski, in the name of his untimely deceased wife, Bina Ceszynski who for many years was devoted to the collection of *seforim* [religious books], books, periodical editions and also archive material.

The collection is strongest in its periodicals. There are such rare periodical editions as: Warsawer Yidishe Zeitung [Warsaw Yiddish Newspaper] 1767-8; Kol Mevaser [Voice of the People], 1869, Odessa; Wiener Yidisher Kikeriki [Viennese Jewish Cock-a-Doodle-Do] 1879; Hatzefira [The Siren] 1881, Warsaw; Hasoef [Zionist literary periodical], 1885 Warsaw; Familien Fraynd [Family Friend] (Dos Spektor [The Specter]), 1888; Yidishes Folks Blat [Jewish People's Paper], 1889, Petersburg; Der Yudishe Biblotek [The Jewish Library] (The I.L. Peretz) 1891; Di Neye Zeit [The New Times]; 1898; Der Yud [The Jew]; 1899, Krakow; Di Yudishe Familie [The Jewish Family], 1902, Krakow; Dos Yudishe Folk [The Jewish People], 1906, Vilna; and many others.

There were also a considerable number of important examples, such as Ben Zav's *Oytser haShishim* [*The Sixty Treasures*], 1817; Chaim Zelig Slonimski's writings, 1866; Lipshitse's Russian-Yiddish Dictionary, 1869; *Tiferes Yisroel* [*Splendid Yisroel*], (Yiddish), 1883, Odessa; Presberger print of Glickel of Hamelin's *Memoirs*, 1836; an old printing of *Guide to the Perplexed* in Hebrew and another in Yiddish and so on.

In addition, there is also a collection of art books and books about art.

It can be seen from the collection that the Ceszynskis devoted themselves to collecting according to a clear plan and, therefore, the collection is of great importance. They succeeded in amassing a fine collection of Soviet publications that is now difficult to obtain.

The management of the Central Library is now busy making a list and preparing a catalogue of the book treasures. All of the Ceszynski books are together in a special place.

Together with the *seforim* [religious books] and archive that was just recently brought over from Frankfurt – YIVO's Central Library and Archive was newly enriched, both with books and with archival material.

[Page LXXXII]

Kof ק
Yakov Kalka

Son of Dovid and Chana. Born in Czenstochow. He is a member of the Stephen Weiss Lodge No. 1. He is now about 84 years old.

———

Shimcha Kalka
(Photo)

Shimcha Kalka was born and spent his childhood years in Nowo-Radomsk. His father, Tuvya, was a Hasidic Jew, always deep in *Ein Yakov* [16th century religious book] or in other Jewish religious books. His mother, Sarah, was known for her honesty and goodness. She shared the meager food with others and was beloved by her neighbors – Jews and Christians.

From his youngest years, Shimcha was a strong, independent and original character. He excelled in his surroundings with his bearing and clothing. While still very young, he became interested in modern literature and in communal problems, carrying out discussions with his father and with Hasidim who would come to his house.

Shimcha Kalka became a printer and settled in Czenstochow. The *S.S.* [Socialist Zionist] movement, into which he threw himself with his entire unrestrained temperament and youthful vigor, won in him one of the most active and devoted workers.

"Comrade Shimcha" did not fear any danger, and despite scores of problems was always ready to carry out any assignment both in the years of the revolutionary tide or, later, during the times of darkest reaction – almost all of the illegal literature printed in Czenstochow was his work that he carried on in Botszan's print shop or in secret print shops.

In May 1913, he married Leah Herszlikowicz, a good comrade in the *S.S.* and, in the same year, left for America. From the start, he worked hard to make a living in his trade. Later, he opened his own printing shop with Josef Kaufman on Delancey Street, New York, that was a gathering place for Czenstochower and Radomsker *landsleit* [people born in the same town or city]. He died in January 1919 at the age of 33 of influenza, leaving a wife and two sons – Yankl and Lou.

His name will always be remembered with deep love and respect.

———

Sarah Kalka

(Photo)

Sarah Kalka (née Grynboim) was born in 1895 in Czenstochow. She married Yehoshua Kalka of Nowo-Radomsk. She was active in Czenstochow in the artisan's club. She emigrated to *Eretz-Yisroel* in 1921 and here mainly provided assistance to the Radomsker *landsleit*. She died in 1943 at the age of 48.

[Page LXXXIII]

When the Radomskers in Tel Aviv founded an aid fund for their city with a managing committee of the following people, Shlomoh Krakowski, Shlomoh Waksman, Moshe Szitenberg, Dovid Krojze, Yehoshua Kalka, Devora Karmoil, Leah Birnboim, Mordekhai Chasom, they decided to name the fund for Sarah Kalka. With this, the name of a rare soul taken away by death in the very bloom of life, and who left an inconsolable sorrow in the hearts of her husband and her many friends, was immortalized.

Honor her memory!

Josef (Arueli) Kalaszynski

(Photo)

Born in Czenstochow in 1888. In 1902, he began his communal activities as a *Poalei-Zionist*. In 1903, he took part in the *Poalei-Zion* conference in Krakow, in which Josef Kruk also took part. A split developed at the conference between the *S.S.* group and *Poalei-Zion*. Josef Kalaszynski remained in *Poalei-Zion* and there carried out his activities until 1908. He left Czenstochow in 1908 because of persecutions by the Czarist government and emigrated to *Eretz-Yisroel*.

Here Josef Kalaszynski (Arueli) took an enthusiastic part in the building of the land. He belonged to the first founders of *Schunat Borokow* [Borokow's residences] and of *Dfus Acduth* [United Press] (*Histadrut*'s cooperative printing house and bookbinding shop). He was the director of the printing shop for 10 years. Later, he opened his own printing shop, where the most beautiful works in the trade still are printed.

Josef Kalaszynski has not stopped his communal activities to this day. He gives a great deal of energy to the Free Masons movement. In 1943, his book abut the Free Masons movement was published. He published articles in the monthly Free Masons journal under the title "Brother to Brother." In general, he is one of the people of whom the Czenstochower *landsleit* can be proud.

Meir Kalman Kaminski

(Photo)

Son of Zaynwel and Zelda. Born in 1866 in Kaminsk, near Piotrkow. He died in Czenstochow on 17 October 1903 (25 Tishrei).

Chaya Sara Kaminski

(Photo)

Daughter of Haim and Mariam Frydman. Born in Czenstochow in 1868 (at the end of Yom-Kippur). She died on 5 December 1936 (22 Kislev 5697).

Arthur Kaminski

Son of Kalman and Chaya Sara. Born on 27 March 1895 in Czenstochow. Came to America from Germany in 1913. He is a member of the Jewish National Workers Union and Regional Czenstochower Union in Detroit.

Mordekhai (Marcus) Kaminski

(Photo)

Born on 5 September 1897 in Czenstochow. He is a descendent of the Kaminski family that had a shop on Fabriczszna, opposite the Igliarnia [a needle factory]. To the older generation, he was known as Haim Laskowski's grandson. His grandfather, Haim Frydman, of blessed memory, of Senatorska Street, in Niedszele's house, was known in Czenstochow as Reb Haim Laskowski. He was a pious Jew, a scholar, a member of the *khevra-kadishe* [burial society] and one of the founders of the *khevra h'tilim* [group of men who recite psalms for those who are sick or who have died] in Shimon the baker's house on Motsova. Such eminent men as Avraham Meir Blater; Reb Yehoshua Dovid Davidowicz – Engineer Davidowicz's father; Reb Shimon Klabucker ("*der gruber*" [the fat] Shimon); Reb Feiwel Alter – father of Mikhal Alter; Yehezkeil Szmulewicz, father of the photographer and active *Lira* worker Heniek Szmulewicz, belonged to the *khevra h'tilim*.

His father – Meir Kalman – was born in Kaminsk (near Radomsk); his grandfather and great grandfather lived there during the time of his father. The name Kaminski comes from there.

At three years of age, M. Kaminski began to study with Little Idesl who was known in Czenstochow. Later, Kaminski met her in Paris selling nuts from *Eretz-Yisroel*.

The school years were spent with Yeheil the *malamed* (Yeheil Klobucker or Yeheil Landsman) on Warsawer Street. He was a tall Jew with a large dark reddish beard, taught us *Yiddishkeit* with the good and bad. That is – with a whip. Later he taught in Leder's School.

His first job was in the bank house of Henrik Zorski.

[Page LXXXIV]

He won many friends and acquaintances among the people there, who would come about communal matters.

He belonged to the *S.S.* Party in the freedom movement.

During the time of the First World War, Kaminski, together with Rafal Federman and other comrades from the trade employees union, helped organize the strike of the trade employees in Czenstochow. From 1916 to the end of the First World War, he was a railroad employee. During the last year, he was actually the chief of the ticket window on the railway car ramp. When, in the end, the Germans were repelled and Poland took over the management of the railroads, he was fired on the morning of the liberation with the words "*Idsz do Berlina*" ("Go to Berlin"), along with scores of other Jewish train workers. He, like other Jews, was prohibited from appearing at the railroad. It should be understood that Polish train workers and clerks, who had previously worked on the trains, remained in their positions.

M. Kaminski was one of the two delegates who traveled to Warsaw to demand that the approximately 200 fired train workers should be paid at least 300 *zlotes* compensation for the time of their work as all of the Christians workers had been (the second was Bialek – a Christian worker who came from Lithuania and was one of the leaders of the "independents"). In Warsaw, Kaminski and Bialek conferred with the railroad minister, Eberhardt, who accepted the demand. This was achieved in large part with the help of the *S.S.* Party representative in Warsaw, who steered them through all of the offices and ministries.

A little later, he left for Dusseldorf. He met many comrades there who were taken to work in the coal mines and factories during the wartime. There they created a union of Polish Jews, where he worked for 20 years, for the entire time he lived in Germany. He also joined the Zionist movement, was active in the local Zionist managing committee and went to national conferences and congresses. He also took part in *kehile* life in Germany and later was elected as a representative to the managing committee. He spent many years until Polish Jews – payers of *kehile* taxes, like the German Jews – achieved the passive voting rights, that is, the right to be elected to the *gemeinde* managing committee. In 1924, he and others helped to found the sports union, *Makabee*, in Dusseldorf.

In 1936 he visited *Eretz-Yisroel* where in Tel Aviv he met his brother, Daniel, and his wife who had emigrated from Germany a year earlier. Daniel had worked with him on the railroad in Czenstochow.

On the night of 28 October 1938, the Nazis pulled 30,000 Polish Jews out of their homes all over Germany, old and young, women and children, also those who were born in Germany, but remained Polish citizens. They packed them in railway trains and trucks and sent them away to the Polish border. Nearly 600 Jews were sent out of Germany with Kaminski and brought to Zbaszyn under police guard. There they met thousands of Jews from all corners of Germany – many naked and barefoot – all became beggars overnight. The Jews were "quartered" in horse stalls in Zbaszyn. It was cold at night and there was nothing to use as a cover. This is how the new "home" looked. In Zbaszyn itself, there were only five Jewish families. One of them was Dovid Yelin from Czenstochow (Kaminski's cousin). He and his wife and her sister did everything that was in their power to do to help the refugees. The first help was bread and tea that warmed and nourished the refugees. Kaminski traveled to Lodz the same day (*Shabbos* at night), where his brother, Dr. Yehuda Kaminski lived.

Mordekhai Kaminski went from Lodz to Warsaw. There he contacted Senator Professor Szor and helped with the rescue activities for the Jewish refugees from Germany. He held negotiations with the Polish Foreign Ministry with the help of Dr. Emil Zomersztajn, the Jewish *Sejm* Deputy, about the return to Germany to liquidate the homes and enterprises. Meanwhile, in Germany, the pogroms of 9 November 1938 [*Kristlnacht*] took place when all of the Jewish houses and synagogues were destroyed. He traveled from Warsaw to Czenstochow to see his sister, Miriam (Manja) Mojer, the only remaining member of his family. Here he met many refugees who were supported by the Jewish *kehile* [community].

He traveled to America through Germany and Holland and arrived in New York on 10 November 1939.

Today, he lives in Detroit and again takes part in Jewish communal life. He is a member of the Zionist organization and the Jewish Congress, of the Jewish National Worker's Union and supports aid work to the Polish Jews in general and of those in Czenstochow in particular in every way possible.

——————

Libby (Ratner) Kaminski
(Photo)

Daughter of Harold and Frieda. Born on the 10 of April 1885 in Zawiercie. Came to America in March 1906. Died on 4 January 1928 in New York.

——————

[Page LXXXV]

Arush Kaminski

Son of Mordekhai and Faygl. Born in Czenstochow on 25 June 1877. He is a tailor. He married Liba Ratner of Zawiercie in Czenstochow. Came to America in 1904. He is a member of the Czenstochower Young Men and of United Czenstochower Relief in New York.

——————

Dovid Koniecpoler
Czenstochow
(Photo)

Born on 27 February 1897 in Czenstochow. Representative of the Zionist organization, *Ichud* [Union], and the Jewish Committee. In 1915 he carried on political-communal work in Radomsk and was active until and during the Second World War. Today, he is active again in the support of worthy Jewish communal work in Czenstochow.

Leon Kapinski
(Photo, caption: The Kapinski Family)

Born in either 1881 or 1882. Studied in *kheder* [religious school], in the *yeshiva*, then studied in Germany. In his youngest years, he was a member of the *S.D.K.F.L.* (Social Democrats), later he went over to the Zionists and was one of the strongest fighters for Hebraism [the movement to make Hebrew the language of the Jewish people].

In 1908 he took part in the founding of *Lira* [a singing society] and was one of its most active workers during its entire existence. He often held meetings and led discussions with the Yiddishists [proponents of Yiddish and Yiddish culture], representing the ideas of *"Khoveve Ofas Eiver"* [Lovers of the Hebrew Language].

(Photo, caption: Kapinski family members at the grave of Leon and Mauritz Kapinski)

(Photo, caption: The headstone of the Kapinskis' mother)

(Photo, caption: The mother of the Kapinskis and her children)

(Photo, caption: A fragment of the headstone on the grave of Leon and Mauritz Kapinski)

Although he, himself, spoke Yiddish and took part in the Yiddish press in Czenstochow – his slogan was: *Polnis v ervit* (Polish or Hebrew).

His Zionism was more spiritual than territorial. In words and in writing, he preached the Ahad Haamist [Ahah Haam, pen name of Asher Ginzburg, a Hebrew writer and thinker] ideas. He was one of the few who studied in depth the Talmudist and modern Hebrew literature.

[Page LXXXVI]

He was active in a whole series of communal institutions until the Second World War. He was appointed as the chief of the *Judenrat* under the Nazi regime, and later, was murdered by the Nazis in the Czenstochower cemetery together with all of the members of the *Judenrat* and the Jewish intelligentsia.

(Photo, caption: The Kott Family)
Nakhum Kott
(Photo)

Son of Shlomoh Hersh and Bluma. Born in Czenstochow on 27 November 1902.

Rywka Kott
(Photo)

Dovid Kolin

Son of Mendl and Chana. Born in New York on 14 July 1895. He is a professor at New York University and a member of the American Economic Association.

Shlomoh Kolin
(Photo)

Son of Haim Josef and Mariam. Born in Kromolow (Poland). He is 74 years old.

Berish Kolin
Detroit

Son of Shlomoh and Ester. Born in Myszkow (Poland) 1895. Came to America on 13 May 1913. He is a member of the Pinsker Society, executive member of the Czenstochower Regional Union in Detroit. He was also one of the most active members of the Czenstochower Union. His two sons – Norman and Arthur – served in the American Army.

Izrael Korpiel

Died March 1881 in Czenstochow at the age of 42.

Fradl Korpiel
(Née Zeigermakher)

Died on 6 February 1920 in Czenstochow at the age of 75.

Sam Korpiel

Son of Izrael and Fradl. Born on 23 November 1876 in Czenstochow. He married Martha Kory in November 1904. Came to America on 25 December 1887.

Sam Korpiel has been an active member for many years and former vice president of the Czenstochower Young Men in New York. He is active in the Czenstochower Relief Committee and in the *Czenstochower Yidn* book committee. His sons, Julian and Seymour, served in the American army.

(Photo)

Martha Korpiel

Born on 4 January 1881. Member of the Young Man's, United Czenstochower Relief and of the *Czenstochower Yidn* book committee.

Jacob and Sara Kory

Abraham Koffy
Chicago
(Photo)

Son of Shmuel and Hinda Leah. Born in Czenstochow on 15 July 1895. He married Chava Wajnrib. Came from England to America on 21 May 1921. He is a member of the Lubliner Educational Society and of the Czenstochower Educational Society.

Mordekhai (Max) Kuszminski

Born in 1894. His father, Berish, and his mother, Chana, headed a religious home and lived in Czenstochow. From age 14 on, he studied tailoring with his father. He belonged to the tailor's union and to the Polish Socialist Party. He married Esther Rozenblat.

Max Kuszminski came to America in 1919. He is a member of the Cloakmakers Union and also was a member of the Czenstochower branch 26, *A.R.* [*Arbeter Ring*] and of the Relief Committee. When the Czenstochower *Patronat* existed, he was active in it and was also a member of its executive.

[Page LXXXVII]

Esther Kuszminski is a member of the Czenstochower Ladies Auxiliary.

Their son, Haimy, volunteered to join the American army.

Morris Kutner
(Photo)

Son of Hershl and Liba. Born in Czenstochow on 15 April 1897. Came to America in 1913. He is a member of the Czenstochower branch 261 *Arbeter Ring* in New York.

Henry Kuperman

Son of Shlomoh Dovid and Sara. Born in Bedzin. He married Regina Rozenfeld. Came to America on 22 June 1922. He was a member of the Czenstochower branch 261 *Arbeter Ring* in New York. Today he is a member of the Piotrkow and Bedzin Society.

Regina Rozenfeld-Kuperman (Ryfka)
(Photo, caption: Regina Kuperman with her mother)

Daughter of Dovid Rozenfeld, a craftsman. She did not know her father because when she was born he was a Russian soldier in the Russo-Japanese War in which he perished. She always thought of him with love in her heart.

At age 18, her mother, Nacha (née Gryn), was left alone with three children: her brother Itzik Leib, R. Rozenfeld and her sister, Ruszka (Reizl). Her mother did everything in order to give her children a good upbringing and spared herself no difficulty. The hard work resulted in her having a lung disease.

Her brother, Itzik Leib, became an upholsterer and belonged to the *Bund*. He married Bukhla Frydman. They had one daughter, Jadja (Itka).

Her younger sister, Ruszka, began working as a seamstress at age 12. She belonged to the youth organization, *Shtral* [sunbeam] in the worker's club, *Fareinikte* [United] and studied at the evening courses for the young workers. Later, she joined the communists, was one of the most active workers in the movement. And spent many years in the Polish jails.

Regina Rozenfeld studied at the elementary Russian school, led by Mrs. Wajzer on Teatralne Street. She learned Yiddish on Garncarska Street with the lame Ruchl. She began to work at age 12 as a hairdresser in the little house factory of Mrs. Wajzman at First Avenue 8, where the main employment was in the production of *sheitlekh* [wigs worn by pious women]. In 1916 the *S.S.* [Socialist Zionists] began to organize the hairdresser workers and R.R. was drawn into the movement. In addition to her, Max Khapot, S. Moszkowicz and a whole series of other people among the hairdresser workers, were active.

She was fired from her work because of her activity in organizing the hairdresser workers and began to work for herself. This led to the bettering of her and her mother's circumstance.

Although they were a poor working family, without a father, and suffered from need, life after work among many close friends and comrades was interesting and rich in content. R.R. belonged to *Fareinikte* [United] and took part in all of the activities of the organization and celebrated every holiday. Abraham Wenger, Hela Wenger, Manya Herszlikowicz (later the wife of Moshe Szjan), Feigl Szliwinska (later Mrs. Linkinska) Karala Szokher (married Max Khropat), Bejla Liberowicz (married Dovid Khropat), Helfgot, Regina Gors, Sara'le Opatszinski Gerszon Muntowicz, and a series of others, belong to the circle of her closest friends. When the Rozenfeld family lived in Ostrow during the summer because of their mother's weak physical condition, Mikhal Alter, Cesza Federman, Abraham Brat, Rusza Plawner, Rayzele Feirtag, Moshe Berkensztat, Regina Waszekha and other comrades would spend time in their house.

She left for America in 1922.

In 1926, she married Henry Kuperman. They have three children: a son, Danny, 19 years old – a university student (served in the American army), a 14-year old daughter, Audrey (Altera) and a six-year old boy, Joel (Gershon).

She visited Czenstochow in 1931. Life in Czenstochow was normal then. She saw her mother and cousins for the last time. They perished during the years 1939-1945. The only one who was saved, due to her good knowledge of the Polish prisons, was her younger sister, Ruszka. She is now in Warsaw and is again active in communal activities as she was earlier.

Jacob Kuklinski
Chicago
(Photo)

Son of Josef and Rayzel. Born in Olsztyn on 18 July 1894. He married Roza Mylsztajn. Came to America in 1922. He is a member of the Czenstochower Educational Union in Chicago.

[Page LXXXVIII]

Mendl Kaufman

Son of Abo (Abele the *shoykhet* [ritual slaughterer]) and Yenta. Born in Czenstochow 1873. He married Ita Lebenhof, daughter of Khasriel *Shenker* [Khasriel the tavern proprietor] and Brandl Lebenhof. Perished in Czenstochow during the years 1939-1945.

(Photos, captions:
Mendl Kaufman
Yenta Kaufman
Khasriel Lebenhof
Brandl Lebenhof
Reb Berish the religious judge, of blessed memory
Father of Abo and Josef Kaufman
Malka Kaufman, may she rest in peace
Mother of Abo and Josef Kaufman

Abo Kaufman
(Photo)

Son of Reb Berish (religious judge and rabbi) and Malka. Born in Czenstochow in 1882. During his childhood, he studied with the teachers, Harcka Gotlib, Leibl Landoy, Yeheil Landsman (Klobucker) and Yitzhak Rozenberg. At 13, he began to study in the city *Beis-Midrash* [house of study] with Josef Gliksman, the son of Berl Gliksman (known as "*der groiser Berl* [the large Berl]," with Yekl Kornberg (Podmorek), who later became the *shoykhet* [ritual slaughterer] in Rotterdam, Holland, with Hershl Gancwajkh, with Nota Gerszonowicz (son of Reb Yehezkeil the teacher) and with Henekh Granek. He also studied with his father, Reb Berish the religious judge and every morning [he studied] a lesson in the Talmud with the city rabbi, Rabbi Reb Nukhem Asz, may he rest in peace.

He read Hebrew and Yiddish books and newspapers, such as *Hamalitz* and *Hatzfire*, in addition to studying *Tanakh* [the bible consisting of the Five Books of Moses, the Prophets and the Writings], Talmud and post Talmudic commentaries. He was a member of the religious Zionist organization, *Mizrakhi*, of the organization, *Khoveve Sfas Ayver* [Lovers of the Hebrew Language] under the leadership of the famous follower of the enlightenment and pedagogue, Klinicki.

In 1904 he entered the military. He spent eight months there and, after coming to Czenstochow from the Caucasus, he became a member of the *S.S.* Party.

In May 1906, on a *Shabbos* afternoon, when a bomb was thrown from Szmulwicz's house on Warszawer Street where his parents lived, he left Czenstochow with Herszl Gotayner and Bem. He was a janitor for several months in Antwerp (Belgium) and on 22 January he came to New York.

He founded the Czenstochower Progressive Young Men's Society in 1908 with several *landsleit* [countrymen]. The main purpose of the society was to help newly arrived *landsleit* find employment and to help them in case of need.

In February 1909, he founded the Czenstochower branch 261 *Arbeter Ring* with comrade and friend, Haim Leib Szwarc and was secretary there for many years.

In July 1914, with the same comrade Szwarc, he founded the Czenstochower Relief Union that later became the Czenstochower Relief Committee.

In 1929, with other comrades, he founded the Czenstochower branch 11 International Workers Order, the only Jewish fraternal people's order.

In 1930, he was a member of the Communist Party. He was an executive member of ICOR (Organization for Jewish Colonization in Russia) for many years during this time; several years secretary of the Czenstochower Patronet (to help the political arrestees in Poland).

[Page LXXXIX]

Today he is an executive member and secretary of the Czenstochower branch 11 of the Jewish Fraternal Peoples Order and executive member and Protocol Secretary of the United Czenstochower Relief Committee.

Josef Kaufman
(Photo)

Son of Reb Berish the religious judge, of blessed memory, and Malka (neé Brakhner). Born in Czentochow on 24 December 1892. Like every Jewish child at that time, he received a national-religious upbringing in his parents' house and went along the road from *kheder* to private religious scholars. However, he did not study for a long time because of his preference for practical work and, while still a young man, he began to learn the printing trade.

The hope for greater satisfaction and the atmosphere that then held sway in Jewish middleclass circles in Poland woke in him the thought of leaving Czenstochow for the wider world. As a result of this, he came to America in 1909.

However, the threads that bound him to his old home were not torn by the distance that separated him from there. He began to seek an approach to his *landsleit* [townspeople] who had arrived here earlier with the aim of founding a Czenstochower *landsmanschaftn* in New York and thus again establish a connection with his birthplace. He began on the first step of his communal activity on American soil.

In 1910 he became a member of branch 261 of the *Arbeter Ring* and remains there today.

At a later time, he had the opportunity to show his connection to his birthplace and his dedication as a communal worker.

This was in 1914 when the Czenstochower Aid Society was founded in New York.

Our contemporaries say that Josef Kaufman took the most difficult work as secretary upon himself and put his private and communal business aside in order to come to a Czenstochower meeting in time. His printing shop at 154 Delancey Street in New York was the place to which Czenstochowers "made a pilgrimage." This was the place of connection to the old home.

In 1917 he became a member of the Young Men and for a time in 1918 he occupied the office of Vice President. Today he is Chairman of the Cemetery Committee and one of the most active members.

However, at the same time as his work in Young Men, he is also very active with the Czenstochowers in New York and from 1936 until today, he has occupied the office of Financial Secretary.

It is enough to remember that on 18 September 1938 United Czenstochower Relief organized a banquet for him and his wife to acknowledge all of his work on behalf of Czenstochow and Czenstochowers in America, at which the thanks of other Czenstochower organizations in New York was expressed.

Today his printing shop, at 416 Fourth Avenue is a small Czestochow in New York. All deliberations occur there and Josef Kaufman serves and welcomes everyone with comradely love and neighborly devotion.

He was particularly active as a member of the *Czenstochower Yidn* book committee. His professional advice and instruction were valuable and helpful.

He stands with other members in the front row of United Czenstochower Relief.

Ray Kaufman

Born in Czenstochow in 1897. Came to America in 1906 and married Josef Kaufman in 1917. She is active in the Ladies Auxiliary,

Ray and Josef Kaufman have three daughters.

Shimshon Klajner, may he rest in peace

Son of Nusan Yakov and Feigl. Born in Czenstochow in 1882. Was known as a small industrialist and honest merchant in Czenstochow. Was a member of *Mizrakhi*. Shared the fate of the martyrs during the years 1939-1945.

May their souls be bound up in the bond of eternal life.

Charles (Kopl) Kleinfeld
(Photo)

Son of Nekhamia and Feigl. Born in Czenstochow on 12 November 1902; came to America on 1 July 1921. Lives in Chelsea, Mass., 18 Maverick Street.

At age 16, Kopl joined the *Bund* youth, where he remained until leaving for America. After arriving in America, he stood aside from political activity. However, after two years in America, learning about the workers' movement here in this country, he joined the *Arbeter Ring*. In the struggle between the "right" and "left" in the *Arbeter Ring*, Kopl was part of the "left," leaving the *Arbeter Ring*. He became a member of the International Workers Order and recording secretary of branch 1702. Later, he was the cultural director for several years and a member of the district committee of the Order. At the same time, he was a member of Labor Lyceum Assn. (a workers institution), became a member of the board and director and later, recording secretary.

During 1925-1930, he was the librarian of the Labor Lyceum Library, which is a wide ranging cultural institution and served a great mass in the cultural area. In 1932 he became the chief manager of the library; during those years, he was also very active in ICOR, created a branch in Chelsea that does good work and he became a member of the city committee for ICOR.

[Page XC]

For the last two years he has been very busy in Russian War Relief, taking part in a campaign to sell war bonds. In general, he is a person who has been occupied in communal work since his arrival in America and is active in many areas.

Berl Kielcziglowski

Son of Yekl and Ruchl. Born in Czenstohow in 1882. Lived in Danzig and, in the end, in Czenstochow. He marred Rywka Reizl Berkowicz. Shared the fate of the martyrs in 1939-1945.

(Photo)

Rywka Reizl Kielcziglowski

Daughter of Mendl and Frimet Berkowicz. Born in Dzialoszyn (Poland) in 1881. Shared the fate of the martyrs in 1939-1945.

Haim Yeshayahu Kielcziglowski (Kiel)
(Photo)

Son of Berl and Ryfka Reizl. Born in Czenstochow on 9 September 1901. Came to America from Danzig on 9 February 1929. He is a member of the Brooklyn Jewish Center, Zionist Organization, Czenstochower Young Men and United Czenstochower Relief in New York. He married Jenny Kaufman in July, 1923, in Berlin.

(Photo, top right, caption: Liza Kutner-Kielcziglowska, second wife of Chona Kielcziglowski)

(Photo, bottom right, caption: Rutka Kielciglowski, daughter of Chona and Sara)

(Photo, top left, caption: Chona Kielcziglowski)

(Photo, bottom left, caption: Sara Kelciglowski, first wife of Chona Kielcziglowski)

(Photo, caption, the Kaufman family)

Jenny (Kielcziglowski) Kiel
(Photo)

Daughter of Mendl and Ita Kaufman. Born in Czenstochow on 26 August 1899. Came to America from Danzig on 12 May 1939. She is a member of the Brooklyn Jewish Center, Zionist Organization, Czenstochower Young Men and of the United Czenstochower Relief in New York.

[Page XCI]

Moshe Kornberg
Philadelphia

Son of Alter and Gnendl.

He is treasurer of the Philadelphia Baker's Union, local 201.

Itshe Leib Knobler

Son of Yerakhmial and Ester. Born in Czenstochow. Came to America in 1922. Belongs to the *Zaloshiner Chevra Anshei Bnei Achim.*

Max (Krzepicki) Kepp

Son of Kalman and Hinda. Born in Czenstochow on 25 October 1891. Came to America on 11 June 1911. He married Ester Fajersztajn.

Max Kepp is an executive member of Czenstochow branch 261 *Arbeter Ring*, member of the Czenstochower Aid Union, of United Czenstochower Relief and of the *Czenstochower Yidn* book committee.

His son-in-law – Albert Broiner and his two sons – Louis and Kalvin served in the American army.

(Photo)

Esther Kepp

Daughter of Shmuel Zanwel and Ruchl Fajersztajn. Born in Brody (Poland) on 25 October 1913. Came to America on 25 October 1913 (Translator's note: There is an obvious error in one of the two dates given.) She is a member of Czenstochower branch 261 of the *Arbeter Ring* and a trustee of the Czenstochower Ladies Auxiliary in New York.

Rose Kuper

Daughter of Shlomoh and Ester. Born on 10 April 1895 in Krzepice. Came to America on 23 May 1914 from Czenstochow. She is a member of the Opeler Society in New York and of the Czenstochower Ladies Auxiliary.

Hinda (Krzepicki) Kepp
(Photo)

Daughter of Leizer and Rosza Szimkowicz. Born in Czenstochow. Came to America in 1928.

She died on 3 May 1944 at the age of 83.

Moshe Krakowski
Detroit
(Photo)

Son of Leibish and Toyba. Born in Wolbrom (Poland). Came to Canada from Czenstochow in 1913, from there to America in 1915. He is a member of the Polish Synagogue in Detroit.

Dwoyra Krakowski
(Photo)

Daughter of Josef and Nakha Beila Zajdman. Born in Czenstochow. She was a member of the Czenstochower Regional Union in Detroit, active in various Jewish communal institutions and gave a great deal of charity. She died at the age of 49 in Detroit, on 2 March 1928.

Josef Krakowski
(Photo)

Son of Moshe and Dworya. Born in Czenstochow. Came to America in January 1922. Died here.

Herman Krak
(Photo)

Born 1860 in Konin (Poland) as the only son of his parents. There he graduated from the gymnasium with distinction and then – from the teacher seminar in Leczyca. In 1900 he moved to Czenstochow, first worked as a teacher and later had his own private school, where a large number of children from the Czenstochower middle class were among his students.

Herman Krak was one of the most educated people in Czenstochow. Hebrew, Russian, Polish and German were taught in his school. He was also a teacher in the Craftworkers' School in Czenstochow for a number of years. He was the father of five sons and two daughters. In 1911 he died at age 52 in Czenstochow. His wife, Matilda, died at the age of 92 in 1938.

[Page XCII]

Irving Kremsdorf
(Photo)

Son of Eidl and Chava. Born on 12 March 1893 in Czenstochow. Came to America in 1904. Member and trustee of Noakh Benevolent Society and of Jupiter Lodge I. A. O. P.

His son, Julian Kremsdorf was a sergeant in the American army.

Greetings from Kremsdorf Family Circle

Our family circle was founded by the children and in memory of Eidl and Chava Kremsdorf. The purpose of our circle is to hold all of the members of the family together in unity and love and jointly to support each other. The number of members, which consists of children, grandchildren and great grandchildren along with their husbands and wives, has now reached approximately 70 people. In the last war, 11 members of our circle served in the American army.

The experiences of the first 13 years have justified the existence of our circle. Under the leadership of Irving Kremsdorf, who was president for the first five years, our circle sank deep roots and fulfilled the hopes of the founders. Through these years, we had successful undertakings, supported each needy member with money and advice and were together in sorrow and joy. Our circle is now led by the younger members and we hope that they will do their work and make their parents proud.

The founders of the circle were:
Louis and Mary Lefkowicz
Louis and Sara Zinger
Abraham and Helen Frydman
Dovid and Roza Kremsdorf
Louis and Hanna Kremsdorf
Irving and Mary Kremsdorf

Eidl Kremsdorf

Son of Shmuel Yehezkeil and Hinda. Born in Czenstochow. Came to America in March 1903. Was a member of the *Zaloshiner* (Dzialoszyn) *Erste Chevra Anshei Bnei Achim.* He died in December 1912 in New York.

(Photo)

Chava Kremsdorf

Daughter of Hershl and Ruchl Szif. Born in Czenstochow. Came to America in March 1903. Was a member of the Zaloshiner Ladies Auxiliary of the *Zaloshiner* (Dzialoszyn) *Erste Chevra Anshei Bnei Achim.* She died in November 1933 in New York.

Efraim Kremsdorf

He was a good friend of *Poalei-Zion* in Czenstochow, a brother-in-law of Leon Altman, who had a café on the Teatralna Street.

When the working masses, under the leadership of Bela Kun, took power in Hungary, Efraim Kremsdorf took part in the struggle with his comrades from the *P.Z.* Party. Later, he returned to Czenstochow and worked temporarily in the cooperative, "Workers Home." In time, he returned to Vienna and came to *Eretz-Yisroel* during the 4th *aliyah*. Here he started as an agricultural worker, which was his ideal. However, after a few years of a life of drudgery, he came to Tel Aviv and settled in Eir Gamim and his material situation began to get better. However, it did not last long and it is known that one night Efraim Kremsdorf was burned. How this happened is not known to this day.

———

Dr. Josef Kruk
(Photo)

"My Grandfather," writes Dr. Josef Kruk in his article, *The End*, "fought in the fields of freedom for Poland." He was set completely in the tradition of the struggle by the Jewish intelligentsia for freedom and justice – [that was] older than his grandfathers and great grandfathers. However, it is certain that his grandfather, the ancient Polish revolutionary, the rebel and fighter lived in Josef Kruk's soul.

However, most children of the former Jewish progressive intelligentsia and fighters for Polish freedom were brought up and grew in an assimilated environment. Yiddish, the language of the people, was loathsome to them. It was called *Shvargatshen* dem jargon [twisting the jargon; jargon was the word used in describing Yiddish by those who held it in contempt]. Still further separation from the Jewish people was called progressive by them. When the liberation movement, after the 1890's, led those with more feeling to join the masses, it was respectable to be cosmopolitan, social democratic, or – when more of a Polish patriot – *Pepesowtses* [members of the Polish Socialist Party].

Josef Kruk also grew up in an assimilated environment. His revolutionary activity began on the school bench in the Russian *gymnazie*, in the tradition of his grandfathers: against the Russification of the school. Beginning his activity among the Jewish workers – he still could not speak any Yiddish, and even in the later years, his Yiddish was a little *fargoyisht* [gentile sounding].

And yet he is – Josef Kruk – whether as a leader or guide of a large part of the Jewish intelligentsia in Czenstochow or as a founder of the first group of worker-Zionists, later one of the leaders of the *S.S.* [Socialist Zionist Party – *Fareinikte* [United] – Independent – became the fiery prophet of Jewish rebirth. The pillar of fire, who always led, inspired and summoned the Jewish masses to struggle for their ethnic and national right there where they live and to struggle for a healthy and secure Jewish life on a territorial bases.

[Page XCIII]

Like many great personalities and leaders in human history, he was not afraid of being alone. Like a heroic captain, he did not lose his ship in the most difficult times, did not give up his ideals. The jails and prisons did not frighten him, as in the old Russian times, as in independent Poland. He belongs to the small camp of "twelve martyrs, twelve rulers."

He details the beginning of his revolutionary Jewish-socialistic activity in a chapter of his memoirs, "How we printed and smuggled the first declaration," with the following words:

"It was the 'romantic, heroic time' when each revolutionary felt like a hero, who creates miracles. A time of revolutionary dreaming, a time of love and belief; a time when each illegal brochure awoke new thoughts – and each proclamation – a soul; a time when each revolutionary word was the greatest action, the heroic action – It was the time when people were ready to sacrifice themselves for a cause.

"It was still more romantic, still a more romantic time for the group of Jewish workers and intellectuals who strove so passionately with their entire soul to find a harmonious synthesis between the general revolutionary-socialistic ideals and the Jewish national requirements, a synthesis between socialism and territorialism. This was a true period of *sturm un drang* [German: storm and stress, in other words, turmoil] for them; for them each printed party word had the power of a spell; for them each printed attempt to prove the new principles of the new creative socialism signified a new epoch."

This was in 1905. Josef Kruk already had "seniority" from several years of revolutionary activity, the *S.S.* [Socialist Zionist] pioneer of the Czenstochow revolutionary movement and the recognized leader among the members of *Ts.K.* The *Ts.K.* entrusted to him the printing in Krakow of the first party declaration and he smuggled them across the border with Dovid Maljarski. It was not easy, but he achieved his goal through "miracles" and fearless iron will.

Josef Kruk left Czenstochow in 1906 and began his activity as leader of the party groups abroad. He entered the University of Bern and graduated with the title, doctor. In 1911 when he returned from an emigrant congress in Kiev – a group of Czenstochower comrades: Hela Bimran, Jakub Goldsztajn, A. Khrabalowski, met in Gutek Bornsztajn's house in Zawiercie. (Traveling through Czenstochow was still dangerous for him.)

He and his wife, Dr. Roza Kruk, were in London at the time of the First World War. He was one of the closest friends of Dr. Izrael Zangwil, and with his wide acquaintance with the problems of international workers, he was active in the development of the Labor Party. Later, now in Poland, he was invited to London by the leaders of the Labor Party to give lectures about international problems.

With the outbreak of the revolution, he returned to Russia. In 1918 he came to Poland, settled in Warsaw and again stood at the head of the *Fareinikte* [United] Party.

It has been just 15 years since he founded the first group of worker-Zionists in Czentochow with a bunch from the intelligentsia and issued the first hectographic [Translator's note: copies created through the use of a gelatin plate] appeal to the Czenstochower Jewish workers.

The Jewish masses and intelligentsia of Czenstochow welcomed him with solemn enthusiasm, joy and love. The light of a heroic personality radiated from him, carrying the great humane idea of liberation and the struggle for the right of the Jewish masses to live as a people equal with all of the people of the world.

This triple light never left him. His personality shone in articles and lectures with broad focus and deep analysis that were always important events in the cities of Poland, where they took place: in Warsaw, Czenstochow, Vilna, Bialystok, etc. With this light, he went through all seven divisions of hell of party struggle and persecution by the police.

He was not afraid to tell the truth to the Polish reactionaries and the militaristic cliques that had taken over the regime. And this was rare in Poland and very dangerous, particularly when he later appeared as an "independent" at the mass meetings of the Polish workers.

He savored his first taste of Polish "freedom," for which he had struggled from his youth on, in 1919, when on the way to Czenstochow in a train station, he threw himself into saving a Jew from the hands of uniformed hooligans and himself had his head split.

He almost received a split head a second time when he called Pilsudski a traitor to the workers at a *Pepesowtse* [Polish Socialist Party] meeting in the firefighters' room in Czenstochow after the Pilsudski "revolution."

And if trouble was still lacking, some sort of police functionary moved into his apartment in Warsaw and was a burden to him for many months.

He lay around in Czenstochow and Piotrkow jails for a long time after a trial at which he was sentenced to a year and a half in jail

The last – the "best." After the independent party was liquidated by the colonels of the Polish government – he was exiled to the well-known concentration camp, Kartuz Bereza, from which he was saved barely alive.

[Page XCIV]

One of his accomplishments that should be described in more detail was the founding of the "Worker-Emigrant Union." This was the first attempt to organize the Jewish emigrant on a wider communal basis after the creation of the "Emigrant Society" in Kiev by Dr. Makhelman. Dr. Sziper, of the right *Poalei-Zion*, characteristically helped him in this work. Party rivalry and denunciations by blackmailers caused the closure by the government of this important institution.

In 1938, Dr. Josef Kruk and a group of close friend joined the "Committee for Working *Eretz-Yisroel*." At the same time, he secured the right to continue working with the "Freeland League," which was organized a few years earlier by the old leaders of the *S.S.* [Socialist Zionists] such as Zalman (Birszoy) Majzel in Warsaw and D. Szerniszewski in Vilna.

After the occupation of Poland, Dr. Josef Kruk saved himself by going to *Eretz- Yisroel*. The Czenstochower *landsleit* there welcomed him with enthusiasm and elected him as honorary chairman of their land council. As in Poland, he occupied a respected place among the communal workers and journalists in *Eretz-Yisroel* and takes part in a wide range of communal committees and important institutions.

———

[Page XCIV]

Resh ר

Moshe Zalman Rusak
(Photo)

Son of Jakov. Born in Dzialoszyn and died there at age 60 in 1919.

———

Chaya Rusak
(Photo)

Daughter of Kojfman and Nakha Lewkowicz. Born in Dzialoszyn. She died at age 68 in Dzialoszyn in 1928.

———

Jack Rozen

Son of Isidore and Mary. Born in New York on 24 June 1915. He married Annie Drajz on 4 February 1938. Their son, Matthew, was born on 12 March 1941 and their daughter, Margie, on 11 June 1941, both in New York.

Jack Rozen has been a member of the *Zaloshiner* (Dzialoszyn) *Erste Chevra Anshei Bnei Achim* in New York for many years.

———

Isidore Rozen (Yitzhak Risak) and Mary
(Photo, Isidore Rozen)
(Photo, Mary Rozen)

Son of Moshe and Chaya. Born in Dzialoszyn on 10 October 1890. He married Mary Staszewski, the daughter of Josef and Ruda, at age 19. She was born on 10 July 1892 in Dzialoszyn.

He was forced to emigrate by the trouble in his small *shtetl* endured by all of the young men who through the reactionary times in the period of 1905 as well as by the difficulty of achieving a respected life enabling him to support a wife.

He left Dzialoszyn with 10 rubles in his pocket and with the address of cousins in America whom he did not know. He came to America in November 1919. The telegram that he had sent to his cousins had been put aside and forgotten by them because it was then the season* and none of them had time to come to take him from the ship. He sat for three days in Castle Garden** until a *landsman* [man from the same town], Zuken Rozental, took mercy on him and took him from there.

(Photo, Annie Druz Rozen)

*[Translator's note: probably a reference to a heavy work period for the clothing industry]

**[Translator's note: Immigration to Castle Garden ended in December 1891; he most likely was kept on Ellis Island.]

When he arrived in New York, he began to work in a shop for three dollars a week and, as was usual, not having any trade, began by cleaning up the shop and very quickly became a foreman in his cousins' ladies waists [garment covering the shoulders to the bottom of the hips] shop.

[Page XCV]

His parents wanted him to return to Poland and appear for Russian military conscription. However, he decided not to do so and used all means to remain in America and decided to bring his wife, who had remained in Poland, to America. And on 10 October 1913***, his wife, Mary, did come to New York. For a time, they both worked and started a small business. The business did not begin so well. More than once they had to give up and start anew. His family grew with three children during this time – two sons and a daughter. Later, Rozen went into business with a partner and after a certain period of difficulty, business grew better from day to day.

***(The date must be incorrect because it is stated that her husband arrived in 1919.)

After the First World War his wife kept the promise that she had given to her parents and she traveled to her home city with her children to see her parents and rejoice with them.

All three children received a college education and today they are in business partnership with the Rozen family.

They were only able to bring over three sisters and brothers from the large family they had left in Poland.

The Rozen family generously supports all Jewish institutions and they have never forgotten their old home.

Isidore Rozen is a long time active member of the First *Zaloshiner* (Dzialoszyn) *Erste Chevra Anshei Bnei Achim*, treasurer of the Dzialoszyner Relief Committee and Chairman of the Loan Fund of the Progressive Friends in the Bronx.

Mary Rozen was the first president of the Dzialosyner Ladies Auxiliary, first president of the Star Charity Sisters, member of the Board of Directors of the Ladies Society for Friendship (a home for girls).

The Rozens responded warmly and generously to every appeal by the Czenstochower Relief Committee.

Their son Rubin was a lieutenant in the American army.

––––––––––

Chaya Waga-Rotman
(Photo)

Daughter of Jakov Tzwi and Beila Gitl Waga. Born in Czenstochow in September 1898. Her parents were middle class, pious people, particularly her mother, who placed a stamp of piety on her family, which consisted of two sons and two daughters. Her mother greatly helped the poor and needy. She herself would give charity and was an example for neighbors and friends. She hoped that her good deeds would give her a great reward in the other world. She would tell her children various stories from Jewish history to influence them to uphold the Jewish religious customs. And although she very much wanted to see her children [become] people with a worldly education, she was overcome with fear that they would be "spoiled" and, therefore it was difficult for Chaya Waga to obtain this education in a Jewish school, later at a Polish *gymnasie*.

Chaya Waga's father had a toy factory. He would sell his products in Russia. With the outbreak of the First World War, the factory had to close. After the war, he began to produce mirrors. He also showed his capabilities in this area. He had a strongly developed sense of invention; he loved to do everything himself. During the later years, his two grown sons helped him. The older one – Moshe – was a yeshiva student until age 15. Later he began to study bookkeeping and still other professions. He had an inclination toward singing and dreamed of becoming a *khazan* [cantor]. He studied with the city *khazan*, Ziskind Rozenblat, later in Abraham Ber Birmboim's school for *khazonim*. However, he ended his studies and again began to work with his father. But, years later, after he married Preger's daughter, Chana, and already had grown children, he again tried to become a *khazan*. He left for Warsaw and there studied in a school for *khazonim*. Coming back to Czenstochow, he prayed in the German *shul* on *Shabbas Chanukah*. A large audience came to hear him and his mother was very proud of her son.

[Page XCVI]

Chaya Waga's young years began with the outbreak of the First World War. The belief that the war would end quickly held the young people back from every cultural activity. The Jewish cultural life of Jewish Czenstochow began some time later, and as Chaya Waga says, the first Jewish lecture by Rafal Federman about Dr. Chaim Szitlowski's, *Jew and Man*, made a deep impression on her. From that moment on, she began reading Yiddish books, was interested in Jewish problems and became close to the Yiddish language. She experienced this period together with her friend, Ester Fuks (today a teacher in Soviet Russia). The professional union of leatherworkers was organized in Czenstochow then. The secretary of the union was Shaul Landa. Under his influence, Chaya Waga and her friend began to help the union with its work. They became librarians in the union library and, in general, took part in the communal work of the union. A large number of the Jewish workers came together around the union, which was then located on Spadek Street. They were involved with varied cultural activities, in which Chaya Waga took an active part. Later an "education union for Jewish workers" was established in Czenstochow. Literary evenings, adult courses and a library and reading room were organized. She worked with her friends, Rafal Federman, Shaul Landa, Jakov Josef Szarnonowiecki, Alkanah Khrabalowski, Mikhal Szlezinger (Dudek), Mikhal Alter, Moshe Weksler, Josef, Szajnweksler, Moshe Berkensztat, Leibish Berkowicz, Fradl Brat, Hershl Gotajner, Shmuel Frank, the Finkelsztajn brothers, Rayzel Frajtag and others. One of the most important tasks was to organize a children's home that later was named after Y. L. Peretz. Chaya Waga was a teacher's aide to Josze Shtam. At the same time, she completed two Frobel courses in Polish under Majge Zalcman. [Friedrich Froebel is the German educator credited with founding kindergarten education.] A year later she took over the leadership of the second children's home – *Fareinikte* ["United"]. She was connected with the children's homes and with the Jewish secular schools in Czenstochow for four years.

(Photo, caption: Leyzer Rotman)

(Photo, caption: the Waga Family)

Chaya Waga met Rafal Federman while doing communal work and became an intimate friend of his and this had a great effect on her and broadened her horizons for communal work. For many years, the mutual friendship strengthened and encouraged her. However, further chances in life changed her way of life. The communal work helped her bear and softened her hard experiences. She led the children's home in Warsaw for three years, one year in Nowo-Radomsk and one year in Grodno, where she also established the children's home.

Chaya Waga also took part in political life simultaneously with her cultural work. She was a member of the *S.S.* [Social Zionists], later *Fareinikte* [United], took part in the professional movement, was a member of the political council and participated in the meetings of the party. She was a candidate in the election to the city council in Czenstochow. After the dissolution of the *Fareinikte* party, she withdrew from political life. The growth and flourishing of the Jewish school system was her ideal. She thought of this period as the finest of her youth.

In 1927 she met B. M. Rotman in Poland, whom she married. They came to America the same year. She worked here for a time in the Sholom-Aleichem Children's Home. Later she traveled to Europe with her husband and they also visited Czenstochow.

Today she lives in New York with her husband and son, Leyzer, who was born in August 1934.

By a miracle, of her family in Poland, her brother, Shlomoh, and his wife, Rena and their son, Ludwig, who hid for 22 months in one of the Czenstochower bunkers, were saved from Hitler's beasts. Her brother also wrote a diary* of over 300 pages about his survival during the Hitler regime in Czenstochow. The remaining members of her family – her parents, her brother, Moshe, and his wife and two children perished during the war. Her youngest sister, Feygele, died after a difficult illness in Bialystok in 1937. Of her hundreds of friends from her hometown, Czenstochow, with whom she was connected for more than half her life, only a few individuals survived.

For her, the coming of Rafal Federman to America at the time of the Second World War as a refugee thanks to the Jewish Workers Committee was a moment of rejoicing in sincere, devoted friendship. She in now active in the United Czenstochower Relief Committee in New York and took part in the publication of the book, *Czenstochower Yidn.*

Max Rozenblat

Son of Haim Shimeon and Chava. Born in Nowo-Radomsk on 1 October 1888. He came to Czenstochow in 1902.

Max Rozenblat lived in Paris for several years; there he married Rochel Gutman and came to America in 1915. He is a member of the Czenstochower Young Men's Society in New York. Their two sons – Haimy, Ph.D. and Benny volunteered to join the American army.

Joe Rozenblat

Son of Haim Shimeon and Chava. Born in Nowo-Radomsk in 1896. He moved to Czenstochow and he came to America on 16 January 1921. He is an active executive member of A.F.F.O. Br. 11, Czentochower United Relief Committee in New York and of the *Czenstochower Yidn* Book Committee, as well as the Kerman-Rozenblat Family Circle. He married Bella Rid.

[Page XCVII]

Sidney Rubin

Son of Yitzhak and Lena. Born on 15 November 1902 in Czenstochow. Came to America in December 1912.

Irving Rubin

Son of Yitzhak and Lena. Born on 14 July 1910 in Czenstochow. Came to America in December 1911.

———

Saul Rubin

Son of Yitzhak and Lena. Born in May 1907 in Czenstochow. Came to America in December 1912.

———

Dovid Rozenfeld
(Photo)

Born in Lodz. He died at the age of 31, while serving in the Russian army in Mukden during the Russo-Japanese War.

Dovid Rozenfeld was the father of Regina Rozenfeld-Kuperman.

———

Moshe Rubel
(Photo)

Son of Zelig and Leah. Died at the age of 82 in Czenstochow.

———

Feyga Rukhel
(Photo)

Daughter of Wolf and Dobra. Died at the age of 82 in Piotrokow.

———

Ziser and Sheindl Rudnicki
(Née Fayner)

They died in Czenstochow.

———

Shlomoh (Sam) Rabinowicz

Son of Mordekhai Yisroel and Sara Gela. Born in 1896 in Sieradz. Came to America from Czenstochow in 1913. He married Yehudis Jarow. His son-in-law, Yitzhak Flekman, served in the American army as a lieutenant.

Klara and Moshe Radosz

Son of Mendel and Breindl. Born in Czenstochow in 1883. Member of the *Arbeter Ring* branch 471. His sons – Alan and Herbert – served in the American army.

(Photo, caption: Moshe Zalman Rozen)

Shmuel Ruk
(Photo)

Born in Czenstochow. His father was a tailor and taught his son the same trade. During the First World War, he, like many others, left for Germany to work. He came to America in 1923. Here he took part in the work of the Czenstochower Relief Committee in New York and also organized and led the Czenstochower Youth Club.

When the Central Committee of *Patronat* was founded in New York in 1933 to support the political arrestees in Poland he was elected secretary and remained in this office until 1935.

A severe illness cut short his young life. He died in May 1935.

Honor his memory!

Yitzhak Rikman
(Photo)

Son of Haim Leib and Meita. Born on 26 December 1880. Came to America in 1900. Member and Vice President of Young Men.

[Page XCVIII]

Ruchl Rikhter
(Photo)

Daughter of Leibish and Brandl Altman. Born in Przyrow on 10 July 1894. Came to America from Canada in September 1914. She was one of the active members of the executive of Czenstochower branch 261 *Arbeter Ring* in New York. Chairlady for a long time of the Czenstochower Ladies Auxiliary and a member of the *Czenstochower Yidn* book committee. She died on 17 December 1944 in New York.

Meir Rembak
(Photo)

Son of Aizik and Keila. Born in Rebielice (Poland) on 25 February 1886. He came to America from London in 1921. In America, he was active in communal life and in the worker's movement. Was involved in the divisions within the Yiddish press on various communal and worker questions. He was an active member of the Czenstochower branch 261 of the *Arbeter Ring* in New York, United Czenstochower Relief in New York and other organizations. He died on 13 December 1943. At his death, the following organizations published resolutions of mourning: Loc. 9, I.L.G.W.U., the Calfiral Mutual Aid Society, *Arbeter Ring*, B. Schlesinger Cloak Finisher Br. Yid. Soc. Union and Medem Club in New York. Before leaving Poland, he lived in Czenstochow and was active in the professional workers movement and for a long time in the General Jewish Worker's *Bund –the Bund*, in Poland.

———

Nathan Rikhter
(Photo)

Son of Hershl and Frimet. Born in Czenstochow on 5 June 1894. Came to America on 25 November 1913. He is an active executive member of the Czenstochower Regional Union in Detroit. His son, Eli, served in the American army.

———

Zalman and Chana Rikhter

In Memory!

———

Dovid Rikhtiger
Chicago
(Photo)

Son of Mordekhai and Ruchl. Born in Czenstochow on 16 October 1890. Came to America in 1909. He is a member of the Bendiner [Bedzin] Society, *Arbeter Ring* branch 176 and the Czenstochower Independent Union in Chicago.

He gave blood to the Red Cross eight times and wife, Roza, four times during the last war. His son, Louis, was a lieutenant in the American army.

———

Broyna Rajch
Detroit
(Photo)

Daughter of Shlomoh and Ester Kolin. Born in 1900 in Myszkow (Poland). Came to America from Czenstochow in 1922. She is a member of the Jewish Fraternal People's Order in Detroit. Her son, Sam, served in the American army.

———

Yehoshua Rikhter
(Photo)

Son of Ezriel and Blima Reyzl. Born in Lisowice (Poland) on 12 October 1913 and came to America in September 1914. He is a member of the Czenstochower branch 261 of the *Arbeter Ring* and of United Czenstochower Relief in New York.

[Page XCIX]

Shin 𝕎

Joe Szaja
Passaic, N.J.
Mordekhai Szaja and his sons

by Morris Szaja

The Szaja family was counted among the oldest families in Czenstochow. Mordekhai "the lathe operator," Szaja's father, presided over a large factory with approximately 50 workers. The factory operated in a primitive manner according to the circumstances of those times. A number of the workers ate and slept at the boss' place, and his wife, who was called "the mother," took care of them.

Mordekhai Szaja was himself an experienced professional and tried to make his children into good professional people. He encouraged his five sons to open their own factories and received assurances from them that they would never become partners nor competitors, because only in this way could they live in peace. Indeed, the oldest son, Itsekl, manufactured chairbacks, rings and medals; Herman – glasses and games; Shayush – tobacco pouches and lighters; Matush – writing pens and pen holders, and Berish – thimbles. They actually remained friends, consulted each other about the conduct of their factories and helped each other.

Hundreds of Jewish workers were employed by the Szajas.

Of the Szajas, only two emigrated to America. One, Moshe (Morris) Szaja, the writer of these lines, a son of Itsekl Szaja, has been in New York since 1920. Here he married a Czenstochower girl – Sera Wajn, a daughter of Grunem Wajn. The second son married Mas' daughter, Nety, here.

There has been no news so far from Czenstochow that someone from the widespread Szaja family saved himself from extinction.

Mota Szapiro
(Photo)

Son of Mendl and Masha. Born in Nowo-Radomsk on 2 January 1893. Came to America in 1913. He married Leah'ke Wales of Kozlowa Ruda [Kazlu Ruda] (Lithuania).

Mota Szapiro is an active member of the Nowo-Radomsker Society, in charge of hospitality for many years; executive member of the Relief Committee since its creation. Was an active member of Patronat for political arrestees in Poland. He belonged to the *S.S.* [Socialist Zionist] party in Radomsk.

(Photo, caption: Leah Szapiro)

(Photo, caption: Szapiro's family in Radomsk)

(Photo: caption: The Szapiro family)

Meir (Szerpinski) Sharp
Chicago

Son of Asher Anshel and Haya. Born in Warsaw on 9 February 1892. He married Lina Granek. Came to America in 1913. He is a member of the *Arbeter Ring* and of the Czenstochower Educational Union.

(Photo, caption: Lina Sharp)

Feigl Szikman

Daughter of Shmuel Borukh and Rywtsha Staszevski. Born in Zarki, Poland. Died in 1918 at the age of 47 in Zurich (Switzerland).

[Page C]

His two sons in Chicago – Sidney and Nathan served in the American army. [Translator's note: this sentence seems to be part of an incomplete entry.]

Mendl Shapiro

Son of Max and Lina. Born in New York on 19 March 1923. Killed in action on 30 June 1944 in India.

The Nowo-Radomsker Society decided to create a Relief Committee in his memory, a fund for orphan children in Europe. The fund already possesses around 1,500 dollars.

It is of added interest that in 1928, while Mendl Shapiro was in Metropolitan Hospital with a serious illness, he helped with the work of publishing the hospital's monthly publication, entitled "Echo." Every month an article of fiction was published about the life of the sick in the hospital. His literary work was praised several times with awards.

Samuel (Shimkhah) Szhukhter
(Photo)

Born in Czenstochow in 1893. He came to America in 1910 and settled in Chicago. He graduated from elementary school, then from high school and in 1914 entered the University of Chicago as a student. He interrupted his education during the First World War and joined the American army with which he fought in France and Germany from 1917 to 1918. In the army, he achieved the rank of lieutenant and was assigned to the "intelligence" division.

In September 1919 he reentered the University of Chicago and graduated as a Doctor of Philosophy with awards in Romance languages in December of the same year.

He later joined the clothing industry where he was active as a labor representative in the executive committee of various well-known clothing firms.

He now lives in Cincinnati, Oh., and is vice president of a large clothing manufacturing business.

During this entire time, he did not forget Czenstochow and on various occasions took part in the aid work for the home of his young years with smaller or larger contributions.

Mendl Szukhter

(Photo)

Mendl Szukhter, the child of a poor shoemaker from Tepergas [Pottery Street] 70 (Garncarska) in Czenstochow, with his intellectual development, education and place in communal life with the Jewish masses in Czenstochow, and then in America – occupies a place of honor among his brothers, comrades, friends and fellow fighters.

His name was a symbol of idealism, friendship and bond with his people and devotion to his ideal until the last minute of his life.

In the middle of all of the currents and storms of life that swept right and left – from S.S. (Socialist Zionists) to the general *Poalei-Zion* Party to the left *Poalei-Zion* and in the end – to the Communist Party – he remained the same: Prometheus, who is riveted to the earth of Jewish life, the dreams in the ghetto, the struggle for the survival of the Jewish people and for a new, free and healthy Jewish life.

He was the type from the Jewish multitudes who tore himself from the suffocating conditions and narrowness of the ghetto to a freer place on God's earth, equal to all of the people of the world.

* * *

Mendl Szukhter was born in 1890 or 1891. His father was already an old man. And his mother died when he was still a young boy. He literally became a child of loneliness and need.

When still in his youth, Mendl began to study to be a tailor. In 1905, at age 15 or 16, he became one of the pioneers in the workers' group *S.S.* [Socialist Zionists] that was organized by Josef Kruk and Yitzhak Gurski. He left for London during the same year. He returned to Czenstochow a year later.

He was arrested in 1908 during an ambush by the police at the *S.S.* printing shop and in 1909 exiled to Siberia. He succeeded in escaping from there and after a short time arrived in America and settled in Chicago. Here he began to work with cloaks and threw himself into union activity with fervor, where he became one of the leaders.

(Photo, caption: Moshe Szwajcer)

At the same time he became active in the American *S.T.* (Socialist Territorialist) organization and one of the first pioneers of the Yiddish Radical School that the *S.S.* and *P.Z.* created. After the Balfour Declaration, he and the majority of the *S.T.* organization in America joined the *Poalei-Zion* party and, after the split, moved to the left *Poalei-Zion* and became one of its leaders.

The difficult situation of the Jewish masses in Europe after the First World

[Page CI]

War – the pogroms in Ukraine and in Poland – caused him to throw himself into the work of organizing public meetings in America against the pogroms and persecution. He became one of the most important leaders in the relief work and occupied an eminent place on the People's Relief Committee. In 1920 he was sent as a delegate to an aid conference in Berlin, visited Poland and brought along aid for a large number of people and communal institutions.

His visit to Europe – where he met face to face with the misfortune that the First World

(Photo: Mendl Szukhter at a meeting with *landsleit*)

War had left behind and with the need and suffering of the masses – made a deep impression on him and pushed him toward the left in the workers' movement. He became one of the organizers of the Jewish Workers Aid Committee and a fervid supporter of the Soviet Union. The Jewish colonization in the Soviet Union and the proclamation of a Jewish Autonomous Region in Biro-Bidjan inspired him. He became one of the founders of ICOR [organization of Yiddish speaking working class immigrants] and a member of its national executive.

However, simultaneously with communal work, he did not stop educating himself. He entered the University of Chicago. At first, he intended to study agronomy, but he later studied law (jurisprudence) – until he graduated as a lawyer in 1924. He was a teacher in a Yiddish school in a town near Chicago during the last of his studies.

As a lawyer, his popularity as a communal activist and campaigner for workers grew from day to day. He became an advocate and fighter for the rights of the masses, of the trade union movement and of everyone who needed legal help.

The Jewish masses in those years were more predisposed to the leftist movement. Mendl Szukhter, like hundreds of others, went with the storm, and in 1927 officially joined the Communist Party.

His glory and name as a communal activist and devoted comrade grew with the waves of the leftist movement. However, the year of crisis came in 1929 and the beginning of his tragic end.

During the attacks by Arabs on the Jewish settlements in *Eretz-Yisroel*, he had to appear at a mass meeting to justify the stand of the Communist Party in connection with the events there. However, he refused to do so and, therefore, was barred from the party. As a result he lost all of his communal support and began to fall from his communal pedestal.

However, later he again was taken into the party. Broken both spiritually and physically, he spent several months in a sanitorium, stopped practicing law and could no longer regain his strength.

His last salvation, where he believed he had found his footing, was his activity as a field organizer for ICOR. While in a town near New York, he did not feel so well and was taken to a hospital and there immediately died.

His name, his memory as a dear comrade from whom always radiated idealism, comradely love and boundless devotion to his people will never be forgotten.

Tovya Szuldinger
Detroit

Son of Dovid and Feigl. Born in Czenstochow on 15 September 1901. He came to America in 1920. He is a member of the Czenstochower Regional Union in Detroit.

Ahron Szuldinger
Detroit

Son of Moshe and Ruchl. Born in Janow in 1988 [Translator's note: most likely the date should be 1898.]. Came to America from Czenstochow on 29 March 1906. He is a member of the Zionist Organization. Married Gitl (Katy) Balantsow.

Joe Shumer
(Godl Szmulewicz)
Detroit

Son of Mordekhai and Mali. Born in Czenstochow in 1906. Came to America in 1921. He is a member of the Jewish National Union in Detroit.

Sam Shumer
(Shmuel Szmulewicz)
Detroit

Son of Mordekhai and Mali. Born in Czenstochow in 1907. Came to America in 1921. He is a member of the Jewish National Union in Detroit.

[Page CII]

Sholom Shumer (Szmulewicz)
Chicago

Son of Mordekhai Beinish and Mata. Born in Czenstochow on 5 July 1901. He married Gitl Gritz. Came to America in 1923. He is a member of the Czenstochower Education Society in Chicago.

Haim Leib Szwarc
(Photo)

Born in Rozprza, near Czenstochow, on 15 August 1883. The information is not certain because at that time for various reasons his parents neglected to report his birth at the correct moment. However, Haim Leib comes from Czentochow. The fact that he was born in Rozprza is the result of this: his father, Avigdor *Brukasz* [paver], at the time when Haim Leib's mother was in her last months of pregnancy, was at the court of the Rozpra rebbe paving the courtyard [Translator's note: most likely with cobblestones] and she came there to bring Haim Leib into the world. His *bris* [ritual circumcision] took place in the rebbe's court.

Haim Leib is descended from the Zigases. One of his uncles was a cantonist [forced to serve in the Russian army for 25 years]. A part of his family, as well as his brother, who received the name Bruder at a hearing in a Russian customs office, emigrated to America in the 1880's and here the divided clan branched out. This was the time when the Czenstochower *shul* named *Chasam Sopher* and the organization, Young Men, were founded. In 1904/05, additional members of the Zigas family came to America, many of them brought over by their relatives and parents. In the end they were held in great reverence and respect by their children. There has been no sign of life from those who remained in Poland.

(Photo, caption: Lina Szwarc)

(Photo, caption: Haim Leib Swarc's mother)

(Photo, caption: H. L. Swarc's wife and their daughter)

Only one, Harcke Zigar (Mendl's son), was saved. He was brought to America by the Jewish Worker's Committee and today he is in New York.

Haim Leibele raised himself in the streets of Czenstochow. It was during his childhood on Czike Street that he first showed his mischievousness and agility. He received the nickname Jaba [frog in Polish]. Haim Leibele began to go to *kheder* at age five. His *malamed* [teacher] was Yitzhak Kraser, a strict, angry Jew. However, Haim Leibele did not study with him for long. Instead of sitting in the *kheder*, he went around on the streets, to the old market and there hid himself as an assistant. This led to his father taking him away from Yitzhak the *malamed* and taking him to the new *Talmud Torah* to Tovya the *malamed*. However, Toyva did not have time to teach the children and in the meantime Haim Leibele helped a Christian potter make clay whistles. At age eight Haim Leibele became an assistant to another *malamed* – Reb Abraham'le. However, here, too, he exhibited his mischievousness and performed various pranks. At 11 he began to work in Mordekhai Dreksler's and Godl Wajnberg's factory for 45 *kopeks* a week for a workday from 6 in the morning to 9 at night.

In 1896, still not 13 years old, Haim Leibele began to work with a house painter – Ahron Goldberg. After a year of working, he already demonstrated the ability to paint a house and at age 14 he was earning three rubles a week. A short time later, a master painter took him to work in Bendin (Bedzin). Because of a grievance over wages that Haim Leibele had with the master painter and because of disputes that arouse from this, he crossed the Austrian border illegally and after wandering for a short time, he went to Krakow. Here he became a suspect and was detained by the police. However, after questioning in Czenstochow, he was freed. Despite the difficult winter, he traveled further, to Vienna. On the way he worked for a short time in Bilitz [Bielsko-Biala]. Then he arrived in Vienna. On Rosh Hashanah, he returned to Czenstochow. Absorbed with socialism and ideals of freedom from the other side of the border, Haim Leibele began to look for literature of this kind. His first step was to Henokh Lapidus. And here he met his current friend, Abo Kojfman. Haim Leibele began to write songs. This prevented him from being persecuted by the Czenstochower scoundrels. In addition, he was protected by his friends: Josef Hirsz Grajcer, Khasriel Stodola, Yakov Ber Zilber, Lipa Goldblum and Mordekha'le Beker. Haim Leibele began to take an interest in Yiddish theater. He would give recitations in the garden and even play roles. He brought actors – Pjornik, the blond Tzlava and Akslerod. He then began to write, to read and to paint. From this he earned money to support his sick father.

[Page CIII]

In 1904 he married Moshe Poznanski's daughter, Odl, and settled in Zurich. A short time later, he came back to Czenstochow. He led the first strike of the painters and won it. During the same year, when the Russian-Japanese War broke out, Haim Leibele escaped to his wife's uncle in Katowice. However, he was only there for a few days and he traveled further – to Mahrisch Ostrau [now Moravska Ostrava in Moravia, the Czech Republic] (then Austria). There he was welcomed by a committee for emigrants and after a short time became an active worker; he helped many of his own *landsleit*, who would pass through on their way to England, America, and so on. However, he did not remain in Mahrisch Ostrau for very long and in 1905 he arrived in London. He spent difficult days there. However, by chance he met several *landsleit*: Stadala – Ratbard, Yakov Ber Silver, Dovid Gotlib and others. He began to work as a painter with Gostinski (a brother of Gostinski in Czenstochow), at first earned three, then eight shillings a day and brought his friend Dovid Gotlib to work with him. Although there already were Czenstochower *landsleit* in London, such as Jankl Szakher's son, Avraham Wolf, Avraham Ber Muszin, Rivek Kantor and others, Haim Leibele joined with others and, in 1906, he was one of the co-founders of the Jewish Socialist Club. He gave theater performances among other activities organized by the club.

In 1906, Haim Leibele traveled to Canada. He came to Toronto where he met his friends, Moshe Dovid and Ahron – Czenstochower painters. He worked a short time in Toronto and in 1907 he came to New York. From the start, he went through very difficult times here. First he worked as a bread hauler, took part in a strike to bring the bread haulers into the bakery union and was one of those who led the strike to victory.

In 1908 he met Abo Kojfman and together they founded branch 251 of the *Arbeter Ring*. In 1914 he was one of the co-founders of the Czenstochower Aid Union and in 1916 he became its chairman. In 1922 he traveled as a delegate to Czenstochow with L. Szimkowicz with instructions to research conditions in the Jewish school-children's home named for Y. L. Peretz.

He moved to Chicago after 1925. Here he was one of the co-founders of the Czenstochower Aid Union; he was also in Detroit with instructions from the Relief Committee in New York.

In 1932 he moved to Los Angeles. Here he began his literary activity in the *Arbeter [Ring]* – he was very active in creating a dramatic section. He was one of the co-founders of an aid committee for Polish arrestees in Czenstochow with Joe Sztibl, Dovid and Yochoved Izrael, Harry Grauman, Fefer and Lina Szwarcz. Dr. Zanwil Klein joined later. The first organizing meeting took place on 10 May 1933. He also took part in the founding of the Food Workers Union. He was arrested for organizing a strike. However, after the trial, he was freed. He and his wife, Leah*, were very active in founding the Czenstochower Aid Union in Los Angeles. In 1936 he visited Honolulu and wrote a series of songs. He returned to Honolulu eight weeks later.

[*Translator's note: Earlier, her name is given as Odl.]

In 1938 he became one of the directors of the Central Jewish Committee and editor of the newspaper, *Town Fair News*.

In 1939 he visited Portland. Here he created more songs.

In 1941 he was in Chicago again.

Today he lives in Seattle, Washington with his wife, Leah, and his daughter, Beverly. Although far from his Czenstochower *landsleit* [countrymen], he is still bound with his most noble feelings to his birthplace and he dedicates much of his literary work to her and supports the Czentochowers in every way possible.

Yakob Stiller
Chicago

Son of Haim and Elka. Born in Klobutzk [Klobuck] on 10 September 1884. He marred Miriam Livak. Came to America in September 1910. He is a member of the Czenstochower Educational Society in Chicago.

Beverly Szwarc
(Photo)

Daughter of Haim-Leib and Leah. Born in 1930. She graduated from high school and is now studying in college.

Beverly Szwarc shows great poetic abilities. One of her poems is *Rosh Hashanah*, written in English and translated by H.L. Szwarc.

I

Today is *yom-tom* [holiday] across the world
There is a shiver in every heart
Rosh Hashanah:
My people stream from every street
And wish *l'shana tova tikatevu* [may you be inscribed for a good year]!

II

Tears appear pearl-like
From a people who struggle for their land:
The witness remains today
The *koysel-maarovi* [Western or Wailing] Wall.

III

The land of milk and honey
In the land of my holy patriarchs;
In the land where blood flowed,
Slaughtered, burned without compassion.

Morris Szwarc
(Pen name – Morris Swan)
(Photo)

Son of Louis Szwarc. Born in New York on 19 January 1908. Joined the American army on 22 May 1943. Chosen to write biographies of military leaders in Washington. In 1944 chosen as the editor of the army newspaper, *Wings*. Held this post for seven months. In addition to this, Morris Swan wrote the editorials in the newspaper, *Keep Them Flying* and various articles for the newspaper, *Alert*. An artist and the daughter of a famous musician, Mr. Leo Birchanski, and Mrs. Betty Birchanski, a former principal in a high school in Odessa, Nora is the wife of Morris Swan.

[Page CIV]

(Photo, caption: Morris Szwarc with his wife and child)

Morris Swan was the literary editor of the *News Press* in Santa Barbara from 1937 to 1939. Simultaneously he was the editor of the Y.P. Rouny publishing house in the same state. Later he was called to *The New York Times* to be the literary critic. He held this post until he was called into the army.

He recently completed the historical novel, *Margin of Ruin*, which will soon be published.

Zanwel Szwiderski
(Photo)

Son of Yakov and Dobra. Born in Sieradz (Poland). Died at age 78, two days before Yom Kippur in 1937 in Czenstochow.

Odel Szwiderski
(Photo)

Daughter of Lipman and Feiga Lurisz. Born in Praszka (Poland). Died at age 81 in 1938 in Czenstochow.

Abraham Sztibel
Los Angeles, Cal.

Son of Wolf and Beila. Born on 22 October 1892 in Czenstochow. Came to America in 1912. As a result of serving in the American army during the First World War, he became the commandant of the American Legion Post 394 in the state of Iowa. He supported the Czenstochower Relief Committee and the institutions that were assisted by it during his time in America. He is one of the founders of the Czentochower Aid Union in Los Angeles.

His son, Sidney, was a corporal in the American army.

Jack Sztibel
(Photo)

Son of Wolf and Beila. Born in Czenstochow on 28 August 1898. Came to America in 1928. His only son is named Joseph Barry.

In Czenstochow, Jack Sztibel belonged to the socialist Zionist party, *Fareinikte* [United]. In America, he became active in the Chicago Relief Committee in Los Angeles – one of the organizers of the Czenstochower *Patronat* for political prisoners in Poland and treasurer until the last minute of his life. He died on 30 May 1940 in Los Angeles.

Mordekhai Sztajer
Chicago

Son of Dovid and Ruchl. Born in Czenstochow in 1887. Came to American in 1911. His son, Henry David, served in the American army.

Hirshl Sztencel
(Photo)

The father of Mordekhai and Kopel. Died in Czenstochow in 1927.

Hana Sztencel

The mother of Mordekhai and Kopel. Died in Czenstochow in 1927.

Kopel Sztencel
(Photo)

Son of Hershl and Hany Ita. Born in Czenstochow on 5 July 1884. Came to America from Krakow in 1911. He is a member of the Independent Lodzer Society in Brooklyn.

[Page CV]

Mordekhai Josef Sztencel

Son of Hershl and Hana Ita. Born in Czenstochow on 4 May 1877. He married Ruchl Gliksman in 1902. Came to America on 31 July 1914. He is a member of the Independent Lodzer Society in Brooklyn. His son, Hyman, was a sergeant in the American army.

A. Sztencel

A Czenstochower poet celebrates *oyneg Shabbos* [Translator's note: literally, joy of *Shabbos*; often a gathering at which lectures are given or discussions are held] in London's Whitechapel

...It would be a sin for me, if I did not give special honor to the few individuals in London who toil with heartbreaking drudgery in order to maintain a burning literary light in the darkness of Jewish life in England.

The caring A. Sztencel is such a passionate toiler for Yiddish.

He is a Don Quixote of Yiddish, a *lamed-vovnik* [Translator's note: according to tradition, one of the 36 secret saints upon whom the survival of the world depends] of Yiddish.

He is the water carrier and wood chopper of the Yiddish word in London.

He is extremely eloquent in his love for Yiddish, zeal for Yiddish and, as a poet himself, in his Yiddish misery.

A believer in Yiddish literature, he feels, however, as a poet, the tragedy of the Yiddish language.

He publishes monthly notebooks, *Loshn un Lebn* [*Language and Life*] with great effort and financial hardship and the title itself indicates his great effort in its preparation with the help of Moshe Over and his devotion to the struggle to strengthen the position of the neglected Yiddish language in London.

I saw the embodiment of his passionate, self-sacrificing devotion to Yiddish and to Yiddish literature when we unexpectedly came to his small salon somewhere in devastated Whitechapel on the day of *Shabbos*, during the week of Passover, where he, Sztencel, led a weekly *oyneg Shabbos*.

He has been holding an interesting *oyneg Shabbos* for a long time, week in and week out. There could be thunder and lightening; bombs could fall on Whitechapel – he, Sztencel would not relinquish the hour when an audience of 100 people gathered as a result of his persistence to spend time with him in an atmosphere of Yiddish language, of Yiddish literature and of Yiddish music.

He organizes lectures on Jewish history for the group, celebrates literary holidays with the group, etc.

This picture, which was revealed before me, when we entered unexpectedly, was both stirring and emotionally moving.

The audience – 100 people, as said – consisted principally of the strata of older, ordinary Jews. The majority of them sat in caps. Women, several of them almost old women, wore kerchiefs.

Particularly from this fact alone, one can and one must be moved:

Simple people, Jewish people, come during the day on *Shabbos* to hear a Yiddish work from a Yiddish poet as they would once come to hear a preacher.

Halevay [may God grant] that there were more such gatherings. However the distress actually lies in the *halevay*.

Barely, 100 elderly people in a large London community.

We cannot fill our hearts with optimism concerning Yiddish in London from this.

I felt a cutting compassion for our Yiddish.

I also feel it in New York. But in New York the writers permit themselves, may they be strengthened, to display self confidence as if greatly insulted, like the stubbornness of captains who will not give up their ships even when mortal danger hovers over their ships. They believe after all in the ship and in the strength of their own belief more than in the power of the danger.

The Yiddish gathering of huddled together old Jews, from around the crushed streets, made an impression on me of a homeless multitude of souls who want to revive each other with their own little bit of loneliness.

I said to myself bluntly and harshly:

This, it seems, is the situation.

When I left, my heart quickly became filled more and more with deep respect and limitless reverence for the knight of Yiddish – for Sztencel, who was left behind in the little salon –

although he strongly wanted to accompany me – to complete until the end the love-deprived, sweet-lonely *oyneg Shabbos*.

H. Levik

Yakov Szternberg
(Photo)

Son of Sholem and Ruchl. Born in Czenstochow. Came to America in 1922. He was a member of the Czenstochower Neighborhood Educational Society in Chicago and was active in the Czenstochower Relief Committee. Died at the age of 38 in Chicago in 1935. He was married to Mrs. Jonel.

Haim Szternberg

Son of Sholem and Ruchl. Born in Czenstochow in 1899. Came to America (Chicago) in 1920 and married his wife, Miriam, here. They have three children. He is a member of the Chicago Painter's Union local 275, member of the Chicago Czenstochower Independent Union and the International People's Order.

Natan (Nathan) Szternberg
Chicago
(Photo)

Son of Sholem and Ruchl. Born in Czenstochow on 12 May 1902. He married Sylvia Lipman. Came to America from *Eretz-Yisroel* on the 15th August 1923. He is a member of the People's Order and of the Czenstochower Independent Union in Chicago.

[Page CVI] (mistakenly printed as CXVI in book)

Morris Stern

Son of Shimkha Binem and Reizl. Born in Tomaszow Mazowiecki (Poland) on 17 July 1893. Came to America on 15 August 1912. He is the financial secretary of the Czenstochower branch 261 *Arbeter Ring* in New York. His two sons – Sidney and Louis – served in the American army.

Kopel Szczekacz
(Photo)

Born in Czenstochow in 1848. When he was 20 years old he was taken into the Russian army in the times of Aleksander II. There he graduated from non-commissioned officer's school and became a sergeant-major. Took part in the Russian-Turkish War. When he was about 33 years old, he returned and became the *shamos* [sexton] in the old synagogue, where he remained for 45 years. He loved to speak about military things and was happy when people listened to his stories. He also took upon himself the duty of teaching children how to say *kaddish* [prayer for the dead]. In this way, he taught about 250 children. Under the Nazis he became the *Juden-Eltster* [Nazi term for the head of the area *Judenrat*]. Greetings still arrived from him in February 1941. Since then there has been no further news about him. He could have still lived for many years. He has a son, Mikhal Szczekacz, in Tel Aviv.

Grunem Szimkowicz

Born in Czenstochow in 1876. Came to America in 1886.

Harold Szimkowicz

(Photo)

Son of Grunem and Cilia. Born on 4 April 1915, died on 30 July 1940.

Was a member of the George Hamilton Lodge 456 of the Knights of Pythias.

Leibl (Lou) Szimkowicz

[Translator's note: The names Leibl and Lou are used interchangeably in this biography.]

(Photo)

Son of Aizik and Chana. Born in Czenstochow in 1866. His parents were middle class people. His father was a tailor. In 1883 his father left Czenstochow and went to America. Leibl Szimkowicz was born in Czentochow and received an elementary education in a Russian public school. His teachers were Sapocznik and Meyerson. After graduating from the school, he learned a trade – as a goldsmith – and worked until he was drafted into the Russian army. His uncle, Haim, sent ship tickets and Leibl and his mother, Chana, brother, Grunem and sisters, Ruchl and Bentshe left for America in the summer of 1886.

Leibl Szimkowicz belongs to the Czenstochower synagogue on Clinton Street, New York, to which his father also belonged.

His was forced to leave his father's house because he had to work on *Shabbos*. He worked with jewelry. At age 25, he married Chaya Gotayner, born in Czenstochow, who died on 26 February 1920, leaving four orphans (two sons and two daughters). [Translator's note: the Yiddish word for orphan is *yosem* and can refer to someone who has lost one parent.]

Later, Lou Szimkowicz joined the Yiddish theater business, managed the vaudeville theater and movie house on Sutter Avenue, Brownsville and in 1898 he managed the Yiddish theater on Delancey Street, New York. He attracted benefits to Brooklyn, Sigel Street, and the Lyric Theater in 1918-1919. The famous artists Jacob Adler, Kessler, Scheingold, [Helen] Bida of Czenstochow, Mr. and Mrs. Goldberg, Mr. and Mrs. Jacobs and others performed in his theaters. He is still involved in the Yiddish theater business.

Leibl Szimkowicz was one of the founders of the Czenstochower Young Men, member of the Czenstochower Synagogue, founder of the Czenstochower Relief Committee and of the Ladies Auxiliary. He was elected as delegate to Czenstochow after the First World War to plan the rebuilding the Y. L. Peretz House children's homes and the Jewish public school. He is a member of the *Czentochower Yidn* book committee and ex-chairman of the Relief Committee.

His two grandsons served in the American army.

George Szimkowicz
(Photo)

Son of Louis and Hela. Died at the age of 21 in New York on 15 September 1916.

———

[Page CVII]

Celia Szimkowicz
(née Gotayner)

Born in Czenstochow in 1877. Married Louis Szimkowicz in 1901.

———

Khanina Szajer
(Photo)

Son of Yehuda Meir and Leah Szajer. Born in Czenstochow on 15 May 1882. Came to America 1906. Married Reizl Silver, the daughter of Yeshayahu Eleizer Silver, 1908. He is a member of the Zionist Organization in Passaic, New Jersey. His son, Julius, was a doctor in the American army.

———

Leah Szajer

Born in Krzepice, near Czenstochow in 1859. Died 1921. Mother of Khanina, Fradl, Mordekhai, Dovid, Rachel, Ester, Moshe and Josef.

Honor her memory.

———

Shlomoh Meir Szlingboim
Jackson Heights, N.J.*
(Photo)

[*Translator's note: Jackson Heights is located in New York City, in the borough of Queens, not in New Jersey]

Son of Yehoshya and Ester-Malka. Born on 14 December 1893 in Warsaw. He lived in Czenstochow for a long time and came to America on 28 August 1912.

Shlomoh Szlingboim is a member of the Czenstochower branch of the International Workers Order.

———

Shlomoh Szlezinger
Chicago

Son of Avraham Leib and Haya. Born in Czenstochow on 7 February 1885. He married Hendl Przerowski. He came to America from Germany in 1921.

Shlomoh Szlezinger is a member of the Czenstochower Educational Union in Chicago. His wife, Hendl, is active in the Bendiner (Bedzin) Ladies Auxiliary and is the treasurer of the

Czenstochower Aid Society in Chicago. She is among the most active workers. Their two sons – Kurt and Morris – served in the American army.

Golda Szmulewicz
Chicago
(Photo)

Daughter of Morton and Elise Szeradski. Born in Radomsk on 18 September 1889. Lived for many years in Czenstochow. Came to America July 1904. Member of the Ladies Support and Sisterhood *Bnei Yisroel.*

Feitl Szmulewicz
(Photo)

In 1904 – at age 16-17 (a worker in Wajnberg's factory), he was drawn into the movement for freedom and became a member of the *S.S* [Social Zionist] Party. He excelled with his earnestness and dedication to the Jewish socialist ideals.

(Photo, caption: Mendl Szmulewicz)

(Photo, caption: F. Szmulewicz's mother)

(Photo, caption: Feitl Szmulewicz in the service of the Home Guard)

After the years 1905-6, when only a small group of the great *S.S.* masses remained, Feitl Szmulewicz was still devoted to idea [of Social Zionism] and was one of the most active in the group. He was a person of deeds. He was one of the founders and most active member of the Yiddish Literary Society and later – *Lira* [a singing organization]. Helped found the Jewish library and for many years was its librarian. He also eagerly helped with the creation of the Yiddish press in Czenstochow. One of his feature articles in the *Czenstochower Vokhnblat* [*Czenstochow Weekly Newspaper*] was: "In What Do Jews Rejoice."

[Page CVII]

F. Sz. was one of the founders of and a committee member of the communal bakery at the time of the First World War and the secretary of the "educator's union" that was the cover of the Social Zionists under the German occupation.

In 1916 he was sent to work by the Germans and arrived in Breslau [Wroclaw]. He met many Jewish workers there, founded a cultural union with a reading room, arranged readings and so on.

In 1918 when Jewish mass emigration through Germany began, he contacted the Jewish delegation in Paris and founded an information bureau for emigrants.

When *O.R.T.* was moved to Berlin, he founded a division in Breslau, with the help of Ahron Singalowski.

In 1920 he founded a division of the Berlin *Mizrekh Yidishn Farband* [Eastern Jewish Union], became its longtime president, arranged one gathering, was elected a delegate to all of the meetings of the union, founded a Yiddish newspaper for eastern Jews – *Undzer Lebn* [*Our Life*] – took an active part in the *kehile* elections where a Czenstochower Jew was elected as the representative of the eastern Jews and F. Sh. became a member of the cultural commission of the Breslauer Jewish community.

In 1922, when the Polish government deprived a number of Jewish emigrants of their civil rights, he took part in the founding of an association of the homeless and with the help of Matskin, the representative of the People's Bund, of the Jewish National Council in Warsaw and personal intervention by the Polish Consul – succeeded in restoring the civil rights for many of the Polish Jews who were then living in Germany.

In 1933, when Hitler came to power and the expulsion of Polish Jews from Germany began, he traveled to Warsaw to intervene with the refugee committee concerning the matter. When he returned, he, too, was expelled and he decided to go to *Eretz-Yisroel.*

Employed in the glass trade – here he became the chairman of the section for many years and wrote a series of articles about the problems of the craftworkers for the only Yiddish newspaper – *Ney Velt* [*New World*]. He became a member of the Yiddish literary and journalist club; worked with the country's YIVO committee; took an active part in the activities of the Czenstochower *landsmanschaftn* [organization of people from the same town] as secretary of the national council under the chair of Dr. Josef Kruk.

One of the first in its service, he joined the "Home Guard" at its creation for national protection and remains there.

His two sons serve the community – one as a *gapir* [Turkish word meaning unofficial armed guard], the second, a member of an agricultural *kibbutz.*

He took an active part in the publication of the book, *Czenstochower Yidn,* as the secretary of the Czenstochower "Home Guard," both with his own articles and by editing the articles of a whole series of *landsleit* in *Eretz-Yisroel.*

————

Louis (Leizer) Szklarczik
Chicago

Son of Hershl and Leah. Born in Radomsk in 1894. Came from Czenstochow to America in 1912. He is an executive member of the Educational Society in Chicago.

————

Yehieil Szpic

Son of Josef and Fradl. Born in Dzialoszyn. He died in Breslau (Germany).

————

Race Szpic

Daughter of Yitzhak and Reizl Khaskel. Died in Krzepice (Poland).

————

Wolf and Hana Szpigelman

(Photo, caption: Wolf Szpigelman)

(Photo, caption: Hana Szpigelman)

Both were born in Czenstochow. Their name was well known in Czenstochow because of their charitable work. Wolf died in 1912 and Hana in 1932.

————

Josef Szpigelman

Son of Wolf and Hana. Born in Czenstochow. He now lives in Detroit. Received a *gymnazie* education, also studied Yiddish and Hebrew with the famous pedagogue, Reb Eliezer Klinecki, of blessed memory, author of the books *Songs of Praise* and *HaHaim haKhodeshim*.

He left Czenstochow in 1910, because he did not want to serve in the Russian army. He visited Czenstochow in 1931.

Max Szpigelman
Detroit

Son of Wolf and Hana. Born on 5 May 1905 in Czenstochow. Came to America June 1921. In Czenstochow, he was a managing committee member of the Jewish Tour and Sports Union.

[Page CIX]

Supplementary [Biographies]

Shlomoh Zalman Goldberg
(Photo)

Born in Czenstochow in 1862; died there in 1916.

Bluma Goldberg
(Photo)

Born in 1866; died in America in 1940.

Parent of Louis Goldberg.

Barnet Gross
(Photo)

Son of Wolf and Gitl Gric. Born in Czenstochow on 4 May 1883. Came to America in 1906. Died in Los Angeles on 9 July 1937. Husband of Szprinca and father of Gladys, Fritzy, Lila and Willy.

Wolf Grosman
(Photo)

Born in Lelew (Poland). He died in 1925 at the age of 60 in Czenstochow.

Shlomoh (Sol) Grynberg
(Photo)

His closeness to Czenstochow comes not only because his wife, Nekha Szpic, may she rest in peace, was a Czenstochower, but also because Sol Grynberg, the communal worker, the philanthropist, the Jew, the man – is always here, when there is aid activity for Jews, all the more when it is for Czenstochow.

Born in Noworadomsk [Radomsko] in 1873, the fourth son of Shmuel and Sheindl, he experienced want, need and poverty. The poverty of his parents in his home was so great that Shlomoh'le had to stop studying at the *kheder* [religious elementary school] at age 12 because the tuition could not be paid for him. He was forced to leave his home and go into the world to seek a purpose.

Shlomoh'le came to Lodz, studied the goldsmith trade for three years, and being by nature very capable, he later found work in Bendin [Bedzin] where he spent a long time. He took his first step in communal and cultural work in Bendin, organizing a theater troupe and, after a time, returned to Noworadomsk.

In 1899 he married Nekha Szpic of Czenstochow, settled in Radomsk, took an active part in the communal life of the city and won many friends.

An incident that took place in Noworadomsk during the Russo-Japanese War in the years 1904-05 made a strong impression on Shlomoh Grynberg and as a result of this, he decided to leave his birthplace and go to America. He came here in 1905 with his wife, Nekha. Like every immigrant at that time, he went through the thorny road of the "shop." His persistence, his energy did not let him remain at the "shop" for long and after a short time, he became independent – he became the pioneer and founder of the Diamond Center on the Bowery in New York.

In time Sol Grynberg attained his financial position and this gave him the ability to develop widespread philanthropic and communal activities.

It is impossible to enumerate in a short biography the support and help that Sol Grynberg gave. A part of his work:

Beginning with individual support for friends, acquaintances and family in general and individual members in particular, there is almost no philanthropic institution in New York that did not share in his support for Jews in general and for his *landsleit* in particular throughout the years. We will state by virtue of the Noworadomsker Relief documents and bulletins that even non-Jews from his birthplace found in Sol Grynberg a person with a heart and through his generosity he won the friendship of the Christian population in Radomsk. Sol Grynberg's high ethical position can be shown by the fact that he even forgave the people with whom he had grievances because they were purely business matters.

[Page CX]

(Photos, caption: Signs of appreciation for S. Grynberg)

The Noworadomsker Relief has not yet reported fully in its publications on the activities of Sol Grynberg as a relief worker. It is first being written and will shortly be published.

We will provide here several extracts from the Golden [Anniversary] Book of the Noworadomsker Society, in which Sol Grynberg was celebrated:

38 *landsleit* and friends wrote about just a small part of his activities as a relief worker.

Hundreds of greetings from Jewry and from organizations; also a personal greeting from the late President, Franklin Delano Roosevelt, to Grynberg, for his help in selling War Bonds.

35 Jewish soldiers with a connection to Noworadomsk thanked Grynberg for his activity on their behalf during the time of war and after their return from the army.

The Federation of Polish Jews in America sent him a thank you letter (signed by Binyamin Winter) for his activity on behalf of Polish Jews.

Various pictures by artists as acknowledgement of his work decorate his house.

Talmud Torahs [schools for the poor], poor and bare footed children, *gmiles khesed* [interest-free loan] funds and other institutions were and today are still supported by him.

Here in America he belongs to the following organizations:

Founder and father of *Beis Lekhem Eni'im* [organization to provide food for the poor] in Manhattan and the Bronx; American Jewish Congress; *Madiner Bal Tzedakah*; Hebrew House for Invalids; Ladies Old Age Home; Bronx Society; *Va'ad Hatzalah* [Rescue Committee]; Hebrew Children's House; Congregation *Beis Yosef*; Congregation *Sher Tefilah* and a series of other, approximately 41, institutions.

Shortly after the liberation of Radomsk, he contributed $5,000 to a fund drive to rebuild his birthplace, Noworadomsk.

Today he lives in New York.

[Page CXI]

Nekha Grynberg

Daughter of Mordekhai and Ita Szpic. Born in 1871 in Czenstochow. Came to America in 1905. She belonged to Radomsker Relief, to the Radomsker Society and to various philanthropic societies. Died in 1836 in New York.

Samuel Gryn

Son of Josef and Cyrl. Born in Klobuck on 28 November 1881. He marred Frances Kawa. Came to America from Warsaw in 1907. He is a member of the Proszker Society and of United Czenstochower Relief in New York. His son, Jacob was a lieutenant and his second son, Arthur, a private in the American army.

Gershon Gryn
(Photo)

Son of Leib and Chana. Born in Czenstochow on 29 February 1896. Came to America in 1912. He married Sara Mularcz. Was a member of the Czentochower Young Men and of United Czenstochower Relief in New York. He died on 29 April 1939 in New York.

Sara Gryn

Daughter of Henekh and Beila Mularcz. Born in Koniecpol on 30 November 1896. Came to America on 17 February 1914. Married Joe Gryn [Translator's note: Joe is probably the name Gershon assumed in America]. She is a member of the Czenstochow Young Men's Society and one of the active co-workers of United Czenstochower Relief in New York and the Ladies Auxiliary. Her sons, Jesse, a sergeant, and Bernard, private, served in the American army.

Bernard (Bronek) Horowicz

Son of Yitzhak and Sheva Gliksman-Horowicz. Born on 14 February 1935. Suffered the fate of the martyrs during the years 1939-1945.

Aleksander Z. Haptka
(Photo)

Son of Tuvya and Salomea. Born in Czenstochow in 1893. Came to America in 1941. Belongs to the National Organization of Polish Jews. In Poland, he was a speaker about Jewish matters at the Interior Ministry until the war.

(Photo, caption: Ala Haptka)

Born in Zarki (Poland) in 1907.

Israel Warszawski
Chicago

Son of Dovid Shmuel and Bluma. Born in Czenstochow on 13 August 1891. Came to America in 1913.

Mendl Warszawski

Son of Avraham and Malka. Born in Koniecpol (Poland) in 1865. Came to America in 1922. He died on 7 May 1932 in Chicago.

Shimkhah Wiewiora (Yura)

Born in Klomnice. Came to America in 1914. He was a member of the Czenstochower Regional Union in Detroit. Died at age 64 in Flint, Mich.

Haim Hirsz Tanski
(Photo)

Son of Berish and Ester Toba. Born in Radomsk in 1871. Was a teacher in Czenstochow. Came to America in 1923.

Father of Avraham, Yitzhak, Dovid, Moshe, Harry and Tilly Kepp.

Chava Tanski
(Photo)

(Née Dukart) From Czenstochow. Came to America in 1923. Died in 1942 in New York.

Honor her memory!

Dovid Tanski

Son of Haim Hirsh Tanski
(Photo)

Ellen Tanski

Daughter of Dovid and Sara Czarni.

[Page CXII]

Jakob Zajdman
(Photo)

Born in Czenstochow on 12 February 1874. Came to America in 1886. Married Betty Cohen in 1900.

A member since 1893 of Czenstochower Young Men. Held several offices in the organization and is now an honorary member. He is also a member of several other organizations.

Henekh (Haimy) Yoskowicz

Son of Josef and Feigl. Born in Piotrkow. Came to America in 1914. He was a member of the *Arbeter Ring* and of the Jewish People's Union in Detroit. Was one of the founders of the Czenstochower Regional Union in Detroit. Died on 20 August 1939 in Detroit.

Mendl Pakula

Son of Leibish and Nakha. Died in 1911 at age 54 in Warsaw. The father of Iser, Welwl and Ita.

Fishl Koziwoda
(Photo)

Koniecpolski
(Photo)

An active worker with *Poale-Zion* in Czenstochow.

Dovid Fajnrajkh
(Photo)

Former member of the *S.S.* [Zionist Socialists]. Spent several years in jail. The brother of Meir Fajnrajkh and Fela Biro.

Makhl Storozum and his wife
(Photo)

Now in America.

Sam Goldberg
(Photo)

Wajsberg
Lynn, Mass.
(Photo)

Shmuel Leser
London
(Photo)

Zelda Leser
(Photo)

Josef Hirsh Grajcer
(Photo)

[Page CXIII]

Abraham Gotlib
(Photo)

Worker for *Poale-Zion* in Czenstochow. Today he is in *Eretz-Yisroel*.

L. Szpicer
(Photo)

Adolf Furman
(Photo)

Dovid Wajnholc
Argentina

Worker with the Aid Union

(Photo)

———

Wajsman
Argentina

Worker with the Aid Union

(Photo)

———

Yosokhar Gricer
(Photo)

———

Adolf Epsztajn
(Photo)

The brother of Hershl Epsztajn (Los Angeles). Chairman of the Retailers Union in Czenstochow. Belonged to the *P.P.S.* [*Polska Partia Socjalistynczna* – Polish Socialist Party] in his youth.

Blanche Willinger
(Photo)

Moshe Szwarc and his wife (Photos)

Devoted active worker for Noworadomsker Relief in New York. Editor of the *Noworadomsker Almanac.*

———

Mrs. Nowid
(Photo)

———

Rywka Frajmowicz and her daughter
(Photo)

The sister of Max Peper, Los Angeles.

[Page CXIV]

Lili Brener
(Photo)

The child of the chairman of the Jewish Committee in Czenstochow, Liber Brener.

To the article: Rozenblat-Dykerman Circle.

(Photo, caption: Dykerman)

(Photo, caption: Chava Rozenblat)

(Photo with no identification)

(Photo, caption: Fajersztajn's daughter with her husband)

(Photo, caption: Finkl's parents)

————

Efriom Kremsdorf
(Photo)

Born in Czenstochow in 1893. Died in 1936 in *Eretz-Yisroel*. Founder of the public school in the Nachlat Ganim area of Tel Aviv.

————

Jack Rozen
(Photo, caption: son of Isidor Rozen)

————

Chena Kolin
(Photo)

(Photo with no identification)

(Photo with no identification)

(Photo, right, caption: Helen Tempelhof Khrobaloski, wife of Alkanan Khrobaloski)

(Photo, left, caption: Chava Khrobaloski, daughter of Alkanan Khrobaloski)

————

Remembering Those Who
Left Us for Their Eternal Rest
To their eternal memory

The list that is published here contains only a small percentage of the people who conducted the communal work of our city and deserve to have their names illuminated in the history of Jewish Czenstochow.

— — — — • — — — —

Translated by Miriam Lebenstein

Edited by Gloria Berkenstat Freund

Mikhal and Tseshe Alter

Mikhal Alter was a member of the Zionist Socialist Workers Party from his early youth to old age; he did not know any Yiddish. He was a practical activist and planner for the party.

(Photo, caption: Mikhal Alter)

(Photo, right, caption: Tseshe Alter)

(Photo, left, caption: Hankele Alter)

Tseshe Federman, whom he married in the years following World War I, was employed in the Neufeld office. She distinguished herself by her modesty and her distinctive aristocratic appearance.

Mikhal Alter, Tseshe and their daughter, Hankele, perished during the period from 1939–1945.

Dov Ber Boczan

Berl Boczan was born in Czenstochow in 1877. In 1898 he and his father, Reb Moshe Boczan, established the Yiddish printing ship on Allee 6. After his father's death, he ran the printing shop in partnership with his brother, the typesetter and printer, Shimon Boczan.

Berl Boczan was a managing member of several Jewish social institutions, and publisher of the *Czenstochower Tageblat* [*Czenstochower Daily Newspaper*] and the *Czenstochower Zeitung* [*Czenstochower Daily*].

He died on the 23 of Sivan, 5699 [10 June 1939], at the age of 62.

Avraham Ber Birnbaum

Avraham Ber Birnbaum was born on the third day of Shevat in 1865 [January 30th] in Pultusk (Poland), into the religious family of a Kotsher Hasid, a religious scholar.

Until the age of 12, he studied in *kheders* [religious elementary schools], and then in the *beis midrash* [religious house of study]. His father married him off at the age of 17. He was one of the greatest *tish zingers* [table singers] at the rebbe's table, but he dedicated his soul to music. This displeased his father-in-law, and he was divorced. Birnbaum married for the second time at 19.

(Photo, caption: Avraham Ber Birnbaum with his family)

In 1890, he became *khazen* [cantor] and *shoykhet* [ritual slaughterer] in Przasnysz. In 1893, he gave up his work as *shoykhet* and accepted an invitation to become chief cantor in the newly built synagogue in Czenstochow. Here, a whole new world opened up for Birnbaum. He became seriously interested in music, began to write articles about music in Hebrew and German.

In 1906, he opened a school for cantors in Czenstochow, where he strove to combine cantorial arts with secular musical education. The school attracted tens of cantors, and later great opera singers, and was renowned in all of Poland and Russia. After 13 years at the cantors' school, he also became a lecturer in the German school.

In 1913, he resigned from his position as chief cantor of Czenstochow and moved to Lodz.

On a visit to Czenstochow, he suddenly fell ill with a brain inflammation, and died on Friday, 11 November 1922, at the age of 58.

[Page CXL]

Makhl Birncwajg

Makhl Birncwajg was born in 1907, his parents' youngest son. He received a Jewish religious education in *kheder*, then attended the Jewish *gymnazia*, where he was drawn into the Zionist youth groups. He soon became disappointed with Zionism and joined the illegal Communist party.

Under the Nazi's bloody regime, Makhl Birncwajg and his brother, Pinkhas, were employed by the Germans as upholsterers. A "furniture *lager* [work camp]" was set up in the building of Wajnberg's factory.

There came the saddest day for the Jewish community in Czenstochow – 22 September 1942, Ukrainians and Nazis were posted all along the streets. The way to the *zamlplatz* [gathering place for deportation] led through the gate and the furniture *lager* where a German guard stood. At a certain moment, Birncwajg managed to divert the attention of the supervisor and of the guards and a stream of driven and persecuted Jews was able to escape into the furniture *lager*, their number reaching 600.

This was one of the most difficult feats

(Photo, caption: Makhl Birncwajg)

carried out under the noses of the Germans and of the two Jewish spies, *Kulibayke* [Editor's note: possibly a corruption of the Russian work *kulebyaka* or *coulibiac* – a Russian main dish pastry often made with salmon] and Gnat, sent in especially by the Gestapo. But it was made possible by the persistence and the steel nerves of Makhl Birncwajg.

Yakov Pat, describing the destruction of the Jewish population, wrote of him:

"The secret underground fighting organization under the direction of the heroic Makhl Birncwajg, also drove out the wagons of cupboards, shelves and chests, but inside there lay Jewish mothers and children who had been smuggled out under the noses of the Germans. They were taken to underground bunkers that had been prepared for them. Some of the children today live in children's homes."

On 8 July 1943, Czenstochow's German executioner, Degenhard, entered the furniture *lager* with a band of police and ordered Birncwajg to gather his entire family, that is, his mother, brother and wife. He quickly realized that the Angel of Death was standing before him. Somehow he managed to escape, jumping over a fence. His 72-year-old mother was shot on the spot. Makhl Birncwajg hid with well known "honorable" Poles, who constantly blackmailed him and finally turned him over to the executioners. He no longer had the will to escape. On 28 July he was shot to death with 60 other Jews in the Jewish cemetery.

Leibish Berkowicz

Leibl Berkowicz was one of the young generation of Jewish workers who were awakened by the freedom movement of 1905 to the struggle for a new and healthy Jewish life. His served the ideal of the Zionist Socialist Workers party, Socialist Territorialism his entire life. He married

Yentl Sliwinski and the five children they raised: Ruzhe, Shimshon, Dalia, Genia and Matush, were in the first ranks of the beauties, the singers and the artists of the I.L. Peretz Children's Home and public school that Leibish and Yentl helped to establish.

(Photos: right, caption: Leibish Berkowicz; left, caption: Genia Berkowicz)

Leibish and Yentl Berkowicz and their daughter, Rushe, and her child, as well as Shimshon, were killed during the Nazi era. Remaining was Genia (today a teacher in the I.L. Peretz school) with her husband and Matush.

Leyzer Berkowicz

He followed the "rabbi," Rafal Federman. Starting together in the *S.D.K.P.L.* [Social Democratic Party of the Kingdom of Poland and Lithuania], they went on to the Zionist Socialist Workers party, took part in the choruses of the literary society, *Lira*, then later in the *Fareinikte* [United] party. He was a shoemaker and worked for a long time in Dzialowski's workshop; later he ran his own workshop in the Second Allee. No trace remains of him, his wife from Noworadomsk and their children.

Dr. Batawia and Dr. Kihan Kulin

In addition to their activities in a whole range of charitable and communal organization, they distinguished themselves with their administration of the Jewish hospital. It should be noted that Dr. Mikulski, a Christian, contributed greatly to the development of the Jewish hospital.

Avram Brat

Quiet, calm, keeping his thoughts to himself, Avram Brat began his career in communal organizations practically in childhood during the First World War, in the office of the Zionist Socialist Workers organization in Allee 43. He later became the treasurer of the large *Fareinikte* [United] party, *Melukhe* [State] in Czenstochow, administrator of *Dos Neye Vort* [*The New Word*] and tens of other administrative positions in various institutions.

[Pages CXLI]

In 1924, he married comrade Ruzhe Plawner.

In 1926 he took over the directorship of the I.L. Peretz Children's Home and *Folkshul* [public elementary school], an honor bestowed on very few, but also a heavy burden and superhuman strain, under the conditions of internal party struggle from the inside and Fascist reaction from the outside.

Under the Nazi regime he and Wolf Fajge also continued to run the I.L. Peretz House, which was a shelter for refugees from Lodz and Plotsk. Letters from him kept coming in the first few years of World War II. In one letter he advised that he had lost his home, along with his furniture and clothing. The Nazis took everything he had and, along with thousands of others, confined him in the ghetto.

(Photo, caption: Abram Brat)

(Photos, captions, right: Ruzhe Plawner Brat; left: daughter of A. and R. Brat)

Shortly thereafter, he and his daughter, then already 16 years old, went the way of the millions of Jewish martyrs.

Brom, Dr. Arnold

Longtime chairman of the Zionist organization in Czenstochow. He was also a member of the community leadership and a member of the city council

Gotajner, Hershl

His main characteristic was his involvement in philosophy. He began as a schoolboy in the local commercial school, wearing a hat with blue bands. He then belonged to the group of Zionist Socialist Workers Party amateur intellectuals. Later, he studied in Krakow. In his years of cultural activities, he would go on walks through the streets and avenues of Czenstochow, philosophizing about Nietzsche, Kant, Hegel and Spinoza.

He married Miss Rajkher and ran his own business. He was an original person and a strong character, hard to beat in a discussion on social issues. He is no longer among the living.

Gajsler, Dr. Hipolit

Dr. Gajsler for the most part dedicated his communal activities to the Jewish artisan and for many years was involved with the artisans club.

Goldsztajn, Shmuel

As early as 1914, Shmuel Goldsztajn was considered first among the candidates for leadership of the Jewish community, on the slate put forward in opposition to the "assimilationists."

During World War I, he became president of the Jewish community, and held this office for a long time.

He was in Warsaw until 1940 under the Nazi occupation. Then he returned to Czenstochow, where he was killed by the German murderers at Treblinka.

Gelber, Meir

Son of Haim Hirsh and Royze. Born in 1890. Shared the fate of the martyrs of 1939–1945.

Wilenberg, Peretz

Peretz Wilenberg was well known in Czenstochow as an artist. Some of his works earned him a name and recognition throughout Poland. He was skilled in drawing, ran an art school in his home and taught drawing in the Artisans School, the Jewish *gymnazie* [high school] and the I.L. Peretz *Folkshul* [public school].

(Drawing by P. Wilenberg in the distinct Jewish style, honoring the Jewish martyrs and personalities.)

[Pages CXLII]

During the Nazi regime he was in Warsaw, pretending to be deaf and dumb so as not to betray himself with his accent in Polish. After Hitler's defeat, he lived in Lodz, where he died 17 February, at the age of 73.

Winsztok, Haim; Epsztajn, Adolf; Filipowicz, Dovid

They ran the association of small businessmen and gave a lot of time and energy to the struggle to protect the Jewish market merchants and small businessmen.

Czarnowiecki, Yakov Yitzhak

His whole life was work and poverty, from his earliest years to his martyr's death. He began as a worker making toys and a simple soldier in the ranks of the Zionist Socialists in the years 1904-05. He did not abandon his party during the reactionary years. During World War I he was a railroad worker, and during that time, he married Dorka Szacher. He was "liberated" from his work when Poland was liberated, and was the secretary of the Central Bureau of the Central Council of the Professional Associations. But he continued to struggle financially and suffered poverty. He fathered two children and his poverty grew. When the Czenstochow city administration established an omnibus route between Rakow and the city, he became, by some miracle, the only Jewish contractor among the otherwise non-Jewish city appointees. He was almost the only one in Czenstochow who went over to *Poale-Zion* with Dr. Kruk. His martyr's death is described in the report of *Khurbn Czenstochow.*

So lived and died a modest man of the people.

Fojgl, Mendl; Krel, Yitzhak Meir

They were activists in the *Agudah* [Orthodox political party]. The latter [Krel] was also a member of the Czenstochow city council.

Koniarski, Lawyer Mendl; Szeriker, William; Dr. Asz
(a son of Rabbi Nakhum Asz)

They distinguished themselves by their activities on behalf of the Jews of Czenstochow. Dr. Asz was also one of the founders and, for many years, the president of *Makabi* [Jewish sports organization].

Koblinc, Rabbi Josef Shimeon, of blessed memory

Josef Shimeon Klobinc was one of the most unusual religious Jews found in Czenstochow. In his youth, he joined the *Hovevei Zion [Lovers of Zion]* movement, and since he was a talented speaker and great religious scholar, his famous sermons about *Eretz Yisroel* drew a large audience.

During the 45 years he lived in Czenstochow, he was active in a large number of social and religious organizations. He died November 1937. His death evoked great sorrow among the Jews of Czenstochow. Thousands of people took part in his funeral.

The *Vad haMizrakhi* [council of *Mizrakhi* – Religious Zionists] of Czenstochow decided to memorialize the name of Josef Shimeon Klobinc in the Golden Book of the Jewish National Fund.

Rozenberg, Yankev

Yankev Rozenberg came to Czenstochow from Warsaw in 1912 and soon became active, first in the Yiddish Literary Society, then in *Lira* [singing society]. He actively participated in and supported Jewish culture and social institutions, was one of the founders of *gymnazie* founded by Dr. Akser. He helped to create the Medem Bibliotheque and fought for Yiddish and for the rights of the Jewish masses and their own institutions in the times of the assimilationist leaders.

As a longtime resident of the Jewish community, he gained the love and appreciation if all segments of the Jewish population in Czenstochow.

Yankev Rozenberg died during the terrible time of the Nazi occupation. Not a trace remains of his family (wife and only daughter).

Fajge, Wolf

He was a worker at Fajge's candle factory. He devoted all of his free time to the party, and to the professional movement. In addition, he still found time to establish a library in Szarik [Zarki], and to participate in running the schools. In 1938, when the "Independents" were liquidated, he joined the *Bund.* He and his wife were murdered. His son survived and is in a D.P. camp in Germany.

Markusfeld, Henrik

It seems that no other name is as strongly associated with the industrial development of Czenstochow as the name Markusfeld.

(Photo, caption: Henrik Markusfeld)

The brothers, Henrik and Dr. Josef Markusfeld, developed and expanded the efforts in industrial, social and philanthropic fields that their father, Adolf Markusfeld, had begun.

[Pages CXLIII]

The artisans school in Czenstochow was built at the initiative and with the support of the brothers, Henrik and Josef Markusfeld in the name of their parents, Adolf and Astina. The horticulture farm and a whole array of other philanthropic institutions were established with their participation. Of the two brothers, it was the eldest, Henrik, whose communal activities were the most outstanding.

There was hardly a social institution in Czenstochow in which he was not an official – president, chairman, or member of the management. The evening he was not occupied, he enjoyed at the *Lira* [singing society]. He often used to stand in front of the warm oven surrounded by a group of *Liristn* [members of the singing society, *Lira*]. He would pronounce words of wisdom and sometimes would lecture the extreme Yiddishists [advocates of Yiddish and Yiddish culture]. But even more than the oven, he was warmed by the ardor of the youth who came to *Lira*.

His manifold duties and pursuits never prevented him from participating in the meetings of the management of tens of institutions. He rarely missed a meeting.

He was once late for a meeting of *Lira*. He apologized, explaining that he had just arrived on the express train from Breslau. "I feel more comfortable with you than with the Germans," he added.

A whole array of Jewish cultural and professional institutions that were always financially shaky continued to exist thanks to his power and assistance. He paid rent; he covered the deficits for their programs. "What is happening with the rent," he would ask the dentist, Ahron Peretz, president of *Lira*. "Drop in and see me tomorrow."

When Henrik Markusfeld died, he was mourned by all of Czenstochow, which gave him the largest funeral ever held there.

Nirenberg, Yehoshua

The Nirenbergs were known for their stationery store in the Second Allee. Their two sons, Henekh and Yehoshua, were members of the Zionist Socialist Workers Party. Henekh made his first appearance in the arena of community affairs during the first elections for the Czenstochow city council during the German occupation in 1917. Along with three others he was elected on the Zionist Socialist Workers Party slate in the sixth district. He was again elected city councilman in "free" Poland and his making public the "hard facts" about anti-Semitism among the leaders of the city council did not please them at all. Nevertheless, he later became the only Jew employed by city hall.

No trace remains of him, his wife and his only son, Marek.

Nemirowski, Shmuel

One of the most energetic social activists in the time following the First World War. Chairman of the homeless shelter, member of *Makabi*, chairman of the Revisionist Party and active in other institutions. Killed during the Nazi era.

Erlikh, Hershele

He was the quiet dreamer from Kamyk, his small *shtetl*. The dream of his life was to see Kamyk brought to life, busy at work, progressive. His greatest achievement was the children's home and *folkshul* [Editor's note: secular public school with Yiddish as the language of instruction] in Kamyk. He was a member of the Zionist Socialist Workers Party and of *Fareinikte* [United], and a *Fraylandist* [Editor's note: possibly a follower of Nakhman Rozensztajn, a resident of Piotrkow Trybunalski, who was a *Bundist* leader known as *Frayland* – free country]. His ambitions reflected his quiet nature – to do something for his Kamyk, to help out the editors of *Dos Naye Vort* [*The New Word*] in Czenstochow. He was the same when he was in Warsaw.

(Photo, caption: Hershele Erlikh)

He was married in Warsaw, had a child and lived in terrible poverty somewhere in the corner of a kitchen. He and his wife and child went hungry, but in the little time left to him, he gave to others. He perished during the years 1939–1945.

Rotbard, Zelig and Chesha (Sztajn)

Zelig Rotbard, a son of Itshe Ber and Szprinca, who ran a leather business at number 23 at the Old Market, was well known in Czenstochow. While still young, he belonged to the Social Democratic Party (S.D.K.P.L.); later, he became an active member of the Jewish Literary Society, where he met and married Chesha Sztajn. They raised two daughters, the older, Lola (Laya) and the younger, Sela (Feygl).

(Photo, caption: Zelig Rotbard)

Under the Nazi regime, Zelig Rotbard was a member of the *Judenrat* and he, his wife and younger daughter were killed with a group of Jews who were taken on Purim to the cemetery and murdered there.

[Pages CXLIV]

In 1940 their older daughter married Henry (Henekh) Helman. Both survived and now live in New York.

Rikhter, Dovid

In the revolutionary world of pre-war Poland, Dovid Rikhter held one of the most important places in the movement. Born in Czenstochow, he achieved exceptional mastery of the Polish language, and was also active as a journalist and editor in the Polish proletarian press. But he was still greatly drawn to Yiddish, Yiddish culture and to Jewish revolutionary activities. He came out of the old Polish Social Democratic Party (*S.D.K.P.L.*), and together with the best elements of the party, poured himself into the Communist Party of Poland. Amazingly, coming from the *S.D.K.P.L.*, where the assimilationist and nationalist-nihilist tendencies were considerable, he nevertheless continued to focus directly on Jewish issues in the Communist movement. Dovid Rikhter remained true to this work until the end.

Dovid Rikhter shone as a splendid journalist, as a basic and uniquely keen and logical polemicist, as a fine pamphleteer and theater critic, with taste and judgment.

His serious published works in the *Literarishe Tribune*, his theoretical pamphlets (under the name, L. Hankes), his brilliant articles in *Fraynd* [*Friend*], (under the name D. Leybin), his brochures and literary works, brought him into the ranks of the foremost journalists.

Dovid Rikhter had a unique style, with a light touch, elegant writing, love of wordplay, and distaste for hackneyed phrases; he was consistently argumentative with tact.

Years of imprisonment in pre-war Poland, the continual bitter worries about making a living, his troubled life, did not make him angry or bitter or heavy hearted. He always had a joke, a *bon mot* on his lips, was always congenial, had time to discuss new artistic forms or an interesting theater production. This was a life-affirming person who loved life and friends.

In 1940 he became editor of the Yiddish newspaper, *Di Bialystoker Shtern* in Bialystok and devoted himself to social and literary endeavors.

He perished during the slaughter in Slonim in 1941.

Szlezinger, Dudek

He was the son of rich parents, who had a big house and a ribbon factory on Spodek Street. He studied engineering in Belgium, but did not complete the course. He began his communal activities during World War I. He worked with the workers' council with Joshek Finkelsztajn. His energy, like an endless volcano, flowed over activities of *Fareinikte* [United] and later, *Umophendike* [Independent]. He met Regina Gros, the unique beauty who grew up in the basement of the house on the corner of Spodek and Onrodow, in the party and he married her. During the Nazi regime, they tried to save their only child by entrusting it to a Christian acquaintance, who betrayed them. The Gestapo brought the child to their house and murdered it before its parents' eyes. Dudek and Regina were both killed along with all of the martyrs of Czenstochow.

Szlezinger, Dovid; Sztiller, Zigmund; Borzykowski, Dovid; the Dykman Brothers; Neufeld, Moritz

They distinguished themselves by their work with the factory owners and merchants association. Moritz Neufeld, previously an "assimilator*," also distinguished himself with his courageous exploits against the *Endekes** in the city council.

*[Editor's notes: "Assimilator" – a Jew who totally assimilated into the surrounding cultural environment. *Endekes* – members of the anti-Semitic National Democratic Party.]

Szapiro, Feliks

At first he was one of the leaders of the business employees, later a Zionist activist with the aldermen in city hall. He distinguished himself by his fight against anti-Semitism in the city council.

Weksler, Haim

He was an activist in *Mizrakhi*. He was president of the *kehile* and for many years, a member of the Czenstochow city council. He was beloved in the city as a good hearted person and philanthropist.

Sztarke, Mrs. Salomea

The home for the elderly and for orphans named for Mina Verde in Czenstochow was one of its most popular institutions and Mrs. Salomea Sztarke, with her exceptional energy, almost single-handedly took on the burden of sustaining the institution for over twenty years. She was able to obtain subsidies for the institution from the city government, amounting to 2,000 *zlotys* a month, from the Jewish community, and most interestingly, from philanthropy. This made it possible to establish a kitchen for the orphans and elderly and, in 1928, a new floor was added to the old building. The number of elderly and orphans in the home began to grow and a teaching staff was hired for the children.

(Photo, caption: Salomea Sztarke)

Representatives of the Czenstochow Jewish community published their thanks and appreciation to Mrs. Sztarke. She was killed during the period of 1939–1945.

Index of Names Mentioned in
The Jews of Czestochowa
Translated by Tamar Grizim

Please note that the pages indicated in this Index of Names are the page numbers in the orginal yizkor book, not the page numbers in this translation. One can find the original page numbers indicated as "[Page 456]" throughout the text.

In the book *The Jews of Czestochowa* (which we the people from Czestochowa have published in the year 1947), for technical reasons, no index of all the names of the people mentioned in that important historical book was included. We consider it important to publish such an index now. The complete list of these names will no doubt be of great help to all historians, researchers, and other readers of the book *The Jews of Czestochowa*.

On the same occasion we publish also herewith the index of names included in the book *Czestochowa*. All the names and lists concerning these books were established by MOTEL BERKOVITZ.

Bibliographic information:

Title: *Tshenstokhov* (Tshenstokhover) *Yidn* or *Czenstochover Yidn*

Author(s): Mahler, Raphael, 1899–

Publication: New York: Aroysgegebn fun Yunaited Tshenstokhover relif komitet un Leydis okzileri in Nyu York, 1947

This index contains the page numbers of the Original Yizkor book, not this translation. For this index that has the page numbers of this translation, refer to the index at the end of this book starting on page 766.

Motolsky, Yidel	125
Mottel, Sh.	329
Mozart	43
Muchanov	23
Mukeikovsky	84
Munovitch, Nehemia	177
Munovitch, Shlomo	302, 303
Mushinska	91, 366
Mushkat, Zygmunt	392
Mussolini	157
Muzshin, Avraham-Ber	34, 41

N

Nachtigal, A.	332
Nachtigal, Dor	336
Nachtigal, Joseph-Ber	181
Nachtigal, Willi	275, 303, 332, 333, 334, 337
Nachum	40
Nachum, Yankelsxi Nehama	89
Nadir, Moshe	184
Naparte	63
Napman	298
Napoleon	10
Nathanson	50
Nathan-Yaakov	336
Ndet, Alfred	164
Neiberg, Frieda	286, 295
Neifeld, Bronislav	22
Neifeld, Clara	386
Neifeld, Daniel-Joseph	17, 18, 19, 20, 22, 23, 29, 30
Neifeld, Maurizi	37, 38, 109, 113, 116, 117, 177, 384, 386, 387
Neifeld, Wanda	386
Neiman	181
Neimintz, Joseph B"R Moshe	29
Neitigal, Darre	337
Neitigal, William	318
Nelson	337
Nemirovsky, Shmuel	103, 207
Nestin, L.	296
Newmark, Aryeh	99
Niedziela, Aharon	130
Nieger, Shmuel	81, 116, 359
Nierenberg	77
Nierenberg, Hennia	185
Nierenberg, Abie	
Nierenberg, Anna	286, 288
Nierenberg, Florence	286, 288
Nierenberg, Heniech	61, 347

INDEX

Please Note: The names on pages 704 – 765 are <u>not</u> included in this index

Kolobus, 514

Kolton, 73

Komissarzhevsky, 476

Kon, 8, 19, 20, 22, 23, 25, 26, 29, 70, 164, 459, 460, 483

Konarski, 47

Kongreci, 458

Kongrecki, 104

Koniarksi, 148

Koniarski, 142, 147, 148, 159, 210, 258, 560, 570, 700

Konicepolski, 537

Koniecpoler, 80, 201, 250, 298, 313, 335, 341, 654

Koniecpolski, 330, 483, 692

Kon-Kolin, 141, 148, 149, 484

Konopnicka, 8, 168

Kop, 388

Kopecka, 626

Koperczuk, 503

Kopertszki, 503

Kopin, 366, 370, 377

Kopin (Kopinsk), 102

Kopinski, 108, 109, 110, 111, 267, 310, 347, 348, 475

Kopinski (Kopin), 2

Kopinsky, 406

Kopl, 44, 48, 53, 120, 356

Koplewicz, 250

Koplowicz, 137

Kordecki, 8, 10

Korek, 52

Kornberg, 658, 661

Korpiel, 42, 366, 370, 375, 378, 386, 387, 656

Kory, 656

Kosczewo, 190

Kostek, 162

Kostek-Biernacki, 217

Koszczol, 56

Kot, 244

Kotarbinski, 241

Kotlarcz, 202

Kotlicki, 47

Kott, 655

Kovner, 389

Kowal, 507, 508

Kozak, 643

Kozewoda, 623

Koziwoda, 692

Kozlowski, 244

Krak, 113, 122, 134, 662, 663

Krakauer, 251

Krakower, 357

Krakowiak, 135

Krakowski, 356, 358, 575, 639, 651, 662

Kramalowska, 113, 122

Kramalowski, 330

Kramer, 247

Kraser, 43, 677

Kraserkes, 538

Krasziner, 582

Kratka, 507

Kraus, 389, 403, 548

Krause, 304

Krauskop, 134

Krauskopf, 485

Krauz, 453

Krawczyk, 355

Krawizki, 559

Krel, 250, 700

Kremsdorf, 406, 565, 643, 663, 664, 695

Kremski, 77, 107, 123, 134, 136, 629, 630, 642

Kricer, 96

Krieger, 256

Lubrowicz, 457

Luks, 178, 415, 417, 529

Luksenburg, 104

Luria, 109, 110, 111, 113

Lurisz, 680

Lustigman, 589

Luszczewski, 18

Lux, 253

Luxemburg, 504, 506

M

Macoch, 8, 24, 544

Madzelewski, 372

Mahler, 63, 203, 426, 429, 527, 529, 532, 533, 704

Maiorczik, 246

Majarczik, 120

Majerczak, 601

Majerczik, 160

Majerczyk, 357

Majerowicz, 224, 470

Majlich, 251

Majman, 28

Majmon, 36, 38

Majorczyk, 33, 113

Majtles, 240

Majzel, 138, 666

Makhelman, 666

Makowski, 357

Makrojer, 79, 104, 160, 619

Makroyer, 122

Malarcz, 44, 594

Malarnja, 576

Malarski, 346, 418, 419, 420, 489, 490, 491, 492, 493, 494, 495, 496, 540, 631

Malarski-Goodman, 494

Malarskis, 407, 489, 490, 491, 493, 494

Malarsz, 594

Maljarski, 665

Mamlak, 146

Mandel, 398

Mandelsberg, 167

Mandelsburg, 37

Manhajt, 296

Manhejt, 249

Manishewicz, 618

Mankowski, 145

Manowicz, 72, 116

Manuszewicz, 386

Marcus, 648

Marcusfeld, 536

Marczak, 570

Marczun, 460

Marek, 305, 309

Marglius, 250

Margolis, 512

Margoshes, 401

Margulis, 514

Markisfeld, 56

Markowicz, 52, 134, 146, 178, 249, 250, 296, 307, 356, 357, 441, 442, 443, 444, 445, 446, 447, 469, 525, 618, 619

Markusfeld, 32, 33, 34, 40, 41, 43, 47, 56, 58, 61, 70, 78, 83, 86, 87, 88, 89, 111, 112, 113, 117, 128, 134, 142, 145, 146, 147, 148, 206, 210, 560, 645, 701

Marlarski, 491

Marlaskis, 491

Marmor, 649

Marquis De Espinos, 214

Marx, 164, 193, 479

Mas, 178, 460, 673

O

www.ingramcontent.com/pod-product-compliance
Lightning Source LLC
Chambersburg PA
CBHW062021090426

42811CB00005B/917